VELÁZQUEZ WORLD WIDE Spanish English Dictionary

English - Spanish / Inglés - Español

Original compiled by
IDA NAVARRO HINOJOSA
R.J. NELSON, Ph.D.

Newly revised by

Velázquez Press
www.VelazquezPress.com

Library of Congress Control Number: 2004109749
ISBN 1594950016 Paper

Printed in the United States of America

PREFACE

Comprehensiveness, relevance, convenience: these are the traits of any good dictionary and were the guiding principals behind this newly revised edition of the *Velázquez World Wide Spanish English Dictionary* (formerly the *World Wide Spanish Dictionary*).

In keeping with the first of these principals, our editors have included hundreds of new entries and expansions on existing entries. Thanks to these additions, words of such recent provenance as ATM, AIDS, and globalization are now included in this dictionary. Our editors' foremost concern in selecting such entries was to ensure that our dictionary continues to be of relevance to our modern reader.

In addition to an expanded lexicon, this edition features a new 2-color layout that not only differentiates dictionary sections, but also calls attention to entry words. Our editors hope that this format adjustment will make our dictionary much more convenient to use. The three-column formatting in the Traveler's Conversation Guide serves this same purpose.

Finally, our editors have added new reference apparatus at the back of the dictionary. Weights and measures charts and a listing of monetary units provide the user of this dictionary with indispensable supplementary information.

Other practical advantages:

1.) modern American English usage and spelling and recognition of Spanish regional variations;

2.) for the English speaker, pronounced Spanish entry words using a simple but accurate system of phonetic spelling;

3.) complete listing of Spanish verb conjugations, both regular and irregular;

4.) an abundance of idiomatic phrases, each under its appropriate key entry;

5.) an indication of the gender of Spanish nouns in both sections;

6.) guide words in Spanish to help the user select the best translation;

7.) a durable vinyl soft cover (good for travelers and students).

Carina Carriedo, *Editor*

For more information on this and other Velázquez Press publications, visit our web site at www.VelazquezPress.com or visit our support site at www.AskVelazquez.com

PREFACIO

Exhaustividad, relevancia, conveniencia: éstas son las características de cualquier buen diccionario y fueron los principios rectores detrás de esta edición nuevamente revisada del *Velázquez World Wide Spanish English Dictionary* (anteriormente el *World Wide Spanish Dictionary*).

En conformidad con el primero de estos principios, nuestros editores han incluido cientos de nuevas entradas y la ampliación de las ya existentes. Gracias a estas adiciones, palabras y frases de tan reciente proveniencia como cajero automático, SIDA, y globalización están ahora incluidas en este diccionario. La preocupación sobresaliente de nuestros editores al seleccionar tales palabras fue asegurar que nuestro diccionario siga teniendo relevancia para nuestro lector moderno.

Además de un léxico ampliado, esta edición luce un nuevo diseño de dos colores que no solamente sirve para diferenciar las secciones del diccionario, sino además para resaltar las palabras de entrada. Nuestros editores esperan que esta modificación del formato vuelva mucho más accesible el uso de nuestro diccionario. El diseño de tres columnas en el Traveler´s Conversation Guide tiene el mismo fin.

Finalmente, nuestros editores han agregado nuevo material de referencia al final del diccionario. Las tablas de pesas y medidas y una lista de monedas nacionales proporcionan al usuario de este diccionario información suplementaria indispensable.

Otras ventajas prácticas

1.) el uso y la ortografía del inglés moderno de los Estados Unidos y reconocimiento de las variaciones regionales del español.

2.) para los lectores de habla inglesa, pronunciaciones para cada vocablo en español que se sirven de un sistema de ortografía fonética simple y preciso.

3.) un listado completo de las conjugaciones de los verbos en español, tanto regulares como irregulares.

4.) una abundancia de modismos, cada uno bajo una entrada apropiada

5.) una indicación del género de los nombres en español en las dos secciones

6.) acotaciones entre paréntesis que ayudan a seleccionar la mejor traducción

7.) una encuadernación en rústica de vinilo durable (excelente para los viajeros y los estudiantes).

Carina Carriedo, *Editora*

Para más información sobre ésta y otras publicaciones de Velázquez Press, visite nuestro sitio web www.VelazquezPress.com o visite nuestro sitio de apoyo www.AskVelazquez.com

CONTENTS

User's guide

Main Entry Words
The entry words in the *Velázquez World Wide Spanish English Dictionary* are in blue bold type.

Pronunciation
Following the main entry appears the phonetic spelling of the word. The black dots between letters represent the syllabic division of the word. The raised diacritic marks indicate where in the word the stress should fall.

Parts of Speech
These appear in italics after the pronunciation. If the word is a noun, then the gender of the noun will be indicated with an abbreviation. For a full list of abbreviations used in this dictionary, turn to pages 24 and 350.

olla, (oˊyâ) *f.* pot, kettle; stew *(guisado);* eddy *(remolino);* — **a presión,** pressure cooker; — **express**, (Mex.) pressure cooker; — **podrida**, potpourri.

Spanish Guide Words
These appear in parenthesis following the translations. They help the user to select the most appropriate translation in a given context.

Examples of Usage
Before some translations appear words or phrases in bold. These are examples of the most common uses of the entry word.

Translations
Each Spanish entry word may have more than one English translation. Each translation is separated by a semicolon.

Regional Variations
A note in parenthesis indicates if a sense of the word is used only in certain countries of the Spanish-speaking world.

Guía del usuario

Entradas
Las palabras de entrada en el *Velázquez World Wide Spanish English Dictionary* son azules.

Traducciones
Cada entrada puede tener varias traducciones. Las traducciones están separadas por un punto y coma.

Género de los nombres
Indicación del género de los nombres en español. Aparece como abreviatura en letra cursiva.

corn, *n.* grano, *m.;* callo, *m.;* maíz, *m.;* — **meal,** harina de maíz; **sweet**— maíz tierno; (Mex.) elote, *m.;* — **popper**, tostador de maíz; *vt.* salpresar; salar; granular.

Ejemplos de uso
Encabezando ciertas traducciones aparecen palabras o frases en letra negrita. Éstas son ejemplos de los usos más comunes de la palabra de entrada.

Categorías gramaticales
Aparecen después de las entradas como abreviaturas en letra cursiva. Para una lista completa de las abreviaturas que aparecen en este diccionario, vea las páginas 24 y 350.

Regionalismos
Una anotación entre paréntesis indica si una traducción se emplea solamente en algunos paises del mundo hispano.

8

The Spanish Alphabet and Its Sounds

Spanish Letter	English Sound	Phonetic Symbol	Spanish Word	Phonetic Respelling
a	father	â	para	(pâ´râ)
b	bad	b	basta	(bâs´tâ)
	save	v	sabe	(sâ´ve)
c	kid	k	casa	(kâ´sâ)
	say	s	cinco	(sēng´ko)
	get	g	anécdota	(â•neg´tho•tâ)
ch	chip	ch	chico	(chē´ko)
d	day	d	dama	(dâ´mâ)
	though	th	mudo	(mū´tho)
e	they	e	leve	(le´ve)
	ten	e	el	(el)
f	few	f	finca	(fēng´kâ)
g	go	g	gana	(gâ´nâ)
	hot	h	gente	(hen´te)
h	(silent)		hacer	(â•ser´)
í	police	ē	Isla	(ēz´lâ)
	yes	y	bien	(byen)
j	hot	h	eje	(e´he)
k	kick	k	kilo	(kē´lo)
l	lamp	l	lana	(lâ´nâ)
ll	yes	y	llama	(yâ´mâ)
m	mama	m	mano	(mâ´no)
n	none	n	nota	(no´ta)
o	go	o	ocho	(o´cho)
	gone	o	ostra	(os´tra)
p	pop	p	papel	(pâ•pel´)
q	quit	k	aquí	(â•ke´)
r	very	r	clero	(kle´ro)
	(none)	rr	río	(rrē´o)
rr	(none)	rr	sierra	(sye´rrâ)
s	see	s	saco	(sâ´ko)
	rose	z	desde	(dez´the)
t	tip	t	todo	(to´tho)
	though	th	atleta	(âth•le´tâ)
u	food	ū	luna	(lū´nâ)
	quit	w	huevo	(we´vo)
	silent		guerra	(ge´rrâ)
v	bad	b	vaca	(bâ´kâ)
	save	v	grave	(grâ´ve)
x	ax	ks	taxi	(tâk´sē)
	see	s	sexto	(ses´to)
Y	yes	y	ya	(yâ)
	police	ē	ley	(leē)
z	see	s	zapa	(sâ´pâ)
	zero	z	biznieto	(bēz•nye´to)

Explanation of the Sounds

a   always has the sound of English *ah*, but shorter. *Symbol*: â. *Example*: **para** (pâ′râ).

b   has a sound somewhat softer than English *b* when it occurs at the beginning of a setence or breath group, and when it follows m or n. *Symbol*: b. *Examples*: **basta** (bâs′ta), **cambio** (kâm′byo).

Everywhere else it has the sound of English *v*, but with the lips lightly touching. *Symbol*: v. *Examples*: **sabe** (sâ′ve), **habla** (â′vlâ), **orbe** (or′ve).

c   has the sound of *k* in *kid* before a, o, u, or a consonant. *Symbol*: k. *Examples*: **casa** (kâ′sâ), **clave** (klâ′ve), **pacto** (pâk′to).

has the sound of *s* in *say* before e or i. *Symbol*: s. *Examples*: **cena** (se′nâ), **cinco** (sēng′ko).

has the sound of *g* in *big* before d or n. Symbol: g. Examples: **anécdota** (â•neg′tho•tâ), **técnica** (teg′nē•kâ).

ch   is a single letter in Spanish and always has the sound of *ch* in *chip*. *Symbol*: ch. *Examples*: **chico** (chē′ko), **mucho** (mū′cho).

d   has a sound somewhat softer than English *d* when it occurs at the start of a sentence or breath group, and when it follows 1 or n. *Symbol*: d. *Examples*: **dama** (dâ′mâ), **calda** (kâl′dâ), **bando** (bân′do).

has the sound of *th* in *though* everywhere else. *Symbol*: th. *Examples*: **mudo** (mū′tho), **verdad** (ber•thath′).

e   has the open sound of *e* in ten before consonants in the same syllable, except m, n, or s. *Symbol*: e. *Examples*: **el** (el), **comer** (ko•mer′).

has the closed sound of *ey* in *they* everywhere else (but without the vanish into *ee*). *Symbol*: e. *Examples*: **mesa** (me′sâ), **buen** (bwen), **reinar** (rreē•nâr′).

NOTE: In English these two sounds signal a complete change of meaning in many word pairs, such as *gate - get, braid - bread, freight - fret*. Linguists speak of the change as "phonemic" (involving a difference in meaning). The same difference in Spanish sounds is non-phonemic. **Mesa**, for example, conveys exactly the same meaning whether the **e** is pronounced open or closed, and the same is true wherever **e** occurs in other Spanish words. One symbol (e) therefore suffices for both sounds.

However, for students of Spanish who want to speak the language "like a native", the two rules above for the sounds of **e** are a useful—though not a sufficient—guide. Attention must also be paid to regional differences in pronunciation. In a few northern parts of Spanish America (Mexico and Cuba, for example) the open e sound is used more often than in most other Spanish-speaking regions, including Spain itself.

f   always has the sound of *f* in *few* or if. *Symbol*: f. *Examples*: **finca** (fēng′kâ), **efecto** (e•fek′to).

g   has the hard sound of *g* in *go* or big before a, o, or u, and before consonants. *Symbol*: g. *Examples*: **gana** (gâ′nâ), **agua** (â′gwâ), **grande** (grân′de).

has a sound between English *g* and *h* before e and i, and is made by pronouncing h with the back of the tongue raised as for the sound of g. *Symbol*: h. *Examples*: **gente** (hen′te), **digesto** (dē•hes′to).

h   is always silent. *Examples*: **hacer** (â•ser′), **bahía** (bâ•ē′â).

i   has the sound of *i* in police except unstressed before vowels. *Symbol*: ē. *Examples*: **rico** (rrē′ko), **isla** (ēz′lâ).

has the sound of *y* in *yes* when unstressed before vowels. *Symbol*: y. *Examples*: **bien** (byen), **hierba** (yer′vâ).

j   always has the second sound described above for **g**. *Symbol*: h. *Examples*: **hijo** (ē′ho), **juego** (hwe′go).

k   occurs only in words of foreign origin and always has the sound of *k* in *kick*. *Symbol*: k. *Examples*: **kilo** (kē′lo), **kerosina** (ke•ro•sē′nâ).

l   always has the sound of *l* in *lamp*. *Symbol*: l. *Examples*: **lana** (lâ′nâ), **bala** (bâ′lâ).

ll   is a single letter in the Spanish alphabet and always has the sound of *y* in *yes*. *Symbol*: y. *Examples*: **calle** (kâ′ye), **llama** (yâ′mâ).

m   has the sound of *m* in *mama* except at the end of a word. *Symbol*: m. *Examples*: **mano** (mâ′no), **campo** (kâm′po).

has the sound of *n* in *none* at the end of a word. *Symbol*: n. *Example*: **álbum** (âl′būn).

n   has the sound of n in none, except before b, f, p, and v. *Symbol*: n. *Examples*: **nota** (no′tâ), **quinto** (kēn′to).

has the sound of *m* before b, f, p, and v. *Symbol*: m. *Examples*: **infante** (ēm•fân′te), **invicto** (ēm•vēk′to).

has the sound of *ng* in *sing* before hard c, hard g, k, and qu. *Symbol*: ng. *Examples*: **finca** (fēng′ka), **tengo** (teng′go).

ñ   always has the sound of *ny* in *canyon*. *Symbol*: ny. *Examples*: **ñapa** (nyâ′pâ), **niña** (nē′nyâ).

o   has the open sound of *o* in gone before consonants in the same syllable. *Symbol*: o. *Examples*: **ostra** (os′trâ), **contar** (kon•târ′).

has the closed sound of *o* in go everywhere else (but without the vanish into *oo*). *Symbol*: o. *Examples*: **todo** (to′tho), **ocho** (o′cho).

NOTE: As in the case of the two sounds of **e**, Spanish-speaking people attach little or no importance to the different sounds of **o**, and one symbol (o) therefore suffices for both.

p   always has a sound slightly softer than *p* in *pop*. *Symbol*: p. *Examples*: **papel** (pâ•pel′), **captura** (kâp•tū′râ).

q   always has the sound of *k* as in *quit*. As in English words, it is always spelled with a following **u**. *Symbol*: k. *Examples*: **que** (ke), **aquí** (â•kē′).

r   has two sounds in Spanish, both different from English *r*.

1. resembles the *r* of very, but with an added flip of the tongue which gives it a slight trill. It occurs only inside words and when not preceded by l, n, or s. *Symbol:* r. Examples: **clero** (kle′ro), **bravo** (brä′vo).

2. has no English counterpart. It is produced by rapidly vibrating the tongue while trying to make the sound of *r*. It has this sound only at the start of words and when preceded by 1, n, or *s*. *Symbol:* rr. *Examples:* **río** (rrē′o), **enredo** (en•rre′tho).

rr   always has the second sound described above for **r**. *Symbol:* rr. *Examples;* ***sierra*** (sye′rrä), **perro** (pe′rro).

s   has the sound of *s* in *see* at the end of a word and when followed by a vowel or one of the following consonants: c f, h, j, p, q, and t. *Symbol:* s. *Examples:* **dos** (dos), **saco** (sä′ko), **descubrir** (des · kū•vrēr′), **deshecho** (de•se′cho).

has the sound of *s* in *rose* when followed by b, d, hard g, 1, m, n r, v or y. *Symbol:* z. *Examples:* **desde** (dez′the), **rasgo** (rräz′go), **disyuntiva** (dēz•yūn•tē′vä).

t   has a sound slightly softer than *t* in *tip*, except before 1, m, and *n*. *Symbol:* t. *Examples:* **todo** (to′tho), **entre** (en′tre).

has the sound of *th* in *though* before 1, m, and n. *Symbol:* th. *Examples:* **atleta** (äth•le′tä), **atmósfera** (äth•mos′fe•rä).

u   has the sound of *oo* in *food* except when followed by a vowel. *Symbol:* ū. *Examples:* **luna** (lū′nä), **use** (ū′so), **luz** (lūs).

has the sound of *w* in *way* before vowels, except when combined with g or q and followed by e or i. *Symbol:* w. *Examples:* **hueso** (we′so), **bueno** (bwe′no).

has no sound at all when combined with g or q and followed by e or i. *Examples:* **guerra** (ge′rrä), **guía** (gē′ä), **que** (ke).

ü   always has the sound of *w* in *way*. *Symbol:* w. It occurs only in the combinations güe or güi. *Examples:* **vergüenza** (ber•gwen′sä), **argüir** (är•gwēr′).

v   has the same two sounds as Spanish **b**. *Symbols:* b and v. *Examples:* **vaca** (bä′kä), **grave** (grä′ve).

x   has two sounds in Spanish:
between **vowels** it has the sound of *x* in *ax*. *Symbol:* ks. *Examples:* **examinar** (ek•sä•mē•när′), **taxi** (täk′sē).

NOTE: In **México** and **mexicano x** has the sound of Spanish **j**: (me′hē•ko), (me•hē•kä′no).

elsewhere it has the sound of *s* in see. *Symbol:* s. *Examples:* **sexto** (ses′to), **extraño** (es•trä′nyo).

y   has the sound of y in yes before vowels. *Symbol:* y. *Examples:* **ya** (yä), **suyo** (sū′yo). elsewhere it has the sound of *i* in po*lí*ce. *Symbol:* ē. *Examples:* **y** (ē), **ley** (leē).

z   has the sound of *z* in *zero* before b, d, hard g, 1, m, n, r, v, and y. *Symbol:* **z**. *Examples:* **biznieto (bēz•nye′to), noviazgo** (no•vyäz′go).
has the sound of *s* in *see* in all other situations. *Symbol:* s. *Examples:* **zapa** (sä′pä), **vez** (ves).

Diphthongs

When two vowels occur together in words, they are usually pronounced as one syllable. Such one-syllable combinations are known as *diphthongs*. Some well-known English examples are *oi* in *boil* and *ou* in *house.* Diphthongs are frequent occurrences in Spanish, and it is therefore important to know how to pronounce them.

The five vowels occur in just about every possible combination. But the more common diphthongs combine *a strong* vowel with *a weak* one. Strong vowels (**a, e,** and **o**) are so called because they usually *sound* stronger (louder) than weak vowels (**i** and **u**) when combined. *Examples:* **aire** (â´ē•re), **causa** (kâ´ū•sâ), **diez** (dyes), **nueve** (nwe´ve), **boina** (bo´ē•nâ).

When two weak vowels combine to form a diphthong, the stress always falls on the second. *Examples:* **viuda** (byū´thâ), **huir** (wēr).

The combination of two strong vowels (**a, e, o**) results, not in a diphthong, but in two syllables. *Examples:* **nao** (nâ´o), **real** (rre · âl´), **boa** (bo´â), **poeta** (po•e´tâ), **caer** (kâ•er´).

When a weak vowel in combination with a strong vowel bears a written accent, the weak vowel is the one that is stressed and two syllables result. *Examples:* **día** (dē´â), **caído** (kâ•ē´tho), **dúo** (dū´o).

When a word ending in **i, u,** or **y** is followed in the same sentence by a second word beginning with a vowel, the two vowels are sometimes pronounced as a diphthong. *Examples:* **mi amor** (myâ•mor´), **su obra** (swo´vrâ), **y usted** (yūs•teth´).

Triphthongs

When three vowels occur together they are usually pronounced as one syllable, with the middle vowel (always a or e) bearing the stress. *Examples:* **buey** (bwe´ē), **Paraguay** (pâ•râ•gwâ´ē).

Accentuation

Words ending in a vowel or in **n** or **s** are accented on the next-to-the-last syllable. *Examples:* **negro** (ne´gro), **hablan** (â´vlân), **comidas** (ko•mē´thâs).

Words ending in a consonant other than **n** or **s** are accented on the last syllable. *Examples:* **papel** (pâ•pel´), **escribir** (es•krē•vēr´), **feroz** (fe•ros´).

Words whose pronunciations do not conform to these rules are spelled with a written accent to indicate the stressed syllable. *Examples:* **francés** (frân•ses´), **lección** (lek•syon´), **ánimo** (â´nē•mo).

Syllabication

Spanish words have no silent vowels (except **u** preceded by **g** or **q** and followed by **e** or **i**), as many English words do *(were, fair, buy).* This means that there are as many syllables as there are sounded vowels (counting diphthongs and triphthrongs as one-vowel sounds).

Single consonants between vowels (and that includes **ch, ll,** and **rr**) belong with the following vowel. *Examples:* **casa** (kâ´sâ), **viuda** (vyū´thâ), **echar** (e•châr).

The following two-consonant combinations are never divided between syllables: **bl, br, cl, cr, dr, fl, fr, gl, gr, pl, pr, tr.** They always start the syllable to which they belong. *Examples:* **hablar** (â•vlâr´), **copla** (ko´plâ), **madre** (mâ´thre), **otro** (o´tro).

All other two-consonant combinations (including **dl** and **tl**) are divided. *Examples:* **manta** (mân´tâ), **orbe** (or´ve), **atleta** (âth•le´tâ).

When vowels are separated by three consonants (except as noted below), the syllable division occurs after the first two. *Examples:* **instinto** (ēns•tēn´to), **obstaculizar** (ovs•tâ•kū•lē•sâr´).

When vowels are separated by three or more consonants the last two of which are **bl, br, cl, cr, dr, fl, gl, gr, pl, pr,** or **tr,** the syllable division occurs before the aforesaid inseparable two-consonant combinations. *The examples:* **estrecho** (es•tre´cho), **instrumento** (ēns•trū•men´to), **implicar** (ēm•plē•kâr´).

CONJUGATION OF SPANISH VERBS

1 Regular Verbs
All regular verbs entered in the dictionary conform to one of the following basic patterns.

In the regular conjugations below, the verb forms are given in the following order: first, second, and third person singular; followed by first, second, and third person plural.

—**AR** VERBS *Example:* **hablar** (â•vlär´) to speak

PRESENT PARTICIPLE **hablando** (â•vlän´do)
PAST PARTICIPLE **hablado** (â•v1â´tho)
PRESENT **hablo** (â´vlo), **hablas** (â´vlâs), **habla** (â´vla), **hablamos** (â•vlä´mos), **habláis** (â•vlä´ēs), **hablan** (a´vlän)
FUTURE **hablaré** (â•vlâ•re´), **hablarás** (â•vlâ•râs´), **hablará** (â•vlâ•râ´), **hablaremos** (â•vlâ•re´mos), **hablaréis** (â•vlâ•re´ēs), **hablarán** (â•vlâ•rân´)
CONDITIONAL **hablaría** (â•vlâ•rē´â), **hablarías** (â•vlâ•rē´âs), **hablaría** (â•vlâ•rē´â), **hablaríamos** (â•vlâ•rē´â•mos), **hablaríais** (â•vlâ•rē´âēs), **hablarían** (â•vlâ•rē´ân)
PRESENT SUBJUNCTIVE **hable** (â´vle), **hables** (âvles), **hable** (â´vle), **hablemos** (â•vle´mos), **habléis** (â•vle´ēs), **hablen** (â´vlen)
IMPERFECT **hablaba** (â•vlä´vâ), **hablabas** (â•vlä´vâs), **hablaba** (â•vlä´vâ), **hablábamos** (â•vlä´vâ•mos), **hablabais** (â•vlä´vâēs) **hablaban** (â•vlä´van)
PRETERITE **hablé** (â•vle´), **hablaste** (a.vlâs´te), **habló** (â•vlo´), **hablamos** (â•vlä´mos), **hablasteis** (â•vlâs´teēs), **hablaron** (â•vlä´ron)
PAST SUBJUNCTIVE (I) **hablase** (â•vlä´se) **hablases** (â•vlä´ses), **hablase** (â•vlä´se), **hablásemos** (â•vlä´se•mos), **hablaseis** (â•vla´seēs), **hablasen** (â•vlä´sen)
PAST SUBJUNCTIVE (II) **hablara** (â•vlä´râ), **hablaras** (â•vlä´râs), **hablara** (â•vlä´râ), **habláramos** (â•vlä´râ•mos), **hablarais** (â•vlä´râēs), **hablaran** (â•vlä´rân)
IMPERATIVE **habla** (â´vlä), **hablad** (â•vlâth´)

—**ER** VERBS Example: **comer** (ko•mer´) to eat

PRESENT PARTICIPLE **comiendo** (ko•myen´do)
PAST PARTICIPLE **comido** (ko•mē´tho)
PRESENT **como** (ko´mo), **comes** (ko´mes), **come** (ko´me), **comemos** (ko•me´mos), **coméis** (ko•me´ēs), **comen** (ko´men)
FUTURE **comeré** (ko•me•re´), **comerás** (ko•me•râs´) **comerá** (ko•me•râ´), **comeremos** (ko•me•re´mos), **comeréis** (ko•me•re´ēs), **comerán** (ko•me•ran´)
CONDITIONAL **comería** (ko•me•rē´â), **comerías** (ko•me•rē´âs), **comería** (ko•me•rē´â), **comeríamos** (ko•me•rē´â•mos), **comeríais** (ko•me•rē´âēs), **comerían** (ko•me•rē´ân)
PRESENT SUBJUNCTIVE **coma** (ko´mâ), **comas** (ko´mâs), **coma** (ko´mâ), **comamos** (ko•mâ´mos), **comáis** (ko•mâ´ēs), **coman** (ko´mân)
IMPERFECT **comía** (komē´â), **comías** (ko•mē´âs), **comía** (ko•mē´â), **comíamos** (ko•miâ•mos), **comíais** (ko•mē´âēs), **comían** (ko • mē´ân)
PRETERITE **comí** (ko•mē´), **comiste** (ko•mēs´te), **comió** (ko•myo´), **comimos** (ko •mē´mos), **comisteis** (ko•mēs´teēs), **comieron** (ko•mye´ron)
PAST SUBJUNCTIVE (I) **comiese** (ko•mye´se), **comieses** (ko•mye´ses), **comiese** (ko•mye´se), **comiésemos** (ko•mye´se•mos), **comieseis** (ko•mye´seēs), **comiesen** (ko•mye´sen)
PAST SUBJUNCTIVE (II) **comiera** (ko•mye´râ), **comieras** (ko•mye´râs), **comiera** (ko mye´-râ), **comiéramos** (ko•mye´râ•mos), **comierais** (ko•mye´râes), **comieran** (ko•mye´´rân)
IMPERATIVE **come** (ko me), **comed** (ko•meth´)

—**IR** VERBS *Example:* **vivir** (bē•vēr´) to live

PRESENT PARTICIPLE **viviendo** (bē•vyen´do)

PAST PARTICIPLE **vivido** (bē•vē´tho)

PRESENT VIVO (bē´vo), **vives** (bē´ves), **vive** (bē´ve), **vivimos** (bē•vē´mos), **vivís** (bē•vēs´), **viven** (bē´ven)

FUTURE **viviré** (bē•vē•re´), **vivirás** (bē•vē•râs´), **vivirá** (bē•vē•râ´), **viviremos** (bē•vē•re´-mos), **viviréis** (bē•vē•re´ēs), **vivirán** (bē•vē•rân´)

CONDITIONAL **viviría** (bē•vē•rē´â), **vivirías** (bē•vē•re´âs), **viviría** (bē•vē•rē´â), **viviríamos** (bē•ve•rē´â•mos), **viviríais** (bē•vē•rē´âēs), **vivirían** (bē•ve•rē´ân)

PRESENT SUBJUNCTIVE **viva** (bē´vâ), **vivas** (bē´vâs), **viva** (bē´vâ), **vivamos** (bē•vâ´mos), **viváis** (bē•vâ´ēs), **vivan** (bē´vân)

IMPERFECT **vivía** (bē•vē´â), **vivías** (bē•vē´âs), **vivía** (bē•vē´â), **vivíamos** (bē•vē´â•mos), **vivíais** (bē•vē´aēs), **vivían** (bē•ve´ân)

PRETERITE **viví** (bē•vē´), **viviste** (bē•ves´te), **vivió** (bē•vyo´), **vivimos** (bē•vē´mos), **vivisteis** (bē•vēs´teēs) **vivieron** (bē•vye´ron)

PAST SUBJUNCTIVE (I) **viviese** (bē•vye´se), **vivieses** (bē•vye´ses), **viviese** (bē•vye´se), **viviésemos** (bē•vye´se•mos), **vivieseis** (bē•vye´seēs), **viviesen** (bē•vye´sen)

PAST SUBJUNCTIVE (n) **viviera** (bē•vye´râ), **vivieras** (bē•vye´râs), **viviera** (bē•vye´râ), **viviéramos** (bē•vye´râ•mos), **vivierais** (bē•vye´râes), **vivieran** (bē•vye´rân)

IMPERATIVE **vive** (bē´ve), **vivid** (bē•vēth´)

2 Irregular Verbs

The following list contains all the irregular Spanish verbs entered in this dictionary. The reader is referred to this list by an asterisk following the irregular verb at the point of entry. In the case of verb families all of whose conjugations follow one basic pattern, only one model verb is given and the others of the family are referred to the model (for example, **pertenecer** see **abastecer**.

In the conjugations offered below, only those tenses containing one or more irregular forms are given. Other tenses can be formed on the model of the regular verbs given previously.

The present subjunctive is not given when the regular subjunctive endings are used with the stem of the first-person singular of the present indicative (for example, **diga**, **digas**, **diga**, **digamos**, **digáis**, **digan** from **diga**). Since the past subjunctive is always formed with regular endings using the stem of the third-person plural of the preterite, no past subjunctive forms are given in the following list (for example, **dijera**, **dijeras**, **dijera**, **dijéramos**, **dijerais**, **dijeran** from **dijeron**). Nor are verbs given that are strictly orthographic changing (for example, **cojo** from **coger** or **venzo** from **vencer**).

Space does not permit including the pronunciation of inflected forms of irregular verbs. But comparison with the pronunciation already given for the inflected forms of regular verbs plus the rules of pronunciation set forth on pages 8-13, should enable the reader to supply his own pronunciation for the verbs listed here.

The verb forms are given in the following order: first, second, and third person singular; followed by first, second, and third person plural.

abastecer to purvey
    PRESENT **abastezco, abasteces, abastece, abastecemos, abastecéis, abastecen**
abnegar to renounce, see **cegar**
abolir to abolish, see **blandir**
aborrecer to hate, see **abastecer**
abrir, to open
    PAST PARTICIPLE **abierto**
absolver to absolve, see **volver**
abstenerse to abstain, see **tener**
abstraer to abstract, see **traer**

acaecer to happen, see acontecer
acertar to hit the mark
　PRESENT acierto, aciertas, acierta,
　acertamos, acertáis, aciertan
　PRESENT SUBJUNCTIVE acierte, acier-
　tes, acierte, acertemos, acertéis, acier-
　ten
aclocarse to brood
　PRESENT aclueco, acluecas, aclueca,
　aclocamos, aclocáis, acluecan
　PRESENT SUBJUNCTIVE aclueque,
　aclueques, aclueque, acloquemos, aclo-
　quéis, acluequen
acontecer to happen
　PRESENT SUBJUNCTIVE acontezca,
　acontezcan
　DEFECTIVE VERB: Used only in the
　third person singular and plural.
acordar to resolve, see mostrar
acostar to put to bed, see mostrar
acrecentar to increase, see acertar
acrecer to augment, see abastecer
adherir to stick, see invertir
adolecer to be ill, see abastecer
adormecer to lull to sleep see abastecer
adquirir to acquire, see inquirir
aducir to adduce, see conducir
advertir to notice, see invertir
afluir to flow, see diluir
agorar to divine
　PRESENT agüero, agüeras, agüera,
　agoramos, agoráis, agüeran
　PRESENT SUBJUNCTIVE agüere,
　agüeres, agüere, agoremos, agoréis
　agüeren
agradecer to appreciate, see abastecer
alentar to breathe, see acertar
almorzar to eat lunch, see forzar
amanecer to dawn, see abastecer
amolar to whet, see mostrar
andar to walk
PRETERITE anduve, anduviste, anduvo,
　anduvimos, anduvisteis, anduvieron
aneblar to cloud, see acertar
anochecer to grow dark, see abastecer
anteponer to prefer, see poner
apacentar to pasture, see acertar
aparecer to appear, see abastecer
apetecer to long for, see abastecer
apostar to bet, see mostrar
apretar to squeeze, see acertar
aprobar to approve, see mostrar
argüir to argue, see diluir
arrendar to rent, see acertar
arrepentirse to repent, see
invertir
ascender to ascend, see hender
asentar to seat, see acertar
asentir to acquiesce, see invertir
aserrar to saw, see acertar

asir to grasp
　PRESENT asgo, ases, ase, asimos, asís,
　asen
asolar to destroy, see mostrar
atender to heed, see hender
atenerse to depend, see tener
atentar to attempt, see acertar
atestar to stuff, see acertar
atraer to attract, see traer
atravesar to cross, see acertar
atribuir to attribute, see diluir
atronar to deafen, see mostrar
avenir to reconcile, see venir
aventar to fan, see acertar
avergonzar to shame
　PRESENT avergüenzo, avergüenzas,
　avergüenza, avergonzamos, avergonzáis,
　avergüenzan
　PRESENT SUBJUNCTIVE avergüence,
　avergüences, avergüence, avergoncemos,
　avergoncéis, avergüencen
　PRETERITE avergoncé, avergonzaste,
　avergonzó, avergonzamos, avergonzas-
　teis, avergonzaron

balbucir to stutter, see blandir
bendecir to bless
　PRESENT PARTICIPLE bendiciendo
　PRESENT bendigo, bendices, bendice,
　bendecimos, bendecís, bendicen
　PRETERITE bendije bendijiste bendijo,
　bendijimos, bendijisteis, bendijeron
bienquerer to regard highly, see querer
blandir to brandish
　DEFECTIVE VERB: Used only in forms
　whose endings begin with i.
blanquecer to blanch, see abastecer
bruñir to burnish, see plañir

caber to fit
　PRESENT quepo, cabes, cabe, cabemos,
　cabéis, caben
　FUTURE cabré, cabrás, cabrá, cabre-
　mos, cabréis, cabrán
　CONDITIONAL cabría, cabrías, cabría,
　cabríamos, cabríais, cabrían
　PRETERITE cupe, cupiste, cupo, cupi-
　mos, cupisteis, cupieron
caer to fall
　PRESENT PARTICIPLE cayendo
　PAST PARTICIPLE caído
　PRESENT caigo, caes, cae, caemos,
　caísteis, caen
　PRETERITE caí, caíste, cayó, caímos,
　caísteis, cayeron
calentar to warm, see acertar
carecer to lack, see abastecer
cegar to go blind

PRESENT ciego, ciegas, ciega, cega-
mos, cegáis, ciegan
PRESENT SUBJUNCTIVE ciegue, cie-
gues, ciegue, ceguemos, ceguéis, cie-
guen
ceñir to surround, see teñir
cerner to sift, see hender
cerrar to close, see acertar
cimentar to found, see acertar
circunscribir to circumscribe, see escribir
cocer to boil
PRESENT cuezo, cueces, cuece, coce-
mos, cocéis, cuecen
PRESENT SUBJUNCTIVE cueza, cue-
zas, cueza, cozamos, cozáis, cuezan
colar to strain, see mostrar
colgar to hang, see rogar
comedirse to restrain oneself, see pedir
comenzar to commence, see empezar
compadecer to pity, see abastecer
comparecer to appear, see abastecer
competir to contend, see pedir
complacer to please, see placer
componer to compose, see poner
comprobar to verify, see mostrar
concebir to conceive, see pedir
concernir to regard
PRESENT concierne, conciernen
DEFECTIVE VERB: Used only in the
third person singular and plural.
concertar to concert, see acertar
concluir to conclude, see diluir
concordar to accord, see mostrar
condescender to consent, see hender
condolerse to condole, see mover
conducir to convey
PRESENT conduzco, conduces, conduce, conducimos, conducís, condu-
cen
PRETERITE conduje, condujiste, con-
dujo, condujimos, condujisteis, con-
dujeron
conferir to confer, see invertir
confesar to confess, see acertar
confluir to join, see diluir
conmover to touch, see mover
conocer to know, see abastecer
conseguir to obtain, see seguir
consentir to consent to, see invertir
consolar to console, see mostrar
constituir to constitute, see diluir
constreñir to constrain, see teñir
construir to build, see diluir
contar to count, see mostrar
contender to contend, see hender
contener to contain, see tener
contorcerse to writhe, see cocer
contradecir to contradict, see decir

contraer to catch, see traer
contravenir to contravene, see venir
contribuir to contribute, see diluir
convalecer to convalesce, see abastecer
convenir to agree, see venir
convertir to transform, see invertir
corregir to correct, see elegir
costar to cost, see mostrar
crecer to grow, see abastecer
creer to believe, see leer
cubrir to cover
PAST PARTICIPLE cubierto

dar to give
PRESENT doy, das, da, damos, dais,
dan
PRESENT SUBJUNCTIVE dé, des, dé,
demos, deis, den
PRETERITE dí, diste, dio, dimos, disteis,
dieron
decaer to decay, see caer
decentar to cut the first piece of, see acertar
decir to say
PRESENT PARTICIPLE diciendo
PAST PARTICIPLE dicho
PRESENT digo, dices, dice, decimos,
decís, dicen
FUTURE diré, dirás, dirá, diremos,
diréis, dirán
CONDITIONAL diría, dirías, diría, diría-
mos, diríais, dirían
PRETERITE dije, dijiste, dijo, dijimos,
dijisteis, dijeron
IMPERATIVE di, decid
deducir to deduce, see conducir
defender to defend, see hender
degollar to behead, see agorar
demoler to demolish, see mover
demostrar to prove, see mostrar
denegar to deny, see cegar
dentar to tooth, see acertar
deponer to depose, see poner
derrengar to twist, see cegar
derretir to melt, see pedir
derruir to demolish, see diluir
desaforar to violate the rights of, see
mostrar
desalentar to wind, see acertar
desandar to retrace, see andar
desaparecer to disappear, see abastecer
desaprobar to disapprove of, see mostrar
desasir to let go of, see asir
desatender to disregard, see hender
desavenir to put at odds, see venir
descabullirse to escape, see engullir
descender to descend, see hender
descolgar to take down, see rogar
descollar to excel, see mostrar

descomedirse to be rude, see **pedir**
descomponer to decompose, see **poner**
desconcertar to disconcert, see **acertar**
desconocer to disown, see **abastecer**
desconsolar to grieve, see **mostrar**
descontar to deduct, see **mostrar**
descornar to dehorn, see **mostrar**
descreer to disbelieve, see **leer**
describir to describe, see **escribir**
descubrir to uncover, see **cubrir**
desdecir to go counter, see **decir**
desencordar to unstring, see **mostrar**
desentenderse to pretend ignorance, see **hender**
desenterrar to disinter, see **acertar**
desenvolver to unwrap, see **volver**
desfallecer to weaken, see **abastecer**
desfavorecer to disfavor, see **abastecer**
desguarnecer to strip of ornaments, see **abastecer**
deshacer to undo, see **hacer**
deshelar to thaw, see **acertar**
desherbar to weed, see **acertar**
desherrar to unchain, see **acertar**
deshumedecer to dehumidify, see **abastecer**
desleir to dissolve, see **reir**
deslucir to offset, see **lucir**
desmembrar to dismember, see **acertar**
desmentir to contradict, see **invertir**
desmerecer to be unworthy of, see **abastecer**
desobedecer to disobey, see **abastecer**
desolar to desolate, see **mostrar**
desollar to skin, see **mostrar**
desovar to spawn, see **mostrar**
despedir to dismiss, see **pedir**
despertar to wake, see **acertar**
desplegar to unfold, see **cegar**
despoblar to depopulate, see **mostrar**
desposeer to dispossess, see **leer**
desteñir to discolor, see **teñir**
desterrar to banish, see **acertar**
destituir to deprive, see **diluir**
destruir to destroy, see **diluir**
desvanecer to dispel, see **abastecer**
detener to stop, see **tener**
devolver to return, see **volver**
diferir to defer, see **invertir**
digerir to digest, see **invertir**
diluir to dilute
    PRESENT PARTICIPLE diluyendo
    PRESENT diluyo diluyes, diluye, diluimos, diluís, diluyen
    PRETERITE diluí, diluiste, diluyó, diluimos, diluisteis, diluyeron
discernir to discern
    PRESENT discierno, disciernes, discierne, discernimos, discernís, disciernen
    PRESENT SUBJUNCTIVE discierna, discier-

nas, discierna, discernamos, discernáis, disciernan
discordar to disagree, see **mostrar**
disentir to dissent, see **invertir**
disolver to dissolve, see **volver**
disonar to be in disharmony, see **mostrar**
disponer to dispose, see **poner**
distender to distend, see **hender**
distraer to distract, see **traer**
distribuir to distribute, see **diluir**
divertir to amuse, see **invertir**
doler to hurt, see **mover**
dormir to sleep
    PRESENT PARTICIPLE durmiendo
    PRESENT duermo, duermes, duerme, dormimos, dormís, duermen
    PRESENT SUBJUNCTIVE duerma, duermas, duerma, durmamos, durmáis, duerman
    PRETERITE dormí, dormiste, durmió, dormimos, dormisteis, durmieron

elegir to choose
    PRESENT PARTICIPLE eligiendo
    PRESENT elijo, eliges, elige, elegimos, elegís, eligen
    PRETERITE elegí, elegiste, eligió, elegimos, elegisteis, eligieron
embellecer to embellish, see **abastecer**
embestir to attack, see **pedir**
emblandecer to soften, see **abastecer**
embobecer to stupefy, see **abastecer**
embrutecer to make brutish, see **abastecer**
emparentar to become related by marriage, see **acertar**
empedernir to harden, see **blandir**
empedrar to pave with stones, see **acertar**
empequeñecer to belittle, see **abastecer**
empezar to begin
    PRESENT empiezo, empiezas, empieza, empezamos, empezáis, empiezan
    PRESENT SUBJUNCTIVE empiece, empieces, empiece, empecemos, empecéis, empiecen
    PRETERITE empecé, empezaste, empezó, empezamos, empezasteis, empezaron
emplumecer to grow feathers, see **abastecer**
empobrecer to impoverish, see **abastecer**
emporcar to soil, see **aclocarse**
enaltecer to praise, see **abastecer**
enardecer to inflame, see **abastecer**
encalvecer to get bald, see **abastecer**
encandecer to bring to a white heat, see **abastecer**
encanecer to turn gray, see **abastecer**
encarecer to raise the price of, see **abastecer**

encender to light, see **hender**
encerrar to confine, see **acertar**
encomendar to recommend, see **acertar**
encontrar to meet, see **mostrar**
encorar to heal, see **mostrar**
encrudecer to exasperate, see **abastecer**
endurecer to harden, see **abastecer**
enflaquecer to weaken, see **abastecer**
enfurecer to infuriate, see **abastecer**
engrandecer to augment, see **abastecer**
engreir to make proud, see **reir**
engrosar to thicken, see **mostrar**
engullir to gobble up
  PRESENT PARTICIPLE **engullendo**
  PRETERITE **engullí, engulliste, engulló,**
  engullimos, engullisteis, engulleron
enloquecer to madden, see **abastecer**
enmendar to correct, see **acertar**
enmohecer to mold, see **abastecer**
enmudecer to silence, see **abastecer**
ennegrecer to blacken, see **abastecer**
ennoblecer to ennoble, see **abastecer**
enorgullecer to fill with pride, see **abaste-**
  cer
enriquecer to enrich, see **abastecer**
enrojecer to redden, see **abastecer**
enronquecer to make hoarse, see **abaste-**
  cer
ensangrentar to bloody, see **acertar**
ensordecer to deafen, see **abastecer**
entender to understand, see **hender**
enternecer to soften, see **abastecer**
enterrar to inter, see **acertar**
entontecer to stupefy, see **abastecer**
entorpecer to dull, see **abastecer**
entreabrir to leave ajar, see **abrir**
entreoír to barely hear, see **oir**
entretener to amuse, see **tener**
entrever to catch a glimpse of, see **ver**
entristecer to sadden, see **abastecer**
entullecerse to be crippled, see **abastecer**
entumecer to numb, see **abastecer**
envanecer to make vain, see **abastecer**
envejecer to age, see **abastecer**
envestir to invest, see **pedir**
envilecer to degrade, see **abastecer**
envolver to involve, see **volver**
equivaler to be of equal value, see **salir**
erguir to raise
  PRESENT PARTICIPLE **irguiendo**
  PRESENT **yergo** or **irgo, yergues** or
  irgues, yergue or **irgue, erguimos,**
  erguís, yerguen or **irguen**
  PRESENT SUBJUNCTIVE **yerga** or **irga,**
  yergas or **irgas, yerga** or **irga, irgamos,**
  igáis, yergan or **irgan**
  PRETERITE **erguí, erguiste, erguimos,**
  erguisteis, irguieron
errar to miss
  PRESENT **yerro, yerras, yerra, erramos,**

  erráis, yerran
  PRESENT SUBJUNCTIVE **yerre, yerres,**
  yerre, erremos, erréis, yerren
escabullirse to escape, see **engullir**
escarmentar to take warning, see **acertar**
escarnecer to mock, see **abastecer**
esclarecer to illuminate, see **abastecer**
escribir to write
  PAST PARTICIPLE **escrito**
esforzar to strengthen, see **forzar**
establecer to establish, see **abastecer**
estar to be
  PRESENT **estoy, estás, está, estamos,**
  estáis, están
  PRESENT SUBJUNCTIVE **esté, estés, esté,**
  estemos, estéis, estén
  PRETERITE **estuve, estuviste, estuvo,**
  estuvimos, estuvisteis, estuvieron
estatuir to establish, see **diluir**
estregar to rub, see **cegar**
estremecer to shake, see **abastecer**
estreñir to constipate, see **teñir**
excluir to exclude, see **diluir**
expedir to expedite, see **pedir**
exponer to expose, see **poner**
extender to extend, see **hender**
extraer to extract, see **traer**

fallecer to die, see **abastecer**
favorecer to favor, see **abastecer**
fenecer to finish, see **abastecer**
florecer to blossom, see **abastecer**
fluir to flow, see **diluir**
fortalecer to fortify, see **abastecer**
forzar to force
  PRESENT **fuerzo, fuerzas, fuerza,**
  forzamos, forzáis, fuerzan
  PRESENT SUBJUNCTIVE **fuerce, fuer-**
  ces, fuerce, forcemos, forcéis, fuercen
  PRETERITE **forcé, forzaste, forzó, forza-**
  mos, forzasteis, forzaron
fregar to scrub, see **cegar**
freir to fry
  PRESENT PARTICIPLE **friendo**
  PAST PARTICIPLE **frito**
  PRESENT **frío, fríes, fríe, freímos, freís,**
  fríen
  PRETERITE **freí, freíste, frió, freímos,**
  freísteis, frieron

garantir to guarantee, see **blandir**
gemir to groan, see **pedir**
gobernar to govern, see **acertar**
gruñir to grunt, see **plañir**
guarnecer to set, see **abastecer**

haber to have

PRESENT **he, has, ha, hemos, habéis, han**
FUTURE **habré, habrás, habrá, habremos, habréis, habran**
CONDITIONAL **habría, habrías, habría, habríamos, habríais, habrían**
PRESENT SUBJUNCTIVE **haya, hayas, haya, hayamos, hayáis , hayan**
PRETERITE **hube, hubiste, hubo, hubimos, hubisteis hubieron**
IMPERATIVE **hé, habed,**
hacer to make, to do
PAST PARTICIPLE **hecho**
PRESENT **hago, haces, hace, hacemos, hacéis, hacen**
FUTURE **haré, harás, hará, haremos, haréis, harán**
CONDITIONAL **haría, harías, haría, haríamos, haríais, harían**
PRETERITE **hice, hiciste, hizo, hicimos, hicisteis, hicieron**
IMPERATIVE **haz, haced**
heder to smell bad, see **hender**
helar to freeze, see **acertar**
henchir to fill, see **pedir**
hender to split
PRESENT **hiendo, hiendes, hiende, hendemos, hendéis, hienden**
PRESENT SUBJUNCTIVE **hienda, hiendas, hienda, hendamos, hendáis, hiendan**
herir to wound, see **invertir**
herrar to shoe, see **acertar**
hervir to boil, see **invertir**
holgar to rest, see **rogar**
hollar to trample, see **mostrar**
huir to flee, see **diluir**
humedecer to moisten, see **abastecer**

imbuir to imbue, see **diluir**
impedir to impede, see **pedir**
imponer to impose, see **poner**
incluir to include, see **diluir**
indisponer to indispose, see **poner**
inducir to induce, see **conducir**
inferir to infer, see **invertir**
influir to influence, see **diluir**
ingerir to ingest, see **invertir**
inquirir to investigate
PRESENT **inquiero, inquieres, inquiere, inquirimos, inquirís, inquieren**
PRESENT SUBJUNCTIVE **inquiera, inquieras, inquiera, inquiramos, inquiráis, inquieran**
inscribir to inscribe, see **escribir**
instituir to institute, see **diluir**
instruir to instruct, see **diluir**
interponer to interpose, see **poner**
intervenir to happen, see **venir**

introducir to introduce, see **conducir**
invertir to invert
PRESENT PARTICIPLE **invirtiendo**
PRESENT **invierto, inviertes, invierte, invertimos, invertís, invierten**
PRESENT SUBJUNCTIVE **invierta, inviertas, invierta, invirtamos, invirtáis, inviertan**
PRETERITE **invertí, invertiste, invirtió, invertimos, invertisteis, invirtieron**
investir to invest, see **pedir**
ir to go
PRESENT PARTICIPLE **yendo**
PRESENT **voy, vas, va, vamos, vais, van**
PRESENT SUBJUNCTIVE **vaya, vayas, vaya, vayamos, vayáis, vayan**
IMPERFECT **iba, ibas, iba, íbamos, ibais, iban**
PRETERITE **fui, fuiste, fue, fuimos, fuisteis, fueron**
IMPERATIVE **vé, id**

jugar to play
PRESENT **juego, juegas, juega, jugamos, jugáis, juegan**
PRESENT SUBJUNCTIVE **juegue, juegues, juegue, juguemos, juguéis, jueguen**

languidecer to languish, see **abastecer**
leer to read
PRESENT PARTICIPLE **leyendo**
PAST PARTICIPLE **leído**
PRETERITE **leí, leíste, leyó, leímos, leísteis, leyeron**
lucir to shine
PRESENT **luzco, luces, luce, lucimos, lucís, lucen**
llover to rain, see **mover**

maldecir to curse, see **bendecir**
malquerer to have a grudge against, see **querer**
manifestar to manifest, see **acertar**
mantener to maintain, see **tener**
medir to measure, see **pedir**
mentar to mention, see **acertar**
mentir to lie, see **invertir**
merecer to deserve, see **abastecer**
merendar to have a snack, see **acertar**
moler to grind, see **mover**
morder to bite, see **mover**
morir to die
PRESENT PARTICIPLE **muriendo**
PAST PARTICIPLE **muerto**
PRESENT **muero, mueres, muere, morimos, morís, mueren**
PRESENT SUBJUNCTIVE **muera, mue**

ras, muera, muramos, muráis, mueran
PRETERITE morí, moriste, murió, morimos, moristeis, murieron
mostrar to show
PRESENT muestro, muestras, muestra, mostramos, mostráis, muestran
PRESENT SUBJUNCTIVE muestre, muestres, muestre, mostremos, mostréis, muestren
mover to move
PRESENT muevo, mueves, mueve, movemos, movéis, mueven
PRESENT SUBJUNCTIVE mueva, muevas, mueva, movamos, mováis, muevan
mullir to fluff up, see engullir

nacer to be born, see abastecer
negar to deny, see cegar
nevar to snow, see acertar

obedecer to obey, see abastecer
obstruir to obstruct, see diluir
obtener to obtain, see tener
ofrecer to offer, see abastecer
oir to hear
PRESENT PARTICIPLE oyendo
PAST PARTICIPLE oído
PRESENT oigo, oyes, oye, oímos, oís, oyen
PRETERITE oí, oíste, oyó, oímos, oísteis, oyeron
IMPERATIVE oye, oíd
oler to smell
PRESENT huelo, hueles, huele, olemos, oléis, huelen
PRESENT SUBJUNCTIVE huela, huelas, huela, olamos, oláis, huelan
oponer to oppose, see poner
oscurecer to darken, see abastecer

pacer to pasture, see abastecer
padecer to suffer, see abastecer
palidecer to turn pale, see abastecer
parecer to appear, see abastecer
pedir to ask
PRESENT PARTICIPLE pidiendo
PRESENT pido, pides, pide, pedimos, pedís, piden
PRETERITE pedí, pediste, pidió, pedimos,pedisteis, pidieron
pensar to think, see acertar
perder to lose, see hender
perecer to perish, see abastecer
permanecer to remain, see abastecer
perseguir to persecute, see seguir
pertenecer to belong, see abastecer
pervertir to pervert, see invertir
placer to please

PRESENT plazco, places, place, placemos, placéis, placen
PRETERITE placé, placiste, plació or plugo, placimos, placisteis, placieron or pluguieron
PAST SUBJUNCTIVE placiera, placieras, placiera or pluguiera, placiéramos, placierais, placieran
plañir to lament
PRESENT PARTICIPLE plañendo
PRETERITE plañí, plañiste, plañó, plañimos, plañisteis, plañeron
plegar to fold, see cegar
poblar to populate, see mostrar
poder to be able
PRESENT PARTICIPLE pudiendo
PRESENT puedo, puedes, puede, podemos, podéis, pueden
FUTURE podré, podrás, podrá, podremos, podréis, podrán
CONDITIONAL podría, podrías, podría, podríamos, podríais, podrían
PRESENT SUBJUNCTIVE pueda, puedas, pueda, podamos, podáis, puedan
PRETERITE pude, pudiste, pudo, pudimos, pudisteis, pudieron
podrir to rot, see pudrir
poner to put
PAST PARTICIPLE puesto
PRESENT pongo, pones, pone, ponemos, ponéis, ponen
FUTURE pondré, pondrás, pondrá, pondremos, pondréis, pondrán
CONDITIONAL pondría, pondrías, pondría, pondríamos, pondríais, pondrían
PRETERITE puse, pusiste, puso, pusimos, pusisteis, pusieron
IMPERATIVE pon, poned
poseer to possess, see leer
posponer to postpone, see poner
predecir to foretell, see decir
predisponer to predispose, see poner
preferir to prefer, see invertir
prescribir to prescribe, see escribir
presentir to have a premonition of, see invertir
presuponer to presuppose, see poner
prevalecer to prevail, see abastecer
prevenir to prepare, see venir
prever to foresee, see ver
probar to try, see mostrar
producir to produce, see conducir
proferir to utter, see invertir
promover to promote, see mover
proponer to propose, see poner
proscribir to exile, see escribir
proseguir to pursue, see seguir
proveer to provide, see leer
provenir to arise, see venir
pudrir to putrefy

Conjugation of Verbs

PAST PARTICIPLE **podrido**

quebrar to break, see **acertar**
querer to wish
  PRESENT **quiero, quieres, quiere, queremos, queréis, quieren**
  FUTURE **querré, querrás, querrá, querremos, querréis, querrán**
  CONDITIONAL **querría, querrías, querría, querríamos, querríais, querrían**
  PRESENT SUBJUNCTIVE **quiera, quieras, quiera, queramos, queráis, quieran**
  PRETERITE **quise, quisiste, quiso, quisimos, quisisteis, quisieron**

reaparecer to reappear, see **abastecer**
recaer to fall back, see **caer**
recalentar to reheat, see **acertar**
recluir to shut in, see **diluir**
recomendar to recommend, see **acertar**
reconocer to recognize, see **abastecer**
reconstruir to reconstruct, see **diluir**
reconvenir to retort with, see **venir**
recordar to remember, see **acertar**
recostar to lean, see **mostrar**
recrudecer to flare up, see **abastecer**
recubrir to cover, see **cubrir**
reducir to reduce, see **conducir**
reelegir to reelect, see **elegir**
referir to refer, see **invertir**
reforzar to strengthen, see **forzar**
regar to water, see **cegar**
regir to rule, see **elegir**
rehacer to repair, see **hacer**
rehuir to avoid, see **diluir**
reir to laugh
  PRESENT PARTICIPLE **riendo**
  PAST PARTICIPLE **reído**
  PRESENT **río, ríes, ríe, reímos, reís, ríen**
  PRETERITE **reí, reíste, rió, reímos, reísteis, rieron**
rejuvenecer to rejuvenate, see **abastecer**
relucir to shine, see **lucir**
remendar to repair, see **acertar**
remover to remove, see **mover**
renacer to be born again, see **abastecer**
rendir to yield, see **pedir**
renegar to deny, see **cegar**
renovar to renovate, see **mostrar**
reñir to wrangle, see **teñir**
repetir to repeat, see **pedir**
reponer to replace, see **poner**
reprobar to fail, see **mostrar**
reproducir to reproduce, see **conducir**
requerir to notify, see **invertir**
resentirse to weaken, see **invertir**
resolver to resolve, see **volver**
resollar to breathe hard, see **mostrar**
resonar to resound, see **mostrar**
resplandecer to shine, see **abastecer**

resquebrar to start to break, see **acertar**
restablecer to restore, see **abastecer**
restituir to restore, see **diluir**
restregar to scrub hard, see **cegar**
restriñir to constrict, see **plañir**
retener to retain, see **tener**
retorcer to twist, see **cocer**
retraer to bring back, see **traer**
retribuir to repay, see **diluir**
reventar to break, see **acertar**
reverdecer to grow green again, see **abastecer**
revestir to don, see **pedir**
revolcarse to wallow, see **aclocarse**
revolver to shake, see **volver**
robustecer to strengthen, see **abastecer**
rodar to roll, see **mostrar**
roer to gnaw
  PRESENT PARTICIPLE **royendo**
  PAST PARTICIPLE **roído**
  PRESENT **roo** or **roigo** or **royo, roes, roe, roemos, roéis, roen**
  PRESENT SUBJUNCTIVE **roa, roiga** or **roya, roas, roa, roamos, roáis, roan**
  PRETERITE **roí, roíste, royó, roímos, roísteis, royeron**
rogar to entreat
  PRESENT **ruego, ruegas, ruega, rogamos, rogáis, ruegan**
  PRESENT SUBJUNCTIVE **ruegue, ruegues, ruegue, roguemos, roguéis, rueguen**
romper to break
  PAST PARTICIPLE **roto**

saber to know
  PRESENT **sé, sabes, sabe, sabemos, sabéis, saben**
  FUTURE **sabré, sabrás, sabrá, sabremos, sabréis, sabrán**
  CONDITIONAL **sabría, sabrías, sabría, sabríamos, sabríais, sabrían**
  PRESENT SUBJUNCTIVE **sepa, sepas, sepa, sepamos, sepáis, sepan**
  PRETERITE **supe, supiste, supo, supimos, supisteis, supieron**
salir to go out
  PRESENT **salgo, sales, sale, salimos, salís, salen**
  FUTURE **saldré, saldrás, saldrá, saldremos, saldréis, saldrán**
  CONDITIONAL **saldría, saldrías, saldría, saldríamos, saldríais, saldría**
  IMPERATIVE **sal, salid**
satisfacer to satisfy, see **hacer**
seducir to seduce, see **conducir**
segar to reap, see **cegar**
seguir to follow
  PRESENT **sigo, sigues, sigue, seguimos, seguís, siguen**

PRETERITE seguí, seguiste, siguió, seguimos, seguisteis, siguieron

sembrar to sow, see **acertar**

sementar to seed, see **acertar**

sentar to seat, see **acertar**

sentir to feel, see **invertir**

ser to be
PRESENT **soy, eres, es, somos, sois, son**
PRESENT SUBJUNCTIVE **sea, seas, sea, seamos, seáis, sean**
IMPERFECT **era, eras, era, éramos, erais, eran**
PRETERITE **fui, fuiste, fue, fuimos, fuisteis, fueron**
IMPERATIVE **sé, sed**

servir to serve, see **invertir**

sobrentender to understand, see **hender**

sobreponer to superimpose, see **poner**

sobresalir to excel, see **salir**

sobrevenir to happen unexpectedly, see **venir**

solar to put a floor in, see **mostrar**

soldar to solder, see **mostrar**

soler to be accustomed to, see **mover**

soltar to untie, see **mostrar**

sonar to sound, see **mostrar**

sonreír to smile, see **reír**

soñar to dream, see **mostrar**

sorber to sip, see **mover**

sosegar to calm, see **cegar**

sostener to sustain, see **tener**

subarrendar to sublet, see **acertar**

sugerir to suggest, see **invertir**

suponer to suppose, see **poner**

sustituir to replace, see **diluir**

sustraer to subtract, see **traer**

tañer to play, see **plañir**

temblar to tremble, see **acertar**

tender to stretch out, see **hender**

tener to have
PRESENT **tengo, tienes, tiene, tenemos, tenéis, tienen**
FUTURE **tendré, tendrás, tendrá, tendremos, tendréis, tendrán**
CONDITIONAL **tendría, tendrías, tendría, tendríamos, tendríais, tendrían**
PRETERITE **tuve, tuviste, tuvo, tuvimos, tuvisteis, tuvieron**
IMPERATIVE **ten, tened**

tentar to touch, see **acertar**

teñir to dye
PRESENT PARTICIPLE **tiñiendo**
PRESENT **tiño, tiñes, tiñe, teñimos, teñís, tiñen**
PRETERITE **teñí, teñiste, tiñó, teñimos, teñisteis, tiñeron**

torcer to twist, see **cocer**

tostar to toast, see **mostrar**

traducir to translate, see **conducir**

traer to bring
PRESENT PARTICIPLE **trayendo**
PAST PARTICIPLE **traído**
PRESENT **traigo, traes, trae, traemos, traéis, traen**
IMPERFECT **traía, traías, traía, traíamos, traíais, traían**
PRETERITE **traje, trajiste, trajo, trajimos, trajisteis, trajeron**

trascender to spread, see **hender**

trascribir to transcribe, see **escribir**

trasferir to transfer, see **invertir**

traslucirse to be transparent, see **lucir**

trasponer to transfer, see **poner**

trocar to exchange, see **aclocarse**

tronar to thunder, see **mostrar**

tropezar to stumble, see **empezar**

valer to be worth, see **salir**

venir to arrive
PRESENT PARTICIPLE **viniendo**
PRESENT **vengo, vienes, viene, venimos, venís, vienen**
FUTURE **vendré, vendrás, vendrá, vendremos, vendréis, vendrán**
CONDITIONAL **vendría, vendrías, vendría, vendríamos, vendríais, vendrían**
PRETERITE **vine, viniste, vino, vinimos, vinisteis, vinieron**
IMPERATIVE **ven, venid**

ver to see
PAST PARTICIPLE **visto**
PRESENT **veo, ves, ve, vemos, veis, ven**
IMPERFECT **veía, veías, veía, veíamos, veíais, veían**
PRETERITE **vi, viste, vio, vimos, visteis, vieron**

verter to spill, see **hender**

vestir to clothe, see **pedir**

volar to fly, see **mostrar**

volcar to upset, see **aclocarse**

volver to return
PAST PARTICIPLE **vuelto**
PRESENT **vuelvo, vuelves, vuelve, volvemos, volvéis, vuelven**
PRESENT SUBJUNCTIVE **vuelva, vuelvas, vuelva, volvamos, volváis, vuelvan**

yacer to lie
PRESENT **yazco or yazgo or yago, yaces, yace, yacemos, yacéis, yacen**
PRESENT SUBJUNCTIVE **yazca or yazga or yaga, yazcas, yazca, yazcamos, yazcáis, yazcan**
IMPERATIVE **yaz or yace, yaced**

zambullirse to dive, see **engullir**

23

PART I

SPANISH – ENGLISH

ESPAÑOL - INGLÉS

ABBREVIATIONS

adj.	adjective, *adjetivo*	min.	mining, *minería*
adv.	adverb, *adverbio*	mus,	music, *música*
avi.	aviation, *aviación*	n.	noun, *sustantivo*
agr.	agriculture, *agricultura*	naut.	nautical, *náutico* or
anat.	anatomy, *anatomía*		*marino*
arch,	architecture, *arquitectura*	orn.	ornithology, *ornitología*
Arg.	Argentina, *Argentina*	phot.	photography, *fotografía*
art.	article, *artículo*	phy.	physics, *física*
ast.	astronomy, *astronomía*	pl.	plural, *plural*
auto.	automobile, *automóvil*	poet.	poetry, *poética*
biol.	biology, *biología*	pol.	politics, *política*
Bol.	Bolivia, *Bolivia*	p.p.·	past participle, *participio*
bot.	botany, *botánica*		*pasado*
chem.	chemistry, *química*	P.R.	Puerto Rico, *Puerto Rico*
Col.	Columbia, *Colombia*	prep.	preposition, *preposición*
coll.	colloquial, *familiar*	print,	printing, *imprenta*
com.	commerce, *comercio*	pron.	pronoun, *pronombre*
conj.	conjunction, *conjunción*	rad.	radio, *radiocomunicación*
dent.	dentistry, *dentistería*	rail.	railway, *ferrocarril*
eccl.	ecclesiastic, *eclesiástico*	rhet.	rhetoric, *retórica*
Ecu.	Ecuador, *Ecuador*	sing.	singular, *singular*
elec.	electricity, *electricidad*	Sp.Am.	Spanish America,
ent.	entomology, *entomología*		*Hispanoamérica*
f.	feminine, *femenino*	theat.	theater, *teatro*
fig.	figurative(ly), *figurado*	TV.	television, *televisión*
geog.	geography, *geografía*	Urug.	Uruguay, *Uruguay*
geol.	geology, *geología*	v.	verb, *verbo*
gram.	grammar, *gramática*	va.	transitive verb, *verbo*
Guat.	Guatemala, *Guatemala*		*activo*
ichth.	ichthyology, *ictiología*	Ven.	Venezuela, *Venezuela*
inter/.	interjection, *interjección*	vet.	veterinary, *veterinaria*
interr.	interrogative, *interrogativo*	vi., vn.	intransitive verb, *verbo*
m.	masculine, *masculino*		*neutro*
math.	mathematics, *matemáticas*	vr.	reflexive verb, *verbo*
mech.	mechanics, *mecánica*		*reflexivo*
med.	medicine, *medicina*	vt.	transitive verb, *verbo*
Mex.	Mexico, *Méjico*		*activo*
mil.	military art, *milicia*	zool.	zoology, *zoología*

Spanish-English

A

a, (â) *prep.* to; in, at *(lugar);* according to *(según);* by, through *(por);* for *(para);* toward *(hacia);* with *(con);* — **pie,** on foot; — **mi izquierda,** on my left.

ab.: abad, abbot.

ábaco, (á′vâ·ko) *m.* abacus.

abad, (â·vâth′) *m.* abbot.

abadejo, (â·vâ·the′ho) *m.* codfish *(bacalao);* yellow wren *(reyezuelo);* Spanish fly *(cantárida).*

abadía, (â·vâ·the′â) *f.* abbey; abbacy *(dignidad).*

abajo, (â·vâ′ho) *adv.* under, underneath, below; downstairs; **calle —,** down the street; **hacia —,** downward.

abalorio, (â·vâ·lo′ryo) *m.* glass bead.

abanderado, (â·van·de·râ′tho) *m.* (mil.) ensign, standard bearer.

abanderar, (â·vân·de·râr′) *va.* to register.

abandonamiento, (â·vân·do·nâ·myen′to) *m.* abandonment; carelessness *(descuido);* debauchery *(vicio).*

abandonar, (â·van·do·nâr′) *va.* to abandon, to desert, to leave; **—se,** to despond, to despair.

abandono, (â·van·do′no) *m.* abandonment, carelessness *(descuido);* loneliness *(soledad);* debauchery *(vicio).*

abanicar, (â·vâ·nê·kâr′) *va.* to fan.

abanico, (â·vâ·nê′ko) *m.* fan: small crane, derrick *(cabria);* — **neumático,** suction fan.

abaratar, (â·vâ·râ·tar′) *va.* to cheapen, to reduce in cost.

abarcar, (â·vâr·kâr′) *va.* to clasp, to em-brace *(ceñir);* to contain, to comprise *(entrañar).*

abarrancadero, (â·vâ·rrâng·kâ·the′ro) *m.* boggy place *(atascadero);* precipice *(risco);* predicament *(estorbo).*

abarrancar, (â·va·rrâng·kâr′) *va.* to dig holes; **—se,** to get into a tight fix, to get into a predicament.

abarrote, (â·vâ·rro′te) *m.* (naut.) small wedge; **—s,** *pl.* groceries; **tienda de —s,** grocery store.

abastecedor, ra, (â·vâs·te·se·thor′, râ) *n.* purveyor, caterer.

abastecer*, (â·vâs·te·ser′) *va.* to purvey, to supply.

abastecimiento, (â·vas·te·sê·myen′to) *m.* provisioning, supplying with provisions.

abate, (â·vâ′te) *m.* abbé.

abatimiento, (â·vâ·tê·myen′to) *m.* low spirits, depression.

abatir, (â·vâ·têr′) *va.* to tear down, to knock down *(derribar);* to take down, to take apart *(desarmar);* to lower *(bajar);* to humble *(humillar);* to depress *(desanimar);* —, *vn. to* descend, to go down; **—se,** to be dejected or crestfallen *(humillarse);* to abate *(disminuir).*

abdicación, (âv·thê·kâ·syon′) *f.* abdication.

abdicar, (âv·thê·kâr′) *va.* to abdicate.

abdomen, (âv·tho′men) *m.* abdomen.

abecé, (â·ve·se′) *m.* ABC′s, alphabet.

abecedario, (â·ve·se·thá′ryo) *m.* alphabet; spelling book, primer *(librito).*

abedul, (â·ve·thũl′) *m.* birch tree.

abeja, (â·ve′hâ) *f.* bee; — **maestra** or

â arm, **e** they, **ē** bē, **o** fore, **ū** blūe, **b** bad, **ch** chip, **d** day, **f** fat, **g** go, **h** hot, **k** kid, **l** let **m** met, **n** not, **p** pot, **r** very, **rr** (none), **s** so, **t** toy, **th** with, **v** eve, **w** we, **y** yes, **z** zero

madre, queen bee.

abejar, (â·ve·hâr´) *m.* beehive.

abejarrón (â·ve·hâ·rron´) or abejorro, (â·ve·ho´rro) *m.* cockchafer *(coleóptero);* bumblebee *(himenóptero).*

abejero, (â·ve·he´ro) *m.* beekeeper.

abejón, (â·ve·hon´) *m.* hornet; drone *(zángano).*

aberración, (â·ve·rrâ·syon´) *f.* aberration.

abertura, (â·ver·tū´râ) *f.* cleft, opening.

abeto, (â·ve´to) *m.* fir tree.

abierto, ta, (â·vyer´to, tâ) *adj.* open; sincere, frank *(sincero).*

abigarrado, da, (â·vē·gâ·rrâ´tho, thâ) *adj.* flecked, dappled.

abigarrar, (â·vē·gâ·rrâr´) *va.* to variegate, to dapple.

abismar, (â·vēz·mâr´) *va.* to throw into an abyss; to depress *(deprimir);* to humble *(humillar);* to confound *(confundir);* — se, (Sp. Am.) to be astonished.

abismo, (â·vēz´mo) *m.* chasm, abyss, gulf; hell *(infierno).*

abjurar, (âv·hū·râr´) *va.* to abjure, to recant upon oath.

ablandamiento, (â·vlân·dâ·myen´to) *m.* mollification, softening.

ablandar, (â·vlân·dâr´) *va.* and *vn.* to mollify, to soften.

ablativo, (â·vlâ·tē´vo) *m.* (gram) ablative.

abnegación, (ây·ne·gâ·syon´) *f.* abnegation, self-denial.

abnegar*, (ây·ne·gâr´) *va.* to renounce.

abobar, (â·vo·vâr´) *va.* to stupefy.

abochornar, (â·vo·chor·nâr´) *va.* to swelter, to overheat *(sobrecalentar);* to mortify *(avergonzar);* —se, to be embarrassed, to blush *(sonrojarse);* to be sweltering *(padecer del calor).*

abofetear, (â·vo·fe·te·âr´) *va.* to slap one's face.

abogacía, (â·vo·gâ·sē´â) *f.* legal profession.

abogado, (â·vo·gâ´tho) *m.* lawyer; advocate, mediator *(defensor).*

abogar, (â·vo·gâr´) *vn.* to mediate, to intercede.

abolengo, (â·vo·leng´go) *m.* ancestry; inheritance *(patrimonio).*

abolición, (â·vo·lē·syon´) *f.* abolition, abrogation.

abolicionista, (â·vo·lē·syo·nēs´tâ) *m.* abolitionist.

abolir*, (â·vo·lēr´) *va.* to abolish.

abolladura, (â·vo·yâ·thū´râ) *f.* dent; embossing *(realce).*

abollar, (â·vo·yâr´) *va.* to dent; to emboss *(realzar).*

abombado, da, (â·vom·bâ´tho, thâ) *adj.*

stunned, confused.

abombarse, (â·vom·bâr´se) *vr.* to begin to spoil or decompose (foods).

abominable, (â·vo·mē·nâ´vle) *adj.* abominable.

abominación, (â·vo·mē·nâ·syon´) *f.* abomination.

abominar, (â·vo·mē·nâr´) *va.* to abominate, to detest.

abonar, (â·vo·nâr´) *va.* to improve *(mejorar);* to make good an assertion *(acertar);* to fertilize *(fertilizar);* (com.) to credit *(acreditar);* to pay (on an account); —se, to subscribe to; — en cuenta, to credit to one's account.

abonaré, (â·vo·nâ·re´) *m.* (com.) check, promissory note, due bill.

abono, (â·vo´no) *m.* fertilizer *(fertilizante);* (com.) payment, installment *(pago);* season ticket (to a theatre) *(suscripción);* — de pasaje, commutation ticket.

abordar, (â·vor·thâr´) *va.* (naut.) to come alongside; to broach, to take up *(entablar);* —, *vn.* to put into port, to dock, to land.

aborigen, (â·vo·rē´hen) *adj.* aboriginal, indigenous; —, *m.* aborigine.

aborrecer*, (â·vo·rre·ser´) *va.* to hate, to abhor; to abandon, to desert *(las aves).*

aborrecimiento, (â·vo·rre·sē·myen´to) *m.* abhorrence, hatred.

abortar, (â·vor·târ´) *vn.* to miscarry, to have an abortion.

aborto, (â·vor´to) *m.* miscarriage, abortion.

abotonar, (â·vo·to·nâr´) *va.* and *vr.* to button; —, *vn.* to bud.

abovedar, (â·vo·ve·thâr´) *va.* to arch, to vault.

abr.: abreviatura, abbr. abbreviation.

abrasador, ra, (â·vrâ·sâ·thor´, râ) *adj.* burning, very hot.

abrasar, (â·vrâ·sâr´) *va.* to burn, to scorch *(quemar);* to parch *(secar);* tierra abrasada, scorched earth.

abrazadera, (â·vrâ·sâ·the´râ) *f.* bracket *(corchete);* loop *(sortija);* binding *(atadura).*

abrazar, (â·vrâ·sâr´) *va.* to embrace, to hug; to surround *(rodear);* to comprise, to contain *(entrañar).*

abrazo, (â·vrâ´so) *m.* embrace, hug.

abrebrechas, (â·vre·vre´châs) *m.* bulldozer.

abrelatas, (â·vre·lâ´tâs) *m.* can opener.

abrevadero, (â·vre·vâ·the´ro) *m.* watering place for cattle.

abreviación, (â·vre·vyâ·syon´) *f.* abbreviation, abridgment, shortening.

abreviar, (â·vre·vyâr´) va. to abridge, to cut short *(acortar);* to accelerate *(acelerar).*

abreviatura, (â·vre·vyâ·tū´râ) f. abbreviation.

abridor, (â·vrē·thor´) m. opener; **— de latas,** can opener.

abrigar, (â·vrē·gâr´) va. to shelter, to protect *(amparar);* to hold, to cherish *(tener);* **— la esperanza,** to hope; **—se,** to take shelter *(refugiarse);* to protect oneself against the cold *(arroparse).*

abrigo, (â·vrē´go) m. shelter, protection, aid *(amparo);* wrap, overcoat *(sobretodo);* **— de pieles,** fur coat.

abril, (â·vrēl´) m. April.

abrillantar, (a·vrē·yân·târ´) va. to cut, to face; to give luster to, to make brilliant *(iluminar).*

abrir*, (â·vrēr´) va. and vr. to open; to unlock, to open up *(soltar);* to disclose, to reveal *(descubrir).*

abrochador, (â·vro·châ·thor´) m. buttonhook.

abrochar, (a·vro·châr´) va. to button on, to clasp on.

abrojo, (â·vro´ho) m. (bot.) thistle, thorn; (mil.) caltrop; **—s,** pl. hidden rocks in the sea.

abrumador, ra, (â·vrū·mâ·thor´, râ) adj. troublesome, annoying *(fastidioso);* overwhelming *(agobiador).*

abrumar, (â·vrū·mâr´) va. to overwhelm *(agobiar);* to importune *(molestar).*

absceso, (âvs·se´so) m. abscess.

absentismo, (âv·sen ·tēz´mo) m. absenteeism.

absolución, (âv·so·lū·syon´) f. forgiveness, absolution.

absolutamente, (âv·lū·tâ·men´te) adv. absolutely.

absolutismo, (âv·so·lū·tēz´mo) m. absolutism, despotism.

absoluto, ta, (âv·so·lū´to, tâ) adj. absolute, unconditional, sole; **en —,** at all, absolutely not.

absolutorio, ria, (âv·so·lū·to´ryo, ryâ) adj. absolving.

absolver*, (ây·sol·ver´) va. to absolve, to pardon.

absorbente, (âv·sor·ven´te) m. and adj. (med.) absorbent, absorbing.

absorber, (ây·sor·ver´) va. to absorb.

absorción, (âv·sor·syon´) f. absorption.

absorto, ta, (âv·sor´to, tâ) adj. absorbed, engrossed *(cautivo);* amazed *(pasmado).*

abstemio, mia, (âvs·te´myo, myâ) adj.

abstemious; **—,** n. teetotaler.

abstención, (âys·ten·syon´) f. abstention.

abstenerse*, (âvs·te·ner´se) vr. to abstain, to refrain from.

abstinencia, (âvs·te·nen´syâ) f. abstinence.

abstinente, (âys·tē·nen´te) adj. abstinent, abstemious.

abstracción, (âvs·trâk·syon´) f. abstraction.

abstracto, ta, (âvs·trâk´to, ta) adj. abstract.

abstraer*, (âvs·trâ·er´) va. to abstract, to leave out, to leave aside; **—se,** to be lost in thought.

abstraído, da (âvs·trâ·ē´tho, thâ) adj. abstracted; absorbed *(absorto).*

absuelto, ta, (ây·swel´to, ta) adj. absolved, acquitted.

absurdo, da, (âv·sūr´tho, thâ) adj. absurd; **—,** m. absurdity.

abuela, (â·vwe´lâ) f. grandmother.

abuelo, (â·vwe´lo) m. grandfather; **—s,** pl. ancestors, forefathers.

abultar, (â·vūl·târ´) va. to make bulky, to enlarge; **—,** vn. to be bulky.

abundancia, (â·vūn·dân´syâ) f. abundance.

abundante, (â·vūn·dân´te) adj. abundant, copious.

abundar, (â·vūn·dâr´) vn. to abound.

aburrido, da, (â·vū·rrē´tho, thâ) adj. bored, weary *(fastidiado);* boresome, tedious *(pesado).*

aburrimiento, (â·vū·rrē·myen´to) m. tediousness, boredom.

aburrir, (â·vū·rrēr´) va. to vex, to weary, to bore; **—se,** to be bored.

abusar, (â·vū·sâr´) vn. to take advantage of, to abuse; **— de,** to impose upon.

abusivo, va, (â·vū·sē´vo, vâ) adj. abusive.

abuso, (â·vū´so) m. abuse, misuse, harsh treatment; **— de confianza,** breach of trust.

abyecto, ta, (âv·yek´to, tâ) adj. abject, low, dejected.

a/c: a cuenta, (corn.) on account, in part payment; **a cargo,** (corn.) drawn on *(girado);* in care of *(a manos de).*

A.C. or A. de C.: Año de Cristo, A.D. in the year of Our Lord.

acá, (â·kâ´) adv. here, this way.

acabado, da, (â·kâ·vâ´tho, thâ) adj. finished, perfect, accomplished *(consumado);* concluded, terminated *(concluido).*

acabar, (â·kâ·vâr´) va. to finish, to complete *(completar);* to achieve *(alcanzar);* **—,** vn. to die *(morir);* to expire, to run out *(expirar)*; **acaba de hacerlo,** he has just done it; **—se,** to grow feeble, to become run down.

academia, (â·kâ·the´myâ) *f.* academy; literary society.

académico, (â·kâ·the´mē·ko) *m.* academician; **—, ca,** *adj.* academic.

acaecer*, (â·kâ·e·ser´) *vn.* to happen.

acaecimiento, (â·kâ·e·sē·myen´to) *m.* event, incident.

acalambrado, da, (â·kâ·lâm·brá´tho, thâ) *adj.* cramped.

acalenturarse, (â·kâ·len·tū·râr´se) *vr.* to be feverish.

acalorar, (â·kâ·lo·râr´) *va.* to heat; **—se,** to get excited *(irritarse)*; to become warm.

acallar, (â·kâ·yâr´) *va.* to quiet, to hush *(aquietar)*; to soften, to assuage, to appease *(aliviar)*

acampamento, (â·kâm·pâ·men´to) *m.* (mil.) encampment.

acampar, (â·kâm·pâr´) *va.* to camp; (mil.) to encamp.

acanalar, (â·kâ·nâ·lâr´) *va.* to make a channel in, to flute, to groove.

acanelado, da, (â·kâ·ne·lâ´tho, thâ) *adj.* cinnamon-colored.

acantonamiento, (â·kân·to·nâ·myen´to) *m.* cantonment.

acantonar, (â·kân·to·nâr´) *va.* (mil.) to quarter, to canton.

acaparar, (â·kit·pa·râr´) *va.* to monopolize, to corner.

acaramelar, (â·kâ·râ·me·lâr´) *va.* to ice, to candy; **—se,** to be cloying, to be overly attentive (toward).

acardenalar, (â·kâr·the·nâ·lâr´) *va.* to beat black and blue; **—se,** to be covered with bruises.

acariciar, (â·kâ·rē·syâr´) *va.* to fondle, to caress; to cherish *(abrigar)*.

acarrear, (â·kâ·rre·âr´) *va.* to convey in a cart, to transport *(trasportar)*; to bring about, to occasion, to cause *(causar)*.

acarreo, (â·kâ·rre´o) *m.* carriage, portage, cartage.

acaso, (â·kâ´so) *m.* chance, happenstance, accident; **—,** *adv.* perhaps, by chance; **por si —.** just in case.

acatar, (â·kâ·târ´) *va.* to revere, to respect, to show willingness to obey.

acatarrarse, (â·kâ·tâ·rrâr´se) *vr.* to catch cold.

acaudalado, da, (â·kâū·thâ·lâ´tho, thâ) *adj.* rich, wealthy.

acaudalar, (â·kâū·thâ·lâr´) *va.* to hoard up, to store up.

acceder, (âk·se·ther´) *vn.* to accede, to

agree.

accesibilidad, (âk·se·sē·vē·lē·thâth´) *f.* accessibility.

accessible, (âk·se·sē´vle) *adj.* attainable, accessible.

acceso, (âk·se´so) *m.* access, approach; **— de tos,** coughing fit; **— dirigido desde tierra,** ground-control approach.

accesorio, ria, (âk·se·so´ryo, ryâ) *adj.* accessory, additional; **—,** *m.* accessory, addition, attachment.

accidental, (âk·sē·then·tâl´) *adj.* accidental, casual.

accidentarse, (âk·sē·then·târ´se) *vr.* to faint, to lose consciousness, to pass out.

accidente, (âk·sē·then´te) *m.* accident *(desgracia)*; attack, fit *(síncope)*.

acción, (âk·syon´) *f.* act, action; operation *(operación)*; battle *(combate)*; (com.) share, stock; **—ones ordinarias,** common stock.

accionar, (âk·syo·nâr´) *vn.* to gesticulate.

accionista, (âk·syo·nēs´tâ) *m. and f.* share-holder, stockholder.

acebo, (â·se´vo) *m.* holly tree.

acechador, (â·se·châ·thor´) *m.* spy.

acechar, (â·se·châr´) *va.* to watch closely, to spy on.

acecho, (â·se´cho) *m.* lying in ambush, waylaying.

aceitar, (â·see·târ´) *va.* to oil.

aceite, (â·se´ē·te) *m.* oil; **— de comer** or **de oliva,** olive oil; **— de hígado de bacalao,** cod-liver oil; **— de ricino,** castor oil.

aceitera, (â·seē·te´râ) *f.* oil cruet, oil jar.

aceitoso, sa, (â·seē·to´so, sâ) *adj.* oily, greasy.

aceituna, (â·seē·tu´nâ) *f.* olive.

aceituno, (â·seē·tū´no) *m.* olive tree.

aceleración, (â·se·le·râ·syon´) *f.* acceleration.

acelerador, (â·se·le·râ·thor´) *m.* accelerator; (auto.) gas pedal.

acelerar, (â·se·le·râr´) *va.* to accelerate, to hurry.

acelerómetro, (â·se·le·ro´me·tro) *m.* accelerometer.

acémila, (â·se´mē·l â) *f.* beast of burden.

acemita, (â·se·mē´tâ) *f.* graham bread.

acendrado, da, (â·sen·drâ´tho, thâ) *adj.* pure, spotless.

acendrar, (â·sen·drâr´) *va.* to refine (metals); (fig.) to purify, to make flawless.

acento, (â·sen´to) *m.* accent.

acentuación. (â·sen·twâ·syon´) *f.* accentuation.

acentuar, (â·sen·twâr´) *va.* to accentuate,

to emphasize.

acepción, (â·sep·syon´) *f.* meaning of a word, import.

acepillar, (â·se·pē·yâr´) *va.* to plane *(alisar);* to brush *(cepillar);* to polish *(pulir).*

aceptable, (â·sep·tá´vle) *adj.* acceptable.

aceptación, (â·sep·tâ·syon´) *f.* acceptance, approbation; (com.) acceptance (of a bill); **presentar a la —,** to present for acceptance; **falta de —,** nonacceptance.

aceptar, (â·sep·târ´) *va.* to accept, to admit; (com.) to honor.

acequia (â·se´kyä) *f.* canal, channel, drain, trench.

acera, (â·se´rä) *f.* sidewalk.

acerado, da, (â·se·rá´tho, thâ) *adj.* made of steel; (fig) mordant, caustic, biting.

acerar, (â·se·rar´) *va.* to steel.

acerbo, ba, (â·ser´vo, vâ) *adj.* bitter, sharptasting; (fig.) harsh, cruel.

acerca de, (â·ser´kä the) *prep.* about, relating to.

acercar, (â·ser·kâr´) *va.* to bring near together; to approach; **—se,** to accost, to approach.

acería, (a·se·rē´ä) *f.* steelwork.

acero, (â·se´ro) *m.* steel; *(arma)* blade; **— dulce,** soft steel; **— de aleación,** alloy steel; **— colado,** cast steel; **— fundido,** hard steel; **— inoxidable,** stainless steel; **— recocido,** tempered steel; **— al carbono,** carbon steel; **— al cromo,** chrome steel; **— al vanadio,** vanadium steel; **— en barras,** bar steel; **— bruto,** raw steel; **pulmón de —,** iron lung.

acérrimo, ma, (â·se´rrē·mo, mâ) *adj.* very strong, very vigorous.

acerrojar, (â·se·rro·hâr´) *va.* to bolt, to lock.

acertado, da, (â·ser·tâ´tho, thâ) *adj.* accurate *(preciso);* skillful *(hábil).*

acertar*, (â·ser·târ´) *va.* to hit (the mark) *(dar en);* to conjecture correctly *(adivinar);* **—,** *vn.* to chance, to happen, to turn out right; **— con,** to discover.

acertijo, (â·ser·tē´ho) *m.* riddle, conundrum.

acervo, (â·ser´vo) *m.* heap, pile.

acetato, (â·se·tâ´to) *m.* (chem.) acetate.

acético, ca, (â·se´tē·ko, kâ) *adj.* acetic.

acetileno, (â·se·tē·le´no) *m.* acetylene.

acetona, (â·se·to´nä) *f.* (chem.) acetone.

acetosa, (â·se·to´sä) *f.* (bot.) sorrel.

aciago, ga, (â·syä´go, gä) *adj.* unlucky, ominous, unhappy.

acial, (â·syál´) *m.* barnacle.

acicaladura, (â·sē·kâ·lâ·thū´râ) *f.,* **acicala-**

miento, (â·sē·kâ·lâ·myen´to) *m.* burnishing.

acicalar, (â·sē·kâ·lâr´) *va.* to polish, to furbish; **—se,** to dress elegantly, to spruce up.

acidez, (â·sē·thes´) *f.* acidity.

acidímetro, (â·sē·thē´me·tro) *m.* acidimeter.

ácido, (á´sē·tho) *m.* (chem.) acid; **exento de —,** acid-free; **— deoxiribonucleico,** deoxyribonucleic acid; **—, da,** *adj.* acid, sour.

acidulo, la, (â·sē´thū·lo, lâ) *adj.* (chem.) acidulous.

acierto, (â·syer´to) *m.* accuracy, exactness *(exactitud);* dexterity, ability, knack *(habilidad).*

acitrón, (â·sē·tron´) *m.* candied lemon.

aclamación, (â·klâ·mâ·syon´) *f.* acclamation; **por —** unanimously.

aclamar, (â·klâ·mâr´) *va.* to applaud, to acclaim.

aclaración, (â·klâ·ra·syon´) *f.* explanation.

aclarar, (â·klâ·râr´) *va.* to clear, to brighten; to explain, to clarify *(clarificar);* **—,** *vn.* to clear up (weather); **—se,** to become clear.

aclimatar, (â·klē·mâ·târ) *va.* to acclimatize.

aclocarse*, (â·klo·kâr´se) *vr.* to brood, to hatch.

acné, (âg·ne´) *f.* (med.) acne.

acobardar, (â·ko·vâr·thâr´) *va.* to intimidate; **— se,** to lose courage, to be afraid.

acogedor, ra, (â·ko·he·thor´, râ) *adj.* cozy, inviting.

acoger, (â·ko·her´) *va.* to receive *(recibir);* to protect, to harbor *(amparar);* **—se,** to resort to.

acogida, (â·ko·hē´thä) *f.* reception; asylum, protection *(amparo);* confluence, meeting place *(concurrencia);* **dar — a una letra,** to honor a draft; **tener excelente —,** to meet with favor, to be well received.

acogimiento, (â·ko·hē·myen´to) *m.* reception, good acceptance.

acolchar, (â·kol·châr´) *va.* to quilt.

acólito, (â·ko´lē·to) *m.* acolyte *(monaguillo)* follower *(satélite).*

acometedor, ra, (a·ko·me·te·thor´, râ) *n.* aggressor; enterpriser *(emprendedor);* **—,** *adj.* aggressive, enterprising.

acometer, (â·ko·me·ter´) *va.* to attack *(atacar);* to undertake *(emprender);* to overtake, to overcome, to steal over *(alcanzar).*

---

m met, **n** not, **p** pot, **r** very, **rr** (none), **s** so, **t** toy, **th** with, **v** eve, **w** we, **y** yes, **z** zero

acometida, (â·ko·me·tē´thâ) f., **acometi-
miento,** (â·ko·me·te·myen´to) m. attack,
assault.
acomodadizo, za, (â·ko·mo·thâ·thē´so, sâ)
adj. accommodating.
acomodado, da, (â·ko·mo·thâ´tho, thâ)
adj. wealthy (rico); suitable, convenient,
fit (conveniente).
acomodador, (â·ko·mo·thâ·thor´) m.
usher.
acomodamiento, (â·ko·mo·thâ·myen´to) m.
transaction; convenience (conveniencia); adaptation (ajuste).
acomodar, (â·ko·mo·thâr´) va. to accommodate, to arrange; —, vn. to fit, to
suit; —se, to make oneself comfortable.
acomodo, (â·ko·mo´tho) m. adjustment,
arrangement (ajuste); employment
(empleo).
acompañador, ra, (â·kom·pâ·nyâ·thor´, râ)
n. companion (compañero); chaperon
(dueña); (mus.) accompanist.
acompañamiento,
(â·kom·pâ·nyâ·myen´·to) m. accompaniment, escort; (mus.) accompaniment.
acompañante, ta, (â·kom·pâ·nyân´te, tâ)
n. attendant (asistente); companion;
(mus.) accompanist.
acompañar, (â·kom·pâ·nyâr´) va. to
accompany, to join; (mus.) to accompany; (com.) to attach, insert.
acompasado, da, (â·kom·pâ·sâ´tho, thâ)
adj. measured, well-proportioned,
cadenced.
acondicionado, da, (â·kon·dē·syo·nâ´tho,
thâ) adj. conditioned; **bien** or **mal —,**
well- or ill-prepared, well- or ill-quali-
fied.
acondicionar, (â·kon·dē·syo·nâr´) va. to
prepare, to arrange, to fit, to put in
condition; **— para uso invernal,** to winterize.
acongojar, (â·kong·go·hâr´) va. to oppress,
to afflict; **—se,** to become sad, to grieve.
aconsejable, (â·kon·se·hâ´vle) adj. advisable.
aconsejar, (â·kon·se·hâr´) va. to advise; **—
se,** to take advice.
acontecer*, (â·kon·te·ser´) vn. to happen.
acontecimiento, (â·kon·te·sē·myen´to) m.
event, incident.
acopado, da, (â·ko·pâ´tho, thâ) adj. cup-
shaped, bell-shaped.
acopiamiento (â·ko·pyâ·myen´to) or **aco-
pio,** (â. ko´pyo) m. gathering, storing.
acopiar, (â·ko·pyâr´) va. to gather, to store
up.
acoplado, da, (â·ko·plâ´tho, thâ) adj. cou-

pled; fitted; —, m. trailer (vehicle).
acoplamiento, (â·ko·plâ·myen´to) m. coupling, connection; (auto.) clutch.
acoplar, (â·ko·plâr´) va. to couple, to
adjust, to fit.
acoquinar, (â·ko·kē·nâr´) va. to intimidate.
acorazado, da, (â·ko·râ·sâ´tho, thâ) adj.
iron-clad; —, m. battleship; **—do de
bolsillo,** pocket battleship.
acorazonado, da (â·ko·râ·so·nâ´tho, thâ)
adj. heart-shaped.
acordado, da, (â·kor·thâ´tho, thâ) adj.
deliberate (intencional); agreed upon
(convenido).
acordar*, (â·kor·thâr´) va. to resolve
(resolver); to tune (afinar); —, vn. to
agree; **—se,** to come to an agreement;
to remember (recordar); **no — mal,** to
remember rightly.
acorde, (â·kor´the) adj. conformable, in
agreement; —, m. accord; (mus.) chord.
acordeón, (â·kor·the·on´) m. accordion.
acordonar, (â·kor·tho·nâr´) va. (mil.) to
form a cordon around; to lace, put
laces on.
acorralar, (â·ko·rrâ·lâr´) va. to corral
(encerrar); to intimidate (acobardar).
acortar, (â·kor·târ´) va. to abridge, to
shorten; **— el paso,** to slow down.
acosar, (â·ko·sâr´) va. to pursue closely
(perseguir); to annoy, to harass
(molestar).
acostar*, (â·kos·târ´) va. to put to bed; **—
se,** to go to bed, lie down (tenderse); to
incline to one side (inclinarse).
acostumbrado, da, (â·kos·tūm·brâ´tho,
thâ) adj. customary, accustomed.
acostumbrar, (â·kos·tūm·brâr´) va. to
make accustomed; —, vn. and vr. to be
accustomed.
acotar, (â·ko·târ´) va. to set bounds (fijar);
to annotate (apuntar); to watch for
(aguardar); to select (elegir).
acre, (â´kre) adj. acid, sharp, bitter; —,
m. acre.
acrecentar* (â·kre·sen·târ´) or **acrecer*,**
(â·kre·ser´) va. to increase, to augment.
acreditado, da, (â ·kre·thē·tâ´tho, thâ) adj.
accredited, authorized, creditable.
acreditar, (â·kre·thē·târ´) va. to assure
(asegurar): to authorize (autorizar); to
credit (abonar); to accredit, to give
credit (elogiar); **—se,** to gain credit, to
get a good reputation.
acreedor, ra, (â·kre·e·thor´, râ) n. creditor;
—, adj. worthy, creditable; **saldo —,**
credit balance.

â arm, **e** they, **ē** bē, **o** fore, **ū** blūe, **b** bad, **ch** chip, **d** day, **f** fat, **g** go, **h** hot, **k** kid, **1** let

acribillar, (â·krē·vē·yâr´) *va.* to perforate *(perforar);* to annoy *(molestar);* to torment *(atormentar).*

acrílico, ca (â·krē´lē·ko, kâ) *adj.* acrylic.

acriminación, (â·krē·mē·nâ·syon´) *f.* accusation.

acriminar, (â·krē·mē·nâr´) *va.* to accuse, to impeach.

acrisolar, (â·krē·so·lâr´) *va.* to refine, to purify.

acrobacia, (â·kro·vâ´syâ) *f.* acrobatics; — **aérea,** stunt flying.

acróbata, (â·kro´vâ·tâ) *m.* and *f.* acrobat.

acta, (âk´tâ) *f.* act; minutes of proceedings; — **de venta,** bill of sale; — **de nacimiento,** birth certificate.

ACTH: hormona adrenocorticotropa, ACTH, adrenocorticotrophic hormone.

actina, (âk·tē´nâ) *m.* actin.

actitud, (âk·tē·tūth´) *f.* attitude, outlook; position, posture *(postura).*

activador, (âk·tē·va·thor´) *m.* (chem.) activator.

activar, (âk·tē·vâr´) *va.* to make active *(animar);* to expedite, to hasten *(acelerar);* to activate.

actividad, (âk·tē·vē·thâth´) *f.* activity *(acción);* liveliness *(animación).*

activo, va, (âk·tē´vo, vâ) *adj.* active, diligent; —, *m.* (com.) assets.

acto, (âk´to) *m.* act, action; function; sexual intercourse *(coito);* — **continuo,** immediately; **en el —,** at once, immediately.

actor, (âk·tor´) *m.* actor, player, comedian; plaintiff *(demandante).*

actriz, (âk·trēs´) *f.* actress.

actuación, (âk·twâ·syon´) *f.* action, performance.

actual, (âk·twâl´) *adj.* present, of the present moment.

actualidad, (âk·twâ·lē·thâth´) *f.* present time; current event *(suceso);* **en la —,** at present.

actuar, (âk·twâr´) *vn.* to act, to take action, to proceed.

actuario. (âk·twâ´ryo) *m.* actuary, notary.

acuafortista, (â·kwâ·for·tēs´tâ) *m.* and *f.* etcher.

acuarela, (â·kwâ·re´lâ) *f.* water coloring, water color.

acuarelista, (â·kwâ·re·lēs´tâ) *m.* and *f.* watercolorist.

acuario, (â·kwâ´ryo) *m.* aquarium, tank; Aquarius *(del Zodiaco).*

acuartelar, (â·kwâr·te·lâr´) *va.* (mil.) to quarter troops; (naut.) to furl sails.

acuático, ca, (â·kwâ´tē·ko, kâ) *adj.* aquatic.

acuatizar, (â·kwâ·tē·sâr´) *vn.* (avi.) to land (seaplane).

acucioso, sa, (â·kū·syo´so, sâ) *adj.* zealous, eager.

acuchillar, (â·kū·chē·yâr´) *va.* to stab, to knife; —**se,** to fight with knives.

acudimiento, (â·kū·thē·myen´to) *m.* aid, assistance.

acudir, (â·kū·thēr´) *vn.* to assist, to succor *(socorrer);* to be present *(asistir);* — **a,** to resort to, to hasten to *(recurrir).*

acueducto, (â·kwe·thūk´to) *m.* aqueduct.

acuerdo, (â·kwer´tho) *m.* agreement, consent; resolution, court decision *(juicio);* **de —,** unanimously, by agreement; **de — con,** in accordance with; **ponerse de —,** to reach an agreement.

acuitar, (â·kwē·târ´) *va.* to afflict, to oppress; —**se,** to grieve, to feel depressed.

acullá, (â·kū·yâ´) *adv.* on the other side, yonder.

acumulación, (â·kū·mū·lâ·syon´) *f.* accumulation.

acumulador, (â·kū·mū·lâ·thor´) *m.* battery, electric storage battery; accumulator.

acumular, (â·kū·mū·lâr´) *va.* to accumulate, to heap together *(juntar);* to impute *(atribuir).*

acuñar, (â·kū·nyâr´) *va.* to coin, to mint *(amonedar);* to wedge in, to secure with wedges *(apoyar).*

acuoso, sa, (â·kwo´so, sâ) *adj.* watery.

acurrucado, da, (â·kū·rrū·kâ´tho, thâ) *adj.* huddled, squatted.

acurrucarse, (â·kū·rrū·kâr´se) *vr.* to huddle up.

acusación. (â·kū·sâ·syon´) *f.* accusation.

acusado, da, (â·kū·sâ´tho, thâ) *n.* defendant, accused.

acusador, ra, (â·kū·sâ·thor´, râ) *n.* accuser.

acusar, (â·kū·sâr´) *va.* to accuse, to reproach *(denunciar);* to meld *(anunciar);* — **recibo de,** to acknowledge receipt of; —**se,** to make one´s confession, to confess.

acusativo, (â·kū·sâ·tē´vo) *m.* (gram.) accusative.

acusatorio, ria, (â·kū·sâ·to´ryo, ryâ) *adj.* accusing.

acuse, (â·kū´se) *m.* melding (in cards); — **de recibo,** acknowledgment of receipt.

acústica, (â·kūs´tē·kâ) *f.* acoustics.

acústico, ca, (â·kūs´tē·ko, kâ) *adj.* acoustic.

m met, **n** not, **p** pot, **r** very, **rr** (none), **s** so, **t** toy, **th** with, **v** eve, **w** we, **y** yes, **z** zero

achacar, (â·châ·kâr´) *va.* to impute, to blame.

achacoso, sa, (â·châ·ko´so, sâ) *adj.* sickly, habitually ailing.

achaque, (â·châ´ke) *m.* unhealthiness, sickliness, ill health; (coll.) menstrual period; (fig.) excuse, pretext.

achatar, (â·châ·târ´) *va.* to flatten.

achicar, (â·chē·kâr´) *va.* to diminish *(disminuir);* to bail *(desaguar);* **—se,** to become smaller *(reducirse);* to humble oneself *(humillarse).*

achicharrar, (â·chē·châ·rrâr´) *va.* to burn in frying *(quemar);* to overheat *(sobrecalentar).*

adagio, (â·thâ´hyo) *m.* adage, proverb; (mus.) adagio.

adamado, da, (â·thâ·mâ´tho, thâ) *adj.* effeminate, ladylike.

adamascado, da, (â·thâ·mâs·kâ´tho, thâ) *adj.* damasklike.

Adán, (â·thân´) *m.* Adam.

adaptabilidad, (â·thâp·tâ·vē·lē·thâth´) *f.* adaptability.

adaptable, (â·thâp·tâ´vle) *adj.* adaptable.

adaptar, (â·thâp·târ´) *va.* to adapt, to fit, to adjust.

adecuado, da, (â·the·kwâ´tho, thâ) *adj.* adequate, fit, able.

adecuar, (â·the·kwâr´) *va.* to fit, to accommodate, to proportion.

A. de J.C.: antes de Jesucristo, B.C. before Christ.

adelantadamente, (â·the·lân·tâ·thâ·men´te) *adv.* beforehand.

adelantado, da, (â·the·lân·tâ´tho, thâ) *adj.* anticipated *(anticipado);* forward, bold *(atrevido);* advanced *(avanzado);* **por — do,** in advance.

adelantar, (â·the lân·târ´) *va.* and *vn.* to advance, to further, to accelerate *(promover);* to ameliorate, to improve *(mejorar);* **— la paga,** to pay in advance; **— se,** to take the lead, to outdo, to outstrip.

adelante, (â·the·lân´te) *adv.* onward, further off; **en —,** from now on, henceforth; **más —,** farther on; later *(después);* **salir —,** to go ahead, to come through; **¡—!** come in! go on! proceed!

adelanto, (â·the·lân´to) *m.* progress, advance.

adelgazar, (â·thel·gâ·sâr´) *va.* to make thin or slender; **—se,** to lose weight.

ademán, (â·the·mân´) *m.* gesture *(gesto);* attitude *(actitud).*

además, (â·the·mas´) *adv.* moreover, also, in addition; **— de,** besides, aside from.

adentro, (â·then´tro) *adv.* within, inwardly; **tierra —,** inland.

adepto, ta, (â·thep´to, tâ) *adj.* adept; **—,** *n.* follower.

aderezar, (â·the·re·sâr´) *va.* to dress, to adorn *(hermosear);* to prepare *(disponer);* to season *(condimentar).*

aderezo, (â·the·re´so) *m.* adornment, finery; set of jewels; seasoning; dressing *(para ensaladas).*

adeudado, da, (â·theū·thâ´tho, thâ) *adj.* indebted.

adeudar, (â·theū·thâr´) *va.* to owe; **— en cuenta,** to charge to one´s account; **— se,** to be indebted.

adeudo, (â·the´ū·tho) *m.* indebtedness; (com.) debit.

adherencia, (â·the·ren´syâ) *f.* adherence, cohesion, adhesion; (fig.) connection, relationship.

adherente, (â·the·ren´te) *adj.* adherent, cohesive.

adherir*, (â ·the·rēr´) *vn.* and *vr.* to stick *(pegarse);* to believe, to be faithful, to belong *(afiliarse);* to hold, to cling to *(guardar).*

adhesión, (â·the·syon´) *f.* adhesion, cohesion, adherence.

adición, (â·the·syon´) *f.* addition.

adicional, (â·thē·syo·nâl´) *adj.* additional, supplementary.

adicionar, (â·thē·syo·nâr´) *va.* to add.

adicto, ta, (â·thēk´to, tâ) *adj.* addicted *(apegado);* devoted to *(dedicado);* **—,** *n.* follower, supporter; addict.

adiestrar, (â·thyes·trâr´) *va.* to guide, to teach, to instruct, to train; **—se,** to practice.

adinerado, da, (â·thē·ne·râ´tho, thâ) *adj.* moneyed, rich, wealthy.

adintelado, da, (â·thēn·te·lâ´tho) *adj.* straight, flat.

adiós, (â·thyos´) *interj.* good-bye, adieu.

aditamento, (â·thē·tâ·mento) *m.* addition, attachment.

adivinador, ra, (â·thē·vē·nâ·thor´, râ) *n.* diviner, soothsayer.

adivinanza, (â·thē·vē·nân´sâ) *f.* riddle, conundrum.

adivinar, (â·thē·vē·nâr´) *va.* to foretell *(predecir);* to conjecture, to guess *(conjeturar).*

adivino, na, (â·thē·vē´no, nâ) *n.* diviner, soothsayer, fortuneteller.

adj.: adjetivo, adj. adjective.

adjetivo, (âth·he·tē´vo) *m.* adjective.

adjudicación, (âth·hū·thē·kâ·syon´) f. award, adjudication.

adjudicar, (âth·hū·thē·kâr´) va. to award; —se, to appropriate to oneself.

adjuntar, (âth·hūn·târ´) va. to enclose, to attach.

adjunto, ta, (âth·hūn´to, ta) adj. united, joined, attached, annexed; —, m. attaché.

ad lib.: a voluntad, ad lib. at pleasure, at will.

administración, (âth·mē·nēs·trâ·syon´) f. administration, management, direction (manejo); headquarters (jefatura); en —, in trust.

administrador, ra, (âth·mē·nēs·trâ·thor´, râ) n. administrator, trustee, manager; —de aduanas, collector of customs; — de correos, postmaster.

administrar, (âth·mē·nēs·trâr´) va. to administer, to manage.

administrativo, va, (âth·mē·nēs·trâ·tē´vo, vâ) adj. administrative.

admirable, (âth·mē·râ´vle) adj. admirable, marvelous.

admiración, (âth·mē·râ·syon´) f. admiration, wonder; (gram.) exclamation point.

admirador, ra, (âth·mē·râ·thor´, râ) admirer.

admirar, (âth·mē·râr´) va. to admire; —se, to be amazed, to be surprised.

admisible, (âth·mē·sē´vle) adj. admissible, acceptable.

admisión, (âth·mē·syon´) f. admission, acceptance.

admitir, (âth·mē·tēr´) va. to admit, to accept (aceptar); to acknowledge (reconocer); to let in (recibir); to concede (conceder).

admonición, (âth·mo·nē·syon´) f. Admonition, warning.

A.D.N.: ácido desoxirribonucleico, D.N.A., deoxyribonucleic acid.

adobar, (â·tho·vâr´) va. to dress (aderezar); to pickle (encurtir); to stew (guisar); to tan (curtir).

adobe, (â·tho´ve) m. adobe, sun-dried brick.

adobo, (â·tho´vo) m. stew (guisado); pickle sauce (salsa); rouge (afeite); ingredients for dressing leather or cloth (curtiente).

adolecer*, (â·tho·le·ser´) vn. to be ill; — de, to suffer or ail from, to be subject to.

adolescencia, (â·tho·les·sen´syâ) f. adolescence, youth.

adolescente, (â·tho·les·sen´te) adj. adolescent, young; —, m. and f. adolescent,

teen-ager.

adonde, (â·thon´de) adv. whither, where.

adondequiera, (â·thon·de·kye´râ) adv. wherever.

adopción, (â·thop·syon´) f. adoption.

adoptar, (â·thop·târ´) va. to adopt.

adoptivo, va, (â·thop·tē´vo, vâ) adj. adoptive, adopted.

adoquín, (â·tho·kēn´)m. paving stone.

adoquinar, (â·tho·kē´·nâr´) va. to pave.

adoración, (â·tho·râ·syon´) f. adoration, worship.

adorar, (â·thó·râr´) va. to adore, to worship.

adormecer*, (â·thor·me·ser´) va. to lull to sleep; —se, to fall asleep.

adormecido, da, (â·thor·me·sē´tho, thâ) adj. drowsy, stilled, sleepy.

adormecimiento, (â·thor·me·sē·myen´to)m. drowsiness, sleepiness.

adormitarse, (â·thor·mē·târ´se) vr. to become drowsy.

adornar, (â·thor·nâr´) va. to embellish, to ornament, to trim.

adorno, (â·thor´no) m. adornment, ornament, decoration.

adquirir*, (âth·kē·rēr´) va. to acquire, to gain.

adquisición, (âth·kē·sē·syon´) f. acquisition, attainment; poder de —, purchasing power.

adrede, (â·thre´the) adv. purposely.

adrenalina, (â·thre·nâ·lē´nâ) f. adrenalin.

aduana, (â·thwâ´nâ) f. customhouse; derechos de —, customhouse duties.

aduanero, (â·thwâ·ne´ro) m. Customhouse officer; —, ra, adj. pertaining to customs or customhouse.

aduar, (â·thwâr´) m. nomadic village of Arabs; gypsy camp (de gitanos).

aducción, (â·thūk·syon´) f. adduction.

aducir*, (â·thū·sēr´) va. to adduce, to cite, to allege.

adueñarse, (â·thwe·nyâr´se) vr. to take possession (of).

adulación, (â·thū·lâ·syon´) f. adulation, flattery.

adulador, ra, (â·thu·lâ·thor´, râ) n. flatterer.

adular, (â·thū·lâr´) va. to flatter, to admire excessively.

adulterar, (â·thūl·te·râr´) va. and vn. to adulterate.

adulterio, (â·thūl·te´ryo) m. adultery.

adúltero, ra, (â·thūl´te·ro, râ) n. adulterer, adulteress.

adulto, ta, (â·thūl´to, tâ) n. and adj. adult, grown-up, mature.

adusto, ta, (â·thūs´to, tä) *adj.* excessively hot, scorching; (fig.) intractable, austere, gloomy.

adv.: adverbio, adv. adverb.

advenedizo, za, (âth·ve·ne·thē´so, sä) *adj.* parvenu *(nuevo rico);* foreign *(extranjero);* —, *n.* upstart, parvenu.

advenimiento, (âth·ve·nē·myen´to) *m.* arrival, long-awaited advent; Advent.

adverbial, (âth·ver·vyäl´) *adj.* adverbial.

adverbio, (âth·ver´vyo) *m.* adverb.

adversario, (âth·ver·sä´ryo) *m.* adversary, antagonist.

adversidad, (âth·ver·sē·thäth´) *f.* adversity, calamity.

adverso, sa, (âth·ver´so, sä) *adj.* adverse, calamitous.

advertencia, (âth·ver·ten´syä) *f.* admonition, warning *(admonición);* notice *(reparo).*

advertido, da, (âth·ver·tē´tho, thä) *adj.* forewarned *(avisado);* skillful *(capaz);* intelligent, clever, alert, aware *(listo).*

advertir*, (âth·ver·tēr´) *va.* to advert, to notice *(reparar);* to call attention to, to warn *(avisar).*

adyacente, (âth·yä·sen´te) *adj.* adjacent.

aéreo, rea, (â·e´re·o, re·ä) *adj.* air, aerial; **correo —,** air mail.

aerodinámica, (â·e·ro·thē·nä´mē·kä) *f.* aerodynamics.

aerodinámico, ca, (â·e·ro·thē·nä´mē·ko, kä) *adj.* streamlined.

aeródromo, (â·e·ro´thro·mo) *m.* airdrome.

aeroembolismo, (â·e·ro·em·bo·lēz´mo) *m.* aeroembolism.

aerograma, (â·e·ro·grä´mä) *m.* wireless message.

aeromedicina, (â·e·ro·me·thē·sē´nä) *f.* aeromedicine.

aeronauta, (â·e·ro·nä´ū·tä) *m.* aeronaut, airman, aviator.

aeronáutica, (â·e·ro·nä´ū·tē·kä) *f.* aeronautics.

aeronave, (â·e·ro·nä´ve) *f.* airship, dirigible, aircraft.

aeroplano, (â·e·ro·plä´no) *m.* airplane; **— de combate,** fighter plane.

aeropostal, (â·e·ro pos·täl´) *adj.* airmail.

aeropuerto, (â·e·ro·pwer´to) *m.* airport; **— para helicópteros,** heliport.

aerosol, (â·e·ro·sol´) *m.* aerosol.

aerospacio, (â·e·ros·pä´syo) *m.* aerospace.

aerotermodinámica, (â·e·ro·ter·mo·thē·nä´mē·kä) *f.* aerothermodynamics.

afabilidad, (â·fä·vē·lē·thäth´) *f.* affability, graciousness.

afable, (â·fä´vle) *adj.* affable, pleasant, courteous.

afamado, da, (â·f â·mä´tho, thä) *adj.* noted, famous.

afamar, (â·fä·mär´) *va.* to make famous.

afán, (â·fän´) *m.* anxiety, solicitude, worry *(ansia);* physical toil *(labor).*

afanar, (â·fä·när´) *va.* to press, to hurry; **—se,** to toil, to overwork *(fatigarse);* to work eagerly, to take pains *(esmerarse).*

afanoso, sa, (â·fä·no´so, sä) *adj.* solicitous, painstaking.

afear, (â·fe·ar´) *va.* to deform, to mar, to misshape, to make ugly.

afección, (â·fek·syon´) *f.* affection fondness, attachment; (med.) affection, disease.

afectación, (â·fek·tä·syon´) *f.* affectation.

afectar, (â·fek·tär´) *va.* to affect *(conmover);* to feign *(fingir).*

afectísimo, ma, (â·fek·tē´sē·mo, mä) *adj.* very affectionate, devoted; yours truly, very truly yours.

afecto, (â·fek´to) *m.* affection, fondness, love; **—, ta,** *adj.* fond of, inclined to.

afectuoso, sa, (â·fek·two´so, sä) *adj.* affectionate, tender.

afeitada, (â·feē·tä´thä) *f.* shave, shaving.

afeitar, (â·feē·tär´) *va.* and *vr.* to shave; to apply make-up, to put on cosmetics *(poner afeites).*

afeite, (â·fe´ē·te) *m.* paint; make-up, cosmetics *(maquillaje).*

afelpado, da, (â·fel·pä´tho, thä) *adj.* plushlike, velvetlike.

afeminado, da, (â·fe·mē·nä´tho, thä) *adj.* effeminate.

afeminar, (â·fe·mē·när´) *va.* to make effeminate.

aferrado, da, (â·fe·rrä´tho, thä) *adj.* stubborn, headstrong.

aferrar, (â·fe·rrär´) *va.* to grapple, to grasp, to seize.

afestonado, (â·fes·to·nä´tho) *adj.* festooned.

afianzar, (â·fyän·sär´) *va.* to bail, to guarantee, to become security for *(garantizar);* to prop, to fix, to secure *(asegurar).*

afición, (â·fē·syon´) *f.* affection *(cariño);* preference, fondness, fancy, liking *(inclinación);* hobby *(pasatiempo).*

aficionado, da, (â·fē·syo·nä´tho, thä) *n.* devotee, fan, amateur.

aficionar, (â·fē·syo·när´) *va.* to inspire affection; **—se,** to be devoted to, to be fond of, to have a taste for, to have an inclination for.

â arm, **e** they, **ē** bē, **o** fore, **ū** blūe, **b** bad, **ch** chip, **d** day, **f** fat, **g** go, **h** hot, **k** kid, **l** let

afijo, ja, (â·fē´ho, hâ) *adj.* suffixed; —, *m.* suffix.

afiladera, (â·fē·lâ·the´râ) *f.* whetstone.

afilado, da, (â·fē·lâ´tho, thâ) *adj.* sharp, clear-cut *(marcado);* thin *(adelgazado).*

afilador, (â·fē·lâ·thor´) *m.* sharpener, grinder.

afilar, (â·fē·lâr´) *va.* to whet, to sharpen, to grind.

afiliado, da, (â·fē·lyâ´tho, thâ) *adj.* affiliated; —, *n.* subsidiary.

afiligranado, da, (â·fē·lē·grâ·nâ´tho, thâ) *adj.* filigreelike.

afin, (â·fēn´) *m.* and *f.* relation, relative; —, *adj.* contiguous *(próximo);* related *(relacionado).*

afinación, (â·fē·nâ·syon´) *f.* refining *(refinación);* tuning *(acuerdo).*

afinado, da, (â·fē·nâ´tho, thâ) *adj.* refined *(purificado);* well-finished *(perfeccionado);* tuned *(acordado).*

afinador, (â·fē·nâ·thor´) *m.* tuner.

afinar, (â·fē·nâr´) *va.* to finish, to perfect *(perfeccionar);* to tune *(acordar);* to refine *(purificar).*

afinidad, (â·fē·nē·thâth´) *f.* affinity, attraction *(atracción);* relationship, kinship *(parentesco);* analogy *(analogía).*

afirmación, (â·fēr·mâ·syon´) *f.* affirmation *(aseguramiento);* statement *(declaración).*

afirmar, (â·fēr·mâr´) *va.* to secure, to fasten *(fijar);* to affirm, to assure *(asegurar).*

afirmativo, va, (â·fēr·mâ·tē´vo, vâ) *adj.* affirmative.

aflicción, (â·flēk·syon´) *f.* affliction, grief, heartache, pain *(pena);* misfortune *(desgracia).*

afligido, da, (â·flē·hē´tho, thâ) *adj.* afflicted, sad, despondent

afligir, (â·flē·hēr´) *va.* to afflict, to grieve, to torment; —se, to grieve *(entristecerse);* to lose heart *(desanimarse).*

aflojar, (â·flo·hâr´) *va.* to loosen, to slacken, to relax *(soltar);* to relent *(ceder);* —, *vn.* to grow weak *(debilitarse);* to abate, to lose intensity *(moderarse).*

afluencia, (â·flwen´syâ) *f.* inflow; plenty, abundance, affluence, *f. (copia).*

afluente, (â·flwen´te) *adj.* affluent, abundant; tributary *(secundario);* loquacious *(hablador);* —, *m.* tributary stream.

afluir*, (â·flwēr´) *vn.* to flow; to congregate, to assemble *(acudir).*

aflujo, (â·flū´ho) *m.* (med.) influx.

afmo, or af.mo: afectisimo: yours truly, very truly yours.

afofarse, (â·fo·fâr´se) *vr.* to fluff up.

afondar, (â·fon·dâr´) *va.* to sink; —, *vn.* to go to the bottom.

aforar, (â·fo·râr´) *va.* to gauge, to measure *(medir);* (com.) to appraise *(valuar).*

afortunadamente, (â·for·tū·nâ·thâ·men´·te) *adv.* fortunately, luckily.

afortunado, da, (â·for´tū·nâ´tho, thâ) *adj.* fortunate, lucky; successful *(exitoso).*

afrancesar, (â·frân·se·sâr´) *va.* to Frenchify

afrecho, (â·fre´cho) *m.* bran.

afrenta, (â·fren´tâ) *f.* outrage, insult, injury *(ultraje);* infamy, disgrace *(deshonor).*

afrentar, (â·fren·târ´) *va.* to affront, to offend

africano, na, (â·frē·kâ´no, nâ) *n.* and *adj.* African.

afrontar, (â·fron·târ´) *va.* to confront.

aftoso, sa, (âf·to´so, sâ) *adj.* (med.) aphthous; **fiebre —sa** (vet.) hoof-and-mouth disease.

afuera, (â·fwe´râ) *adv.* out, outside, outward; ¡—! *interj.* out of the way!

afueras, (â·fwe´râs) *f. pl.* environs, suburbs, outskirts.

agachar, (â·gâ·châr´) *va.* to lower; —, *vn.* to crouch; —se, to stoop, to squat, to duck down.

agalla, (â·gâ´yâ) *f.* gallnut; —s, *pl.* tonsils *(amígdalas);* fish gills.

ágape, (á´gâ·pe) *m.* banquet, testimonial dinner.

agarradera, (â·gâ·rrâ·the´râ) *f.* holder, handle.

agarrado, da, (â·gâ·rrâ´tho, thâ) *adj.* miserable, stingy.

agarrar, (â·gâ·rrâr´) *va.* to grasp, to seize; —se, to hold on.

agarrotar, (â·gâ·rro·târ´) *va.* to fasten tightly with ropes *(amarrar);* to garrote, to strangle *(estrangular).*

agasajar, (â·gâ·sâ·hâr´) *va.* to regale, to entertain, to treat affectionately.

agasajo, (â·gâ·sâ´ho) *m.* kind attention, entertainment.

ágata, (á´gâ·tâ) *f.* agate.

agazapar, (â·gâ·sâ·pâr´) *va.* (coll.) to catch, to grab; —se, to hide *(esconderse);* to crouch down *(agacharse).*

agencia, (â·hen´syâ) *f.* agency; — de turismo, travel agency.

agenciar, (â·hen·syâr´) *va.* to solicit, to endeavor to obtain.

agenda, (â·hen´dâ) *f.* agenda.

agente, (â·hen´te) *m.* agent, representative

(intermediario); attorney *(abogado);* —
viajero, traveling salesman; — de bolsa,
broker; — de cambios, bill broker; —
de cobros, collector; — publicitario,
adman; — de seguros, insurance agent.

ágil, (â´hĕl) *adj.* nimble, fast, active, agile.

agilidad, (â·hē·lē·thâth´) *f.* agility, nimble-
ness.

agio, (â´hyo) *m.* agio; stockjobbing, speculation.

agiotador (â·hyo·tâ·thor´) or agiotista,
(â·hyo·tĕs´tä) *m.* (corn.) money changer;
stockjobber, speculator.

agiotaje, (â·hyo·tâ´he) *m.* agiotage; stockjobbing.

agitación, (â·hē·tâ·syon´) *f.* agitation, excitement.

agitado, da, (â·hē·tâ´tho, thä) *adj.* excited,
agitated.

agitar, (â·hē·târ´) *va.* to agitate, to move;
—se, to become excited.

aglomerar, (â·glo·me·râr´) *va.* and *vr.* to
agglomerate.

agnosticismo, (âg·nos·tē·sēz´mo) *m.*
agnosticism.

agobiar, (â·go·vyâr´) *va.* to weigh down, to
oppress, to burden.

agolparse, (â·gol·pâr´se) *vr.* to assemble in
crowds.

agonía, (â·go·nē´â) *f.* agony, anguish.

agonizante, (â·go·nē·sân´te) *m.* and *f.*
dying person; —, *adj.* dying, agonizing.

agonizar, (â·go·nē·sâr´) *va.* to assist dying
persons; (coll.) to harass; —, *vn.* to be
in the agony of death, to agonize.

agorar*, (â·go·râr´) *va.* to divine, to augur.

agorero, ra, (â·go·re´ro, râ) *n.* diviner.

agorgojarse, (â·gor·go·hâr´se) *vr.* (agr.) to
be infested with grubs or weevils.

agostar, (â·gos·târ´) *va.* to parch with
heat; to blight; —, *vn.* to be in summer
pasture; to spend August; —se to fade
away, to be crushed.

agosto, (â·gos´to) *m.* August; harvest
time.

agotado, da, (â·go·tâ´tho, thä) *adj.* sold
out *(terminado);* exhausted, spent, tired
(rendido).

agotamiento, (â·go·tâ·myen´to) *m.* exhaustion.

agotar, (â·go·târ´) *va.* to misspend *(malgastar);* to exhaust, to use up *(gastar);*
—se, to become run-down, to become
exhausted *(rendirse);* to be sold out
(terminarse).

agraciado, da, (â·grâ·syâ´tho, thä) *adj.*
graceful *(donairoso);* refined *(refinado);*
gifted *(donado).*

agraciar, (â·grâ·syâr´) *va.* to embellish
(embellecer); to grace, to favor *(favorecer).*

agradable, (â·grâ·thâ´vle) *adj.* agreeable,
pleasant.

agradar, (â·grâ·thâr´) *va.* to please, to
gratify.

agradecer*, (â·grâ·the·ser´) *va.* to be grateful for, to appreciate.

agradecido, da, (â·grâ·the·sē´tho, thä) *adj.*
thankful, grateful.

agradecimiento, (â·grâ·the·sē·myen´to) *m.*
gratitude, gratefulness.

agrado, (â·grâ´tho) *m.* agreeableness,
courteousness *(afabilidad);* pleasure
(placer); liking *(preferencia);* ser de su
—, to be satisfactory.

agrandamiento, (â·gran·dâ·myen´to) *m.*
enlargement.

agrandar, (â·grân·dâr´) *va.* to enlarge; to
extend.

agrario, da, (â·grâ´ryo, ryâ) *adj.* agrarian.

agravante, (â·grâ·vân´te) *adj.* aggravating,
trying.

agravar, (â·grâ·vâr´) *va.* to oppress
(oprimir); to aggravate *(irritar);* to make
worse, to exaggerate *(empeorar).*

agraviar, (â·grâ·vyâr´) *va.* to wrong, to
injure, to hurt *(afrentar);* to make
worse *(empeorar);* —se, to take offense.

agravio, (â·grâ´vyo) *m.* offense, injury.

agregación, (â·gre·gâ·syon´) *f.* aggregation;
collection.

agregado, (â·gre·gâ´tho) *m.* aggregate
(conjunto); attaché *(funcionario).*

agregar, (â·gre·gâr´) *va.* to aggregate, to
heap together, to collect, to add.

agremiar, (â·gre·myâr´) *va.* to organize
into a union; —se, to unionize.

agresión, (â·gre·syon´) *f.* aggression,
attack.

agresivo, va, (â·gre·sē´vo, vâ) *adj.* aggressive.

agresor, (â·gre·sor´) *m.* aggressor,
assaulter.

agreste. (â·gres´te) *adj.* wild, rude, rustic,
rough.

agriar, (â·gryâr´) *va.* to sour, to acidify;
(fig.) to exasperate.

agricola, (â·grē´ko·lâ) *adj.* agricultural.

agricultor, (â·grē·kūl·tor´) *m.* agriculturist,
farmer.

agricultura, (â·grē·kūl·tū´râ) *f.* agriculture.

agridulce, (â·grē·thūl´se) *adj.* bittersweet.

agrietado. da, (â·grye·tâ´tho, thä) *adj.*
cracked, cleft.

agrietarse, (â·grye·târ´se) *vr.* to crack.

â arm, e they, ē bē, o fore, ū blūe, b bad, ch chip, d day, f fat, g go, h hot, k kid, 1 let

agrimensor, (â·grē·men·sor´) *m.* land surveyor.

agrimensura, (â·grē·men·sū´rä) *f.* land surveying.

agrio, ria, (ä´gryo, gryä) *adj.* sour, acrid; rough, rocky, craggy *(peñascoso);* sharp, rude, unpleasant *(áspero).*

agrónomo, (â·gro´no·mo) *m.* agronomist.

agrupación, (â·grū·pâ·syon´) *f.* group, association, crowd.

agrupar, (á· grū·pâr´) *va.* to group, to place together; —**se,** to cluster, to crowd together.

agrura (â·grū´rä) *f.* acidity.

Agte. Gral.: Agente General, G.A. General Agent.

agto. or **ag.to : agosto,** Aug. August.

agua, (ä´gwä) *f.* water; slope *(vertiente);* — **arriba,** upstream; — **delgada,** soft water; — **gorda,** hard water; — **de soda,** soda water; — **fresca,** cold or fresh water; — **jabonosa,** suds; — **llovediza** or — **lluvia,** rain water; — **potable,** drinking water; — **tibia,** lukewarm water.

aguacate, (â·gwâ·kâ´te) *m.* avocado, alligator pear.

aguacero, (â·gwâ·se´ro) *m.* short, heavy shower of rain.

aguada, (â· gwä´thä) *f.* flood in a mine *(inundación);* (naut.) fresh-water supply; wash *(pintura).*

aguadero, (â·gwâ·the´ro) *m.* watering place for cattle, horsepond.

aguado, da, (â·gwä´tho, thä) *adj.* watered down, watery, mixed with water; not firm, flaccid.

aguador, ra, (â·gwä·thor´, rä) *n.* water carrier.

aguafiestas, (â·gwâ·fyes´tâs), *m.* and *f.* killjoy, spoilsport.

aguafuerte, (â·gwâ·fwer´te) *m.* or *f.* etching.

aguamanil, (â·gwâ·mâ·nēl´) *m.* washstand *(lavabo);* pitcher *(jarro).*

aguamarina, (â·gwâ·mâ·rē´nâ) *f.* aquamarine.

aguamiel, (â·gwâ·myel´) *f.* hydromel, honey and water.

aguanieve, (â·gwâ·nye´ve) *f.* sleet; (orn.) lapwing.

aguantar, (â·gwân·târ´) *va.* to sustain, to suffer, to endure, to bear.

aguante, (â·gwân´te) *m.* patience, endurance.

aguar, (â·gwâr´) *va.* to dilute with water *(diluir);* to spoil *(turbar).*

aguardar, (â·gwâr·thâr´) *va.* to expect, to await, to wait for.

aguardiente, (â·gwâr·thyen´te) *m.* distilled liquor.

aguarrás, (â·gwâ··rrâs´) *m.* turpentine.

agudeza, (â·gū·the´sä) *f.* keenness, sharpness; acuteness, smartness.

agudo, da, (â·gū´tho, thä) *adj.* sharppointed, keen-edged, fine *(afilado);* acute, witty, bright *(perspicaz);* (fig.) shrill, glaring, loud.

aguerrido, da, (â·ge·rrē´tho, thä) *adj.* inured to war.

aguijada, (â·gē·hâ´thä) *f.* spur, goad.

aguijón, (â·gē·hon´) *m.* stinger of a bee or wasp *(dardo);* stimulation *(estímulo).*

aguijonear, (â·gē·ho·ne·âr´) *va.* to prick; to spur on, to stimulate, to goad *(estimular).*

águila, (ä´gē·lä) *f.* eagle; (fig.) sharp, clever person.

aguileño, ña, (â·ge·le´nyo, nyâ) *adj.* aquiline; hawk-nosed.

aguilucho, (â·gē·lü´cho) *m.* eaglet.

aguinaldo, (â·gē·nâl´do) *m.* Christmas gift.

aguja, (â·gū´hä) *f.* needle; (rail.) switch; — **de coser,** sewing needle; — **de tejer,** knitting needle; — **de zurcir,** darning needle.

agujerear, (â·gū·he·re·âr´) *va.* to pierce, to bore.

agujero, (â·gū·he´ro) *m.* hole *(abertura);* needlemaker *(fabricante);* needle seller *(vendedor).*

agujeta, (â·gū·he´tä) *f.* shoelace *(cordón);* muscular twinge *(punzada).*

aguoso, sa, (â·gwo´so, sä) *adj.* aqueous, watery.

agusanarse, (â·gū·sâ·nâr´se) *vr.* to become worm-eaten.

Agustín, (â·gūs·tēn´) Augustine, Austin.

agustiniano (â·gūs·tē·nya´no) or **agustino,** (â·gūs·tē´no) *m.* monk of the order of St. Augustine.

aguzadera, (â·gū·sâ·the´rä) *f.* whetstone.

aguzar, (â·gū·sâr´) *va.* to whet, to sharpen *(afilar);* to stimulate *(estimular).*

aherrojar, (â·e·rro·hâr´) *va.* to put in chains or irons.

ahí, (â·ē´) *adv.* there; **de — que,** for this reason; **por —,** that direction; more or less.

ahijada, (â·ē·hâ´thä) *f.* goddaughter.

ahijado, (â·ē·hâ´tho) *m.* godson.

ahínco, (â·hēng´ko) *m.* zeal, earnestness, eagerness.

ahogar, (â·o·gâr´) *va.* and *vr.* to smother, to suffocate *(sofocar);* to drown *(en agua);* —, *va.* to oppress *(oprimir);* to quench *(apagar).*

ahogo, (â·o´go) *m.* suffocation; anguish

---

m met, **n** not, **p** pot, **r** very, **rr** (none), **s** so, **t** toy, **th** with, **v** eve, **w** we, **y** yes, **z** zero

(angustia).

ahondar, (â·on·dâr´) *va.* to sink, to deepen; —, *vn.* to penetrate deeply *(penetrar);* to go into thoroughly *(profundizar).*

ahora, (â·o´râ) *adv.* now, at present; —, *conj.* whether, or; — **mismo,** right now; **hasta** —, thus far; **por** —, for the present; — **bien,** now, then; **de** — **en adelante,** from now on.

ahorcajarse, (â·or·kâ·hâr´se) *vr.* to sit astride.

ahorcar, (â·or·kâr´) *va.* to kill by hanging; **—se,** to hang oneself, to commit suicide by hanging.

ahorita, (â·o·rē´tâ) *adv.* (Sp. Am.) right now, in just a minute.

ahorquillado, da, (â·or·kē·yâ´tho, thâ) *adj.* forked.

ahorrar, (â·o·rrâr´) *va.* to economize, to save.

ahorrativo, va, (â·o·rrâ·tē´vo, vâ) *adj.* frugal, parsimonious, sparing.

ahorro, (â·o´rro) *m.* saving, thrift; **caja** or **banco de —s,** savings bank.

ahuecar, (â·we·kâr´) *va.* to hollow, to scoop out.

ahumadero, (âū·ma·the´ro) *m.* smokehouse.

ahumar, (âū·mâr´) *va.* to smoke, to cure in smoke; **—se** (coll.) to get high, to become tipsy.

ahusar, (âū·sâr´) *va.* to make thin as a spindle; —. *va.* and *vr.* to taper.

ahuyentar, (âū·yen·târ´) *va.* to put to flight, to banish; **—se,** to flee; to escape.

airarse, (âē·râr´se) *vr.* to become irritated, to become angry.

aire, (â´ē·re) *m.* air; wind *(viento);* atmosphere; gracefulness, charm *(gracia);* aspect, countenance *(apariencia);* musical composition, melody *(melodía);* (auto.) choke; — **viciado,** foul air; **con** — **acondicionado,** air-conditioned; **al** — **libre,** outdoors.

airear, (âē·re·âr´) *va.* to air, to ventilate.

airoso, sa, (âē·ro´so, sâ) *adj.* airy, windy; graceful, charming *(garboso);* successful *(lucido).*

aislacionismo, (âēz·lâ·syo·nēz´mo) *m.* isolationism.

aislacionista, (âēz·lâ·syo·ne´s´tâ) *m.* and *f.* isolationist.

aislado, da, (âēz·lâ´tho, thâ) *adj.* isolated, cut off, insulated.

aislador, (âēz·lâ·thor´) *m.* (elec.) insulator.

aislamiento, (âēz·lâ·myen´to) *m.* isolation,

insulation; (fig.) solitude, loneliness; privacy.

aislante, (âēz·lân´te) *adj.* insulating.

aislar, (âēz·lâr´) *va.* to surround with water; to isolate, to insulate.

¡ajá! (â·hâ´) *interj.* aha!

ajar, (â·hâr´) *va.* to rumple, to crumple.

ajedrecista, (â·he·thre·sēs´tâ) *m.* or *f.* chess player.

ajedrez, (â·he·thres´) *m.* chess; (naut.) netting, grating.

ajenjo, (â·hen´ho) *m.* wormwood; absinthe *(licor).*

ajeno, na, (â·he´no, nâ) *adj.* another´s, not one´s own; strange, improper, contrary, foreign *(impropio);* unknown to.

ajetrearse, (â·he·tre·âr´se) *vr.* to exert oneself, to bustle, to toil.

ají, (â·hē´) *m.* chili pepper, chili.

ajo, (â´ho) *m.* garlic; garlic sauce *(salsa);* (coll.) shady deal, dishonest business transaction; **¡—!** *interj.* darn! heck!

ajolote, (â·ho·lo´te) *m.* (zool.) axolotl.

ajuar, (â·hwâr´) *m.* bridal apparel and furniture, trousseau *(de boda);* household furnishings *(muebles).*

ajustable, (â·hūs·tâ´vle) *adj.* adjustable.

ajustar, (â·hūs·târ´) *va.* to regulate, to adjust, to repair; — **cuentas,** to settle matters, to settle accounts; **—se,** to adjust or adapt oneself.

ajuste, (â·hūs´te) *m.* agreement, adjustment, settlement, accommodation.

ajusticiar, (â·hūs·tē·syâr´) *va.* to execute.

al, (âl) to the; — **fin,** at last; — **instante,** at once.

ala, (â´lâ) *f.* wing; brim *(parte lateral);* **—s,** *pl.* (naut.) upper studding sails.

alabanza, (â·lâ·vân´sâ) *f.* praise, applause.

alabar, (â·lâ·vâr´) *va.* to praise, to applaud, to extol.

alabastrino, na, (â·lâ·vâs·trē´no, nâ) *adj.* of alabaster.

alabastro, (â·lâ·vâs´tro) *m.* alabaster.

alabearse, (â·lâ·ve·âr´se) *vr.* to warp.

alacena, (â·lâ·se´nâ) *f.* cupboard.

alacrán, (â·lâ·krân´) *m.* scorpion; ring of the mouthpiece of a bridle *(de freno).*

alacridad, (â·lâ·krē·thâth´) *f.* alacrity.

alado, da. (â·lâ´tho, thâ) *adj.* winged.

alambicado, da, (â·lâm·bē·kâ´tho, thâ) *adj.* given sparingly or grudgingly; pedantic, overly subtle *(rebuscado).*

alambicar, (â·lâm·bē·kâr´) *va.* to distil; to scrutinize, to examine closely *(escudriñar).*

alambique, (â·lâm·bē´ke) *m.* still, distillery.

alambrado, (â·lâm·brá'tho) *m.* wire fence, wire screen.

alambrar, (â·lâm·brâr') *va.* to fence with wire.

alambre, (â·lâm'bre) *m.* wire, copper wire; **— de púas,** barbed wire.

alameda, (â·lâ·me'thâ) *f.* poplar grove; tree-lined promenade *(paseo).*

álamo, (â'lâ·mo) *m.* poplar, poplar tree; cottonwood tree *(chopo);* **— temblón,** aspen tree.

alarde, (â·lâr'the) *m.* military review *(desfile);* display, show, exhibition *(ostentación);* **hacer —,** to boast, to brag.

alardear, (â·lâr·the·âr') *vn.* to brag, to boast.

alargado, da, (â·lâr·gá'tho, thâ) *adj.* elongated.

alargar, (â·lâr·gâr') *va.* to lengthen, to extend, to prolong.

alarido, (â·lâ·rē'tho) *m.* outcry, shout, howl; **dar —s,** to howl.

alarma, (â·lâr'mâ) *f.* alarm; **— de incendios,** fire alarm; **— contra ladrones,** burglar alarm.

alarmante, (â·lâr·mân'te) *adj.* alarming.

alarmar, (â·lâr·mâr') *va.* to alarm; **—se** to be alarmed.

alarmista, (â·lâr·mēs'tâ) *m.* and *f.* alarmist.

a la v/: **a la vista,** (com.) at sight.

alba, (âl'vâ) *f.* dawn of day, daybreak; alb, surplice *(vestidura).*

albacea, (âl·vâ·se'â) *m.* executor; **—,** *f.* executrix.

albañal, (âl·vâ·nyâl') *m.* sewer, drain.

Albañil, (âl·vâ·nyēl') *m.* mason, bricklayer.

albarda, (âl·vâr'thâ) *f.* packsaddle.

albaricoque, (âl·vâ·rē·ko'ke) *m.* apricot.

albatros, (âl·vâ'tros) *m.* albatross.

albedrío, (âl·ve·thrē'o) *m.* free will.

albéitar, (âl·ve'ē·tar) *m.* veterinary surgeon.

alberca, (âl·ver'kâ) *f.* swimming pool *(piscina);* reservoir, cistern *(cisterna);* pond *(estanque).*

albergar, (âl·ver·gâr') *va.* to lodge, to house, to harbor; **—se,** to take shelter.

albergue, (âl·ver'ge) *m.* shelter, refuge.

albillo, (â·vē'yo) *m.* white grape *(uva);* white-grape wine *(vino).*

albino, na, (âl·vē'no, nâ) *n.* albino.

albo, ba, (âl'vo, vâ) *adj.* (poet.) white.

albóndiga, (âl·von'dē·gâ) *f.* meatball.

albor, (âl·vor') *m.* (poet.) dawn; **—es,** *pl.* beginnings.

alborada, (âl·vo·râ'thâ) *f.* first dawn of day; (mus.) aubade.

alborotadizo, za, (âl·vo·ro·tâ·thē'so, sâ) *adj.* easily upset, easily perturbed.

alborotado, da, (âl·vo·ro·tá'tho, thâ) *adj.* rash, thoughtless, heedless.

alborotar, (âl·vo·ro·târ') *va.* to upset, to stir up, to disturb.

alboroto, (âl·vo·ro'to) *m.* noise, disturbance, tumult, riot.

alborozado, da, (âl·vo·ro·sá'tho, thâ), *adj.* excited.

alborozar, (âl·vo·ro·sâr') *va.* to exhilarate.

alborozo, (âl·vo·ro'so) *m.* joy, gaiety, rejoicing.

¡albricias! (âl·vrē'syâs) *interj.* good news!

álbum, (âl'vūn) *m.* album; **— de recortes,** scrap book.

albumen, (âl·vū'men) *m.* **albúmina,** (âl. vu'mē·nâ) *f.* albumen.

albuminuria, (âl·vū·mē·nū'ryâ) *f.* (med.) Bright's disease.

albur, (âl·vūr') *m.* chance, hazard; **jugar** or **correr un —,** to leave to chance, to take a risk.

albura, (âl·vū'râ) *f.* whiteness; sapwood *(madera).*

alcachofa, (âl·kâ·cho'fâ) *f.* artichoke.

alcahuete, ta, (âl·kâ·we'te, tâ) *n.* pimp, bawd, procurer.

alcahuetería, (âl·kâ·we·te·rē'â) *f.* bawdry, pandering.

alcaide, (âl·kâ'ē·the) *m.* jailer, warden.

alcaldía, (âl·kâl·thē'â) *f.* office of a warden or jailer.

alcalde, (âl·kâl'de) *m.* mayor.

alcaldía, (âl·kâl·dē'â) *f.* mayor's office.

álcali, (âl'kâ·lē) *m.* (chem.) alkali.

alcalino, na, (âl·kâ·lē'no, nâ) *adj.* alkaline.

alcance, (âl·kân'se) *m.* reach, scope, range; ability, grasp *(talento);* (fig.) import, significance; **— del oído,** earshot.

alcancía, (âl·kân·sē'â) *f.* piggy bank; (eccl.) alms box.

alcanfor, (âl·kâm·for') *m.* camphor.

alcantarilla, (âl·kân·tâ·rē'yâ) *f.* small bridge, culvert *(puentecillo);* drain, sewer, conduit *(albañal).*

alcantarillado, (âl·kân·tâ·rē·yâ'tho) *m.* sewage.

alcanzar, (âl·kan·sâr') *va.* to overtake, to catch up with, to reach *(emparejar);* to get, to obtain *(obtener);* to perceive *(percibir);* **— a oir,** to overhear; **—,** *vn.* to suffice, to reach, to be enough.

alcaparra, (âl·kâ·pá'rrâ) *f.* caper (condiment) fled, stunned.

alcatraz, (âl·kâ·trâs'), *m.* pelican; (Mex.)

calla ily.

alcázar, (âl·kä´sär), *m.* castle; fortress; (naut.) quarterdeck.

alce, (âl´se), *m.* the cut (in cards); (zool.) elk or moose.

alcoba, (âl·ko´vä), *f.* bedroom.

alcohol, (âl·ko·ol´), *m.* alcohol.

alcohólico, ca, (âl·ko´olē·ko, kâ), *adj.* alcoholic.

Alcorán, (âl·ko·rân´), *m.* Koran.

alcornoque, (âl·kor·no´ke), *m.* cork tree; (coll.) dunce, blockhead.

alcrebite, (âl·kre·vē´te), *f.* lineage, race, ancestry.

alcurnia, (âl·kūr´nyä), *f.* lineage, race, ancestry.

alcuza, (âl·kū´sä), *f.* oil jar, vinegar and oil cruet.

aldaba, (âl·dä´vä), *f.* knocker, clapper of a door (llamador); crossbar, latch (travesaño).

aldea, (âl·de´ä), *f.* hamlet, small village.

aldeano, na, (âl·de·ä´no, nä), *adj.* rustic, countried, uncultured; —, *n.* Peasant, countryman.

aleación, (â·le·â·syon´), *f.* metal alloy.

alear, (â·le·âr), *vn.* to flutter; —, *va.* to alloy.

aledaño, ña, (â·le·thä´nyo, nyä), *adj.* bordering, pertaining to a boundary line; —, *m.* border, boundary.

alegación, (â·le·gä·syon´), *f.* allegation.

alegar, (â·le·gär), *va.* to allege, to maintain, to affirm.

alegato, (â·le·gä´to), *m.* allegation, statement of plaintiff's case.

alegoría, (â·le·go·rē´ä), *f.* allegory.

alegórico, ca, (â·le·go´rē·ko, kâ), *adj.* allegorical.

alegrar, (â·le·grâr´), *va.* to gladden (regocijar); to lighten (aliviar); to exhilarate, to enliven (avivar); to beautify (hermosear); **—se,** to rejoice (regocijarse); to grow merry with drinking (achisparse).

alegre, (â·le´gre), *adj.* glad, merry, joyful, content.

alegría, (â·le·grē´ä), *f.* mirth, gaiety, delight, cheer.

alegrón, (â·le·gron´), *m.* (coll.) sudden joy; sudden outburst of flame (llamarada).

alejamiento, (â·le·hä·myen´to), *m.* distance, remoteness; removal, separation.

alejar, (â·le·hâr´), *va.* To remove to a greater distance, to separate, to take away; **—se,** to withdraw, to move away.

Alej.o: Alejandro, Alex, Alexander.

alelado,da, (â·le·lä´tho, thâ), *adj.* stupefied, stunned.

alelarse, (â·le·lâr´se) *vr.* to become stupid.

aleluya, (â·le·lū´yä) *m.* or *f.* hallelujah; —, *m.* Easter time.

alemán, ana, (â·le·mân´, ä´nä) *adj.* and *n.* German; —, *m.* German language.

Alemania, (â·le·mä´nyä) *f.* Germany.

alentador, ra, (â·len·tä·thor´, râ) *adj.* encouraging.

alentar*, (â·len·târ´) *vn.* to breathe; —, *va.* to animate, to cheer, to encourage, — **se,** to recover.

alergia, (â·ler´hyä) *f.* (med.) allergy.

alérgico, ca, (â·ler´hē·ko, kâ) *adj.* allergic.

alergista, (â·ler·hēs´tä) *m.* or *f.* allergist.

alergólogo, (â·ler·go´lo·go) *m.* allergist.

alero, (â·le´ro) *m.* eaves.

alerón, (â·le·ron´) *m.* (avi.) aileron.

alerta, (â·ler´tä) *adv.* vigilantly; **estar —,** to be on the alert; **¡—!** *interj.* take care! watch out!

alertar, (â·ler·târ´) *va.* to alert.

alerto, ta, (â·ler´to, tä) *adj.* alert, vigilant, open-eyed.

aleta, (â·le´tä) *f.* fin (de pez); (mech.) blade (de hélice).

aletargarse, (â·le·târ·gâr´se) *vr.* to fall into a lethargic state, to become torpid.

aletazo, (â·le·tä´so) *m.* blow, hit, from a wing.

aletear, (â·le·te·âr´) *vn.* to flutter, to flap, to flick.

aleteo, (â·le·te´o) *m.* flapping of wings, fluttering.

aleve, (â·le´ve) *adj.* treacherous, perfidious.

alevosía, (â·le·vo·sē´ä) *f.* treachery, perfidy; **con — y ventaja,** with malice aforethought.

alevoso, sa, (â·le·vo´so, sä) *adj.* treacherous, perfidious.

alfa, (âl´fä) *f.* alpha, first letter of the Greek alphabet; **— y omega,** beginning and end.

alfabéticamente, (âl·fâ·ve·tē·kâ·men´te) *adv.* alphabetically.

alfabético, ca, (âl·fâ·ve´tē·ko, kâ) *adj.* alphabetical.

alfabeto. (âl·fa·ve´to) *m.* alphabet.

alfajor, (âl·fâ·hor´) *m.* sweet paste made of corn and honey.

alfarería, (âl·fâ·re·rē´ä) *f.* art of pottery, ceramics.

alfarero, (âl·fâ·re´ro) *m.* potter.

alfeñique, (âl·fe·nyē´ke) *m.* sugar paste; weakling (canijo).

alferecía, (âl·fe·re·sē´ä) *f.* epilepsy.

alférez, (âl·fe´res) *m.* ensign (abanderado); second lieutenant (subteniente).

alfil, (âl·fēl´) *m.* bishop (in chess).

â arm, **e** they, **ē** bē, **o** fore, **ū** blūe, **b** bad, **ch** chip, **d** day, **f** fat, **g** go, **h** hot, **k** kid, **1** let

alfiler, (âl·fē·ler´) *m.* pin; **—es,** *pl.* pin money; **— de corbata,** stickpin; **— imperdible,** safety pin.

alfilerazo, (â·fē·le·râ´so) *m.* prick of a pin; large pin.

alfiletero, (âl·fē·le·te´ro) *m.* pincushion.

alfombra, (âl·fom´brâ) *f.* carpet, rug.

alfombrar, (âl·fom·brâr´) *va.* to carpet.

alfombrilla, (âl·fom·brē´yâ) *f.* (med.) measles.

alforja, (âl·for´hâ) *f.* saddlebag, knapsack.

alforza, (âl·for´sâ) *f.* tuck, pleat.

alga, (âl´gâ) *f.* (bot.) alga, seaweed.

algarabía, (âl·ga·râ·vē´â) *f.* Arabic tongue *(idioma);* babble, jargon *(babilonia);* clamor, din *(alboroto).*

algarada, (âl·gâ·râ´thâ) *f.* uproar *(vocería);* sudden attack *(ataque).*

algazara, (âl·gâ·sâ´râ) *f.* din, hubbub, uproar.

álgebra, (âl´he·vrâ) *f.* algebra.

algebraico, ca, (âl·he·vrâ´ē·ko, kâ) *adj.* algebraic.

álgido, (âl´hē·tho) *adj.* icy, chilly.

algo, (âl´go) *pron.* some, something; any-thing; **— de,** a little; **— que comer,** something to eat; **en —,** somewhat, in some way, a bit; **por —,** for some reason; **—,** *adv.* a little, rather.

algodón, (âl·go·thon´) *m.* cotton, cotton plant; cotton material *(tela);* **— en bruto** or **en rama,** raw cotton.

algodonado, da, (âl·go·tho·nâ´tho, thâ) *adj.* filled with cotton, wadded, padded.

algodonal, (âl·go·tho·nâl´) *m.* cotton plantation.

algodonero, (âl·go·tho·ne´ro) *m.* cotton plant; dealer in cotton, cotton broker *(negociante);* **—, ra,** *adj.* pertaining to the cotton industry.

algoso, sa, (âl·go´so, sâ) *adj.* full of algae or seaweed.

alguacil, (âl·gwâ·sēl´) *m.* bailiff, constable.

alguien, (âl´gyen) *pron.* someone, some-body, anyone, anybody.

algún, (âl·gūn´), **alguno, na,** (âl·gū´no, nâ) *pron.* somebody, someone, some person, anybody, anyone; **—,** *adj.* some, any; **en modo —,** in any way; **— cosa,** anything; **en —na parte,** anywhere; **—s,** *pl.* a few.

alhaja, (â·lâ´hâ) *f.* jewel, gem.

alharaca, (â·lâ·râ´kâ) *f.* clamor, vociferation, ballyhoo.

alhóndiga, (â·lon´dē·gâ) *f.* public granary.

aliado, da, (â·lyâ´tho, thâ) *adj.* allied; **—,** *n.* ally.

alianza, (â·lyân´sâ) *f.* alliance, league.

aliarse, (â·lyâr´se) *vr.* to ally oneself, to become allied.

alias, (â´lyâs) *adv.* alias, otherwise known as.

alicaído, da, (â·lē·kâ·ē´tho, thâ) *adj.* weak, drooping, extenuated.

alicates, (â·lē·kâ´tes) *m. pl.* pincers, nippers, pliers.

aliciente, (â·lē·syen´te) *m.* attraction, incitement, inducement.

alícuota, (â·lē´kwo·tâ) *adj.* aliquot (number).

alienista, (â·lye·nēs´tâ) *m. and f.* alienist.

aliento, (â·lyen´to) *m.* breath;. (fig.) support, encouragement; **dar —,** to encourage; **sin —,** without vigor, spiritless, dull.

aligar, (â·lē·gâr´) *va.* to tie, to unite.

aligerar, (â·lē·he·râr´) *va.* to lighten, to alleviate *(aliviar);* to hasten, quicken *(acelerar).*

alijador, (â·lē·hâ·thor´) *m.* (naut.) lighter *(lanchón);* longshoreman.

alijo, (â·lē´ho) *m.* (naut.) lightening, unloading.

alimentación, (â·lē·men·tâ·syon´) *f.* maintenance, feeding, nourishment, meals.

alimentar, (â·lē·men·târ´) *va.* to feed, to nourish.

alimenticio, cía, (â·lē·men·tē´syo, syâ) *adj.* nutritious, nutritive.

alimento, (â·lē·men´to) *m.* nourishment, food; **—s,** *pl.* alimony, allowance.

alindar, (â·lēn·dâr´) *va.* to fix limits.

alineación, (â·lē·ne·â·syon´) *f.* alignment.

alinear, (â·lē·ne·âr´) *va.* to align, to arrange in a line, to line up; **—se,** to fall in line, to fall in.

aliñar, (â·lē·nyâr´) *va.* to adorn *(adornar);* to season *(condimentar).*

aliño, (â·lē´nyo) *m.* dress, ornament, decoration *(adorno);* dressing, seasoning *(condimento).*

alisar, (â·lē·sâr´) *va.* to plane, to smooth; to polish *(pulir).*

alisios, (â·lē´syos) *m. pl.,* trade winds.

aliso, (â·lē´so) *m.* alder tree.

alistado, da, (â·lēs·tâ´tho, thâ) *adj.* striped.

alistar, (â·lēs·târ´) *va.* to enlist, to enroll; **—se,** to get ready, to make ready.

aliviar, (â·lē·vyâr´) *va.* to lighten, to ease, to mollify, to alleviate.

alivio, (â·lē´vyo) *m.* alleviation, mitigation, comfort.

aljibe, (âl·hē´ve) *m.* cistern.

alma, (âl´mâ) *f.* soul; human being *(individuo);* principal part, heart *(ánimo);* (fig.) conscience, motivating force.

almacén, (âl·mâ·sen´) *m.* department store *(tienda);* warehouse, magazine *(depósito);* tener en —, to have in stock.

almacenaje, (âl·ma·se·nä´he) *m.* warehouse rent.

almacenar, (âl·mâ·se·nâr´) *va.* to store, to lay up, to warehouse.

almacenista, (âl·mâ·se·nēs´tâ) *m.* shop owner; salesman *(dependiente);* wholesaler *(mayorista).*

almadén, (âl·mâ·then´) *m.* mine.

almagre, (âl·mâ´gre) *m.* red ochre.

almanaque, (âl·ma·nâ´ke) *m.* almanac.

almazara (âl·ma·sä´râ) *f.* oil mill.

almeja, (âl·me·hâ) *f.* clam.

almena, (âl·me´nä) *f.* battlement.

almenado, da, (âl·me·nâ´tho, thâ) *adj.* embattled.

almendra, (âl·men´drä) *f.* almond; — garapiñada, sugared, honeyed almond.

almendrera, (âl·men·dre´râ) *f.* almendrero (âl·men·dre´ro) or almendro, (âl·men´-dro) *m.* almond tree.

almez (âl·mes´) or almezo, (âl·me´so) *m.* lotus tree.

almiar, (âl·myâr´) *m.* haystack.

almíbar, (âl·mē´vâr) *m.* sirup.

almibarar, (âl·mē·vä·râr´) *va.* to preserve fruit in sugar; (fig.) to ply with soft and endearing words.

almidón, (âl·mē·thon´) *m.* starch, farina.

almidonado, da, (âl·mē·tho·nâ´tho, thâ) *adj.* starched; (fig.) affected, stiff in mannerisms, overly prim.

almidonar, (âl·mē·tho·nâr´) *va.* to starch.

almirantazgo, (âl·mē·rân·tâz´go) *m.* admiralty.

almirante, (âl·mē·rân´te) *m.* admiral.

almirez, (âl·mē·res´) *m.* brass mortar; — y mano, mortar and pestle.

almizcle, (âl·mēs´kle) *m.* musk.

almizclera, (âl·mēs·kle´râ) *f.* muskrat.

almodrote, (âl·mo·thro´te) *m.* (coll.) hodgepodge.

almohada, (âl·mo·â´thä) *f.* pillow, cushion.

almohadilla, (âl·mo·â·thē´yâ) *f.* small pillow, sewing cushion.

almohadón, (âl·mo·â·thon´) *m.* large cushion.

almojábana, (âl·mo·hâ´vä·nä) *f.* type of cheesecake.

almoneda, (âl·mo·ne´thä) *f.* auction.

almorranas, (âl·mo·rrâ´nâs) *f. pl.* hemorrhoids, piles.

almorzar*, (âl·mor·sâr´) *vn.* to eat lunch, to have lunch.

almuerzo, (âl·mwer´so) *m.* lunch, lunch-

eon.

alocado, da, (â·lo·kâ´tho, thâ) *adj.* crackbrained, foolish, reckless.

alocución, (â·lō·kū·syon´) *f.* address, speech.

áloe (â´lo·e) or aloe, (â·lo´e) *m.* (bot.) aloe.

aloja, (â·lo´hâ) *f.* mead.

alojamiento, (â·lo·hâ·myen´to) *m.* lodging, accommodation; (naut.) steerage.

alojar, (â·lo·hâr´) *va.* to lodge; —se, to reside in lodgings, to board.

alón, (â·lon´) *m.* plucked wing.

alondra, (â·lon´drä) *f.* lark.

alosa, (â·lo´sä) *f.* shad.

alpaca, (âl·pa´kâ) *f.* (zool.) alpaca; alpaca fabric *(tela).*

alpargata, (âl·pâr·gä´tâ) *f.* hempen shoe.

Alpes, (âl´pes) *m. pl.* Alps.

alpinismo, (âl·pē·nēz´mo) *m.* mountain climbing.

alpinista, (âl·pē·nēs´tâ) *m.* and *f.* mountain climber.

alpino, na, (âl·pē´no, nâ) *adj.* Alpine.

alpiste, (âl·pē´ste) *m.* canary seed.

alquería, (âl·ke·rē´â) *f.* farmhouse.

alquilar, (âl·kē·lâr´) *va.* to let, to hire, to rent.

alquiler, (âl·kē·ler´) *m.* hire; rent *(de casa);* de —, for hire, for rent.

alquimia, (âl·kē´myâ) *f.* alchemy.

alquimista, (âl·kē·mēs´tâ) *m.* alchemist.

alquitrán, (âl·kē·trân´) *m.* tar, liquid pitch; — de hulla, coal tar; — de madera, pine tar.

alrededor, (âl·rre·the·thor´) *adv.* around; — de, about, around.

alrededores, (âl·rre·the·tho´res) *m. pl.* environs, neighborhood, surroundings.

alt.: altitud, alt. altitude; altura, ht. height.

alta, (âl´tâ) *f.* new member; dar de —, to dismiss, to discharge.

altanería, (âl·tâ·ne·rē´â) *f.* haughtiness.

altanero, ra, (âl·tâ·ne´ro, râ) *adj.* haughty, arrogant, vain, proud.

altar, (âl·târ´) *m.* altar; — mayor, high altar.

altavoz, (âl·tâ·vos´) *m.* loudspeaker; — para sonidos agudos, tweeter; — para sonidos graves, woofer.

alterable, (âl·te·râ´vle) *adj.* alterable, mutable.

alteración, (âl·te·râ·syon´) *f.* alteration, change, mutation; emotional upset, disturbance *(trastorno).*

alterar, (âl·te·râr´) *va.* to alter, to change *(cambiar);* to disturb, to upset *(trastornar);* —se, to become angry.

â arm, e they, ē bē, o fore, ū blūe, b bad, ch chip, d day, f fat, g go, h hot, k kid, 1 let

altercación, (âl·ter·kâ·syon´) *f.* altercation, controversy, quarrel, contention, strife.

altercado, (âl·ter·kâ´tho) *m.* disagreement, quarrel.

altercar, (âl·ter·kâr´) *va.* to dispute, to altercate, to quarrel.

alternar, (âl·ter·nâr´) *va.* and *vn.* to alternate.

alternativa, (âl·ter·nâ·tē´vä) *f.* alternative.

Alteza, (âl·te´sä) *f.* Highness (title).

alteza (âl·te´sä) *f.* height, elevation.

altibajos, (âl·tē·vä´hos) *m. pl.* unevenness of the ground; (fig.) ups and downs of life.

altímetro, (âl·tē´me·tro) *m.* altimeter.

altiplanicie, (âl·tē·plä·nē´sye) *f.* highland.

altiplano, (âl·tē·plä´no) *m.* high plateau.

altísimo, ma, (âl·tē´sē·mo, ma) *adj.* extremely high; **el A—,** the Most High, God.

altisonante (âl·tē·so·nân´te) or **altísono, na,** (âl·tē·so·no, nä) *adj.* high-sounding, pompous.

altitonante, (âl·tē·to·nân´te) *adj.* (poet.) thundering from on high.

altitud, (âl·tē·tūth´) *f.* altitude; **— absoluta,** (äer.) absolute altitude.

altivez, (âl·tē·ves´) *f.* pride, haughtiness, huff.

altivo, va, (âl·tē´vo, vä) *adj.* haughty, proud.

alto, ta, (âl´to, tä) *adj.* tall, high, elevated; loud *(fuerte);* **—,** *m.* height; story, floor *(piso);* highland *(meseta);* (mil.) halt; (mus.) tenor, tenor notes; **¡—!** or **¡—ahí!** *interj.* stop there!

altoparlante, (âl·to·pâr·lân´te) *m.* loudspeaker.

altruismo, (âl·trwēz´mo) *m.* altruism, unselfishness.

altruista, (âl·trwēs´tä) *adj.* altruistic, unselfish; **—,** *m.* and *f.* altruist, unselfish person.

altura, (âl·tū´rä) *f.* height, highness, altitude; peak, summit *(cumbre);* **—s,** *pl.* the heavens.

alubia, (ä·lū´vyä) *f.* string bean.

alucinación, (ä·lū·sē·nä·syon´) *f.,* **alucinamiento,** (ä·lū·sē·nä·myen´to) *m.* hallucination.

alucinar, (ä·lū·sē·nâr´) *va.* to delude, to deceive; to hallucinate; **—se,** to deceive oneself, to be deceived.

alud, (ä·lūth´) *m.* avalanche.

aludido, da, (ä·lū·thē´tho, thä) *adj.* referred to, above-mentioned.

aludir, (ä·lū·thēr´) *vn.* to allude, to refer to.

alumbrado, da, (ä·lūm·brä´tho, thä) *adj.* illuminated; **—,** *m.* lighting; (avi.) flare.

alumbramiento, (ä·lūm·brä·myen´to) *m.* illumination; childbirth *(parto).*

alumbrar, (ä·lūm·brâr´) *va.* to light, to illuminate; (fig.) to enlighten.

alumbre, (ä·lūm´bre) *m.* alum.

aluminio, (ä·lū·mē´nyo) *m.* aluminum.

alumno, na, (ä·lūm´no, nä) *n.* student, pupil; (fig.) disciple, follower.

alusión, (ä·lū·syon´) *f.* allusion, hint.

aluvión, (ä·lū·vyon´) *m.* alluvion, flood; (fig.) crowd of people.

álveo, (äl´ve·o) *m.* bed of a river.

alveolo, (äl·ve·o´lo) or **alvéolo,** (äl·ve´o·lo) *m.* socket of a tooth; honeycomb cell *(de panal).*

alverjas, (äl·ver´hâs) *f. pl.* peas.

alza, (äl´sä) *f.* advance in price; lift.

alzado, da, (äl·sä´tho, thä) *adj.* raised, lifted; (coll.) proud, insolent *(engreído);* fraudulent *(negociante).*

alzamiento, (äl·sä·myen´to) *m.* raising, elevation; uprising.

alzaprima, (äl·sä·prē´mä) *f.* lever.

alzar, (äl·sar´) *va.* to raise, to lift up; to heave *(levantar);* to construct, to build *(construir);* to hide, to lock up *(guardarse);* to cut cards *(cortar);* **— cabeza,** to recover from a calamity; **— se,** to rise in rebellion.

allá, (ä·yä´) *adv.* there; thither; **más —,** further on, beyond; **más — de,** beyond.

allanar, (ä·yä·nar´) *va.* to level, to flatten *(aplanar);* to overcome, to rise above *(superar);* to pacify, to subdue *(sujetar);* **— se,** to submit, to abide by.

allegado, da, (ä·ye·gä´tho, thä) *adj.* related, similar, close; **—,** *n.* follower, ally.

allegar, (ä·ye·gâr´) *va.* to collect, to gather.

allende, (ä·yen´de) *adv.* on the other side, beyond.

allí, (ä·yē´) *adv.* there, in that place; **por —,** yonder, over there.

A.M.: antemeridiano, A.M. or a.m., before noon.

ama, (ä´mä) *f.* mistress; **— de casa,** house-wife; **— de llaves,** housekeeper.

amabilidad, (ä·mä·vē·lē·thâth´) *f.* amiability, kindness.

amable, (ä·mä´vle) *adj.* amiable, kind.

amado, da, (ä·mä´tho, thä) *n.* and *adj.* beloved, darling, loved.

amaestrado, da, (ä·mä·es·trä´tho, thä) *adj.* taught, trained, drilled.

amaestrar, (ä·mä·es·trâr´) *va.* to teach, to train.

amagar, (ä·mä·gâr´) *va.* and *vn.* to threat-

---

m met, **n** not, **p** pot, **r** very, **rr** (none), **s** so, **t** toy, **th** with, **v** eve, **w** we, **y** yes, **z** zero

en, to hint at, to smack of.

amago, (â·mä´go) *m.* threat, indication, symptom.

amainar, (â·mäē·när´) *va.* (naut.) to lower; *vn.* to die down, to lose its strength; — **se,** to give up, to withdraw from.

amalgama, (â·mäl·gä´mä) *f.* amalgam, alloy; (fig.) mixture, blend.

amalgamar, (â·mäl·gä·mär´) *va.* (chem.) to amalgamate, to mix.

amamantar, (â·mä·man·tar´) *va.* to suckle, to nurse.

amancebarse, (â·man·se·vâr´se) *vr.* to live in concubinage.

amancillar, (â·man·sē·yär´) *va.* to stain, to defile, to taint, to injure.

amanecer, (â·mä·ne·ser´) *m.* dawn, daybreak; **al —,** at daybreak; **—*,** *vn.* to dawn; to appear at daybreak *(aparecer);* to reach at daybreak *(llegar).*

amanerado, da, (â·mä·ne·rä´tho, thä) *adj.* affected, artificial.

amaneramiento, (â·mä·ne·rä·myen´to) *m.* mannerism.

amanerarse, (â·mä·ne·râr´se) *vr.* to become affected, to acquire undesirable mannerisms.

amansar, (â·män·sär´) *va.* to tame, to domesticate *(domesticar);* to soften, to pacify *(apaciguar).*

amante, (â·män´te) *m.* and *f.* lover.

amanuense, (â·mä·nwen´se) *m.* and *f.* amanuensis, clerk, copyist.

amañar, (â·mä·nyär´) *va.* to do cleverly; — — **se,** to become accustomed, to adapt oneself, to become expert.

amapola, (â·mä·po´lä) *f.* (bot.) poppy.

amar, (â·mär´) *va.* to love.

amargar, (â·mär·gär´) *va.* to make bitter; (fig.) to exasperate; —, *vn.* to be bitter; — **se,** to become bitter.

amargo, ga, (â·mär´go, gä) *adj.* bitter, acrid; (fig.) painful, unpleasant; —, *m.* bitterness; —**s,** *m. pl.* bitters.

amargor, (â·mar·gor´) *m.* bitterness; (fig.) sorrow, distress.

amargura, (â·mar·gü´rä) *f.* bitterness; (fig.) sorrow, affliction.

amarillento, ta, (â·ma´·rē·yen´to, tä) *adj.* yellowish.

amarillo, lla, (â·mä·rē´yo, yä) *adj.* yellow.

amarrar, (â·mä·rrär´) *va.* to tie, to fasten.

amarre, (â·mä´rre) *m.* mooring; mooring line or cable.

amartillar, (â·mär·tē·yär´) *va.* to hammer; to cock *(disparador).*

amasar, (â·mä·sär´) *va.* to knead; (fig.) to arrange, to prepare, to plot.

amasijo, (â·mä·sē´ho) *m.* mixed mortar *(argamasa);* bread dough *(harina).*

amatista, (â·mä·tēs´tä) *f.* amethyst.

amazona, (â·mä·so´nä) *f.* amazon, masculine woman.

ambages, (âm·bä´hes) *m. pl.* circumlocution; **sin —,** in plain language.

ámbar, (âm´bâr) *m.* amber; — **gris,** amber-gris.

ambarino, na, (âm·bä·rē´no, nä) *adj.* amber, amberlike.

Amberes, (âm·be´res) *f.* Antwerp.

ambición, (âm·bē·syon´) *f.* ambition; drive, desire *(pasión).*

ambicionar, (âm·bē·syo·när´) *va.* to covet, to aspire to.

ambicioso, sa, (âm·bē·syo´so, sä) *adj.* ambitious.

ambidextro, tra, (âm·bē·des´tro, trä) *adj.* ambidextrous.

ambiental, (âm·byen·tâl´) *adj.* environmental.

ambientalismo, (âm·byen·tâ·lēz´mo) *m.* environmentalism.

ambiente, (âm·byen´te) *m.* environment.

ambigú, (âm·bē·gü´) *m.* light meal, buffet lunch.

ambigüedad, (âm·bē·gwe·thâth´) *f.* ambiguity.

ambiguo, gua, (âm·bē´gwo, gwä) *adj.* ambiguous, equivocal.

ámbito, (âm´bē·to) *m.* border, limit, enclosed area, realm.

ambivertido, (âm·bē·ver·tē´tho) *m.* ambivert.

ambos, bas, (âm´bos, bäs) *pron.* and *adj. pl.* both.

ambrosia, (âm·bro·sē´ä) *f.* ambrosia.

ambulancia, (âm·bü·1ân´syä) *f.* ambulance.

ambulante, (âm·bü·lân´te) *adj.* ambulatory, roving; **músico —,** street musician; **vendedor —,** peddler.

amedrentar. (â·me·thren·tar´) *va.* to frighten, to intimidate.

amelga, (â·mel´gä) *f.* ridge between two furrows.

ameliorar, (â·me·lyo·râr´) *va.* to better, to improve.

amén, (â·men´) *interj.* amen, so be it; —, *n.* acquiescence, consent; **en un decir —,** in an instant; **— de,** besides, in addition to.

amenaza, (â·me·nä´sä) *f.* threat, menace.

amenazador, ra, (â·me·nä·sä·thor´, rä) *adj.* menancing, threatening.

amenazar, (â·me·nä·sär´) *va.* to threaten, to menace.

amenidad, (â·me·nē·thâth´) *f.* amenity, agreeableness.

amenizar, (â·me·nē·sâr´) *va.* to make pleasant.

ameno, na, (â·me´no, nâ) *adj.* pleasant, amusing, entertaining.

América del Norte, (â·me´rē·kâ thel nor´te) *f.* North America.

América del Sur, (â·me´rē·kâ thel sūr) *f.* South America.

americana, (â·me·rē·kâ´nâ) *f.* sackcoat, coat.

americanismo, (â·me·rē·kâ·nēz´mo) *m.* Americanism; an expression or word used in Latin-American Spanish.

americanizado, da, (â·me·rē·kâ·nē·sâ´·tho, thâ) *adj.* Americanized.

americano, na, (â·me·rē·kâ´no, nâ) *n.* and *adj.* American.

ametralladora, (â·me·trâ·y´â·tho´râ) *f.* machine gun.

amianto, (â·myân´to) *m.* asbestos.

amiba, (â·mē´vâ) *f.* ameba or amoeba.

amigable, (â·mē·gâ´vle) *adj.* amiable, friendly.

amígdala, (â·mēg´thâ·lâ) *f.* tonsil.

amigo, ga, (â·mē´go, gâ) *n.* friend, comrade; devotee, fan, lover *(aficionado)*; **—, ga,** *adj.* friendly; fond, devoted.

amilanar, (â·mē·lâ·nâr´) *va.* to frighten, to terrify; **—se,** to become terrified.

aminoácido, (â·mē·no·â´sē·tho) *m.* amino acid.

aminorar, (â·mē·no·râr´) *va.* to reduce, to lessen.

amistad, (â·mēs·tâth´) *f.* friendship; **hacer —,** to become acquainted.

amistoso, sa, (â·mēs·to´so, sâ) *adj.* friendly, cordial.

amnesia, (âm·ne´syâ) *f.* amnesia.

amnistía, (âm·nēs·tē´â) *f.* amnesty.

amo, (â´mo) *m.* master, proprietor, owner.

amodorramiento, (â·mo·tho·rrâ·myen´to) *m.* stupor, sleepiness.

amodorrarse, (â·mo·tho·rrâr´se) *vr.* to grow sleepy.

amoladera, (â·mo·lâ·the´râ) *f.* whetstone, grindstone.

amolador, (â·mo·lâ·thor´) *m.* grinder.

amolar*, (â·mo·lâr´) *va.* to whet, to grind, to sharpen.

amoldar, (â·mol·dâr´) *va.* to mold; to adapt, to adjust *(ajustar);* **—se,** to adapt oneself to, to live up to, to pattern oneself after.

amonestación, (â·mo·nes·tâ·syon´) *f.* advice, admonition, warning; **—ones,** pl. publication of marriage bans.

amonestar, (â·mo·nes·târ´) *va.* to advise, to admonish, to warn; to publish, to make public *(anunciar).*

amonio, (â·mo´nyo) *m.* (chem.) ammonium.

amontonar, (â·mon·to·nâr´) *va.* to heap together, to accumulate.

amor, (â·mor´) *m.* love; **por — de,** for the sake of; **por — de Dios,** for God´s sake; **— propio,** dignity, pride; **—es,** pl. love affair.

amoratado, da, (â·mo·râ·tâ´tho, thâ) *adj.* livid, black and blue, purplish.

amorcillo, (â·mor·sē´yo) *m.* flirtation.

amordazar, (â·mor·thâ·sâr´) *va.* to gag, to muzzle.

amorfo, fa, (â·mor´fo, fâ) *adj.* amorphous.

amorío, (â·mo·rē´o) *m.* love-making, love.

amoroso, sa, (â·mo·ro´so, sâ) *adj.* affectionate, loving.

amortiguador, (â·mor·tē·gwâ·thor´) *m.* shock absorber.

amortiguar, (â·mor·tē·gwâr´) *va.* to lessen, to mitigate, to soften *(apaciguar);* to deaden *(amortecer);* to temper *(moderar).*

amortizable, (â·mor·tē·sâ´vle) *adj.* redeemable.

amortización, (â·mor·tē·sâ·syon´) *f.* amortization.

amortizar, (â·mor·tē·sâr´) *va.* to amortize.

amotinador, ra, (â·mo·tē·nâ·thor´, râ) *n.* mutineer.

amotinamiento, (â·mo·tē·nâ·myen´to) *m.* mutiny.

amotinar, (â·mo·tē·nâr´) *va.* to excite rebellion; **—se,** to mutiny.

amovible, (â·mo·vē´vle) *adj.* removable.

amparar, (âm·pâ·râr´) *va.* to shelter, to favor, to protect; **—se,** to claim protection.

amparo, (âm·pâ´ro) *m.* protection, help, support; refuge, asylum *(abrigo);* (Mex.) habeas corpus.

amperio, (âm·pe´ryo) *m.* (elec.) ampere.

ampliación, (âm·plyâ·syon´) *f.* amplification, enlargement.

ampliar, (âm·plyâr´) *va.* to amplify, to enlarge, to extend, to expand, to increase.

amplificador, (âm·plē·fē·kâ·thor´) *m.* amplifier.

amplio, plia, (âm´plyo, plyâ) *adj.* ample, vast, spacious.

amplitud, (âm·plē·tūth´) *f.* amplitude, extension, largeness; **— de miras,** broadmindedness.

ampo (âm´po) *m.* dazzling whiteness.

---

m met, **n** not, **p** pot, **r** very, **rr** (none), **s** so, **t** toy, **th** with, **v** eve, **w** we, **y** yes, **z** zero

ampolla, (ȧm·po´yȧ) f. blister; vial, flask (frasco); (med.) ampoule.

ampollar, (ȧm·po·yȧr´) va. to raise blisters; **—se,** to rise in bubbles; **—,** adj. bubble-shaped; blister-like.

ampolleta, (ȧm·po·ye´tȧ) f. hourglass.

ampuloso, sa, (ȧm·pū·lo´so, sȧ) adj. affected, bombastic.

amputación, (ȧm·pū·tȧ·syon´) f. amputation.

amputar, (ȧm·pū·tȧr´) va. to amputate.

amueblar, (ȧ·mwe·vlȧr´) va. to furnish.

amuleto, (ȧ·mū·le´to) m. amulet.

amurallar, (ȧ·mū·rȧ·yȧr´) va. to surround with walls.

ana, (ȧ´nȧ) f. ell (measure).

anacardo, (ȧ·nȧ·kȧr´tho) m. cashew tree or fruit.

anaconda, (ȧ·nȧ·kon´dȧ) f. anaconda, South American boa.

anacoreta, (ȧ·nȧ·ko·re´tȧ) m. anchorite, hermit, recluse.

anacronismo, (ȧ·nȧ·kro·nēz´mo) m. anachronism.

ánade, (ȧ´nȧ·the) m. or f. duck.

anadino, na, (ȧ·nȧ·thē´no, nȧ) n. duckling.

anadón, (ȧ·nȧ·thon´) m. mallard.

anafe, (ȧ·nȧ´fe) m. portable stove.

anagrama, (ȧ·nȧ·grȧ´mȧ) m. anagram.

anales, (ȧ·nȧ´les) m. pl. annals.

analfabetismo, (ȧ·nȧl·fȧ·ve·tēz´mo) m. illiteracy.

analfabeto, ta, (ȧ·nȧl·fȧ·ve´to, tȧ) n. illiterate person.

análisis, (ȧ·nȧ´lē·sēs) m. or f. analysis.

analítico, ca, (ȧ·nȧ·lē´tē·ko, kȧ) adj. analytical.

analizar, (ȧ·nȧ·lē·sȧr´) va. to analyze.

analogía, (ȧ·nȧ·lo·hē´ȧ) f. analogy.

análogo, ga, (ȧ·nȧ´lo·go, gȧ) adj. analogous, similar.

anaquel, (ȧ·nȧ·kel´) m. shelf in a bookcase.

anaranjado, da, (ȧ·nȧ·rȧn·hȧ´tho, thȧ) adj. orange-colored.

anarquía, (ȧ·nȧr·kē´ȧ) f. anarchy.

anarquismo, (ȧ·nȧr·kēz´mo) m. anarchism.

anarquista, (ȧ·nȧr·kēs´tȧ) m. and f. anarchist.

anatema, (ȧ·nȧ·te´mȧ) m. or f. anathema.

anatomía, (ȧ·nȧ·to·mē´ȧ) f. anatomy. .

anatómico, ca, (ȧ·nȧ·to´mē·ko, kȧ) adj. anatomical.

anca, (ȧng´kȧ) f. buttock (nalga); hindquarter, haunch.

ancianidad, (ȧn·syȧ·nē·thȧth´) f. old age, great age.

anciano, na, (ȧn·syȧ´no, nȧ) adj. aged, ancient; **—,** n. ancient.

ancla, (ȧng´klȧ) f. anchor; echar **—s,** to anchor.

anclaje, (ȧng·klȧ´he) m. anchorage.

anclar, (ȧng·klȧr´) vn. to anchor.

áncora, (ȧng´ko·rȧ) f. anchor.

ancorar, (ȧng·ko·rȧr´) vn. to cast anchor.

ancho, cha, (ȧn´cho, chȧ) adj. broad, wide, large; **—,** m. breadth, width.

anchoa, (ȧn·cho´ȧ) f. anchovy; **—s,** (Mex.) pin curls.

anchura, (ȧn·chū´rȧ) f. width, breadth.

andaderas, (ȧn·dȧ·the´rȧs) f. pl. gocart.

Andalucía, (ȧn·dȧ·lū·sē´ȧ) f. Andalusia.

andamio, (ȧn·dȧ´myo) m. scaffold, scaffolding; (naut.) gangplank, gangway.

andana, (ȧn·dȧ´nȧ) f. row, rank, line; llamarse **—,** (coll.) to unsay, to retract a promise.

andanada, (ȧn·dȧ·nȧ´thȧ) f. grandstand (gradería); (fig.) volley of insults; (naut.) broadside.

andaniño, (ȧn·dȧ·nē´nyo) m. child´s walker.

andante, (ȧn·dȧn´te) adj. walking, errant; (mus.) andante.

andar*, (ȧn·dȧr´) vn. to go, to walk; to do, to fare (estar); to proceed, to behave (proceder); to work, to function, to move (funcionar); **— a tientas,** to grope; ¡ándale! hurry up! move on! ¡anda! you don´t say!

andarín, (ȧn·dȧ·rēn´) m. fast walker, good walker.

andas, (ȧn´dȧs) f. pl. bier with shafts; stretcher (camilla).

andén, (ȧn·den´) m. pavement, sidewalk (acera); (rail.) platform; foot path (senda); dock, landing.

andrajo, (ȧn·drȧ´ho) m. rag, tatter of clothing.

andrajoso, sa, (ȧn·drȧ·ho´so, sa) adj. ragged.

Andrés, (ȧn·dres´) Andrew.

andrógeno, (ȧn·dro´he·no) m. androgen; **—, na,** adj. androgenic.

andurriales, (ȧn·dū·rryȧ´les) m. pl. byways.

aneblar*, (ȧ·ne·vlȧr´) va. to cloud, to darken; **—se,** to become cloudy.

anécdota, (ȧ·neg´tho·tȧ) f. anecdote.

anegación, (ȧ·ne·gȧ·syon´) f. overflowing, inundation.

anegar, (ȧ·ne·gȧr´) va. to inundate, to submerge **—se,** to drown or to be flooded—

anemia, (â·ne′myâ) f. (med.) anemia.
anémico, ca, (â·ne′mē·ko, kâ) adj. anemic.
anemómetro, (â·ne·mo′me′tro) m. anemometer.
anestesia, (â·nes·te′syâ) f. (med.) anesthesia.
anestésico, ca, (â·nes·te′sē·ko, kâ) m. and adj. anesthetic.
anexar, (â·nek·sâr′) va. to annex, to join (añadir); to enclose (adjuntar).
anexidades, (â·nek·sē·thá′thes) f. pl. annexes, appurtenances.
anexión, (â·nek·syon′) f. annexation.
anexo, xa, (â·nek′so, sa) adj. annexed, joined; —, m. attachment on a letter or document; —s, m. pl. belongings.
anfibio, bia, (âm·fē′vyo, vyá) adj. amphibious; —, m. amphibian.
anfiteatro, (âm·fē·te·â′tro) m. amphitheater, auditorium (auditorio); (theat.) balcony; — anatómico, (med.) dissecting room.
anfitrión, (âm·fē·tryon′) m. host.
anfitriona, (âm·fē·tryo′ná) f. hostess.
ánfora, (âm′fo·râ) f. amphora; (Mex.) voting box.
angarillas, (âng·gâ·rē′yâs) f. pl. stretcher.
ángel, (ân·hēl) m. angel; tener —, to have a pleasing personality.
angelical, (ân·he·lē·kâl′) adj. angelic.
angina, (ân·hē′ná) f. (med.) angina; — de pecho, angina pectoris.
anglicismo, (âng·glē·sēz′mo) m. Anglicism.
anglosajón, ona, (âng·glo·sâ·hon′, o′ná) n. and adj. Anglo-Saxon.
angostar, (âng·gos·târ′) va. to narrow, to contract.
angosto, ta, (âng·gos′to, ta) adj. narrow, close.
angostura, (âng·gos·tū′râ) f. narrowness; narrow passage (paso).
anguila, (âng·gē′lâ) f. (zool.) eel.
angular, (âng·gū·lâr′) adj. angular; piedra —. cornerstone.
ángulo, (âng′gū·lo) m. angle, comer.
anguloso, sa, (âng·gūl·lo′so, sa) adj. angular, cornered.
angustia, (âng·gūs′tyâ) f. anguish, heartache.
angustiado, da, (ân·gūs·tyâ′tho, thâ) adj. worried, miserable.
angustiar, (âng·gūs·tyâr′) va. to cause anguish; —se, to feel anguish, to grieve.
angustioso, sa, (ân·gūs·tyo′so, sa) adj. distressing, alarming.
anhelante, (â·ne·lân′te) adj. eager.
anhelar, (â·ne·lâr′) vn. to long for, to desire (ansiar); to breathe with difficulty (jadear).
anhelo, (â·ne′lo) m. vehement desire, longing.
anheloso, sa, (â·ne·lo′so, sa) adj. very desirous.
anidar, (â·nē·thâr′) va. to inhabit; —, vn. to nestle, to make a nest.
anillo, (â·nē′yo) m. ring, small circle; — de empaquetadura del émbolo, piston ring; — de boda, wedding ring.
ánima, (á′nē·mâ) f. soul; bore of a gun (de fusil); —s, pl. church bells ringing at sunset.
animación, (â·nē·mâ·syon′) f. animation, liveliness.
animado, da, (â·nē·mâ′tho, thâ) adj. lively; animated.
animal, (â·nē·mâl′) m. and adj. animal; brute.
animar, (â·nē·mâr′) va. to animate, to enliven (avivar); to comfort, to encourage (alentar); —se, to cheer up, to be encouraged.
ánimo, (á′nē·mo) m. soul, spirit; (fig.) energy, determination. ¡—! interj. cheer up!
animosidad, (â·nē·mo·sē·thâth′) f. animosity.
animoso, sa, (â·nē·mo′so, sâ) adj. courageous, spirited.
aniñarse, (â·nē·nyâr′se) vr. to act in a childish manner.
aniquilar, (â·nē·kē·lâr′) va. to annihilate, to destroy; —se, to decay, to be consumed; (fig.) to be crushed, to be nonplussed.
anís, (â·nēs′) m. (bot.) anise.
aniversario, (â·nē·ver·sâ′ryo) m. anniversary; —, ria, adj. annual.
ano, (á′no) m. anus.
anoche, (â·no′che) adv. last night.
anochecer*, (â·no·che·ser′) vn. to grow dark; to arrive by nightfall (llegar).
anodizar, (â·no·thē·sar′) va. to anodize.
ánodo, (á′no·tho) m. (elec.) anode.
anomalía, (â·no·ma·lē′â) f. anomaly.
anómalo, la, (â·no′mâ·lo, lâ) adj. anomalous.
anon, (â·non′) m. (bot.) custard apple.
anonadar, (â·no·nâ·thâr′) va. to annihilate (aniquilar); to crush, to humiliate (humillar); to lessen (apocar); —se, to feel crushed, humiliated.
anónimo, ma, (â·no′nē·mo, ma) adj. anonymous; —, m. anonymous message.
anormal, (â·nor·mâl′) adj. abnormal.

anotación, (â·no·tâ·syon´) f. annotation, note.

anotar, (â·no·târ´) va. to jot down, to note.

anoxia, (â·nok´syâ) f. anoxia.

ansia, (ân´syâ) f. anxiety, worry *(inquietud)*; eagerness, yearning *(anhelo)*.

ansiar, (ân·syâr´) va. to desire exceedingly, to long for.

ansiedad, (ân·sye·thâth´) f. anxiety, worry.

ansioso, sa, (ân·syo´so, sâ) adj. anxious, eager.

anta, (ân´tâ) f. (zool.) elk; moose *(de América)*.

antagónico, ca, (ân·tâ·go´nē·ko, kâ) adj. antagonistic.

antagonista, (ân·tâ·go·nēs´tâ) m. and f. antagonist.

antaño, (ân·tâ´nyo) adv. long ago; of old.

antártico, ca, (ân·târ´tē·ko, kâ) adj. Antarctic.

ante, (ân´te) m. (zool.) elk; elk skin; —, *prep.* before, in the presence of; — **todo,** above all else.

anteayer, (ân·te·â·yer´) adv. day before yesterday.

antebrazo, (ân·te·vrâ´so) m. forearm.

antecámara, (ân·te·kâ´mâ·râ) f. antechamber, lobby, hall.

antecedente, (ân·te·se·then´te) m. and adj. antecedent.

anteceder, (ân·te·se·ther´) va. to precede, to antecede.

antecesor, ra, (ân·te·se·sor´, râ) n. predecessor; forefather *(antepasado)*.

antedatar, (ân·te·thâ·tar´) va. to antedate.

antedicho, cha, (ân·te·thē´cho, châ) adj. aforesaid.

antediluviano, na, (ân·te·thē·lū·vyâ´no, nâ) adj. antediluvian.

antelación, (ân·te·lâ·syon´) f. precedence.

antemano, (ân·te·mâ´no) **de —,** adv. beforehand, in advance.

antemeridiano, na, (ân·te·me·rē·thyâ´no, nâ) adj. in the forenoon.

antena, (ân·te´nâ) f. feeler; antenna, aerial.

antenoche, (ân·te·no´che) adv. the night before last.

antenombre, (ân·te·nom´bre) m. title prefixed to a proper name.

anteojera, (ân·te·o·he´râ) f. eyeglass case.

anteojo, (ân·te·o´ho) m. spyglass, eyeglass; **— de larga vista,** telescope; **—s,** pl. spectacles, glasses.

antepagar, (ân·te·pâ·gâr´) va. to pay in advance.

antepasado da, (ân·te·pâ·sâ´tho, thâ) adj. passed, elapsed; **semana —,** week

before anti last; **—dos,** m. pl. ancestors.

anteponer*, (ân·te·po·ner´) va. to place before; to prefer *(preferir)*.

anterior, (ân·te·ryor´) adj. anterior, fore *(delantero)*; former, previous *(antecedente)*; **año —,** preceding year.

anterioridad, (ân·te·ryo·rē·thâth´) f. precedence; **pagar con —,** to pay in advance.

antes, (ân´tes) adv. first *(primero)*; formerly *(anteriormente)*; before, before-hand *(de antemano)*; rather *(más bien)*; **— bien,** on the contrary; **— de,** before (time); **— que,** before (position) ; **cuanto —,** as soon as possible; **— de J.C. B.C.,** before Christ.

antesala, (ân·te·sâ´lâ) f. antechamber, waiting room; **hacer —,** to wait one's turn in an office.

antiaéreo, rea, (ân·tē·â·e´re·o, re·â) adj. pertaining to antiaircraft; **—s,** m. pl. antiaircraft.

antibiótico, (ân·tē·vyo´tē·ko) m. antibiotic.

anticipación, (ân·tē·sē·pâ·syon´) f. anticipation; advance *(adelanto)*; **pagar con —,** to pay in advance.

anticuado, da, (ân·tē·kwâ·´tho thâ) adj. anticipated, in advance; **gracias —das,** thanks in advance.

anticipar, (ân·tē·sē·pâr´) va. to anticipate; to forestall *(prevenir)*.

anticipo, (ân·tē·sē´po) m. advance; **— de pago,** payment in advance, retainer.

anticonceptivo, (ân·tē·kon·sep·tē´vo) m. contraceptive.

anticuado, da, (ân·tē·kwâ´tho, thâ) adj. antiquated; obsolete *(desusado)*.

anticuario, (ân·tē·kwâ´ryo) m. antiquary, antiquarian.

antidetonante, (ân·tē·the·to·nân´te) adj. antiknock.

antídoto, (ân·tē´tho·to) m. antidote.

antier, (ân·tyer´) adv. day before yesterday.

antiguamente, (ân·tē·gwâ·mente) adv. anciently, formerly.

antigüedad, (ân·tē·gwe·thâth´) f. antiquity, oldness; ancient times *(tiempo)*; **— es,** f. pl. antiques.

antiguo, gua, (ân·te´gwo, gwâ) adj. antique, old, ancient.

antihigiénico, ca, (ân·tē·e·hye´nē·ko, kâ) adj. unsanitary.

antihistamina, (ân·tē·ēs·tâ·mē´nâ) f. antihistamine.

antílope, (ân·tē´lo·pe) m. antelope.

Antillas, (ân·tē´yas) f. pl. Antilles or West Indies.

antiparras, (ân·tē·pä´ rrâs) *f. pl.* (coll.) spectacles.

antipatía, (ân·tē·pä·tē´ä) *f.* antipathy, dislike.

antipático, ca, (ân·tē·pä´ tē·ko, kâ) *adj.* disagreeable, displeasing.

antípodas, (ân·tē´ po·thâs) *m. pl.* antipodes.

antisemítico, ca, (ân·tē·se·mē´ tē·ko, kâ) *adj.* anti-Semitic.

antiséptico, ca, (ân·tē·sep´ tē·ko, kâ) *adj.* antiseptic.

antisocial, (ân·tē·so·syâl´) *adj.* antisocial.

antitanque, ´(ân·tē·tang´ke) *adj.* antitank.

antítesis, (ân·tē´ te·sēs) *f.* (gram.) antithesis.

antitoxina, (ân·tē·tok·sē´ nâ) *f.* antitoxin.

antojadizo, za, (ân·to·hâ·thē´ so, sâ) *adj.* capricious, fanciful.

antojarse, (ân·to·hâr´ se) *vr.* to long, to desire earnestly, to take a fancy.

antojo, (ân·to´ ho) *m.* whim, fancy, longing, craving.

antología, (ân·to·lo·hē´ä) *f.* anthology.

antónimo, (ân·to´ nē·mo) *m.* antonym.

antorcha, (ân·tor´ châ) *f.* torch, taper.

antracita, (ân·trâ·sē´ tâ) *f.* anthracite, hard coal.

antropófago, (ân·tro·po´ fâ·go) *m.* maneater, cannibal.

antropoide, (ân·tro·po´ ē·the) *m.* and *adj.* anthropoid.

antropología, (ân·tro·po·lo·hē´ä) *f.* anthropology.

anual, (â·nwâl´) *adj.* annual.

anualidad, (â·nwâ·lē·thâth´) *f.* yearly recurrence; annuity *(renta).*

anuario, (â·nwâ´ ryo) *m.* annual, yearbook.

anubarrado, da, (â·nū·vâ·rra´ tho, thâ) *adj.* clouded, covered with clouds.

anublar, (â·nū·vlâr´) *va.* to cloud, to obscure; **—se** to become clouded *(obscurecerse);* (fig.) to fall through, to fail *(fracasar).*

anudar, (â·nū·thâr´) *va.* to knot, to tie, to join.

anuente, (â·nūen´te) *adj.* agreeing, yielding.

anular, (â·nū·lâr´) *va.* to annul, to render void, to void; **—**, *adj.* annular; **dedo —**, ring finger, fourth finger.

anunciador, (â·nūn·syâ·thor´) *m.* announcer.

anunciante, (â·nūn·syân´te) *m.* advertiser.

anunciar, (â·nūn·syâr´) *va.* to announce, to advertise.

anuncio, (â·nūn´ syo) *m.* advertisement, announcement.

anverso, (âm·ber´ so) *m.* obverse (in coins).

anzuelo, (ân·swe´ lo) *m.* fishhook; (fig.) allurement, attraction.

añadidura, (â·nyâ·thē·thū´ râ) *f.* addition; **por —**, in addition, besides.

añadir, (â·nyâ·thēr´) *va.* to add, to join, to attach.

añejar, (â·nye·hâr´) *va.* to make old; **—se**, to get old, to become stale; to age *(mejorar).*

añejo, ja, (â·nye´ ho, hâ) *adj.* old, stale, musty, aged.

añicos, (â·nyē´ kos) *m. pl.* bits, small pieces; **hacer —**, to break into small pieces; **hacerse —**, to overexert oneself.

añil, (â·nyēl´) *m.* indigo plant; indigo.

año, (â´ nyo) *m.* year; **— bisiesto**, leap year; **al** or **por —**, per annum; **cumplir —s**, to reach one´s birthday; **día de A— Nuevo**, New Year´s; **el — pasado**, last year; **el — que viene**, next year; **entrado en —s**, middle-aged; **hace un —**, a year ago; **tener dos —s**, to be two years old.

añojo, (â·nyo´ ho) *m.* a yearling calf.

añoranza, (â·nyo·rân´ sâ) *f.* melancholy, nostalgia.

añublo, (â·nyū´ vlo) *m.* mildew.

apacentar*, (â·pâ·sen·tar´) *va* to pasture, to graze.

apacibilidad, (â·pâ·sē·vē·lē·thâth´) *f.* placidity.

apacible, (â·pâ·sē´ vle) *adj.* affable, gentle, placid.

apaciguador, (â·pâ·sē·gwâ·thor´) *m.* pacifier, appeaser.

apaciguamiento, (â·pâ·sē·gwâ·myen´to) *m.* appeasement.

apaciguar, (â·pâ·sē·gwâr´) *va.* to appease, to pacify, to calm; **—se**, to calm down.

apachurrar (â·pâ·chū·rrâr´) *va.* to crush, to flatten.

apadrinar, (â·pâ·thrē·nâr´) *va.* to act as godfather to, to sponsor; to support, to favor, to patronize *(patrocinar).*

apagado, da, (â·pâ·gä´ tho, thâ) *adj.* put out, turned off *(extinguido);* low, dull, muffled *(amortiguado);* submissive *(sumiso).*

apagador, (â·pâ·gä·thor´) *m.* extinguisher, damper; **— de incendios**, fire extinguisher.

apagar, (â·pâ·gâr´) *va.* to quench, to extinguish, to put out, to turn off; to soften *(aplacar).*

apagón, (â·pâ·gon´) *m.* blackout.

apalabrar, (â·pâ·lâ·vrâr´) *va.* to bespeak, to speak for.

apalear, (â·pâ·le·âr´) *va.* to whip, to beat

---

m met, **n** not, **p** pot, **r** very, **rr** (none), **s** so, **t** toy, **th** with, **v** eve, **w** we, **y** yes, **z** zero

with a stick.

apañar, (â·pâ·nyâr´) va. to catch, to grasp, to seize; to pilfer (ratear); —se, (coll.) to be skillful.

aparador, (â·pâ·râ·thor´) m. buffet; sideboard; workshop (taller); store window (escaparate); estar de —, to be dressed for receiving visitors.

aparar, (â·pâ·râr´) va. to prepare, to set up, to ready (preparar); to till, to cultivate, to work (cultivar).

aparato, (â·pâ·râ´to) m. apparatus, appliance (máquina); preparation, ostentation, show.

aparatoso, sa, (â·pâ·râ·to´so, sâ) adj. pompous showy.

aparcero, (â·pâr·se´ro) m. sharecropper.

aparear, (â·pâ·re·âr´) va. to match, to pair; —se, to be paired off by twos.

aparecer*, (â·pâ·re·ser´) vn. to appear, to be found.

aparecido, (â·pâ·re·sê´tho) m. apparition, ghost.

aparejar, (â·pâ·re·hâr´) va. to prepare; to harness (arrear); (naut.) to rig.

aparejo, (â·pâ·re´ho) m. preparation; harness (arreo); sizing (del lienzo); (naut.) tackle, rigging; —s, pl. tools, implements.

aparentar, (â·pâ·ren·târ´) va. to assume, to simulate, to affect, to feign, to pretend, to sham.

aparente, (â·pâ·ren´te) adj. apparent; fit, suitable (conveniente); evident; seeming, ilusory, deceptive (engañoso).

aparición, (â·pâ·rê·syon´) f. apparition (fantasma); appearance (manifestación).

apariencia, (â·pâ·ryen´syâ) f. appearance, looks.

apartadero, (â·pâr·tâ·the´ro) m. (rail.) siding, side track; wide roadbed for passing.

apartado, (â·pâr·tâ´tho) m. post-office box; —, da, adj. secluded, separated; (fig.) reserved, aloof.

apartamiento, (â·par·tâ·myen´to) m. secluded place (retiro); apartment, flat; — amueblado, furnished apartment; — sin muebles, unfurnished apartment.

apartar, (â·pâr·târ´) va. to separate, to divide (separar); to dissuade (disuadir) to remove (sacar); to sort (clasificar); —se, to withdraw; to desist.

aparte, (â·pâr´te) m. (theat.) aside; new paragraph (acápite); —, adv. apart, separately.

apasionado, da, (â·pâ·syo·nâ´tho, thâ) adj. passionate, impulsive; devoted to, fond of (aficionado).

apasionar, (â·pâ·syo·nâr´) va. to excite apassion; —se, to become very fond (of), to be prejudiced (about).

apatía, (â·pâ·tê´â) f. apathy.

apático ca, (â·pâ´tê·ko, kâ) adj. apathetic, indifferent.

apeadero, (â·pe·â·the´ro) m. horse block (poyo); rest stop, resting place; (rail.) flag stop, whistle-stop.

apear, (â·pe·âr´) va. to dismount, to alight (desmontar); to survey, to measure lands (amojonar); to dissuade, to change someone´s mind (disuadir); — se, to get off a train, horse, etc., to alight.

apedreado, da, (â·pe·thre·â´tho, thâ) adj. stoned, pelted.

apedrear, (â·pe·thre·âr´) va. to throw stones at; to stone to death, to lapidate (lapidar); —, vn. to hail; —se, to be injured by hail.

apegarse, (â·pe·gâr´se) vr. to become attached, to become fond.

apego, (â·pe´go) m. attachment, fondness.

apelación, (â·pe·lâ·syon´) f. supplication, entreaty; appeal (jurídica).

apelante, (â·pe·lân´te) m. appellant.

apelar, (â·pe·lar´) vn. to appeal, to have recourse, to supplicate.

apelativo, (â·pe·lâ·tê´vo) adj. appelative; nombre —, generic name.

apelmazar, (â·pel·mâ·sâr´) va. to compress, to condense, to make compact.

apellidar, (â·pe·yê·thâr´) va. to call by one´s last name; (mil.) to call to arms; —se, to be surnamed, to be one´s last name.

apellido, (â·pe·yê´tho) m. surname, family name.

apenar, (â·pe·nâr´) va. to cause pain; — se, to grieve.

apenas, (â·pe´nâs) adv. scarcely, hardly.

apéndice, (â·pen´dê·se) m. (med.) appendix; supplement (suplemento).

apendicitis, (â·pen·dê·sê´tês) f. appendicitis.

apeo, (â·pe´o) m. survey (amojonamiento); act of dismounting (desmonte).

aperar, (â·pe·râr´) va. to repair or equip (farming vehicles).

apercibir, (â·per·sê·vêr´) va. to prepare to provide (disponer); to warn, to advise (avisar); to sense.

aperitivo, (â·pe·rê·tê´vo) m. appetizer, apéritif.

apero, (â·pero) m. farm implements (aparejo); outfit, equipment (aparejo); (Sp. Am.) riding outfit; (Ven.) saddle.

apertura, (â·per·tū´râ) f. opening, inauguration.

apesadumbrar, (â·pe·sâ·thúm·brâr´) va. to cause trouble; **—se**, to be grieved *(afligirse);* to lose heart *(desanimarse).*

apestar, (â·pes·târ´) vn. to produce an offensive smell, to smell bad, to stink.

apetecer*, (â·pe·te·ser´) va. to long for, to crave.

apetecible, (â·pe·te·sē´vle) adj. desirable.

apetito, (â·pe·tē´to) m. appetite; **entrar en —**, to get hungry, to work up an appetite.

apetitoso, sa, (â·pe·tē·to·so, sâ) adj. appetizing.

apiadarse, (â·pyâ·thâr´se) vr. to commiserate (with), to take pity (on).

ápice, (á´pē·se) m. summit, point; (fig.) smallest part.

apilar, (â·pē·lâr´) va. to pile up.

apiñado, da, (â·pē·nyâ´tho, tha) adj. cone-shaped; crowded, packed tightly *(apretado).*

apiñar, (a·pē·nyâr´) va. to press, to crowd close together; **—se**, to clog, to crowd.

apio, (â´pyo) m. (bot.) celery.

apisonar, (â·pē·so·nâr´) va. to tamp, to drive down.

aplacar, (â·plâ·kâr´) va. to appease, to pacify; **—se**, to calm down.

aplanadora, (â·plâ·nâ·tho´râ) f. steamroller.

aplanar, (â·plâ·nâr´) va. to level, to flatten; to astonish *(pasmar);* **—se**, to fall to the ground.

aplanchado, (â·plân·chá´tho) = planchado.

aplanchadora, (â·plân·châ·tho´râ) = planchadora.

aplanchar, (â·plân·chár´) = planchar.

aplastado, da, (â·plâs·tâ´tho, thâ) adj. crushed, flattened; (fig.) dispirited.

aplastar, (â·plâs·târ´) va. to flatten, to crush; (fig.) to squelch or crush (an opponent); **—se**, to collapse; to feel squelched.

aplaudir, (â·lâū·thēr´) va. to applaud; to extol *(celebrar).*

aplauso, (â·plâ´ū·so) m. applause, approbation, praise.

aplazamiento, (â·plâ·sâ·myen´to) m. postponement; summons.

aplazar, (â·plâ·sâr´) va. to call together, to call into session; to defer, to put off, to postpone *(diferir).*

aplicable, (â·plē·ká´vle) adj. applicable.

aplicación, (â·plē·kâ·syon´) f. application; attention, care, industriousness *(esmero).*

aplicado, da, (â·plē·kâ´tho, thâ) adj. studious, industrious.

aplicar, (â·plē·kâr´) va. to apply, to stick; (fig.) to adapt, to make use of; **—se**, to devote oneself, to apply oneself.

aplomado, da, (â·plo·mâ´tho, thâ) adj. lead-colored, leaden; (fig.) heavy, dull.

aplomo, (â·plo´mo) m. composure, self-possession, poise.

apocado, da, (â·po·ká´tho, thâ) adj. pusillanimous, cowardly *(cobarde);* low, mean *(vil).*

apocar, (â·po·kâr´) va. to lessen, to diminish, to limit; **—se**, to humble oneself.

apócope, (â·po´ko·pe) m. apocope.

apodar, (â·po·thâr´) va. to give nicknames.

apoderado, da, (â·po·the·râ´tho, thâ) adj. authorized, empowered; **—**, m. legal representative, proxy, attorney in fact.

apoderar, (â·po·the·râr´) va. to empower *(autorizar);* to grant power of attorney; **—se**, to take possession.

apodo, (â·po´tho) m. nickname.

apogeo, (â·po·he´o) m. (ast.) apogee; (fig.) apex, culmination; **estar en su —**, to be at the height of one´s fame or popularity.

apolillar, (â·po·lē·yâr´) va. to gnaw or eat (of moths); **—se**, to get moth-eaten.

apología, (â·po·lo·hē´á) f. eulogy, apology.

apoltronarse, (â·pol·tro·nâr´se) vr. To grow lazy, to remain inactive.

apoplejía, (â·po·ple·hē´á) f. apoplexy.

aporreado, da, (â po·rre·â´tho, thâ) adj. cudgeled, beaten; **—**, m. (Cuba) kind of beef stew.

aporrear, (â·po·rre·âr´) va. to thrash, to slug.

aportar, (â·por·târ´) va. to bring, to contribute; **—**, vn. to land at a port.

aposento, (â·po·sen´to) m. room, chamber; inn *(posada).*

aposición, (â·po·sē·syon´) f. (gram.) apposition.

apostar*, (â·pos·târ´) va. to bet, to lay a wager; (mil.) to station; **—se**, to station oneself.

apóstata, (â·pos´tâ·ta) m. apostate.

apostema, (â·pos·te´mâ) f. abscess, tumor.

apóstol, (â·pos´tol) m. apostle.

apostólico, ca, (â·pos·to´lē·ko, kâ) adj. apostolic.

apostrofar, (â·pos·tro·far´) va. to apostrophize.

apóstrofe, (â·pos´tro·fe) m. (rhet.) apostrophe.

apóstrofo, (â·pos´tro·fo) *m.* (gram.) apostrophe.

apostura, (â·pos·tū´râ) *f.* neatness.

apoteosis, (â·po·te·o´sēs) *f.* apotheosis.

apoyar, (â·po·yâr´) *va.* to favor, to support; —, *vn.* to rest, to lie; —**se,** to lean upon.

apoyo, (â·po´yo) *m.* prop, rest, stay, support *(sostén);* (fig.) protection, aegis.

apreciable, (â·pre·syâ´vle) *adj.* appreciable, valuable, respectable; **su** —, (corn.) your favor (letter).

apreciación, (â·pre·syâ·syon´) *f.* estimation, evaluation, appreciation.

apreciar, (â·pre·syâr´) *va.* to appreciate, to value.

aprecio, (â·pre´syo) *m.* appreciation, esteem, regard.

aprehender, (â·pre·en·der´) *va.* to apprehend, to seize.

aprehensión, (â·pre·en·syon´) *f.* apprehension, seizure.

aprehensivo, va, (â·pre·en·sē´vo, vâ) *adj.* apprehensive, fearful; quick to understand, bright *(listo).*

apremiante, (â·pre·myân´te) *adj.* urgent, pressing.

apremiar, (â·pre·myâr´) *va.* to hurry, to urge, to press; to oppress *(oprimir).*

apremio, (â·pre´myo) *m.* pressure, urging; enjoinder *(jurídico).*

aprender, (â·pren·der´) *va.* to learn; — **de memoria,** to learn by heart.

aprendiz, za, (â·pren·dēs´, sâ) *n.* apprentice.

aprensar, (â·pren·sâr´) *va.* to press, to calender.

aprensión, (â·pren·syon´) *f.* apprehension, fear, misgiving.

apresar, (â·pre·sâr´) *va.* to seize, to grasp *(agarrar);* to capture *(aprisionar).*

aprestar, (â·pres·târ´) *va.* to prepare, to make ready.

apresurado, da, (â·pre·sū·râ´tho, thâ) *adj.* hasty.

apresuramiento, (â·pre·sū·râ·myen´to) *m.* haste.

apresurar, (â·pre·sū·râr´) *va.* to accelerate, to hasten, to expedite; —**se,** to hurry, to hasten.

apretado, da, (â·pre·tâ´tho, thâ) *adj.* tight, squeezed; mean, miserable, closehanded *(mezquino);* hard, difficult *(difícil).*

apretar* (â·pre·târ´) *va.* to close tight, to tighten, to squeeze *(estrechar);* to bother, to harass *(afligir);* to pinch, to be too tight *(calzado);* to urge, to entreat *(instar).*

apretón, (â·pre·ton´) *m.* pressure; — **de manos,** strong handshake.

aprieto, (â·prye´to) *m.* crowd *(gentío);* predicament, difficulty *(apuro);* **estar en un** —, to be in a pickle, to be in a jam.

aprisa, (â·pre´sâ) *adv.* in a hurry, swiftly

aprisionar, (â·prē·syo·nâr´) *va.* to imprison.

aprobación, (â·pro·vâ·syon´) *f.* approbation, approval.

aprobado, da, (â·pro·vâ´tho, thâ) *adj.* well-thought-of; *(en un examen)* passed; —, *m.* pass, passing grade.

aprobar*, (â·pro·vâr´) *va.* to approve, to approve of, to OK.

aprontar, (â·pron·târ´) *va.* to prepare hastily, to get ready.

apropiación, (â·pro·pyâ·syon´) *f.* appropriation, assumption.

apropiado, da, (â·pro·pyâ´tho, thâ) *adj.* appropriate, adequate.

apropiar, (â·pro·pyâr´) *va.* to appropriate; —**se,** take possession of.

aprovechable, (â·pro·ve·châ´vle) *adj.* available, usable.

aprovechamiento, (â·pro·ve·châ·myen´to) *m.* taking advantage, profiting.

aprovechar, (â·pro·ve·châr´) *va.* to avail oneself of, to make use of; —, *vn.* to make progress; —**se de,** to take advantage of, to avail oneself of.

aproximación, (â·prok·sē·ma·syon´) *f.* approximation, approach.

aproximar, (â·prok·sē·mar´) *va.* and *vr.* to approach, to move near, to approximate.

aptitud, (âp·tē·tūth´) *f.* aptitude, fitness, ability, talent.

apto, ta, (âp´to, tâ) *adj.* apt, fit, able, clever.

apuesta, (â·pwes´tâ) *f.* bet, wager.

apuesto, ta, (â·pwes´to, ta) *adj.* smart, elegant.

apuntado, da, (â·pūn·tâ´tho, thâ) *adj.* pointed *(puntiagudo);* jotted, written down *(anotado).*

apuntador, (â·pūn·tâ·thor´) *m.* (theat.) prompter; (naut.) gunner; — **electrónico,** teleprompter.

apuntalamiento, (â·pūn·tâ·lâ·myen´to) *m.* propping, pinning; — **por la base,** underpinning.

apuntalar, (â·pūn·tâ·lâr´) *va.* to prop, to pin; (naut.) to shore (a vessel).

apuntar, (â·pūn·târ´) *va.* to aim, to level *(asestar);* to point out, to note *(señalar);* to write down *(anotar);* (theat.) to prompt; —, *vn.* to begin to appear; — **se,** to register, to enroll *(alistarse);* to begin to turn (of wine) *(agriarse).*

apunte, (â·pūn′te) *m.* annotation, note; sketch *(boceto);* (theat.) stage prompting.

apurado, da, (â·pū·râ′tho, thâ) *adj.* financially embarrassed, in need of cash *(falto de caudal);* in a hurry *(apresurado);* **verse —,** to be in difficulties.

apurar, (â·pū·râr′) *va.* to rush, to hurry *(apresurar);* to annoy *(afligir);* to exhaust (as patience) *(agotar);* to purify (as gold) *(purificar);* **—se,** to hurry oneself *(apresurarse);* to worry, to grieve *(inquietarse).*

apuro, (â·pū′ro) *m.* want, lack *(escasez);* affliction, vexation, embarrassment *(aflicción);* **salir de un -,** to get out of a difficulty.

aquel, lla, (â·kel′, yâ) *adj.* **aquél, lla,** *pron.* that; the former; **—llos, llas,** *pl.* those.

aquello, (â·ke′yo) *pron.* that, the former, the first mentioned, that matter.

aquí, (â·kē′) *adv.* here, in this place; **de —,** hence; **por —,** this way.

aquietar, (â·kye·târ′) *va.* to quiet, to appease, to lull; **—se,** to become calm.

aquilatar, (â·kē·lâ·târ′) *va.* to assay, to appraise; (fig.) to evaluate, to appraise, to test.

aquilón, (â·kē·lon′) *m.* north wind.

ara, (â′râ) *f.* altar; **en —s de,** for the sake of.

árabe, (â′râ·ve) *m.* and *f.* Arab; —, *adj.* Arabic; —, *m.* Arabic language.

arabesco, (â·râ·ves′ko) *m.* arabesque; —, **ca,** *adj.* Arabic.

arábico, ca, (â·râ′vē·ko, kâ) or **arábigo, ga,** (â·râ′vē·go, gâ) *adj.* Arabian, Arabic.

arado, (â·râ′tho) *m.* plow; **— de azada,** hoe plow; **— de discos,** disc plow; **— giratorio,** rotary plow; **— múltiple,** gang plow.

arador, (â·râ·thor′) *m.* plowman.

aragonés, esa, (â·râ·go·nes′, esâ) *n.* and *adj.* Aragonese.

arancel, (â·rân·sel′) *m.* customs rates, duty rates.

arancelario, ria, (â·rân·se·lâ′ryo, ryâ) *adj.* pertaining to tariff rates; **derechos —s,** customs duties.

arandela, (â·rân·de′lâ) *f.* drip catcher on a candlestick *(de candelero);* (Sp. Am.) ruffles *(chorrera);* screw washer *(chapa).*

araña, (â·râ′nyâ) *f.* (ent.) spider; chandelier *(candelabro).*

arañar, (â·râ·nyâr′) *va.* to scratch, to scrape.

arañazo, (â·râ·nyâ′so) *m.* deep scratch.

arar, (â·râr′) *va.* to plow, to till.

arbitraje, (âr·vē·trâ′he) *m.* arbitration.

arbitrar, (âr·vē·trâr′) *va.* to arbitrate.

arbitrario, ria, (âr·vē·trâ′ryo, ryâ) *adj.* arbitrary.

arbitrio, (âr·vē′tryo) *m.* free will *(albedrío);* means, expedient, way *(medio);* arbitration; **—s,** *pl.* excise taxes.

árbitro? (âr′vē·tro) *m.* arbiter, arbitrator; umpire *(del juego).*

árbol, (âr′vol) *m.* tree; (mech.) shaft; (naut.) mast; **— de eje,** or de manivela, crankshaft; **— de levas,** camshaft.

arbolado, da, (âr·vo·lâ′tho, thâ) *adj.* forested, wooded; —, *m.* woodland.

arboladura, (âr·vo·lâ·thū′râ) *f.* (naut.) masting, masts.

arboleda, (âr·vo·le′thâ) *f.* grove.

arbusto, (âr·vūs′to) *m.* shrub.

arca, (âr′kâ) *f.* chest, wooden box; **— de hierro,** strongbox, safe.

arcada, (âr·kâ′thâ) *f.* (ârch.) arcade, row of arches; retching *(vómito).*

arcaico, ca, (âr·kâ′ē·ko, kâ) *adj.* archaic, ancient.

arcángel, (âr·kân′hel) *m.* archangel.

arcano, na, (âr·kâ′no, nâ) *adj.* secret, mysterious; —, *m.* very important secret, mystery.

arce, (âr′se) *m.* maple tree.

arcilla, (âr·sē′yâ) *f.* argil, clay.

arco, (âr′ko) *m.* arc; (ârch.) arch; (mus.) fiddle bow; hoop *(aro);* **— iris,** rainbow; **soldadura con —,** arc welding; **adintelado,** straight, fiat arch.

arcón, (âr·kon′) *m.* large chest, bin.

archiduque, (âr·chē·thū′ke) *m.* archduke.

archipiélago, (âr·chē·pye′lâ·go) *m.* archipelago.

archivar, (âr·chē·vâr′) *va.* to file, to place in the archives.

archivero, ra (âr·chē·ve′ro, râ) *n.* or **archivista,** (âr·chē·vēs′tâ) *m.* and *f.* keeper of the archives; file clerk.

archivo, (âr·chē′vo) *m.* archives, files.

arder, (âr·ther′) *vn.* to burn, to blaze.

ardid, (âr·thēth′) *m.* stratagem, cunning, trick.

ardiente, (âr·thyen′te) *adj.* ardent, fiery, intense.

ardilla, (âr·thē′yâ) *f.* squirrel.

ardor, (âr·thor′) *m.* great heat; energy, vivacity *(eficacia);* anxiety, longing *(anhelo);* fervor, zeal *(esfuerzo).*

ardoroso, sa, (âr·tho·ro′so, sâ) *adj.* fiery,

---

m met, **n** not, **p** pot, **r** very, **rr** (none), **s** so, **t** toy, **th** with, **v** eve, **w** we, **y** yes, **z** zero

restless.

arduo, dua, (âr´thwo, dwâ) *adj.* arduous, difficult.

área, (á´re·â) *f.* area.

arena, (â·re´nâ) *f.* sand, grains; arena *(palenque).*

arenal, (â·re·nâl´) *m.* sandy ground, sand pit.

arenga, (â·reng´gâ) *f.* harangue, speech.

arengar, (â·reng·gâr´) *vn.* to harangue.

arenilla, (â·re·ne´yâ) *f.* molding sand; (med.) calculus stone; fine sand for drying ink *(secante);* **—s,** *pl.* refined saltpeter.

arenoso, sa, (â·re·no´so, sa) *adj.* sandy.

arenque, (â·reng´ke) *m.* herring; **— ahumado,** smoked herring; **— en escabeche,** pickled herring.

aretes, (â·re´tes) *m. pl.* earrings.

argamasa, (âr·gâ·mâ´sâ) *f.* mortar.

argentado, da, (âr·hen·tâ´tho, thâ) *adj.* silverlike.

argentino, na, (âr·hen·te´no, na) *adj.* silvery *(argénteo);* Argentine.

argolla, (â·go´yâ) *f.* large metal ring.

argucia, (âr·gû´syâ) *f.* subtlety, trickery.

argüir*, (âr·gwêr´) *vn.* to argue, to dispute, to oppose; **—,** *va.* to infer.

argumentar, (âr·gû·men·târ´) *vn.* to argue, to dispute.

argumento, (âr·gû·mento) *m.* argument; (theat.) plot, intrigue.

aria, (á´ryâ) *f.* (mus.) aria.

aridez, (â·rē·thes´) *f.* aridity, dryness; (fig.) barrenness.

árido, da, (á´rē·tho, thâ) *adj.* arid, dry; barren *(estéril).*

ariete, (â·rye´te) *m.* battering ram; **— hidráulico,** hydraulic ram.

arillo, (â·rē´yo) *m.* earring.

ario, ria, (á´ryo, ryâ) *n.* and *adj.* Aryan.

arisco, ca, (â·rēs´ko, kâ) *adj.* fierce, rude, surly.

aristocracia, (â·res·to·krâ´syâ) *f.* aristocracy.

aristócrata, (â·rēs·to´krâ·tâ) *m.* and *f.* aristocrat.

aristocrático, ca, (â·rēs·to·krâ´tē·ko, kâ) *adj.* aristocratic.

aritmética, (â·rēth·me´tē·kâ) *f.* arithmetic.

arlequín, (âr·le·kēn´) *m.* harlequin, buffoon.

arma, (âr´mâ) *f.* weapon, arm; **—s blancas,** side arms; **alzarse en —s,** to revolt.

armada, (âr·mâ´thâ) *f.* fleet, armada.

armadillo, (âr·mâ·the´yo) *m.* armadillo.

armado, da, (âr·mâ´tho, thâ) *adj.* armed; assembled, put together *(montado).*

armador, (âr·mâ·thor´) *m.* (naut.) ship outfitter, shipbuilder; shipowner *(naviero);* jacket, jerkin *(jubón).*

armadura, (âr·mâ·thû´râ) *f.* armor; (arch.) framework.

armamento, (âr·mâ·men´to) *m.* armament.

armar, (âr·mâr´) *va.* to furnish with arms or troops; to put together, to set up, to assemble *(montar);* to cause, to bring about *(provocar).*

armario, (âr·mâ´ryo) *m.* wall cabinet, cupboard.

armatoste, (âr·mâ·tos´te) *m.* white elephant; (fig.) clumsy, useless individual.

armazón, (âr·ma·son´) *f.* framework, skeleton; (naut.) hulk of a ship; **—,** *m.* (anat.) skeleton.

armella, (âr·me´yâ) *f.* staple, screweye.

armero, (âr·me´ro) *m.* armorer, keeper of arms.

armiño, (âr·mē´nyo) *m.* ermine.

armisticio, (âr·mēs·tē´syo) *m.* armistice.

armonía, (âr·mo·nē´â) *f.* harmony.

armónico, ca, (âr·mo´nē·ko, kâ) *adj.* harmonious, harmonic; **—,** *f.* harmonica, mouth organ.

armonioso, sa, (âr·mo·nyo´so, sâ) *adj.* harmonious, sonorous.

armonizar, (âr·mo·nē·sâr´) *va.* to harmonize.

árnica, (âr´nē·kâ) *f.* arnica, medicinal plant.

aro, (á´ro) *m.* hoop; (auto.) rim.

aroma, (â·ro´mâ) *f.* flower of the aromatic myrrh tree; **—,** *m.* aroma, fragrance.

aromático, ca, (â·ro·mâ´tē·ko, kâ) *adj.* aromatic.

aromatizar, (â·ro·mâ·tē·sâr´) *va.* to perfume.

arpa, (âr´pâ) *f.* (mus.) harp.

arpía, (âr·pē´â) *f.* (poet.) harpy; (fig.) hag, witch.

arpillera, (âr·pē·ye´râ) *f.* burlap, sackcloth.

arpista, (âr·pēs´tâ) *m.* harpist.

arpón, (âr·pon´) *m.* harpoon.

arponar, (âr·po·nâr´) *va.* to harpoon.

arqueada, (âr·ke·â´thâ) *f.* (mus.) bowing.

arqueado, da, (âr·ke·â´tho, thâ) *adj.* arched, vaulted; bent.

arquear, (âr·ke·âr´) *va.* to arch.

arqueo, (âr·ke´o) *m.* act of arching, system of arches; (naut.) tonnage; (com.) checking of money and pavers in a safe.

arqueología, (âr·ke·o·lo·hē´â) *f.* archaeology.

arquero, (âr·ke´ró) *m.* archer *(soldado);* bow maker; goalkeeper *(portero);*

â arm, **e** they, **ē** bē, **o** fore, **ū** blūe, **b** bad, **ch** chip, **d** day, **f** fat, **g** go, **h** hot, **k** kid, **1** let

cashier *(cajero).*

arquitecto, (ar·kē·tek´to) *m.* architect.

arquitectura, (ar·kē·tek·tū´ra) *f.* architecture.

arrabal, (â·rrâ·vâl´) *m.* suburb; **—es,** *pl.* outskirts, outlying districts.

arrabalero, ra, (â·rrâ·vâ·le´ro, râ) *adj.* (coll.) uncouth, common, vulgar.

arraigar, (â·rrâê·gâr´) *vn.* to take root; (fig.) to become established, to become deepseated, to become fixed; **costumbre arraigada,** settled habit, second nature.

arraigo, (â·rrâ´ē·go) *m.* landed property, real estate *(bienes raíces);* settlement, establishment *(establecimiento).*

arrancador, (â·rrâng·kâ·thor´) *m.* starter (of a motor).

arrancar, (â·rrâng·kâr´) *va.* to pull up by the roots, to pull out; (fig.) to wrest from, to drag from; —, *vn.* to start; (naut.) to set sail.

arranque, (â·rrâng´ke) *m.* extirpation, pulling out; burst of rage, scene, tantrum *(ímpetu);* (auto.) ignition, starter; (fig.) bright idea *(ocurrencia);* — **automático,** self-starter; **motor de —,** self-starting motor.

arrasar, (â·rrâ·sâr´) *va.* to demolish, to destroy, to raze; —, *vn.* to clear up (of the sky).

arrastrado, da, (â·rrâs·trâ´tho, thâ) *adj.* dragged along; (fig.) miserable, destitute.

arrastrar, (â·rrâs·trâr´) *vn.* to creep, to crawl; to lead a trump in card playing; — *va.* to drag along the ground.

arrastre, (â·rrâs´tre) *m.* dragging; creeping; lead of a trump in cards; (Mex.) mining mill.

¡arre! (â´rre) *interj.* giddap!

arrear, (â·rre·âr´) *va.* to drive (horses, mules); to urge on, hurry *(dar prisa).*

arrebatado, da, (â·rre·vâ·tâ´tho, thâ) *adj.* rapid, violent, impetuous, rash, inconsiderate.

arrebatar, (â·rre·vâ·târ´) *va.* to carry off, to snatch hurriedly; (fig.) to enrapture, to thrill.

arrebato, (â·rre·vâ´to) *m.* surprise; sudden attack; (fig.) thrill, rapture, ecstasy.

arrebol, (â·rre·vol´) *m.* redness in the sky; rouge *(colorete).*

arreciar, (â·rre·syâr´) *vn.* to increase in intensity.

arrecife, (â·rre·sē´fe) *m.* reef; causeway *(calzada).*

arredrar, (â·rre·thrâr´) *va.* to remove to a greater distance *(alejar);* to terrify *(ate-*

rrorizar); **—se,** to lose courage.

arreglado, da, (â·rre·glâ´tho, thâ) *adj.* regular, moderate; (fig.) neat, organized *(ordenado).*

arreglar, (â·rre·glâr´) *va.* to regulate, to adjust; to arrange *(disponer);* — **una cuenta,** to settle an account; **arreglárselas,** to manage, to make out, to get by.

arreglo, (â·rre´glo)*m.* adjustment,arrangement,settlement;**con — a,** according to.

arrellanarse, (â·rre·yâ·nâr´se) *vr.* to stretch out, to make oneself comfortable.

arremangar, (â·rre·mâng·gâr´) *va.* to roll up, to tuck up; **—se,** to resolve firmly.

arremeter, (â·rre·me·ter´) *va.* to assail, to attack.

arremetida, (â·rre·me·tē´thâ) *f.* attack, assault.

arrendado, da, (â·rren·dâ´tho, thâ) *adj.* manageable, tractable, easily reined.

arrendador, (â·rren·dâ·thor´) *m.* tenant, lessee *(inquilino);* lessor, hirer.

arrendajo, (â·rren·dâ´ho) *m. (om.)* mockingbird; (fig.) mimic, buffoon.

arrendamiento, (â·rren·dâ·myen´to) *m.* lease, leasing, rental; **contrato de —,** lease.

arrendar*, (â·rren·dâr´) *va.* to rent, to let out, to lease; to tie, to bridle *(atar);* to mimic, to imitate *(remedar).*

arrendatario, ria, (â·rren·dâ·tâ´ryo, ryâ) *n.* tenant, lessee.

arreo, (â·rre´o) *m.* grooming, preparation, adornment; **—s,** *pl.* appurtenances, accessories; **—,** *adv.* successively, uninterruptedly.

arrepentido, da, (â·rre·pen·tē´tho, thâ) *adj.* repentant.

arrepentimiento, (â·rre·pen·tē·myen´to) *m.* remorse, penitence.

arrepentirse*, (â·rre·pen·tēr·se)*vr.* to repent.

arrestado, da, (â·rres·tâ´tho, thâ) *adj.* intrepid, bold.

arrestar, (â·rres·târ´) *va.* to arrest, to imprison; **—se,** to be bold and enterprising.

arresto, (â·rres´to)*m.* boldness, vigor, enterprise; imprisonment, arrest *(detención).*

arriar, (â·rrē·âr´) *va.* (naut.) to lower, to strike, to haul down; **—se,** (fig.) to flag, to wane.

arriata, (â·rryâ´tâ) *f.,* **arriate,** *m.* flowerbed; roadway, causeway *(calzada).*

arriba, (â·rrē´vâ) *adv.* up above, on high, overhead, upstairs; (naut.) aloft; **de — abajo,** from head to foot; **para —,** up, upwards.

arribar, (â·rrē·vâr´) *vn.* to arrive; (naut.) to put into port; to fall off to leeward *(sotaventarse).*

arribista, (â·rrē·vēs´tâ) *m.* or *f.* social climber, parvenu, upstart.

arribo, (â·rrē´vo) *m.* arrival.

arriendo, (â·rryen´do) *m.* lease, farm rent.

arriero, (â·rrye´ro) *m.* muleteer.

arriesgado, (â·rryez·gâ´tho) *adj.* risky, dangerous.

arriesgar, (â·rryez·gâr´) *va.* and *vr.* to risk, to hazard, to expose to danger.

arrimar, (â·rrē·mâr´) *vá.* to approach, to draw near *(acercar);* (naut.) to stow; to lay aside, to pigeonhole; to shelve *(arrinconar);* to relinquish, to renounce *(abandonar);* **—se a,** to lean against, (fig.) to seek the protection of, to join the banner of.

arrinconar, (â·rrēng·ko·nâr´) *va.* to put in a corner *(poner);* (fig.) to corner, to tree *(acosar);* to lay aside, to neglect, to forget; **—se,** to retire, to withdraw.

arriscado, da, (â·rrēs·kâ´tho, thâ) *adj.* forward, bold, audacious, intrepid.

arrizar, (â·rrē·sâr´) *va.* (naut.) to reef, to tie or lash.

arroba, (â·rro´vâ) *f.* weight of twenty-five pounds *(peso);* measure of thirty-two pints *(capacidad).*

arrobador, ra, (â·rro·vâ·thor´, ra) *adj.* enchanting, entrancing, captivating.

arrobamiento, (â·rro·vâ·myen´to) *m.* rapture, amazement, rapturous admiration.

arrocero, (â·rro·se´ro) *m.* rice grower *(cultivador);* rice merchant *(vendedor).*

arrodillar, (â·rro·thē·yâr´) *va.* to cause to kneel down; **—se,** to kneel.

arrogancia, (â·rro·gân´syâ) *f.* arrogance, haughtiness.

arrogante, (â·rro·gân·te) *adj.* haughty, proud, assuming, arrogant *(altanero);* bold, valiant, stout *(valiente).*

arrojadamente, (â·rro·hâ·thâ·men´te) *adv.* daringly.

arrojado, da, (â·rro·hâ´tho, thâ) *adj.* rash, inconsiderate *(arrebatado);* bold, fearless, unflinching *(resuelto).*

arrojar, (â·rro·hâr´) *va.* to dart, to fling, to hurl, to dash *(lanzar);* to shed, to emit, to give off *(emitir);* **— un saldo,** (com.) to show a balance.

arrojo, (â·rro´ho) *m.* boldness, intrepidity, fearlessness.

arrollar, (â·rro·yâr´) *va.* to wind, to roll up, to coil *(enrollar);* to roll along, to sweep

away *(arrebatar);* to overwhelm, to defeat *(derrotar);* to confuse, to confound *(confundir).*

arropar, (â·rro·pâr´) *va.* to dress warmly, to bundle up.

arrostrar, (â·rros·trâr´) *va.* to undertake bravely, to confront with determination, to face; **—se,** to fight face to face.

arroyo, (â·rro´yo) *m.* creek; (Sp. Am.) gully, dry creek bed.

arroz, (â·rros´) *m.* rice.

arrozal, (â·rro·sal´) *m.* rice field.

arruga, (â·rrū´gâ) *f.* wrinkle, rumple.

arrugar, (â·rrū·gâr´) *va.* to wrinkle, to rumple, to fold; **— el ceño,** to frown; **— la frente,** to knit one's brow; **—se,** to shrivel.

arruinado, da, (â·rrwē·nâ´tho, thâ) *adj.* fallen.

arruinar, (â·rrwē·nâr´) *va.* to demolish, to ruin; **—se,** to lose one's fortune.

arrullador, ra, (â·rrū·yâ·thor´, râ) *adj.* flattering, cajoling.

arrullar, (â·rrū·yâr´) *va.* to lull to rest; to court, to woo *(cortejar).*

arrullo, (â·rrū´yo) *m.* cooing of pigeons; (fig.) lullaby.

arsenal, (âr·se·nâl´) *m.* arsenal; (naut.) dockyard.

arsénico, (âr·se´nē·ko) *m.* arsenic.

arte, (âr´te) *m.* and *f.* art; skill, artfulness *(habilidad);* **bellas —s,** fine arts.

artefacto, (âr·te·fâk´to) *m.* artifact, mechanism, device.

arteria, (âr·te´ryâ) *f.* artery.

arterial, (âr·te·ryâl´) *adj.* arterial; **presión —,** blood pressure.

artesano, (âr·te·sâ´no) *m.* artisan, workman.

ártico, ca, (âr´tē·ko, kâ) *adj.* Arctic.

articulación, (âr·tē·kū·lâ·syon´) *f.* articulation, enunciation, way of speaking; (anat.) joining, joint; **— universal,** (mech.) universal joint.

articular, (âr·tē·kū·lâr´) *va.* to articulate, to pronounce distinctly.

articulistas, (âr·tē·kū·lēs´tâ) *m.* newspaper columnist.

artículo, (âr·tē´kū·lo) *m.* article; clause, point *(subdivisión);* (gram.) article; **— de fondo,** editorial; **—s de fantasia,** novelties; **—s de tocador,** toilet articles; **—s para escritorio,** office supplies.

artífice, (âr·tē·fē·se) *m.* artisan, artist.

artificial, (âr·tē·fē·syâl´) *adj.* artificial.

artificio, (âr·tē·fē´syo) *m.* workmanship, craft *(arte);* device, artifice *(mecanismo);* trickery, cunning, subterfuge *(disimulo).*

artificioso, sa, (âr·tē·fē·syo′so, sâ) adj. skillful, ingenious; artful, cunning (astuto).

artillería, (âr·tē·ye·rē′â) f. gunnery, artillery; ordnance (material).

artillero, (âr·tē·ye′ro) m. artilleryman.

artimaña, (âr·tē·mä′nyâ) f. stratagem, deception (astucia); trap (trampa).

artisela, (âr·tē·se′lâ) f. (Max.) synthetic silk, type of rayon.

artista, (âr·tēs′tâ) m. and f. artist.

artístico, ca, (âr·tēs′tē·ko, kâ) adj. artistic.

artritis, (âr·trē′tēs) f. (med.) arthritis.

arveja, (âr·ve′hâ) f. (bot.) vetch; (Sp. Am.) green pea.

arzobispado, (âr·so·vēs·pä′tho) m. archdiocese.

arzobispo, (âr·so·vēs′po) m. archbishop.

as, (âs) m. ace; as (moneda).

asa, (ä′sä) f. handle, haft.

asado, da, (ä·sä′tho, thâ) adj. roasted; —, m. roast.

asador, (ä·sä·thor′) m. tumspit (varilla); barbecue (aparato).

asadura, (ä·sä·thū′râ) f. entrails, chitterlings.

asalariado, da, (ä·sä·lä·ryä′tho, thâ) adj. and n. salaried, salaried person.

asaltador, (ä·sal·tä·thor′) m. assailant, highwayman.

asaltar, (ä·sal·tär′) va. to attack, to storm, to assail, to fall upon; — a mano armada, to commit assault with a deadly weapon.

asalto, (ä·sâl′to) m. assault, holdup.

asamblea, (ä·sâm·ble′â) f. assembly, meeting.

asar, (ä·sâr′) va. to roast.

asbesto, (äz·ves′to) m. asbestos.

ascendencia, (âs·sen·den′syâ) f. ascending line, line of ancestors.

ascendente, (âs·sen·den′te) adj. ascending.

ascender*, (âs sen·der′) va. and vn. to ascend, to climb; (corn.) to amount to.

ascendiente, (âs·sen·dyen′te) m. ascendant, forefather; (fig.) influence.

ascensión, (âs·sen·syon′) f. (eccl.) feast of the Ascension; ascent.

ascenso, (âs·sen′so) m. promotion, advance.

ascensor, (âs·sen·sor′) m. elevator, lift.

ascetismo (âs·se·tēz′mo) m. asceticism.

asco, (âs′ko) m. nausea; (fig.) loathing, disgust.

ascua, (âs′kwä) f. red-hot coal; estar en —s, (coll.) to be restless or excited; ¡—!

interj. ouch!

aseado, da, (ä·se·ä′tho, thâ) adj. clean; well-groomed, neat.

asear, (ä·se·âr′) va. to clean, to groom, to make neat.

asechanza, (ä·se·chân′sâ) f. snare.

asediar, (ä·se·thyâr′) va. to besiege; (fig.) to annoy, to nag.

asedio, (ä·se′thyo) m. siege; nagging.

asegurado, da, (ä·se·gū·râ′tho, thâ) adj. assured, secured; (corn.) insured; —, n. policyholder.

asegurador, (ä·se·gū·râ·thor′) m. fastener; (corn.) insurer, underwriter.

asegurar, (ä·se·gū·râr′) va. to secure, to fasten; (fig.) to assure, to affirm; (corn.) to insure.

asemejar, (ä·se·me·hâr′) va. to make similar; —se, to resemble.

asenso, (ä·sen′so) m. assent, consent.

asentaderas, (ä·sen·ta·the′râs) f. pl. buttocks.

asentador, (ä·sen·tâ·thor′) m. razor strop.

asentar*, (ä·sen·târ′) va. to seat, to place; (fig.) to assure, to establish, to base; — al crédito de, to place to the credit of; —, vn. to be becoming; —se, to settle, to distill (liquid).

asentimiento, (ä·sen·tē·myen′to) m. assent.

asentir*, (ä·sen·tēr′) vn. to acquiesce, to concede.

aseo, (ä·se′o) m. cleanliness, neatness.

asequible, (ä·se·kē′vle) adj. attainable, obtainable.

aserción, (ä·ser·syon′) m. assertion, affirmation.

aserradero, (ä·se·rrâ·the′ro) m. sawmill.

aserraduras, (ä·se·rrâ·thū′râs) f. pl. sawdust.

aserrar*, (ä·se·rrâr′) va. to saw.

aserrín, (ä·se·rrēn′) m. sawdust.

asesinar, (ä·se·sē·nâr′) va. to assassinate.

asesinato, (ä·se·sē·nä′to) m. assassination.

asesino, na, (ä·se·sē′no, nâ) m. assassin.

asesor, (ä·se·sor′) m. counselor, assessor.

asesorar, (ä·se·so·râr′) va. to give legal advice to; —se, to employ counsel; to take advice.

asestar, (ä·ses·târ′) va. to aim, to point; to fire, to let go with (descargar).

aseverar, (ä·se·ve·râr′) va. to asseverate, to affirm solemnly.

asfalto, (âs·fâl′to) m. asphalt.

asfixia, (âs·fēk′syä) f. (med.) asphyxia,

asfixiante, (âs·fēk·syân′te) adj. asphyxiating, suffocating.

asfixiar, (âs·fēk·syâr′) va. and vr. to

m met, n not, p pot, r very, rr (none), s so, t toy, th with, v eve, w we, y yes, z zero

asphyxiate, to suffocate.

así, (â·sē´) adv. so, thus, in this manner; therefore, as a result (por esto); even though (aunque); — **que,** as soon as, just after; **por decirlo —,** so to speak.

asiático, ca, (â·syä´tē·ko,·kâ) n. and adj. Asiatic.

asidero, (â·sē·the´ro) m. handle; (fig.) occasion, pretext.

asido, da, (â·sē´tho, thâ) adj. fastened, tied, attached.

asiduidad, (â·se·thwē·thâth´) f. assiduity, diligence.

asiduo, dua, (â·sē´thwo, thwâ) adj. assiduous, devoted, careful.

asiento, (â·syen´to) m. chair, seat; (corn.) entry; (fig.) stability, permanence; — **trasero,** back seat.

asignación, (â·sēg·nâ·syon´) f. allocation, distribution, destination.

asignar, (â·sēg·nâr´) va. to allocate, to apportion, to assign, to distribute.

asignatura, (â·sēg·nâ·tū´râ) f. subject of a school course.

asilo, (â·sē´lo) m. asylum, refuge.

asimetría, (â·sē·me·trē´â) f. asymmetry.

asimilar, (â·sē·mē·lâr´) vn. to resemble; —. va. to assimilate.

asimismo, (â·sē·mēz´mo) adv. similarly, likewise.

asir*, (â·sēr´) va. and vn. to grasp, to seize, to hold, to grip; (fig.) to take root, to take hold.

asistencia, (â·sēs·ten´syâ) f. presence, attendance; assistance, help (ayuda); **falta de —,** absence (from class, etc.); — **social,** social work.

asistente, (â·sēs·ten´te) m. assistant, helper; (mil.) orderly; **los —s,** those present.

asistir, (â·sēs·tēr´) vn. to be present, to attend; —, va. to help, to further; to attend, to take care of (atender).

asma, (âz´mâ) f. asthma.

asmático, ca, (âz·mâ´tē·ko, kâ) adj. asthmatic.

asno, (âz´no) m. ass.

asociación, (â·so·syâ·syon´) f. association; partnership (conjunto).

asociado, da, (â·so·syâ´tho, thâ) n. associate; —, adj. associated.

asociar, (â·so·syâr´) va. to associate; —**se,** to form a partnership.

asolar*, (â·so·lâr´) va. to destroy, to devastate; —**se,** to settle, to clear (liquids).

asoleado, da, (â·so·le·â´tho, thâ) adj.

sunny; suntanned (bronceado).

asolear, (â·so·le·âr´) va. to expose to the sun; —**se,** to bask in the sun.

asomar, (â·so·mâr´) vn. to begin to appear, to become visible, to show; —**se,** to look out, to lean out, to peer over, to peek.

asombrar, (â·som·brâr´) va. to amaze, to astonish.

asombro, (â·som´bro) m. amazement, astonishment.

asombroso, sa, (â·som·bro´so, sâ) adj. astonishing (sorprendente); marvelous (admirable).

asomo, (â·so´mo) m. mark, token, indication; **ni por —,** nothing of the kind, far from it, I wouldn't dream of it.

asonancia, (â·so·nân´syâ) f. assonance, harmony.

aspa, (âs´pâ) f. reel; Saint Andrew's cross; — **de hélice,** propeller blade; — **de molino,** wing of a windmill.

aspar, (âs·pâr´) va. to reel; to martyr on a Saint Andrew's cross; (fig.) to vex, to plague; —**se a gritos,** to cry out loudly, to yell.

aspaviento, (âs·pâ·vyen´to) m. exaggerated astonishment or fear, histrionics.

aspecto, (âs·pek´to) m. appearance; aspect (punto).

aspereza, (âs·pe·re´sâ) f. asperity, harshness, acerbity.

áspero, ra, (âs´pe·ro, râ) adj. rough, rugged, craggy; (fig.) harsh, gruff.

aspiración, (âs·pē·râ·syon´) f. aspiration, ambition.

aspirado, da, (âs·pē·râ´tho, thâ) adj. indrawn.

aspiradora, (âs·pē·râ·tho´râ) f. vacuum cleaner.

aspirante, (âs·pē·rân´te) m. and f. aspirant.

aspirar, (âs·pē·râr´) va. (gram.) to aspirate; to suck in, to draw in.

aspirina, (âs·pē·rē´nâ) f. aspirin.

asqueroso, sa, (âs·ke·ro´so, sâ) adj. loathsome, repugnant.

asta, (âs´tâ) f. lance; horn (cuerno); handle (mango); staff, pole (palo).

aster, (âs·ter´) m. (bot.) aster.

asterisco, (âs·te·rēs´ko) m. asterisk.

astigmatismo, (âs·tēg·mâ·tēz´mo) m. astigmatism.

astilla, (âs·tē´yâ) f. chip, splinter, fragment.

astillar, (âs·tē·yâr´) va. to chip.

astillero, (âs·tē·ye´ro) m. (naut.) dock-yard, shipyard; rack for weapons (percha).

â arm, **e** they, **ē** bē, **o** fore, **ū** blūe, **b** bad, **ch** chip, **d** day, f fat, **g** go, **h** hot, **k** kid, **1** let

astringente, (ās·trēn·hen´te) *adj.* and *m.* astringent.

astro, (ās´tro) *m.* star.

astrobiología, (ās·tro·vyo·lo·hē´ā) *f.* astrobiology.

astrofísica, (ās·tro·fē´sē·kā) *f.* astrophysics.

astrología, (ās·tro·lo·hē´ā) *f.* astrology.

astrólogo, (ās·tro´lo·go) *m.* astrologer.

astronauta, (ās·tro·nā´ū·tā) *m.* astronaut.

astronavegación, (ās·tro·nā·ve·gā·syon´) *f.* astronavigation.

astronomía, (ās·tro·no·mē´ā) *f.* astronomy.

astronómico, ca, (ās·tro·no´mē·ko, kā) *adj.* astronomical.

astrónomo (ās·tro´no·mo) *m.* astronomer.

astucia, (ās·tū´syā) *f.* cunning, slyness *(maña);* finesse *(sutileza).*

asturiano, na, (ās·tū·ryā´no, nā) *n.* and *adj.* Asturian.

astuto, ta, (ās·tū´to, tā) *adj.* cunning, sly, astute, foxy.

asueto, (ā·swe´to) *m.* holiday, vacation.

asumir, (ā·sū·mēr´) *va.* to assume.

Asunción, (ā·sūn·syon´) *f.* (eccl.) Assumption.

asunto, (ā·sūn´to) *m.* subject, matter *(materia);* affair, business deal *(negocio).*

asustadizo, za, (ā·sūs·tā·thē´so, sā) *adj.* easily frightened, shy.

asustar, (ā·sūs·tār´) *va.* to frighten; **—se,** to be frightened.

atacado, da, (ā·tā·kā´tho, thā) *adj.* irresolute, timid; (fig.) petty, mean.

atacar, (ā·tā·kār´) *va.* to attack, to assail; to ram in, to jam in *(apretar);* to button *(abrochar);* to fit *(ceñir).*

atadura, (ā·tā·thū´rā) *f.* knot, fastening.

atajar, (ā·tā·hār´) *va.* to cut off, to intercept; to stop, to obstruct *(detener);***—,** *vn.* to take a short cut.

atajo, (ā·tā´ho) *m.* bypass, short cut.

atalaya, (ā·tā·lā´yā) *f.* watchtower; **—,** *m.* guard in a watchtower.

ataque, (ā·tā´ke) *m.* attack, assault; (mil.) trenches; (med.) siege of illness.

atar, (ā·tār´) *va.* to tie, to bind, to fasten; (fig.) to hamstring, to impede; **—se,** to be frustrated, to be baffled.

atarantado, da, (ā·tā·ran·tā´tho, thā) *adj.* bitten by a tarantula; frightened, bewildered *(aturdido);* noisy and restless *(bullicioso).*

atareado, da, (ā·tā·re·ā´tho, thā) *adj.* busy.

atarear, (ā·tā·re·ār´) *va.* to impose a task; **—se,** to work diligently.

atarugar, (ā·tā·rū·gār´) *va.* to wedge, to

plug; to stuff, to fill *(atestar);* (coll.) to silence, to nonplus.

atasajar, (ā·tā·sā·hār´) *va.* to jerk (meat).

atascar, (ā·tās·kār´) *va.* to stop (a leak); (naut.) to caulk; (fig.) to obstruct, to impede; **—se,** to become clogged, to become blocked, to become stuffed.

ataúd, (ā·tā·ūth´) *m.* coffin.

ataviar, (ā·tā·vyar´) *va.* to trim, to adorn, to ornament.

atavío, (ā·tā·vē´o) *m.* dress, ornament, finery.

atediar, (ā·te·thyār´) *va.* to disgust; **—se,** to be bored.

ateísmo, (ā·te·ēz´mo) *m.* atheism.

ateísta, (ā·te·ēs´tā) *m.* and *f.* atheist.

atemorizar, (ā·te·mo·rē·sār´) *va.* to strike with terror, to daunt, to frighten; **—se,** to become frightened.

Atenas, (ā·te´nās) *f.* Athens.

atención, (ā·ten·syon´) *f.* attention, heedfulness, concentration; civility, politeness *(urbanidad);* thing to do, thing on one's mind *(preocupación);* consideration; **en — a,** in consideration of, as regards; **llamar la —,** to attract one's attention, to make one take notice; **prestar —,** to give one's attention, to pay attention.

atender*, (ā·ten·der´) *vn.* to be attentive, to heed, to hearken; **—,** *va.* to wait for *(esperar);* to look after *(cuidar).*

atenerse*, (ā·te·ner´se) *vr.* to depend, to rely.

atenido, da, (ā·te·nē´tho, thā) *adj.* dependent.

atentado, da, (ā·ten·tā´tho, thā) *adj.* sensible, moderate; careful, skillful *(con tiento);* **—,** *m.* aggression, offense, crime.

atentar*, (ā·ten·tār´) *va.* to attempt an illegal act, to try to commit a crime.

atento, ta, (ā·ten´to, tā) *adj.* attentive, heedful, observant, mindful; courteous, considerate *(comedido).*

atenuar, (ā·te·nwār´) *va.* to attenuate, to diminish, to lessen.

ateo, a, (ā·te´o, ā) *n.* and *adj.* atheist, atheistic.

aterciopelado, da, (ā·ter·syo·pe·lā´tho, tha) *adj.* velvetlike.

aterrado, da, (ā·te·rrā´tho, thā) *adj.* terrified, appalled.

aterrador, ra, (ā·te·rrā·thor´, rā) *adj.* terrifying, frightful.

aterrar, (ā·te·rrār´) *va.* to terrify; (fig.) to prostrate, to humble; **—se,** to be terrified.

aterrizaje, (ā·te·rrē·sā´he) *m.* (avi.) landing

---

m met, **n** not, **p** pot, **r** very, **rr** (none), **s** so, **t** toy, **th** with, **v** eve, **w** we, **y** yes, **z** zero

(of airplane); — **accidentado,** crash landing; — **ciego,** blind landing; — **de emergencia,** crash landing; — **forzoso,** forced landing; **campo de** —, landing field; **pista de** —, landing strip; **tren de** —, landing gear.

aterrizar, (â·te·rrē·sâr´) vn. (avi.) to land.

aterrorizar, (â·te·rro·rē·sâr´) va. to frighten, to terrify.

atesorar, (â·te·so·râr´) va. to save up, to put away.

atestación, (â·tes·tâ·syon´) f. testimony, evidence; affidavit (declaración).

atestado, da, (â·tes·tâ´tho, thâ) adj. stubborn (testarudo); crowded; —, m. certificate, affidavit.

atestamiento, (â·tes·tâ·myen´to) m. cramming, crowding.

atestar, (â·tes·târ´) va. to attest, to testify, to witness.

atestar*, (â·tes·târ´) va. to cram, to stuff, to crowd; **—se,** to overeat.

atestiguar, (â·tes·tē·gwâr´) va. to witness, to attest.

ático, (â´tē·ko) m. (arch.) attic; Attic.

atiesar, (â·tye·sâr´) va. to make stiff, to make rigid.

atildado, da, (â·tēl·dâ´tho, thâ) adj. correct, neat.

atildar, (â·tēl·dâr´) va. to punctuate, to underline, to accent; to censure (censurar); to deck out, to dress up, to adorn (asear).

atinar, (â·tē·nâr´) va. and vn. to hit (the mark) (acertar); to guess (adivinar).

atisbadero, (â·tēz·vâ·the´ro) m. peephole, eyehole.

atisbar, (â·tēz·vâr´) va. to examine closely, to delve into.

atizar, (â·tē·sâr´) va. to stir with a poker; (fig.) to stir up, to roil.

Atlántico, ca, (âth·lân´tē·ko, kâ) m. and adj. Atlantic.

atlas, (âth´lâs) m. atlas.

atleta, (âth·le´tâ) m. and f. athlete.

atlético, ca, (âth·le´tē·ko, kâ) adj. athletic.

atmósfera, (âth·mos´fe·râ) f. atmosphere.

atmosférico, ca, (âth·mos·fe´rē·ko, kâ) adj. atmospheric.

atole, (â·to´le) m. corn-flour gruel; **dar — con el dedo,** (Mex. coll.) to deceive, to cheat.

atolondramiento, (â·to·lon·drâ·myen´tō) m. stupefaction, confusion, perplexity.

atolondrar, (â·to·lon·drâr´) va. to confuse, to stupefy; **—se,** to be befuddled, to be confused.

atolladero, (â·to·yâ·the´ro) m. miry place,

bog; (fig.) difficulty, obstacle.

atollar, (â·to·yâr´) vn. and vr. to get stuck in the mud.

atómico, ca, (â·to´mē·ko, kâ) adj. atomic.

átomo, (â´to·mo) m. atom.

atónito, ta, (â·to´nē·to, tâ) adj. astonished, amazed.

átono, na, (â´to·no, nâ) adj: atonic, unaccented.

atontar, (â·ton·târ´) va. to stun, to stupefy; **—se,** to grow stupid.

atorarse, (â·to·râr´se) vr. to choke (atragantarse); to stick in the mud (atascarse).

atormentar, (â·tor·men·târ´) va. to torment, to give pain.

atornillar, (â·tor·nē·yâr´) va. to screw.

atracadero, (â·trâ·kâ·the´ro) m. landing place.

atracar, (â·trâ·kâr´) va. (naut.) to overhaul a ship; to cause to overeat; —, vn. (naut.) to make shore, to dock,

atracción, (â·trâk·syon´) f. attraction.

atractivo, va, (â·trâk·tē´vo, vâ) adj. attractive, magnetic; —, m. charm, grace.

atraer*, (â·trâ·er´) va. to attract, to allure.

atragantarse, (â·trâ·gân·târ´se) vr. to choke; (fig.) to get mixed up in conversation (turbarse).

atrancar, (â·trâng·kâr´) va. to barricade.

atrapar, (â·trâ·pâr´) va. (fig.) to get, to obtain; to catch, to nab; to deceive, to take in (engañar).

atrás, (â·trâs´) adv. backwards, back; behind (detrás); past (pasado); **hacerse** —, to fall back; **hacia** —, backwards, back; **echarse** —, to change one's mind, to go back on one's word.

atrasado, da, (â·trâ·sâ´tho, thâ) adj. (fig.) backward, behind the times; late, tardy (tardío); in arrears (adeudado); slow (de reloj).

atrasar, (â·trâ·sâr´) va. to outstrip, to leave behind; to postpone, to delay (demorar); **— el reloj,** to set a watch back; **—se,** to be late, to fall behind; (corn.) to be in arrears.

atraso. (â·trâ´so) m. delay, falling behind.

atravesado, da, (â·trâ·ve·sâ´tho, thâ) adj. squint-eyed (bizco); of mixed breed. mongrel (híbrido); (fig.) degenerate, perverse.

atravesar*, (â·trâ·ve·sâr´) va. to lay across, to put across; to run through, to pierce (penetrar); to go across, to cross (cruzar); to trump (meter triunfo); **—se,** to get in the way, to thwart one's purpose.

atreverse, (â·tre·ver´se) *vr.* to dare, to venture.

atrevido, da, (â·tre·vē´tho, thâ) *adj.* bold, audacious, daring.

atrevimiento, (â·tre·vē·myen´to) *m.* boldness, audacity.

atribución (â·trē·vū·syon´) *f.* attribution, imputation.

atribuir*, (â·trē·vwēr´) *va.* to attribute, to ascribe, to impute; **—se** to assume.

atribular, (â·tre·vū·lâr´) *va.* to vex, to afflict; **—se,** to grieve, to carry on.

atributo, (â·trē·vū´to) *m.* attribute.

atrición, (â·trē·syon´) *f.* contrition.

atril, (â·trēl´) *m.* lectern, reading desk.

atrincherar, (â·trēn·che·râr´) *va.* to entrench.

atrio, (â´tryo) *m.* porch; portico.

atrocidad, (â·tro·sē·thâth´) *f.* atrocity.

atrofia, (â·tro´fyâ) *f.* atrophy.

atrofiado, da, (â·tro·fyâ´tho, thâ) *adj.* atrophied, emaciated.

atronar, (â·tro·nâr´) *va.* to deafen, to stun, to din; **—se** to be thunderstruck.

atropellado, da, (â·tro·pe·yâ´tho, thâ) *adj.* hasty, precipitate; **—,** *n.* person who has been run over.

atropellar, (â·tro·pe·yâr´) *va.* to trample, to run down, to knock down; **—se,** (fig.) to fall all over oneself, to overdo it.

atropello, (â·tro·pe´yo) *m.* trampling, knocking down; (fig.) abusiveness; **— de automóvil,** automobile collision.

atroz, (â·tros´) *adj.* atrocious; (coll.) enormous.

attmo. or att.ᵐᵒ: atentísimo, very kind, very courteous; **attmo. y seguro servidor,** yours very truly (in a letter).

atto. or att.o: atento, kind, courteous; atto. servidor, yours truly (in a letter).

atuendo, (â·twen´do) *m.* attire, garb *(vestido);* pomp, ostentation.

atún, (â·tūn´) *m.* tuna, tunny fish.

aturdido, da, (â·tūr·thē´tho, thâ) *adj.* harebrained, rattled.

aturdimiento, (â·tūr·thē·myen´to) *m.* stupefaction, dazed condition; (fig.) astonishment, bewilderment.

aturdir, (â·tūr·thēr´) *va* (fig.) to bewilder, to confuse; to stupefy, to daze.

atusar, (â·tū·sâr´) *va.* to trim, to even (the hair); **—se el bigote,** to twist one´s mustache.

audacia, (â,thâ´syâ) *f.* audacity, boldness.

audaz, (âū·thâs´) *adj.* audacious, bold.

audible, (âū·thē´vle) *adj.* audible.

audición, (âū·thē·syon´) *f.* audition, hearing

audiencia, (âū·thyen´syâ) *f.* audience, hearing; hearing in court; circuit court; appellate court *(tribunal),*

audífono, (âū·thē´fo·no) *m.* radio earphone.

audiófilo, (âū·thyo´fē·lo) *m.* audiophile.

audiofrecuencia, (âū·thyo·fre·kwen´syâ) *f.* audiofrequency.

audiología, (âū·thyo·lo·hē´â) *f.* audiology.

audiómetro, (âū·thyo´me·tro) *m.* audiometer.

audiovisual, (âū·thyo·vē·swâl´) *adj.* audiovisual.

auditivo, va, (âū·thē·tē´vo·va) *adj.* auditory.

auditorio, (âū·thē·to´ryo) *m.* assembly, audience.

auge, (â´ū·he) *m.* the pinnacle of power, height of success.

augurar, (âū·gū·râr´) *va.* to tell in advance, to predict.

augusto, ta, (âū·gūs´to, tâ) *adj.* august, majestic, magnificent, stately.

aula, (â´ū·la) *f.* lecture room, classroom.

aullar, (âū·yâr´) *vn.* to howl.

aullido, (âū·yē´tho) or **aúllo,** (â·ū´yo) *m.* howling, wailing, cry.

aumentar, (âū·men·târ´) *va.* to augment, to increase; **—,** *vn.* to grow larger.

aumento, (âū·men´to) *m.* increase, growth; promotion, advancement, progress *(adelantamiento).*

aun, (â´ūn) *adv.* even, the very; **— cuando,** even though.

aún, (â·ūn´) *adv.* still, yet.

aunar, (âū·nâr´) *va.* to unite, to assemble.

aunque, (â´ūn·ke) *conj.* though, notwithstanding.

¡aúpah! (â·ū´pâ) *interj.* up! up!

aura, (â´ū·râ) *f.* gentle breeze; **— popular,** popularity.

áureo, rea, (â´ū·re·o, re·â) *adj.* golden, gilt.

aureola (âū·re·o´lâ) or **auréola,** (âū·re´o lâ) *f.* halo; (fig.) glory, heavenly bliss; (ast.) corona.

aureomicina, (âū·re·o·mē·sē´nâ) *f.* (marca registrada) Aureomycin (trademark).

auricular, (âū·re·kū·lâr´) *adj.* within hearing, auricular; **—,** *m.* earphone; **— de casco,** headset.

aurora, (âū·ro´râ) *f.* dawn, daybreak; (poet.) dawn, first beginnings.

auscultar, (âūs·kul·târ´) *va.* (med.) to auscultate.

ausencia, (âū·sen´syâ) *f.* absence.

ausentarse, (âū·sen·târ´se) *vr.* to absent oneself.

---

m met, **n** not, **p** pot, **r** very, **rr** (none), **s** so, **t** toy, **th** with, **v** eve, **w** we, **y** yes, **z** zero

ausente, (āū·sen´te) *adj.* absent.
austeridad, (āūs·te·rē·thāth´) *f.* rigor, austerity.
austero, ra, (āūs·te´ro, rä) *adj.* austere, severe.
austral, (āūs·trāl´) *adj.* austral, southern.
austriaco, ca (āūs·tryä´ko, kä) or **austríaco, ca,** (āūs·trē´ä·ko, kä) *n.* and *adj.* Austrian.
austro, (á´ūs·tro) *m.* south wind.
autarquía, (āū·tár·ke´ä) *f.* autarchy, economic self-sufficiency.
autenticar, (āū·ten·tē·kár´) *va.* to authenticate.
autenticidad, (āū·ten·tē·sē·thäth´) *f.* authenticity.
auténtico, ca, (āū·ten´tē·ko, kä) *adj.* authentic, true, genuine.
auto, (á´ū·to) *m.* judicial decree, edict, ordinance; auto, car; — **de auxilio,** wrecker, tow car; — **de fe,** auto-da-fé; — **sacramental,** religious or allegorical play.
autobiografía, (āū·to·vyo·grä·fē´ä) *f.* autobiography.
autobús, (āū·to·vūs´) *m.* motorbus, bus.
autocamión, (āū·to·kä·myon´) *m.* auto truck, motor truck.
autocarril, (āū·to·kä·rrēl´) *m.* (Sp. Am.) automotive railroad car.
autocinema, (āū·to·sē·ne´mä) *m.* drive-in theatre.
autoclave, (āū·to·klä´ve) *f.* autoclave, sterilizer.
autocracia, (āū·to·krä´syä) *f.* autocracy.
autócrata, (āū·to´krä·tä) *m.* and *f.* autocrat.
autogiro, (āū·to·hē´ro) *m.* autogyro.
autógrafo, (āū·to´grä·fo) *m.* autograph.
autohotel, (āū·to·o·tel´) *m.* motel.
autoinfamación, (āū·toēn·flä·mä·syon´) *f.* spontaneous combustion.
autómata, (āū·to´mä·ta) *m.* automaton, robot.
automático, ca, (āū·to·mä´tē·ko, ka) *adj.* automatic.
automatización, (āū·to·ma·tē·sä·syon´) *f.* automation.
automotor, ra, (āū·to·mo·tor´, rä) *adj.* automotive.
automotriz, (āū·to·mo·trēs´) *f. adj.* automotive.
automóvil, (āū·to·mo´vēl) *m.* automobile; — **acorazado,** armored car.
automovilista, (āū·to·mo·vē·lē´stä) *m.* motorist.
automovilístico, ca, (āū·to·mo·vē·lēs´tē ko, kä) *adj.* automobile.

autonomía, (āū·to·no·mē´ä) *f.* autonomy.
autónomo, ma, (āū·to´no·mo, mä) *adj.* autonomous.
autopiano, (āū·to·pyä´no) *m.* player piano.
autopista, (āū·to·pēs´tä) *f.* superhighway, expressway; — **de acceso limitado,** freeway.
autopsia, (āū·top´syä) *f.* autopsy, post mortem.
autor, (āū·tor´) *m.* author.
autora, (āū·to´rä) *f.* authoress.
autoridad, (āū·to·rē·tháth´) *f.* authority.
autoritativo, va, (āū·to·rē·tä·tē´vo, vá) *adj.* authoritative.
autorización, (āū·to·rē·sä·syon´) *f.* authorization.
autorizado, da, (āū·to·rē·sä´tho, thä) *adj.* competent, reliable.
autorizar, (āū·to·rē·sär´) *va.* to authorize.
autorretrato, (āū·to·rre·trä´to) *m.* self-portrait.
autoviuda, (āū·to·vyū´thä) *f.* killer of her own husband.
auxiliar, (āūk·sē·lyär´) *va.* to aid, to help, to assist; to keep a deathwatch with; —, *adj.* auxiliary.
auxilio, (āūk·sē´lyo) *m.* aid, help, assistance; **acudir en — de,** to go to the assistance of; **primeros —s,** first aid.
a/v.: a la vista, (corn.) at sight.
aval, *m.* backing, countersignature, collateral.
avalorar, (ä·vä·lo·rär´) *va.* to enhance the value of; (fig.) to inspire, to enthuse.
avaluar, (ä·vä·lwär´) *va.* to estimate, to value, to evaluate, to appraise, to set a price on.
avalúo, (ä·vä·lū´o) *m.* appraisal.
avance, (ä·vän´se) *m.* (mil.) advance, attack.
avanzada, (ä·vän·sä´thä) *f.* (mil.) vanguard.
avanzar, (ä·vän·sär´) *va.* and *vn.* to advance, to push forward.
avaricia, (ä·vä·rē´syä) *f.* avarice.
avariento, ta, (ä·vä·ryen´to, tä) *adj.* avaricious, covetous.
avaro, ra, (ä·vä´ro, rä) *adj.* avaricious, miserly; —, *m.* miser.
avasallar, (ä·vä·sä·yär´) *va.* to subdue, to enslave.
ave, (ä´ve) *f.* bird; — **de corral,** fowl.
avejigar, (ä·ve·hē·gár´) *va.* and *vn.* to blister
avellana, (ä·ve·yä´nä) *f.* filbert, hazelnut.
avellanarse, (ä·ve·yä·när´se) *vr.* to shrivel,

â arm, **e** they, **ē** bē, **o** fore, **ū** blūe, **b** bad, **ch** chip, **d** day, f fat, **g go, h** hot, **k** kid, **1** let

to dry up.

avemarías, (â·ve mâ·rē´ä) f. Ave Maria, salutation of the Virgin Mary.

¡Ave María! (â·ve mâ·rē´ä) interj. my goodness! golly!

avena, (â·ve´nä) f. oats.

avenencia, (â·ve·nen´syâ) f. agreement, bargain (convenio); union, concord (conformidad).

avenida, (â·ve·nē´thä) flood, inundation; (fig.) coming together, concurrence, conjunction; avenue, boulevard.

avenir*, (â·ve·nēr´) va. to reconcile, to bring into agreement; —se to be reconciled, to come to an agreement.

aventador, (â·ven·tâ·thor´) m. (agr.) winnower; fan.

aventajado, da, (â·ven·tâ·hä´tho, thä) adj. advantageous, excelling, superior.

aventajar, (â·ven·tâ·hâr´) va. to surpass, to excel, to have the advantage.

aventar*, (â·ven·târ´) va. to fan; (agr.) to winnow; to blow along; (fig.) to cast out, to expulse; —se, to puff up, to fill with air.

aventura, (â·ven·tū´râ) f. adventure, event, incident, chance.

aventurar, (â·ven·tū·râr´) va. to venture, to risk, to take chances with.

aventurero, ra, (â·ven·tū·re´ro, râ) adj. adventurous; —, n. adventurer, free lance.

avergonzado, da, (â·ver·gon·sâ´tho, thä) adj. embarrassed, sheepish.

avergonzar*, (â·ver·gon·sâr´) va. to shame, to abash; —se, to be ashamed.

avería, (â ve·rē´ä) f. damage to goods; (orn.) aviary; (naut.) average.

averiado, da, (â·ve·ryä´tho, thä) adj. damaged by sea water.

averiarse, (â·ve·ryâr´se) vr. to suffer damage at sea.

averiguación, (â·ve·rē·gwä·syon´) f. investigation.

averiguar, (â·ve·rē·gwâr´) va. to inquire into, to investigate, to ascertain, to find out.

aversión, (â·ver·syon´) f. aversion, dislike, antipathy.

avestruz, (â·ves·trūs´) m. ostrich.

avezar, (â·ve·sâr´) va. to accustom, to habituate.

aviación, (â·vyä·syon´) f. aviation.

aviador, ra, (â·vyä·thor´, râ) n. aviator.

aviar, (â·vyâr´) va. to provision, to provide for, to supply, to equip; to hasten, to speed up (apresurar); —se, to equip oneself, to fit oneself out.

avidez, (â·vē·thes´) f. covetousness.

ávido, da, (â´vē·tho, thä) adj. greedy, covetous.

avillanar, (â·vē·yâ·nâr´) va. to debase.

avío, (â·vē´o) m. preparation, provision.

avión, (â·vyon´) m. (orn.) martin, swallow; airplane; — **radioguiado,** drone; — **de bombardeo,** bomber; — **de combate,** pursuit plane; — **de turbohélice,** turboprop; — **de turborreacción,** turbo-jet; **por —,** by plane, by air mail.

avisar, (â·vē·sâr´) va. to inform, to notify; to admonish, to advise (aconsejar).

aviso, (â·vē´so) m. information, notice; advertisement (anuncio); warning, hint (advertencia); prudence, discretion; counsel, advice (consejo); **sin otro —,** without further advice; **según —,** as per advice.

avispa, (â·vēs´pä) f. wasp.

avispado, da, (â·vés·pä´tho, thä) adj. lively, brisk, vivacious.

avispar, (â·vēs·pâr´) va. to spur, to incite to alertness; —se,to grow restless.

avispero, (â·vēs·pe´ro) m. wasps' nest.

avivar, (â·vē·vâr´) va. to quicken, to encourage.

axila, (âk·sē´lä) f. armpit.

axioma, (âk·syo´mä) m. axiom, maxim.

axiomático, ca, (â·syo·mä´tē·ko, kä) adj. axiomatic.

¡ay! inter. alas!; **¡— de mí!** alas! poor me!

aya, (ä´ya) f. governess, instructress.

ayer, (â·yer´) adv. yesterday; (fig.) lately; — **mismo,** only yesterday; — **por la mañana,** yesterday morning; — **por la tarde,** yesterday afternoon.

ayes, (ä´yes) m. pl. lamentations, sighs.

ayuda, (â·yū´thä) f. help, aid, assistance, support; —, m. assistant; — **de cámara,** valet.

ayudante, (â·yū·thân´te) m. assistant; (mil.) adjutant, aide-de-camp.

ayudar, (â·yū·thâr´) va. to aid, to help, to assist; to further, to contribute to (alentar).

ayunar, (â·yū·nâr´) vn. to fast, to abstain from food.

ayunas, (â·yū´nâs) **en —,** adv. before breakfast, not having had breakfast; (fig.) unprepared, lacking information, ignorant (of a situation).

ayuno, (â·yū´no) m. fast, abstinence from food.

ayuntamiento, (â·yūn·tâ·myen´to) m. town council (junta); city hall, town hall; city government (corporación).

azabache, (â·sä·vä´che) m. jet.

---

m met, **n** not, **p** pot, **r** very, **rr** (none), **s** so, **t** toy, **th** with, **v** eve, **w** we, **y** yes, **z** zero

azada, (â·sä´thä) f. spade, hoe.

azadón, (â·sä·thon´) m. pickax; hoe.

azafata, (â·sä·fä´tä) f. plane stewardess.

azafrán, (â·sä·frän´) m. saffron.

azahar, (â·sä·är´) m. orange or lemon blossom.

azar, (â·sär´) m. unforeseen disaster, unexpected accident *(desgracia)*; chance, happenstance *(casualidad);* al —, at random.

azaroso, sa, (â·sä·ro´so, sä) adj. ominous, hazardous, foreboding.

ázoe, (â´so·e) m. (chem.) nitrogen.

azogar, (â·so·gär´) va. to overlay with mercury; — la cal, to slake lime; —se, to be in a state of agitation.

azogue, (â·so´ge) m. mercury.

azorar, (â·so·rär´) va. to frighten, to terrify; —se, to be terrified.

azotar, (â·so·tär´) va. to whip, to lash.

azote, (â·so´te) m. whip, scourge; lash given with a whip *(azotazo);* (fig.) calamity, great misfortune.

azotea, (â·so·te´ä) f. flat roof; roof garden.

azteca, (äs·te´kä) m. and f. and adj. Aztec; —, m. Mexican gold coin.

azúcar, (â·sü´kär) m. or f. sugar; — blanco, ca, refined sugar; — cubicado, da, cube sugar; — de remolacha, beet sugar; — morena, brown sugar.

azucarado, da, (â·sü·kä·rä´tho, thä) adj. sugared; sugary.

azucarar, (â·sü·kä·rär´) va. to sugar, to sweeten.

azucarera, (â·sü·kä·re´rä) f. sugar bowl.

azucarero, (â·sü·kä·re´ro) m. sugar bowl; confectioner.

azucena, (â·sü·se´nä) f. white lily.

azufre, (â·sü´fre) m. sulphur, brimstone.

azul, (â·sül´) adj. blue; — celeste, sky blue; — subido, bright blue; — turquí, turquoise blue.

azulado, da, (â·sü·lä´tho, thä) adj. azure, bluish.

azulejo, (â·sü·le´ho) m. glazed tile; (orn.) bluebird.

azumbre, (â·süm´bre) f. liquid measure (half a gallon).

azur, (â·sür´) adj. (poet.) blue.

azuzar, (â·sü·sär´) va. to sic, to set on; (fig.) to irritate, to stir up.

B

baba, (bä´vä) f. driveling, drooling, slobbering; (zool.) mucus, slime.

babear, (bä·ve·är´) vn. to drivel, to drool, to slobber.

babel, (bä·vel´) m. babel, confusion.

babero, (bä·ve´ro) m. bib.

babieca, (bä·vye´kä) m. and f. ignorant, stupid person.

babor, (bä·vor´) m. (naut.) larboard, port; de — a estribor, athwart ship.

babosear, (bä·vo·se·är´) va. and vn. to drool, to slobber.

baboso, sa, (bä·vo´so, sä) adj. driveling, slobbery; (fig.) foolish, silly; —, n. (Sp. Am.) fool, idiot.

bacalao, (bä·kä·lä´o) m. codfish.

bacanales, (bä·kä·nä´les) f. pl. bacchanals.

bacía, (bä·sē´ä) f. basin; shaving bowl *(de barbero).*

bacilo, (bä·sē´lo) m. bacillus.

bacinica (bä·sē·nē´kä) or bacinilla, (bä·sē·nē´yä) chamber pot.

bacteria (bak·te´ryä) f. bacteria.

bactericida, (bäk·te·rē·sē´thä) adj. germici-

dal; —, m. germicide.

bacteriología, (bäk·te·ryo·lo·hē´ä) f. bacteriology.

bacteriólogo, ga, (bäk·te·ryo´lo·go, gä) n. bacteriologist.

bache, (bä´che) m. rut, hole, pothole; (avi.) air pocket.

bachiller, (bä·chē·yer´) m. and f. holder of a bachelor's degree.

bachiller, ra, (bä·chē·yer´, rä) adj. prating, babbling.

bachillerato, (bä·chē·ye·rä´to) m. bachelor's degree.

badajo, (bä·thä´ho) m. clapper of a bell; (fig.) idle, foolish talker.

badana, (bä·thä´nä) f. dressed sheepskin.

badil, (bä·thēl´) m. fire shovel.

bagatela, ((bä·gä·te´lä) f. bagatelle, trifle.

bagazo, (bä·gä´so) m. bagasse.

bahía. (bä·ē´ä) f. bay.

bailador, ra, (bäē·lä·thor´, rä) n. dancer.

bailar, (bäē·lär´) vn. to dance.

bailarín, (bäē·lä·rēn´) m. male dancer.

bailarina, (bäē·lä·rē´nä) f. ballerina, female, dancer.

baile, (bâ´ē·le) *m.* dance, ball; bailiff *(magistrado);* **— de etiqueta,** dress ball; **— de máscaras,** masked ball.

baja, (bâ´hâ) *f.* drop in prices, loss of value; (mil.) loss, casualty; withdrawal, resignation *(de una sociedad);* **dar de —** to discharge, to release; **darse de —** to withdraw, to resign, to drop out.

bajada, (bâ·hâ´thâ) *f.* incline, slope; descent, going down *(acción).*

bajamar, (bâ·hâ·mâr´) *f.* low water, low tide, ebb.

bajar, (bâ·hâr´) *va.* to lower, to decrease *(precio);* to take down, to let down, to lead down; to lean down, to bend down *(inclinar);* to humble, to humiliate *(humillar);* **—,** *vn.* to go down, to descend; **— de** to get out of, to descend from, to alight from.

bajel, (bâ·hel´) *m.* vessel, ship.

bajeza, (bâ·he´sâ) *f.* meanness, littleness, pettiness.

bajío, (bâ·hē´o) *m.* shoal, sandbank; (Sp. Am.) lowland.

bajista, (bâ·hēs´tâ) *m.* (com.) bear (in stocks).

bajo, ja, (bá´ho, hâ) *adj.* low *(altura);* short *(persona);* abject, humble *(abatido);* coarse, common *(tosco);* dull, faint *(color);* downcast, cast down, bent over *(inclinado);* **tierra —,** lowland; **piso** or **planta —,** ground floor; **—jo,** *adv.* under; **—jo,** *prep.* underneath, below; **— par,** under or below par; **— techo,** indoors; **— cuerda,** underhandedly; **—,** *m.* (mus.) bass.

bajón, (bâ·hon´) *m.* bassoon.

bajorrelieve, (bâ·ho·rre·lye´ve) *m.* bas-relief.

bala, (bá´lâ) *f.* bullet, shot *(proyectil);* bale *(de mercancías);* (print.) inking roller.

balacera, (bâ·lâ·se´râ) *f.* (Mex.) shooting at random.

balada, (bâ·lâ´thâ) *f.* ballad.

baladí, (bâ·lâ·thē´) *adj.* mean, despicable, worthless.

baladronada, (bâ·lâ·thro·nâ´thâ) *f.* boast, brag, bravado.

baladronear, (bâ·lâ·thro·ne·âr´) *vn.* to boast, to brag.

balance, (bâ´lân´se) *m.* swaying, swinging; (fig.) indecisiveness, hesitation; (com.) balancing accounts, balancing the books; balance sheet *(estado);* **hacer un —,** to draw (or strike) a balance.

balancear, (bâ·lân·se·âr´) *va.* to balance, to

put in balance; **—se,** to rock, to sway, to swing; (fig.) to hesitate, to be doubtful.

balanceo, (bâ·lân·se´o) *m.* rocking, swing; (avi. and naut.) rolling, pitching.

balancín, (bâ·lân·sēn´) *m.* whiffletree *(de carruaje);* coining die *(volante);* tightrope walker´s pole *(de volantinero);* (mech.) rocker arm.

balanza, (bâ·lân´sâ) *f.* scale, balance, (fig.) evaluation, comparison; **— de comercio,** balance of trade.

balar, (bâ·lâr´) *vn.* to bleat.

balasto, (bâ·lâs´to) *m.* (rail.) ballast.

balaustrada, (bâ·lâūs·trâ´thâ) *f.* balustrade.

balaustre (bâ·lâ´ūs·tre) or **balaústre,** (bâ·lâ·us´tre)) *m.* banister.

balazo, (bâ·lâ´so) *m.* shot; bullet wound *(herida).*

balboa, (bâl·vo´â) *m.* monetary unit of Panama.

balbucear, (bâl·vū·se·âr´) *va.* and *vn.* to speak indistinctly, to stammer.

balbucir*, (bâl·vū·sēr´) *va.* and *vn.* To stammer, to stutter.

balcón, (bâl·kon´) *m.* balcony.

baldar, (bâl·dâr´) *va.* to cripple.

balde, (bâl´de) *m.* bucket, pail; **de —,** gratis, for nothing; **en —,** in vain.

baldear, (bâl·de·âr´) *va.* to wash down with pailfuls of water *(regar);* to bail out with a bucket *(achicar).*

baldío, día, (bâl·dē´o, dē´â) *adj.* (agr.) untilled, uncultivated; idle, shiftless *(vagabundo);* fruitless, useless *(vano).*

baldosa, (bâl·do´sâ) *f.* fine paving bricks or tile.

balido, (bâ·lē´tho) *m.* bleating, bleat.

balín, (bâ·lēn´) *m.* buckshot.

balística, (bâ·lēs´tē·kâ) *f.* ballistics.

baliza, (bâ·lē´sâ) *f.* buoy.

balneario, (bâl·ne·â´ryo) *m.* bathing resort.

balompié, (bâ·lom·pye´) *m.* football.

balón, (bâ·lon´) *m.* balloon; bale *(fardo);* **— de fútbol,** football.

baloncesto, (bâ·lon·ses´to) *m.* basketball.

balonvolea, (bâ·lom·bo·le´â) *m.* volleyball.

balsa, (bâl´sâ) *f.* raft, float, pool, large puddle *(charca).*

balsadera, (bâl·sâ·the´râ) *f.* ferry landing.

bálsamo, (bâl´sâ·mo) *m.* balsam, balm.

balsear, (bâl·se·âr´) *va.* to cross by ferry.

balsero, (bâl·se´ro) *m.* ferryman.

baluarte, (bâ·lwâr´te) *m.* bastion, bulwark,

rampart.

ballena, (bâ·ye´nä) *f.* whale; whalebone *(producto).*

ballenato, (bâ·ye·nä´to) *m.* whale calf.

ballesta, (bâ·yes´tä) *f.* crossbow.

ballestear, (bâ·yes·te·âr´) *va.* to shoot with a crossbow.

bambolear, (bâm·bo·le·âr´) *vn.* to reel, to sway, to stagger.

bamboleo, (bâm·bo·le´o) *m.* reeling, staggering.

bambolla, (bâm·bo´yä) *f.* (coll.) ostentation vain show.

bambú, (bâm·bū´) *m.* bamboo.

bambuco, (bâm·bū´ko) *m.* Colombian popular tune and dance.

banana, (bâ·nä´nä) *f.* banana tree or fruit.

bananero, (bâ·nä·ne´ro) *m.* banana tree or fruit; **—, ra,** *adj.* pertaining to the banana.

banano, (bâ·nä´no) *m.* banana tree or fruit.

banasto, (bâ·näs´to) *m.* large round basket.

banca, (bâng´kä) *f.* bench; (corn.) banking.

bancario, ria, (bang·kä´ryo, ryä) *adj.* banking.

bancarrota, (bang·kâ·rro´tä) *f.* bankruptcy.

banco, (bâng´ko) *m.* bench; bank, shoal *(bajo);* (ichth.) school; (corn.) bank; **— agrícola,** agricultural (or farmers') bank; **— de ahorros,** savings bank; **— de depósito,** trust bank; **— de emisión,** bank of issue; **— del estado,** state bank; **— de liquidación,** clearinghouse; **— de préstamos,** loan bank; **— de sangre,** blood bank; **— de taller,** workbench; **— hipotecario,** mortgage bank; **billete de —,** banknote; **empleado de —,** bank clerk; **libro de —,** passbook; **poner en el —,** to deposit in the bank.

banda, (bân´dä) *f.* band; sash, ribbon *(faja);* faction, party *(partido);* side, edge *(lado).*

bandada, (bân·dä´thä) *f.* covey, flock.

bandearse, (bân·de·âr´se) *vr.* to shift for oneself.

bandeja, (bân·de´hä) *f.* tray;— **de entrada,** in-box *(internet);*— **de salida,** out-box *(internet).*

bandera, (bân·de´râ) *f.* banner, standard *(estandarte);* flag; **a —s desplegadas,** freely, openly.

banderilla, (bân·de·rē´yä) *f.* small decorated dart used at a bullfight.

banderola, (bân·de·ro´lä) *f.* streamer, pennant.

bandido, (bân·dē´tho) *m.* bandit, outlaw;

highwayman *(bandolero).*

bandido, da, (ban·dē´tho, thä) *adj.* bandit like, lawless.

bando, (bân´do) *m.* faction, party; proclamation, decree *(edicto).*

bandola, (ban·do´lä) *f.* mandolin.

bandolero, (bân·do·le´ro) *m.* highway-man, robber.

bandolín, (bân·do·lēn´) *m.* mandolin.

bandolina, (ban·do·lē´nä) *f.* mandolin; hair pomade *(mucílago).*

banquero, ra, (bang·ke´ro, ra) *n.* banker.

banqueta, (bang·ke´tä) *f.* stool; (Max. and Guat.) sidewalk.

banquete, (bang·ke´te) *m.* banquet; feast.

bañar, (bâ·nyâr´) *va.* to bathe; to dip *(sumergir);* to coat, to apply a coat (of a liquid) to *(cubrir);* **por —se,** to take a bath.

bañera, (bâ·nye´râ) *f.* bathtub.

baño, (bä´nyo) *m.* bath; bathtub *(pila);* bathroom *(cuarto);* coat, coating *(capa);* **— de ducha,** shower bath; **— de regadera,** shower bath.

baquelita, (bâ·ke·lē´tä) *f.* bakelite.

baqueta, (bâ·ke´tä) *f.* ramrod; (taus.) drumstick; (mil.) gauntlet *(castigo).*

baquetazo, (bâ·ke·tä´so) *m.* blow with a ramrod.

baraja, (bâ·râ´hä) *f.* deck of playing cards; **jugar con dos —s** to deal from the bottom of the deck, to be a double-crosser.

barajar, (bâ·râ·hâr´) *va.* to shuffle (cards); (fig.) to entangle, to mix up, to envolve.

baranda, (bâ·rân´dä) *f.* banister, railing.

barandal, (bâ·ran·dâl´) *m.* railing.

baratero, ra, (bâ·râ·te´ro, ra) *adj.* selling at a low price, offering bargains.

baratijas, (bâ·râ·tē´häs) *f. pl.* trifles, toys.

baratillero, (bâ·râ·tē·ye´ro) *m.* peddler.

baratillo, (bâ·râ·tē´yo) *m.* secondhand shop; sale of secondhand goods, bargain sale *(venta).*

barato, ta, (bâ·râ´to, tä) *adj.* cheap, low-priced; **—to,** *adv.* cheaply; **—,** *m.* bargain sale, sale at low prices; part of the take given the bystanders by the winning gambler.

baratura, (bâ·râ·tū´rä) *f.* cheapness.

baraúnda, (bâ·râ·ūn´dä) *f.* noise, confusion.

barba, (bâr´vä) *f.* chin; beard, whiskers *(pelo);* **— a —,** face to face; **hacer la —,** to fawn on, to play up to; to bother, to annoy *(fastidiar);* **por —,** per person.

barbacoa, (bar·vâ·ko´â) *f.* barbecue.

barbada, (bâr·vâ´thä) *f.* lower jaw of a horse: (ichth.) dab.

barbaridad. (bâr·vâ·rē·thâth´) *f.* barbarity,

â arm, **e** they, **ē** bē, **o** fore, **ū** blūe, **b** bad, **ch** chip, **d** day, f fat, **g go, h** hot, **k** kid, **1** let

cruelty *(fiereza)*; rudeness, grossness *(grosería)*; piece of foolishness, harebrained action *(disparate)*; (coll.) tremendous amount, awful lot; ¡qué —! how terrible!

barbarie, (bâr·vä´rye) *f.* barbarism, cruelty; lack of culture, grossness.

barbarismo, (bâr·vä·rēz´mo) *m.* barbarism.

bárbaro, ra, (bâr´vä·ro, rä) *adj.* cruel, savage, barbaric *(fiero)*; rash, headstrong, impetuous *(arrojado)*; rude, unpolished, gross *(inculto)*.

barbería, (bâr·ve·rē´ä) *f.* barbershop.

barbero, (bâr·ve´ro) *m.* barber.

barbicano, na, (bâr·vē·kä´no, nä) *adj.* gray-bearded.

barbilla, (bâr·vē·yä) *f.* point of the chin.

barbital, (bar·vē·tä´l) *m.* barbital.

barbitúrico, (bâr·vē·tū´rē·ko) *m.* barbiturate.

barbudo, da, (bâr·vū´tho, thä) *adj.* long-bearded.

barbulla, (bar·vū´yä) *f.* confused noise.

barca, (bâr´kä) *f.* boat, barge.

barcaza, (bâr·kä´sä) *f.* barge, lighter.

barco, (bâr´ko) *m.* boat, (poet.) bark, ship; — de guerra, warship.

bardo, (bâr´tho) *m.* bard, poet.

bario, (bä´ryo) *m.* barium.

barítono, (bâ·rē´to·no) *m.* (mus.) baritone.

barlovento, (bâr·lo·ven´to) *m.* (naut.) windward; ganar el —, to get to windward.

barniz, (bâr·nēs´) *m.* varnish; — para uñas, nail polish.

barnizar, (bar·nē·sâr´) *va.* to varnish.

barómetro, (bâ·ro´me·tro) *m.* barometer; indicación del —, barometric reading.

barón, (bâ·ron´) *m.* baron.

baronesa, (bä·ro·ne´sä) *f.* baroness.

barquero, (bâr·ke´ro) *m.* boatman.

barquillo, (bâr·kē´yō) *m.* cone-shaped wafer; ice-cream cone *(de helado)*.

barra, (bä´rrä) *f.* bar; crowbar, lever *(palanca)*; large ingot *(lingote)*; sandbar *(alfaque)*.

barraca, (bä·rrä´kä) *f.* hut, cabin; (Sp. Am.) depository, warehouse, storage shed.

barranca, (bä·rräng´kä) *f.* precipice, cliff; ravine, gully *(quiebra)*.

barranco, (bä·rräng´ko) *m.* ravine, gorge; cliff; (fig.) difficult situation, predicament.

barrancoso, sa, (bä·rräng·ko´so, sä) *adj.* uneven, rugged, gullied, full of holes.

barredor, ra, (bä·rre·thor´, rä) *n.* sweeper.

barrena, (bä·rre´nä) *f.* borer, gimlet, auger.

barrenar, (bä·rre·nâr´) *va.* to bore holes in; (naut.) to scuttle; (fig.) to frustrate, to undermine, to undo.

barrendero, ra, (bä·rren·de´ro, rä) *n.* sweeper, dustman or woman.

barreno, (bä·rre´no) *m.* large borer, large auger; hole bored, bore *(agujero)*.

barrer, (bä·rrer´) *va.* to sweep; (fig.) to sweep away, to clear away, to rid of.

barrera, (bä·rre´rä) *f.* clay pit *(de barro)*; bar, barrier, barricade *(valla)*; (fig.) obstruction; — antiaérea, flak; — sónica, sound barrier.

barriada, (bä·rryä´thä) *f.* quarter, section, part.

barrica, (bä·rrē´kä) *f.* cask containing about 60 gallons, hogshead.

barricada, (bä·rrē·kä´thä) *f.* barricade.

barrido, (bä·rrē´thō) *m.* sweep; —, da, *adj.* swept.

barriga, (bä·rrē´gä) *f.* abdomen, belly; belly *(de vasija)*; (fig.) bulge in a wall.

barrigón, (bä·rrē·gon´) *m.* (Cuba) small child; —, ona, *adj.* big-bellied.

barrigudo, da, (bä·rrē·gū´tho, thä) *adj.* big-bellied.

barril, (bä·rrēl´) *m.* barrel, cask.

barrilero, (bä·rrē·le´ro) *in.* barrelmaker, cooper.

barrio, (bä´rryo) *m.* district or section of a town, neighborhood; —s bajos, slums.

barro, (bä´rro) *m.* clay *(arcilla)*; mud *(lodo)*; pimple *(granillo)*; — cocido, terra cotta, baked clay.

barroco, (bä·rro´ko) *m.* baroque.

barroso, sa, (bä·rro´so, sä) *adj.* muddy; like clay; pimpled, pimply.

barrote, (bä·rro´te) *m.* heavy bar, metal brace.

barruntamiento, (bä·rrün·tä·myen´to) *m.* conjecturing, guessing, inkling.

barruntar, (bä·rrün·târ´) *va.* to conjecture, to suspect, to have an inkling.

barrunto, (bä·rrün´to) *m.* conjecture, inkling, suspicion.

basalto, (bä·säl´to) *m.* basalt.

basar, (bä·sâr´) *va.* to base, to found, to support; — se en, to rely on, to have confidence in.

báscula, (bäs´kū·lä) *f.* platform scale.

base, (bä´se) *f.* base, basis;— de datos, database.

básico, ca, (bä´sē·ko, kä) *adj.* basic, fundamental.

basílica, (bä·sē´lē·kä) *f.* basilica.

básquetbol, (bäs´ket·vol) *m.* basketball.

---

basquetbolista, (bâs·ket·vo·lēs´tâ) *m.* and *f.* basketball player.

basta, (bâs´tâ) *f.* basting, loose stitching; ¡—! *interj.* enough!

bastante, (bâs·tân´te) *adj.* sufficient, enough; considerable; —, *adv.* enough, sufficiently; quite a bit, quite, rather *(no poco).*

bastar, (bâs·târ´) *vn.* to suffice, to be enough.

bastardilla, (bâs·târ·thē´yâ) *f.* italic.

bastardo, da, (bâs·târ´tho, thâ) *adj.* bastard, spurious; —, *m.* bastard.

bastear, (bâs·te·âr´) *va.* to stitch loosely, to baste.

bastidor, (bâs·tē·thor´) *m.* frame; stretcher *(de cuadro);* (auto.) chassis; (phot.) plateholder; —**es,** *pl.* (theat.) wings; **tras —es,** backstage; — **de ventana** or **puerta,** sash.

bastilla, (bâs·tē·yâ) *f.* hem, seam.

bastimento, (bas·tē·men´to) *m.* provisions, supplies; (naut.) vessel.

basto, (bâs´to) *m.* packsaddle; club *(naipe);* —, **ta,** *adj.* coarse, rude, unpolished.

bastón, (bâs·ton´) *m.* staff, cane.

bastoncillo, (bâs·ton·sē´yo) *m.* small cane; narrow braid trimming *(galoncillo).*

bastonero, (bâs·to·ne´ro) *m.* cane maker or seller; dance director, dance manager *(de baile);* assistant jailer *(de la cárcel).*

bastos, (bâs´tos) *m. pl.* clubs.

basura, (bâs·sū´râ) *f.* dirt, dust, sweepings; trash; horse manure *(estiércol).*

basurero, (bâs·sū·re´ro) *m.* garbage man, trash collector; garbage dump, trash pile *(muladar).*

bata, (bâ´tâ) *f.* dressing gown, robe; — **de mujer,** housecoat.

batahola or **bataola,** (bâ·tâ·o´lâ) *f.* hurlyburly, bustle.

batalla, (bâ·tâ´yâ) *f.* battle, combat, fight; — **campal,** pitched battle.

batallador, ra, (bâ·tâ·yâ·thor´, râ) *adj.* battling, combative; —, *m.* combatant, warrior.

batallar, (bâ·tâ·yâr´) *vn.* to battle, to fight, to struggle; to fence with foils *(esgrimir);* to dispute, to wrangle *(disputar)* ; to fluctuate, to waver *(vacilar).*

batallón, (bâ·tâ·yon´) *m.* (mil.) battalion.

batata, (bâ·tâ´tâ) *f.* sweet potato.

batea, (bâ·te´â) *f.* painted wooden tray *(bandeja);* flatcar *(vagón);* rounded trough *(dornajo);* square flat-bottomed

boat *(barco).*

batear, (bâ·te·âr´) *va* and *vn.* (baseball) to bat.

batería, (bâ·te·rē´â) *f.* battery; (mus.) percussion instruments; — **de acumuladores,** storage battery; — **de cocina,** kitchen utensils; — **de teatro,** stage lights; — **líquida,** wet battery; — **seca,** dry battery.

batey, (bâ·te´ē) *m.* (Cuba) premises of a sugar refinery; (P.R.) front yard.

batido, da, (ba·tē´tho, thâ) *adj.* beaten; with a changeable luster, chatoyant *(tejido);* well-beaten, well-traveled *(camino);* —, *m.* batter.

batidor, (bâ·tē·thor´) *m.* beater.

batidora, (bâ·tē·tho´râ) *f.* beater; — **eléctrica,** mixmaster, electric beater.

batín, (bâ·tēn´) *m.* smoking jacket.

batir, (bâ·tēr´) *va.* to beat; to beat down, knock down, to demolish *(derribar);* to flap violently, to beat *(las alas);* to coin, to mint *(moneda);* to rout, to defeat *(derrotar);* —**se,** to fight, to struggle; — **banderas,** to salute with colors; — **palmas,** to clap, to applaud; —**se a muerte,** to fight to the death; — **tiendas,** to strike camp.

batiscafo, (bâ·tēs·kâ´fo) *m.* bathyscaphe.

batista, (bâ·tēs´tâ) *f.* batiste, cambric.

baturrillo, (bâ·tū·rrē´yo) *m.* hodgepodge, potpourri, medley.

batuta, (bâ·tū´tâ) *f.* baton; **llevar la —,** to lead, to preside.

baúl, (bâ·ūl´) *m.* trunk, chest; — **ropero,** wardrobe trunk.

bautismal, (bâū·tēz·mâl´) *adj.* baptismal.

bautismo, (bâū·tēz´mo) *m.* baptism.

bautizar, (bâū·tē·sâr´) *va.* to baptize, to christen.

bautizo, (bâū·tē´so) *m.* baptism, christening.

baya, (bâ´yâ) *f.* berry.

bayeta, (bâ·ye´tâ) *f.* woolen baize.

bayetón, (bâ·ye·ton´) *m.* heavy wool baize, bearskin.

bayo, ya, (bâ´yo, yâ) *adj.* bay.

bayoneta, (bâ·yo·ne´tâ) *f.* bayonet.

baza, (ba´sâ) *f.* card trick; **meter —,** to butt into a conversation.

bazar, (bâ·sâr´) *m.* bazaar; department store *(tienda).*

beata, (be·â´tâ) *f.* lay woman in charity work; (coll.) very devout woman, saintly woman.

beatería, (be·â·te·rē´â) *f.* affected piety.

beatificar, (be·â·tē·fē·kâr´) *va.* to beatify, to

hallow, to sanctify, to make blessed.

beatifico, ca, (be·â·tē´fē·ko, kâ) *adj.* beatific.

beatisimo, ma, (be·â·tē´sē·mo, mâ) *adj.* most holy; **B— Padre,** Most Holy Father (the Pope).

beatitud, (be·â·tē·tûth´) *f.* beatitude, blessedness.

beato, ta, (be·â´to, tâ) *adj.* fortunate, blessed *(bienaventurado);* devout *(piadoso);* hypocritical, sanctimonious *(santurrón);* —, *n.* pious person, devout individual.

bebedero, (be·ve·the´ro) *m.* drinking dish; watering trough *(abrevadero);* bird bath *(para aves);* —, **ra,** *adj.* drinkable, potable.

bebedor, ra, (be·ve·thor´, râ) *n.* drinker; (fig.) tippler, drunkard.

beber, (be·ver´) *va.* and *vn.* to drink; —, *m.* drinking.

bebible, (be·vē´vle) *adj. (coll.)* drinkable, pleasant to the taste.

bebida, (be·vē´thâ) *f.* drink, beverage; — **alcohólica,** intoxicant.

bebido, da, (be·vē´tho, thâ) *adj.* intoxicated.

beca, (be´kâ) *f.* scholarship, fellowship.

becerra, (be·se´rrâ) *f.* female calf; (bot.) snapdragon.

becerrillo, (be·se·rrē´yo) *m.* dressed calfskin.

becerro, (be·se´rro) *m.* yearling calf; calfskin *(piel);* — **marino,** (zool.) seal.

beduino, na, (be·thwē´no, nâ) *adj.* and *n.* Bedouin; —, *m.* ungovernable, barbaric individual.

befar, (be·fâr´) *va.* to mock, to ridicule.

béisbol, (be´ēz·vol) *m.* baseball.

bejucal, (be·hû·kâl´) *m.* reed bank.

bejuco, (be·hû´ko) *m.* liana.

bejuquillo, (be·hû·kē´yo) *m.* small gold chain; (bot.) ipecacuanha.

beldad, (bel·dâth´) *f.* beauty.

Belén, (be·len´) *m.* Bethlehem; **estar en** —, not to pay attention, to have one's mind elsewhere; **b—,** *m.* creche *(nacimiento);* bedlam *(confusión);* **meterse en —enes,** to do things at the wrong time.

belga, (bel´gâ) *adj.* and *n.* Belgian.

Bélgica, (bel´hē·kâ) *f.* Belgium.

bélico, ca, (be´lē·ko, kâ) *adj.* warlike, martial.

belicoso, sa, (be·lē·ko´so, sâ) *adj.* martial, pugnacious, aggressive.

beligerancia, (be·lē·he·rân´syâ) *f.* belligerency.

beligerante, (be·lē·he·rân´te) *adj.* belligerent.

Belice, (be·lē´se) *f.* British Honduras; Belize *(ciudad).*

bellacada, (be·yâ·kâ´thâ) *f.* knavery, rascality.

bellaco, ca, (be·yâ´ko, kâ) *adj.* sly, cunning, roguish; —, *m.* knave.

belladona, (be·yâ·tho´nâ) *f.* (bot.) deadly nightshade; (med.) belladonna.

bellaquería, (be·yâ·ke·rē´â) *f.* knavery, roguery.

belleza, (be·ye´sâ) *f.* beauty.

bello, lla, (be´yo, yâ) *adj.* beautiful, handsome, fair, fine; **—llas artes,** fine arts.

bellota, (be·yo´tâ) *f.* acorn.

bemol, (be·mol´) *m.* (mus.) flat.

bencedrina, (ben·se·thrē´nâ) *f.* benzedrine.

bencina, (ben·sē´nâ) *f.* (chem.) benzine.

bendecir*, (ben·de·sēr´) *va.* to consecrate, to bless *(consagrar);* to praise, to exalt *(alabar).*

bendición, (ben·dē·syon´) *f.* benediction, blessing.

bendito, ta, (ben·dē´to, tâ) *adj.* sainted, blessed; simple, naive, simpleminded *(sencillo);* fortunate, happy *(dichoso);* **dormir como un —,** to sleep soundly; **¡—s sean!** bless their hearts!

benedictino (be·ne·dēk·tē´no) or **benito,** (be·nē´to) *m.* Benedictine.

benefactor, (be·ne·fâk·tor´) *m.* benefactor.

beneficencia, (be·ne·fē·sen´syâ) *f.* beneficence, charity.

beneficiado, da, (be·ne·fē·syâ´tho, thâ) *n.* person or charity receiving proceeds from a benefit performance; —, *m.* (eccl.) incumbent.

beneficiar, (be·ne·fē·syâr´) *va.* to profit, to benefit; to work, to cultivate *(tierras);* to exploit, to work *(minas);* **—se con** or **por,** to profit by, to benefit from.

beneficiario, ria, (be·ne·fē·syâ´ryo, ryâ) *n.* beneficiary.

beneficio, (be·ne·fē´syo) *m.* benefit, favor, kindness *(bien hecho);* (agr.) working, cultivation; (min.) exploitation, working, profit, gain, advantage *(utilidad);* benefit, benefit performance *(espectáculo);* (eccl.) benefice; **a — de,** for the benefit of; **— marginal,** (com.) fringe benefit.

benéfico, ca, (be·ne´fē·ko, kâ) *adj.* beneficent, kind.

benemérito, ta, (be·ne·me´rē·to, tâ) *adj.* meritorious, worthy.

beneplácito, (be·ne·plâ´sē·to) *m.* good will,

approbation.

benevolencia, (be·ne·vo·len´syâ) *f.* benevolence, kindness, good will, goodness of heart.

benévolo, la, (be·ne´vo·lo, lâ) *adj.* benevolent, charitable, kindhearted.

benignidad, (be·nēg·nē·thâth´) *f.* kindliness, mildness.

benigno, na, (be·nēg´no, nâ) *adj.* benign, kind, mild.

berenjena, (be·ren·he´nâ) *f.* eggplant.

bergantín, (ber·gân·tēn´) *m.* (naut.) brigantine, brig.

bermejizo, za, (ber·me·hē´so, sâ) *adj.* reddish.

bermejo, ja, (ber·me´ho, hâ) *adj.* vermilion, reddish orange.

bermellón, (ber·me·yon´) *m.* vermilion.

berrear, (be·rre·âr´) *vn.* to low, to bellow.

berrenchín, (be·rren chēn´) *m.* snorting of an enraged boar; (fig.) tantrum, fit of temper.

berrido, (be·rrē´tho) *m.* bleating of a calf.

berrinche, (be·rrēn´che) *m.* fit of anger, temper tantrum.

berro, (be´rro) *m.* watercress.

berza, (ber´sâ) *f.* cabbage.

besamanos, (be·sâ·mâ´nos) *m.* levee, court reception.

besar, (be·sâr´) *va.* to kiss; (coll.) to touch, to be in contact; **—se,** (coll.) to bump heads, to knock heads together.

beso, (be´so) *m.* kiss; touching, contact *(objetos);* knocking heads together *(personas).*

bestia, (bes´tyâ) *f.* beast, animal; **—,** *m.* and *f.* dunce, idiot, nitwit.

bestial, (bes·tyâl´) *adj.* bestial, brutal.

bestialidad, (bes·tyâ·lē·thâth´) *f.* bestiality.

besuquear, (be·sū·ke·âr´) *va.* (coll.) to smooch with, to smooch.

besuqueo, (bū·sū·ke´o) *m.* (coll.) smooching.

betabel, (be·tâ·vel´) *m.* (Mex.) beet.

betarraga (be·tâ·rrâ´gâ) or **betarrata,** (be·tâ·rrâ´tâ) *f.* (bet.) beet.

betatrón, (be·tâ·tron´) *m.* betatron.

betún, (be·tūn´) *m.* shoe polish; (Mex.) frosting.

bevatrón, (be·vâ·tron´) *m.* bevatron.

biberón, (bē·ve·ron´) *m.* nursing bottle.

Biblia, (bē´vlyâ) *f.* Bible.

bíblico, ca, (bē´vlē·ko, kâ) *adj.* Biblical.

bibliófilo, la, (bē·vlyo´fē·lo, lâ) *n.* booklover, bibliophile.

bibliografía, (bē·vlyo·grâ·fē´â) *f.* bibliography.

biblioteca, (bē·vlyo·te´kâ) *f.* library.

bibliotecario, ria, (bē·vlyo·te·kâ´ryo, ryâ) *n.* librarian.

bicarbonato, (bē·kâr·vo·nâ´to) *m.* bicarbonate; **— de sosa,** baking soda.

biceps, (bē´seps) *m.* (anat.) biceps.

bicicleta, (bē·sē·kle´tâ) *f.* bicycle; **montar en —**to ride a bicycle.

biciclista,(bē·sē·klēs´tâ) *m.* and *f.* bicyclist.

bicho, (bē´cho) *m.* insect, bug; **todo — viviente,** every living soul, every man jack.

biela, (bye´lâ) *f.* connecting rod.

bien, (byen´) *m.* good; use, benefit *(provecho);* welfare, good *(bienestar);* **— es,** *pl.* property, possessions, goods; **—,** *adv.* well, right, all right; very *(muy);* readily, willingly **(con gusto); ¡—!** *interj.* fine! good! all right! **antes —,** rather, on the contrary; **— de salud,** well, in good health; **—** or **mal acondicionado,** in good or bad condition; **— es muebles,** goods and chattels; **—es raíces** or **inmuebles,** real estate; **¡está —!** very well! good!

bienal, (bye·nâl´) *adj.* biennial.

bienandanza, (bye·nân·dân´sâ) *f.* prosperity, success.

bienaventurado, da, (bye·nâ·ven·tū·râ´·tho, thâ) *adj.* blessed happy, fortunate; simple, naive *(sencillo).*

bienaventuranza, (bye·nâ·ven·tū·rân´sâ) *f.* (eccl.) heavenly bliss, life eternal; happiness, prosperity; **—s,** *pl.* (eccl.) Beatitudes.

bienestar, (bye·nes·târ´) *m.* well-being, welfare, comfort.

bienhablado, da, (bye·nâ·vlâ´tho, thâ) *adj.* courteous, well-spoken.

bienhadado, da, (bye·na·thâ´tho, thâ) *adj.* lucky, fortunate.

bienhechor, ra, (bye·ne·chor´, râ) *adj.* humane; **—,** *n.* benefactor.

bienio, (bye´nyo) *m.* period of two years, biennium.

bienquerer*, (byeng·ke·rer´) *va.* to hold in high esteem, to regard highly.

bienquistar, (byeng·kēs·târ´) *va.* to reconcile, to settle one's differences with; **— se,** to settle their differences, to become reconciled.

bienquisto, ta, (byeng·kēs´to, tâ) *adj.* of good repute, well-thought-of.

bienvenida, (byem·be·nē´thâ) *f.* welcome.

bienvenido, da, (byem·be·nē´tho, thâ) *adj.* welcome.

bienvivir, (byem·bē·vēr´) *vn.* to live in comfort, to live well *(con holgura);* to live an

â arm, e they, ē bē, o fore, ū blūe, b bad, ch chip, d day, f fat, g go, h hot, k kid, 1 let

honest life, to live right.

bifocal, (bē·fo·kál´) *adj.* bifocal; **lentes —es,** bifocal glasses.

bifurcación, (bē·fūr·ká·syon´) *f.* junction forking, branching

bigamia, (bē·gá´myâ) *f.* bigamy.

bígamo, ma, (bē´gä·mo, mâ) *adj.* bigamous; —, *n.* bigamist.

bigardía, (bē·gâr·thē´á) *f.* trickery, deception.

bigornia, (bē·gor´nyä) *f,* anvil.

bigote, (bē·go´te) *m.* mustache; (print.) dash rule; **tener —a,** to be firm and undaunted.

bilateral, (bē´lâ·te·râl´) *adj.* bilateral.

bilingüe, (bē·lēng´gwe) *adj.* bilingual.

bilioso, sa, (bē·lyo´so, sâ) *adj.* bilious.

bilis, (bē´lēs) *f.* bile.

billar, (bē·yâr´) *m.* billiards.

billete, (bē·ye´te) *m.* ticket *(cédula);* bill *(moneda);* note, short letter *(carta);* **— de banco,** banknote; **— de entrada,** admission ticket; **— de ida y vuelta,** round-trip ticket; **— del tesoro,** treasury note; **— directo,** through ticket; **— sencillo,** one-way ticket.

billetera, (bē·ye·te´rä) *f.* billfold.

billetero, ra, (bē·ye·te´ro, râ) *n.* (Sp. Am.) person selling lottery tickets.

billón, (bē·yon´) *m.* billion.

billonario, ria, (bē·yo·nâ´ryo, ryâ) *n.* billionaire.

bimestral, (bē·mes·trâl´) *adj.* bimonthly.

bimestre, (bē·mes´tre) *adj.* bimonthly; —, *m.* period of two months; bimonthly payment *(pago);* bimonthly charge *(cobranza).*

bimotor, ra, (bē·mo·tor´, râ) *adj.* two-motored.

binóculo, (bē·no´kū·lo) *m.* lorgnette.

biofísica, (byo·fē´sē·kâ) *f.* biophysics.

biofísico, ca, (byo·fē´sē·ko, kâ) *adj.* biophysical.

binomio, mia, (bē·no´myo, myâ) *m.* and *adj.* binomial.

biografía, (byo·grâ·fē´á) *f.* biography.

biógrafo, (byo´grâ·fo) *m.* biographer.

biología, (byo·lo·hē´á) *f.* biology; **— molecular,** molecular biology.

biombo, (byom´bo) *m.* screen.

biónica, (byo´nē·kâ) bionics.

bioquímica, (byo·kē´mē·kâ) *f.* biochemistry.

biotina, (byo·tē´nä) biotin.

bípedo, (bē´pe·tho) *m.* and *adj.* biped.

biplano, (bē·plâ´no) *m.* biplane.

birla, (bēr´lâ) *f.* (Arg.) bowling pin.

birlar, (bēr·lâr´) *va.* in bowls, to throw the ball a second time from the place it stopped the first time; (coll.) to kill with one shot *(matar);* to trick out of, to do out of, to make off with *(quitar).*

birrete, (bē·rre´te) *m.* (eccl.) beretta; academic cap, graduation cap.

bisabuela, (bē·sâ·vwe´lä) *f.* great-grandmother.

bisabuelo, (bē·sâ·vwe´lo) *m.* great-grandfather.

bisagra, (bē·sâ´grä) *f.* hinge; shoemaker´s polisher *(de zapatero).*

bisecar, (bē·se·kâr´) *va.* to bisect.

bisección, (bē·sek·syon´) *f.* bisection.

bisel, (bē·sel´) *m.* bevel.

biselar, (bē·se·lâr´) *va.* to bevel.

bisemanal, (bē·se·mâ·nâl´) *adj.* semi-weekly.

bisonte, (bē·son´te) *m.* bison.

bisoño, ña, (bē·so´nyo, nyâ) *adj.* raw, green, inexperienced; —, *n.* novice, greenhorn; (mil.) raw recruit.

bistec, (bēs·tek´) *m.* beefsteak; **— de filete,** tenderloin steak.

bisutería, (bē·sū·te·rē´á) *f.* cheap or imitation jewelry.

bituminoso, sa, (be·tū·mē·no´so, sâ) *adj.* bituminous.

bizarría, (bē·sâ·rrē´á) *f.* gallantry, valor; liberality, generosity, magnanimity *(generosidad).*

bizarro, rra, (bē·sâ´rro, rrâ) *adj.* brave, gallant; generous, liberal.

bizco, ca, (bēs´ko, kâ) *adj.* squint-eyed, cross-eyed.

bizcocho, (bēs·ko´cho) *m.* biscuit; cake, ladyfinger, sponge cake *(pastel).*

biznieta, (bēz·nye´tâ) *f.* great-granddaughter.

biznieto, (bēz·nye´to) *m.* great-grandson.

blanca, (blâng´kâ) *f.* an old Spanish copcoin; ca; (mus.) minim.

blanco, â, *adj.* white, blank; **ropa —** linens; —, *m.* blank; (print.) blank form; target; **— directo,** direct hit; **carta en — co,** blank credit; **dar en el —,** to hit the target; **en —co,** blank.

blancura, (blâng·kū´râ) *f.* whiteness.

blancuzco, ca, (blâng·kūs´ko, kâ) *adj.* whitish.

blandir*, (blân·dēr´) *va.* to brandish, to swing.

blando, da, (blân´do, dâ) *adj.* soft, smooth, bland; (fig.) mild, gentle, mellow; cowardly, soft, unmanly *(cobarde).*

blandura, (blân·dū´râ) *f.* softness; daintiness, delicacy, mildness; cowardice, weakness.

m met, **n** not, **p** pot, **r** very, **rr** (none), **s** so, **t** toy, **th** with, **v** eve, **w** we, **y** yes, **z** zero

blanquear, (blâng·ke·âr´) va. to bleach, to whiten; to whitewash *(dar de yeso)*; (ent.) to wax, to put wax on *(panales)*; —, vn. to show whiteness, to turn white; to verge on white *(tirar a blanco)*.

blanquecer*, (blâng·ke·ser´) va. to blanch *(metales)*; to whiten, to bleach.

blanqueo, (blâng·ke´o) m. whitening, bleaching; whitewash.

blasfemador, ra, (blâs·fe·ma·thor´, râ) n. blasphemer.

blasfemar, (blâs·fe·mâr´) vn. to blaspheme.

blasfemia, (blâs·fe´myâ) f. blasphemy; oath; (fig.) gross insult, vituperation.

blasfemo, ma, (blâs·fe´mo, ma) adj. blasphemous· —, n. blasphemer.

blasón, (bla·son´) m. heraldry, blazonry; (fig.) honor, glory; escutcheon, coat of arms *(escudo)*.

blasonar, (blâ·so·nâr´) va. to blazon; —, vn. to blow one´s own horn, to boast.

bledo, (ble´tho) m. (bot.) wild amaranth; **no me importa un —,** I don´t give a rap, I just don´t care.

blindado, da, (blēn·dâ´tho, thâ) adj. ironclad, ironplated, armored.

blondo, da, (blon´do, dâ) adj. light-haired, fair.

bloque, (blo´ke) m. block; (poi.) bloc; **— comunista,** Communist bloc.

bloquear, (blo·ke·âr´) va. to blockade.

bloqueo, (blo·ke´o) m. blockade.

blusa, (blü´sâ) f. blouse.

boa, (bo´â) f. (zool.) boa; boa *(prenda)*.

boato, (bo·â´to) m. ostentation, pompous show.

bobada, (bo·vâ´thâ) f. folly, foolish action.

bobería, (bo·ve·rē´â) f. folly, foolishness.

bobina, (bo·vē´nâ) f. bobbin, spool; (elec.) coil.

bobo, ba, (bo´vo, va) n. dunce, fool; stage clown *(gracioso)*; —, adj. stupid, silly, foolish; naive *(cándido)*.

boca, (bo´kâ) f. (anat.) mouth; entrance, opening, mouth *(entrada)*; (fig.) taste; **a pedir de —,** to one´s heart´s content; **de — en —,** by word of mouth; **— abajo,** face down, on the stomach; **hacerse agua la —,** to make one´s mouth water; **a — de farro,** point blank.

bocacalle, (bo·kâ·kâ´ye) f. street intersection.

bocadillo, (bo·kâ·thē´yo) m. snack; sandwich, stuffed roll *(panecillo)*; narrow ribbon *(cinta)*; very thin linen *(lienzo)*.

bocado, (bo´kâ´tho) m. morsel, mouthful.

bocamanga, (bo·kâ·mâng´gâ) f. cuff, wristband, lower sleeve.

bocanada, (bo·kâ·nâ´thâ) f. mouthful of liquid *(sorbo)*; puff of smoke *(de humo)*; **— de gente,** crowd of people; **— de viento,** gust of wind.

boceto, (bo·se´to) m. sketch.

bocina, (bo·sē´nâ) f. horn, trumpet; megaphone *(tornavoz)*; (zool.) triton; (auto.) horn; (Chile and Col.) blowgun; (Sp. Am.) hearing trumpet; speaker *(del radio)*; receiver *(del teléfono)*.

bocio, (bo´syo) m. goiter.

bocón, ona, (bo·kon´, o´nâ) n. (coll.) wide-mouthed individual *(bocudo)*; braggart *(fanfarrón)*.

bocoy, (bo·ko´ē) m. large barrel.

bocudo, da, (bo·kü´tho, thâ) adj. large-mouthed.

bochorno, (bo·chor´no) m. sultry weather, dog days, scorching heat *(vulturno)*; flush, blush *(del rostro)*; (fig.) humiliation, embarrassment.

bochornoso, sa, (bo·chor·no´so, sâ) adj. sultry, scorching; (fig.) shameful, reproachful.

boda, (bo´thâ) f. nuptials, wedding; **—s de plata** or **de oro,** silver or golden wedding.

bodega, (bo·the´gâ) f. wine cellar; harvest of wine *(cosecha)*; dock warehouse *(almacén)*; wine shop, tavern *(taberna)*; (naut.) hold of a ship; pantry *(despensa)*

bodegón, (bo·the·gon´) m. chophouse, lunchroom; still life of food and kitchenware *(cuadro)*.

bodoque, (bo·tho´ke) m. pellet; (fig.) dunce, idiot, dolt.

bofes, (bo´fes) m. pl. lungs.

bofetada, (bo·fe·tâ´thâ) f. slap in the face, box on the ear.

bofetón, (bo·fe·ton´) m. hard slap in the face; (theat.) revolving flat.

boga, (bo´gâ) f. (fig.) vogue, popularity; (ichth.) boce; rowing; —, m. and f. rower; **estar en —,** to be fashionable, to be in vogue.

bogador, ra, (bo·gâ·thor´, râ) n. rower.

bogar, (bo·gâr´) vn. to row, to paddle.

bohemio, mia, (bo·e´myo, myâ) n. and adj. Bohemian.

bohío, (bo·e´o) m. (Sp. Am.) Indian hut.

boicot, (boē·kot´) m. boycott.

boicotear, (boē·ko·te·âr´) va. to boycott.

boina, (bo´ē·nâ) f. beret.

bola, (bo´lâ) f. ball, globe; shoe polish

(betun); bowling (juego); (coll.) tall tale, fib; (Mex.) disturbance, row; **hacerse —s,** to get confused.

bolchevique, (bol•che•vē´ke) *m.* and *f.* and *adj.* Bolshevik.

bolchevismo, (bol•che•vēz´mo) *m.* Bolshevism.

bolchevista, (bol•che•vēs´tä) *m.* and *f.* and *adj.* Bolshevik.

bolear, (bo•le•är´) *vn.* to play billiards without keeping score; **—,** *va.* to cast, to throw *(arrojar);* to blackball, to reject *(reprobar);* (Mex.) to polish, to put a shine on; (Arg.) to rope with bolas; (fig.) to play a mean trick on, to do a bad turn.

bolero, (bo•le´ro) *m.* bolero; (Mex.) bootblack, shoeshine boy.

boletín, (bo•le•tēn´) *m.* bulletin; pay warrant *(libranza);* ticket, permit, *(cédula);* (Cuba) railroad ticket; **— meteorológico,** weather report.

boleto, (bo•le´to) *m. (Sp.* Am.) ticket; **— de entrada,** admission ticket; **— de ferrocarril,** railroad ticket; **— de avión,** airplane ticket; **— de ida y vuelta,** round-trip ticket; **— sencillo,** one-way ticket.

boliche, (bo•lē´che) *m.* bowling; jack; small dragnet *(jábega).*

bolígrafo, (bo•lē´grä•fo) *m.* ball-point pen.

bolillo, (bo•lē´yo) *m.* bobbin used in lace making *(palito);* form for lace cuffs *(horma);* (zool.) coffin bone.

bolina, (bo•lē´nä) *f.* noise, uproar *(alboroto);* (naut.) bowline; flogging, lashing *(azotes);* **ir a la —,** to sail on a wind.

bolívar, (bo•le´vär) *m.* monetary unit of Venezuela.

boliviano, na, (bo•lē•vyä´no, nä) *adj.* and *n.* Bolivian; **—,** *m.* monetary unit of Bolivia.

bolo, (bo´lo) *m.* tenpin or ninepin; bolo *(cuchillo);* (arch.) newel *(nabo);* ignoramus, fool *(necio);* **—s,** pl. bowling, game of tenpins or ninepins.

bolsa, (bol´sä) *f.* purse, handbag *(de mujer);* pouch; (com.) stock exchange; (min.) main lode; **— de aire,** air pocket; **— de comercio** or **financiera,** stock exchange; **corredor de —,** stockbroker, exchange broker, **jugar a la —,** to speculate in stocks, to play the stock market.

bolsillo, (bol•sē´yo) *m.* pocket; money, funds *(caudal).*

bolsista, (bol•sēs´tä) *m.* speculator, stock-broker; jobber.

bollo (bo´yo) *m.* sweet roll, muffin *(panecillo);* dent *(hueco);* lump, bump *(chichón);* (coll.) tight spot, mess.

bomba, (bom´bä) *f.* pump; bomb, bombshell *(proyectil);* **a prueba de —,** bombproof; **— atómica,** atomic bomb; **— de alimentación,** feed pump; **— de apagar incendios,** fire engine; **— de carena,** bilge pump; **— de cobalto,** cobalt bomb; **— de profundidad,** depth charge; **— de vacio,** vacuum pump; **— de vapor,** steam pump; **— de hidrógeno,** hydrogen bomb; **— de neutrones,** neutron bomb.

bombachos, (bom•bä´chos) *m. pl.* slacks.

bombardear, (bom•bär•the•är) *va.* to bombard.

bombardeo, (bom•bär•the´o) *m.* bombardment.

bombardero, (bom•bär•the´ro) *m.* bomber; bombardier *(artillero);* **— de pique,** dive bomber.

bombeo, (bom•be´o) *m.* convexity, bulge.

bombero, (bom•be´ro) *m.* fireman *(matafuego);* pumper; (mil.) howitzer.

bombilla, (bom•bē´yä) *f.* light bulb; (Sp. Am.) a tube to sip maté; **— de destello,** photoflash bulb.

bombo, (bom´bo) *m.* large drum, bass drum.

bombón, (bom•bon´) *m.* bonbon, candy.

bonachón, ona, (bo•nä•chon´, o´nä) *adj.* good-natured, easy to get along with.

bonaerense, (bo•nä•e•ren´se) *m.* and *f.* and *adj.* native of or pertaining to Buenos Aires.

bonancible, (bo•nän•sē´vle) *adj.* calm, fair, serene.

bonanza, (bo•nän´sä) *f.* (naut.) fair weather, calm seas; (min.) bonanza; (fig.) good fortune, success.

bondad, (bon•däth´) *f.* goodness, bounty kindness; **tenga la — de,** please be good enough to, please have the kindness to, please.

bondadoso, sa, (bon•dä•tho´so, sä) *adj.* bountiful, kind, good; **poco —,** unkind.

bonete, (bo•ne´te) *m.* (eccl.) secular biretta; (fig.) member of the secular clergy; graduation cap, academic cap *(de graduado).*

boniato, (bo•nyä´to) *m.* sweet potato.

bonificación (bo•nē•fē•kä•syon´) *f.* allowance, bonus.

bonito, ta, (bo•nē´to, tä) *adj.* quite good, pretty good *(bueno);* pretty, nice looking *(lindo);* **—,** *m.* tuna, bonito.

---

m met, **n** not, **p** pot, **r** very, **rr** (none), **s** so, **t** toy, **th** with, **v** eve, **w** we, **y** yes, **z** zero

bono, (bo´no) *m.* (com.) bond, certificate; **—s de gobierno,** government bonds.

boñiga, (bo·nye´gá) *f.* cow dung.

boquear, (bo·ke·âr´) *vn.* to gape, to gasp; to be breathing one´s last, to be dying *(expirar);* (fig.) to be winding up, to be just about finished; —, *va.* to pronounce, to utter.

boquerón, (bo·ke·ron´) *m.* (ichth.) anchovy; large hole or opening *(abertura).*

boquete, (bo·ke´te) *m.* gap, narrow entrance.

boquiabierto, ta, (bo·kyâ·vyer´to, tâ) *adj.* open-mouthed.

boquiancho, cha, (bo·kyân´cho, châ) *adj.* wide-mouthed.

boquiangosto, ta, (bo·kyâng·gos´to, tâ) *adj.* narrow-mouthed.

boquiduro, ra, (bo·kē·thū´ro, râ) *adj.* hard-mouthed (of horses).

boquilla, (bo·kē´yâ) *f.* mouthpiece *(de instrumento);* stem *(de pipa);* cigarette holder, cigar holder *(de cigarro);* burner, jet *(de llama).*

bórax, (bo´râks) *m.* borax.

borbotón, (bor·bo·ton´) *m.* bubbling, gushing of water; **hablar a —ones,** to speak in torrents, to ramble on.

borceguí, (bor·se·gē´) *m.* buskin, half boot.

bordado, (bor·thâ´tho) *m.* embroidery.

bordador, ra, (bor·thâ·thor´, râ) *n.* embroiderer.

bordar, (bor·thâr´) *va.* to embroider; (fig.) to embellish, to elaborate; **seda de —,** embroidery silk.

borde, (bor´the) *m.* border, edge; rim *(de vasija);* (naut.)board;— **de la acera,** curb.

bordear, (bor·the·âr´) *vn.* to go along the edge, to stay on the outskirts; (naut.) to ply to windward; —, *va.* to skirt along the edge of.

bordo, (bor´tho) *m.* (naut.) board; tack *(bordada);* **a —,** on board; **franco a —,** free on board (f.o.b.).

bordonear, (bor·tho·ne·âr´) *va.* (avi.) to buzz.

Boreal, (bo·re·âl´) *adj.* boreal, northern.

borgoña, (bor·go´nyâ) *m.* Burgundy wine; **B—,** Burgundy.

bórico, (bo´rē·ko) *adj.* boric; **ácido —,** boric acid.

borinqueño fia, (bo·rēng·ke´nyó, nyâ) *n.* and *adj.* Puerto Rican.

borla, (bor´lâ) *f.* tassel; **— de empolvarse,** powder puff; **tomar la —,** to receive one´s doctorate.

borra, (bo´rrâ) *f.* yearling ewe *(cordera);*

goat´s hair *(de cabra);* nap, fuzz, lint *(pelusa);* thick wool *(lana);* (fig.) dross, junk.

borrachera, (bo·rrâ·che´râ) *f.* drunkenness; bacchanal, carousing, revelry *(función);* (fig.) excess, exaltation.

borracho, cha, (bo·rrâ´cho, châ) *adj.* drunk, intoxicated; (fig.) frenzied, infuriated.

borrachón, ona, (bo·rrâ·chon´, o´nâ) *n.* great drinker, tippler.

borrador, (bo·rrâ·thor´) *m.* rough draft, first draft; rubber eraser *(goma).*

borrar, (bo·rrâr´) *va.* to erase *(con goma);* to scratch out, to strike out *(tachar)* to blot, to blur *(manchar);* (fig.) to strike, to delete, to erase.

borrasca, (bo·rrâs´kâ) *f.* violent storm, squall; wind; (fig.) hazard, danger, risk.

borrascoso, sa, (bo·rrâs·ko´so, sâ) *adj.* stormy.

borregada, (bo·rre·gâ´thâ) *f.* flock of lambs.

borrego, ga, (bo·rre´go, gâ) *n.* lamb; (fig.) simpleton, easy mark.

borrica, (bo·rrē´kâ) *f.* she-ass, jenny.

borricada, (bo·rrē·kâ´thâ) *f.* drove of asses; group outing on donkeyback

borrico (bo·rrē´ko) *m.* donkey, ass; (fig.) donkey, blockhead.

borrón, (bo·rron´) *m.* ink blot, splotch of ink, ink smudge; (fig.) blemish, imperfection; rough draft, first copy *(borrador);* preliminary sketch, outline of a painting *(de cuadro).*

borronear, (bo·rro·ne·âr´) *va.* to sketch, to scribble.

borroso, sa, (bo·rro´so, sâ) *adj.* indistinct, blurred.

boruca, (bo·rū´kâ) *f.* noise, clamor, excitement.

bosque, (bos´ke) *m.* forest, grove, woods.

bosquejar, (bos·ke·hâr´) *va.* to make a sketch of *(pintura);* to sculpt rough *(escultura);* (fig.) to rough in, to do the preliminary work on; to outline, to sketch out hazily *(concepto).*

bosquejo, (bos·ke´ho) *m.* outline, sketch.

bostezar, (bos·te·sâr´) *vn.* to yawn, to gape.

bostezo, (bos·te´so) *m.* yawn, yawning.

bota, (bo´tâ) *f.* wine bag *(odre);* water cask *(cuba);* boot *(calzado).*

botana, (bo·tâ´nâ) *f.* plug, stopper *(remiendo);* (coll.) healing plaster *(parole);* (coll.) scar *(cicatriz);* (Mex.) appetizer.

botánica, (bo·tâ´nē·kâ) *f.* botany.

botar, (bo·târ´) *va.* to cast, to throw; to launch *(buque).*

â arm, **e** they, **ē** bē, **o** fore, **ū** blūe, **b** bad, **ch** chip, **d** day, **f** fat, **g go, h** hot, **k** kid, **1** let

botarate (bo·tâ·râ′te) *m.* and *f.* madcap; (Sp. Am.) spendthrift *(malgastador).*

bote, (bo′te) *m.* rowboat, small boat; *(barco);* thrust blow *(de arma);* prance, caper *(de caballo);* rebound, bounce *(de pelota);* (Mex.) jail; — **de salva-vidas,** lifeboat; **de — en —,** jammed, overcrowded.

botella, (bo·te′yâ) *f.* bottle, flask.

botica, (bo·tē′kâ) *f.* drugstore, pharmacy.

boticario, (bo·tē·kâ′ryo) *m.* druggist, pharmacist.

botija, (bo·tē′hâ) *f.* earthen jar with a short and narrow neck.

botijo (bo·tē′ho) or **botijón,** (bo·tē·hon′) *m.* round earthen jar.

botín, (bo·tēn′) *m.* half boot *(botina);* short gaiter *(polaina);* booty, loot, spoils *(despojo);* (Chile) sock.

botiquín, (bo·tē·kēn′) *m.* first-aid kit.

boto, ta, (bo′to, tâ) *adj.* blunt; (fig.) slow in understanding, dull, dense.

botón, (bo·ton′) *m.* button; bud *(yema);* — **de contacto,** push button; — **de llamada,** call button; — **eléctrico,** push button.

botonadura, (bo·to·nâ·thu·′râ) *f.* set of buttons.

bóveda, (bo′ve·thâ) *f.* dome, vault; crypt, vault *(cripta).*

bovino na, (bo·vē′no, nâ) *adj.* bovine.

boxeador, (bok·se·â·thor′) *m.* boxer, pugilist; — **profesional,** prizefighter.

boxear, (bok·se·âr′) *vn.* to box.

boxeo, (bok·se′o) *m.* boxing, pugilism.

boya, (bo′yâ) *f.* (naut.) buoy; float *(de red).*

boyar, (bo·yâr′) *vn.* to float, to be afloat; (naut.) to be returned to service, to be floated again.

bozal, (bo·sâl′) *m.* muzzle; —, *adj.* green, inexperienced; foolish, stupid *(necio).*

braceaje, (brâ·se·â′he) *m.* coinage, minting; (naut.) ocean depth.

bracear, (brâ·se·âr′) *vn.* to swing the arms; (naut.) to brace the yards.

bracero, (brâ·se′ro) *m.* day laborer *(peón);* man with a good throwing arm.

bracete, (brâ·se′te) *m.* small arm; **de —,** arm in arm.

braco ca, (brâ′ko, kâ) *adj.* flat-nosed; —, *m.* pointer (dog).

braguero, (brâ·ge′ro) *m.* truss, bandage for a rupture.

bragueta, (brâ·ge′tâ) *f.* trousers' fly.

brama, (brâ′mâ) *f.* rut, mating time.

bramadero, (brâ·mâ·the′ro) *m.* rutting place, mating spot.

bramante, (brâ·mân′te) *m.* packthread,

twine; Brabant linen *(lienzo);* —, *adj.* roaring.

bramar, (brâ·mâr′) *vn.* to roar, to bellow; (fig.) to storm, to bluster; to be in a fury.

bramido, (brâ·mē′tho) *m.* roar, bellow; furious outcry, shriek of rage *(del hombre).*

brasa, (bra′sâ) *f.* live coal.

brasero, (brâ·se′ro) *m.* brazier.

Brasil, (brâ·sē·l′) *m.* Brazil.

brasileño, ña, (brâ·sē·le′nyo, nyâ) *n.* and *adj.* Brazilian.

bravata, (brâ·vâ′tâ) *f.* bravado, boasting, braggadocio, swaggering.

bravear, (brâ·ve·âr′) *vn.* to bully, to hector, to bluster, to swagger.

bravío, via, (brâ·vē′o, vē′â) *adj.* ferocious, savage, wild; (fig.) coarse, uncultured *(rústico);* —, *m.* fierceness, savageness.

bravo, va, (brâ′vo, vâ) *adj.* brave, valiant; blustering, bullying *(valentón);* savage, fierce *(fiero);* angry, enraged *(enojado);* very good, excellent, fine *(excelente);* ¡— **vo!** *interj.* bravo! well done!

bravura, (brâ·vu·′râ) *f.* ferocity *(fiereza);* bravery, courage *(valentía);* bravado, boasting *(bravata).*

braza, (brâ′sâ) *f.* fathom; breast stroke *(natación).*

brazada, (brâ·sâ′thâ) *f.* rowing motion of the arms; armful *(brazado).*

brazado, (brâ·sâ′tho) *m.* armful.

brazaje, (brâ·sâ′he) *n.* (naut.) depth of water.

brazalete, (brâ·sâ·le′te) *m.* bracelet.

brazo, (brâ′so) *m.* arm; branch *(del árbol);* foreleg *(de cuadrúpedo);* (fig.) stamina, strength, power *(brío);* — **a —** man to man; **a — partido,** with bare hands; — **s,** *pl.* hands, man power; **huelga de —s caídos,** sit-down strike.

brea, (bre′â) *f.* pitch, tar.

brebaje, (bre·vâ′he) *m.* unpalatable brew; (naut.) grog.

brecha, (bre′châ) *f.* breach, gap; (fig.) vivid impression, marked effect; **batir en —,** (mil.) to make a breach; (fig.) to impress on someone's mind, to get through to someone; (Mex.) dirt road.

brega, (bre′gâ) *f.* strife, struggle; joke, trick *(chasco).*

bregar, (bre·gâr′) *vn.* to contend, to struggle; —, *va.* to knead.

breña, (bre′nyâ) *f.* craggy, brambly ground.

breñal (bre·nyâl′) or **breñar,** (bre·nyâr′) *m.* craggy, brambly area.

---

m met, **n** not, **p** pot, **r** very, **rr** (none), **s** so, **t** toy, **th** with, **v** eve, **w** we, **y** yes, **z** zero

bresca, (bres·kä) f. honeycomb.
brescar, (bres·kär´) va. to take out the honeycombs from.
Bretaña, (bre·tá´nyä) f. Brittany; **Gran —,** Great Britain.
bretones, (bre·to´nes) m. pl. Brussels sprouts.
breve, (bre´ve) m. apostolic brief; **—,** f. (mus.) breve; **—,** adj. brief, short; **en —,** shortly.
brevedad, (bre·ve·thäth´) f. brevity, shortness, conciseness; **a la mayor — posible,** as soon as possible.
breviario, (bre·vyä´ryo) m. (eccl.) breviary; abridgement, breviary (compendio).
brezal, (bre·säl´) m. heath.
bribón, ona, (brē·von´, o´nä) adj. mischievous, impish; rascally roguish, scoundrel (bellaco); **—,** n. imp; rascal, rogue, scoundrel.
bribonada, (brē·vo·nä´thä) f. mischievous trick, impish action; roguery.
brida, (brē´thä) f. bridle; (fig.) restraint, check, curb; flange (de tubo).
brigada, (brē·gä´thä) f. brigade.
brillante, (brē·yän´te) adj. brilliant, bright, shining; **—,** m. brilliant, diamond.
brillantez, (brē·yän·tes´) f. brilliancy, brightness.
brillantina, (bre·yän·tē´nä) f. brilliantine.
brillar, (brē·yär´) vn. to shine, to sparkle, to glisten; (fig.) to stand out, to be preeminent, to be outstanding.
brillo, (brē´yo) m. brilliancy, brightness, splendor.
brincar, (brēng·kär´) vn. to leap, to jump; (fig.) to get upset, to flare up (resentirse); (fig.) to gloss over the details, to skip over the details (pasar por alto).
brinco, (brēng´ko) m. leap, jump; **dar —s,** to leap, to jump around.
brindar, (brēn·där´) va. to offer, to provide with; **— a,** to drink to the health of, to toast (beber); to invite to, to offer to (ofrecer); **—se** to offer one's help.
brindis, (brēn´dēs) m. health, toast.
brío, (brē´o) m, strength, vigor; (fig.) spirit, verve, vivacity.
brioso, sal (bryo´so, sä) adj. strong, vigorous; spirited, lively, vivacious.
brisa, (brē´sä) f. breeze.
británico, ca, (brē·tä´nē·ko, kä) adj. British.
brizna, (brēz´na) f. wisp, thin strip, shred.
brocado, (bro·kä´tho) m. brocade; **—, da,** adj. brocaded.

brocal, (bro·käl´) m. curbstone.
brocatel, (bro·kä·tel´) m. brocatelle.
bróculi, (bro´kū·lē) m. broccoli.
brocha, (bro´chä) f. paintbrush; shaving brush (para enjabonar).
brochada, (bro·chä´thä) f. brush stroke.
broche, (bro´che) m. clasp, brooch.
broma, (bro´mä) f. hilarity, noisy fun; joke, jest prank (chanza); **dar —,** to tease, to have fun with; **tomar a —,** to take as a joke, to take in fun.
bromear, (bro·me·är´) vn. to jest, to joke, to play pranks.
bromista, (bro·mēs´tä) m. and f. joker, prankster; **—,** adj. fond of playing jokes.
bromuro, (bro·mū´ro) m. bromide.
bronce, (bron´se) m. bronze.
bronceado, da, (bron·se·ä´tho, thä) adj. bronzed; suntanned (piel); **—,** m. bronze-color finish.
broncear, (bron·se·är´) va. to bronze; **—se,** to get a suntan, to get sun-tanned.
bronco, ca, (brong´ko, ka) adj. rough, coarse, unfinished; brittle, easily broken (metal); harsh, gruff (voz); (fig.) crabby, vile-tempered (genio); (Mex.) untamed.
broncoscopio, (brong·kos·ko´pyo) m. bronchoscope.
bronquio, (brong´kyo) m. bronchial tube.
bronquitis, (brong·kē´tēs) f. bronchitis.
broquel, (bro·kel´) m. (mil.) buckler; (fig.) shield; protection; **rajar —es,** to play the bully, to lord it.
brotar, (bro·tär´) vn. (bot.) to bud, to germinate, to sprout; to gush, to rush out (agua); (fig.) to erupt, to break out, to crop out; **—,** va. (bot.) to shoot out, to shoot forth; (fig.) to give rise to.
brote, (bro´te) m. bud, shoot; (fig.) outbreak, rash, outcrop.
broza, (bro´sä) f. plant trash (vegetal); rubbish, trash (escoria); underbrush (maleza); (print.) brush.
brozar, (bro·sär´) va. to brush (type).
bruces, (bru·´ses) **a —** or **de —,** head-long, face downward.
bruja, (brū´hä) f. witch, hag; **—,** adj. (Mex.) temporarily broke.
brujería, (bru·he·rē´ä)f. witchcraft.
brujo, (brū´ho) m. sorcerer.
brújula, (brū´hū·lä) f. compass; magnetic needle (aguja); **— giroscópica,** gyrocompass.
bruma, (brū´mä) f. mist, haze.

â arm, **e** they, **ē** bē, **o** fore, **ū** blūe, **b** bad, **ch** chip, **d** day, **f** fat, **g** go, **h** hot, **k** kid, **1** let

brumoso, sa, (brū·mo´so, sâ) *adj.* misty,

bruno, na, (brū´no, nâ) *adj.* dark brown.

bruñido, (brū·nyē´tho) *m.* polish, burnish; **—, da,** *adj.* polished, burnished.

bruñir*, (brū·nyēr´) *va.* to burnish, to polish; (fig.) to put makeup on, to paint *(el rostro).*

brusco, ca, (brūs´ko, kâ) *adj.* rude, gruff, brusque; abrupt, sudden *(súbito).*

Bruselas, (brū·se´lâs) *f.* Brussels.

brusquedad, (brūs·ke·thâth´) *f.* rudeness; abruptness, suddenness.

brutal, (brū·tâl´) *adj.* brutal, brutish; (coll.) colossal, terrific; **—,** *m.* brute, beast.

brutalidad, (brū·tâ·lē·thâth´) *f.* brutality; (fig.) brutal action.

bruto, (brū´to) *m.* brute, beast, blockhead; **—, ta,** *adj.* brutal; stupid *(torpe);* (min.) crude; (com.) gross; coarse, unpolished, unrefined *(tosco);* **en —to,** in a raw, unmanufactured state, as **lino en —to,** raw flax; **peso —,** gross weight.

¡bu! (ha) *interj.* boo!

bubilla, (bū·vē´yâ) *f.* pimple, pustule.

bubónico, ca, (bū·vo´nē·ko, kâ) *adj.* bubonic.

bucanero, (bū·kâ·ne´ro) *m.* buccaneer.

bucear, (bū·se·âr´) *vn.* to skin-dive; to deepsea-dive *(con escafandra).*

buceo, (bū·se´o) *m.* skin-diving; deepsea diving.

bucle, (bū´kle) *m.* curl.

bucólico, ca, (bū·ko´lē·ko, kâ) *adj.* pastoral, rural, bucolic; **—,** *f.* pastoral poetry; (coll.) food.

buche, (bū´che) *m.* craw, crop, gullet *(de ave);* stomach *(de cuadrúpedo);* mouthful *(bocanada);* suckling ass *(borrico);* pucker, crease *(de ropa);* (fig.) bosom, heart.

buen, (bwen) *adj.* apocope of bueno (good); used only before a masculine noun or before an infinitive, i.e., **el — comer,** good eating; **hacer — tiempo,** to be good weather; **tener — éxito,** to be successful.

buenaventura, (bwe·nâ·ven·tū´râ) *f.* fortune, good luck.

bueno, na, (bwe´no, nâ) *ad´.* good; fair, pleasant *(de genio);* kind, sociable *(bondadoso);* strong; well, fit, healthy *(de salud);* large, good-sized *(de tamaño);* **dar — acogida,** to honor (a draft); **de — gana,** freely, willingly; **—no,** *adv.* enough, sufficiently; **—no está,** enough, no more; **¡ —no!** *interj.* all right! that's enough!

buey, (bwe´ē) *m.* ox, bullock.

bufa, (bū´fâ) *f.* jeer, scoff, taunt, mock; (Cuba) drunkenness.

búfalo, (bū´fâ·lo) *m.* buffalo.

bufanda, (bū·fân´dâ) *f.* scarf.

bufar, (bū·fâr´) *vn.* to snort; (fig.) to snort, to rage.

bufete, (bū·fe´te) *m.* desk; (fig.) lawyer's office *(despacho);* practice, clients *(clientela).*

bufido, (bū·fē´tho) *m.* snort.

bufo, (bū´fo) *m.* (theat.) buffoon, clown; **—, fa,** *adj.* comic; **ópera —,** comic opera.

bufón, (bū·fon´) *m.* buffoon, jester; **—, ona,** *adj.* funny, comical.

bufonada, (bū·fo·nâ´thâ) *f.* buffoonery; raillery *(chanza).*

buganvilia, (bū·gan·vē´lyâ) *f.* (bot.) bugainvillea.

buhardilla, (bwâr·thē´yâ) *f.* dormer; small garret, attic *(desván).*

búho, (bū´o) *m.* owl; (fig.) unsociable individual.

buhonero, (bwo·ne´ro) *m.* peddler, hawker.

buitre, (bwē´tre) *m.* vulture.

bujía, (bū·hē´a) *f.* candle; candlestick *(candelero);* (auto.) spark plug; candle, international candle *(medida);* **— de cera,** wax candle.

bula, (bū´lâ) *f.* papal bull.

bulbo, (būl´vo) *m.* (bot.) bulb.

bulevar, (bū·le·vâr´) *m.* boulevard, parkway.

bulto, (būl´to) *m.* bulk, mass; parcel, pack-age, bundle *(fardo);* lump, swelling *(hinchazón);* bust *(busto);* piece of luggage *(maleta);* **en —,** in bulk.

bulla, (bū´yâ) *f.* confused noise, clatter; crowd *(gentío).*

bullanguero, ra, (bū·yâng·ge´ro, râ) *adj.* noisy, boisterous; **—,** *n.* noisy, loud person.

bullicio, (bū·yē´syo) *m.* bustle, tumult, uproar.

bullicioso, sa, (bū·yē·syo´so, sâ) *adj.* lively, restless *(desasosegado);* noisy, clamorous, turbulent; boisterous, riotous *(alborotador).*

bumerang (bū·me·rân´) *m.* boomerang.

buñuelo, (bū·nywe´lō) *m.* doughnut.

buque, (bū´ke) *m.* ship, vessel; capacity *(cabida);* hull *(casco);* **— explorador,** scouting ship; **— fanal,** lightship; **— petrolero,** tanker; **— taller,** repair ship; **— de vela,** sailboat.

burdel, (būr·thel´) *m.* brothel.

burdo, da, (būr´tho, thâ) *adj.* coarse, rough.

m met, **n** not, **p** pot, **r** very, **rr** (none), **s** so, **t** toy, **th** with, **v** eve, **w** we, **y** yes, **z** zero

bureta, (bū·re´tâ) f. (chem.) burette.

burgomaestre, (būr·go·mâ·es´tre) m. burgomaster.

burgués, esa, (būr·ges´, e´sâ) adj. and n. bourgeois.

burguesía, (būr·ge·sē´â) f. bourgeoisie.

buril, (bū·rēl´) m. burin, graver.

burla, (būr´lâ) f. scoffing, mockery, sneering (mofa); trickery (engaño); joke, jest (chanza); de —, in jest; hacer una —, to play a joke.

burlar, (būr·lâr´) va. to play a trick on, to deceive (engañar); to frustrate, to disappoint (frustrar); to mock; —se de, to make fun of.

burlesco, ca, (būr·les´ko, kâ) adj. burlesque, comical, funny.

burlete, (būr·le´te) m. weather stripping.

burlón, ona, (būr·lon´, o´nâ) n. mocker, scoffer; —, adj. mocking, scoffing, sarcastic.

buró, (bū·ro´) m. writing desk; (Mex.) night table.

burocracia, (bū·ro·krâ´syâ) f. bureaucracy.

burocrático, ca, (bū·ro·krâ´tē·ko, kâ) adj. bureaucratic.

burrada, (bū·rrâ´thâ) f. drove of asses; (fig.) stupidity, asininity.

burro, (bū´rro) m. ass, donkey; (fig.) workhorse; sawhorse (armazón); — de planchar, ironing board.

bursátil, (būr·sâ´tēl) adj. relating to the stock exchange.

busca, (būs´kâ) f. search, examination.

buscapiés, (būs·kâ·pyes´) m. firecracker.

buscar, (būs·kâr´) va. to seek, to search for, to look for; ir a —, to get, to go after.

buscón, (būs·kon´) m. searcher; pilferer, petty robber (ratero).

búsqueda, (būs´ke·thâ) f. search.

busto, (būs´to) m. bust.

butaca, (bū·tâ´kâ) f. armchair; (theat.) orchestra seat.

butifarra, (bū·tē·fâ´rrâ) f. Catalonian sausage; (coll.) wide, loose-fitting stocking; (Peru) ham sandwich.

buzo, (bū´so) m. skin diver (de superficie); deepsea diver (con escafandra).

buzón, (bū·son´) m. mailbox, letter drop; conduit, canal (de desagüe).

C

C.: centígrado, C. Centigrade.

c : cargo, (com.) cargo, charge.

C.A.: corriente alterna, A.C. alternating current.

c/a : cuenta abierta, (com.) open account.

cabal, (kâ·vâl´) adj. precise, exact; perfect, complete, accomplished (acabado).

cabalgada, (kâ·vâl·gâ´thâ) f. mounted foray into the countryside.

cabalgadura, (kâ·vâl·gâ·thū´râ) f. beast of burden.

cabalgar, (kâ·vâl·gâr´) vn. to ride horseback.

cabalgata, (kâ·vâl·gâ´tâ) f. cavalcade.

caballar, (kâ·vâ·yâr´) adj. equine.

caballeresco, ca, (kâ·va·ye·res´ko, kâ) adj. knightly, chivalrous; (fig.) lofty, sublime.

caballería, (kâ·vâ·ye·rē´â) f. (mil.) cavalry; mount (animal); chivalry, knighthood; — andante, knight-errantry.

caballeriza, (kâ·vâ·ye·rē´sâ) f. stable; mounts owned by one individual.

caballero, (kâ·vâ·ye´ro) m. gentleman; nobleman, knight (hidalgo); cavalier, rider, horseman (jinete).

caballerosidad, (kâ·va·ye·ro·sē·thâth´) f. chivalry, nobleness, knightliness.

caballeroso, sa, (kâ·vâ·ye·ro´so, sâ) adj. noble, gentlemanly, chivalrous.

caballete, (kâ·vâ·ye´te) m. ridge (de tejado); trestle, sawhorse (asnilla); horse (de tormento); easel (de pintor); (avi.) gantry tower.

caballitos, (kâ·vâ·yē´tos) m. pl. merry-go-round (tiovivo); miniature mechanical horse race (juego).

caballo, (kâ·vâ´yo) m. horse; knight (de ajedrez); a —, on horseback; — de fuerza, horsepower.

cabaña, (kâ·vâ´nyâ) f. hut, cabin, cottage (choza); cabana (de playa); large number of livestock (de ganado); balkline (de billar).

cabaret,(kâ·vâ·ret´) m. cabaret, night club.

cabecear, (kâ·ve·se·âr´) vn. to nod with sleep; to shake one's head (de nega-

ción); (naut., avi.) to pitch; to hit with one's head *(deportes).*

cabeceo, (kâ·ve·se´o) *m.* nod; shaking of the head; pitching.

cabecera, (kâ·ve·se´râ) *f.* head; head, headboard *(de la cama);* pillow *(almohada);* headwaters *(del río);* heading *(del libro);* **médico de —,** attending physician.

cabecilla, (kâ·ve·sē´yâ) *m.* ringleader.

cabellera, (kâ·ve·ye´râ) *f.* long hair falling to the shoulders; wig *(peluca);* (ast.) coma.

cabello, (kâ·ve´yo) *m.* hair of the head.

cabelludo, da, (kâ·ve·yū´tho, thâ) *adj.* hairy, overgrown with hair; **cuero —,** scalp.

caber*, (kâ·ver´) *vn.* to fit; to be possible, to be likely *(ser posible);* to be admitted, to be allowed in *(tener entrada);* **el libro no cabe,** there isn´t room for the book.

cabestrar, (kâ·ves·trâr´) *va.* to halter.

cabestrear, (kâ·ves·tre·âr´) *vn.* to be led easily by the halter.

cabestrillo, (kâ·ves·trē´yo) *m.* sling; necklace, chain.

cabestro, (kâ·ves´tro) *m.* halter; lead ox *(buey).*

cabeza, (kâ·ve´sâ) *f.* head.

cabezada, (kâ·ve·sâ´thâ) *f.* blow on the head *(recibida);* butt with the head *(dada);* nod; headstall *(correaje);* instep *(de bota).*

cabezal, (kâ·ve·sâl´) *m.* small pillow; bolster *(de la cama);* (med.) surgical compress.

cabezón, ona, (kâ·ve·son´, o´nâ) *adj.* bigheaded; (fig.) stubborn; —, *m.* hole for the head.

cabezudo, da, (kâ·ve·sū´tho, thâ) *adj.* bigheaded; (fig.) headstrong, obstinate, stubborn.

cabida, (kâ·vē´thâ) *f.* content, capacity.

cabildear, (kâ·vēl·de·âr´) *vn.* to lobby.

cabildeo, (kâ·vēl·de´o) *m.* lobbying.

cabildo, (kâ·vēl´do) *m.* (eccl.) cathedral chapter; (eccl.) chapter meeting; town council *(ayuntamiento).*

cabina, (kâ·vé´nâ) *f.* cockpit; **— a presión,** pressurized cabin; **— cerrada trasparente,** (avi.) canopy; **— telefónica,** telephone booth.

cabizbajo, ja, (kâ·vēz·vâ´ho, ha´) *adj.* crestfallen.

cable, (kâ´vle) *m.* cable, rope; **— conductor,** electric cable; **— de remolque,** towline.

cablegrafiar, (kâ·vle·grâ·fyâr´) *va.* to cable.

cablegráfico, ca, (kâ·vle·grâ´fē·ko, kâ) *adj.*

cable; **dirección —ca,** cable address.

cablegrama, (kâ·vle·grâ´mâ) *m.* cable.

cabo,((kâ´vo) *m.* (geog.) cape, headland; end *(fin);* tip, extremity *(extremo);* (mil.) corporal; **al —,** at last; **al — de,** at the end of; **llevar a** or **al —,** to finish, to carry out, to accomplish.

Cabo de Buena Esperanza, (kâ´vo the vwe´nâ es·pe·rân´sa) *m.* Cape of Good Hope.

Cabo de Hornos, (kâ´vo the or´nos) *m.* Cape Horn.

cabra, (kâ´vrâ) *f.* goat.

cabrestante, (kâ·vres·tân´te) *m.* (naut.) capstan.

cabrio, (kâ·vrē´o) *m.* flock of goats; **macho —,** buck.

cabriola, (kâ·vryo´lâ) *f.* caper, gambol; pirouette.

cabriolar (kâ·vryo·lâr´) or **cabriolear,** (kâ·vryo·le·âr´) *vn.* to caper, to curvet; to pirouette.

cabriolé, (kâ·vryo·le´) *m.* cabriolet.

cabritilla, (kâ·vrē·tē´yâ) *f.* dressed kidskin.

cabrito, (kâ·vrē´to) *m.* kid.

cabrón, (kâ·vron´) *m.* buck, he-goat; (fig.) cuckold.

cabronada, (kâ·vro·nâ´thâ) *f.* cuckoldry.

cacahual (ka·kâ·wâl´) or **cacaotal,** (kâ·o·tâl´) *m.* cocoa plantation.

cacahuate (kâ·kâ·wâ´te) or **cacahuete,** (kâ·kâ·we´te) *m.* peanut.

cacao, (kâ·kâ´o) *m.* (bot.) cacao; cocoa seed *(semilla).*

cacarear, (kâ·kâ·re·âr´) *vn.* to crow *(gallo);* to cackle, to cluck *(gallina);* (fig.) to brag, to boast.

cacareo, (kâ·kâ·re´o) *n.* crowing; cackling; (fig.) boasting, bragging.

cacera, (ka·se´râ) *f.* irrigation canal.

cacería, (kâ·se·rē´â) hunting party.

cacerola, (kâ·se·ro´lâ) *f.* casserole.

cacique, (kâ·sē´ke) *m.* cacique; (fig.) political boss.

caciquismo, (kâ·sē·kēz´mo) *m. (poi.)* bossism.

cacofonía, (kâ·ko·fo·nē´â) *f.* cacophony, dissonance.

cacto, (kâk´to) *m.* cactus.

cacumen, (kâ·kū´men) *m.* acumen, keenness, discernment.

cacha, (kâ´châ) *f.* knife handle; grip.

cacharro, (kâ·châ´rro) *m.* piece of crockery, crock; pottery fragment, potsherd *(pedazo).*

cachaza, (kâ·châ´sâ) *f.* (coll.) deliberateness, unhurriedness *(sosiego);* coldness, indifference *(flema)*; foam of impurities on juice of sugar cane *(del guarapo)*.

cachete, (kâ·che´te) *m.* chubby cheek *(carrillo)*; sock in the face *(golpe)*.

cachetudo, da, (kâ·che·tũ´tho, thâ) *adj.* chubby-cheeked.

cachimba, (kâ·chēm´bâ) *f.*, cachimbo, (kâ·chēm´bo) *m.* pipe.

cachiporra, (kâ·chē·po´rrâ) *f.* cudgel, club, bludgeon.

cachivache, (kâ·chē·vâ´che) *m.* junky kitchen utensil, old piece of kitchen-ware; *(fig.)* phony, fake.

cacho, (kâ´cho) *m.* slice, piece; (Sp. Am.) horn *(cuerno)*.

cachondo, da, (kâ·chon´do, dâ) *adj.* in heat, in rut.

cachorro, rra, (kâ·cho´rro, rrâ) *n.* puppy *(perro)*; cub.

cachucha, (kâ·chũ´châ) *f.* cachucha, Andalusian solo dance *(baile)*; rowboat *(bote)*; cap *(gorra)*.

cachupín, ina, (kâ·chũ·pēn´, ē´nâ) *n.* Spanish settler in America.

cada, (kâ´thâ) *adj.* each, every; every *(con numeral absoluto)*; — cual, everyone, everybody; — uno, everyone, each one; — vez, every time; — vez más, more and more.

cadalso, (kâ·thâl´so) *m.* scaffold, platform.

cadáver, (kâ·thâ´ver) *m.* corpse, cadaver.

cadavérico, ca, (kâ·thâ·ve´rē·ko, kâ) *adj.* cadaveric; *(fig.)* cadaverous.

cadena, (kâ·the´nâ) *f.* chain; chain gang *(de galeotes)*; network, series *(conjunto)*; — antideslizante, nonskid chain; — de montañas, range of mountains; — perpetua, life sentence; life imprisonment.

cadencia, (kâ·then´syâ) *f.* cadence.

cadente, (kâ·then´te) *adj.* cadent, rythmical *(cadencioso)*; declining, failing.

cadera, (kâ·the´râ) *f.* hip.

cadete, (kâ·the´te) *m.* (mil.) cadet.

caducar, (ka·thũ·kar´) *vn.* to be senile, to dote *(chochear)*; to lose effect, to lapse *(perder fuerza)*; *(fig.)* to fall into disuse, to be outmoded *(acabarse)*.

caduco, ca, (kâ·thũ´ko, kâ) *adj.* senile, in one´s dotage; perishable, fleeting *(perecedero)*.

C.A.E.: cóbrese al entregar, C.O.D. or c.o.d. cash on delivery.

caer*, (kâ·er´) *vn.* to fall, to tumble down; to diminish, to lag *(debilitarse)*; to be fall, to happen *(una desgracia)*; to come by chance, to happen to come *(llegar)*; (com.) to fall due; to catch on, to

understand *(comprender)*; — bien, to suit, to be pleasing; — de bruces, to fall headlong; — en gracia, to be liked, to win favor; —se de suyo, to be self-evident; dejar —, to drop.

café, (kâ·fe´) *m.* coffee tree *(cafeto)*; coffee; coffeehouse, café *(sitio)*; — cargado, strong coffee; — claro, weak coffee; — molido, ground coffee; —, *adj.* coffee-colored.

cafeína, (kâ·fe·ē´nâ) *f.* caffeine.

cafetal, (kâ·fe·tâl´) *m.* coffee plantation.

cafetalero, ra, (kâ·fe·tâ·le´ro, râ) *n.* coffee grower, coffee planter.

cafetera, (kâ·fe·te´râ) *f.* coffee pot *(vasija)*; (coll.) jalopy *(automóvil)*.

cafetería, (kâ·fe·te·rē´â) *f.* coffeehouse, coffee shop; cafeteria *(de autoservicio)*.

cafetero, ra, (kâ·fe·te´ro, râ) *adj.* pertaining to coffee; (coll.) very fond of coffee; —, *n.* coffee picker *(que cosecha)*; coffee seller *(que vende)*; coffeehouse owner *(dueño del café)*.

cafeto, (kâ·fe´to) *m.* coffee tree.

cafre, (kâ´fre) *adj.* savage, inhuman *(cruel)*; uncouth, rough *(rústico)*.

caída, (kâ·ē´thâ) *f.* fall, falling; slope, descent *(declive)*; — de agua, waterfall; — de la tarde, nightfall; — incontrolada, free fall.

caído, da, (kâ·ē´tho, thâ) *adj.* fallen.

caimán, (kaē·mân´) *m.* caiman, cayman; (fig.) crafty, tricky individual.

caja, (kâ´hâ) *f.* box; case *(de instrumento)*; casket, coffin *(ataúd)*; strong box, cashbox *(para valores)*; cashier´s desk *(del cajero)*; — alta, upper case; — baja, lower case; — de ahorros, savings bank; — de cambios, gear box, transmission; — de cartón, carton; — de herramientas, tool chest; — de interrupción, switch box; — de reclutamiento, recruiting branch; — de seguridad, safe-deposit box; — fuerte, safe vault; — registradora, (cash register); libro de —, cashbook.

cajero, ra, (kâ·he´ro, râ) *n.* cashier;— automático, automatic teller machine (ATM).

cajeta, (kâ·he´tâ) *f.* (Sp. Am.) small box; jelly jar *(para jaleas)*.

cajetilla, (kâ·he·tē´yâ) *f.* pack *(de cigarillos)*; (Arg.) city swell, city slicker *(elegante)*.

cajista, (kâ·hēs´tâ) *m.* compositor.

cajón, (kâ·hon´) *m.* space between shelves *(de estante)*; drawer *(gaveta)*; (Sp. Am.)grocery store; ser de —, (coll.) to be

the usual thing, to be customary.
cajuela, (kâ·hwe'lä) *f.* auto trunk.
cal, (kâl) *f.* lime; — **viva,** quicklime.
cala, (kä'lä) *f.* cove, inlet, small bay.
calabaza, (kâ·lâ·vä'sä) *f.* pumpkin, gourd;
 dar —s, to reject, to give the cold shoulder *(a un pretendiente);* to fail, to flunk
 (en los exámenes).
calabozo, (kâ·lâ·vo'so) *m.* dungeon *(subte-*
 rráneo); isolated cell *(de cárcel).*
calada, (kâ·lâ'thä) *f.* dive, swoop *(ave de*
 rapiña); soaking; laying, sinking *(artes*
 de pesca).
calado, (ka·lâ'tho) *m.* openwork, drawn
 work *(en tela);* (naut.) draft *(del barco);*
 depth *(profundidad).*
calador, (kâ·lâ·thor') *m.* probe.
calafate, (kâ·lâ·fâ'te) *m.* (naut.) calker.
calamar, (kâ·la·mar') *m.* squid.
calambre, (kâ·lâm'bre) *m.* cramp.
calamidad, (kâ·lâ·mē·thâth') *f.* calamity,
 general disaster.
calamita, (kâ·lâ·mē'tä) *f.* magnetic needle.
calamitoso, sa, (kâ·lâ·mē·to'so, sä) *adj.*
 calamitous, disastrous.
calar, (kâ·lâr') *va.* to soak *(un líquido);* to
 pierce *(traspasar);* to plug *(un melón);*
 to fix, to ready *(una arma);* to lay, to
 sink *(artes de pesca);* —, *vi.* (naut.) to
 draw; to pounce, to swoop down; **—se,**
 to be soaked through *(mojarse);* **—se el**
 sombrero, to pull down one's hat.
calavera, (kâ·lâ·ve'râ) *f.* skull; *m.* reckless
 individual, daredevil, madcap.
calaverada, (kâ·lâ·ve·râ'thä) *f.* prank,
 escapade, reckless action.
calcañal (kâl·kâ·nyâl') or **calcañar,**
 (kâl·kâ·nyâr') *m.* heel bone *(calcáneo);*
 heel *(talón).*
calcar, (kâl·kâr') *va.* to trace, to copy; to
 trample on, to step on *(con el pie);* (fig.)
 to copy slavishly.
calcáreo, rea, (kâl·kâ're·o, re·â) *adj.*
 chalky.
calceta, (kâl·se'tä) *f.* stocking.
calcetín, (kâl·se·tēn') *m.* sock.
calcificar, (kâl·sē·fē·kâr') *va.* to calcify.
calcinar, (kâl·sē·nâr') *va.* to calcine; (fig.)
 to char, to reduce to ashes.
calcio, (kâl'syo) *m.* calcium.
calcomanía, (kâl·ko·mâ·nē'â) *f.* decalcomania, sticker.
calculable, (kâl·kū·lâ'vle) *adj.* calculable.
calculador, (kâl·kū·lâ·thor') *m.* calculator,
 computer; estimator; —, **ra,** *adj.* calculating, scheming.
calculadora, (kâl·kū·lâ·tho'râ) *f.* calculating machine, calculator.

calcular, (kâl·kū·lâr') *va.* to calculate, to
 compute; to estimate, to judge *(apre-*
 ciar).
cálculo, (kâl'kū·lo) *m.* calculation, computation; estimate, judgment; — **biliario,**
 (med.) gallstone.
calda, (kâl'dä) *f.* warming up, heating up;
 —s, *pl.* hot baths, thermal springs.
caldear, (kâl·de·âr') *va.* to make red-hot
 (hacer ascua); to warm up, to heat up;
 (fig.) to cheer up, to brighten up.
caldera, (kâl·de'râ) *f.* kettle; — **de vapor,**
 steam boiler; — **tubular,** hot-water boiler.
calderón, (kâl·de·ron') *m.* large kettle, cal-
 dron; (print.) paragraph sign; (mus.)
 pause.
caldo, (kâl'do) *m.* broth, bouillon; salad
 dressing *(de la ensalada);* — **de carne,**
 beef consommé.
calefacción, (kâ·le·fâk·syon') *f.* heating.
calendario, (kâ·len·dâ'ryo) *m.* calendar.
calentador, (kâ·len·tâ·thor') *m.* heater,
 heating apparatus; — **de agua,** water
 heater.
calentar*, (kâ·len·târ') *va.* to warm, to
 heat; **—se,** (fig.) to get hot under the
 collar; (zool.) to be in rut.
calentura, (kâ·len·tū'râ) *f.* fever.
calenturiento, ta, (kâ·len·tū·ryen'to, tâ)
 adj. feverish.
calesa, (kâ·le'sä) *f.* calash.
calesín, (kâ·le·sēn') *m.* light calash.
calibración, (kâ·lē·vrâ·syon') *f.* calibration.
calibrador, (kâ·lē'·vrâ·thor') *m.* gauge.
calibrar, (kâ·lē·vrâr') *va.* to calibrate.
calibre, (kâ·lē'vre) *m.* bore, caliber, gauge
 (de un cañón); caliber *(de un proyectil);*
 diameter *(de un alambre);* (fig.) caliber.
calicanto, (kâ·lē·kân'to) *m.* stone masonry.
calidad, (kâ·lē·thâth') *f.* quality; type, kind
 (índole); qualities, qualifications *(para*
 un cargo); term, condition *(para un*
 contrato); **en — de,** in one's position
 as.
cálido, da, (kâ'lē·tho, thâ) *adj.* hot, warm.
calidoscopio, (kâ·lē·thos·ko'pyo) *m.* kaleidoscope.
caliente, (kâ·lyen'te) *adj.* hot, warm; (fig.)
 fiery, vehement *(acalorado);* **en —,** at
 once, immediately.
calificación, (kâ·lē·fē·kâ·syon') *f.* rating,
 classification, evaluation; grade, mark
 (nota de examen).
calificar, (kâ·lē·fē·kâr') *va.* to rate, to classify, to evaluate; to grade, to mark *(al*
 alumno); (fig.) to ennoble; **—se,** to prove

m met, **n** not, **p** pot, **r** very, **rr** (none), **s** so, **t** toy, **th** with, **v** eve, **w** we, **y** yes, **z** zero

one's noble birth.

caligrafía, (kä·lē·grä·fē´ä) *f.* calligraphy, penmanship.

calisténica, (kä·lēs·te´nē·kä) *f.* calisthenics.

cáliz (kä´lēs) *m.* chalice, goblet; (bot.) calyx.

caliza, (kä·lē´sä) *f.* limestone.

calma, (käl´mä) *f.* calm, stillness; lull, let-up *(cesación);* (fig.) peace, quiet *(tranquilidad).*

calmante, (käl·män´te) *m.* (med.) sedative; tranquilizer.

calmar, (käl·mär´) *va.* to calm, to quiet; **—se,** to quiet down, to calm down.

calmoso, sa, (käl·mo´so, sä) *adj.* calm; tranquil, peaceful.

caló, (kä·lo´) *m.* gypsy argot.

calofriarse, (kä·lo·fryär´se) *vr.* to be chilled, to have a chill.

calofrío, (kä·lo·frē´o) *m.* shivering, chill.

calor, (kä·lor´) *m.* heat, warmth; (fig.) ardor, enthusiasm *(ardimiento);* heat, flush *(de una acción);* **hacer —,** to be hot or warm, to be hot weather; **tener —,** to be hot or warm.

caloría, (kä·lo·rē´ä) *f.* calorie.

calorífero, ra, (kä·lo·rē´fe·ro, rä) *adj.* heat producing; **—,** *m.* furnace; **— de aire caliente,** hot-air furnace.

calumnia, (kä·lūm´nyä) *f.* calumny, slander.

calumniador, ra, (kä·lūm·nyä·thor´, rä) *n.* slanderer.

calumniar, (kä·lūm·nyär´) *vn.* to slander, to smear.

calumnioso, sa, (kä·lūm·nyo´so, sä) *adj.* calumnious, slanderous.

caluroso, sa, (kä·lū·ro´so, sä) *adj.* warm, hot; **— bienvenida,** cordial welcome.

calva, (käl´vä) *f.* bald spot, bald place *(de la cabeza);* clearing *(del bosque).*

Calvario, (käl·vä´ryo) *m.* Calvary; via dolorosa *(vía crucis);* **c—,** (fig.) cross to bear, via dolorosa.

calvicie, (käl·vē´sye) *f.* baldness.

calvo, va, (käl´vo, vä) *adj.* bald; barren, bare *(terreno).*

calzada, (käl·sä´thä) *f.* causeway, highway.

calzado, (käl·sä´tho) *m.* footwear.

calzador, (käl·sä·thor´) *m.* shoe horn.

calzar, (käl·sär´) *va.* to put on *(calzado);* to put a wedge under *(cuña);* to take *(calibre de bala);* to wear, to take *(número de zapato).*

calzón, (käl·son´) *m.* ombre *(tresillo);* (Mex.) sugar-cane blight; **—ones,** *pl.*

breeches, knee-length shorts *(hasta la rodilla);* trousers, pants *(pantalones).*

calzoncillos, (käl·son·sē´yos) *m. pl.* drawers, shorts.

¡calla!, (kä´yä) *interj.* no! you don't say! you don't mean it!

callado, da, (kä·yä´tho, thä) *adj.* silent, noiseless, quiet *(silencioso);* tight-lipped, close-mouthed, quiet *(taciturno).*

callar, (kä·yär´) *vn.* to keep quiet, to be silent *(guardar silencio);* to become quiet, to stop talking *(dejar de hablar);* **—,** *va.* not to mention, to keep quiet about; **hacer —,** to silence, to hush up.

calle, (kä´ye) *f.* street; lane *(en una competición);* **— trasversal,** crossroad; **cruce de —,** street crossing; **doblar la —,** to turn the corner; **—s céntricas,** downtown.

calleja, (kä·ye´hä) *f.* lane, narrow street, alley.

callejear, (kä·ye·he·är´) *vn.* to wander the streets.

callejero, ra, (kä·ye·hero, rä) *adj.* fond of wandering the streets.

callejón, (kä·ye·hon´) *m.* short street; **— sin salida,** dead-end street; blind alley.

callejuela, (kä·ye·hwe´lä) *f.* lane, narrow street; (fig.) subterfuge, shift.

callista, (kä·yēs´tä) *m.* or *f.* chiropodist.

callo, (kä´yo) *m.* corn, callus; **—s,** *pl.* tripe.

calloso, sa, (kä·yo´so, sä) *adj.* callous.

cama, (kä´mä) *f.* bed; litter *(para el ganado);* den, lair *(de animales);* **— plegadiza,** folding bed; **guardar —,** to stay in bed; **hacer la —,** to make the bed.

camada, (kä·mä´thä) *f.* litter, brood *(cría);* layer *(de huevos);* gang of thieves, robber's den *(de ladrones).*

camafeo, (kä·mä·fe´o) *m.* cameo.

camaleón, (kä·mä·le·on´) *m.* chameleon.

cámara, (kä´mä·rä) *f.* hall, chamber; (pol.) house; (phot.) camera; (avi.) cockpit; (mech.) chamber; **— de aire,** inner tube; **— de combustión,** combustion chamber; **— de comercio,** chamber of commerce; **— de compensación,** clearing house; **— de escape,** exhaust; **— frigorífica,** cold-storage locker.

camarada, (kä·mä·rä´thä) *m.* comrade, companion.

camaradería, (kä·mä·rä·the·rē´ä) *f.* fellowship.

camarera, (kä·mä·re´rä) *f.* waitress *(de restaurante);* maid.

camarero, (kä·mä·re´ro) *m.* waiter *(de restaurante);* valet; (naut. and avi.) steward.

camarilla, (kâ·mä·rē′yä) *f.* hidden clique of advisers to a government.

camarista, (kâ·mä′rēs′tä) *m.* member of the supreme council; —, *f.* maid of honor of the queen.

camarógrafo, (kâ·mâ·ro′grä·fo) *m.* cameraman.

camarón, (kâ·mä·ron′) *m.* (ichth.) shrimp; **coctel de —ones,** shrimp cocktail.

camarote, (kâ·mä·ro′te) *m.* cabin, stateroom.

cambalachear, (kâm·bâ·lä·che·âr′) *va.* (coll.) to trade, to exchange.

cambiable, (kâm·byä′vle) *adj.* changeable.

cambiante, (kâm·byän′te) *adj.* changeable; iridescent *(tela);* —, *m.* iridescence.

cambiar, (kâm·byâr′) *va.* to change; to exchange *(una cosa por otra);* to alter *(modificar);* to turn *(convertir);* to convert *(divisas);* to make change for *(billetes).*

cambiavía, (kâm·byä·vē′ä) *f.* (rail.) switchman.

cambija, (kâm·bē′hä) *f.* reservoir.

cambio, (kâm′byo) *m.* exchange; change; alteration; — **exterior** or **extranjero,** foreign exchange; — **de marchas** or **de velocidad,** gearshift; — **de moneda,** money exchange; **a — de,** in exchange for; **al — de,** at the rate of exchange of; **en —,** on the other hand; **agente de —,** stockbroker; **casa de —,** exchange office; **corredor de —,** exchange broker; **letra de —,** bill of exchange; **tipo de —,** rate of exchange.

cambista, (kâm·bēs′tä) *m.* money changer; banker *(banquero).*

cambray, (kâm·brä′ē) *m.* cambric.

camelia, (kâ·me′lyä) *f.* (bot.) camellia.

camelo, (kâ·me′lo) *m.* courting, flirting *(galanteo);* joke, trick *(burla).*

camello, (kâ·me′yo) *m.* camel.

camilla, (kâ·mē′yä) *f.* stretcher.

caminador, ra, (kâ·mē·nä·thor′, rä) *adj.* prone to walking a great deal.

caminante, (kâ·mē·nân′te) *m.* traveler, wayfarer; walker.

caminar, (kâ·mē·nâr′) *vn.* to travel; to walk *(andar).*

caminata, (kâ·mē·nä′tä) *f.* long walk.

camino, (kâ·mē′no) *m.* road; — **trillado,** beaten path; — **de acceso,** access road; **en —,** on the way; **ponerse en —,** to start out.

camión, (kâ·myon′) *m.* truck; (Mex.) bus.

camioneta, (kâ·myo·ne′tä) *f.* station wagon; small truck *(para mercancías).*

camisa, (kâ·mē′sä) *f.* shirt; chemise *(de señora);* — **de fuerza,** straitjacket.

camisería, (kâ·mē·se·rē′ä) *f.* haberdashery.

camiseta, (kâ·mē·se′tä) *f.* undershirt.

camisola, (kâ·mē·so′lä) *f.* ruffled shirt.

camisón, (kâ·mē·son′) *m.* nightgown *(de dormir);* chemise.

camorra, (kâ·mo′rrä) *f.* quarrel, dispute.

camorrista, (kâ·mo·rrēs′tä) *m.* and *f.* quarrelsome person.

camote, (kâ·mo′te) *m.* sweet potato.

campal, (kâm·pâl′) *adj.* pertaining to the field; **batalla —,** pitched battle.

campamento, (kâm·pâ·men′to) *m.* (mil.) encampment, camp.

campana, (kâm·pâ′nä) *f.* bell; — **de buzo,** diving bell; — **de chimenea,** funnel of a chimney; **juego de —s,** chimes.

campanada, (kâm·pâ·nä′thä) *f.* peal, stroke of a bell; (fig.) scandal.

campanario, (kâm·pâ·nä′ryo) *m.* belfry, steeple.

campaneo, (kâm·pâ·ne′o) *m.* tolling of bells, pealing of bells; (fig.) affected walk, strut *(contoneo).*

campanero, (kâm·pâ·ne′ro) *m.* bell founder *(artífice);* bell ringer.

campanilla, (kâm·pâ·nē′yä) *f.* hand bell; (anat.) uvula.

campanillazo, (kâm·pâ·nē·yä′so) *m.* loud ring of a bell.

campaña, (kâm·pâ′nyä) *f.* level countryside, flat country; campaign *(serie de actos).*

campear, (kâm·pe·âr′) *vn.* to go out into the countryside *(animales);* to turn green *(sementeras);* to excel, to stand out *(sobresalir);* (coll.) to look for *(ganado).*

campechano, na, (kâm·pe·chä′no, nä) *adj.* (coll.) good-natured, cheerful.

campeón, ona, (kâm·pe·on′, o′nä) *n.* champion.

campeonato, (kâm·pe·o·nä′to) *m.* championship.

campesino, na, (kâm·pe·sē′no, nä) *adj.* rural; —, *n.* peasant.

campestre, (kâm·pes′tre) *adj.* rural, rustic; **merienda —,** picnic lunch.

campiña, (kâm·pē′nyä) *f.* large tract of arable land.

campo, (kâm′po) *m.* country, countryside; field *(terreno);* (mil.) camp; — **de deportes,** playing field; — **de juegos,** playground; — **minado,** mine field.

camposanto, (kâm·po·sân′to) *m.* cemetery.

camuflaje, (kâ·mū·flä′he) *m.* camouflage.

can, (kân) *m.* dog; — **mayor,** Canis Major; — **menor,** Canis Minor.

---

m met, **n** not, **p** pot, **r** very, **rr** (none), **s** so, **t** toy, **th** with, **v** eve, **w** we, **y** yes, **z** zero

cana, (kä´nä) f. gray hair; **peinar —s,** to grow old.

Canadá, (kä·nä·thä´) m. Canada.

canadiense, (kä·nä·thyen´se) m. and f. and adj. Canadian.

canal, (kä·näl´) m. channel; canal (artificial); gutter (del tejado).

Canal de la Mancha, (kä·näl´ the lä män´chä) m. English Channel.

canalización, (kä·nä·lē·sä·syon´) f. channeling; (elec.) wiring.

canalizar, (kä·nä·lē·sär´) va. to channel; (elec.) to wire.

canalón, (kä·nä·lon´) m. large gutter.

canalla, (kä·nä´yä) f. mob, rabble; —, m. scoundrel, heel, despicable person.

canallada, (kä·nä·yä´thä) f. despicable act.

canana, (kä·nä´nä) f. cartridge box.

canapé, (kä·nä·pe´) m. lounge, settee.

Canarias, (kä·nä´ryäs) f. pl. Canary Islands.

canario, (kä·nä´ryo) m. canary; (Sp. Am.) liberal tipper; —, **ria,** adj. from the Canary Islands.

canasta, (kä·näs´tä) f. basket, hamper; canasta (juego).

canastilla, (kä·näs·tē´yä) f. small basket; layette (ropa).

canasto, (kä·näs´to) m. large basket.

¡canastos! (kä·näs´tos) interj. confound it! darn it!

cáncamo, (käng´kä·mo) m. (naut.) ring-bolt; — **de mar,** heavy wave.

cancelación, (kän ·se·lä·syon´) f. cancellation; erasure; settlement.

cancelar, (kän·se·lär´) va. to annul, to void (un documento); to pay, to liquidate (una deuda); to break, to cancel (un compromiso).

cáncer, (kän´ser) m. (med.) cancer.

cancerarse, (kan·se·rär´se) vr. to become cancerous.

canceroso, sa, (kän·se·ro´so, sä) adj. cancerous.

canciller, (kan·sē·yer´) m. chancellor; attaché (de consulado).

canción, (kän·syon´) f. song.

cancionero, (kän·syo·ne´ro) m. collection of songs and poetry.

cancha, (kän´chä) f. playing field; **— de tenis,** tennis court.

candado, (kän·dä´tho) m. padlock.

candela, (kän·de´lä) f. (coll.) a light (lumbre); candle.

candelabro, (kän·de·lä´vro) m. candelabrum.

candelero, (kän·de·le´ro) m. candlestick.

candente, (kän·den´te) adj. red-hot.

candidato, ta, (kän·dē·thä´to, tä) n. candidate, applicant.

candidatura, (kän·dē·thä·tū´rä) f. candidacy.

candidez, (kän·dē·thes´) f. candor, frankness; whiteness (blancura).

cándido, da, (kän´dē·tho, thä) adj. frank, open, candid; white.

candil, (kän·dēl´) m. oil lamp; (Mex.) chandelier (araña).

candilejas, (kän·dē·le´häs) f. pl. stage lights.

candongo, ga, (kän·dong´go, gä) adj. cajoling, fawning.

candor, (kän·dor´) m. candor, frankness.

caneca, (kä·ne´kä) f. glazed earthen bottle; liquid measure of 19 liters (medida).

canela, (ca·ne´lä) f. cinnamon; **— en raja,** cinnamon stick; **— en polvo,** powdered cinnamon.

canelón, (kä·ne·lon´) m. large gutter; icicle (carámbano); cinnamon candy (confite); **—ones,** pl. hollow noodles for stuffing.

cangilón, (kän·hē·lon´) m. dipper.

cangrejo, (käng·gre´ho) m. crawfish, crab.

canguro, (käng·gū´ro) m. kangaroo.

caníbal, (kä·nē´väl) m. cannibal.

canilla, (kä·nē´yä) f. (anat.) shinbone; tap, spigot (de la cuba); bobbin (de la máquina de coser).

canino, na, (kä·nē´no, nä) adj. canine.

canje, (kän´he) exchange, interchange.

canjear, (kän·he·är´) va. to exchange, to interchange.

cano, na, (kä´no, nä) adj. hoary, gray-haired.

canoa, (kä·no´ä) f. canoe; (Sp. Am.) wooden trough (artesa); (Sp. Am.) wooden aqueduct (canal).

canon, (kä´non) m. catalogue, list; (eccl.) canon; **cánones,** pl. canon law.

canónico, ca, (kä·no´nē·ko, kä) adj. canonical.

canónigo, (kä·no´nē·go) m. (eccl.) canon, prebendary.

canonizar, (kä·no·nē·sär´) va. to canonize.

canoso, sa, (kä·no´so, sä) adj. white-haired.

cansado, da, (kän·sä´tho, thä) adj. weary, wearied, tired; tedious, tiresome (fastidioso).

cansancio, (kan·sän´syo) m. lassitude, fatigue, weariness.

cansar, (kän·sär´) va. to weary, to fatigue; to annoy, to bore (fastidiar); **—se,** to grow weary, to get tired.

cantable, (kän·tä´vle) adj. singable.

cantaleta, (kän·tä·le´tä) f. shivaree (a los

recién casados); mocking singsong.

cantante, (kân·tân´te) *m.* and *f.* singer.

cantar, (kân·târ´) *m.* song; —, *va.* and *vn.* to sing.

cántara, (kân´tâ·râ) *f.* pitcher; a liquid measure of 32 pints *(medida).*

cántaro, (kân´tâ·ro) *m.* pitcher; ballot box *(electoral);* **llover a —s,** to rain heavily, to pour.

cantera, (kân·te´râ) *f.* quarry.

cantería, (kân·te·rē´â) *f.* stonecutting trade *(arte);* piece of hewn stone.

cantero, (kân·te´ro) *m.* stonecutter.

cántico, (kân´tē·ko) *m.* song, canticle.

cantidad, (kân·tē·thâth´) *f.* quantity, amount, number.

cantilena, (kân·tē·le´nâ) *f.* humdrum, same old thing, monotony.

cantimplora, (kân·têm·plo´râ) *f.* siphon *(sifón);* decanter *(garrafa);* water bottle, canteen *(frasco).*

cantina, (kân·tē´nâ) *f.* barroom, cantina; wine cellar *(sótano);* canteen *(caja).*

cantinero, (kân·tē·ne´ro) *m.* bartender.

canto, (kân´to) *m.* song; (eccl.) chant; edge *(de mesa);* chunk, piece *(de piedra);* canto *(del poema épico).*

cantón, (kân·ton´) *m.* corner *(esquina);* (mil.) quarters; region, area *(región).*

cantonera, (kân·to·ne´râ) *f.* corner table *(rinconera);* corner brace *(refuerzo);* corner ornamentation *(adorno).*

cantor, ra, (kân·tor´, râ) *n.* singer; —, *adj.* singing.

canturrear, (kân·tū·rre·âr´) *vn.* to hum, to sing in a low voice.

caña, (kâ´nyâ) *f.* cane, reed *(planta);* stalk *(tallo);* (Sp. Am.) rum; **— del timón,** helm; **— de azúcar,** sugar cane.

cañada, (kâ·nyâ´thâ) *f.* ravine; livestock path *(para ganado).*

cañal, (kâ·nyâl´) *m.* cane plantation *(plantío);* reed bank, canebrake.

cañamar, (kâ·nyâ·mâr´) *m.* hemp field.

cañamiel, (kâ·nyâ·myel´) *f.* sugar cane.

cáñamo, (kâ´nyâ·mo) *m.* hemp; hempen cloth *(lienzo).*

cañamón, (kâ·nyâ·mon´) *m.* hemp seed.

cañavera, (kâ·nyâ·ve´râ) *f.* reed.

cañaveral, (kâ·nyâ·ve·râl´) *m.* sugar-cane plantation.

cañería, (kâ·nye·rē´â) *f.* pipe line; gas main *(del gas);* water main *(de las aguas).*

cañiza, (kâ·nyē´sâ) *f.* coarse linen.

cañizo, (kâ·nyē´so) *m.* reed frame.

caño, (kâ´nyo) *m.* tube, pipe; drain *(albañal)*

cañón, (kâ·nyon´) *m.* pipe *(de órgano);*

gorge, canyon *(paso estrecho);* cannon, gun *(de artillería);* barrel *(de fusil).*

cañonazo, (kâ·nyo·nâ´so) *m.* cannon shot.

cañoneo, (kâ·nyo·ne´o) *m.* cannonade.

cañonera, (kâ·nyo·ne´râ) *f.* cannon emplacement.

cañonería, (kâ·nyo·ne·rē´â) *f.* organ pipes; (mil.) battery of cannons.

cañonero, ra, (kâ·nyo·ne´ro, râ) *adj.* carrying guns; —, *m.* gunboat.

cañutillo, (kâ·nyū·tē´yo) *m.* slender glass tubing.

caoba, (kâ·o´vâ) *f.* mahogany.

caos, (kâ´os) *m.* chaos, confusion.

caótico, ca, (kâ·o´tē·ko, kâ) *adj.* chaotic.

capa, (kâ´pâ) *f.* cloak, cape *(prenda de vestir);* layer, coating *(de azucar);* stratum *(del terreno);* cover *(cubierta);* (fig.) pretext; **defender a — y espada,** to defend at all costs.

capacidad, (kâ·pâ·sē·thâth´) *f.* capacity.

capacitar, (kâ·pâ·sē·târ´) *va.* to enable *(habilitar);* to empower, to authorize *(facultar).*

capar, (kâ·pâr´) *va.* to geld, to castrate; (fig.) to curtail, to curb.

capataz, (kâ·pâ·tâs´) *m.* overseer *(de hacienda);* foreman *(de operarios).*

capaz, (kâ·pâs´) *adj.* spacious, roomy *(grande);* capable *(apto);* able, competent *(diestro).*

capeador, (kâ·pe·â·thor´) *m.* bullfighter who executes maneuvers with his cape.

capear, (kâ·pe·âr´) *va.* to steal the cape of; to execute maneuvers with the cape in front of *(al toro);* **— el temporal,** to battle the storm; (fig.) to battle adversity.

capellán, (kâ·pe·yân´) *m.* chaplain; clergyman *(eclesiástico);* **— castrense,** army chaplain; **— de navío,** navy chaplain.

caperuza, (kâ·pe·rū´sâ) *f.* hood; **Caperucita Roja,** Little Red Riding Hood.

capilar, (kâ·pē·lâr´) *adj.* capillary.

capilla, (kâ·pē´yâ) *f.* hood *(capucha);* chapel.

capiller (kâ·pē·yer´) or **capillero,** (kâ·pē·ye´ro) *m.* sexton, church warden.

capirote, (kâ·pē·ro´te) *adj.* with the head of a different color than the body; —, *m.* hood; **tonto de —,** simpleton, blockhead.

capitación, (kâ·pē·tâ·syon´) *f.* poll tax.

capital, (kâ·pē·tâl´) *m.* capital *(valor permanente);* principal; estate, assets *(caudal);* **— circulante,** rolling capital; **— fluctuante,** floating capital; **colocar un**

—, to invest capital; —, *f.* capital; *adj.* capital; principal, main.

capitalismo, (kâ·pē·tâ·lēz´mo) *m.* capitalism.

capitalista; (kâ·pē·tâ·lēs´tâ) *m.* and *f.* and *adj.* capitalist; **socio** —, investor, investing member.

capitalización, (kâ·pē·tâ·lē·sâ·syon´) *f.* capitalization.

capitalizar, (kâ·pē·tâ·lē·sâr´) *va.* to capitalize.

capitán, (kâ·pē·tân´) *m.* captain; chief, leader *(de forajidos);* — **de corbeta,** lieutenant commander; — **del puerto,** harbor master.

capitanear, (kâ·pē·tâ·ne·âr´) *va.* to captain, to lead.

capitel, (kâ·pē·tel´) *m.* steeple *(de una torre);* capital *(de una columna).*

capitolio, (kâ·pē·to´lyo) *m.* capitol.

capitular, (kâ·pē·tū·lâr´) *vn.* to reach an agreement, to come to an understanding; (mil.) to capitulate; (eccl.) to sing canons in the Mass; —, *va.* to charge, to impeach.

capítulo, (kâ·pē´tū·lo) *m.* chapter; charge, count, allegation *(cargo).*

capón, (kâ·pon´) *m.* capon.

caporal, (kâ·po·râl´) *m.* chief, ringleader.

capota, (kâ·po´tâ) *f.* bonnet *(de carruaje);* top; short cape *(capa).*

capote, (kâ·po´te) *m.* long cloak, capote; bullfighter´s cape *(de torero);* (coll.) stern look, frown *(ceño);* **decir para su** —, to say to oneself.

capotudo, da, (kâ·po·tū´tho, thâ) *adj.* frowning.

capricho, (kâ·prē´cho) *m.* caprice, whim, fancy.

caprichoso, sa, (kâ·prē·cho´so, sâ) *adj.* capricious, whimsical, fickle.

cápsula, (kâp´sū·lâ) *f.* capsule *(envoltura);* top, cap *(de botella);* cartridge *(del arma de fuego);* — **de escape** or **de emergencia,** escape capsule; — **espacial,** space capsule; — **fulminante,** detonator, percussion cap.

captar, (kâp·târ´) *va.* to captivate; (rad.) to tune in; to understand, to perceive *(comprender).*

captura, (kâp·tū´râ) *f.* capture, seizure.

capturar, (kâp·tū·râr´) *va.* to capture.

capucha, (kâ·pū´châ) *f.* (print.) circumflex accent; hood, cowl.

capuchina, (kâ·pū·chē´nâ) *f.* Capuchin nun.

capuchino, (kâ·pū·chē´no) *m.* Capuchin monk; —, **na,** *adj.* pertaining to the Capuchins.

capullo, (kâ·pū´yo) *m.* cocoon *(de oruga);* bud *(de flor).*

caqui, (kâ´kē) *adj.* khaki.

cara, (kâ´râ) *f.* face, visage *(del hombre);* front *(fachada);* surface *(superficie);* — **a** —, face to face; — **o cruz** or — **o sello,** heads or tails; **de** —, opposite, facing; **buena** —, cheerful mien; **mala** —, frown; **tener mala** —, to look bad.

carabina, (kâ·râ·vē´nâ) *f.* carbine; **ser como la** — **de Ambrosio,** to be good for nothing, to be worthless.

carabinero, (kâ·râ·vē·ne´ro) *m.* carabineer.

caracol, (kâ·râ·kol´) *m.* snail; **escalera de** —, winding staircase, spiral staircase.

caracoles! (kâ·râ·ko´les) *interj.* blazes! confound it!

carácter, (kâ·râk´ter) *m.* character; nature, disposition *(genio);* characteristic *(rasgo);* position, rank *(condición).*

característica, (kâ·râk·te·rēs´tē·kâ) *f.* characteristic; trait *(de una persona).*

característico, ca, (kâ·râk·te·rēs´tē·ko, kâ) *adj.* characteristic.

caracterizar, (kâ·râk·te·rē·sâr´) *va.* to characterize.

caradura, (kâ·râ·thū´râ) *adj.* shameless, brazen.

¡caramba! (kâ·râm´bâ) *interj.* heck! dam it!

carámbano, (kâ·râm´bâ·no) *m.* icicle.

carambola, (kâ·râm·bo´lâ) *f.* carom; trick *(embuste);* fluke, chance *(casualidad);* **por** —, indirectly, by chance.

caramelo, (kâ·râ·me´lo) *m.* caramel.

carapacho, (kâ·râ·pâ´cho) *m.* shell; (Cuba) shellfish stew.

carátula, (kâ·râ´tū·lâ) *f.* mask; (fig.) theater, stage; (Sp. Am.) title page *(de un libro).*

caravana, (kâ·râ·vâ´nâ) *f.* caravan; — **de automóviles,** autocade, motorcade.

¡caray! (kâ·râ´ē) *interj.* confound it! darn it!

carbohidrato, (kâr·voē·thrâ´to) *m.* carbohydrate.

carbón, (kâr·von´) *m.* coal; (elec.) carbon; **copia al** —, carbon copy; — **de leña,** charcoal; — **de piedra,** mineral coal; **papel** —, carbon paper; — **vegetal,** charcoal.

carbonera, (kâr·vo·ne´râ) *f.* coal mine *(mina de hulla);* coal bin *(depósito).*

carbonero, (kâr·vo·ne´ro) *m.* collier; —, **ra,** *adj.* pertaining to coal.

carbónico, ca, (kâr·vo´nē·ko, kâ) *adj.* carbonic.

â arm, **e** they, **ē** bē, **o** fore, **ū** blūe, **b** bad, **ch** chip, **d** day, **f** fat, **g go, h** hot, **k** kid, **1** let

carbonífero, ra, (kär·vo·nē´fe·ro, rä) *adj.* carboniferous, coal producing.

carbonizar, (kär·vo·nē·sär´) *va.* to carbonize, to char.

carbono, (kär·vo´no) *m.* (chem.) carbon.

carbunclo (kär·vūng´klo) or **carbunco,** (kär·vūng´ko) *m.* carbuncle.

carburador, (kär·vū·rä·thor´) *m.* carburetor.

carcacha, (kär·kä´chä) *f.* (coll. *Mex.*) jalopy, old dilapidated car.

carcajada, (kär·kä·hä´thä) *f.* hearty laughter; **soltar una —,** to burst out laughing.

carcañal (kär·kä·nyäl´) or **carcaño** (kär·kä´nyo) *m.* heel bone.

cárcel, (kär´sel) *f.* jail; prison *(presidio).*

carcelero, (kär·se·le´ro) *m.* jailer.

carcinógeno, (kär·sē·no´he·no)*m.*carcinogen.

cárcola, (kär´ko·lä) *f.* treadle.

carcoma, (kär·ko´mä) *f.* wood louse; (fig.) deep concern vexing problem.

carcomer, (kär·ko·mer´) *va.* to gnaw; (fig.) to corrode, to waste, to eat away.

carcomido, da, (kär·ko·mē´tho, thä) *adj.* worm-eaten.

carda, (kär´thä) *f.* teasel *(para los paños);* card *(para la lana);* (fig.) reprimand, rebuke.

cardador, ra, (kär·thä·thor´, rä) *n.* carder.

cardar, (kär·thär´) *va.* to card; to teasel.

cardenal, (kär·the·näl´) *m.* cardinal; (orn.) cardinal; bruise *(equimosis).*

cardenillo, (kär·the·nē´yo) *m.* Paris green.

cárdeno, na, (kär´the·no, nä) *adj.* livid, purple.

cardiaco, ca (kär·thyä´ko, kä) or **cardiaco, ca,** (kär·thēä·ko, kä) *adj.* cardiac; **síncope —co,** heart attack.

cardinal, (kär·thē·näl´) *adj.* cardinal.

cardiógrafo, (kär·thyo´grä·fo) *m.* (med.) cardiograph.

cardiograma, (kär·thyo·grä´mä) *m.* (med.) cardiogram.

cardo, (kär´tho) *m.* thistle.

carducha, (kär·thū´chä) *f.* large iron card.

carear, (kä·re·är´) *va.* to confront, to bring face to face; to compare *(cotejar);* to lead *(el ganado);* **—se,** to get together in person.

carecer*, (kä·re·ser´) *vn.* to want, to lack.

carena, (kä·re´nä) *f.* (naut.) careening ship.

carencia, (kä·ren´syä) *f.* lack, scarcity.

carero, ra, (kä·re´ro, rä) *adj.* high-priced.

carestía, (kä·res·tē´ä) *f.* food shortage *(de los víveres);* high cost of living.

careta, (kä·re´tä) *f.* mask.

carey, (kä·re´ē) *m.* sea turtle, hawksbill turtle; tortoise shell *(concha).*

carga, (kär´gä) *f.* load; burden, pack *(en hombros);* freight, cargo *(en vehículo);* load, charge *(de pólvera);* impost, tax *(gravamen);* (fig.) responsibility, obligation *(obligación);* worry, problem *(cuidado);* — **inútil** useless burden; — **de profundidad,** (mil.) depth charge; — **útil,** payload.

cargadero, (kär·gä·the´ro) *m.* loading dock.

cargado, da, (kär·gä´tho, thä) *adj.* loaded, full; — **de espaldas,** round shouldered.

cargador, (kär·gä·thor´) *m.* stoker *(fogonero);* stevedore, longshoreman *(estibador);* rammer, ramrod *(para armas de fuego);* carrier, porter *(portador).*

cargamento, (kär·gä·men´to) *m.* (naut.) load, cargo.

cargar, (kär·gär´) *va.* to load, to freight *(un vehículo);* to charge *(una batería);* to impose, to charge *(imponer);* to assault, to attack *(al enemigo);* to impute, to charge *(imputar);* (fig.) to worry, to vex *(incomodar);* — **en cuenta,** to charge on account, to debit to one´s account; — **con,** to assume the responsibility for.

cargo, (kär´go) *m.* (com.) debits; charge, accusation *(falta);* position, office *(oficio);* care, responsibility *(obligación);* weight, load *(peso);* **a — de,** in care of; to the account of *(a expensas de);* **a mi —,** to my account; — **de conciencia,** remorse, sense of guilt; **girar a nuestro (mi) —,** to draw on us (me); **hacerse — de,** to take into consideration, to realize; **librar a — de una persona,** to draw on a person.

cariancho, cha, (kä·ryän´cho, chä) *adj.* broad-faced, chubby-cheeked.

cariarse, (kä·ryär´se) *vr.* to become decayed.

caribe, (kä·rē´ve) *adj.* Caribbean.

caricatura, (kä·rē·kä·tū´rä) *f.* caricature, cartoon; — **animada,** animated cartoon.

caricia, (kä·rē´syä) *f.* caress.

caridad, (kä·rē·thäth´) *f.* charity, benevolence; alms *(limosna).*

caries, (kä´ryes) *f.* (med.) caries, decay.

carigordo, da, (kä·rē·gor´tho, thä) *adj.* full-faced.

carilargo, ga, (kä·rē·lär´go, gä) *adj.* long-faced.

carilla, (kä·rē´yä) *f.* sheet, page *(página);* beekeeper´s mask *(de colmenero).*

carilleno, na, (kä·rē·ye´no, nä) *adj.* full-faced.

carillón, (kâ·rē·yon´) *m.* carillon.

carinegro, gra, (kâ·rē·ne´gro, grâ) *adj.* swarthy-complexioned.

cariño, (kâ·rē´nyo) *m.* fondness, affection; term of endearment *(manifestación).*

cariñoso, sa, (kâ·rē·nyo´so, sâ) *adj.* affectionate, fond, endearing.

carirredondo, da, (kâ·rē·rre·thon´do, dâ) *adj.* roundfaced.

caritativo, va, (kâ·rē·tâ·tē´vo, vâ) *adj.* charitable.

carmelita, (kâr·me·lē´tâ) *f.* and *adj.* Carmelite.

carmenar, (kâr·me·nâr´) *va.* to card *(cardar);* to untangle, to unravel *(desenmarañar);* to fleece, to cheat *(defraudar).*

carmesí, (kâr·me·sē´) *adj.* crimson; —, *m.* cochineal powder.

carmín, (kâr·mēn´) *m.* and *adj.* carmine.

carnada ((kâr·nâ´thâ) *m.* and *f.* bait, lure.

carnal, (kâr·nâl´) *adj.* carnal, fleshy; sensual *(lascivo);* blood, related by blood; **primo** —, first cousin; —, *m.* time of year other than Lent.

carnaval, (kâr·nâ·vâl´) *m.* carnival.

carne, (kâr´ne) *f.* flesh, meat; pulp *(de la fruta);* — **asada en horno,** baked meat; — **asada en parrilla,** broiled meat; — **de gallina,** (fig.) gooseflesh; — **de vaca,** beef.

carnero, (kâr·ne´ro) *m.* sheep; mutton *(carne);* family vault *(sepulcro).*

carnet, (kâr·net´) *m.* notebook, memorandum book.

carnicería, (kâr·nē·se·rē´â) *f.* meat market, butcher shop; (fig.) massacre, shambles.

carnicero, (kâr·nē·se´ro) *m.* butcher; —, **ra,** *adj.* fond of eating meat.

carnívoro, ra, (kâr·nē´vo·ro, râ) *adj.* carnivorous.

carnosidad, (kâr·no·sē·thâth´) *f.* scar tissue; obesity *(gordura).*

carnoso, sa, (kar·no´so, sâ) or **carnudo, da,** (kâr·nū´tho, thâ) *adj.* fleshy; full of marrow *(meduloso).*

caro, ra, (kâ´ro, râ) *adj.* expensive, dear; —**ra mitad,** better half.

carpa, (kâr´pâ) *f.* (ichth.) carp; (Sp. Am.) camping tent.

carpe, (kâr´pe) *m.* (bot.) witch hazel.

carpeta, (kâr·pe´tâ) *f.* table cover; folder *(de un legajo).*

carpintear, (kâr·pēn·te·âr´) *vn.* to carpenter.

carpintería, (kâr·pēn·te·rē´â) *f.* carpentry; carpenter´s shop *(taller).*

carpintero, (kâr·pēn·te´ro) *m.* carpenter;

pájaro —, woodpecker.

carpo, (kâr´po) *m.* (anat.) carpus, wristbones.

carraleja, (kâ·rrâ·le´hâ) *f.* black beetle.

carrasca, (kâ·rrâs´kâ) *f.,* **carrasco,** (kâ·rrâs´ko) *m.* live oak.

carraspera, (kâ·rrâs·pe´râ) *f.* hoarseness, roughness in the throat.

carrera, (kâ·rre´râ) *f.* running *(acción);* run *(espacio);* track *(sitio);* race *(certamen);* row, line *(hilera);* course of one´s life *(de la vida humana);* career, profession *(profesión);* **a** — **abierta,** at full speed; — **de armamentos,** arms race.

carreta, (kâ·rre´tâ) *f.* long narrow cart or wagon.

carretada, (kâ·rre·tâ´thâ) *f.* cartload; **a** —**s,** in great numbers.

carretaje, (kâ·rre·tâ´he) *m.* cartage.

carrete, (kâ·rre´te) *m.* spool, bobbin *(de hilo);* reel *(del sedal);* (elec.) coil; (phot.) cartridge.

carretel, (kâ·rre·tel´) *m.* reel.

carretera, (kâ·rre·te´râ) *f.* highway, main road.

carretero, (kâ·rre·te´ro) *m.* cartwright; carter *(el que guía).*

carretilla, (kâ·rre·tē´yâ) *f.* go-cart, handcart; wheelbarrow *(con una rueda);* — **elevadora,** fork-lift truck.

carretón, (kâ·rre·ton´) *m.* small cart, small wagon.

carril, (kâ·rrēl´) *m.* wheel rut *(huella);* furrow *(surco);* rail *(del ferrocarril);* lane, narrow road *(camino).*

carrilera, (kâ·rrē·le´râ) *f.* track, wheel rut.

carrillo, (kâ·rrē´yo) *m.* (anat.) cheek; pully *(polea).*

carrilludo, da, (kâ·rrē·yū´tho, thâ) *adj.* round-cheeked.

carro, (kâ´rro) *m.* (rail.) freight car; chariot *(de guerra);* cart, wagon *(de transporte);* (Sp. Am.) auto, car; carriage *(de la máquina de escribir);* — **entero,** carload; — **lateral,** side car of a motor-cycle; **C— Mayor,** Big Dipper; **C— Menor,** Little Dipper.

carrocería, (kâ·rro·se·rē´â) *f.* body *(del coche automóvil);* body shop, auto-repair pair shop *(taller).*

carroña, (kâ·rro´nyâ) *f.* carrion.

carroza, (kâ·rro´sâ) *f.* state coach; (naut.) awning.

carruaje, (kâ·rrwâ´he) *m.* wheeled vehicle.

carrusel, (kâ·rrū·sel´) *m.* merry-go-round.

carta, (kâr´tâ) *f.* letter; charter *(constitución);* (avi. and naut.) chart; card *(naipe);* — **aérea,** airmail letter; — **certi-**

ficada, registered letter; **— credencial** or **de crédito,** letter of credit; **— de amparo,** safe conduct; **— de ciudadanía** citizenship papers; **— de porte,** bill of lading; **— de presentación,** letter of introduction; **— en lista,** general delivery letter; **— general,** form letter.

cartapacio, (kâr·tâ·pâ´syo) *m.* notebook *(cuaderno);* portfolio *(funda).*

cartear, (kâr·te·âr´) *vn.* to play low cards; **—se,** to correspond, to carry on a correspondence.

cartel, (kâr·tel´) *m.* poster; show bill *(de teatro);* (poi.) cartel, organized crime; **no fijar —es,** post no bills.

cartelera, (kâr·te·le´râ) *f.* billboard.

cárter, (kâr´ter) *m.* gear case; **— del cigüeñal,** automobile crankcase.

cartera, (kâr·te´râ) *f.* brief case; flap *(del bolsillo);* **— de bolsillo,** billfold, wallet.

cartero, (kâr·te´ro) *m.* letter carrier, postman, mailman.

cartílago, (kâr·tē´lâ·go) *m.* cartilage.

cartilla, (kâr·tē´yâ) *f.* primer.

cartografia, (kâr·to·grâ·fē´â) *f.* cartography.

cartón, (kâr·ton´) *m.* pasteboard, cardboard.

cartuchera, (kâr·tū·che´râ) *f.* cartridge case *(caja);* cartridge belt *(canana).*

cartucho, (kâr·tū´cho) *m.* cartridge; **— en blanco,** blank cartridge.

cartulina, (kâr·tū·lē´nâ) *f.* bristol.

casa, (kâ´sâ) *f.* house; home *(hogar);* (corn.) firm, concern; **— al por mayor,** wholesale house; **— de banca,** banking house; **— de cambio,** exchange office; **— de campo,** country house; **— de correos,** post office; **— de comercio,** business house; **— de comisiones,** commission house; **— de compensación,** clearing house; **— de huéspedes,** boarding-house; **— de locos,** madhouse; **— de máquinas,** engine house; **— de maternidad,** maternity hospital; **— de moneda,** mint; **— de préstamos or empeños,** pawnshop; **— editorial,** publishing house; **— matriz,** main office; **— mortuoria,** funeral parlor; **en —,** at home; **poner —,** to set up housekeeping.

casaca, (kâ·sâ´kâ) *f.* frock coat.

casadero, ra, (kâ·sâ·the´ro, râ) *adj.* marriageable.

casamiento, (kâ·sâ·myen´to) *m.* marriage, wedding.

casar, (kâ·sâr´) *va.* to marry, to wed; (fig.) to join, to combine; to abrogate, to annul *(anular);* **—se,** to get married.

cascabel, (kâs·kâ·vel´) *m.* sleigh bell; (zool.) rattlesnake.

cascabelear, (kâs·kâ·ve·le·âr´) *va.* (fig.) to lead on, to entice; **—,** *vn.* to behave foolishly.

cascada, (kâ·kâ´thâ) *f.* cascade, waterfall.

cascajal, (kâs·kâ·hâl´) *m.* gravel bed.

cascajo, (kâs·kâ´ho) *m.* gravel; (coll.) piece of junk *(trasto).*

cascanueces, (kâs·kâ·nwe´ses) *m.* nutcracker.

cascar, (kâs·kâr´) *va.* to crack, to break into pieces; (coll.) to lick, to beat *(pegar);* **—se,** to break open.

cáscara, (kâs´kâ·râ) *f.* rind, peel *(de la fruta);* husk; bark *(del árbol);* skin *(piel de fruta).*

¡cáscaras! (kâs´kâ·râs) *interj.* gosh! golly!

cascarón, (kâs·kâ·ron´) *m.* eggshell.

cascarrón, ona, (kâs·kâ·rron´, o´nâ) *adj.* rough, harsh, tough.

casco, (kâs´ko) *m.* skull, cranium *(cráneo);* fragment, piece *(fragmento);* helmet *(armadura);* (naut.) hulk; crown *(del sombrero);* hoof *(de caballería).*

casera, (kâ·se´râ) *f.* housekeeper.

caserío, (kâ·se·rē´o) *m.* village.

casero, ra (kâ·se´ro, râ) *adj.* domestic, homey; homemade *(hecho en casa);* **—,** *m.* landlord; **—,** *f.* landlady.

casi, (kâ´sē) *adv.* almost, nearly; **— que,** or **—,** very nearly.

casilla, (kâ·sē´yâ) *f.* booth, shelter; box office *(taquilla);* square *(del tablero);* postal box *(apartado);* **— de correos,** mailbox; **—s,** *pl.* pigeonholes; **sacar de sus —s,** to get out of one's rut, to make change one's ways; to infuriate, to exasperate *(irritar).*

casillero, (kâ·sē·ye´ro) *m.* pigeonhole desk.

casimir, (kâ·sē·mēr´) *m.* cashmere.

casino, (kâ·sē´no) *m.* casino; clubhouse *(centro de recreo).*

caso, (kâ´so) *m.* case *(punto de consulta);* event *(circunstancia);* occurrence, happening *(acontecimiento);* (gram.) case; **— que,** in case; **en — de,** in case of; **en — de fuerza,** in case of emergency; **en ese —,** in that case; **en todo —,** at all events; **no hacer —,** to pay no attention; **poner por —,** to state as an example.

casorio, (kâ·so´ryo) *m.* hasty marriage.

caspa, (kâs´pâ) *f.* dandruff; scab *(de una llaga).*

¡cáspita! (kâs´pē·tâ) *interj.* confound it! gracious!

casquetazo, (kâs·ke·tâ´so) *m.* butt with the head.

---

m met, **n** not, **p** pot, **r** very, **rr** (none), **s** so, **t** toy, **th** with, **v** eve, **w** we, **y** yes, **z** zero

casquete, (kâs·ke'te) m. helmet, cap; — polar, polar cap.

casquijo, (kâs·kē'ho) m. gravel.

casquillo, (kâs·kē'yo) m. (mech.) ferrule; arrowhead *(de la saeta);* (Sp. Am.) horseshoe.

casquivano, na, (kâs·kē·vâ'no, nâ) adj. feather-brained.

casta, (kâs'tâ) f. caste *(clase);* race, lineage *(linaje);* (fig.) kind, quality *(especie).*

castaña, (kâs·tâ'nyâ) f. chestnut; demijohn *(damajuana);* bun *(de pelo).*

castañal (kâs·tâ·nyál') or castañar, (kâs·tâ·nyâr') m. chestnut grove.

castañazo, (kâs·tâ·nyâ'so) m. blow with the fist.

castañetear, (kâs·tâ·nye·te·âr') vn. to shake the castanets; to chatter, to knock together *(dientes).*

castaño, (kâs·tâ'nyo) m. chestnut tree; —, ña, adj. chestnut.

castañuela, (kâs·tâ·nywe'lâ) f. castanet.

castellano, na, (kâs·te·yâ'no, nâ) n. and adj. Castilian; —, m. Spanish language.

castidad, (kâs·tē·thâth') f. chastity.

castigador, ra, (kâs·tē·gâ·thor', râ) n. punisher; —, adj. punishing.

castigar, (kâs·tē·gâr') va. to chastise, to punish.

castigo, (kâs·tē'go) m. chastisement, punishment.

Castilla, (kâs·tē'yâ) f. Castile.

castillejo, (kâs·tē·ye'ho) m. walker, gocart *(para niño);* scaffolding *(andamio).*

castillo, (kâs·tē'yo) m. castle, fortress; cell of the queen bee *(maestril).*

castizo, za, (kâs·tē'so, sâ) adj. of noble descent; pure, uncorrupt *(de lenguaje).*

casto, ta, (kâs'to, tâ) adj. pure, chaste.

castor, (kâs·tor') m. beaver.

castración, (kâs·trâ·syon') f. castration, emasculation.

castrar, (kâs·trâr') va. to geld, to castrate *(capar);* to prune *(podar);* to remove the honey from *(a las colmenas).*

casual, (kâ·swâl') adj. accidental, happenstance.

casualidad, (kâ·swâ·lē·thâth') f. accident, chance, coincidence; por —, by chance, by coincidence.

casucha, (kâ·sū'châ) f. hut, shack.

cata, (kâ'tâ) f. tasting; (Sp. Am.) parrakeet *(cotorra).*

catabolismo, (kâ·tâ·vo·lēz'mo) m. catabolism.

cataclismo, (kâ·tâ·klēz'mo) m. cataclysm.

catacumbas, (kâ·tâ·kūm'bâs) f. pl. catacombs.

catadura, (kâ·tâ·thū'râ) f. act of tasting; countenance, appearance *(semblante).*

catalán, ana, (kâ·tâ·lân', â'nâ) n. and adj. Catalan, Catalonian.

catalizador, (kâ·tâ·lē·sâ·thor') m. catalyst.

catalogar, (kâ·tâ·lo·gâr') va. to catalogue, to list.

catálogo, (kâ·tâ'lo·go) m. catalogue, list.

Cataluña, (kâ·tâ·lū'nyâ) f. Catalonia.

cataplasma, (kâ·tâ·plâz'mâ) f. poultice, plaster.

catar, (kâ·târ') va. to taste *(saborear);* to inspect, to examine *(observar).*

catarata, (kâ·tâ·râ'tâ) f. cataract, waterfall, cascade; (med.) cataract.

catarro, (kâ·tâ'rro) m. catarrh, cold.

catártico, ca, (ca·târ'tē·ko, kâ) adj. (med.) cathartic, purging.

catastro, (kâ·tâs'tro) m. cadastre.

catástrofe, (kâ·tâs'tro·fe) f. catastrophe, disaster.

catecismo, (kâ·te·sēz'mo) m. catechism.

catecúmeno, (kâ·te·kū'me·no) m. catechumen.

cátedra, (kâ'te·thrâ) f. professorate; class, course *(clase).*

catedral, (kâ·te·thrâl') adj. and f. cathedral.

catedrático, (kâ·te·thrâ'tē·ko) m. professor.

categoría, (kâ·te·go·rē'â) f. category, class.

categórico, ca, (kâ·te·go'rē·ko, kâ) adj. categorical, decisive.

catequismo, (kâ·te·kēz'mo) m. catechism.

caterva, (kâ·ter'vâ) f. multitude, flock, great number.

cátodo, (kâ'to·tho) m. cathode.

catolicismo, (kâ·to·lē·sēz'mo) m. Catholicism.

católico, ca, (kâ·to'lē·ko, kâ) adj. and n. Catholic.

catorce, (kâ·tor'se) m. and adj. fourteen.

catre, (kâ'tre) m. fieldbed, cot.

caucásico, ca, (kâū·kâ'sē·ko, kâ) adj., Caucasian.

cauce, (kâ'ū·se) m. irrigation ditch *(acequia);* riverbed *(del río).*

caución, (kâū·syon') f. precaution; security, guaranty *(fianza).*

caucionar, (kâū·syo·nâr') va. to guarantee.

cauchal, (kâū·châl') m. stand of rubber plants.

cauchera, (kâū·che'râ) f. rubber plant.

caucho, (ka'ū·cho) m. rubber; — artificial, synthetic rubber; — endurecido, hard rubber.

caudal, (kâū·thâl') m. property, fortune, wealth *(hacienda);* (com.) funds; abun-

caud
91 **cela**

dance, plenty *(abundancia);* flow, discharge *(de agua).*

caudaloso, sa, (kāū·thâ·lo´so, sâ) *adj.* carrying much water.

caudillo, (kāū·thē´yo) *m.* chief, leader.

causa, (kā´ū·sâ) *f.* cause, origin *(fundamento);* motive, reason *(motivo);* case, lawsuit *(pleito);* **a — de,** owing to, because of, on account of, by reason of.

causante, (kāū·sán´te) *m.* and *f.* originator, causer.

causar, (kāū·sâr´) *va.* to cause, to produce, to occasion.

cáustico, (kā´ūs·tē·ko) *m.* caustic; **—, ca,** *adj.* caustic.

cautela, (kāū·te´lâ) *f.* caution, prudence, heedfulness.

cautelar, (kāū·te·lâr´) *va.* to guard against; **—,** *vn.* to take precautions.

cauteloso, sa, (kāū·te·lo´so, sâ) *adj.* cautious, prudent.

cauterizar, (kāū·te·rē·sâr´) *va.* to cauterize; (fig.) to reproach severely.

cautivador, ra, (kāū·tē·vâ·thor´, râ) *adj.* captivating, fascinating.

cautivar, (kāū·tē·vâr´) *va.* to take prisoner, to capture; (fig.) to captivate, to charm, to attract.

cautiverio, (kāū·tē·ve´ryo) *m.* captivity, confinement.

cautivo, va, (kāū·tē´vo, vâ) *n.* captive, prisoner.

cauto, ta, (kā´ū·to, tâ) *adj.* cautious, wary, prudent.

cavar, (kâ·vâr´) *va.* to dig, to excavate; **—,** *vn.* to penetrate deeply, to study thoroughly *(profundizar).*

caverna, (kâ·ver´nâ) *f.* cavern, cave.

caviar, (kâ·vyâr´) *m.* caviar.

cavidad, (kâ·vē·thâth´) *f.* cavity, hollow.

cavilar, (kâ·vē·lâr´) *va.* to mull over, to ponder over excessively.

caviloso, sa, (kâ·vē·lo´so, sâ) *adj.* ponderous, overly given to detail.

cayo, (kâ´yo) *m.* cay, key.

caza, (kâ´sâ) *f.* game *(animales);* hunting, hunt *(acción);* (avi.) pursuit plane, fighter plane.

cazador, (kâ·sâ·thor´) *m.* hunter, huntsman; **— furtivo,** poacher.

cazar, (kâ·sâr´) *va.* to hunt.

cazasubmarinos, (kâ·sâ·sūb·mâ·rē´nos) *m.* submarine chaser.

cazatorpedero, (kâ·sâ·tor·pe·the´ro) *m.* torpedo-boat chaser.

cazo, (kâ´so) *m.* saucepan.

cazuela, (kâ·swe´lâ) *f.* stewpan.

cazuz, (kâ·sūs´) *m.* (bot.) ivy.

C.C.: corriente continua, D.C. or d.c. direct current.

c/cta.: cuya cuenta, (corn.) whose account.

CD: disco compacto, CD, compact disk; **reproductor de —,** CD player.

ceba, (se´vâ) *f.* fattening of livestock; (fig.) stoking *(de los hornos).*

cebada, (se·vâ´thâ) *f.* barley; **— fermentada,** malt.

cebadera, (se·vâ·the´râ) *f.* nosebag, feed-bag.

cebador, (se·vâ·thor´) *m.* primer.

cebar, (se·vâr´) *va.* to feed, to fatten *(alimentar);* (mech.) to stoke, to fuel; (fig.) to incite, to provoke, to motivate; to prime *(arma de fuego);* **—,** *vn.* to start, to engage, to catch.

cebo, (se´vo) *m.* feed *(para engordar);* bait, lure *(para atraer);* priming *(del arma de fuego).*

cebolla, (se·vo´ya) *f.* onion; bulb *(bulbo).*

cebollar, (se·vo·yâr´) *m.* onion patch.

cebollino, (se·vo·yē´no) *f.* seedling onion.

cebra or **zebra,** (se´vrâ) *f.* zebra.

cebruno, na, (se·vrū´no, nâ) *adj.* reddish brown.

cecear, (se·se·âr´) *vn.* to lisp.

cecina, (se·sē´nâ) *f.* jerked meat, jerky.

cedazo, (se·thâ´so) *m.* sieve, strainer.

cedente, (se·then´te) *m.* and *f.* transferor, assigner.

ceder, (se·ther´) *va.* to cede, to yield; to transfer, to assign *(transferir);* **—,** *vn.* to submit, to comply, to give in *(rendirse);* to abate, to diminish *(disminuir).*

cedro, (se´thro) *m.* cedar.

cédula, (se·thū·lâ) *f.* slip, ticket; card *(documento);* **— de cambio,** bill of exchange; **— personal** or **de vecindad,** identification papers; **—s hipotecarias,** bank stock in the form of mortgages.

céfiro, (se´fē·ro) *m.* zephyr, breeze.

cegar,* (se·gâr´) *vn.* to go blind; **—,** *va.* to blind; to shut *(cerrar).*

cegato, ta, (se·gâ´to, tâ) *adj.* (coll.) nearsighted.

ceguedad, (se·ge·thâth´) *f.* blindness.

ceguera, (se·ge´râ) *f.* blindness.

ceja, (se´hâ) *f.* eyebrow *(del ojo);* edge, rim.

ceo, (se´ho) *m.* river fog, river mist.

cejudo, da, (se·hu´tho, thâ) *adj.* having bushy eyebrows.

celada, (se·lâ´thâ) *f.* sallet; ambush *(emboscada);* trick, trap *(engaño).*

celaje, (se·lâ´he) *m.* cloud formation *(de nubecillas);* bull's-eye, small window *(ventana);* (fig.) indication, presage *(indicio).*

m met, **n** not, **p** pot, **r** very, **rr** (none), **s** so, **t** toy, **th** with, **v** eve, **w** we, **y** yes, **z** zero

celar, (se·lâr´) va. to fulfill carefully, to carry out to the letter *(esmerarse);* to watch over, to guard *(vigilar);* to hide, to conceal *(ocultar);* to engrave *(esculpir).*

celda, (sel´dä) f. cell.

celdilla, (sel·dē´yâ) f. cellule; cell *(de abeja).*

celebérrimo, ma, (se·le·ve´rrē·mo, ma) adj. most famous.

celebración, (se·le·vrâ·syon´) f. celebration; praise, acclamation *(aplauso).*

celebrar, (se·le·vrâr´) va. to celebrate *(una ceremonia);* to praise, to acclaim, to be glad of *(aplaudir);* —, vi. to take place; — misa, to say mass.

célebre, (se´le·vre) adj. famous, renowned; humorous witty *(gracioso).*

celebridad, (se·le·vrē·thâth´) f. fame, renown; celebrity, famous person *(personaje).*

celemín, (se·le·mēn´) m. one-half peck.

celeridad, (se·le·rē·thâth´) f. celerity, velocity.

celerímetro, (se·le·rē´me·tro) m. speedometer.

celeste, (se·les´te) adj. heavenly, celestial; sky-blue *(color).*

celestial, (se·les·tyâl´) adj. celestial, heavenly.

célibe, (se´lē·ve) adj. single, unmarried; —, m. and f. celibate, single person.

celo, (se´lo) m. zeal *(entusiasmo);* care *(esmero);* rut, heat *(de los animales);* — s, pl. jealousy; tener — s de, to be jealous of.

celofán, (se·lo·fân´) m. cellophane.

celosía, (se·lo·sē´â) f. jalousie.

celoso, sa, (se·lo´so, sâ) adj. zealous, eager; jealous.

celta, (sel´tâ) adj. Celtic; —, m. or f. Celt.

céltico, ca, (sel´tē·ko, kâ) adj. Celtic.

célula, (se´lū·lâ) f. cell; — fotoeléctrica, electric eye.

celular, (se·lū·lâr´) adj. cellular.

celuloide, (se·lū·lo´e·the) m. celluloid.

celulosa, (se·lū·lo´sâ) f. (chem.) cellulose.

cementar, (se·men·târ´) va. to case harden.

cementerio, (se·men·te´ryo) m. cemetery.

cemento, (se·men´to) m. cement; — armado, reinforced concrete.

cena, (se´nâ) f. supper.

cenador, (se´·nâ·thor´) m. arbor *(pabellón);* diner.

cenagal, (se·nâ·gâl´) m. slough, quagmire, marsh.

cenagoso, sa, (se·nâ·go´so, sâ) adj. miry, marshy.

cenar, (se·nâr´) vn. to have supper, to dine.

cencerrear, (sen·se·rre·âr´) vn. *to* jangle *(los cencerros);* to squeak *(los herrajes).*

cencerro, (sen·se´rro) m. cowbell; a — s tapados, (fig.) quietly, unobtrusively.

cenefa, (se·ne´fâ) f. border, trimming.

cenicero, (se·nē·se´ro) m. ash dump; ash pit *(del hogar);* ash tray *(platillo).*

ceniciento, ta, (se·nē·syen´to, tâ) adj. ash, ash-colored; La C—, Cinderella.

cenit, (se´nēt) m. zenith, pinnacle.

ceniza, (se·nē´sâ) f. ashes; Miércoles de C—, Ash Wednesday.

cenote, (se·no´te) m. cenote, limestone sinkhole.

censo, (sen´so) m. census *(lista);* ground rent paid under contract and redeemable *(contrato).*

censor, (sen·sor´) m. censor; critic, fault-finder *(crítico);* proctor, monitor *(en los colegios).*

censura, (sen·sū´râ) f. censorship; censure *(reprobación).*

censurar, (sen·sū·râr´) va. to censor *(notar por malo);* to judge, to estimate *(formar juicio);* to censure, to find fault with *(criticar).*

centavo, (sen·tâ´vo) m. hundredth; cent *(moneda).*

centella, (sen·te´yâ) f. thunderbolt *(rayo);* spark *(chispa).*

centellar (sen·te·yâr´) or centellear, (sen·te·ye·âr´) vn. to sparkle, to glitter.

centelleo, (sen·te·ye´o) m. glitter, sparkle.

centena, (sen·te´nâ) f. hundred.

centenal, (sen·te·nâl´) m. rye field.

centenar, (sen·te·nâr´) m. hundred.

centenario, ria, (sen·te·nâ´ryo, ryâ) adj. and n. centenarian; —. m. centennial.

centeno, (sen·te´no) m. (bot.) rye; —, na, adj. hundredth.

centésimo, ma, (sen·te´sē·mo, ma) adj. centesimal, hundredth.

centígrado, da, (sen·tē´grâ·tho, thâ) adj. and m. centigrade.

centigramo, (sen·tē·grâ´mo) m. centigram.

centímetro, (sen·tē´me·tro) m. centimeter.

céntimo, (sen´tē·mo) m. cent; centime *(moneda francesa).*

centinela (sen·tē·ne´lâ) m. and f. sentinel; estar de or hacer —, (mil.) to be on guard.

central, (sen·trâl´) adj. central, centric; f. headquarters; (Sp. Am.) sugar refinery *(de azúcar);* — de electricidad, power-house; — telefónica, telephone central.

centralización, (sen·trâ·lē·sâ·syon´) f. centralization.

centralizar, (sen·trâ·lē·sâr´) *va.* to centralize.

centrar, (sen·trâr´) *va.* to center.

céntrico, ca, (sen´trē·ko, kâ) *adj.* central, centric.

centrífugo, ga, (sen·trē´fū·go, gâ) *adj.* centrifugal.

centro, (sen´tro) *m.* center; downtown *(de una población);*— **comercial,** mall, shopping center.

Centroamérica, (sen·tro·â·me´rē·kâ) *f.* Central America.

centuria, (sen·tū´ryâ) *f.* century.

ceñidor, (se·nyē·thor´) *m.* belt, sash.

ceñir*, (se·nyēr´) *vn.* to gird, to surround, to encircle *(rodear);* to curtail *(abreviar);* to fit around one´s waist; **—se,** to limit oneself, to take in one´s sails.

ceño, (se´nyo) *m.* frown.

ceñudo, da, (se·nyū´tho, thâ) *adj.* frowning, stern, gruff.

cepa, (se´pâ) *f.* tree stump; (fig.) lineage, family; **de buena —,** of good stock.

CEPAL, (se´pâl´) **Comisión Económica para la América Latina,** Latin American Economic Commission.

cepillo, (se·pē´yo) *m.* brush; plane *(de carpintero);* collection box *(para donativos);* **— de dientes,** toothbrush; **— para el cabello** or **para la cabeza,** hairbrush; **— para ropa,** clothesbrush.

cepo, (se´po) *m.* trap *(de caza);* branch, limb *(de árbol);* stock *(de yunque);* poor box, collection box *(para donativos);* stocks *(para el reo).*

cera, (se´râ) *f.* wax; **— s,** *pl.* honeycomb.

cerámica, (se·râ´mē·kâ) *f.* ceramics.

cerca, (ser´kâ) *f.* enclosure, fence; **—,** *adv.* near, at hand, close by; **— de,** close to, near; about *(aproximadamente).*

cercado, (ser·kâ´tho) *m.* fenced-in garden *(huerto);* enclosure, fence *(cerca).*

cercanía, (ser·kâ·nē´â) *f.* neighborhood, vicinity.

cercano, na, (ser·kâ´no, nâ) *adj.* nearby, neighboring.

cercar, (ser·kâr´) *va.* to enclose, to surround, to fence in; (mil.) to lay siege to.

cercenar, (ser·se·nâr´) *va.* to pare off, to trim off, to cut off; to cut down, to reduce *(disminuir).*

cerciorar, (ser·syo·râr´) *va.* to assure, to reassure, to convince; **— se,** to make certain.

cerco, (ser´ko) *m.* siege *(asedio);* hoop, ring *(aro);* circular motion *(movimiento);* enclosure.

cerda, (ser´thâ) *f.* bristle.

cerdo, (ser´tho) *m.* hog, pig.

cereal, (se·re·âl´) *m.* cereal, grain.

cerebelo, (se·re·ve´lo) *m.* (anat.) cerebellum.

cerebral, (se·re·vrâl´) *adj.* cerebral; **parálisis —,** cerebral palsy.

cerebro, (se·re´vro) *m.* brain.

ceremonia, (se·re·mo´nyâ) ceremony.

ceremonial, (se·re·mo·nyâl´) *adj.* and *m.* ceremonial.

ceremonioso, sa, (se·re·mo·nyo´so, sâ) *adj.* ceremonious.

cerero, (se·re´ro) *m.* candlemaker.

cereza, (se·re´sâ) *f.* cherry.

cerezo, (se·re´so) *m.* cherry tree.

cerilla, (se·rē´yâ) *f.* taper; wax *(de los oídos);* wax match *(fósforo).*

cerillo, (se·rē´yo) *m.* (Mex.) wax match.

cernedera, (ser·ne·the´râ) *f.* sifter.

cerner*, (ser·ner´) *va.* to sift, to strain; (fig.) to examine closely; **—,** *vn.* to blossom; to drizzle *(llover);* **—se,** to sway, to waddle; to hover *(las aves).*

cernidura, (ser·nē·thū´râ) *f.* sifting.

cero, (se´ro) *m.* zero; **ser un — a la izquierda,** to be insignificant, to be of no account.

cerote, (se·ro´te) *m.* shoemaker´s wax; (coll.) panic, fear.

cerrado, da, (se·rrâ´tho, thâ) *adj.* closed; closemouthed, reserved *(callado);* abstruse *(obscuro);* stupid, dense *(torpe)..*

cerradura, (se·rrâ·thū´râ) *f.* act of locking; lock *(mecanismo);* **— de golpe** or **de muelle,** spring lock.

cerrajero, (se·rrâ·he´ro) *m.* locksmith.

cerrar*, (se·rrâr´) *va.* and *vn.* to close, to shut; to obstruct, to block off *(impedir la entrada);* to lock *(con cerradura);* to shut up, to wall in *(tapar);* to seal *(una carta);* to bring to an end, to close *(terminar);* **— una operación,** to close a transaction, to arrange a deal; **—se,** to close ranks *(un batallón);* to persist.

cerrero, ra, (se·rre´ro, râ) *adj.* running wild; **caballo —,** unbroken horse, bronco.

cerril, (se·rrēl´) *adj.* mountainous, rough; untamed *(ganado).*

cerro, (se´rro) *m.* hill; neck *(del animal);* backbone *(espinazo);* **en —,** bareback.

cerrojo, (se·rro´ho) *m.* bolt, latch.

certamen, (ser·tâ´men) *m.* literary contest.

certero, ra, (ser·te´ro, râ) *adj.* certain, sure; well-aimed, accurate *(en el tiro).*

certeza, (ser·te´sâ) *f.* certainty, assurance.

certidumbre, (ser·tē·thūm´bre) *f.* certainty,

certitude.

certificación, (ser·tē·fē·kä·syon´) f. certification.

certificado, (ser·tē·fē·kä´tho) m. certificate; —, da, adj. certified; registered *(una carta)*.

certificar, (ser·tē·fē·kär´) va. to certify, to affirm; to register *(una carta)*.

cerval (ser·väl´) or cervario, ria, (ser·vä´r·yo, ryä) adj. deer-like.

cervato, (ser·vä´to) m. fawn.

cervecería, (ser·ve·se·rē´ä) f. brewery.

cervecero, (ser·ve·se´ro) m. brewer; —, ra, adj. fond of beer.

cerveza, (ser·ve´sä) f. beer.

cerviz, (ser·vēs´) f. (anat.) cervix, nape of the neck; doblar or bajar la —, to humble oneself.

cesación, (se·sä·syon´) f. cessation, ceasing, pause, discontinuation.

cesante, (se·sän´te) m. dismissed public official; —, adj. jobless, out of a job.

cesar, (se·sär´) vn. to cease, to quit, to stop.

cesáreo, rea, (se·sä´re·o, re·ä) adj. Caesarean; operación —rea, Caesarean section.

cesión, (se·syon´) f. cession, transfer.

cesionario, ria, (se·syo·nä´ryo, ryä) n. assignee, transferee.

cesionista, (se·syo·nēs´tä) m. and f. assignor, transferor.

césped, (ses´peth) m. grass, lawn.

cesta, (ses´tä) f. basket; scoop *(del pelotari)*.

cestero, ra, (ses·te´ro, rä) n. basketmaker.

cesto, (ses´to) m. large basket; cestus *(de pugilista)*.

cetrino, na, (se·trē´no, nä) adj. citrine; jaundiced *(de rostro); (fig.)* melancholy, somber.

cetro, (se´tro) m. scepter.

cf: costo de flete, freight cost; caballo de fuerza, h.p. horsepower; confesor, confessor.

cg.: centigramo, cg. centigram.

Cía.: Compañía, Co. Company. cía, (sē´ä) f. hip bone.

cianosis, (syä·no´ses) f. (med.) cyanosis.

cianotipia, (syä·no·tē´pyä) f. blueprint; copiar a la —, to blueprint.

ciática, (syä´tē·kä) f. (med.) sciatica.

cibernética, (sē·ver·ne´tē·kä) f. cybernetics.

cicatriz, (sē·kä·trēs´) f. scar.

ciclismo, (sē·klēz´mo) m. bicycling.

ciclista, (sē·klēs´tä) m. and f. cyclist, bicyclist.

ciclo, (sē´klo) m. cycle.

ciclón, (sē·klon´) m. cyclone.

ciclotrón, (sē·klo·tron´) m. cyclotron.

cicuta, (sē·sü´tä) f. (bot.) hemlock.

cidra, (sē´thrä) f. citron.

cidro, (sē´thro) m. citron tree.

ciego, ga, (sye´go, gä) adj. blind; —, n. blind person; a —gas, blindly; vuelo a —gas, blind flying.

cielo, (sye´lo) m. sky, heaven; climate, weather; — de la cama, bed canopy; — de la boca, roof of the mouth, palate; — máximo, (avi.) ceiling.

ciempiés, (syem·pyes´) m. centipede.

cien, (syen´) adj. one hundred (used before a noun).

ciencia, (syen´syä) f. science; —s físicas, physical science; a — cierta, with certainty; hombre de —, scientist.

cieno, (sye´no) m. mud, mire.

científicamente, (syen·tē·fē·kä·men´te) adv. scientifically.

científico, ca, (syen·tē´fē·ko, kä) adj. scientific; m. scientist.

ciento, (syen´to) adj. one hundred; —, m. a hundred; por —, per cent; tanto por —, percentage.

cierne, (syer´ne) m. act of blossoming; en —, in blossom; (fig.) just beginning.

cierre, (sye´rre) m. closing; — relámpago, zipper; — de los libros, (com.) closing of the books.

cierto, ta, (syer´to, tä) adj. certain; confident, sure *(seguro);* noticias —s, definite news; por — to, certainly.

cierva, (syer´vä) f. (zool.) hind.

ciervo, (syer´vo) m. deer, stag; — volante, stag beetle.

c.i.f.: costo, seguro y flete, c.i.f. (com.) cost, insurance, and freight.

cifra, (sē´frä) f. cipher, number *(número);* abbreviation *(abreviatura);* monogram *(monograma);* code *(escritura secreta)*.

cifrado, da, (sē·frä´tho, thä) adj. dependent; — en, dependent upon.

cifrar, (sē·frär´) va. to write in code, to code; to abridge *(resumir);* — la esperanza en, to place one's hope in.

cigarra, (sē·gä´rrä) f. cicada, locust.

cigarrera, (se·gä·rre´rä) f. humidor; cigarette case *(para cigarrillos)*.

cigarrero, ra, (sē·gä·rre´ro, rä) m. cigar maker.

cigarrillo, (sē·gä·rrē´yo) m. cigarette.

cigarro, (sē·gä´rro) m. cigar; cigarette *(de papel)*.

cigarrón, (sē·gä·rron´) m. grasshopper.

cigüeña, (sē·gwe´nyä) f. (orn.) stork; (mech.) crank.

â arm, e they, ē bē, o fore, ū blūe, b bad, ch chip, d day, f fat, g go, h hot, k kid, 1 let

cigüeñal, (sē·gwe·nyâl´) m. crankshaft.

cilantro (sē·lân´tro) or culantro, (kū·lân´tro) m. (bot.) coriander.

cilicio, (sē·lē´syo) m. sackcloth.

cilíndrico, ca, (sē·lēn´drē·ko, kâ) adj. cylindncal.

cilindro, (sē·lēn´dro) m. cylinder.

cima, (sē´mâ) f. summit, peak, top.

cimborio (sēm·bo´ryo) or cimborrio, (sēm·bo´rryo) m. cupola.

cimbra, (sēm´brâ) f. (arch.) intrados.

cimbrar (sēm·brâr´) or cimbrear, (sēm·bre·âr´) va. to swing, to shake, to sway; to bend (doblar); — a alguno, to give someone a beating.

cimentado, (sē·men·tâ´tho) m. refinement of gold.

cimentar*, (sē·men·târ´) va. to lay the foundation of; to found, to establish (fundar); (fig.) to affirm; (min.) to refine.

cimera, (sē·me´râ) f. crest.

cimiento, (se·myen´to) m. (fig.) foundation, base; —s, pl. (arch.) foundation.

cinc, (sēngk) m. zinc.

cincel, (sēn·sel´) m. chisel.

cincelar, (sēn·se·lâr´) va. to chisel.

cinco, (sēng´ko) adj. and m. five.

cincuenta, (sēng·kwen´tâ) m. and adj. fifty.

cincha, (sēn´châ) f. girth, cinch.

cinchar, (sēn·châr´) va. to girth.

cine (sē´ne) or cinematógrafo, (se·ne·mâ·to´grâ·fo) m. motion-picture projector (aparato); movie theater (sala); — sonoro, sound motion-picture projector.

cinematografia, (sē·ne·mâ ·to·grâ·fē´â) f. cinematography.

cinescopio, (sē·nes·ko´pyo) m. kinescope.

cinética, (sē·ne´tē·kâ) f. kinetics.

cínico, ca, (sē´nē· ko, kâ) adj. cynical.

cinta, (sēn´tâ) f. ribbon, band; — de medir, tape measure; — de teletipo, (com.) ticker tape; — trasportadora, conveyor belt.

cintillo, (sēn·tē´yo) m. hatband.

cinto, (sēn´to) m. belt, girdle.

cintura, (sēn·tū´râ) f. waist; belt (ceñidor).

cinturón, (sēn·tū·ron´) m. belt; — salvavidas, life belt; — de seguridad, safety belt; — Van Allen de radiación, Van Allen radiation belt.

ciprés, (sē·pres´) m. cypress tree.

circo, (sēr´ko) m. circus.

circuito, (sēr·kwē´to) m. circuit; hookup, network (de comunicaciones).

circulación, (sēr·kū·lâ·syon´) f. circulation; traffic (del tráfico).

circular, (sēr·kū·lâr´) adj. circular, round; carta —, circular letter; —, va. and vn. to circulate.

círculo, (sēr´kū·lo) m. circle; circumference (circumferencia); sphere, province (extensión); club (sociedad).

circuncidar, (sēr·kūn·sē·thâr´) va. to circumcise.

circuncisión, (sēr·kūn·sē·syon´) f. circumcision.

circundar, (sēr·kūn·dâr´) va. to surround, to encircle.

circunferencia, (sēr·kūm·fe·ren´syâ) f. circumference.

circunnavegar, (sēr·kūn·nâ·ve·gâr´) va. to circumnavigate.

circunscribir*, (sēr·kūns·krē·vēr´) va. to circumscribe.

circunspecto, ta, (sēr·kūns·pek´to, ta) adj. circumspect, cautious.

circunstancia, (sēr·kūns·tân´syâ) f. circumstance.

circunstancial, (sēr ·kūns·tân·syâl´) adj. circumstantial.

circunstante, (sēr·kūns·tân´te) adj. surrounding, attending; —s, m. pl. bystanders, audience.

circunvalar, (sēr·kūm·bâ·lâr´) va. to surround, to encircle.

circunvecino, na, (sēr·kūm·be·sē´no, nâ) adj. neighboring, adjacent.

cirio, (sē´ryo) m. wax candle.

ciruela, (sē·rwe´lâ) f. plum; — seca or — pasa, prune.

ciruelo, (sē·rwe´lo) m. plum tree.

cirugía, (sē·rū·hē´â) f. surgery.

cirujano, (sē·rū·hâ´no) m. surgeon.

cisco, (sēs´ko) m. coal dust; (coll.) hubbub, row.

cisne, (sēz´ne) m. swan; (fig.) outstanding poet or musician.

cisquero, (sēs·ke´ro) m. coal-dust dealer; pounce bag (muñequilla).

cisterna, (sēs·ter´nâ) f. cistern, tank, reservoir.

cita, (sē´tâ) f. date, appointment; citation, quotation (nota).

citación, (sē·tâ·syon´) f. summons, citation.

citado, da, (sē·tâ´tho, thâ) adj. mentioned, quoted.

citar, (sē·tar´) va. to make an appointment with; to call together, to convoke (convocar); to cite, to quote (alegar); (law) to summon, to cite.

cítara, (sē´tâ·râ) f. zither; cithara (lira).

cítrico, ca, (sē´trē·ko, kâ) adj. citric.

ciudad, (syū·thâth´) f. city; — natal, city of

birth, home town.

ciudadanía, (syū·thâ·thâ·nē´â) f. citizenship.

ciudadano, na, (syū·thâ·thá´no, nâ) n. citizen; —, adj. civic, city.

ciudadela, (syū·thâ·the´lâ) f. citadel.

cívico, ca, (sē´vē·ko, kâ) adj. civic.

civil, (sē·vēl´) adj. civil; polite, courteous (sociable).

civilización, (sē·vē·lē·sâ·syon´) f. civilization.

civilizador, ra, (sē·vē·lē·sâ·thor´, râ) adj. civilizing.

civilizar, (sē·vē·lē·sâr´) va. to civilize.

civismo, (sē·vēz´mo) m. patriotism.

cizaña, (sē·sá´nyâ) f. (bot.) darnel; bad influence, rotten apple (lo que daña); unrest, disagreement (disensión); meter —, to sow discord.

clamar, (klâ·mâr´) vn. to cry out, to call out.

clamor, (klâ·mor´) m. clamor, outcry; death knells (de campanas).

clamoroso, sa, (klâ·mo·ro´so, sâ) adj. clamorous; éxito —, howling success.

clan, (klân) m. clan.

clandestino, na, (klân·des·tē´no, nâ) adj. clandestine, secret, concealed.

clara, (klâ´râ) f. egg white; brief letup in the rain (de la lluvia).

claraboya, (klâ·râ·vo´yâ) f. skylight (en el techo); bull´s-eye.

clarear, (klâ·re·âr´) vn. to dawn; to clear up (el tiempo); —se, to be transparent.

clarete (klâ·re´te) or vino —, m. claret wine.

claridad, (klâ·rē·thâth´) f. clearness, clarity.

clarificar, (klâ·rē·fē·kâr´) va. to illuminate, to brighten; to clarify, to clear up (aclarar).

clarín, (klâ·rēn´) m. bugle, trumpet; trumpeter (el que toca).

clarinete, (klâ·rē·ne´te) m. clarinet; clarinet player (músico).

clarividencia, (klâ·rē·vē·then´syâ) f. clairvoyance.

claro, ra, (klâ´ro, râ) adj. clear; bright (luminoso); light (de color); thin (ralo); evident, obvious (evidente); poner en —ro, to set right; —, m. opening (abertura); space (espacio); ¡—ro! interj. of course!

clase, (klâ´se) f. class; classroom (aula); kind (especie); — acomodada, well-to-do, wealthy class; — culta, intelligentsia, cultured class; — media, middle class.

clásico, ca, (klâ´sē·ko, kâ) adj. classical, classic.

clasificación, (klâ·sē·fē·kâ· syon´) f. classification.

clasificar, (klâ·sē·fē·kâr´) va. to classify, to class, to put in order.

claustro, (klâ´ūs·tro) m. cloister.

cláusula, (klâ´ū·sū·lâ) f. clause.

clausura, (klâū·sū´râ) f. cloister (recinto); cloistered life (vida religiosa); vows of seclusion (obligación); closing (cierre).

clausurar, (klâū·sū·râr´) va. to close, to suspend operation of.

clavado, da. (klâ·vâ´tho, thâ) adj. exact precise (fijo); a perfect fit, well-suited (pintiparado); just like, very similar (parecido); dive (natación).

clavar, (klâ·vâr´) va. to drive in, to stick (introducir); to nail (asegurar); (fig.) to cheat, to deceive (engañar); — la mirada en, — la vista en, to stare at, to fix one´s gaze on.

clave, (klâ´ve) f. key; (mus.) clef; palabra —, key word; —, m. harpsichord, clavichord.

clavel, (klâ·vel´) m. (bot.) pink, carnation.

clavicordio, (klâ·vē·kor´thyo) m. clavichord, harpsichord.

clavícula, (klâ·vē´kū·lâ) f. (anat.) clavicle, collarbone.

clavija, (klâ·vē´hâ) f. pin; (elec.) plug; (mus.) peg.

clavo, (klâ´vo) m. nail; corn (callo); — de olor, — de especia, clove.

claxon, (klâk´son) m. (Mex.) auto horn.

clemencia, (kle·men´syâ) f. clemency, mercy.

cleptomania, (klep·to·mâ·nē´â) f. kleptomania.

cleptómano, na, (klep·to´mâ·no, nâ) adj. and n. kleptomaniac.

clerical, (kle·rē·kâl´) adj. clerical, pertaining to the clergy.

clérigo, (kle´rē·go) m. clergyman.

clero, (kle´ro) m. clergy.

cliente, (klyen´te) m. and f. client, customer.

clientela, (klyen·te´lâ) f. clientele, patronage.

clima, (klē´mâ) m. climate; — artificial, air conditioning.

climatérico, ca, (klē·mâ·te´rē·ko, kâ) adj. climacteric.

climático, ca, (klē·má´tē·ko, kâ) adj. climatic.

climatológico, ca, (klē·mâ·to·lo´hē·ko, kâ) adj. climatological.

clínica, (klē´nē·kâ) f. clinic.

clínico, ca, (klē´nē·ko, kâ) *adj.* clinical.

clíper, (klē´per) *m.* clipper.

clisé, (klē·se´) (print.) plate, cut.

cloaca, (klo·â´kâ) *f.* sewer.

cloquear, (klo·ke·âr´) *vn.* to cluck.

cloqueo, (klo·ke´o) *m.* cluck, clucking.

cloquera, (klo·ke´râ) *f.* brooding time.

cloramfenicol, (klo·râm·fe·nē·kol´) *m.* chloramphenicol.

cloro, (klo´ro) *m.* (chem) chlorine.

clorofila, (klo·ro·fē´lâ) *f.* chlorophyll.

cloroformo, (klo·ro·for´mo) *m.* chloroform.

cloromicetina, (klo·ro·mē·se·tē´nâ) *f.*(marca registrada) Chloromycetin (tm).

cloruro, (klo·rū´ro) *m.* (chem.) chloride.

club, (klūv) *m.* club, association.

clueca, (klwe´kâ) *adj.* brooding; —, *f.* brooder.

clueco, ca, (klwe´ko, kâ) *adj.* (coll.) decrepit.

cm. or c/m: centímetro, cm. centimeter.

Co.: Compañía, Co. Company

c/o: a cargo de, c/o or c.o. in care of.

coacción, (ko·âk·syon´) *f.* coaction, compulsion.

coadyutor (ko·âth·yū·tor´) or coadjutor, (ko·âth·hū·tor´) *m.* coadjutor.

coadyuvar, (ko·âth·yū·vâr´) *va.* to help, to assist.

coagular, (ko·â·gū·lâr´) *va.* and *vr.* to coagulate, to curd.

coágulo, (ko·â´gū·lo) *m.* blood clot *(de sangre);* coagulum, clot.

coalición, (ko·â·lē·syon´) *f.* coalition, confederacy.

coartación, (ko·âr·tâ·syon´). *f.* limitation, restriction.

coartada, (ko·âr·tâ´thâ) *f.* (law) alibi.

coartar, (ko·âr·târ´) *va.* to limit, to restrict, to restrain.

coate, ta, (ko·â´te, tâ) *n.* and *adj. (Max.)* twin; —, *n.* chum pal, close friend.

cobarde, (ko·vâr´the) *adj.* cowardly, timid; —, *n.* and *f.* coward.

cobardía, (ko·vâr·thē´â) *f.* cowardice.

cobayo, (ko·vâ´yo) *m.* guinea pig.

cobertizo (ko·ver·tē´so) *m.* shed; — para automóvil, carport.

cobija, (ko·vē´hâ) *f.* gutter tile *(teja);* covering *(cubierta);* (Max.) blanket *(manta);* (Sp. Am.) thatch *(de paja).*

cobijar, (ko·vē·hâr´) *va.* to cover; (fig.) to shelter, to protect; (Sp. Am.) to thatch, to cover with thatch *(con paja).*

cobra, (ko´vrâ) *f.* (zool.) cobra.

cobrador, (ko·vrâ·thor´) *m.* collector; conductor *(de tranvía).*

cobranza,(ko·vrân´sâ)*f.* recovery; collection.

cobrar, (ko·vrâr´) *va.* to collect *(una cantidad);* to recover *(recuperar);* to charge *(un precio);* to cash *(un cheque);* to acquire *(adquirir);* to pull in *(una soga);* — ánimo, to take courage; — fuerzas, to gain strength; — impuestos, to tax; letras or efectos a —, bills receivable.

cobre, (ko´vre) *m.* copper; set of copper kitchenware *(batería de cocina);* moneda de —, copper coin.

cóbrese al entregar,(ko´vre· se·âl·en·tre·gâr´) cash on delivery, C.O.D.

cobrizo, za (ko·vrē´so, sâ) *adj.* coppery.

cobro, (ko´vro) *m.* collection; presentar al —, to present for payment or collection.

coca, (ko´kâ) *f.* (bot.) coca; (coll.) head.

cocaína, (ko·kâ·ē´nâ) *f.* cocaine.

cocción, (kok·syon´) *f.* cooking.

coceador, ra, (ko·se·â·thor´, râ) *adj.* kicking, apt to kick.

cocear, (ko·se·âr´) *vn.* to kick; (fig.) to resist, to balk.

cocer*, (ko·ser´) *va.* to boil *(el té);* to cook; to bake *(el pan);* —, *vn.* to boil; to ferment; —se, to suffer for a long time.

cocido, da, (ko·sē´tho, thâ) *adj.* cooked; boiled; (fig.) skilled, experienced *(experimentado);* —, *m.* Spanish stew.

cociente, (ko·syen´te) *m.* quotient.

cocimiento, (ko·sē·myen´to) *m.* cooking; first bath *(de la lana).*

cocina, (ko·sē´nâ) *f.* kitchen; cuisine *(arte);* — económica, cooking range.

cocinar, (ko·sē·nâr´) *va.* to cook; —, *vn.* to meddle.

cocinero, ra, (ko·sē·ne´ro, râ) *n.* cook.

cocinilla, (co·sē·nē´yâ) *f.* kitchenette; chafing dish *(infiernillo).*

coco, (ko´ko) *m.* coconut *(fruto);* coconut palm *(árbol);* bogeyman *(fantasma);* agua de —, coconut water; hacer —s, to flirt.

cocodrilo, (ko·ko·thrē´lo) *m.* crocodile.

coctel, (kok·tel´) *m.* cocktail.

cocuyo (ko·kū´yo) or cucuyo, (kū·kū´yo) *m.* firefly.

coche, (ko´che) *m.* coach, carriage; automobile, car *(automóvil);* — de alquiler, cab; — cama, sleeping car; — comedor, diner; — directo, through coach; — fumador, smoking car; — restaurante, dining car; — salón, parlor car.

cochecillo, (ko·che·sē´yo) *m.* small carriage; — de niño, baby carriage.

cochera, (ko·che´râ) *f.* coach house *(para carruajes);* garage.

cochina, (ko·chē´nâ) *f.* sow.

m met, n not, p pot, r very, rr (none), s so, t toy, th with, v eve, w we, y yes, z zero

cochinilla, (ko·chē·nē´yâ) f. wood louse; cochineal *(colorante)*.

cochino, na, (ko·chē´no, nâ) *adj.* dirty, nasty, filthy, messy; —, *m.* pig.

coctelera, (kok·te·le´ra) f. cocktail shaker.

codazo, (ko·thâ´so) *m.* blow with the elbow.

codear, (ko·the·âr´) *vn.* to elbow; —se con, to hobnob with.

códice, (ko´thē·se) *m.* codex.

codicia, (ko·thē´syâ) f. covetousness, greed, cupidity.

codiciar, (ko·thē·syâr´) *va.* to covet, to desire eagerly.

codicioso, sa, (ko·thē·syo´so, sâ) *adj.* greedy, covetous; diligent, laborious *(hacendoso)*.

código, (ko´thē·go) *m.* code.

codo, (ko´tho) *m.* elbow; dar de —, to elbow; charlar hasta por los —s, to talk a blue streak.

codo, da, (ko´tho, thâ) *adj.* (Mex. coll.) stingy, cheap.

codorniz, (ko·thor·nēs´) f. (orn.) quail.

coeficiente, (ko·e·fē·syen´te) *m.* coefficient; — de seguridad, safety factor.

coerción, (ko·er·syon´) f. coercion, restraint.

coercitivo, va, (ko·er·sē·tē´vo, vâ) *adj.* coercive.

coexistencia, (ko·ek·sēs·ten´syâ) f. coexistence.

coexistir, (ko·ek·sēs·tēr´) *vn.* to coexist.

cofia, (ko´fyâ) f. hair net.

cofre, (ko´fre) *m.* coffer, chest.

cogedor, (ko·he·thor´) *m.* collector, gatherer; dustbin *(cajón)*; dustpan *(cucharón)*.

coger, (ko·her´) *va.* to catch, to get hold of, to grab *(asir)*; to occupy *(ocupar)*; to gather *(recoger)*; to catch by surprise *(sorprender)*.

cogollo, (ko·go´yo) *m.* heart *(de la lechuga)*; shoot *(brote)*.

cogote, (ko·go´te) *m.* nape of the neck.

cogulla, (ko·gū´ yâ) f. cowl.

cohabitar, (ko·â·vē·târ´) *vn.* to cohabit, to live together.

cohecho, (ko·e´cho) *m.* bribery; (agr.) plowing season.

coheredero, ra, (ko·e·re·the´ro, râ) *n.* joint heir or heiress.

coherencia, (ko·e·ren´syâ) f. coherence.

coherente, (ko·e·ren´te) *adj.* coherent; cohesive *(cohesivo)*.

cohesión, (ko·e·syon´) f. cohesion.

cohete, (ko·e´te) *m.* skyrocket *(artificio de fuego)*; rocket; — espacial, space rocket;

— de ignición múltiple, multi-stage rocket; — impulsor, booster rocket; — de señales, (avi.) flare; — de sondeo, probe rocket.

cohibir, (ko·ē·vēr´) *va.* to restrain, to curb.

cohorte, (ko·or´te) f. cohort; — de males, series of misfortunes, streak of bad luck.

coincidencia, (ko·ēn·sē·then´syâ) f. coincidence.

coincidente, (ko·ēn·sē·then´te) *adj.* coincident.

coincidir, (ko·ēn·sē·thēr´) *vn.* to coincide.

coito, (ko´ē·to) *m.* coitus.

cojear, (ko·he·âr´) *vn.* to halt, to limp; to wobble *(un mueble)*; (coll.) to get off the straight and narrow.

cojera, (ko·he´râ) f. lameness, limping.

cojín, (ko·hēn´) *m.* cushion.

cojinete, (ko·hē·ne´te) *m.* (mech.) bearing; small cushion; — de bolas, ball bearing; — de rodillos, roller bearing.

cojo, ja, (ko´ho, hâ) *adj.* lame, crippled.

cojudo, da, (ko·hū´tho, thâ) *adj.* not gelded, not castrated.

cok, (kok) *m.* coke.

col, (kol) f. cabbage.

cola, (ko´lâ) f. tail; train *(de vestido)*; line *(hilera de personas)*; glue *(pasta)*; — de pescado, isinglass; a la —, behind; hacer —, to stand in line.

colaboración, (ko·lâ·vo·râ·syon´) f. collaboration.

colaborar, (ko·lâ·vo·râr´) *vn.* to collaborate.

colación, (ko·lâ·syon´) f. collation *(comparación)*; light lunch, snack *(merienda)*; traer a —, to present as proof.

coladera, (ko·lâ·the´râ) f. strainer, colander.

coladero, (ko·lâ·the´ro) *m.* colander; narrow passage *(paso estrecho)*.

colador, (ko·lâ·thor´) *m.* colander, strainer.

colapso, (ko·lâp´so) *m.* (med.) prostration, collapse.

colar*, (ko·lâr´) *va.* to strain; to confer *(beneficio o grado)*; to pass off *(en virtud de engaño)*; —, *vi.* to squeeze through; —se, to crash, to sneak in.

colateral, (ko·lâ·te·râl´) *adj.* collateral.

colcha, (kol´châ) f. bedspread, quilt.

colchón, (kol·chon´) *m.* mattress; — de muelles, spring mattress; — de pluma, feather mattress; — de viento, air mattress.

colección, (kol·lek·syon´) f. collection.

colecta, (ko·lek´tâ) f. assessment *(de tributos)*; offering *(caritativa)*; collect *(oración)*.

colectar, (ko·lek·târ´) va. to collect.
colectividad, (ko·lek·tē·vē·thâth´) f. collectivity.
colectivismo, (ko·lek·tē·vēz´mo) m. collectivism.
colectivista, (ko·lek·tē·vēs´tâ) m. collectivist.
colectivo, va, (ko·lek·tē´vo, vâ) adj. collective, aggregated; contrato —, group contract; sociedad —va, general partnership.
colector, (ko·lek·tor´) m. collector, gatherer; (elec.) commutator.
colega, (ko·le´gâ) m. and f. colleague.
colegial, (ko·le·hyâl´) m. collegian, student; —, adj. collegiate, college.
colegiala, (ko·le·hyâ´lâ) f. woman collegian.
colegio, (ko·le´hyo) m. college; private school, academy (escuela).
cólera, (ko´le·râ) f. anger, rage, fury; montar en —, to fly into a rage; —, m. (med.) cholera.
colérico, ca, (ko·le´rē·ko, kâ) adj. choleric; suffering from cholera (enfermo de cólera).
colesterol, (ko·les·te·rol´) m. (med.) cholesterol.
coleta, (ko·le´tâ) f. queue; postscript (a un escrito).
coleto, (ko·le´to) m. buff jacket; (coll.) insides, inner man; deck decir para su —, to say to oneself.
colgadero, (kol·gâ·the´ro) m. hook; clothesline
colgadizo, (kol·gâ·thē´so) m. shed; —, za, adj. hanging, suspended.
colgadura, (kol·gâ·thū´râ) f. hangings.
colgante, (kol·gân´te) adj. suspended, hanging; puente —, suspension bridge.
colgar*, (kol·gâr´) va. to hang, to suspend; to decorate with hangings (adornar); —, vn. to be suspended.
colibrí, (ko·lē·vrē´) m. hummingbird.
cólico, (ko´lē·ko) m. colic.
coliflor, (ko·lē·flor´) f. cauliflower.
colilla, (ko·lē´yâ) f. cigarette butt.
colina, (ko·lē´nâ) f. hill.
colinabo, (ko·lē·nâ´vo) m. turnip.
colindar, (ko·lēn·dâr´) vn. to be contiguous; — con, to be adjacent to.
coliseo, (ko·lē·se´o) m. coliseum.
colmar, (kol·mâr´) va. to heap up, to fill up; — con, (fig.) to shower with.
colmena, (kol·me´nâ) f. beehive.
colmenar, (kol·me·nâr´) m. apiary.
colmillo, (kol·mē´yo) m. eyetooth; tusk (del elefante); tener—, to be sly.
colmo, (kol´mo) m. overflowing; (fig.)

height, high point; eso es el —, that is the limit; a —, plentifully.
colocación, (ko·lo·kâ·syon´) f. placement (acción); situation, position.
colocar, (ko·lo·kâr´) va. to situate, to place; — dinero, to invest money.
colon, (ko´lon) m. (anat.) colon, large intestine.
Colón, (ko·lon´) Columbus.
colón, (ko·lon´) m. monetary unit of Costa Rica and El Salvador.
colonia, (ko·lo´nyâ) f. colony; (Cuba) sugar-cane field (de azúcar); (Mex.) subdivision, neighborhood (barrio).
colonial, (ko·lo·nyâl´) adj. colonial.
colonización, (ko·lo·nē·sâ·syon´) f. colonization.
colonizar, (ko·lo·nē·sâr´) va. to colonize.
colono, (ko·lo´no) m. colonist; tenant farmer (labrador).
coloquio, (ko·lo´kyo) m. colloquy; chat, conversation (plática).
color, (ko·lor´) m. color; rouge (colorete); so —, under pretext; este — destiñe, this color fades.
colorado,da,(ko·lo·râ´tho, thâ)adj. ruddy, red.
colorante, (ko·lo·rân´te) m. coloring.
colorar, (ko·lo·râr´) va. to color; to tint, to dye (teñir).
colorear, (ko·lo·re·âr´) va. to color; (fig.) to palliate, to cover up (disimular); —, vn. to grow red.
colorete, (ko·lo·re´te) m. rouge.
colorido, (ko·lo·rē´tho) m. coloring; pretext, pretense (pretexto).
colorín, (ko·lo·rēn´) m. (orn.) linnet; bright color.
colosal, (ko·lo·sâl´) adj. colossal, great.
coloso, (ko·lo´so) m. colossus.
columbrar, (ko·lūm·brâr´) va. to glimpse, to barely make out; (fig.) to guess.
columna, (ko·lūm´nâ) f. column.
columnata, (ko·lūm·nâ´tâ) f. colonnade.
columpiarse, (ko·lūm·pyâr´se) vr. to swing to and fro.
columpio, (ko·lūm´pyo) m. swing.
collado, (ko·yâ´tho) m. hillock.
collar, (ko·yâr´) m. necklace (adorno); collar.
coma, (ko´mâ) f. comma; —, m. (med.) coma.
comadre, (ko·mâ´thre) f. midwife (partera); godmother of one´s child (madrina); close friend, crony (amiga).
comadreja, (ko·mâ·thre´hâ) f. weasel.
comadrería, (ko·mâ·thre·rē´â) f. gossiping.
comadrona, (ko·mâ·thro´nâ) f. midwife.

comandancia, (ko·mân·dân´syâ) f. command.

comandante, (ko·mân·dân´te) m. commander, chief; major (de batallón).

comandar, (ko·mân·dâr´) va. (mil.) to command.

comandita, (ko·mân·dē´tâ) f. (com.) silent partnership.

comanditario, ria, (ko·mân·dē·tâ´ryo, ryâ) adj. relating to a silent partnership; socio —, silent partner.

comando, (ko·mân´do) m. (mil.) commando.

comarca, (ko·mâr´kâ) f. territory, district, region.

comatoso, sa, (ko·mâ·to´so, sâ) adj. (med.) comatose.

combar, (kom·bâr´) va. to bend; —se, to warp, to twist.

combate, (kom·bâ´te) m. combat, struggle; (fig.) conflict; fuera de —, out of action; (fig.) out of the running; aeroplano de—, fighter plane.

combatidor, (kom·bâ·tē·thor´) m. combatant.

combatiente, (kom·bâ·tyen´te) m. combatant; no —, non-combatant.

combatir, (kom·bâ·tēr´) va. and vn. to combat, to struggle, to fight.

combinación, (kom·bē·nâ·syon´) f. combination.

combinar, (kom·bē·nâr´) va. and vr. to combine.

combo, ba, (kom´bo, bâ) adj. bent, twisted, warped; —, m. cask stand.

combustible, (kom·būs·tē´vle) adj. combustible; —, m. fuel; — de alta potencia, exotic fuel.

combustión, (kom·būs·tyon´) f. combustion.

comebolas, (ko·me·vo´lâs) m. and f. (Cuba) one who believes everything he hears.

comedia, (ko·me´thyâ) f. comedy, play.

comedianta, (ko·me·thyân´tâ) f. actress, comedienne.

comediante, ta, (ko·me·thyân´te, tâ) n. actor, comedian.

comedido, da, (ko·me·thē´tho, thâ) adj. polite, courteous.

comedirse*, (ko·me·thēr´se) vr. to restrain or control oneself; — a, to offer to, to be willing to.

comedor, ra, (ko·me·thor´, râ) n. eater; —, m. dining room.

comején, (ko·me·hen´) m. white ant, termite.

comendador, (ko·men·dâ·thor´) m. knight commander (de orden militar); com-

mander.

comentador, ra, (ko·men·tâ·thor´, râ) n. commentator.

comentar, (ko·men·târ´) va. to comment on, to remark, to speak of.

comentario, (ko·men·tâ´ryo) m. comment, commentary.

comenzar*, (ko·men·sâr´) va. and vn. to commence, to begin.

comer, (ko·mer´) va. to eat; to eat away, to consume (gastar); to take (ajedrez y damas); —, vn. to have dinner; dar de —, to feed; —se, to skip over, to jump.

comercial, (ko·mer·syâl´) adj. commercial.

comerciante, (ko·mer·syân´te) m. trader, merchant, tradesman.

comerciar, (ko·mer·syâr´) va. to trade, to do business, to have dealings; — en, to deal in.

comercio, (ko·mer´syo) m. trade, commerce, business; communication, intercourse (comunicación); en el —, in the shops; junta de —, board of trade.

comestible, (ko·mes·tē´vle) adj. edible; —s, m. pl. foodstuffs, groceries, food; tienda de —s, grocery store.

cometa, (ko·me´tâ) m. comet; —, f. kite.

cometer, (ko·me·ter´) va. to commit; to entrust, to charge (encargar).

cometido, (ko·me·tē´tho) m. task, assignment.

comezón, (ko·me·son´) f. itch; (fig.) burning desire, fervent wish.

comicios, (ko·mē´syos) m. pl. election, voting.

cómico, ca, (ko´mē·ko, kâ) adj. comic, comical, funny; —, m. actor, comedian; —, f. actress, comedienne.

comida, (ko·mē´thâ) f. eating; food (alimento); meal (habitual); dinner (principal); — chatarra, junk food;— para llevar, take-out;— rápida, fast food.

comidilla, (ko·mē·thē´yâ) f. food and drink; talk of the town (objeto de conversación).

comienzo, (ko·myen´so) m. beginning.

comillas, (ko·mē´yâs) f. pl. quotation marks; entre —, in quotation marks.

comino, (ko·mē´no) m. cumin; no valer un —, to be absolutely worthless.

comisaría, (ko·mē·sâ·rē´â) f. commissariat (oficina); commissioner´s duties.

comisario, (ko·mē·sâ´ryo) m. commissary, deputy, commissioner; (Sp. Am.) police inspector (de policía).

comisión, (ko·mē·syon´) f. commission; errand (encargo); —, on commission.

comisionado, (ko·mē·syo·nâ´tho) m. commissioner.

comisionar, (ko·mē·syo·nâr´) va. to commission.

comisionista, (ko·mē·syo·nēs´tâ) m. commission agent, salesman on commission.

comité, (ko·mē·te´) m. committee.

comitiva, (ko·mē·tē´va) f. suite, retinue, cortege, followers.

como, (ko´mo) adv. and conj. (interr. cómo) as (lo mismo que); such as, like (tal como); almost (casi); how (de qué manera); why (por qué); — quiera que, whereas, inasmuch as; however, no matter how; ¿a cómo estamos? what is the date?

cómoda (ko´mo·thâ) f. chest of drawers.

comodidad, (ko·mo·thē·thâth´) f. comfort, ease, convenience; profit, interest (interés).

cómodo, da, (ko´mo·tho, thâ) adj. convenient, commodious, comfortable.

compacto, ta, (kom·pâk´to, tâ) adj. compact, close; (fig.) thick, dense (apiñado).

compadecer*, (kom·pâ·the·ser´) va. to pity, to sympathize with; —se de, to take pity on.

compadrar, (kom·pâ·thrâr´) vn. to become godfather to someone´s child; to become a close friend.

compadre, (kom·pâ´thre) m. godfather of one´s child (padrino); close friend, crony (amigo).

compaginar, (kom·pâ·hē·nâr´) va. (print.) to page; to put in order (ordenar).

compañero, ra, (kom·pâ·nye´ro, râ) n. companion, comrade; fellow, mate; — de cuarto roommate; — de destierro, fellow exile; — de viaje, traveling companion.

compañía, (kom·pâ·nyē´â) f. company.

comparable, (kom·pâ·râ´vle) adj. comparable.

comparación, (kom·pâ·râ·syon´) f. comparison.

comparar, (kom·pâ·râr´) va. to compare.

comparecer*, (kom·pâ·re·ser´) vn. to appear.

comparendo, (kom·pâ·ren´do) m. summons.

comparsa, (kom·pâr´sâ) m. and f. extra, walk-on, supernumerary; —, f. walk-ons, extras.

compartir, (kom·pâr·tēr´) va. to divide, to share.

compás, (kom·pâs´) m. pair of compasses; calipers; (mus.) measure, time; (naut.) compass; (fig.) rule, guide; — de cali-

bres, inside calipers; — de espesores, outside calipers.

compasión, (kom·pâ·syon´) f. compassion, pity.

compasivo, va, (kom·pâ·sē´vo, va) adj. compassionate.

compatible, (kom·pâ·tē´vle) adj. compatible.

compatriota, (kom·pâ·tryo´tâ) m. and f. fellow countryman, compatriot.

compeler, (kom·pe·ler´) va. to compel, to constrain.

compendiar, (kom·pen·dyâr´) va. to summarize.

compendio, (kom·pen´dyo) m. summary, compendium.

compendioso, sa, (kom·pen·dyo´so, sâ) adj. compendious, concise.

compensación, (kom·pen·sâ·syon´) f. compensation, recompense; casa de —, clearing house.

compensar, (kom·pen·sâr´) va. and vn. to compensate, to make amends, to recompense.

competencia, (kom·pe·ten´syâ) f. competition, rivalry; competence (aptitud).

competente, (kom·pe·ten´te) adj. competent; sufficient, adequate, just (propio).

competer, (kom·pe·ter´) vn. to be one´s due, to be incumbent on one, to be in one´s competence.

competidor, ra, (kom·pe·tē·thor´, râ) n. competitor, rival.

competir*, (kom·pe·tēr´) vn. to vie, to contend, to compete, to rival.

compilar, (kom·pē·lâr´) va. to compile.

compinche, (kom·pēn´che) m. (coll.) comrade, confidant, crony.

complacencia, (kom·plâ·sen´syâ) f. pleasure, complaisance.

complacer*, (kom·plâ·ser´) va. to please; — se, to be pleased, to be happy.

complaciente, (kom·plâ·syen´te) adj. pleasing, pleasurable; accommodating, complaisant (propenso a complacer).

complejidad, (kom·ple·hē·thâth´) f. complexity.

complejo, (kom·ple´ho) m. complex; —, ja, adj. complex, intricate.

complementario, ria, (kom·ple·men·tâ·ryo, ryâ) adj. complementary.

complemento, (kom·ple·men´to) m. complement; completion (plenitud); (gram.) object.

completar, (kom·ple·tar´) va. to complete.

completo, ta, (kom·ple´to, tâ) adj. complete; perfect, all-round (acabado); por —to, completely.

complexión, (kom·plek·syon´) f. constitution, physique.

complicación, (kom·plē·kâ·syon´) f. complication; complexity *(estado de complejo)*.

complicar, (kom·plē·kâr´) va. to complicate.

cómplice, (kom´plē·se) m. and f. accomplice.

complicidad, (kom·plē·sē·thâth´) f. complicity.

complot, (kom·plot´) m. plot, conspiracy.

componer*, (kom·po·ner´) va. to compose; (math.) to compound; to form, to make up *(formar);* to mend, to repair *(reparar);* to strengthen, to restore *(restaurar);* to prepare, to mix *(aderezar);* to adjust, to settle, to reconcile *(reconciliar);* to calm *(moderar);* —se, to make up, to put on makeup; —se de, to be composed of.

comportar, (kom·por·târ´) va. to suffer, to tolerate; —se. to behave, to comport oneself; —se bien, to behave well; —se mal, to behave badly.

composición, (kom·po·sē·syon´) f. composition; composure *(mesura);* adjustment, agreement *(ajuste).*

compositor, ra, (kom·po·sē·tor´, râ) n. composer; (print.) compositor.

compostura, (kom·pos·tū´râ) f. composition *(construcción);* mending, repair *(reparo);* neatness *(aseo);* agreement, adjustment *(convenio);* composure, circumspection *(mesura).*

compota, (kom·po´tâ) f. preserve, compote.

compra, (kom´prâ) f. purchase; day´s shopping *(para el gasto diario);* —s, pl. purchases; —s al contado, cash purchases; ir de —s, to go shopping.

comprador, ra, (kom·prâ·thor´, râ) n. buyer, purchaser.

comprar, (kom·prâr´) va. to buy, to purchase; — al contado, to buy for cash; — al crédito or al fiado, to buy on credit; — al por mayor (menor), to buy at wholesale (retail); — de ocasión, to buy secondhand.

comprender, (kom·pren·der´) va. to include, to contain, to comprise *(contener);* to comprehend, to understand *(entender).*

comprendido, da, (kom·pren·dē´tho, thâ) adj. including; understood.

comprensible, (kom·pren·sē´vle) adj. understanding, comprehensible.

comprensión, (kom·pren·syon´) f. comprehension, understanding.

comprensivo, va, (kom·pren·sē´vo, vâ) adj. comprehensive.

compresión, (kom·pre·syon´) f. compression, pressure.

compresor, (kom·pre·sor´) m. compressor.

comprimir, (kom·prē·mēr´) va. to compress, to condense; to repress, to restrain *(reprimir);* —se, to restrain oneself, to control oneself.

comprobación, (kom·pro·vâ·syon´) f. checking, verification.

comprobante, (kom·pro·vân´te) adj. proving; —, m. voucher, receipt.

comprobar*, (kom·pro·vâr´) va. to verify, to check, to confirm, to prove.

comprometedor, ra, (kom·pro·me·te·thor´, râ) adj. compromising.

comprometer, (kom·pro·me·ter´) va. to compromise; to oblige *(obligar);* to endanger, to risk *(exponer);* —se, to commit oneself, to envolve oneself.

compromiso, (kom·pro·mē´so) m. engagement *(esponsales);* compromise *(convenio);* pledge, commitment *(obligación);* compromising position *(embarazo).*

compuerta, (kom·pwer´tâ) f. floodgate, sluice; half door *(media puerta).*

compuesto, (kom·pwes´to) m. compound; —, ta, adj. compound, composed.

compulsión, (kom·pūl·syon´) f. compulsion.

compulsivo, va, (kom·pūl·sē´vo, vâ) adj. compulsive.

compulsorio, ria, (kom·pūl·so´ryo, ryâ) adj. compulsory.

compunción, (kom·pūn·syon´) f. compunction, remorse.

compungido, da, (kom·pūn·hē´tho, thâ) adj. having compunctions, remorseful.

computación, (kom·pū·tâ·syon´) f. computation.

computador, ra, (kom·pu·tâ·thor´, râ) n. computer; —ra digital, digital computer.

computar, (kom·pū·târ´) va. to compute.

cómputo, (kom´pū·to) m. computation, calculation.

comulgar, (ko·mūl·gâr´) va. to administer Communion to; —, vn. to take Communion.

común, (ko·mūn´) adj. common; acciones en —, common stock; de — acuerdo, by mutual consent; en —, jointly; poco —, unusual; por lo —, in general, generally; —, m. community, people; watercloset *(retrete).*

comuna, (ko·mū´nâ) f. town hall, municipality.

comunal, (ko·mū·nâl´) m. commonalty, common people; —, adj. community, communal.

comunicación, (ko·mū·nē·kâ·syon′) *f.* communication, message; — **radioeléctrica,** radio message.

comunicado, (ko·mū·nē·kâ′tho) *m.* communiqué.

comunicar, (ko·mū·nē·kâr′) *va.* and *vr.* to communicate.

comunicativo, va, (ko·mū·nē·kâ·te′vo, vâ) *adj.* communicative.

comunidad, (ko·mū·nē·thâth′) *f.* community.

comunión, (ko·mū·nyon′) (eccl.) Communion; communication, intercourse.

comunismo, (ko·mū·nēz′mo) *m.* communism.

comunista, (ko·mū·nēs′tâ) *m.* and *f.* communist.

comunistoide, (ko·mū·nēs·to′ē·the) *m.* (pol.) fellow traveler.

con, (kon) *prep.* with; despite *(a pesar de)*; — **que,** then, therefore; — **tal que,** on condition that; **dar** —, to find; **tratar** —, to do business with, to deal with.

conato, (ko·nâ′to) *m.* endeavor, effort *(esfuerzo)*; attempt *(intento)*.

concavidad, (kong·kâ·vē·thath′) *f.* concavity.

cóncavo, va, (kong′kâ·vo, va) *adj.* concave.

concebir*, (kon·se·vēr′) *va.* and *vn.* to conceive.

conceder, (kon·se·ther′) *va.* to grant, to concede.

concejal, (kon·se·hâl′) *m.* councilman, councilor.

concejo, (kon·se′ho) *m.* town council.

concentración, (kon·sen·trâ·syon′) *f.* concentration; **campo de** —, concentration camp.

concentrado, da, (kon·sen·trâ′tho, thâ) *adj.* concentrated.

concentrar, (kon·sen·trâr′) *va.* and *vr.* to concentrate.

concepción, (kon·sep·syon′) *f.* conception *(acción)*; idea, concept *(producto)*.

concepto, (kon·sep′to) *m.* concept, idea thought; judgment, opinion *(juicio)*; witticism *(agudeza)*; reason *(motivo)*; **por todos** —**s,** by and large.

conceptuar, (kon·sep·twâr′) *va.* to repute, to judge, to think.

conceptuoso, sa t (kon·sep·two′so, sâ) *adj.* keen, witty.

concerniente, (kon·ser·nyen′te) *adj.* concerning, relating.

concernir*, (kon·ser·nēr′) *vn.* to regard, to concern.

concertar*, (kon·ser·târ′) *va.* to concert; (mus.) to harmonize; to arrange, to settle on *(un negocio)*; to reconcile *(intenciones)*; to set *(un hueso)*; — *vn.* to agree, to be in accord.

concertina, (kon·ser·tē′nâ) *f.* concertina.

concertista, (kon·ser·tēs′tâ) *m.* and *f.* concert performer.

concesión, (kon·se·syon′) *f.* concession; grant *(otorgamiento)*.

concesionario, (kon·se·syo·nâ′ryo, ryâ) *n.* grantee.

conciencia, (kon·syen′syâ) *f.* conscience; awareness *(conocimiento)*.

concienzudo, da, (kon·syen·sū′tho, thâ) *adj.* conscientious.

concierto, (kon·syer′to) *m.* concert, agreement; (mus.) concert; **de** —, with one accord, in concert.

conciliación, (kon·sē·lyâ·syon′) *f.* conciliation, reconciliation.

conciliar, (kon·sē·lyâr′) *va.* to conciliate. to reconcile; —, *adj.* conciliar, council.

conciliatorio, ria, (kon·sē·lyâ·to′ryo, ryâ) *adj.* conciliatory

concilio, (kon·sē′lyo) *m.* (eccl.) council.

conciso, sa, (kon·sē′so, sâ) *adj.* concise, brief.

conciudadano, na, (kon·syū·thâ·thâ′no, nâ) *n.* fellow citizen, fellow countryman.

cónclave (kong′klâ·ve) or **conclave,** (kong·klâ′ve) *m.* conclave.

concluir*, (kong·klwēr′) *va.* to conclude; to convince *(convencer)*.

conclusión, (kong·klū·syon′) *f.* conclusion.

concluso, sa, (kong·klū′so, sâ) *adj.* closed, concluded.

concluyente, (kong·klū·yente) *adj.* conclusive.

concordancia, (kong·kor·thân′syâ) *f.* (gram.) agreement; (mus.) harmony; concord; —**s,** *pl.* concordance.

concordar*, (kong·kor·thâr′) *va.* to accord; —, *vn.* to agree.

concordia, (kong·kor′thyâ) *f.* concord, agreement; (mus.) harmony; **de** —, by common consent.

concretar, (kong·kre·târ′) *va.* to combine, to unite; to make concrete, to reduce to essentials *(reducir)*; —**se,** to limit oneself.

concreto, ta, (kong·kre′to, tâ) *adj.* concrete, definite; **en** —**to,** in short.

concubina, (kong·kū·vē′nâ) *f.* concubine, mistress.

concuñada, (kong·kū·nyâ′thâ) *f.* sister of one's brother-in-law or sister-in-law.

concuñado, (kong·kū·nyâ′tho) *m.* brother

of one's brother-in-law or sister-in-law.

concurrencia, (kong·kū·rren´syä) concurrence; coincidence *(simultaneidad);* gathering *(junta).*

concurrentes, (kong·kū·rren´tes) *m. pl.* those gathered, those assembled.

concurrido, da, (kong·kū·rrē´tho, thâ) *adj.* crowded, well attended.

concurrir, (kong·kū·rrēr´) *vn.* to concur; to assemble, to gather *(juntarse);* to participate, to take part *(en un concurso);* to coincide *(coincidir);* — **con,** to contribute, to give.

concurso, (kong·kūr´so) *m.* concourse, crowd, assembly; help, aid *(ayuda);* presence *(asistencia);* contest *(competencia);* — **aéreo,** air meet; — **de acreedores,** meeting of creditors; — **de belleza,** beauty contest; — **deportivo,** athletic meet.

concusión, (kong·kū·syon´) *f.* (med.) concussion; shake, shock.

concha, (kon´chä) *f.* shell; tortoise shell *(carey);* (theat.) prompter's box.

conchudo, da, (kon·chū´tho, thâ) *adj.* covered by a shell, shelled; (fig.) astute, cunning.

condado, (kon·dâ´tho) *m.* earldom, county.

conde, (kon´de) *m.* earl, count; gypsy chief *(de los gitanos).*

condecorar, (kon·de·ko·râr´) *va.* to decorate, to award a decoration.

condenable, (kon·de·nâ´vle) *adj.* condemnable.

condena, (kon·de´nä) *f.* condemnation.

condenar, (kon·de·nâr´) *va.* to condemn; to sentence *(pronunciar sentencia);* (eccl.) to damn; to board up, to close up *(cerrar);* **—se,** (eccl.) to be damned.

condensación, (kon·den·sâ·syon´) *f.* condensation.

condensador, (kon·den·sâ·thor´) *m.* condenser.

condensar, (kon·den·sâr´) *va.* and *vr.* to condense.

condesa, (kon·de´sä) *f.* countess.

condescendencia, (kon·des·sen·den´syä) *f.* affability, complaisance.

condescender*, (kon·des·sen·der´) *vn.* to consent, to agree.

condescendiente, (kon·des·sen·dyen´te) *adj.* complaisant, obliging.

condición, (kon·dē·syon´) *f.* condition; quality *(calidad);* basis *(base);* station, position *(posición);* character, nature *(carácter);* **a — de que,** provided that; **—ones de pago,** terms of payment; **reunir las —ones necesarias,** to possess the

necessary qualifications.

condicional, (kon·dē·syo·nâl´) *adj.* conditional.

condimentar, (kon·dē·men·tar´) *va.* to season.

condimento, (kon·dē·men´to) *m.* condiment, seasoning.

condiscípulo, la, (kon·dēs·sē´pū·lo, lâ) *n.* fellow-student.

condolerse*, (kon·do·ler´se) *vr.* to condole, to sympathize.

condominio, (kon·do·mē´nyo) *m.* condominium.

condón, (kon·don´) *m.* condom.

condonar, (kon·do·nâr´) *va.* to pardon, to forgive, to condone.

cóndor, (kon´dor) *m.* (orn.) condor.

conducción, (kon·dūk·syon´) *f.* conduction; (auto.) driving; conducting, guiding *(de personas);* conveying, transport *(de mercancías).*

conducente, (kon·dū·sen´te) *adj.* conducive, contributive.

conducir*, (kon·dū·sēr´) *va.* to transport, to convey *(cosas);* to conduct; to lead *(a personas);* — **un automóvil,** to drive an automobile; **—se** to conduct oneself, to behave oneself.

conducta, (kon·dūk´tâ) *f.* leading. guiding *(conducción);* conduct, management *(gobierno);* behavior, conduct *(comportamiento).*

conductivo, va, (kon·dūk·tē´vo, vâ) *adj.* conductive.

conducto, (kon·dūk´to) *m.* conduit, tube; (anat.) channel, drain; **por — de,** through, by means of.

conductor, ra, (kon·dūk·tor´, râ) *adj.* conductive; **hilo** or **alambre —,** electric wire; **—,** *m.* conductor; (auto.) motorist, driver; (rail.) engineer.

condueño, ña, (kon·dwe´nyo, nyâ) *n.* joint owner, partner.

conectar, (ko·nek·târ´) *va.* to connect.

conejera, (ko·ne·he´râ) *f.* warren.

conejo, ja, (ko·ne´ho, hâ) *n.* rabbit.

conejillo, (ko·ne·hē´yo) *m.* small rabbit; — **de Indias,** guinea pig.

conexión, (ko·nek·syon´) *f.* connection.

conexo, xa, (ko·nek´so, sâ) *adj.* connected, united.

confección, (kom·fek·syon´) *f.* (med.) confection; making up, preparation.

confeccionado, da, (kom·fek·syo·nâ´tho, thâ) *adj.* ready-made.

confeccionar, (kom·fek·syo·nâr´) *va.* to make up, to put together; to prepare *(un medicamento).*

confederación, (kom·fe·the·rä·syon´) f. confederacy, confederation.

confederado, da, (kom·fe·the·rä´tho, thä) n. and adj. confederate.

conferencia, (kom·fe·ren·syä) f. conference, talk (plática); lecture (lección); — de larga distancia, long-distance call.

conferenciante, (kom·fe·ren·syän´te) m. and f. lecturer.

conferenciar, (kom·fe·ren·syâr´) vn. to consult together, to confer.

conferencista, (kom·fe·ren·sēs´tä) m. and f. lecturer, speaker.

conferir*, (kom·fe·rēr´) va. to confer, to grant.

confesar*, (kom·fe·sâr´) va. to confess, to avow, to admit.

confesión, (kom·fe·syon´) f. confession, avowal.

confesionario, (kom·fe·syo·nä´ryo) m. confessional; rules for the confessional (reglas).

confeso, sa, (kom·fe´so, sä) n. confessed criminal.

confesor, (kom·fe·sor´) m. confessor.

confeti, (kom·fe´tē) m. confetti.

confiado, da, (kom·fyä´tho, thä) adj. unsuspecting, credulous (crédulo); presumptuous.

confianza, (kom·fyän´sä) f. confidence, reliance (seguridad); self-reliance (en sí mismo); presumption, overconfidence (presunción); familiarity, informality (familiaridad); de —, informal; digno de —, reliable, trustworthy; en —, confidentially; tener — en, to trust.

confiar, (kom·fyär´) va. to entrust, to confide (encargar); —, vn. to have faith, to rely.

confidencia, (kom·fē·then´syä) f. confidence.

confidencial, (kom·fē·then·syäl´) adj. confidential.

confidente, ta, (kom·fē·then´te, tä) n. confidant; —, adj. faithful, trustworthy.

confín, (kom·fēn´) m. limit, boundary.

confinar, (kom·fē´när´) va. to confine; —, vn. to border.

confirmación, (kom·fēr·mä·syon´) f. confirmation.

confirmar, (kom·fēr·mär´) va. to confirm, to corroborate.

confiscación, (kom·fēs·kä·syon´) f. confiscation.

confiscar, (kom·fēs·kär´) va. to confiscate.

confite, (kom·fē´te) m. candy, bonbon.

confitera, (kom·fē·te´rä) candy box.

confitería, (kom·fē·te·rē´ä) f. confectioner´s

shop.

confitura, (kom·fē·tū´rä) f. jam, preserve.

conflagración, (kom·flä·grä·syon´) f. conflagration.

conflicto, (kom·flēk´to) m. conflict, fight, struggle.

confluir*, (kom·flwēr´) vn. to join, to flow together (rim); to meet, to come together (caminos); to flock together, to crowd together (gente).

conformar, (kom·for·mär´) va. to conform, to make agree; —, vn. to conform, to agree; —se, to submit, to resign oneself.

conforme, (kom·for´me) adj. conformable; estar —, to be in agreement; —, adv. according to.

conformidad, (kom·for·mē·thäth´) f. conformity; patience, resignation (tolerancia); de —, by common consent; de — con, in accordance with.

confort, (kom·fort´) m. comfort.

confortante, (kom·for·tän´te) adj. comforting; —, m. sedative.

confortar, (kom·for·tär´) va. to console, to comfort; to strengthen, to liven (dar vigor).

confraternidad, (kom·frä·ter·nē·thäth´) f. brotherhood.

confrontar, (kom·fron·tär´) va. to confront (carear); to compare (cotejar).

confundir, (kom·fūn·dēr´) va. to confuse; to confound (turbar).

confusión, (kom·fū·syon´) f. confusion; shame (vergüenza).

confuso, sa, (kom·fū´so, sä) adj. confused, confounded.

conga, (kong´gä) f. conga; (Col.) large poisonous ant.

congelación, (kon·he·lä·syon´) f. freezing, — rápida, quick freezing.

congelador, (kon·he·lä·thor´) m. freezer.

congeladora, (kon·he·lä·tho´rä) f. deep freeze; almacenar en —, to deepfreeze.

congelar, (kon·he·lär´) va. and vr. to freeze, to congeal; (com.) to freeze, to immobilize.

congeniar, (kon·he·nyär´) vn. to be congenial, to get along well.

congénito, ta, (kon·he´nē·to, tä) adj. congenital.

congestión, (kon·hes·tyon´) f. (med.) congestion.

conglomeración, (kong·glo·me·rä·syon´) f. conglomeration.

conglomerado, (kong·glo·me·rä´tho) m. conglomerate.

congoja, (kong·go´hä) f. anguish, grief, heartbreak.

m met, n not, p pot, r very, rr (none), s so, t toy, th with, v eve, w we, y yes, z zero

congratulación, (kong·grâ·tū·lâ·syon´) *f.* congratulation.

congratular, (kong·grâ·tū·lâr´) *va.* to congratulate.

congregación, (kong·gre·gâ·syon´) *f.* congregation, assembly.

congregar, (kong·gre·gâr´) *va.* to congregate, to assemble, to call together.

congreso, (kong·gre´so) *m.* congress.

congruencia, (kong·grwen´syâ) *f.* appropriateness, suitableness, congruity *(conveniencia):* congruence.

cónico, ca, (ko´nē·ko, kâ) *adj.* conical.

conjetura, (kon·he·tū´râ) *f.* conjecture.

conjeturar, (kon·he·tū·râr´) *va.* to conjecture.

conjugación, (kon·hū·gâ·syon´) *f.* (gram.) conjugation.

conjugar, (kon·hū·gâr´) *va.* (gram.) to conjugate.

conjunción, (kon·hūn·syon´) *f.* conjunction.

conjuntivitis, (kon·hūn·tē·vē´tēs) *f.* (med.) conjunctivitis, pink eye.

conjunto, ta, (kon·hūn´to, tâ) *adj.* united, joint, conjunct; **el —,** the whole, the ensemble.

conjuración, (kon·hū·râ·syon´) *f.* conspiracy, plot.

conjurado, da, (kon·hū·râ´tho, thâ) *n.* conspirator; **—,** *adj.* conspiring.

conjurar, (kon·hū·râr´) *va.* to swear in *(juramentar);* to entreat *(suplicar);* **—,** *vn.* to plot, to conspire.

conjuro, (kon·hū´ro) *m.* entreaty *(ruego);* incantation.

conllevar, (kon·ye·vâr´) *va,* to stand, to put up with *(tolerar);* to help out with, to help bear *(ayudar).*

conmemoración, (kon·me·mo·râ·syon´) *f.* commemoration.

conmemorar, (kon·me·mo·râr´) *va.* to commemorate.

conmemorativo, va, (kon·me·mo·râ·tē´vo, va) *adj.* memorial.

conmensurar, (kon·men·sū·râr´) *va.* to commensurate.

conmigo, (kon·mē´go) *pron.* with me.

conmiseración, (kon·mē·se·râ·syon´) *f.* commiseration.

conmoción, (kon·mo·syon´) *f.* tremor, quake *(sacudimiento);* shock *(del ánimo);* reaction, excitement, commotion *(tumulto).*

conmovedor, ra, (kon·mo·ve·thor´, râ) *adj.* touching, moving; exciting, breathtaking, stirring.

conmover*, (kon·mo·ver´) *va.* to touch, to move *(enternecer);* to stir, to excite *(inquietar).*

conmutación, (kon·mū·tâ·syon´) *f.* commutation.

conmutador, (kon·mū·tâ·thor´) *m.* electric switch; **— telefónico,** switchboard.

conmutar, (kon·mū·târ´) *va.* to commute.

connatural, (kon·nâ·tū·râl´) *adj.* inborn, ingrained, natural.

connivencia, (kon·nē·ven´syâ) *f.* connivance.

connotación, (kon·no·tâ·syon´) *f.* connotation; distant relationship *(parentesco).*

connotar, (kon·no·târ´) *va.* to connote, to imply.

cono, (ko´no) *m.* cone; **— de aire,** (avi.) air sleeve, air sock.

conocedor, ra, (ko·no·se·thor´, râ) *n.* expert, connoisseur; **—,** *adj.* knowing, aware; **— de,** familiar with, expert in.

conocer*, (ko·no·ser´) *va.* to know, to be acquainted with; to meet *(encontrar);* to recognize *(reconocer).*

conocido, da, (ko·no·sē´tho, thâ) *n.* acquaintance; **—** *adj.* known.

conocimiento, (ko·no·sē·myen´to) *m.* knowledge, understanding; consciousness *(facultad);* acquaintance *(conocido);* (com.) bill of lading; **poner en —,** to inform, to advise.

conque, (cong´ke) *conj.* so then, well then *(después de punto final);* therefore, as a result.

conquista, (kong·kēs´tâ) *f.* conquest.

conquistador, (kong·kēs·tâ·thor´) *m.* conqueror.

conquistar, (kong·kēs·târ´) *va.* to conquer; (fig.) to convince, to win over.

consabido, da, (kon·sâ·vē´tho, thâ) *adj.* well known; previously mentioned.

consagración, (kon·sâ·grâ·syon´) *f.* consecration.

consagrar, (kon·sâ·grâr´) *va.* to consecrate, to hallow; to dedicate *(dedicar);* **—se,** to devote oneself.

consciente, (kons·syen´te) *adj.* conscious.

conscripción, (kons·krēp·syon´) *f.* conscription.

conscripto, (kons·krep´to) *m.* draftee.

consecución, (kon·se·kū·syon´) *f.* attainment.

consecuencia, (kon·se·kwen´syâ) *f.* consequence, result; consistency *(correspondencia);* **como —,** in consequence, consequently; **en —,** therefore.

consecuente, (kon·se·kwen´te) *m.* consequent; **—,** *adj.* consequent; consistent.

consecutivo, va, (kon·se·kū·tē´vo, vâ) *adj.*

consecutive.

conseguir*, (kon·se·gēr´) va. to obtain, to get, to attain.

consejero, ra, (kon·se·he´ro, rä) n. counselor, advisor; councilor (de algún consejo).

consejo, (kon·se´ho) m. counsel, advice; council (cuerpo); — **de guerra,** court-martial; — **directivo,** board of directors.

consenso (kon·sen´so) m. consensus.

consentido, da, (kon·sen·tē´tho, thä) adj. pampered, spoiled.

consentimiento, (kon·sen·tē·myen´to) m. consent, assent; pampering, spoiling.

consentir*, (kon·sen·tēr´) va. to consent to, to allow (permitir); to tolerate, to permit (tolerar); to spoil, to pamper (mimar).

conserje, (kon·ser´he) m. concierge, janitor.

conserva, (kon·ser´vä) f. conserve, preserve; —**s,** pl. canned goods.

conservación, (kon·ser·vä·syon´) f. conservation; upkeep, maintenance; canning.

conservador, (kon·ser·vä·thor´) m. conservator, curator; (pol.) conservative; —, **ra,** adj. conservative.

conservar, (kon·ser·vär´) va. to can, to preserve (hacer conservas); to keep up, to maintain (mantener); to conserve (cuidar de la permanencia de).

conservatorio, (kon·ser·vä·to´ryo) m. conservatory; —, **ria,** adj. preservative.

considerable, (kon·sē·the·rä´vle) adj. considerable; great, large (muy grande).

consideración, (kon·sē·the·rä·syon´) f. consideration, regard; **ser de** —, to be of importance.

considerado, da, (kon·sē·the·rä´tho, thä) adj. prudent considerate; esteemed, respected, highly considered (respetado).

considerando, (kon·sē·the·rän´do) conj. whereas.

considerar, (kon·sē·the·rär´) va. to consider, to think over; to respect, to think highly of (respetar).

consigna, (kon·sēg´nä) f. (mil.) watchword, countersign; (rail.) checkroom.

consignación, (kon·sēg·nä·syon´) f. consignation, consignment; **a la** — **de,** consigned to.

consignador, (kon·sēg·nä·thor´) m. consigner.

consignar, (kon·sēg·när´) va. to consign.

consignatario, (kon·sēg·nä·tä´ryo) m. trustee, consignee.

consigo, (kon·se´go) pron. with oneself.

consiguiente, (kon·sē·gyen´te) adj. consequent, resulting; —, m. consequence, effect; **por** —, consequently, as a result.

consistencia, (kon·sēs·ten´syä) f. consistence, consistency.

consistir, (kon·sēs·tēr´) vn. to consist, to be comprised.

consocio, (kon·so´syo) m. fellow member, associate.

consola, (kon·so´lä) f. console table.

consolación, (kon·so·lä·syon´) f. consolation.

consolador, ra, (kon·so·lä·thor´, rä) adj. consoling, soothing; —, n. consoler.

consolar*, (kon·so·lär´) va. to console, to comfort, to soothe.

consolidación, (kon·so·lē·thä·syon´) f. consolidation, merger.

consolidar, (kon·so·lē·thär´) va. to consolidate; (fig.) to cement, to assure; — **se,** to become consolidated.

consomé, (kon·so·me´) m. consomme, broth.

consonante, (kon·so·nän´te) f. (gram.) consonant; —, m. rhyme word; —, adj. consonant.

consorte, (kon·sor´te) m. and f. consort (marido); companion, fellow; —, m. and f. pl. accomplices.

conspicuo, cua, (kons·pē´kwo, kwä) adj. conspicuous, prominent, outstanding.

conspiración, (kons·pē·rä·syon´) f. conspiracy, plot.

conspirador, ra, (kons·pē·rä·thor´, rä) n. conspirator, plotter.

conspirar, (kons·pē·rär´) vn. to conspire, to plot.

constancia, (kons·tän´syä) f. constancy, perseverance; proof (prueba); certainty (certeza); **dejar** — **de,** to establish, to prove.

constante, (kons·tän´te) adj. persevering, constant; certain, sure (cierto).

constar, (kons·tär´) vn. to be evident, to be clear (ser evidente); to be composed, to consist (estar compuesto); **hacer** —, to state; **me consta,** I know positively, it is clear to me.

constelación, (kons·te·lä·syon´) f. constellation.

consternación, (kons·ter·nä·syon´) f. consternation.

consternar, (kons·ter·när´) va. to dismay, to consternate.

constipación, (kons·tē·pä·syon´) f. cold, head cold; — **de vientre,** constipation.

constipado, (kons·tē·pä´tho) m. cold in the head; —**do, da,** adj. having a head cold.

constiparse, (kons·tē·pär´se) vr. to catch

cold.

constitución, (kons·tē·tū·syon´) f. constitution.

constitucional, (kons·tē·tū·syo·nâl´) adj. constitutional.

constituir*, (kons·tē·twēr´) va. to constitute.

constitutivo, va, (kons·tē·tū·tē´vo, vâ) adj. constituent; —, m. essential, component.

constituyente, (kons·tē·tū·yen´te) n. and adj. constituent.

constreñimiento, (kons·tre·nyē·myen´to) m. constraint.

constreñir*, (kons·tre·nyēr´) va. to constrain, to force; (med.) to constipate.

construcción, (kons·trūk·syon´) f. construction; building, structure (obra construida).

constructor, ra, (kons·trūk·tor´, râ) n. builder; —, adj. building.

construir*, (kons·trwēr´) va. to build, to construct; (gram.) to construe.

consuelo, (kon·swe´lo) m. consolation, comfort; joy, merriment (alegría).

cónsul, (kon´sūl) m. consul.

consulado, (kon·sū·lâ´tho) m. consulate.

consulta, (kon·sūl´tâ) f. consultation; opinion, appraisal (opinión).

consultar, (kon·sūl·târ´) va. to consult; to discuss, to deal with (deliberar).

consultivo, va, (kon·sūl·tē´vo, vâ) adj. consultative; **consejo** —, advisory board.

consultor, ra, (kon·sūl·tor´, râ) n. adviser, consultant; —, adj. consulting, advisory.

consultorio, (kon·sūl·to´ryo) m. consultant´s office; clinic (de médico).

consumación, (kon·sū·mâ·syon´) f. consummation; termination, extinction (acabamiento).

consumado, da, (kon·sū·mâ´tho, thâ) adj. consummate; —, m. thick broth, consommé.

consumar, (kon·sū·mâr´) va. to consummate, to perfect.

consumidor, ra, (kon·sū·mē·thor´ râ) n. consumer; —, adj. consuming.

consumir, (kon·sū·mēr´) va. to consume, to use up; to consume, to destroy (destruir); —se, to waste away, to languish.

consumo, (kon·sū´mo) m. consumption.

consunción, (kon·sūn·syon´) f. (med.) consumption.

contabilidad, (kon·tâ·vē·lē·thâth´) f. accounting, bookkeeping; — **por partida doble,** double-entry bookkeeping.

contacto, (kon·tâk´to) m. contact, touch; —**del magneto,** (avi.) ignition switch.

contado, da, (kon·tâ´tho, thâ) adj. scarce, rare; **de** —**do,** instantly; in hand; **al** —**do,** in cash, in ready money; **$50 al** —**do,** $50 down; **tanto al** —**do,** so much down.

contador, (kon·tâ·thor´) m. accountant, bookkeeper; meter, gauge (aparato); — **Geiger,** Geiger counter.

contaduría, (kon·tâ·thū·rē´â) f. accounting (contabilidad); accountancy (oficio).

contagiar, (kon·tâ·hyâr´) va. to infect; —**se,** to become infected.

contagio, (kon·tâ´hyo) m. contagion.

contagioso, sa, (kon·tâ·hyo´so, sâ) adj. contagious, catching.

contaminación, (kon·tâ·mē·nâ·syon´) f. contamination; (fig.) defilement, corruption.

contaminar, (kon·tâ·mē·nâr´) va. to contaminate; (fig.) to defile, to corrupt.

contante, (kon·tân´te) adj. ready, cash; **dinero** — **y sonante,** ready cash.

contar*, (kon·târ´) va. to count; to charge, to debit (meter en cuenta); to relate, to tell (referir); — **con,** to rely upon, to count on.

contemplación, (kon·tem·plâ·syon´) f. contemplation.

contemplar, (kon·tem·plâr´) va. to contemplate, to meditate; to indulge, to be lenient with (complacer).

contemplativo, va, (kon·tem·plâ·tē´vo, vâ) adj. contemplative.

contemporáneo, nea, (kon·tem·po·râ´ne·o, ne·â) n. and adj. contemporary.

contemporizar, (kon·tem·po·rē·sâr´) vn. to temporize.

contender*, (kon·ten·der´) vn. to struggle, to contend; (fig.) to compete, to vie.

contendiente, (kon·ten·dyen´te) m. and f. competitor, contender.

contener*, (kon·te·ner´) va. to contain, to be comprised of; to hold back, to restrain (reprimir).

contenido, da, (kon·te·nē´tho, thâ) adj. moderate, restrained; —, m. contents.

contentadizo, za, (kon·ten·tâ·thē´so, sâ) adj. easily satisfied, easy to please; **mal** —, hard to please.

contentar, (kon·ten·târ´) va. to content, to satisfy, to please; —**se,** to be pleased or satisfied.

contento, ta, (kon·ten´to, tâ) adj. glad, pleased, content; —, m. contentment.

conteo, (kon·te´o) m. (coll.) count, counting; — **regresivo,** countdown.

â arm, **e** they, **ē** bē, **o** fore, **ū** blūe, **b** bad, **ch** chip, **d** day, f fat, **g go,** h hot, **k** kid, **1** let

contestación, (kon·tes·tâ·syon´) f. answer, reply; argument *(disputa)*.

contestar, (kon·tes·târ´) va. to answer; to confirm, to substantiate *(atestiguar)*; vn. to agree, to be in accord.

contienda, (kon·tyen´dâ) f. contest, dispute, struggle, fight.

contigo, (kon·tē´go) pron. with thee, with you.

contigüidad, (kon·tē·gwē·thâth´) f. contiguity.

contiguo, gua, (kon·tē´gwo, gwâ) adj. contiguous, bordering.

continencia, (kon·tē·nen´syâ) f. continence, moderation.

continental, (kon·tē·nen·tâl´) adj. continental.

continente, (kon·tē·nen´te) m. continent; mien, bearing *(aspecto)*; container *(cosa que contiene)*; —, adj. abstinent, moderate.

contingencia, (kon·tēn·hen´syâ) f. contingency, contingence; risk *(riesgo)*.

contingente, (kon·tēn·hen´te) adj. fortuitous, accidental; —, m. contingent; quota, share *(cuota)*.

continuación, (kon·tē·nwâ·syon´) f. continuation, continuance *(acción)*; continuity *(efecto)*; a —, below, hereafter.

continuadamente, (kon·tē·nwâ·thâ·men´te) adv. continuously.

continuamente, (kon·tē·nwâ·men´te) adv. continuously, continually.

continuar, (kon·tē·nwâr´) va. and vn. to continue.

continuidad, (kon·tē·nwē·thâth´) f. continuity; **sistema de —**, follow-up system.

continuo, nua, (kon·tē´nwo, nwâ) adj. continuous, continual, ceaseless; **de —nuo**, continually.

contómetro, (kon·to´me·tro) m. comptometer.

contonearse, (kon·to·ne·âr´se) vr. to strut, to swagger.

contorcerse*, (kon·tor·ser´se) vr. to writhe.

contorno, (kon·tor´no) m. environs; contour, outline *(de una figura)*; **en —**, round about; **cultivo en —**, contour plowing.

contorsión, (kon·tor·syon´) f. contortion.

contra, (kon´trâ) prep. against; facing *(enfrente)*; **seguro — incendio**, fire insurance; **ir en —**, to go against.

contraalmirante, (kon·trâ·âl·mē·rân´te) m. rear admiral.

contraataque, (kon·trâ·â·tâ´ke) m. counterattack.

contrabajo, (kon·trâ·vá´ho) m. double bass, contrabass.

contrabandista, (kon·trâ·vân·dēs´tâ) m. and f. smuggler, dealer in contraband.

contrabando, (kon·trâ·vân´do) m. contraband, smuggling.

contracandela, (kon·trâ·kân·de´lâ) f. (Cuba) backfire.

contracción, (kon·trâk·syon´) f. contraction; — **económica**, recession.

contraceptivo, (kon·trâ·sep·tē´vo) m. contraceptive; — **bucal**, oral contraceptive.

contracorriente, (kon·trâ·ko·rryen´te) f. countercurrent, backwater.

contradanza, (kon·trâ·thân´sâ) f. contredanse, folk dance.

contradecir*, (kon·trâ·the·sēr´) va. to contradict, to gainsay.

contradicción, (kon·trâ·thēk·syon´) f. contradiction.

contradictorio, ria, (kon·trâ·thēk·to´ryo, ryâ) adj. contradictory, opposite.

contraer*, (kon·trâ·er´) va. to catch *(una enfermedad)*; to acquire *(una costumbre)*; to limit, to restrict *(reducir)*.

contraespionaje, (kon·trâ·es·pyo·nâ´he) m. counterespionage.

contrafuerte, (kon·trâ·fwer´te) m. counterfort, buttress.

contragancho, (kon·trâ·gân´cho) m. (golf) slice.

contrahecho, cha, (kon·trâ·e´cho, châ) adj. deformed, humpbacked *(deforme)*; counterfeit *(falsificado)*.

contrahílo (kon·trâ·ē´lo) a —, against the grain.

contralmirante, (kon·trâl·mē·rân´te) m. rear admiral.

contralor, (kon·trâ·lor´) m. controller, inspector.

contralto, (kon· trâl´to) m. and f. (mus.) contralto.

contramaestre, (kon·trâ·mâ·es´tre) m. (naut.) boatswain; foreman *(de taller)*.

contramarca, (kon·trâ·mâr´kâ) f. countermark.

contramarcha, (kon·trâ·mâr´châ) f. (mil.) countermarch; (auto.) reverse; going back, return over the same route.

contramarea, (kon·trâ·mâ·re´â) f. (naut.) springtide.

contraofensiva, (kon·trâ·o·fen·sē´vâ) f. counteroffensive.

contraorden, (kon·trâ·or´then) f. countermand.

contrapartida, (kon·trâ·pâr·tē´thâ) f. corrective entry, offsetting entry.

contrapaso, (kon·trâ·pá´so) m. back step; (mus.) countermelody.

contrapelo, (kon·trâ·pe´lo) **a —,** against the grain.

contrapeso, (kon·trâ·pe´so) *m.* counterbalance; counterweight; tightrope walker´s pole *(balancín);* (Chile) uneasiness *(inquietud);* **hacer — a,** to counterbalance, to offset.

contraposición, (kon·trâ·po·sē·syon´) *f.* contrast.

contraproducente, (kon·trâ·pro·thū·sen´te) *adj.* self-defeating.

contraproyectil, (kon·trâ·pro·yek·tēl´) *m.* countermissile.

contraprueba, (kon·trâ·prwe´vâ) *f.* counterproof.

contrapuerta, (kon·trâ·pwer´tâ) *f.* inner door.

contrapunto, (kon·trâ·pūn´to) *m.* (mus.) counterpoint.

contrariar, (kon·trâ·ryâr´) *va.* to oppose *(oponerse a);* to vex, to annoy *(enfadar);* to resist *(estorbar).*

contrariedad, (kon·trâ·rye·thâth´) *f.* opposition, resistance; vexation, annoyance.

contrario, ria, (kon·trâ´ryo, ryâ) *n.* opponent, antagonist; **llevar la —,** to take the opposite side; **—,** *adj.* contrary, opposite; adverse, hostile *(adverso);* **al —rio,** on the contrary.

contrarrestar, (kôn·trâ·rres·târ´) *va.* to hit back, to return *(pelota);* to resist, to offset, to counteract *(resistir).*

contrarrevolución, (kon·trâ·rre·vo·lū·syon´) counterrevolution.

contraseña , (kon·trâ·se´nyâ) *f.* countersign; (mil.) watchword, password.

contrastar, (kon·trâs·târ´) *va.* to face, to resist *(hacer frente);* to assay, to analyze *(moneda);* to verify, to check *(pesas);* **—,** *vn.* to contrast.

contraste, (kon·trâs´te) *m.* contrast; opposition, resistance; assayer *(almotacén);* (naut.) sudden reversal of the wind.

contratación, (kon·trâ·tâ·syon´) *f.* trade, dealings *(acción);* business transaction, deal *(efecto).*

contratante, (kon·trâ·tân´te) *adj.* contracting; **partes —s,** contracting parties; **—,** *m.* contractor.

contratar, (kon·trâ·târ´) *va.* to contract, to hire *(un servicio);* to negotiate, to agree on, to contract for.

contratiempo, (kon·trâ·tyem´po) *m.* mishap, accident, misfortune.

contratista, (kon·trâ·tēs´tâ) *m.* contractor, lessee.

contrato, (kon·trâ´to) *m.* contract; **celebrar un —,** to draw up a contract.

contraveneno, (kon·trâ·ve·ne´no) *m.* antidote.

contravenir*, (kon·trâ·ve·nēr´) *va.* to contravene, to go against.

contraventana, (kon·trâ·ven·tâ´nâ) *f.* window shutter.

contravidriera, (kon·trâ·vē·thrye´râ) *f.* storm window.

contribución, (kon·trē·vū·syon´) *f.* contribution; tax *(impuesto).*

contribuir*, (kon·trē·vwēr´) *va.* to contribute.

contribuyente, (kon·trē·vū·yen´te) *adj.* contributing, contributory; **—,** *m.* and *f.* contributor; taxpayer.

contrición, (kon·trē·syon´) *f.* contrition, penitence.

contrincante, (kon·trēng·kân´te) *m.* competitor, opponent.

contrito, ta, (kon·trē´to, tâ) *adj.* contrite, penitent.

control, (kon·trol´)*m.* control, check; **— remoto,** remote control; **— de natalidad,** birth control; **— de precios,** price control.

controlar, (kon·tro·lâr´) *va.* to control.

controversia, (kon·tro·ver´syâ) *f.* controversy, dispute.

contumacia, (kon·tū·mâ´syâ) *f.* contempt of court *(del reo);* obstinacy.

contumaz, (kon·tū·mâs´) *adj.* obstinate, stubborn.

conturbar, (kon·tūr·vâr´) *va.* to perturb, to disquiet.

contusión, (kon·tū·syon´) *f.* contusion, bruise.

convalecencia, (kom·bâ·le·sen´syâ) *f.* convalescence.

convalecer*, (kom·bâ·le·ser´) *vn.* to convalesce; (fig.) to be out of danger, to be out of harm´s way.

convaleciente, (kom·bâ·le·syen´te) *adj.* convalescing; **—,** *m.* and *f.* convalescent.

convecino, na, (kom·be·sē´no, nâ) *adj.* neighboring.

convencer, (kom·ben·ser´) *va.* to convince.

convencimiento, (kom·ben·sē·myen´tō) *m.* conviction.

convención, (kom·ben·syon´) *f.* convention; agreement *(conveniencia).*

convencional, (kom·ben·syo·nâl´) *adj.* conventional.

convenido, da, (kom·be·nē´tho, thâ) *adj.* agreed, decided.

conveniencia, (kom·be·nyen´syâ) *f.* advantage, profit *(utilidad);* convenience, ease, comfort *(comodidad);* agreement *(conve-*

nio); suitability *(conformidad).*

conveniente, (kom·be·nyen´te) *adj.* profitable, advantageous; convenient, easy; suitable; advisable, desirable *(oportuno).*

convenio, (kom·be´nyo) *m.* compact, covenant; (com.) bankruptcy settlement.

convenir*, (kom·be·nēr´) *vn.* to agree, to be in agreement *(estar de acuerdo);* to convene, to assemble *(juntarse);* to be suitable, to be becoming *(corresponder);* to be important, to be desirable *(ser a propósito).*

convento, (kom·ben´to) *m.* convent *(de religiosas);* monastery *(de religiosos).*

conventual, (kom·ben·twäl´) *adj.* monastic; conventual.

convergencia, (kom·ber·hen´syâ) *f.* convergence.

conversación, (kom·ber·sâ·syon´) *f.* conversation; **amigo de la —,** given to good conversation.

conversador, ra, (kom·ber·sâ·thor´, râ) *n.* good conversationalist.

conversar, (kom·ber·sâr´) *vn.* to converse; cope to live, to dwell *(habitar);* to deal, to have to do *(comunicar).*

conversor, (kom·ber·sor´) *m.* (rad.) converter.

conversión, (kom·ber·syon´) *f.* conversion.

converso, sa, (kom·ber´so, sâ) *n.* convert.

convertible, (kom·ber·tē´vle) *adj.* and *m.* convertible.

convertidor, (kom·ber·tē·thor´) *m.* converter.

convertir*, (kom·ber·tēr´) *va.* to convert; to change, to transform *(mudar);* **—se,** to become, to change.

convexo, xa, (kom·bek´so, sâ) *adj.* convex.

convicción, (kom·bēk·syon´) *f.* conviction.

convicto, ta, (kom·bēk´to, tâ) *adj.* convicted, found guilty; **—,** *n.* convict.

convidado, da, (kom·bē·thâ´tho, thâ) *adj.* invited; **—,** *n.* guest.

convidar, (kom·bē·thâr´) *va.* to invite; (fig.) to urge, to entreat; **— a uno con,** to treat someone to **—se,** to offer one's services.

convincente, (kom·bēn·sen´te) *adj.* convincing.

convite, (kom·bē·te) *m.* invitation; party *(función).*

convocar, (kom·bo·kâr´) *va.* to convoke, to assemble.

convocatoria, (kom·bo·kâ·to´ryâ) *f.* notification, notice of a meeting.

convoy, (kom·bo´ē) *m.* convoy; (coll.) retinue, following *(séquito);* (fig.) table cruets *(taller).*

convulsión, (kom·būl·syon´) *f.* convulsion.

conyugal, (kon·yū·gâl´) *adj.* conjugal.

cónyuges, (kón·yū·hes) *m. pl.* married couple, husband and wife.

coñac, (ko·nyâk´) *m.* cognac.

cooperación, (ko·o·pe·râ·syon´) *f.* cooperation.

cooperar, (ko·o·pe·râr´) *vn.* to cooperate.

cooperativo, va, (ko·o·pe·râ·tē´vo, vâ) *adj.* cooperative; **—,** *f.* cooperative.

coordinación, (ko·or·thē·nâ·syon´) *f.* coordination.

coordinar, (ko·or·thē·nâr´) *va.* to harmonize, to coordinate.

copa, (ko´pâ) *f.* goblet, glass, wineglass; treetop *(del árbol);* crown *(del sombrero);* **—s,** *pl.* hearts; **tomar una —,** to have a drink.

Copenhague, (ko·pen·hâ´ge) *f.* Copenhagen.

copete, (ko·pe´te) *m.* pompadour *(cabello),* crest, tuft *(del ave);* forelock *(del caballo);* top, summit *(cima).*

copetudo, da, (ko·pe·tū´tho, thâ) *adj.* tufted, crested.

copia, (ko´pyâ) *f.* plenty, abundance *(muchedumbre);* copy.

copiar, (ko·pyâr´) *va.* to copy.

copioso, sa, (ko·pyo´so, sâ) *adj.* copious, abundant.

copista, (ko·pēs´tâ) *m.* and *f.* copyist.

copla, (ko´plâ) *f.* ballad, popular song; stanza *(estrofa);* couplet *(pareja).*

copo, (ko´po) *m.* snowflake.

copra, (ko´prâ) *f.* copra.

copudo, da, (ko·pū´tho, thâ) *adj.* bushy, thick.

cópula, (ko´pū·lâ) *f.* (arch.) cupola; (gram.) copula; joining, union; copulation *(sexual).*

copulativo, va, (ko·pū·lâ·tē´vo, vâ) *adj.* copulative.

coqueta, (ko·ke´tâ) *f.* coquette, flirt.

coquetear, (ko·ke·te·âr´) *vn.* to coquet, to flirt.

coquetería, (ko·ke·te·rē´â) *f.* coquetry, flirtation.

coquetón, ona, (ko·ke·ton´, o´nâ) *adj.* flirtatious, coquettish.

coquito, (ko·kē´to) *m.* face made to amuse a baby.

coraje, (ko·râ´he) *m.* courage *(valor);* anger *(ira).*

corajudo, da, (ko·râ·hū´tho, thâ) *adj.* ill-tempered, cross.

coral, (ko·râl´) *m.* coral; **—es,** *pl.* coral necklace, coral beads; **—,** *adj.* choral.

---

m met, **n** not, **p** pot, **r** very, **rr** (none), **s** so, **t** toy, **th** with, **v** eve, **w** we, **y** yes, **z** zero

coraza, (ko·râ´sâ) *f.* cuirass; (naut.) armor; (zool.) shell.

corazón, (ko·râ·son´) *m.* heart; de —, wholeheartedly, with all one´s heart; **enfermedad del —,** heart trouble.

corazonada, (ko·râ·so·nâ´thâ) *f.* feeling *(presentimiento);* rash impulse, thoughtless move *(impulso).*

corbata, (kor·vâ´tâ) *f.* cravat, necktie.

corcel, (kor·sel´) *m.* charger, courser.

corcova, (kor·ko´vâ) *f.* hump, protuberance.

corcovado, da, (kor·ko·vâ´tho, thâ) *adj.* humpbacked, hunchbacked.

corcheta, (kor·che´tâ) *f.* eye of a hook and eye.

corchete, (kor·che´te) *m.* clasp *(broche);* bench hook *(de carpintero);* bracket *(signo);* (coll.) constable.

corcho, (kor´cho) *m.* cork; beehive *(colmena).*

cordel, (kor·thel´) *m.* string, cord.

cordero, (kor·the´ro) *m.* lamb; lambskin *(piel).*

cordial, (kor·thyâl´) *adj.* cordial, hearty, affectionate; —, *m.* cordial.

cordialidad, (kor·thyâ·lē·thâth´) *f.* cordiality.

cordillera, (kor·the·ye´râ) *f.* range of mountains.

córdoba, (kor´tho·vâ) *m.* monetary unit of Nicaragua.

cordón, (kor·thon´) *m.* cord, string; cordon *(de personas).*

cordura, (kor·thû´râ) *f.* prudence, wisdom, judgment.

coreografía, (ko·re·o·grâ·fē´â) *f.* choreography.

corista, (ko·rēs´tâ) *m.* (eccl.) choir brother; —, *m.* and *f.* (theat.) member of the chorus; —, *f.* chorine, chorus girl.

cornada, (kor·nâ´thâ) *f.* butt, goring with the horns, thrust of the horns.

cornamenta, (kor·nâ·men´tâ) *f.* horns; antlers *(del venado).*

córnea, (kor´ne·â) *f.* cornea.

cornear, (kor·ne·âr´) *va.* to butt, to gore.

cornejo, (kor·ne´ho) *m.* (bot.) dogwood.

córneo, nea, (kor´ne·o, ne·â) *adj.* horny, hornlike.

corneta, (kor·ne´tâ) *f.* cornet; hunting horn *(de caza);* (mil.) bugle; pennant *(banderita);* —, *m.* bugler.

cornisa, (kor·nē´sâ) *f.* cornice, molding.

corno, (kor´no) *m.* (Mex.) French horn.

cornucopia, (kor·nû·ko´pyâ) *f.* cornucopia, horn of plenty; ornate mirror with candelabra *(espejo).*

cornudo, da, (kor·nû´tho, thâ) *adj.* horned; —, *m.* cuckold.

coro, (ko´ro) *m.* (eccl.) choir; chorus; **en —,** all together, in unison.

corola, (ko·ro´lâ) *f.* corolla.

corona, (ko·ro´nâ) *f.* crown; (eccl.) tonsure; (ast.) corona.

coronación, (ko·ro·nâ·syon´) *f.* coronation.

coronar, (ko·ro·nâr´) *va.* to crown; to reward *(premiar);* to climax, to culminate *(perfeccionar).*

coronario, ria, (ko·ro·nâ´ryo, ryâ) *adj.* relating to the crown; (med.) coronary

coronel, (ko·ro·nel´) *m.* (mil.) colonel.

coronilla, (ko·ro·nē´yâ) *f.* crown of the head.

corpiño, (kor·pē´nyo) *m.* bodice; (Sp. Am.) brassiere *(sostén).*

corporación, (kor·po·râ·syon´) *f.* corporation, society.

corporal, (kor·po·râl´) *adj.* corporal, bodfly; —, *m.* (eccl.) corporal.

corpóreo, rea, (kor·po´re·o, re·â) *adj.* corporeal.

corpulencia, (kor·pû·len´syâ) *f.* corpulence.

corpulento, ta, (kor·pû·len´to, tâ) *adj.* corpulent, bulky.

Corpus, (kor´pûs) *m.* Corpus Christi.

corpuscular, (kor·pûs·kû·lâr´) *adj.* corpuscular.

corpúsculo, (kor·pûs´kû·lo) *m.* corpuscle.

corral, (ko·rrâl´) *m.* yard; court theater *(de comedias);* **corral** *(en el campo);* **aves de —,** poultry; **hacer —es,** (coll.) to play hooky.

correa, (ko·rre´â) *f.* leather strap, thong; pliancy *(flexibilidad);* belt *(cinturón);* **tener —,** to be a good sport, to be able to take it.

corrección, (ko·rrek·syon´) *f.* correction; correctness *(calidad);* refinement *(urbanidad).*

correcto, ta, (ko·rrek´to, tâ) *adj.* correct; refined, proper *(fino).*

corrector, ra, (ko·rrek·tor´, râ) *n.* corrector; (print.) proofreader.

corredizo, za, (ko·rre·thē´so, sâ) *adj.* easily untied; **nudo —,** slipknot; **puerta —,** sliding door.

corredor, ra, (ko·rre·thor´, râ) *adj.* running; —, *n.* runner; —, *m.* (com.) broker; (mil.) scout; corridor, hall *(pasillo);* trackman *(de pista y campo);* **—s,** *f. pl.* (orn.) flightless birds.

corregir*, (ko·rre·hēr´) *va.* to correct; to

punish *(castigar);* to lessen, to mitigate *(disminuir).*

correlación, (ko·rre·lâ·syon´) *f.* correlation.

correlacionar, (ko·rre·lâ·syo·nâr´) *va.* to correlate.

correo, (ko·rre´o) *m.* mail; postman, mail-man *(cartero);* post office *(casa);* accomplice *(responsable);* **a vuelta de —,** by return mail.

correoso, sa, (ko·rre·o´so, sâ) *adj.* flexible, pliable; (fig.) tough, like leather.

correr, (ko·rrer´) *vn.* to run, to race; to flow *(el agua);* to blow *(el viento);* to go by, to pass *(el tiempo);* —, *vt.* to race *(un caballo);* to run *(un riesgo);* to slide *(deslizar);* to cover, to traverse *(recorrer);* to hunt down to pursue *(perseguir);* **a todo —,** at full speed; **— parejas,** to be a good match, to be on an equal footing; **—se,** to become embarrassed, to get flustered.

correría, (ko·rre·rē´â) *f.* excursion; (mil.) raid, incursion; **—s,** youthful escapades.

correspondencia, (ko·rres·pon·den´syâ) *f.* correspondence; relationship, harmony *(relación);* communication, contact *(comunicación);* mail *(correo);* transfer, connection *(entre vehículos);* **estar en — con,** to correspond with; **llevar la —,** to be in charge of the correspondence.

corresponder (ko·rres·pon·der´) *vn.* to correspond; to be connected, communicate *(habitaciones);* to repay, reciprocate *(recompensar);* to concern *(tocar);* **— con,** to repay for; **—se con,** to correspond with.

correspondiente, (ko·rres·pon·dyen´te) *adj.* corresponding; **—,** *m.* and *f.* correspondent.

corresponsal, (ko·rres·pon·sâl´) *m.* correspondent.

corretaje, (ko·rre·tâ´he) *m.* brokerage; broker´s fee *(comisión).*

corretear, (ko·rre·te·âr´) *vn.* (coll.) to rove, to wander; to run back and forth, to run about *(jugando);* to pursue.

correvedile, (ko·rre·ve·thē´le) *m.* talebearer, gossip; pander, procurer *(alcahuete).*

corrida, (ko·rrē´thâ) *f.* race; **— de toros,** bullfight; **de —,** at full speed.

corrido, da, (ko·rrē´tho, thâ) *adj.* expert; artful; ashamed.

corriente, (ko·rryen´te) *f.* current; stream, flow, course, progression *(curso);* **— alterna,** (elec.) alternating current; **— continua,** direct current; **del —,** of the current month; **poner al —,** to inform; **tener al —,** to keep advised; **—** *adj.* current *(del tiempo);* fluent *(fluido);* running *(que corre);* well-known, generally known *(sabido);* permissible, customary *(admitido);* run-of-the-mill, common *(ordinario).*

corrillo, (ko·rrē´yo) *m.* spot where people gather for a chat.

corro, (ko´rro) *m.* circle of people.

corroborar, (ko·rro·vo·râr´) *va.* to corroborate; to strengthen *(fortificar).*

corroer, (ko·rro·er´) *va.* to corrode.

corromper, (ko·rrom·per´) *va.* (fig.) to corrupt; to spoil, to ruin *(echar a perder);* to seduce *(seducir);* —, *vn.* to smell bad; **—se,** to rot, to spoil.

corrosión, (ko·rro·syon´) *f.* corrosion.

corrte, cte. or **corr.te:** corriente, current.

corrupción, (ko·rrūp·syon´) *f.* corruption; putrefaction, spoilage; seduction.

corruptivo, va, (ko·rrūp·tē´vo, vâ) *adj.* corruptive.

corruptor, ra, (ko·rrūp·tor´, râ) *n.* corrupter; —. *adj.* corrupting.

corsé, (kor·se´) *m.* corset.

cortacircuitos, (kor·tâ·sēr·kwē´tos) *m.* (elec.) circuit breaker.

cortado, da, (kor·tâ´tho, thâ) *adj.* disconnected, choppy *(estilo);* adapted, proportioned *(ajustado).*

cortador, ra, (kor·tâ·thor´, râ) *adj.* cutting; **—,** *m.* butcher *(carnicero);* cutter; (anat.) incisor; **—,** *f.* slicing machine.

cortadura, (kor·tâ·thū´râ) *f.* cut; clipping *(recortado);* **—s,** *pl.* shreds, trimmings.

cortafuego, (kor·tâ·fwe´go) *m.* firebreak.

cortapapel, (kor·tâ·pâ·pel´) *m.* paper cutter, paper knife.

cortaplumas, (kor·tâ·plū´mâs) *m.* penknife, pocket knife.

cortar, (kor·târ´) *va.* to cut; to cut off *(separar);* to cut out *(suprimir);* to interrupt, to break into *(una conversación);* **—se,** to stop short, to be at a loss for words; to coagulate *(coagularse).*

cortaúñas, (kor·tâ·ū´nyâs) *m.* nail clippers.

corte, (kor´te) *m.* edge, cutting edge *(filo);* cross section *(de un edificio);* material *(para una prenda);* cut *(lesión);* edge *(de libro);* cutting down, felling *(de árboles);* cut, cutting; **—,** *f.*

court; court-yard *(patio);* **hacer la —,** to court, to woo.

cortedad, (kor·te·tháth´) *f.* shortness *(poca extensión);* smallness *(pequeñez);* (fig.) lack, want *(escasez);* timidness, lack of spirit *(timidez).*

cortejante, (kor·te·hán´te) *m.* courtier, gallant.

cortejar, (kor·te·hár´) *va.* to woo, to court *(a una mujer);* to fete, to treat royally.

cortejo, (kor·te´ho) *m.* courtship, wooing; gift, present *(regalo);* entourage *(comitiva).*

Cortes, (kor´tes) *f. pl.* Spanish Parliament.

cortés, (kor·tes´) *adj.* courteous, genteel, polite.

cortesanía, (kor·te·sá·nē´á) *f.* courtesy, politeness.

cortesano, na, (kor·te·sá´no, ná) *adj.* court, of the court; courteous, urbane *(cortés);* —, *m.* courtier; —, *f.* courtesan.

cortesía, (kor·te·sē´á) *f.* courtesy, politeness *(cortesanía);* (com.) days of grace; expression of respect *(tratamiento);* gift, present *(regalo).*

corteza, (kor·te´sá) *f.* (anat.) cortex; bark *(de árbol);* peel *(de fruta);* crust *(de pan);* (fig.) outward appearance; grossness, roughness *(grosería).*

cortijo, (kor·tē´ho) *m.* farmhouse.

cortina, (kor·tē´ná) *f.* curtain; — **de hieno,** iron curtain; — **de humo,** smoke screen.

cortinaje, (kor·tē·ná´he) *m.* set of curtains.

cortisona, (kor·tē·so´ná) *f.* (med.) cortisone.

corto, ta, (kor´to, tá) *adj.* short; scanty *(escaso);* small *(pequeño);* limited, lacking in ability *(de escaso talento);* shy, timid *(tímido)* **a la —ta o a la larga,** sooner or later.

cortocircuito, (kor·to·sēr·kwē´to) *m.* (elec.) short circuit.

corva, (kor´vá) *f.* hollow of the knee, ham.

corvadura, (kor·vá·thū´rá) *f.* curvature; (arch.) bend of an arch.

corveta, (kor·ve´tá) *f.* curvet.

corvo, va, (kor´vo, vá) *adj.* bent, crooked.

corzo, za, (kor´so, sá) *n.* roe deer.

cosa, (ko´sá) *f.* thing; **no hay tal —,** there is no such thing; **otra —,** something else; **ninguna —,** nothing; — **de cajón,** matter of course, routine.

cosecha, (ko·se´chá) *f.* harvest, crop; harvest time *(tiempo);* **de su —,** of one´s own invention.

cosechar, (ko·se·chár´) *va.* to reap, to harvest.

cosechero, (ko·se·che´ro) *m.* harvester, gatherer.

coser, (ko·ser´) *va.* to sew; (fig.) to join *(unir);* **máquina de —,** sewing machine.

cosmético, (koz·me´tē·ko) *m.* cosmetic.

cósmico, ca, (koz´mē·ko, ká) *adj.* cosmic.

cosmonauta, (koz·mo·ná´ū·tá) *m.* cosmonaut, astronaut.

cosmopolita, (koz·mo·po·lē´tá) *m.* and *f.* cosmopolite; —, *adj.* cosmopolitan.

cosquillas, (kos·kē´yás) *f. pl.* tickling; **hacer —,** to tickle.

cosquillear, (kos·kē·ye·ár´) *va.* to tickle.

cosquilloso, sa, (kos·kē·yo´so, sá) *adj.* ticklish.

costa, (kos´tá) *f.* cost, price; coast, shore *(litoral);* **a toda —,** at any cost; **a lo largo de la —,** coastwise.

costado, (kos·tá´ho) *m.* side; (mil.) flank; (naut.) ship´s side.

costal, (kos·tál´) *m.* sack, large bag; tamper *(pisón);* —, *adj.* (anat.) costal.

costanera, (kos·tá·ne´rá) *f.* slope; —**s,** pl. rafters, beams.

costanero, ra, (kos·tá·ne´ro, rá) *adj.* coastal; sloping *(en cuesta).*

costar*, (kos·tár´) *vn.* to cost; —, *vt.* to cause, to give.

costarricense, (kos·tá·rrē·sen´se) *m.* and *f.* and *adj.* Costa Rican.

coste, (kos´te) *m.* price.

costear, (kos·te·ár´) *va.* to pay the cost of; *vn.* to sail along the coast.

costero, ra, (kos·te´ro, rá) *adj.* coastal; —, *f.* hill, slope; —, *n.* coastal inhabitant.

costilla, (kos·tē´yá) *f.* rib; rung *(de silla);* stave *(de barril).*

costillaje (kos·tē·yá´he) or costillar, (kostē·yár´) *m.* ribbing; (anat.) rib cage.

costo, (kos´to) *m.* cost, expense; — **de fabricación,** production cost; **precio de —,** cost price.

costoso, sa, (kos·to´so, sá) *adj.* costly, dear, expensive.

costra, (kos´trá) *f.* crust; scab *(postilla).*

costumbre, (kos·tūm´bre) *f.* custom, habit; **de —,** usually; **tener por —,** to be in the habit of.

costura, (kos·tū´rá) *f.* sewing; seam *(sutura);* (naut.) splice; **medias sin —,** seamless hose.

costurera, (kos·tū·re´râ) f. seamstress, dressmaker.

costurero, (kos·tū·re´ro) m. sewing room (cuarto); sewing box (cajón).

cotejar, (ko·te·hâr´) va. to compare, to collate.

cotejo, (ko·te´ho) m. comparison, collation.

cotidiano, na, (ko·tē·thyâ´no, nâ) adj. daily.

cotización, (ko·tē·sâ·syon´) f. (com.) quotation; boletín de —, list of quotations.

cotizar, (ko·tē·sâr´) va. (com.) to quote.

coto, (ko´to) m. enclosed pasture (terreno); (zool.) howler monkey; landmark (mojón); (med.) goiter.

cotón, (ko·ton´) m. printed cotton.

cotorra, (ko·to´rrâ) f. magpie (urraca); parrakeet (loro); (coll.) chatterbox (charlatán).

coyote, (ko·yo´te) m. coyote.

coyunda, (ko·yūn´dâ) f. yoke strap; (fig.) marriage, matrimony.

coyuntura, (ko·yūn·tū´râ) f. (anat.) joint, articulation; occasion, moment (oportunidad); economic picture (estado económico).

coz, (kos) f. kick; recoil (del arma de fuego) back flow (del agua); butt (culata).

C.P.T.: Contador Público Titulado, C.P.A. Certified Public Accountant.

cráneo, (krâ´ne·o) m. skull, cranium.

crápula, (krâ´pū·lâ) f. intoxication; (ag.) licentiousness (licencia).

craquear, (krâ·ke·âr´) va. to crack, to subject to cracking.

craqueo, (krâ·ke´o) m. cracking of petroleum.

craso, sa, (krâ´so, sâ) adj. thick, heavy; (fig.) crass.

cráter, (krâ´ter) m. crater.

crátera, (krâ´te·râ) f. krater.

creación, (kre·â·syon´) f. creation.

Creador, (kre·â·thor´) m. Creator, Maker.

creador, ra, (kre·â·thor´, râ) adj. creative; —, n. originator, creator.

crear, (kre·âr´) va. to create, to originate; to establish, to found (fundar).

crecer*, (kre·ser´) vn. to grow; to increase to swell (por nueva materia).

creces, (kre´ses) f. pl. augmentation, increase; pagar con —, to pay back generously, to pay more than is due.

crecida, (kre·sē´thâ) f. swell, floodtide.

crecido, da, (kre·sē´tho, thâ) adj. grown,

increased, large.

creciente, (kre·syen´te) f. swell, floodtide (crecida); crescent (de la luna); —, adj. growing, swelling.

crecimiento, (kre·sē·myen´to) m. increase; growth.

credencial, (kre·then·syâl´) f. credential.

credibilidad, (kre·thē·vē·lē·thâth´) f. credibility.

crédito, (kre´thē·to) m. credit; — mercantil, good will; a —, on credit; —s activos, assets; —s pasivos, liabilities.

credo, (kre´tho) m. creed; en menos de un —, in less than a jiffy.

credulidad, (kre·thū·lē·thâth´) f. credulity.

crédulo, la, (kre´thū·lo, lâ) adj. credulous.

creencia, (kre·en´syâ) f. credence; belief (opinión); faith, religious persuasion (fe religioso).

creer*, (kre·er´) va. to believe; to think (tener por probable); ¡ya lo creo! I should say so! you bet! of course!

creíble, (kre·ē´vle) adj. credible, believable.

crema, (kre´mâ) f. cream; skin cream (para el cutis); — batida, whipped cream; — de afeitar, shaving cream; — dental, toothpaste.

cremación, (kre·mâ·syon´) f. cremation.

crémor (kre´mor) or crémor tártaro, (kre·´mor târ´tâ·ro) m. cream of tartar.

crencha, (kren´châ) f. part of one´s hair.

crepuscular, (kre·pūs·kū·lâr´) adj. twilight.

crepúsculo, (kre·pūs´kū·lo) m. twilight.

crespo, pa, (kres´po, pâ) adj. crisp (hojas); curly (cabello); (fig.) bombastic, turgid (estilo); (fig.) upset, angry (alterado); —, m. curl.

crespón, (kres·pon´) m. crepe.

cresta, (kres´tâ) f. crest; — de gallo, cockscomb.

creyente, (kre·yen´te) adj. believing; —, m. and f. believer.

cría, (krē´â) f. raising; breeding (de animales); offspring, young (conjunto).

criada, (kryâ´thâ) f. maid.

criadero, (kryâ·the´ro) m. tree nursery (de arbolillos); breeding ground (de animales); —, ra, adj. prolific, productive.

criadilla, (kryâ·thē´yâ) f. (anat.) testicle; small bread roll (panecillo); — de tierra, truffle.

criado, (kryâ´tho) m. servant; —, da, adj. bred, brought up.

criador, (kryâ·thor´) *m.* creator; breeder; —, **ra,** *adj.* nourishing; creating, creative; fruitful.

crianza, (kryân´sâ) *f.* raising, rearing *(acción);* breeding *(efecto);* nursing *(lactancia);* **dar** —, to bring up, to rear.

criar, (kryâr´) *va.* to create *(dar motivo);* to produce *(producir);* to breed, to rear *(animales);* to nurse, to suckle *(nutrir):* to raise, to bring up *(a los niños).*

criatura, (kryâ·tū´râ) *f.* creation, work, thing created *(cosa criada);* small child, baby *(niño);* creature *(hechura).*

criba, (krē´vâ) *f.* sieve.

cribado, (krē·vâ´tho) *m.* sifting.

cribar, (krē·vâr´) *va.* to sift, to screen.

crimen, (krē´men) *m.* crime.

criminal, (krē·mē·nâl´) *m.* and *f.* and *adj.* criminal.

criminalista, (krē·mē·nâ·lēs´tâ) *adj.* pertaining to criminal law; **abogado** —, criminal lawyer.

criminología, (krē·mē·no·lo·hē´â) *f.* criminology.

crin, (krēn) *f.* mane.

criogenia, (kryo·he´nyâ) *f.* cryogenics.

criollo, lla, (kryo´yo, yâ) *n.* and *adj.* Creole *(de padres europeos);* —, *adj.* native, indigenous.

cripta, (krēp´tâ) *f.* crypt.

criptografía, (krēp·to·grâ·fē´â) *f.* cryptography.

crisantemo, (krē·sân·te´mo) *m.* chrysanthemum.

crisis, (krē´sēs) *f.* crisis; attack *(ataque);* mature decision *(juicio).*

crisma, (krēz´mâ) *m.* or *f.* chrism; —, *f.* (coll.) head.

crisol, (krē·sol´) *m.* crucible, melting pot.

crispar, (krēs·pâr´) *va.* to contract, to twitch; (coll.) to put on edge, to make nervous.

cristal, (krēs·tâl´) *m.* crystal; pane of glass *(hoja de vidrio);* — **tallado,** cut crystal.

cristalería, (krēs·tâ·le·rē´â) *f.* glassware.

cristalino, na, (krēs·tâ·lē´no, nâ) *adj.* crystalline, clear.

cristalización, (krēs·tâ·lē·sâ·syon´) *f.* crystallization.

cristalizar, (krēs·tâ·lē·sâr´) *va.* to crystallize.

cristiandad, (krēs·tyân·dâth´) *f.* Christianity, Christendom.

cristianismo, (krēs·tyâ·nēz´mo) *m.* Christianity, Christendom.

cristiano, na, (krēs·tyâ´no, nâ) *n.* and *adj.* Christian.

Cristo, (krēs´to) *m.* Christ.

Cristóbal Colón, (krēs·to´vâl ko·lon´) Christopher Columbus.

criterio, (krē·te´ryo) *m.* criterion *(regla);* judgment *(juicio).*

crítica, (krē´tē·kâ) *f.* criticism.

criticable, (krē·tē·kâ´vle) *adj.* open to criticism.

criticar, (krē·tē·kâr´) *va.* to criticize, to find fault with; to evaluate *(analizar).*

crítico, (krē´tē·ko) *m.* critic; —, **ca,** *adj.* critical.

criticón, ona, (krē·tē·kon´, o´nâ) *n.* faultfinder.

cromo, (kro´mo) *m.* chromium, chrome.

cromosoma, (kro·mo·so´mâ) *m.* (biol.) chromosome.

crónica, (kro´nē·kâ) *f.* chronicle; news feature, news story *(de prensa).*

crónico, ca, (kro´nē·ko, kâ) *adj.* chronic.

cronista, (kro·nēs´tâ) *m.* and *f.* chronicler; news writer, feature writer.

cronógrafo, (kro·no´grâ·fo) *m.* stop watch.

cronología, (kro·no·lo·hē´â) *f.* chronology.

cronológicamente, (kro·no·lo·hē·kâ men´te) *adv.* chronologically.

cronológico, ca, (kro·no·lo´hē·ko, kâ) *adj.* chronological.

croqueta, (kro·ke´tâ) *f.* croquette.

croquis, (kro´kēs) *m.* sketch.

cruce, (krū´se) *m.* crossing; intersection *(punto);* — **en trébol,** highway cloverleaf.

crucero, (krū·se´ro) *m.* cruise.

crucial, (krū·syâl´) *adj.* crucial, critical.

crucificar, (krū·sē·fē·kâr´) *va.* to crucify; (fig.) to torment.

crucifijo, (krū·sē·fē´ho) *m.* crucifix.

crucigrama, (krū·sē·grâ´mâ) *m.* crossword puzzle.

crudeza, (krū·the´sâ) *f.* crudeness.

crudo, da, (krū´tho, thâ) *adj.* raw *(sin cocer);* green, unripe *(no maduro);* unprocessed, crude *(sin preparación);* hard *(agua);* raw, cold *(tiempo);* (fig.) harsh, sharp *(áspero);* (coll.) hung over *(tras una borrachera);* hard to digest *(de difícil digestión).*

cruel, (krwel) *adj.* cruel, heartless *(despiadado);* savage, bloodthirsty *(sanguinario);* intense, bitter *(riguroso).*

crueldad, (krwel·dâth´) *f.* cruelty; savageness; intensity.

cruento, ta, (krwen´to, tâ) *adj.* bloody, savage.

crujía, (krū·hē´â) *f.* corridor, passage-way; — de hospital, hospital ward.

crujido, (krū·hē´tho) *m.* crack; crackling, crunch; chattering; rustling.

crujir, (krū·hēr´) *vn.* to crack *(la madera);* to crackle, to crunch *(hojas secas);* to chatter *(los dientes);* to rustle *(la seda).*

cruz, (krūs) *f.* cross; tail, reverse *(de una moneda).*

Cruz del Sur, (krūs thel sūr) *f.* Southern Cross.

cruzada, (krū·sâ´thâ) *f.* crusade.

cruzado, da, (krū·sâ´tho, thâ) *adj.* crossed; mixed-breed *(animal);* double-breasted *(saco);* —, *m.* crusader.

cruzamiento, (krū·sâ·myen´to) *m.* crossing; — de calle, street crossing; — de vía, (rail.) junction.

cruzar, (krū·sâr´) *va.* to cross; to come across *(encontrar);* (naut.) to cruise.

c. s. f.: costo, seguro y flete, c. i. f. cost, insurance, and freight.

cta. or cᵗᵃ: cuenta, (com.) a/c or acct. account.

cta. cte. or cta. corr.te: cuenta corriente, (com.) current account.

cte. or corr.te: corriente, current.

c/u: cada uno, each one, every one.

cuaderno, (kwâ·ther´no) *m.* notebook; — de bitácora, logbook.

cuadra, (kwâ´thrâ) *f.* city block.

cuadrado, da, (kwâ·thrâ´tho, thâ) *adj.* square; (fig.) perfect, flawless *(cabal);* *m.* (math.) square; die *(troquel);* clock *(de las medias);* gusset *(de la camisa);* (print.) quad.

cuadragésimo, ma, (kwâ·thrâ·he´sē·mo, ma) *adj.* fortieth.

cuadrangular, (kwâ·thrâng·gū·lâr´) *adj.* quadrangular; —, *m.* home run.

cuadrángulo, (kwâ·thrâng´gū·lo) *m.* quadrangle.

cuadrante, (kwâ·thrân´te), *m.* quadrant; face *(del reloj).*

cuadrar, (kwâ·thrâr´) *va.* to square; to rule in squares *(cuadricular);* —, *vi.* to agree, to measure up *(conformarse);* to please, to be fine *(agradar);* to come out right *(cuentas);* —se, to square one´s shoulders.

cuadricular, (kwâ·thrē·kū·lâr´) *vt.* to mark off in squares, to rule in squares.

cuadrilátero, ra, (kwâ·thrē·lâ´te·ro, râ) *adj.* and *m.* quadrilateral.

cuadrilongo, ga, (kwâ·thrē·long´go, gâ) *adj.* oblong, rectangular.

cuadrilla, (kwâ·thrē´yâ) *f.* gang, crew *(en una obra);* quadrille *(baile);* band, company *(banda).*

cuadrimotor, (kwâ·thrē·mo·tor´) *adj.* four-motor.

cuadro, (kwâ´thro) *m.* square; picture; painting *(pintura);* frame *(marco);* (theat.) scene; (mil.) cadre; (naut.) ward-room; — de control, (elec.) switch-board.

cuadrúpedo, da, (kwâ·thrū´pe·tho, thâ) *adj.* quadruped.

cuajada, (kwa·hâ´thâ) *f.* curd; cottage cheese *(requesón).*

cuajar, (kwâ·hâr´) *va.* to coagulate, to curdle; —, *vn.* to jell, to come through *(lograr);* to suit, to please *(gustar);* —se, to coagulate, to curdle; to fill up *(llenarse).*

cuajarón, (kwâ·hâ·ron´) *m.* grume, clot.

cuajo, (kwâ´ho) *m.* rennet.

cual, (kwâl) *pron.* which, which one; just as, like *(usado con tal);* —, *adv.* such as, according to how.

cuál, (kwâl) *interr. pron.* which one, which; some *(disyuntivo);* —, *adv.* how.

cualidad, (kwâ·lē·thâth´) *f.* quality.

cualquier, (kwâl·kyer´) *adj.* any.

cualquiera, (kwâl·kye´râ) *adj.* any; —, *pron.* anyone, someone, anybody, somebody.

cuan, (kwân´) *adv.* as.

cuán, (kwân) *adv.* how; — grande es Dios! how great is God!

cuando, (kwân´do) *(interr.* cuándo), *adv.* when; in case, if *(en caso de que);* —, *conj.* even if, although even though; since *(puesto que);* de — en —, from time to time; — más, — mucho, at most, at best; — menos, at least; ¿de cuándo acá? since when? aun —, even though; de vez en —, from time to time, now and then; — quiera que, whenever that.

cuantía, (kwân·tē´â) *f.* quantity; rank, distinction *(importancia).*

cuantioso, sa, (kwân·tyo´so, sâ) *adj.* numerous, abundant.

cuanto, ta, (kwân´to, tâ) *adj.* as much as, all, whatever.

cuanto, (kwân´to) *adv.* as soon as; — antes, at once; — más, the more; all the more; en —, as soon as; while *(mientras);* en — a, with regard to; por —, inasmuch as.

cuánto, ta, (kwân'to, tâ) *interr. adj.* how much.

cuánto, (kwân'to) *adv.* how much; how, to what degree *(de qué manera).*

cuarenta, (kwâ·ren'tâ) *adj.* forty.

cuarentena, (kwâ·ren·te'nâ) *f.* Lent; quarantine.

cuaresma, (kwâ·rez'mâ) *f.* Lent.

cuarta, (kwâr'tâ) *f.* quarter; run of four cards *(de naipes);* (naut.) rhumb, point.

cuartear, (kwâr·te·âr') *va.* to quarter; to divide up *(dividir);* to make the fourth for *(un juego);* to drive from side to side *(un carruaje);* —se, to split, to crack.

cuartel, (kwâr·tel') *m.* quarter, fourth; district, section *(barrio);* (mil.) quarters; plot *(de terreno);* quarter, mercy *(gracia);* (naut.) hatch; — general, head-quarters.

cuarteto, (kwâr·te'to) *m.* quartet.

cuartilla, (kwâr·te'yâ) *f.* fourth part of an **arroba;** quarter sheet of paper *(de un pliego);* pastern *(de caballería).*

cuartillo, (kwâr·te'yo) *m.* pint *(para líquidos);* quart *(para áridos).*

cuarto, (kwâr'to) *m.* fourth part, quarter; room *(aposento).*

cuarzo, (kwâr'so) *m.* quartz.

cuate, ta, (kwâ'te, tâ) or **coate, ta,** *n.* and *adj.* (Mex.) twin; —, *n.* chum, pal, close friend.

cuatrero, (kwâ·tre'ro) *m.* cattle rustler; horse thief *(de caballos).*

cuatro, (kwâ'tro) *adj.* four; —, *m.* figure four; **las —,** four o'clock.

cuba, (kū'vâ) *f.* cask, barrel *(cerrada);* tub, vat *(abierta);* (coll.) tubby person; toper, tippler *(borrachón).*

cubano, na, (kū·vâ'no, nâ) *adj.* and *n.* Cuban.

cubeta, (kū·ve'tâ) *f.* bucket; (phot.) tray.

cúbico, ca, (kū'vē·ko, kâ) *adj.* cubic.

cubierta, (kū·vyer'tâ) *f.* cover; envelope *(sobre);* dust jacket *(de libro);* pretext; (naut.) deck.

cubierto (kū·vyer'to) *m.* protection, shelter *(abrigo);* setting, cover *(servicio de mesa);* table d'hote *(comida).*

cubil, (kū·vēl') *m.* den, lair, cave.

cubilete, (kū·vē·le'te) *m.* copper pan; dice box *(para dados);* (Sp. Am.) high hat *(sombrero).*

cubo, (kū'vo) *m.* (math.) cube; millpond *(estanque);* pail *(balde);* socket *(de candelero);* hub *(de rueda).*

cubrecama, (kū·vre·kâ'mâ) *f.* bedspread.

cubrir*, (kū·vrēr') *va.* to cover; (fig.) to drown out *(ahogar);* to cover up, to hide *(disimular);* — **una cuenta,** to balance an account; —se, to put on one's hat.

cucaña, (kū·kâ'nyâ) *f.* greased pole; (coll.) snap, cinch, cakewalk *(ganga).*

cucaracha, (kū·kâ·râ'châ) *f.* cockroach.

cuclillo, (kū·klē'yo) *m.* cuckoo; (fig.) cuckold.

cuco, ca, (kū'ko, kâ) *adj.* (coll.) pretty, nice; sly, crafty *(taimado);* —, *m.* cuckoo.

cucurucho, (kū·kū·rū'cho) *m.* paper cone.

cuchara, (kū·châ'râ) *f.* spoon.

cucharada, (kū·châ·râ'thâ) *f.* spoonful.

cucharita, (kū·châ·rē'tâ) *f.* teaspoon.

cucharón, (kū·châ·ron') *m.* soup ladle, soup spoon.

cuchichear, (kū·chē·che·âr') *vn.* to whisper.

cuchicheo, (kū·chē·che'o) *m.* whispering.

cuchilla, (kū·chē'yâ) *f.* large knife; cleaver *(de carnicero);* blade *(de la hoja de afeitar).*

cuchillada, (kū·chē·yâ'thâ) *f.* knife cut, gash; slash *(en un vestido);* —s, *pl.* wrangle, quarrel.

cuchillo, (kū·chē'yo) *m.* knife; gusset, gore *(de una prenda);* — **de hoja automática,** switchblade; — **mantequillero,** butter knife; — **de postres,** fruit knife.

cueca, (kwe'kâ) *f.* popular Chilean dance.

cuello, (kwe'yo) *m.* neck; collar *(de una prenda);* **levantar el —,** (coll.) to have one's head above water, to see one's way clear.

cuenca, (kweng'kâ) *f.* wooden bowl; (geog.) valley, river basin; (anat.) eye socket.

cuenta, (kwen'tâ) *f.* account; calculation, count *(cálculo);* (com.) bill; bead *(del rosario);* **abonar en —,** to credit with; **adeudar en —,** to charge to one's account; **caer en la —,** to become aware, to realize; — **abierta** or **corriente,** checking account; — **atrasada,** overdue account; — **inversiva,** countdown; — **en participación,** joint account; — **pendiente,** account due; **dar — de,** to report on; **darse —,** to realize; **llevar —s,** to keep accounts; **tener en —,** to take into account, to bear in mind; **tomar por su —,** to assume responsibility for.

cuentagotas, (kwen·tâ·go'tâs) *m.* medicine dropper.

cuentahabiente, (kwen·tä·â·vyen´te) *m.* and *f.* account holder.

cuentista, (kwen·tēs´tä) *m.* and *f.* storyteller; talebearer, gossip *(chismoso).*

cuento, (kwen´to) *m.* story, account *(relato);* count *(cómputo);* tale, story *(chisme);* — **de viejas,** old wives´ tale.

cuerda, (kwer´thä) *f.* (mus.) string; main-spring *(del reloj);* (math.) chord; rope, cord; — **vocal,** vocal chord; **bajo** —, underhandedly; **dar** —, to wind; (fig.) to give free rein to; **sin** —, unwound; **mozo de** —, porter.

cuerdo, da, (kwer´tho, thä) *adj.* sane; prudent, wise *(sabio).*

cuerno, (kwer´no) *m.* horn; — **de abundancia,** horn of plenty; **levantar hasta los —s de la luna,** to praise to the skies.

cuero, (kwe´ro) *m.* hide, skin; leather *(curtido y preparado);* — **cabelludo,** scalp; **en —s,** stark naked.

cuerpo, (kwer´po) *m.* body; cadaver, corpse; build, physique *(talle);* section, part *(parte);* (mil.) corps; — **de aviación,** air corps; — **a** —, hand to hand.

cuervo, (kwer´vo) *m.* (orn.) crow, raven.

cuesco, (kwes´ko) *m.* stone *(de la fruta);* millstone *(de molino).*

cuesta, (kwes´tä) *f.* hill, slope, decline; **a —s,** on one´s shoulders; **ir — abajo,** to go downhill, to be on the decline; **hacérsele — arriba,** to be hard to do for, to be distasteful to.

cuestación, (kwes·tä·syon´) *f.* collection, charity drive.

cuestión, (kwes·tyon´) *f.* question, matter; problem *(punto dudoso);* argument, quarrel *(riña).*

cuestionar, (kwes·tyo·nâr´) *va.* to question, to dispute.

cuestionario, (kwes·tyo·nä´ryo) *m.* questionnaire.

cueva, (kwe´vä) *f.* cave, cavern; cellar *(sótano).*

cuezo, (kwe´sō) *m.* trough.

cuidado, (kwē·thä´tho) *m.* care *(esmero);* concern, problem *(a cargo de uno);* anxiety, worry *(recelo);* **estar con** —, to be worried; **estar de** —, to be dangerously ill; **tener** —, to be careful; **¡— !** *interj.* watch out! be careful!

cuidadosamente, (kwē·thä·tho·sâ·men´te) *adv.* carefully.

cuidadoso, sa, (kwē·thä·tho´so, sä) *adj.* careful, observant, watchful *(vigilan-*

te).

cuidaniños, (kwē·thä·nē´nyos) *m.* and *f.* baby-sitter.

cuidar, (kwē·thâr´) *va.* to take care of, to look after *(asistir);* to be careful with *(of) (poner cuidado);* —**se,** to be careful of one´s health.

cuita, (kwē´tä) *f.* grief, sorrow, suffering.

cuitado, da, (kwē·tä´tho, thä) *adj.* griefstricken, sorrowful; (fig.) cowardly, irresolute *(apocado).*

culantro (kū·lân´tro) or **cilantro,** (sē·lân´tro) *m.* (bot.) coriander.

culata, (kū·lä´tä) *f.* hindquarter *(de caballería);* butt *(de escopeta);* breech *(del cañón);* (fig.) back end, tail end; — **de cilindro,** cylinder head.

culebra, (kū·le´vrä) *f.* snake; — **de cascabel,** rattlesnake.

culebreo, (kū·le·vre´o) *m.* wiggling.

culminación, (kūl·mē·nä·syon´) *f.* culmination.

culminante, (kūl·mē·nân´te) *adj.* predominant; **punto** —, high point, highwater mark.

culo, (kū´lo) *m.* buttocks; hindquarters *(del animal);* anus *(ano);* bottom *(de botella).*

culpa, (kūl´pä) *f.* wrong, fault, defect *(falta);* guilt, blame *(responsabilidad);* **tener la** —, to be at fault, to be to blame.

culpabilidad, (kūl·pä·vē·lē·thäth´) *f.* guiltiness.

culpable, (kūl·pä´vle) *adj.* guilty, at fault.

culpar, (kūl·pâr´) *va.* to accuse, to blame.

culterano, na, (kūl·te·rä´no, nä) *adj.* overly refined, affected.

cultivado, da, (kul·tē·vä´tho, thä) *adj.* cultivated, cultured; **perlas —s,** cultured pearls.

cultivar, (kūl·tē·vâr´) *va.* to cultivate; to grow *(plantar).*

cultivo, (kūl·tē´vo) *m.* cultivation; culture *(de microbios).*

culto, ta, (kūl´to, tä) *adj.* cultured, cultivated; affected, overly refined *(culterano);* —, *m.* veneration, worship *(homenaje);* religion, form of worship *(religión);* (fig.) cult *(admiración).*

cultura, (kūl·tū´rä) *f.* cultivation, culture.

cumbre, (kūm´bre) *f.* summit, peak; highpoint, height *(punto culminante);* **conferencia en la** —, summit conference.

cumpleaños, (kŭm·ple·á´nyos´) *m.* birthday.

cumplido, da, (kŭm·plē´tho, thâ) *adj.* full, complete; long, full *(vestido);* courteous *(cortés);* —, *m.* courtesy, attention.

cumplimentar, (kŭm·plē·men·târ´) *va.* to compliment; to fulfill, to carry out *(poner en ejecución).*

cumplimiento, (kŭm·plē·myen´to) *m.* compliment *(parabién);* accomplishment, fulfillment; expiration *(vencimiento).*

cumplir, (kŭm·plēr´) *va.* to execute, to fulfill, to carry out *(ejecutar);* — **años,** to have a birthday; —, *vn.* to fall due, to expire *(vencer);* to be fitting, to be proper *(convenir).*

cumular, (kŭ·mū·lâr´) *va.* to accumulate.

cúmulo, (kŭ´mū·lo) *m.* heap, pile *(montón);* (fig) lot, great deal; cumulus cloud *(nube).*

cuna, (kŭ´nâ) *f.* cradle; homeland *(patria);* birthplace *(lugar de nacimiento);* foundling home *(de expósitos);* source, cause *(origen);* **de humilde —,** of lowly birth.

cundir, (kŭn·dēr´) *vn.* to spread out *(extenderse);* to grow, to spread *(propagarse);* to swell, to puff up *(dar mucho de sí);* to be going well *(un trabajo).*

cuneta, (kŭ·ne´tâ) *f.* gutter, dìtch.

cuña, (kŭ´nyâ) *f.* wedge; (coll.) support, backing *(apoyo).*

cuñada, (kŭ·nyá´thâ) *f.* sister-in-law.

cuñado, (kŭ·nyá´tho) *m.* brother-in-law.

cuño, (kŭ´nyo) *m.* stamping die; (fig.) seal, stamp *(huella).*

cuociente, (kwo·syen´te) *m.* quotient.

cuota, (kwo´tâ) *f.* quota, share.

cupé, (kŭ·pe´) *m.* coupé, coupe.

cupo, (kŭ´po) *m.* quota, share.

cupón, (kŭ·pon´) *m.* (com.) coupon.

cuprífero, ra, (kŭ·prē´fe·ro, râ) *adj.* copper-bearing; **minas —s,** copper mines.

cúpula, (kŭ´pū·lâ) *f.* cupola, dome; — **geodésica,** geodesic dome.

cuquillo (kŭ·ké´yo) *m.* (orn.) cuckoo.

cura, (kŭ´·râ) *m.* parish priest; —, *f.* healing *(curación);* cure, remedy *(método curativo).*

curable, (kŭ·râ´vle) *adj.* curable.

curandero, (kŭ·rân·de´ro) *m.* quack, medicaster: medicine man.

curar, (kŭ·râr´) *va.* to cure, to heal; **—se,** to be cured, to recover.tive, healing.

curativo, va, (kŭ·râ·tē´vo, vâ) *adj.* curative, healing.

curato, (kŭ·râ´to) *m.* parish *(parroquia);* pastorate, ministry *(cargo de cura).*

curca, (kŭr´kâ) *f.* (Chile) hump.

curda, (kŭr´thâ) *f.* (coll.) drunk.

cureña (kŭ·re´nyâ) *f.* gun carriage *(del cañón);* stay of a crossbow *(de ballesta).*

curio, (kŭ´ryo) *m.* curite.

curiosear, (kŭ·ryo·se·âr´) *vn.* to pry, to snoop, to meddle.

curiosidad, (kŭ·ryo·sē·thâth´) *f.* curiosity; neatness *(aseo);* object of curiosity, rarity *(cosa curiosa).*

curioso, sa, (kŭ·ryo´so; sâ) *adj.* curious; tidy, neat; careful *(cuidadoso).*

cursado, da, (kŭr·sâ´tho, thâ) *adj.* skilled, versed.

cursar, (kŭr·sâr´) *va.* to take, to study *(una materia);* to haunt, to frequent *(un paraje);* to engage in frequently *(una cosa);* to follow through with *(una solicitud).*

cursi, (kŭr´sē) *adj.* tawdry, cheap, in bad taste.

cursivo, va, (kŭr·sē´vo, vâ) *adj.* cursive; **letra —,** cursive.

curso, (kŭr´so) *m.* course; circulation, currency *(de una moneda);* — **de repaso,** refresher course; — **de verano,** summer course; — **legal,** legal tender; **perder el —,** to fail the course.

curtidor, (kŭr·tē·thor´) *m.* tanner.

curtir, (kŭr·tēr´) *va.* to tan *(las pieles);* to sunburn, to tan *(el cutis);* to inure, to harden *(acostumbrar a la vida dura).*

curucú, (kŭ·rū·kŭ´) *m.* quetzal.

curul, (kŭ·rūl) *f.* legislative seat.

curva, (kŭr´vâ) *f.* curve; — **cerrada,** sharp bend; — **doble,** S-curve.

curvatura. (kŭr·vâ·tū´râ) *f.* curvature.

curvear, (kŭr ve·âr´) *vn.* to curve.

curvilíneo, nea, (kŭr·vē·lē´ne·o, ne·â) *adj.* curvilinear.

curvo, va, (kŭr´vo, vâ) *adj.* curved, bent.

cúspide, (kŭs´pē·the) *f.* cusp *(de diente);* peak *(de montaña);* (math.) apex.

custodia, (kŭs·to´thyâ) *f.* custody; custodian *(persona);* (eccl.) monstrance.

custodiar, (kŭs·to·thyâr´) *va.* to guard, to keep in custody.

cutáneo, nea, (kŭ·tá´ne·o, ne·â) *adj.* cutaneous.

cúter, (kŭ´ter) *m.* (naut.) cutter.

cutícula, (kŭ·tē´kū·lâ) *f.* or *f.* cuticle.

cutis, (kŭ´tēs) *m.* or *f.* skin, complexion.

cuyo, ya, (kŭ´yo, yâ) *pron.* of which, of whom, whose.

czar, (sâr) = **zar.**

â arm, **e** they, **ē** bē, **o** fore, **ū** blüe, **b** bad, **ch** chip, **d** day, f fat, **g** go, **h** hot, **k** kid, **l** let

CH

chabacano, na, (châ·vâ·kâ´no, nâ) *adj.* in poor taste, vulgar.

chacal, (châ·kâl´) *m.* jackal.

chacarero, ra, (châ·kâ·re´ro, râ) *n.* (Amer.) truck farmer.

chacota, (châ·ko´tâ) *f.* hilarity, noisy mirth; **hacer — de,** to make fun of.

chacra, (châ´krâ) *f.* (Amer.) truck farm.

cháchara, (châ´châ·râ) *f.* (coll.) chitchat, chatter, idle talk; **—,** *pl.* trinkets, trifles.

chal, (châl) *m.* shawl.

chalán, ana, (châ·lân´, â´nâ) *f.* horsetrader, shrewd businessman; **—,** *adj.* shrewd.

chalana, (châ·lâ´nâ) *f.* lighter, scow, barge.

chaleco, (châ·le´ko) *m.* waistcoat, vest.

chalina, (châ·lē´nâ) *f.* scarf.

chalupa, (châ·lū´pâ) *f.* (naut.) shallop.

chamaco, ca, (châ·mâ´ko, kâ) *n.* (Mex.) youngster, kid.

chamarra, (châ·mâ´rrâ) *f.* sheepskin jacket, mackinaw.

chambergo, (châm·ber´go) *m.* slouch hat.

chambón, ona, (châm·bon´, o´nâ) *adj.* awkward, bungling; **—,** *n.* poor player.

champaña, (châm·pâ´nyâ) *m.* champagne.

champiñones, (châm·pē·nyo´nes) *m. pl.* mushrooms.

champú, (châm·pū´) *m.* shampoo.

champurrar, (châm·pū·rrâr´) *va.* (coll.) to mix, to mix in.

chamuscado, da, (châ·mūs·kâ´tho, thâ) *adj.* singed, scorched; (coll.) slightly hipped, slightly obsessed.

chamuscar, (châ·mūs·kâr´) *va.* to singe.

chancear, (chân·se·âr´) *vn.* and *vr.* to joke, to jest.

chancero, ra, (chân·se´ro, râ) *adj.* given to joking.

chancla, (châng´klâ) *f.* old shoe.

chancleta, (châng·kle´tâ) *f.* house slipper.

chanclo, (châng´klo) *m.* patten; rubber, overshoe *(zapato de goma);* **zapato de —,** wedge shoe.

chanchullo, (chân·chū´yo) *m.* crooked deal, underhanded affair.

chantaje, (chân·tâ´he) *m.* blackmail.

chantajista, (chân·tâ·hēs´tâ) *m.* and *f.* blackmailer.

chanza, (chân´sâ) *f.* joke, jest, fun.

chapa, (châ´pâ) *f.* thin sheet *(hoja);* color, flush *(del rostro);* veneer *(de madera).*

chaparreras, (châ·pâ·rre´râs) *f. pl.* (Mex.) chaps.

chaparro, (châ·pâ´rro) *m.* dwarf evergreen oak; **—, rra,** *adj.* short and stocky.

chaparrón, (châ·pâ·rron´) *m.* downpour.

chapear, (châ·pe·âr´) *va.* to sheet, to plate; to veneer; **—se,** (Chile) to feather one's nest.

chapitel, (châ·pē·tel´) *m.* (arch.) capital.

chapotear, (châ·po·te·âr´) *va.* to sponge down, to wet down; **—,** *vn.* to splash in the water; to splash *(sonar el agua batida).*

chapucear, (châ·pū·se·âr´) *va.* to botch.

chapucería, (châ·pū·se·rē´â) *f.* botched job, mess.

chapucero, (châ·pū·se´ro) *m.* blacksmith *(herrero);* poor craftsman; **—, ra,** *adj.* rough, clumsy, bungling.

chapulín, (châ·pū·lēn´) *m.* grasshopper.

chapurrar, (châ·pū·rrâr´) or **chapurrear,** (châ·pū·rre·âr´) *va.* to speak badly, to speak brokenly *(un idioma);* (coll.) to mix in, to mix.

chapuz, (châ·pūs´) *m.* bungled job, mess *(chapucería);* secondrate job *(de poca importancia);* ducking.

chapuzar, (châ·pū·sâr´) *va.* to duck under water.

chaqueta, (châ·ke´tâ) *f.* jacket, coat.

chaquetear, (châ·ke·te·âr´) *vn.* to turn tail; to change camps, to change viewpoints *(de opiniones).*

charada, (châ·râ´thâ) *f.* charade.

charanga, (châ·râng´gâ) *f.* brass band.

charca, (châr´kâ) *f.* pool, pond.

charco, (châr´ko) *m.* puddle; **cruzar el —,** (coll.) to cross the pond.

charla, (châr´lâ) *f.* idle chitchat, chatter; conversation, chatting; informal talk *(conferencia).*

charlador, ra, (châr·lâ·thor´, râ) *n.* chatterbox, great talker; **—,** *adj.* talkative.

charladuría, (châr·lâ·thū·rē´â) *f.* compulsion to talk, garrulousness.

charlar, (châr·lâr´) *vn.* to chatter, to chitchat; to chat, to talk *(conversar).*

charlatán, ana, (châr·lâ·tân´, â´nâ) *n.* windbag; gossip, idle talker *(indiscreto);* charlatan, medicine man, quack *(curandero).*

charlatanería, (châr·lâ·tâ·ne·rē´â) *f.* idle talk; quackery, spellbinding.

charnela, (châr·ne´lâ) *f.* hinge.

charol, (châ·rol´) *m.* lacquer, enamel; patent leather *(cuero).*

charrada, (châ·rrâ´thâ) *f.* boorish action;

uncouth remark *(dicho);* example of poor taste, showy, overdone display *(obra charra).*

charro, (châ´rro) *m.* Mexican horseman in fancy dress; —, **rra,** *adj.* gaudy, overdone, in poor taste *(de mal gusto);* boorish, uncouth *(rústico).*

chasco, (chisto) *m.* joke, prank *(broma);* disappointment; **llevarse —,** to be disappointed.

chasis, (châ´sēs) *m.* chassis.

chasquear, (châs·ke·âr´) *va.* to crack to snap *(el látigo);* to play a joke on *(burlarse);* to fail, to disappoint *(faltar);* —, *vn.* to crack, to snap.

chasquido, (châs·kē´tho) *m.* snap, crack.

chato, ta, (châ´to, tâ) *adj.* flat; pugnosed *(de nariz).*

chaveta, (châ·ve´tâ) *f.* pin, cotter pin; **perder la —,** (fig.) to go out of one´s head, to go off the deep end.

checoslovaco, ca, (che·koz·lo·vâ´ko, kâ) *adj.* and *n.* Czechoslovakian.

chelín, (che·lēn´) *m.* shilling.

cheque, (che´ke) *m.* (corn.) check; **— al portador,** check to bearer; **— de caja,** cashier´s check; **— de viajeros,** traveler´s check.

chicle, (chē´kle) *m.* chicle; chewing gum *(goma de masticar).*

chico, ca, (chē´ko, kâ) *adj.* little, small; *n.* child; (coll.) young person *(joven).*

chicoria, (chē·ko´ryâ) *f.* chicory.

chicote, ta, (chē·ko´te, tâ) *n.* lively youngster; —, *m.* (naut.) cable end; (coll.) cigar *(cigarro);* (Sp. Am.) whip *(látigo).*

chícharo, (chē´châ·ro) *m.* pea.

chicharra, (chē·châ´rrâ) *f.* cicada.

chicharrón, (chē·châ·rron´) *m.* food burned to a crisp *(manjar requemado);* cracklings *(del cerdo).*

chichón, (chē·chon´) *m.* lump on the head, bump on the head.

chifladera, (chē·flâ·the´râ) *f.* whistling; booing.

chiflar, (chē·flâr´) *vn.* to whistle; —, *va.* to boo, **to jeer; —se,** to go half out of one´s mind; **—se con,** to be enfatuated with, to be mad about.

chiflido, (chē·flē´tho) *m.* whistle; boo.

chile, (chē´le) *m.* (bot.) chili, red pepper.

chileno, na, (chē·le´no, nâ) *n.* and *adj.* Chilean.

chillar, (chē·yâr´) *vn.* to scream, to shriek, to howl, to sob.

chillido, (chē·yē´tho) *m.* scream, shriek; **dar un —,** to utter a shriek, scream.

chillón, ona, (chē·yon´, o´nâ) *adj.* scre-

achy, shrill *(sonido);* loud, flashy, showy *(color); n.* bawler, screamer; —, *m.* nail.

chimenea, (chē·me·ne´â) *f.* chimney; smokestack *(de una fábrica);* (naut.) funnel.

chimpancé, (chēm·pân·se´) *m.* chimpanzee.

china, (chē´nâ) *f.* pebble; (Cuba and P.R.) orange; **— poblana,** national costume of Mexico; **la C —,** China.

chinche, (chēn´che) *f.* bedbug; thumbtack *(clavito);* —, *m.* and *f.* pill, boring person.

chinchilla, (chēn·chē´yâ) *f.* chinchilla.

chinchona, (chēn·cho´nâ) *f.* quinine.

chinchorro, (chēn·cho´rro) *m.* very small rowboat *(embarcación);* fish net *(red).*

chinela, (chē·ne´lâ) *f.* house slipper.

chino, na, (chē´no, nâ) *n.* and *adj.* Chinese; —, *m.* Chinese language.

chiquero, (chē·ke´ro) *m.* pigsty.

chiquillo, lla, (che·kē´yo, yâ) *n.* child, youngster, moppet.

chiquito, ta, (chē·kē´to, tâ) *adj.* little, small; —, *m.* little boy; —, *f.* little girl.

chirinola, (chē·rē·no´lâ) *f.* trifle, mere nothing.

chiripa, (chē·rē´pâ) *f.* fluke; **de —,** by mere chance, due to luck.

chirla, (chēr´lâ) *f.* mussel.

chirriar, (chē·rryâr´) *vn.* to sizzle *(de un calor);* to squeak, to creak *(al ludir);* to chirp *(los pájaros).*

chirrido, (chē·rrē´tho) *m.* chirping; sizzling; creaking, squeaking.

chisme, (chēz´me) *m.* gossip.

chismear, (chēz·me·âr´) *vn.* to carry tales, to gossip.

chismoso, sa, (chēz·mo´so, sâ) *adj.* gossipy, talebearing; —, *n.* gossip, talebearer.

chispa, (chēs´pâ) *f.* spark; tiny diamond *(diamante);* tiny bit, little bit *(partícula);* liveliness, sparkle *(viveza);* tipsiness *(borrachera);* **¡—!,** *interj.* my gosh! for goodness sake!; **echar —s,** to be furious, to rant and rave.

chispeante, (chēs·pe·ân´te) *adj.* sparkling; witty, bright.

chispear, (chēs·pe·âr´) *vn.* to spark *(echar chispas),* to glitter, to sparkle *(relucir);* to sprinkle *(llover).*

chisporrotear, (chēs·po·rro·te·âr´) *vn.* to sputter.

chistar, (chēs·târ´) *vn.* to open one´s mouth, to say a word; **sin — ni mistar,** (coll.) without saying boo.

chiste, (chēs´te) *m.* joke, funny story;

humor *(gracia).*

chistera, (chēs•te´râ) *f.* creel; top hat *(sombrero);* scoop *(del pelotari).*

chistoso, sa, (chēs•to´so, sâ) *adj.* funny, comical, humorous.

¡chito! (chē´to) or **¡chitón!** (chē•ton´) *interj.* hush!

chivo, va, (chē´vo, vâ) *n.* kid, young goat.

¡cho! (cho) *interj.* whoa!

chocante, (cho•kân´te) *adj.* shocking, offensive.

chocar, (cho•kâr´) *vn.* to smash, to crash; (fig.) to collide, to clash *(pelear);* to shock, to upset *(irritar).*

chocarrero, (cho•kâ•rre´ro) *m.* off-color joketeller, shocker; —, **ra,** *adj.* off-color, dirty.

chocolate, (cho•ko•lâ´te) *m.* chocolate.

chocolatera, (cho•ko•lâ•te´râ) *f.* chocolate pot.

chochear, (cho•che•âr´) *vn.* to dote.

chochera, (cho•che´râ) *f.* second childhood.

chocho, cha, (cho´cho, châ) *adj.* doting.

chofer (cho•fer) or **chófer,** (cho´fer) *m.* chauffeur, driver.

choque, (cho´ke) *m.* collision, crack-up, crash *(impacto);* (mil.) clash, encounter, conflict, dispute *(contienda);* shock *(conmoción).*

chorizo, (cho•rē´so) *m.* pork sausage.

chorrear, (cho•rre•âr´) *vn.* to gush, to pour out; to drip *(goteando);* (fig.) to flow steadily.

chorrillo, (cho•rrē´yo) *m.* steady stream, continual flow.

chorro, (cho´rro) *m.* gush, flow; jet *(de vapor);* a **—s,** heavily, copiously.

chotear, (cho•te•âr´) *va.* to rib, to kid, to poke fun at.

choza, (cho´sâ) *f.* hut, cabin.

chubasco, (chū•vâs´ko) *m.* rainsquall, rainstorm.

chuchería, (chū•che•rē´â) *f.* bauble, gewgaw.

chufleta, (chū•fle´tâ) *f.* jest, joke.

chulear, (chū•le•âr´) *va.* to make fun of good-naturedly, to kid; (Mex.) to flatter, to pay compliments *(requebrar).*

chuleta, (chū•le´tâ) *f.* chop; **— de cordero,** lamb chop; **— de puerco,** pork chop; **— de ternera,** veal chop.

chulo, (chū´lo) *m.* sporty Madrid lowlife; pimp *(rufián);* bullring assistant *(en la corrida)* —, **la,** *adj.* (Sp. Am.) pretty, charming.

chumacera, (chū•mâ•se´râ) *f.* (mech.) journal bearing; (naut.) oarlock.

chupada, (chū•pâ´thâ) *f.* suction, sucking.

chupado, da, (chū•pâ´tho, thâ) *adj.* lean, drawn.

chupador, (chū•pâ•thor´) *m.* teething ring.

chupar, (chū•pâr´) *va.* to suck; (fig.) to sponge on, to drain, to sap *(quitar a uno);* **—se** to grow weak and thin.

chupón (chū•pon´) *m.* (bot.) sucker; (mech.) piston, sucker; —, **ona,** *n.* swindler; drain; —, *adj.* fond of sucking.

churrasco, (chū•rrâs´ko) *m.* charcoal broiled meat.

churrigueresco, ca, (chū•rrē•ge•res´ko, kâ) *adj.* churrigueresque.

chus ni mus, (chūs nē mūs) (coll.) **no decir —,** not to say a word.

chusco, ca, (chūs´ko, kâ) *adj.* droll, clever, funny.

chusma, (chūz´mâ) *f.* rabble, mob.

chuzo, (chū´so) *m.* pike; **llover a —s,** to rain heavily, to pour, to rain cats and dogs.

chuzón, ona, (chū•son´, o´nâ) *adj.* sly.

D

D., Dn. or **D.n: Don,** Don, title equivalent to Mr., but used before given name.

Da. or **Dña.: Doña,** Donna, title equivalent to Mrs. or Miss but used before given name.

dable, (dâ´vle) *adj.* feasible, possible.

dacrón, (dâ•kron´) *m.* dacron.

dactilografía, (dâk•tē•lo•grâ•fē´â) *f.* typewriting, typing.

dactilógrafo, (dâk•tē•lo´grâ•fo, fâ) *n.* typist.

dádiva, (dâ´thē•vâ) *f.* gift, present.

dadivoso, sa, (dâ•thē•vo´so, sâ) *adj.* generous, open-handed.

dado, (dâ´tho) *m.* die; **—s,** *pl.* dice; —, **— da,** *adj.* given; **—do que** or **—do caso que,** on condition that, provided that.

dador, ra (da•thor´, râ) *n.* giver, donator;

(com.) endorser; bearer *(portador);* — **de sangre,** blood donor.

daga, (dä´gä) *f.* dagger.

dalia, (dâ´lyä) *f.* (bot.) dahlia.

daltoniano, na, (dâl·to·nyä´no, nä) *adj.* color-blind.

daltonismo, (dâl·to·nēz´mo) *m.* color blindness.

dama, (dä´mä) *f.* lady; mistress *(manceba);* king *(en damas);* queen *(en ajedrez);* (theat.) leading lady; —*s, pl.* checkers.

damasco, (dä·mäs´ko) *m.* damask *(tejido);* damson *(fruta).*

damisela, (dä·mē·se´lä) *f.* sweet young thing, young lady.

damnificar, (dâm·nē·fē·kâr´) *va.* to hurt, to damage, to harm.

danés, esa, (dä·nes´, e´sä) *adj.* Danish; —, *n.* Dane.

Danubio, (dä·nū´vyo) *m.* Danube.

danza, (dân´sä) *f.* dance.

danzante, (dân·sân´te) *m.* dancer; giddy, lightheaded individual *(atolondrado).*

danzar, (dân·sâr´) *va.* to dance; —, *vn.* (coll.) to meddle, to butt in.

danzarín, ina, (dân·sä·rēn´, ē´nä) *n.* dancer; (coll.) meddler, meddlesome individual.

dañar, (dä·nyâr´) *va.* to damage, to injure; to spoil, to ruin *(echar a perder).*

dañino, na, (dä·nyē´no, nä) *adj.* harmful, dangerous.

daño, (dä´nyo) *m.* damage, injury; ruin; —s **y perjuicios,** damages; **hacer** —, to hurt, to injure.

dañoso, sa, (dä·nyo´so, sä) *adj.* injurious, harmful, detrimental.

dar*, (dâr) *va.* to give; to consider *(considerar);* to strike *(la hora);* —, *vn.* to matter *(importar);* to fall *(caer);* to insist *(empeñarse);* to arise *(ocurrir);* to tell *(presagiar);* — **a conocer,** to make known; — **a la calle,** to face the street; — **a luz,** to give birth; — **de comer,** to feed; — **con,** to find, to come upon; — **fe,** to certify, to attest; — **fianza,** to go good for, to give security; — **los buenos días,** to say good morning; — **memorias** or **saludos,** to give regards; — **un paseo,** to take a walk; — **prestado,** to lend; — **que decir,** to give cause to criticize; — **que pensar,** to make suspicious, to cause to think; — **razón de,** to inform; —**se por vencido,** to give up; —**se cuenta de,** to realize; —**se prisa,** to hurry.

dardo, (dâr´tho) *m.* dart, arrow.

dársena, (dâr´se·nä) *f.* dock.

data, (dä´tä) *f.* date; (com.) item.

datar, (dâ·târ´) *va.* to date.

dátil, (dä´tēl) *m.* (bot.) date.

dativo, (dâ·tē´vo) *m.* (gram.) dative.

dato, (da´to) *m.* datum; —*s, pl.* data, information.

D. de J.C.: después de Jesucristo, A.D. after Christ.

de, (de) *prep.* of *(posesión);* from *(origen);* for *(para);* by *(por);* with *(con).*

deán, (de·ân´) *m.* (eccl.) dean.

debajo, (de·vä´ho) *adv.* underneath, below; — **de,** beneath, under.

debate, (de·vä´te) *m.* debate, discussion; contest, struggle *(contienda).*

debatir, (de·vä·tēr´) *va.* to debate, to discuss; to contest, to struggle for *(combatir).*

debe, (de´ve) *m.* (com.) debits; — **y haber,** debits and credits.

deber, (de·ver´) *m.* obligation, duty; —, *va.* to owe.

debidamente, (de·vē·thâ·men´te) *adv.* duly, properly.

debido, da, (de·vē´tho, thä) *adj.* due, proper, just.

débil, (de´vēl) *adj.* weak.

debilidad, (de·vē·lē·thâth´) *f.* weakness.

debilitar, (de·vē·lē·târ´) *va.* to debilitate, to weaken; —**se,** to become weak.

debitar, (de·vē·târ´) *va.* (com.) to debit.

débito, (de´vē·to) *m.* debt.

debut, (de·vūt´) *m.* debut.

debutar, (de·vū·târ´) *vn.* to make one´s debut.

década, (de´kä·thä) *f.* decade.

decadencia, (de·kä·then´syä) *f.* decline, decadence.

decadente, (de·kä·then´te) *adj.* decadent, declining.

decaer*, (de·kä·er´) *vn.* to decline, to fail, to decay.

decaído, da, (de·kä·ē´tho, thä) *adj.* decadent, in decline; weakened, spiritless *(abatido).*

decaimiento, (de·käē·myen´to) *m.* decay, decline; lack of vitality *(desaliento).*

decano, (de·kä´no) *m.* dean *(con titulo);* senior member.

decapitar, (de·kä·pē·târ´) *va.* to behead.

decasílabo, ba, (de·kä·sē´lä·vo, vä) *adj.* decasyllabic; —, *m.* decasyllable.

deceleración, (de·se·le·râ·syon´) *f.* deceleration.

decencia, (de·sen´syä) *f.* decency.

decentar*, (de·sen·târ´) *va.* to cut the first piece of; — **la salud,** to begin to lose one´s health; —**se,** to get bedsores.

decente, (de·sen´te) *adj.* decent; appropriate, proper *(conveniente);* neat, tidy *(aseado).*

decepción, (de·sep·syon´) *f.* disappointment *(desengaño);* deception *(engaño).*

decibel (de·sē·vel´) or decibelio, (de·sē·ve´l-yo) *m.* decibel.

decible, (de·sē´vle) *adj.* expressible.

decididamente, (de·sē·thē·thâ·men´te) *adv.* decidedly.

decidido, da, (de·sē·thē´tho, thâ) *adj.* determined, resolute, energetic.

decidir, (de·sē·thēr´) *va.* to decide, to determine; to make decide, to cause to make a decision *(mover a decidirse);* — se, to decide, to make a decision.

decigramo, (de·sē·grá´mo) *m.* decigram.

decimal, (de·sē·mâl´) *adj.* decimal; (eccl.) tithing.

décimo, ma, (de´sē·mo, mâ) *adj.* and *m.* tenth.

decimoctavo, va, (de·sē·mok·tá´vo, vâ) *m.* and *adj.* eighteenth.

decimonono, na (de·sē·mo·no´no, nâ) or decimonoveno, na, (de·sē·mo·no ve´no, nâ) *m.* and *adj.* nineteenth.

decimoquinto, ta, (de·sē·mo·kēn´to, tâ) *m.* and *adj.* fifteenth.

decimoséptimo, ma, (de·sē·mo·sep´tē·mo, ma) *m.* and *adj.* seventeenth.

decimotercio, cia (de·sē·mo·ter´syo, syâ) or decimotercero, ra, (de·sē·mo·ter·se´ro, râ) *m.* and *adj.* thirteenth.

decir*, (de·sēr´) *va.* to say; to tell *(relatar);* to talk *(hablar);* to call *(nombrar);* to mean *(significar);* querer —, to mean; por lo así, as it were; —, *m.* familiar saying.

decisión, (de·sē·syon´) *f.* decision; determination *(ánimo).*

decisivo, va, (de·sē·sē´vo, vâ) *adj.* decisive.

declamación, (de·klâ·mâ·syon´) *f.* elocution, public speaking *(arte);* (fig.) wordiness, rhetoric.

declamador, ra, (de·klâ·mâ·thor´, râ) *n.* declaimer.

declamar, (de·klâ·mâr´) *va.* to declaim, to deliver; —, *vn.* to harangue, to rail.

declaración, (de·klâ·râ·syon´) declaration; testimony, evidence *(del testigo).*

declarar, (de·klâ·râr´) *va.* to declare; —, *vi.* to give evidence, to give testimony; —se, to break out, to take place *(manifestarse);* to declare oneself.

declinable, (de·klē·nâ´vle) *adj.* declinable.

declinación, (de·klē·nâ·syon´) *f.* descent, slope *(bajada);* falling off, decline *(menoscabo);* (gram.) declension.

declinar, (de·klē·nâr´) *vn.* to decline; to

bend, to slope *(inclinarse);* —, *va.* (gram.) to decline; to refute.

declive, (de·klē´ve) *m.* declivity, slope.

decomisar, (de·ko·mē·sâr´) *va.* to confiscate.

decomiso, (de·ko·mē´so) *m.* confiscation.

decoración, (de·ko·râ·syon´) *f.* decoration; (theat.) setting, stage set; decorating *(arte);* memorizing *(de memoria).*

decorado, (de·ko·râ´tho) *m.* decoration; stage set; decorating.

decorador, ra, (de·ko·râ·thor´, râ) *n.* decorator; —, *adj.* decorating.

decorar, (de·ko·râr´) *va.* to decorate; to memorize, to learn by heart.

decoro, (de·ko´ro) *m.* honor, respect; decorum *(recato).*

decoroso, sa, (de·ko·ro´so, sâ) *adj.* decorous, decent.

decremento, (de·kre·men´to) *m.* decrease, diminution.

decrépito, ta, (de·kre´pē·to, tâ) *adj.* decrepit.

decrepitud, (de·kre·pē·tūth´) *f.* decrepitude.

decretar, (de·kre·târ´) *va.* to decree.

decreto, (de·kre´to) *m.* decree.

dechado, (de·châ´tho) *m.* example, model.

dedal, (de·thâl´) *m.* thimble.

dedicación, (de·thē·kâ·syon´) *f.* dedication.

dedicado, da, (de·thē·kâ´tho, thâ) *adj.* dedicated; devoted.

dedicar, (de·thē·kâr´) *va.* to dedicate; to devote, to apply *(emplear).*

dedicatoria, (de·thē·kâ·to´ryâ) *f.* dedication.

dedillo, (de·thē´yo) *m.* little finger; saber una cosa al —, to know a thing perfectly.

dedo, (de´tho) *m.* finger *(de la mano);* toe *(del pie);* finger´s breadth *(medida);* — índice, index finger; — meñique, little finger; — pulgar, thumb; — del corazón, middle finger; — anular, ring finger.

deducción, (de·thūk·syon´) *f.* deduction; derivation, source *(derivación).*

deducir*, (de·thū·sēr´) *va.* to deduce; to deduct *(rebajar).*

defectivo, va, (de·fek·tē´vo, vâ) *adj.* defective.

defecto, (de. fek´to) *m.* defect; lack *(carencia).*

defectuoso, sa, (de·fek·two´so, sâ) *adj.* defective.

defender*, (de·fen·der´) *va.* to defend; to protect *(proteger).*

defensa, (de·fen´sâ) *f.* defense; protection;

tusk *(colmillo);* , *m.* linebacker; — **civil,** civil defense.

defensiva, (de·fen·sē´vä) *f.* defensive, guard.

defensivo, va, (de·fen·sē´vo, vä) *adj.* defensive.

defensor, ra, (de·fen·sor´, rä) *n.* defender, supporter; —, *m.* lawyer for the defense.

deferencia, (de·fe·ren´syä) *f.* deference.

deferente, (de·fe·ren´te) *adj.* deferential; deferent *(que lleva fuera).*

deficiencia, (de·fē·syen´syä) *f.* deficiency.

deficiente, (de·fē·syen´te) *adj.* deficient.

déficit, (de´fē·sēt) *m.* deficit.

definición, (de·fē·nē·son´) *f.* definition; decision, finding *(determinación).*

definido, da, (de·fē·ne´tho, thä) *adj.* definite.

definir, (de·fē·nēr´) *va.* to define; to decide, to find on; to finish *(una obra).*

definitivo, va, (de·fē·nē·tē´vo, vä) *adj.* definitive; **en —va,** definitely, decisively.

deformación, (de·for·mä·syon´) *f.* deformation.

deformado, da, (de·for·mä´tho, thä) *adj.* deformed.

deformar, (de·for·mar´) *va.* to deform; (fig.) to distort *(alterar).*

deforme, (de·for´me) *adj.* deformed, misshapen.

deformidad, (de·for·mē·thäth´) *f.* deformity; gross blunder *(error).*

defraudar, (de·fräu·thär´) *va.* to defraud, to cheat; (fig.) to ruin, to spoil *(frustrar).*

defunción, (de·fūn·syon´) *f.* demise, passing.

degeneración, (de·he·ne·rä·syon´) *f.* degeneracy *(efecto);* degeneration *(acción).*

degenerado, da, (de·he·ne·rä´tho, thä) *adj.* degenerated; —, *n.* and *adj.* degenerate.

degenerar, (de·he·ne·rär´) *vn.* to degenerate.

degollar*, (de·go·yär´) *va.* to behead; (fig.) to ruin, to destroy *(destruir).*

degradación, (de·grä·thä·syon´) *f.* degradation.

degradar, (de·grä·thär´) *va.* to degrade, to demean; to demote *(a un militar);* to tone down *(color);* to scale down *(tamaño).*

degüello, (de·gwe´yo) *m.* beheading.

dehesa, (de·e´sä) *f.* pasture, grazing land.

deidad, (deē·thäth´) *f.* deity; divinity *(esencia divina).*

deificar, (deē·fē·kär´) *va.* to deify.

deiforme, (deē·for´me) *adj.* (poet.) godlike.

deísta (de·ēs´tä) *m.* deist.

dejadez, (de·hä·thes´) *f.* negligence, carelessness.

dejado, da, (de·hä´tho, thä) *adj.* careless, negligent; dejected, spiritless *(abatido).*

dejamiento, (de·hä·myen´to) *m.* carelessness; dejection; relinquishment, giving up *(abandono).*

dejar, (de·här´) *va.* to leave; to let, to allow, to permit *(consentir);* to loan, to let have *(prestar);* to stop *(cesar);* — **atrás,** to leave behind, to excel, to surpass; — **de,** to fail to; —**se,** to abandon oneself, to give oneself over.

dejo, (de´ho) *m.* end, termination; negligence, carelessness *(descuido);* aftertaste *(gustillo);* aftereffect *(sentimiento).*

del, (del) of the.

delación, (de·lä·syon´) *f.* accusation.

delantal, (de·län·täl´) *m.* apron.

delante, (de·län´te) *adv.* ahead; — **de,** in front of.

delantero, ra, (de·län·te´ro, rä) *adj.* foremost, first; —, *m.* front mule runner; —, *f.* front part; lead, advantage *(distancia);* (theat.) first row; **tomar la —,** to get ahead, to take the lead.

delatar, (de·lä·tär´) *va.* to accuse, to denounce.

delator, ra, (de·lä·tor´, rä) *n.* accuser, denouncer.

delectación, (de·lek·tä·syon´) *f.* pleasure, delight.

delegación, (de·le·gä·syon´) *f.* delegation.

delegado, da, (de·le·gä´tho, thä) *n.* delegate.

delegar, (de·le·gär´) *va.* to delegate.

deleitable, (de·leē·tä´vle) *adj.* delightful.

deleitar, (de·leē·tar´) *va.* to delight.

deleite, (de·le´ē·te) *m.* pleasure, delight.

deletrear, (de·le·tre·är´) *va.* and *vn.* to spell; to decipher, to interpret *(adivinar).*

deletreo, (de·le·tre´o) *m.* spelling.

deleznable, (de·lez·nä´vle) *adj.* weak, fragile; slippery *(resbaladizo).*

delfín, (del·fēn´) *m.* dauphin; (zool.) dolphin.

delgadez, (del·gä·thes´) *f.* leanness, slenderness, thinness.

delgado, da, (del·gä´tho, thä) *adj.* thin, slender, lean; sharp, acute *(agudo);* fine, thin *(tenue).*

deliberación, (de·lē·ve·rä·syon´) *f.* deliberation; resolution, decision *(resolución).*

deliberadamente, (de·lē·ve·rä·thä·men´te) *adv.* deliberately, willfully.

deliberar, (de·lē·ve·rär´) *vn.* to deliberate, to consider carefully; —, *va.* to resolve,

---

â arm, **e** they, **ē** bē, **o** fore, **ū** blūe, **b** bad, **ch** chip, **d** day, f fat, **g go, h** hot, **k** kid, **1** let

to decide.

delicadeza, (de·lē·kâ·the´sâ) *f.* delicacy; scrupulousness, exactitude *(escrupulosidad).*

delicado da, (de·lē·kâ´tho, thâ) *adj.* delicate; keen, quick *(ingenioso);* scrupulous.

delicia, (de·lē´syâ) *f.* delight, pleasure.

delicioso, sa, (de·lē·syo´so, sâ) *adj.* delicious *(placer sensual);* delightful.

delimitar, (de·lē·mē·târ´) *va.* to delimit, to define.

delincuencia, (de·lēng·kwen´syâ) *f.* delinquency.

delincuente, (de·lēng·kwen´te) *m.* and *f.* and *adj.* delinquent, criminal.

delineación, (de·lē·ne·â·syon´) *f.* delineation, sketch, portrayal.

delineamiento, (de·lē·ne·â·myen´to) *m.* delineation.

delinear, (de·lē·ne·âr´) *va.* to delineate, to sketch, to portray.

delinquir, (de·lēng·kēr´) *vn.* to violate the law.

delirante, (de·lē·rân´te) *adj.* delirious.

delirar, (de·lē·râr´) *vn.* to be delirious, to rant; (fig.) to talk out of one´s head, to talk foolishness.

delirio, (de·lē´ryo) *m.* delirium; nonsense *(disparate).*

delito, (de·lē´to) *m.* crime, infraction.

delta, (del´tâ) *f.* delta.

delusorio, ria, (de·lū·so´ryo ryâ) *adj.* deceiving, deceptive, misleading.

demacrado, da, (de·mâ·krâ´tho, thâ) *adj.* emaciated.

demacrarse, (de·mâ·krâr´se) *vr.* to waste away, to become emaciated.

demanda, (de·mân´dâ) *f.* (com.) demand; endeavor *(empresa);* request, petition *(súplica);* charge, complaint *(del litigante)* **oferta y —,** supply and demand.

demandado, da, (de·man´dâ´tho, thâ) *n.* defendant.

demandante, (de·mân·dân´te) *m.* and *f.* plaintiff.

demandar, (de·mân·dâr´) *va.* to request, to petition; to bring charges against, to lodge a complaint against *(ante el juez).*

demarcar, (de·mâr·kâr´) *va.* to mark off the limits of, to demarcate.

demás, (de·mâs´) *adj.* other, remainder of the; **los** or **las —,** the rest, the others; **— adv.** besides; **y —,** and so forth, and so on; **estar —,** to be more than needed, to be superfluous; **por —,** in vain, to no purpose; excessively, too much *(en demasía).*

demasía, (de·mâ·sē´â) *f.* excess, extreme;

daring, boldness *(atrevimiento);* insolence, rudeness *(insolencia);* **en —,** excessively.

demasiado, da, (de·mâ·syâ´tho, thâ) *adj.* excessive, too much; **—do,** *adv.* too much, excessively.

demencia, (de·men´syâ) *f.* madness, insanity, dementia; **— precoz,** dementia praecox.

demente, (de·men´te) *adj.* mad, insane, demented.

demérito, (de·me´rē·to) *m.* demerit.

democracia, (de·mo·krâ´syâ) *f.* democracy.

demócrata, (de·mo´krâ·tâ) *m.* and *f.* democrat.

democrático, ca, (de·mo·krâ´tē·ko, kâ) *adj.* democratic.

democratizar, (de·mo·krâ·tē·sâr´) *va.* to democratize.

demoler*, (de·mo·ler´) *va.* to demolish, to destroy, to tear down.

demonio, (de·mo´nyo) *m.* devil, demon; ¡—! *interj.* darn it!

demora, (de·mo´râ) *f.* delay; (com.) demurrage; (naut.) bearing.

demorar, (de·mo·râr´) *vn.* to delay, to tarry; **—,** *va.* to delay, to slow up.

demostración, (de·mos·trâ·syon´) *f.* demonstration; display, show *(manifestación).*

demostrar*, (de·mos·trâr´) *va.* to prove, to demonstrate.

demostrativo, va, (de·mos·trâ·tē´vo, vâ) *adj.* demonstrative.

denegación, (de·ne·gâ·syon´) *f.* denial, refusal.

denegar*, (de·ne·gâr´) *va.* to deny, to refuse.

denigración, (de·nē·grâ·syon´) *f.* defamation, maligning.

denigrante, (de·nē·grân´te) *adj.* defamatory.

denigrar, (de·nē·grâr´) *va.* to malign, to defame.

denodado, da, (de·no·thâ´tho, thâ) *adj.* bold intrepid.

denominación, (de·no·mē·nâ·syon´) *f.* denomination.

denominador, (de·no·mē·nâ·thor´) *m.* (math.) denominator.

denominar, (de·no·mē·nâr´) *va.* to name, to mention.

denotar, (de·no·târ´) *va.* to denote, to indicate.

densidad, (den·sē·thâth´) *f.* density; **— específica,** specific gravity.

denso, sa, (den´so, sâ) *adj.* dense.

dentado, da, (den·ta´tho, thâ) *adj.* dentated, dentate; **rueda** —, cogwheel.

dentadura, (den·tâ·thū′rä) f. set of teeth; denture, false teeth (la postiza).

dental, (den·täl′) m. (agr.) plowshare beam (del arado); metal tooth (del trillo); —, adj. dental; **pasta** —, tooth-paste.

dentar*, (den·tar′) va. to tooth, to indent; —, vn. to teethe, to cut one's teeth.

dentellada, (den·te·yä′thä) f. gnashing (sin mascar nada); tooth mark (huella); bite (acción); **a** —s, with one's teeth.

dentición, (den·tē·syon′) f. dentition, teething.

dentífrico, (den·tē′frē·ko) m. dentifrice; — **ca**, adj. for cleaning the teeth; **polvo** —, tooth powder; **pasta** —, toothpaste.

dentista, (den·tēs′tä) m. and f. dentist.

dentistería, (den·tēs·te·rē′ä) f. dentistry.

dentro, (den′tro) adv. within, inside; — **de**, inside of; — **de poco**, shortly; **hacia** —, in, inward, inside; **por** —, on the inside, within.

denuedo, (de·nwe′tho) m. valor, daring, courage.

denuesto, (de·nwes′to) m. affront, abuse.

denuncia, (de·nūn′syä) f. denunciation; announcement.

denunciación, (de·nūn·syä·syon′) f. denunciation, denouncement.

denunciador, ra, (de·nūn·syä·thor′, rä) n. denouncer.

denunciar, (de·nūn·syâr′) va. to announce, to declare (declarar); to denounce (acusar); to predict, to foretell (pronosticar).

deparar, (de·pâ·râr′) va. to furnish, to provide (proporcionar); to afford, to present (poner delante).

departamental, (de·pâr·tâ·men·tâl′) adj. departmental.

departamento, (de·pâr·tâ·men′to) m. department; compartment (compartimiento); apartment (apartamento); administrative divisions of a territory; province (en algunos paises de latinoamérica).

departir, (de·pâr·tēr′) vn. to chat.

dependencia. (de·pen·den′syä) f. dependency; relationship, connection (relación); business, affair (negocio).

depender, (de·pen·der′) vn. to depend, to be dependent; — **de,** to be contingent on, to depend on.

dependiente, (de·pen·dyen′te) m. dependent; employee, clerk (empleado); —, adj. dependent.

depilatorio, (de·pē·1ä·to′ryo) m. depilatory.

deplorable, (de·plo·râ′vle) adj. deplorable, regrettable.

deplorar, (de·plo·râr′) va. to deplore, to regret.

deponer*, (de·po·ner′) va. to put aside (apartar de sí); to depose (a un rey); to testify, to assert (afirmar); to lower, to remove (bajar); —, vi. to have a movement.

deportación, (de·por·tâ·syon′) f. deportation.

deportar, (de·por·târ′) va. to deport.

deporte, (de·por′te) m. sport.

deportivo, va, (de·por·tē′vo, vä) adj. sport, sporting; **club** —**vo,** athletic club.

deposición, (de·po·sē·syon′) f. deposition; movement (del vientre); deposal (privación).

depositante, (de·po·sē·tân′te) m. and f. depositor.

depositar, (de·po·sē·tar′) va. to deposit; (fig.) to confide, to entrust (encomendar).

depositario, ria, (de·po·sē·tâ′ryo, ryä) depositary; —, adj. depository.

depósito, (de·po′sē·to) m. deposit, depository.

depravación, (de·prâ·vâ·syon′) f. depravity.

depravar, (de·prâ·vâr′) va. to deprave, to corrupt.

deprecación, (de·pre·kâ·syon′) f. petition, earnest entreaty.

deprecar, (de·pre·kâr′) va. to beg, to implore.

depreciación, (de·pre·syä·syon′) f. depreciation.

depreciar, (de·pre·syâr′) va. to depreciate.

depresión, (de·pre·syon′) f. depression.

deprimente, (de·prē·men′te) adj. depressing.

deprimir, (de·prē·mēr′) va. to depress; to compress (reducir el volumen); to weaken (quitar las fuerzas); to disparage, to belittle (humillar).

depuración, (de·pū·râ·syon′) f. purification.

depurador, (de·pū·râ·thor′) m. purifier.

depurar, (de·pū·râr′) va. to purify.

derecha, (de·re′chä) f. right hand (mano); right side (lado); (pol.) right wing; **a**—**s**, properly, correctly; **a la** —, to the right.

derechista, (de·re·chēs´tä) *m.* and *f.* (pol.) rightist, conservative.

derecho cha, (de·re´cho, chä) *adj.* right; straight *(recto o vertical);* just, legitimate, right *(justo);* — cho, *adv.* straight ahead; —, *m.* law *(leyes);* right *(facultad);* right side *(lado labrado);* dar — cho, to entitle; —os consulares, consular fees; —os de aduana or arancelarios, customs duties; —os de entrada, import duties; —os de autor, royalties; — humanos, human rights, —os reservados, all rights reserved; facultad de — cho, law school.

deriva, (de·rē´vä) *f.* drift; indicador de —, drift indicator; a la —, drifting.

derivación, (de·rē·vä·syon´) *f.* derivation.

derivado, (de·rē·vä´tho) *m.* by-product; (gram.) derivative; —, da, *adj.* derived.

derivar, (de·rē·vär´) *va.* to derive; to direct, to focus *(encaminar);* —, *vn.* (naut.) to drift; to derive, to be derived.

dermatología, (der·mä·to·lo·hē´ä) *f.* dermatology.

derogación, (de·ro·gä·syon´) *f.* abrogation, abolishment; decrease, reduction *(disminución).*

derogar, (de·ro·gär´) *va.* to abrogate, to abolish.

derramamiento, (de·rrä·mä·myen´to) *m.* overflow; scattering; outpour; — de sangre, bloodshed.

derramar, (de·rrä·mär´) *va.* to pour, to splash *(un líquido);* to scatter *(cosas menudas);* to spread *(una noticia);* — se, to run over, to overflow *(un líquido);* to scatter, to fan out *(desparramarse).*

derrame (de·rrä´me) *m.* loss, waste; leakage *(del recipiente);* — cerebral, (med.) stroke.

derredor, (de·rre·thor´) *m.* boundary, outer edge; al — or en —, about, around.

derrelicto, ta, (de·rre·lēk´to, tä) *adj.* and *m.* derelict.

derrengado, da, (de·rreng·gä´tho, thä) *adj.* bent, twisted.

derrengar*, (de·rreng·gär´) *va.* to dislocate the hip of *(descaderar);* to injure the back of *(despaldar);* to bend, to twist *(torcer).*

derretimiento, (de·rre·tē·myen´to) *m.* melting.

derretir*, (de·rre·tēr´) *va.* to melt *(liquidar);* (fig.) to run through, to burn up *(gastar);* —se, to fall hard, to fall head over heels *(enamorarse);* to fall apart, to be all broken up *(deshacerse).*

derribar, (de·rrē·vär´) *va.* to knock down *(un edificio);* to throw down *(a una persona);* to overthrow *(trastornar);* —se, to throw oneself on the ground.

derribo, (de·rrē´vo) *m.* demolition, knocking down; overthrow; rubble, debris *(materiales).*

derrocar, (de·rro·kär´) *va.* to hurl, to dash *(despeñar);* (fig.) to tear down, to demolish *(derribar);* to unseat, to pull down *(a uno en poder).*

derrochador, ra, (de·rro·chä·thor´, rä) *n.* prodigal, squanderer, wastrel.

derrochar, (de·rro·chär´) *va.* to squander, to waste.

derroche, (de·rro´che) *m.* squandering, waste.

derrota, (de·rro´tä) *f.* (naut.) course, route; (mil.) defeat, rout; road, path *(camino).*

derrotar, (de·rro·tär´) *va.* (naut.) to throw off course; (mil.) to defeat, to rout; to ruin *(destruir).*

derrotero, (de·rro·te´ro) *m.* (naut.) course *(ruta);* (naut.) chart book *(libro);* (fig.) plan of action *(modo de obrar).*

derrotismo, (de·rro·tēz´mo) *m.* defeatism.

derrotista, (de·rro·tēs´tä) *m.* and *f.* defeatist.

derruir*, (de·rrwēr´) *va.* to demolish, to tear down, to wreck.

derrumbar, (de·rrūm·bär´) *va.* to throw headlong, to dash; (Sp. Am.) to knock down, to throw down *(derribar);* —se, to cave in, to collapse.

derrumbe, (de·rrūm´be) *m.* collapse, cave-in.

desabotonar, (de·sä·vo·to·när´) *va.* to unbutton; —, *vn.* to blossom.

desabrido, da, (de·sä·vrē´tho, thä) *adj.* tasteless, insipid; peevish, sharp *(áspero).*

desabrigado, da, (de·sä·vrē·gä´tho, thä) *adj.* without one´s coat; (fig.) shelterless *(desamparado).*

desabrigar, (de·sä·vrē·gär´) *va.* to take off one´s coat, to remove one´s outer clothing.

desabrochar, (de·sä·vro·chär´) *va.* to unbutton, to unfasten; —se con, to confide in.

desacato, (de·sä·kä´to) *m.* disrespect, rudeness; excess *(acción).*

desacertado, da, (de·sä·ser·tä´tho, thä) *adj.* mistaken, wrong, in error.

desacierto, (de·sä·syer´to) *m.* error, mistake, blunder.

desacomodado, da,(de·sä·ko·mo·thä´·tho, thä) *adj.* unemployed, out of work *(sin* acomodo); uncomfortable (incómodo); without means, in want (sin medios).

desacomodar, (de·sâ·ko·mo·thâr´) va. to inconvenience; to discharge (quitar el empleo); —se, to lose one´s job.

desacomodo, (de·sâ·ko·mo´tho) m. loss of one´s job; inconveniencing.

desacordado, da, (de·sâ·kor´thâ´tho, thâ) adj. poorly matched, unharmonious.

desacorde, (de·sâ´kor´the) adj. discordant, inharmonious.

desacostumbrado, da,(de·sâ·kos·trüm·brâ´ tho, thâ) adj. uncustomary, unusual (insólito); unaccustomed.

desacostumbrarse, (de·sâ·kos·tüm·brâ·r´se) vr. to become unaccustomed.

desacreditar, (de·sâ·kre·the·târ´) va. to discredit.

desactivar, (de·sâk·te·vâr´) va. to deactivate.

desacuerdo, (de·sâ·kwer´tho) m. disagreement, discord; failure to remember (falta de memoria).

desafecto, (de·sâ fek´to) m. disaffection, ill will, enmity.

desafiar, (de·sâ·fyâr´) va. to challenge; (fig.) to defy, to brave (oponerse).

desafinar, (de·sâ·fē·nâr´) vn. and vr. to be off key (la voz); to be out of tune (un instrumento); (fig.) to talk out of turn.

desafio, (de·sâ·fē´o) m. challenge (acción); duel (efecto); rivalry, contest (competencia).

desaforado, da, (de·sâ·fo·râ´tho, thâ) adj. lawless, heedless (sin ley); unearthly, extraordinary (excesivo).

desaforar*, (de·sâ·fo·râr´) va. to violate the rights of; —se, to get beside oneself, to go to pieces.

desafortunado, da, (de·sâ·for·tü·nâ´tho, thâ) adj. unfortunate.

desafuero, (de·sâ·fwe´ro) m. excess (desacato); lawless act (contra ley); violation of someone´s rights.

desagradable, (de·sâ·grâ·thâ´vle) adj. disagreeable, unpleasant.

desagradar, (de·sâ·grâ·thâr´) va. to displease, to offend.

desagradecido, da, (de·sâ·grâ·the·sē´tho, thâ) adj. ungrateful; —, n. ingrate.

desagrado, (de·sâ·grâ´tho) m. displeasure.

desagraviar, (de·sâ·grâ·vyâr´) va. to make amends for.

desagravio, (de·sâ·grâ´vyo) m. satisfaction, amends.

desaguadero, (de·sâ·gwâ·the´ro) m. drain pipe (conducto); drainage canal.

desaguar, (de·sâ·gwâr´) va. and vn. o drain.

desagüe (de·sâ´gwe) m. draining, drainage; drain pipe, drain (conducto).

desahogado, da, (de·sâ·o·gâ´tho, thâ) adj. impudent (descarado); comfortable (cómodo).

desahogar, (de·sâ·o·gâr´) va. to ease, to relieve (aliviar); to give free rein to (dar rienda suelta); —se, to get relief; to unburden oneself, to get a problem off one´s chest (expansionarse).

desahogo, (de·sâ·o´go) m. relief (alivio); relaxation (ensanche); ease, comfort (comodidad); freedom, lack of restraint (libertad).

desahuciar, (de·sâü·syâr´) va. to evict (al inquilino); to declare incurable (al enfermo); to make despair of (quitar la esperanza).

desairado, da, (de·sâē·râ´tho, thâ) adj. slighted, offended; rebuffed; mediocre, poor (desgarbado).

desairar, (de·sâē·râr´) va. to disregard to rebuff (rechazar); to slight, to offend (desatender); to detract from (deslucir).

desaire, (de·sâ´ē·re) m. rebuff, disregard; offense, slight; awkwardness (falta de garbo).

desajuste, (de·sâ·hüs´te) m. breakdown, collapse.

desalentar*, (de·sâ·len·târ´) va. to wind (dificultar el aliento); (fig.) to discourage; —se, to lose hope, to be discouraged.

desaliento, (de·sâ·lyen´to) m. dispair, discouragement, dejection.

desaliñado, da, (de·sâ·lē·nyâ´tho, thâ) adj. slipshod, messy.

desaliñar, (de·sâ·lē·nyâr´) va. to disarrange, to mess up.

desalmado da, (de·sâl·mâ´tho, thâ) adj. cruel, inhuman, heartless.

desalojar, (de·sâ·lo·hâr´) va. to dislodge; to abandon, to evacuate (abandonar); to displace (desplazar); —, vn. to move out.

desalumbrado, da, (de·sâ·lüm·brâ´tho, thâ) adj. dazzled; (fig.) groping in the dark, off the track (que ha perdido el tino).

desamarrar, (de·sâ·mâ·rrâr´) va. to unmoor; (fig.) to let loose of (desasir).

desamparar, (de·sâm·pâ·râr´) va. to forsake, to abandon; to relinquish (con *renuncia de derecho).*

desamparo, (de·sãm·pä´ro) *m.* abandonment, forlornness, desolation; relinquishment.

desandar*, (de·sãn·dâr´) *va.* to retrace, to go back over.

desangrar, (de· sãng·grär´) *va.* to remove a large amount of blood from; (fig.) to drain *(un estanque);* to impoverish slowly *(empobrecer).*

desanimado, da, (de·sä·nē·mä´tho, thä) *adj.* downhearted; dull, spiritless *(poco animado).*

desanimar, (de·sä·nē·mär´) *va.* to discourage; **—se,** to become discouraged.

desanudar, (de·sä·nū·thär´) *va.* to untie; (fig.) to disentangle, to unravel *(disolver).*

desapacible, (de·sä·pä·sē´vle) *adj.* disagreeable, unpleasant.

desapadrinar, (de·sä·pä· thrē·när´) *va.* to disapprove of *(desaprobar);* to disavow, to disclaim, to disown *(retirar el apoyo).*

desaparecer*, (de·sä·pä·re·ser´) *va.* to whisk out of sight; **—,** *vn.* to disappear.

desaparecimiento, (de·sä·pä·re·sē· myen´to) *m.* disappearance.

desaparejar, (de·sä·pä·re·här´) *va.* to unharness *(una caballería);* (naut.) to unrig.

desaparición, (de·sä·pä·rē·syon´) *f.* disappearance.

desapasionar, (de·sä·pä·syo·när´) *va.* to make objective, to remove one´s prejudice *(volver imparcial);* to root out one´s passion.

desapercibido, da, (de·sä·per·sē·vē´tho, thä) *adj.* unprepared, not ready.

desaplicado, da, (de·sä·plē·kä´tho, thä) *adj.* careless, lazy, indifferent.

desaprobación, (de·sä·pro·vä·syon´) *f.* disapproval.

desaprobar*, (de·sä ·pro·vär´) *va.* to disapprove of.

desapropiar, (de·sä·pro·pyär´) *vt.* to expropriate, to take from; **—se de,** to give up ownership of, to alienate.

desaprovechado, da (de·sä·pro·ve·chä´tho, thä) *adj.* lacking drive, lacking ambition, indifferent *(persona);* wasted, untapped, unused.

desaprovechamiento, (de·sä·pro·ve·chä·myen´to) *m.* misuse, waste; lack of drive.

desaprovechar, (de·sä·pro·vechâr´) *va.* to misuse, to waste.

desapuntar, (de·sä·pūn·tär´) *va.* to unstitch; to make lose one´s aim *(quitar la puntería).*

desarbolar, (de·sâr·vo·lär´) *va.* (naut.) to dismast.

desarmable, (de·sâr·mä´vle) *adj.* collapsible, dismountable.

desarmados, (de·sâr·mä·thor´) *m.* hammer of a gun.

desarmar, (de ·sâr·mär´) *va.* to disarm; to take apart, to dismount, to disassemble *(desmontar);* (naut.) to unrig; (mil.) to disband; (fig.) to pacify, to assuage *(templar).*

desarme, (de· sâr´me) *m.* disarmament, disassembly; pacifying.

desarraigar, (de·sä· rräê· gâr´) *va.* to uproot; (fig.) to root out, to eradicate.

desarraigo, (de·sä·rrä´ē·go) *m.* (fig.) eradication; uprooting.

desarreglado, da, (de·sä·rre·glä´tho, thä) *adj.* immoderate, intemperate; disorderly *(desordenado).*

desarreglar, (de·sä·rre·glär´) *va.* to put out of order, to upset.

desarreglo, (de·sä·rre´glo) *m.* disorder.

desarrimar, (de· sä·rrē·mär´) *va.* to push back, to pull back; (fig.) to get out of.

desarrollar, (de·sä·rro·yär´) *va.* to unroll, to unwrap; (fig.) to develop *(acrecentar).*

desarrollo, (de·sä·rro´yo) *m.* development, growth.

desarropar, (de· sä·rro·pâr´) *va.* to undress.

desarrugar, (de·sä·rrū·gâr´) *va.* to take out the wrinkles from.

desaseado, da, (de·sä·se·ä´tho, thä) *adj.* untidy, careless.

desasear, (de·sä·se·âr´) *va.* to mess up, to make untidy.

desaseo, (de·sä·se´o) *m.* lack of neatness, slovenliness.

desasir*, (de· sä·sēr´) *va.* to let loose of, to let go of; **—se de,** to get rid of.

desasosiego, (de·sä·so·sye´go) *m.* restlessness, uneasiness.

desastrado, da, (de·sâs·trä´tho, thä) *adj.* wretched, miserable; ragged, slovenly, sloppy *(desarreglado).*

desastre, (de· sâs´tre) *m.* disaster, misfortune.

desastroso, sa, (de ·sâs·tro´so, sä) *adj.* disastrous.

desatar, (de·sä·tär´) *va.* to untie, to loosen *(deshacer);* to figure out, to clear up *(aclarar);* **—se,** to break out *(descomedirse);* to come out of one´s shell *(perder la timidez).*

desatascar, (de·sä·tâs·kär´) *va.* to pull out of the mud; to unplug *(una cañería);*

(fig.) to get out of a jam *(de un apuro).*

desataviar, (de·sâ·tâ·vyâr´) *va.* to strip of decorations.

desatención, (de· sâ·ten·syon´) *f.* lack of attention, absentmindedness; slight, impoliteness *(descortesía).*

desatender*, (de·sâ·ten· der´) *va.* to pay no attention to, to disregard, to neglect, to slight.

desatento, ta, (de· sâ·ten´to, tâ) *adj.* inattentive, careless; rude, uncivil *(descortés).*

desatinado, da, (de·sâ·tē ·nâ´tho, thâ) *adj.* senseless, foolish; off-the-mark.

desatinar, (de·sâ·tē·nâr´) *va.* to drive out of one´s mind, to drive to distraction; —, *vn.* to talk nonsense.

desatino, (de·sâ·tē´no) *m.* foolishness, nonsense.

desatornillar, (de·sâ·tor·nē·yâr´) *va. to* unscrew.

desautorizar, (de·sâū·to·rē·sâr´) *va.* to wrest authority from.

desavenencia, (de·sâ·ve·nen´syâ) *f.* discord, disagreement.

desavenir*, (de· sâ·ve·nēr´) *va.* to put at odds, to make disagree.

desayunador, (de·sâ·yū·nâ·thor´) *m.* breakfast room.

desayunarse, (de·sâ·yū·nâr´se) *vr.* to breakfast, to eat breakfast.

desayuno, (de·sâ´yū no) *m.* breakfast.

desazón, (de· sâ·son´) *f.* tastelessness; poor quality *(de las tierras);* (fig.) trouble, bad time *(molestia);* queasiness, upset *(de salud).*

desazonado, da, (de· sâ·so ·nâ´tho, thâ) *adj.* queasy; poor; upset, bothered.

desazonar, (de·sâ·so·nâr´) *va.* to take away the taste of; (fig.) to upset, to bother *(molestar);* —se, to feel indisposed.

desbancar, (dez·vâng·kâr´) *va.* (fig.) to supplant, to take the place of.

desbandarse, (dez·vân·dâr´se) *vr.* to disband, to disperse.

desbarajuste, (dez·vâ·râ·hūs´te) *m.* confusion, jumble.

desbaratado, da, (dez·vâ·râ·tâ´tho, thâ) *adj.* broken; upset.

desbaratar, (dez·vâ·râ·târ´) *va.* to break, to ruin *(arruinar);* to run through, to waste *(disipar);* (fig.) to spoil, to upset *(estorbar);* (mil.) to rout; —, *vn.* to talk nonsense.

desbarato, (dez·vâ·râ´to) *m.* waste, squandering; ruin, breaking; rout.

desbarrar, (dez·vâ·rrâr´) *vn.* to slip away,

to steal away; (fig.) to wander aimlessly *(sin razón).*

desbastar, (dez ·vâs·târ´) *va.* to rough in, to work roughly; to use up, to diminish *(desgastar);* (fig.) to smooth out, to give some polish *(educar).*

desbastecido, da, (dez ·vâs·te·sē´tho, thâ) *adj.* without sufficient provisions, out of supplies.

desbocado, da, (dez·vo·kâ´tho, thâ) *adj.* widemouthed *(cañón);* runaway *(caballería);* (fig.) foul-mouthed *(grosero).*

desbordar, (dez ·vor·thâr´) *vn.* to overflow, to spill over, to run over; (fig.) to know no bounds *(rebosar).*

desbordamiento, (dez·vor·thâ·myen´to) *m.* overflowing.

desbuchar, (dez ·vū·châr´) *va.* to disgorge; (coll.) to unbosom, to reveal *(confesar).*

descabellado da, (des·kâ·ve·yâ´tho,thâ) *adj.* disorderly, unruly, unrestrained.

descabellar, (des· kâ·ve·yâr´) *va.* to muss, to dishevel; to kill instantly with a drive to the neck *(al toro).*

descabello, (des·kâ·ve´yo) *m.* driving in the sword to the neck, dispatch.

descabezado, da, (des·kâ·ve·sâ´tho, thâ) *adj.* (fig.) out of one´s head; headless.

descabezar, (des·kâ·ve·sâr´) *va.* to behead; to lop off the top of *(un árbol);* —se, to rack one´s brains.

descabullirse*, (des·kâ· vū·yēr´se) *vr.* to escape, to get away; (fig.) to get oneself off the hook.

descalabrar, (des·kâ·lâ·vrâr´) *va.* to injure in the head; to hurt, to injure *(herir).*

descalabro, (des·kâ·lá´vro) *m.* calamity, misfortune.

descalificar, (des·kâ·lē ·fē·kâr´) *va.* to disqualify.

descalzar, (des·kâl·sâr´) *va.* to pull off, to take off; to take off one´s shoes *(quitar el calzado).*

descalzo, za, (des·kâl´so, sâ) *adj.* barefooted.

descaminar, (des· kâ·mē·nâr´) *va.* to misguide, to lead astray, to mislead.

descampado, da, (des·kâm·pâ´tho, thâ) open, clear.

descampar, (des·kâm·pâr´) *vn.* to stop raining; —, *va.* to clear off.

descansadamente, (des·kân·sâ·thâ·men´te) *adv.* easily, effortlessly.

descansado, da, (des·kân·sâ´tho, thâ) *adj.* peaceful, quiet, restful.

descansar, (des·kân·sâr´) *va.* to rest *(apo-*

yar); to spell, to relieve *(ayudar)*; vn. to rest.

descanso, (des·kän´so) *m.* rest, repose.

descarado, da, (des·kä·rá´tho, thä) *adj.* impudent, barefaced, cheeky.

descararse, (des·kä·râr´se) *vr.* to behave insolently.

descarga, (des·kär´gä) *f.* unloading; (mil.) volley; discharge, firing.

descargadero, (des·kär·gä·the´ro) *m.* wharf, dock.

descargar, (des·kär·gär´) *va.* to unload *(la carga)*; to discharge, to fire *(un arma)*; to free, to relieve *(de una obligación)*; to let go with, to let have *(un golpe)*; **—se,** to be cleared of the charges, to be acquitted.

descargo, (des· kär´go) *m.* discharge; acquittal; unloading.

descarnar, (des·kär· när´) *va.* to remove the flesh from; to chip away part of *(desmoronar)*.

descaro, (des·kä´ro) *m.* impudence, audacity.

descarriar, (des·kä·rryär´) *va.* to lead astray *(desviar)*; to separate, to keep separately *(reses)*; **—se** to go astray.

descarrilar, (des·kä·rrē ·lär´) *vn.* (rail.) to jump the track, to derail.

descartar, (des·kär·tär´) *va.* to cast aside, to throw off *(apartar)*; to count out, to leave out *(de un proyecto)*; to discard *(un naipe)*.

descarte, (des·kär´te) *m.* discard; excuse, reason *(evasiva)*.

descasar, (des·kär´sär) *va.* to separate; to annul the marriage of *(anular el matrimonio)*; to throw out of balance *(cosas que casaban bien)*.

descascar, (des·käs·kär´) *va.* to peel; to shell; to husk, to shuck.

descascarar, (des·käs·kä·rär´) *va.* to skin *(una manzana)*; to peel *(una naranja)*; to shell *(una nuez)*; to shuck, to husk *(la espiga)*.

descendencia, (des·sen·den´syä) *f.* descent *(linaje)*; descendants.

descendente, (des·sen·den´te) *adj.* descending.

descender*, (des·sen·der´) *vn.* to descend; to derive, to originate *(derivarse)*; **—,** *va.* to lower, to take down.

descendiente, (des·sen·dyen´te) *adj.* descending; **—,** *m.* descendant.

descendimiento, (des·sen·dē·myen´to) *m.* descent; lowering.

descensión, (des·sen·syón) *m.* descent.

descenso, (des·sen´so) *m.* descent; (fig.)

degradation.

descentralización, (des·sen·trä· lē·sä· syon´) *f.* decentralization.

descentralizar, (des·sen·trä·lē·sär´) *va.* to decentralize.

descentrar, (des·sen·trär´) *va.* to put off center; **—se,** to be off center.

descepar, (des·se·pär´) *va.* to uproot; (fig.) to weed out, to get rid of *(extirpar)*.

descerrajar, (des·se·rrä·här´) *va.* to rip the lock from *(arrancar)*; to break the lock on *(violentar)*; (coll.) to shoot, to fire *(disparar)*.

descifrar, (des·sē· frär´) *va.* to decipher, to decode.

descinchar, (des·sēn·chär´) *va.* to loosen the saddle straps of.

desclavar, (des·klä·vär´) *va.* to pull out the nails from.

descobijar, (des·ko·vē·här´) *va.* to uncover, to remove the blankets from.

descolgar*, (des· kol·gär´) *va.* to take down *(algo colgado)*; to lower with a rope *(bajar)*; to take down the hangings from *(una iglesia)*; to take down the draperies from *(una casa)*; **—se,** to slide down a rope; (fig.) to slip down, to descend.

descolorar, (des·ko·lo·rär´) *va.* to discolor.

descolorido, da, (des·ko·lo·rē´tho, thä) *adj.* faded, discolored.

descollar*, (des·ko·yär´) *vn.* to excel, to be outstanding.

descombrar, (des·kom· brär´) *va.* to disencumber.

descomedido, da, (des ·ko·me·thē´tho, thä) *adj.* excessive, out of proportion *(excesivo)*; rude, disrespectful *(descortés)*.

descomedirse*, (des·ko·me·thēr´se) *vr.* to be rude, to be disrespectful.

descompasado, da, (des·kom·pä·sä´tho, thä) *adj.* excessive, immoderate.

descomponer*, (des·kom·po·ner´) *va.* (chem.) to decompose, to break down; to put out of order *(desordenar)*; to put at odds, to hurt the friendship of *(dos personas)*; **—se,** to decompose, to rot *(corromperse)*; to lose one´s composure *(perder la serenidad)*.

descomposición, (des·kom·po·sē·syon´) *f.* falling out; (chem.) decomposition, breakdown; decay, rotting; loss of composure.

descompuesto, ta, (des·kom·pwes´to, tä) *adj.* decomposed rotten; out of order; distorted *(alterado)*; (fig.) discourteous, insolent *(descortés)*.

descomunal, (des· ko·mū·nâl′) *adj.* most unusual, extraordinary, highly uncommon.

desconcertado, da, (des·kon·ser·tâ′tho, thä) *adj.* disconcerted; dislocated; out of order; (fig.) evil *(de mala vida).*

desconcertar*, (des· kon·ser·târ′) *va.* to put out of order *(desordenar);* to dislocate *(un hueso);* to disconcert *(confundir);* —se, to have a falling out *(enemistarse);* (fig.) to be rude, to be disrespectful.

desconcierto, (des·kon·syer′to) *m.* disrepair *(desarreglo):* disorder, confusion *(desorden);* (fig.) lack of restraint *(falta de medida);* recklessness *(falta de gobierno).*

desconectar, (des·ko·nek·târ′) *va.* (elec.) to disconnect; (fig.) to detach, to separate *(desunir).*

desconfiado, da, (des·kom·fyä′tho, thä) *adj.* suspicious, distrustful.

desconfianza, (des·kom·fyän′sä) *f.* distrust, lack of confidence, mistrust.

desconfiar, (des·kom·fyâr′) *vn.* to lack confidence, to be distrustful; — de, to mistrust, to distrust.

desconforme, (des·kom·for′me) *adj.* in disagreement; unresigned, dissatisfied *(no satisfecho).*

desconformidad, (des·kom·for·mē·thâth′) *f.* disagreement *(desacuerdo);* impatience, dissatisfaction.

descongelador, (des·kon·he·lä·thor′) *m.* defroster, deicer.

descongelar, (des·kon·he·lâr′) *va.* to defrost.

desconocer*, (des·ko·no·ser′) *va.* to disown, to disavow *(rechazar);* not to know *(no conocer);* not to recognize *(no reconocer);* to have forgotten *(no recordar);* to pretend unawareness of *(darse por desentendido).*

desconocido, da. (des·ko·no·sē′tho, thä) *adj.* ungrateful *(ingrato);* unknown, foreign *(ignorado);* unrecognizable *(muy cambiado);* —, *n.* stranger.

desconsiderado, da, (des·kon·sē·the·rä′-tho, thä) *adj.* inconsiderate.

desconsolado, da, (des·kon·so·lä′tho, thä) *adj.* disconsolate, grieving.

desconsolador, ra, (des·kon·so·lä·thor′, rä) *adj.* depressing, dejecting, disconsolate.

desconsolar*, (des·kon·so·lâr′) *va.* to grieve, to hurt, to pain.

desconsuelo. (des·kon·swe′lo) *m.* dejection, grief, suffering.

descontaminación, (des·kon·tâ·mē·nä·syon′) *f,* decontamination.

descontaminar, (des·kon·tâ·mē·nâr′) *va.* to decontaminate.

descontar*, (des·kon·târ′) *va.* to discount; to grant, to assume to be true *(dar por cierto);* to deduct *(rebajar).*

descontentar, (des·kon·ten·târ′) *va.* to displease, to dissatisfy.

descontento, (des·kon·ten′to) *m.* discontent, dissatisfaction, displeasure; —, ta, *adj.* dissatisfied, discontented, displeased.

descontinuar, (des·kon·tē·nwâr′) *va.* to discontinue.

descorazonado, da, (des·ko·râ·so·nä′tho, thä) *adj.* depressed, in low spirits, glum.

descorazonar, (des·ko·râ·so·nâr′) *va.* to remove the heart of; (fig.) to dishearten, to discourage *(desanimar).*

descornar*, (des·kor·nâr′) *va.* to dehorn.

descorrer, (des·ko·rrer′) *vn.* to run, to flow; —, *va.* to retravel, to go back over; — la cortina, to draw open the curtain.

descortés, (des·kor·tes′) *adj.* impolite, discourteous.

descortesía, (des·kor·te·sē′ä) *f.* discourtesy, impoliteness.

descortezar, (des·kor·te·sâr′) *va.* to remove the bark from *(un árbol);* to remove the crust from *(un pan);* (fig.) to refine, to cultivate *(desbastar).*

descoser, (des·ko·ser′) *va.* to rip, to unstitch; —se, (fig.) to let slip out, to let out of the bag.

descosido, (des·ko·sē′tho) *m.* ripped seam, rip; — da, *adj.* ripped, unstitched; indiscreet, given to revealing confidences *(imprudente).*

descostrar, (des·kos·trâr′) *va.* to take off the crust from.

descotado, (des·ko·tâ′tho) *adj.* décolleté; vestido —, décolleté gown.

descote, (des·ko′te) *m.* low neck, décolletage.

descoyuntar, (des·ko·yūn·târ′) *va.* to dislocate; (fig.) to bother, to annoy *(molestar).*

descrédito, (des·kre′thē·to) *m.* discredit.

descreer*, (des·kre·er′) *va.* to disbelieve, to fail to believe.

descreído, da, (des·kre·ē′tho, thä) *n.* and *adj.* infidel.

descreimiento, (des·kreē·myen′to) *m.* lack of faith, disbelief.

describir*, (des·krē·vēr′) *va.* to describe.

descripción, (des·krēp·syon′) *f.* descrip-

descriptivo, va, (des·krēp·tē´vo, vä) *adj.* descriptive.

descrito, ta, (des·krē´to, tä) *adj.* described.

descuartizar, (des·kwâr·tē·sâr´) *va,* to quarter; (coll.) to divide up, to split up *(hacer pedazos).*

descubierto, ta, (des·kū·vyer´to, tä) *adj.* uncovered; bareheaded (destocado); —, *m.* (com.) deficit; (eccl.) showing of the sacrament; **al —to,** sincere, aboveboard; **girar en —to,** to overdraw.

descubridor, ra, (des·kū·vrē·thor´, rä) *n.* discoverer; —, *m.* (mil.) scout.

descubrimiento, (des·kū·vrē·myen´to) *m.* discovery.

descubrir*, (des·kū·vrēr´) *va.* to uncover (destapar); to disclose (manifestar); to discover *(lo ignorado); ;* to invent *(inventar);* to make out, to have a view of *(alcanzar a ver);* **—se,** to take off one's hat.

descuello, (des·kwe´yo) *m.* towering height, imposing height; (fig.) superiority, distinction, preeminence *(eminencia);* haughtiness *(altivez).*

descuento, (des·kwen´to) *m.* discount; deduction.

descuidado, da, (des·kwē·thä´tho, thä) *adj.* careless, negligent.

descuidar, (des·kwē·thâr´) *va.* to relieve, to free *(de una obligación);* to distract *(distraer);* to neglect, to be careless of *(no cuidar de).*

descuido, (des·kwē´tho) *m.* carelessness, neglect; slip; oversight *(desliz).*

desde, (dez´the) *prep.* since *(de tiempo);* from *(de espacio);* **— luego,** of course, **— entonces,** since then; **— que,** since; **— ahora,** from now on; **— un principio,** from the beginning.

desdecir*, (dez·the·sēr´) *vn.* to go counter, to be out of keeping *(no corresponder);* **—se,** to retract a remark, to take back what one has said.

desdén, (dez·then´) *m.* disdain, contempt.

desdentado da, (dez·then·tä´tho, thä) *adj.* toothless.

desdeñar, (dez·the·nyâr´) *va.* to disdain, to look down on; **—se,** to be disdainful.

desdeñoso, sa, (dez·the·nyo´so, sä) *adj.* disdainful, contemptuous.

desdicha, (dez·thē´chä) *f.* misfortune; dire poverty *(pobreza).*

desdichado, da, (dez·thē·chä´tho, thä) *adj.* unfortunate, miserable.

desdoblar, (dez·tho·vlâr´) *va.* to unfold, to spread out.

desdoro, (dez·tho´ro) *m.* slur, blemish, blot.

deseable (de·se·ä´vle) *adj.* desirable.

desear, (de·se·âr´) *va.* to desire, to wish; **— saber,** to wonder.

desecar, (de·se·kâr´) *va.* to dry; (fig.) to harden.

desechable, (de·se·chä´vle) *adj.* disposable.

desechar, (de·se·châr´) *va.* to reject *(rechazar);* to throw out *(arrojar);* to depreciate, to underrate *(menospreciar);* to cast off *(apartar de sí).*

desecho, (de·se´cho) *m.* residue, remainder *(residuo);* discard, castoff *(cosa que no sirve);* low opinion, low regard *(menosprecio).*

desembalar, (de·sem·bä·lâr´) *va.* to unpack, to open.

desembarazar, (de·sem·bä·rä·sâr´) *va.* to clear, to disencumber; to clear out, to empty *(desocupar).*

desembarazo, (de·sem·bä·rä´so) *m.* ease, facility, freedom of movement.

desembarcadero, (de·sem·bâr·kä·the´ro) *m.* landing place.

desembarcar, (de·sem·bâr·kâr´) *va.* to unload; —, *vn.* to disembark, to land.

desembarco, (de·sem·bâr´ko) *m.* landing, disembarkment.

desembarque, (de·sem·bâr´ke) *m.* landing, unloading.

desembocadero, (de·sem·bo·kä·the´ro) *m.* outlet, exit; entrance *(de una calle);* mouth *(de un río).*

desembocar, (de·sem·bo·car´) *vn.* to run, to end *(una calle);* to flow, to empty *(un río).*

desembolsar, (de·sem·bol·sâr´) *va.* to empty out from a purse; (fig.) to expend, to disburse.

desembolso, (de·sem·bol´so) *m.* disbursement, expenditure.

desembozar, (de· sem·bo·sâr´) *va.* to unmuffle, to uncover.

desembragar, (de·sem·brä·gâr´) *va.* (mech.) to disengage; (auto.) to put in neutral; —, *vn.* to depress the clutch pedal.

desembrollar, (de·sem·bro·yâr´) *va.* to disentangle, to unravel, to untangle.

desembuchar, (de·sem·bū·châr´) *va.* to disgorge; (coll.) to unbosom, to reveal *(confesar).*

desemejante, (de·se·me·hän´te) *adj.* dissimilar, different, unlike.

desemejanza, (de·se·me·hän´sä) *f.* dissimilarity, difference, unlikeness.

desempacar, (de·sem·pâ·kâr´) va. to unpack, to unwrap.

desempacho, (de·sem·pâ´cho) m. unconcern, ease.

desempapelar, (de·sem·pâ·pe·lâr´) va. to take the paper off.

desempaquetar, (de·sem·pâ·ke·târ´) va. to unpack, to unwrap.

desemparejar, (de·sem·pâ·re·hâr´) va. to unmatch, to make uneven.

desempatar, (de·sem·pâ·târ´) va. to break the tie in.

desempeñar, (de·sem·pe·nyâr´) va. to redeem (una garantía); to get out of debt (librar de deudas); to play (un papel); to fulfill, to carry out (cumplir); to get out of a difficult situation (sacar airoso).

desempeño. (de·sem·pe´nyo) m. redeeming; fulfillment, performance.

desempleado, da, (de·sem·ple·â´tho, thâ) adj. unemployed.

desempleo, (de·sem·ple´o) m. unemployment.

desempolvar, (de·sem·pol·vâr´) va. to dust off; to brush up on (traer a la memoria); —se, to brush up.

desencabestrar. (de·seng·kâ·ves·trâr´) va. to disentangle from the halter.

desencadenar, (de·seng·kâ·the·nâr´) va. to unchain; (fig.) to unleash, to set abroad; —se, to break out, to be unleashed.

desencajar, (de·seng·kâ·hâr´) va. to pull out of place, to pull from its socket or fitting; —se, to become contorted.

desencallar, (de·seng·kâ·yâr´) va. to float, to set afloat.

desencantar, (de·seng·kân·târ´) va. to disenchant, to disillusion.

desencanto, (de·seng·kân´to) m. disenchantment, disillusion.

desencolerizarse, (de·seng·ko·le·rē·sâr´se) vr. to grow calm, to get over one s anger.

desenconar, (de·seng·ko·nâr´) va. to reduce (la inflamación); to appease, to calm (el ánimo); —se, to abate, to subside.

desencono, (de·seng·ko´no) m. calming down; abatement.

desencordar*, (de·seng·kor·thâr´) va. to unstring.

desencordelar, (de·seng·kor·the·lâr´)va. to unbind, to unfasten.

desencorvar, (de·seng·kor·vâr´) va. to straighten.

desenfadado, da, (de·sem·fâ·thâ´tho, thâ)

adj. unencumbered, free; spacious, roomy (un sitio).

desenfadar, (de·sem·fâ·thâr´) va. to calm the anger of, to appease.

desenfado, (de·sem·fâ´tho) m. freedom, ease, facility (despejo); relaxation, change (diversión).

desenfrenado, da, (de·sem·fre·nâ´tho, thâ) adj. wanton, unbridled; debauched.

desenfrenar, (de·sem·fre·nâr´) va. to unbridle; —se, to become completely debauched; to be unleashed (los elementos).

desenfreno, (de·sem·fre´no) m. debauchery (libertinaje); unbridling; unleashing.

desenganchar, (de·seng·gân·châr´) va. to unhook; to unhitch (caballerías).

desengañado, da, (de·seng·gâ·nyâ´tho, thâ) adj. disillusioned; disabused.

desengañar, (de·seng·gâ·nyâr´) va. to open one´s eyes to, to undeceive; to disillusion, to disappoint (quitar ilusiones).

desengaño, (de·seng·gâ´nyo) m. disillusionment, disappointment; naked truth, fact of the matter (claridad).

desengranar, (de·seng·grâ·nâr´) va. to throw out of gear, to disengage.

desenhebrar, (de·se·ne·vrâr´) va. to unthread.

desenjaular, (de·sen·hâū·lâr´) va. to let out of the cage.

desenlace, (de·sen·lâ´se) m. denouement, outcome.

desenlazar, (de·sen·lâ·sâr´) va. to untie; (fig.) to unravel, to resolve, to clear up (solucionar).

desenmarañar, (de·sen·mâ·râ·nyâr) va. to disentangle.

desenmascarar, (de·sen·mâs·kâ·râr´) va. to unmask; (fig.) to expose, to reveal; —se, to unmask.

desenojo, (de·se·no´ho) m. calming down, quieting down.

desenredar, (de·sen·rre·thâr´) va. to disentangle; —se, to extricate oneself, to free oneself.

desenrollar, (de·sen·rro·yâr´) va. to unroll.

desenroscar, (de·sen·rros·kâr´) va. to untwist, to unroll.

desensartar, (de·sen·sâr·târ´) va. to unthread.

desensillar, (de·sen·sē·yâr´) va. to unsaddle.

desentenderse*, (de·sen·ten·der´se) vr. to pretend ignorance, to pretend not to notice; — de, to disregard, to ignore; to have nothing to do with (prescindir de).

desentendido, da, (de·sen·ten·dē´tho, thä) *adj.* unmindful; **hacerse el —** or **la —** to feign ignorance, to pretend to be unaware.

desenterrar*, (de·sen·te·rrär´) *va.* to disinter, to dig up.

desentonar, (de·sen·to·när´) *va.* to humble; —, *vn.* to have poor tone; **—se,** (fig.) to raise one´s voice, to snap.

desentono, (de·sen·to´no) *m.* poor tone; (fig.) rude tone of voice.

desentrañar, (de·sen·trä·nyär´) *va.* to eviscerate; (fig.) to ferret out, to figure out *(averiguar).*

desenvainar, (de·sem·bäē·när´) *va.* to unsheathe; (fig.) to bring to light *(sacar);* to stretch out *(las garras).*

desenvoltura, (de·sem·bol·tū´rä) *f.* ease, effortlessness, self-assurance, freedom; articulateness *(de elocución).*

desenvolver*, (de·sem·bol·ver´) *va.* to unwrap, to unroll *(desarrollar);* to clear up, to unravel *(desenredar);* to develop *(acrecentar);* **—se,** to act with assurance, to get along well.

desenvuelto, ta, (de· sem·bwel´to, tä) *adj.* poised self-assured; articulate.

deseo, (de·se´o) *m.* desire, wish.

deseoso, sa, (de·se·o´so, sa) *adj.* desirous.

desequilibrio, (de·se·kē·lē´vryo) *m.* unsteadiness, lack of balance.

deserción, (de·ser·syon´) *f.* desertion.

desertar, (de·ser·tär´) *va.* to desert; to withdraw, to abandon *(la apelación).*

desertor, (de·ser·tor´) *m.* deserter.

desescarchador, (de·ses·kär·chä·thor´) *m.* defroster.

desesperación, (de·ses·pe·rä·syon´) *f.* despair, desperation; anger, fury *(cólera).*

desesperadamente, (de·ses·pe·rä·thä·men´-te) *adv.* desperately.

desesperado, da, (de·ses·pe·rä´tho, thä) *adj.* desperate, hopeless.

desesperanzar, (de·ses·pe·rän· sär´) *va.* to deprive of hope, to make desperate.

desesperar, (de·ses·pe·rär´) *va.* to make desperate; (coll.) to annoy, to get on one s nerves *(impacientar);* **—se,** to grow desperate.

desfalcar, (des·fäl·kär´) *va.* to embezzle.

desfalco, (des· fäl´ko) *m.* embezzlement.

desfallecer* (des·fä·ye·ser´) *vn.* to weaken, to fall away; to faint *(desmayarse);* —, *va.* to weaken; **— de hambre,** to starve, to weaken by lack of food.

desfallecido, da, (des·fä·ye·sē´tho, thä) *adj.* weak, faint; unconscious.

desfallecimiento, (des·fä·ye·sē·myen´to) *m.*

weakening, faintness; swoon, fainting *(desmayo).*

desfavorable, (des·fä·vo·rä´vle) *adj.* unfavorable.

desfavorecer*, (des·fä·vo·re·ser´) *va.* to disfavor.

desfigurar, (des·fē·gū·rär´) *va.* to disfigure, to deform; to cover, to disguise *(disimular);* to distort *(alterar);* **—se,** to become disfigured; to be distorted.

desfigurado, da, (des·fē·gū·rä´tho, thä) *adj.* deformed, disfigured; hidden, covered; distorted.

desfiladero, (des·fē·lä·the´ro) *m.* pass, gorge.

desfilar, (des·fē·lär´) *vn.* to march, to parade; (coll.) to troop out, to file out *(salir uno tras otro);* (mil.) to march in review.

desfile, (des·fē´le) *m.* parade.

desflorar, (des·flo·rär´) *va.* to deflower; to skim, to deal with superficially *(tratar de).*

desfondar, (des·fon·där´) *va.* to stave in; **—se,** to go in over one´s head, to flounder.

desganado, da, (dez·gä·nä´tho, thä) *adj.* having no appetite; without will.

desganar, (dez·gä·när´) *va.* to make lose one´s taste for; **—se,** to lose one´s appetite; (fig.) to be fed up.

desgano, (dez·gä´no) *m.* lack of appetite *(inapetencia);* lack of interest *(tedio).*

desgarbado, da, (dez·gär·vä´tho, thä) *adj.* ungraceful, gawky, awkward.

desgarrado, da, (dez·gä·rrä´tho, thä) *adj.* (coll.) licentious, dissolute *(desvergonzado);* ripped, torn *(rasgado).*

desgarrador, ra, (dez·gä·rrä·thor´, rä) *adj.* piercing; (fig.) heartrending.

desgarrar, (dez·gä·rrär´) *va.* to tear, to rip; to rend, to hurt deeply *(los sentimientos);* **—se,** to tear oneself away.

desgastar, (dez·gäs·tär´) *va.* to consume, to wear away slowly; (fig.) to ruin, to spoil *(echar a perder);* **—se** (fig.) to lose one´s vigor, to lose one´s verve.

desgaste, (dez·gäs´te) *m.* wearing away, eating away.

desgobierno, (dez·go·vyer´no) *m.* misgovernment, mismanagement.

desgoznar, (dez·goz·när´) *va.* to unhinge; **— se.** (fig.) to gyrate.

desgracia, (dez·grä´syä) *f.* misfortune, mishap *(acontecimiento);* disgrace *(pérdida de favor);* bad luck, adversity *(mala suerte);* sharpness, disagreeableness *(aspereza);* **por —,** unfortunately.

---

m met, **n** not, **p** pot, **r** very, **rr** (none), **s** so, **t** toy, **th** with, **v** eve, **w** we, **y** yes, **z** zero

desgraciado, da, (dez·grâ·syâ´tho, thâ) *adj.* unfortunate; out of favor *(desfavorecido);* disagreeable, unpleasant *(desagradable).*

desgramar, (dez·grâ ·mar´) *va.* to remove the grass from.

desgranar, (dez·grâ·nâr´) *va.* to remove the kernels from *(el maíz) ;* to seed *(las uvas);* to remove the grains from *(el trigo).*

desgrasar, (dez·grâ·sâr´) *va.* to remove the grease from.

desgreñar, (dez·gre·nyâr´) *va.* to dishevel one´s hair, to muss the hair of.

desguarnecer*, (dez·gwâr·ne·ser´) *va.* to strip of adornments, to remove the trimmings from; (mech.) to strip down; to disarm *(una plaza).*

deshabitado, da (de·sâ·vē·tâ´tho, thâ) *adj.* deserted, desolate.

deshabitar, (de·sâ·vē·tar´) *va.* to move out of *(una casa);* to depopulate *(un territorio).*

deshabituar, (de·sâ·vē ·twâr´) *va.* to disaccustom.

deshacer*, (de·sâ·ser´) *va.* to undo; to rout, to defeat *(derrotar);* to take apart *(despedazar);* to dissolve *(liquidar);* to break up *(descomponer);* —**se,** to break, to be smashed; to be on edge, to be on pins and needles *(estar inquieto);* to outdo oneself *(trabajar mucho);* to injure, to damage *(maltratarse);* to wear oneself out, to overwork *(extenuarse);* —**se en,** to break into; —**se de,** to get rid of.

deshebrar, (de·se·vrâr´) *va.* to unravel; (fig.) to shred, to make mincemeat of.

deshecha, (de·se´châ) *f.* dissembling, pretense, front *(disimulo);* formal leavetaking *(despedida);* crossover step; **hacer la —,** to feign, to pretend.

deshecho, cha, (de·se´cho, châ) *adj.* undone; broken; enormous; torrential; routed; **borrasca —,** violent storm.

deshelador, (de·se·lâ ·thor´) *m.* deicer.

deshelar*, (de·se·lâr´) *va.* to thaw; —**se,** to thaw, to melt.

desherbar*, (de·ser·vâr´) *va.* to weed.

desheredar, (de·se·re·thâr´) *va.* to disinherit; —**se,** to be a black sheep; to get away from one´s family.

desherrar*, (de·se·rrâr´) *va.* to unchain; to unshoe *(la caballería).*

deshielo, (de·sye´lo) *m.* thaw.

deshilachar, (de·sē·lâ·châr´) *va.* to unravel.

deshilado, (de·sē·lâ´tho) *m.* openwork.

deshilar, (de·sē·lâr´) *va.* to do openwork on.

deshinchar, (de·sēn·châr´) *va.* to reduce the swelling on; (fig.) to appease, to calm down; —**se,** to go down, to be reduced; (fig.) to come down a notch, to have one´s pride deflated.

deshojar, (de·so·hâr´) *va.* to strip off the leaves from.

deshollinar, (de·so·yē·nâr´) *va.* to clean, to sweep *(las chimeneas);* (fig.) to sift through, to comb through *(registrar).*

deshonesto, ta, (de·so·nes´to, tâ) *adj.* indecent, lewd.

deshonor, (de·so·nor´) *m.* disgrace, shame.

deshonra, (de·son´rrâ) *f.* dishonor.

deshonrar, (de·son·rrâr´) *va.* to disgrace, to dishonor *(hacer perder la honra);* to affront, to insult *(injuriar);* to ravish, to violate *(a una mujer).*

deshonroso, sa, (de·son·rro´so, sâ) *adj.* dishonorable, vile, infamous.

deshora, (de·so´râ) *f.* inopportune moment, wrong time.

deshuesar, (de·swe·sâr´) *va.* to bone *(la carne);* to pit *(un fruto).*

deshumedecer*, (de·su·me·the·ser´) *va.* to dehumidify.

desidia, (de·sē´thyâ) *f.* idleness, indolence.

desidioso, sa, (de·sē·thyo´so, sâ) *adj.* lazy, idle.

desierto, ta, (de·syer´to, tâ) *adj.* deserted, solitary; —, *m.* desert, wilderness; **predicar en el —,** to be a voice crying in the wilderness.

designación, (de·sēg·nâ·syon´) *f.* designation.

designar, (de·sēg·nâr´) *va.* to designate; to plan, to project *(formar designio).*

designio, (de·sēg´nyo) *m.* plan, course of action, scheme.

desigual, (de·sē·gwâl´) *adj.* unequal, unlike; uneven, rough *(barrancoso);* difficult, thorny *(arduo);* changeable *(vario).*

desigualar, (de·sē·gwâ·lâr´) *va.* to make unequal; —**se,** to surpass, to excel.

desigualdad, (de·sē·gwâl·dâth´) *f.* unlikeness, unequalness; unevenness, roughness *(de un terreno);* (math.) inequality.

desilusión, (de·sē·lū·syon´) *f.* disillusion.

desilusionar, (de·sē·lū·syo·nâr´) *va.* to disillusion; —**se,** to become disillusioned.

desinfectante, (de·sēm ·fek·tân´te) *m.* disinfectant.

desinfectar, (de·sēm·fek·târ´) *va.* to disinfect.

â arm, **e** they, **ē** bē, **o** fore, **ū** blūe, **b** bad, **ch** chip, **d** day, **f** fat, **g** go, **h** hot, **k** kid, **l** let

desinflable, (de·sēm·flä´vle) adj. deflatable.

desinflaclón, (de·sēm·flä·syon´) f. deflation.

desinflamar, (de·sēm·flä·mâr´) va. to soothe the inflammation in.

desinflar, (de·sēm·flâr´) va. to deflate.

desintegrable, (de·sēn·te·grä´vle) adj. fissionable.

desintegración, (de·sēn·te·grä·syon´) f. disintegration; — nuclearia, nuclear fission.

desintegrador de átomos, (de·sēn·te·grä ·thor´ the â´to·mos) m. atom smasher.

desintegrar, (de·sēn·te·grâr´) va. and vn. to disintegrate.

desinterés, (de·sēn·te·res´) m. unselfishness, disinterestedness.

desinteresado, da, (de·sēn·te·re·sä´tho, thä) adj. disinterested, unselfish.

desistir, (de·sēs·tēr´) vn. to desist, to cease, to stop.

desjuntar, (des·hūn·târ´) va. to divide, to separate.

deslave, (dez·lä´ve) m. washout, landslide.

desleal, (dez·le·âl´) adj. disloyal, perfidious.

deslealtad, (dez·le·âl·tâth´) f. disloyalty, breach of faith.

desleír*, (dez ·le·ēr´) va. to dilute, to dissolve.

deslenguado, da, (dez·leng·gwä´tho, thä) adj. foul-mouthed.

desliar, (dez·lyâr´) va. to untie.

desligar, (dez·lē·gâr´) va. to loosen, to unbind; (fig.) to untangle, to clear up (desenredar).

deslindar, (dez·lēn·dâr´) va. to mark off the boundaries of, to demarcate.

deslinde, (dez·lēn´de) m. demarcation.

desliz, (dez·lēs´) m. slip, sliding; (fig.) slip, mistake, false step (falta).

deslizamiento, (dez·lē ·sä·myen´to) m. slide, slip.

deslizar, (dez·lē·sâr´) va. to slide; to do without thinking (por descuido); —, vn. to slip, to slide; —se, to scurry away, to slip away; (fig.) to make a false step.

deslucido, da, (dez·lū·sē´tho, thä) adj. second-rate, poor, unaccomplished; quedar or salir —, to be a failure.

deslucir*, (dez·lū·sēr´) va. to offset, to spoil, to ruin the effect of (quitar la gracia); to discredit, to ruin the reputation of (desacreditar).

deslumbrador, ra, (dez·lūm·brä·thor´, rä) adj. dazzling.

deslumbrante, (dez·lūm·brân´te) adj. dazzling.

deslumbrar, (dez·lūm·brâr´) va. to dazzle; (fig.) to puzzle, to perplex (dejar en la incertidumbre); to overwhelm (producir una impresión excesiva).

deslustrar, (dez·lūs·trâr´) va. to tarnish; to frost (el vidrio); to ruin the reputation of (desacreditar).

deslustre, (dez·lūs´tre) m. tarnish; (fig.) stain, discredit blemish (descrédito).

desmán, (dez·mân´) m. misbehavior (demasía); misfortune, disaster (desgracia).

desmandar, (dez·mân·dâr´) va. to countermand, to revoke; —se, to stray (el ganado); to be insubordinate (descomedirse).

desmanotado, da, (dez·mä ·no·tä´tho, thä) adj. unhandy, awkward.

desmantelado, da, (dez·mân·te·lä´tho, thä) adj. dilapidated, in bad repair.

desmantelar, (dez·mân·te·lâr´) va. to dismantle, to tear down (derribar); (fig.) to abandon, to desert; (naut.) to dismast.

desmañado, da, (dez·mä·nä´tho, thä) adj. clumsy, awkward, unskillful.

desmarañar, (dez·mä·râ·nyâr´) va. to disentangle; (fig.) to clear up (aclarar).

desmayado, da, (dez·mä·yä´tho, thä) adj. pale, soft (color); wan, weak (sin fuerzas).

desmayar, (dez·mä·yâr´) va. to daunt, to dishearten, to dismay; —, vn. (fig.) to fail, to falter; —se, to faint, to swoon.

desmayo, (dez·mä´yo) m. disheartenment, dismay; failure, faltering (desfallecimiento); swoon, faint.

desmedido, da, (dez·me·thē´tho, thä) adj. out of proportion, excessive.

desmedrado, da, (dez·me·thrä´tho, thä) adj. deteriorated, worsened; thin, skinny (flaco).

desmejorado, da, (dez·me·ho·rä´tho, thä) adj. sickly, wan.

desmejorar, (dez·me·ho·râr´) va. to worsen, to deteriorate; —, vn. to lose one´s health.

desmelenar, (dez·me·le·nâr´) va. to dishevel, to muss; —se, to give way, to give in.

desmembrar*, (dez·mem·brâr´) va. to dismember, to cut up.

desmemoriado, da, (dez·me·mo·ryä´tho, thä) adj. forgetful.

desmentir*, (dez· men·tēr´) va. to contradict (contradecir); to give the lie to.

desmenuzar, (dez·me·nū·sâr´) va. to tear into small pieces, to shred; (fig.) to pick

m met, **n** not, **p** pot, **r** very, **rr** (none), **s** so, **t** toy, **th** with, **v** eve, **w** we, **y** yes, **z** zero

to pieces *(criticar severamente).*

desmerecer*, (dez·me·re·ser´) *va.* to be unworthy of; —, *vn.* to compare unfavorably.

desmesurado, da, (dez·me·sū·râ´tho, thâ) *adj.* excessive, unwarranted; discourteous *(insolente).*

desmigajar, (dez·mē·gâ·hâr´) *va.* to crumble, to break into bits.

desmochar, (dez·mo·châr´) *va.* to lop off the top of.

desmontable, (dez ·mon·tâ´vle) *adj.* collapsible, dismountable.

desmontar, (dez ·mon·târ´) *va.* to clear *(los árboles);* to level *(el terreno);* to clear away *(un montón);* to take down, to dismantle *(una máquina);* to dismount *(al jinete);* —, *vn.* and *vr.* to dismount, to alight.

desmoralizar, (dez·mo·râ ·lē·sâr´) *va.* to demoralize.

desmoronar, (dez·mo·ro·nâr´) *va.* to chip away, to wear away; —se, to decay, to crumble.

desmovilizar, (dez·mo·vē·lē·sâr´) *va.* to demobilize.

desnatado, da, (dez·nâ·tâ´tho, thâ) *adj.* skimmed.

desnatadora, (dez·nâ·tâ·tho´râ) *f.* cream separator.

desnatar, (dez·nâ·târ´) *va.* to skim; to take the flower of *(sacar lo mejor).*

desnaturalizado, da, (dez·nâ·tū·râ·lē·sâ´-tho, thâ) *adj.* unnatural, inhuman.

desnaturalizar, (dez·nâ·tū·râ·lē·sâr´) *va.* to denaturalize; to twist, to give a false slant, to misconstrue *(desfigurar).*

desnivel, (dez·nē·vel´) *m.* unevenness *(falta de nivel);* difference in elevation *(entre dos puntos);* paso a —, underpass.

desnucar, (dez·nū·kár´) *va.* and *vr.* to break one´s neck.

desnudar, (dez·nū·thâr´) *va.* to strip; (fig.) to denude, to strip bare; —se de, to get rid of, to free oneself of.

desnudez, (dez·nū·thes´) *f.* nakedness, bareness.

desnudismo, (dez·nū·thēz´mo) *m.* nudism.

desnudista, (dez·nū·thēs´ta) *m.* and *f.* nudist.

desnudo, da, (dez·nū´tho, thâ) *adj.* naked, bare; (fig.) lacking *(falto de);* half naked, destitute *(muy pobre);* plain, unadulterated *(sin rebozo).*

desnutrición, (dez·nū·trē·syon´) *f.* malnutrition.

desnutrido, da, (dez·nū·trē´tho, thâ) *adj.* suffering from malnutrition.

desobedecer*, (de·so·ve·the·ser´) *va.* to disobey.

desobediencia, (de·so·ve·thyen´syâ) *f.* disobedience; — civil, civil disobedience.

desobediente, (de·so·ve·thyen´te) *adj.* disobedient.

desocupar, (de·so·kū·pâr´) *va.* to empty, to clear out; —se, to get out, to be freed.

desodorante, (de ·so ·tho·rân´te) *m.* deodorant.

desolación, (de·so·lâ ·syon´) *f.* desolation.

desolado, da, (de·so·lâ´tho, thâ) *adj.* desolate.

desolar*, (de·so·lâr´) *va.* to desolate; —se, (fig.) to become overwrought, to get very upset.

desollar*, (de·so·yâr´) *va.* to skin; (fig.) to fleece, to take to the cleaners.

desorden, (de·sor´then) *m.* disorder.

desordenado, da, (de·sor·the·nâ´tho, thâ) *adj.* disorderly, unruly.

desordenar, (de ·sor·the ·nâr´) *va.* to disarrange, to put out of order; —se, to live a disorderly life.

desorganización, (de·sor·gâ·nē·sâ·syon´) *f.* disorganization.

desorganizar, (dâ·sor·gâ·nē·sâr´) *va.* to disorganize.

desorientado, da, (de·so·ryen·tâ´tho, thâ) *adj.* having lost one's bearings; (fig.) confused, disconcerted.

desovar, (de·so·vâr´) *vn.* to spawn.

desovillar, (de·so·vē·yâr´) *va.* to unwind, to unravel; (fig.) to solve, to clear up *(aclarar).*

despabilar, (des·pâ·vē·lâr´) *va.* to snuff; (fig) to run through hurriedly *(despachar);* to steal *(robar);* to rouse, to stir up *(exitar el ingenio);* —se, to wake up, to spring to attention.

despacio, (des·pâ´syo) *adv.* slowly; ¡—! *interj.* slow up! hold on there!

despacito, (des·pâ ·sē´to) *adv.* very slowly; ¡—! *interj.* slow up! hold your horses!

despachar, (des·pâ·châr´) *va.* to dispatch; to sell *(mercaderías);* to take care of, to wait on *(a los compradores);* to send away *(despedir);* —se, to hurry up; — se uno a su gusto, (coll.) to say whatever one pleases.

despacho, (des·pâ´cho) *m.* dispatch; dismissal *(despedida);* store *(tienda);* office *(oficina).*

desparejar, (des·pâ·re·hâr´) *va.* to make uneven.

desparpajo, (des·pâr·pâ´ho) *m.* (coll.) pertness, boldness, flippancy.

desparramar, (des·pâ·rrâ·mâr´) *va.* to scatter, to spread out; (fig.) to squander, to waste *(el caudal);* —**se,** to lead a reckless life.

despavesar, (des·pâ·ve·sâr´) *va.* to snuff.

despavorido, da, (des·pâ·vo·re´tho, thâ) *adj.* frightened, terrified.

despecho, (des·pe´cho) *m.* rancor, resentment, bitterness *(disgusto);* despair, desperation *(desesperación);* **a — de,** in spite of.

despedazar, (des·pe·thâ·sâr´) *va.* to tear into pieces; (fig.) to break, to shatter; — **se de risa,** to burst into fits of laughter.

despedida, (des·pe·the´thâ) *f.* good-bye, leave-taking; giving off; dismissal; discharge; loosening.

despedir*, (des·pe·ther´) *va.* to loosen, to free *(soltar);* to discharge, to fire *(quitar el empleo);* to dismiss, to send away *(apartar de si);* to give off, to emit *(esparcir);* to say good-bye to *(acompañar al que se va);* —**se,** to take one´s leave, to say good-bye.

despegado, da, (des·pe·gá´tho, thâ) *adj.* (fig.) unpleasant, disagreeable.

despegar, (des·pe·gár´) *va.* to unglue; —, *vn.* (avi.) to take off; —**se,** to come unstuck; not to go well, to be unbecoming *(caer mal).*

despego, (des·pe´go) *m.* (fig.) coolness, indifference, detachment.

despegue, (des·pe´ge) *m.* takeoff; blast-off *(de un cohete);* — **de emergencia,** (avi.) emergency take-off.

despeinado, (des·peê·nâ´tho, thâ) *adj.* uncombed, unkempt, tousled.

despeinar, (des·peê·nâr´) *va.* to tousle the hair off, to mess up one´s hairdo.

despejado, da, (des·pe·hâ´tho, thâ) *adj.* quick, able *(listo);* clear, cloudless *(libre de nubes);* bright, ready *(inteligente);* broad, roomy *(espacioso).*

despejar, (des·pe·hâr´) *va.* to clear *(desocupar);* (math.) to solve; (fig.) to clear up, to clarify *(aclarar);* —**se,** to be at ease; to clear up *(el tiempo).*

despejo, (des·pe´ho) *m.* clearing; openness, easy manner *(en el trato);* (fig.) brightness, ability *(talento).*

despeluzar, (des·pe·lũ·sâr´) *va.* to make one´s hair stand on end.

despellejar, (des·pe·ye·hâr´) *va.* to skin.

despensa, (des·pen´sâ) *f.* pantry; provi-

sions, food supply *(provisiones).*

despensero, (des·pen·se´ro) *m.* butler, steward.

despeñadero, (des·pe·nyâ·the´ro) *m.* precipice; (fig.) great danger, risky undertaking.

despeñar, (des·pe·nyâr´) *va.* to cast, to throw, to hurl; —**se,** to fall headlong, to hurtle.

despepitar, (des·pe·pē·târ´) *va.* to seed; — **se,** to scream, to carry on violently.

despercudir, (des·per·kũ·ther´) *va.* to clean thoroughly of grime.

desperdiciar, (des·per·thē·syâr´) *va.* to squander, to waste, to lose.

desperdicio, (des·per·thē´syo) *m.* waste loss, squandering; —**s,** *pl.* waste, odd bits.

desperezarse, (des·pe·re·sâr´se) *vr.* to stretch oneself.

despertador, (des·per·tâ·thor´) *m.* alarm clock.

despertar*, (des·per·târ´) *va.* to wake, to awake; (fig.) to awaken; —**se,** to wake up, to waken.

despiadado, da, (des·pyâ·thâ´tho, thâ) or **desapiadado, da,** (de·sâ·pyâ·thâ´tho, thâ) *adj.* pitiless, merciless, inhuman.

despierto, ta, (des·pyer´to, tâ) *adj.* awake; (fig.) quick, alert *(vivo).*

despilfarrar, (des·pēl·fâ·rrâr´) *va.* to squander, to spend recklessly.

despilfarro, (des·pēl·fâ´rro) *m.* wastefulness, mismanagement *(descuido);* reckless expense *(gasto).*

despintar, (des·pēn·târ´) *va.* to wash the paint from; (fig.) to ruin, to alter *(desfigurar);* —, *vn.* not to take after one´s family; —**se,** to become discolored, to fade.

despiojar, (des·pyo·hâr´) *va.* to delouse; (fig.) to remove from one´s sordid surroundings.

desplantar, (des·plân·târ´) *va.* to uproot *(desarraigar);* to put out of plumb *(desviar del vertical);* —**se,** to lose one´s stance.

desplante, (des·plân´te) *m.* poor stance; (fig.) impropriety, insolence *(descaro).*

desplazado, da, (des·plâ·sâ´tho, thâ) *adj.* displaced; **persona —,** displaced person.

desplazar, (des·plâ·sâr´) *va.* to displace.

desplazamiento, (des·plâ·sâ·myen´to) *m.* displacement.

desplegar*, (des·ple·gár´) *va.* to unfold; (fig.) to display *(hacer alarde);* to explain *(aclarar);* to unfurl *(una bande-*

ra); (mil.) to deploy.
desplomar, (des·plo·mâr´) va. to knock over; —se, to fall over, to collapse; to plummet to the ground, to plunge to the ground (caer a plomo).
desplome, (des·plo´me) m. collapse; plunge.
desplumar, (des·plū·mâr´) va. to deplume, to pluck; (fig.) to fleece.
despoblado, (des·po·vlâ´tho) m. uninhabited region.
despoblar*, (des·po·vlâr´) va. to depopulate; (fig.) to lay waste, to strip.
despojar, (des·po·hâr´) va. to strip, to rob; to remove from, to take off (quitar); —se, to strip; to give up, to renounce (voluntariamente).
despojo, (des·po´ho) m. robbing, stripping (acción); plunder, spoil (botín); offal (de un animal); ravages (del tiempo); —s, pl. mortal remains (cadáver); debris, rubble (derribos).
desposado, da, (des·po·sâ´tho, thâ) adj. newly married; handcuffed (aprisionado).
desposar, (des·po·sâr´) va. to publish the marriage bans of; —se, to be married.
desposeer*, (des·po·se·er´) va. to dispossess; —se, to renounce one´s possessions.
desposorios, (des·po·so´ryos) m. pl. engagement, betrothal.
déspota, (des´po·tâ) m. despot; (fig.) tyrant.
despótico, ca, (des·po´tē·ko, kâ) adj. despotic.
despotismo, (des·po·tēz´mo) m. despotism.
despreciable, (des·pre·syâ´vle) adj. contemptible, despicable.
despreciar, (des·pre·syâr´) va. to despise, to scorn.
desprecio, (des·pre´syo) m. scorn, contempt.
desprender, (des·pren·der´) va. to unfasten, to loosen; —se, to come loose, to come unfastened; to be shown, to be manifest (inferirse).
desprendimiento, (des·pren·dē·myen´to) m. unloosening, unfastening; disinterest, coolness (desapego); (fig.) generosity (largueza).
despreocupado, da, (des·pre·o·kū·pâ´tho, thâ) n. nonconformist, freethinker; —, adj. unconventional, nonconformist; without a worry in the world, worryfree (sin preocupaciones).
despreocuparse, (des·pre·o·kū·pâr´se) vr.

to forget one´s worries; to lose one´s interest (desentenderse).
desprestigiar, (des·pres·tē·hyâr´) va. to discredit, to bring into disrepute, to lose one´s reputation.
desprestigio, (des·pres·tē´hyo) m. loss of prestige, discredit, disrepute.
desprevenido, da, (des·pre·ve·nē´tho, thâ) adj. unprepared, unaware.
desproporción, (des·pro·por·syon´) f. disproportion.
despropósito, (des·pro·po´sē·to) m. absurdity, nonsense.
desprovisto, ta, (des·pro·vēs´to, tâ) adj. unprovided, devoid, lacking.
después, (des·pwes´) adv. afterward, later; — de after.
despuntar, (des·pūn·târ´) va. to blunt; (naut.) to round; —, vn. to sprout (las plantas); to sparkle, to show wit (una persona); to start, to begin (empezar); al — del día, at break of day.
desquiciar, (des·kē·syâr´) va. to unhinge; (fig.) to throw into disorder, to turn upside down.
desquitar, (des·kē·târ´) va. to recoup (una pérdida); to avenge (un disgusto); —se, to recoup one´s losses; to take revenge.
desquite, (des·kē´te) m. revenge; recoup.
desrielarse, (dez·rrye·lâr´se) vr. (Sp. Am.) to jump the track, to derail.
destacamento, (des·tâ·kâ·men´to) m. (mil.) detachment.
destacar, (des·ta·kâr´) va. to make stand out, to highlight; (mil.) to detach; —se, to be prominent, to stand out.
destajo, (des·tâ´ho) m. piecework; a —, by the piece; (fig.) hurriedly (apresuradamente).
destapar, (des·tâ·pâr´) va. to uncover; —se, (fig.) to unburden oneself; —se con, to confide in.
destartalado, da, (des·târ·tâ·lâ´tho, thâ) adj. shabby, tumble-down.
destello, (des·te´yo) m. gleam, glimmer, flash.
destemplado, da, (des·tem·plâ´tho, thâ) adj. (mus.) out of tune; intemperate.
destemplanza, (des·tem·plân´sâ) f. intemperateness; (med.) slight fever.
destemplar, (des·tem·plâr´) va. (mus.) to put out of tune; to upset, to put out of order; —se, (med.) to have a slight fever; to lose its temper (el acero); (fig.) to lose one´s temper.
desteñir*, (des·te·nyēr´) va. to discolor, to fade.
desternillarse, (des·ter·nē·yâr´se) vr. —

â arm, e they, ē bē, o fore, ū blūe, b bad, ch chip, d day, f fat, g go, h hot, k kid, 1 let

de risa, to split one's sides with laughter.

desterrado, da, (des·te·rrá'tho, thâ) n. exile; —, adj. exiled, banished.

desterrar*, (des·te·rrâr') va. to banish, to exile; (fig.) to expel, to drive away *(alejar)*; to remove the earth from *(quitar la tierra)*.

destetar, (des·te·târ') va. to wean.

destierro, (des·tye'rro) m. exile, banishment.

destilación, (des·tē·lâ·syon') f. distillation.

destilar, (des·tē·lâr') va. and vn. to distil.

destilería, (des·tē·le·rē'â) f. distillery.

destinar, (des·tē·nâr') va. to destine, to intend; to send *(enviar)*.

destinatario, ria, (des·tē·nâ·tâ'ryo, ryâ) n. addressee.

destino, (des·tē'no) m. destiny, fate; destination *(destinación)*; post, position *(empleo)*; con — a, bound for.

destitución, (des·tē·tū·syon') f. destitution, abandonment.

destituir*, (des·tē·twēr') va. to deprive *(privar)*; to dismiss from office *(de un cargo)*.

destornillador, (des·tor·nē·yâ·thor') m. screwdriver.

destornillar, (des·tor·nē·yâr') va. to unscrew; —se, (fig.) to go off the deep end, to lose one's head.

destreza, (des·tre'sâ) f. dexterity, skill, ability.

destronamiento, (des·tro·nâ·myen'to) m. dethronement.

destronar, (des·tro·nâr') va. to dethrone; (fig.) to depose.

destroncar, (des·trong·kâr') va. to lop off the top of, to cut short *(un árbol)*; (fig.) to mutilate *(el cuerpo)*; to wear out, to bush *(cansar)*; to ruin *(en los negocios)*.

destrozado, da, (des·tro·sâ'tho, thâ) adj. tattered, torn.

destrozar, (des·tro·sâr') va. to destroy, to rip to pieces; (fig.) to ruin; (mil.) to crush.

destrozo, (des·tro'so) m. destruction, ripping to pieces; (mil) rout, severe defeat.

destrucción, (des·trūk·syon') f. destruction, ruin.

destructivo, va, (des·trūk·tē'vo, vâ) adj. destructive.

destructor, (des·trūk·tor') m. (naut.) destroyer; —, ra, adj. destroying, destructive.

destruir*, (des·trwēr') va. to destroy, to ruin; —se, (math.) to cancel out.

desuncir, (de·sūn·sēr') va. to unyoke.

desunión, (de·sū·nyon') f. separation; (fig.) discord, dissension, disunion.

desunir, (de·sū·nēr') va. to separate; (fig.) to disunite.

desusar, (de·sū·sâr') va. to drop from use, to stop using.

desuso, (de·sū'so) m. disuse, obsoleteness.

desvaído, da, (dez·vâ·ē'tho, thâ) adj. ungainly, gawky; dull, dark *(apagado)*.

desvalido, da, (dez·vâ·lē'tho, thâ) adj. helpless, destitute.

desvalorizar, (dez·vâ·lo·rē·sâr') va. to devaluate.

desván, (dez·vân') m. garret.

desvanecer*, (dez·vâ·ne·ser') va. to dispel; —se, to evaporate, to be dissipated; to lose one's senses, to black out, to faint *(desmayarse)*; to grow proud, to become haughty *(envanecerse)*.

desvanecimiento, (dez·vâ·ne·sē·myen'to) m. pride, haughtiness *(vanidad)*; blackout, fainting spell *(desmayo)*; (rad.) fade-out.

desvarío, (dez·vâ·rē'o) m. delirium; (fig.) aberration.

desvelar, (dez·ve·lâr') va. to keep awake; —se, (fig.) to make great sacrifices, to go out of one's way.

desvelo, (dez·ve'lo) m. keeping awake; staying awake *(acción de desvelarse)*; great pains, sacrifices *(solicitud)*.

desventaja, (dez·ven·tâ'hâ) f. disadvantage.

desventura, (dez·ven·tū'râ) f. misfortune, bad luck.

desventurado, da, (dez·ven·tū·râ'tho, thâ) adj. unfortunate.

desvergonzado, da, (dez·ver·gon·sâ'tho, thâ) adj. shameless, insolent, cheeky.

desvergüenza, (dez·ver·gwen'sâ) f. shamelessness, cheek, effrontery.

desviación, (dez·vyâ·syon') f. deviation, diversion; (auto.) detour.

desviar, (dez·vyâr') va. to divert; (fig.) to draw away, to separate *(apartar)*; —se, to deviate, to change direction.

desvío, (dez·vē'o) m. deviation, diversion; (auto.) bypass, detour; (fig.) indifference, aversion *(desapego)*.

desvirtuar, (dez·vēr·twâr') va. to rob of its strength; —se, to lose its strength.

detallar, (de·tâ·yâr') va. to detail.

detalle, (de·tâ'ye) m. detail; (com.) retail; vender al —, to retail.

detallista, (de·tâ·yēs'tâ) m. person fond of details; (com.) retailer.

detective, (de·tek·tē've) m. detective.

detector, (de·tek·tor´) *m.* detector.

detención, (de·ten·syon´) *f.* arresting, stopping; delay *(tardanza);* detention *(encarcelamiento).*

detener*, (de·te·ner´) *va.* to stop, to arrest; to retain, to keep *(guardar);* — se, to stop; to delay, to go slowly *(retardarse).*

detenido, da, (de·te·nē´tho thâ) *adj.* sparing, scant *(escaso);* careful, painstaking *(minucioso);* under arrest *(preso).*

detenimiento, (de·te·nē·myen´to) *m.* thoroughness, care *(cuidado);* detainment.

detergente, (de·ter·hen´te) *m. and adj.* detergent.

deteriorar, (de·te·ryo·râr´) *va. and vr.* to deteriorate.

deterioro, (de·te·ryo´ro) *m.* deterioration.

determinación, (de·ter·mē·nâ·syon´) *f.* determination; resolution, boldness *(osadía);* tomar la —, to make the decision.

determinado, da, (de·ter·mē·nâ´tho, thâ) *adj.* bold, resolute *(atrevido);* definite, specific *(preciso);* artículo —, definite article.

determinar, (de·ter·mē·nâr´) *va.* to determine; to fix, to decide on *(señalar).*

detestable, (de·tes·tâ´vle) *adj.* detestable; frightful, beastly *(muy malo).*

detestar, (de·tes·târ´) *va.* to detest.

detonación, (de·to·nâ·syon´) *f.* detonation.

detonador, (de·to·nâ·thor´) *m.* detonator, blasting cap.

detractor, (de·trâk·tor´) *m.* slanderer.

detrás, (de·trâs´) *adv.* behind; (fig.) behind one´s back, in one´s absence; por —, from behind; — de, in back of, behind.

detrimento, (de·trē·men´to) *m.* detriment, damage.

deuda, (de´ū·thâ) *f.* debt; fault, offense *(falta).*

deudo, (de´ū·tho) *m.* relationship; —, da, *n.* relative.

deudor, ra, (deū·thor´, râ) *n.* debtor.

devanador, ra, (de·vâ·nâ·thor´, râ) *n.* winder.

devanar, (de·vâ·nâr´) *va.* to wind, to reel.

devaneo, (de·vâ·ne´o) *m.* delirium; idle pursuit, frivolous pastime *(distracción);* crush *(amorío).*

devastación, (de·vâs·tâ·syon´) *f.* devastation.

devastador, ra, (de·vâs·tâ·thor´, râ) *n.* devastator, ravager; —, *adj.* devastating, ravaging.

devastar, (de·vâs·târ´) *va.* to devastate, to ravage.

devengar, (de·veng·gâr´) *va.* to earn, to draw, to receive.

devoción, (de·vo·syon´) *f.* devotion; special fondness *(afición);* wont, habit *(costumbre);* estar a la — de, to be under the thumb of.

devocionario, (de·vo·syo·nâ´ryo) *m.* prayer book.

devolución, (de·vo·lū·syon´) *f.* return, restitution.

devolutivo, va, (de·vo·lū·tē´vo, vâ) *adj.* to be returned; con carácter —vo, on a loan basis.

devolver*, (de·vol·ver´) *va.* to return *(al dueño);* to restore *(al estado primitivo);* (coll.) to throw up *(vomitar).*

devorar, (de·vo·râr´) *va.* to devour; — sus lágrimas, to hold back one´s tears.

devoto, ta, (de·vo´to, tâ) *adj.* devout; devoted *(a una persona);* devotional *(que mueve a devoción).*

D.F.: Distrito Federal, Federal District.

d/f or d/fha.: días fecha, (com.) d.d. days after date.

día, (dē´â) *m.* day; al otro —, on the following day; — de trabajo, workday, working day; al —, up to date; a treinta —s vista, at thirty days´ sight; — quebrado, half holiday; — feriado, — festivo or — de fiesta, holiday; dentro de ocho —a, within a week; de hoy en ocho —s, a week from today; el — siguiente, the next day.

diabetes, (dyâ·vetes) *f.* diabetes.

diabético, ca, (dyâ·ve´tē·ko, kâ) *adj.* diabetic.

diablillo, (dyâ·vlē´yo) *m.* (fig.) troublemaker, schemer.

diablo, (dyâ´vlo) *m.* devil; más sabe el — por viejo que por —, experience is the best teacher.

diablura, (dyâ·vlū´râ) *f.* deviltry.

diabólico, ca, (dyâ·vo´lē·ko, kâ) *adj.* diabolical, devilish.

diácono, (dyâ´ko·no) *m.* deacon.

diadema, (dyâ·the´mâ) *f.* diadem.

diáfano, nit, (dyâ´fâ·no, nâ) *adj.* diaphanous.

diagnosticar, (dyâg·nos·tē·kâr´) *va.* to diagnose.

diagnóstico, (dyâg·nos´tē·ko) *m.* diagnosis; —, ca, *adj.* diagnostic.

diagonal, (dyâ·go·nâl´) *adj.* oblique.

diagrama, (dyâ·grâ´mâ) *m.* diagram, graph.

dialéctica, (dyâ·lek´tē·kâ) *f.* dialectic.

dialecto, (dyâ·lek´to) *m.* dialect.

diálogo, (dyâ´lo·go) *m.* dialogue.

â arm, e they, ē bē, o fore, ū blūe, b bad, ch chip, d day, f fat, g go, h hot, k kid, 1 let

diamante, (dyâ·mân´te) *m.* diamond; — **en bruto,** rough diamond.

diametral, (dyâ·me·trâl) *adj.* diametrical.

diámetro, (dyâ´me·tro) *m.* diameter.

diana, (dyâ´nä) *f.* (mil.) reveille.

diantre, (dyân´tre) *m.* (coll.) deuce, dickens.

diapasón, (dyâ·pâ·son´) *m.* (mus.) diapason, tuning fork.

diario, (dyâ´ryo) *m.* daily *(publicación);* diary *(relación);* daily earnings *(ganancia);* daily expenses *(gasto);* — **hablado,** news report; — **de navegación,** logbook; —, **ria,** *adj.* daily.

diarrea, (dyâ·rre´ä) *f.* diarrhea.

diatriba, (dyâ·trē´vä) *f.* diatribe.

dibujante, (dē·vū·hân´te) *m.* draftsman.

dibujar, (dē·vū·hâr´) *va.* to draw; (fig.) to sketch, to indicate.

dibujo, (dē·vū´ho) *m.* drawing; (fig.) sketch, outline; **—s animados,** animated cartoon; **no meterse en —s** , not to get off the track.

dicción, (dēk·syon´) *f.* diction; expression, word *(palabra).*

diccionario, (dēk·syo·nä´ryo) *m.* dictionary.

diciembre, (dē·syem´ bre) *m.* December.

dictado, (dēk·tâ´tho) *m.* dictation; title *(título);* **—s** , *pl.* dictates.

dictador, (dēk·tâ·thor´) *m.* dictator.

dictadura, (dēk·tâ·thū´râ) *f.* dictatorship.

dictáfono, (dēk·tâ´fo·no) *m.* dictaphone.

dictamen, (dēk·tâ´men) *m.* advice, counsel.

dictar, (dēk·târ´) *va.* to dictate.

dicha, (dē´châ) *f.* happiness, good fortune; **por —,** luckily, fortunately.

dicharacho, (dē·châ·râ´cho) *m.* vulgar expression.

dicho, (dē´cho) *m.* saying; remark *(ocurrencia);* testimony *(del testigo);* —, **cha,** *adj.* said; **dejar —cho,** to leave word.

dichoso, sa, (dē´cho´so, sâ) *adj.* happy, joyful.

diecinueve or diez y nueve, (dye·sē·nwe´ve) *m.* and *adj.* nineteen.

dieciocho or diez y ocho, (dye·syo´cho) *m.* and *adj.* eighteen.

dieciséis or diez y seis, (dye·sē·se´ēs) *m.* and *adj.* sixteen.

diecisiete or diez y siete, (dye·sē·sye´te) *m.* and *adj.* seventeen.

Diego, (dye´go) *m.* James.

diente, (dyen´te) *m.* tooth; (arch.) projection; **—s postizos,** false teeth; **hablar** or **decir entre —s** , to mumble, to mut-

ter.

diestra, (dyes´trâ) *f.* right hand.

diestro, tra, (dyes´tro, trâ) *adj.* right; skillful, expert *(hábil);* **a —o y siniestro** higgledy-piggledy, haphazardly; —, *m.* matador.

dieta, (dye´tâ) *f.* diet; **—s** , *pl.* fee.

dietética, (dye·te´tē·kä) *f.* dietetics.

diez, (dyes´) *adj.* and *m.* ten.

diezmar, (dyez·mâr´) *va.* to decimate; (eccl.) to tithe.

diezmo, (dyez´mo) *m.* tithe; —, **ma,** *adj.* tenth.

difamación, (dē·fâ·mâ·syon´) *f.* defamation.

difamar, (dē·fâ·mâr´) *va.* to defame, to libel.

diferencia, (dē·fe·ren´syä) *f.* difference; **a — de,** unlike.

diferencial, (dē·fe·ren·syâl´) *adj.* differential; —, *m.* (auto.) differential; —, *f.* (math.) differential.

diferenciar, (dē·fe·ren·syâr´) *va.* to differentiate; to change, to vary *(variar);* —, *vn.* to differ; **—se,** to stand out, to distinguish oneself.

diferente, (dē·fe·ren´te) *adj.* different, unlike.

diferir*, (dē·fe·rēr´) *va.* to defer, to put off; —, *vn.* to differ.

difícil, (dē·fē´sēl) *adj.* difficult; unlikely *(improbable).*

difícilmente, (dē·fē·sēl·men´te) *adv.* with difficulty.

dificultad, (dē·fē·kūl·tâth´) *f.* difficulty.

dificultar, (dē·fē·kūl·târ´) *va.* to make difficult; **—se,** to become difficult.

dificultoso, sa, (dē·fē·kūl·to´so, sâ) *adj.* difficult.

difteria, (dēf·te´ryä) *f.* diphtheria.

difundido, da, (dē·fūn·dē´tho, thâ) *adj.* spread, diffused.

difundir, (dē·fūn·dēr´) *va.* to spread, to diffuse.

difunto, ta, (dē·fūn´to, tâ) *adj.* dead, deceased; —, *n.* deceased, dead person.

difusamente, (dē·fū·sâ·men´te) *adv.* at great length.

difusión, (dē·fū·syon´) *f.* diffusion.

difusivo, va, (dē·fū·sē´vo, vâ) *adj.* diffusive.

difuso, sa, (dē·fū´so, sâ) *adj.* diffuse; **orador —so,** long-winded speaker.

difusora, (dē·fū·so´râ) *f.* broadcasting station.

digerible, (dē·he·rē´vle) *adj.* digestible.

digerir*, (dē·he·rēr´) *va.* to digest; (fig.) to swallow, to take *(sobrellevar).*

digestión, (dē·hes·tyon´) f. digestion.

digestivo, va, (dē·hes·tē´vo, vâ) adj. digestive.

digesto, (dē·hes´to) m. digest.

digital, (dē·hē·tâl´) f. (hot.) digitalis, foxglove; —, adj. digital; **impresiones** or **huellas —es,** fingerprints.

dignarse, (dēg·nâr´ se) vr. to condescend, to deign.

dignatario, (dēg·nâ·tâ´ryo) m. dignitary, high official.

dignidad, (dēg·nē·thâth´) f. dignity.

digno, na, (dēg´no, nâ) adj. worthy; — **de confianza,** trustworthy, dependable, reliable.

digresión, (dē·gre·syon´) f. digression.

dije, (dē´je) m. charm, amulet; (fig.) jewel, treasure (persona).

dilación, (dē·lâ·syon´) f. delay.

dilapidar, (dē·lâ·pē·thâr´) va. to dilapidate.

dilatación, (dē·lâ·tâ·syon´) f. expansion, dilation; (fig.) calmness under stress (serenidad); **bala de —,** dumdum bullet.

dilatado, da, (dē·lâ·tâ´tho, thâ) adj. extensive, numerous.

dilatar, (dē·lâ·târ´) va. to expand, to dilate; (fig.) to delay (retrasar); to spread (propagar); **—se,** to talk at great length, to be long-winded.

dilatoria, (dē·lâ·to´ryâ) f. delay; **traer a uno en —s ,** to keep one waiting; **andar con —s ,** to waste time with red tape.

dilecto, ta, (dē·lek´to, tâ) adj. beloved, greatly loved.

dilema, (dē·le´mâ) m. dilemma.

diligencia, (dē·lē·hen´syâ) f. effort, care (esmero); speed (prisa); stagecoach (coche); (coll.) matter, job (negocio).

diligenciar, (dē·lē·hen·syâr´) va. to process, to expedite.

diligente, (dē·lē·hen´te) adj. diligent; prompt, swift (pronto).

dilucidación, (dē·lū·sē·thâ·syon´) f. explanation.

dilucidar, (dē·lū·sē·thâr´) va. to elucidate, to explain.

diluir*, (dē·lwēr´) va. and vr. to dilute.

diluvio, (dē·lū´vyo) m. deluge.

dimanar, (dē·mâ·nâr´) vn. to spring, to originate, to be due.

dimensión, (dē·men·syon´) f. dimension; dimensions (tamaño).

dimes, (dē´mes) m. pl. **andar en — y diretes.** (coll.) to contend, to argue back and forth.

diminución, (dē·mē·nū·syon´) f. diminution, decrease.

diminutivo, va, (dē·mē·nū·tē´vo, vâ) m. and adj. (gram.) diminutive.

diminuto, ta, (dē·mē·nū´to, tâ) adj. defective, faulty; diminutive, very tiny (muy pequeño).

dimisión, (dē·mē·syon´) f. resignation, resigning.

dimitir, (dē·mē·tēr´) va. and vn. to resign.

Dinamarca, (dē·nâ·mâr´kâ) f. Denmark.

dinámica, (dē·nâ´mē·kâ) f. dynamics.

dinámico, ca, (dē·nâ´mē·ko, kâ) adj. dynamic.

dinamismo, (dē·nâ·mēz´mo) m. dynamism; (fig.) energy, vigor.

dinamita, (dē·nâ·mē´tâ) f. dynamite.

dínamo, (dē´nâ·mo) or **dinamo,** (dē·nâ´mo) f. dynamo.

dinastía, (dē·nâs·tē´â) f. dynasty.

dineral, (dē·ne·râl´) m. large sum of money; **costar un —,** to cost a fortune.

dinero, (dē·ne´ro) m. money; — **contante y sonante,** ready money, cash.

dinosaurio, (dē·no·sâ´ū·ryo) m. dinosaur.

dintel, (dēn·tel´) m. transverse, lintel.

diócesis, (dyo´se·sēs) f. diocese.

diorama, (dyo·râ´mâ) m. diorama.

Dios, (dyos) m. God; — **es grande,** let us trust in God, God will help us; — **mediante,** with the help of God; — **quiera, — lo permita,** God grant.

dios, (dyos) m. god, deity.

diosa, (dyo´sâ) f. goddess, female deity.

dióxido de carbono, (dyok´sē·tho·the·kar·vo´no) m. carbon dioxide.

diplejia espástica, (dē·ple´hyâ·es·pâs´te·kâ) f. cerebral palsy.

diploma, (dē·plo´mâ) m. diploma (título); license, certificate.

diplomacia (dē·plo·mâ´syâ) or **diplomática,** (dē·plo·mâ´tē·kâ) f. diplomacy.

diplomarse, (dē·plo·mâr´se) vr. to be graduated, to receive one´s diploma.

diplomático, ca, (dē·plo·mâ´tē·ko, kâ) adj. diplomatic; —, m. diplomat.

dipsomania, (dēp·so·mâ·nē´â) f. dipsomania.

dipsómano, na, (dēp·so´mâ·no, nâ) n. dipsomaniac.

diptongo, (dēp·tong´go) m. diphthong.

diputación. (dē·pū·tâ·syon´) f. delegation.

diputado, (dē·pū·tâ´tho) m. delegate, deputy.

diputar, (dē·pū·târ´) va. to delegate.

dique, (dē´ke) m. dike; — **de carena,** dry dock; — **flotante,** floating dock.

dirección, (dē·rek·syon´) f. direction, directorship *(cargo);* directorate, board of directors *(junta);* address *(morada);* — **telegráfica** or **cablegráfica,** cable address; **de dos —ones,** two-way.

directivo, va, (dē·rek·tē'vo, vä) *adj.* managing; —, *f.* directive; board of directors *(junta).*

directo, ta, (dē·rek'to, tä) *adj.* direct; —, *m.* straight *(blow).*

director, ra, (dē·rek·tor', rä) *adj.* directing, directive; —, *n.* director; principal *(de escuela);* — **de escena,** stage manager;— **ejecutivo,** chief executive officer.

directorio, ria, (dē·rek·to'ryo, ryä) *adj.* directory; —, *m.* directory, guide; board, directorate *(junta).*

directriz, (dē·rek·trēs') *adj. f.* **línea —,** (math.) directrix.

dirigente, (dē·rē·hen'te) *adj.* leading.

dirigible, (dē·rē·hē'vle) *m.* dirigible; —, *adj.* controllable.

dirigir, (dē·rē·hēr') *va.* to direct; to address *(una carta);* to dedicate *(una obra);* — **la palabra,** to address; **—se,** to go; **—se a,** to speak to, to address.

discerniente, (dēs·ser·nyen'te) *adj.* discerning.

discernimiento, (dēs·ser·nē·myen'to) *m.* discernment; appointment as guardian.

discernir*, (dēs·ser·nēr') *va.* to discern; to appoint as guardian *(encargar la tutela).*

disciplina, (dēs·sē·plē'nä) *f.* discipline.

disciplinado, da, (dēs·sē·plē·nä'tho, thä) *adj.* disciplined.

disciplinar, (dēs·sē·plē·när') *va.* to discipline.

discípulo, la, (dēs·sē'pū·lo, lä) *n.* disciple; pupil *(alumno).*

disco, (dēs'ko) *m.* disk; record *(grabación);* discus *(atlético).*

díscolo, la, (dēs'ko·lo, lä) *adj.* disobedient, unmanageable.

discordancia, (dēs·kor·thän'syä) *f.* difference.

discordante, (dēs·kor·thän'te) *adj.* discordant, different.

discordar*, (dēs·kor·thär') *vn.* to be at variance, to disagree; (mus.) to be out of harmony.

discorde, (dēs·kor'the) *adj.* in disagreement, at variance; (mus.) out of harmony.

discordia, (dēs·kor'thyä) *f.* discord; **manzana de la —,** bone of contention.

discoteca, (dēs·ko·te'kä) *f.* phonograph record collection; discotheque *(local).*

discreción, (dēs·kre·syon') *f.* discretion; quick mind, ready wit *(agudeza);* **a —,** at discretion, as much as one thinks best.

discrepancia, (dēs·kre'pän'syä) *f.* discrepancy.

discrepar, (dēs·kre·pär') *vn.* to differ, to disagree.

discreto, ta, (dēs·kre'to, tä) *adj.* discreet; discrete *(discontinuo);* witty *(agudo).*

disculpa, (dēs·kūl'pä) *f.* apology, excuse.

disculpar, (dēs·kūl·pär') *va.* to excuse, to pardon; — **se,** to apologize, to excuse oneself.

discurrir, (dēs·kū·rrēr') *vn.* to ramble about *(andar);* to flow *(fluir),* to pass *(transcurrir);* to ponder *(reflexionar);* —, *va.* to figure out; to draw *(inferir).*

discursear, (dēs·kūr·se·är') *vn.* (coll.) to talk on, to ramble.

discurso, (dēs·kūr'so) *m.* reasoning power *(facultad);* speech *(charla);* sentence *(oración);* **hilo del —,** train of thought.

discusión, (dēs·kū·syon') *f.* discussion.

discutible, (dēs·kū·tē'vle) *adj.* debatable.

discutir, (dēs·kū·tēr') *va.* and *vn.* to discuss, to argue.

disecar, (dē·se·kär') *va.* to dissect.

disección, (dē·sek·syon') *f.* dissection.

diseminación, (dē·se·mē·nä·syon') *f.* dissemination.

diseminar, (dē·se·mē·när') *va.* to disseminate.

disensión, (dē·sen·syon') *f.* dissension.

disentería, (dē·sen·te·rē'ä) *f.* dysentery.

disentimiento, (dē·sen·tē·myen'to) *m.* dissent, disagreement.

disentir*, (dē·sen·tēr') *vn.* to dissent, to disagree.

diseñar, (dē·se·nyär') *va.* to draw, to design.

diseño, (dē·se'nyo) *m.* design, drawing; description, word portrayal *(descripción).*

disertación, (dē·ser·tä·syon') *f.* dissertation.

disertar, (dē·ser·tär') *vn.* to dissertate.

disforme, (dēs·fôr'me) *adj.* deformed.

disfraz, (dēs·frás') *m.* disguise.

disfrazar, (dēs·frä·sär') *va.* to disguise.

disfrutar, (dēs·frū·tär') *va.* to enjoy *(gozar de);* to have the use of, to make use of *(aprovechar).*

disfrute, (dēs·frū'te) *m.* enjoyment; use.

disgregación, (dēz·gre·gä·syon') *f.* disintegration.

disgregar, (dēz·gre·gär') *va.* to disintegrate.

m met, n not, p pot, r very, rr (none), s so, t toy, th with, v eve, w we, y yes, z zero

disgustar, (dēz·gŭs·târ´) va. to displease, to bother; **—se con,** to quarrel with, to have a falling out with.

disgusto, (dēz·gŭs´to) m. displeasure, bother *(molestia);* quarrel *(disputa);* worry *(inquietud);* **a —,** against one´s will; **llevarse un —,** to be disappointed.

disidente, (dē·sē·then´te) adj. dissident, dissenting; **—,** m. and f. dissenter.

disimetría, (dē·sē·me·trē´á) f. lack of symmetry.

disímil, (dē·sē´mēl) adj. dissimilar.

disimuladamente, (dē·sē·mū·lá·thá men´te) adv. pretending ignorance; on the sly *(a hurtadillas).*

disimulado, da, (dē·sē·mū·lá´tho, thá) adj. false, hypocritical.

disimular, (dē·sē·mū·lár´) va. to hide, to cover up; to pretend to know nothing about *(desentenderse de);* **—,** vn. to dissemble.

disimulo, (dē·sē·mū´lo) m. hiding, covering up; pretense.

disipación, (dē·sē·pá·syon´) f. dissipation.

disipado, da, (dē·sē·pá´tho, thá) adj. dissipated, prodigal.

disipador, ra, (dē·sē·pá·thor´, rá) n. spendthrift.

disipar, (dē·sē·pár´) va. to dissipate.

dislate, (dēz·lá´te) m. nonsense, foolishness.

dislocación, (dēz·lo·ká·syon´) f. dislocation.

dislocar, (dēz·lo·kár´) va. to dislocate; to break up *(dispersar);* (fig.) to carve up *(dismembrar).*

disminución, (dēz·mē·nū·syon´) f. lessening, reduction.

disminuir, (dēz·mē·nwēr´) va. to diminish.

disolución, (dē·so·lū·syon´) f. dissolution; dissoluteness *(desenfreno).*

disoluto, ta, (dē·so·lū´to, tá) adj. dissolute, licentious.

disolver*, (dē·sol·ver´) va. to dissolve; **— se,** to dissolve, to break up.

disonante, (dē·so·nán´te) adj. dissonant, inharmonious.

disonar*, (dē·so·nár´) vn. to be in discord, to be dissonant.

dispar, (dēs·pár´) adj. unlike, unequal.

disparar, (dēs·pá·rár´) va. to throw hard, to heave *(arrojar);* to fire *(una escopeta);* **—se,** to dart off, to rush off.

disparatado, da, (dēs·pá·rá·tá´tho, thá) adj. absurd, nonsensical; (coll.) huge, enormous *(excesivo).*

disparate, (dēs·pá·rá´te) m. nonsense, absurdity; (coll.) excess, enormity.

disparejo, ja, (dēs·pá·re´ho, há) adj. unequal, uneven.

disparidad, (dēs·pá·rē·tháth´) f. disparity.

disparo, (dēs·pá´ro) m. shot.

dispensa, (dēs·pen´sá) f. (eccl.) dispensation; exemption.

dispensación, (dēs·pen·sá·syon´) f. dispensation; exemption.

dispensar, (dēs·pen·sár´) va. to dispense *(administrar);* to exempt, to excuse *(eximir);* to forgive, to excuse *(absolver).*

dispensario, (dēs·pen·sá´ryo) m. dispensary.

dispepsia, (dēs·pep´syá) f. dyspepsia.

dispersar, (dēs·per·sár´) va. and vr. to scatter, to disperse.

disperso, sa, (dēs·per´so, sá) adj. dispersed, scattered.

displicencia, (dēs·plē·sen´syá) f. displeasure, disdain *(desagrado);* slacking off, slowing up *(desaliento).*

displicente, (dēs·plē·sen´te) adj. disagreeable.

disponer*, (dēs·po·ner´) va. to dispose *(prevenir);* to ready, to make ready *(preparar);* to determine, to decide *(determinar);* **— de,** to have at one´s disposal, to have the use of; **—se,** to get ready, to prepare.

disponible, (dēs·po·nē´vle) adj. available.

disponibilidad, (dēs·po·nē·vē·lē·tháth´) f. availability.

disposición, (dēs·po·sē·syon´) f. disposition; disposal; plan, arrangement *(arreglo);* preparation *(preparativo).*

dispuesto, ta, (dēs·pwes´to, tá) adj. disposed, fit, ready; **bien —,** favorably inclined; **mal —,** unfavorably disposed.

disputa, (dēs·pū´tá)f. dispute, controversy.

disputar, (dēs·pū·tar´) va. to dispute, to argue; **—,** vn. to quarrel.

disquete, (dēs·ke´te) m. diskette.

distancia, (dēs·tân´syá) f. distance; (fig.) difference.

distante, (dēs·tân´te) adj. removed, at a distance; far-off, distant, remote *(remoto).*

distar, (dēs·târ´) vn. to be distant; (fig.) to be different *(diferenciarse).*

distender*, (dēs·ten·der´) va. and vr. to distend.

distinción, (dēs·tēn·syon´) f. distinction; division *(separación).*

distinguido, da, (dēs·tēng·gē´tho, thá) adj. distinguished.

distinguir, (dēs·tēng·gēr´) va. to distinguish; to honor *(otorgar).*

distintivo, va, (dēs·tēn·tē´vo, vá) adj. dis-

â arm, **e** they, **ē** bē, **o** fore, **ū** blūe, **b** bad, **ch** chip, **d** day, **f** fat, **g** go, **h** hot, **k** kid, **1** let

tinctive; —, m. distinction, distinguishing feature; insignia, mark, badge *(marca)*.

distinto, ta, (dēs·tēn´to, tâ) adj. distinct; different *(diferente)*.

distracción, (dēs·trâk·syon´) f. distraction; misappropriation *(de fondos)*.

distraer*, (dēs·trâ·er´) va. to distract; to misappropriate *(malversar)*; —se, to enjoy oneself, to have fun.

distraído, da, (dēs·trâ·ē´tho, thâ) adj. distracted; dissolute *(licencioso)*.

distribución, (dēs·trē·vū·syon´) f. distribution; arrangement *(arreglo)*.

distribuidor, (dēs·trē·vwē·thor´) m. (mech.) slide valve; (auto.) distributor; — automático, vending machine.

distribuir*, (dēs·trē·vwēr´) va. to distribute; to lay out; to arrange *(disponer)*.

distributivo, va, (dēs·trē·vū·tē´vo, vâ) adj. distributive.

distrito, (dēs·trē´to) m. district.

distrofia, (dēs·tro´fyâ) f. distrophy; — muscular, muscular distrophy.

disturbar, (dēs·tūr·vâr´) va. to bother, to disturb.

disturbio, (dēs·tūr´vyo) m. disturbance, interruption, bother.

disuadir, (dē·swâ·thēr´) va. to dissuade.

disuasión, (dē·swâ·syon´) f. dissuasion.

disyuntiva, (dēz·yūn·tē´va) f. choice of two alternatives.

disyuntor, (dēz·yūn·tor´) m. (elec.) circuit breaker.

diurético, ca, (dyū·re´tē·ko, kâ) adj. diuretic; —, m. diuretic.

diurno, na, (dyūr´no, nâ) adj. diurnal.

diva, (dē´vâ) f. prima donna, diva.

divagación, (dē·vâ·gâ·syon´) f. wandering; digression, rambling.

divagar, (dē·vâ·gâr´) vn. to digress, to ramble; to wander *(vagar a la ventura)*.

diván, (dē·vân´) m. sofa.

divergencia, (dē·ver·hen´syâ) f. divergence.

diversidad, (dē·ver·sē·thâth´) f. diversity, variety.

diversificar, (dē·ver·sē·fē·kâr´) va. to diversify, to vary.

diversión, (dē·ver·syon´) f. diversion.

diverso, sa, (dē·ver´so, sâ) adj. diverse, different.

divertido, da, (dē·ver·tē´tho, thâ) adj. amusing, enjoyable.

divertir*, (dē·ver·tēr´) va. to amuse, to entertain; to divert *(apartar)*; —se, to have a good time, to enjoy oneself.

dividendo, (dē·vē·then´do) m. (math. and com.) dividend.

dividir, (dē·vē·thēr´) va. to divide; —se, to part company, to separate.

divieso, (dē·vye´so) m. (med.) boil.

divinidad, (dē·vē·nē·thâth´) f. divinity; (fig.) exceptional beauty *(persona)*.

divino, na, (dē·vē´no, nâ) adj. divine.

divisa, (dē·vē´sâ) f. motto *(lema)*; badge *(señal)*; foreign currency *(papel moneda)*.

divisar, (dē·vē·sâr´) va. to just make out, to barely see.

división, (dē·vē·syon´) f. division.

divisor, (dē·vē·sor´) m. (math.) divisor.

divisorio, ria, (dē·vē·so´ryo, ryâ) adj. dividing; linea — de las aguas, watershed, water parting.

divorciar, (dē·vor·syâr´) va. to divorce; —se, to get a divorce.

divorcio, (dē·vor´syo) m. divorce; (fig.) divorcement.

divulgación, (dē·vūl·gâ·syon´) f. divulgence; spreading, circulation.

divulgar, (dē·vūl·gâr´) va. to divulge *(un secreto)*; to spread, to circulate *(una noticia)*.

dizque, (dēs´ke) m. (Sp. Am.) hearsay, gossip; —, adv. possibly, they say that.

dls.: dólares, $ dollars.

dm.: decímetro, dm. decimeter.

do, (do) m. (mus.) do.

dobladillo, (do·vlâ·thē´yo) m. fold, reinforcement; heavy thread *(hilo)*.

doblado, (do·vlâ´tho) m. dubbing of a film; —, da, adj. wiry, strong *(recio)*; uneven broken *(quebrado)*; folded *(plegado)*; (fig.) double-dealing, artful *(taimado)*.

doblar, (do·vlâr´) va. to double *(aumentar)*; to fold up *(un mantel)*; to bend *(torcer)*; to round *(un cabo)*; to dub *(una película)*; to sway *(inclinar a una persona)*; —, vn. to toll.

doble, (do´vle) adj. double; brawny, tough *(fornido)*; two-faced *(disimulado)*; —, m. crease, fold *(doblez)*; tolling *(de campanas)*; copy *(reproducción)*; (theat.) double.

doblegable, (do·vle·gâ´vle) adj. flexible, pliant.

doblez, (do·vles´) m. crease, fold; —, m. or f. duplicity *(disimulo)*.

doce, (do´se) adj. and m. twelve.

docena, (do·se´nâ) f. dozen; — del fraile, (coll.) baker's dozen.

doceno, na, (do·se´no, nâ) adj. twelfth.

docente, (do·sen´te) adj. teaching; personal —, teaching staff.

dócil, (do´sēl) adj. docile, obedient; malleable, tractable *(dúctil)*.

docilidad, (do·sē·lē·thâth´) f. docility, obedience.

docto, ta, (dok´to, tâ) adj. learned.

doctor, (dok·tor´) m. doctor.

doctorado, (dok·to·râ´tho) m. doctorate.

doctorar, (dok·to·râr´) va. to confer a doctorate upon; —se, to receive one´s doctorate.

doctrina, (dok·trē´nâ) f. doctrine; dominical, Sunday school.

doctrinar, (dok·trē·nâr´) va. to indoctrinate.

documentación, (do·kū·men·tâ·syon´) f.
documentation.

documental, (do·kū·men·tâl´) adj. and
documentary.

documento, (do·kū·men´to) m. document.

dogal, (do·gâl´) m. halter; noose (cuerda
para ahorcar).

dogma, (dog´mâ) m. dogma.

dogmático, ca, (dog·mâ´tē·ko, kâ) adj.
dogmatic.

dogo, (do´go) m. bulldog.

dólar, (do´lâr) m. dollar.

dolencia, (do·len´syâ) f. affliction, sickness.

doler*, (do·ler´) vn. to hurt, to ache; to
grieve, to pain (causar disgusto); —se,
to regret, to be sorry; to complain (quejarse).

doliente, (do·lyen´te) adj. painful (dolorido); sick (enfermo).

dolor, (do·lor´) m. ache, pain; regret
(arrepentimiento).

dolorido, da, (do·lo·rē´tho, thâ) adj. painful sore; grieving, bereaved (desconsolado).

doloroso, sa, (do·lo·ro´so, sâ) adj. lamentable, regrettable (lastimoso); painful
(que causa dolor).

doloso, sa, (do·lo´so, sâ) adj. fradulent.

domable, (do·mâ´vle) adj. tamable.

domador, ra, (do·mâ·thor´, râ) n. Animal
tamer; horsebreaker, bronco buster.

domar, (do·mâr´) va. to tame; (fig.) to subdue, to master (vencer); sin —,
untamed, unbroken.

domesticar, (do·mes·tē·kâr´) va. to domesticate.

domesticidad, (do·mes·tē·sē·thâth´) f.
domesticity.

doméstico, ca, (do·mes´tē·ko, kâ) adj. and
m. domestic.

domiciliado, da, (do·mē·sē·lyâ´tho, thâ)
adj. residing.

domiciliarse, (do·mē·sē·lyâr´se) vr. to
establish one´s residence.

domicilio, (do·mē·sē´lyo) m. domicile,

home; — social, place of business.

dominación, (do·mē·nâ·syon´) f. dominion,
domain; domination (acción).

dominador, ra, (do·mē·nâ·thor´, râ) adj.
dominating; —, n. dominator.

dominante, (do·mē·nân´te) adj. dominant;
domineering (avasallador).

dominar, (do·mē·nâr´) va. to dominate; —
se, to control oneself.

dómine, (do´mē·ne) m. Latin instructor;
pedagogue (maestro anticuado).

domingo, (do·mēng´go) m. Sunday.

dominicano, na, (do·mē·nē·kâ´no, nâ) adj.
and n. Dominican.

dominio, (do·mē´nyo) m. dominance;
domain, dominion (territorio).

dominó, (do·mē·no´) m. domino; dominoes
(juego).

don, (don) m. gift, quality; Don (título); —
de la palabra, ability with words; — de
gentes, savoir-faire, ability to get along.

donación, (do·nâ syon´) f. donation, giving.

donador, ra, (do·nâ·thor´, râ) n. giver,
donor; — de sangre, blood donor.

donaire, (do·nâ´ē·re) m. grace, charm, elegance.

donante, (do·nân´te) m. and f. donor,
giver.

donar, (do·nâr´) va. to donate.

donativo, (do·nâ·tē´vo) m. donation.

doncella, (don·se´yâ) f. virgin, maiden.

donde, (don´de) adv. where; which (lo
cual).

dónde, (don´de) adv. where?¿por —? with
what reason?

dondequiera, (don·de·kye´râ) adv. anywhere, wherever.

donoso, sa, (do·no´so, sâ) adj. pleasant,
charming.

doña, (do´nyâ) f. Doña.

doquier (do·kyer´) or doquiera, (do·kye´râ)
adv. anywhere, wherever.

dorado, da, (do·râ´tho, thâ) adj. gilded; —,
m. gilding.

dorar, (do·râr´) va. to gild; (fig.) to sugar-
coat (paliar); to brown lightly (tostar).

dormido, da, (dor·mē´tho, thâ) adj. asleep.

dormilón, ona, (dor· mē·lon´, o´nâ) n.
(coll.) sleepyhead; —, adj. fond of sleeping.

dormir*, (dor·mēr´) vn. to sleep; —se, to
fall asleep; hacer —, to put to sleep.

dormitar, (dor·mē·târ´) vn. to doze, to be
half asleep.

dormitorio, (dor·mē·to´ryo) m. bedroom.

dorsal, (dor·sâl´) adj. dorsal; espina —,
spinal column, backbone.

â arm, e they, ē bē, o fore, ū blūe, b bad, ch chip, d day, f fat, g go, h hot, k kid, 1 let

dorso, (dor´so) *m.* back.

dos, (dos) *adj.* and *m.* two; **de — en —,** two abreast, two by two.

doscientos, tas, (dos·syen´tos, tâs) *m.* and *adj.* two hundred.

dosel, (do·sel´) *m.* canopy.

dosis, (do´sēs) *f.* dose, (fig.) some, degree.

dotación, (do·tâ·syon´) *f.* endowment; (naut.) complement; staff, crew *(personal).*

dotal, (do·tâl´) *adj.* endowment; **seguro —,** endowment insurance.

dotar, (do·târ´) *va.* to endow; (fig.) to staff, to provide *(asignar).*

dote, (do´te) *m.* and *f.* dower, dowry; **llevarse —,** to receive a dowry; **—,** *f.* quality, good point.

dovela, (do·ve´lâ) *f.* arch stone.

draga, (drâ´gâ) *f.* dredge.

dragado, (drâ·gâ´tho) *m.* dredging.

dragaminas, (drâ·gâ·mē´nâs) *m.* (naut.) mine sweeper .

dragón, (drâ·gon´) *m.* dragon; (mil.) dragoon.

drama, (drâ´mâ) *m.* drama.

dramático, ca, (drâ·mâ´tē·ko, kâ) *adj.* dramatic.

dramatizar, (drâ·mâ·tē·sâr´) *va.* to dramatize.

dramaturgo, (drâ·mâ·tūr´go) *m.* dramatist, playwright.

drástico, ca, (drâs´tē·ko, kâ) *adj.* drastic.

drenaje, (dre·nâ´he) *m.* (med.) drainage.

dril, (drēl) *m.* drill, drilling.

droga, (dro´gâ) *f.* drug; (fig.) trick, ruse *(embuste);* nuisance, pill *(cosa molesta);* (Mex.) debt.

droguería, (dro·ge·rē´â) *f.* drugstore; drug trade *(comercio).*

droguero, (dro·ge´ro) *m.* druggist.

droguista, (dro·gēs´tâ) *m.* druggist.

dromedario, (dro·me·thâ´ryo) *m.* dromedary.

ducado, (dū·kâ´tho) *m.* duchy, dukedom; ducat *(moneda).*

ducho, cha, (dū´cho, châ) *adj.* dexterous, accomplished; **—,** *f.* shower.

duda, (dū´thâ) *f.* doubt; **poner en —,** to question; **no cabe —,** there is no doubt; **en la — vale más abstenerse,** when in doubt, don´t.

dudable, (dū·thâ´vle) *adj.* dubious, doubtful.

dudar, (dū·thâr´) *va.* to doubt; **—,** *vn.* to be undecided, not to know.

dudoso, sa, (dū·tho´so, sâ) *adj.* doubtful, dubious.

duela, (dwe´lâ) *f.* stave.

duelo, (dwe´lo) *m.* duel *(combate);* suffe-ring, woe, grief *(aflicción);* mourning *(por la muerte de uno);* mourners *(los que asisten a los funerales).*

duende, (dwen´de) *m.* elf, goblin.

dueño, ña, (dwe´nyo, nyâ) *n.* owner, proprietor; **— de sí mismo,** self-controlled; **hacerse —,** to take possession; *f.* duenna, chaperon; **— de casa,** homemaker; lady of the house.

dueto, (dwe´to) *m.* duet.

dulce, (dūl´se) *adj.* sweet; malleable *(dúctil);* fresh *(agua);* **—,** *m.* piece of candy.

dulcedumbre, (dūl·se·thūm´bre) *f.* sweetness; mildness.

dulcería, (dūl·se·rē´â) *f.* candy shop.

dulcificante, (dūl·sē·fē·kân´te) *m.* sweetener.

dulcificar, (dūl·sē·fē·kâr´) *va.* to sweeten.

dulzura, (dūl·sū´râ) *f.* sweetness; gentleness, mildness *(suavidad).*

dúo, (dū´o) *m.* (mus.) duo, duet.

duodécimo, ma, (dwo·the´sē·mo, mâ) *adj.* twelfth.

duodeno, (dwo·the´no) *m.* duodenum; **úlcera del —,** duodenal ulcer.

duplicación, (dū·plē·kâ·syon´) *f.* duplication; doubling.

duplicado, (dū·plē·kâ´tho) *m.* duplicate.

duplicador, ra, (dū·plē·kâ·thor´, râ) *adj.* duplicating; **—,** *m.* duplicator.

duplicar, (dū·plē·kâr´) *va.* to duplicate; to double *(multiplicar por dos).*

duplicidad, (dū·plē·sē·thâth´) *f.* duplicity, falseness.

duque, (dū´ke) *m.* duke.

duquesa, (dū·ke´sâ) *f.* duchess.

durabilidad, (dū·râ·vē·lē·thâth´) *f.* durability.

durable, (dū·râ´vle) *adj.* durable, lasting.

duración, (dū·râ·syon´) *f.* duration.

duradero, ra (dū·râ·the´ro, râ) *adj.* lasting, durable.

durante, (dū·rân´te) *adv.* during.

durar, (dū·râr´) *vn.* to last, to endure; to remain *(subsistir);* to wear well (la ropa).

durazno, (dū·râz´no) *m.* peach; peach tree *(árbol).*

dureza, (dū·re´sâ) *f.* hardness; (med.) hardening.

durmiente, (dūr·myen´te) *adj.* sleeping; **—,** *m.* (arch.) sleeper, stringer; (rail.) crosstie.

duro, ra, (dū´ro, râ) *adj.* hard; strong, vigorous *(resistente);* rough, cruel *(violento);* harsh *(áspero);* **—ro,** *adv.* hard; **—,** *m.* dollar, peso.

d/v.: días vista, (com.) days´ sight.

E

e, (e) *conj.* and.
E.: Este, E. East.
¡ea! (e´â) *interj.* very well! well then! let´s just see!
ebanista, (e·vâ·nēs´tâ) *m.* cabinetmaker.
ébano, (e´vâ·no) *m.* ebony.
ebonita, (e·vo·nē´tâ) *f.* ebonite, vulcanite.
ebriedad, (e·vrye·thâth´) *f.* intoxication, drunkenness.
ebrio, bria, (e´vryo, vryâ) *adj.* intoxicated, drunk; (fig.) blind.
ebullición, (e·vū·yē·syon´) *f.* boiling, ebullition; (fig.) turmoil, ferment, frenzy.
eclesiástico, (e·kle·syâs´tē·ko) *m.* clergyman, ecclesiastic; —, ca, *adj.* ecclesiastical.
eclipsar, (e·klēp·sâr´) *va.* (ast.) to eclipse; to blot out, to hide *(ocultar);* —se, to drop out of sight.
eclipse, (e·klēp´se) *m.* eclipse.
eco, (e´ko) *m.* echo.
ecología, (e·ko·lo·hē´â) *f.* ecology.
economía, (e·ko·no·mē´â) *f.* economy; — política, economics, political economy; — dirigida, planned economy; — doméstica, home economics, domestic science.
económico, ca, (e·ko·no´mē·ko, kâ) *adj.* economic; economical, saving *(ahorrador).*
economista, (e·ko·no·mēs´tâ) *m.* economist.
economizar, (e·ko·no·mē·sâr´) *va.* to save, to economize.
ecoturismo, (e·ko·tū·rēz´mo) *m.* ecotourism.
ectoplasma, (ek·to·plâz´mâ) *m.* ectoplasm.
ecuación, (e·kwâ·syon´) *f.* equation.
ecuador, (e·kwâ·thor´) *m.* equator; E—, Ecuador.
ecuánime, (e·kwâ´nē·me) *adj.* eventempered, level-headed *(templado);* fair, impartial *(imparcial).*
ecuatorial, (e·kwâ·to·ryâl´) *adj.* equatorial.
ecuatoriano, na, (e·kwâ·to·ryâ´no, nâ) *n.* Ecuadorian; —, *adj.* from Ecuador.
ecuestre, (e·kwes´tre) *adj.* equestrian.
eczema. (ek·se´mâ) *f.* eczema.
echar, (e·châr´) *va.* to throw *(echar);* to discharge *(despedir);* to throw out *(arrojar);* to attribute *(imponer);* to go

(ir); — a correr, to start running; — a perder, to ruin, to spoil; — a pique, to scuttle; — carnes, to grow fat; — de menos, to miss; — de ver, to notice; — la de, to pride oneself on being; — raíces, to take root; — las cartas en el correo, to mail the letters; —se, to throw oneself; to stretch out *(acostarse);* —se para atrás, to jump back;, (fig.) to go back on one´s word.
echazón, (e·châ·son´) *f.* throw, throwing; (naut.) jettison.
edad, (e·thâth´) *f.* age; time *(época);* — atómica, atomic age; — de la aviación, air age; — media, Middle Ages; mayor —, majority; ser mayor de —, to be of age; menor —, minority, infancy; ser menor de — to be a minor.
edecán, (e·the·kân´) *m.* (mil.) aide.
Edén (e·then´) *m.* Eden.
edición, (e·thē·syon´) *f.* edition; publication *(impresión).*
edicto, (e·thēk´to) *m.* edict.
edificación, (e·thē·fē·kâ·syon´) *f.* building, construction; buildings *(edificios);* (fig.) edification.
edificante (e·thē·fē·kân´te) *adj.* edifying.
edificar, (e·thē·fē·kâr´) *va.* to build, to construct; to set up *(fundar);* (fig.) to edify, to set an example for.
edificio, (e·thē·fē´syo) *m.* building, structure.
editor, ra, (e·thē·tor´, râ) *n.* publisher; editorial writer *(que escribe editoriales);* —, *adj.* publishing; casa —, publishing house.
editorial, (e·thē·to·ryâl´) *adj.* publishing; *m.* editorial; —, *f.* publishing house.
educación, (e·thū·kâ·syon´) *f.* education, upbringing, rearing.
educado, da, (e·thū·kâ´tho, thâ) *adj.* wellmannered, refined.
educando, da. (e·thū·kân´do, dâ) *n.* pupil.
educar, (e·thū·kâr´) *va.* to educate, to instruct, to rear, to bring up.
educativo, va, (e·thū·kâ·tē´vo, vâ) *adj.* educational.
EE. UU. or E.U.A.: Estados Unidos, Estados Unidos de América, U.S. or U. S. A. United States of America.
efectivamente, (e·fek·tē·vâ·men´te) *adv.*

â arm, e they, ē bē, o fore, ū blūe, b bad, ch chip, d day, f fat, g go, h hot, k kid, 1 let

actually, really, certainly.

efectividad, (e·fek·tē·vē·thâth´) f. reality, truth, certainty.

efectivo, va, (e·fek·tē´vo, vâ) adj. true, real, actual; —, m. cash, specie; — en caja, cash on hand; hacer —vo, to cash; valor —vo, real value.

efecto, (e·fek´to) m. effect, result; piece of merchandise (artículo); purpose, end (fin); —s, pl. goods, belongings; —s a cobrar or —s a recibir, bills receivable; —s a pagar, bills payable; —s comerciales or —s de comercio, commercial papers; —s de escritorio, stationery; —s públicos, public securities; en —to, in fact, in truth.

efectuar, (e·fek·twâr´) va. to effect, to produce, to accomplish; — un pago, to make a payment.

efervescencia, (e·fer·ves·sen´syâ) f. effervescence; (fig.) fervor, unrest.

eficacia, (e·fē·kā´syâ) f. effectiveness.

eficaz, (e·fē·kâs´) adj. effective.

eficiente, (e·fē·syen´te) adj. efficient.

efigie, (e·fē´hye) f. effigy; image (en una moneda); (fig.) personification.

efímero, ra, (e·fē´me·ro, râ) adj. ephemeral, short-lived.

efluvio, (e·flū´vyo) m. effluvium.

efugio, (e·fū´hyo) m. evasion, ruse.

efusión, (e·fū·syon´) f. effusion, gush.

efusivo, va, (e·fū·sē´vo, vâ) adj. effusive, gushing.

égida, (e´hē·thâ) f. aegis.

egipcio, cia, (e·hēp´syo, syâ) n. and adj. Egyptian.

Egipto, (e·hēp´to) m. Egypt.

egoísmo, (e·go·ēz´mo) m. selfishness, egoism.

egoísta, (e·go·ēs´tâ) adj. egoistic, selfish, self-centered; —, m. and f. egoist, self-seeker.

egregio, gia, (e·gre´hyo, hyâ) adj. eminent, illustrious.

egreso, (e·gre´so) m. debit.

eje, (e´he) m. axle (barra); axis; — de levas, (mech.) camshaft; — vertical, (avi.) vertical axis.

ejecución, (e·he·kū·syon´) f. execution.

ejecutante, (e·he·kū·tân´te) m. and f. performer; distrainer (judicial); —, adj. distraining.

ejecutar (e·he·kū·târ´) va. to execute; to distrain (por via legal); to play (tocar).

ejecutivo, va, (e·he·kū·tē´vo, vâ) adj. demanding (apremiante); executive; —, n. executive; —, f. board of directors.

ejecutor, ra, (e·he·kū·tor´, râ) adj. executive; —n. executer.

ejemplar, (e·hem·plâr´) m. copy; pattern, original (normal); —, adj. exemplary.

ejemplificar, (e·hem·plē·fē·kâr´) va. to exemplify.

ejemplo, (e·hem´plo) m. example; — casero, everyday example; por —, for instance.

ejercer, (e·her·ser´) va. to exercise, to perform (una facultad); to practice (una profesión); — la medicina, to practice medicine.

ejercicio, (e·her·sē´syo) m. exercise, practice; (mil.) drill; — de tiro, target practice.

ejercitar, (e·her·sē·târ´) va. to practice (una arte); to train (a uno); —se, to become proficient.

ejército, (e·her´sē·to) m. army.

ejido, (e·hē´tho) m. common land; (Mex.) communal farm.

ejote, (e·ho´te) m. (Mex.) string bean. el—, (el) art. (m. sing.) the.

él, (el) pron. he; him (con preposición), it (cosa o animal). — mismo, he himself.

elaboración, (e·lâ·vo·râ·syon´) f. elaboration; processing; secretion.

elaborado, da, (e·lâ·vo·râ´tho, thâ) adj. processed, worked.

elaborar, (e·lâ·vo·râr´) va. to elaborate; to work, to process (preparar); (anat.) to secrete.

elasticidad, (e·lâs·tē·sē·thâth´) f. elasticity; (fig.) laxity.

elástico, ca, (e·lâs´tē·ko, kâ) adj. elastic; —, m. elastic.

elección, (e·lek·syon´) f. freeedom of action; (pol.) election; selection (escogido).

electivo, va, (e·lek·tē´vo, vâ) adj. elective.

electo, ta, (e·lek´to, tâ) n. and adj. elect.

elector, (e·lek·tor´) m. elector.

electorado, (e·lek·to·râ´tho) m. electorate.

electoral, (e·lek·to·râl´) adj. electoral.

electricidad, (e·lek·trē·sē·thâth´) f. electricity.

electricista, (e·lek·trē·sēs´tâ) m. electrician.

eléctrico, ca, (e·lek´trē·ko, kâ) adj. electric, electrical.

electrificación, (e·lek·trē·fē·kâ·syon´) f. electrification.

electrificar, (e·lek·trē·fē·kâr´) va. to electrify.

electrizar, (e·lek·trē·sâr´) va. to electrify.

electrocardiógrafo, (e·lek·tro·kar·thyo´grâ·fo) m. electrocardiograph.

electrocardiograma,

(e·lek·tro·kär·thyo·grä' mä) *m.* electrocardiogram.

electrocución, (e·lek·tro·kū·syon') *f.* electrocution.

electrodo, (e·lek·tro'tho) *m.* electrode.

electrólisis, (e·lek·tro'lē·sēs) *f.* electrolysis.

electromagnético, ca, (e·lek·tro·mäg·ne' tē·ko, kä) *adj.* electromagnetic.

electromotor, ra, (e·lek·tro·mo·tor', rä) *adj.* electromotive.

electromotriz, (e·lek·tro·mo·trēs') *f. adj.* electromotive.

electrón (e·lek·tron') *m.* electron.

electrónica, (e·lek·tro'nē·kä) *f.* electronics.

electrónico, ca, (e·lek·tro'nē·ko, kä) *adj.* electronic.

electroplatear, (e·lek·tro·plä·te·är') *va.* to electroplate.

electrotecnia, (e·lek·tro·teg'nyä) *f.* electrical engineering.

electroterapia, (e·lek·tro·te·rä'pyä) *f.* electrotherapy.

electrotipo, (e·lek·tro·tē'po) *m.* electrotype.

elefante, (e·le·fän'te) *m.* elephant.

elegancia, (e·le·gän'syä) *f.* elegance.

elegante, (e·le·gän'te) *adj.* elegant, fashionable.

elegía, (e·le·jē'ä) *f.* elegy.

elegible, (e·le·hē'vle) *adj.* eligible.

elegir*, (e·le·hēr') *va.* to elect; to choose *(escoger)*.

elemental, (e·le·men·täl') *adj.* elemental; elementary *(fundamental).*

elemento, (e·le·men'to) *m.* element; integral part *(fundamento).*

elenco, (e·leng'ko) *m.* catalogue, table, index; (theat.) cast.

elevación, (e·le·va·syon') *f.* raising; (fig.) elevation; (geog.) height; (fig.) ecstasy, rapture *(enajenamiento).*

elevado da, (e·le·vä'tho, thä) *adj.* high, tall; (fig.) lofty, elevated.

elevador, (e·le·vä·thor') *m.* hoist, lift; (Sp. Am.) elevator *(ascensor).*

elevar, (e·le·vär') *va.* to lift, to raise *(alzar);* (fig.) to elevate; —se, (fig.) to be carried away, to be enraptured *(trasportarse);* to swell up with pride *(envanecerse).*

eliminación, (e·lē·mē·nä·syon') *f.* elimination.

eliminar, (e·lē·mē·när') *va.* to eliminate.

elipse, (e·lēp'se) *f.* (math.) ellipse.

elixir, (e·lēk'sēr) or **elixir,** (e·lēk·sēr') *m.* elixir.

elocución, (e·lo·kū·syon') *f.* elocution *(parte de la retórica);* speaking style,

self-expression.

elocuencia, (e·lo·kwen'syä) *f.* eloquence.

elocuente, (e·lo·kwen'te) *adj.* eloquent.

elogiar, (e·lo·hyär') *va.* to eulogize, to extol.

elogio, (e·lo'hyo) *m.* eulogy, extolling.

elucidar, (e·lū·sē·thär') *va.* to elucidate, to clarify.

eludir, (e·lū·thēr') *va.* to elude, to avoid.

ella, (e'yä) *pron.* she; her *(con preposición);* it *(cosa o animal);* — misma, she herself.

ello, (e'yo) *pron.* it, that.

ellos, ellas, (e'yos, e'yäs) *pron. pl.* they.

emaciación, (e·mä·syä·syon') *f.* emaciation.

emanación, (e·mä·nä·syon') *f.* emanation; (fig.) indication, expression.

emanar, (e·mä·när') *vn.* to emanate.

emancipación, (e·män·sē·pä·syon') *f.* emancipation.

emancipar, (e·män·sē·pär') *va.* to emancipate, to set free.

embadurnar, (em·bä·thūr·när') *va.* to daub, to smear.

embajada, (em·bä·hä'thä) *f.* embassy.

embajador, (em·bä·hä·thor') *m.* ambassador.

embalaje, (em·bä·lä'he) *m.* packing, packaging.

embalar, (em·bä·lär') *va.* to pack, to package.

embaldosar, (em·bäl·do·sär') *va.* to tile, to floor with tiles.

embalsamar, (em·bäl·sä·mar') *va.* to embalm; to perfume *(perfumar).*

embalsar, (em·bäl·sär') *va.* to put on a raft; —se, to dam up, to back up.

embanderar, (em·bän·de·rär') *va.* to decorate with flags.

embarazada, (em·bä·rä·sä'thä) *f. adj.* pregnant; —, *f.* pregnant woman.

embarazar, (em·bä·rä·sär') *va.* to obstruct, to block *(impedir);* to make pregnant *(poner encinta);* —se, to get pregnant; to be hindered, to be held back *(hallarse impedido).*

embarazo, (em·bä·rä'so) *m.* obstruction; pregnancy; awkwardness, embarrassment *(falta de soltura).*

embarazoso, sa, (em·bä·rä·so'so, sä) *adj.* awkward, troublesome, hindering.

embarcación, (em·bär·kä·syon') *f.* vessel, ship; embarkation *(embarco).*

embarcadero, (em·bär·kä·the'ro) *m.* wharf, dock, pier; (rail.) platform.

embarcar, (em·bär·kär') *va.* to embark; — se to embark, to go on board; —se en, (fig.) to embark on, to launch on.

embarco, (em·bâr´ko) *m.* boarding, embarkation.

embargar, (em·bâr·gâr´) *va.* (naut.) to embargo; (fig.) to affect, to bother; to attach *(retener judicialmente).*

embargo, (em·bâr´go) *m.* embargo; bother, trouble; attachment; **sin —,** nevertheless, however.

embarque, (em·bâr´ke) *m.* shipment, embarkment.

embarrar, (em·bâ·rrâr´) *va.* to daub with mud, to muddy *(de barro);* to smear, to daub.

embaucador, (em·bâū·kâ·thor´) *m.* swindler, huckster.

embaucamiento, (em·bâū·kâ·myen´to) *m.* trickery, deception, hoodwinking.

embaucar, (em·bâū·kâr´) *va.* to deceive, to trick, to hoodwink.

embeber, (em·be·ver´) *va.* to absorb, to soak up *(absorber);* to contain, to hold *(contener);* to shorten (recoger); to soak *(empapar);* to insert *(encajar);* —, *vn.* to shrink; **—se,** to be wrapped up, to be absorbed; **—se en,** to imbibe, to drink in, to ground oneself thoroughly in.

embelesamiento, (em·be·le·sâ·myen´to) *m.* rapture.

embelesar, (em·be·le·sâr´) *va.* to enrapture, to enthrall.

embeleso, (em·be·le´so) *m.* rapture, enchantment, bliss; delight, joy *(cosa).*

embellecer*, (em·be·ye·ser´) *va.* to embellish, to beautify.

embellecimiento, (em·be·ye·sē·myen´to) *m.* embellishment, beautifying.

embestida, (em·bes·tē´thâ) *f.* assault, violent attack.

embestir*, (em·bes·tēr´) *va.* to attack, to assault.

emblandecer*, (em·blân·de·ser´) *va.* to soften, to make tender; **—se,** to be moved to pity, to soften.

emblanquecer, (em·blâng·ke·ser´) *va.* to whiten, to turn white.

emblema, (em·ble´mâ) *m.* emblem.

embobar, (em·bo·vâr´) *va.* to distract, to absorb; **—se,** to stand gaping, to be enthralled.

embobecer*, (em·bo·ve·ser´) *va.* to stupefy, to benumb.

embocadura, (em·bo·kâ·thū´râ) *f.* mouthpiece; mouth *(de río);* taste *(de vino);* squeezing in, forcing through *(acción),* (coll.) **tomar la —,** to get the hang of it, to catch on.

embodegar, (em·bo·the·gâr´) *va.* to store

in a cellar.

embolar, (em·bo·lâr´) *va.* to blunt the horns of with wooden balls *(al toro);* to shine, to polish *(el calzado).*

embolismo, (em·bo·lēz´mo) *m.* embolism.

émbolo, (em´bo·lo) *m.* (mech.) piston; **anillo de empaquetadura del —,** piston ring; **vástago del —,** piston rod.

embolsar, (em·bol·sâr´) *va.* to take in, to make *(cobrar);* to put in one´s purse.

emborrachar, (em·bo·rrâ·châr´) *va.* to intoxicate, to make drunk; **—se,** to get drunk, to become intoxicated.

emborronar, (em·bo·rro·nâr´) *va.* to blot, to smudge; (fig.) to dash off, to scribble *(escribir de prisa).*

emboscada, (em·bos·kâ´thâ) *f.* ambush.

embotado, da, (em·bo·tâ´tho, thâ) *adj.* dull, blunt.

embotar, (em·bo·târ´) *va.* to blunt; (fig.) to dull, to weaken; **—se,** to wear boots.

embotellar, (em·bo·te·yâr´) *va.* to bottle.

embozado, da, (em·bo·sâ´tho, thâ) *adj.* concealed, hidden, disguised.

embozo, (em·bo´so) *m.* scarf or muffler across the lower part of the face; border, upper fold *(de la sábana);* (fig.) duplicity, equivocation.

embragar, (em·brâ·gâr´) *vn.* to let out or release the clutch pedal; —, *va.* (naut.) to sling; (auto.) to put in gear; (mech.) to engage.

embrague, (em·brâ´ge) *m.* clutch *(mecanismo);* letting out the clutch *(acción).*

embriagar, (em·bryâ·gâr´) *va.* to intoxicate, to make drunk; (fig.) to enrapture, to carry away.

embriaguez, (em·bryâ·ges´) *f.* intoxication, drunkenness; (fig.) rapture, bliss.

embrión, (em·bryon´) *m.* embryo.

embrionario, ria, (em·bryo·nâ´ryo, ryâ) *adj.* embryonic.

embrollado, da, (em·bro·yâ´tho, thâ) *adj.* tangled, confused.

embrollar, (em·bro´yâr´) *va.* to entangle, to confuse.

embrollo, (em·bro´yo) *m.* tangle, confusion; trick, ruse *(embuste);* (fig.) tight spot.

embromado, da, (em·bro·mâ´tho, thâ) *adj.* vexed, annoyed.

embromar, (em·bro·mâr´) *va.* to trick; to trip up *(engañar);* to fool with, to banter *(chancear);* to joke with *(dar broma).*

embrujar, (em·brū·hâr´) *va.* to bewitch.

embrutecer*, (em·brū·te·ser´) *va.* to make brutish, to stupefy.

embudo, (em·bū´tho) *m.* funnel *(instru-*

---

m met, **n** not, **p** pot, **r** very, **rr** (none), **s** so, **t** toy, **th** with, **v** eve, **w** we, **y** yes, **z** zero

mento); trap, trick *(trampa).*

embuste, (em·būs'te) *m.* trick, wile, artifice; **—s,** *pl.* gewgaws, trinkets.

embustero, ra, (em·bus·te'ro, râ) *n.* cheat, liar, trickster; — *adj.* tricky, deceitful.

embutido, da, (em·bu·tē'tho, thâ) *adj.* inlaid *(taraceado);* stuffed *(rellenado);* —, *m.* inlaid work; **fábrica de —dos,** sausage factory.

embutir, (em·bū·tēr') *va.* to inlay *(taracear)* ; to stuff *(meter);* (fig.) to cram *(incluir);* (fig.) to stuff, to wolf down, to gobble up *(tragar).*

emergencia, (e·mer·hen'syâ) *f.* emergency *(urgencia);* emergence *(salida);* **campo de** —, (avi.) emergency landing field; **sala de —,** emergency room.

emérito, (e·me'rē·to) *adj.* emeritus.

emersión, (e·mer·syon') *f.* emersion.

emigración, (e·mē·grä·syon') *f.* emigration.

emigrado, da, (e·mē·grä'tho, thâ) *adj.* emigrated; —, *n.* emigrant, émigré.

emigrante, (e·mē·grän'te) *m. and f.* emigrant.

emigrar, (e·mē·grär') *vn.* to emigrate.

eminencia, (e·mē·nen'syâ) *f.* eminence.

eminente, (e·mē·nen'te) *adj.* eminent.

emisario, (e·mē·sä'ryo) *m.* emissary.

emisora, (e·mē·so'râ) *f.* broadcasting station.

emitir, (e·mē·tēr') *va.* to issue *(poner en circulación);* to emit, to give off *(arrojar);* (rad. and T.V.) to transmit, to broadcast; to give out, to express *(manifestar).*

emoción, (e·mo·syon') *f.* emotion, feeling.

emocionante, (e·mo·syo·nân'te) *adj.* thrilling, exciting.

emocionar, (e·mo·syo·nâr') *va.* to excite, to thrill, to affect.

emolumento, (e·mo·lū·men'to) *m.* emolument, fee.

emotivo, va, (e·mo·tē'vo, vâ) *adj.* emotional, emotive.

empacar, (em·pâ·kâr') *va.* to pack.

empachar, (em·pâ·chär') *va.* to surfeit, to stuff; **—se,** to be at a loss, to be confused.

empacho, (em·pâ'cho) *m.* overfull feeling, indigestion *(ahíto);* confusion, perplexity *(turbación);* **sin —,** unconcernedly, unceremoniously.

empadronamiento, (em·pâ·thro·nâ·myen'- to) *m.* census.

empadronar, (em·pâ·thro·nâr') *va.* to take a census of.

empajar, (em·pâ·hâr') *va.* to cover with straw; to thatch *(techar).*

empalagar, (em·pâ·lâ·gâr') *va.* to stuff, to cloy, to surfeit *(empachar);* to weary, to get on one's nerves *(fastidiar).*

empalago, (em·pâ·lá'go) *m.* stuffed feeling; disgust.

empalagoso, sa, (em·pâ·lâ·go'so, sâ) *adj.* cloying, sickeningly sweet *(meloso);* wearisome, troublesome *(pesado).*

empalmadura (em·pâl·mâ·thū'râ) *f.* splice, connection.

empalmar, (em·pâl·mâr') *va.* to splice; (fig.) to hook up, to connect *(unir);* —, *vi.* to join, to hook up; to follow right after *(suceder a continuación).*

empalme, (em·pâl'me) *m.* (rail.) junction; (rad.) hookup.

empanada, (em·pâ·nâ'thâ) *f.* meat pie.

empanado, da, (em·pâ·nâ'tho, thâ) *adj.* breaded.

empanar, (em·pâ·nâr') *va.* to put crust on *(masa);* to bread *(pan rallado);* (agr.) to sow with wheat.

empantanar, (em·pân·tâ·nâr') *va.* to swamp *(inundar);* (fig.) to bog down, to block.

empañar, (em·pâ·nyâr') *va.* to swaddle, to wrap *(a las criaturas);* to blur, to cloud *(oscurecer);* (fig.) to tarnish, to sully *(manchar).*

empapar, (em·pâ·pâr') *va.* to saturate, to soak, to drench *(remojar);* to absorb *(absorber);* **—se,** to become thoroughly grounded, to go into deeply.

empapelar, (em·pâ·pe·lâr') *va.* to paper; to wrap in paper *(envolver).*

empaque, (em·pâ'ke) *m.* packing.

empaquetadura, (em·pâ·ke·tâ·thū'râ) *f.* packing, packaging.

empaquetar, (em·pâ·ke·târ') *va.* to pack, to package.

emparchar, (em·pâr·châr') *va.* to put a plaster cast on.

emparedado, (em· pâ·re·thâ'tho) *m.* sandwich; —, **da,** *adj.* walled-in, secluded.

emparedar, (em·pâ·re·thâr') *va.* to confine, to wall in.

emparejar, (em·pâ·re·hâr') *va.* to match *(formar, pareja);* to level, to equalize *(poner al nivel);* —, *vn.* to be level, to catch up.

emparentar*, (em·pâ·ren·târ') *vn.* to become related by marriage.

emparrado, (em·pâ·rrâ'tho) *m.* arbor, trellis.

empastar, (em·pâs·târ') *va.* to fill with dough, to cover with paste; to fill *(un diente);* to hard-bind *(un libro).*

empatar, (em·pâ·târ´) va. to tie; to tie up, to delay (estorbar).

empate, (em·pâ´te) m. tie; delay, tie-up.

empavesar, (em·pâ·ve·sâr´) va. to deck out with flags; (naut.) to dress.

empedernir*, (em·pe·ther·nēr´) va. to harden; —se, to become insensitive, to become hardened.

empedrado, (em·pe·thrâ´tho) m. stone pavement.

empedrar*, (em·pe·thrâr´) va. to pave with stones.

empeine, (em·pe´ē·ne) m. lower abdomen; instep (del pie).

empellar, (em·pe·yâr´) va. to push, to shove.

empellejar, (em·pe·ye·hâr´) va. to cover with skins.

empellón, (em·pe·yon´) m. forceful push, heavy shove; a —ones, roughly, violently.

empeñar, (em·pe·nyâr´) va. to pawn (dar en prenda); to obligate, to pledge (poner por empeño); to compel, to require (precisar); —se, to insist, to persist, to go into debt (endeudarse).

empeño, (em·pe´nyo) m. determination, resolve (deseo vehemente); obligation, pledge (obligación); backer (padrino); (Mex.). pawn shop.

empeoramiento, (em·pe·o·râ·myen´to) m. deterioration, worsening.

empeorar, (em·pe·o·râr´) va. to make worse, to worsen, —, vn. to grow worse, to worsen, to deteriorate.

empequeñecer*, (em·pe·ke·nye·ser´) va. to belittle, to minimize.

emperador, (em·pe·râ·thor´) m. emperor.

emperatriz, (em·pe·râ·trēs´) f. empress.

emperifollar, (em·pe·rē·fo·yâr´) va. and vr. to dress up elaborately, to spruce up.

empero, (em·pe´ro) conj. however, nevertheless.

empezar*, (em·pe·sâr´) va. to begin, to commence.

empinado, da, (em·pē·nâ´tho, thâ) adj. steep (escarpado); lofty, towering (muy alto); stiff (estirado).

empinar, (em·pē·nâr´) va. to raise, to lift; —se, to stand on tiptoe; (fig.) to tower.

empírico, (em·pē´rē·ko) m. empiric, empiricist; —, ca, adj. empirical.

empirismo, (em·pē·rez´mo) m. empiricism.

empizarrar, (em·pē·sâ·rrâr´) va. to slate, to cover with slate.

emplastar, (em·plâs·târ´) va. (med.) to put a plaster on; (fig.) to put makeup on; to delay, to foul up (un negocio); —se, to

get all sticky, to get messed up.

emplasto, (em·plâs´to) m. plaster.

emplazamiento, (em·plâ·sâ·myen´to) m. site, location; summons, citation (cita).

emplazar, (em·plâ·sâr´) va. to summon; to place, to locate (colocar).

empleado, da, (em·ple·â´tho, thâ) n. employee.

emplear, (em·ple·âr´) va. to employ (ocupar); to use (usar); to spend (gastar).

empleo, (em·ple´o) m. employment, occupation.

emplomar, (em·plo·mâr´) va. to line with lead.

emplumar, (em·plü·mâr´) va. to feather, to put feathers on; to tar and feather (a una persona); —se, to grow feathers.

emplumecer*, (em·plü·me·ser´) vn. to grow feathers.

empobrecer*, (em·po·vre·ser´) va. to impoverish, to reduce to poverty; —se, to grow poor.

empobrecimiento, (em·po·vre·sē·myen´to) m. impoverishing.

empolvado, da, (em·pol·vâ´tho, thâ) adj. powdered; dusty; (Mex.) out of practice, rusty.

empolvar, (em·pol·vâr´) va. to powder (el rostro); to cover with dust; —se, to become dusty; (Mex.) to be out of practice (perder la práctica).

empollar, (em·po·yar´) va. to brood, to hatch.

emponzoñar, (em·pon·so·nyâr´) va. to poison; (fig.) to infect.

emporcar*, (em·por·kâr´) va. to soil, to dirty.

emprendedor, ra, (em·pren·de·thor´, râ) adj. enterprising.

emprender, (em·pren·der´) va. to initiate, to undertake.

empresa, (em·pre´sâ) f. enterprise, undertaking; symbol, motto (lema); company, firm (sociedad); libre —, free enterprise.

empresario, (em·pre·sâ´ryo) m. contractor (por contrata); (theat.) impresario, manager.

empréstito, (em·pres´tē·to) m. loan.

empujar, (em·pü·hâr´) va. to push, to shove; to press (hacer presión); (fig.) to oust, to remove.

empuje, (em·pü´he) m. push, shove; (avi.) thrust; (fig.) drive, energy.

empujón, (em·pü·hon´) m. shove, forceful push; rapid strides (avance rápido); a — ones, roughly, carelessly.

empuñadura, (em·pü·nyâ·thü´râ) f. hilt (de espada); handle (de paraguas).

empuñar, (em·pū·nyâr´) va. to grasp, to clutch, to grip *(por el puño);* to hold, to take hold of *(con la mano).*

emulación, (e·mū·lâ·syon´) f. rivalry, competition.

emular, (e·mū·lâr´) va. to rival, to compete with.

emulsión, (e·mūl·syon´) f. emulsion.

en (en) prep. at, in; on *(encima de);* — **adelante,** in the future; — **cuanto,** as soon as; — **cuanto a,** as to, in regard to; — **domingo,** on Sunday; — **casa,** at home; — **la clase,** in class.

enagua, (e·nâ´gwâ) f. or **enaguas,** (e·nâ·gwâs) *pl.* underskirt, petticoat.

enajenable, (e·nâ·he·nâ´vle) adj. alienable.

enajenación, (e·nâ·he·nâ·syon´) f. alienation (fig.) absentmindedness, inattention.

enajenamiento, (e·nâ·he·nâ·myen´to) m. alienation; (fig.) lack of attention, absentmindedness.

enaltecer*, (e·nâl·te·ser´) va. to praise, to exalt.

enamoradizo, za, (e·nâ·mo·râ·thē´so, sâ) adj. inclined to falling in love easily.

enamorado, da, (e·nâ·mo·râ´tho, thâ) adj. in love, enamored, lovesick.

enamoramiento, (e·nâ·mo·râ·myen´to) m. falling in love.

enamorar, (e·nâ·mo·râr´) va. to enamor, to inspire love in; to court, to woo *(decir requiebros);* —**se,** to fall in love.

enano, na, (e·nâ´no, nâ) adj. dwarfish; —, n. dwarf, midget.

enarbolar, (e·nâr·vo·lâr´) va. to hoist, to raise; —**se,** to become angry, to lose one´s temper.

enardecer*, (e·nâr·the·ser´) va. to inflame, to kindle, to excite.

encabestrar, (eng·kâ·ves·trâr´) va. to put a halter on; to guide by the halter *(guiar);* (fig.) to bring in line, to keep in tow.

encabezamiento, (eng·kâ·ve·sâ·myen´to) m. census *(registro);* heading *(de una carta);* foreword, preface *(de un libro).*

encabezar, (eng·kâ·ve·sâr´) va. to make a census of; to put a heading on; to write a preface to; (fig.) to lead, to head up.

encabritarse, (eng·kâ·vrē·târ´se) vr. to tear.

encadenamiento, (eng·kâ·the·nâ·myen´to) m. linking together; chaining together; connecting.

encadenar, (eng·kâ·the·nâr´) va. to chain; (fig.) to link together, to connect.

encajar, (eng·kâ·hâr´) va. to fit in, to

attach *(meter);* to throw in, to bring in *(una cosa inoportuna);* to pass off, to fob off *(con engaño);* —, vn. to fit in; (fig.) to be to the point, to be relevant *(venir al caso);* —**se,** to squeeze in.

encaje, (en·kâ´he) m. lace *(tejido);* fitting, socket *(hueco);* inlay *(labor de taracea);* — **de aguja,** needlepoint.

encajetillar, (eng·kâ·he·tē·yâr´) va. to package.

encajonamiento, (eng·kâ·ho·nâ·myen´to) m. packaging in boxes.

encajonar, (eng·kâ·ho·nâr´) va. to box, to case; to squeeze *(estrechar);* (fig.) to put in close quarters.

encalvecer*, (eng·kâl·ve·ser´) vn. to get bald, to lose one´s hair.

encallar, (eng·kâ·yâr´) vn. (naut.) to run aground; (fig.) to be at an impasse, to be stalled.

encaminar, (eng·kâ·mē·nâr´) va. to show the way, to start out; to direct *(dirigir);* —**se,** to start out; to be on the way.

encandecer*, (eng·kân·de·ser´) va. to bring to a white heat, to make red-hot.

encandilar, (eng·kân·dē·lâr´) va. to dazzle, to daze; (fig.) to confuse, to perplex; — **se,** to become bloodshot.

encanecer*, (eng·kâ·ne·ser´) vn. to turn gray; (fig.) to grow old.

encantador, ra, (eng·kân·tâ·thor´, râ) adj. charming, delightful, enchanting; —, m. enchanter, sorcerer, magician; —, f. sorceress, enchantress.

encantamiento, (eng·kân·tâ·myen´to) m. enchantment.

encantar, (eng·kân·târ´) va. to enchant, to cast a spell on; (fig.) to charm, to captivate.

encanto, (eng·kân´to) m. enchantment, spell; (fig.) charm, delightfulness.

encapado, da, (eng·kâ·pâ´tho, thâ) adj. cloaked.

encapotar, (eng·kâ·po·târ´) va. to cloak; — **se,** to put on one´s cape; (fig.) to cloud over, to become overcast *(el cielo);* to grow sullen, to frown *(una persona).*

encapricharse, (eng·kâ·prē·châr´se) vr. to be stubborn, to persist.

encapuchar, (eng·kâ·pū·châr´) va. to put a hood on.

encaramar, (eng·kâ·râ·mâr´) va. to raise; —**se,** to climb.

encarar, (eng·kâ·râr´) va. to aim at *(apuntar);,* to face, to come face to face with.

encarcelar, (eng·kâr·se·lâr´) va. to imprison.

encarecer*, (eng·kâ·re·ser´) va. to raise

the price of; (fig.) to praise, to rate highly *(alabar);* to urge, to recommend strongly *(recomendar).*

encarecidamente, (eng·kä·re·sē·thä·men´te) *adv.* most earnestly, strongly.

encarecimiento, (eng·ka·re·sē·myen´to) *m.* raising the price; high praise, enhancement; strong recommendation, urging; **con —,** earnestly.

encargar, (eng·kär·gär´) *va.* to give the job, to entrust; **—se de,** to take upon oneself, to take charge of, to take care of.

encargo, (eng·kär´go) *m.* entrusting, giving the job *(acción);* job, responsibility; position *(empleo).*

encariñar,(eng·kä·rē·nyär´)*va.* to inspire affection in; **—se con,** to become fond of.

encarnación, (eng·kär·nä·syon´) *f.* incarnation.

encarnado, da, (eng·kär·nä´tho, thä) *adj.* incarnate; incarnadine *(color);* **—,** *m.* flesh color.

encarnar, (eng·kär·när´) *vn.* to become incarnate; to grow new flesh *(una herida);* (fig.) to make a tremendous impression; **—,** *vt.* to embody, to personify; **—se,** to mix, to fuse.

encarnizado, da, (eng·kär·nē·sä´tho, thä) *adj.* bloodshot, inflamed *(encendido);* savage, without quarter *(porfiado).*

encarnizar, (eng·kär·nē·sär´) *va.* to flesh; (fig.) to make bloodthirsty, to brutalize; **—se,** to become bloodthirsty; to take out one´s wrath *(una persona).*

encarrilar, (eng·kä·rrē·lär´) *va.* to channel, to direct; (fig.) to put to rights, to set right.

encartar, (eng·kär·tär´) *va.* to proscribe *(a un reo);* to register *(en un padrón);* to insert, to inclose *(incluir);* to involve *(implicar);* to play into the hand of *(un naipe).*

encartonar, (eng·kär·to·när´) *va.* to bind in boards *(un libro);* to cover with cardboard.

encascabelado, da, (eng·kâs·kä·ve·lä´tho, thä) *adj.* trimmed with bells.

encasillado, (eng·kä·sē·yä´tho) *m.* set of pigeonholes; (poi.) slate of candidates.

encasillar, (eng·kä·sē·yär´) *va.* to pigeonhole; to classify, to sort out *(clasificar).*

encasquetar, (eng·käs·ke·tär´) *va.* to put on tight, to jam down *(el sombrero);* (fig.) to get into someone´s skull; to make listen to *(hacer oir).*

encastar, (eng·käs·tär) *va.* to crossbreed;

—, *vn.* to breed, to reproduce.

encastillar, (eng·käs·tē·yär´) *va.* to fortify with castles; to stack up *(apilar).*

encausar, (eng·käū·sär´) *va.* to indict, to prosecute.

encauzar, (eng·käū·sär´) *vt.* to channel, to direct.

encefalitis, (en·se·fä·lē´tēs) *f.* encephalitis; **— letárgica,** sleeping sickness.

encelamiento, (en·se·lä·myen´to) *m.* jealousy; rut.

encelarse, (en·se·lär´se) *vr.* to become jealous; to be in rut *(los animales).*

encenagarse, (en·se·nä·gär´se) *vr.* to get covered with mud; (fig.) to wallow in vice.

encendedor, (en·sen·de·thor´) *m.* lighter; **— de cigarrillos,** cigarette lighter.

encender*, (en·sen·der´) *va.* to light *(pegar fuego);* to ignite, to set on fire *(incendiar);* to turn on, to switch on *(la luz);* (fig.) to kindle, to inflame *(excitar);* **—se,** to blush, to turn red.

encendido, da, (en·sen·dē´tho, thä) *adj.* red-hot *(hecho ascua);* flushed, red *(encarnado);* **—,** *m.* ignition; **— prematuro,** backfiring.

encendimiento, (en·sen·dē·myen´to) *m.* lighting, kindling *(acción);* (fig.) ardor, burning, heat, intensity *(ardor).*

encerado, da, (en·se·rá´tho, thä) *adj.* waxen; **—,** *m.* oilcloth; blackboard *(pizarra).*

encerar, (en·se·rär´) *vn.* to wax.

encerrar*, (en·se·rrär´) *va.* to shut up, to confine, to lock up; to hold, to contain *(contener);* **—se,** to go into seclusion.

encía, (en·sē´ä) *f.* (anat.) gum.

enciclopedia, (en·sē·klo·pe´thyä) *f.* encyclopedia.

enciclopédico, ca, (en·se·klo·pe´thē·ko, kä) *adj.* encyclopedic.

encierro, (en·sye´rro) *m.* confinement, locking up; enclosure *(lugar);* seclusion, retirement *(clausura);* narrow cell *(prisión);* pen for fighting bulls *(toril).*

encima, (en·sē´mä) *adv.* above, over; on top *(en la parte superior);* as well, morever *(además);* **— de,** on top of, on; **por — de,** over.

encina, (en·sē´nä) *f.* holm oak, ilex.

encinta, (en·sēn´tä) *f. adj.* pregnant.

enclaustrado, da, (eng·klâūs·trä´tho, thä) *adj.* cloistered; (fig.) hidden away.

enclavadura, (eng·klä·vä·thū´rä) *f.* groove *(hueco);* nail piercing the hoof *(de la caballería).*

enclavar, (eng·klä·vär´) *va.* to nail.

---

m met, **n** not, **p** pot, **r** very, **rr** (none), **s** so, **t** toy, **th** with, **v** eve, **w** we, **y** yes, **z** zero

enclavijar, (eng·klâ·vē·hâr´) va. to pin, to join with dowels; (mus.) to peg.

enclenque, (eng·kleng´ke) adj. feeble, sickly; —, m. and f. weakling.

encofrado, (eng·ko·frá´tho) m. wooden form (para el hormigón); wall support (de galería).

encoger, (eng·ko·her´) va. to draw back, to pull back; (fig.) to make timid, to impede, to hold back: —se, to shrink; —se de hombros, to shrug one´s shoulders.

encogido, da, (eng·ko·hē´tho, thâ) adj. timid, fearful.

encogimiento, (eng·ko·hē·myen´to) m. shrinkage; (fig.) timidness, lack of resolve.

encolar, (eng·ko·lâr´) va. to flue.

encolerizar, (eng·ko·le·rē·sar´) va. to anger, to infuriate.

encomendar*, (eng·ko·men·dâr´) va. to recommend, to entrust; —se, to commit oneself, to rely.

encomiar, (eng·ko·myâr´) va. to praise.

encomiástico, ca, (eng·ko·myâs´tē·ko, kâ) adj. complimentary, high in praise.

encomienda, (eng·ko·myen´dâ) f. commission, trust (encargo); (Sp. Am.) package by mail (envío); praise (elogio); — postal, parcel post.

encomio, (eng·ko´myo) m. praise, commendation.

enconar, (eng·ko·nâr´) va. to inflame, to irritate; (fig.) to vex, to anger (irritar); to weigh heavily on, to hurt (la conciencia).

encono, (eng·ko´no) m. malevolence, rancor, ill-will.

enconoso, sa, (eng·ko·no´so, sâ) adj. quick to anger, irritable; inflamed (una llaga).

encontrar*, (eng·kon·trâr´) va. to meet by chance, to come upon (tropezar con); to find, to locate (hallar); —se, to run into each other; to meet (concurrir); to clash,to be at odds (las opiniones); to be, to find oneself (estar); —se con, to meet.

encontrón, (eng·kon·tron´) m. jolt, bump.

encopetado, da, (eng·ko·pe·tâ´tho, thâ) adj. presumptuous, boastful.

encorajar, (eng·ko·râ·hâr´) va. to give courage; —se, to be in a rage.

encorar*, (eng·ko·râr´) va. to cover with leather; —, vn. to heal, to grow new skin.

encorchar, (eng·kor·châr´) va. to hive (las abejas); to cork (una botella).

encorvar, (eng·kor·vâr´) va. to bend, to curve.

encrespar, (eng·kres·pâr´) va. to curl (ensortijar); to ruffle (el plumaje); to make stand on end (por emoción fuerte); to stir up (irritar); —se, to grow rough (las olas); to become complicated (un asunto).

encrestado, da, (eng·kres·tâ´tho, thâ) adj. (fig.) haughty, high and mighty.

encrucijada, (en·krū·sē·hâ´thâ) f. crossroads (de caminos); intersection (de calles).

encrudecer*, (eng·krū·the·ser´) va. to make rough and raw; (fig.) to rub the wrong way, to exasperate (irritar).

encuadernación, (eng·kwâ·ther·nâ·syon´) f. binding (resultado); bookbinding (acción); bindery (taller); — en rústica, paper binding; — en tela, cloth binding.

encuadernador, (eng·kwâ·ther·nâ·thor´) m. bookbinder.

encuadernar, (eng·kwâ·ther·nâr´) va. to bind.

encuadrar, (eng·kwâ·thrâr´) va. to frame; to insert, to fit (encajar).

encubar, (eng·kū·vâr´) va. to cask, to barrel.

encubridor, ra, (eng·kū·vrē·thor´,râ) adj. covering, concealing; —, n. (fig.) cover, shield.

encubrir, (eng·kū·vrēr´) va. to hide, to conceal.

encuentro, (eng·kwen´tro) m. collision, crash (choque); meeting, encounter (acto de encontrarse); disagreement, opposition (en el parecer); match, game (deportivo); (mil.) encounter, clash; find (hallazgo); salir a —, to go out to meet; to face (hacer).

encuesta, (eng·kwes´tâ) f. investigation, poll.

encumbrado, da, (eng·kūm·brâ´tho, thâ) adj. high, elevated.

encumbramiento, (eng·kūm·brâ·myen´to) m. elevation, height.

encumbrar, (eng·kūm·brâr´) va. to raise, to elevate; to reach the top of (un monte); —se, to grow vain, to swell with pride (envanecerse); to tower, to loom.

encurtido, (eng·kūr·tē´tho) m. pickle; — con eneldo, dill pickle.

enchapar, (en·châ·pâr´) va. to veneer, to plate.

encharcar, (en·châr·kâr´) va. to flood, to cover with water.

enchilada, (en·chē·lâ´thâ) f. (Mex.) tortilla

seasoned with chili and stuffed with cheese and meat.

enchilar, (en·chē·lär´) va. (Sp. Am.) to put chili on; (Mex.) to throw into a rage *(emberrenchinar);* (Costa Rica) to let down, to disappoint *(dar chasco).*

enchufe, (en·chū´fe) m. (elec.) outlet *(conexión);* plug *(aparato);* connection *(de cañerías);* tener —, (coll.) to have pull.

endeble, (en·de´vle) adj. feeble, weak; flimsy *(tela).*

endemoniado, da, (en·de·mo·nyä´tho, thä) adj. possessed, bedeviled; (coll.) devilish, fiendish.

enderezamiento, (en·de·re·sä·myen´to) m. straightening.

enderezar, (en·de·re·sär´) va. to straighten; to rectify *(enmendar);* to direct, to send straight *(encaminar).*

endeudarse, (en·deū·thär´se) vr. to get into debt.

endiablado, da (en·dyä·vlä´tho, thä) adj. devilish, diabolical.

endiosar, (en·dyo·sär´) va. to deify; —se, (fig.) to puff up with pride *(engreírse);* to be absorbed, to be deeply engrossed *(enajenarse).*

endorso, (en·dor´so) m. endorsement.

endosante, (en·do·sän´te) m. endorser.

endosar, (en·do·sär´) va. to endorse; (fig.) to load with, to throw on *(una carga).*

endoso, (en·do´so) m. endorsement.

endulzar, (en·dūl·sär´) va. to sweeten *(dulcificar);* to soften *(suavizar).*

endurecer*, (en·dū·re·ser´) va. to harden; —se, to become cruel, to grow hard.

endurecido, da, (en·dū·re·sē´tho, thä) adj. inured, hardened.

endurecimiento, (en·dū·re·sē·myen´to) m. hardening; (fig.) obstinacy *(obstinación).*

eneldo, (e·nel´do) m. dill; **encurtido con** —, dill pickle.

enemigo, ga, (e·ne·mē´go, gä) adj. unfriendly, hostile; —, n. enemy.

enemistad, (e·ne·mes·täth´) f. enmity, hatred.

enemistar, (e·ne·mēs·tär´) va. to estrange, to make enemies; —se, to become enemies.

energía, (e·ner·hē´ä) f. power, force *(potencia);* strength *(eficacia);* (phy.) energy; **— atómica,** atomic energy; — **nuclear** or **nuclearia,** nuclear power; — **solar,** solar power; — **vatimétrica,** wattage.

enérgico, ca, (e·ner´hē·ko, kä) adj. energetic; powerful, strong *(eficaz).*

energúmeno, na, (e·ner·gū´me·no, nä) n. (fig.) one possessed whirling dervish.

enero, (e·ne´ro) m. January.

enervar, (e·ner·vär´) va. to enervate.

enésimo, ma, (e·ne´sē·mo, mä) adj. umpteenth; **por —ma vez,** for the umpteenth time.

enfadado, da, (em·fä·thä´tho, thä) adj. angry, irate; annoyed, vexed.

enfadar, (em·fä·thär´) va. to anger, to make angry; to annoy, to vex *(fastidiar);* —se, to get angry; to be annoyed.

enfado, (em·fä´tho) m. vexation, annoyance; anger, ire *(enojo).*

enfadoso, sa, (em·fä·tho´so, sä) adj. annoying, vexing.

enfardar, (em·fär·thär´) va. to pack, to bale, to package.

énfasis, (em´fä·sēs) m. emphasis.

enfático, at, (em·fä´tē·ko, kä) adj. emphatic.

enfermar, (em·fer·mar´) va. to sicken, to make sick; (fig.) to weaken *(debilitar);* —, vn. to get sic ; —se, (Sp. Am.) to get sick.

enfermedad, (em·fer·me·thäth´) f. illness, sickness, disease.

enfermería, (em·fer·me·rē´ä) f. infirmary.

enfermero, ra, (em·fer·me´ro, rä) n. nurse.

enfermizo, za, (em·fer·mē´so, sä) adj. infirm, sickly; unhealthful *(que ocasiona enfermedades);* twisted, sick *(alterado).*

enfermo, ma, (em·fer´mo, ma) adj. sick; diseased *(atacado);* —, n. sick person, patient; **ponerse —,** to get sick.

enfilar, (em·fē·lär´) va. to line up; to string *(ensartar);* to follow the course of *(seguir);* (mil.) to enfilade.

enflacar, (em·flä·kär´) vn. to get thin, to lose weight.

enflaquecer*, (em·flä·ke·ser´) va. to make lose weight; (fig.) to weaken *(enervar);* —se, to lose weight, to get thin.

enfocar, (em·fo·kär´) va. to focus.

enfoque, (em·fo´ke) m. focus.

enfrascar, (em·fräs·kär´) va. to bottle; — se, to become entangled; (fig.) to become deeply involved, to give oneself over *(aplicarse).*

enfrenar, (em·fre·när´) va. to bridle *(el caballo);* (mech.) to brake; (fig.) to curb, to check.

enfrentar, (em·fren·tär´) va. to bring face to face, to confront *(poner frente a frente);* to face *(hacer frente).*

enfrente, (em·fren´te) adv. across, opposite; in front; opposed *(en contra).*

enfriador, ra, (em·fryâ·thor´, râ) *adj.* cooling; —, *m.* cool spot.

enfriamiento, (em·fryâ·myen´to) *m.* refrigeration, cooling; (med.) chill; — **por aire,** air-cooling.

enfriar, (em·fryâr´) *va.* to cool, to refrigerate; (fig.) to chill, to dampen *(amortiguar);* —, *vn.* to cool off.

enfurecer*, (em·fû·re·ser´) *va.* to infuriate, to enrage; —**se,** to grow furious; (fig.) to get rough; to become wild *(alborotarse).*

enfurruñarse, (em·fû·rrû·nyâr´se) *vr.* to pout, to sulk.

engalanar, (eng·gâ·lâ·nâr´) *va.* to adorn, to deck out.

enganchador, ra, (eng·gân·châ·thor´, râ) *adj.* hitching, connecting; —, *m.* (mil.) recruiter.

enganchar, (eng·gân·châr´) *va.* to hook, to connect; to hang *(en una percha);* to hitch *(la caballería);* (mil.) to recruit; (coll.) to hook, to trap *(obligar con maña).*

enganche, (eng·gân´che) *m.* connection, hook; (Mex.) down payment.

engañabobos, (eng·gâ·nyâ·vo´vos) *m.* (coll.) fake.

engañadizo, za, (eng·gâ·nyâ·thē´so, sâ) *adj.* easily deceived.

engañador, ra, (eng·gâ·nyâ·thor´, râ) *n.* cheat, deceiver, fake; —, *adj.* deceiving, tricky.

engañar, (eng·gâ·nyâr´) *va.* to deceive, to cheat; to mislead, to take advantage of *(abusar de);* to wile away, to pass *(entretener);* —**se,** to be mistaken, to be wrong.

engaño, (eng·gâ´nyo) *m.* mistake; deceit *(trampa).*

engañoso, sa, (eng·gâ·nyo´so, sâ) *adj.* deceitful, misleading.

engarrotar, (eng·gâ·rro·târ´) *va.* to garrote.

engarzar, (eng·gâr·sâr´) *va.* to curl *(rizar);* to thread, to wire *(reunir con un hilo).*

engastar, (eng·gâs·târ´) *va.* to enchase, to mount.

engaste, (eng·gâs´te) *m.* setting, mounting.

engatusar, (eng·gâ·tû·sâr´) *va.* to wheedle, to coax.

engazar, (eng·gâ·sâr´) *va.* to curl *(rizar);* to thread, to wire *(unir);* to dye after weaving *(un paño).*

engendrar, (en·hen·drâr´) *va.* to engender, to beget.

englobar, (eng·glo·vâr´) *va.* to lump together.

engolfar, (eng·gol·fâr´) *vn.* to go far out to sea; —**se,** to throw oneself heart and soul, to devote all one´s time.

engomar, (eng·go·mâr´) *va.* to gum; to rubberize *(de caucho).*

engordar, (eng·gor·thâr´) *va.* to fatten; —**se,** to get fat; (coll.) to grow rich *(hacerse rico).*

engorro, (eng·go´rro) *m.* obstacle, impediment.

engorroso, sa, (eng·go·rro´so, sâ) *adj.* troublesome, bothersome.

engranaje, (eng·grâ·nâ´he) *m.* gear, gears; meshing *(acción).*

engranar, (eng·grâ·nâr´) *vn.* to mesh, to gear.

engrandecer*, (eng·grân·de·ser´) *va.* to increase, to augment; to aggrandize, to extol *(alabar).*

engrandecimiento, (eng·gran·de·sē·myen´-to) *m.* increase, augment; aggrandizement, exaltation.

engrasar, (eng·grâ·sâr´) *va.* to grease, to oil.

engreimiento, (eng·grē·myen´to) *m.* presumption, vanity; (Sp. Am.) overindulgence, spoiling *(consentimiento).*

engreir*, (eng·gre·ēr´) *va.* to make vain, to make proud; (Sp. Ant) to spoil, to overindulge *(mimar).*

engrosar*, (eng·gro·sâr´) *va.* to thicken; (fig.) to swell; —, *vn.* to put on weight.

engrudo, (eng · grû´ tho) *m.* library paste.

engullidor, ra, (eng·gû·yē·thor´, râ) *adj.* gulping, gobbling.

engullir*, (eng·gû·yēr´) *va.* to gobble up, to gulp down.

enhebrar, (e·ne·vrâr´) *va.* to thread.

enhorabuena, (e·no·râ·vwe´nâ) *f.* congratulations; —, *adv.* safely, well.

enhoramala, (e·no·râ·mâ´lâ) *adv.* cursed be the time, unluckily.

enigma, (e·nēg´mâ) *m.* riddle, enigma.

enigmático, ca, (e·nēg·mâ´tē·ko, kâ) *adj.* enigmatical.

enjabonadura, (en·hâ·vo·nâ·thû´râ) *f.* soaping.

enjabonar, (en·hâ·vo·nâr´) *va.* to soap, to lather.

enjaezar, (en·hâe·sâr´) *va.* to put fancy trappings on.

enjalma, (en·hâl´mâ) *f.* packsaddle.

enjambrar, (en·hâm·brâr´) *va.* to remove a new bee colony from; —, *vn.* to swarm.

enjambre, (en·hâm´bre) *m.* swarm of bees; (fig.) throng, swarm *(multitud).*

enjardinar, (en·hâr·thē·nâr´) *va.* to set

out, to plant in regular patterns.

enjaretar, (en·hâ·re·târ´) va. to run through the hem; (fig.) to reel off, to dash off *(decir atropelladamente);* to palm off, to fob off *(encajar).*

enjaular, (en·hâū·lâr´) va. to cage; (coll.) to jail.

enjoyar, (en·ho·yâr´) va. to put jewels on; (fig.) to embellish.

enjuagar, (en·hwâ·gar´) va. to rinse, to rinse out.

enjuague, (en·hwâ´ge) m. rinse, rinsing; mouthwash *(para la boca).*

enjugar, (en·hū·gâr´) va. to dry off *(secar);* to wipe off *(la humedad);* (com.) to wipe out *(cancelar).*

enjuiciar, (en·hwē·syâr´) va. to pass judgment on; to try *(instruir);* to sue, to bring to trial *(sujetar a juicio).*

enjundioso, sa, (en·hūn·dyo´so, sâ) adj. substantial, meaty.

enjuto, ta, (en·hū´to, tâ) adj. dry *(seco);* skinny, sparse *(flaco).*

enlace, (en·lâ´se) m. connection, link *(conexión);* relationship *(parentesco);* (rail.) junction; wedding *(casamiento).*

enladrillado, (en·lâ·thrē·yâ´tho) m. brick paving.

enladrillar, (en·lâ·thrē·yâr´) va. to pave with bricks.

enlatado, da, (en·lâ·tâ´tho, thâ) adj. canned, preserved; **productos —s,** canned goods.

enlatar, (en·lâ·târ´) va. to can, to tin.

enlazar, (en·lâ·sâr´) va. to link, to connect; to lasso *(un animal);* to tie, to bind *(coger con lazos);* **—se,** to be united by marriage.

enlistonado, (en·lēs·to·nâ´tho) m. lathing.

enlodar, (en·lo·thâr´) va. to cover with mud; **—se,** to get muddy.

enloquecer*, (en·lo·ke·ser´) va. to madden, to drive mad; **—se,** to go mad; (fig.) to be mad, to be wild.

enloquecido, da, (en·lo·ke·sē´tho, thâ) adj. deranged, mad.

enloquecimiento, (en·lo·ke·sē·myen´to) m. madness, insanity.

enlosar, (en·lo·sâr´) va. to set flagstones on, to lay with flagstone.

enlutar, (en·lū·târ´) va. to dress in mourning; **—se,** to go into mourning.

enllantar, (en·yân·târ´) va. to put a tire on.

enmaderar, (en·mâ·the·râr´) va. to board, to timber.

enmarañar, (en·mâ·râ·nyâr´) va. to entangle, to snarl up (fig.) to confuse, to mix

up.

enmarcar, (en·mâr·kâr´) va. to frame.

enmascarar, (en·mâs·kâ·râr´) va. to mask.

enmendar*, (en·men·dâr´) va. to amend, to correct *(corregir);* to make restitution for *(subsanar);* to revise *(una sentencia).*

enmienda, (en·myen´dâ) f. correction; revision, amendment; restitution.

enmohecer*, (en·mo·e·ser´) va. to mold; to rust *(herrumbrar);* **—se,** to grow moldly; to rust, to get rusty.

enmohecido, da, (en·mo·e·sē´tho, thâ) adj. moldy; rusty.

enmudecer*, (en·mū·the·ser´) va. to silence, to keep silent; **—,** vn. to be struck dumb, to lose one's speech; (fig.) to keep quiet, to say nothing *(callarse).*

ennegrecer*, (en·ne·gre·ser´) va. to blacken.

ennoblecer*, (en·no·vle·ser´) va. to ennoble.

ennoblecimiento, (en·no·vle·sē·myen´to) m. ennoblement.

enojadizo, za, (en·o·hâ·thē´so, sâ) adj. touchy, quick-tempered.

enojado, da, (e·no·hâ´tho, thâ) adj. angry, cross.

enojar, (e·no·hâr´) va. to anger, to make angry; to peeve, to irritate *(desazonar);* **—se,** to get angry.

enojo (e·no´ho) m. anger; irritation, bother *(molestia).*

enojón, ona, (e·no·hon´, o´nâ) adj. (Sp. Am.) quick-tempered, irritable.

enojoso, sa, (e·no·ho´so, sâ) adj. irritating, vexing.

enorgullecer*, (e·nor·gū·ye·ser´) va. to fill with pride; **—se,** to swell with pride.

enorme, (e·nor´me) adj. enormous, huge; **—mente,** adv. enormously.

enormidad, (e·nor·mē·thâth´) f. enormity.

enramada, (en·rrâ·mâ´thâ) f. boughs *(ramaje);* bower, leafy retreat *(cobertizo).*

enredadera, (en·rre·thâ·the´râ) f. climbing plant, vine.

enredar, (en·rre·thâr´) va. to net *(prender con red);* to twist up, to tangle *(enmarañar);* to stir up, to start *(discordia);* to mix up, to entangle *(en un mal negocio);* **—se,** to have an affair *(amancebarse);* to present problems, to run afoul *(un negocio).*

enredo, (en·rre´tho) m. tangle, snarl *(maraña);* prank *(travesura);* trick, trap *(engaño);* problem, difficulty *(complica-*

ción); plot (trama).

enrejado, (en·rre·hâ´tho) m. grillwork, grating; openwork (labor de mano).

enrejar, (en·rre·hâr´) va. to put grillwork over.

enrevesado, da, (en·rre·ve·sâ´tho, thâ) adj. intricate, complicated; (fig.) contrary, headstrong (travieso).

enriquecer*, (en·rrē·ke·ser´) va. to enrich; —, vn. to grow rich.

enriscar, (en·rrēs·kâr´) va. (fig.) to elevate, to raise, —se, to take refuge among the rocks.

enrizar, (en·rrē·sâr´) va. to curl.

enrojecer*, (en·rro·he·ser´) va. to make red-hot (en el fuego); to redden, to make red; —se, to blush, to redden.

enrollar, (en·rro·yâr´) va. to wind, to roll.

enronquecer*, (en·rrong·ke·ser´) va. to make hoarse; —, vn. to grow hoarse.

enroscar, (en·rros·kâr´) va. to twist; to screw in (introducir).

ensalada, (en·sâ·lâ´thâ) f. salad; (fig.) hodgepodge.

ensaladera, (en·sâ·lâ·the´râ) f. salad bowl.

ensalzar, (en·sâl·sâr´) va. to exalt, to praise; —se, to boast, to make much of oneself.

ensamblador, (en·sâm·blâ·thor´) m. assembler.

ensamblar, (en·sâm·blâr´) va. to assemble, to fit together.

ensamble, (en·sâm´ble) m. assembly, fitting together.

ensanchar, (en·sân·châr´) va. to widen, to enlarge; —se, to assume an air of importance.

ensanche, (en·sân´che) m. widening, enlargement; seam allowance (tela).

ensangrentar*, (en·sâng·gren·târ´) va. to bloody, to make bloody; —se, (fig.) to rage, to seethe; —se con, to take out one's wrath on.

ensañar, (en·sâ·nyâr´) va. to enrage, to infuriate; —se en to vent one's rage on, to do unnecessary violence.

ensartar, (en·sâr·târ´) va. to string; to stick, to drive (introducir).

ensayar, (en·sâ·yâr´) va. to experiment with, to try out (probar); to teach, to train (adiestrar): (theat.) to rehearse; to assay (un metal).

ensayo, (en·sâ´yo) m. trying out, experiment; essay (escrito); (theat.) rehearsal; assay; — **general,** dress rehearsal.

ensebar, (en·se·vâr´) va. to grease.

ensenada, (en·se·nâ´thâ) f. cove, small bay.

enseña, (en·se´nyâ) f. standard, ensign, colors.

enseñanza, (en·se·nyân´sâ) f. teaching, instruction; **primera** —, primary grades; **segunda** —, high school grades.

enseñar, (en·se·nyâr´) va. to teach, to instruct (instruir); to show (mostrar); to point out (indicar).

enseres, (en·se´res) m. pl. implements, equipment; — **domésticos,** household goods.

enseriarse, (en·se·ryâr´se) vr. (Sp. Am.) to become sober, to get serious.

ensilladura, (en·sē·yâ·thū´râ) f. back of a mount under the saddle; saddling (acción).

ensillar, (en·sē·yâr´) va. to saddle.

ensimismarse, (en·sē·mēz·mâr´se) vr. to be lost in thought (absorberse); to be stuck on oneself (engreírse).

ensordecer*, (en·sor·the·ser´) va. to deafen; —, vn. to grow deaf; to keep quiet, not to answer (enmudecer).

ensortijar, (en·sor·tē·hâr´) va. to curl.

ensuciar, (en·sū·syâr´) va. to dirty, to soil; (fig.) to tarnish, to stain (deslustrar); — **se,** (fig.) to accept bribes, to be able to be bought.

ensueño, (en·swe´nyo) m. dream, reverie, illusion.

entablado, da, (en·tâ·vlâ´tho, thâ) adj. boarded, made of boards; —, m. wooden flooring.

entablar, (en·tâ·vlâr´) va. to board over; to splint (entabillar); to broach (comenzar).

entablillar, (en·tâ·vlē·yâr´) va. to splint.

entalladura, (en·tâ·yâ·thū´râ) f. carving; tap, notch (en el árbol); groove (en las maderas).

entallar, (en·tâ·yâr´) va. to carve; to tap, to notch; to groove; —, vn. to fit.

entapizar, (en·tâ·pē·sâr´) va. to hang with tapestries.

entarimado, (en·tâ·rē·mâ´tho) m. wooden flooring.

entarimar, (en·tâ·rē·mâr´) va. to cover with wooden flooring.

ente, (en´te) m. entity, being; (coll.) character.

entenado, da, (en·te·nâ´tho, thâ) n. stepson, stepdaughter.

entender*, (en·ten·der´) va. to understand (comprender); to know (conocer);. to intend, to mean (querer); to believe (creer).

entendido, da, (en·ten·dē´tho, thâ) adj. wise, learned, skilled; **valor —do,** value agreed on.

entendimiento, (en·ten·dē·myen´to) *m.*
understanding; good judgment *(juicio).*

enteramente, (en·te·rä´men´te) *adv.*
entirely, completely.

enterar, (en·te·râr´) *va.* to inform, to notify, to let know; **—se de,** to find out
about, to be informed of.

entereza, (en·te·re´sä) *f.* entirety, perfection; (fig.) perseverance, steadfastness
(fortaleza).

enteritis, (en·te·rē´tēs) *f.* (med.) enteritis.

enterizo, za, (en·te·rē´so, sä) *adj.* entire,
complete.

enternecer*, (en·ter·ne·ser´) *va.* to soften;
(fig.) to affect, to move *(conmover);* **—se,**
to be touched, to be moved.

enternecimiento, (en·ter·ne·sē·myen´to) *m.*
compassion, pity.

entero, ra, (en·te´ro, rä) *adj.* whole, entire;
(fig.) just, upstanding *(recto);* resolute
(firme); virtuous honest *(incorruptible);*
por —ro, entirely, completely.

enterrador, (en·te·rrä·thor´) *m.* gravedigger.

enterrar*, (en·te·rrâr´) *va.* to inter, to
bury.

entibiar, (en·tē·vyâr´) *va.* to cool.

entidad, (en·tē·thäth´) *f.* entity, being;
importance, value *(valor).*

entierro, (en·tye´rro) *m.* burial, interment.

entomología, (en·to·mo·lo·hē´ä) *f.* entomo-
logy.

entonación, (en·to·nä·syon´) *f.* intonation;
(fig.) presumption, airs *(presunción).*

entonar, (en·to·nâr´) *va.* to intone; to sing
in tune *(afinando la voz);* (med.) to tone
up; to harmonize *(armonizar).*

entonces, (en·ton´ses) *adv.* then, at that
time.

entontecer*, (en·ton·te·ser´) *va.* to stupefy,
to dull; **—se,** to grow stupid.

entorchado, (en·tor·chä´tho) *m.* braid.

entorchar, (en·tor·châr´) *va.* to braid, to
twist.

entornar, (en·tor·nâr´) *va.* to leave ajar, to
leave half-open.

entorpecer*, (en·tor·pe·ser´) *va.* to stupefy,
to dull; (fig.) to block, to hinder *(estorbar).*

entorpecimiento, (en·tor·pe·sē·myen´to) *m.*
torpor, numbness.

entrada, (en·trä´thä) *f.* entry *(acción);*
entrance *(sitio);* attendance *(concurrencia);* admission, ticket *(billete);* beginning *(principio);* first course *(de una
comida);* (com.) receipt; ear, access
(favor).

entrambos, bas, (en·trâm´bos, bäs) *adj.
pl.* both.

entrampar, (en·trâm·pâr´) *va.* to trap, to
snare; (fig.) to trick, to deceive
(engañar); to complicate, to confuse
(enredar); **—se,** (coll.) to go deeply into
debt.

entrante, (en·trân´te) *adj.* next, incoming,
coming.

entrañable, (en·trä·nyä´vle) *adj.* intimate,
very dear.

entrañas, (en·trä´nyäs) *f. pl.* intestines;
(fig.) bowels *(lo más oculto);* very heart,
life blood *(lo más íntimo).*

entrar, (en·trâr´) *vn.* to enter; to pierce, to
penetrate *(penetrar);* to fit *(caber);* to be
used *(emplearse);* to start up *(manifestarse);* **—,** *va.* to bring in *(introducir);* to
get through to *(pegar).*

entre, (en´tre) *prep.* between; among *(en
medio de);* within *(dentro);* **— manos,** at
hand, on hand.

entreabierto, ta, (en·tre·ä·vyer´to, tä) *adj.*
ajar, half-open.

entreabrir*, (en·tre·ä·vrēr´) *va.* to open
half-way, to leave ajar.

entreacto, (en·tre·äk´to) *n.* (theat.) intermission.

entrecano, na, (en·tre·kä´no, nä) *adj.* grayish, graying.

entrecejo, (en·tre·se´ho) *m.* space between
the eyebrows; (fig.) frown *(ceño).*

entrecoger, (en·tre·ko·her´) *va.* to catch, to
intercept, to grab hold of.

entrecortado, da, (en·tre·kor·tä´tho, thä)
adj. faltering, intermittent, broken.

entrecubiertas, (en·tre·kü·vyer´täs) *f. pl.*
(naut.) between decks.

entredicho, (en ·tre·thē´cho) *m.* prohibition.

entrega, (en·tre´gä) *f.* delivery, handing
over; surrender; **— inmediata,** special
delivery; **novela por —s,** serial or installment novel.

entregar, (en·tre·gâr´) *va.* to deliver, to
hand over; **—se,** to surrender, to give
up; to devote oneself, to give oneself
over *(dedicarse).*

entrelazado, da, (en·tre·lä·sä´tho, thä) *adj.*
interlaced, entwined.

entrelazar, (en·tre·lä·sâr´) *va.* to interlace,
to entwine.

entremés, (en·tre·mes´) *m.* (theat.) scene
of comic relief; appetizer *(en la comida).*

entremeter, (en·tre·me·ter´) *va.* to insert,
to place between; **—se,** to meddle, to
intrude.

entremetido da, (en·tre·me·tē´tho, thä) *n.*

meddler, kibitzer; —, **da,** *adj.* meddling, meddlesome.

entremezclar, (en·tre·mes·klâr´) *va.* to mix together.

entrenador, (en·tre·nâ·thor´) *m.* trainer, coach.

entrenar, (en·tre·nâr´) *va.* to train, to coach.

entreoir*, (en·tre·o·ēr´) *va.* to barely hear, to catch snatches of.

entrepaño, (en·tre·pâ´nyo) *m.* panel.

entrepiernas, (en·tre·pyer´nâs) *f. pl.* inner-part of the thighs; (Chile) swim trunks.

entresacar, (en·tre·sâ·kâr´) *va.* to thin out.

entresuelo, (en·tre·swe´lo) *m.* mezzanine.

entretanto, (en·tre·tân´to) *adv.* meanwhile.

entretejer, (en ·tre·te·her´) *va.* to inter-weave.

entretela, (en·tre·te´lâ) *f.* interlining.

entretener*, (en·tre·te·ner´) *va.* to enter-tain, to amuse *(divertir);* to delay to put off *(demorar);* to allay *(hacer más lleva-dero).*

entretenido, da, (en·tre·te·nē´tho, thâ) *adj.* pleasant, amusing.

entretenimiento, (en·tre·te·nē·myen´to) *m.* amusement, entertainment.

entretiempo, (en·tre·tyem´po) *m.* seasons of spring and fall.

entrevenado, da, (en·tre·ve·nâ´tho, thâ) *adj.* intravenous.

entrevenarse, (en·tre·ve·nâr´se) *vr.* to spread through the veins.

entrever*, (en·tre·ver´) *va.* to catch a glimpse of, to barely see.

entrevista, (en·tre·vēs´tâ) *f.* interview.

entrevistar, (en·tre·vēs·tar´) *va.* to inter-view.

entristecer*, (en·trēs·te·ser´) *va.* to sad-den, to grieve; —**se,** to grieve, to be sad.

entrometimiento, (en·tro·me·tē·myen´to) *m.* interference, meddling.

entronar, (en·tro·nâr´) *va.* to enthrone.

entroncar, (en·trong·kâr´) *va.* to establish a relationship with; —, *vn.* to have a common ancestry, to be related; (rail.) to meet, to join.

entronque, (en·trong´ke) *m.* (rail.) junc-tion; common ancestry, relationship.

entubar, (en·tū·vâr´) *va.* to pipe.

entuerto, (en·twer´to) *m.* affront, insult; —**s,** *pl.* afterpains.

entullecerse*, (en·tū·ye·ser´se) *vr.* to be crippled.

entumecer*, (en·tū·me·ser´) *va.* to numb, to make numb; —**se,** (fig.) to swell, to rise *(hincharse).*

entumecimiento, (en·tū·me·sē·myen´to) *m.* numbness; numbing *(acción).*

entumirse, (en·tū·mēr´se) *vr.* to become numb.

enturbiar, (en·tūr·vyâr´) *va.* to muddy, to stir up; (fig.) to spoil, to upset *(turbar).*

entusiasmar, (en·tū·syâz·mâr´) *va.* to enthuse, to make enthusiastic; —**se,** to enthuse.

entusiasmo, (en·tū·syâz´mo) *m.* enthu-siasm.

entusiasta, (en·tū·syâs´tâ) *m. and f.* enthusiast, fan; —, *adj.* enthusiastic.

enumeración, (e·nū·me·râ·syon´) *f.* enu-meration.

enumerar, (e·nū·me·râr´) *va.* to enume-rate.

enunciación, (e·nūn·syâ·syon´) *f.* enuncia-tion, declaration, clear statement.

enunciar, (e·nūn·syâr´) *va.* to enunciate, to declare, to state clearly.

envainar, (em·bâê·nâr´) *va.* to sheathe.

envalentonar, (em·ba·len·to·nâr´) *va.* to give the courage, to make bold enough; —**se,** to pluck up courage; to consider oneself quite a hero *(jactarse de valiente).*

envanecer*, (em·bâ·ne·ser´) *va.* to make vain, to swell up, to puff up; —**se,** to become vain.

envararse, (em·bâ·râr´se) *vr.* to become numb.

envasar, (em·bâ·sâr´) *va.* to bottle *(en vasijas);* to package; to drink too much *(beber con exceso).*

envase, (em·bâ´se) *m.* bottling; packaging; container *(recipiente).*

envejecer*, (em·be·he·ser´) *va.* to age; —, *vn.* to age, to grow older.

envejecido da, (em·be·he·sē´tho,thâ) *adj.* aged, old; (fig.) veteran, experienced *(acostumbrado).*

envejecimiento, (em·be·he·sē·myen´to) *m.* aging.

envenenamiento, (em·be·ne·nâ·myen´to) *m.* poisoning.

envenenar, (em·be·ne·nâr´) *va.* to poison.

envestir*, (em·bes·tēr´) *va.* to invest.

enviado, (em·byâ´tho) *m.* envoy, messen-ger.

enviar, (em·byâr´) *va.* to send.

enviciar, (em·bē·syâr´) *va.* to vitiate, to corrupt; —**se en** to spend too much time at, to go overboard on.

envidia, (em·bē´thyâ) *f.* envy; desire *(emu-lación).*

envidiable, (em·bē·thyyâ´vle) *adj.* enviable.

envidiar, (em·bē·thyâr´) *vn.* to envy, to begrudge; to wish one had, to long for *(desear).*

envidioso, sa, (em·bē·thyo´so, sâ) *adj.* envious.

envilecer*, (em·bē·le·ser´) *va.* to degrade, to debase; **—se,** to degrade oneself, to be debased.

envío, (em·bē´o) *m.* shipment, remittance.

envite, (em·bē´te) *m.* bid, offer.

enviudar, (em·byū·thâr´) *vn.* to be widowed; to be left a widower *(quedarse viudo).*

envoltorio, (em·bol·to´ryo) *m.* bundle.

envoltura, (em·bol·tū´râ) *f.* covering, wrapping; swaddling clothes *(del niño).*

envolver*, (em·bol·ver´) *va.* to wrap, to cover, to involve *(mezclar);* to swaddle *(al niño);* to complicate to hide *(ocultar);* **—se,** to have an affair.

envolvimiento, (em·bol·vē·myen´to) *m.* involvement; covering; complication.

enyesar, (en·ye·sâr´) *va.* to plaster; (med.) to put in a cast.

enzima, (en·sē´mâ) *f.* (biol.) enzyme.

eón, (e·on´) *m.* aeon.

epicentro, (e·pē·sen´tro) *m.* epicenter.

épico, ca, (e´pē·ko, kâ) *adj.* epic.

epicúreo, rea, (e·pē·kū´re·o, re·â) *adj.* epicurean; **—,** *n.* epicure.

epidemia, (e·pē·the´myâ) *f.* epidemic.

epidermis, (e·pē·ther´mēs) *f.* epidermis.

epígrafe, (e·pē´grâ·fe) *m.* epigraph.

epigrama, (e·pē·grâ´mâ) *m.* epigram.

epilepsia, (e·pē·lep´syâ) *f.* epilepsy.

epilogar, (e·pē·lo·gâr´) *va.* to conclude, to sum up.

epilogo, (e·pē´lo·go) *m.* epilogue.

episcopado, (e·pēs·ko·pâ´tho) *m.* bishopric; episcopate *(conjunto de obispos).*

episodio, (e·pē·so´thyo) *m.* episode.

epístola, (e·pēs´to·lâ) *f.* epistle; (eccl.) Epistle.

epistolar, (e·pēs·to·lâr´) *adj.* epistolary.

epitafio, (e·pē·tâ´fyo) *m.* epitaph.

epíteto, (e·pē´te·to) *m.* epithet.

epitome, (e·pē´to·me) *m.* epitome.

época, (e´po·kâ) *f.* epoch, age, era, period.

epopeya, (e·po·pe´yâ) *f.* epic poem; (fig.) saga, epic.

equidad, (e·kē·thâth´) *f.* equity; moderation *(templanza).*

equidistar, (e·kē·thēs·târ´) *vn.* to be equidistant.

equilátero, ra, (e·kē·lâ´te·ro, râ) *adj.* equilateral.

equilibrado, da, (e·kē·lē·vrâ´tho, thâ) *adj.* sensible, well-balanced.

equilibrar, (e·kē·lē·vrâr´) *va.* to balance, to equilibrate.

equilibrio, (e·kē·lē´vryo) *m.* equilibrium, balance; (fig.) poise *(ecuanimidad);* **— político,** balance of power.

equinoccio, (e·kē·nok´syo) *m.* equinox.

equipaje, (e·kē·pâ´he) *m.* baggage, luggage; (naut.) crew; **coche de —,** baggage car; **— de mano,** hand baggage, carry-on.

equipar, (e·kē·pâr´) *va.* to fit out, to equip, to furnish.

equipo, (e·kē´po) *m.* equipment, outfit, team *(grupo);* **— corriente,** standard equipment; **— de novia,** trousseau.

equis, (e´kēs) *f.* name of the letter x.

equitación, (e·kē·tâ·syon´) *f.* horsemanship.

equitativo, va, (e·kē·tâ·tē´vo, va) *adj.* equitable, just; **trato —,** square deal.

equivalencia, (e·kē·vâ·len´syâ) *f.* equivalence.

equivalente, (e·kē·vâ·len´te) *adj.* equivalent.

equivaler*, (e·kē·vâ·ler´) *vn.* to be of equal value, to have the same value.

equivocación, (e·kē·vo·kâ·syon´) *f.* error, misunderstanding.

equivocar, (e·kē·vo·kâr´) *va.* to mistake; **— se,** to be mistaken.

era, (e´râ) *f.* era *(época);* plot, patch *(de hortalizas);* threshing floor *(para la trilla).*

erario, (e·râ´ryo) *m.* government treasury, treasury department.

erección, (e·rek·syon´) *f.* erection; foundation, establishment *(fundación).*

eremita, (e·re·mē´tâ) *m.* hermit.

erguir*, (er·gēr´) *va.* to raise, to straighten up; **—se,** (fig.) to be puffed up, to become haughty.

erigir, (e·rē·hēr´) *va.* to erect, to build *(construir);* to found, to establish *(instituir);* to elevate, to raise *(elevar).*

erisipela, (e·rē·sē·pe´lâ) *f.* (med.) erysipelas.

erizar, (e·rē·sâr´) *va.* to bristle; (fig.) to make thorny; **—se,** to stand on end, to bristle.

erizo, (e·rē´so) *m.* hedgehog; (bot.) bur.

ermita, (er·mēta) *f.* hermitage.

ermitaño, (er·mē·tâ´nyo) *m.* hermit *(eremita);* hermit crab *(crustáceo).*

erosión, (e·ro·syon´) *f.* erosion; abrasion, scrape *(abrasión).*

erótico, ca, (e·ro´tē·ko, kâ) *adj.* erotic.

erradicación, (e·rrâ·thē·kâ·syon´) *f.* eradication.

erradicar, (e·rrâ·thē·kâr´) *va.* to eradicate.

errante, (e·rrân´te) *adj.* errant, wandering, roving.

---

errar*, (e·rrâr´) va. to miss, to fall short of; —, vn. to wander, to rove; — el blanco, to miss the mark.

errata, (e·rrä´tä) f. printing error.

erre, (e´rre) f. name of the double letter rr and of the single letter r when initial in a word or following 1, n, or s; — que , (coll.) obstinately, stubbornly.

erróneo, nea, (e·rro´ne·o, ne·â) adj. erroneous.

error, (e·rror´) m. error, mistake.

eructar, (e·rūk·târ´) vn. to belch.

eructo, (e·rūk´to) m. belch.

erudición, (e·rū·thē·syon´) f. erudition, learning.

erudito, ta, (e·rū·thē´to, tâ) adj. learned, erudite; —, m. scholar, man of erudition; — a la violeta, superficial scholar.

erupción, (e·rūp·syon´) f. eruption.

erutar, (e·rū·târh) eruto,(e·rū´to)= eructar, eructo.

esbelto, ta, (ez·vel´to, tâ) adj. slender, graceful, svelte.

esbirro, (ez·vē´rro) m. bailiff.

esbozar, (ez·vo·sâr´) va. to sketch, to outline.

esbozo, (ez·vo´so) m. outline, sketch.

escabeche, (es·kâ·ve´che) m. pickle; pescado en —, pickled fish.

escabel, (es·kâ·vel´) m. footstool.

escabroso, sa, (es´kâ·vro´so, sâ) adj. rough, uneven; (fig.) harsh (áspero); scabrous (obsceno).

escabullirse*, (es·kâ·vū·yēr´se) vr. to escape, to get away.

escafandra, (es·kâ·fân´drâ) f. diving suit; — espacial, spacesuit; — autónoma, Scuba.

escala, (es·kâ´lâ) f. ladder (escalera); scale (sucesión); (mus.) scale; (naut.) port of call; hacer — en, to stop at, to call at.

escalar, (es·kâ·lâr´) va. to climb, to scale.

escalafón, (es·kâ·lâ·fon´) m. seniority scale, grade scale.

escaldado, da, (es·kâl·dâ´tho, thâ) adj. cautious, suspicious, wary.

escaldar, (es·kâl·dâr´) va. to scald.

escalera, (es·kâ·le´râ) f. stairs, stairway; run (de naipes); — de mano stepladder; — mecánica escalator.

escalfar, (es·kâl·fâr´) va. to poach.

escalofrío, (es·kâ·lo·frē´o) m. chill.

escalón, (es·kâ·lon´) m. step, tread (peldaño); (fig.) grade, rank; (mil.) echelon.

escalonar, (es·kâ·lo·nâr´) va. to stagger (en tiempos sucesivos); to space out, to place at intervals (de trecho en trecho).

escama, (es·kâ´mâ) f. scale; (fig.) resent-

ment (desazón).

escamar, (es·kâ·mâr´) va. to scale; (fig.) to make wary, to teach; —se, to become wary, to learn from experience.

escamoso, sa, (es·kâ·mo´so, sâ) adj. scaly.

escampar, (es·kâm·pâr´) vn. to stop rain.

escandalizar, (es·kân·dâ·lē·sâr´) va. to scandalize, to shock; —se, to be scandalized, to be outraged.

escándalo, (es·kân´dâ·lo) m. scandal; (fig.) uproar (alboroto).

escandaloso, sa, (es·kân·dâ·lo´so, sâ) adj. scandalous; boisterous (revoltoso)

escaño, (es·kâ´nyo) m. (Sp. Am.) par bench; (poi.) seat.

escapada, (es·kâ·pá´thâ) f. escape, flight.

escapar, (es·kâ·pâr´) va. to race, to run at high speed; —, vn. to escape; to flee (salir a todo escape); —se, to escape, to get free; to run out, to escape (un liquido).

escaparate, (es·kâ·pâ·râ´te) m. show window (en la fachada); display cabinet, showcase (alacena).

escapatoria, (es·kâ·pâ·to´ryâ) f. escape, flight; (fig.) way out, loophole, excuse (pretexto).

escape, (es·kâ´pe) m. escape, flight (fuga); leak (de un liquido); (mech.) exhaust; escapement, (del reloj); a todo —, at top space.

escapism, (es·kâ·pēz´mo) m. escapism.

escapulario, (es·kâ·pū·lâ´ryo) m. scapulary.

escarabajo, (es·kâ·râ·vâ´ho) m. dung beetle, scarab; (coll.) twerp.

escaramuza, (es·kâ·râ·mū´sâ) f. skirmish.

escaramuzar, (es·kâ·râ·mū·sâr´) vn. to skirmish.

escarapela, (es·kâ·râ·pe´lâ) f. cockade.

escarbadientes, (es·kâr·vâ·thyen´tes) m. toothpick.

escarbar, (es·kâr·vâr´) va. to scratch; to clean, to pick (los dientes); to stir, to poke (la lumbre); (fig.) to sift through, to dig into (inquirir).

escarcha, (es·kâr´châ) f. hoarfrost.

escarchar, (es ·kâr·châr´) va. to sugar; —, vn. to be frost.

escardador, ra, (es·kâr·thâ·thor´, râ) n. weeder.

escardar, (es·câr·thâr´) va. to weed.

escarlata, (es·câr·lâ´tâ) f. scarlet.

escarlatina, (es·kâr·lâ·tē´nâ) f. scarlet fever.

escarmentar*, (es·kâr·men·târ´) vn. to profit by experience, to take warning; —, va. to punish severely.

â arm, e they, ē bē, o fore, ū blūe, b bad, ch chip, d day, f fat, g go, h hot, k kid, 1 let

escarmiento, (es·kâr·myen´to) *m.* caution, profit from experience *(cautela);* punishment *(castigo).*

escarnecer*, (es·kâr·ne·ser´) *va.* to mock, to ridicule, to scoff at.

escarnio, (es·kâr´nyo) *m.* ridicule, mocking, scoffing.

escarola, (es·kä·ro´lä) *f.* (bot.) endive.

escarpado, da, (es·kâr·pâ´tho, thä) *adj.* sloping steeply; steep *(empinado).*

escarpia, (es·kâr´pyä) *f.* hook.

escarpín, (es·kâr·pēn´) *m.* pump.

escasear, (es·kâ·se·âr´) *va.* to skimp on, to spare, to give grudgingly; —, *vn.* to be scarce, to be in short supply.

escasez, (es·kâ·ses´) *f.* niggardliness *(mezquindad);* shortage *(poca cantidad);*

escaso, sa, (es·kâ´so, sâ) *adj.* limited, in short supply, scanty *(poco abundante);* stingy, niggardly *(mezquino).*

escatimar, (es·kâ·tē·mar´) *va.* to hold back, to begrudge.

escayola, (es·kä·yo´lä) *f.* stucco.

escena, (es·se´na) *f.* stage *(escenario);* scene; **poner en —,** to stage.

escenario, (es·se·nä´ryo) *m.* stage.

escenografia, (es·se·no·grâ·f· ē´ä) *f.* set design.

escepticismo, (es·sep·tē·sēz´mo) *m.* skepticism.

escéptico, ca, (es·sep´tē·ko, kä) *adj.* skeptic, skeptical.

esclarecer*, (es·klâ·re·ser´) *va.* to illuminate, to light up; (fig.) to ennoble *(ilustrar);* to clear up, to explain *(dilucidar);* —, *vn.* to begin to dawn.

esclarecido, da, (es·klâ·re·sē´tho, thä) *adj.* illustrious, noble.

esclavitud, (es·klâ·vē·tūth´) *f.* slavery.

esclavizar, (es·klâ·vē·sâr´) *va.* to enslave.

esclavo, va, (es·klâ´vo, vä) *n.* slave, captive.

esclerosis, (es·kle·ro´sēs) *f.* (med.) sclerosis; **— múltiple,** multiple sclerosis.

esclusa, (es·klū´sä) *f.* lock, floodgate.

escoba, (es·ko´vä) *f.* broom.

escobilla, (es·ko·vē´yä) *f.* brush.

escocés, esa, (es·ko·ses´, e´sä) *n.* Scot; —, *adj.* Scotch, Scottish.

escoger, (es·ko·her´) *va.* to choose, to select.

escogido, da, (es·ko·hē´tho, thä) *adj.* chosen, selected *(selecto);* choice *(excelente).*

escolar, (es·ko·lâr´) *m.* pupil, student; —, *adj.* student, scholastic; **sistema —,** school system.

escolástico, ca, (es·ko·lâs´tē·ko, kä) *adj.* scholastic.

escolta, (es·kol´tä) *f.* escort.

escoltar, (es·kol·târ´) *va.* to escort.

escollo, (es·ko´yo) *m.* sunken rock; (fig.) snare, pitfall.

escombrar, (es·kom·brâr´) *va.* to clean up, to clear of rubble.

escombro, (es·kom´bro) *m.* rubble, debris; (ichth.) mackerel.

escondedero, (es·kon·de·the´ro) *m.* hiding place.

esconder, (es·kon·der´) *va.* to hide, to conceal.

escondidas (es·kon·dē´thäs) or escondidillas, (es·kon·dē·thē´yas) a secretly; **a — de,** without the knowledge of.

escondido, da, (es·kon·dē´tho, thä) *adj.* hidden.

escondite, (es·kon·dē´te) *m.* hiding place; hide-and-seek *(juego).*

escondrijo, (es·kon·drē´ho) *m.* hiding place.

escopeta, (es·ko·pe´tä) *f.* shotgun; **a tiro de —,** within gunshot; **aquí te quiero —,** this is it! it´s now or never!

escopetero, (es·ko·pe·te´ro) *m.* musketeer *(soldado);* gunsmith *(fabricador).*

escoplo, (es·ko´plo) *m.* chisel.

escorbuto, (es·kor·vū´to) *m.* scurvy.

escoria, (es·ko´ryä) *f.* slag; (fig.) dregs.

escorial, (es·ko·ryäl´) *m.* slag deposit, slag heap.

escorpión, (es·kor·pyon´) *m.* scorpion.

escotado, da, (es·ko·tä´tho, thä) *adj.* low-necked, décolleté.

escote, (es·ko´te) *m.* décolletage; share, part *(de un gasto común).*

escotilla, (es·ko·tē´yä) *f.* hatchway.

escotillón, (es·ko·tē·yon´) *m.* trapdoor.

escozor, (es·ko·sor´) *m.* smart, sting; (fig.) grief, pain.

escribanía, (es·krē·vä·nē´ä) *f.* clerk´s office.

escribano, (es·krē·vâ´no) *m.* clerk.

escribidor, ra, (es·krē·vē·thor´, râ) *n.* (coll.) poor writer.

escribiente, (es·krē·vyen´te) *m. and f.* clerk, secretary.

escribir*, (es·krē·vēr´) *va.* to write; to spell *(ortografiar);* **— a máquina,** to typewrite.

escrito, (es·krē´to) *m.* writing; written document *(papel manuscrito);* writ, brief *(alegato);* **por —,** in writing; —, **ta,** *adj.* written.

escritor ra, (es·krē·tor´, râ) *n.* writer.

escritorio, (es·krē·to´ryo) *m.* writing desk

(mueble); office; desktop *(computación).*

escritura, (es·krē·tū´rä) *f.* penmanship, handwriting *(caligrafía);* writing *(acción);* document *(escrito);* script, alphabet *(caracteres);* deed *(instrumento público);* **Sagrada —,** Holy Writ.

escrúpulo, (es·krū´pū·lo) *m.* scruple.

escrupuloso, sa, (es·krū·pū·lo´so, sä) *adj.* scrupulous; (fig.) precise, exact.

escrutinio, (es·krū·tē´nyo) *m.* scrutiny; polling and counting votes *(en las elecciones).*

escuadra, (es·kwä´thrä) *f.* square; bracket, brace *(de ensambladura);* (naut.) squadron; (mil.) squad.

escuadrón, (es·kwä·thron´) *m.* cavalry squadron.

escuálido, da, (es·kwä´le·tho, thä) *adj.* squalid.

escuchar, (es·kū·chär´) *va.* to listen to.

escudar, (es·kū·thär´) *va.* to shield.

escudero, (es·kū·the´ro) *m.* squire, shield bearer.

escudo, (es·kū´tho) *m.* shield; escutcheon, coat of arms *(cuerpo de blasón).*

escudriñar, (es·kū·thrē·nyär´) *va.* to scrutinize.

escuela, (es·kwe´lä) *f.* school; **— de párvulos,** kindergarten; **— dominical,** Sunday school; **— para externos,** day school; **— para internos,** boarding school.

escueto, ta, (es·kwe´to, tä) *adj.* unadorned, plain, bare.

esculpir, (es·kūl·pēr´) *va.* to sculpture, to sculpt; to engrave *(grabar).*

escultor, (es·kūl·tor´) *m.* sculptor.

escultura, (es·kūl·tū´rä) *f.* sculpture.

escupidera, (es·kū·pē·the´rä) *f.* spittoon.

escupir, (es·kū·pēr´) *va.* to spit; (fig.) to cast off *(echar de sí).*

escurriduras, (es·kū·rrē·thū´räs) *f. pl.* dregs, lees.

escurrimiento, (es·kū·rrē·myen´to) *m.* run-off, dripping, flow.

escurrir, (es·kū·rrēr´) *va.* to drain; to let drain *(los platos fregados);* **—,** *vn.* to drip *(caer gota a gota);* to slip *(deslizar);* **—se,** to slip.

ESE: estesudeste, ESE or E.S.E. east southeast.

ese, sa, (e´se, sä) *adj.* ése, sa, *pron.* that; **—sos, sas,** *pl.* those.

esencia, (e·sen´syä) *f.* essence.

esencial, (e·sen·syäl´) *adj.* essential.

esfera, (es·fe´rä) *f.* sphere; dial *(del reloj).*

esférico, ca, (es·fe´rē·ko, kä) *adj.* spherical.

esforzado, da, (es·for·sä´tho, thä) *adj.* strong, vigorous.

esforzar*, (es·for·sär´) *va.* to strengthen; to encourage *(alentar);* **—se,** to exert oneself, to make an effort.

esfuerzo, (es·fuer´so) *m.* effort; spirit, vigor, courage *(vigor).*

esfumarse, (es·fū·mär´se) *vr.* to disappear, to vanish.

esgrima, (ez·grē´mä) *f.* fencing.

esgrimir, (ez·grē·mēr´) *vn.* to fence; **—,** *va.* to wield.

eslabón, (ez·lä·von´) *m.* link.

eslabonar, (ez·lä·vo·när´) *va.* to link; (fig.) to compose, to put together.

esmaltar, (ez·mäl·tär´) *va.* to enamel; (fig.) to adorn, to brighten.

esmalte, (ez·mäl´te) *m.* enamel; **— para las uñas,** nail polish.

esmerado, da, (ez·me·rä´tho, thä) *adj.* painstaking, careful.

esmeralda, (ez·me·räl´dä) *f.* emerald.

esmerar, (ez·me·rär´) *va.* to polish; **—se,** to do one´s best, to take pains.

esmeril, (ez·me·rēl´) *m.* emery.

esmero, (ez·me´ro) *m.* great care, painstaking.

esnobismo, (ez·no·vēz´mo) *m.* snobbery.

eso, (e´so) *pron.* that, that matter; **— de,** that matter of; **a — de,** about; **por —,** for that reason, therefore; **nada de —,** not at all, absolutely not.

esófago, (e·so´fä·go) *m.* esophagus.

espaciador, (es·pä·syä·thor´) *m.* spacer.

espacial, (es·pä·syäl´) *adj.* spatial; **cápsula —,** space capsule.

espaciar, (es·pä·syär´) *va.* to space out, to spread out.

espacio, (es·pä´syo) *m.* space; period *(de tiempo);* piece *(de terreno);* slowness *(lentitud).*

espaciosidad, (es·pä·syo·sē·thäth´) *f.* spaciousness, roominess.

espacioso, sa, (es·pä·syo´so, sä) *adj.* spacious, roomy.

espada, (es·pä´thä) *f.* sword; spade *(de naipes);* swordsman *(persona);* **—,** *m.* matador.

espadachín, (es·pä·thä·chēn´) *m.* good swordsman, fine blade; trigger-happy individual *(amigo de pendencias).*

espadín, (es·pä·thēn´) *m.* rapier.

espalda, (es·päl´dä) *f.* back; backstroke *(en la natación);* **—s,** *pl.* back, shoulders; **a —s,** behind one´s back; **cargo de —s,** round-shouldered; **dar la —,** to turn one´s back on; **tener buenas —s,** to have strong shoulders, to be able to take it.

espaldar, (es·pâl·dâr´) m. back; carapace (de la tortuga); trellis (armazón).

espaldilla, (es·pal·dē´yä) f. shoulder blade.

espantadizo, za, (es·pân·tâ·thē´so, sâ) adj. skittish (caballo); easily frightened.

espantajo, (es·pân·tâ´ho) m. scarecrow; (fig.) bugbear, bugaboo.

espantamoscas, (es·pân·tâ·mos´kâs) m. fly swatter.

espantapájaros, (es·pân·tâ·pâ´hä·ros) m. scarecrow.

espantar, (es·pân·târ´) va. to frighten, to terrify; to frighten away, to chase away (ahuyentar).

espanto, (es·pân´to) m. fright, terror (terror); menace, threat (amenaza); specter (fantasma).

espantoso, sa, (es·pân·to´so, sâ) adj. frightful, terrible.

España, (es·pâ´nyä) f. Spain.

español, la, (es·pâ·nyol´, lâ) adj. Spanish; —, n. Spaniard; —, m. Spanish language.

esparavel, (es·pâ·râ·vel´) m. casting net, dragnet.

esparcimiento, (es·pâr·sē·myen´to) m. spreading out, fanning out; opening up, enjoyment (alegría).

esparcir, (es·pâr·sēr´) va. to scatter, to spread out (derramar); to spread (divulgar); —se, to open up, to enjoy oneself.

espárrago, (es·pâ´ rrä·go) m. asparagus.

espasmo, (es·pâz´mo) m. spasm.

espasmódico, ca, (es·pâz·mo´thē·ko, kâ) adj. spasmodic.

espástico, ca, (es·pâs´tē·ko, kâ) adj. spastic.

espátula, (es·pâ´tü·lâ) f. spatula.

especias, (es·pe´syâs) f. pl. spices.

especial, (e·spe·syâl´) adj. special, particular; en —, specially.

especialidad, (es·pe·syâ·lē·thâth´) f. specialty.

especialista, (es·pe·syâ·lēs´tâ) m. and f. specialist.

especializarse, (es·pe·syâ·lē·sâr´se) vr. to specialize.

especialmente, (es·pe·syâl·men´te) adv. specially.

especie, (es·pe´sye) f. species; kind, quality (calidad); (fig.) case, instance (caso).

especiería, (es·pe·sye·rē´â) f. spice shop.

especiero, (es·pe·sye´ro) m. dealer m. spices.

especificación, (es·pe·sē·fē·kâ·syon´) f. specification.

especificar, (es·pe·se·fē·kâr´) va. to specify.

específico, ca, (es·pe·sē´fē·ko, kâ) adj. specific; —, m. patent medicine.

espécimen, (es·pe´sē·men) m. specimen.

espectacular, (es·pek·tâ·kū·lâr´) adj. spectacular.

espectáculo, (es·pek·tâ´kū·lo) m. show, public amusement; spectacle, display (lo que atrae la atención).

espectador, ra, (es·pek·tâ·thor´, râ) n. spectator, onlooker.

espectral, (es·pek·trâl´) adj. spectral, ghostly.

espectro, (es·pek´tro) m. specter, ghost; (phy.) spectrum.

especulación, (es·pe·kū·lâ·syon´) f. speculation.

especulador, ra, (es·pe·kū·lâ·thor´, râ) n. speculator.

especular, (es·pe·kū·lâr´) va. to speculate on; —, vn. to speculate.

especulativo, va, (es·pe·kū·lâ·tē´vo, vâ) adj. speculative.

espejismo, (es·pe·hēz´mo) m. mirage.

espejo, (es·pe´ho) m. looking glass, mirror; — de retrovisión, rearview mirror; — ustorio, burning glass.

espeluznante, (es·pe·luz·nân´te) adj. hair-raising.

espeluznar, (es·pe·lūz·nâr´) va. to set one´s hair on end.

espera, (es·pe´râ) f. wait; stay, delay (jurídica); patience, restraint (paciencia); sala de —, waiting room.

esperanto, (es·pe·rân´to) m. Esperanto.

esperanza, (es·pe·rân´sâ) f. hope, expectation; áncora de —, (naut.) sheet anchor.

esperanzar, (es·pe·rân·sâr´) va. to give hope.

esperar, (es·pe·râr´) va. to hope for, to wait for, to await (aguardar); to expect (creer).

esperma, (es·per´mâ) f. sperm.

espesar, (es·pe·sâr´) va. to thicken, to close up, to tighten (apretar).

espeso, sa, (es·pe´so, sâ) adj. thick, dense.

espesor, (es·pe·sor´) m. thickness, density.

espetar, (es·pe·târ´) va. to spit, to skewer; to pierce (atravesar); —se, (fig.) to become stiff, to grow very formal.

espía, (es·pē´â) m. and f. spy.

espiar, (es·pyâr´) va. to spy on, to observe carefully.

espiga, (es·pē´gä) f. ear (del trigo); peg (clavo); fuse (espoleta).

espigado, da, (es·pē·gä´tho, thâ) adj. (fig.)

tall and willowy.

espigador, ra, (es·pē·gâ·thor´, râ) *n.* gleaner.

espigar, (es·pē·gâr´) *va.* to research, to glean; —, *vn.* to ear; —**se,** to shoot up.

espigón, (es·pē·gon´) *m.* ear of corn *(mazorca);* sting *(aguijón);* point *(punta).*

espina, (es·pē´nâ) *f.* (bot.) thorn; sliver *(astilla);* (ichth.) bone; (anat.) spine; (fig.) thorn in one´s side *(pesar);* **estar en** —**s,** to be on needles and pins.

espinaca, (es·pē·nâ´kâ) *f.* (bot.) spinach.

espinar, (es·pē·nâr´) *va.* to prick; —, *m.* brier patch; (fig.) rub, difficulty *(enredo).*

espinazo, (es·pē·nâ´so) *m.* spine, backbone.

espinilla, (es·pē·nē´yâ) *f.* shinbone; pimple *(barrillo).*

espino, (es·pē´no) *m.* hawthorn.

espinoso, sa, (es·pē·no´so, sâ) *adj.* spiny; thorny; (fig.) tricky, complicated *(enredado).*

espiral, (es·pē·râl´) *adj.* spiral; —, *f.* spiral; —, *m.* spiral spring.

espirar, (es·pē·râr´) *va.* to give off; to cheer, to inspire *(animar);* —, *vn.* to exhale; to breathe *(alentar).*

espiritismo, (es·pē·rē·tēz´mo) *m.* spiritualism, spiritism.

espíritu, (es·pē´rē·tū) *m.* spirit; **el E— Santo,** the Holy Ghost.

espiritual, (es·pē·rē·twâl´) *adj.* spiritual.

espiritualidad, (es·pē·rē·twâ·lē·thâth´) *f.* spirituality.

esplendente, (es·plen·den´te) *adj.* resplendent, shining.

esplendidez, (es·plen·dē·thes´) *f.* splendor, magnificence.

espléndido, da, (es·plen´dē·tho, thâ) *adj.* splendid, magnificent; brilliant, bright *(resplandeciente).*

esplendor, (es·plen·dor´) *m.* radiance, splendor.

esplín, (es·plēn´) *m.* melancholy.

espolón, (es·po·lon´) *m.* (orn.) spur; (naut.) prow, cutwater; dike *(malecón);* spur *(de una sierra).*

esponja, (es·pon´hâ) *f.* sponge.

esponjar, (es·pon·hâr´) *va.* to make spongy, to fluff up; —**se,** to puff up with pride.

esponjoso, sa, (es·pon·ho´so, sâ) *adj.* spongy.

esponsales, (es·pon·sâ´les) *m. pl.* betrothal.

espontaneidad, (es·pon·tâ·neē·thâth´) *f.* spontaneity.

espontáneo, nea, (es·pon·tâ´ne·o, ne·â) *adj.* spontaneous.

espora, (es·po´râ) *f.* spore.

esposa, (es·po´sâ) *f.* wife; —**s,** *pl.* manacles, handcuffs.

esposo, (es·poso) *m.* husband; —**s,** *pl.* married couple.

espuela, (es·pwe´lâ) *f.* spur; (bot.) larkspur.

espuma, (es·pū´mâ) *f.* foam, froth; (fig.) cream *(flor);* **hule** —, foam rubber.

espumar, (es·pū·mâr´) *va.* to skim; —, *vn.* to foam, to froth.

espumarajo, (es·pū·mâ·râ´ho) *m.* foam, froth.

espumoso, sa, (es·pū·mo´so, sâ) *adj.* frothy, foamy.

espurio, ria, (es·pū´ryo, ryâ) *adj.* spurious, adulterated.

esputo, (es·pū´to) *m.* spit, sputum.

esquela, (es·ke´lâ) *f.* note, short letter *(carta);* announcement, notice *(que comunica noticias).*

esquelético, ca, (es·ke·le´tē·ko, kâ) *adj.* skeletal.

esqueleto, (es·ke·le´to) *m.* skeleton.

esquema, (es·ke´mâ) *m.* diagram, outline.

esquí, (es·kē´) *m.* ski.

esquiador, ra, (es·kyâ·thor´, râ) *n.* skier.

esquiar, (es·kyâr´) *vn.* to ski.

esquicio, (es·kē´syo) *m.* thumbnail sketch.

esquife, (es·kē´fe) *m.* skiff; small boat *(barco pequeño).*

esquilar, (es·kē·lâr´) *va.* to shear.

esquimal, (es·kē·mâl´) *adj. and n.* Eskimo.

esquina, (es·kē´nâ) *f.* corner; **doblar la** —, to turn the corner; **hacer** —, to be on the corner.

esquinado, da, (es·kē·nâ´tho, thâ) *adj.* hard to get along with, troublesome.

esquinazo, (es·kē·nâ´so) *m.* corner; (Chile) serenade; **dar** —, (coll.) to lose, to shake off.

esquirol, (es·kē·rol´) *m.* strikebreaker.

esquivar, (es·kē·vâr´) *va.* to avoid, to dodge; —**se,** to get out, to retract.

esquivo, va, (es·kē´vo, vâ) *adj.* diffident, aloof.

estabilidad, (es·tâ·vē · lē· thâth´) *f.* stability.

estabilización, (es·tâ·vē·lē·sâ·syon´) *f.* stabilization.

estabilizador, (es·tâ·vē·lē·sâ·thor´) *m.* stabilizer.

estabilizar, (es·tâ·vē·lē·sâr´) *va.* to stabilize.

estable, (es·tâ´vle) *adj.* stable.

establecer*, (es·tâ·vle·ser´) va. to establish; —se, to settle, to establish oneself.

establecimiento, (es·tâ·vle·sē·myen´to) m. establishment; statute (ley).

establo, (es·tâ´vlo) m. stable.

estaca, (es·tâ´kâ) f. stake; club (garrote); spike (clavo largo).

estacar, (es·tâ·kâr´) va. to stake (atar); to stake out (señalar).

estacazo, (es·tâ·ka´so) m. blow with a club.

estación, (es·tâ·syon´) f. station; residence (morada); stay, stopover (paraje); season (temporada); — astral, (avi.) space station; — de servicio, (auto.) service station; red de —ones, network.

estacionamiento, (es·tâ·syo·nâ·myen´to) m. (auto.) parking.

estacionar, (es·tâ·syo·nâr´) va. (auto.) to park; to position, to station (colocar).

estacionario, ria, (es·tâ·syo·nâ´ryo, ryâ) adj. stationary.

estadía, (es·tâ·thē´â) f. stay, sojourn; (naut.) demurrage.

estadio (es·tâ´thyo) m. stadium; furlong (medida); phase, period (fase).

estadista, (es·tâ·thēs´tâ) m. statesman.

estadística, (es·tâ·thēs´tē·kâ) f. statistics; — demográfica, vital statistics.

estadístico, (es·tâ·thēs´tē·ko) m. statistician; —, ca, adj. statistical.

estado, (es·tâ´tho) m. state; statement (cuenta); — de cuenta, statement of account; — de guerra, martial law; — de sitio, state of siege; — mayor, military staff; hombre de —, statesman; — protector, welfare state; ministro de E —, Secretary of State.

Estados Unidos de América, (es·tâ´thos ū·nē´thoz the â·me´rē·kâ) m. pl. United States of America.

estadounidense (es·tâ·tho·ū·nē·then´se) or estadunidense, (es·tâ·thū·nē·then´se) adj. American, United States; —, m. and f. American, United States resident.

estafa, (es·tâ´fâ) f. swindle.

estafador, ra, (es·tâ·fâ·thor´, râ) n. swindler.

estafar, (es·tâ·fâr´) va. to swindle.

estafeta, (es·tâ·fe´tâ) f. branch post office.

estalactita, (es·tâ·lâk·tē´tâ) f. stalactite.

estalagmita, (es·tâ·lâg·mē´tâ) f. stalagmite.

estallar, (es·tâ·yâr´) vn. to blow up (reventar); to crack (el látigo); (fig.) to break out (un incendio, la guerra).

estallido, (es·tâ·yē´tho) m. crack; report

(explosión); outbreak (de la guerra); blowing up.

estambre, (es·tâm´bre) m. wool yarn; (bot.) stamen; — de la vida, (fig.) fabric of life.

estameña, (es·tâ·me´nyâ) f. serge.

estampa, (es·tâm´pâ) f. printed image; (fig.) looks, appearance (aspecto); press (imprenta); mark (huella).

estampar, (es·tâm·pâr´) va. to print, to stamp; to press, to imprint (una medalla); (coll.) to throw, to dash (arrojar).

estampida, (es·tâm·pē´thâ) f. stampede.

estampido, (es·tâm·pē´tho) m. report, explosion.

estampilla, (es·tâm·pē´yâ) f. signet, seal (Sp. Am.) postage stamp.

estancamiento, (es·tâng·kâ·myen´to) m. standstill; delay; sales controls.

estancar, (es·tâng·kâr´) va. to stem, to hold back (detener); to subject to sales controls (las mercaderías); to hold up, to delay (suspender la marcha).

estancia, (es·tân´syâ) f. stay, sojourn; (Sp. Am.) ranch, country estate (finca).

estanciero, ra, (es·tân·sye´ro, râ) n. farmer, rancher.

estanco, (es·tâng´ko) m. government control of sales; government outlet (tienda); —, ca, watertight.

estandardización, (es·tân·dâr·thē·sâ syon´) f. standardization.

estandarte, (es·tân·dâr´te) m. banner, standard.

estanque, (es·tâng´ke) m. reservoir, pond.

estanquillo, (es·tâng·kē´yo) m. tobacco shop, cigar store.

estante, (es·tân´te) m. bookcase.

estañar, (es·tâ·nyâr´) va. to tin; to solder (soldar).

estaño, (es·tâ´nyo) m. (chem.) tin.

estaquilla, (es·tâ·kē´yâ) f. cleat; spike (estaca).

estar*, (es·tar´) vn. to be; — de prisa, to be in a hurry; — sobre sí, to be cautious, to be alert; — por, to be in favor of; ¿estamos? agreed? is that alright? — bien, to be well; — de, to be in the middle of; — de pie, to be standing; — mal, to be ill; — en sí, to be fully aware of one's actions; — para, to be about to; — de receso, to be adjourned.

estarcido, (es·târ·sē´tho) m. stencil.

estarcir, (es·târ·sēr´) va. to stencil.

estática, (es·tâ´tē·kâ) f. statics.

estático, ca, (es·tâ´tē·ko, kâ) adj. static.

estatua, (es·tâ´twâ) f. statue.

estatuario, (es·tâ·twâ´ryo) m. statuary.

estatuir*, (es·tâ·twēr´) va. to establish, to enact.

estatura, (es·tâ·tū´râ) f. stature.

estatuto, (es·tâ·tū´to) m. statute.

este, (es´te) m. east.

este, ta, (es´te, tâ) adj. éste, ta, pron. this; the latter; —ta noche, tonight; —tos, tas, pl. these.

esteatita, (es·te·â·tē´tâ) f. soapstone.

estela, (es·te´lâ) f. wake (de buque de vapor); trail (de estrella); — de vapor, contrail.

estenografia, (es·te·no·grâ·fē´â) f. stenography, shorthand.

estenógrafo, fa, (es·te·no´grâ·fo, fâ) n. stenographer.

estenomecanografia, (es·te·no·me·kâ·no·grâ·fē´â) f. stenotyping.

estenomecanógrafo, fa, (es·te·no·me·kâ·no´grâ·fo, fâ) n. stenotypist.

estera, (es·te´râ) f. matting.

esterar, (es·te·râr´) va. to cover with matting.

estereofónico, ca, (es·te·re·o·fo´nē·ko, kâ) adj. stereophonic.

estereoscopio, (es·te·re·os·ko´pyo) m. stereoscope.

estereotipar, (es·te·re·o·tē·pâr´) va. to stereotype.

estéril, (es·te´rēl) adj. sterile, barren.

esterilidad, (es·te·rē·lē·thâth´) f. sterility, barrenness.

esterilización, (es·te·rē·lē·sâ·syon´) f. sterilization.

esterilizador, (es·te·rē·lē·sâ·thor´) m. sterilizer; —, ra, adj. sterilizing.

esterilizar, (es·te·rē·lē·sâr´) va. to sterilize.

esterilla, (es·te·rē´yâ) f. gold braid (de oro); silver braid (de plata); fine straw matting (pleita).

esterlina, (es·ter·lē´nâ) adj. sterling; libra —, pound sterling.

estero, (es·te´ro) m. matting; estuary (estuario); (Arg.) swampy lowland.

esteroide, (es·te·ro´ē·the) m. steroid.

estética, (es·te´tē·kâ) f. aesthetics.

estetoscopio, (es·te·tos·ko´pyo)m.stethoscope.

esteva, (es·te´vâ) f. plow handle.

estiércol, (es·tyer´kol) m. manure.

estigma, (es·tēg´mâ) m. stigma; —s, pl. stigmata.

estilo, (es·tē´lo) m. style; stylus (para escribir); por el —, like that, of that kind.

estilográfico, ca, (es·tē·lo·grâ´fē·ko, kâ) adj. stylographic; —, f. stylograph.

estima, (es·tē´mâ) f. esteem.

estimable, (es·tē·mâ´vle) adj. estimable; perceptible, appreciable (que admite estimación).

estimación, (es·tē·mâ·syon´) f. esteem, estimation; estimate (evaluación).

estimar, (es·tē·mâr´) va. to esteem, to value; to estimate (evaluar).

estimulante, (es·tē·mū·lân´te) m. stimulant; —, adj. stimulating.

estimular, (es·tē·mū·lâr´) va. to stimulate.

estímulo, (es·tē´mū·lo) m. stimulus; (fig.) impulse, motivation.

estío, (es·tē´o) m. summer.

estipendio, (es·tē·pen´dyo) m. stipend.

estipulación,(es·te·pū·lâ·syon´)f. stipulation.

estipular, (es·tē·pū·lâr´) va. to stipulate.

estirado, da, (es·tē·râ´tho, thâ) adj. stiff, prim; high-handed (orgulloso); tight-fisted (económico).

estirador, (es·tē râ·thor´) m. stretcher.

estirar, (es·tē·râr´) va. to stretch out, to pull out; (fig.) to stretch to the limit, to draw out; — la pata, (coll.) to kick the bucket.

estirón, (es·tē·ron´) m. pull, jerk; dar un —, to grow rapidly, to shoot up.

estirpe, (es·tēr´pe) f. origin, stock, family.

estivador, (es·tē·vâ·thor´) m. stevedore, longshoreman.

esto, (es´to) pron. this, this matter; a —, hereto; con —, herewith; en —, at that moment; por —, for this reason; — es, that is, that is to say.

estocada, (es·to·kâ´thâ) f. stab, blow (golpe); stab wound (herida).

estofado, da, (es·to·fâ´tho, thâ) adj. quilted; stewed.

estofar, (es·to·fâr´) va. to quilt (bordar); to stew (guisar).

estoico, ca, (es·to´ē·ko, kâ) adj. stoic; (fig.) cold, indifferent.

estola, (es·to´lâ) f. stole.

estolidez, (es·to·lē·thes´) f. stupidity, denseness.

estólido, da, (es·to´lē·tho, thâ) adj. stupid, dense.

estomacal, (es·to·mâ·kâl´) adj. stomachic, stomach; malestar —, upset stomach.

estómago, (es·to´mâ·go) m. stomach.

estopa, (es·to´pâ) m. (naut.) oakum; tow (hilaza); burlap (tela).

estorbar, (es·tor·vâr´) va. to hinder, to obstruct; (fig.) to bother, to annoy (incomodar).

estorbo, (es·tor·vo) m. hindrance, obstruction; bother, annoyance.

estornudar, (es·tor·nū·thâr´) vn. to

sneeze.

estornudo, (es·tor·nū´tho) *m.* sneeze.

estrabismo, (es·trâ·vēz´mo) *m.* squint, strabismus.

estrado, (es·trä´tho) *m.* drawing room; — s, *pl.* lawcourts.

estrafalario, ria, (es·trâ·fâ·lä´ryo, ryâ) *adj.* slovenly, unkempt; (fig.) outlandish, weird.

estrago, (es·trä´go) *m.* ravage, havoc.

estrambótico, ca, (es·trâm·bo´tē·ko, kâ) *adj.* (coll.) oddball, bizarre, weird.

estrangulación, (es·trâng·gū·lä·syon´) *f.* strangulation; **cuello de —,** bottleneck.

estrangulador, ra, (es·trâng·gū·lä·thor´, râ) *adj.* choking, strangling.

estrangular, (es·trâng·gū·lâr´) *va.* to choke, to strangle; (med.) to strangulate.

estratagema, (es·trâ·tâ·he´mâ) *f.* stratagem; (fig.) trickiness, craftiness *(astucia).*

estrategia, (es·trâ·te´hyâ) *f.* strategy.

estratégico, ca, (es·trâ·te´hē·ko, kâ) *adj.* strategic.

estrato, (es·trä´to) *m.* stratum; (anat.) layer; stratus cloud *(nube).*

estratosfera, (es·trâ·tos·fe´râ) *f.* stratosphere.

estraza, (es·trä´sâ) *f.* rag; **papel de —,** brown paper.

estrechar, (es·tre·châr´) *va.* to tighten, to narrow; (fig.) to press, to close in on *(apretar);* to force, to make *(precisar a uno);* to hug, to hold tight *(abrazar);* — se, to squeeze in *(ceñirse);* to cut expenses *(reducir el gasto).*

estrechez, (es·tre·ches´) *f.* tightness, narrowness *(angostura);* (fig.) close relationship *(enlace);* close friendship *(amistad);* tight spot, ticklish situation *(apuro);* lean time *(escasez).*

estrecho, (es·tre´cho) *m.* (geog.) straits; period of want *(escasez);* —, **cha,** narrow *(angosto);* tight *(apretado);* (fig.) narrow, mean *(apocado);* close *(íntimo);* severe, harsh *(rígido).*

estregar*, (es·tre·gâr´) *va.* to rub.

estrella, (es·tre´yâ) *f.* star.

estrellado, da, (es·tre·yä´tho, thâ) *adj.* starry; dashed to pieces; **huevos —s,** friend eggs.

estrellar, (es·tre·yâr´) *va.* to dash to pieces, to smash to bits; to fry *(los huevos);* —**se,** to smash, to crash; (fig.) to fail *(fracasar);* to fill with stars *(el cielo).*

estremecer*, (es·tre·me·ser´) *va.* to jolt, to

shake; —**se,** to quake, to shake, to tremble.

estremecimiento, (es·tre·me·sē·myen´to) *m.* trembling, quaking; jolt, shake.

estrenar, (es·tre·nâr´) *va.* to inaugurate; to use for the first time *(una prenda);* to premiere *(una comedia);* —**se,** to make one's debut; to premiere.

estreno, (es·tre´no) *m.* inauguration; first time in use; premiere; debut.

estrenuo, nua, (es·tre´nwo, nwâ) *adj.* strenuous, rigorous.

estreñimiento, (es·tre·nyē·myen´to) *m.* constipation.

estreñir*, (es·tre·nyēr´) *va.* to constipate; —**se,** to become constipated.

estrépito, (es·tre´pē·to) *m.* crash, loud noise; show, splash *(ostentación).*

estrepitoso, sa, (es·tre·pē·to´so, sâ) *adj.* noisy, loud.

estreptococo, (es·trep·to·ko´ko) *m.* streptococcus.

estreptomicina, (es·trep·to·mē·sē´nâ) *f.* (med.) streptomycin.

estría, (es·trē´â) *f.* groove.

estribar, (es·trē·vâr´) *vn.* to rest, to lie; — **en,** to be supported by, to be grounded on.

estribillo, (es·trē·vē´yo) *m.* refrain; (fig.) favorite word.

estribo, (es·trē´vo) *m.* (arch.) buttress; running board *(del coche);* stirrup; **perder los —s,** to act foolishly, to lose one's head.

estribor, (es·trē·vor´) *m.* (naut.) starboard.

estricto, ta, (es·trēk´to, tâ) *adj.* strict.

estridente, (es·trē·then´te) *adj.* strident, piercing *(agudo);* clamorous, noisy *(ruidoso).*

estroboscopio, (es·tro·vos·ko´pyo) *m.* stroboscope.

estrofa, (es·tro´fâ) *f.* stanza; strophe *(del canto griego).*

estrógeno, (es·tro´he·no) *m.* estrogen.

estroncio, (es·tron´syo) *m.* strontium.

estropajo, (es·tro´pä´ho) *m.* dishrag; (fig.) old shoe.

estropajoso, sa, (es·tro·pâ·ho´so, sâ) *adj.* (coll.) tough, like leather *(carne);* unkempt, slovenly *(desaseado).*

estropear, (es·tro·pe·âr´) *va.* to cripple *(dejar lisiado);* to misuse, to abuse *(maltratar);* to spoil, to ruin *(echar a perder).*

estropeo, (es·tro·pe´o) *m.* crippling; use, abuse, rough treatment; ruin, spoiling.

estructura, (es·trūk·tū´râ) *f.* structure.

estruendo, (es·trwen´do) *m.* blast, din

m met, **n** not, **p** pot, **r** very, **rr** (none), **s** so, **t** toy, **th** with, **v** eve, **w** we, **y** yes, **z** zero

(ruido); confusion, hullabaloo, uproar *(alboroto);* great pomp and circumstance *(pompa).*

estrujar, (es·trū·hâr´) *va.* to squeeze *(exprimir);* to bruise, to crush *(magullar);* (fig.) to drain, to bleed *(agotar).*

estrujón, (es·trū·hon´) *m.* last pressing of grapes; pressing, squeezing *(estrujadura).*

estuco, (es·tū´ko) *m.* stucco.

estuche, (es·tū´che) *m.* kit; **ser un —,** (coll.) to be handy, to be very versatile.

estudiantado, (es·tū·thyân·ta´tho) *m.* student body.

estudiante, (es·tū·thyân´te) *m.* student.

estudiantil. (es·tū·thyân·tēl´) *adj.* student, scholastic.

estudiar, (es·tū·thyâr´) *va.* to study.

estudio, (es·tū´thyo) *m.* study; studio *(aposento).*

estudioso, sa, (es·tū·thyo´so, sâ) *adj.* studious.

estufa, (es·tū´fâ) *f.* stove *(fogón);* heater *(calorífero);* greenhouse *(invernáculo).*

estupefacción, (es´tū´pe·fâk·syon´) *f.* astonishment, great surprise, amazement.

estupefacientes, (es·tū·pe·fâ·syen´tes) *m. pl.* drugs, narcotics.

estupefacto, ta, (es·tū·pe·fâk´to, tâ) *adj.* amazed, astonished.

estupendo, da, (es·tū·pen´do,dâ) *adj.* stupendous, marvelous.

estupidez, (es·tū·pē·thes´) *f.* stupidity.

estúpido, da, (es·tū´pē·tho, thâ) *adj.* stupid.

estupor, (es·tū·por´) *m.* stupor; (fig.) daze.

estupro, (es·tū´pro) *m.* rape.

esturión, (es·tū·ryon´) *m.* (ichth.) sturgeon.

etapa, (e·tâ´pâ) *f.* phase, stage *(fase);* leg *(distancia entre altos);* stop, pause *(escala);* (mil.) ration.

éter, (e´ter) *m.* ether.

etéreo. rea, (e·te´re·o, re·â) *adj.* ethereal.

eternidad, (e·ter·nē·thâth´) *f.* eternity.

eternizar, (e·ter·nē·sâr´) *va.* to eternize, to make endless.

eterno, na, (e·ter´no, nâ) *adj.* eternal.

ética, (e´tē·kâ) *f.* ethics.

ético, ca, (e´tē·ko, kâ´) *adj.* ethical.

etileno, (e·tē·le´no) *m.* (chem.) ethylene.

etilo, (e·tē´lo) *m.* ethyl.

etimología, (e·tē·mo·lo·hē´â) *f.* etymology.

etiope, (e·tyo´pe) *n.* and *adj.* Ethiopian.

etiqueta, (e· tē· ke´ tâ) *f.* etiquette; formality *(ceremonia);* tag, label *(marbete);* **de —,** in formal dress.

étnico, ca, (eth´nē·ko, kâ) *adj.* ethnic.

etnógrafo, (eth·no´grâ·fo) *m.* ethnographer.

etnológico, ca, (eth·no·lo´hē·ko, kâ) *adj.* ethnological.

etnólogo, (eth·no´lo·go) *m.* ethnologist.

etrusco, ca, (e·trūs´ko , kâ) *n.* and *adj.* Etruscan.

E.U.A.: Estados Unidos de América, U.S.A. United States of America.

eucalipto, (eū·kâ·lēp´to) *m.* eucalyptus.

Eucaristía, (eū·kâ·rēs·tē´â) *f.* Lord´s Supper.

eufonía, (eū·fo·nē´â) *f.* euphony.

eufónico, ca, (eū·fo´nē·ko, kâ) *adj.* euphonic.

eugenesia, (eū·he·ne´syâ) *f.* eugenics.

Europa, (eū·ro´pâ) *f.* Europe.

europeo, pea, (eū·ro·pe´o, pe´â) *n.* and *adj.* European.

eutanasia, (eū·tâ·nâ´syâ) *f.* euthanasia.

evacuación, (e·vâ·kwâ·syon´) *f.* evacuation; carrying out; emptying; movement.

evacuar, (e·vâ·kwâr´) *va.* to evacuate; to empty *(desocupar);* to carry out *(cumplir);* **—se el vientre,** to have a bowel movement.

evadir, (e·vâ·thēr´) *va.* to evade, to avoid; **—se,** to flee, to escape.

evaluación, (e·vâ·lwâ·syon´) *f.* evaluation.

evaluar, (e·vâ·lwâr´) *va.* to evaluate.

evangélico, ca, (e·vân·he´lē·ko, kâ) *adj.* evangelical.

evangelio, (e·vân·he´lyo) *m.* Gospel.

evangelista, (e·vân·he·lēs´tâ) *m.* Evangelist; (Mex.) public letter writer, scribe.

evaporar, (e·vâ·po·râr´) *va.* and *vr.* To evaporate.

evasión, (e·vâ·syon´) *f.* evasion, escape *(fuga);* subterfuge *(evasiva).*

evasivo, va, (e·vâ·sē´vo, vâ) *adj.* evasive, elusive; **—,** *f.* subterfuge, evasion.

eventual, (e·ven·twâl´) *adj.* possible, contingent; fringe *(emolumento).*

evicción, (e·vēk·syon´) *f.* loss, damages.

evidencia, (e·vē·then´syâ) *f.* evidence, manifestation; **poner en —,** to make clear, to demonstrate.

evidente, (e·vē·then´te) *adj.* evident, clear, manifest.

evitable, (e·vē·tâ´vle) *adj.* avoidable.

evitar, (e·vē·târ´) *va.* to avoid.

evocación, (e·vo·kâ·syon´) *f.* evocation.

evocar, (e·vo·kâr´) *va.* to evoke.

evolución, (e·vo·lū·syon´) *f.* evolution: change *(mudanza).*

evolucionar, (e·vo·lū·syo·nâr´) *vn.* to

evolve, to undergo evolution.

exacerbar, (ek·sâ·ser·vâr´) va. to exasperate, to irritate.

exactitud, (ek·sâk·tē·tūth´) f. exactness.

exacto, ta, (ek·sâk´to, tâ) adj. exact; ¡—!
interj. fine! perfect!

exageración, (ek·sâ·he·râ·syon´) f. exaggeration.

exagerar, (ek·sâ·he·râr´) va. to exaggerate.

exaltación, (ek·sâl·tâ·syon´) f. exaltation.

exaltado, da, (ek·sâl·tâ´tho, thâ) adj. hotheaded, fanatic.

exaltar, (ek·sâl·târ´) va. to exalt; —se, to
become highly excited, to get carried
away.

examen, (ek·sâ´men) m. examination.

examinador, ra, (ek·sâ·mē·nâ·thor´, râ) n.
examiner.

examinar, (ek·sâ·mē·nâr´) va. to examine.

exánime, (ek·sâ´nē·me) adj. lifeless; faint
(desmayado).

exasperación, (ek·sâs·pe·râ·syon´) f. exasperation; intensity (de una enfermedad).

exasperar, (ek·sâs·pe·râr´) va. to exasperate; —se, to become intense (un dolor).

excavación, (es·kâ·vâ·syon´) f. excavation.

excavadora, (es·kâ·vâ·tho´râ) f. power shovel.

excavar, (es·kâ·vâr´) va. to excavate.

excedente, (ek·se·then´te) adj. excessive,
excess; —, m. surplus, excess.

exceder, (ek·se·ther´) va. to excede; —se,
to overdo, to overstep the limit, to go
too far.

excelencia, (ek·se·len´syâ) f. excellence;
E—, Excellency (tratamiento).

excelente, (ek·se·len´te) adj. excellent.

excelso, sa, (ek·sel´so, sâ) adj. elevated,
sublime, lofty.

excentricidad, (ek·sen·trē·sē·thâth´) f.
eccentricity.

excéntrico, ca, (ek·sen´trē·ko, kâ) adj.
eccentric.

excepción, (ek·sep·syon´) f. exception.

excepcional, (ek·sep´syo·nâl´) adj. exceptional.

excepto, (ek·sep´to) adv. with the exception of.

exceptuar, (ek·sep·twâr´) va. to except, to
exclude.

excesivo, va, (ek·se·sē´vo, vâ) adj. excessive.

exceso, (ek·se´so) m. excess; — de peso or
de equipaje, excess baggage.

excitable, (ek·sē·tâ´vle) adj. excitable.

excitación, (ek·sē·tâ·syon´) f. excitement.

excitante, (ek·sē·tân´te) adj. exciting;

(med.) stimulating; —, m. stimulant.

excitar, (ek·sē·târ´) va. to excite; to stimulate.

exclamación, (es·klâ·mâ·syon´) f. exclamation.

exclamar, (es·klâ·mâr´) vn. to exclaim.

excluir*, (es·klwēr´) va. to exclude.

exclusión, (es·klū·syon´) f. exclusion.

exclusivamente, (es·klū·sē·vâ·men´te) adv.
exclusively.

exclusive, (es·klū·sē´ve) adv. exclusively.

exclusivo, va, (es·klū·sē´vo, vâ) adj. exclusive; —, f. (com.) exclusive rights, sole
dealership.

excomulgar, (es·ko·mūl·gâr´) va. to
excommunicate.

excomunión, (es·ko·mū·nyon´) f. excommunication.

excoriar, (es·ko·ryâr´) va. to skin.

excremento, (es·kre·men´to) m. excrement.

excretar, (es·kre·târ´) va. to excrete.

excursión, (es·kūr·syon´) f. excursion;
ómnibus de —, sight-seeing bus.

excursionista, (es·kūr·syo·nēs´tâ) m. and
f. sightseer, excursionist.

excusa, (es·kū´sâ) f. excuse.

excusable, (es·kū·sâ´vle) adj. excusable.

excusado, da, (es·kū·sâ´tho, thâ) adj.
exempt (por privilegio); unnecessary
(superfluo); private (reservado); —, m.
washroom, lavatory, toilet.

excusar, (es·kū·sâr´) va. to excuse; to
avoid (evitar); to exempt (eximir).

execrar, (ek·se·krâr´) va. to execrate.

exención, (ek·sen·syon´) f. exemption.

exento, ta, (ek·sen´to, tâ) adj. exempt,
free.

exequias, (ek·se´kyâs) f. pl. funeral rites,
obsequies.

exhalación, (ek·sâ·lâ·syon´) f. exhalation;
falling star (estrella fugaz); vapor
(vaho); flash (centella).

exhalar, (ek·sâ·lâr´) va. to exhale; to emit
(un suspiro).

exhausto, ta, (ek·sâ´ūs·to, tâ) adj.
exhausted, depleted.

exhibición, (ek·sē·vē·syon´) f. exhibition.

exhibicionista, (ek·sē·vē·syo·nēs´tâ) m.
and f. exhibitionist.

exhibir, (ek·sē·vēr´) va. to exhibit.

exhortación, (ek·sor·tâ·syon´) f. exhortation.

exhortar, (ek·sor·târ´) va. to exhort.

exhumar, (ek·sū·mâr´) va. to exhume.

exigencia, (ek·sē·hen´syâ) f. demand, exigency; unreasonable demand (pretensión desmedida).

m met, n not, p pot, r very, rr (none), s so, t toy, th with, v eve, w we, y yes, z zero

exigente, (ek·sē·hen′te) *adj.* exacting, demanding, exigent.

exigir, (ek·sē·hēr′) *va.* to demand, to necessitate; to exact, to collect *(percibir).*

exiguo, gua, (ek·sē′gwo, gwâ) *adj.* small, tiny.

exiliado, da, (ek·sē·lyá′tho, thâ) *n.* exile.

exiliar, (ek·sē·lyâr′) *va.* to exile.

eximio, mia (ek·sē′myo, myâ) *adj.* superior, choice.

eximir, (ek·sē·mēr′) *va.* to exempt, to excuse.

existencia, (ek·sēs·ten′syâ) *f.* existence, being; en —, in stock; —s, *pl.* stock on hand.

existencialismo, (ek·sēs·ten·syâ·lēz′mo) *m.* existentialism.

existente, (ek·sēs·ten′te) *adj.* existent.

existir, (ek·sēs·tēr′) *vn.* to exist; to be in existence *(durar).*

éxito, (ek′sē·to) *m.* result, outcome *(fin);* success *(resultado feliz);* — de librería, best seller.

ex libris, (eks lē′vrēs) *m.* ex libris, bookplate.

éxodo, (ek′so·tho) *m.* exodus.

exoneración, (ek·so·ne·râ·syon′) *f.* exoneration.

exonerar, (ek·so·ne·râr′) *va.* to exonerate; to dismiss, to relieve *(de un empleo).*

exorbitancia, (ek·sor·vē·tân′syâ) *f.* exorbitance, excessiveness.

exorbitante, (ek·sor·vē·tân′te) *adj.* exorbitant, excessive.

exótico, ca, (ek·so′tē·ko, kâ) *adj.* exotic.

expansión, (es·pân·syon′) *f.* expansion; expansiveness *(manifestación efusiva).*

expansivo, va, (es·pân·sē′vo, vâ) *adj.* expansive.

expatriación, (es·pâ·tryâ·syon′) *f.* expatriation.

expatriarse, (es·pâ·tryâr′se) *vr.* to expatriate.

expectación, (es·pek·tâ·syon′) *f.* expectation.

expectativa, (es·pek·tâ·tē′vâ) *f.* expectancy.

expectorar, (es·pek·to·râr′) *va.* to expectorate.

expedición, (es·pe·thē·syon′) expedition; promptness *(prontitud);* *(com.)* shipment; gastos de —, shipping expenses.

expedicionario, ria, (es·pe·thē·syo·ná′ryo, ryâ) *adj.* expeditionary.

expedidor, (es·pe·thē·thor′) *m.* shipper.

expediente, (es·pe·thyen′te) *m.* expedient *(pretexto);* file, dossier *(conjunto de*

papeles); dispatch, ease *(prontitud).*

expedir*, (es·pe·thēr′) *va.* to expedite; to issue *(un documento);* to dispatch, to ship *(enviar).*

expedito, ta, (es·pe·thē′to, tâ) *adj.* prompt, speedy.

expeler, (es·pe·ler′) *va.* to expel.

expendio, (es·pen′dyo) *m.* (Sp. Am.) retail selling; (Mex.) cigar shop.

expensas, (es·pen′sâs) *f. pl.* expenses, charges; a — de, at the expense of.

experiencia, (es·pe·ryen′·syâ) *f.* experience.

experimentado, da, (es·pe·rē·men·tâ′tho, thâ) *adj.* experienced.

experimental, (es·pe·rē·men·tal′) *adj.* experimental.

experimentar, (es·pe·rē·men·târ′) *va.* to experience; to try out, to experiment with *(probar).*

experimento, (es·pe·rē·men′to) *m.* experiment.

experto, ta, (es·per′to, tâ) *n.* and *adj.* expert.

expiación, (es·pyâ·syon′) *f.* expiation.

expiar, (es·pyâr′) *va.* to expiate, to atone for.

expiatorio, ria, (es·pyâ·to′ryo, ryâ) *adj.* expiatory.

expirar, (es·pē·râr′) *vn.* to expire.

explanada, (es·plâ·nâ′thâ) *f.* esplanade.

explanar, (es·plâ·nâr′) *va.* to level, to grade *(allanar);* to explain *(explicar).*

explayar, (es·plâ·yâr′) *va.* to extend, to enlarge; —se, to dwell at great lengths, to go on and on.

explicable, (es·plē·kâ′vle) *adj.* explainable.

explicación, (es·plē·kâ·syon′) *f.* explanation.

explicar, (es·plē·kâr′) *va.* to explain; —se, to understand, to comprehend.

explicativo, va, (es·plē·kâ·tē′vo, vâ) *adj.* explanatory.

explícito, ta, (es·plē′sē·to, tâ) *adj.* explicit.

exploración, (es·plo·râ·syon′) *f.* exploration.

explorador, ra, (es·plo·râ thor′, râ) *n.* explorer; —, *m.* scanner *(del televisor);* —, *adj.* exploratory; niño —, boy scout.

explorar, (es·plo·râr′) *va.* to explore.

exploratorio, ria, (es·plo·râ·to′ryo, ryâ) *adj.* exploratory.

explosión, (es·plo·syon′) *f.* explosion.

explosivo, va, (es·plo·se′vo, vâ) *adj.* and *m.* explosive.

explotación, (es·plo·tâ·syon′) *f.* exploitation.

explotar, (es·plo·târ′) *va.* to exploit; —, *vn.*

to explode.

exponente, (es·po·nen´te) *m.* and *f.* exponent; —, *m.* (math.) exponent.

exponer*, (es·po·ner´) *va.* to expose; to exhibit *(un cuadro);* to risk *(poner en peligro).*

exportación, (es·por·tâ·syon´) *f.* exportation, export.

exportador, ra, (es·por·tâ·thor´, râ) *adj.* exporting; **casa —,** export company; —, exporter.

exportar, (es·por·târ´) *va.* to export.

exposición, (es·po·sē·syon´) *f.* exposition; exposure *(orientación);* danger, exposure to risk *(riesgo).*

expósito, ta, (es·po´sē·to, tâ) *adj.* abandoned; —, *n.* foundling.

expositor, ra, (es·po·sē·tor´, râ) *n.* expositor; exhibitor *(en una exposición pública).*

expresar, (es·pre·sâr´) *va.* to express.

expresión, (es·pre·syon´) *f.* expression.

expresivo, va, (es·pre·sē´vo, vâ) *adj.* expressive; affectionate, demonstrative *(afectuoso).*

expreso, sa, (es·pre´so, sâ) *adj.* and *m.* express; — **aéreo,** air express.

exprimidor, (es·prē·mē·thor´) *m.* squeezer.

exprimir, (es·prē·mēr´) *va.* to squeeze out; (fig.) to drain, to wring out *(agotar);* to express clearly, to make clear *(expresar).*

ex profeso, (eks pro· fe´so) *adv.* on purpose, purposely.

expropiar, (es·pro·pyâr´) *va.* to expropriate.

expuesto, ta, (es·pwes´to, tâ) *adj.* dangerous; **lo —to,** what has been said.

expulsar, (es·pūl·sâr´) *va.* to expel, to expulse.

expulsión, (es·pūl·syon´) *f.* expulsion.

expurgar, (es·pūr·gâr´) *va.* to purge, to purify; (fig.) to expurgate *(un escrito).*

exquisito, ta, (es·kē·sē´to, tâ) *adj.* exquisite.

éxtasis, (es´tâ·sēs) *m.* ecstasy.

extático, ca, (es·tâ´tē·ko, kâ) *adj.* ecstatic.

extender*, (es·ten·der´) *va.* to extend, to spread; to draw up, to make out *(un documento);* **—se,** to spread (propagarse); to reach (alcanzar).

extensión, (es·ten·syon´) *f.* extension; extent *(importancia).*

extensivo, va, (es·ten·sē´vo, vâ) *adj.* extensive; **sentido —,** extended meaning.

extenso, sa, (es·ten´so, sâ) *adj.* extensive, vast.

extenuación, (es·te·nwâ·syon´) *f.* near

collapse, extreme weakness.

extenuar, (es·te·nwâr´) *va.* to debilitate, to weaken.

exterior, (es·te·ryor´) *adj.* exterior, outer; overseas, foreign *(con el extranjero);* —, *m.* outward look, appearance; abroad *(países extranjeros).*

exterioridad, (es·te·ryo·rē·thâth´) *f.* outer appearance *(apariencia);* outer show, –hollow demonstration *(pompa).*

exteriorizar, (es·te·ryo·rē·sâr´) *va.* to externalize, to express.

exterminador, (es·ter·mē·nâ·thor´) *m.* exterminator.

exterminar, (es·ter·mē·nâr´) *va.* to exterminate.

exterminio, (es·ter·mē´nyo) *m.* extermination.

externo, na, (es·ter´no, nâ) *adj.* external; —, *n.* day pupil.

extinción, (es·tēn·syon´) *f.* extinction.

extinguir, (es·tēng·gēr´) *va.* to extinguish.

extinto, ta, (es·tēn´to, tâ) *adj.* extinguished, extinct; (Sp. Am.) passed on, dead.

extirpación, (es·tēr·pâ·syon´) *f.* uprooting; extirpation.

extirpador, (es·tēr·pâ·thor´) *m.* cultivator.

extirpar, (es·tēr·pâr´) *va.* to root out, to uproot; (fig.) to extirpate.

extorsión, (es·tor·syon´) *f.* obtaining by force, wresting; (fig.) turmoil, upset *(daño).*

extra, (es´trâ) *adj.* special, superior; —, *m.* and *f.* (theat.) extra; —, *m.* extra edition *(de periódico);* bonus, added payment *(gaje);* — **de,** (coll.) in addition to, besides.

extracción, (es·trâk·syon´) *f.* extraction.

extractar, (es·trâk·târ´) *vn.* to make an extract of.

extracto, (es·trâk´to) *m.* extract.

extractor, ra, (es·trâk·tor´, râ) *n.* extractor; —, *adj.* extracting.

extraer*, (es·trâ·er´) *va.* to extract.

extralimitarse, (es·trâ·lē·mē·târ´se) *vr.* To overstep one´s authority, to take advantage of one´s position.

extramuros, (es·trâ·mū´ros) *adv.* outside town, out of the city.

extranjero, ra, (es·trân·he´ro, râ) *adj.* foreign; **cambio —,** foreign exchange; —, *n.* foreigner; —, *m.* foreign lands; **ir al —ro,** to go abroad.

extrañar, (es·trâ·nyâr´) *va.* to be lonesome for, to miss *(echar de menos);* to exile *(desterrar);* to estrange *(privar del trato);* to be surprised by *(notar con* *extrañeza);* to find hard to get used to *(sentir la novedad de);* to surprise *(causar sorpresa);* **—se de,** to be surprised at.

extrañeza, (es·trâ·nye′sâ) *f.* wonderment, surprise *(asombro);* strangeness *(rareza).*

extraño, ña, (es·trâ′nyo, nyâ) *n.* stranger; **—,** *adj.* strange; not a party, disassociated *(que no tiene que ver).*

extraoficial, (es·trâ·o·fē·syâl′) *adj.* unofficial, off the record.

extraordinario, ria, (es·trâ·or·thē·nâ′ryo, ryâ) *adj.* extraordinary; **—,** *m.* specialty *(manjar);* special edition *(de un periódico).*

extrasensorio, ria, (es·trâ·sen·so′ryo, ryâ) *adj.* extrasensory.

extraterrestre, (es·trâ·te·rres′tre) *adj.* from outer space.

extraterritorial, (es·trâ·te·rrē·to·ryâl′) *adj.* extraterritorial.

extravagancia, (es·trâ·vâ·gân′syâ) *f.* eccentricity.

extravagante, (es·trâ·vâ·gân′te) *adj.* eccentric.

extravertido, da, (es·trâ·ver·tē′tho, thâ) *n.* extrovert; **—,** *adj.* extroverted.

extraviar, (es·trâ·vyâr′) *va.* to mislead, to lead astray; to misplace, to mislay *(una cosa);* **—se,** (fig.) to stray from the straight and narrow.

extravio, (es·trâ·vē′o) *m.* misleading; misplacing; (fig.) bad habits, going astray; (coll.) trouble, bother *(molestia).*

extremado, da, (es·tre·mâ′tho, thâ) *adj.* extreme.

extremar, (es·tre·mâr′) *va.* to carry to extremes; **—se,** to outdo oneself.

extremidad, (es·tre·mē·thâth′) *f.* extremity.

extremista, (es·tre·mēs′tâ) *m.* and *f.* and *adj.* extremist.

extremo, ma, (es·tre′mo, ma) *adj.* extreme, last; **—,** *m.* end, tip; extreme *(grado último);* great care *(esmero);* **de —mo a —mo,** from one end to the other; **en —mo, por —mo,** extremely

F

f.: franco, (com.) free.

f/: fardo, bl. bale; bdl. bundle.

f.a.b.: franco a bordo, (com.) f.o.b. free on board.

fábrica, (fâ′vrē·kâ) *f.* factory, mill; manufacture *(fabricación);* construction *(edificio).*

fabricación, (fâ·vrē·kâ·syon′) *f.* manufacture; **costo de —,** production cost; **— en serie** or **en gran escala,** mass production.

fabricador, ra, (fâ·vrē·kâ·thor′, râ) *n.* (fig.) fabricator.

fabricante, (fâ·vrē·kân′te) *m.* manufacturer; factory owner *(dueño).*

fabricar, (fâ·vrē·kâr′) *va.* to manufacture, to produce; to construct *(construir);* (fig.) to fabricate, to create.

fabril, (fâ·vrēl′) *adj.* manufacturing.

fábula, (fâ·vū′lâ) *f.* fable; gossip, hearsay *(hablilla);* **la — del pueblo,** the talk of the town.

fabuloso, sa, (fâ·vū·lo′so, sâ) *adj.* fabulous.

facción, (fâk·syon′) *f.* faction; (mil.) action; **—ones,** *pl.* features.

faccioso, sa, (fâk·syo′so, sâ) *adj.* and *n.* partisan, rebel.

faceta, (fâ·se′tâ) *f.* facet *(cara);* phase, aspect *(aspecto).*

facial, (fâ·syâl′) *adj.* facial; (fig.) perceptive; **valor —,** face value.

fácil, (fâ′sēl) *adj.* easy likely *(probable).*

facilidad, (fâ·sē·lē·thath′) *f.* facility, ability *(destreza);* easiness *(calidad de fácil);* overindulgence *(complacencia);* **—es,** *pl.* advantages, convenience.

facilitar, (fâ·sē·lē·târ′) *va.* to facilitate; to supply, to provide with *(proporcionar).*

fácilmente, (fâ·sēl·men′te) *adv.* easily.

facineroso, sa, (fâ·sē·ne·ro′so, sâ) *adj.* wicked, evil, vicious; **—,** *m.* villain, scoundrel.

facsímile, (fâk·sē′mē·le) *m.* facsimile.

factible, (fâk·tē′vle) *adj.* feasible, practical.

factor, (fâk·tor′) *m.* factor; (rail.) shipping agent; **— Rh,** Rh factor, **— de seguridad,** safety factor.

factoría, (fâk·to·rē′â) *f.* colonial trading post, factory.

factura, (fâk·tū′râ) *f.* invoice, bill; **— simulada,** pro forma invoice; **— de remesa** or

de expedición, shipping invoice.

facturar, (fâk·tū·râr´) *va.* to invoice; (rail.) to check.

facultad, (fa·kūl·tâth´) *f.* faculty; property *(propiedad);* school *(de una universidad);* authority *(derecho).*

facultado, da, (fa·kūl·tâ´tho, thâ) *adj.* authorized.

facultativo, va, (fâ·kūl·tâ·tē´vo, vâ´) *adj.* optional; — *m.* doctor.

facundia (fâ·kūn´dyâ) *f.* eloquence.

facha, (fâ´châ) *f.* appearance, aspect, mien; **ponerse en** — to dress shabbily.

fachada, (fa·cha´thâ) *f.* facade.

fachenda, (fa·chen´dâ) *m.* braggart; —, *f.* bragging.

fachendear, (fâ·chen·de·âr´) *vn.* to brag, to boast.

faena, (fâ·e´nâ) *f.* labor; job, duty, chore *(quehacer).*

fagocito, (fâ·go·sē´to) *m.* phagocyte.

faisán, (fâē·sân´) *m.* pheasant.

faja, (fâ´hâ) *f.* band, strip; sash *(ceñidor);* **— de radiación Van Allen,** Van Allen radiation belt.

fajar, (fâ·hâr´) *va.* to wrap, to bandage; to put a sash on *(ceñir).*

fajina, (fâ·hē´nâ) *f.* toil, chore *(faena);* kindling wood *(leña).*

fajo, (fâ´ho) *m.* bundle.

falacia, (fâ·lá´syâ) *f.* trickery, deceit.

falange, (fâ·lân´he) *f.* phalanx.

falangista, (fâ·lân·hēs´tâ) *m.* Falangist.

falaz, (fâ·lâz´) *adj.* deceitful, false.

falda, (fâl´dâ) *f.* skirt; lap *(regazo);* lower slope, foothill *(de un monte);* **perrillo de** —, lap dog.

faldero, ra, (fâl·de´ro, râ) *adj.* (fig.) fond of women´s company; **perro** —, lap dog.

faldón, (fâl·don´) *m.* short, full skirt *(de levita);* shirt tail *(de camisa).*

falsarregla, (fâl·sâ·rre´glâ) *f.* bevel square, bevel rule.

falsear, (fâl·se·âr´) *va.* to falsify; to pierce *(la armadura);* to force, to break open *(una cerradura);* —, *vn.* to be off tune *(disonar)* to weaken *(flaquear).*

falsedad, (fâl·se·thâth´) *f.* falsehood, untruth.

falsete, (fâl·se´te) *m.* falsetto; plug *(corcho).*

falsificación, (fâl·sē·fē·kâ·syon´) *f.* falsification.

falsificador, ra, (fâl·sē·fē·kâ·thor´, râ) *n.* falsifier; counterfeiter *(de moneda).*

falsificar, (fâl·sē·fē·kâr´) *va.* to falsify; to counterfeit *(la moneda).*

falso, sa, (fâl´so, sâ) *adj.* false; counterfeit;

unsteady, unstable *(caballo);* **en** —**so,** falsely.

falta, (fâl´tâ) *f.* lack, want *(privación);* mistake, error *(equivocación);* breach, infraction *(en el obrar);* — **de aceptación,** nonacceptance; — **de pago,** non-payment; **hacer** —, to be necessary, to be needed; **poner** —**s,** to find fault; **a** — **de,** by lack of, by want of; **sin** —, without fail.

faltar, (fâl·tar´) *vn.* to be lacking; to run short, to run out *(acabar);* to fail to show up *(a una cita);* to fail, to fall short *(no cumplir);* to be absent, to be missing *(estar ausente);* **¡no faltaba más!** (coll.) not on your life! that´s the last straw!

falto, ta, (fâl´to, tâ) *adj.* wanting, lacking, short.

faltriquera, (fâl·trē·ke´râ) *f.* pocket.

fallar, (fâ·yâr´) *va.* to decide, to find on, to judge *(un proceso);* to trump *(poner triunfo);* —, *vn.* to fail, to fall through *(frustrarse);* to weaken *(flaquear).*

fallecer*, (fâ·ye·ser´) *vn.* to die, to pass on.

fallecimiento, (fâ·ye·sē·myen´to) *m.* death, passing.

fallo, (fâ´yo) *m.* finding, verdict; lack of a suit *(en los juegos);* —, **lla,** *adj.* out of, lacking.

fama, (fâ´ma) *f.* reputation *(reputación);* fame *(celebridad);* talk, rumor *(voz pública);* **es** —, they say, it´s said.

familia, (fâ·mē´lya) *f.* family; servants *(servidumbre).*

familiar, (fâ·mē·lyâr´) *adj.* familiar; colloquial *(corriente);* — *m.* relative, relation *(miembro de la familia);* familiar.

familiaridad, (fâ·mē·lya·rē·thâth´) *f.* familiarity.

familiarizar, (fâ·mē·lya·rē·sâr´) *va.* to familiarize; —**se,** to become familiar, to acquaint oneself.

famoso, sa, (fâ·mo´so, sâ) *adj.* famous; (coll.) first-rate, excellent, top-notch.

fanal, (fâ·nâl´) *m.* lighthouse; bell jar *(campana de cristal).*

fanático, ca, (fâ·nâ´tē·ko, kâ) *adj.* fanatic.

fanatismo, (fâ·nâ·tēz´mo) *m.* fanaticism.

fandango, (fan·dâng´go) *m.,* fandango; (coll.) mess, muddle *(lío).*

fanfarrón, ona, (fan·fâ·rron´, o´nâ) *adj.* boasting, bragging; —, *n.* braggart, boaster.

fanfarronada, (fan·fâ·rro·nâ´thâ) *f.* bravado, boasting.

fanfarronear, (fân·fâ·rro·ne·âr´) *vn. to* boast, to bluster, to swagger.

m met, **n** not, **p** pot, **r** very, **rr** (none), **s** so, **t** toy, **th** with, **v** eve, **w** we, **y** yes, **z** zero

fango, (fång'go) *m.* mire, mud.

fangoso, sa, (fång·go'so, så) *adj.* muddy, miry.

fantasear, (fan·tå·se·år') *vn.* to daydream, to let one's mind wander.

fantasia, (fån·tå·sē'å) *f.* fantasy; fancy *(imaginación).*

fantasma, (fån·tåz'må) *m.* phantom; (fig.) stuffed shirt *(persona entonada).*

fantástico, ca, (fån·tås'tē·ko, kå) *adj.* fantastic; (fig.) stuffy *(presuntuoso).*

faramalla, (få·rå·må'yå) *f.* hocus-pocus, rigmarole.

farándula, (få·rån'dū·lå) *f.* profession of the farceur; hocus-pocus, rigmarole *(faramalla.)*

farandulero, ra, (få·rån·dū·le'ro, rå) *n.* farceur; —, *adj.* tricky, sly, deceitful.

Faraón, (få·rå·on') *m.* Pharoah; **f—,** faro.

fardo, (får'tho) *m.* bale, bundle.

faringe, (få·rēn'he) *f.* (anat.) pharynx.

fariseo, (fa·rē·se'o) *m.* Pharisee; pharisee *(hipócrita).*

farmacéutico, ca, (får·må·se'ū·tē·ko, kå) *adj.* pharmaceutical; —, *m.* pharmacist.

farmacia, (får·må'syå) *f.* pharmacy.

faro, (få'ro) *m.* lighthouse; (fig.) beacon; (auto.) headlight.

farol, (få·rol') *m.* lantern; (naut.) light.

farola, (få·ro'lå) *f.* street light.

farolear, (få·ro·le·år') *vn.* (coll.) to boast, to brag, to toot one's own horn.

farolero, (få·ro·le'ro) *m.* lamplighter; —, **ra,** *adj.* boastful, cocky; —, **ra,** *n.* braggart, cocky individual.

farsa, (får'så) *f.* farce; company of farceurs *(compañia)*

farsante, (får·sån'te) *m.* and *f.* farceur; —, *m.* and *f.* and *adj.* humbug.

fascinación, (fås·sē·nå·syon') *f.* fascination.

fascinador, ra, (fås·sē·nå·thor', rå) *adj.* fascinating.

fascinar, (fas·sē·når') *va.* to fascinate; to bewitch *(hacer mal de ojo).*

fascismo, (fås·sēz'mo) *m.* fascism.

fascista, (fås·sēs'tå) *m.* and *f.* fascist.

fase, (fa'se) *f.* phase, aspect.

fastidiar, (fås·tē·thyår') *va.* (fig.) to annoy, to bother, to bore.

fastidio, (fas·tē'thyo) *m.* annoyance, boredom, bother.

fastidioso, sa, (fas·tē·thyo'so, så) *adj.* annoying, boring, bothersome.

fatal, (få·tål') *adj.* fatal; terrible, very bad *(malo).*

fatalidad, (få·tå·lē·thåth') *f.* fate; disaster, misfortune *(desgracia).*

fatalismo, (få·tå·lēz'mo) *f.* fatalism.

fatalista, (få·tå·lēs'tå) *m.* and *f.* fatalist; —, *adj.* fatalistic.

fatiga, (få·tē'gå) *f.* fatigue; toil, labor *(trabajo);* difficulty in breathing *(respiración dificultosa);* nausea.

fatigado, da, (få·tē·gá'tho, thå) *adj.* fatigued, worn out.

fatigar, (få·tē·går') *va.* to tire, to wear out.

fatigoso, sa, (få·tē·go'so, så) *adj.* wearysome, tiresome.

fatuo, tua, (få'two, twå) *adj.* fatuous, inane, silly.

fauna, (få'ū·nå) *f.* fauna.

fausto, ta, (få'ūs·to, tå) *adj.* happy, lucky, fortunate; —, *m.* luxury, splendor.

favor, (få·vor') *m.* favor; **a — de,** by means of, due to *(por medio de);* in favor of.

favorable, (få·vo·rå'vle) *adj.* favorable.

favorecer*, (få·vo·re·ser') *va.* to favor; to help *(amparar).*

favoritismo, (få·vo·rē·tēz'mo) *m.* favoritism.

favorito, ta, (få·vo·rē'to, tå) *adj.* favorite.

faz, (fås') *f.* face; side *(lado).*

F.C. or f.c.: ferrocarril, R.R. or r.r. railroad.

F. de T.: Fulano de Tal, John Doe.

fe, (fe) *f.* faith; faithfulness *(fidelidad);* testimony *(testimonio);* **a — mía,** on my honor; **dar —,** to certify, to testify.

fealdad, (fe·ål·dåth') *f.* ugliness.

Feb. or feb.: febrero, Feb. February.

febrero, (fe·vre'ro) *m.* February.

febril, (fe·vrēl') *adj.* feverish.

fecal, (fe·kål') *adj.* (med.) fecal.

fecundar, (fe·kūn·dår') *va.* (biol.) to fertilize; to make fertile, to make fruitful.

fecundidad, (fe·kūn·dē·thåth') *f.* fecundity, prolificness.

fecundo, da, (fe·kūn'do, då) *adj.* fruitful, prolific *(productivo);* fertile.

fecha, (fe'chå) *f.* date; day *(día transcurrido);* **a treinta días —,** at thirty days' sight; **hasta la —,** to date; **con —,** under date.

fechar, (fe·chår') *va.* to date.

fechoría, (fe·cho·rē'å) *f.* misdeed, villainy.

federación, (fe·the·rå·syon') *f.* federation.

federal, (fe·the·rål') *adj.* federal.

fehaciente, (fe·å·syen'te) *adj.* authentic.

felicidad, (fe·lē·sē·thåth') *f.* happiness.

felicitación, (fe·lē·sē·tå·syon') *f.* congratulation.

felicitar, (fe·lē·sē·tår') *va.* to congratulate, to felicitate.

feligrés, esa, (fe·lē·gres', e'så) *n.* parishioner.

å arm, **e** they, **ē** bē, **o** fore, **ū** blūe, **b** bad, **ch** chip, **d** day, **f** fat, **g** go, **h** hot, **k** kid, **1** let

felino, na, (fe·lē´no, nâ) *adj.* feline.
feliz, (fe·lēs´) *adj.* happy, fortunate; — **idea,** clever idea.
felón, ona, (fe·lon´ o´nä) *n.* traitor.
felonía, (fe·lo·nē´ä) *f.* disloyalty, treachery.
felpa, (fel´pâ) *f.* plush; (coll.) good drubbing, beating.
felpilla, (fel·pē´yä) *f.* chenille.
femenino, na, (fe·me·nē´no, nä) *adj.* feminine; (biol.) female.
feminista, (fe·mē·nēs´tä) *m. and f.* feminist.
fémur, (fe´mūr) *m.* femur, thighbone.
fenecer*, (fe·ne·ser´) *va.* to finish, to conclude; —, *vn.* to come to an end; to pass on, to die *(fallecer).*
fénico, ca, (fe´nē·ko, kâ) *adj.* carbolic; **ácido —,** carbolic acid.
fenomenal, (fe·no·me·nâl´) *adj.* phenomenal.
fenómeno, (fe·no´me·no) *m.* phenomenon; (coll.) freak *(monstruo).*
feo, fea, (fe´o, fe´â) *adj.* ugly.
feracidad, (fe·râ·sē·thâth´) *f.* richness, fertileness.
feraz, (fe·râz´) *adj.* fertile, agriculturally rich.
féretro, (fe´re·tro) *m.* bier, coffin.
feria, (fe´ryâ) *f.* weekday fair *(mercado);* day off *(suspensión del trabajo).*
feriado, da, (fe·ryâ´tho, thä) *adj.* off, free; **día —do,** holiday, day off.
feriar, (fe·ryâr´) *va.* to buy at the fair; to treat to *(regalar);* —, *vn.* to suspend work.
ferino, na, (fe·rē´no, nä) *adj.* savage; **tos — na,** whooping cough.
fermentación, (fer·men·tâ·syon´) *f.* fermentation.
fermentar, (fer·men·târ´) *va. and vn.* to ferment.
ferocidad, (fe·ro·sē·thâth´) *f.* ferocity, ferociousness.
feroz, (fe·ros´) *adj.* ferocious.
férreo, rrea, (fe´rre·o, rre·â) *adj.* iron, ferrous; **vía —,** railroad.
ferrete, (fe·rre´te) *m.* sulfate of copper; iron punch *(punzón).*
ferretería, (fe·rre·te·rē´â) *f.* hardware store.
ferrocarril, (fe·rro·kâ·rrēl´) *m.* railroad; — **de cable,** cable railroad; — **funicular,** funicular railroad; — **subterráneo,** subway; **por —,** by rail.
ferrocarrilero, ra, (fe·rro·kâ·rrē·le´ro, râ) *adj.* (Sp. Am.) railroad; —, *m.* railroad man.
ferroviario, ria, (fe·rro·vyâ´ryo, ryâ) *adj.* railroad.

ferruginoso, sa, (fe·rrū·hē·no´so, sâ) *adj.* containing iron; iron *(agua).*
fértil, (fer´tēl) *adj.* fertile, fruitful.
fertilidad, (fer·tē·lē·thâth´) *f.* fertility, fruitfulness.
fertilización, (fer·tē·lē·sâ·syon´) *f.* fertilization.
fertilizante, (fer·tē·lē·sân´te) *m.* fertilizer.
fertilizar, (fer·tē·lē·sâr´) *va.* to fertilize.
férula, (fe´rū·lâ) *f.* ferule; **estar bajo la — de otro,** to be under somebody else's domination.
férvido, da, (fer´vē·tho, thâ) *adj.* fervent, ardent.
ferviente, (fer·vyen´te) *adj.* fervent.
fervor, (fer·vor´) *m.* fervor.
fervoroso, sa, (fer·vo·ro´so, sâ) *adj.* fervent, ardent, eager.
festejar, (fes·te·hâr´) *va.* to celebrate, to fete, to entertain *(agasajar);* to court, to woo *(galantear);* to court.
festejo, (fes·te´ho) *m.* fete, entertainment; courtship, wooing.
festín, (fes·tēn´) *m.* feast banquet.
festividad, (fes·tē·vē·thath´) *f.* festivity.
festivo, va, (fes·tē´vo, vâ) *adj.* festive; **día —vo,** holiday.
festonear, (fes·to·ne·âr´) *va.* to festoon.
fetiche, (fe·tē´che) *m.* fetish.
fétido, da, (fe´tē·tho, thâ) *adj.* fetid, stinking.
feto, (fe´to) *m.* fetus.
feúcho, cha, (fe·ū´cho, châ) *adj.* frightfully ugly.
feudal, (feū·thâl´) *adj.* feudal.
feudo, (fe´ū·tho) *m.* fief, feud, fee.
fiable, (fyâ´vle) *adj.* responsible, trustworthy.
fiado, da, (fyâ´tho, thä) *adj.* on trust; **al — do,** on credit charged.
fiador, ra, (fyâ·thor´, râ) *n.* bondsman, surety; —, *m.* fastener; safety catch *(de la escopeta);* snap *(de la capa).*
fiambre, (fyâm´bre) *adj.* cold, served cold; **—s,** *pl.* cold cuts.
fiambrera, (fyâm·bre´râ) *f.* lunch basket.
fianza, (fyân´sä) *f.* surety, guarantee; bond *(prenda);* **dar** or **prestar —,** to go good for.
fiar, (fyâr´) *va.* to go good for; to sell on credit *(vender a crédito);* to trust with *(dar en confianza);* —, *vn.* to trust.
fiasco, (fyâs´ko) *m.* failure.
fibra, (fē´vrâ) *f.* fiber; grain *(de madera);* (fig.) vigor, toughness *(energía);* **—s del corazón,** heartstrings.
fibroma, (fē·vro´mâ) *m.* fibroid tumor.
fibroso, sa, (fē·vro´so, sâ) *adj.* fibrous.

---

m met, **n** not, **p** pot, **r** very, **rr** (none), **s** so, **t** toy, **th** with, **v** eve, **w** we, **y** yes, **z** zero

ficción, (fĕk·syon') f. fiction.

ficticio, cia (fĕk·tē'syo, syâ) adj. fictitious.

ficha, (fē'châ) f. chip (en el juego); token (en substitución de moneda); index card (cédula).

fichero, (fē·che'ro) m. card index, card file.

fidedigno, na, (fē·the·thēg'no, nâ) adj. trustworthy, believable.

fideicomiso, (fe·theē·ko·mē'so) m. trust.

fidelidad, (fē·the·lē·thâth') f. fidelity; accuracy, care (exactitud).

fideos, (fē·the'os) m. pl. vermicelli, thin noodles.

fiebre, (fye'vre) f. fever; — amarilla, yellow fever; — cerebral, brain fever, meningitis; — de Malta, undulant fever; — aftosa, hoof-and-mouth disease.

fiel, (fyel') adj. faithful; —, m. public inspector; indicator (de las balanzas); los — es, the faithful.

fieltro, (fyel'tro) m. felt.

fiera, (fye'râ) f. beast, wild animal; (fig.) fiend, monster (persona).

fiereza, (fye·re'sâ) f. fierceness, ferociousness.

fiero, ra, (fye'ro, râ) adj. bestial; hard, cruel (duro); huge, monstrous (excesivo) (fig.) horrible, frightful.

fiesta, (fyes'tâ) f. (eccl.) feast, festival; holiday (día sagrado); party, festivity (regocijo); aguar la —, (fig.) to spoil the fun; no estar para —s, (coll.) to be in no mood for jokes.

fig.: figura, fig. figure.

figura, (fē·gū'râ) f. figure; countenance, face (rostro); representation (símbolo); face card (naipe); (mus.) note.

figurado, da, (fē·gū·râ'tho, thâ) adj. figurative.

figurar, (fe·gū·râr') va. to portray, to figure; to feign, to pretend (fingir); —, vn. to figure, to be counted; —se, to imagine.

figurín, (fe·gū·rēn') m. model; (fig.) dude, fashion plate (petimetre).

fijar, (fē·hâr') va. to fix, to fasten; (fig.) to determine, to fix (precisar); (phot.) to fix; —se, to notice, to take notice; se prohibe — carteles post no bills.

fijeza, (fē·he'sâ) f. firmness, stability; persistence (continuidad).

fijo, ja, (fē'ho, hâ) adj. fixed; de —jo, certainly, surely.

fila, (fē'lâ) f. row, line.

filantropía, (fē·lân·tro·pē'â) f. philanthrophy.

filantrópico, ca, (fe·lân·tro'pē·ko, kâ) adj. philanthropic.

filántropo, (fē·lân'tro·po) m. philanthropist.

filarmónico, ca, (fē·lâr·mo'nē·ko, kâ) adj. philharmonic.

filatelia, (fē·lâ·te'lyâ) f. philately.

filatélico, ca, (fē·lâ·te'lē·ko, kâ) adj. philatelic.

filatelista, (fē·lâ·te·lēs'tâ) m. and f. philatelist.

filete, (fē·le'te) m. fillet; small spit (asador).

filiación, (fē·lyâ·syon') f. filiation; description (señas personales).

filial, (fē·lyâl') adj. filial.

filigrana, (fē·lē·grâ'nâ) f. filigree; watermark (en el papel).

filipino, na, (fē·lē·pē'no, nâ) n. and adj. Filipino; —, adj. Philippine.

filisteo, tea, (fē·lēs·te'o, te'â) n. and adj. Philistine.

filmar, (fēl·mâr') va. to film.

filme, (fēl'me) m. film.

filmoteca, (fēl·mo·te'kâ) f. film library.

filo, (fē'lo) m. cutting edge; dividing line, division (línea).

filocomunista, (fē·lo·ko·mū·nēs'tâ) m. and f. (poi.) fellow traveler.

filología, (fē·lo·lo·hē'â) f. philology.

filólogo, (fē·lo'lo·go) m. philologist.

filosofar, (fe·lo·so·fâr') vn. to philosophize.

filosofia, (fe·lo·so·fē'â) f. philosophy.

filosófico, ca, (fē·lo·so'fē·ko, kâ) adj. philosophical.

filósofo, (fē·lo'so·fo) m. philosopher.

filtración, (fēl·trâ·syon') f. filtration.

filtrar, (fēl·trâr') va. to filter; —se, to filter, to seep.

filtro, (fēl'tro) m. filter; love potion (bebida); — de vacío, vacuum filter.

fin, (fēn) m. end; al —, at last; en —, in conclusion, in short; sin — endless number.

finado, da, (fē·nâ'tho, thâ) n. dead, deceased.

final, (fē·nâl') adj. final; —, m. end; —, f. finals, main event.

finalidad, (fē·nâ·lē·thâth') f. end, purpose.

finalista, (fē·nâ·lēs'tâ) m. and f. finalist.

finalizar, (fē·nâ·lē·sâr') va. to finish, to conclude.

finalmente, (fē·nâl·men'te) adv. finally, at last.

financiamiento, (fē·nân·syâ·myen'to) m. financing.

financiar, (fē·nân·syâr') va. to finance.

financiero, ra, (fē·nân·sye'ro, râ) adj. financial; —, n. financeer.

â arm, e they, ē bē, o fore, ū blūe, b bad, ch chip, d day, f fat, g go, h hot, k kid, 1 let

finc

flor

finca, (fēng´kâ) f. piece of land, property; (Sp. Am.) ranch, country place.

fineza, (fē·ne´sâ) f. fineness; token of friendship (dádiva); refinement (delicadeza); good turn (acción amistosa).

fingido, da, (fēn·hē´tho, thâ) adj. false, feigned, not genuine.

fingimiento, (fēn·hē·myen´to) m. feigning, pretense.

fingir, (fēn·hēr´) va. to feign, to fake, to pretend; —se, to pretend to be.

finiquitar, (fē·nē·kē·târ´) va. to settle, to liquidate (una cuenta); to finish (acabar).

fino, na, (fē´no, nâ) adj. fine; polite, courteous (cortés); true (fiel); cunning (astuto).

finura, (fē·nū´râ) f. delicacy (delicadeza); excellence (primor); courtesy, politeness.

fiordo, (fyor´tho) m. fiord.

firma, (fēr´mâ) f. signature; company, firm (razón social); signing (acto de firmar).

firmamento, (fēr·mâ·men´to) m. firmament.

firmar, (fēr·mâr´) va. to sign.

firme, (fēr´me) adj. firm stable.

firmeza, (fēr·me´sâ) f. firmness, stability.

fiscal, (fēs·kâl´) m. public prosecutor, district attorney; treasurer (agente del fisco); —, adj. fiscal.

fiscalizar, (fēs·kâ·lē·sâr´) va. (fig.) to meddle in, to pry into.

fisco, (fēs´ko) m. treasury department.

física, (fē´sē·kâ) f. physics; — de altas energías, high-energy physics; — de bajas temperaturas, low-temperature physics; — del estado sólido, solid state physics; — del plasma, plasma physics.

físico, ca, (fē´sē·ko, kâ) adj. physical; —, m. physicist; outward appearance, looks (de una persona).

fisiografía, (fē·syo·grâ·fē´â) f. physiography.

fisiología, (fē·syo·lo·hē´â) f. physiology.

fisión, (fē·syon´) f. fission; — nuclear, nuclear fission.

fisionable, (fē·syo·nâ´vle) adj. fissionable.

fisioterapia, (fē·syo·te·râ´pyâ) f. physiotherapy.

fisonomía, (fē·so·no·mē´â) f. look, countenance, features.

fisonomista, (fē·so·no·mēs´tâ) m. and f. person who has a good memory for faces.

flaco, ca, (flâ´ko, kâ) adj. thin; (fig.) feeble.

flagrante, (flâ·grân´te) adj. flagrant; en —, in the act red-handed.

flamante, (flâ·mân´te) adj. flaming, bright; brand-new (nuevo).

flamear, (flâ·me·âr´) vn. (naut.) to flutter, to wave (ondear); to flame, to blaze (echar llamas).

flamenco, ca, (flâ·meng´ko, kâ) n. and adj. Flemish; baile —co, Andalusian gypsy dance; —, m. flamingo.

flan, (flân) m. custard.

flanco, (flâng´ko) m. flank, side.

flanquear, (flâng·ke·âr´) va. (mil.) to flank, to outflank.

flaquear, (flâ·ke·âr´) vn. to flag, to weaken, to lose spirit, to slacken.

flaqueza, (flâ·ke´sâ) f. leanness (delgadez); meagerness (pobreza); feebleness, weakness (debilidad); failing (fragilidad).

flatulento, ta, (flâ·tū·len´to, tâ) adj. flatulent.

flauta, (flâ´ū·tâ) f. (mus.) flute.

flautín, (flâū·tēn´) m. piccolo, fife.

flautista, (flâū·tēs´tâ) m. and f. flutist, flautist.

fleco, (fle´ko) m. flounce, fringe; —s, pl. gossamer.

flecha, (fle´châ) f. arrow.

fleje, (fle´he) m. iron arrow.

flema, (fle´mâ) f. phlegm; (fig.) apathy.

flemático, ca, (fle·mâ´tē·ko, kâ) adj. phlegmatic.

flequillo, (fle·kē´yo) m. bangs.

fletador, (fle·tâ·thor´) m. freighter, charterer.

fletamento, (fle·tâ·men´to) m. chartering, charter (contrato).

fletar, (fle·târ´) va. to freight, to load (embarcar); to charter (alquilar).

flete, (fle´te) m. freight; — aéreo, airfreight.

flexibilidad, (flek·sē·vē·lē·thâth´) f. flexibility, mobility.

flexible, (flek·sē´vle) adj. flexible.

flirtear, (flēr·te·âr´) vn. to flirt.

flirteo, (flēr·te´o) m. flirting, flirtation.

flojedad, (flo·he·thâth´) f. weakness (debilidad); (fig.) laziness, negligence (pereza).

flojera, (flo·he´râ) f. laziness, slackness.

flojo, ja, (flo´ho, hâ) adj. loose, slack; weak (sin fuerza ; (fig.) lazy, idle (perezoso).

flor, (flor) f. flower; echar —es, to compliment, to flatter; — de la edad, prime of life.

flora, (flo´râ) f. (bot.) flora.

florear, (flo·re·âr´) va. to take the best part of; —, vn. to be always paying compliments.

florecer*, (flo·re·ser´) vn. to blossom, to flower, to bloom; (fig.) to flourish.

m met, n not, p pot, r very, rr (none), s so, t toy, th with, v eve, w we, y yes, z zero

floreciente, (flo·re·syen'te) *adj.* in bloom, flowering; (fig.) flourishing *(próspero).*

Florencia, (flo·ren'syâ) *f.* Florence.

florentino, na, (flo·ren·tē'no, nâ) *n.* and *adj.* Florentine.

floreo, (flo·re'o) *m.* frivolous chitchat; (mus.) flourish; triviality, banality *(dicho vano).*

florero, (flo·re'ro) *m.* vase for flowers.

floresta, (flo·res'tâ) *f.* grove; florilegium, anthology *(colección).*

florete, (flo·re'te) *m.* foil.

floricultor, ra, (flo·rē·kūl·tor', râ) *n.* floriculturist.

floricultura, (flo·rē·kūl·tū'râ) *f.* floriculture.

florido, da, (flo·rē'tho, thâ) *adj.* florid, flowery; choice, select *(selecto).*

florista, (flo·rēs'tâ) *m.* and *f.* florist.

florón, (flo·ron') *m.* (print.) vignette; (fig.) flower, crowning grace.

flota, (flo'tâ) *f.* fleet; — **aérea,** air fleet.

flotación, (flo·tâ·syon') *f.* floating.

flotante, (flo·tân'te) *adj.* floating.

flotar, (flo·târ') *vn.* to float.

flote, (flo'te) *m.* floating; **a —,** buoyant, afloat.

flotilla, (flo·tē'yâ) *f.* flotilla.

fluctuación, (flūk·twâ·syon') *f.* fluctuation.

fluctuar, (flūk·twâr') *vn.* to fluctuate.

fluidez, (flwē·thes') *f.* fluidity; (fig.) fluency.

fluido, da, (flwē'tho, thâ) *adj.* fluid; (fig.) fluent; —, *m.* fluid.

fluir*, (flwēr') *vn.* to flow, to run.

flujo, (flū'ho) *m.* flow; — **de risa,** outburst of laughter.

fluorescencia, (flwo·res·sen'syâ) *f.* fluorescence.

fluorescente, (flwo·res·sen'te) *adj.* fluorescent.

fluoroscopio, (flwo·ros·ko'pyo) *m.* fluoroscope.

fluoruración, (flwo·rū·râ·syon') *f.* fluoridation.

fluvial, (flū·vyâl') *adj.* fluvial; **vías —es,** waterways.

foca, (fo'kâ) *f.* (zool.) seal; **piel de —,** sealskin.

focal, (fo·kâl') *adj.* focal.

foco, (fo'ko) *m.* focus; lightbulb.

fofo, fa, (fo'fo, fâ) *adj.* soft, fluffy.

fogón, (fo·gon') *m.* stove; vent *(en el arma de fuego).*

fogonazo, (fo·go·nâ'so) *m.* flash of powder.

fogonero, (fo·go·ne'ro) *m.* fireman, stoker.

fogosidad, (fo·go·sē·thâth') *f.* heatedness, fieriness, fervor.

fogoso, sa, (fo·go'so, sâ) *adj.* fiery, ardent, heated.

foliación, (fo·lyâ·syon') *f.* foliation.

folio, (fo'lyo) *m.* folio.

folklore, (fol·klor') *m.* folklore.

folklórico, ca, (fol·klo'rē·ko, kâ) *adj.* folkloric.

folklorista, (fol·klo·rēs'tâ) *m.* student of folklore.

follaje, (fo·yâ'he) *m.* foliage.

folletín, (fo·ye·tēn') *m.* special supplement.

folleto, (fo·ye'to) *m.* pamphlet.

follón, ona, (fo·yon', o'nâ) *adj.* indolent, good-for-nothing; —, *m.* dud.

fomentador, ra, (fo·men·tâ·thor', râ) *n.* promoter, inciter; furtherer.

fomentar, (fo·men·târ') *va.* to heat, to warm; (fig.) to incite, to foment *(excitar);* to promote, to further *(dar auxilio).*

fomento, (fo·men'to) *m.* heat, warmth; (fig.) promotion, foment.

fonda, (fon'dâ) *f.* inn.

fondear, (fon·de·âr') *va.* (naut.) to sound; to search *(una embarcación);* —, *vn.* to anchor.

fondillos, (fon·dē'yos) *m. pl.* seat of trousers.

fondo, (fon'do) *m.* bottom *(parte más baja);* depth *(hondura);* back, back part *(de un salón);* background *(campo);* fund *(caudal);* qualities *(índole);* — **doble,** false bottom; **artículo de —,** editorial; **dar —,** to cast anchor; **a —,** completely, fully.

fonética, (fo·ne'tē·kâ) *f.* phonetics.

fonético, ca, (fo·ne'tē·ko, kâ) *adj.* phonetic.

fonógrafo, (fo·no'grâ·fo) *m.* phonograph.

forajido, da, (fo·râ·hē'tho, thâ) *n.* outlaw, highwayman.

foráneo, nea, (fo·râ'ne·o, ne·â) *adj.* foreign, strange.

forastero, ra, (fo·ras·te'ro, râ) *adj.* strange; —, *n.* stranger.

fórceps, (for'seps) *m.* forceps.

forense, (fo·ren'se) *adj.* forensic.

forestal, (fo·res·tâl') *adj.* forest.

forjador, (for·hâ·thor') *m.* smith; (fig.) inventor, fabricator.

forjadura, (for·hâ·thū'râ) *f.* forging; (fig.) fabrication.

forjar, (for·hâr') *va.* to forge, to work; (fig.) to invent, to coin, to fabricate.

forma, (for'mâ) *f.* form, shape ; way *(modo de proceder);* (print.) format.

formación, (for·mâ·syon') *f.* formation.

formal, (for·mâl') *adj.* formal; reliable, serious *(cumplido).*

formalidad, (for·mâ·lē·thâth') *f.* formality; reliability, seriousness *(exactitud).*

â arm, e they, ē bē, o fore, ū blūe, b bad, ch chip, d day, f fat, g go, h hot, k kid, 1 let

formalizar, (for·mâ·lē·sâr´) va. to formalize; —se, to grow stiff, to get very formal *(darse por ofendido);* to become serious, to grow up.

formar, (for·mâr´) va. to form, to shape; — causa, to bring suit.

formativo, va, (for·mâ·tē´vo, vâ) adj. formative.

formato, (for·mâ´to) m. (print.) format.

formidable, (for·mē·thâ´vle) adj. formidable, terrific.

formón (for·mon´) m. chisel *(escoplo);* punch *(sacabocados).*

fórmula, (for´mū·lâ) f. formula.

formulación, (for·mū·lâ·syon´) f. formulation.

formular, (for·mū·lâr´) va. to formulate.

formulario, (for·mū·lâ´ryo) m. form, blank.

fornicación, (for·nē·kâ·syon´) f. fornication.

fornicar, (for·nē·kâr´) vn. to commit fornication, to fornicate.

foro, (fo´ro) m. forum; bar *(jurisprudencia);* (theat.) back of the stage.

forraje, (fo·rrâ´he) m. forage, fodder.

forrar, (fo·rrâr´) va. to line; to cover *(cubrir).*

forro, (fo´rro) m. lining; cover.

fortalecer*, (for·tâ·le·ser´) va. to fortify, to strengthen.

fortaleza, (for·tâ·le´sâ) f. fortitude; fortress, stronghold *(recinto fortificado).*

fortificación, (for·tē·fē·kâ·syon´) f. fortification.

fortificar, (for·tē·fē·kâr´) va. to fortify.

fortín, (for·tēn´) m. small fort; bunker *(en los atrincheramientos).*

fortuito, ta, (for·twē´to, tâ) adj. fortuitous, unforseen.

fortuna, (for·tū´nâ) f. fortunes *(azar);* luck *(buena suerte);* fortune *(hacienda);* storm *(tempestad);* por —, luckily, fortunately.

forzado, da, (for·sâ´tho, thâ) adj. forced, compelled; —, m. convict.

forzar*, (for·sâr´) va. to force; to ravish *(una mujer);* to force one´s way in, to storm *(entrar por violencia).*

forzosamente, (for·so·sâ·men´te) adv. of necessity.

forzoso, sa, (for·so´so, sâ) adj. unavoidable.

fosa, (fo´sâ) f. grave; (anat.) cavity; — séptica, septic tank.

fosfato, (fos·fâ´to) m. phosphate.

fosforescente, (fos·fo·res·sen´te) adj. phosphorescent.

fosfórico, ca, (fos·fo´rē·ko, kâ) adj. phosphoric.

fósforo (fos´fo·ro) m. phosphorus; match *(cerillo);* — de seguridad, safety match.

fósil, (fo´sēl) adj. and m. fossil.

foso, (fo´so) m. pit; (mil.) moat, trench; (auto.) grease pit.

fotocélula, (fo·to·se´lū·lâ) f. electric eye.

fotocopiar, (fo·to·ko·pyâr´) va. xerox, copy.

fotoeléctrico, ca, (fo·to·e·lek´trē·ko, kâ) adj. photoelectric.

fotostático, ca, (fo·to·stá´tē·ko, kâ) adj. photogenic.

fotograbado, (fo·to·grâ·vâ´tho) m. photoengraving, photogravure.

fotografía, (fo·to·grâ·fē´â) f. photograph *(reproducción);* photography *(arte);* — aérea, aerial photography.

fotografiar, (fo·to·gra·fyâr´) va. to photograph.

fotógrafo, (fo·to´grâ·fo) m. photographer.

fotómetro, (fo·to´me·tro) m. photometer; (phot.) light meter.

fotón (fo·ton´) m. photon.

fotosíntesis, (fo·to·sēn´te·sēs) f. (chem.) photosynthesis.

fotostático, ca, (fo·tos·tâ´tē·ko, kâ) adj. photostatic.

F.P.S.: factor de protección solar, SPF, sun protection factor.

frac, (frâk) m. full dress, tails.

fracasar, (frâ·kâ·sâr´) vn. to be wrecked, to be dashed.

fracaso, (frâ·kâ´so) m. collapse, ruin; fiasco *(malogro).*

fracción, (frâk·syon´) f. fraction; division, cutting up *(división).*

fraccionamiento, (frâk·syo·nâ·myen´to) m. cutting up, dividing up.

fraccionario, ria, (frâk·syo·nâ´ryo, ryâ) adj. fractional.

fractura, (frâk·tū´râ) f. fracture *(de un hueso);* break, rupture.

fracturar, (frâk·tū·râr´) va. to fracture; to break open, to smash.

fragancia, (fra·gân´syâ) f. fragrance, perfume.

fragante, (frâ·gân´te) adj. fragrant; flagrant *(flagrante).*

fragata, (fra·gâ´tâ) f. (Haut.) frigate.

frágil, (frâ´hēl) adj. fragile; (fig.) weak, frail.

fragilidad, (frâ·hē·lē·thâth´) f. fragility; (fig.) frailty.

fragmento, (frâg·men´to) m. fragment.

fragor, (frâ·gor´) m. noise, clamor.

fragoso, sa, (frâ·go´so, sâ) adj. craggy, rough; loud, noisy *(ruidoso).*

fragua, (frâ´gwâ) f. forge.

m met, n not, p pot, r very, rr (none), s so, t toy, th with, v eve, w we, y yes, z zero

fraguar, (frä·gwär´) *va.* to forge ; to contrive *(idear)*; —, *vn.* to solidify, to harden.

fraile, (frä´ē·le) *m.* friar.

frambuesa, (främ·bwe´sä) *f.* raspberry.

frambueso, (främ·bwe´so) *m.* raspberry bush.

francachela, (fräng·kä·che´lä) *f.* (coll.) festive gathering, high old time.

francés, esa, (frän·ses´, e´sa) *adj.* French; —, *m.* French language *(idioma)*; Frenchman; —, *f.* French woman.

Francia, (frän´syä) *f.* France.

franco, ca, (fräng´ko, kä) *adj.* free *(exento)*; liberal, generous *(dadivoso)*; frank, open *(sincero)*; **— a bordo,** free on board; **— de porte,** postpaid, prepaid; —, *m.* franc; —, *n.* Frank.

franela, (frä·ne´lä) *f.* flannel.

franja, (frän´hä) *f.* fringe; strip, band *(lista)*.

franquear, (fräng·ke·är´) *va.* to exempt *(eximir)*; to permit, to give *(conceder)*; to clear *(desembarazar)*; to stamp *(una carta)*; to free *(dar libertad)*; **—se,** to be easily swayed; to reveal one's true feelings *(descubrir los pensamientos)*.

franqueo, (fräng·ke´o) *m.* postage *(de una carta)*; exemption; freeing.

franqueza, (fräng·ke´sä) *f.* frankness *(sinceridad)*; liberty, freedom *(exención)*; liberality *(generosidad)*.

franquicia, (fräng·kē´syä) *f.* immunity from customs payments; franchise; free mailing privileges *(de correo)*.

frasco, (fräs´ko) *m.* flask; powder horn *(para la pólvora)*.

frase, (frä´se) *f.* phrase; sentence *(oración)*; **— en sentido figurado,** figure of speech.

frasear, (frä·se·är´) *va.* to phrase.

fraseología, (frä·se·o·lo·hē´ä) *f.* phraseology.

fraternal, (frä·ter·näl´) *adj.* fraternal, brotherly.

fraternidad, (frä·ter·nē·thäth´) *f.* fraternity, brotherhood.

fratricida, (frä·trē·sē´thä) *m.* and *f.* fratricide.

fratricidio, (frä·trē·sē´thyo) *m.* fratricide.

fraude, (fra´ū·the) *m.* fraud, cheating.

fraudulento, ta, (fräū·thū·len´to, tä) *adj.* fraudulent.

fray, (frä´ē) *m.* friar.

frazada, (frä·sä´thä) *f.* blanket.

frecuencia, (fre·kwen´syä) *f.* frequency; **con —,** frequently.

frecuentar, (fre·kwen·tär´) *va.* to frequent; to frequent the company of *(una persona)*.

fregadero, (fre·gä·the´ro) *m.* kitchen sink.

fregado, (fre·gä´tho) *m.* scouring, washing; scrubbing.

fregador, (fre·gä·thor´) *m.* scrub brush; —, **ra,** *n.* dishwasher.

fregar*, (fre·gär´) *va.* to scrub *(estregar)*; to scour, to wash *(los platos)*; (coll.) to rub the wrong way, to annoy *(fastidiar)*.

fregona, (fre·go´nä) *f.* kitchen maid.

freir*, (fre·ēr´) *va.* to fry.

fréjol, (fre´hol) *m.* kidney bean.

frenar; (fre·när´) *va.* to brake.

frenesí, (fre·ne·sē´) *m.* frenzy.

frenético, ca, (fre·ne´tē·ko, kä) *adj.* frenzied.

frenillo, (fre·nē´yo) *m.* (anat.) frenum; **no tener — en la lengua,** to have a loose tongue.

freno, (fre´no) *m.* bridle; (mech.) brake; **— de aire,** air brake; **—s,** braces *(odontología)*.

frenópata, (fre·no´pä·tä) *m.* alienist.

frenopatía, (fre·no·pä·tēa) *f.* study of mental diseases.

frente, (fren´te) *f.* forehead; (fig.) face; **— a —,** face to face; —, *m.* front; **— obrero,** labor front; **en —.** in front; **— a,** in front of; **hacer —,** to face, to stand up to.

fresa, (fre´sä) *f.* strawberry.

fresco, ca, (fres´ko, kä) *adj.* cool; fresh *(reciente)*; (fig.) healthy, ruddy *(de buen color)*; unruffled *(sereno)*; (coll.) fresh, cheeky *(descarado)*.

frescura, (fres·kū´rä) *f.* freshness; coolness; calmness, steadiness *(desenfado)*; smart remark, jibe *(chanza)*; (fig.) carelessness *(descuido)*.

fresno, (frez´no) *m.* ash tree.

frialdad, (fryäl·däth´) *f.* coldness; indifference *(indiferencia)*; (med.) frigidity; (fig) stupidity *(necedad)*.

fricasé, (frē·kä·se´) *m.* fricassée.

fricción, (frēk·syon´) *f.* friction.

friccionar, (frēk·syo·när´) *va.* to rub.

friega, (frye´gä) *f.* massage; whipping.

frígido, da, (frē´hē·tho, thä) *adj.* frigid.

frigorífero, (frē·go·rē´fe·ro) *m.* refrigerator.

frigorífico, (frē·go·rē´fē·ko) *m.* cold-storage plant; refrigerator *(nevera)*; —, **ca,** *adj.* refrigerating.

frijol, (frē·hol´) *m.* kidney bean.

frío, fria, (frē´o, frē´ä) *adj.* and *m.* cold; **hacer — or tener —,** to be cold.

friolera, (fryo·le´rä) *f.* trifle.

frisar, (frē·sär´) *va.* to tease *(un tejido)*; to rub *(refregar)*; —, *vn.* to be very much alike *(congeniar)*; to approach *(acercarse)*.

friso, (frē′so) *m.* frieze.

fritada, (frē·tá′thä) *f.* fry.

frito, ta, (frē′to, tä) *adj.* fried.

fritura, (frē·tū′rä) *f.* fry; — **de pescado,** fish fry.

frivolidad, (frē·vo·lē·tháth′) *f.* frivolity.

frívolo, la, (frē′vo·lo, lä) *adj.* frivolous.

frondosidad, (fron·do·sē·thäth′) *f.* thick foliage.

frondoso, sa (fron·do′so, sä) *adj.* thick, dense, leafy.

frontera, (fron·te′rä) *f.* frontier, border.

fronterizo, za, (fron·te·rē′so, sä) *adj.* frontier, border; opposite, on the other side *(que está en frente).*

frontis, (fron′tēs) *m.* face, facade.

frontispicio, (fron·tēs·pē′syo) *m.* frontispiece.

frontón, (fron·ton′) *m.* pelota court *(cancha);* court wall *(pared);* (arch.) pediment.

frotación, (fro·tä·syon′) or **frotadura,** (fro·tä·tū′rä) *f.* friction, rubbing.

frotar, (fro·tär′) *va.* to rub.

fructífero, ra, (frūk·tē′fe·ro, rä) *adj.* fruitful.

fructificar, (frūk·tē·fē·kär′) *vn.* to yield fruit.

fructosa, (frūk·to′sä) *f.* fructose.

fructuoso, sa, (fruk·two′so, sä) *adj.* fruitful.

frugal, (frū·gäl′) *adj.* frugal, sparing.

frugalidad, (frū·gä·lē·thäth′) *f.* frugality, parsimony.

fruición, (frwē·syon′) *f.* fruition.

fruncimiento (frūn·sē·myen′to) *m.* gathering, ruffling; (fig.) ruse, trick *(embuste).*

fruncir, (frūn·sēr′) *va.* to gather, to ruffle *(una tela); (fig.)* to press together *(recoger);* — **las cejas,** to knit one′s eyebrows, to frown; — **los labios,** to purse one′s lips; — **el ceño,** to frown.

fruslería, (frūz·le·rē′ä) *f.* trifle, mere nothing.

frustrar, (frūs·trär′) *va.* to frustrate, to thwart; to fail in the attempt of *(un delito);* —**se,** to miscarry, to fall through.

fruta, (frū′tä) *f.* fruit; — **del tiempo,** fruit in season; — **azucarada,** candied fruit.

frutal, (frū·täl′) *m.* fruit tree; —, *adj.* fruit-bearing.

frutería, (frū·te·rē′ä) *f.* fruit store.

frutero, ra, (frū·te′ro, rä) *adj.* fruit, holding fruit; —, *n.* fruit vendor; —, *m.* fruit dish; still life of fruit *(cuadro).*

fruto, (frū′to) *m.* fruit.

fuego, (fwe′go) *m.* fire; burning sensation

(picazón); dwelling *(hogar);* — **fatuo,** ignis fatuus, will-o′-the-wisp; —**s artificiales,** fireworks.

fuelle, (fwe′ye) *m.* bellows; (coll.) gossip, tale-bearer *(soplón).*

fuente, (fwen′te) *f.* fountain *(construcción);* source *(principio);* spring *(manantial);* platter *(plato).*

fuer, (fwer) *m.* **a — de,** by means of, by dint of.

fuera, (fwe′rä) *adv.* without, outside; — **de,** outside of; over and above *(además de);* — **de sí,** frantic, beside oneself; — **de alcance,** beyond reach; — **de ley,** lawless, outside the law; ¡—! *interj.* out of the way! make way!

fuero, (fwe′ro) *m.* jurisdiction; code *(de leyes);* special right, concession *(privilegio);* — **interior,** heart, innermost conscience; —**s,** *pl.* (coll.) arrogance, presumption.

fuerte, (fwer′te) *m.* small fortification; —, *adj.* strong; considerable *(grande);* —, *adv.* loud; hard (con fuerza).

fuerza, (fwer′sä) *f.* force; strength *(solidez);* power *(poderío);* **a — de,** by dint of; — **electromotriz,** electromotive force; — **mayor,** act of God; —**s,** *pl.* (mil.) forces.

fuete, (fwe′te) *m.* (Sp. Am.) horsewhip.

fuga, (fū′gä) *f.* flight; exuberance *(ardor);* leak, escape *(de un liquido); (mus.)* fugue.

fugarse, (fū·gär′se) *vr.* to escape, to flee.

fugaz, (fū·gäs′) *adj.* fleeting, momentary.

fugitivo, va, (fū·hē·tē′vo, va) *adj.* and *n.* fugitive.

fulano, na, (fū·lä′no, nä) *n.* so-and-so, what′s his (her) name; — **de tal,** John Doe, Jane Doe.

fulgor, (fūl·gor′) *m.* glow, brilliance, splendor.

fulgurante, (fūl·gū·rän′te) *adj.* resplendent, brilliant.

fulgurar, (fūl·gū·rär′) *vn.* to flash, to shine brilliantly.

fulminante, (fūl·mē·nän′te) *m.* percussion cap, primer; —, *adj.* fulminating *(amenazador);* explosive *(que estalla);* killing, that strikes dead.

fulminar, (fūl·mē·när′) *va.* to strike dead; to throw off *(arrojar)* ; (fig.) to thunder *(dictar);* —, *vn.* to fulminate.

fumada, (fū·mä′thä) *f.* puff.

fumadero, (fū·ma·the′ro) *m.* smoking room, smoker.

fumador, ra, (fū·mä·thor′, rä) *n.* smoker; —, *adj.* given to smoking.

fumar, (fū·mär′) *va.* and *vn.* to smoke.

m met, **n** not, **p** pot, **r** very, **rr** (none), **s** so, **t** toy, **th** with, **v** eve, **w** we, **y** yes, **z** zero

fumigación, (fū·mē·gâ·syon´) *f.* fumigation.
fumigador, (fū·mē·gâ·thor´) *m.* fumigator.
función, (fūn·syon´) *f.* function; (theat.) performance; (mil.) engagement.
funcional, (fūn·syo·nâl´) *adj.* functional.
funcionamiento, (fūn·syo·nâ·myen´to) *m.* performance, function, running.
funcionar, (fūn·syo·nâr´) *vn.* to function, to work, to run.
funcionario, (fūn·syo·nâ´ryo) *m.* official, functionary.
funda, (fūn´dâ) *f.* case, cover; slip cover *(de butaca);* **— de almohada,** pillowcase.
fundación, (fūn·dâ·syon´) *f.* foundation.
fundador, ra, (fūn·dâ·thor´, râ) *n.* founder.
fundamental, (fūn·dâ·men·tâl´) *adj.* fundamental.
fundamento, (fūn·dâ·men´to) *m.* foundation, base; seriousness, levelheadedness *(formalidad);* grounds *(motivo).*
fundar, (fūn·dâr´) *va.* to found, to establish.
fundición, (fūn·dē·syon´) *f.* melting, fusion; founding, casting; foundry *(fábrica);* (print.) font.
fundidor, (fūn·dē·thor´) *m.* foundryman, caster.
fundir, (fūn·dēr´) *va.* to found, to cast *(un objeto);* to fuse, to melt; **—se,** (fig.) to fuse, to join.
fúnebre, (fū´ne·vre) *adj.* funeral, funereal.
funeral, (fū·ne·râl´) *adj.* funereal; **—es,** *m. pl.* funeral.
funerario, ria, (fū·ne·râ´ryo, ryâ) *adj.* funeral, funereal; **—,** *f.* funeral parlor; **—,** *m.* undertaker.
funesto, ta, (fū·nes´to, tâ) *adj.* mournful, dismal; ill-fated, disastrous *(fatal).*
furgón, (fūr·gon´) *m.* (rail.) boxcar, freight-car; (auto.) trailer truck, van.
furia, (fū´ryâ) *f.* fury, rage; (fig.) haste *(prisa);* **a toda —,** with the utmost speed.
furioso, sa, (fū·ryo´so, sâ) *adj.* furious.
furor, (fū·ror´) *m.* fury.
furtivo, va, (fūr·tē´vo, vâ) *adj.* furtive, sly; **cazador —vo,** poacher.
fuselado, da, (fū·se·lâ´tho, thâ) *adj.* streamlined.
fuselaje, (fū·se·lâ´he) *m.* fuselage.
fusible, (fū·sē´vle) *m.* (elec.) fuse; **caja de —s,** fuse box.
fusil, (fū·sēl´) *m.* rifle.
fusilar, (fū·sē·lâr´) *va.* to shoot, to execute; (coll.) to plagiarize, to steal.
fusilazo, (fū·sē·lâ´so) *m.* rifle shot.
fusión, (fū·syon´) *f.* fusion; **temperatura de —,** melting point.
fuste, (fūs´te) *m.* shaft *(vara);* saddletree *(de la silla del caballo);* (fig.) importance, matter *(fundamento);* backbone, character *(nervio);* **hombre de —,** man of character, man of initiative.
fustigar, (fūs·tē·gâr´) *va.* to lash; (fig.) to rake over the coals *(criticar).*
fútbol, (fūt´bol) *m.* soccer; football *(de Estados Unidos).*
futbolista, (fūt·bo·lēs´tâ) *m.* football player; soccer player.
fútil, (fū´tēl) *adj.* useless, trifling, unimportant.
futilidad, (fū·tē·lē·thâth´) *f.* futility.
futurismo, (fū·tū·rēz´mo) *m.* futurism.
futuro, ra, (fū·tū´ro, râ) *adj.* and *m.* future; **en un — próximo,** in the near future.

G

g/: gramo, gr. gram; **giro,** draft.
gabacho, cha, (gâ·vâ´cho, châ) *n.* and *adj.* (coll.) Frenchie; **—,** *adj.* awkward *(desgarbado);* **—,** *m.* (coll.) French; Frenchified Spanish *(lleno de galicismos).*
gabán, (gâ·vân´) *m.* overcoat.
gabardina, (gâ·vâr·thē´nâ) *f.* gabardine *(tela);* trench coat *(abrigo).*
gabarra, (gâ·vá´rrâ) *f.* (naut.) lighter.
gabela, (gâ·ve´lâ) *f.* tax, duty.
gabinete, (gâ·vē·ne´te) *m.* (poi.) cabinet; study *(aposento);* exhibition hall, exhibit *(colección).*
gacela, (gâ·se´lâ) *f.* gazelle.
gaceta, (gâ·se´tâ) *f.* newspaper.
gacetero, (gâ·se·te´ro) *m.* newswriter, newspaper writer, journalist.
gacetilla, (gâ·se·tē´yâ) *f.* news in brief; short news item *(noticia);* (fig.) news hound.
gachas, (gâ´châs) *f. pl.* porridge, mush.

gacho, cha, (gä´cho, chä) *adj.* curved down, bent down.

gafa, (gä´fä) *f.* hook; —s, *pl.* spectacles, glasses.

gaguear, (gä·ge·är´) *vn.* (Sp. Am.) to stutter.

gaita, (gä´ē·tä) *f.* bagpipe.

gajes, (gä´hes) *m. pl.* salary, wages; — **del oficio,** bad part of a job, worries attached to a position.

gajo, (gä´ho) *m.* broken branch *(rama);* section *(de fruta);* spur *(de una cordillera).*

gala, (gä´lä) *f.* finery, elegant dress; grace, refinement *(garbo);* pride *(lo más selecto);* **hacer —,** to glory in.

galán, (gä·län´) *m.* gallant, suitor, swain *(novio);* dandy, swell; **primer —,** (theat.) leading man.

galano, na, (gä·lä´no, nä) *adj.* elegantly dressed; (fig.) elegant, polished *(gallardo).*

galante, (gä·län´te) *adj.* gallant; coquettish *(mujer).*

galanteador, (gä·län·te·ä·thor´) *adj.* attentive, courting; —, *m.* suitor, swain.

galantear, (gä·län·te·är´) *va.* to court, to woo.

galanteo, (gä·län·te´o) *m.* courtship, wooing.

galantería, (gä·län·te·rē´ä) *f.* gallantry, elegance *(elegancia);* liberality, generosity *(liberalidad).*

galápago, (gä·lä´pä·go) *m.* sea turtle; light saddle *(silla).*

galardón, (gä·lär·thon´) *m.* reward, recompense.

galeno, (gä·le´no) *m.* (coll.) doctor.

galeón, (gä·le·on´) *m.* (naut.) galleon.

galeote, (gä·le·o´te) *m.* galley slave.

galera, (gä·le´rä) *f.* (naut.) galley; covered wagon *(carro);* women´s prison *(cárcel);* (print.) galley.

galerada, (gä·le·rä´thä) *f.* (print.) galley proof; wagonload.

galería, (gä·le·rē´ä) *f.* gallery.

Gales, (gä´les) *m.* Wales.

galgo, (gäl´go) *m.* greyhound.

galicismo, (gä·lē·sēz´mo) *m.* Gallicism.

galimatías, (gä·lē·mä·tē´äs) *m.* (coll.) gobbledygook, gibberish.

galón, (gä·lon´) *m.* braid; gallon *(medida).*

galopar, (gä·lo·pär´) *vn.* to gallop.

galope, (gä·lo´pe) *m.* gallop; **a —,** in a hurry, in great haste.

galopear, (gä·lo·pe·är´) = **galopar.**

galladura, (gä·yä·thū´rä) *f.* tread.

gallardear, (gä·yär·the·är´) *vn.* to acquit oneself extremely well, to do a top-notch job.

gallardete, (gä·yär·the´te) *m.* pennant, streamer.

gallardía, (gä·yär·thē´ä) *f.* grace ease, effortlessness *(gracia);* resourcefulness, spirit *(ánimo).*

gallardo, da, (gä·yär´tho, thä) *adj.* graceful, elegant; spirited, resourceful; (fig.) splendid *(hermoso).*

gallego, ga, (gä·ye´go, gä) *n.* and *adj.* Galician.

galleta, (gä·ye´tä) *f.* hardtack, sea biscuit; cracker *(bizcocho seco).*

gallina, (gä·yē´nä) *f.* hen; — **ciega,** blindman´s bluff; —, *m.* and *f.* (coll.) chicken, coward.

gallinazo, (gä·yē·nä´so) *m.* (zool.) turkey buzzard.

gallinero, ra, (gä·yē·ne´ro, rä) *n.* poulterer; —, *m.* chicken coop; (theat.) peanut gallery; (coll.) bedlam, madhouse *(gritería).*

gallipavo, (gä·yē·pä´vo) *m.* (coll.) sour tone, false note.

gallito, (gä·yē´to) *m.* (fig.) smart aleck, cocky individual.

gallo, (gä´yo) *m.* cock; **misa de —,** midnight mass.

gama, (gä´mä) *f. (mus.)* gamut; (zool.) doe.

gamuza, (gä·mū´sä) *f.* chamois.

gana, (gä´nä) *f.* desire, wish; **tener —s de,** to feel like; **de buena —,** with pleasure, willingly, gladly; **de mala —,** unwillingly, with reluctance.

ganadería, (gä·nä·the·rē´ä) *f.* cattle raising *(cría);* stock cattle *(ganado).*

ganadero, ra, (gä·nä·the´ro, rä) *n.* cattle dealer, cattle raiser; —, *adj.* cattle, livestock.

ganado, (gä·nä´tho) *m.* cattle, livestock; **— de cerda,** swine; — **mayor,** bulls, cows, mules, and mares; — **menor,** sheep and goats.

ganador, ra, (gä·nä·thor´, rä) *n.* winner; earner; —, *adj.* winning; earning.

ganancia, (gä·nän´syä) *f.* gain, profit, earnings; — **líquida,** net profit; —**s y pérdidas,** profit and loss.

ganancioso, sa, (gä·nän·syo´so, sä) *adj.* gainful, winning *(que gana).*

ganar, (gä·när´) *va.* to earn; to win *(por lucha o casualidad);* to reach *(alcanzar);* to win over *(captar la voluntad);* to be ahead of *(aventajar);* to deserve, to earn *(merecer);* —, *vn.* to improve.

m met, **n** not, **p** pot, **r** very, **rr** (none), **s** so, **t** toy, **th** with, **v** eve, **w** we, **y** yes, **z** zero

gancho, (gan´cho) *m.* hook; wheedler, coaxer *(que solicita con maña);* charm, allure *(atractivo).*

gandul, la, (gân·dūl´, lâ) *n.* (coll.) idler, tramp, loafer.

ganga, (gâng´gâ) *f.* (orn.) European sand grouse; bargain; windfall *(ventaja inesperada).*

ganglio, (gâng´glyo) *m.* (anat.) ganglion.

gangoso, sa, (gâng·go´so, sâ) *adj.* snuffling, sniveling.

gangrena, (gâng·gre´nâ) *f.* gangrene.

gangrenarse, (gâng·gre·nâr´se) *vr.* to become gangrenous.

ganguear, (gang·ge·âr´) *vn.* to snuffle, to snivel.

ganoso, sa, (gâ·no´so, sâ) *adj.* desirous.

ganso, sa, (gân´so, sâ) *n.* goose; —, *m.* gander.

garabatear, (gâ·râ·vâ·te·âr´) *va.* to hook; to scrawl, to scribble *(garrapatear).*

garabato, (gâ·râ·vâ´to) *m.* hook, scrawl, scribbling; —s, *pl.* fidgeting of the hands.

garaje, (gâ·râ´he) *m.* garage.

garante, (ga·rân´te) *m.* guarantor.

garantía, (gâ·ran·tē´â) *f.* guarantee, pledge.

garantir*, (gâ·rân·tēr´) *va.* to guarantee.

garantizar, (gâ·rân·tē·sâr´) *va.* to guarantee.

garapiña, (gâ·râ·pē´nyâ) *f.* sugar-coating, icing, frosting.

garapiñado, da, (gâ·râ·pē·nyâ´tho, thâ) *adj.* candied, frosted, glace; **almendras —s,** sugar-coated almonds.

garbanzo, (gâr·vân´so) *m.* chick-pea.

garbo, (gâr´vo) *m.* gracefulness, elegance, grace; gallantry, generous nature *(desinterés).*

garboso, sa, (gâr·vo´so sâ) *adj.* sprightly, graceful, elegant; gallant, liberal, attentive *(generoso).*

gardenia, (gâr·the´nyâ) *f.* (bot.) gardenia.

gargajear, (gâr·gâ·he·âr´) *vn.* to spit, to clear one´s throat.

gargajo, (gâr·gâ´ho) *m.* phlegm, spittle.

garganta, (gâr·gân´tâ) *f.* throat; instep *(del pie);* neck *(de una botella);* narrows *(de un río);* narrow pass *(entre montañas).*

gárgara, (gâr´gâ·râ) *f.* gargle; **hacer —s,** to gargle.

gárgola, (gâr´go·lâ) *f.* gargoyle.

garita, (gâ·rē´tâ) *f.* sentry box; (rail.) lineman´s box; (auto.) cab.

garito, (gâ´·rē´to) *m.* gambling den.

garlito, (gâr·lē´to) *m.* fish net; (fig.) trap, snare.

garra, (gâ´rrâ) *f.* claws; (orn.) talons; **caer en las —s de,** to fall in the clutches of.

garrafa, (gâ·rrâ´fâ) *f.* decanter, carafe.

garrafón, (gâ·rrâ·fon´) *m.* demijohn, large water jar.

garrapata, (gâ·rrâ·pâ´tâ) *f.* (ent.) tick.

garrapato, (gâ·rrâ·pâ´to) *m.* scrawl, doodle.

garrocha, (gâ·rro´châ) *f.* goad.

garrote, (gâ·rro´te) *m.* cudgel, club *(palo);* garrote.

gárrulo, la, (gâ´rrū·lo, lâ) *adj.* (orn.) chirping, twittering; (fig.) babbling, murmuring.

garza, (gâr´sâ) *f.* heron.

garzo, (gâr´so) *m.* agaric; —, **za,** *adj.* bluish grey.

gas, (gâs) *m.* gas; **— lacrimógeno,** tear gas.

gasa, (ga´sâ) *f.* gauze, chiffon.

gaseoso, sa, (gâ·se·o´so, sâ) *adj.* gaseous; —, *f.* soft drink, soda water.

gasolina, (gâ·so·lē´nâ) *f.* gasoline; **tanque de —,** gasoline tank.

gasolinera, (gâ·so·lē·ne´râ) *f.* (naut.) motor launch; (auto.) gas station.

gastado, da, (gâs·tâ´tho, thâ) *adj.* wornout, tired out; worn down *(borrado);* used up, spent *(desgastado).*

gastador, ra, (gâs·tâ·thor´, râ) *n.* and *adj.* spendthrift; —, *m.* convict laborer; (mil.) sapper, pioneer.

gastar, (gâs·târ´) *va.* to spend *(el dinero);* to use up, to go through *(consumir);* to lay waste *(un territorio);* to waste *(echar a perder);* to have always *(tener habitualmente);* to use *(usar);* —las, (coll.) to behave, to act.

gasto, (gâs´to) *m.* expense, cost; waste; consumption.

gastrónomo, (gâs·tro´no·mo) *m.* gourmet, epicure.

gastrorrectomía, (gâs·tro·rrek·to·mē´â) *f.* gastrorectomy

gastrotomía, (gas·tro·to·mē´â) *f.* gastrostomy.

gata, (gâ´tâ) *f.* she-cat, tabby; **a —s,** on all fours.

gatear, (gâ·te·âr´) *vn.* to creep, to go on all fours *(andar a gatas);* to climb up, to clamber up *(trepar);* —, *va.* to scratch; (coll.) to snatch, to pilfer *(hurtar).*

gatillo, (gâ·tē´yo) *m.* pincers, tooth extractor; trigger *(del arma de fuego).*

gato, (gâ´to) *m.* cat, tomcat; car jack, lifting jack *(enganche);* hooking tong *(garfio);* (fig.) sneak thief *(ladrón);* — **montés,** wildcat.

gaucho, (gâ´ū·cho) *m.* Argentine cowboy.

gaveta, (gâ·ve´tâ) *f.* desk drawer.

gavia, (gâ´vyâ) *f.* (naut.) tops´l, topsail; drainage ditch *(zanja);* (orn.) sea gull.

gavilán, (gâ·vē·lân´) *m.* (orn.) sparrow hawk.

gaviota, (gâ·vyo´tâ) *f.* (orn.) gull, sea gull.

gavota, (gâ·vo´tâ) *f.* gavotte.

gazapo, (gâ·sâ´po) *m.* young rabbit *(conejo);* (fig.) sly fox, shrewd individual *(hombre taimado);* (coll.) slip, mistake *(error).*

gaznate, (gâz·nâ´te) *m.* throttle, windpipe.

géiser, (ge´ē·ser) *m.* geyser.

gelatina (he·lâ·tē´nâ) *f.* gelatine.

gema, (he´mâ) *f.* gem, precious stone.

gemelo, la, (he·me´lo, lâ) *n.* twin; **—s,** *m. pl.* cuff links *(juego de botones);* opera glasses *(de teatro);* binoculars *(prismáticos).*

gemido, (he·mē´tho) *m.* groan, moan, wail; **dar —s,** to groan.

gemir*,(he·mēr´) *vn.* to groan, to moan, to wail.

gen, (hen) *m.* gene.

gendarme, (hen·dâr´me) *m.* gendarme.

genealogía, (he·ne·â·lo·hē´â) *f.* genealogy.

generación, (he·ne·râ·syon´) *f.* generation.

generador, (he·ne·râ·thor´) *m.* generator.

general, (he·ne·râl´) *m.* general; **—,** *adj.* general, usual; **en —,** generally, in general; **por lo —,** as a rule; **cuartel —,** headquarters; **procurador —,** Attorney General.

generalidad, (he·ne·râ·lē·thâth´) *f.* generality.

generalísimo, (he·ne·râ·lē´sē·mo) *m.* generalissimo.

generalizar, (he·ne·râ·lē·sâr´) *va.* to generalize; to spread, to make common *(hacer público).*

genérico, ca, (he·ne´rē·ko, kâ) *adj.* generic.

género, (he´ne·ro) *m.* (biol.) genus; kind, sort *(clase);* (gram.) gender; — **humano,** mankind; **—s,** *pl.* goods, commodities.

generosidad, (he·ne·ro·sē·thâth´) *f.* generosity.

generoso, sa, (he·ne·ro´so, sâ) *adj.* generous.

Génesis, (he´ne·sēs) *m.* Genesis; **g—,** *f.* genesis, origin.

genética, (he·ne´tē·kâ) *f.* genetics.

genial, (he·nyâl´).*adj.* genial, cheerful *(agradable);* outstanding, inspired *(sobresaliente).*

genio, (he´nyo) *m.* sort, kind *(indole);* temper, disposition *(inclinación);* genius *(talento).*

genital, (he·nē·tâl´) *adj.* genital.

genocidio, (he·no·sē´thyo) *m.* genocide.

gente, (hen´te) *f.* people; — **bien,** well-to do; — **menuda,** children, young fry; — **de trato,** tradespeople; **ser buena —,** (Sp. Am.) to be likable, to be nice.

gentecilla, (hen´te·sē´yâ) *f.* mob, rabble.

gentil, (hen·tēl´) *m.* and *f.* and *adj.* pagan; **—,** *adj.* refined, genteel *(gracioso);* obvious, evident *(notable).*

gentileza, (hen·tē·le´sâ) *f.* gentility, elegance; kindness *(amabilidad).*

gentilhombre, (hen·tē·lom´bre) *m.* gentleman.

gentilicio, cia, (hen·tē·lē´syo, syâ) *adj.* national; family *(perteneciente al linaje).*

gentío, (hen·tē´o) *m.* crowd, multitude.

gentuza, (hen·tū´sâ) *f.* rabble, mob.

genuino, na, (he·nwē´no, nâ) *adj.* genuine, pure.

geodésico, ca, (he·o·the´sē·ko, kâ) *adj.* geodesic; **cúpula —,** geodesic dome.

geofísico, ca, (he·o·fē´sē·ko, kâ) *adj.* geophysical; **año —,** geophysical year.

geofísica, (he·o·fē´sē·kâ) *f.* geophysics.

geografía, (he·o·grâ·fē´â) *f.* geography.

geográfico ca, (he·o·grâ´fē·ko, kâ) *adj.* geographical.

geógrafo, (he·o´grâ·fo) *m.* geographer.

geología, (he·o·lo·hē´â) *f.* geology.

geólogo, (he·o´lo·go) *m.* geologist.

geometría, (he·o·me·trē´â) *f.* geometry; — **del espacio,** solid geometry; — **plana,** plane geometry.

geométrico, ca, (he·o·me´trē·ko, kâ) *adj.* geometrical, geometric.

geranio, (he·râ´nyo) *m.* (bot.) geranium.

gerencia, (he·ren´syâ) *f.* management, administration.

gerente, (he·ren´te) *m.* manager.

geriatría, (he·ryâ·trē´â) *f.* geriatrics.

germen, (her´men) *m.* germ; origin, source *(principio).*

germicida, (her·mē·sē´thâ) *adj.* germicidal.

germinación, (her·mē·nâ·syon´) *f.* germination.

germinar, (her·mē·nâr´) *vn.* to germinate.

gerundio, (he·rūn´dyo) *m.* (gram.) present participle.

gestación, (hes·tâ·syon´) *f.* gestation.

gesticular, (hes·tē·kū·lâr´) *vn.* to gesticulate.

gestión, (hes·tyon´) *f.* management; effort, measure *(diligencia).*

gestionar, (hes·tyo·nâr ´) *va.* to carry out, to implement.

gesto, (hes´to) *m.* face *(semblante)* look, expression *(expresión);* movement, gesture *(ademán).*

gestor, ra, (hes·tor´, râ) *adj.* managing; **socio —,** active partner; **—,** *m.* manager.

giba, (hē´vâ) *f.* hump, hunch; (coll.) annoyance, bother.

giganta, (hē·gân´tâ) *f.* giantess.

gigante, (hē·gân´te) *m.* giant; **—,** *adj.* gigantic.

gigantesco, ca, (hē·gân·tes´ko, kâ) *adj.* gigantic huge.

gigote, (hē·go´te) *m.* hash.

gimnasia, (hēm·nâ´syâ) *f.* gymnastics.

gimnasio, (hēm·nâ´syo) *m.* gymnasium.

gimnasta, (hēm·nâs´tâ) *m.* and *f.* gymnast.

gimnástica, (hēm·nâs´tē·kâ) *f.* gymnastics.

gimnástico, ca, (hēm·nâs´tē·ko, kâ) *adj.* gymnastic.

gimotear, (hē·mo·te·âr´) *vn.* (coll.) to whine.

ginebra, (hē·ne´vrâ) *f.* gin; (fig.) confusion, bedlam *(confusión).*

ginecología, (hē·ne·ko·lo·hē´â) *f.* (med.) gynecology.

ginecólogo, (hē·ne·ko´lo·go) *m.* gynecologist.

gingivitis, (hēn·hē·vē´tēs) *f.* (med.) gingivitis.

gira (hē´râ) = **jira.**

girado, (hē·râ´tho) *m.* drawee (of a draft).

girador, (hē·râ·thor´) *m.* drawer (of a draft).

girafa, (hē·râ´fâ) *f.* giraffe.

girar, (hē·râr´) *vn.* to rotate, to revolve; to turn, to revolve *(desarrollarse);* to turn *(desviarse);* **—,** *va.* (com.) to draw; **— contra,** to draw on.

girasol, (hē·râ·sol´) *m.* sunflower.

giratorio, ria, (hē·râ·to´ryo, ryâ) *adj.* rotating, revolving; **silla —,** swivel chair.

giro, (hē´ro) *m.* rotation, rovolution; turn, tack *(de un asunto);* (com.) draft; **— a la vista,** sight draft; **— postal,** money order.

gitanesco, ca, (hē·tâ·nes´ko, kâ) *adj.* gypsylike.

gitano, na, (hē·tâ´no, nâ) *n.* gypsy; **—,**

adj. fawning, sly, tricky.

glacial, (glâ´syâl) *adj.* glacial.

glaciar, (glâ·syâr´) *m.* glacier.

gladiador, (glâ·thyâ·thor´) or **gladiator,** (glâ·thyâ·tor´) *m.* gladiator.

gladiolo, (glâ·thē´o·lo) or **gladiolo,** (glâ·thyo´lo) *m.* (bot.) gladiolus, gladiola.

glándula, (glân´dū·lâ) *f.* gland.

glanduloso, sa, (glân·dū·lo´so, sâ) *adj.* glandulous.

glaucoma, (glâū·ko´mâ) *f.* (med.) glaucoma.

glicerina, (glē·se·rē´nâ) *f.* glycerine.

glicina, (glē·sē´nâ) *f.* (bot.) wisteria.

global, (glo·vâl´) *adj.* total, lump, allinclusive.

globalización, (glo·vâ·lē·sâ·syon´), *f.* globalization.

globo, (glo´vo) *m.* globe, sphere; **en —,** as a whole, in a lump sum; **— aerostático,** (avi.) balloon; **— de barrera,** barrage balloon; **— del ojo,** eyeball.

globulina gamma, (glo·vū·lē´nâ gâm´mâ) *f.* (med.) gamma globulin.

glóbulo, (glo´vū·lo) *m.* globule; **—s rojos,** red blood corpuscles; **—s blancos,** white blood corpuscles.

gloria, (glo´ryâ) *f.* glory; **saber a —,** to taste delicious; **oler a —,** to smell delightful.

gloriarse, (glo·ryâr´se) *vr.* to glory, to take delight.

glorieta, (glo·rye´tâ) *f.* bower, arbor; circle *(en una encrucijada).*

glorificación, (glo·rē·fē·kâ·syon´) *f.* glorification.

glorificar, (glo·rē·fē·kâr´) *va.* to glorify; **— se,** to boast, to vaunt.

glorioso, sa, (glo·ryo´so, sâ) *adj.* glorious.

glosa, (glo´sâ) *f.* gloss, commentary.

glosar, (glo·sâr´) *va.* to gloss, to comment on; (fig.) to find fault with.

glosario, (glo·sâ´ryo) *m.* glossary.

glotón, ona, (glo·ton´, o´nâ) *n.* glutton; **—,** *adj.* gluttonous.

glotonería, (glo·to·ne·rē´â) *f.* gluttony.

glucosa, (glū·ko´sâ) *f.* glucose.

gluten, (glū´ten) *m.* gluten.

glutinoso, sa, (glū·tē·no´so, sâ) *adj.* glutinous, viscous.

gnomo, (no´mo) *m.* gnome.

gobernación, (go·ver·nâ·syon´) *f.* government, governing.

gobernador, ra, (go·ver·nâ·thor´, râ) *adj.* governing; **—,** *m.* governor; **—,** *f.* governor's wife.

gobernante, (go·ver·nân´te) *m.* governor;

(coll.) self-appointed authority; —, adj. governing.

gobernar*, (go·ver·när´) va. to govern; to guide, to direct (guiar); (naut.) to steer; —, vn. to steer.

gobierno, (go·vyer´no) m. government; direction; (naut.) helm.

goce, (go´se) m. enjoyment, possession.

gol, (gol) m. goal.

goleta, (go·le´tä) f. schooner.

golf, (golf) m. golf; **campo de** —, golf course, links.

golfo, (gol´fo) m. gulf.

golilla, (go·lē´yä) f. ruff; (mech.) sleeve, flange.

golondrina, (go·lon·drē´nä) f. (orn.) swallow.

golosina, (go·lo·sē´nä) f. tidbit, delicacy; (fig.) frill, trifle (chuchería).

goloso, sa, (go·lo´so, sä) adj. gluttonous.

golpe, (gol´pe) m. blow; large quantity (copia); beat (del corazón); flap (del bolsillo); blow, calamity (desgracia); shock, surprise (admiración): **de** —, all at once; **— de estado**, coup d´état; **— de mar**, heavy surge, strong wave; **— de gracia**, death blow.

golpear, (gol·pe·är´) va. to beat, to hit.

goma, (go´mä) f. gum, rubber; **— de mascar**, chewing gum; **— laca**, shellac; **— vulcanizada**, ebonite, hard rubber; **— para borrar**, eraser; **— para pegar**, mucilage.

gomorresina, (go·mo·rre·sē´nä) f. gum resin.

gomoso, sa, (go·mo´so, sä) adj. gummy.

góndola, (gon´do·lä) f. gondola.

gonorrea, (go·no·rre´ä) f. gonorrhea.

gordiflón, ona, (gor·thē·flon´, o´nä) adj. (coll.) pudgy, roly-poly.

gordo, da (gor´tho, thä) adj. fat; stocky (muy abultado).

gordura, (gor·thū´rä) f. grease (grasa); fatness (corpulencia).

gorgojo, (gor·go´ho) m. grub, weevil.

gorila, (go·rē´lä) m. (zool.) gorilla.

gorjear, (gor·he·är´) vn. to warble, to trill.

gorjeo, (gor·he´o) m. trilling, warbling.

gorra, (go´rrä) f. cap; **de** —, (coll.) at others´ expense, by sponging.

gorrión, (go·rryon´) m. sparrow.

gorrista, (go·rrēs´tä) m. and f. parasite, sponger, cadger.

gorro, (go´rro) m. cap.

gorrón, ona, (go·rron´, o´nä) n. sponger, parasite; —, adj. sponging, parasitic, cadging.

gorronear, (go·rro·ne·är´) vn. to sponge,

to cadge.

gota, (go´tä) f. drop; (med.) gout.

gotear, (go·te·är´) vn. to drip; to trickle.

goteo, (go·te´o) m. dripping, trickling; **a prueba de** —, leakproof.

gotera, (go·te´rä) f. leak (hendedura); dripping water; water stains (señal).

gozar, (go·sär´) va. to enjoy; **— de**, to possess; **—se**, to enjoy, to have fun.

gozne, (goz´ne) m. hinge.

gozo, (go´so) m. joy, pleasure, delight.

gozoso, sa, (go·so´so, sä) adj. joyful, cheerful.

gr.: **gramo**, gr. gram.

grabación, (grä·vä·syon´) f. recording, cutting; **— en cinta**, tape recording.

grabado, (grä·vä´tho) m. engraving; print, picture (estampa); **— al agua fuerte**, etching.

grabador, (grä·vä·thor´) m. engraver; recorder (de discos).

grabadora, (grä·vä·tho´rä) f. tape recorder.

grabar, (grä·vär´) va. to engrave; to record, to cut (un disco); (fig.) to etch, to impress; **— al agua fuerte**, to etch.

gracia, (grä´syä) f. grace (garbo); boon (beneficio); pardon (perdón); witty remark (chiste); name (nombre); **hacer** —, to amuse, to strike as funny; **tener** —, to be amusing; **—s**, pl. thanks; **dar —s**, to thank.

gracioso, sa, (grä·syo´so, sä) adj. graceful, charming (garboso); funny, witty; gratuitous (gratuito); —, n. comic.

grada, (grä´thä) f. step (peldaño); row, tier (de anfiteatro); (agr.) harrow; **—s**, pl. steps.

grado, (grä´tho) m. degree; grade (sección de escuela); step (grada).

graduación, (grä·thwä·syon´) f. graduation; (mil.) rank, grade.

graduado, da, (grä·thwä´tho, thä) n. graduate, alumnus; —, adj. graduated.

gradual, (gra·thwäl´) adj. gradual.

graduar, (grä·thwär´) va. to graduate; to classify (clasificar); **—se**, to graduate, to be graduated.

gráfico, ca, (grä´fē·ko, kä) adj. graphic; —, m. (math.) graph; —, f. scale, graph.

grama, (grä´mä) f. Bermuda grass.

gramática, (grä·mä´tē·kä) f. grammar.

gramatical, (grä·mä·tē·käl´) adj. grammatical.

gramático, (grä·mä´tē·ko) m. grammarian.

gramo, (grä´mo) m. gram.

gramófono, (grä·mo´fo·no) m. phono-

m met, **n** not, **p** pot, **r** very, **rr** (none), **s** so, **t** toy, **th** with, **v** eve, **w** we, **y** yes, **z** zero

graph.

gran, (gran) *adj.* apocope of **grande,** great; large, big,

grana, (grä´nâ) *f.* seeding; cochineal *(cochinilla);* kermes *(quermes);* red fabric *(tela).*

granada, (grâ·nâ´thâ) *f.* (mil.) grenade; pomegranate; **— de metralla,** shrapnel.

granadero (grâ·nâ·the´ro) *m.* (mil.) grenadier.

granadilla, (grâ·nâ·thẽ´yâ) *f.* passion flower; passion fruit *(fruto).*

granadino, na, (grâ·nâ·thẽ´no, nâ) *adj.* of Granada.

granado, da, (grâ·nâ´tho, thâ) *adj.* select, illustrious; experienced, mature *(experto);* —, *m.* pomegranate tree.

granar, (grâ·nâr´) *vn.* to go to seed, to seed.

granate, (grâ·nâ´te) *m.* garnet.

Gran Bretaña, (grâm·bre·tâ´nyâ) *f.* Great Britain.

grande, (grân´de) *adj.* large, big; great *(notable);* —, *m.* grandee.

grandeza, (gran·de´sâ) *f.* largeness, large size; grandeur *(nobleza);* vastness *(magnitud).*

grandiosidad, (grân·dyo·sẽ·thâth´) *f.* splendor, magnificence.

grandioso, sa, (grân·dyo´so, sâ) *adj.* magnificent, splendid.

granel, (grâ·nel´) *m.* **a —,** in bulk, loose.

granero, (grâ·ne´ro) *m.* granary.

granito, (grâ·nẽ´to) *m.* granite.

granizada, (grâ·nẽ·sâ´thâ) *f.* hailstorm; (fig.) downpour, torrent.

granizar, (grâ·nẽ·sâr´) *vn.* to hail.

granizo, (grâ·nẽ´so) *m.* hail.

granja, (grân´hâ) *f.* grange, farm; country home *(quinta de recreo);* **— modelo,** model farm.

granjear, (grân·he·âr´) *va.* to earn; to win *(la voluntad).*

grano, (grâ´no) *m.* grain; (med.) pimple; **ir al —,** to get to the point.

granuja, (grâ·nũ´hâ) *f.* loose grape; —, *m.* (coll.) urchin, rascal.

grapa, (grâ´pâ) *f.* staple.

grapador, (grâ·pâ·thor´) *m.* stapler.

grasa, (grâ´sâ) *f.* fat; grease *(manteca);* dirt *(mugre);* **— de ballena,** whale blubber.

grasiento, ta, (grâ·syen´to, tâ) *adj.* greasy.

gratificación, (grâ·tẽ·fẽ·kâ·syon´) *f.* gratification; bonus *(de servicio extraordinario);* gratuity *(propina).*

gratificar, (grâ·tẽ·fẽ·kâr´) *va.* to reward, to recompense *(recompensar);* to gratify,

to please *(agradar).*

gratis, (grâ´tēs) *adv.* gratis, free.

gratitud, (grâ·tē·tũth´) *f.* gratitude, gratefulness.

grato, ta, (grâ´to, tâ) *adj.* pleasant, pleasing; **me es —to,** I have the pleasure of, I am pleased to; **su —ta,** (com.) your letter.

gratuito, ta, (grâ·twē´to, tâ) *adj.* gratuitous; unwarranted *(arbitrario).*

gravamen, (grâ·vâ´men) *m.* burden, obligation *(obligación);* lien, encumbrance *(sobre un inmueble).*

gravar, (grâ·vâr´) *va.* to burden, to oppress; to encumber *(un inmueble).*

grave, (grâ´ve) *adj.* heavy; grave *(serio);* weighty *(importante);* (gram.) grave; very sick *(enfermo).*

gravedad, (grâ·ve·thâth´) *f.* gravity; seriousness *(importancia);* **fuerza de —,** force of gravity; **ausencia de —,** weightlessness.

grávido, da, (grâ´vē·tho, thâ) *adj.* filled, laden; pregnant *(encinta);* **en estado —,** in the family way.

gravitación, (grâ·vē·tâ·syon´) *f.* gravitation.

gravitar, (grâ·vē·târ´) *vn.* to gravitate.

graznar, (grâz·nâr´) *vn.* to cackle, to caw.

graznido, (grâz·nẽ´tho) *m.* cawing, cackling.

Grecia, (gre´syâ) *f.* Greece.

greda, (gre´thâ) *f.* fuller´s earth.

gremio, (gre´myo) *m.* guild, union, society.

greña, (gre´nyâ) *f.* matted hair, snarled hair; (fig.) tangle, snarl *(maraña).*

greñudo, da, (gre·nyũ´tho, thâ) *adj.* with one´s hair in snarls.

gresca, (gres´kâ) *f.* clatter, confusion *(jaleo);* wrangle, quarrel *(riña).*

grey, (gre´ē) *f.* flock.

griego, ga, (grye´go, gâ) *n.* and *adj.* Greek.

grieta, (grye´tâ) *f.* crack, chink.

grifo, fa, (grē´fo, fâ) *adj.* kinky, curly; —, *m.* griffin; faucet *(llave).*

grillo, (grē´yo) *m.* cricket; **—s,** *pl.* fetters, irons.

gringo, ga, (gring´go, gâ) *n.* (Sp. Am.) Yankee; Limey *(inglés).*

gripe, (grē´pe) *f.* grippe.

gris, (grēs) *adj.* gray; —, *m.* (coll.) cold, sharp wind.

gritar, (grē·târ´) *vn.* to cry out, to shout, to scream.

gritería, (grē·te·rē´â) *f.* shouting, screaming, hubbub.

grito, (grē´to) *m.* shout, outcry, scream.

gro, (gro) *m.* grosgrain.

Groenlandia, (gro·en·lân′dyâ) *f.* Greenland.

grosella, (gro·se′yâ) *f.* currant.

grosería, (gro·se·rē′â) *f.* coarseness, illbreeding.

grosero, ra, (gro·se′ro, râ) *adj.* coarse, rude, unpolished.

grotesco, ca, (gro·tes′ko, kâ) *adj.* grotesque.

grúa, (grū′â) *f.* crane, derrick; **— de pórtico,** (avi) gantry tower.

gruesa, (grwe′sa) *f.* gross.

grueso, sa, (grwe′so, sâ) *adj.* thick; large *(abultado);* dense *(de entendimiento);* **—,** *m.* heaviness; thickness *(espesor).*

grulla, (grū′yâ) *f.* (orn.) crane.

grumoso, sa, (grū·mo′so, sâ) *adj.* clotted, curdled.

gruñido, (grū·nye′tho) *m.* grunt; grumble; creak.

gruñidor, ra, (grū·nyē·thor′, râ) *adj.* grumbling, complaining.

gruñir*, (grū·nyēr′) *vn.* to grunt; to grumble *(murmurar);* to creak *(chirriar).*

grupa, (grū′pâ) *f.* rump, croup.

grupo, (grū′po) *m.* group.

gruta, (grū′tâ) *f.* grotto.

gsa.: gruesa, gro. gross.

gte.: gerente, mgr. manager.

guacamayo, ya, (gwâ·ka·mâ′yo, yâ) *n.* macaw.

guachinango, (gwâ·chē·nâng′go) *m.* (ichth). red snapper.

guadaña, (gwâ·thá′nyâ) *f.* scythe.

guadañero, (gwa·thâ·nye′ro) *m.* mower.

guajolote, (gwâ·ho·lo′te) *m.* (Mex.) turkey.

gualdrapa, (gwâl·drâ′pâ) *f.* trappings; (coll.) tatter, rag *(calandrajo).*

guanaco, (gwâ·nâ′ko) *m.* (zool.) guanaco.

guano, (gwâ′no) *m.* guano.

guante, (gwân′te) *m.* glove; **—s,** *pl.* tip.

guapo, pa, (gwâ′po, pâ) *adj.* good-looking, handsome *(bien parecido);* stouthearted, brave *(valiente);* showy *(ostentoso);* **—,** *m.* bully, tough guy; beau, gallant *(galán).*

guarapo, (gwâ·râ′po) *m.* sugar-cane juice.

guarda, (gwâr′thâ) *m.* and *f.* custodian; **—,** *f.* custody, care; endpaper *(de libro).*

guardabarreras, (gwâr·thâ·vâ·rre′râs) *m.* (rail.) lineman.

guardabosque, (gwâr·thâ·vos′ke) *m.* forest ranger.

guardabrisa, (gwâr·thâ·vrē′sâ) *m.* windshield.

guardacostas, (gwâr·thâ·kos′tâs) *m.* coast guard cutter.

guardaespaldas, (gwâr·thâ·es·pâl′dâs) *m.* bodyguard.

guardafango, (gwâr·thâ·fâng′go) *m.* mudguard, fender.

guardafrenos, (gwâr·thâ·fre′nos) *m.* brakeman.

guardafuego, (gwâr·thâ·fwe′go) *m.* fender, fire screen.

guardagujas, (guâr·thâ·gū′hâs) *m.* (rail.) switchman.

guardalmacén, (gwâr·thâl·mâ·sen′) *m.* warehouseman.

guardapelo, (gwâr·thâ ·pe′lo) *m.* locket.

guardapolvo, (gwâr·thâ·pol′vo) *m.* dust cover *(cubierta);* duster, smock *(vestido).*

guardar, (gwâr·thâr′) *va.* to keep; to guard *(vigilar);* to protect *(preservar de daño);* **—se,** to avoid *(evitar);* to protect oneself *(preservarse);* **— rencor,** to hold a grudge.

guardarropa, (gwâr·thâ·rro′pâ) *m.* wardrobe; checkroom *(en local público),* **—,** *f* (theat.) wardrobe mistress; check girl.

guardarropía, (gwâr·thâ·rro·pē′â) *f.* (theat.) wardrobe, costumes.

guardasellos, (gwâr·thâ ·se′yos) *m.* keeper of the seal.

guardavía, (gwâr·thâ·vē′â) *m.* (rail.) lineman.

guardavidas, (gwâr·thâ·vē′thâs) *m.* lifeguard.

guardería, (guar·the·rē′â) *f.* day nursery.

guardia, (guâr′thyâ) *f.* guard; keeping, care *(custodia);* (naut.) watch; **—,** *m.* guardsman; **— civil,** national guardsman.

guardián, ana, (gwâr·thyân′, â′nâ) *n.* keeper, guardian.

guardilla, (gwâr·thē′yâ) *f.* garret.

guarida, (gwâ·rē′thâ) *f.* den, lair; refuge, shelter *(amparo).*

guarismo, (gwa·rēz′mo) *m.* cipher, number.

guarnecer*, (gwâr·ne·ser′) *va.* to set *(engastar);* to garnish, to decorate *(adornar);* (mil.) to garrison; to provide, to supply *(suministrar).*

guarnición, (gwâr·nē·syon′) *f.* setting; decoration, garnishment; (mil.) garrison.

guasa, (gwâ′sâ) *f.* (ichth.) jewfish; (coll.) stupidity, dullness *(pesadez);* fun, jest *(broma).*

guasón, ona, (gwâ·son′, o′na) *adj.* (coll.) dull, boring *(soso);* humorous, witty, sharp, fond of jokes *(bromista);* **—,** *n.* joker.

guatemalteco, ca, (gwâ·te·mâl·te′ko, kâ) *n.* and *adj.* Guatemalan.

guayaba, (gwâ·yâ′vâ) *f.* guava.

---

m met, **n** not, **p** pot, **r** very, **rr** (none), **s** so, **t** toy, **th** with, **v** eve, **w** we, **y** yes, **z** zero

guayabo, (gwâ·yä´vo) *m.* guava tree.

gubernamental, (gü·ver·na·men·täl´) *adj.* governmental.

gubernativo, va, (gü·ver·nä·tē´vo, vä) *adj.* governmental.

guedeja, (ge·the´hä) *f.* long hair; mane *(de león).*

güero, ra, (gwe´ro, rä) *adj.* (Mex.) blond, fair-haired; —, *n.* towhead; light-skinned.

guerra, (ge´rrä) *f.* war; hostility *(discordia);* —fría, cold war; — nuclear, nuclear war; — química, chemical warfare; — relámpago, blitzkrieg; — de escaramuzas, brushfire war; — de guerrillas, guerrilla warfare; hacer la —, to wage war; dar —, to cause trouble, to be a nuisance.

guerrear, (ge·rre·är´) *vn.* to war, to wage war.

guerrero, (ge·rre´ro) *m.* warrior; —, ra, *adj.* martial, warlike.

guerrilla, (ge·rre´yä) *f.* guerilla warfare; guerrilla party *(partida).*

guía, (gē´ä) *m.* and *f.* guide; —, *m.* guide; —, *f.* guide; guidebook *(libro).*

guiar, (gyär) *va.* to guide, to lead; (auto.) to drive.

guijarro, (gē·hä´rro) *m.* cobblestone.

Guillermo, (gē·yer´mo) *m.* William.

guillotina, (gē·yo·tē´nä) *f.* guillotine.

guinda, (gēn´dä) *f.* sour cherry.

guindar, (gēn·där´) *va.* to hang.

guindola, (gēn·do´lä) *f.* (naut.) life buoy.

guinda, (gēng´dä) *f.* gingham.

guiñada, (gē·nyä´thä) *f.* wink; (naut.) yaw.

guiñapo, (gē·nyä´po) *m.* tatter, rag.

guiñar, (gē·nyär´) *va.* to wink; (naut.) to yaw.

guión, (gyon) *m.* banner, standard; (fig.)

leader *(guía);* outline *(escrito breve);* script *(argumento);* (gram.) hyphen.

guirnalda, (gēr·näl´dä) *f.* garland, wreath.

güiro, (gwē´ro) *m.* bottle gourd.

guisa, (gē´sä) *f.* manner, fashion; a — de, in the manner of, like.

guisado, (gē·sä´tho) *m.* meat stew *(de carne);* stew.

guisante, (gē·sän´te) *m.* (bot.) pea.

guisar, (gē·sär´) *va.* to cook, to stew; (fig.) to prepare, to ready *(aderezar).*

guiso, (gē´so) *m.* stewed dish, stew.

guitarra, (gē·tä´rrä) *f.* guitar.

guitarrero, ra, (gē·tä·rre´ro, rä) *n.* guitar maker; guitar dealer *(vendedor).*

guitarrista, (gē·tä·rrēs´tä) *m.* and *f.* guitar player.

gula, (gü´lä) *f.* gluttony.

gusano, (gü·sä´no) *m.* worm; — de luz, glowworm, — de seda, silkworm.

gusarapo, (gü·sa·rä´po) *m.* waterworm.

gustación, (güs·tä·syon´) *f.* tasting.

gustar, (güs·tär´) *va.* to taste; —, *vn.* to be pleasing, to be enjoyable; — de, to have a liking for, to take pleasure in.

gusto, (güs´to) *m.* taste; pleasure, delight *(placer);* decision, choice *(voluntad);* a —, to one's liking, however one wishes; tener — en, to be glad to; tanto —, glad to meet you.

gustosamente, (güs·to·sä·men´te) *adv.* tastefully *(con garbo);* gladly, willingly *(de buena gana).*

gustoso, sa, (güs·to´so, sä) *adj.* tasty *(sabroso);* glad, happy.

gutagamba, (gü·tä·gäm´bä) *f.* gamboge.

gutapercha, (gü·tä·per´chä) *f.* gutta-percha.

gutural, (gü·tü·räl´) *adj.* guttural.

H

h.: habitantes, *pop.* population.

haba, (ä´vä) *f.* (bot.) broad bean.

Habana, (ä·vä´nä) *f.* Havana.

habanero, ra, (ä·vä·ne´ro, rä) *n.* and *adj.* Havanan; —, *f.* habanera.

habano, (ä·vä´no) *m.* Havana cigar.

haber*, (ä·ver´) *va.* to get hold of; —, *v.* auxiliary to have; —, *vn.* there to be; va a —, there is going to be; — de to have to; —, *m.* (com.) credit side; —es, *pl.* property, goods; hay, there is, there are.

habichuela, (ä·vē·chwe´lä) *f.* kidney bean; — verde, string bean.

hábil, (ä´vēl) *adj.* capable, qualified *(capaz);* skillful, clever *(ingenioso).*

habilidad, (ä·vē·lē·thäth´) *f.* qualification, capacity; aptitude, skillfulness, ability.

habilitación, (ä·vē·lē·tä·syon´) *f.* qualification.

habilitado, da, (ä·vē·lē·tä´tho, thä) *adj.* qualified; —, *m.* paymaster.

habilitar, (ä·vē·lē·tär´) *va.* to qualify, to

enable; to equip, to furnish *(proveer)*.

habitación, (â·vē·tâ·syon´) *f.* dwelling, residence *(domicilio);* room *(aposento);* (zool.) habitat.

habitante, (â·vē·tân´te) *m.* and *f.* inhabitant.

habitar, (â·vē·târ´) *va.* to inhabit, to live in.

hábito, (a´vē·to) *m.* dress *(vestido);* custom, habit *(costumbre).*

habitual, (â·vē·twâl´) *adj.* habitual, customary, usual.

habituar, (â·vē·twâr´) *va.* to accustom; — **se,** to accustom oneself, to get used.

habla, (á´vlâ) *f.* speech; **sin** —, speechless.

hablador, ra, (â·vlâ·thor´, râ) *n.* chatterbox *(parlanchín);* gossip *(murmurador);* —, *adj.* talkative; gossipy.

habladuría, (â·vlâ·thü·rē´â) *f.* sarcasm; gossip, chatter *(murmuración).*

hablanchín, china, (â·vlân·chēn´, chē´nâ) *adj.* (coll.) talkative; gossipy.

hablar, (a·vlâr´) *vn.* to talk; to speak *(conversar);* —, *va.* to say *(decir);* to speak *(un idioma).*

hablilla, (â·vlē´yâ) *f.* rumor, gossip.

hacedero, ra, (a·se·the´ro, râ) *adj.* feasible, practicable.

hacedor, ra, (â·se·thor´, râ) *n.* maker, creator; manager *(de una hacienda).*

hacendado, (â ·sen·dâ´tho) *m.* landowner, property owner; (Sp. Am.) rancher; —, **da,** *adj.* landed.

hacendoso, sa, (a·sen·do´so, sâ) *adj.* domestic, good around the house.

hacer*, (â·ser´) *va.* to make *(crear);* to work *(obrar);* to make up *(arreglar);* to contain *(contener);* to get used *(acostumbrar);* to do *(ocuparse en);* to make *(obligar);* to play *(aparentar);* —, *vn.* to matter; — **alarde,** to boast; — **alto,** to halt; — **burla,** to poke fun at; — **calor,** to be warm; — **caso de,** to pay attention to — **daño,** to hurt; — **de,** to act as; — **falta,** to be lacking; — **frío,** to be cold; — **fuego,** (mil.) to open fire; — **la prueba,** to try out; — **muecas,** to make faces; — **un papel,** to play a role; — **presente,** to notify; — **saber,** to inform; **hace poco,** a short time ago; —**se,** to become.

hacia, (á´syâ) *prep.* toward; about *(cerca de);* — **acá,** this way, over here; — **atrás,** backward; — **abajo,** down, downward; — **arriba,** up, upward.

hacienda, (â·syen´dâ) *f.* holdings, possessions *(fortuna);* farm, country place *(finca).*

hacinar, (â·sē·nâr´) *va.* to stack up, to pile

up.

hacha, (á´châ) *f.* ax *(herramienta);* torch *(tea de esparto).*

hachero, (â·che´ro) *m.* torch stand; (mil.) pioneer; woodcutter, lumberjack *(leñador).*

hada, (á´thâ) *f.* fairy; **cuento de** —**s,** fairy tale.

hado, (á´tho) *m.* fate, destiny.

haitiano, na, (âē·tyâ´no, nâ) *n.* and *adj.* Haitian.

halagar, (â·lâ·gâr´) *va.* to please; to cajole, to flatter *(lisonjear).*

halago, (â·lá´go) *m.* pleasure, appeal *(agrado);* flattery *(lisonja).*

halagüeño, ña, (a·lâ·gwe´nyo, nyâ) *adj.* pleasing, appealing; flattering.

halar, (â·lâr´) *va.* to pull.

halcón, (âl·kon´) *m.* falcon, hawk.

hálito, (â´lē·to) *m.* breath; (poet.) gentle breeze.

halo, (á´lo) *m.* halo.

haltera, (âl·te´râ) *f.* barbell, weight.

hallar, (â·yâr´) *va.* to find; **no** —**se,** to be out of sorts.

hallazgo, (â·yâz´go) *m.* finding, location *(acción);* find, discovery *(cosa hallada);* reward *(recompensa).*

hamaca, (â·mâ´kâ) *f.* hammock.

hambre, (âm´bre) *f.* hunger; famine *(escasez);* **tener** —, to be hungry; **matar el** —, to satisfy one´s hunger.

hambriento, ta, (âm·bryen´to, tâ) *adj.* hungry.

hamburguesa, (âm·bür·ge´sâ) *f.* hamburger.

hampa, (âm´pâ) *f.* underworld.

hangar, (âng·gâr´) *m.* hangar.

haragán, ana, (â·râ·gân´, á´nâ) *n.* idler, loafer, good-for-nothing; —, *adj.* lazy, idle.

haraganear, (â·râ·gâ·ne·âr´) *vn.* to loaf, to laze, to idle.

haraganería, (a·râ·gâ·ne·rē´â) *f.* idleness, laziness.

harapiento, ta, (â·râ·pyen´to, tâ) *adj.* ragged, in tatters.

harapo, (â·râ´po) *m.* rag, tatter.

haraposo, sa, (â·râ·po´so, sâ) *adj.* ragged.

harén, (â·ren´) *m.* harem.

harina, (â·rē´nâ) *f.* flour; fine powder *(polvo menudo);* — **de maíz,** corn meal.

harinero, (â·rē·ne´ro) *m.* flour dealer; —, **ra,** *adj.* flour.

harinoso, sa, (â·rē·no´so, sâ) *adj.* mealy, floury.

harmonía, (âr·mo·nē´â) *f.* harmony.

hartar, (ar·târ´) va. to stuff, to satiate *(saciar)*; (fig.) to satisfy, to appease *(satisfacer)*; to bore, to tire *(molestar)*; **—se**, to be fed up.

harto, ta, (âr´to, tâ) adj. satiated; sufficient *(bastante)*; **—to**, adv. enough.

hartura, (âr·tū´râ) f. fill *(saciedad)*; plenty, abundance *(abundancia)*.

hasta, (âs´tâ) prep. until, till *(tiempo)*; as far as *(espacio)*; as much as *(cantidad)*; **— ahora** or **— aquí**, till now; **— luego** or **— después**, see you later; **— no más**, to the very limit; **— la vista**, I´ll be seeing you; **—** conj. even.

hastío, (âs·tē´o) m. aversion, disgust.

hato, (â´to) m. clothes *(ropa)*; herd *(de ganado)*; (fig.) gang *(de gente)*; flock, bunch *(montón)*.

haya, (â´yâ) f. beech tree.

haz, (âs) m. bundle; beam *(de rayos)*; **—**, f. face; (fig.) surface *(de una tela)*.

hazaña, (â·sâ´nyâ) f. exploit, achievement, feat.

hazmerreir, (âz·me·rre·ēr´) m. laughing-stock.

he; (e) adv. **— allí**, there is; **— aquí**, here is; **—me aquí**, here I am.

hebilla, (e·vē´yâ) f. buckle.

hebra, (e´vrâ) f. thread, fiber; stringiness *(de la carne)*; (min.) vein.

hebraico, ca, (e·vrâ´ē·ko, kâ) adj. Hebraic.

hebreo, ea, (e·vre´o, e´â) n. and adj. Hebrew; **—**, m. Hebrew language.

hecatombe, (e·kâ·tom´be) f. hecatomb.

hectárea, (ek·tâ´re·â) f. hectare.

hectógrafo, (ek·to´grâ·fo) m. hectograph.

hechicería, (e ·chē·se·rē´â) f. witchcraft; enchantment *(encanto)*.

hechicero, ra, (e·chē·se´ro, râ) adj. bewitching; **—**, f. witch, sorceress; **—**, m. warlock, sorcerer.

hechizar, (e·chē·sâr´) va. to bewitch, to enchant.

hechizo, (e·chē´so) m. enchantment, spell.

hecho, cha, (e´cho, châ.) adj. made; done; used, accustomed *(acostumbrado)*; **bien —**, well done; **mal —**, poorly done; **—**, m. happening *(acontecimiento)*; matter *(asunto)*; act *(acción)*.

hechura, (e·chū´râ) f. construction, workmanship *(composición)*; creature, creation *(criatura)*; shape, appearance *(forma)*; making *(acción)*.

heder*, (e·ther´) vn. to stink, to smell bad.

hediondez, (e·thyon·des´) f. stench, evil smell.

hediondo, da, (e·thyon´do, dâ) adj. fetid, stinking, malodorous.

hedor, (e·thor´) m. stench, stink.

helada, (e·lâ´thâ) f. freezing.

heladería, (e·lâ·the·rē´â) f. ice-cream parlor.

helado, da, (e ·lâ´tho, thâ) adj. freezing, like ice; (fig.) cold *(desdeñoso)*; astounded, thunderstruck *(atónito)*; **—**, m. ice cream.

helar*, (e·lâr´) va. to freeze; (fig.) to strike *(dejar suspenso)*; to discourage *(desanimar)*; **—se**, to freeze.

helecho, (e·le´cho) m. (bot.) fern.

hélice, (e´lē·se) f. helix; (avi.) propeller.

helicóptero, (e·lē·kop´te·ro) m. helicopter.

helio, (e´lyo) m. helium.

heliotropo, (e·lyo·tro´po) m. heliotrope.

hembra, (em´brâ) f. female; eye *(de un corchete)*; nut *(de tornillo)*.

hemeroteca, (e·me·ro·te´kâ) f. periodical library.

hemisferio, (e·mēs·fe´ryo) m. hemisphere.

hemoglobina, (e·mo·glo·vē´nâ) f. (med.) hemoglobin.

hemorragia, (e·mo·rrâ´hyâ) f. (med.) hemorrhage.

hemorroides, (e·mo·rro´ē·thes) f. pl. piles, hemorrhoids.

henar, (e·nâr´) m. hay field.

henchir*, (en·chēr´) va. to fill, to stuff; **— se**, to overeat, to stuff oneself.

hendedura, (en·de·thū´râ) = **hendidura.**

hender* (en·der´) va. to split; to cut one´s way through *(abrirse paso)*.

hendidura, (en·dē·thū´râ) f. crack, split.

henequén, (e·ne·ken´) m. (bot.) henequen.

heno, (e´no) m. hay.

heparina, (e·pâ·rē´nâ) f. heparin.

hepático, ca, (e·pâ´tē·ko, kâ) adj. hepatic.

hepatitis, (e·pâ·tē´tēs) f. (med.) hepatitis.

heraldo, (e·râl´do) m. herald.

herbaje, (er·vâ´he) m. herbage, pasture.

hercúleo, ea, (er·kū´le·o, e·â) adj. herculean.

heredad, (e·re·thâth´) f. farm, country place.

heredar, (e·re·thâr´) va. to inherit.

hereditario, ria, (e·re·thē·tâ´ryo, ryâ) adj. hereditary.

heredero, ra, (e·re·the´ro, râ) n. heir, heiress.

hereje, (e·re´he) m. and f. heretic.

herejía. (e·re·hē´â) f. heresy.

herencia, (e·ren´syâ) f. inheritance, heritage; (biol.) heredity.

herético, ca, (e·re´tē·ko, kâ) adj. heretic.

herida, (e·re´thâ) f. wound, injury.

herido, da, (e·rē´tho, thâ) adj. wounded, injured.

herir*, (e·rēr´) va. to wound, to injure; (fig.)

to hurt; to touch *(el corazón).*

hermafrodita, (er·mâ·fro·thē´tä) *adj.* hermaphrodite.

hermanar, (er·mâ·nâr´) *va.* to match, to mate; **—se,** to become brothers.

hermanastra, (er·mâ·nâs´trä) *f.* stepsister, half sister.

hermanastro, (er·mâ·nâs´tro) *m.* stepbrother, half brother.

hermandad, (er·man·dâth´) *f.* fraternity, brotherhood; (fig.) affinity, likeness *(correspondencia).*

hermano, na, (er·mâ´no, nâ) *n.* brother; sister; mate *(de cosas);* **primo —** or **prima —,** first cousin; **—na de la Caridad,** Sister of Charity.

hermético, ca, (er·me´tē·ko, kâ) *adj.* hermetic, airtight.

hermosear, (er·mo·se·âr´) *va.* to beautify, to make handsome.

hermoso, (er·mo´so, sâ) *adj.* beautiful, handsome.

hermosura, (er·mo·sū´râ) *f.* beauty.

hernia, (er´nyä) *f.* hernia.

héroe, (e´ro·e) *m.* hero.

heroicidad, (e·roē·sē·thâth´) *f.* heroism.

heroico, ca, (e·ro´ē·ko, kâ) *adj.* heroic; **drogas —s,** narcotics.

heroína, (e·ro·ē´nä) *f.* heroine; (chem.) heroin.

heroísmo, (e·ro·ēz´mo) *m.* heroism.

herpes, (er´pes) *m.* or *f. pl.* (med.) shingles.

herrada, (e·rrâ´thä) *f.* pail, bucket.

herrador, (e·rrâ·thor´) *m.* farrier.

herradura, (e·rrâ·thū´râ) *f.* horseshoe; **camino de —,** bridle path.

herramienta, (e·rrâ·myen´tä) *f.* tool, implement *(instrumento);* set of tools *(conjunto);* (coll.) choppers, grinders *(dentadura).*

herrar*, (e·rrâr´) *va.* to shoe; to brand *(marcar).*

herrería, (e·rre·rrē´â) *f.* smithy; ironworks *(fábrica);* clamor, din *(alboroto).*

herrero, (e·rre´ro) *m.* blacksmith.

herrumbre, (e·rrūm´bre) *f.* rust, rustiness.

hervidero, (er·vē·the´ro) *m.* boiling, bubbling; (fig.) bubbling spring *(manantial);* rattle, wheeze *(del pecho);* swarm, throng *(muchedumbre).*

hervir* (er·vēr´) *vn.* to boil; (fig.) to be teeming *(abundar).*

hervor, (er·vor´) *m.* boiling, boil; (fig.) fire, spirit *(ardor).*

heterogéneo, nea, (e·te·ro·he´ne·o, ne·â) *adj.* heterogeneous.

hético, ca, (e´tē·ko, kâ) *adj.* tubercular, consumptive; (fig.) skin and bones *(delgaducho).*

hexágono, (ek·sâ´go·no) *m.* hexagon.

hexámetro, (ek·sâ´me·tro) *m.* hexameter.

hez, (es) *f.* dregs.

híbrido, da, (e´vrē·tho, thâ) *adj. and n.* hybrid.

hidalgo,ga, (ē·thâl´go, gâ) **—,** *adj.* noble, illustrious; **—,** *m.* nobleman; **—,** *f.* noblewoman.

hidalguía, (ē·thâl·gē´â) *f.* nobility.

hidratación, (ē·thrâ·tâ·syon´) *f.* hydration.

hidráulica, (ē·thrâ´ū·lē·kâ) *f.* hydraulics.

hidráulico ca, (ē·thrâ´ū·lē·ko, kâ) *adj.* hydraulic.

hidroavión, (ē·thro·â·vyon´) *m.* seaplane.

hidrocarburo, (ē·thro·kâr·vū´ro) *m.* (chem.) hydrocarbon.

hidroeléctrico, ca, (ē·thro·e·lek´trē·ko, kâ) *adj.* hydroelectric.

hidrofobia, (ē·thro·fo´vyä) *f.* hydrophobia, rabies.

hidrógeno, (ē·thro´he·no) *m.* (chem.) hydrogen; **— liquido,** liquid hydrogen.

hidromático, ca, (ē·thro·mâ´tē·ko, kâ) *adj.* hydromatic.

hidrónica, (ē·thro´nē·kâ) *f.* hydronics.

hidropesía, (ē·thro·pe·sē´â) *f.* dropsy.

hidroplano, (ē·thro·plâ´no) *m.* hydroplane.

hidropónica, (ē·thro·po´nē·kâ) *f.* hydroponics.

hidrostática, (ē·thros·tâ´tē·kâ) *f.* hydrostatics.

hidroterapia, (ē·thro·te·râ´pyä) *f.* hydrotherapy.

hiedra, (ye´thrä) *f.* ivy.

hiel, (yel´) *f.* gall, bile.

hielo, (ye´lo) *m.* ice; (fig.) coldness *(frialdad);* **— seco,** dry ice.

hiena, (ye´nä) *f.* hyena.

hierba, (yer´vä) *f.* grass; **— mate,** (bot.) maté; **mala —,** weed; **— medecinal,** herb.

hierbabuena, (yer·vâ·vwe´nä) *f.* (bot.) mint.

hierro, (ye´rro) *m.* iron; brand *(marca);* **—s,** *pl.* fetters; **— colado** or **de fundición,** or **fundido,** cast iron; **— forjado** or **de fragua,** wrought iron.

hígado, (ē´gâ·tho) *m.* liver; (coll.) guts, courage *(valentía).*

higiene, (ē·hye´ne) *f.* hygiene.

higiénico, ca, (ē·hye´nē·ko, kâ) *adj.* hygienic, sanitary; **papel —co,** toilet paper, bathroom tissue.

higo, (ē´go) *m.* fig.

higuera, (ē·ge´râ) *f.* fig tree.

---

m met, **n** not, **p** pot, **r** very, **rr** (none), **s** so, **t** toy, **th** with, **v** eve, **w** we, **y** yes, **z** zero

hijastro, tra, (ē·hâs´tro, trâ) *n.* stepchild.
hijo, ja, (ē´ho, hâ) *n.* child, offspring *(de un animal);* brainchild *(obra);* —, *m.* son; —, *f.* daughter.
hila, (ē´lä) *f.* row, line; spinning *(acción).*
hilacha, (ē·lä´chä) *f.* ravel, shred.
hilado, (ē·lä´tho) *m.* spinning; thread, yarn *(producto).*
hilador, ra, (ē·lä·thor´, râ) *n.* spinner; —, *adj.* spinning.
hilandero, ra, (ē·lan·de´ro, râ) *n.* spinner.
hilar, (ē·lär´) *va.* to spin.
hilaridad, (ē·lä·rē·thäth´) *f.* hilarity, mirth, gaiety.
hilera, (ē·le´rä) *f.* row, line, file.
hilo, (ē´lo) *m.* thread *(hebra);* linen *(tela);* wire *(alambre);* thin stream, trickle *(chorro);* thread *(del discurso);* **cortar el** —, (fig.) to interrupt; **al** —, with the grain; **telegrafía sin** —, wireless.
hilván, (ēl·vän´) *m.* basting.
hilvanar, (ēl·vä·när´) *va.* to baste; (fig.) to tie together *(enlazar);* (coll.) to throw together.
himno, (ēm´no) *m.* hymn; anthem *(canto nacional).*
hincapié, (ēng·kä·pye´) *m.* getting a foothold, taking a firm stance; **hacer — en,** to stress, to emphasize, to underline.
hincar, (ēng·kär´) *va.* to thrust in, to drive in; **— el diente,** to bite; **—se,** to kneel down.
hinchar, (ēn·chär´) *va.* to swell; (fig.) to puff up *(exagerar);* **—se,** to swell up; to puff up *(envanecerse).*
hinchazón, (ēn·chä·son´) *f.* swelling; ostentation, vanity *(ostentación).*
hindú, (ēn´dū´) *m.* and *f.* and *adj.* Hindu.
hinojo, (ē·no´ho) *m.* knee; (bot.) fennel; **ponerse de —s,** to kneel down.
hipérbole, (ē·per´vo·le) *f.* hyperbole.
hipergólico, ca, (ē·per·go´lē·ko, kâ) *adj.* hypergolic.
hipersónico, ca, (ē·per·so´nē·ko, kâ) *adj.* hypersonic.
hipertensión, (ē·per·ten·syon´) *f.* hypertension.
hípico, ca, (ē´pē·ko, kâ) *adj.* equine.
hipnótico, ca, (ēp·no´tē·ko, kâ) *adj.* hypnotic.
hipnotismo, (ēp·no·tēz´mo) *m.* hypnotism.
hipnotizar, (ēp·no·tē·sär´) *va.* to hypnotize.
hipo, (ē´po) *m.* hiccough.
hipocondría, (ē·po·kon·drē´ä) *f.* hypochondria.
hipocresía, (ē·po·kre·sē´ä) *f.* hypocrisy.
hipócrita, (ē·po´krē·tä) *adj.* hypocritical; —, *m.* and *f.* hypocrite.

hipodérmico, ca, (ē·po·ther´mē·ko, kâ) *adj.* hypodermic.
hipódromo, (ē·po´thro·mo) *m.* race track.
hipopótamo, (ē·po·po´tä·mo) *m.* hippopotamus.
hipoteca, (ē·po·te´kä) *f.* mortgage.
hipotecar, (ē·po·te·kär´) *va.* to mortgage.
hipotecario, ria, (ē·po·te·kä´ryo, ryä) *adj.* mortgage; **juicio —,** mortgage foreclosure.
hipotensión, (ē·po·ten·syon´) *f.* hypotension.
hipotenusa, (ē·po·te·nū´sä) *f.* hypotenuse.
hipótesis, (ē·po´te·sēs) *f.* hypothesis.
hipotético, ca, (ē·po·te´tē·ko, kâ) *adj.* hypothetical.
hirviente, (ēr·vyen´te) *adj.* boiling.
hispano, na (ēs·pâ´no, nä) *adj.* Hispanic.
Hispanoamérica, (ēs·pâ·no·â·me´rē·kä) *f.* Spanish America.
hispanoamericano, na, (ēs·pâ·no·â·me·rē·kä´no, nä) *adj.* and *n.* Spanish American.
histamina, (ēs·tâ·mē´nä) *f.* histamine.
histérico, ca, (ēs·te´rē·ko, kâ) *adj.* hysterical.
histerismo, (ēs·te·rēz´mo) *m.* hysteria.
historia, (ēs·to´ryä) *f.* history; tale, story *(cuento).*
historiado, da, (ēs·to·ryä´tho, thä) *adj.* ornate.
historiador, ra, (ēs·to·ryâ·thor´, râ) *n.* historian.
historial, (ēs·to·ryäl´) *adj.* historical; —, *m.* background.
historiar, (ēs·to·ryär´) *va.* to tell the history of.
histórico, ca, (ēs·to´rē·ko, kâ) *adj.* historical, historic.
historieta, (ēs·to·rye´tä) *f.* short story, anecdote; **cómica,** comic strip.
hito, (ē´to) *m.* landmark, guidepost; (fig.) target *(blanco);* **a —,** fixedly; **mirar de — en —,** to stare at, to fix one's gaze on.
Hno.: Hermano, Bro. Brother.
hocico, (o·sē´ko) *m.* snout, muzzle; (coll.) face; **meter — en todo,** (coll.) to stick one's nose into everything.
hogar, (o·gâr´) *m.* hearth, fireplace; home *(casa).*
hogareño, ña, (o·gâ·re´nyo, nyä) *adj.* home-loving.
hoguera, (o·ge´rä) *f.* bonfire, huge blaze.
hoja, (o´hä) *f.* leaf; blade *(cuchilla);* sheet **hoja** *(de papel);* **— de afeitar,** razor blade; **— de apunte,** tally sheet; **— de cálculo,** spreadsheet; **— de lata,** tin; —

â arm, **e** they, **ē** bē, **o** fore, **ū** blūe, **b** bad, **ch** chip, **d** day, f fat, **g** go, **h** hot, **k** kid, **1** let

de ruta, (avi.) flight plan; — **en blanco,** blank sheet.

hojalata, (o·hâ·lá´tä) *f.* tinplate, tin.

hojalatero, (o·hâ·lâ·te´ro) *m.* tinsmith.

hojaldre, (o·hâl´dre) *f.* puff paste.

hojarasca, (o·hâ·râs´kâ) *f.* dead leaves; excess leafage *(de un árbol);* (fig.) dross, froth.

hojear, (o·he·âr´) *va.* to skim through, to scan.

¡hola! (o´lâ) *interj.* hello! hi!

Holanda, (o·lân´dä) *f.* Holland.

holandés, esa, (o·lân·des´, e´sâ) *adj.* Dutch.

holgachón, ona, (ol·gâ·chon´, o´nâ) *adj.* lazy, idling.

holgado, da, (ol·gä´tho, thä) *adj.* unoccupied, idle; roomy, ample, wide *(ancho);* (fig.) leisurely, worry-free.

holganza, (ol·gân´sä) *f.* leisure, relaxation; laziness *(pereza);* pleasure, joy *(placer).*

holgar*, (ol·gâr´) *vn.* to rest *(descansar);* to be useless *(ser inútil);* —**se,** to amuse oneself.

holgazán, ana, (ol·gâ·sân´, â´nâ) *n.* idler, loafer; —, *adj.* lazy, do-nothing.

holgazanear, (ol·gâ·sâ·ne·âr´) *vn.* to idle, to loaf.

holgazanería, (ol·gâ·sâ·ne·rē´â) *f.* idleness, indolence, loafing.

holgura, (ol·gū´rä) *f.* frolic, merrymaking; roominess *(anchura);* ease, comfort *(bienestar).*

holocausto, (o·lo·kâ´ūs·to) *m.* holocaust.

hollar*, (o·yär´) *va.* to trample, to tread upon.

hollín, (o·yēn´) *m.* soot.

hombre, (om´bre) *m.* man; omber *(juego de naipes);* — **de bien,** honorable man; — **de negocios,** businessman; — **de letras,** literary man; — **de Estado,** statesman; — **de ciencia,** scientist; — **rana,** frogman.

hombrera, (om·bre´rä) *f.* shoulder pad.

hombría, (om·brē´â) *f.* manhood; — **de bien,** probity, honesty.

hombro, (om´bro) *m.* shoulder.

hombruno, na, (om·brū´no, nâ) *adj.* mannish.

homenaje, (o·me·nâ´he) *m.* homage, tribute; **rendir** —, to pay homage, to honor.

homeopatía, (o·me·o·pâ·tē´â) *f.* (med.) homeopathy.

homicida, (o·mē·sē´thâ) *m.* and *f.* homicide; —, *adj.* homicidal.

homicidio, (o·mē·sē´thyo) *m.* homicide.

homogéneo, nea, (o·mo·he´ne·o, ne·â) *adj.* homogeneous.

homogenizar, (o·mo·he·nē·sâr´) *va.* to homogenize.

homosexual, (o·mo·sek·swâl´) *adj.* and *m.* and *f.* homosexual.

honda, (on´dä) *f.* slingshot.

hondear, (on·de·âr´) *va.* (naut.) to sound.

hondo, da, (on´do, dä) *adj.* deep; (fig.) profound.

hondonada, (on·do·nâ´thä) *f.* bottom land.

hondura, (on·dū´rä) *f.* depth, profundity; **meterse en** —**s,** (coll.) to get into deep water, to go over one's head.

hondureño, na, (on·dū·re´nyo, nyâ) *n.* and *adj.* Honduran.

honestidad, (o·nes·tē·thâth´) *f.* integrity, decency; politeness, decorum *(urbanidad).*

honesto, ta, (o·nes´to, tâ) *adj.* decent; polite, polished, refined.

hongo, (ong´go) *m.* mushroom; fungus; derby *(sombrero).*

honor, (o·nor´) *m.* honor.

honorable, (o·no·râ´vle) *adj.* honorable.

honorario, ria, (o·no·râ´ryo, ryâ) *adj.* honorary; —**s,** *m. pl.* fees.

honorífico, ca, (o·no·rē´fē·ko, kâ) *adj.* honorable; **mención** —**ca,** honorable mention.

honra, (on´rrä) *f.* honor, self-respect; repute, acclaim *(buena fama).*

honradez, (on·rrâ·thes´) *f.* honesty.

honrado, da, (on·rrä´tho, thâ) *adj.* honest.

honrar, (on·rrâr´) *va.* to honor; —**se,** to deem it an honor.

honroso, sa, (on·rro´so, sâ) *adj.* honorable.

hora, (o´rä) *f.* hour; time *(momento de terminado);* — **de comer,** mealtime; **media** —, half an hour.

horadar, (o·râ·thâr´) *va.* to drill a hole through.

horario, ria, (o·râ´ryo, ryâ) *adj.* hourly; —, *m.* hour hand *(de reloj);* timetable, schedule.

horca, (or´kâ) *f.* gallows; (agr.) pitchfork.

horcajadas (or·kâ·hâ´thâs) or **horcajadillas,** (or·kâ·hâ·thē´yâs) **a** —, astride.

horchata, (or·châ´tä) *f.* orgeat.

horizontal, (o·rē·son·tâl´) *adj.* horizontal.

horizonte, (o·rē·son´te) *m.* horizon.

horma, (or´mä) *f.* mold, form; — **de zapatos,** shoe last.

hormiga, (or·mē´gâ) *f.* ant.

hormigón, (or·mē·gon´) *m.* concrete; — **armado,** reinforced concrete.

hormiguear, (or·mē·ge·âr´) *vn.* to itch, to crawl *(picar);* (fig.) to swarm, to flock.

hormiguero, (or·mē·ge´ro) *m.* anthill.

hormona, (or·mo'nâ) f. hormone; — **adre-nocorticotropa,** adrenocorticotrophic hormone.

hornada, (or·nâ'thâ) f. batch.

hornear, (or·ne·âr') va. to bake; —, vn. to be a baker.

hornilla, (or·nē'yâ) f. burner.

horno, (or'no) m. oven; **alto —,** blast furnace; **— de ladrillo,** brick kiln; **— Siemens-Martin,** open-hearth furnace.

horóscopo, (o·ros'ko·po) m. horoscope.

horquilla, (or·kē'yâ) f. forked stick (sostén); (agr.) pitchfork; hairpin (alfiler).

horrendo, da, (o·rren'do, dâ) adj. horrible, hideous.

horrible, (o·rrē'vle) adj. horrid, horrible.

horror, (o·rror') m. horror.

horrorizar, (o·rro·rē·sâr') va. to horrify.

horroroso, sa, (o·rro·ro'so, sâ) adj. horrible, hideous.

hortaliza, (or·tâ·lē'sâ) f. vegetable.

hortelano, (or·te·lâ'no) m. gardener.

hortensia, (or·ten'syâ) f. (bot.) hydrangea.

horticultura, (or·tē·kŭl·tū'râ) f. horticulture.

hosco, ca, (os'ko, kâ) adj. dark (oscuro); sullen, gloomy (severo).

hospedaje, (os·pe·thâ'he) m. lodging.

hospedar, (os·pe·thâr') va. to lodge, to put up; **—se en,** to lodge at, to put up at.

hospicio, (os·pē'syo) m. home, asylum; **— de huérfanos,** orphanage.

hospital, (os·pē·tâl') m. hospital.

hospitalario, ria, (os·pē·tâ·lâ'ryo, ryâ) adj. hospitable.

hospitalidad, (os·pē·tâ·lē·thâth') f. hospitality

hospitalización, (os·pē·tâ·lē·sâ·syon') f. hospitalization.

hostería, (os·te·rē'â) f. inn.

hostia, (os'tyâ) f. wafer; (eccl.) Host.

hostigar, (os·tē·gâr') va. to whip (azotar); to harass, to keep after (acosar).

hostil, (os·tēl') adj. hostile, adverse.

hostilidad, (os·tē·lē·thâth') f. hostility, enmity.

hostilizar, (os·tē·lē·sâr') va. to inflict damage on, to make telling inroads on.

hotel, (o·tel') m. hotel.

hotelero, ra, (o·te·le'ro, râ) n. innkeeper; **—,** adj. hotel; **industria —,** hotel industry.

hoy, (o'ē) adv. today; **de — en adelante,** henceforth, from now on; **— día,** nowadays.

hoyo, (o'yo) m. hole; pit (en una superficie); grave (tumba).

hoyuelo, (o·ywe'lo) m. dimple.

hoz, (os) f. sickle.

huarache, (wâ·râ'che) m. (Mex.) sandal.

huaso, (wâ'so) m. Chilean cowboy.

hueco, ca (we'ko, kâ) adj. hollow; deep (voz); fluffy, soft (mullido); pretentious (afectado); —, m. hollow; space (intervalo); (coll.) opening (empleo vacante).

huelga, (wel'gâ) f. strike; **— de brazos caídos,** sit-down strike.

huella, (we'yâ) f. track, trace; **—s digitales,** fingerprints.

huérfano, na, (wer'fâ·no, nâ) n. and adj. orphan.

huero, ra, (we'ro, râ) adj. empty, void; **huevo —,** rotten egg.

huerta, (wer'tâ) f. large orchard; vast irrigated area (terreno de regadío).

huerto, (wer'to) m. vegetable garden, kitchen garden; orchard (de árboles frutales).

hueso, (we'so) m. bone; stone (del fruto); (fig.) hard job (cosa dificultosa).

huésped, da, (wes'peth, thâ) n. innkeeper (mesonero); guest, roomer, boarder (persona alojada); (biol.) host, **—,** m. host; **—,** f. hostess.

hueste, (wes'te) f. host, force.

huesudo, da, (we·sū'tho, thâ) adj. bony.

huevero, ra, (we·ve'ro, râ) n. egg dealer; **—,** f. (orn.) oviduct.

huevo (we'vo) m. egg; (biol.) ovum; **— cocido,** hard-boiled egg; **— condimentado con picantes,** deviled egg; **— frito** or **estrellado,** fried egg; **— pasado por agua,** or **— tibio,** soft-boiled egg; **—s revueltos,** scrambled eggs.

huida, (wē'thâ) f. flight, escape.

huidizo, za, (wē·thē'so, sâ) adj. taking flight easily, evasive.

huir*, (wēr) vn. to flee, to escape.

hule, (ū'le) m. rubber; oilcloth (tela); **— espuma,** foam rubber.

hulla, (ū'yâ) f. soft coal; **— blanca,** water power; **— verde,** river power.

humanidad, (ū·mâ·nē·thâth') f. humanity.

humanitario, ria, (ū·mâ·nē·tâ'ryo, ryâ) n. and adj. humanitarian.

humano, na, (ū·mâ'no, nâ) adj. human; humane, kind (bondadoso).

humeante, (ū·me·ân'te) adj. smoking; steaming.

humear, (ū·me·âr') vn. to smoke; to steam (despedir vapor).

humedad, (ū·me·thâth') f. humidity, moisture.

â arm, e they, ē bē, o fore, ū blūe, b bad, ch chip, d day, f fat, g go, h hot, k kid, l let

humedecedor, (ū·me·the·se·thor´) *m.* humidifier.

humedecer*, (ū·me·the· ser´) *va.* to moisten, to wet.

húmedo, da, (ū´me·tho, thä) *adj.* humid, damp, moist; wet *(cargado de liquido).*

humildad, (ū·mēl·däth´) *f.* humility; humbleness *(sumisión).*

humilde, (ū·mēl´de) *adj.* humble; **de — cuna,** of humble birth.

humillación, (ū·mē·yâ·syon´) *f.* humiliation.

humillar, (ū·mē·yâr´) *va.* to humble, to humiliate; to bend down, to bow down *(doblar);* **—se,** to humble oneself.

humo, (ū´mo) *m.* smoke; fume, steam *(vapor).*

humor, (ū·mor´) *m.* humor; **buen —,** good humor; **mal —,** moodiness; **estar de buen —,** to be in good spirits, to be in a good mood.

humorada, (ū·mo·râ´thä) *f.* witticism, joke.

humorismo, (ū·mo·rēz´mo) *m.* humor.

humorista, (ū·mo·rēs´tä) *m.* and *f.* humorist.

hundimiento, (ūn·dē·myen´to) *m.* sinking.

hundir, (ūn·dēr´) *vn.* to sink; (fig.) to stump *(confundir);* to ruin, to defeat *(abrumar);* **—se,** (fig.) to be wrecked, to be ruined; (coll.) to drop out of sight *(desaparecer).*

húngaro, ra, (ūng´gâ·ro, rä) *adj.* and *n.* Hungarian.

Hungría, (ūng·grē´ä) *f.* Hungary.

huracán, (ū·rä´·kän´) *m.* hurricane.

huraño, ña, (ū·rä´nyo, nyä) *adj.* unsociable, shy, retiring.

hurgón, (ūr·gon´) *m.* poker.

hurtadillas, (ūr·tä·thē´yâs) **a —,** stealthily.

hurtar, (ūr·târ´) *va.* to steal, to pilfer; (fig.) to move aside *(apartar).*

hurto, (ūr´to) *m.* theft, robbery.

husillo, (ū·sē´yo) *m.* clamp screw *(tornillo);* drain *(canal).*

husmear, (ūz·me·âr´) *va.* to scent; to pry into, to poke into *(averiguar).*

husmeo, (ūz·me´o) *m.* prying.

huso, (ū´so) *m.* spindle.

I

ib.: ibídem, ib. or ibid. ibidem.

ibérico, ca, (ē·ve´rē·ko, kä) *adj.* Iberian.

iberoamericano,na, (ē·ve·ro·â·me·rē·kä´no, nä) *adj.* and *n.* Ibero-American.

ibídem, (ē·vē´then) *adv.* ibidem.

iconoclasta, (ē·ko·no´klâs´tä) *m.* iconoclast.

iconoscopio, (ē·ko·nos·ko´pyo) *m.* iconoscope.

ictericia, (ēk·te·rē´syä) *f.* jaundice.

íd.: ídem, id. idem.

ida, (ē´thä) *f.* going; (fig.) dash, start *(impetu);* **—s y venidas,** comings and goings; **billete** or **boleto de — y vuelta,** round-trip ticket.

idea, (ē·the´ä) *f.* idea; **cambiar de —,** to change one´s mind.

ideal, (ē·the·âl´) *m.* and *adj.* ideal.

idealismo, (ē·the·â·lēz´mo) *m.* idealism.

idealista, (ē·the·â·lēs´tä) *m.* and *f.* idealist; **—,** *adj.* idealistic.

idealización, (ē·the·â·lē·sâ·syon´) *f.* idealization.

idealizar, (ē·the·â·lē·sâr´) *va.* to idealize.

idear, (ē·the·âr´) *va.* to think up, to plan.

ideario, (ē·the·â´ryo) *m.* ideas, set of ideas.

ídem, (ē´then) *adv.* idem.

idéntico, ca, (ē·then´tē·ko, kä) *adj.* identical.

identidad, (ē·then·tē·thâth´) *f.* identity; **cédula de —,** identification card.

identificar, (ē·then·tē·fē·kâr´) *va.* to identify; **—se,** to identify oneself.

ideología, (ē·the·o·lo·hē´ä) *f.* ideology.

ideológico, ca, (ē·the·o·lo´ hē·ko, kä) *adj.* ideological.

idilio, (ē·thē´lyo) *m.* idyl.

idioma, (ē·thyo´mä) *m.* language.

idiomático, ca, (ē·thyo·mä´tē·ko, kä) *adj.* idiomatic.

idiosincrasia, (ē·thyo·sēng·krä´syä) *f.* individual temperament, own ways, idiosyncrasy.

idiota, (ē·thyo´tä) *m.* and *f.* idiot; **—,** *adj.* idiotic.

idiotez, (ē·thyo·tes´) *f.* idiocy.

idiotismo, (ē·thyo·tēz´mo) *m.* ignorance *(ignorancia);* (gram.) idiom, idiotism.

idólatra, (ē·tho´lä·trä) *m.* and *f.* idolater.

idolatrar, (ē·tho·lä·trâr´) *va.* to idolize.

idolatría, (ē·tho·lä·trē´ä) *f.* idolatry.

ídolo, (ē´tho·lo) *m.* idol.

---

idóneo, nea, (ē·tho'ne·o, ne·â) *adj.* fit, suitable.

iglesia, (ē·gle'syâ) *f.* church.

ignición, (ēg·nē·syon') *f.* ignition.

ignominioso, sa, (ēg·no·mē·nyo'so, sâ) *adj.* ignominious.

ignorancia, (ēg·no·rân'syâ) *f.* ignorance.

ignorante, (ēg·no·rân'te) *adj.* ignorant.

ignorar, (ēg·no·râr') *va.* to be unaware of, not to know.

ignoto, ta, (ēg·no'to, tâ) *adj.* unknown.

igual, (ē·gwâl') *adj.* equal; like (muy parecido); the same (de la misma clase); constant *(que no varía);* smooth *(liso).*

iguala, (ē·gwâ'lâ) *f.* smoothing; equating; equalizing; fee *(convenio).*

igualar, (ē·gwâ·lar') *va.* to smooth out *(allanar);* to equalize, to make equal *(hacer igual);* (fig.) to equate *(juzgar igual);* —, *vn.* to be equal.

igualdad, (ē·gwâl·dâth') *f.* equality.

igualmente, (ē·gwâl·men'te) *adv.* equally.

iguana, (ē·gwâ'nâ) *f.* iguana.

ilegal, (ē·le·gâl') *adj.* illegal, unlawful.

ilegalidad, (ē·le·gâ·lē·thâth') *f.* illegality, unlawfulness.

ilegítimo, ma, (ē·le·hē'tē·mo, mâ) *adj.* illegitimate.

ileso, sa, (ē·le'so, sâ) *adj.* unhurt.

ilícito, ta, (ē·lē'sē·to, tâ) *adj.* illicit, unlawful.

ilimitado, da, (ē·lē·mē·tâ'tho, thâ) *adj.* unlimited, boundless.

iliterato, ta, (ē·lē·te·râ'to, tâ) *adj.* illiterate, unlearned.

ilógico, ca, (ē·lo'hē·ko, kâ) *adj.* illogical.

iluminación, (ē·lū·mē·nâ·syon') *f.* illumination.

iluminar, (ē·lū·mē·nâr') *va.* to illuminate.

ilusión, (ē·lū·syon') *f.* illusion.

ilusionarse, (ē·lū·syo·nâr'se) *vr.* to daydream, to indulge in wishful thinking.

iluso, sa, (ē·lū'so, sâ) *adj.* deluded; visionary *(soñador).*

ilusorio, ria, (ē·lū·so'ryo, ryâ) *adj.* illusory.

ilustración, (ē·lūs·trâ·syon') *f.* illustration *(grabado);* enlightenment *(movimiento);* learning *(instrucción).*

ilustrar, (ē·lūs·trâr') *va.* to illustrate; to enlighten *(instruir).*

ilustre, (ē·lūs'tre) *adj.* illustrious, eminent.

imagen, (ē·mâ'hen) *f.* image.

imaginación, (ē·mâ'·hē·nâ·syon') *f.* imagination; fancy, figment *(cosa imaginada).*

imaginar, (ē·mâ·hē·nâr') *va.* to imagine.

imaginario, ria, (ē·mâ·hē·nâ'ryo, ryâ) *adj.* imaginary.

imaginativo, va, (ē·mâ·hē·nâ·tē'vo, vâ) *adj.* imaginative.

imán, (ē·mân') *m.* magnet.

imbécil, (ēm·be'sēl) *m.* and *f.* imbecile; —, *adj.* imbecilic; idiotic, foolish *(tonto).*

imberbe, (ēm·ber've) *adj.* beardless.

imbuir*, (ēm·bwēr') *va.* to imbue.

imitable, (ē·mē·tâ'vle) *adj.* imitable.

imitación, (ē·mē·tâ·syon') *f.* imitation.

imitador, ra, (e·mē·tâ·thor', râ) *n.* imitator; —, *adj.* imitative.

imitar, (ē·mē·târ') *va.* to imitate.

impaciencia, (ēm·pâ·syen'syâ) *f.* impatience.

impacientar, (ēm·pâ·syen·târ') *va.* to make impatient; —se, to become impatient, to lose one's patience.

impaciente, (ēm·pâ·syen'te) *adj.* impatient.

impacto, (ēm·pâk'to) *m.* impact.

impala, (ēm·pâ'lâ) *f.* impala.

impar, (ēm·pâr') *adj.* odd, uneven *(número);* unmatched.

imparcial, (ēm·pâr·syâl') *adj.* impartial.

imparcialidad, (ēm·pâr·syâ·lē·thâth') *f.* impartiality.

impartir, (ēm·pâr·tēr') *va.* to impart.

impasible, (ēm·pâ·sē'vle) *adj.* impassible; impassive *(insensible).*

impávido, da, (ēm·pâ'vē·tho, thâ) *adj.* fearless, intrepid.

impecable, (ēm·pe·kâ'vle) *adj.* impeccable.

impedimento, (ēm·pe·thē·men'to) *m.* impediment.

impedir*, (ēm·pe·thēr') *va.* to impede.

impeler, (ēm·pe·ler') *va.* to propel *(empujar);* (fig.) to impel *(estimular).*

impenetrable, (ēm·pe·ne·trâ'vle) *adj.* impenetrable.

impensado da, (ēm·pen·sâ'tho, thâ) *adj.* unthought-of, unforeseen.

imperar, (ēm·pe·râr') *vn.* to reign.

imperativo, va, (ēm·pe·râ·tē'vo, vâ) *adj.* and *m.* imperative.

imperceptible, (ēm·per·sep·tē'vle) *adj.* imperceptible.

imperdible, (ēm·per·thē'vle) *m.* safety pin.

imperdonable, (ēm·per·tho·nâ'vle) *adj.* unpardonable.

imperecedero, ra, (ēm·pe·re·se·the'ro, râ) *adj.* imperishable.

imperfección, (ēm·per·fek·syon') *f.* imperfection.

imperfecto, ta, (ēm·per·fek'to, tâ) *adj.* imperfect.

imperial, (ēm·pe·ryâl') *adj.* imperial.

imperialismo, (ēm·pe·ryâ·lēz'mo) *m.* imperialismo.

imperialista, (ēm·per·yâ·lēs'tâ) *adj.* imperialistic.

imperio, (ēm·pe´ryo) *m.* empire.

imperioso, sa, (ēm·pe·ryo´so, sâ) *adj.* imperious; imperative *(apremiante).*

impermeable, (ēm·per·me·ä´vle) *adj.* impermeable, waterproof; —, *m.* raincoat.

impersonal, (ēm·per·so·nâl´) *adj.* impersonal.

impertinencia, (ēm·per·tē·nen´syä) *f.* impertinence.

impertinente, (ēm·per·tē·nen´te) *adj.* impertinent.

impertinentes, (ēm·per·tē·nen´tes) *m. pl.* lorgnette.

imperturbable, (ēm·per·tūr·vä´vle) *adj.* imperturbable.

ímpetu, (ēm´pe·tū) *m.* impetus; impetuousness *(violencia).*

impetuoso, sa, (ēm·pe·two´so, sâ) *adj.* impetuous.

impío, pía, (ēm·pē´o, pē´â) *adj.* impious.

implacable, (ēm·plä·kä´vle) *adj.* implacable.

implicación, (ēm·plē·kâ·syon´) *f.* implication.

implicar, (ēm·plē·kâr´) *va.* to imply; to contain, to hold *(contener).*

implícito, ta, (ēm·plē´sē·to, tâ) *adj.* implicit.

implorar, (ēm·plo·râr´) *va.* to implore.

impolítico, ca, (ēm·po·lē´tē·ko, kâ) *adj.* impolite.

imponderable, (ēm·pon·de·râ´vle) *adj.* imponderable.

imponente, (ēm·po·nen´te) *adj.* imposing.

imponer*, (ēm·po·ner´) *va.* to impose; to deposit *(poner a rédito);* to instruct *(instruir);* to charge falsely with *(atribuir falsamente).*

importación, (ēm·por·tâ·syon´) *f.* importation.

importador, ra, (ēm·por·tâ·thor´, râ) *n.* importer; —, *adj.* importing

importancia, (ēm·por·tân´sya) *f.* importance.

importante, (ēm·por·tân´te) *adj.* important.

importar, (ēm·por·târ´) *vn.* to be important, to matter; to import *(géneros);* **no** —, not to matter.

importe, (ēm·por´te) *m.* amount; — **bruto** or — **total,** gross amount; — **líquido** or — **neto,** net amount.

importunar, (ēm·por·tū·nâr´) *va.* to importune, to bother.

importuno, na, (ēm·por´tū´no, nâ) *adj.* importunate; inopportune *(inoportuno).*

imposibilidad, (ēm·po·sē·vē·lē·thâth´) *f.* impossibility.

imposibilitar, (ēm·po·sē·vē·lē·târ´) *va.* to make impossible; —**se,** to become crippled.

imposible, (ēm·po·sē´vle) *adj.* impossible.

imposición, (ēm·po·sē·syon´) *f.* imposition.

impostor, ra, (ēm·pos·tor´, râ) *n.* impostor, fraud.

impotencia, (ēm·po·ten´sya) *f.* impotence.

impotente, (ēm·po·ten´te) *adj.* impotent.

impracticable, (ēm·prâk·tē·kâ´vle) *adj.* impracticable.

imprecar, (ēm·pre·kâr´) *va.* to imprecate, to curse.

imprecatorio, ria, (ēm·pre·kâ·to´ryo, ryâ) *adj.* imprecatory, punctuated with curses.

impregnarse, (ēm·preg·nâr´se) *vr.* to become impregnated.

impremeditado, da, (ēm·pre·me·thē·tâ´·tho, thâ) *adj.* unpremeditated.

imprenta, (ēm·pren´tâ) *f.* printing *(arte);* printing office *(edificio);* (fig.) press.

imprescindible, (ēm·pres·sēn·dē´vle) *adj.* indispensable, essential.

impresión, (ēm·pre·syon´) *f.* printing *(acción);* presswork *(calidad del impreso);* impression *(huella);* — **digital,** fingerprint.

impresionable, (ēm·pre·syo·nâ´vle) *adj.* impressionable.

impresionar, (ēm·pre·syo·nâr´) *va.* to impress.

impresionismo, (ēm·pre·syo·nēz´mo) *m.* impressionism.

impreso, (ēm·pre´so) *m.* printed matter; —, **sa,** *adj.* printed.

impresor, ra, (ēm·pre·sôr´, râ) *n.* printer.

imprevisión, (ēm·pre·vē·syon´) *f.* lack of foresight, negligence.

imprevisto, ta, (ēm·pre·vēs´to, tâ) *adj.* unforeseen, unexpected, unprovided-for.

imprimir, (ēm·prē·mēr´) *va.* to press, to imprint *(huellas);* to print *(un libro);* (fig.) to impart.

improbable, (ēm´pro·vâ·vle) *adj.* improbable, unlikely.

ímprobo, ba, (ēm´pro·vo, vâ) *adj.* corrupt, wicked; excessive, oppressive *(muy duro).*

improductivo, va, (ēm·pro´thūk·tē´vo, vâ) *adj.* unproductive.

improperio, (ēm·pro·pe´ryo) *m.* grave insult.

impropio, pia, (ēm·pro´pyo, pyâ) *adj.* improper, unfit.

improvisación, (em·pro·vē·sâ·syon´) f. improvisation.

improvisar, (ēm·pro·vē·sâr´) va. to improvise.

improviso, sa, (ēm·pro·vē´so, sâ) adj. unforeseen; de —so, unexpectedly.

imprudente, (ēm·prū·then´te) adj. imprudent, unwise.

impudente, (ēm·pū·then´te) adj. impudent, shameless.

impúdico, ca, (ēm·pū´thē·ko, kâ) adj. immodest, indecent.

impuesto, (ēm·pwes´to) m. tax; — sobre la renta, income tax; cobrar —s, to tax; tarifa de —s, tax schedule.

impugnar, (ēm·pūg·nâr´) va. to impugn, to oppose.

impulsar, (ēm·pūl·sâr´) va. to drive, to propel.

impulsivo, va, (ēm·pūl·sē´vo, vâ) adj. impulsive.

impulso, (ēm·pūl´so) m. impulse.

impune (ēm·pū´ne) adj. unpunished.

impunidad, (ēm·pū·nē·thâth´) f. impunity.

impureza, (ēm·pū·re´sâ) f. impurity.

impuro, ra, (ēm·pū´ro, râ) adj. impure.

imputar, (ēm·pū·târ´) va. to impute, to attribute.

inaccesible, (ē·nâk·se·sē´vle) adj. inaccessible; (fig.) incomprehensible.

inacción, (ē·nâk·syon´) f. inaction, inactivity.

inaceptable, (ē·nâ·sep·tâ´vle) adj. unacceptable.

inactividad, (ē·nâk·tē·vē·thâth´) f. inactivity.

inadaptable, (e·nâ·thâp·tâ´vle) adj. unadaptable.

inadecuado, da, (ē·nâ·the·kwâ´tho, thâ) adj. inadequate.

inadmisible, (ē·nâth·mē·sē´vle) adj. inadmissible.

inadvertencia, (ē·nâth·ver·ten´syâ) f. oversight.

inadvertido, da, (ē·nâth·ver·tē´tho, thâ) adj. inattentive; unnoticed, unobserved (no advertido).

inagotable, (ē·nâ·go·tâ´vle) adj. inexhaustible.

inaguantable, (ē·nâ·gwân·tâ´vle) adj. insufferable, intolerable.

inajenable; (ē·nâ·he·nâ´vle) adj. inalienable.

inalámbrico, ca, (ē·nâ·lâm´brē·ko, kâ) adj. wireless.

inalienable, (ē·nâ·lye·nâ´vle) adj. inalienable.

inalterable, (ē·nâl·te·râ´vle) adj. unaltera-

ble.

inanimado, da, (ē·nâ·nē·mâ´tho, thâ) adj. lifeless, inanimate.

inarrugable, (ē·nâ·rrū·gâ´vle) adj. wrinkleproof.

inastillable, (ē·nâs·tē·yâ´vle) adj. shatterproof.

inaudito, ta, (ē·nâū·thē´to, tâ) adj. unheard-of.

inauguración, (ē·nâū·gū·râ·syon´) f. inauguration.

inaugurar, (ē·nâū·gū·râr´) va. to inaugurate.

inca, (ēng´kâ) m. Inca.

incandescencia, (ēng·kân·des·sen´syâ) f. incandescence.

incansable, (ēng·kân·sâ´vle) adj. tireless, indefatigable.

incapacidad, (ēng·kâ·pâ·sē·thâth´) f. incapacity; (fig.) lack of ability, stupidity (rudeza).

incapacitar, (ēng·kâ·pâ·sē·târ´) va. to incapacitate.

incapaz, (ēng·kâ·pâz´) adj. incapable; (fig.) incompetent (falto de talento).

incauto, ta, (ēng·kâ´ū·to, ta) adj. incautious, unwary.

incendiar, (ēn·sen·dyâr´) va. to set on fire; —se, to catch fire.

incendiario, ria, (ēn·sen·dyâ´ryo, ryâ) n. and adj. incendiary.

incendio, (ēn·sen´dyo) m. fire; compañia de seguros contra —s, fire insurance company; boca de —, fireplug.

incentivo, (ēn·sen·tē´vo) m. inducement, incentive.

incertidumbre, (ēn·ser·tē·thūm´bre) f. uncertainty.

incesante, (ēn·se·sân´te) adj. incessant, unceasing.

incesto, (ēn·ses´to) m. incest.

incidencia, (ēn·sē·then´syâ) f. incidence; (fig.) incident (lo que sobreviene); por —, by chance, accidentally.

incidente, (ēn·sē·then´te) m. incident, event.

incidir, (ēn·sē·thēr´) vn. to fall into, to run into; (med.) to make an incision.

incienso, (ēn·syen´so) m. incense.

incierto, ta, (ēn·syer´to, tâ) adj. uncertain, doubtful.

incinerador, (ēn·sē·ne·râ·thor´) m. incinerator.

incinerar, (ēn·sē·ne·râr´) va. to incinerate.

incipiente, (ēn·sē·pyen´te) adj. incipient, beginning.

incisión, (ēn·sē·syon´) f. incision.

incisivo, va, (ēn·sē·sē´vo, vâ) adj. incisive.

â arm, e they, ē bē, o fore, ū blūe, b bad, ch chip, d day, f fat, g go, h hot, k kid, 1 let

inciso, (ēn·sē´so) *m.* clause.

incitar, (ēn·sē·tär´) *va.* to incite.

incivil, (ēn·sē·vēl´) *adj.* uncivil.

inclemencia, (ēng·kle·men´syä) *f.* inclemency, seventy; **a la —,** exposed, without shelter.

inclinación, (ēng·klē·nä·syon´) *f.* inclination.

inclinar, (ēng·klē·när´) *va.* to incline; **—se,** to be inclined.

incluir*, (ēng·klwēr´) *va.* to include.

inclusión, (ēng·klū·syon´) *f.* inclusion.

inclusive, (ēng·klū·sē´ve) *adv.* inclusively.

incluso, sa, (ēng·klū´so, sä) *adj.* enclosed.

incógnito, ta, (ēng·kog´nē·to, tä) *adj.* unknown; **de —,** incognito.

incoherente, (ēng·ko·e·ren´te) *adj.* incoherent.

incoloro, ra, (ēng·ko·lo´ro, rä) *adj.* colorless.

incólume, (ēng·ko´lū·me) *adj.* unharmed, safe.

incomible, (ēng·ko·mē´vle) *adj.* inedible.

incomodar, (ēng·ko·mo·thär´) *va.* to inconvenience, to bother, to annoy.

incomodidad, (ēng·ko·mo·thē·thäth´) *f.* inconvenience, annoyance, discomfort.

incómodo, da, (ēng·ko´mo·tho, thä) *adj.* uncomfortable, inconvenient.

incomparable, (ēng·kom·pâ·rä´vle) *adj.* incomparable, matchless.

incompatibilidad, (ēng·kôm·pâ·tē·vē·lē·thäth´) *f.* incompatibility.

incompatible, (ēng·kom·pâ·tē´vle) *adj.* incompatible.

incompetencia, (ēng·kom·pe·ten´syä) *f.* incompetency.

incompetente, (ēng·kom·pe·ten´te) *adj.* incompetent.

incompleto, ta, (ēng·kom·ple´to, tä) *adj.* incomplete.

incomprensible, (ēng·kom·pren·sē´vle) *adj.* incomprehensible.

incomunicado, da,(ēng·ko·mū·nē·kä´tho, thä) *adj.* incommunicado.

inconcebible, (ēng·kon·se·vē´vle) *adj.* inconceivable.

inconexo, xa, (ēng·ko·nek´so, sä) *adj.* unconnected.

inconforme, (ēng·kom·for´me) *adj.* in disagreement; unsatisfied.

incongelable, (ēng·kon·he·lä´vle) *adj.* **solución —,** antifreeze.

incongruencia, (ēng·kong·grwen´syä) *f.* incongruity.

incongruo, grua, (ēng·kong´grwo, grwâ) *adj.* incongruous.

inconocible, (ēng·ko·no·sē´v1e) *adj.* (Sp.

Am.) unrecognizable.

inconsciencia, (eng·kons·syen´syâ) *f.* unconsciousness.

inconsciente, (ēng·kons·syen´te) *adj.* unconscious.

inconsecuencia, (ēng·kon·se·kwen´syâ) *f.* inconsistency, illogic.

inconsecuente, (ēng·kon·se·kwen´te) *adj.* inconsistent, illogical.

inconsiderado, da, (ēng·kon·se·the·râ tho, thâ) *adj.* inconsiderate.

inconsolable, (en·kon·so·lâ´vle) *adj.* inconsolable.

inconstante, (ēng·kons·tân´te) *adj.* inconstant, variable.

inconstitucional, (ēng·kons·tē·tū·syo·nâl´) *adj.* unconstitutional.

inconveniencia, (ēng·kom·be·nyen´syâ) *f.* inconvenience *(descomodidad);* unsuitability.

inconveniente, (ēng·kom·be·nyen´te) *adj.* inconvenient; unsuitable; **—,** *m.* objection, disadvantage *(impedimento);* resulting damage, harm done *(daño).*

incorporación, (ēng·kor·po·râ·syon´) *f.* incorporation; joining.

incorporar, (ēng·kor·po·râr´) *va.* to incorporate; to sit up, to straighten up *(el cuerpo);* **—se,** to join; to sit up, to straighten up.

incorrecto, ta, (eng·ko·rrek´to, tâ) *adj.* incorrect.

incorregible, (eng·ko·rre·hē´vle) *adj.* incorrigible.

incorruptible, (ēng·ko·rrūp·tē´vle) *adj.* incorruptible.

incredulidad, (ēng·kre·thū·lē·thäth´) *f.* incredulity.

incrédulo, la, (ēng·krē´thū·lo, lâ) *adj.* incredulous.

increíble, (ēng·kre·ē´vle) *adj.* incredible.

incremento, (ēng·kre·men´to) *m.* increment.

incubación, (ēng·kū·vâ·syon´) *f.* incubation, hatching.

incubadora, (ēng·kū·vâ·tho´râ) *f.* incubator.

incubar, (ēng·kū·vâr´) *va.* to hatch, to incubate.

inculcar, (ēng·kūl·kâr´) *va.* to inculcate.

inculpar, (ēng·kūl·pâr´) *va.* to accuse.

inculto, ta, (ēng·kūl´to, tâ) *adj.* uncultivated.

incumbencia, (ēng·kūm·ben´syâ) *f.* incumbency, duty; **eso no es de mi —,** that isn´t my responsibility.

incumbir, (ēng·kūm·bēr´) *vn.* to be incum-

m met, **n** not, **p** pot, **r** very, **rr** (none), **s** so, **t** toy, **th** with, **v** eve, **w** we, **y** yes, **z** zero

bent, to be the responsibility.

incumplido, da, (ēng·kūm·plē´tho, thâ) *adj.* unreliable.

incurable, (ēng·kū·rä´vle) *adj.* incurable.

incurrir, (ēng·kū·rrēr´) *vn.* to incur.

incursión, (ēng·kūr·syon´) *f.* incursion; — **aérea,** air raid.

indagación, (ēn·dâ·gâ·syon´) *f.* investigation, research.

indagar, (en·dâ·gâr´) *va.* to investigate, to research.

indebido, da, (ēn·de·vē´tho, thâ) *adj.* undue; illegal, unlawful *(ilícito).*

indecencia, (ēn·de·sen´syâ) *f.* indecency.

indecente, (ēn·de·sen´te) *adj.* indecent.

indecible, (ēn·de·sē´vle) *adj.* inexpressible, unutterable.

indecisión, (ēn·de·sē·syon´) *f.* irresolution, indecision.

indeciso, sa, (en·de·sē´so, sâ) *adj.* irresolute, undecided; vague, imprecise *(vago).*

indecoroso, sa, (ēn·de·ko·ro´so, sâ) *adj.* unbecoming, indecorous, improper.

indefenso, sa, (ēn·de·fen´so, sâ) *adj.* defenseless.

indefinible, (ēn·de·fē·nē´vle) *adj.* indefinable.

indefinido, da, (ēn·de·fē·nē´tho, thâ) *adj.* indefinite.

indeleble, (ēn·de·le´vle) *adj.* indelible.

indelicado, da, (ēn·de·lē·kâ´tho, thâ) *adj.* indelicate.

indemnización, (ēn·dem·nē·sâ·syon´) *f.* indemnity, compensation.

indemnizar, (ēn·dem·nē·sâr´) *va.* to indemnify.

independencia, (ēn·de·pen·den´syâ) *f.* independence.

independiente, (ēn·de·pen·dyen´te) *adj.* independent.

indescriptible, (ēn·des·krēp·tē´vle) *adj.* indescribable.

indestructible, (ēn·des·trūk·tē´vle) *adj.* indestructible.

indeterminado, da, (ēn·de·ter·mē·nâ´tho, thâ) *adj.* undetermined; irresolute, undecided *(indeciso).*

Indias Occidentales, (ēn´dyâs ok·sē·then·tâ´les) *f. pl.* West Indies.

Indias Orientales, (ēn´dyâs o·ryen·tâ´les) *f. pl.* East Indies.

indicación, (ēn·dē·kâ·syon´) *f.* indication.

indicador, (ēn·dē·kâ·thor´) *m.* indicator; — **de dirección,** (avi.) direction indicator.

indicar, (ēn·dē·kâr´) *va.* to indicate.

indicativo, va, (ēn·dē·kâ·tē´vo, vâ) *adj.* and *m.* indicative.

índice, (ēn´dē·se) *m.* index; hand *(del*

reloj); index finger *(dedo);* table of contents *(de capítulos).*

indicio, (en·dē´syo) *m.* indication, sign.

índico, ca, (ēn´dē·ko, kâ) *adj.* East Indian; **Océano I—,** Indian Ocean.

indiferencia, (ēn·dē·fe·ren´syâ) *f.* indifference, unconcern.

indiferente, (ēn·dē·fe·ren´te) *adj.* indifferent.

indígena, (ēn·dē´he·nâ) *adj.* indigenous, native; —, *m.* and *f.* native.

indigencia, (ēn·dē·hen´syâ) *f.* indigence.

indigente, (ēn·dē·hen´te) *adj.* indigent.

indigestión, (ēn·dē·hes·tyon´) *f.* indigestion.

indigesto, ta, (ēn·dē·hes´to, tâ) *adj.* indigestible; undigested *(sin digerir).*

indignación, (ēn·dēg·nâ·syon´) *f.* indignation.

indignado, da, (ēn·dēg·nâ´tho, thâ) *adj.* indignant.

indignar, (ēn·dēg·nâr´) *va.* to anger, to make indignant.

indigno, na, (ēn·dēg´no, nâ) *adj.* unworthy, undeserving; disgraceful, contemptible *(ruin).*

indio, dia, (ēn´dyo, dyâ) *n.* and *adj.* Indian, native.

indirecta, (ēn·dē·rek´ta) *f.* innuendo, hint, cue, insinuation.

indirecto, ta, (ēn·dē·rek´to, tâ) *adj.* indirect.

indisciplinado, da, (ēn·dēs·sē·plē·nâ´tho, thâ) *adj.* undisciplined.

indiscreción, (ēn·dēs·kre·syon´) *f.* indiscretion.

indiscreto, ta, (ēn·dēs·kre´to, tâ) *adj.* indiscreet.

indiscutible, (ēn·dēs·kū·tē´vle) *adj.* unquestionable.

indisoluble, (ēn·dē·so·lū´vle) *adj.* indissoluble.

indispensable, (ēn·dēs·pen·sâ´vle) *adj.* indispensable.

indisponer*, (ēn·dēs·po·ner´) *va.* to make feel under the weather *(alterar la salud);* to put at odds *(malquistar);* to indispose.

indisposición, (ēn·dēs·po·sē·syon´) *f.* indisposition; unwillingness *(para una cosa).*

indispuesto, ta, (ēn·dēs·pwes´to, tâ) *adj.* indisposed.

individual, (ēn·dē·vē·thwâl´) *adj.* individual.

individualizar, (ēn·dē·vē·thwâ·lē·sâr) *va.* to individualize.

individuo, (ēn·dē·vē´thwo) *m.* individual.

indivisible, (ēn·dē·vē·sē´vle) *adj.* indivisi-

â arm, **e** they, **ē** bē, **o** fore, **ū** blūe, **b** bad, **ch** chip, **d** day, **f** fat, **g** go, **h** hot, **k** kid, **1** let

ble.

índole, (ēn´do•le) *f.* temperament, inclination *(genio);* class, kind, nature *(clase).*

indolencia, (ēn•do•len´syā) *f.* indolence.

indolente, (ēn•do•len´te) *adj.* indolent.

indomable, (ēn•do•mā´vle) *adj.* untamable, wild.

indómito, ta, (ēn•do´mē•to, tā) *adj.* untamed; (fig.) indomitable, uncontrollable.

inducción, (ēn•dūk•syon´) *f.* induction; **carrete de —** or **bobina de —,** induction coil.

inducir*, (ēn•dū•sēr´) *va.* to induce.

indudable, (ēn•dū•thā´vle) *adj.* unquestionable, certain.

indulgencia, (ēn•dūl•hen´syā) *f.* indulgence.

indulgente, (ēn•dūl•hen´te) *adj.* indulgent.

indultar, (ēn•dūl•tār´) *va.* to pardon; to exempt *(eximir).*

indulto, (ēn•dūl´to) *m.* pardon; exemption.

indumentaria, (ēn•dū•men•tā´ryā) *f.* clothing, attire.

industria, (ēn•dūs´tryā) *f.* industry; ability, knack *(destreza).*

industrial, (ēn•dūs•tryāl´) *adj.* industrial.

industrioso, sa, (ēn•dūs•tryo´so, sā) *adj.* industrious; skillful, able *(diestro).*

inédito, ta, (ē•ne´thē•to, tā) *adj.* unpublished.

inefable, (ē•ne•fā´vle) *adj.* ineffable.

ineficacia, (ē•ne•fē•kā´syā) *f.* inefficacy.

ineptitud, (ē•nep•tē•tūth´) *f.* ineptitude.

inepto, ta, (ē•nep´to, tā) *adj.* inept, unfit; stupid *(necio).*

inequívoco, ca, (ē•ne•kē´vo•ko, kā) *adj.* unmistakable.

inercia, (ē•ner´syā) *f.* inertia.

inerte, (ē•ner´te) *adj.* inert; (fig.) dull, sluggish.

inesperado, da, (ē•nes•pe•rā´tho, thā) *adj.* unexpected, unforeseen.

inevitable, (ē•ne•vē•tā´vle) *adj.* unavoidable, inevitable.

inexacto, ta, (ē•nek•sāk´to, tā) *adj.* inaccurate, inexact.

inexcusable, (ē•nes•kū•sā´vle) *adj.* inexcusable, unpardonable.

inexorable, (ē•nek•so•rā´vle) *adj.* inexorable.

inexperto, ta, (ē•nes•per´to, tā) *adj.* inexperienced; **—,** *n.* novice.

inexplicable, (ē•nes•plē•kā´vle) *adj.* inexplicable.

infalible, (ēm•fā•lē´vle) *adj.* infallible.

infame, (ēm•fā´me) *adj.* infamous; terrible *(vil);* **—,** *m.* and *f.* wretch, scoundrel.

infamia, (ēm•fā´myā) *f.* infamy.

infancia, (ēm•fān´syā) *f.* early childhood, infancy.

infanta, (ēm•fān´tā) *f.* infanta; little girl *(niña pequeña).*

infante, (ēm•fān´te) *m.* (mil.) infantryman; infante; little boy *(niño pequeño).*

infantería, (ēm•fān•te•rē´ā) *f.* infantry; — **de marina,** marines.

infanticidio, (ēm•fān•tē•sē´thyo) *m.* infanticide.

infantil, (ēm•fān•tēl´) *adj.* infantile; **parálisis —,** infantile paralysis, poliomyelitis.

infarto, (ēm•fār´to) *m.* (med.) infarct, heart attack.

infatigable, (ēm•fā•tē•gā´vle) *adj.* indefatigable.

infatuación, (ēm•fā•twā•syon´) *f.* infatuation.

infausto, ta, (ēm•fā´ūs•to, tā) *adj.* unlucky, unfortunate.

infección, (ēm•fek•syon´) *f.* infection.

infeccioso, sa, (ēm•fek•syo´so, sā) *adj.* infectious, contagious.

infectar, (ēm•fek•tār´) *va.* to infect.

infeliz, (ēm•fe•lēs´) *adj.* unhappy, unfortunate.

inferior, (ēm•fe•ryor´) *adj.* lower *(colocado debajo);* (fig.) inferior.

inferioridad, (ēm•fe•ryo•rē•thāth´) *f.* inferiority; **complejo de —,** inferiority complex.

inferir*(ēm•fe•rēr´) *va.* to infer; to cause, to bring about *(ocasionar).*

infernal, (ēm•fer•nāl´) *adj.* infernal.

infestar, (ēm•fes•tār´) *va.* to infest.

infidelidad, (ēm•fē•the•lē•thāth´) *f.* infidelity.

infiel, (ēm•fyel´) *adj.* unfaithful; inaccurate *(falto de exactitud).*

infierno, (ēm•fyer´no) *m.* hell.

infiltración, (ēm•fēl•trā•syon´) *f.* infiltration.

infiltrar, (ēm•fēl•trār´) *va.* and *vr.* to infiltrate.

ínfimo, ma, (ēm´fē•mo,mā) *adj.* lowest, most abject.

infinidad, (ēm•fē•nē•thāth´) *f.* infinity; (fig.) great number.

infinitivo, (ēm•fē•nē•tē´vo) *m.* (gram.) infinitive.

infinito, ta, (ēm•fē•nē´to, tā) *adj.* infinite; **—to,** *adv. a* great deal; immensely; **—,** *m.* (math. and phot.) infinity.

inflación, (ēm•flā•syon´) *f.* inflation.

inflamable, (ēm•flā•mā´vle) *adj.* inflammable.

inflamación, (ēm•flā•mā•syon´) *f.* inflammation.

inflamar, (ēm·flâ·mâr´) va. to set fire to *(encender);* (fig.) to inflame *(el ánimo);* **—se,** to catch fire.

inflar, (ēm·flâr´) va. to inflate.

inflexible, (ēm·flek·sē´vle) adj. inflexible.

influencia, (ēm·flwen´syâ) f. influence.

influenza, (ēm·flwen´sa) f. influenza.

influir*, (ēm·flwēr´) vn. to influence.

influjo, (ēm·flū´ho) m. influence.

influyente, (ēm·flū·yen´te) adj. influential.

información, (ēm·for·mâ·syon´) f. information; inquiry, investigation *(averiguación).*

informal, (ēm·for·mâl´) adj. informal; unreliable *(falto de seriedad).*

informalidad, (ēm·for·ma·lē·thâth´) f. unreliability; informality.

informante (ēm·for·mân´te) m. and f. informer, informant.

informar, (ēm·for·mâr´) va. to inform, to report.

informe (ēm·for´me) m. report, account *(acción de informar);* piece of information *(noticia);* —, adj. shapeless.

infortunio, (ēm·for·tū´nyo) m. misfortune.

infracción, (ēm·frâk·syon´) f. infraction, violation; **— de tránsito,** traffic violation.

infrarrojo, ja, (ēm·frâ·rro´ho, hâ) adj. infrared.

infrecuente, (ēm·fre·kwen´te) adj. infrequent, unusual.

infringir, (ēm·frēn·hēr´) va. to infringe on, to violate.

infructuoso, sa, (ēm·frūk·two´so, sâ) adj. fruitless, unproductive, unprofitable.

infundado, da, (ēm·fūn·dâ´tho, thâ) adj. groundless.

infundir, (ēm·fūn·dēr´) va. to infuse, to instill.

infusión, (ēm·fū·syon´) f. infusion.

ingeniar, (ēn·he·nyâr´) va. to conceive, to contrive; **—se,** to contrive a way, to manage.

ingeniero, (ēn·he·nye´ro) m. engineer.

ingenio, (ēn·he´nyo) m. ingenuity; talent *(sujeto ingenioso);* creativity *(don creador);* ability, cleverness *(industria);* machine, contrivance *(máquina);* **— de azúcar,** sugar mill.

ingenioso, sa, (ēn·he·nyo´so, sâ) adj. ingenious; talented; creative; clever.

ingenuidad, (ēn·he·nwē·thâth´) f. ingenuousness.

ingenuo, nua, (ēn·he´nwo, nwâ) adj. ingenuous.

ingerencia, (ēn·he·ren´syâ) f. interference,

meddling.

ingerir*, (ēn·he·rēr´) va. to ingest; **— se,** to mix, to meddle.

Inglaterra, (ēng·glâ·te´rrâ) f. England.

ingle, (ēng´gle) f. groin.

inglés, esa, (ēng·gles´, e´sâ) adj. English; **—,** n. Briton; **—,** m. Englishman; **—,** f. Englishwoman; **—,** m. English language.

ingratitud, (ēng·grâ·tē·tūth´) f. ingratitude.

ingrato, ta, (ēng·grâ´to, tâ) adj. ungrateful *(desagradecido);* disagreeable, unpleasant *(áspero);* unproductive, unrewarding.

ingravidez, (ēn·grâ·vē·thes´) f. weightlessness.

ingrediente, (ēng·gre·thyen´te) m. ingredient.

ingreso, (ēng·gre´so) m. entrance *(entrada);* (com.) receipt.

inhabilitar, (ē·nâ·vē·lē·târ´) va. to disqualify.

inhabitable, (ē·nâ·vē·tâ´vle) adj. uninhabitable.

inhalador, (ē·nâ·lâ·thor´) m. inhaler.

inherente, (ē·ne·ren´te) adj. inherent.

inhibición, (ē·nē·vē·syon´) f. inhibition.

inhumación, (ē·nū·mâ·syon´) f. burial, interment; **agencia de —ones,** funeral parlor.

inhumano, na, (ē·nū·mâ´no, nâ) adj. inhuman, cruel.

inicial, (ē·nē·syâl´) f. and adj. initial.

iniciar, (ē·nē·syâr´) va. to initiate, to begin; **—se,** to be initiated; (eccl.) to receive one´s first orders.

iniciativo, va, (ē·nē·syâ·tē´vo, vâ) adj. first, preliminary; **—,** f. initiative.

inicuo, cua, (ē·nē´kwo, kwâ) adj. iniquitous; unjust *(falto de equidad).*

inigualado, da, (ē·nē·gwâ·lâ´tho, thâ) adj. unequaled.

inimitable, (ē·nē·mē·tâ´vle) adj. inimitable.

iniquidad, (ē·nē·kē·thâth´) f. iniquity; injustice.

injertar, (ēn·her·târ´) va. to graft.

injerto, (ēn·her´to) m. graft; grafting *(acción);* **— de órganos,** medical transplant.

injuria, (ēn·hū´ryâ) f. offense, insult; harm, damage *(daño).*

injuriar, (ēn·kū·ryâr´) va. to insult; to harm *(dañar).*

injusticia, (ēn·hūs·tē´syâ) f. injustice.

injusto, ta, (ēn·hūs´to, ta) adj. unjust.

inmaculado, da, (ēn·mâ·kū·lâ´tho, thâ) adj. immaculate.

inmaduro, ra, (ēn·mâ·thū´ro, râ) adj.

â arm, **e** they, **ē** bē, **o** fore, **ū** blūe, **b** bad, **ch** chip, **d** day, **f** fat, **g** go, **h** hot, **k** kid, **l** let

immature.

inmaturo, ra, (ēn·mâ·tū´ro, râ) *adj.* immature.

inmediación, (ēn·me·thyâ·syon´) *f.* nearness *(proximidad);* immediacy.

inmediatamente, (ēn·me·thyâ·tâ·men´te) *adv.* immediately, at once.

inmediato, ta, (ēn·me·thyâ´to, tâ) *adj.* immediate; **de —to,** immediately.

inmejorable, (ēn·me·ho·râ´vle) *adj.* unsurpassable.

inmemorial, (ēn·me·mo·ryâl´) *adj.* immemorial.

inmensidad, (ēn·men·sē·thâth´) *f.* immensity.

inmenso, sa, (ēn·men´so, sâ) *adj.* immense.

inmensurable, (ēn·men·sū·râ´vle) *adj.* immeasurable.

inmersión, (ēn·mer·syon´) *f.* immersion.

inmigración, (ēn·mē·grâ·syon´) *f.* immigration.

inmigrar, (ēn·mē·grâr´) *vn.* to immigrate.

inminente, (ēn·mē·nen´te) *adj.* imminent.

inmoderado, da, (ēn·mo·the·râ´tho, thâ) *adj.* immoderate.

inmodesto, ta, (ēn·mo·thes´to, tâ) *adj.* immodest.

inmoral, (ēn·mo·râl´) *adj.* immoral.

inmoralidad, (ēn·mo·râ·lē·thâth´) *f.* immorality.

inmortal, (ēn·mor·tâl´) *adj.* immortal.

inmortalidad, (ēn·mor·tâ·lē·thâth´) *f.* immortality.

inmortalizar, (ēn·mor·tâ·lē·sâr´) *va.* to immortalize.

inmóvil, (ēn·mo´vēl) *adj.* immovable; motionless *(que no se mueve);* firm, resolute *(constante).*

inmovilidad, (ēn·mo·vē·lē·thâth´) *f.* immobility.

inmueble, (ēn·mwe´vle) *adj.* real; **bienes —s,** real estate, immovables.

inmundicia, (ēn·mūn·dē´syâ) *f.* dirt, filth; (fig.) indecency.

inmundo, da, (ēn·mūn´do, dâ) *adj.* filthy, dirty; (fig.) indecent.

inmune, (ēn·mū´ne) *adj.* immune.

inmunidad, (ēn·mū·nē·thâth´) *f.* immunity.

inmunizar, (ēn·mū·nē·sâr´) *va.* to immunize.

inmutable, (ēn·mū·tâ´vle) *adj.* immutable, unchangeable.

inmutar, (ēn·mū·târ´) *va.* to change; **—se,** to change countenance.

innato, ta, (ēn·nâ´to, tâ) *adj.* inborn, innate.

innecesario, ria, (ēn·ne·se·sâ´ryo, ryâ) *adj.* unnecessary,

innovación, (ēn·no·vâ·syon´) *f.* innovation.

innovar, (ēn·no·vâr´) *va.* to innovate.

innumerable, (ēn·nū·me·râ´vle) *adj.* innumerable.

inocencia, (ē·no·sen´syâ) *f.* innocence.

inocente, (ē·no·sen´te) *adj.* innocent.

inocular, (ē·no·kū·lâr´) *va.* to inoculate.

inocuo, cua, (ē·no´kwo, kwâ) *adj.* harmless.

inodoro, ra, (ē·no·tho´ro, râ) *adj.* odorless; **—,** *m.* water closet.

inofensivo, va, (ē·no·fen·sē´vo, vâ) *adj.* inoffensive, harmless.

inolvidable, (ē·nol·vē·thâ´vle) *adj.* unforgettable.

inoxidable, (ē·nok·sē·thâ´vle) *adj.* rustproof; **acero —,** stainless steel.

inquebrantable, (ēng·ke·vrân·tâ´vle) *adj.* unbreakable; (fig.) unswerving, unshakable.

inquietar, (ēng·kye·târ´) *va.* to disturb, to concern, to worry.

inquieto, ta, (ēng·kye´to, tâ) *adj.* restless, anxious, uneasy.

inquietud, (ēng·kye·tūth´) *f.* restlessness, worry, anxiety.

inquilino, na, (ēng·kē·lē´no, nâ) *n.* tenant, renter.

inquirir*, (ēng·kē·rēr´) *va.* to inquire into, to investigate.

inquisición, (ēng·kē·sē·syon´) *f.* (eccl.) inquisition; inquiry, investigation.

insaciable, (ēn·sâ·syâ´vle) *adj.* insatiable.

insalubre, (ēn·sâ·lū´vre) *adj.* unhealthful.

insano, na, (ēn·sâ´no, nâ) *adj.* insane, mad.

inscribir*, (ēns·krē·vēr´) *va.* to inscribe; **— se,** to register.

inscripción, (ēns·krēp·syon´) *f.* inscription; registration.

insecticida, (ēn·sek·tē·sē´thâ) *m.* insecticide.

insecto, (ēn·sek´to) *m.* insect.

inseguridad, (ēn·se·gū·rē·thâth´) *f.* insecurity; uncertainty *(incertidumbre).*

inseguro, ra, (ēn·se·gū´ro, râ) *adj.* uncertain; unsteady, insecure *(inestable).*

insensatez, (ēn·sen·sâ·tes´) *f.* stupidity, folly.

insensato, ta, (ēn·sen·sâ´to, tâ) *adj.* stupid, senseless.

insensibilidad, (ēn·sen·sē·vē·lē·thâth´) *f.* insensibility.

insensible, (ēn·sen·sē´vle) *adj.* insensible; (fig.) insensitive *(impasible);* imperceptible.

inseparable, (ēn·se·pâ·râ´vle) *adj.* inseparable.

inserción, (ēn·ser·syon´) *f.* insertion.

insertar, (ēn·ser·târ´) *va.* to insert.

inservible, (ēn·ser·vē´vle) *adj.* unserviceable, useless.

insigne, (ēn·sēg´ne) *adj.* notable, famous.

insignia, (ēn·sēg´nyâ) *f.* badge; **—s,** *pl.* insignia.

insignificancia, (ēn·sēg·nē·fē·kân´syâ) *f.* insignificance.

insignificante, (ēn·sēg·nē·fē·kân´te) *adj.* insignificant.

insinuación, (ēn·sē·nwâ·syon´) *f.* insinuation, hint.

insinuar, (ēn·sē·nwâr´) *va.* to insinuate, to imply, to hint; **—se,** to steal, to slip, to creep.

insipidez, (ēn·sē·pē·thes´) *f.* insipidity.

insípido, da, (ēn·sē´pē·tho, thâ) *adj.* insipid.

insistencia, (ēn·sēs·ten´syâ) *f.* insistence.

insistir, (ēn·sēs·tēr´) *vn.* to insist; to rest, to lie *(descansar).*

insociable, (ēn·so·syâ´vle) *adj.* unsociable.

insolente, (ēn·so·len´te) *adj.* insolent.

insólito, ta, (ēn·so´lē·to, tâ) *adj.* unusual, uncommon.

insoluble, (ēn·so·lū´vle) *adj.* insoluble.

insolvente, (ēn·sol·ven´te) *adj.* insolvent.

insomnio, (ēn·som´nyo) *m.* insomnia.

insoportable, (ēn·so·por·tâ´vle) *adj.* intolerable.

inspección, (ēns·pek·syon´) *f.* inspection.

inspeccionar, (ēns·pek·syo·nâr´) *va.* to inspect, to examine.

inspector, (ēns·pek·tor´) *m.* inspector.

inspiración, (ēns·pē·râ·syon´) *f.* inspiration.

inspirar, (ēns·pē·râr´) *va.* to inspire.

instalación, (ēns·tâ·lâ·syon´) *f.* installation.

instalar, (ēns·tâ·lâr´) *va.* to install; **— de nuevo,** to reinstate.

instancia, (ēns·tân´syâ) *f.* entreaty, request; **elevar una —,** to make a request.

instantáneo, nea, (ēns·tân·thâ´ne·o, ne·â) *adj.* instantaneous; **—,** *f.* snapshot.

instante, (ēns·tân´te) *m.* instant; **al —,** immediately.

instar, (ēns·târ´) *va.* to press, to urge; **—,** *vn.* to be urgent.

instaurar, (ēns·tâû·râr´) *va.* to establish *(establecer);* to reestablish, to renew *(restablecer).*

instigación, (ēns·tē·gâ·syon´) *f.* instigation.

instigar, (ēns·tē·gâr´) *va.* to instigate.

instintivo, va, (ēns·tēn·tē´vo, vâ) *adj.* instinctive.

instinto, (ēns·tēn´to) *m.* instinct; **— de conservación,** instinct of self-preservation.

institución, (ēns·tē·tū·syon´) *f.* institution.

instituir*, (ēns·tē·twēr´) *va.* to institute, to establish.

instituto, (ēns·tē·tū´to) *m.* institute.

institutriz, (ēns·tē·tū·trēs´) *f.* governess.

instrucción, (ēns´trūk·syon´) *f.* instruction; education *(enseñanza);* **—ones breves,** (mil.) briefing.

instructivo, va, (ēns·trūk·tē´vo, vâ) *adj.* instructive.

instructor, (ēns·trūk·tor´) *m.* instructor, teacher.

instruido, da, (ēns·trwē´tho, thâ) *adj.* well-educated; well-informed.

instruir*, (ēns·trwēr´) *va.* to instruct, to teach; to let know, to inform *(informar).*

instrumentación, (ēns·trū·men·tâ·syon´) *f.* instrumentation.

instrumento, (ēns·trū·men´to) *m.* implement *(herramienta);* instrument; **— de viento,** wind instrument; **— de cuerda,** string instrument; **aproximación por —s,** (avi.) instrument approach; **tablero de —,** instrument panel; **vuelo con —s,** (avi.) blind flying.

insubordinado, da, (ēn·sū·vor·thē·nâ´tho, thâ) *adj.* insubordinate.

insubordinar, (ēn·sū·vor·thē·nâr´) *va.* to incite to insubordination; **—se,** to rebel.

insuficiencia, (ēn·sū·fē·syen´syâ) *f.* insufficiency, inadequacy.

insuficiente, (ēn·sū·fē·syen´te) *adj.* insufficient, inadequate.

insufrible, (ēn·sū·frē´vle) *adj.* insufferable, intolerable.

insular, (ēn·sū·lâr´) *m. and f.* islander; **—,** *adj.* insular.

insulina, (ēn·sū·lē´nâ) *f.* insulin.

insulso, sa, (ēn·sūl´so, sâ) *adj.* insipid, tasteless.

insultar, (ēn·sūl·târ´) *va.* to insult.

insulto, (ēn·sūl´to) *m.* insult, offense.

insuperable, (ēn·sū·pe·râ´vle) *adj.* insurmountable.

insurrección, (ēn·sū·rrek·syon´) *f.* insurrection.

insurrecto, ta, (ēn·sū·rrek´to, tâ) *n. and adj.* insurgent, rebel.

insustituible, (ēn·sūs·tē·twē´vle) *adj.* irreplaceable.

intacto, ta, (ēn·tâk´to, tâ) *adj.* intact, whole.

intachable, (ēn·tâ·châ´vle) *adj.* blameless,

irreproachable.

integración, (ēn·te·grä·syon´) f. integration.

integral, (ēn·te·grâl´) adj. integral, whole.

integridad, (ēn·te·grē·thâth´) f. integrity; virginity (virginidad).

íntegro, gra, (ēn´te·gro, grâ) adj. integral, whole; (fig.) honest, upright (probo).

intelectual, (ēn·te·lek·twâl´) adj. intellectual.

inteligencia, (ēn·te·lē·hen´syâ) f. intelligence, understanding.

inteligente, (ēn·te·lē·hen´te) adj. intelligent.

inteligible, (ēn·te·lē·hē´vle) adj. intelligible.

intemperancia, (ēn·tem·pe·rân´syâ) f. intemperance.

intemperie, (ēn·tem·pe´rye) f. rough weather; **a la —,** outdoors.

intempestivo, va, (ēn·tem·pes·tē´vo, vâ) adj. inopportune, badly timed.

intención, (ēn·ten·syon´) f. intention, wish; caution (cautela); (fig.) dangerousness (de un animal); **con —,** on purpose.

intencionadamente, (ēn·ten·syo·nâ·thâ·men´te) adv. intentionally.

intencionado, da, (ēn·ten·syo·nâ´tho, thâ) adj. inclined, disposed.

intendente, (ēn·ten·den´te) m. intendant.

intensidad, (ēn·ten·sē·thâth´) f. intensity.

intensificar, (ēn·ten·sē·fē·kâr´) va. to intensify.

intensivo, va, (ēn·ten·sē´vo, vâ) adj. intensive.

intenso, sa, (ēn·ten´so, sâ) adj. intense.

intentar, (ēn·ten·târ´) va. to try, to attempt (procurar); to intend.

intento, (ēn·ten´to) m. intent, purpose.

interamericano, na, (ēn·te·râ·me·rē·kâ´no, nâ) adj. interamerican.

intercalar, (ēn·ter·kâ·lâr´) va. to interpolate, to intercalate.

intercambio, (ēn·ter·kâm´byo) m. interchange.

interceder, (ēn·ter·se·ther´) vn. to intercede.

interceptar, (ēn·ter·sep·târ´) va. to intercept.

intercesión, (ēn·ter·se·syon´) f. intercession.

interés, (ēn·te·res´) m. interest; **tipo de —,** rate of interest.

interesado, da, (ēn·te·re·sâ´tho, thâ) adj. interested; selfish (egoísta) —, n. person concerned.

interesante, (ēn·te·re·sân´te) adj. interesting.

interesar, (ēn·te·re·sâr´) to interest; to

involve (obligar); **—se,** to become interested.

interferencia, (ēn·ter·fe·ren´syâ) f. interference.

interino, na, (ēn·te·rē´no, nâ) adj. provisional; **secretario —,** acting secretary.

interior, (ēn·te·ryôr´) adj. inner; internal (propio de la nación); **ropa —,** underwear; **—,** m. interior, **—es,** pl. entrails, internal parts.

interioridad, (ēn·te·ryo·rē·thâth´) f. inner nature; **—es,** pl. inner secrets.

interjección, (ēn·ter·hek·syon´) f. (gram.) interjection.

interlocutor, ra, (ēn·ter·lo·kū·tor´, râ) n. speaker.

interludio, (ēn·ter·lū´thyo) m. interlude.

intermediar, (ēn·ter·me·thyâr´) va. to interpose, to intervene, to mediate.

intermediario, ria, (ēn·ter·me·thyâ´ryo, ryâ) n. and adj. intermediary.

intermedio, dia, (ēn·ter·me´thyo, thyâ) adj. intermediate; **—,** m. interval; (theat.) intermission; **por —dio de,** through, by means of.

interminable, (ēn·ter·mē·nâ´vle) adj. interminable, endless.

intermitente, (ēn·ter·mē·ten´te) adj. intermittent.

internacional, (ēn·ter·nâ·syo·nâl´) adj. international.

internado, da, (ēn·ter·nâ´tho thâ) adj. interned; **—,** m. boarding school; student body (conjunto de alumnos).

internar, (ēn·ter·nâr´) va. to take inland; to intern (encerrar); **—se,** to penetrate; to curry favor (ganarse la amistad).

internista, (ēn·ter·nēs´tâ) m. and f. (med.) internist.

interno, na, (ēn·ter´no, nâ) adj. internal; boarding (alumno); **—,** n. boarding school student.

interpelar, (ēn·ter·pe·lâr´) va. to request the aid of; to interpellate (exigir explicaciones).

interplanetario, ria, (ēn·ter·plâ·ne·tâ´ryo, ryâ) adj. interplanetary.

interpolar, (ēn·ter·po·lâr´) va. to interpolate; to interrupt momentarily (interrumpir).

interponer*, (ēn·ter·po·ner´) va. to interpose.

interpretación, (ēn·ter·pre·tâ·syon´) f. interpretation.

interpretar, (ēn·ter·pre·târ´) va. to interpret.

intérprete, (ēn·ter´pre·te) m. and f. interpreter.

interrogación, (ēn·te·rro·gâ·syon´) f. question.

interrogante, (ēn·te·rro·gân´te) adj. interrogative; —, m. and f. questioner.

interrogar, (ēn·te·rro·gâr´) va. to question.

interrogativo, va, (ēn·te·rro·gâ·tē´vo, vâ) adj. interrogative.

interrogatorio, (ēn·te´rro·gâ·to´ryo) m. questioning.

interrumpir, (ēn·te·rrūm·pēr´) va. to interrupt.

interrupción, (ēn·te·rrūp·syon´) f. interruption.

interruptor, (ēn·te·rrūp·tor´) m. (elec.) switch.

intersección, (ēn·ter·sek·syon´) f. intersection.

intersectario, ría, (ēn·ter·sek·tâ´ryo, ryâ) adj. interdenominational.

intervalo, (ēn·ter·vâ´lo) m. interval.

intervención, (ēn·ter·ven·syon´) f. intervention; (med.) operation.

intervenir*, (ēn·ter·ve·nēr´) vn. to happen (acontecer); to take part (tomar parte); to intervene, to intercede; —, va. to audit; (med.) to operate on.

intestado, da, (ēn·tes·tâ´tho, thâ) adj. intestate.

intestino, na, (ēn·tes·tē´no, nâ) adj. internal; —, m. intestine.

intimar, (ēn·tē·mâr´) va. to intimate, to declare; —, vn. to become intimate.

intimidación, (ēn·tē·mē·thâ·syon´) f. intimidation.

intimidad, (ēn·tē·mē·thâth´) f. intimacy.

intimidar, (ēn·tē·mē·thâr´) va. to intimidate; —se, to lose courage.

íntimo, ma, (ēn´tē·mo, ma) adj. intimate; ropa —, lingerie.

intocable, (ēn·to·kâ´vle) adj. untouchable.

intolerable, (ēn·to·le·râ´vle) adj. intolerable, insufferable.

intolerancia, (ēn·to·le·rân´syâ) f. intolerance.

intolerante, (ēn·to·le·rân´te) adj. intolerant.

intoxicación, (ēn·tok·sē·kâ·syon´) f. intoxication.

intramuros, (ēn·trâ·mū´ros) adv. in the city, in town.

intranquilo, la, (ēn·trâng·kē´lo, lâ) adj. restless, uneasy.

intransitable, (ēn·trân·sē·tâ´vle) adj. impassable.

intransitivo, va, (ēn·trân·sē·tē´vo, vâ) adj. (gram.) intransitive.

intratable, (ēn·trâ·tâ´vle) adj. intractable; impassable (intransitable).

intravenoso, sa, (ēn·trâ·ve·no´so, sâ) adj. intravenous.

intrepidez, (ēn·tre·pē·thes´) f. daring, courage, intrepidness.

intrépido, da, (ēn·tre´pē·tho, thâ) adj. intrepid, daring.

intriga, (ēn·trē´gâ) f. intrigue, plot.

intrigante, (ēn·trē·gân´te) m. and f. intriguer; —, adj. intriguing, scheming.

intrigar, (ēn·trē·gâr´) va. and vn. to intrigue.

intrínseco, ca, (ēn·trēn´se·ko, kâ) adj. intrinsic.

introducción, (ēn·tro·thūk·syon´) f. introduction.

introducir*, (ēn·tro·thū·sēr´) va. to introduce; to show in (dar entrada); to insert (meter).

introductorio, ría, (ēn·tro·thūk·to´ryo·ryâ) adj. introductory.

introspección, (ēn·tros·pek·syon´) f. introspection.

introspectivo, va, (ēn·tros·pek·tē´vo, vâ) adj. introspective.

intruso, sa, (ēn·trū´so, sâ) adj. intrusive; —, n. intruder, interloper.

intuición, (ēn·twē·syon´) f. intuition.

intuitivo, va, (ēn·twē·tē´vo, vâ) adj. intuitive.

inundación, (ē·nūn·dâ·syon´) f. inundation; (fig.) deluge, flood.

inundar, (ē·nūn·dâr´) va. to inundate, to overflow.

inusitado, da, (ē·nū·sē·tâ´tho, thâ) adj. unusual.

inútil, (ē·nū´tēl) adj. useless needless.

inutilidad, (ē·nū·tē·lē·thâth´) f. uselessness.

inutilizar, (ē·nū·tē·lē·sâr´) va. to make useless.

inútilmente, (ē·nū·tēl·men´te) adv. uselessly.

invadir, (ēm·bâ·thēr´) va. to invade.

invalidar, (ēm·bâ·lē·thâr´) va. to invalidate.

inválido, da, (ēm·bâ´lē·tho, thâ) adj. invalid, null; —, n. invalid.

invariable, (ēm·bâ·ryâ´vle) adj. invariable.

invasión, (ēm·bâ·syon´) f. invasion.

invasor, ra, (ēm·bâ·sor, râ) n. invader; —, adj. invading.

invencible, (ēm·ben·sē´vle) adj. invincible.

invención, (ēm·ben·syon´) f. invention.

inventar, (ēm·ben·târ´) va. to invent.

inventario, (ēm·ben·tâ´ryo) m. inventory.

â arm, e they, ē bē, o fore, ū blūe, b bad, ch chip, d day, f fat, g go, h hot, k kid, 1 let

inventiva, (ēm·ben·tē´vâ) f. inventiveness.

invento, (ēm·ben´to) m. invention.

inventor, ra, (ēm·ben·tor´, râ) n. inventor.

invernadero, (ēm·ber·nâ·the´ro) m. greenhouse.

invernal, (ēm·ber·nâl´) adj. winter.

inverosímil, (ēm·be·ro·sē´mēl) adj. unlikely, improbable.

inversión, (ēm·ber·syon´) f. inversion; (com.) investment.

inversionista, (ēm·ber·syo·nēs´tâ) m. and f. investor.

inverso, sa, (ēm·ber´so, sâ) adj. inverted, inverse; opposite (contrario).

invertebrado, da, (ēm·ber·te·vrâ´tho, thâ) adj. and m. invertebrate.

invertir*, (ēm·ber·tēr´) va. to invert; (com.) to invest; to spend (el tiempo).

investidura, (ēm·bes·tē·thū´râ) f. investiture.

investigación, (ēm·bes·tē·gâ·syon´) f. investigation.

investigar, (ēm·bes·tē·gâr´) va. to investigate.

investir*, (ēm·bes·tēr´) va. to invest, to endow.

invicto, ta, (ēm·bēk´to, tâ) adj. undefeated, never defeated.

invierno, (ēm·byer´no) m. winter; **en pleno** —, in the dead of winter.

inviolable, (ēm·byo·lâ´vle) adj. inviolable.

invisible (ēm·bē·sē´vle) adj. invisible.

invitación, (ēm·bē·tâ·syon´) f. invitation.

invitado, da, (ēm·bē·tâ´tho, thâ) n. guest.

invitar, (ēm·bē·târ´) va. to invite.

invocación, (ēm·bo·kâ·syon´) f. invocation.

invocar, (ēm·bo·kâr´) va. to invoke.

involuntario, ria, (ēm·bo·lūn·tâ´ryo, ryâ) adj. involuntary.

invulnerable, (ēm·būl·ne·râ´vle) adj. invulnerable.

inyección, (ēn·yek·syon´) f. injection; (coll.) shot; — **estimulante**, (med.) booster shot.

inyectar, (ēn·yek·târ´) va. to inject.

inyector, (ēn·yek·tor´) m. (mech.) injector; — **del combustible**, (avi.) afterburner.

ion, (yon) m. ion.

ionosfera, (yo·nos·fe´râ) f. ionosphere.

ir* (ēr) vn. to go; to be (estar); to be diferent (distinguirse); to proceed (proceder); to become, to be fitting (sentar); — **adelante**, to get ahead, to progress; — **y venir**, to go back and forth; — **a lo largo de**, to go along; —**se**, to leak (rezumarse); to slip (deslizarse); to pass on (morrirse); to go away, to leave (moverse).

ira, (ē´râ) f. anger, wrath.

iracundo, da, (ē·râ·kūn´do, dâ) adj. wrathful, enraged.

irascible, (ē·râs·sē´vle) adj. irascible, choleric.

iris, (ē´rēs) m. rainbow; (anat.) iris.

Irlanda, (ēr·lân´dâ) f. Ireland.

irlandés, esa, (ēr·lân·des´ e´sâ) adj. Irish; —, m. Irishman; —, f. Irishwoman.

ironía, (ē·ro·nē´â) f. irony.

irónico, ca, (ē·ro´nē·ko, kâ) adj. ironical, ironic.

irracional, (ē·rrâ·syo·nâl´) adj. irrational.

irradiación, (ē·rrâ·thyâ·syon´) f. irradiation.

irradiado, da, (ē·rrâ·thyâ´tho, thâ) adj. irradiated.

irrazonable, (ē·rrâ·so·nâ´vle) adj. unreasonable.

irrealizable, (ē·rre·â·lē·sâ´vle) adj. unreachable, unattainable.

irrefutable, (ē·rre·fū·tâ´vle) adj. irrefutable.

irregular, (ē·rre·gū·lâr´) adj. irregular.

irremediable, (ē·rre·me·thyâ´vle) adj. beyond help, hopeless.

irreparable, (ē·rre·pâ·râ´vle) adj. irreparable.

irresistible, (ē·rre·sēs·tē´vle) adj. irresistible.

irresoluto, ta, (ē·rre·so·lū´to, tâ) adj. irresolute; unresolved (sin resolver).

irresponsable, (ē·rres·pon·sâ´vle) adj. irresponsible.

irrevocable, (ē·rre·vo·kâ´vle) adj. irrevocable.

irrigación, (ē·rrē·gâ·syon´) f. irrigation.

irrisible, (ē·rrē·sē´vle) adj. laughable.

irrisorio, ria, (ē·rrē·so´ryo, ryâ) adj. ridiculous, laughable.

irritación, (ē·rrē·tâ·syon´) f. irritation.

irritado, da, (ē·rrē·tâ´tho, thâ) adj. irritated.

irritar, (ē·rrē·târ´) va. to irritate; (fig.) to fan, to stir up (aumentar).

irrompible, (ē·rrom·pē´vle) adj. unbreakable.

irrupción, (ē·rrūp·syon´) f. violent attack; invasion (invasión).

isla, (ēz·lâ) f. isle, island.

isleño, ña, (ēz·le´nyo, nyâ) n. islander; —, adj. island.

isobárico, ca, (ē·so·vâ´rē·ko, kâ) adj. isobaric.

isometría, (ē·so·me·trē´â) f. isometrics.

isométrico, ca, (ē·so·me´trē·ko, kâ) adj. isometric.

isotermo, ma, (ē·so·ter´mo, mâ) *adj.* isothermal.

isótopo, (ē·so´to·po) *m.* isotope.

israelí, (ēz·rrâ·e·lē´) *m. and f. and adj.* Israeli.

israelita, (ēz·rrâ·e·lē´tâ) *m. and f. and adj.* Israelite.

istmo, (ēz´mo) *m.* isthmus.

Italia, (ē·tâ´lyâ) *f.* Italy.

italiano, na, (ē·tâ·lyâ´no nâ) *n. and adj.* Italian; —, *m.* Italian language.

itinerario, ría, (ē·tē·ne·râ´ryo, ryâ) *adj.* and *m.* itinerary.

izamiento, (ē·sâ·myen´to) *m.* hoisting, hauling up.

izar, (ē·sâr´) *va.* (naut.) to hoist, to haul up.

izquierdista, (ēs·kyer·thēs´tâ) *m. and f.* (pol.) leftist.

izquierdo, da, (ēs·kyer´tho, thâ) *adj.* left; left-handed *(zurdo);* —, *f.* left; left hand.

J

jaba, (hâ´vâ) *f.* (Sp. Am.) basket.

jabalí, (hâ·vâ·lē´) *m.* wild boar.

jabalina, (hâ·vâ·lē´nâ) *f.* wild sow; javelin *(arma).*

jabón, (hâ·von´) *m.* soap; **pastilla de —,** cake of soap.

jabonadura, (hâ·vo·nâ·thū´râ) *f.* soaping, lathering; **—s,** *pl.* soapsuds, sudsy water.

jaca, (hâ´kâ) *f.* small horse.

jacal, (hâ·kâl´) *m.* (Mex) hut, shack.

jacarandá, (hâ·kâ·rân·dâ´) *m.* (bot.) jacaranda.

jacinto, (hâ·sēn´to) *m.* hyacinth.

jactancia, (hâk·tân´syâ) *f.* boasting.

jactancioso, sa, (hâk·tân·syo´so, sâ´) *adj.* boastful.

jactarse, (hâk·târ´se) *vr.* to boast.

jade, (hâ´the) *m.* jade.

jadeante, (hâ·the·ân´te) *adj.* out of breath, panting.

jadear, (hâ·the·âr´) *vn.* to pant.

jaez, (ha·es´) *m.* harness; (fig.) ilk, kind *(calidad).*

jaguar, (hâ·gwâr´) *m.* jaguar.

jai alai, (hâ´ē â·lâ´ē) *m.* jai alai.

jaiba, (hâ´ē·vâ) *f.* (Sp. Am.) crab.

jalea, (hâ·le´â) *f.* jelly.

jamás, (ha·mas´) *adv.* never; **para siempre —,** for ever and ever; **nunca —,** never again.

jamón, (hâ·mon´) *m.* ham.

Japón, (hâ·pon´) *m.* Japan.

japonés, esa, (hâ·po·nes´, e´sâ) *adj. and n.* Japanese; —, *m.* Japanese language.

jaque, (hâ´ke) *m.* check; bully *(valentón);* **— mate,** checkmate.

jaqueca, (hâ·ke´kâ) *f.* headache.

jarabe, (hâ·râ´ve) *m.* sirup; **— tapatío,**

Mexican national dance.

jarana, (hâ·râ´nâ) *f.* (coll.) lark, fun *(bulla);* noise, din *(alboroto).*

jardín, (hâr·thēn´) *m.* garden; **— de la infancia,** kindergarten.

jardinería, (hâr·thē·ne·rē´â) *f.* gardening.

jardinero, ra, (hâr·thē·ne´ro, râ) *n.* gardener; —, *m.* outfielder.

jaripeo, (hâ·rē·pe´o) *m.* (Sp. Am.) rodeo.

jarra, (hâ´rrâ) *f.* jug, jar, pitcher; **en —s,** with one´s arms akimbo.

jarro, (hâ´rro) *m.* pitcher.

jarrón, (hâ·rron´) *m.* large urn.

jaspeado, da, (hâs·pe·â´tho, thâ) *adj.* marbled, speckled.

jaula, (hâ´ū·lâ) cage.

jauría, (hâū·rē´â) *f.* pack of hounds.

jazz, (yâs) *m.* jazz.

J.C.: Jesucristo, J.C. Jesus Christ.

jefatura, (he·fâ·tū´râ) *f.* headquarters; leadership *(dirección);* **— de policía,** police headquarters.

jefe (he´fe) *m.* chief, head, leader, boss.

jején, (he·hen´) *m.* gnat.

jengibre, (hen·hē´vre) *m.* (bot.) ginger.

jerarquía, (he·râr·kē´â) *f.* hierarchy.

jerez, (he·res´) *m.* sherry.

jerga, (her´gâ) *f.* coarse cloth; (Mex.) mop rag; gibberish *(galimatías);* slang, jargon *(lenguaje especial).*

jerigonza, (he·rē·gon´sâ) *f.* gibberish; (coll.) silly thing to do *(acción ridícula).*

jeringa, (he·rēng´gâ) *f.* syringe; **— hipodérmica,** hypodermic syringe.

jeroglífico ca, (he·ro·glē´fē·ko, kâ) *adj.* and *m.* hieroglyphic.

Jesucristo, (he·sū·krēs´to) *m.* Jesus Christ.

jesuita, (he·swē´tâ) *m. and adj.* Jesuit.

Jesús, (he·sūs´) *m.* Jesus; ¡—! *interj.* good night!

jícara, (hē´kâ·râ) *f.* cup.

jicotea, (hē·ko·te´â) *f.* (Cuba) fresh-water terrapin.

jigote, (hē·go´te) *m.* hash.

jilguero, (hēl·ge´ro) *m.* linnet.

jinete, (hē·ne´te) *m.* horseman, rider.

jipijapa, (hē·pē·hâ´pâ) *f.* jipijapa straw; —, *m.* Panama hat.

jira, (hē´râ) *f.* excursion, tour; — **campestre,** picnic; — **comercial,** business trip.

jirafa, (hē·râ´fâ) *f.* giraffe.

jirón, (hē·ron´) *m.* shred, piece.

jitomate, (hē·to·mâ´te) *m.* (Mex.) tomato.

jiu-jitsu, (hyū·hēt´sū) *m.* jujitsu.

jocoso, sa, (ho·ko´so, sâ) *adj.* humorous, jocular.

jonrón, (hon·rron´) *m.* home run.

jornada, (hor·nâ´thâ) *f.* day´s journey; trip, journey *(todo el viaje);* (mil.) foray; (fig.) lifespan *(vida);* (theat.) act; scene *(episodio).*

jornal, (hor·nâl´) *m.* day´s work *(trabajo);* day´s pay *(pago);* **a —,** by the day.

jornalero, (hor·nâ·le´ro) *m.* day laborer.

joroba, (ho·ro´vâ) *f.* hump; (fig.) nuisance, bother.

jorobado, da, (ho·ro·vâ´tho, thâ) *adj.* hunchbacked.

jorobar, (ho·ro·vâr´) *va.* (coll.) to bother, to annoy.

jota, (ho´ta) *f.* j. *(letra);* jota *(baile);* jota, jot *(pizca);* **no saber ni — de,** to know absolutely nothing about.

joven, (ho´ven) *adj.* young; —, *m.* young man; —, *f.* young woman.

jovial, (ho·vyâl´) *adj.* jovial.

jovialidad, (ho·vyâ·lē·thâth´) *f.* joviality.

joya, (ho´yâ) *f.* jewel *(adorno);* present, gift *(regalo).*

joyel, (ho·yel´) *m.* small jewel.

joyería, (ho·ye·rē´â) *f.* jewelry store.

joyero, (ho·ye´ro) *m.* jeweler; jewel case *(estuche).*

juanete, (hwâ·ne´te) *m.* bunion.

jubilación, (hū·vē·lâ·syon´) *f.* retirement; pension *(renta);* happiness *(alegría).*

jubilar, (hū·vē·lâr´) *va.* to retire, to pension; (coll.) to get rid of, to cast off *(desechar);* —, *vn.* to retire; to be glad *(alegrarse).*

jubileo, (hū·vē·le´o) *m.* jubilee; (coll.) great to do, great bustle.

júbilo, (hū´vē·lo) *m.* merriment; jubilation.

judaico, ca, (hū·thâ´ē·ko, kâ) *adj.* Judaic.

judía, (hū·thē´â) *f.* kidney bean.

judicial, (hū·thē·syâl´) *adj.* judicial.

judío, día, (hū·thē´o, thē´â) *adj.* Jewish; —, *n.* Jew.

juego, (hwe´go) *m.* game; play *(acción de jugar);* set *(conjunto);* — **de damas,** checkers; — **de muebles,** set of furniture; — **de palabras,** play on words; **campo de —s,** playground; **hacer —,** to match to go together.

juerga, (hwer´gâ) *f.* (coll.) spree, carousal.

jueves, (hwe´ves) *m.* Thursday.

juez, (hwes) *m.* judge.

jugada, (hū·gâ´thâ) *f.* play, move; **mala —,** (fig.) dirty deal, underhanded thing to do.

jugador, ra, (hū·gâ·thor´, râ) *n.* player.

jugar*, (hū·gâr´) *vn.* to play; to move *(moverse);* to match *(hacer juego);* to become involved *(intervenir);* —, *va.* to wield *(una arma);* to risk, to gamble *(arriesgar).*

juglar, (hū·glâr´) *m.* minstrel, jester.

jugo, (hū´go) *m.* juice; (fig.) meat *(lo más sustancial).*

jugoso, sa, (hū·go´so, sâ) *adj.* juicy, succulent.

juguete, (hū·ge´te) *m.* toy, plaything.

juguetear, (hū·ge·te·âr´) *vn.* to fool around, to play, to romp.

juguetón, ona, (hu·ge·ton, o´nâ) *adj.* playful.

juicio, (hwē´syo) *m.* judgment; right mind *(sana razón);* trial *(proceso);* **en tela de —,** pending, under consideration; — **hipotecario,** mortgage foreclosure.

juicioso, sa, (hwē·syo´so, sâ) *adj.* judicious.

julio, (hū´lyo) *m.* July.

jumento (hū·men´to) *m.* ass, donkey.

junco, (hung´ko) *m.* (bot.) rush; Chinese junk.

junio, (hū´nyo) *m.* June.

junta, (hūn´tâ) *f.* meeting *(reunión);* board *(de directores);* seam, joint *(juntura);* connection *(unión);* — **directiva,** board of directors.

juntar, (hūn·târ´) *va.* to join, to unite *(unir);* to collect, to gather *(amontonar);* —**se,** to assemble, to gather.

junto, (hūn´to) *adv.* near, close; — **a,** close to; —, **ta,** *adj.* united, joined.

juntura, (hūn·tū´râ) *f.* joint seam.

jura, (hū´râ) *f.* pledge of allegiance; oath *(juramento).*

jurado, (hū·râ´tho) *m.* juror, juryman; jury *(tribunal).*

juramentar, (hū·râ·men·târ´) *va.* to swear in.

---

m met, **n** not, **p** pot, **r** very, **rr** (none), **s** so, **t** toy, **th** with, **v** eve, **w** we, **y** yes, **z** zero

juramento, (hū·râ·men´to) m. oath; **prestar —**, to take oath.

jurar, (hū·râr´) va. to swear; to swear loyalty to *(un país)*; **—**, vn. to swear.

jurídico, ca, (hū·rē´thē·ko, kâ) adj. lawful, legal, juridical.

jurisconsulto, (hū·rēs·kon·sūl´to) m. jurist.

jurisdicción, (hū·rēz·thēk·syon´) f. jurisdiction.

jurisprudencia, (hū·rēs·prū·then´syâ) f. jurisprudence.

jurista, (hū·rēs´tâ) m. jurist.

justicia, (hūs·tē´syâ) f. justice; rightness *(calidad de justo)*; execution *(castigo)*.

justiciero, ra, (hūs·tē·sye´ro, râ) adj. fair, just.

justificación, (hūs·tē·fē·kâ·syon´) f. justification.

justificado, da, (hūs·tē·fē·kâ´tho, thâ) adj. just, right.

justificar, (hūs·tē·fē·kâr´) va. to justify.

justo, ta, (hūs´to, tâ) adj. just; exact, perfect *(exacto)*; **—**, n. righteous person.

juvenil, (hū·ve·nēl´) adj. youthful.

juventud, (hū·ven·tūth´) f. youth.

juzgado, (hūz·gâ´tho) m. tribunal, court.

juzgar, (hūz·gâr´) va. and vn. to judge.

K

kaki, (kâ´kē) m. and adj. khaki.

kaleidoscopio, (kâ·leē·thos·ko´pyo) m. kaleidoscope.

Kc.: kilociclo, kc. kilocycle.

Kg. or kg.: kilogramo, k. or kg. kilogram.

kermés, (ker·mez´) f. bazaar; charity fair; potluck.

kilo, (kē´lo) m. kilo, kilogram.

kilociclo, (kē·lo·sē´klo) m. kilocycle.

kilogramo, (kē·lo·grâ´mo) m. kilogram.

kilometraje, (kē·lo·me·trâ´he) m. mileage.

kilométrico, ca, (kē·lo·me´trē·ko, kâ) adj. kilometric; (coll.) too long; **billete —co,** mileage ticket; **discurso —,** very long speech.

kilómetro, (kē·lo´me·tro) m. kilometer.

kilotón, (kē·lo·ton´) m. kiloton.

kilotonelada, (kē·lo·to·ne·lâ´thâ) f. kiloton.

kilovatio, (kē·lo·vâ´tyo) m. kilowatt.

kilovoltamperio, (kē·lo·vol·tâm·pe´ryo) m. kilovolt-ampere.

kilovoltio, (kē·lo·vol´tyo) m. kilovolt.

kimono, (kē·mo´no) m. kimono.

kinescoplo, (kē·nes·ko´pyo) m. kinescope.

kiosco, (kyos´ko) = **quiosco.**

Km. or km.: kilómetro, km. kilometer.

koala, (ko·â·lâ) m. koala.

kv. or k.w.: kilovatio, kw. kilowatt.

L

l.: ley, law; **libro,** bk. book; **litro,** l. liter.

L/ l.ª, 1.: letra, bill, draft, letter.

libra esterlina, (lē´vrâ es·ter·lē´nâ) ū, pound sterling.

la, (lâ) art. *(f. sing.)* the, as **la señora, la casa; —**, pron. *(accusative f. sing.)* her, it, as **la vio,** he saw her, **la compré,** I bought it **(casa).**

laberinto, (lâ·ve·rēn´to) m. labyrinth, maze.

labia, (lâ´vyâ) f. (coll.) winning eloquence.

labio, (lâ´vyo) m. lip.

labor, (lâ·vor´) f. labor, task *(trabajo)*; needlework *(adorno)*; tilling, working *(aradura)*.

laborar, (lâ·vo·râr´) va. and vn. to work, to till.

laboratorio, (lâ·vo·râ·to´ryo) m. laboratory.

laboriosidad, (lâ·vo·ryo·sē·thâth´) f. laboriousness, assiduity.

laborioso, sa, (lâ·vo·ryo´so, sâ) adj. laborious, industrious.

labrado, da, (lâ·vrâ´tho, thâ) adj. worked; finely carved or wrought; **—**, m. cultivated land.

labrador, ra, (lâ·vrâ·thor´,râ) n. laborer; farmer, farmhand.

labranza, (lâ·vrân´sâ) f. farming, agriculture *(cultivo)*; landholding, farm *(hacienda).*

labrar, (lâ·vrâr´) va. to work *(trabajar)*; to labor, to cultivate *(arar)*; to cause, bring about.

labriego, ga, (lâ·vrye´go, gâ) *n.* peasant.

laca, (lâ´ka) *f.* lac *(resina);* lacquer *(pintura).*

lacayo, (lâ·kâ´yo) *m.* lackey, footman.

lacerar, (lâ·se·râr´) *va.* to tear to pieces, to lacerate.

lacio, cia, (lâ´syo, syâ) *adj.* faded, withered *(marchito);* languid *(flojo);* straight *(cabello).*

lacónico, ca, (lâ·ko´nē·ko, kâ) *adj.* laconic, concise.

lacra, (lâ´krâ) *f.* mark left by an illness *(enfermedad);* fault, vice *(defecto).*

lacrar, (lâ·krâr´) *va.* to damage the health of *(salud);* to hurt financially *(negocios);* to seal with sealing wax *(lacre).*

lacre, (lâ´kre) *m.* sealing wax; —, *adj.* lacquer red.

lacrimoso, sa, (lâ·krē·mo´so, sâ) *adj.* tearful, lachrymose.

lactancia, (lâk·tân´syâ) *f.* time of suckling.

lácteo, tea, (lâk´te·o, te·â) *adj.* lactic, lacteous, milky; **ácido** —, (chem.) lactic acid; **Via** —, Milky Way.

lactosa, (lâk·to´sâ) *f.* (chem.) lactose.

ladear, (lâ·the·âr´) *va.* to move to one side, to lean to one side; —, *vn.* to incline to one side; —se, to incline to an opinion or belief.

ladera, (lâ·the´râ) *f.* declivity, slope.

ladino, na, (lâ·the´no, nâ) *adj.* sagacious, cunning, crafty; adept in a foreign language.

lado, (lâ´tho) *m.* side; facet, aspect; **al otro** —, on the other side; **al** — **de,** by the side of; near to; — **superior,** upper side; **por otro** —, on the other hand; **¡a un —!** to one side, clear the way!

ladrar, (lâ·thrâr´) *vn.* to bark.

ladrido, (lâ·thrē´tho) *m.* bark, barking; (coll.) censure, criticism.

ladrillo, (lâ·thrē´yo) *m.* brick; — **refractario,** firebrick.

ladrón, (lâ·thron´) *m.* thief, robber, highwayman.

lagañoso, (lâ·gâ·nyo´so) = **legañoso.**

lagartija, (lâ·gâr·tē´hâ) *f.* (zool.) small lizard.

lagarto, (lâ·gâr´to) *m.* lizard; alligator *(caimán).*

lago, (lâ´go) *m.* lake.

lágrima, (lâ´grē·mâ) *f.* tear.

lagrimoso, sa, (lâ·grē·mo´so, sâ) *adj.* weeping, shedding tears.

laguna, (lâ·gū´nâ) *f.* lagoon, pond *(lago);* blank space, hiatus *(hueco en blanco);* gap, deficiency *(vacío).*

laico, ca, (lâ´ē·ko, kâ) *adj.* lay, laic.

lamentable, (lâ·men·tâ´vle) *adj.* lamentable, deplorable, pitiable.

lamentación, (lâ·men·tâ·syon´) *f.* lamentation, lament.

lamentar, (lâ·men·târ´) *va.* to lament, to regret; —, *vn.* and *vr.* to lament, to mourn.

lamento, (lâ·men´to) *m.* lamentation, lament, mourning.

lamer, (lâ·mer´) *va.* to lick, to lap.

lámina, (lâ´mē·nâ) *f.* plate, sheet of metal *(plancha);* copper plate, engraving *(grabado);* print plate *(estampa).*

laminación, (lâ·mē·nâ·syon´) *f.* lamination.

laminar, (lâ·mē·nâr´) *va.* to laminate.

lámpara, (lâm´pâ·râ) *f.* lamp; — **de arco,** arc light; — **portátil,** emergency light; — **de radio,** radio tube; — **de rayos ultravioleta,** sunlamp; — **de soldar,** blowtorch.

lamparilla, (lâm·pâ·rē´yâ) *f.* night-light.

lampiño, ña, (lâm·pē´nyo, nyâ) *adj.* beardless.

lana, (lâ´nâ) *f.* wool; (Mex. coll.) money, cash.

lanar, (lâ·nâr´) *adj.* woolly; **ganado** —, sheep.

lance, (lân´se) *m.* cast, throw *(lanzamiento);* critical situation *(trance);* occurrence, happening *(acontecimiento);* sudden quarrel *(riña).*

lancha, (lân´châ) *f.* barge, lighter *(de carga);* launch; — **de carrera,** speedboat; — **de salvavidas,** lifeboat.

lanchón, (lân·chon´) *m.* (naut.) lighter, barge.

langosta, (lâng·gos´tâ) *f.* (ent.) locust; lobster *(crustáceo);* swindler *(estafador).*

langostino, (lâng·gos·tē´no) *m.* prawn.

languidecer*, (lâng·gē·the·ser´) *vn.* to droop, to languish.

lánguido, da, (lâng´gē·tho, thâ) *adj.* languid, faint, weak *(flaco);* languorous, languishing *(abatido).*

lanolina, (lâ·no·lē´nâ) *f.* lanolin.

lanudo, da, (lâ·nū´tho, thâ) *adj.* woolly, fleecy.

lanza, (lân´sâ) *f.* lance, spear *(arma);* tongue, pole *(palo);* nozzle *(tubo).*

lanzabombas, (lân·sâ·vom´bâs) *m.* bomb thrower, bomb release.

lanzacohetes, (lân·sâ·ko·e´tes) *m.* rocket launcher.

lanzadera, (lân·sâ·the´râ) *f.* shuttle.

lanzador, (lân·sâ·thor´) *m.* pitcher (in baseball).

lanzamiento, (lân·sâ·myen´to) *m.* launching.

lanzar, (lân·sâr´) va. to throw, to dart, to launch, to fling; to eject *(despojar);* **—se,** to throw oneself forward or downward; **—se en paracaídas,** to bail out.

lapicero, (lâ·pē·se´ro) m. pencil holder; lead pencil.

lápida, (lâ´pē·thâ) f. tombstone.

lápiz, (lâ´pēs) m. lead pencil; (min.) black lead; **— de labios** or **labial,** lipstick.

larga, (lâr´gâ) f. delay, adjournment; **a la —,** in the long run.

largar, (lâr·gâr´) va. to loosen, to slacken *(aflojar);* to let go of *(soltar);* to dismiss; **—se,** (coll.) to get out, to leave; (naut.) to set sail.

largo, ga, (lâr´go, gâ) adj. long; (coll.) generous, liberal; copious *(abundante);* **de —gometraje,** full-length (applied to films); **—,** m. length; **todo lo o de,** the full length of; **a lo —go,** lengthwise.

laringe, (lâ·rēn´he) f. larynx.

laringitis, (lâ·rēn·hē´tēs) f. (med.) laryngitis.

larva, (lâr´vâ) f. (zool.) larva.

lascivo, va, (lâs·sē´vo, vâ) adj. lascivious, lewd.

lasitud, (lâ·sē·tūth´) f. lassitude, weariness.

lástima, (lâs´tē´mâ) f. compassion, pity; object of pity *(cosa).*

lastimar, (lâs·tē·mâr´) va. to hurt, to wound *(herir);* to grieve, to sadden *(agraviar).*

lastimero, ra, (lâs·tē·me´ro, râ) adj. sad, mournful, lamentable.

lastimoso, sa, (lâs·tē·mo´so, sâ) adj. grievous, mournful.

lastre, (lâs´tre) m. ballast *(peso);* good judgment, sense *(juicio);* handicap *(en el golf).*

lat: latín, Lat. Latin; **latitud,** lat.latitude.

lata, (lâ´tâ) f. tin can *(bote);* (coll.) nuisance, annoyance *(fastidio);* **dar —,** to annoy, to be a nuisance; **productos en —,** canned goods.

latente, (lâ·ten´te) adj. dormant, concealed.

lateral, (lâ·te·râl´) adj. lateral.

latido, (lâ·tē´tho) m. throbbing, palpitation *(del corazón);* yelping of dogs *(ladrido).*

latifundio, (lâ·tē·fūn´dyo) m. large farm, landed estate.

latigazo, (lâ·tē·gâ´so) m. lash, crack of a whip.

látigo,(lâ´tē·go) m. whip.

latín, (lâ·tēn´) m. Latin language.

latino, na, (lâ·tē´no, nâ) adj. and n. Latin.

Latinoamérica, (lâ·tē·no·â·me´rē·kâ) f. Latin America.

latinoamericano, na, (lâ·tē·no·â·me·rē·kâ´no, nâ) n. and adj. Latin American.

latir, (lâ·tēr´) vn. to palpitate; to howl, to yelp *(ladrar).*

latitud, (lâ·tē·tūth´) f. breadth, width *(ancho);* (fig.) latitude.

latón, (lâ·ton´) m. brass.

latoso, sa, (lâ·to´so, sâ) adj. annoying, boring.

latrocinio, (lâ·tro·sē´nyo) m. larceny, theft, robbery.

laudable, (lâü·thâ´vle) adj. laudable, praiseworthy.

laurear, (lâü·re·âr´) va. to crown with laurel *(coronar);* to graduate *(graduar);* to reward *(premiar).*

laurel, (lâü·rel´) m. (bot.) laurel; laurel crown.

lavabo, (lâ·vâ´vo) m. washbowl; sink.

lavadedos, (la·vâ·the´thos) m. finger bowl.

lavadero, (lâ·vâ·the´ro) m. place where gold is panned; laundry.

lavado, (lâ·vâ´tho) m. washing, wash.

lavadora, (lâ·vâ·tho´râ) f. washing machine.

lavamanos, (lâ·vâ·mâ´nos) m. washstand.

lavandera, (lâ·vân·de´râ) f. laundress.

lavandería, (lâ·vân·de·rē´â) f. laundry; **— automática,** laundromat.

lavandero, (lâ·vân de´ro) m. laundryman.

lavaplatos, (lâ·vâ·plâ´tos) m. or f. dishwasher; **—,** f. dishwashing machine.

lavar, (lâ·vâr´) va. to wash; to tint, to give a wash to *(dibujo).*

lavativa, (lâ·vâ·tē´vâ) f. enema.

lavatorio, (lâ·vâ·to´ryo) m. act of washing; medicinal lotion; ceremony of washing the feet on Holy Thursday; lavatory, washroom *(lavabo).*

laxante, (lâk·sân´te) m. and adj. (med.) laxative..

lazarillo, (lâ·sâ·rē´yo) m. boy who guides a blind man.

lazo, (lâ´so) m. lasso, lariat *(cuerda);* slipknot *(nudo);* snare, trick *(ardid);* tie, bond *(vínculo);* bow; **— de zapato,** shoestring.

lb.: libra, lb. pound.

Ldo., L.do or **l.do: Licenciado,** licentiate, master; (Sp. Am.) lawyer.

le, (le) pron. *(dative sing.)* to him, to her, to it.

leal, (le·âl´) adj. loyal, faithful.

lealtad, (le·âl·tâth´) f. loyalty.

lección, (lek·syon´) f. lesson.

lector, ra, (lek·tor´, râ) *adj.* reading; —, *n.* reader; — **de pruebas,** copyreader.
lectura, (lek·tú´ra) *f.* reading.
lechada, (le·châ´thâ) *f.* calcimine.
leche, (le´che) *f.* milk.
lechera, (le·che´râ) *f.* milkmaid, dairymaid.
lechería, (le·che·rē´â) *f.* dairy, dairy barn.
lechero, (le·che´ro) *m.* milkman, dairyman; —, **ra,** *adj.* pertaining to milk, dairy.
lecho, (le´cho) *m.* bed *(cauce);* litter *(capa).*
lechón, ona, (le·chon´, o´nâ) *n.* sucking pig.
lechoso, sa, (le·cho´so, sâ) *adj.* milky.
lechuga, (le·chū´gâ) *f.* lettuce.
lechuza, (le·chū´sâ) *f.* owl.
leer*, (le·er´) *va.* to read; to lecture on *(enseñar).*
legación, (le·gâ·syon´) *f.* legation, embassy.
legajo, (le·gâ´ho) *m.* bundle of loose papers tied together.
legal, (le·gâl´) *adj.* legal, lawful; **moneda** —, legal tender.
legalidad, (le·gâ·lē·thâth´) *f.* legality, fidelity.
legalizar, (le·gâ·lē·sâr´) *va.* to legalize.
legañoso, sa, (le·gâ·nyo´so, sâ) *adj.* bleary, blear-eyed.
legar, (le·gâr´) *va.* to depute; to bequeath *(por testamento).*
legendario, ria, (le·hen·dâ´ryo, ryâ) *adj.* legendary.
legible, (le·hē´vle) *adj.* legible.
legión, (le·hyon´) *f.* legion.
legionario, ria, (le·hyo·nâ´ryo, ryâ) *adj.* legionary.
legislación, (le·hēz·lâ·syon´) *f.* legislation.
legislador, ra, (le·hēz·lâ·thor´, râ) *n.* legislator, lawmaker.
legislar, (le·hēz·lâr´) *vn.* to legislate.
legislativo, va, (le·hēz·lâ·tē´vo, vâ) *adj.* legislative.
legislatura, (le·hez·lâ·tū´râ) *f.* legislature.
legitimar, (le·hē·tē·mar´) *va.* to legitimate, to make lawful.
legitimidad, (le·hē·tē·mē·thâth´) *f.* legitimacy.
legítimo, ma, (le·hē´tē·mo, mâ) *adj.* legitimate, lawful.
lego, (le´go) *m.* (eccl.) layman.
legua, (le´gwâ) *f.* league (measure of length); **a** —**s,** very distant.
legumbre, (le·gūm´bre) *f.* vegetable.
leguminoso, sa, (le·gū·mē·no´so, sâ) *adj.* leguminous; —**s,** *f. pl.* legumes.
leído, da, (le·ē´tho, thâ) *adj.* well-read.
lejanía, (le·hâ·nē´â) *f.* distance, remoteness.
lejano, na, (le·hâ´no, nâ) *adj.* distant, remote, far; **en un futuro no** —, in the near future.
lejía, (le·hē´â) *f.* lye, alkaline solution.
lejos, (le´hos) *adv.* at a great distance, far off.
lema, (le´mâ) *m.* motto, slogan *(mote);* theme of a literary composition *(tema);* (math.) lemma.
lencería, (len·se·rē´â) *f.* linen goods; linen shop *(establecimiento).*
lengua, (leng´gwâ) *f.* tongue; language, tongue *(idioma).*
lenguaje, (leng·gwâ´he) *m.* language, style, choice of words.
lenitivo, va, (le·nē·tē´vo, vâ) *adj.* mitigating; —, *m.* palliative, lenitive.
lente, (len´te) *m.* lens; —**s,** *m. pl.* eyeglasses; reading glasses; —**s contra resplandores,** sunglasses; heat glasses; —**s de contacto,** contact lenses.
lenteja, (len·te´hâ) *f.* (bot.) lentil.
lentejuela, (len·te·hwe´lâ) *f.* spangle, sequin.
lentitud, (len·tē·tūth´) *f.* slowness.
lento, ta, (len´to, tâ) *adj.* slow, tardy, lazy.
leña, (le´nyâ) *f.* firewood, kindling wood.
leñador, ra, (le·nyâ·thor´, râ) *n.* woodman, woodcutter.
leño, (le´nyo) *m.* log, length of tree trunk; (bot.) wood.
León, (le·on´) *m.* Leo, Leon.
león, (le·on´) *m.* lion; — **marino,** sea lion.
leona, (le·o´nâ) *f.* lioness.
leopardo, (le·o·pâr´tho) *m.* leopard.
leopoldina, (le·o·pol·dē´nâ) *f.* fob, short chain.
lepra, (le´prâ) *f.* leprosy.
leproso, sa, (le·pro´so, sâ) *adj.* leprous; —, *n.* leper.
lerdo, da, (ler´tho, thâ) *adj.* slow, heavy *(pesado);* stupid *(torpe).*
lesión, (le·syon´) *f.* damage *(daño);* wound, injury.
lesionar, (le·syo·nâr´) *va.* to injure.
leso, sa, (le´so, sâ) *adj.* hurt, wounded.
letanía, *f.* litany.
letárgico, ca, (le·târ´hē·ko, kâ) *adj.* lethargic.
letargo, (le·târ´go) *m.* lethargy; drowsiness *(modorra).*
letra, (le´trâ) *f.* letter *(carácter);* handwriting *(escritura);* printing type *(tipo);* (com.) draft; words to a song; — **a la vista,** sight draft; — **a plazo,** time draft; —**de cambio,** bill of exchange, draft; **buena** —, good handwriting; **al pie de la**

—, literally; —**s,** pl. learning; **hombre de —s,** literary man.

letrado, da, (le·trä´tho, thâ) adj. learned, lettered; —, m. lawyer.

letrero, (le·tre´ro) m. inscription, label (etiqueta); notice, poster, sign.

letrina, (le·trē´nä) f. outhouse, toilet.

leucocitos, (leū·ko·sē´tos) m. pl. leucocytes, white corpuscles.

leva, (le´vä) f. weighing anchor (salida); (mil.) levy; (mech.) cam.

levadura, (le·vä·thü´rä) f. yeast, leaven, ferment.

levantamiento, (le·vân·tä·myen´to) m. elevation; insurrection, uprising (motín).

levantar, (le·vân·târ´) va. to raise, to lift (alzar); to build, to construct (fabricar); to impute falsely; to promote, to cause (producir); — **el campo,** to break camp; —**se,** to rise; to get up from bed; to stand up.

leve, (le´ve) adj. light trifling.

levita, (le·vē´tä) m. Levite; deacon (diácono); —, f. frock coat.

levulosa, (le·vü·lo´sä) f. levulose.

ley, (le´ē) f. law; loyalty, obligation, devotion (fidelidad); **proyecto de —,** proposed bill; **fuera de —,** lawless.

leyenda, (le·yen´dä) f. inscription; legend.

liar, (lyâr´) va. to tie, to bind.

libélula, (lē·ve´lū·lä) f. dragonfly.

liberación, (lē·ve·râ·syon´) f. liberation, deliverance.

liberal, (lē·ve·râl´) adj. liberal, generous.

liberar, (lē·ve·râr´) va. to free, to release.

liberalidad, (lē·ve·râ·lē·thâth´) f. liberality, generosity.

liberalizar, (lē·ve·râ·lē·sâr´) va. to liberalize.

libertad, (lē·ver·tâth´) f. liberty, freedom, independence; — **académica,** academic freedom; — **de comercio,** free trade.

libertador, ra, (lē·ver·tâ·thor´, râ) n. deliverer, liberator.

libertar, (lē·ver·târ´) va. to free, to set at liberty; to exempt, to clear (eximir).

libertinaje, (lē·ver·tē·nä´he) m. licentiousness.

libertino, na, (lē·ver·tē´no, nä) adj. dissolute, licentious; —, n. libertine.

libra, (lē´vrä) f. pound (weight); — **esterlina,** pound sterling.

librado, da, (lē·vrä´tho, thâ) n. drawee, acceptor of a draft.

libramiento, (lē·vrä·myen´to) m. deliverance; (com.) written order of payment; city by-pass, alternate highway.

libranza, (lē·vrän´sä) f. (com.) draft, order of payment, bill of exchange.

librar, (lē·vrâr´) va. to free, to rid, to deliver; (corn.) to give order for payment of, to draw; to put, to place (confianza); —**bien** or — **mal,** to come off or acquit oneself well or badly; —**se de,** to rid oneself of, to be rid of.

libre, (lē´vre) adj. free; exempt; —**empresa,** free enterprise; — **pensador, ra,** freethinker; —, m. (Mex.) taxicab.

librea, (lē·vre´â) f. livery.

librepensador, (lē·vre·pen·sâ·thor´) m. freethinker.

librería, (lē·vre·rē´â) f. bookstore.

librero, (lē·vre´ro) m. bookseller; (Mex.) bookcase.

libreta, (lē·vre´tä) f. memorandum book, notebook.

libreto, (lē·vre´to) m. (mus.) libretto; (rad.) script.

libro, (lē´vro) m. book; — **de actas,** minute book; — **de caja,** cashbook; — **de cheques,** checkbook.

Lic. or Licdo: licenciado, holder of a master's degree; (Sp. Am.) lawyer.

licencia, (lē·sen·syä) f. permission, license; —**para manejar,** driver's license.

licenciado, (lē·sen·syä´tho) m. holder of a master's degree; (Sp. Am.) lawyer.

licenciar, (lē·sen·syâr´) va. to permit, to allow; to confer the master's degree (grado); (mil.) to discharge; —**se,** to become dissolute; to receive one's master's degree.

licitación, (lē·sē·tâ·syon´) f. bid, bidding (at an auction).

licitador, (lē·sē·tâ·thor´) m. bidder.

licito, ta, (lē´sē·to, tä) adj. lawful, licit.

licor, (lē·kor´) m. liquor (bebida); liquid.

licorera, (lē·ko·re´râ) f. liquor container, liquor bottle.

licuar, (lē·kwâr´) va. to liquefy.

lid, (lēth) f. combat; **en buena —,** by fair means.

líder, (lē´ther) m. and f. leader.

liderear, (lē·the·re·âr´) va. (Sp. Am.) to lead, to be the leader of, to command.

lidiar, (lē·thyâr´) vn. to fight, to struggle; —**con,** to contend, to put up with.

lidiador, (lē·thyâ·thor´) m. combatant.

liebre, (lye´vre) f. hare.

lienzo, (lyen´so) m. linen; canvas, painting (pintura).

liga, (lē´gâ) f. garter; birdlime (visco); coalition; (met) alloy; rubber band.

ligadura, (lē·gâ·thü´râ) f. ligature, binding.

ligar, (lē·gâr´) va. to tie, to bind, to fasten; to alloy (alear); to confederate (confeder-

ar); —**se,** to league; to be allied; to bind oneself to a contract.

ligereza, (lē·he·re′sâ) *f.* lightness; fickleness; swiftness.

ligero, ra, (lē·he′ro, râ) *adj.* light; swift, rapid *(rápido);* fickle *(inconstante).*

lija, (lē′hâ) *f.* sandpaper; (ichth.) dogfish.

lijar, (lē·hâr′) *va.* to smooth, to polish.

lila, (lē′lâ) lilac bush; lilac *(flor).*

lima, (lē′mâ) *f.* file.

limadura, (lē·mâ·thū′râ) *f.* filing.

limar, (lē·mâr′) *va.* to file; to polish *(pulir).*

limbo, (lēm′bo) *m.* limbo.

limeño, ña, (lē·me′nyo nyâ) *n.* native of Lima; —, *adj.* from Lima, of Lima.

limitación, (lē·mē·tâ·syon′) *f.* limitation, restriction.

limitado, da, (lē·mē·tâ′tho, thâ) *adj.* limited.

limitar, (lē·mē·târ′) *va.* to limit; to restrain *(moderar).*

límite, (lē′mē·te) *m.* limit, boundary; — **de velocidad,** speed limit.

limítrofe, (lē·mē′tro·fe) *adj.* limiting, bordering.

limo, (lē′mo) *m.* slime, mud.

limón, (lē·mon′) *m.* lemon.

limonada, (lē·mo·nâ′thâ) *f.* lemonade.

limonar, (lē·mo·nâr′) *m.* grove of lemon trees.

limonero, (lē·mo·ne′ro) *m.* lemon tree.

limosna, (lē·môz′nâ) *f.* alms, charity.

limosnero, ra, (lē·môz·ne′ro, râ) *adj.* charitable; —, *n.* beggar *(pordiosero);* alms giver *(donador).*

limpiabotas, (lēm·pyâ·vo′tâs) *m.* bootblack.

limpiachimeneas, (lēm·pyâ·chē·me·ne′âs) *m.* chimney sweep.

limpiador, (lēm·pyâ·thor′) *m.* cleanser, scourer.

limpiaparabrisas, (lem·pyâ·pâ·râ·vrē′sâs) *m.* windshield wiper.

limpiar, (lēm·pyâr′) *va.* to clean, to cleanse.

limpiaúñas, (lēm·pyâ·ū′nyâs) *m.* nail cleaner.

límpido, da, (lēm′pē·tho, thâ) *adj.* clear, limpid.

limpieza, (lēm·pye′sâ) *f.* cleanliness, neatness *(aseo);* chastity, purity *(pureza);* precision, exactness *(destreza).*

limpio, pia, (lēm′pyo, pyâ) *adj.* clean, neat; pure; exact, precise, **en —o,** clearly; **sacar en —o,** to infer, to understand; to prepare in final form from a rough draft *(copiar).*

linaje, (lē·nâ′he) *m.* lineage, descent.

linaza, (lē·nâ′sâ) *f.* linseed; **aceite de —,** linseed oil.

lince, (lēn′se) *m.* lynx; (fig.) keen person, fox; — *adj.* sharp-eyed, keen-sighted.

linchar, (lēn·châr′) *va.* to lynch.

lindar, (lēn·dâr′) *vn.* to be contiguous.

lindero, (lēn·de′ro) *m.* boundary, edge.

lindeza, (lēn·de′sâ) *f.* prettiness; —s, *pl.* (used ironically) insults.

lindo, da, (lēn′do, dâ) *adj.* handsome, pretty; wonderful, perfect *(exquisito);* —, *m.* (coll.) coxcomb, fop.

línea, (lē′ne·â) *f.* line; (fig.) boundary, limit; — **de montaje,** assembly line.

lineal, (lē·ne·âl′) *adj.* lineal, linear.

linfa, (lēn′fâ) *f.* lymph.

linfático, ca, (lēn·fâ′tē·ko, kâ) *adj.* lymphatic.

lingüística, (lēng·gwēs′tē·kâ) *f.* linguistics.

linimento, (lē·nē·men′to) *m.* liniment.

lino, (lē′no) *m.* flax; linen *(textil);* **semilla de —,** flaxseed.

linóleo, (lē·no′le·o) *m.* linoleum.

linotipo, (lē·no·tē′po) *m.* linotype.

linterna, (lēn·ter′nâ) *f.* lantern; — **de bolsillo,** flashlight; — **delantera,** head-light; — **trasera** or — **de cola,** taillight.

lío, (lē′o) *m.* bundle; scrape *(aprieto);* conspiracy *(conjuración);* **armar un —,** to make a fuss, to start a row; **hacerse un —,** to become confused, to get into a mess.

liquidación, (lē·kē·thâ·syon′) *f.* liquidation, settlement; clearance sale *(venta).*

liquidar, (lē·kē·thâr′) *va.* to liquefy, to melt, to liquidate, to dissolve *(disolver);* to settle, to clear *(ajustar).*

líquido, da, (lē′kē′·tho, thâ) *adj.* liquid, net; **producto —,** net proceeds; **saldo —,** net balance.

lira, (lē′râ) *f.* lyre.

lírico, ca, (lē′rē·ko, kâ) *adj.* lyrical, lyric.

lirio, (lē′ryo) *m.* iris; — **blanco,** lily.

Lisboa, (lēz·vo′â) *f.* Lisbon.

lisiado, da, (lē·syâ′tho, thâ) *adj.* crippled, lame.

lisiar, (lē·syâr′) *va.* to lame, to cripple; to mutilate.

liso, sa, (lē′so, sâ) *adj.* plain, even, flat, smooth.

lisonja, (lē·son′hâ) *f.* adulation, flattery.

lisonjear, (lē·son·he·âr′) *va.* to flatter; to charm, to delight *(deleitar).*

lisonjero, ra (lē·son·he′ro, râ) *n.* flatterer; —, *adj.* flattering; pleasing, delightful.

lista, (lēs′tâ) *f.* slip, narrow strip *(tira);* list, catalogue *(catálogo);* colored stripe *(de tejidos);* — **de correos,** gen-

eral delivery; **— de espera,** wait-list;
— de pagos, payroll; **— de platos,** bill
of fare, menu; **— de precios,** price list;
pasar —, to call the roll.

listado, da, (lĕs·tä´tho, thä) *adj.* striped.

listo, ta, (lĕs´to, tä) *adj.* ready, prepared
(apercibido); prompt, quick *(pronto);*
clever *(sagaz).*

listón, (lĕs·ton´) *m.* ribbon; tape.

litera, (lĕ·te´rä) *f.* litter; berth *(camarote);*
—s, *pl.* bunk beds.

literal, (lĕ·te·räl´) *adj.* literal.

literario, ria, (lē·te·rä´·ryo, ryä) *adj.* literary.

literato, ta, (lē·te·rä´to, tä) *adj.* learned,
lettered; **—,** *n.* literary person, writer.

literatura, (lē·te·rä·tū´rä) *f.* literature.

litigante, (lē·tē·gän´te) *m.* and *f.* litigant.

litigar, (lē·tē·gär´) *va.* to litigate, to take to
court.

litigio, (lē·tē´hyo) *m.* lawsuit.

litografía, (lē·to·grä·fē´ä) *f.* lithography.

litografiar, (lē·to·grä·fyär´) *va.* to lithograph.

litoral, (lē·to·räl´) *m.* littoral, coast; **—,** *adj.*
littoral, coastal.

litro, (lē´tro) *m.* liter.

litúrgico, ca, (lē·tūr´hē·ko, kä) *adj.* liturgi-
cal.

liviandad, (lē·vyän·däth´) *f.* lightness; (fig.)
imprudent action, rash move.

liviano, na, (lē·vyä´no, nä) *adj.* light; fickle
(inconstante); lewd *(lascivo).*

lívido, da, (lē´vē·tho, thä) *adj.* livid, pale.

lo, (lo) *pron. (accusative m.* and *neuters-
ing.)* him, it; **—,** *art. (neuter sing.)* the
(used before a masculine adjective
with noun force); **— bueno,** the good
thing.

loable, (lo·ä´vle) *adj.* laudable.

loar, (lo·är´) *va.* to praise; to approve *(sancionar).*

lobo, (lo´vo) *m.* wolf.

lóbrego, ga, (lo´vre·go, gä) *adj.* murky,
obscure; (fig.) sad, gloomy, glum.

lóbulo, (lo´vū·lo) *m.* lobe.

local. (lo·käl´) *adj.* local: **—,** *m.* place.

localidad, (lo·kä·lē·thäth´) *f.* locality; **—es,**
pl. tickets, seats.

localización, (lo·kä·lē·sä·syon´) *f.* placing,
location.

localizar, (lo·kä·lē·sär´) *va.* to localize; to
locate *(encontrar).*

loción, (lo·syon´) *f.* lotion.

loco, ca, (lo´ko, kä) *adj.* mad, crazy, insane; **casa de —cos,** insane asylum; **—
rematado,** stark raving mad; **volverse
—,** to go mad.

locomoción, (lo·ko·mo·syon´) *f.* locomotion.

locomotora, (lo·ko·mo·to´rä) *f.* locomotive.

locuaz, (lo·kwäs´) *adj.* loquacious, garrulous, long-winded.

locura, (lo·kū´rä) *f.* madness, insanity;
passion, frenzy *(exaltación);* folly, foolishness *(desacierto).*

locutor, ra, (lo·kū·tor´, rä) *n.* announcer;
—de radio or **de televisión,** radio or T.V.
announcer or commentator.

lodazal, (lo·thä·säl´) *m.* muddy place.

lodo, (lo´tho) *m.* mud, mire.

logaritmo, (lo·gä·rēth´mo) *m.* logarithm.

logia, (lo´hyä) *f.* lodge, secret society.

lógica, (lo´hē·kä) *f.* logic.

lógico, ca, (lo´hē·ko, kä) *adj.* logical, reasonable; **—** *m.* logician.

logística, (lo·hēs´tē·kä) *f.* logistics.

lograr, (lo·grär´) *va.* to gain, to obtain, to
succeed in, to attain.

logro, (lo´gro) *m.* gaining, attainment,
accomplishment; usury *(usura).*

loma, (lo´mä) *f.* hillock.

lombriz, (lom·brēs´) *f.* earthworm; **— solitaria,** tapeworm.

lomo, (lo´mo) *m.* (anat.) loin; back, spine
(de libro); crease *(de tejido);* ridge *(entre
surcos);* **llevar a** or **traer a —,** to carry
on one's back.

lona, (lo´nä) *f.* canvas; (naut.) sailcloth.

londinense, (lon·dē·nen´se) *m.* and *f.* and
adj. Londoner, from London.

Londres, (lon´dres) *m.* London.

longaniza, (long·gä·nē´sä) *f.* long, narrow
pork sausege.

longevidad, s (lôn·he·vē·thäth´) *f.* longevity.

longitud, (lon·hē·tūth´) *f.* length; (geog.)
longitude; **— de onda,** (rad.) wave-
length.

lonja, (lon´hä) *f.* (com.) exchange; grocery
store, delicatessen *(tienda);* warehouse
(almacén); slice *(tira);* (Mex. Coll.) roll of
fat, love-handle.

lontananza, (lon·tä·nän´sä) *f.* distance; **en
—,** far off, barely visible.

loquero, (lo·ke´ro) *m.* attendant in an
insane asylum.

loro, (lo´ro) *m.* parrot.

losa, (lo´sä) *f.* flagstone, slab.

lote, (lo´te) *m.* lot, share.

lotería, (lo·te·rē´ä) *f.* lottery; lotto *(juego).*

loza, (lo´sä) *f.* porcelain, chinaware.

lozanía, (lo·sä·nē´ä) *f.* vigor, vivacity.

lozano, na, (lo·sä´no, nä) *adj.* luxuriant;
healthy, ruddy *(sano).*

lubricación, (lū·vrē·kä·syon´) *f.* lubrica-

â arm, **e** they, **ē** bē, **o** fore, **ū** blūe, **b** bad, **ch** chip, **d** day, **f** fat, **g** go, **h** hot, **k** kid, **1** let

lubricador, ra, (lū·vrē·kâ·thor´, râ) *adj.* lubricating.

lubricante, (lū·vre·kân´te) *adj.* lubricating; —, *m.* lubricant.

lubricar, (lū·vrē·kâr´) **lubrificar,** (lū·vrē·fē·kâr´) *va.* to lubricate.

lucero, (lū·se´ro) *m.* morning star, day star.

lucidez, (lū·sē·thes´) *f.* brilliance, splendor.

lúcido, da, (lū´sē·tho, thâ) *adj.* shining, bright; (fig.) clear, lucid.

luciente, (lū·syen´te) *adj.* bright, shining.

luciérnaga, (lū·syer´nâ·gâ) *f.* glowworm, firefly.

lucimiento, (lū·sē·myen´to) *m.* splendor, luster; success, accomplishment.

lucir*, (lū·sēr´) *vn.* to shine, to be brilliant; (fig.) to be of benefit, to be useful; to excel, to do well *(sobresalir);* —, *va.* to light up, to illuminate; to sport, to show off *(alardear);* **—se,** to dress up, to put on one´s Sunday best.

lucrativo, va, (lū·krâ·tē´vo, vâ) *adj.* lucrative.

lucro, (lū´kro) *m.* gain, profit, lucre.

lucha, (lū´châ) *f.* struggle, strife; wrestling *(deporte);* — **libre,** catch-as-catch-can wrestling.

luchador, ra, (lū·châ·thor´, râ) *n.* wrestler; fighter, contender.

luchar, (lū·châr´) *vn.* to wrestle; to struggle, to fight.

luego, (lwe´go) *adv.* at once, immediately *(prontamente);* then, afterwards, later *(después);* **desde —,** of course; **hasta —,** good-by; **— que,** as soon as.

lugar, (lū·gâr´) *m.* place; village *(aldea);* employment, office *(empleo);* cause, motive *(motivo);* (math.) locus; **en — de,** instead of; **— de diversión,** place of amusement; **—es comunes,** commonplaces; **— natal,** birthplace; **en primer —,** in the first place, first; **tener —,** to take place, to occur.

lugarteniente, (lū·gâr·te·nyen´te) *m.* deputy, lieutenant.

lúgubre, (lū´gū·vre) *adj.* gloomy, lugubrious, mournful.

lujo, (lū´ho) *m.* luxury; **de —,** de luxe, elegant.

lujoso, sa, (lū·ho´so, sâ) *adj.* sumptuous, luxurious.

lujuria, (lū·hū´ryâ) *f.* lewdness; (fig.) excess, excessiveness.

lumbre, (lūm´bre) *f.* light; (fig.) brilliance, brightness.

lumbrera, (lūm·bre´râ) *f.* luminary; skylight *(abertura).*

lummoso, sa (lū·mē·no´so, sâ) *adj.* lucid, bright, brilliant.

luna, (lū´nâ) *f.* moon; plate glass *(cristal);* **— de miel,** honeymoon.

lunar, (lū·nâr´) *m.* mole, skin blemish; —, *adj.* lunar.

lunático, ca, (lū·nâ´tē·ko, kâ) *adj.* lunatic, moonstruck.

lunes, (lū´nes) *m.* Monday.

luneta, (lū·ne´tâ) *f.* (theat.) orchestra seat; eyeglass.

lupanar, (lū·pâ·nâr´) *m.* brothel.

lúpulo, (lū´pū·lo) *m.* (bot.) hops.

lustrar, (lūs·trâr´) *va.* to shine, to polish.

lustre, (lūs´tre) *m.* gloss, luster; (fig.) splendor, glory.

lustro, (lūs´tro) *m.* lustrum.

lustroso, sa, (lūs·tro´so, sâ) *adj.* bright, brilliant.

luterano, na, (lū·te·râ´no, nâ) *n.* and *adj.* Lutheran.

luto, (lū´to) *m.* mourning; bereavement *(duelo);* **de —,** in mourning.

luz, (lūs) *f.* light; news, information *(aviso);* guide, example *(modelo);* **dar a —,** to give birth; **— de la luna,** moon-light; **— solar,** sunlight; **— diurna,** **— del día,** daylight; **luces,** *pl.* culture, at tainment, enlightenment; **traje de luces,** bullfighter´s costume.

LL

llaga, (yâ´gâ) *f.* wound, sore.

llama, (yâ´mâ) *f.* flame; (zool.) llama.

llamada, (yâ·mâ´thâ) *f.* call; (mil.) summons; **— de incendios,** fire alarm; **— de larga distancia,** long-distance call.

llamado, da, (yâ·mâ´tho, thâ) *adj.* so-called, by the name of.

llamador, (yâ·mâ·thor´) *m.* door knocker.

llamamiento, (yâ·mâ·myen´to) *m.* call, calling; (eccl.) divine inspiration.

llamar, (yâ·mar´) *va.* to call; to summon, to cite *(convocar);* to call on, to invoke *(invocar);* —, *vn.* to knock; — **con señas,** to motion to, to signal; **¿cómo se llama Ud.?** what is your name?

llamativo, va, (yâ·mâ·tē´vo, vâ) *adj.* showy, conspicuous.

llamear, (yâ·me·âr´) *vn.* to flame, to blaze up.

llanero, ra, (yâ·ne´ro, râ) *n.* plainsman, plainswoman.

llaneza, (yâ·ne´sâ) *f.* simplicity, sincerity, openness.

llano, na, (yâ´no, nâ) *adj.* plain, even, smooth; unassuming, simple *(sencillo);* evident *(claro);* —, *m.* plain, prairie.

llanta, (yân´tâ) *f.* rim *(de rueda);* tire *(neumático);* — **balón,** balloon tire.

llanto, (yân´to) *m.* flood of tears, weeping.

llanura, (yâ·nū´râ) *f.* evenness, level *(calidad);* plain *(superficie).*

llave, (yâ´ve) *f.* key; hammer *(de arma de fuego);* **ama de —s,** housekeeper; **cerrar con —,** to lock; — **inglesa,** monkey wrench; — **maestra,** master key.

llavero, (yâ·ve´ro) *m.* keeper of the keys; key ring, key chain *(anillo).*

llegada, (ye·gâ´thâ) *f.* arrival, coming.

llegar, (ye·gâr´) *vn.* to arrive, to reach; — **a ser,** to become.

llenar, (ye·nâr´) *va.* to fill; to fulfill; to meet *(cumplir);* to fill out *(un formulario).*

lleno, na, (ye´no, nâ) *adj.* full, replete; **de —no,** entirely, fully.

llevadero, ra, (ye·vâ·the´ro, râ) *adj.* tolerable.

llevar, (ye·vâr´) *va.* to carry, to bear, to take; to lead, to take *(conducir);* to wear *(vestir);* to receive, to obtain *(lograr);* to win over, to persuade *(persuadir);* — **a cabo,** to complete, to accomplish; — **la voz por,** to speak for; — **los libros,** to keep books; — **puesto,** to be wearing, to have on; **volver a —,** to carry back, to bring back; **—se,** to take away; **—se bien,** to get along well together; **—se chasco,** to be disappointed.

llorar, (yo·râr´) *va.* and *vn.* to weep, to cry; (fig.) to mourn, to feel deeply.

lloriqueo, (yo·rē·ke´o) *m.* whining, crying.

lloroso, sa, (yo·ro´so, sâ) *adj.* mournful, full of tears.

llover*, (yo·ver´) *vn.* to rain.

lloviznar, (yo·vēz·nâr´) *vn.* to drizzle.

lluvia, (yū´vyâ) *f.* rain; — **nuclear,** fallout.

lluvioso, sa, (yū·vyo´so, sâ) *adj.* rainy.

M

m.: masculino, *m.* masculine; **metro,** *m.* meter; **milla,** *m.* mile.

M.ª: María, Mary.

macabro, bra, (mâ·kâ´vro, vrâ) *adj.* macabre, hideous.

macanudo, da, (mâ·kâ·nū´tho, thâ) *adj.* (Sp. Am. coll.) excellent, fine, grand, first-rate.

macarrones, (mâ·kâ·rro´nes) *m. pl.* macaroni.

maceta, (mâ·se´tâ) *f.* flowerpot.

Mach (mâk) or **número —,** (nū´me·ro mâk) *m.* Mach number.

macilento, ta, (mâ·sē·len´to, tâ) *adj.* lean, withered.

macizo, za, (mâ·sē´so, sâ) *adj.* massive, solid.

machacar, (mâ·châ·kâr´) *va.* to pound, to crush; —, *vn.* to harp on the same thing, to dwell monotonously on one

subject.

machete, (mâ·che´te) *m.* machete, heavy knife.

macho, (mâ´cho) *m.* male animal; hook *(del corchete);* (mech.) male part; —, *adj.* male; masculine, manly, virile *(robusto).*

machucar, (mâ·chū·kâr´) *va.* to pound, to crush.

madeja, (mâ·the´hâ) *f.* skein; hank of hair *(de pelo).*

madera, (mâ·the´râ) *f.* timber, wood; — **aserrada,** lumber; **de —,** wooden; — **contrachapada** or **terciada,** plywood; — **de construcción,** building timber.

maderero, (mâ·the·re´ro) *m.* lumberman.

madero, (mâ·the´ro) *m.* beam of timber; piece of lumber.

madona, (mâ·tho´nâ) *f.* Madonna.

madrastra, (mâ·thrâs´trâ) *f.* stepmother.

madre, (mâ´thre) f. mother; riverbed *(del río);* main sewer line *(alcantarilla).*

madreperla, (mâ·thre·per´lâ) f. mother of pearl.

madreselva, (mâ·thre·sel´vâ) f. honeysuckle.

madriguera, (mâ·thre·ge´râ) f. burrow; den, hiding place *(escondite).*

madrileño, ña, (mâ·thrē·le´nyo, nyâ) n. inhabitant of Madrid; —, adj. from Madrid, of Madrid.

madrina, (mâ·thrē´nâ) f. godmother.

madrugada, (mâ·thrū·gâ´thâ) f. dawn; **de** —, at break of day.

madrugador, ra, (mâ·thrū·gâ·thor´, râ) n. early riser.

madrugar, (mâ·thrū·gâr´) vn. to get up early; (fig.) to be ahead of the game, to be ready ahead of time.

madurar, (mâ·thū·râr´) va. to ripen; —, vn. to ripen, to grow ripe; (fig.) to arrive at maturity, to mature.

madurez, (mâ·thū·res´) f. maturity; prudence, wisdom *(juicio).*

maduro, ra, (ma·thū´ro, râ) adj. ripe, mature; prudent, judicious, wise.

maestra, (mâ·es´trâ) f. schoolmistress, woman teacher.

maestranza, (mâ·es·trân´sâ) f. (mil.) arsenal; (naut.) marine arsenal; arsenal staff *(operarios).*

maestría, (mâ·es·trē´â) f. skill, mastery.

maestro, (mâ·es´tro) m. master, expert; teacher; (mus.) maestro; —, **tra,** adj. masterly; **obra** —, masterpiece.

Magallanes, (mâ·gâ·yâ´nes) m. Magellan.

magia, (mâ´hyâ) f. magic.

mágico, ca, (mâ´hē·ko, kâ) adj. magical; **poder** —**co,** magic power, magic; —, m. magician.

magisterio, (mâ·hēs·te´ryo) m. teaching profession; class control, teaching ability *(gobierno).*

magistrado, (ma·hēs·trâ´tho) m. magistrate.

magistral, (mâ·hēs·trâl´) adj. magisterial; masterful, definitive *(soberano).*

magistratura, (mâ·hēs·trâ·tū´râ) f. magistracy.

magnanimidad, (mâg·nâ·nē·mē·thâth´) f. magnanimity.

magnánimo, ma, (mâg·nâ´nē·mo, mâ) adj. magnanimous.

magnate, (mâg·nâ´te) m. magnate.

magnesia, (mâg·ne´syâ) f. magnesia.

magnético, ca, (mâg·ne´tē·ko, kâ) adj. magnetic.

magnetismo, (mâg·ne·tēz´mo) m. magnetism.

magnetizar, (mâg·ne·tē·sâr´) va. to magnetize.

magneto, (mâg·ne´to) m. magneto.

magnetófono, (mâg·ne·to´fo·no) m. tape recorder.

magnetohidrodinámica, (mâg·ne·to·ē·thro·the·nâ´mē·kâ) f. magnetohydrodynamics.

magnificar, (mâg·nē·fē·kâr´) va. to exalt, to magnify.

magnificencia, (mâg·nē·fē·sen´syâ) f. magnificence, splendor.

magnífico, ca, (mâg·nē´fē·ko, kâ) adj. magnificent, splendid.

magnitud, (mâg·nē·tūth´) f. magnitude, grandeur.

magno, na, (mâg´no, nâ) adj. great.

magnolia, (mâg·no´lyâ) f. (bot.) magnolia.

mago, (mâ´go) n. magician, wizard.

magro, gra, (mâ´gro, grâ) adj. meager, thin.

maguey, (mâ·ge´ē) m. (bot.) maguey, century plant.

magullar, (mâ·gū·yâr´) va. to bruise, to contuse.

mahometano, na, (mâ·o·me·tâ´no, nâ) n. and adj. Mohammedan.

maíz, (mâ·ēs´) m. corn, maize; — **machacado** or **molido,** hominy; **palomitas de** —, (Mex.) popcorn.

maizal, (mâē·sâl´) m. cornfield.

majadería, (mâ·hâ·the·rē´â) f. piece of foolishness, annoying behavior, pestiness.

majadero, ra, (mâ·hâ·the´ro, râ) adj. dull, silly, foolish; annoying, bothersome *(pesado);* —, n. pest, bore; —, m. pestle.

majestad, (mâ·hes·tâth´) f. majesty.

majestuoso, sa, (mâ·hes·two´so, sa) adj. majestic, sublime.

majo, ja, (mâ´ho, hâ) adj. sportily dressed, showily dressed; —, n. flashy dresser.

mal, (mâl) m. evil, bad; pain, ache *(dolencia);* illness *(enfermedad),* misfortune, badluck *(desgracia);* injury, damage *(daño);* — **de garganta,** sore throat; —, adj. (used only before masculine nouns) bad; **ir, caer** or **venir** —, to be unbecoming or displeasing.

malabarista, (mâ·lâ·vâ·rēs´tâ) m. or f. juggler.

malacate, (mâ·lâ·kâ´te) m. hoist, windlass, winch.

malagradecido, da, (mâ·lâ·grâ·the·sē´tho, thâ) adj. ungrateful.

malagueño, ña, (mâ·lâ·ge´nyo, nyâ) adj. pertaining to Malaga; —, f. malaguena.

malaria, (mâ·lâ´ryâ) f. malaria.

malaventurado, da, (mâ·lâ·ven·tū·râ´tho, thâ) *adj.* unfortunate.

malbaratar, (mâl·vâ·râ·târ´) *va.* to sell at a low price; (fig.) to squander, to waste.

malcriado, da, (mâl·kryâ´tho, thâ) *adj.* ill-bred, ill-behaved, unmannerly.

maldad, (mâl·dâth´) *f.* wickedness.

maldecir*, (mâl·de·sēr´) *va.* to curse.

maldición, (mâl·dē·syon´) *f.* malediction, curse, cursing.

maldito, ta, (mâl·dē´to, tâ) *adj.* perverse, wicked; damned, cursed *(condenado);* ¡— sea! *interj.* damn it!

malear, (mâ·le·âr´) *va.* to corrupt.

malecón, (mâ·le·kon´) *m.* sea wall, breakwater *(de mar);* levee, dike.

maledicencia, (mâ·le·thē·sen´syâ) *f.* slander, calumny.

maleficio, (mâ·le·fē´syo) *m.* curse, evil spell.

malentendido (mâ·len·ten·dē´tho) or mal entendimiento, (mâl·en·ten·dē·myen´to) *m.* misunderstanding.

malestar, (mâ·les·târ´)*m.* (med.) queasiness, indisposition; uneasiness, anxiety.

maleta, (mâ·le´tâ) *f.* suitcase, satchel.

maletilla, (mâ·le·tē´yâ) *f.* or maletín, (mâ·le·tēn´) *m.* handbag, satchel.

malevolencia, (mâ·1e·vo·len´syâ) *f.* malevolence.

malévolo, la, (mâ·le´vo·lo, lâ) *adj.* malevolent.

maleza, (mâ·le´sâ) *f.* underbrush.

malgastar, (mâl·gâs·târ´) *va.* to waste, to misuse.

malhablado, da, (mâ·lâ·vlâ´tho, thâ) *adj.* foul-mouthed.

malhecho, (mâ·le´cho) *m.* evil act, wrong; —, cha, *adj.* malformed, deformed.

malhechor, ra, (mâ·le·chor´, râ) *n.* malefactor.

malhumorado, da, (mâ·lū·mo·râ´tho, thâ) *adj.* peevish, ill-humored.

malicia, (mâ·lē´syâ) *f.* malice, perversity; suspicion *(recelo);* cunning, artifice *(maña);* **tener —,** to suspect.

maliciar, (mâ·lē·syâr´) *va.* to suspect, to get a hint of; —se, to smell a rat, to have one's doubts.

malicioso, sa, (mâ·lē·syo´so, sâ) *adj.* malicious, wicked.

malignidad. (mâ·lēg·nē·thâth´) *f.* malignity, malice, evildoing.

maligno, na, (mâ·lēg´no, nâ) *adj.* malignant, malicious.

malinchismo, (mâ·lēn·chēz´mo) *m.* preference for anything foreign.

malintencionado, da, (mâ·lēn·ten·syo·nâ´- tho, thâ) *adj.* ill-disposed.

malnutrido, da, (mâl·nū·trē´tho, thâ) *adj.* undernourished.

malo la, (mâ´lo, lâ) *adj.* bad, wicked; sickly, sick, ill *(de salud).*

malograr, (mâ·lo·grâr´) *va.* to waste, not to take advantage of, to miss; —se, to fail, to fall through.

malparto, (mâl·pâr´to) *m.* abortion, miscarriage.

malquerer*, (mâl·ke·rer´) *va.* to have a grudge against.

malquisto, ta, (mâl·kēs´to, tâ) *adj.* hated, detested.

malsano, na, (mâl·sâ´no, nâ) *adj.* unhealthy, sickly *(enfermizo);* unhealthful, unwholesome, unsanitary.

maltratar, (mâl·trâ·târ´) *va.* to treat badly, to abuse, to mistreat.

malva, (mâl´vâ) *f.* (bot.) mallow.

malvado, da, (mâl·va´tho, thâ) *adj* wicked, perverse; —, *n:* wrongdoer, villain.

malversar, (mâl·ver·sâr´) *va.* to misapply, to misappropriate.

malla, (ma´yâ) *f.* mesh *(de red);* mail *(de cota);* tights *(de gimnasta);* (Sp. Am.) bathing suit.

mamá, (mâ·mâ´) *f.* mamma.

mamadera, (mâ·mâ·the´râ) *f.* nipple; nursing bottle *(biberón).*

mamar, (mâ·mâr´) *va.* and *vn.* to suck.

mamarracho, (mâ·mâ·rrâ´cho) *m.* white elephant, piece of junk.

mameluco, (mâ·me·lū´ko) *m.* child's rompers; (coll.) simpleton, fool.

mamey, (mâ·me´ē) *m.* (bot.) mamey, mammee.

mamífero, ra, (mâ·mē´fe·ro, râ) *adj.* mammalian; —, *m.* mammal.

mampara, (mâm·pâ´râ) *f.* screen.

mampostería, (mâm·pos·te·rē´â) *f.* rough stone work.

maná. (ma·nâ´) *m.* manna.

manada, (mâ·nâ´thâ) *f.* flock, drove, herd; (coll.) crowd, pack; — de lobos, wolf pack.

manantial, (mâ·nân·tyâl´) *m.* spring; (fig.) origin, source.

manar, (mâ·nâr´) *vn.* to spring, to issue, to flow out; to distill *(destilar);* to abound, to be teeming *(abundar).*

mancebo, (mân·se´vo) *m.* youth, young man; salesclerk *(dependiente).*

manco, ca, (mâng´ko, kâ) *adj.* one-handed *(mano);* one-armed *(brazo);* (fig.) incomplete, faulty.

mancomunar, (mâng·ko·mū·nâr´) *va.* to

associate, to unite; **—se,** to act together, to collaborate.

mancuerna, (mäng·kwer′nä) f. pair tied together; **—s,** cuff links.

mancha, (män′chä) f. stain, spot, blot.

manchar, (man·chär′) va. to stain, to soil, to spot.

manchego, ga, (män·che′go, gä) n. a native of La Mancha, Spain; **queso —,** cheese from La Mancha.

mandado, (män·dä′tho) m. mandate; errand *(recado);* message *(mensaje).*

mandamiento, (män·dä·myen′to) m. mandate, command; (eccl.) commandment.

mandar, (män·där′) va. to command, to order; to will, to bequeath *(legar);* to send *(enviar);* **—,** vn. to rule, to govern, to give the orders.

mandatario, (män·dä·tä′ryo) m. mandatory; (Sp. Am) director.

mandato, (män·dä′to) m. mandate, order.

mandíbula, (man·dē′vū·lä) f. jawbone, jaw.

mandil, (män·dēl′) m. apron.

mando, (män′do) m. command, authority, power.

mandolin, (män·do·lēn′) m. or **mandolina,** (män·do·lē′nä) f. mandolin.

mandón, ona, (män·don′, o′nä) adj. imperious, domineering; **—,** n. imperious, haughty person.

mandril, (män·drēl′) m. (zool.) baboon; (mech.) spindle of a lathe.

manecilla, (mä·ne·sē′yä) f. hand of a clock.

manejable, (mä·ne·hä′vle) adj. manageable.

manejar, (mä·ne·här′) va. to manage, to handle; to drive *(un coche);* **—se,** to behave.

manejo, (mä·ne′ho) m. management, direction, administration.

manera, (mä·ne′rä) f. manner, way; kind *(especie);* **de ninguna —,** not at all.

manga, (mäng′gä) f. sleeve; waterspout *(de agua);* hose *(tubo);* **— de aire,** (avi.) jet stream.

mango, (mäng′go) m. handle, haft; (bot.) mango.

manguera, (mäng·ge′rä) f. hose for sprinkling.

manguito, (mäng·gē′to) m. muff; (mech.) bushing sleeve.

maní, (mä·nē′) m. (Cuba) peanut.

manía, (mä·nē′ä) f. frenzy, madness.

maniatar, (mä·nyä·tär′) va. to manacle, to handcuff:

maniático, ca, (mä·nyä′tē·ko, kä) adj. maniac, mad, frantic.

manicero, (mä·nē·se′ro) m. peanut vendor.

manicomio, (mä·nē·ko′myo) m. insane asylum.

manicurista, (mä·nē·kū·rēs′tä) m. and f. manicurist.

manifestación, (mä·nē·fes·tä·syon′) f. manifestation, demonstration, declaration, statement.

manifestar*, (mä·nē·fes·tär′) va. to manifest, to show.

manifiesto, ta, (mä·nē·fyes′to, tä) adj. manifest, open; **—,** m. manifest *(de aduana);* (eccl.) presentation of the Host; (pol) manifesto.

manigua, (ma·nē′gwä) f. (Cuba) thicket, jungle.

manigueta, (mä·nē·ge′tä) f. handle, haft; (naut.) kevel.

manija, (mä·nē′hä) f. handle, crank, hand lever.

maniobra, (mä·nyo′vrä) f. handiwork, handling, operation; (fig.) maneuver, stratagem.

manipular, (mä·nē·pū·lär′) va. to manipulate, to manage.

maniquí, (mä·nē·kē′) m. mannikin.

manirroto, ta, (mä·nē·rro′to, tä) adj. wasteful, prodigious **—,** n. spendthrift.

manivela, (mä·nē·ve′lä) f. (mech.) crank, crankshaft.

manjar, (män·här′) m. choice food, specialty food.

mano, (mä′no) f. hand; coat, layer *(de pintura);* **a —,** at hand; **a —s llenas,** liberally, abundantly; **tener buena —,** to be skillful; **— de obra,** labor, construction work; **de propia —,** with one′s own hand; **venir a las —s,** to come to blows; **¡—s a la obra!** let′s get started! let′s get going!

manojo, (mä·no′ho) m. handful, bundle.

manómetro, (mä·no′me·tro) m. pressure gauge.

manopla, (mä·no′plä) f. gauntlet; short whip *(látigo).*

manosear, (mä·no·se·är′) va. to handle; to muss *(desarreglar).*

manotear, (mä·no·te·är′) vn. to gesture with the hands; **—** va. to slap.

mansedumbre, (män·se·thūm′bre) f. meekness, gentleness.

mansión, (män·syon′) f. sojourn, residence *(detención);* abode, home *(morada);* mansion.

manso, sa, (män′so, sä) adj. tame, gentle, mild.

manta, (män′tä) f. blanket: **— de cielo,** cheesecloth.

manteca, (mân·te′kâ) f. lard.

mantecado, (mân·te·kâ′tho) m. ice cream *(sorbete);* biscuit *(bollo).*

mantel, (mân·tel′) m. tablecloth.

mantelería, (mân·te·le·rē′â) f. table linen.

mantener*, (mân·te·ner′) va. to maintain, to support.

mantenimiento, (mân·te·nē·myen′to) m. maintenance, support.

mantequilla, (mân·te·kē′yâ) f. butter.

mantequillera, (mân·te·kē·ye′râ) f. butter churn; butter dish *(de servicio).*

mantilla, (mân·tē′yâ) f. mantilla; **—s,** *pl.*swaddling clothes; **estar en —s,** to be in its infancy, to be just beginning.

manto, (mân′to) m. mantle, cloak, robe.

mantón, (mân·ton′) m. shawl; **— de Manila,** Spanish shawl.

manuable, (mâ·nwâ′vle) *adj.* easy to handle, handy.

manual, (mâ·nwâl′) *adj.* manual; handy. easy to handle *(manuable);* **—,** m. manual.

manubrio, (mâ·nū′vryo) m. handlebar.

manufactura, (mâ·nū·fâk·tū′râ) f. manufacture.

manufacturar, (mâ·nū·fâk·tū·râr′) va. to manufacture.

manuscrito, (mâ·nūs·krē′to) m. manuscript; **—, ta,** *adj.* handwritten.

manutención, (mâ·nū·ten·syon′) f. maintaining; maintenance *(efecto).*

manzana, (mân·sâ′nâ) f. apple; block *(de casas).*

manzano, (mân·sâ′no) m. apple tree.

maña, (mâ′nyâ) f. dexterity, skill, cleverness, ability *(destreza);* artifice, cunning, trickery *(astucia);* evil way, vice, bad habit *(vicio).*

mañana, (mâ·nyâ′nâ) f. morning; **—,** *adv.* tomorrow; **pasado —,** day after tomorrow.

mañanear, (mâ·nyâ·ne·âr′) vn. to be an early riser, to have the habit of getting up early.

mañoso, sa, (mâ·nyo′sō, sâ) *adj.* skillful, handy; cunning, tricky.

mapa, (mâ′pâ) m. map.

mapache, (mâ·pâ′che) m. (zool.) raccoon.

mapamundi, (mâ·pâ·mūn′dē) m. map of the world.

maqueta, (mâ·ke′tâ) f. mock-up, scale model.

maquiavélico, ca, (mâ·kyâ·ve′lē·ko, kâ) *adj.* Machiavelian.

maquillaje, (mâ·kē·yâ′he) m. makeup.

maquillar, (mâ·kē·yâr′) va. to make up; **— se,** to put on one′s makeup.

máquina, (mâ′kē·nâ) f. machine, engine; **— calculadora digital,** digital computer; **— de calcular,** calculating machine; **— de coser,** sewing machine; **— de escribir,** typewriter; **— de sumar,** adding machine; **— de vapor,** steam engine; **— electoral,** voting machine.

maquinación, (mâ′kē·nâ·syon′) f. machination.

maquinalmente, (mâ·kē·nâl·men′te) *adv.* mechanically.

maquinar, (mâ·kē·nâr′) va. to machinate, to conspire.

maquinaria, (mâ·kē·nâ′ryâ) f. machinery.

maquinista, (mâ·kē·nēs′tâ) m. machinist, mechanician; driver, engineer *(conductor).*

mar, (mâr) m. or f. sea; **en alta —,** on the high seas.

maraña, (mâ·râ′nyâ) f. thicket; snarl *(enredo);* (fig.) perplexity, difficult situation.

maravilla, (mâ·râ·vē′yâ) f. wonder; **a las mil —s,** uncommonly well, exquisitely; **a —,** marvelously.

maravillar, (mâ·rrâ·vē·yâr′) va. to admire: **—se,** to wonder, to be astonished.

maravilloso, sa, (mâ·râ·vē·yo′so, sâ) *adj* wonderful, marvelous.

marca, (mâr′kâ) f. mark, sign; **— de fábrica,** trademark, brand name.

marcar, (mâr·kâr′) va. to mark; to observe, to note *(notar).*

marcial, (mâr·syâl′) *adj.* martial, warlike.

marco, (mâr′ko) m. frame; mark *(moneda).*

marcha, (mâr′châ) f. march; (fig.) course, development; **ponerse en —,** to proceed, to start off; **reducir** or **acortar la —,** to slow down.

marchar, (mâr·châr′) vn. to leave, to go off; (mil) to march; **— al encuentro,** to go to meet; **—se,** to go away.

marchitar, (mâr·chē·târ′) va. to wither; to fade *(desteñir);* (fig.) to deprive of vigor, to devitalize.

marchito, ta, (mâr·chē′to, tâ) *adj.* faded; withered.

marea, (mâ·re′â) f. tide; **— alta,** high tide; **— menguante,** ebb tide.

mareado, da, (mâ·re·â′tho, thâ) *adj.* dizzy; (naut.) seasick.

marearse, (mâ·re·âr′se) vr. to get seasick: to get dizzy; (fig.) to have success go to one′s head.

marejada, (mâ·re·hâ′thâ) f. sea swell, head sea, surf.

â arm, **e** they, **ē** bē, **o** fore, **ū** blūe, **b** bad, **ch** chip, **d** day, **f** fat, **g** go, **h** hot, **k** kid, **l** let

mareo, (mâ·re´o) *m.* seasickness.

marfil, (mâr·fēl´) *m.* ivory.

margarina, (mâr·gâ·rē´nä) *f.* margarine.

margarita, (mâr·gâ·rē´tä) *f.* daisy.

margen, (mâr´hen) *m.* or *f.* margin, border; marginal note *(apostilla).*

mariachi, (mâ·ryä´chē) *m.* (Mex.) street band, mariachi; musician in a mariachi.

mariano, na, (mâ·ryä´no, nä) *adj.* Marian, pertaining to the Virgin Mary.

marica, (mâ·rē´kä) *f.* magpie; —, *m.* effeminate man, milksop.

marido, (mâ·rē´tho) *m.* husband.

marimacho, (mâ·rē·mä´cho) *m.* virago, mannish woman.

marimba, (mâ·rēm´bä) *f.* marimba.

marina, (mâ·rē´nä) *f.* navy; (com.) shipping fleet.

marinero, (mâ·rē·ne´ro) *m.* mariner, sailor.

marino, na, (mâ·rē´no, nä) *adj.* marine; —, *m.* mariner, seaman.

mariposa, (mâ·rē·po´sä) *f.* butterfly.

mariquita, (mâ·rē·kē´tä) *f.* (zool.) lady-bird, ladybug.

mariscal, (mâ·rēs·kâl´) *m.* marshal; horse-shoer, blacksmith *(herrador);* — de campo, field marshal.

marisco, (mâ·rēs´ko) *m.* shellfish.

marital, (mâ·re·tâl´) *adj.* marital.

marítimo, ma, (mâ·rē´tē·mo, mä) *adj.* maritime, marine.

maritornes, (mâ·rē·tor´nes) *f.* (coll.) awkward, gawky woman.

marmita, (mâr·mē´tä) *f.* kettle, pot.

mármol, (mâr´mol) *m.* marble.

marmóreo, rea, (mâr·mo´re·o, re·ä) *adj.* marbled, marble.

marmota, (mâr·mo´tä) *f.* marmot; (Sp. Am.) woodchuck, groundhog.

maroma, (mâ·ro´mä) *f.* rope; (Sp. Am.) feat, stunt.

marqués, (mâr·kes´) *m.* marquis.

marquesa, (mâr·ke´sä) *f.* marchioness.

marquesina, (mâr·ke·sē´nä) *f.* marquee, canopy.

marrana, (mâ·rrä´nä) *f.* sow.

marrano, (mâ·rrä´no) *m.* pig, hog; (fig.) sloppy, unkempt person.

marras, (mä´rräs) *adv.* long ago; de —, of long ago; (coll.) well known, old hat.

marroquí, (mâ·rro·kē´) *m.* and *f.* and *adj.* Moroccan; —, *m.* morocco leather.

marsellés, esa, (mâr·se·yes´, e´sä) *n.* and *adj.* native of Marseilles; of Marseilles; la M— the Marseillaise, French national anthem.

marta, (mâr´tä) *f.* marten.

martes, (mâr´tes) *m.* Tuesday.

martillar, (mâr·tē·yâr´) *va.* to hammer.

martillazo, (mâr·tē·yâ´so) *m.* blow with a hammer.

martillo, (mâr·tē´yo) *m.* hammer.

mártir, (mâr´tēr) *m.* or *f.* martyr.

martirio, (mâr·tē´ryo) *m.* martyrdom; (fig.) torture.

martirizar, (mâr·tē·rē·zâr´) *va.* to martyr; to torture, to wrack.

martirologio, (mâr·tē·ro·lo´hyo) *m.* martyrology.

marzo, (mâr´so) *m.* March.

mas, (mäs) *conj.* but, yet.

más, (mäs) *adv.* more; a —, besides, moreover; — o menos, more or less; a — tardar, at latest; sin — ni —, without more ado; — frío, colder; — caliente, hotter; lo —, the most; — allá, farther; tanto —, so much more; —, *adj.* more — alimento, more food.

masa, (mä´sä) *f.* dough, paste *(pasta);* mass; las —s populares, the lower classes, the masses.

masaje, (mä·sä´he) *m.* massage.

mascar, (mäs·kâr´) *va.* to chew.

máscara, (mäs´kâ·rä) *m.* or *f.* masquerader; —, *f.* mask; baile de —s, masquerade ball.

mascarada, (mäs·kâ·râ´thä) *f.* masquerade.

mascota, (mäs·ko´tä) *f.* mascot.

masculino, na, (mäs·kū·lē´no, nä) *adj,* masculine, male.

masonería, (mä·so·ne·rē´ä) *f.* free-masonry.

masticar, (mäs·tē·kâr´) *va.* to masticate, to chew.

mástil, (mäs´tēl) *m.* (naut.) topmast; pylon.

mastín, (mäs·tēn´) *m.* mastiff.

mastoides, (mäs·to´ē·thes) *f.* and *adj.* mastoid.

mata, (mä´tä) *f.* plant, shrub.

matadero, (mâ·tâ·the´ro) *m.* slaughterhouse.

matador, (mâ·tâ·thor´) *m.* murderer; bullfighter *(torero).*

matamoscas, (mâ·tâ·mos´käs) *m.* flyswatter.

matanza, (mâ·tän´sä) *f.* slaughtering; massacre *(mortandad).*

matar, (mâ·târ´) *va.* to kill; —se, to commit suicide; to be killed.

matasanos, (mâ·tâ·sâ´nos) *m.* quack, charlatan.

matasiete, (mâ·tâ·sye´te) *m.* bully, braggadocio.

mate, (mâ′te) *m.* checkmate *(del ajedrez);* maté.

matemática, (mâ·te·mâ′tē·kâ) *f.* mathematics.

matemático, ca, (ma·te·mâ′tē·ko, kâ) *adj.* mathematical; —, *m.* mathematician.

materia, (mâ·te′ryâ) *f.* matter, material; (fig.) subject, topic, matter; (med.) pus; — **prima,** raw material; **entrar en —,** to lead up to a subject, to broach a topic.

material, (mâ·te·ryâl′) *adj.* material, corporal; (fig.) rude, uncouth; —, *m.* ingredients, materials.

materialismo, (mâ·te·ryâ·lēz′mo) *m.* materialism.

materialista, (mâ·te·ryâ·lēs′tâ) *m.* and *f.* materialist; —, *adj.* materialistic.

maternal, (mâ·ter·nâl′) *adj.* maternal, motherly.

maternidad, (mâ·ter·nē·thâth′) *f.* motherhood, motherliness.

materno, na, (mâ·ter′no, nâ) *adj.* maternal, motherly.

matinal, (mâ·tē·nâl′) *adj.* morning.

matiné, (mâ·tē·ne′) *f.* matinée.

matiz, (mâ·tēs′) *m.* shade, nuance.

matizar, (mâ·tē·sâr′) *va.* to mix well, to blend, to shade.

matón, (mâ·ton′) *m.* bully.

matorral, (mâ·to·rrâl′) *m.* brambles, thicket, dense underbrush.

matraca, (mâ·trâ′kâ) *f.* rattle; **dar —,** to annoy, to tease.

matricida, (mâ·trē·sē′thâ) *m.* or *f.* matricide.

matricidio, (mâ·trē·sē′thyo) *m.* matricide.

matrícula, (mâ·trē′kū·lâ) *f.* register, list; license plate *(placa);* registration, number registered *(conjunto).*

matricular, (ma·trē·kū·lâr′) *va.* to matriculate; **—se,** to register.

matrimonial, (mâ·trē·mo·nyâl′) *adj.* matrimonial.

matrimonio, (mâ·trē·mo′nyo) *m.* marriage, matrimony.

matriz, (mâ·trēs′) *f.* uterus, womb; mold, die *(troquel);* —, *adj.* main, parent; **casa —,** head or main office.

matrona, (mâ·tro′nâ) *f.* matron.

matutino, na, (mâ·tū·tē′no, nâ) *adj.* morning, in the morning.

maullar, (mâū·yâr′) *vn.* to mew, to meow.

maullido, (maū·yē′tho) *m.* mewing, meowing.

mausoleo, (mâū·so·le′o) *m.* mausoleum.

máxima, (mâk′sē·mâ) *f.* maxim, rule.

máxime, (mâk′sē·me) *adv.* principally.

máximo, ma, (mâk′sē·mo, mâ) *adj.* maximum, chief, principal; —, *m.* maximum.

mayo, (mâ′yo) *m.* May.

mayonesa, (mâ·yo·ne′sâ) *f.* and *adj.* mayonnaise.

mayor, (mâ·yor′) *adj.* greater, larger; elder *(edad);* **estado —,** military staff; **— de edad,** of age; —, *m.* superior; (mil.) major; **al por —,** wholesale.

mayoral, (mâ·yo·râl′) *m.* foreman *(de obreros);* head shepherd *(de pastores).*

mayorazgo, (mâ·yo·râz′go) *m.* primogeniture; inheritance of the first born *(bienes).*

mayorista, (mâ·yo·rēs′tâ) *m.* wholesaler.

mayordomo, (mâ·yor·tho′mo) *m.* steward, butler, majordomo.

mayoría, (mâ·yo·rē′â) *f.* majority.

mayúscula, (mâ·yūs′kū·lâ) *f.* capital letter.

maza, (mâ′sâ) *f.* club, mace, mallet; hub *(de una rueda).*

mazamorra, (mâ·sâ·mo′rrâ) *f.* small bits, crumbs; (Col.) thick corn stew; (Arg. and Col.) boiled corn; (naut.) potage made from broken hardtack.

mazapán, (mâ·sâ·pân′) *m.* marzipan.

mazo, (mâ′so) *m.* mallet; bundle *(manojo).*

mazorca, (mâ·sor′kâ) *f.* ear of corn.

mazurca, (mâ·sūr′kâ) *f.* mazurka.

m/c: mi cargo or mi cuenta, (com.) my account.

m/cta.: mi cuenta, (com.) my account.

m/c. m/c.: moneda corriente, cur. currency.

me, (me) *pron.* me, to me; me *(acusativo).*

mear, (me·âr′) *vn.* to urinate.

mecánicamente, (me·kâ·nē·kâ·men′te) *adv.* mechanically, automatically.

mecánica, (me·kâ′nē·kâ) *f.* mechanics; — **celeste,** celestial mechanics.

mecánico, ca, (me·kâ′nē·ko, kâ) *adj.* mechanical; —, *m.* mechanic.

mecanismo, (me·kâ·nēz′mo) *m.* mechanism.

mecanizar, (me·kâ·nē·sâr′) *va.* to mechanize.

mecanografía, (me·kâ·no·grâ·fē′â) *f.* typewriting, typing.

mecanógrafo, fa, (me·kâ·no′grâ·fo, fâ) *n.* typist.

mecate, (me·kâ′te) *m.* (Mex.) rope.

mecedora, (me·se·tho′râ) *f.* rocking chair, rocker.

mecer, (me·ser′) *va.* to swing, to rock.

mecha, (me′châ) *f.* wick; fuse *(cuerda);* match *(fósforo).*

mechar, (me·châr′) *va.* to lard.

mechero, (me·che′ro) *m.* socket *(de candelero);* nozzle, jet *(boquilla);* **— de gas,**

gas burner, gas jet.

mechón, (me·chon´) *m.* shock.

medalla, (me·thä´yä) *f.* medal.

medallón, (me·thä·yon´) *m.* medallion; locket *(relicario).*

media, (me´thyä) *f.* stocking.

mediación, (me·thyä·syon´) *f.* mediation, intervention.

mediado, da, (me·thyä·tho, thä) *adj.* half-full; **a —dos de,** about the middle of, half way through.

mediador, (me·thyä·thor´) *m.* mediator, go-between.

medianía, (me·thyä·nē´ä) *f.* moderation; mediocrity *(mediocridad).*

mediano, na, (me·thyä´no, nä) *adj.* moderate, average, medium; mediocre, passable.

medianoche, (me·thyä·no´che) *f.* midnight.

mediante, (me·thyän´te) *adv.* by means of, through; **Dios —,** God willing.

mediar, (me·thyär´) *vn.* to be in the middle; to intercede, to mediate *(interceder).*

medicamento, (me·thē·kä·men´to) *m.* medicine.

medicastro, (me·thē·käs´tro) *m.* charlatan, quack.

medicina, (me·thē·sē´nä) *f.* medicine; **— espacial,** space medicine.

medicinal, (me·thē·sē·näl´) *adj.* medicinal.

medicinar, (me·thē·sē·när´) *va.* to give medicine, to treat.

médico, (me´thē·ko) *m.* physician; **—, ca,** *adj.* medical.

medida, (me·thē´thä) *f.* measure; **— para líquidos,** liquid measure; **a la —,** madeto-measure, tailor-made; **a — que,** at the same time that, in proportion as, as.

medidor, (me·thē·thor´) *m.* meter, gauge; **— de franqueo,** postage meter; **— del gas,** gas meter; **—, ra,** *n.* measurer.

medieval, (me·thye·väl´) *adj.* medieval.

medio, dia, (me´thyo, thyä) *adj.* half; half-way *(moderado);* middle, average *(usual);* mean, average *(de promedio);* **a — asta,** at halfmast; **a —dias,** by halves; **de peso —,** middle weight; **— hora,** half an hour; **—dia noche,** midnight; **la Edad M—,** the Middle Ages; **—,** *m.* way, method, step *(diligencia);* surroundings, medium *(elemento);* middle *(mitad);* **—s,** *m. pl.* means.

mediocre, (me·thyo´kre) *adj.* middling, mediocre.

mediocridad, (me·thyo·krē·thäth´) *f.* mediocrity.

mediodía, (me·thyo·thē´ä) *m.* noon, midday; south *(sur).*

medir*, (me·thēr´) *va.* to measure; **—se,** to act with moderation.

meditación, (me·thē·tä ·syon´) *f.* meditation.

meditar, (me·thē·tär´) *va.* and *vn.* to meditate, to consider.

Mediterráneo, (me·thē·te·rrä´ne·o) *m.* Mediterranean.

medrar, (me·thrär´) *vn.* to thrive, to prosper.

medroso, sa, (me·thro´so, sä) *adj.* fearful, timorous *(temeroso);* terrible, frightful.

medula, (me·thü´lä) or **médula,** (me´thü lä) *f.* marrow; (fig.) essence, pith, main part.

megaciclo, (me·gä·sē´klo) *m.* megacycle.

megáfono, (me·gä´fo·no) *m.* megaphone.

megalomania, (me·gä·lo·mä·nē´ä) *f.* megalomania.

megatón, (me·gä·ton´) *m.* megaton.

megatonelada, (me·gä·to·ne·lä´thä) *f.* megaton.

mejicano, na, (me·hē·kä´no, nä) = **mexicano, na.**

mejilla, (me·hē´yä) *f.* cheek.

mejor, (me·hor´) *adj.* and *adv.* better, best; **— dicho,** rather, more properly; **a lo —,** when least expected.

mejora, (me·ho´rä) *f.* improvement, melioration.

mejoramiento, (me·ho·rä·myen´to) *m.* improvement, enhancement.

mejorana, (me·ho·rä´nä) *f.* sweet marjoram.

mejorar, (me·ho·rär´) *va.* to improve, to cultivate; to heighten *(realzar);* to mend *(componer);* **—,** *vn.* to recover, to get over a disease; **—se,** to improve, to get better.

mejoría, (me·ho·rē´ä) *f.* improvement; (med.) recovery; advantage *(ventaja).*

melancolía, (me·läng·ko·lē´ä) *f.* melancholy.

melancólico, ca, (me·läng·ko´lē·ko, kä) *adj.* melancholy, sad.

melaza, (me·lä´sä) *f.* molasses.

melena, (me·le´nä) *f.* long, bushy hair; mane *(del león).*

melenudo, da, (me·le·nü´tho, thä) *adj.* having long, bushy hair.

melindroso, sa, (me·lēn·dro´so, sä) *adj.* prudish, finical.

melocotón, (me·lo·ko·ton´) *m.* (bot.) peach.

melodía, (me·lo·thē´ä) *f.* melody.

melodioso, sa, (me·lo·thyo´so, sä) *adj.* melodious.

m met, **n** not, **p** pot, **r** very, **rr** (none), **s** so, **t** toy, **th** with, **v** eve, **w** we, **y** yes, **z** zero

melodrama, (me·lo·thrä´mä) *m.* melodrama.

melodramático, ca, (me·lo·thrä·mä´te·ko, kä) *adj.* melodramatic.

melón, (me·lon´) *m.* melon; — de verano, cantaloupe.

melosidad, (me·lo·sē·thäth´) *f.* sweetness, mellowness.

meloso, sa, (me·lo´so, sä) *adj.* like honey; sweet, mellow *(dulce).*

mella, (me´yä) *f.* notch, gap; hacer —, to affect adversely, to have a telling effect on.

mellizo, za, (me·yē´so, sä) *n.* and *adj.* twin.

membrana, (mem·brä´nä) *f.* membrane.

membrete, (mem·bre´te) *m.* letterhead.

membrillo, (mem·brē´yo) *m.* quince; quince tree *(arbusto).*

memorable, (me·mo·rä´vle) *adj.* memorable.

memorándum, (me·ro·rän´dun) *m.* memorandum; notebook *(librito).*

memoria, (me·mo´ryä) *f.* memory; account, report *(relación);* de —, by heart, from memory; —s, *pl.* compliments, regards; memoirs *(de acontecimientos).*

memorial, (me·mo·ryäl´) *m.* memorandum book; memorial, brief *(relación).*

mención, (men·syon´) *f.* mention.

mencionar, (men·syo·när´) *va.* to mention.

mendicante, (men·dē·kän´te) *adj.* mendicant, begging; —, *m.* mendicant.

mendigar, (men·dē·gär´) *va.* to ask for charity, to beg.

mendigo, (men·dē´go) *m.* beggar.

mendrugo, (men·drū´go) *m.* stale crust of bread.

menear, (me·ne·är´) *va.* to stir, to agitate *(un líquido);* to wiggle, to wag; —se, to wag, to wiggle; (fig.) to bustle about, to bestir oneself.

meneo, (me·ne´o) *m.* stirring, wagging; wiggling.

menester, (me·nes·ter´) *m.* necessity, want; ser —, to be necessary; —es, *pl.* bodily needs, bare necessities.

menesteroso, sa, (me·nes·te·ro´so, sä) *adj.* needy, necessitous.

menestra, (me·nes´trä) *f.* dried legumes.

mengua, (meng´gwä) *f.* decay, decline; poverty *(pobreza);* disgrace *(deshonra).*

menguante, (meng·gwän´te) *adj.* decreasing, diminishing; —, *f.* ebb tide, low water; (fig.) decline, falling off.

menguar, (meng·gwär´) *vn.* to decay, to fall off; to decrease, to diminish *(disminuir);* to fail *(faltar).*

meningitis, (me·nēn·hē´tēs) *f.* (med.)

meningitis.

menor, (me·nor´) *m.* and *f.* minor, person under age; —, *adj.* less, smaller; younger *(edad);* por —, (com.) retail; minutely, detailedly.

menos, (me´nos) *adv.* less; with the exception of *(excepto);* a lo —, or por lo —, at least, in any event; lo — posible, the least possible; venir a —, to decline, to lessen; a — que, unless; echar de —, to miss.

menoscabar, (me·nos·kä·vär´) *va.* to lessen; to worsen, to make worse *(empeorar);* to reduce *(reducir).*

menoscabo, (me·nos·kä´vo) *m.* diminution, deterioration, loss.

menospreciar, (me·nos·pre·syär´) *va.* to undervalue, to underestimate; to despise, to contemn *(desdeñar).*

menosprecio, (me·nos·pre´syo) *m.* contempt, scorn.

mensaje, (men·sä´he) *m.* message, errand; — s no deseados, junk mail, SPAM.

mensajero, ra, (men·sä·he´ro, rä) *n.* messenger.

menstruación, (mens·trwä·syon´) *f.* menstruation.

mensual, (men·swäl´) *adj.* monthly; — mente, *adv.* monthly.

mensualidad, (men·swä·lē·thäth´) *f.* monthly payment.

ménsula, (men´sū·lä) *f.* (arch.) cantilever; bracket, support.

menta, (men´tä) *f.* (bot.) mint.

mental, (men·täl´) *adj.* mental, intellectual.

mentalidad, (men·tä·lē·thäth´) *f.* mentality.

mentalmente, (men·täl·men´te) *adv.* mentally.

mentar*, (men·tär´) *va.* to mention.

mente, (men´te) *f.* mind, understanding.

mentecato, ta, (men·te·kä´to, tä) *adj.* silly, crackbrained; —, *n.* fool, simpleton.

mentir*, (men·tēr´) *vn.* to lie, to tell falsehoods.

mentira, (men·tē´rä) *f.* lie, falsehood; decir —, to lie; parecer —, to seem impossible.

mentirilla, (men·tē·rē´yä) *f.* fib, white lie.

mentiroso, sa, (men·tē·ro´so, sä) *adj.* lying, deceitful; —, *n.* liar.

mentón, (men·ton´) *m.* chin.

menú, (me·nū´) *m.* menu, bill of fare.

menudear, (me·nū·the·är´) *va.* to repeat, to detail; —, *vn.* to occur frequently; to be plentiful *(abundar);* to go into detail *(detallar).*

menudencia, (me·nū·then´syä) *f.* trifle;

â arm, e they, ē bē, o fore, ū blūe, b bad, ch chip, d day, f fat, g go, h hot, k kid, 1 let

great care, minuteness *(esmero)*; **—s**, *pl.* giblets.

menudeo, (me·nū·the′o) *m.* retail; **al —**, at retail.

menudo, da, (me·nū′tho, thâ) *adj.* small, minute; **a —do**, repeatedly, often; **—**, *m.* change, silver; tripe, entrails *(de res)*; tripe soup.

meñique, (me·nyē′ke) *m.* little finger.

mequetrefe, (me·ke·tre′fe) *m.* meddler, blunderbuss.

mercachifle, (mer·kâ·chē′fle) *m.* peddler, hawker.

mercader, (mer·kâ·ther′) *m.* dealer, trader, merchant.

mercadería, (mer·kâ·the·rē′â) *f.* commodity, merchandise.

mercado, (mer·kâ′tho) *m.* market; market place *(sitio)*; **— de valores**, stock market; **M— Común**, Common Market.

mercadotecnia, *f.* (mer·kâ·tho·teg′nyâ)marketing.

mercancía, (mer·kân′sē′â) *f.* trade, traffic *(trato)*; goods, merchandise.

mercante, (mer·kân′te) *adj.* merchant; **buque —**, merchant ship.

mercantil, (mer·kân·tēl′) *adj.* commercial, mercantile; **derecho —, ley —**, business law.

merced, (mer·seth′) *f.* favor, grace; mercy, will, pleasure *(voluntad)*; **estar a — de otro**, to be at another's mercy.

mercenario, (mer·se·nâ′ryo) *m.* day laborer; (mil.) mercenary; **—, ria,** *adj.* mercenary.

mercería, (mer·se·rē′â) *f.* drygoods store.

Mercomún, (mer·ko·mūn′) *m.* European Common Market.

mercurio, (mer·kū′ryo) *m.* mercury, quicksilver.

mercurocromo, (mer·kū·ro·kro′mo) *m.* Mercurochrome (trademark).

merecedor, ra, (me·re·se·thor′, râ) *adj.* deserving, worthy.

merecer*, (me·re·ser′) *va.* to deserve, to merit; **—**, *vn.* to be deserving.

merecido, da, (me·re·sē′tho, thâ) *adj.* deserved; **bien** or **mal —**, well- or ill-deserved; **—**, *m.* just punishment, just deserts.

merecimiento, (me·re·sē·myen′to) *m.* merit, desert.

merendar*, (me·ren·dâr′) *vn.* to have a snack.

merengue, (me·reng′ge) *m.* meringue, typical dance of the Dominican Republic.

meridiano, (me·rē·thyâ′no) *m.* meridian; **pasado —,** afternoon; **—, na,** *adj.* meri-

dional.

meridional, (me·rē·thyo·nâl′) *adj.* southern, meridional.

merienda, (me·ryen′dâ) *f.* light lunch, snack; **— campestre,** picnic lunch.

mérito, (me′rē·to) *m.* merit, desert.

meritorio, ria, (me·rē·to′ryo, ryâ) *adj.* meritorious, laudable.

merma, (mer′mâ) *f.* decrease; shortage *(escasez)*.

mermar, (mer·mâr′) *vn.* to diminish, to decrease.

mermelada, (mer·me·lâ′thâ) *f.* marmalade.

mero, (me′ro) *m.* (ichth.) pollack; **—, ra,** *adj.* mere, pure; (Mex. coll.) real, actual; **—ro,** *adv.* (Mex. coll.) almost.

merodear, (me·ro·the·âr′) *vn.* to pillage, to go marauding.

mes, (mes) *m.* month.

mesa, (me′sâ) *f.* table; **— redonda,** round table; **poner la —,** to set the table; **quitar la —,** to clear the table.

mesada, (me·sâ′thâ) *f.* monthly payment.

meseta, (me·se′tâ) *f.* landing *(de escalera)*; tableland, plateau.

Mesías, (me·sē′âs) *m.* Messiah.

mesón, (me·son′) *m.* inn, hostelry; (phy.) meson.

mesonero, (me·so·ne′ro) *m.* innkeeper.

mestizo, za, (mes·tē′so, sâ) *n.* half-breed; **—,** *adj.* of mixed blood.

mesura, (me·sū′râ) *f.* grave deportment, dignity, politeness *(educación)*; moderation *(moderación)*.

mesurado, da, (me·sū·râ′tho, thâ) *adj.* moderate, modest; gentle, quiet *(apacible)*.

meta, (me′tâ) *f.* goal, finish line; (fig.) end, goal.

metabolismo, (me·tâ·vo·lēz′mo) *m.* metabolism; **— basal,** basal metabolism.

metafísica, (me·tâ·fē′sē·kâ) *f.* metaphysics.

metáfora, (me·tâ′fo·râ) *f.* metaphor.

metafórico, ca, (me·tâ·fo′rē·ko, kâ) *adj.* metaphorical.

metal, (me·tâl′) *m.* metal; brass *(latón)*; tone, timbre *(de la voz)*.

metálico, ca, (me·tâ′lē·ko, kâ) *adj.* metallic, metal.

metalizado, da, (mâ·tâ·lē·sâ′tho, thâ) *adj.* (coll.) mercenary, money-hungry.

metalurgia, (me·tâ·lūr′hyâ) *f.* metallurgy.

metamorfosis, (me·tâ·mor·fo′sēs) *f.* metamorphosis.

metate, (me·tâ′te) *m.* (Mex.) stone for-grinding corn.

meteoro, (me·te·o′ro) *m.* meteor.

meteorología, (me·te·o·ro·lo·hē′â) *f.* meteo-

rology.

meter, (me•ter´) *va.* to place in, to put in, to insert; to cause, to start *(promover);* to smuggle *(contrabandear);* —**se,** to meddle, to interfere.

meticuloso, sa, (me•tē•kū•lo´so, sâ) *adj.* conscientious, meticulous.

metiche, (me•tē´che) *m.* and *f.* (coll.) prier, meddler, kibitzer.

metódico, ca, (me•to´thē•ko, kâ) *adj.* methodical, systematic.

metodista, (me•to•thēs´tâ) *m.* and *f.* and *adj.* Methodist.

método, (me´to•tho) *m.* method.

metraje, (me•trá´he) *m.* length in meters; **de largo** —, full length (film).

métrico, ca, (me´trē•ko, kâ) *adj.* metrical.

metro, (me´tro) *m.* meter; (coll.) subway.

metrópoli, (me•tro´po•lē) *f.* metropolis.

metropolitano, na, (me•tro•po•lē•tâ´no, nâ) *adj.* metropolitan; —, *m.* subway.

Mex. or **Mej. México** or **Méjico, Mex.** Mexico.

mexicano, na, (me•hē•kâ´no, nâ) or **mejicano, na,** *n.* and *adj.* Mexican.

mezcla, (mes´klâ) *f.* mixture, medley.

mezclar, (mes•klâr´) *va.* to mix, to mingle; —**se,** to mix, to take part.

mezclilla, (mes•kle´yâ) *f.* denim.

mezcolanza or **mescolanza,** (mes•ko•lân´sâ) *f.* hodgepodge.

mezquindad, (mes•kēn•dâth´) *f.* penury, poverty; avarice, stinginess *(avaricia);* trifle *(pequeñez).*

mezquino, na, (mes•kē´no, nâ) *adj.* poor, indigent; avaricious, covetous; mean, petty.

mezquita, (mes•kē´tâ) *f.* mosque.

m/f.: mi favor, my favor.

m/fha. meses fecha, (com.) months after today´s date.

mg.: miligramo, mg. milligram.

m/g: mi giro, (com.) my draft.

mi, (mē) *pron.* my; —, *m.* (mus.) mi.

mi, (mē) *pron. (object of prep.)* me.

mico, (mē´ko) *m.* monkey.

micra, (mē•krâ) *f.* micron.

microbio, (mē•kro´vyo) *m.* microbe, germ.

microbiólogo, (mē•kro•vyo´lo•go) *m.* microbiologist.

microcircuito, (mē•kro•sēr•kwē´to) *m.* microcircuit.

microfilme, (mē•kro•fēl´me) *m.* micro-film.

micrófono, (mē•kro´fo•no) *m.* microphone; receiver *(del teléfono).*

micrómetro, (mē•kro´me•tro) *m.* micrometer.

microonda, (mē•kro•on´dâ) *f.* microwave.

microscópico, ca, (mē•kros•ko´pē•ko, kâ) *adj.* microscopic.

microscopio, (mē•kros•ko´pyo) *m.* microscope.

microsurco, (mē•kro•sūr´ko) *m.* microgroove.

miedo, (mye´tho) *m.* fear, dread; **tener** —, to be afraid.

miedoso, sa, (mye•tho´so, sâ) *adj.* afraid, fearful.

miel, (myel) *f.* honey; **luna de** —, honeymoon.

miembro, (myem´bro) *m.* member; (anat.) limb.

mientras, (myen´trâs) *adv.* while; — **tanto,** meanwhile, in the meantime.

miércoles, (myer´ko•les) *m.* Wednesday; **M— de Ceniza,** Ash Wednesday.

mierda, (myer´thâ) *f.* excrement, ordure.

mies, (myes) *f.* harvest.

miga, (mē´gâ) crumb.

migaja, (mē•gâ´hâ) *f.* scrap, crumb, small particle.

migración, (mē•grâ•syon´) *f.* migration.

mil, (mēl) *m.* one thousand; **por** —, per thousand; — **millones,** one thousand million; one billion in U.S.A.

milagro, (mē•lâ´gro) *m.* miracle, wonder; ex-voto *(presentalla).*

milagroso, sa, (mē•lâ•gro´so, sâ) *adj.* miraculous.

milenario, ria, (mē•le•nâ´ryo, ryâ) *adj.* millenary; —, *m.* millennium.

milésimo, ma, (mē•le´sē•mo, mâ) *adj.* thousandth.

milicia, (mē•lé´syâ) *f.* militia.

miligramo, (mē•lē•grâ´mo) *m.* milligram.

milímetro, (mē•lé´me•tro) *m.* millimeter.

militar, (mē•lē•târ´) *adj.* military; —, *vn.* to serve in the army.

militarismo, (mē•lē•tâ•rēz´mo) *m.* militarism.

milpa, (mēl´pâ) *f.* (Sp. Am.) cornfield.

milla, (mē´ya) *f.* mile.

millar, (mē•yâr´) *m.* thousand.

millón, (mē•yon´) *m.* million.

millonario, ria, (mē•yo•nâ´ryo, ryâ) *n.* millionaire.

mimar, (mē•mâr´) *va.* to indulge, to cater to, to spoil *(consentir);* to treat with affection; to gratify.

mimbre, (mēm´bre) *m.* wicker.

mimeógrafo, (mē•me•o´grâ•fo) *m.* mimeograph.

mímica, (mē´mē•kâ) *f.* mimicry.

mimo, (mē´mo) *m.* mime, mimic *(actor);* mimicry, satire *(representación);* gratification, affection; indulgence, spoiling *(del niño).*

mimoso, sa, (mē·mo´so, sä) *adj.* fastidious, finicky, overindulged.

mina, (mē´nä) *f.* mine; (fig.) wealth, goldmine, trove; — **terrestre,** land mine.

minar, (mē·när´) *va.* to mine; to undermine *(destruir);* (fig.) to work hard at, to pursue diligently.

mineral, (mē·ne·räl´) *m.* mineral; fountainhead, wellspring *(de una fuente);* —, *adj.* mineral.

minería, (mē·ne·rē´ä) *f.* mining.

minero, (mē·ne´ro) *m.* miner; —, **ra,** *adj.* mining.

miniatura, (mē·nyä·tū´rä) *f.* miniature.

miniaturización, (mē·nyä·tū·rē·sä·syon´) *f.* miniaturization.

mínima, (mē´nē·mä) *f.* (mus.) minim.

mínimo, ma, (mē´nē·mo, mä) *adj.* least, slightest.

ministerio, (mē·nēs·te´ryo) *m.* ministry, department; function, position *(empleo);* cabinet *(cuerpo).*

ministro, (mē·nēs´tro) *m.* minister; (pol.) secretary, minister; **M— de Estado,** Secretary of State.

minoría, (mē·no·rē´ä) **minoridad,** (mē·no·rē·thäth´) *f.* minority.

minucioso, sa, (mē·nū·syo´so, sä) *adj.* minute, very exact.

minué, (mē·nwe´) *m.* minuet.

minuendo, (mē·nwen´do) *m.* (math.) minuend.

minúscula, (mē·nūs´kū·lä) *adj.* small, lower-case; —, *f.* lower-case letter.

minuta, (mē·nū´tä) *f.* minute, rough draft *(borrador);* bill of fare, menu *(de platos);* note, memorandum *(apuntación);* list, catalogue.

minutero, (mē·nū·te´ro) *m.* minute hand.

minuto, (mē·nū´to) *m.* minute.

mío, (mē´o) **mía,** (mē´ä) *pron.* mine; —, *adj.* of mine.

miocardio, (myo·kär´thyo) *m.* myocardium; **infarto del —,** coronary occlusion.

miope, (myo´pe) *adj.* nearsighted; —, *m.* and *f.* nearsighted person.

miopía, (myo·pē´ä) *f.* nearsightedness.

miosota, (myo·so´tä) *f.* forget-me-not plant.

mira, (mē´rä) *f.* gunsight; purpose, intention *(propósito);* care *(interés);* — **de bombardero,** bombsight; **estar a la —,** to be on the lookout, to be on the alert.

mirada, (mē·rä´thä) *f.* glance *(vistazo);* gaze; **clavar la —,** to peer, to stare.

mirador, ra, (mē·rä·thor´, rä) *n.* spectator, onlooker; —, *m.* enclosed porch *(bal-*

cón); belvedere.

miramiento, (mē·rä·myen´to) *m.* consideration, circumspection, care.

mirar, (mē·rär´) *va.* to behold, to look at, to observe; to spy on *(espiar);* to face, to look over *(estar situado).*

mirasol, (mē·rä·sol´) *m.* (bot.) sunflower.

mirlo, (mēr´lo) *m.* blackbird.

mirón, ona, (mē·ron´, o´nä) *n.* spectator, bystander, kibitzer *(en los juegos);* prier, busybody.

mirto, (mēr´to) *m.* myrtle.

misa, (mē´sä) *f.* mass; — **del gallo,** midnight mass **cantar —,** to say mass.

misal, (mē·säl´) *m.* missal.

misántropo, (mē·sän´tro·po) *m.* misanthrope, misanthropist.

misceláneo, nea, (mēs·se·lä´ne·o, ne·ä) *adj.* miscellaneous; —, *f.* miscellany; (ex.) sundries shop.

miserable (mē·se·rä´vle) *adj.* miserable, wretched; stingy, avaricious *(avariento).*

miseria, (mē·se´ryä) *f.* misery; niggardliness *(tacañería)* ; trifle *(pequeñez).*

misericordia, (mē·se·rē·kor´thyä) *f.* mercy, clemency, pity.

misericordioso, sa, (mē·se·rē·kor·thyo´so, sä) *adj.* merciful, clement.

mísero, ra, (mē´se·ro, rä) *adj.* miserable, poor, wretched.

misión, (mē·syon´) *f.* mission.

misionero, ra, (mē·syo·ne´ro, rä) *n.* missionary.

mismo, ma, (mēz´mo, mä) *adj.* same; **ahora —mo,** just now; **yo —,** I myself; **él —,** he himself; **usted —,** you yourself; **el** or **la —,** the same; **ella —,** she herself; **ellos —s,** they themselves.

misterio, (mēs·te´ryo) *m.* mystery.

misterioso, sa, (mēs·te·ryo´so, sä) *adj.* mysterious.

mística, (mēs´tē·kä) *f.* mysticism.

místico, ca, (mēs´tē·ko, kä) *adj.* mystic, mystical.

mitad, (mē·täth´) *f.* half; middle *(medio).*

mítico, ca, (mē´tē·ko, kä) *adj.* mythical.

mitigación, (mē·tē·gä·syon´) *f.* mitigation.

mitigar, (mē·tē·gär´) *va.* to mitigate.

mitin, (mē´tēn) *m.* meeting.

mito, (mē´to) *m.* myth.

mitología, (mē·to·lo·hē´ä) *f.* mythology.

mitológico, ca, (mē·to·lo´hē·ko, kä) *adj.* mythological.

mitote, (mē·to´te) *m.* Mexican Indian dance; (Sp. Am.) family party *(fiesta);* excitement, clamor *(bulla).*

mitotero, ra, (mē·to·te´ro, rä) *adj.* (Sp.

Am.) enthusiastic, fond of excitement.

mitra, (mē´trä) *f.* (eccl.) miter.

mixto, ta, (mēs´to, tä) *adj.* mixed, mingled.

mixtura, (mēs·tū´rä) *f.* mixture.

m/l or **m/L:** mi letra, my letter, my draft.

ml.: mililitro, ml. milliliter.

mm.; milímetro, mm. millimeter.

m/n: moneda nacional, national currency.

m/o: mi orden, (com.) my order.

mobiliario, (mo·vē·lyä´ryo) *m.* furniture; chattels *(enseres).*

mocedad, (mo·se·thäth´) *f.* youth, adolescence.

moco, (mo´ko) *m.* mucus.

mocosidad, (mo·ko·sē·thäth´) *f.* mucosity.

mocoso, sa, (mo·ko´so, sä) *adj.* sniveling, mucous; —, *n.* brat.

mochar, (mo·chär´) *va.* to lop off, to cut off.

mochila, (mo·chē´lä) *f.* knapsack.

mocho, cha, (mo´cho, chä) *adj.* hornless; shaved *(pelado);* maimed *(mutilado).*

mochuelo, (mo·chwe´lo) *m.* owl; **cargar con el —,** (coll.) to get the worst of the deal.

moda, (mo´thä) *f.* fashion, mode; **a la —,** in style; **de —,** fashionable; **última —,** latest fashion.

modales, (mo·thä´les) *m. pl.* manners, breeding, bearing.

modalidad, (mo·thä·lē·thäth´) *f.* nature, character, quality.

modelar, (mo·the·lär´) *va.* to model, to form.

modelo, (mo·the´lo) *m.* model, pattern.

moderación, (mo·the·rä·syon´) *f.* moderation, temperance.

moderado, da, (mo·the·rä´tho, thä) *adj.* moderate, temperate.

moderar, (mo·the·rär´) *va.* to moderate.

modernismo, (mo·ther·nēz´mo) *m.* modernism.

modernista, (mo·ther·nēs´tä) *adj.* modernistic.

modernización, (mo·ther·nē·sä·syon´) *f.* modernization.

modernizar, (mo·ther·nē·sär´) *va.* to modernize.

moderno, na, (mo·ther´no, nä) *adj.* modern

modestia, (mo·thes´tyä) *f.* humility, diffidence.

modesto, ta, (mo·thes´to, tä) *adj.* unassuming, modest, unpretentious.

módico, ca, (mo´thē·ko, kä) *adj.* moderate, reasonable, modest.

modificación, (mo·thē·fē·kä·syon´) *f.* modification.

modificador, (mo·thē·fē·kä·thor´) *m.* modifier.

modificar, (mo·thē·fē·kär´) *va.* to modify.

modismo, (mo·thēz´mo) *m.* idiom, idiomatic expression.

modista, (mo·thēs´tä) *f.* dressmaker.

modo, (mo´tho) *m.* mode, method, manner; moderation *(templanza);* (gram.) mood; **de — que,** so that; **de ningún —,** by no means; **de todos —s,** by all means.

modorra, (mo·tho´rrä) *f.* drowsiness.

modulación, (mo·thū·lä·syon´) *f.* modulation; **— de frecuencia,** (rad.) frequency modulation.

modulador, ra, (mo·thū·lä·thor´, rä) *n.* modulator.

modular, (mo·thū·lär´) *va.* to modulate.

mofar, (mo·fär´) *va.* and *vr.* to deride, to mock, to scoff.

mogote, (mo·go´te) *m.* knoll; **—s,** *pl.* antlers.

mohín, (mo·ēn´) *m.* grimace, wry face.

moho, (mo´o) *m.* (bot.) mold; rust.

mohoso, sa, (mo·o´so, sä) *adj.* moldy, musty; rusty.

moisés, (moē·ses´) *m.* bassinet.

mojado, da, (mo·hä´tho, thä) *adj.* wet.

mojar, (mo·här´) *va.* to wet, to moisten; **— se,** to get wet.

mojiganga, (mo·hē·gäng´gä) *f.* masquerade, mummery.

mojigato, ta, (mo·hē·gä´to, tä) *adj.* hypocritical; —, *n.* hypocrite; religious fanatic *(gazmoño).*

mojón, (mo·hon´) *m.* boundary mark *(de propiedad);* milestone *(de distancia);* landmark *(guía);* heap, pile *(montón).*

molde, (mol´de) *m.* mold, matrix *(el hueco);* pattern; (fig.) example, model.

moldura, (mol·dū´rä) *f.* molding.

mole, (mo´le) *adj.* soft, mild; —, *f.* mass, bulk; —, *m.* (Mex.) kind of spicy sauce for fowl and meat stews.

molécula, (mo·le´kū·lä) *f.* molecule.

moler*, (mo·ler´) *va.* to grind, to pound; (fig.) to vex, to annoy.

molestar, (mo·les·tär´) *va.* to vex, to annoy, to trouble.

molestia, (mo·les´tyä) *f.* disturbance, annoyance *(fastidio);* discomfort *(incomodidad);* indisposition, ailment *(desazón).*

molesto, ta, (mo·les´to, tä) *adj.* vexatious, troublesome.

molestoso, sa, (mo·les·to´so, sä) *adj.* annoying, bothersome.

â arm, **e** they, **ē** bē, **o** fore, **ū** blūe, **b** bad, **ch** chip, **d** day, **f** fat, **g** go, **h** hot, **k** kid, **1** let

molienda, (mo·lyen´dä) f. grinding, pounding.

molinero, (mo·lē·ne´ro) m. miller.

molinillo, (mo·lē·nē´yo) m. hand mill, hand grinder.

molino, (mo·lē´no) m. mill; — **de viento,** windmill.

molleja, (mo·ye´hä) f. gizzard.

mollera, (mo·ye´rä) f. crown of head; **ser duro de** —, to be headstrong or hardheaded *(testarudo);* to be dense or dull *(duro).*

momentáneo, nea, (mo·men·tä´ne·o, ne·ä) *adj.* momentary.

momento, (mo·men´to) m. moment.

momia, (mo´myä) f. mummy.

mona, (mo´nä) f. female monkey; (fig.) copycat, imitator; drunkenness *(borrachera);* drunkard *(ebrio).*

monada, (mo·nä´thä) f. (coll.) cute child; grimace *(mueca);* monkeyshine *(acción).*

monaguillo, (mo·nä·gē´yo) m. acolyte, altar boy.

monarca, (mo·när´kä) m. monarch.

monarquía, (mo·när·kē´ä) f. monarchy.

monasterio, (mo·näs·te´ryo) m. monastery, cloister.

mondadientes, (mon·dä·thyen´tes) m. toothpick.

mondar, (mon·där´) va. to clean, to cleanse; to trim *(podar);* to husk, to peel *(descascarar);* to deprive of, to strip of *(despojar).*

mondo, da, (mon´do, dä) *adj.* neat, clean, pure; —**do y lirondo,** pure and simple.

mondongo, (mon·dong´go) m. animal intestines.

moneda, (mo·ne´thä) f. money, coinage, currency; — **corriente,** currency; — **falsa,** counterfeit money; — **legal,** legal tender; **casa de** —, mint; **papel** —, paper money.

monedero, (mo·ne·the´ro) m. coiner; coin purse *(portamonedas).*

monería, (mo·ne·rē´ä) f. monkeyshine *(monada);* cute ways *(de un niño);* clowning around, fooling around.

monetario, ria, (mo·ne·tä´ryo, ryä) *adj.* monetary.

mongoloide, (mon·go·lo´ē·the) *adj.* Mongoloid.

monigote, (mo·nē·go´te) m. lay brother; (coll.) bumpkin, dolt, lout *(torpe);* (coll.) poor painting *(pintura);* badly done statue *(estatua).*

monitor, (mo·nē·tor´) m. monitor.

monja, (mon´hä) f. nun.

monje, (mon´he) m. monk.

mono, na, (mo´no, nä) *adj.* (coll.) pretty, cute; —, m. monkey; ape *(antropomorfo).*

monóculo, (mo·no´kŭ·lo) m. monocle.

monogamia, (mo·no·gä´myä) f. monogamy.

monografía, (mo·no·grä·fē´ä) f. monograph.

monograma, (mo·no·grä´mä) m. monogram.

monolito, (mo·no·lē´to) m. monolith.

monólogo, (mo·no´lo·go) m. monologue.

monoplano, (mo·no·plä´no) m. monoplane.

monopolio, (mo·no·po´lyo) m. monopoly.

monorriel, (mo·no·rryel´) m. monorail.

monosílabo, ba, (mo·no·sē´lä·vo, vä) *adj.* monosyllabic; —, m. monosyllable.

monotipo, (mo·no·tē´po) m. monotype.

monotonía, (mo·no·to·nē´ä) f. monotony.

monótono, na, (mo·no´to·no, nä) *adj.* monotonous.

Monseñor, (mon·se·nyor´) m. Monseigneur, Monsignor.

monstruo, (mons´trwo) m. monster.

monstruosidad, (mons·trwo·sē·thäth´) f. monstrosity.

monstruoso, sa, (mons·trwo´so, sä) *adj.* monstrous, freakish.

montacargas, (mon·tä·kär´gäs) m. elevator, hoist.

montaje, (mon·tä´he) m. assembly, setting up, putting up, mounting *(armado);* editing *(de un filme);* —**s,** pl. artillery carriage.

montaña, (mon·tä´nyä) f. mountain.

montañés, esa, (mon·tä·nyes´, e´sä) *adj.* from the mountains, mountain; —, n. mountaineer.

montañoso, sa, (mon·tä·nyo´so, sä) *adj.* mountainous.

montar, (mon·tär´) vn. to climb up, to get up; to mount *(en una cabalgadura);* to ride horseback *(cabalgar);* —, vt. to set up, to put together *(armar);* to amount to, to come to *(una cantidad);* to edit *(un filme).*

montaraz, (mon·tä·räs´) *adj.* mountainous; wild, untamed *(cerril).*

monte, (mon´te) m. mountain; wilds, brush *(sin roturar);* (fig.) stumbling block, obstacle.

monto, (mon´to) m. amount, sum.

montón, (mon·ton´) m. heap, pile, mass, cluster; **a** —**ones,** abundantly, in great quantities.

montura, (mon·tū´rä) f. mount *(cabalgadura);* saddle trappings *(de caballería);* mounting, framework *(armazón).*

monumental, (mo·nŭ·men·täl´) *adj.* monumental.

monumento, (mo·nū·men´to) *m.* monument.

monzón, (mon·son´) *m.* monsoon.

moño, (mo´nyo) *m.* topknot, loop *(del pelo); (orn.)* tuft, crest.

moquillo, (mo·kē´yo) *m.* distemper; pip *(de aves).*

mora, (mo´râ) *f.* blackberry, mulberry.

morada, (mo·râ´thâ) *f.* abode, residence, dwelling.

morado, da, (mo·râ´tho, thâ) *adj.* violet, purple.

morador, ra, (mo·râ·thor´, râ) *n.* lodger, dweller.

moral, (mo·râl´) *m.* mulberry tree; —, *f.* morals, ethics; —, *adj.* moral.

moraleja, (mo·râ·le´hâ) *f.* moral, moral lesson.

moralidad, (mo·râ·lē·thâth´) *f.* morality, morals.

moralista, (mo·râ·lēs´tâ) *m.* moralist.

moralizar, (mo·râ·lē·sâr´) *vn.* to moralize.

morar, (mo·râr´) *vn.* to inhabit, to dwell.

moratoria, (mo·râ·to´ryâ) *f.* moratorium.

mórbido, da, (mor´vē·tho, thâ) *adj.* diseased, morbid.

morcilla, (mor·sē´yâ) *f.* blood sausage.

mordaz, (mor·thâs´) *adj.* biting, sarcastic.

mordaza, (mor·thâ´sâ) *f.* gag.

mordedura, (mor·the·thū´râ) *f.* bite.

morder*, (mor·ther´) *va.* to bite.

mordisco (mor·thēs´ko) or mordiscón, (mor·thēs·kon´) *m.* bite.

morena, (mo·re´nâ) *f.* (ichth.) moray eel; brunette *(mujer);* (geol.) moraine.

moreno, na, (mo·re´no, nâ) *adj.* swarthy, dark brown.

morfina, (mor·fē´nâ) *f.* morphine.

morfinómano, na, (mor·fē·no´mâ·no, nâ) *n.* morphine addict.

moribundo, da, (mo·rē·vūn´do, dâ) *adj.* dying.

morir*, (mo·rēr´) *vn.* to die, to expire; —se, to go out, to be extinguished.

morisco, ca, (mo·rēs´ko, kâ) *adj.* Moorish.

moro, ra, (mo´ro, râ) *adj.* Moorish; —, *n.* Moor; Moslem *(mahometano).*

morosidad, (mo·ro·sē·thâth´) *f.* slowness, delay, tardiness.

moroso, sa, (mo·ro´so, sâ) *adj.* slow, tardy, late.

morral, (mo·rrâl´) *m.* feed bag, nose bag *(para pienso);* sack, provisions sack.

morriña, (mo·rrē´nyâ) *f.* murrain; (fig.) sadness, melancholy.

mortaja, (mor·tâ´hâ) *f.* shroud, winding sheet; mortise *(muesca).*

mortal, (mor·tâl´) *adj.* mortal, fatal, deadly; mortal *(sujeto a la muerte).*

mortalidad, (mor·tâ·lē·thâth´) *f.* mortality; death rate *(cantidad).*

mortandad, (mor·tân·dâth´) *f.* number of dead, death toll.

mortero, (mor·te´ro) *m.* mortar.

mortífero, ra, (mor·tē´fe·ro, râ) *adj.* fatal, deadly.

mortificación, (mor·tē·fē·kâ·syon´) *f.* mortification; vexation, trouble *(preocupación).*

mortificar, (mor·tē·fē·kâr´) *va.* to mortify; to afflict, to vex *(afligir).*

mortuorio, (mor·two´ryo) *m.* burial, funeral; —, rite, *adj.* mortuary.

moruno, na, (mo·rū´no, nâ) *adj.* Moorish.

mosaico, (mo·sâ´ē·ko) *m.* mosaic.

mosca, (mos´kâ) *f.* fly.

moscarda, (mos·kâr´thâ) *f.* horsefly.

moscatel, (mos·kâ·tel´) *m.* muscatel.

Moscú, (mos·kū´) *m.* Moscow.

mosquetero, (mos·ke·te´ro) *m.* musketeer.

mosquitero, (mos·kē·te´ro) *m.* mosquito net.

mosquito, (mos·kē´to) *m.* mosquito.

mostacho, (mos·tá´cho) *m.* mustache.

mostaza, (mos·tâ´sâ) *f.* mustard; mustard seed *(semilla).*

mostrador, (mos·trâ·thor´) *m.* shop counter.

mostrar*, (mos·trâr´) *va.* to show, to exhibit; —se, to appear, to show oneself.

mota, (mo´tâ) *f.* burl *(del paño);* speck; — de empolvarse, powder puff.

moteado, da, (mo·te·â´tho, thâ) *adj.* spotted, mottled.

motín, (mo·tēn´) *m.* mutiny, riot.

motivar, (mo·tē·vâr´) *va.* to motivate, to give a motive for; to justify, to explain the reason for *(explicar).*

motivo, (mo·tē´vo) *m.* motive, cause, reason; con este —, therefore; con — de, by reason of.

motocicleta, (mo·to·sē·kle´tâ) *f.* motorcycle.

motón, (mo·ton´) *m.* (naut.) block, pulley.

motor, ra, (mo·tor´, râ) *adj.* moving, motor; —, *m.* motor, engine; — de búsqueda, search engine; poner en marcha el —, to start the motor.

motriz, (mo·trēs´) *f. adj.* motor, moving.

movedizo, za, (mo·ve·thē´so, sâ) *adj.* moving, movable.

mover*, (mo·ver´) *va.* to move; to stir up, to cause *(suscitar).*

movible, (mo·vē´·vle) *adj.* movable.

móvil, (mo´·vēl) *adj.* movable; —, *m.*

motive, incentive.

movilización, (mo·vē·lē·sâ·syon´) *f.* mobilization.

movilizar, (mo·vē·lē·sâr´) *va.* to mobilize.

movimiento, (mo·vē·myen´·to) *m.* movement.

moza, (mo´·sâ) *f.* girl, lass; maidservant *(sirvienta).*

mozalbete, (mo·sâl·ve´·te) *m.* lad.

mozo, za, (mo´·so, sâ) *adj.* young; —, *m.* youth, lad; manservant *(sirviente);* waiter *(camarero).*

m/r: mi remesa, (com.) my remittance, my shipment.

MS.: manuscrito, Ms. or MS. or ms. manuscript.

MSS.: manuscritos, Mss. or MSS. or mss. manuscripts.

muchacha, (mū·châ´·châ) *f.* girl, lass, young woman.

muchacho, (mū·châ´·cho) *m.* boy, lad, young man; —, **cha,** *adj.* boyish; girlish.

muchedumbre, (mū·che·thūm´·bre) *f.* crowd, multitude.

mucho, cha, (mū´·cho, châ) *adj.* much, abundant; — **tiempo,** a long time; **hay** —**s,** there are many; —**cho** *adv.* much.

muda, (mū´·thâ) *f.* change, alteration; molt, molting *(de plumas).*

mudanza, (mū·thân´·sâ) *f.* change; mutation; inconstancy *(inconstancia);* **estoy de** —, I am moving.

mudar, (mū·thâr´) *va.* to change; to molt; —**se de casa,** to move, to move into a new home; —**se de ropa,** to change clothes.

mudo, da, (mū´·tho, thâ) *adj.* dumb; silent, mute *(callado).*

mueblaje, (mwe·vlâ´·he) *m.* household furniture.

mueble, (mwe´·vle) *m.* piece of furniture; —**s,** *pl.* furniture.

mueblería, (mwe·vle·rē´·â) *f.* furniture store.

mueca, (mwe´·kâ) *f.* grimace, wry face.

muela, (mwe´·lâ) *f.* molar tooth; — **cordal** or **del juicio,** wisdom tooth.

muelle, (mwe´·ye) *adj.* tender, delicate, soft; —, *m.* spring *(resorte);* (naut.) dock, quay, wharf; (rail.) freight dock.

muérdago, (mwer´·thâ·go) *m.* mistletoe.

muerte, (mwer´·te) *f.* death.

muerto, (mwer´·to) *m.* corpse; —, **ta,** *adj.* dead.

muesca, (mwes´·kâ) *f.* notch, groove.

muestra, (mwes´·trâ) *f.* sample *(de mercancía);* sign *(de tienda);* pattern, model *(modelo);* (mil.) muster, inspection; face,

dial *(del reloj);* indication, sample, example *(señal).*

muestrario, (mwes·trâ´·ryo) *m.* samples, sample book.

mugido, (mū·hē´·tho) *m.* lowing, bellowing.

mugir, (mū·hēr´) *vn.* to low, to bellow.

mugre, (mū´·gre) *f.* dirt, grease.

mugriento, ta, (mū·gryen´·to, tâ) *adj.* greasy, dirty, filthy.

mujer, (mū·her´) *f.* woman; wife *(casada).*

mujeriego, (mū·he·rye´·go) *m. adj.* very fond of women; womanizer.

mujeril, (mū·he·rēl´) *adj.* womanish, womanly.

mula, (mū´·lâ) *f.* she-mule.

muladar, (mū·lâ·thâr´) *m.* trash heap.

mulato, ta, (mū·lâ´·to, tâ) *n.* and *adj.* mulatto.

muleta, (mū·le´·tâ) *f.* crutch.

multa, (mūl´·tâ) *f.* fine, penalty.

multar, (mūl·târ´) *va.* to impose a penalty on, to penalize, to fine.

multifacético, ca, (mūl·tē·fâ·se´·tē·ko, kâ) *adj.* multiphase.

multígrafo, (mūl·tē´·grâ·fo) *m.* multigraph.

multimillonario, ria, (mūl·tē·mē·yo·nâ´·ryo, ryâ) *adj.* and *n.* multimillionaire.

múltiple, (mūl´·tē·ple) *adj.* multiple, manifold.

multiplicador, ra, (mū1·tē·plē·kâ·thor´, râ) *n.* multiplier; —, *m.* (math.) multiplier.

multiplicando, (mūl·tē·plē·kân´·do) *m.* multiplicand.

multiplicar, (mūl·tē·plē·kâr´) *va.* to multiply.

multiplicidad, (mūl·tē·plē·sē·thâth´) *f.* multiplicity.

multitud, (mūl·tē·tūth´) *f.* multitude, crowd.

mullir*, (mū·yēr´) *va.* to shake up, to fluff up.

mundano, na, (mūn·dâ´·no, nâ) *adj.* mundane, worldly.

mundial, (mūn·dyâl´) *adj.* world-wide, world.

mundo, (mūn´·do) *m.* world; **todo el** —, everybody.

munición, (mū·nē·syon´) *f.* ammunition.

municipal, (mū·nē·sē·pâl´) *adj.* municipal.

municipio, (mū·nē·sē´·pyo) *m.* city council.

muñeca, (mū·nye´·kâ) *f.* (anat.) wrist; doll *(juguete).*

muñeco, (mū·nye´·ko) *m.* figurine, statuette; (fig.) sissy, effeminate boy.

mural, (mū·râl´) *m.* and *adj.* mural.

muralla, (mū·râ´·yâ) *f.* rampart, wall.

---

m met, **n** not, **p** pot, **r** very, **rr** (none), **s** so, **t** toy, **th** with, **v** eve, **w** we, **y** yes, **z** zero

murciélago, (mūr·sye´·lâ·go) *m.* (zool.) bat.
murmullo, (mūr·mū´·yo) *m.* murmuring.
murmuración, (mūr·mū·râ·syon´) *f.* back-
biting, gossip.
murmurar, (mūr·mū·râr´) *vn.* to murmur;
to backbite, to gossip *(chismear).*
muro, (mū´·ro) *m.* wall.
musa, (mū´·sâ) *f.* Muse.
muscular, (mūs·kū·lâr´) *adj.* muscular.
músculo, (mūs´·kū·lo) *m.* muscle.
muselina, (mū·se·lē´·nâ) *f.* muslin.
museo, (mū·se´·o) *m.* museum.
musgo, (mūz´·go) *m.* moss.
música, (mū´·sē·kâ) *f.* music; — **de
cámara,** chamber music; — **sagrada,**
church music.
musical, (mū·sē·kâl´) *adj.* musical.
músico, (mū´·sē·ko) *m.* musician.

muslo, (muz´·lo) *m.* thigh.
mustio, tia, (mūs´·tyo, tyâ) *adj.* withered
(marchito); sad, sorrowful *(triste).*
musulmán, (mū·sūl·mân´) **musulmano,
na,** (mū·sūl·mâ´·no, nâ) *adj.* and *n.*
Mohammedan.
mutación, (mū·tâ·syon´) *f.* mutation,
change.
mutilación, (mū·tē·lâ·syon´) *f.* mutilation.
mutilar, (mū·tē·lâr´) *va.* to mutilate, to
maim.
mutismo, (mū·tēz´·mo) *m.* muteness.
mutual, (mū·twâl´) *adj.* mutual.
mutuo, tua, (mū´·two, twâ) *adj.* mutual,
reciprocal.
muy, (mwē) *adv.* very; greatly *(altamente).*
Mzo. or mzo.: **marzo,** Mar. March.

N

N.: **norte,** N., No., or no. North.
no: **nacido,** b. born.
n/: **nuestro,** our.
naba, (nâ´·vâ) *f.* rutabaga, Swedish turnip.
nabo, (nâ´·vo) *m.* turnip.
Nac.: **nacional,** nat. national.
nácar, (nâ´·kâr) *m.* mother-of-pearl.
nacarado, da, (nâ·kâ·râ´·tho, thâ) *adj.* set
with mother-of-pearl; pearl-colored
(anacarado).
nacela, (nâ·se´·lâ) *f.* (avi.) nacelle; (arch.)
concave moulding.
nacer*, (nâ·ser´) *vn.* to be born; (bot.) to
bud, to germinate.
nacido, da, (nâ·sē´·tho, thâ) *adj.* born; —,
m. tumor, swelling.
naciente, (nâ·syen´·te) *adj.* rising; **el sol** —,
the rising sun.
nacimiento, (nâ·sē·myen´·to) *m.* birth;
Nativity *(de Jesucristo);* manger, creche
(belén).
nación, (nâ·syon´) *f.* nation.
nacional, (nâ·syo·nâl´) *adj.* national.
nacionalidad, (nâ·syo·nâ·lē·thâth´) *f.* nationality.
nacionalismo, (nâ·syo·nâ·lēz´·mo) *m.*
nationalism.
nacionalista, (nâ·syo·nâ·lēs´·tâ) *m.* and *f.*
nationalist.
Naciones Unidas, (nâ·syo´·nes ū·nē´·thâs)
f. pl. United Nations.
nada, (nâ´·thâ) *f.* nothing; **de** —, don´t
mention it, you´re welcome; — **de eso,**

of course not, not at all; —, *adv.* in no
way, by no means.
nadador, ra, (nâ·thâ·thor´, râ) *n.* swimmer; —, *adj.* swimming.
nadar, (nâ·thâr´) *vn.* to swim.
nadie, (nâ´·thye) *pron.* nobody, no one.
nafta, (nâf´·tâ) *f.* naphtha; (Arg., Uruguay)
gasoline.
naipe, (nâ´·ē·pe) *m.* playing card.
nalga, (nâl´·gâ) *f.* buttock; —**s,** *pl.* rump.
nalgada, (nâl·gâ´·thâ) *f.* spank, slap on the
buttocks.
nana, (nâ´·nâ) *f.* (Mex.) nursemaid.
nao, (nâ´·o) *f.* (poet.) ship, vessel.
Nápoles, (na´·po·les) *f.* Naples.
naranja, (nâ·rân´·hâ) *f.* orange; **jugo de** —,
orange juice.
naranjada, (nâ·rân·hâ´·thâ) *f.* orangeade.
naranjado, da, (nâ·rân·ha´·tho, thâ) *adj.*
orange-colored.
naranjal, (nâ·rân·hâl´) *m.* orange grove.
naranjo, (nâ·rân´·ho) *m.* orange tree.
narciso, (nâr·sē´·so) *m.* (bot.) narcissus;
narcissist.
narcótico, ca, (nâr·ko´·tē·ko, kâ) *adj.* and
m. narcotic.
narigón, ona, (nâ·rē·gon´·, o´·nâ) or **narigu-
do, da,** (nâ·rē·gū´·tho, thâ) *adj.* big-
nosed.
nariz, (nâ·rēs´) *f.* nose; sense of smell
(olfato); nostril *(ventana).*
narración, (nâ·rrâ·syon´) *f.* narration,
account.

narrador, ra, (nâ·rrâ·thor´·, râ) *n.* narrator.

narrar, (nâ·rrâr´) *va.* to narrate, to tell.

N.ª S.ª: Nuestra Señora, Our Lady.

nasal, (nâ·sâl´) *adj.* nasal.

nata, (nâ´·tâ) *f.* thick, rich cream; **la flor y —,** the cream, the elite.

natación, (nâ·tâ·syon´) *f.* swimming.

natal, (nâ·tâl´) *adj.* natal, native; **pueblo —,** home town; **ciudad —,** native city.

natalidad, (nâ·tâ·lē·thâth´) *f.* birth rate.

natalicio, (nâ·tâ·lē´·syo) *m.* birthday.

natilla (nâ·tē´·yâ) *f.* custard.

natividad, (nâ·tē·vē·thâth´) *f.* nativity.

nativo, va, (nâ·tē´·vo, vâ) *adj.* native.

natural, (nâ·tū·râl´) *adj.* natural; native *(originario);* natural, unaffected *(ingenuo);* **al —,** unaffectedly; **del —,** from life.

naturaleza, (nâ·tū·râ·le´·sâ) *f.* nature.

naturalidad, (nâ·tū·râ·lē·thâth´) *f.* naturalness; national origin *(origen);* ingenuity, candor *(sencillez).*

naturalista, (nâ·tū·râ·lēs´·tâ) *m.* naturalist.

naturalmente, (nâ·tū·râl·men´·te) *adv.* naturally, of course.

naufragar, (nâû·frâ·gâr´) *vn.* to be shipwrecked; (fig.) to fail, to be ruined.

naufragio, (nâû·frâ´·hyo) *m.* shipwreck.

náufrago, ga, (nâ´·ū·frâ·go, gâ) *n.* shipwrecked person.

náusea, (nâ´·ū·se·â) *f.* nausea.

náutica, (nâ´·ū·tē·kâ) *f.* navigation, nautical science.

náutico, ca, (nâ´·ū·tē·ko, kâ) *adj.* nautical.

navaja, (nâ·vâ´·hâ) *f.* pocketknife; **— de afeitar,** razor; **— de seguridad,** safety razor.

naval, (nâ·vâl´) *adj.* naval.

nave, (nâ´·ve) *f.* ship; (arch.) nave; **— espacial,** spacecraft, spaceship.

navegable, (nâ·ve·gâ´·vle) *adj.* navigable.

navegación, (nâ·ve·gâ·syon´) *f.* navigation, shipping.

navegante, (nâ·ve·gân´·te) *m.* navigator, seafarer.

navegar, (nâ·ve·gâr´) *vn.* to navigate.

Navidad, (nâ·vē·thâth´) *f.* Christmas.

navideño, ña, (nâ·vē·the´·nyo, nyâ) *adj.* pertaining to Christmas; **espíritu —ño,** Christmas spirit.

naviero, ra, (nâ·vye´·ro, râ) *adj.* shipping; **compañía —,** shipping company; **—,** *m.* shipowner.

N.B.: Nota Bene, N.B. take notice.

n/ c. or n/cta.: nuestra cuenta, our account.

NE: nordeste, NE or N.E. northeast.

neblina, (ne·vlē´·nâ) *f.* mist.

nebuloso, sa, (ne·vū·lo´·so, sâ) *adj.* cloudy; (fig.) nebulous, foggy, hazy.

necedad, (ne·se·thâth´) *f.* gross ignorance; stupidity *(tontería);* nonsense *(disparate).*

necesario, (ne·se·sâ´·ryo, ryâ) *adj.* necessary.

neceser, (ne·se·ser´) *m.* cosmetic case, vanity case, manicure case.

necesidad, (ne·se·sē·thâth´) *f.* necessity, need, want.

necesitado, da, (ne·se·sē·tâ´·tho, thâ) *adj.* needy, indigent.

necesitar, (ne·se·sē·târ´) *va.* to need, to necessitate; **—,** *vn.* to want, to need.

necio, cia, (ne´·syo, syâ) *adj.* ignorant, stupid, foolish.

necroscopia, (ne·kros·ko´·pyâ) *f.* autopsy.

néctar, (nek´·târ) *m.* nectar.

nefasto, ta, (ne·fâs´·to, tâ) *adj.* unlucky, ill-fated.

negar*, (ne·gâr´) *va.* to deny; **—se,** to refuse, to decline.

negativo, va, (ne·gâ·tē´·vo, vâ) *adj.* negative; **—,** *f.* refusal, denial; (phot.) negative.

negligencia, (ne·glē·hen´·syâ) *f.* negligence.

negligente, (ne·glē·hen´·te) *adj.* careless, heedless.

negociación, (ne·go·syâ·syon´) *f.* negotiation; (com.) transaction, business deal, affair.

negociante, (ne·go·syân´·te) *m.* and *f.* trader, dealer, merchant.

negociar, (ne·go·syâr´) *va.* to negotiate; **—,** *vn.* to trade, to deal.

negocio, (ne·go´·syo) *m.* business; **hombre de —s,** businessman.

negro, gra, (ne´·gro, grâ) *adj.* black; **—,** *n.* Negro.

negrura, (ne·grū´·râ) *f.* blackness.

nene, na, (ne´·ne, nâ) *n.* baby.

neófito, (ne·o´·fē·to) *m.* neophyte, novice.

neologismo, (ne·o·lo·hēz´·mo) *m.* neologism.

neón, (ne·on´) *m.* neon; **alumbrado de —,** neon lighting.

neoyorquino, na, (ne·o·yor·kē´·no, nâ) *n.* New Yorker; **—,** *adj.* from New York, of New York.

nepotismo, (ne·po·tēz´·mo) *m.* nepotism.

neptunio, (nep·tū´·nyo) *m.* (chem.) neptunium.

nervio, (ner´·vyo) *m.* nerve.

nervioso, sa, (ner·vyo´·so, sâ) *adj.* nervous.

neto, ta, (ne´·to, tâ) *adj.* net.

neumático, (neû·mâ´·tē·ko) *m.* tire; **—**

balón, balloon tire; — **desinflado,** deflated tire; — **de repuesto,** spare tire; — **recauchado,** retread; —, **ca,** adj. pneumatic.

neumonía, (neū·mo·nē´·â) f. pneumonia.

neuralgia, (neū·rál´·hyâ) f. neuralgia.

neurastenia, (neū·râs·te´nyâ) f. (med.) neurasthenia.

neuritis, (neū·rē´·tēs) f. (med.) neuritis.

neurosis, (neū·ro´·sēs) f. neurosis; — **de guerra,** shell shock, war neurosis.

neurótico, ca, (neū·ro´·tē·ko, kâ) adj. neurotic.

neutral, (neū·trâl´) adj. neutral.

neutralidad, (neū·trâ·lē·thâth´) f. neutrality.

neutralizar, (neū·trâ·lē·sâr´) va. (chem.) to neutralize.

neutro, tra, (ne´·ū·tro, trâ) adj. neuter.

neutrón, (neū·tron´) m. neutron.

nevada, (ne·vâ´·thâ) f. snowfall.

nevado, da, (ne·vâ´·tho, thâ) adj. snow-covered, snow-capped.

nevar*, (ne·vâr´) vn. to snow.

nevera, (ne·ve´·râ) f. refrigerator.

nevería, (ne·ve·rē´·â) f. ice cream store.

n/f.: nuestro favor, our favor.

n/g.: nuestro giro, (com.) our draft.

ni, (nē) conj. neither, nor; — **el uno — el otro,** neither one nor the other.

niacina, (nyâ·sē´·nâ) f. (chem.) niacin.

nicaragüense, (nē·kâ·ra·gwen´·se) m. and f. and adj. Nicaraguan.

nicotina, (nē·ko·tē´·na) f. nicotine.

nicho, (nē´·cho) m. niche.

nido, (nē´·tho) m. nest; den, hangout (de bribones).

niebla, (nye´·vlâ) f. fog.

nieta, (nye´·tâ) f. granddaughter.

nieto, (nye´·to) m. grandson.

nieve, (nye´·ve) f. snow.

nigua, (nē´·gwâ) f. chigoe, jigger, chigger.

Nilo, (nē´·lo) m. Nile.

nimbo, (nēm´·bo) m. nimbus (nube); halo (aureola).

nimiedad, (nē·mye·thâth´) f. excess, superfluousness; trifle, insignificance (pequeñez).

ninfa, (nēm´·fâ) f. nymph.

ningún, (nēng·gūn´) adj. (apocope of ninguno), no, not any (used only before masculine nouns); **de — modo,** in no way, by no means.

ninguno, na, (nēng·gū´·no, nâ) adj. none, not one, neither; **en —na parte,** no place; nowhere.

niña, (nē´·nyâ) f. little girl; — **del ojo,** pupil of the eye; — **de los ojos,** (coll.) apple of

one´s eye.

niñera, (nē·nye´·râ) f. nursemaid; babysitter (por horas).

niñería, (nē·nye·rē´·â) f. puerility, childish action.

niñero, ra, (nē·nye´·ro, râ) adj. fond of children.

niñez, (nē·nyes´) f. childhood.

niño, ña, (ne´·nyo, nyâ) adj. childish; —, n. child, infant; **desde —,** from infancy, since childhood.

N.I.P.: número de identificación personal, P.I.N.: personal identification number.

nipón, ona, (nē·pon´, o´·na) adj. and n. Japanese.

níquel, (nē´·kel) m. nickel.

niquelado, da, (nē·ke·lâ´·tho, thâ) adj. nickel-plated.

níspero, (nēs´·pe·ro) m. medlar tree.

nítido, da, (nē´·tē·tho, thâ) adj. (poet.) bright, pure, shining.

nitrato, (nē·trâ´·to) m. (chem.) nitrate, saltpeter.

nitrógeno, (nē·tro´·he·no) m. nitrogen.

nivel, (nē·vel´) m. level, plane; **a —,** perfectly level.

nivelación, (nē·ve·lâ·syon´) f. grading, leveling.

niveladora, (nē·ve·lâ·tho´·râ) f. bulldozer.

nivelar, (nē·ve·lâr´) va. to level.

n/l. or **n/L.: nuestra letra,** (com.) our letter, our draft.

NNE: nornordeste, NNE or N.N.E. northnortheast.

NNO: nornoroeste, NNW or N.N.W. northnorthwest.

NO:noroeste, NW or N.W. northwest.

No. or **N.o : número,** no. number.

n/o.: nuestra orden, (com.) our order.

no, (no) adv. no (uso absoluto); not.

noble, (no´·vle) adj. noble, illustrious.

nobleza, (no·vle´·sâ) f. nobleness; nobility (de título).

noción, (no·syon´) f. notion, idea.

nocivo, va, (no·sē´·vo, vâ) adj. injurious.

nocturno, na, (nok·tūr´·no, nâ) adj. (zool.) nocturnal; nightly; —, m. nocturn; (mus.) nocturne.

noche, (no´·che) f. night; **esta —,** tonight, this evening; **de —,** at night; **media —,** midnight; **N— Buena,** Christmas Eve; **cada —, todas las —s,** every night; **buenas —s, good evening; good night** (despedida).

nodriza, (no·thrē´·sâ) f. wet nurse.

nogada, (no·gâ´·thâ) f. nougat.

nogal, (no·gâl´) m. walnut tree; walnut (madera).

â arm, **e** they, **ē** bē, **o** fore, **ū** blūe, **b** bad, **ch** chip, **d** day, **f** fat, **g** go, **h** hot, **k** kid, **1** let

nómada, (no'·mâ·thâ) or nómade, (no'·mâ·the) *adj.* nomad, nomadic.

nombradía, (nom·brâ·thē'·â) *f.* fame, reputation.

nombramiento, (nom·brâ·myen'·to) *m.* nomination, appointment *(elección);* mention, naming.

nombrar, (nom·brâr') *va.* to name; to nominate *(nominar);* to appoint *(señalar).*

nombre, (nom'·bre) *m.* name *(de persona);* title; reputation *(fama).*

nomenclatura, (no·meng·klâ·tū'·râ) *f.* nomenclature *(científica);* catalogue.

nomeolvides, (no·me·ôl·vē'·thes) *f.* (bot.) forget-me-not.

nómina, (no'·mē·nâ) *f.* catalogue; pay roll *(de paga);* membership list *(de socios).*

nominador, ra, (no·mē·nâ·thor'·, râ) *n.* nominator, appointer; —, *adj.* nominating.

nominal, (no·mē·nâl') *adj.* nominal.

nominativo, (no·mē·nâ·tē'·vo) *m.* (gram.) nominative.

non, (non) *adj.* odd, uneven.

nonagenario, ria, (no·nâ·he·nâ'·ryo, ryâ) *adj..* ninety years old; —, *n.* nonagenarian.

nonagésimo, ma, (no·nâ·he'·sē·mo, mâ) *adj.* ninetieth.

nono, na, (no'·no, nâ) *adj.* ninth.

non plus ultra, (nom plūs ūltrâ) *m.* absolute limit, very end.

nordeste, (nor·thes'·te) *m.* northeast.

nórdico, ca, (nor'·thē·ko, kâ) *adj.* and *n.* Nordic.

noria, (no'·ryâ) *f.* water wheel, noria.

norma, (nor'·mâ) *f.* norm, standard, model; square *(escuadra).*

normal, (nor·mâl') *adj.* normal.

normalidad, (nor·mâ·lē·thâth') *f.* normality.

nornordeste, (nor·nor·thes'·te) *m.* north-northeast.

nornoroeste, (nor·no·ro·es'·te) *m.* north-northwest.

noroeste, (no·ro·es'·te) *m.* northwest.

norte, (nor'·te) *m.* north; (fig.) rule, guide.

Norte América, (nor'·te·â·me'·rē·kâ) *f.* North America.

norteamericano, na, (nor·te·â·me·rē·kâ'·no, nâ) *n.* and *adj.* North American; a native of U.S.A. *(estadounidense).*

Noruega, (no·rwe'·gâ) *f.* Norway.

noruego, ga, (no·rwe'·go, gâ) *n.* and *adj.* Norwegian.

nos, (nos) *pron.* us, to us.

nosotros, tras, (no·so'·tros, trâs) *pron.* we; us *(con preposición).*

nostalgia, (nos·tâl'·hyâ) *f.* homesickness *(de la patria);* nostalgia.

nota, (no'·tâ) *f.* note; grade *(calificación);* — **bene,** n. B. take notice; — **de entrega,** delivery order; — **musical,** musical note; — **de gastos,** bill of expenses.

notable, (no·tâ'·vle) *adj.* notable, remarkable, distinguished.

notación, (no·tâ·syon') *f.* notation.

notar, (no·târ') *va.* to note, to mark; to remark, to observe *(reparar).*

notaría, (no·tâ·rē'·â) *f.* profession of notary public.

notario, (no·tâ'·ryo) *m.* notary public.

noticia, (no·tē'·syâ) *f.* notice; knowledge, information *(conocimiento);* piece of news *(novedad);* **en espera de sus —s,** (com.) awaiting your reply.

noticiario, (no·tē·syâ'·ryo) *m.* newscast.

noticiero, ra, (no·tē·sye'·ro, râ) *n.* newscaster, news commentator.

notificación, (no·tē·fē·kâ·syon') *f.* notification.

notificar, (no·tē·fē·kâr') *va.* to notify, to inform.

notoriedad, (no·to·rye·thâth') *f.* notoriety.

notorio, ria, (no·to'·ryo, ryâ) *adj.* well-known, known to all.

novato, ta, (no·vâ'·to, tâ) *adj.* new; —, *n.* novice, greenhorn. freshman.

Novbre., nov.^e: noviembre, Nov. November.

novecientos, tas, (no·ve·syen'·tos, tâs) *adj.* and *m.* nine hundred.

novedad, (no·ve·thâth') *f.* novelty, newness; change *(cambio);* news *(noticias);* **—es,** *pl.* notions.

novela, (no·ve'·lâ) *f.* novel; (fig.) he, tale.

novelero, ra, (no·ve·le'·ro, râ) *adj.* fond of novels; news-hungry *(noticias);* newfangled *(novedades);* (fig.) fickle, changeable *(inconstante).*

novelesco, ca, (no·ve·les'·ko, kâ) *adj.* novelesque.

novelista, (no·ve·lēs'·tâ) *m.* and *f.* novelist.

novena, (no·ven'·nâ) *f.* Novena.

noveno, na, (no·ve'·no, nâ) *adj.* ninth.

noventa, (no·ven'·tâ) *m.* and *adj.* ninety.

novia, (no'·vyâ) *f.* newlywed; fiancée, betrothed woman *(prometida);* sweetheart, girlfriend *(querida).*

noviazgo, (no·vyâz'·go) *m.* courtship.

noviciado, (no·vē·syâ'·tho) *m.* novitiate.

novicio, cia, (no·vē'·syo, syâ) *n.* novice.

noviembre, (no·vyem'·bre) *m.* November.

novilla, (no·vē'·yâ) *f.* heifer.

novillada, (no·vē·yâ'·thâ) *f.* drove of young

bulls; fight featuring young bulls *(corrida)*.

novillo, (no·vē´·yo) *m.* young bull; **hacer —s,** (coll.) to play hooky.

novio, (no´·vyo) *m.* fiancé; sweetheart, boyfriend; newlywed *(recién casado).* **viaje de —s,** honeymoon trip.

novísimo, ma, (no·vē´·sē·mo, mä) *adj.* newest.

novocaína, (no·vo·kä·ē´·nä) *f.* novocaine.

n/p: nuestro pagaré, (com.) our promissory note.

n/r: nuestra remesa, (com.) our remittance or our shipment.

N.S.: Nuestro Señor, Our Lord.

N.S.J.C.: Nuestro Señor Jesucristo, Our Lord Jesus Christ.

nubarrón, (nū·vä·rron´) *m.* large dark cloud.

nube, (nū´·ve) *f.* cloud.

nublado, da, (nū·vlä´·tho, thä) *adj.* cloudy.

nublarse, (nū·vlär´·se) *vr.* to cloud over, to become cloudy.

nuca, (nū´·kä) *f.* nape, scruff of the neck.

nuclear, (nū·kle·är´) *adj.* nuclear; **desintegración —,** nuclear fission; **física —,** nuclear physics; **lluvia —,** fallout.

nucleario, ria, (nū·kle·ä´·ryo, ryä) nuclear.

nucleico, ca, (nū·kle´·ē·ko, kä) *adj.* nucleic.

núcleo, (nū´·kle·o) *m.* nucleus *(del átomo);* core *(del fruto).*

nudillo, (nū·thē´·yo) *m.* knuckle *(artejo);* small knot.

nudo, (nū´·tho) *m.* knot; (bot.) knot, gnarl; **— corredizo,** slipknot.

nuera, (nwe´·rä) *f.* daughter-in-law.

nuestro, tra, (nwes´·tro, trä) *adj.* our; **—,** *pron.* ours.

nueva, (nwe´·vä) *f.* news.

nueve, (nwe´·ve) *m.* and *adj.* nine.

nuevo, va, (nwe´·vo, vä) *adj.* new; another *(otro);* **de —vo,** once more, again; **¿qué hay de —vo?** is there any news? what´s new?

nuez, (nwes) *f.* nut; walnut *(del nogal);* (anat.) Adam´s apple; **— moscada** or **de especia,** nutmeg.

nulidad, (nū·lē·thäth´) *f.* nullity, nonentity.

nulo, la, (nū´·lo, lä) *adj.* null, void.

núm.: número, no. number.

numen, (nū´·men) *m.* numen.

numeración, (nū·me·rä·syon´) *f.* numeration, numbering.

numerador, (nū·me·rä·thor´) *m.* numerator.

numeral, (nū·me·räl´) *adj.* numeral.

numerar, (nū·me·rär´) *va.* to number *(marcar);* to numerate, to count.

numérico, ca, (nū·me´·rē·ko, kä) *adj.* numerical.

número, (nū´·me·ro) *m.* number; cipher *(cifra);* **— atrasado,** back number.

numeroso, sa, (nū·me·ro´·so, sä) *adj.* numerous.

numismática, (nū·mēz·mä´·tē·kä) *f.* numismatics.

nunca, (nūng´·kä) *adv.* never.

nuncio, (nūn´·syo) *m.* messenger; (eccl.) nuncio.

nupcial, (nūp·syäl´) *adj.* nuptial.

nupcias, (nūp´·syäs) *f. pl.* nuptials, wedding.

nutria, (nū´·tryä) *f.* otter.

nutrición, (nū·trē·syon´) *f.* nutrition; feeding *(acción).*

nutrir, (nū·trēr´) *va.* to nourish.

nutritivo, va, (nū·trē·tē´·vo, vä) *adj.* nutritive, nourishing.

nylon, (nä´·ē·lon) *m.* nylon.

Ñ

ñame, (nyä´·me) *m.* (bot.) tropical yam.

ñapa, (nyä´·pä) *f.* (Sp. Am.) lagniappe.

O

o, (o) (ó when between numbers) *conj.* or; **el uno — el otro,** either one or the other.

oasis, (o·ä´·sēs) *m.* oasis.

obcecación, (ov·se·kä·syon´) *f.* obduracy, stubbornness.

obedecer*, (o·ve·the·ser´) *va.* to obey.

obediencia, (o·ve·thyen´·syä) *f.* obedience.

obediente, (o·ve·thyen´·te) *adj.* obedient.

obelisco, (o·ve·lēs´·ko) *m.* obelisk.

â arm, **e** they, **ē** bē, **o** fore, **ū** blūe, **b** bad, **ch** chip, **d** day, **f** fat, **g** go, **h** hot, **k** kid, **1** let

obertura, (o·ver·tū´râ) *f.* (mus.) overture.

obesidad, (o·ve·sē·thâth´) *f.* obesity.

obeso, sa, (o·ve´so, sâ) *adj.* obese.

óbice, (o´vē·se) *m.* obstacle.

obispado, (o·vēs·pä´tho) *m.* bishopric; episcopate; diocese *(territorio)*.

obispo, (o·vēs´po) *m.* bishop; (ichth.) ray.

obituario, (o·vē·twä´ryo) *m.* obituary.

objeción, (ov·he·syon´) *f.* objection; **poner —,** to raise an objection.

objetar, (ov·he·târ´) *va.* to raise, to bring up, to object.

objetivo, va, (ov·he·tē´vo, vâ) *adj.* objective; **—,** *m,* objective, purpose; lens *(lente)*.

objeto, (ov·he´to) *m.* object; subject *(asunto)*.

oblea, (o·vle´â) *f.* (med.) pill, tablet; seal *(para cartas);* (fig.) skeleton.

oblicuo, cua, (o·vlē´kwo, kwâ) *adj.* oblique.

obligación, (o·vlē·gâ·syon´) *f.* obligation, duty; debt *(deuda)*.

obligado, da, (o·vlē·gâ´tho, thâ) *adj.* obliged, obligated, beholden; **—,** *m.* city supplier; (mus.) obbligato.

obligar, (o·vlē·gâr´) *va.* to oblige, to force.

obligatorio, ria, (o·vlē·gâ·to´ryo, ryâ) *adj.* compulsory, obligatory.

oblongo, ga, (o·vlong´go, gâ) *adj.* oblong.

oboe, (o·vo´e) *m.* (mus.) oboe.

óbolo, (o´vo·lo) *m.* obolus; pittance *(contribución)*.

obra, (o´vrâ) *f.* work; construction *(edificio);* virtue, power *(medio);* **— maestra,** masterpiece; **manos a la —,** let´s get started.

obrar, (o·vrâr´) *va.* to work; to do, to execute *(hacer);* to build *(edificar);* **—,** *vn.* to be; to have a bowel movement *(del vientre)*.

obrero, ra, (o·vre´ro, râ) *n.* worker; (eccl.) churchwarden.

obreropatronal, (o·vre·ro·pâ·tro·nâl´) *adj.* relating to capital and labor; **relaciones —es,** employer-employee relations.

obscenidad, (ovs·se·nē·thâth´) *f.* obscenity.

obsceno, na, (ovs·se´no, nâ) *adj.* obscene.

obscurecer, (ovs·kū·re·ser´) = **oscurecer.**

obscurecimiento, (ovs·kū·re·sē·myen´to) = **oscurecimiento.**

obscuridad, (ovs·kū·rē·thâth´) = **oscuridad.**

obscuro, (ovs·kū´ro) = **oscuro.**

obsequiar, (ov·se·kyâr´) *va.* to court; to give *(regalar);* to shower with attention *(agasajar)*.

obsequio, (ov·se´kyo) *m.* gift; attention, kindness *(holgazanería)*.

obsequioso, sa, (ov·se·kyo´so, sâ) *adj.*

obsequious, officious; courteous, obliging *(cortesano)*.

observación, (ov·ser·vâ·syon´) *f.* observation.

observador, ra, (ov·ser·vâ·thor´, râ) *n.* observer; **—,** *adj.* observant.

observancia, (ov·ser·vân´syâ) *f.* observance; deference, respect *(respeto)*.

observar, (ov·ser·vâr´) *va.* to observe.

observatorio, (ov·ser·vâ·to´ryo) *m.* observatory.

obsesión, (ov·se·syon´) *f.* obsession.

obstáculo, (ovs·tâ´kū·lo) *m.* obstacle, bar, impediment.

obstante, (ovs·tân´te) *adj.* in the way; **no —,** notwithstanding, nevertheless.

obstar, (ovs·târ´) *vn.* to obstruct, to hinder, to get in the way; to oppose *(oponerse)*.

obstetricia, (ovs·te·trē´syâ) *f.* obstetrics.

obstinación, (ovs·tē·nâ·syon´) *f.* obstinacy, stubbornness.

obstinado, da, (ovs·tē·nâ´tho, thâ) *adj.* obstinate, stubborn.

obstrucción, (ovs·trūk·syon´) *f.* obstruction.

obstruir*, (ovs·trwēr´) *va.* to obstruct; **—se,** to get blocked up, to get stopped up.

obtener*, (ov·te·ner´) *va.* to obtain, to get; to retain, to maintain *(conservar)*.

obturador, (ov·tū·râ·thor´) *m.* (phot.) shutter.

obtuso, sa, (ov·tū´so, sâ) *adj.* obtuse, blunt; (fig.) slow, dense.

obús, (o·vūs´) *m.* (mil.) howitzer.

obviar, (ov·vyâr´) *va.* to obviate; **—,** *vn.* to be in the way.

obvio, via, (ov´vyo, vyâ) *adj.* obvious, evident.

ocasión, (o·kâ·syon´) *f.* occasion; danger, risk *(peligro);* **de —,** used, secondhand.

ocasional, (o·kâ·syo·nâl´) *adj.* occasional; causative, causal *(que ocasiona)*.

ocasionalmente, (o·kâ·syo·nâl·men´te) *adv.* occasionally.

ocasionar, (o·kâ·syo·nâr´) *va.* to cause, to occasion; to move, to motivate *(mover);* to endanger *(poner en peligro)*.

ocaso, (o·kâ´so) *m.* occident; decline *(bajada);* sunset *(puesta del sol)*.

occidental, (ok·sē·then·tâl´) *adj.* occidental, western.

occidente, (ok·sē·then´te) *m.* occident, west.

océano, (o·se´â·no) *m.* ocean.

ocio, (o´syo) *m.* leisure; pastime *(pasatiempo);* idleness *(holgazanería)*.

ociosidad, (o·syo·sē·thâth´) *f.* idleness,

laziness.

ocioso, sa, (o•syo´so, sâ) *adj.* idle, lazy; useless *(inútil).*

ocre, (o´kre) *m.* ochre.

octágono, (ok•tá´go•no) *m.* octagon.

octava, (ok•tá´vä) *f.* octave.

octavo, va, (ok•tá´vo, vä) *adj.* eighth.

Octbre, oct. e: octubre, Oct. October.

octogenario, ria, (ok•to•he•nä´ryo, ryä) *n.* and *adj.* octogenarian.

octubre, (ok•tü´vre) *m.* October.

ocular, (o•kü•lâr´) *adj.* ocular; —, *m.* eyepiece, ocular.

oculista, (o•kü•lēs´tä) *m.* oculist.

ocultar, (o•kül•târ´) *va.* to hide, to conceal.

oculto, ta, (o•kül´to, tä) *adj.* hidden, concealed.

ocupación, (o•kü•pä•syon´) *f.* occupation; employment *(empleo).*

ocupado, da, (o•kü•pä´tho, thä) *adj.* busy, occupied; pregnant *(encinta).*

ocupar, (o•kü•pâr´) *va.* to occupy; to bother *(estorbar);* to attract the attention of *(llamar la atención);* **—se en** to give one´s attention to.

ocurrencia, (o•kü•rren´syä) *f.* occurrence, event, incident; brainstorm *(pensamiento);* witticism *(dicho agudo).*

ocurrente, (o•kü•rren´te) *adj.* witty.

ocurrir, (o•kü•rrēr´) *vn.* to occur, to happen *(suceder);* to occur *(a la mente);* — **a,** to have recourse to.

ochenta, (o•chen´tä) *adj.* and *m.* eighty.

ocho, (o´cho) *m.* and *adj.* eight.

ochocientos, (o•cho•syen´tos) *m.* and *adj.* eight hundred.

oda, (o´thä) *f.* ode.

odiar, (o•thyâr´) *va.* to hate.

odio, (o´thyo) *m.* hatred.

odioso, sa, (o•thyo´so, sä) *adj.* hateful, odious.

odisea, (o•thē•se´ä) *f.* odyssey.

odontología, (o•thon•to•lo•hē´ä) *f.* odontology.

odorífero, ra, (o•tho•rē´fe•ro, rä) *adj.* fragrant.

odre, (o´thre) *m.* wineskin; (coll.) souse, drunkard *(borracho).*

O.E.A.: Organización de Estados Americanos, O.A.S.: Organization of American States.

oeste, (o•es´te) *m.* west; west wind *(viento).*

ofender, (o•fen•der´) *va.* to offend; to injure *(maltratar);* to bother, to annoy *(fastidiar);* **—se,** to get angry, to take offense.

ofensa, (o•fen´sä) *f.* offense; injury *(herida);* annoyance *(fastidio).*

ofensivo, va, (o•fen•sē´vo, vä) *adj.* offensive.

oferta, (o•fer´tä) *f.* offer; offering, gift *(don);* **— y demanda,** supply and demand.

oficial, (o•fē•syäl´) *adj.* official; —, *m.* officer, official; journeyman *(obrero);* clerk *(empleado);* (mil.) officer; **— de sanidad,** health officer; **— mayor,** chief clerk.

oficiar, (o•fē•syâr´) *va.* to officiate; to communicate by an official letter *(por escrito);* **— de,** to act as.

oficina, (o•fē•sē´nä) *f.* office; workshop *(taller);* laboratory *(laboratorio);* (fig.) hotbed.

oficio, (o•fē´syo) *m.* occupation; office *(cargo);* trade *(de artes mecánicas);* official letter *(comunicación);* **—s,** *pl.* divine services.

oficioso, sa, (o•fē•syo´so, sä) *adj.* officious; useful *(útil);* mediative *(de la mediación);* informal *(no oficial);* obliging *(solícito).*

ofrecer*, (o•fre•ser´) *va.* to offer; **—se,** to occur, to happen.

ofrecimiento, (o•fre•sē•myen´to) *m.* offer.

ofrenda, (o•fren´dä) *f.* offering.

ofuscar, (o•füs•kâr´) *va.* to darken, to obscure; to confuse *(confundir);* **—se,** to get confused.

oído, (o•ē´tho) *m.* hearing; (anat.) ear; **hablar al —,** to whisper.

oír*, (o•ēr´) *va.* to hear; to listen to *(atender);* to understand *(entender);* to attend *(asistir).*

ojal, (o•hâl´) *m.* buttonhole; hole *(agujero).*

¡ojalá! (o•hä•lá´) *interj.* would to God! God grant! if only!

ojeada, (o•he•ä´thä) *f.* glance, look.

ojear, (o•he•âr´) *va.* to eye, to look at, to stare at; to give the evil eye to *(aojar);* to raise *(la caza);* (fig.) to frighten.

ojera, (o•he´rä) *f.* eye cup; **—s,** *pl.* dark rings under the eyes.

ojo, (o´ho) *m.* eye; spring *(de agua);* hole *(del pan);* span *(de un puente);* (print.) type size; attention *(atención);* note *(señal);* scrubbing *(mano de jabón);* **en un abrir y cerrar de —s,** in the twinkling of an eye, in a second.

ola, (o´lä) *f.* wave; (fig.) wave, surge.

oleada, (o•le•ä´thä) *f.* large wave; surge *(movimiento);* beating, pounding *(embate);* wave *(gran cantidad);* large crop *(de aceite).*

oleaje, (o•le•ä´he) *m.* running sea, sea swell.

óleo, (o´le•o) *m.* oil; olive oil *(de oliva);* **santo —,** (eccl.) holy oil.

oleoducto, (o·le·o·thūk´to) *m.* oil pipe line.

oleomargarina, (o·le·o·mâr·gâ·rē´nä) *f.* ole-omargarine.

oler*, (o·ler´) *va.* to smell; (fig.) to ferret out; —, *vn.* to smell; to smack *(tener señas).*

olfatear, (ol·fâ·te·âr´) *va.* to smell, to sniff; (fig.) to smell out *(averiguar).*

olfato, (ol·fâ´to) *m.* sense of smell, smell; (fig.) a keen nose, acumen.

oligarquía, (o·lē·gâr·kē´ä) *f.* oligarchy.

Olimpiada, (o·lēm·pyä´thä) *f.* Olympics.

olímpico, ca, (o·lēm´pē·ko, kä) *adj.* Olympic; Olympian *(soberbia).*

oliva, (o·lē´vä) *f.* olive; olive tree *(árbol);* owl *(lechuza);* (fig.) peace.

olivar, (o·lē·var´) *m.* olive grove.

olivo, (o·lē´vo) *m.* olive tree; olive wood *(madera).*

olmo, (ol´mo) *m.* elm tree.

olor, (o·lor´) *m.* odor, scent, smell; hope *(esperanza);* (fig.) reputation.

oloroso, sa, (o·lo·ro´so, sä) *adj.* fragrant, odorous.

olote, (o·lo´te) *m.* (Mex.) corncob.

olvidadizo, za, (ol·vē·thâ·thē´so, sä) *adj.* forgetful, absent-minded; ungrateful *(desagradecido).*

olvidar, (ol·vē·thâr´) *va.* and *vr.* to forget.

olvido, (ol·vē´tho) *m.* forgetfulness; **dar al** —, **echar al** —, to forget completely, to bury.

olla, (o´yä) *f.* pot, kettle; stew *(guisado);* eddy *(remolino);* **—a presión,** pressure cooker; **— express,** (Mex.) pressure cooker; **— podrida,** potpourri.

ombligo, (om·blē´go) *m.* navel; umbilical cord *(cordón).*

O.M.C.: Organización Mundial del Comercio, W.T.O.: World Trade Organization.

ominoso, sa, (o·mē·no´so, sä) *adj.* ominous.

omisión, (o·mē·syon´) *f.* omission; neglect, remissness *(descuido).*

omitir, (o·mē·tēr´) *va.* to omit; to overlook *(pasar en silencio).*

ómnibus, (om´nē·vūs) *m.* omnibus, bus.

omnipotencia, (om·nē·po·ten´syä) *f.* omni-potence.

omnipotente, (om·nē·po·ten´te) *adj.* omni-potent, almighty.

O.M.S.: Organización Mundial de la Salud, W.H.O.: World Health Organization.

once, (on´se) *m.* and *adj.* eleven.

onceno, na, (on·se´no, nä) *adj.* eleventh; elevenman team.

onda, (on´dä) *f.* wave; scallop *(guarnición);*

flicker *(de la llama);* (rad.) wave length; **— corta,** (rad.) short wave; **— de choque,** shock wave; **— sonora,** sound wave.

ondeado, da, (on·de·â´tho ,thâ) *adj.* wavy.

ondear, (on·de·âr´) *vn.* to be wavy, to toss *(el agua);* to wave *(ondular);* to flicker *(una llama).*

ondímetro, (on·dē´me·tro) *m.* ondograph.

ondulación, (on·dū·lä·syon´) *f.* undulation, wave.

ondulado, da, (on·dū·lä´tho, thâ) *adj.* wavy, rippled; rolling *(terreno);* **—do permanente,** permanent wave.

ondular, (on·dū·lâr´) *vn.* to undulate; — *va.* to wave, to make wavy.

oneroso, sa, (o·ne·ro´so, sä) *adj.* onerous.

O.N.G.: Organización No Gubernamental, N.G.O. nongovernmental organization.

onomástico, (o·no·mâs´tē·ko) *m.* saint´s day.

O.N.U.: Organización de las Naciones Unidas, U.N. United Nations.

onz.: onza, oz. ounce.

onza, (on´sä) *f.* ounce.

onzavo, va, (on·sâ´vo, vâ) *m.* and *adj.* eleventh.

opaco, ca, (o·pâ´ko, kä) *adj.* opaque; dark, somber *(oscuro);* melancholy, gloomy *(triste).*

ópalo, (o´pâ·lo) *m.* opal.

opción, (op·syon´) *f.* option.

ópera, (o´pe·râ) *f.* opera.

operación, (o·pe·râ·syon´) *f.* operation; **— cesárea,** Caesarean section.

operar, (o·pe·râr´) *va.* to operate on; —, *vn.* to take effect; to operate *(maniobrar);* **— se,** to have an operation.

operario, ria, (o·pe·râ´ryo, ryâ) *n.* laborer, workman.

opereta, (o·pe·re´tâ) *f.* operetta.

opinar, (o·pē·nâr´) *vn.* to express an opinion, to opine.

opinión, (o·pē·nyon´) *f.* opinion.

opio, (o´pyo) *m.* opium.

opíparo, ra, (o·pē´pâ·ro, râ) *adj.* succulent, sumptuous.

oponer*, (o·po·ner´) *va.* to oppose, to put up; **— se a,** to oppose; to compete for *(pretender un cargo).*

oporto, (o·por´to) *m.* port wine.

oportunidad, (o·por·tū·nē·thâth´) *f.* right moment, opportunity; opportuneness *(calidad de oportuno).*

oportuno, na, (o·por·tū´no, nä) *adj.* opportune, timely; witty *(ocurrente).*

oposición, (o·po·sē·syon´) *f.* opposition; competition *(concurso).*

m met, **n** not, **p** pot, **r** very, **rr** (none), **s** so, **t** toy, **th** with, **v** eve, **w** we, **y** yes, **z** zero

opositor, ra, (o·po·sē·tor´, râ) *n.* opponent.

opresión, (o·pre·syon´) *f.* oppression.

opresor, ra, (o·pre·sor´, râ) *n.* oppressor.

oprimir, (o·prē·mēr´) *va.* (fig.) to oppress *(sujetar);* to press, to squeeze.

oprobio, (ō·pro´vyo) *m.* ignominy, disgrace.

optar, (op·târ´) *va.* to choose, to select.

óptico, ca, (op´tē·ko, kâ) *adj.* optic, optical; —, *m.* optician.

optimismo, (op·tē·mēz´mo) *m.* optimism.

optimista, (op·tē·mēs´tâ) *m. and f.* optimist; —, *adj.* optimistic.

óptimo, ma, (op´tē·mo, mâ) *adj.* best.

optómetra, (op·to´me·trâ) *m.* optometrist.

optometría, (op·to·me·trē´â) *f.* optometry.

opuesto, ta, (o·pwes´to, tâ) *adj.* opposite, contrary.

opulencia, (o·pū·len´syâ) *f.* opulence, wealth, riches.

opulento, ta, (o·pū·len´to, tâ) *adj.* opulent, wealthy, rich.

ora, (o´râ) *conj.* now; — esto, — aquello, at times this, at other times that.

oración, (o·ra·syon´) *f.* oration, speech; prayer *(rezo);* (gram.) sentence.

oráculo, (o·râ´kū·lo) *m.* oracle.

orador, ra, (o´·râ·thor´, râ) *n.* orator, speaker; petitioner *(que pide);* —, *m.* preacher.

oral, (o·râl´) *adj.* oral.

orangután, (o·râng·gū·tân´) *m.* (zool.) orangutan.

orar, (o·râr´) *vn.* to make a speech, to speak; to pray *(rezar);* —, *vt.* to beg, to supplicate.

oratoria, (o·râ·to´ryâ) *f.* oratory, rhetoric.

oratorio, (o·râ·to´ryo) *m.* oratory; oratorio *(composición);* —, ria, *adj.* rhetorical, oratorical.

orbe, (or´ve) *m.* orb; world, sphere *(mundo);* (ichth.) globefish.

órbita (or´ve·ta) *f.* orbit.

orbital, (or·vē·tal´) *adj.* orbital.

orden, (or´then) *m.* order; (eccl.) Holy Orders; — del día, (mil.) order of the day; —, *f.* order, command; (eccl.) order; a sus órdenes, at your service.

ordenado, da, (or·the·nâ´tho, thâ) *adj.* neat, orderly.

ordenador, (or·the·nâ·thor´) *m.* computer.

ordenanza, (or·the·nân´sâ) *f.* order; command *(mandato);* method, system *(arreglo);* ordinance *(regla);* —, *m.* (mil.) orderly.

ordenar, (or·the·nâr´) *va.* to arrange, to put in order *(arreglar);* to order, to command *(mandar);* (eccl.) to ordain; —se, to become ordained.

ordeñar, (or·the·nyâr´) *va.* to milk.

ordinal, (or·the·nâl´) *adj.* ordinal.

ordinario, ria, (or·thē·nâ´ryo, ryâ) *adj.* ordinary; daily *(diario);* acetones —rias, common stock; de —rio, usually, ordinarily; —, *m.* ordinary.

orégano, (o·re´gâ·no) *m.* (bot.) oregano, wild marjoram.

oreja, (o·re´hâ) *f.* ear; hearing *(sentido);* outer ear *(ternilla);* flap *(del zapato);* (fig.) gossip; —s de mercader, deaf ears; con las —s caldas, crestfallen.

orejera, (o·re·he´râ) *f.* ear muff; moldboard *(del arado).*

orejón, (o·re·hon´) *m.* tweak of the ear; (mil.) orillion; preserved peach slice *(melocotón).*

orfandad, (or·fân·dâth´) *f.* orphanage; (fig.) neglect, desertion.

orfebre, (or·fe´vre) *m.* goldsmith; silversmith *(platero).*

orfelinato (or·fe·lē·nâ´to) *m.* orphanage.

organdí, (or·gân·dē´) *m.* organdy.

orgánico, ca, (or·gâ´nē·ko, kâ) *adj.* organic.

organillero, (or·gâ·nē·ye´ro) *m.* organ grinder.

organillo, (or·gâ·nē´yo) *m.* hand organ, hurdy-gurdy.

organismo, (or·gâ·nēz´mo) *m.* organization; organism *(conjunto de órganos).*

organista, (or·gâ·nēs´tâ) *m. and f.* organist.

organización, (or·gâ·nē·sâ·syon´) *f.* organization.

organizador, ra, (or·gâ·nē·sâ·thor´, râ) *n.* organizer; —, *adj.* organizing.

organizar, (or·gâ·nē·sâr´) *va.* to organize.

órgano, (or´gâ·no) *m.* organ; — de cañones, pipe organ.

orgía, (or·hē´a) *f.* orgy.

orgullo, (or·gū´yo) *m.* pride; haughtiness *(altivez).*

orgulloso, sa, (or·gū·yo´so, sâ) *adj.* proud; haughty.

orientación, (o·ryen·tâ·syon´) *f.* orientation; (naut.) trimming; — por inercia, (avi.) inertial guidance; — vocacional, vocational guidance.

oriental, (o·ryen·tâl´) *adj.* (geog.) Oriental; eastern.

orientar, (o·ryen·târ´) *va.* to orient; (naut.) to trim; —se, to get one's bearings, to orient oneself.

â arm, e they, ē bē, o fore, ū blūe, b bad, ch chip, d day, f fat, g go, h hot, k kid, 1 let

oriente, (o·ryen′te) *m.* orient, east; (geog.) Orient.

orificar, (o·rē·fē·kâr′) *vt.* to fill with gold.

orificación, (o·rē·fē·kâ·syon′) *f.* gold filling.

orificio, (o·rē·fē′syo) *m.* orifice, opening.

origen, (o·rē′hen) *m.* origin; descent *(ascendencia).*

original, (o·rē·hē·nâl′) *adj.* original; eccentnc, odd *(extraño);* —, *m.* original, first copy; oddball *(persona extravagante).*

originalidad, (o·rē·hē·nâ·lē·thâth′) *f.* originality; eccentricity, oddness *(extrañez).*

originar, (o·rē·hē·nâr′) *va.* to cause, to be the origin of; —se, to originate.

originario, ria, (o·rē·hē·nâ′ryo, ryâ) *adj.* native, originating; being the cause *(que da origen);* — **de Inglaterra,** native of England.

orilla, (o·rē′yâ) *f.* border, margin *(margen);* edge *(de tela);* sidewalk *(acera);* shore *(ribera);* fresh breeze *(vientecillo).*

orín, (o·rēm′) *m.* rust.

orina, (o·rē′nâ) *f.* urine.

orinal, (o·rē·nâl′) *m.* urinal.

orinar, (o·rē·nâr′) *vn.* to urinate.

orines, (o·rē′nes) *m. pl.* urine.

oriol, (o·ryol′) *m.* (orn.) oriole.

oriundo, da, (o·ryūn′do, dâ) *adj.* native.

orla, (or′lâ) *f.* edge, border, trimming.

orlar, (or·lâr′) *va.* to border, to edge, to trim.

ornamento, (or·nâ·men′to) *m.* ornament, embellishment; (fig.) virtue, asset; —s, *pl.* (eccl.) vestments.

ornar, (or·nâr′) *va.* to trim, to adorn.

ornato, (or·nâ′to) *m.* ornament, decoration.

ornitólogo, (or·nē·to′lo·go) *m.* ornithologist.

oro, (o′ro) *m.* gold; (fig.) wealth, riches; **de** —, golden; **patrón** —, gold standard; —s, *pl.* diamonds.

oropel, (o·ro·pel′) *m.* tinsel.

orozuz, (o·ro·sūs′) *m.* (bot.) licorice.

orquesta, (or·kes′tâ) *f.* orchestra.

orquestación, (or·kes·tâ·syon′) *f.* orchestration.

orquídea, (or·kē′the·â) *f.* orchid.

ortiga, (or·tē′gâ) *f.* (bot.) nettle.

ortodóntico, (or·to·thon′tē·ko) *m.* orthodontist.

ortodoxo, xa, (or·to·thok′so, sâ) *adj.* orthodox.

ortografia, (or·to·grâ·fē′â) *f.* orthography.

ortopédico, ca, (or·to·pe′thē·ko, kâ) *adj.* orthopedic; —, *n.* orthopedist.

oruga, (o·rū′gâ) *f.* (bot.) rocket; (ent. and mech.) caterpillar.

os, (os) *pron.* you; to you *(dativo).*

osa, (o′sâ) *f.* she-bear; **O— Mayor,** (ast.) Great Bear.

osadía, (o·sâ·thē′â) *f.* boldness, courage.

osar (o·sâr′) *vn.* to dare, to venture.

osar (o·sâr′) or **osario,** (o·sâ′ryo) *m.* charnel house.

oscilar, (os·sē′lâr′) *vn.* to oscillate; (fig.) to vacillate.

oscurecer*, (os·kū·re·ser′) *va.* to darken; (fig.) to obscure; (fig.) to confuse *(confundir);* to shade *(pintura);* —, *vi.* to darken, to grow dark; —se, to get cloudy, to cloud over; (fig.) to vanish into thin air.

oscurecimiento, (os·kū·re·sē·myen′to) *m.* darkening; obscuring; confusing; shading.

oscuridad, (os·kū·rē·thâth′) *f.* darkness; (fig.) obscurity; confusion.

oscuro, ra, (os·kū′ro, râ) *adj.* dark; (fig.) obscure; **a —as,** in the dark.

óseo, sea, (o′se·o, se·â) *adj.* bony.

oso, (o′so) *m.* bear; — **pardo,** brown bear; — **hormiguero,** anteater.

ostensible, (os·ten·sē′vle) *adj.* ostensible, apparent.

ostentación, (os·ten·tâ·syon′) *f.* displaying, showing; great display, ostentation *(vanagloria);* pomp *(magnificencia).*

ostentar, (os·ten·târ′) *va.* to show, to display; to show off *(hacer gala de).*

ostentoso, sa, (os·ten·to′so, sâ) *adj.* sumptuous, magnificent.

osteópata, (os·te·o′pâ·tâ) *m. and f.* osteopath.

ostra, (os′trâ) *f.* oyster.

ostracismo, (os·trâ·sēz′mo) *m.* ostracism.

otero, (o·te′ro) *m.* hill, knoll.

otólogo, (o·to′lo·go) *m.* ear specialist.

otoñal, (o·to·nyâl′) *adj.* autumnal.

otoño, (o·to′nyo) *m.* autumn, fall.

otorgamiento, (o·tor·gâ·myen′to) *m.* grant; consent, approval *(aprobación);* closing *(de un contrato).*

otorgar, (o·tor·gâr′) *va.* to consent to *(consentir);* to grant *(conceder).*

otro, otra, (o′tro, o′trâ) *adj.* another, other; **al — lado,** on the other side; **—a vez,** once more, again; **el uno al —,** one to the other, to each other; **el uno o el —,** one or the other; **ni el uno ni el —,** neither one nor the other, neither one; **por —a parte,** on the other hand; **en alguna — parte,** somewhere else.

ovación, (o·vâ·syon′) *f.* ovation.

ovalado, da, (o·vâ·lâ′tho, thâ) *adj.* oval.

---

m met, **n** not, **p** pot, **r** very, **rr** (none), **s** so, **t** toy, **th** with, **v** eve, **w** we, **y** yes, **z** zer′

óvalo, (o´vâ·lo) *m.* oval.
ovario, (o·vâ´ryo) *m.* ovary.
oveja, (o·ve´hâ) *f.* sheep.
ovillo, (o·vē´yo) *m.* ball of yarn; (fig.) snarl, tangle, confused mess *(enredo).*
ovíparo, ra, (o·vē´pâ·ro, râ) *adj.* oviparous.
oxidar, (ok·sē·thâr´) *va.* to oxidize; —se, to rust, to get rusty.
óxido, (ok´sē·tho) *m.* (chem.) oxide; — de

cinc, zinc oxide.
oxigenado, da, (ok·sē·he·nâ´tho, thâ) *adj.* oxygenated; rubia —, peroxide blonde.
oxígeno, (ok·sē´he·no) *m.* (chem.) oxygen; — liquido, lox, liquid oxygen.
oyente, (o·yen´te) *m. and f.* listener; auditor *(alumno);* —s, *pl.* audience.

P

P.A.: por ausencia, in the absence; por autorización, by authority; Prensa Asociada, A. P. Associated Press.
pabellón, (pâ·ve·yon´) *m.* pavilion; flag *(bandera);* stack *(armas);* bell *(de un instrumento);* protection *(protección).*
pabilo, (pâ·vē´lo) or pábilo, (pâ´vē·lo) *m.* wick; snuff *(cordón carbonizado).*
pacer*, (pa·ser´) *vn.* to pasture, to graze; — *vt.* to gobble up; to graze.
paciencia, (pâ·syen´syâ) *f.* patience.
paciente, (pâ·syen´te) *adj. and m. and f.* patient.
pacificador, ra, (pâ·sē·fē·kâ·thor´, râ) *n.* peacemaker.
pacificar, (pâ·sē·fē·kâr´) *va.* to pacify, to make peaceful; —, *vn.* to negotiate for peace; —se, to become peaceful.
pacifico, ca, (pâ·sē´fe·ko, kâ) *adj.* pacific, peaceful.
pacifista, (pâ·sē·fēs´tâ) *n. and adj.* pacifist.
pacotilla, (pâ·ko·tē´yâ) *f.* goods free of freight; merchandise *(mercancías);* hacer uno su —, (coll.) to make one´s pile; de —, (coll.) of inferior quality, trashy.
pactar, (pâk·târ´) *va.* to agree on, to agree to.
pacto, (pâk´to) *m.* pact, agreement.
pachorra, (pâ·cho´rrâ) *f.* indolence, sluggishness.
padecer*, (pâ·the·ser´) *va.* to suffer.
padecimiento, (pa·the·sē·myen´to) *m.* suffering.
padrastro, (pâ·thrâs´tro) *m.* stepfather; bad father *(mal padre);* obstacle *(obstáculo);* hangnail *(pellejo).*
padre, (pâ´thre) *m.* father; sire, stud *(del ganado);* —s, *pl.* parents; forefathers *(antepasados);* santos —s, fathers of the Church.

padrenuestro, (pâ·thre·nwes´tro) *m.* Lord´s Prayer.
padrinazgo, (pâ·thrē·naz´go) *m.* sponsorship.
padrino, (pâ·thrē´no) *m.* godfather; second *(que acompaña);* sponsor *(que favorece);* — de boda, groomsman.
paella, (pâ·e´yâ) *f.* paella.
pág.: página, p. page.
paga, (pá´gâ) *f.* payment; satisfaction *(satisfacción);* fee, wage *(sueldo);* requital *(correspondencia).*
pagadero, ra, (pa·gâ·the´ro, râ) *adj.* payable; —, *m.* time of payment, term´s of payment.
pagador, ra, (pâ·gâ·thor´, râ) *n.* payer; paymaster *(oficial).*
paganismo, (pâ·gâ·nēz´mo) *n.* paganism, heathenism.
pagano, (pâ·gâ´no) *m.* heathen, pagan; (coll.) dupe, easy mark *(de quien se abusa);* —, na, *adj.* heathen, pagan.
pagar, (pâ·gâr´) *va.* to pay, to pay for; to atone for *(satisfacer);* to repay, to return *(corresponder);* —se de, to be pleased with; to boast about *(jactarse).*
pagaré, (pâ·gâ·re´) *m.* promissory note, due bill, I.O.U.
página, (pa´hē·nâ) *f.* page;— inicial, home page.
pago, (pâ´go) *m.* pay, payment; satisfaction, recompense *(recompensa);* region *(distrito);* village *(aldea);* — al contado, cash payment.
pagoda, (pâ·go´thâ) *f.* pagoda.
pagua, (pâ´gwa) *f.* (Mex.) avocado.
paila, (pâ´ē·lâ) *f.* large pan.
país, (pa·ēs´) *m.* country, land; landscape (*pintura).*
paisaje, (pâē·sâ´he) *m.* landscape.
paisano, na, (pâē·sâ´no, nâ) *adj.* of the

same country; —, *n.* countryman, compatriot; rustic *(campesino);* civilian *(que no es militar).*

paja, (pä´hä) *f.* straw; **techo de —,** thatched roof.

pajar, (pä·här´) *m.* hayloft.

pajarera, (pä·hä·re´rä) *f.* bird cage.

pajarero, ra, (pa·hä·re´ro, rä) *adj.* gay, merry; (coll.) loud, flamboyant *(chillón);* —, *m.* birdman.

pájaro, (pä´hä·ro) *m.* bird; (fig.) fox; (fig.) specialist *(especialista);* **vista de —,** bird´s-eye view; **— carpintero,** woodpecker.

paje, (pä´he) *m.* page; caddie *(en el golf);* cabin boy *(marinero);* dressing table *(mueble).*

pala, (pä´la) *f.* shovel; blade *(parte ancha);* racket *(raqueta);* setting *(de las joyas);* (fig.) guile, cunning; vamp *(de un zapato).*

palabra, (pä·lä´vrä) *f.* word; speech *(facultad);* gift of oratory *(oratoria);* floor *(turno);* **de —,** by word of mouth; **dirigir la —,** to address; **libertad de —,** freedom of speech; **pedir la —,** to ask for the floor; **tener la —,** to have the floor; **— por —,** literally, word for word.

palabrería, (pä·lä·vre·rē´ä) *f.* verbosity, wordiness.

palabrota, (pä·lä·vro´tä) *f.* vulgarity; harsh word *(ofensiva).*

palaciego, ga, (pä·lä·sye´go, gä) *adj.* court, palace; —, *n.* courtier.

palacio, (pä´·lä´syo) *m.* palace.

palada, (pä·lä´thä) *f.* shovelful; stroke *(de un remo).*

paladar, (pä·lä·thär´) *m.* palate; taste *(sabor);* fig.) feeling, sensitivity *(gusto).*

paladín, (pä·lä·thēn´) *m.* paladin.

palanca, (pä·läng´kä) *f.* lever; pole *(pértiga);* influence, pull *(influencia);* **— de cambio de marcha,** reverse lever; **— embrague,** clutch lever; **— de impulsión,** driving lever; **— de hierro,** crowbar.

palangana, (pä·läng·gä´nä) *f.* washbowl.

palanqueta, (pä·läng·ke´tä) *f.* (naut.) bar shot; jimmy.

palco, (päl´ko) *m.* theater box; bench *(tabladillo).*

paleontología, (pä·le·on·to·lo·hē´ä) *f.* paleontology.

palero, (pä·le´ro) *m.* (Mex. theat.) stooge.

palestra, (pä·les´trä) *f.* (fig.) literary forum; (poet.) wrestling *(lucha);* palaestra.

paleta, (pä·le´tä) *f.* fire shovel; palette *(del*

pintor); trowel *(llana);* shoulder blade *(omóplato);* lollipop *(dulce);* blade *(álabe)* serving knife *(espátula).*

paletada, (pä·le·tä´thä) *f.* trowelful; shovelful.

paliativo, va, (pä·lyä·tē´vo, vä) *adj.* palliative.

palidecer*, (pä·lē·the·ser´) *vn.* to turn pale, to pale.

palidez, (pä·lē·thes´) *f.* paleness, wanness.

pálido, da, (pä´lē·tho, thä) *adj.* pallid, pale.

palillero, (pä·lē·ye´ro) *m.* toothpick holder.

palillo, (pä·lē´yo) *m.* bobbin *(bolillo);* toothpick *(de dientes);* drumstick *(para tocar);* stem *(del tabaco);* (fig.) chit-chat.

palio, (pä´lyo) *m.* pallium; cloak *(capa);* canopy *(dosel);* prize *(premio).*

palique, (pä·lē´ke) *m.* (coll.) chit-chat.

paliza, (pä·lē´sä) *f.* beating, drubbing.

palma, (päl´mä) *f.* palm; (fig.) victory, triumph; sole *(de un caballo);* **ganar la —,** to carry the day; **—s,** *pl.* applause; **batir —s,** to clap hands.

palmada, (päl·mä´thä) *f.* slap *(golpe);* clap; **—s,** *pl.* clapping.

palmera, (päl·me´rä) *f.* palm tree.

palmeta, (päl·me´tä) *f.* ferule, rod; lick, rap *(palmetazo).*

palmito, (päl·mē´to) *m.* palmetto; shoot *(tallo);* (coll.) face *(cara);* slender figure *(cuerpo).*

palmo, (päl´mo) *m.* palm; **— a —,** inch by inch.

palmotear, (päl·mo·te·är´) *vn.* to applaud.

palmoteo, (päl·mo·te´o) *m.* clapping; lick, rap *(palmetazo).*

palo, (pä´lo) *m.* stick; (naut.) mast; blow *(golpe);* hook *(de letra);* handle *(mango);* suit *(de la baraja);* **pata de —,** wooden leg.

paloma, (pä·lo´mä) *f.* dove, pigeon; (fig.) lamb; high collar *(cuello);* **— torcaz,** ring dove; **— viajera** or **mensajera,** homing pigeon, carrier pigeon; **—zorita,** wood pigeon; **—s,** *pl.* whitecaps.

palomar, (pä·lo·mär´) *m.* pigeon coop.

palomilla, (pä·lo·mē´yä) *f.* young pigeon; butterfly *(mariposa);* back *(de la grupa);* (Mex.) gang, crowd.

palomino, (pä·lo·mē´no) *m.* young pigeon; whippersnapper, stripling *(joven).*

palomita, (pä·lo·mē´tä) *f.* squab; **—s de maíz,** popcorn.

palomo, (pä·lo´mo) *m.* cock pigeon.

---

m met, **n** not, **p** pot, **r** very, **rr** (none), **s** so, **t** toy, **th** with, **v** eve, **w** we, **y** yes, **z** zero

palote, (pa·lo´te) *m.* drumstick.

palpable, (pâl·pá´vle) *adj.* palpable; evident.

palpar, (pâl·pâr) *va.* to feel, to touch; to grope through *(andar a tientas);* to be certain of *(conocer).*

palpitación, (pâl·pē·tâ·syon´) *f.* palpitation.

palpitante, (pâl·pē·tân´te) *adj.* palpitating; **cuestión** —, burning question.

palpitar, (pâl·pē·târ´) *vn.* to palpitate, to beat, to throb.

paludismo, (pâ·lū·thēz´mo) *m.* malaria.

pampa, (pâm´pâ) *f.* pampa, plain.

pámpano, (pâm´pâ·no) *m.* tendril *(pimpollo);* vine leaf *(hoja);* (ichth.) pampano.

pampero, ra, (pâm·pe´ro, râ) *n.* and *adj.* pampean; —, *m.* pampero.

pamplinada, (pâm·plē·nâ´thâ) *f.* nonsense, foolishness.

pan, (pân) *m.* bread; loaf of bread; dough *(masa sobada);* food *(alimento);* (fig.) wheat *(trigo);* foil *(hoja de oro).*

pana, (pâ´nâ) *f.* plush, velveteen; (naut.) plank.

panacea, (pâ·nâ·se´â) *f.* panacea, cure-all.

panadería, (pâ·nâ·the·rē´â) *f.* baking trade *(oficio);* bakery.

panadero, ra, (pâ·nâ·the´ro, râ) *n.* baker.

panal, (pâ·nâl´) *m.* honeycomb; hornet comb *(de las avispas);* lemon meringue *(azucarillo).*

panameño, ña, (pâ·nâ·me´nyo, nyâ) *n.* and *adj.* Panamenian.

panamericanismo, (pâ·nâ·me·rē·kâ·nēz´ - mo) *m.* Panamericanism.

páncreas, (pâng´kre·âs) *m.* pancreas.

panda, (pân´dâ) *m.* (zool.) panda; —, *f.* gallery in a cloister.

pandear, (pan·de·âr) *vn.* to warp, to bulge.

pandemónium, (pân·de·mo´nyūn) *m.* pandemonium.

pandereta, (pân·de·re´tâ) *f.* tambourine.

pandero, (pân·de´ro) *m.* tambourine, timbrel.

pandilla, (pân·dē´yâ) *f.* gang; gathering, group *(que va al campo).*

pando, da, (pân´do, dâ) *adj.* bulging, convex; (fig.) deliberate *(pausado).*

panegírico, ca, (pâ·ne·hē´rē·ko, kâ) *adj.* panegyrical; —, *m.* panegyric.

panera, (pâ·ne´râ) *f.* granary; bread basket *(cesta).*

pánfilo, la, (pâm´fē·lo, lâ) *adj.* slow, sluggish; —, *n.* dawdler.

paniaguado, (pâ·nyâ·gwâ´tho) *m.* servant; protégé *(protegido).*

pánico, (pâ´nē·ko) *m.* panic, terror.

panorama, (pâ·no·râ´mâ) *m.* panorama.

pantalones, (pân·tâ·lo´nes) *m. pl.* trousers, pants; pantaloons *(de mujer).*

pantalla, (pân·tâ´yâ) *f.* screen, fire screen *(para el fuego);* lamp shade *(para la luz);* screen *(telón);* (fig.) blind, front.

pantano, (pân·tâ´no) *m.* swamp, marsh, bog; (fig.) quagmire, morass.

pantanoso, sa, (pân·tâ·no´so, sâ) *adj.* marshy, fenny, boggy; (fig.) sticky, messy.

panteón, (pân·te·on´) *m.* pantheon; cemetery *(cementerio).*

pantera, (pân·te´râ) *f.* panther.

pantomima, (pân·to·mē´mâ) *f.* pantomime.

pantorrilla, (pân·to·rrē´yâ) *f.* calf.

pantufla, (pân·tū´flâ) *f.* slipper.

panza, (pân´sâ) *f.* belly, paunch; belly, bulge *(de vasija);* rumen *(de rumiante).*

panzudo, da, (pân·sū´tho, thâ) *adj.* potbellied.

pañal, (pâ·nyâl´) *m.* diaper; shirttail *(de camisa);* —es, *pl.* infancy *(niñez);* first stages *(principios).*

paño, (pâ´nyo) *m.* cloth; breadth of cloth *(ancho);* tapestry *(tapiz);* growth over eye *(del ojo);* spot *(mancha);* defect *(defecto);* coating, film *(que disminuye el brillo).*

pañoleta, (pâ·nyo·le´tâ) *f.* shawl.

pañolón, (pâ·nyo·lon´) *m.* large shawl.

pañuelo, (pâ·nywe´lo) *m.* handkerchief.

papa, (pâ´pâ) *f.* Pope; (coll.) papa *(papá);* —, *f.* potato; —s, *f. pl.* food, grub.

papá, (pâ·pâ´) *m.* papa, dad.

papada, (pâ·pâ´thâ) *f.* double chin; dewlap *(de animales).*

papado, (pâ·pâ´tho) *m.* papacy.

papagayo, (pâ·pâ·gâ´yo) *m.* parrot.

papal, (pâ·pâl´) *adj.* papal.

papalina, (pâ·pâ·lē´nâ) *f.* sunbonnet; (coll.) drunkenness, drunk *(borrachera).*

papalote, (pâ·pâ·lo´te) *m.* kite.

papamoscas, (pâ·pâ·mos´kâs) *m.* (orn.) flycatcher; (coll.) simpleton.

papaya, (pâ·pâ´yâ) *f.* (hot.) papaya.

papel, (pâ·pel´) *m.* paper; sheet of paper *(hoja);* role, part *(de una obra dramática);* — encerado, waxed paper; — de entapizar, wallpaper; — de escribir, writing paper; — de estraza, brown paper; — de excusado, — higiénico, toilet paper; — de lija, sandpaper; — de seda, tissue paper; — moneda, paper money; — secante, blotter; — sellado, official document paper.

papeleo, (pâ·pe·le´o) m. red tape; leafing through papers *(acción de revolver papeles).*

papelería, (pâ·pe·le·rē´â) f. stationery store *(tienda);* bunch of papers.

papelero, (pâ·pe·le´ro) m. paper manufacturer *(fabricante);* paper dealer; —, **ra,** *adj.* boastful, pretentious.

papeleta, (pâ·pe·le´tâ) f. ballot *(de voto);* slip of paper *(cédula);* paper roll *(cucurucho);* (fig.) difficult job.

papelón, ona, (pâ·pe·lon´, o´nä) *adj.* boastful; —, m. poor quality paper; fine cardboard *(cartelón).*

papera, (pâ·pe´râ) f. goiter; mumps *(parótida);* —s, *pl.* (med.) scrofula.

papilla, (pâ·pē´yä) f. pap; guile, deceit *(astucia).*

papista, (pâ·pēs´tâ) n. and *adj.* papist.

paquete, (pâ·ke´te) m. package, packet, bundle; (naut.) packet boat.

par, (pâr) *adj.* similar, equal, alike; (math.) even; **sin —,** peerless, matchless; **—es o nones,** even or odd; —, f. par; —, m. pair; peer *(título).*

para, (pa´râ) *prep.* for, to, in order to; toward *(hacia);* good for *(capacidad);* **estar —,** to be about to; **— que,** so that, in order that.

parabién, (pâ·râ·vyen´) m. congratulations.

parábola, (pâ·râ´vo·lä) f. parable; parabola *(curva).*

parabrisa, (pâ·râ·vrē´sä) m. windshield.

paracaídas, (pâ·râ·kâ·ē´thäs) m. parachute; **— de frenado,** (avi.) drag chute.

paracaidista, (pâ·râ·kâē·thēs´tâ) m. parachutist; (Mex. coll.) party crasher; **—s,** *pl.* paratroops.

parachoques, (pâ·râ·cho´kes) m. (rail.) buffer, bumper; (auto.) bumper.

parada, (pâ·râ´thä) f. (mil.) parade; (mus.) pause; stop *(del autobús);* end *(fin);* stall *(de res);* dam *(presa);* stake, bet *(en el juego).*

paradero, (pâ·râ·the´ro) m. stopping place; whereabouts *(ubicación);* station, depot *(apeadero);* (fig.) end *(fin).*

parado, da, (pâ·râ´tho, thä) *adj.* stopped; unemployed *(desocupado)* (Sp. Am.) standing up.

paradoja, (pâ·râ·tho´hä) f. paradox.

parador, (pâ·râ·thor´) m. catcher; inn, hostelry *(mesón);* **— para turistas,** tourist court, motel.

parafina, (pâ·râ·fē´nä) f. paraffin.

parafrasear, (pâ·râ·frâ·se·âr´) va. to paraphrase.

paraguas, (pâ·râ´gwâs) m. umbrella.

paraíso, (pâ·râ·ē´so) m. paradise.

paraje, (pâ·râ´he) m. place, location; state *(estado).*

paralelo, la, (pâ·râ·le´lo, lä) *adj.* and *n.* parallel.

paralelogramo, (pâ·râ·le·lo·grâ´mo) m. parallelogram.

parálisis, (pâ·râ´lē·sēs) f. (med.) paralysis.

paralítico, ca, (pâ·râ·lē´tē·ko, kä) *adj.* paralytic.

paralizar, (pâ·râ·lē·sâr´) va. to paralyze.

paramilitar, (pâ·râ·mē·lē·târ´) *adj.* paramilitary.

páramo, (pâ´râ·mo) m. highland desert, wasteland, paramo.

parangón, (pâ·râng·gon´) m. comparison.

parangonar, (pâ·râng·go·nâr´) va. to compare.

parapeto, (pâ·râ·pe´to) m. parapet.

parapléjico, ca, (pâ·râ·ple´hē·ko, kä) paraplegic.

parar, (pâ·râr´) vn. to stop, to halt; to end *(terminar);* to come into the possession of *(propiedad);* to end up *(reducirse);* to stay *(hospedarse);* —, vt. to detain, to impede *(detener);* to put up, to stake *(arriesgar);* to point *(de la caza);* to change *(cambiar);* to prepare *(preparar);* **— en mal,** to come to a bad end; **sin —,** without stopping; **—se,** to stop, to halt· to stand up *(ponerse en pie).*

pararrayo, (pâ·râ·rrâ´yo) m. lightning r◌

parasicología, (pâ·râ·sē·ko·lo·hē´â) f. p◌ psychology.

parásito, (pâ·râ´sē·to) m. parasite.

parasol, (pâ·râ·sol´) m. parasol.

parcial, (pâr·syâl´) *adj.* partial.

parcialidad, (pâr·syâ·lē·thâth´) f. p◌ lity; faction *(confederación);* cir◌ group *(facción);* friendliness *(◌* partisanship *(falta de neutra◌*

parcialmente, (pâr·syâl·men´te◌ tially, in part; passionately◌ *adamente.*

parco, ca, (pâr´ko, kä) *adj.* ◌ gal; temperate, modera◌◌

parche, (pâr´che) m. patc◌ *heridas);* drumhead *(p◌ (tambor);* (fig.) splotc◌

pardo, da, (pâr´tho, th◌ cloudy *(nublado);* fl◌ mulato *(mulato);* ◌

pardusco, ca, (pâr·t◌ yish, grizzly.

parear, (pâ·re·âr´) ◌ *parar);* to match,◌

parecer, (pâ·re·ser´)◌

ment; mien; demeanor *(aspecto);* **al —,** apparently; **—*,** *vn.* to appear; to show up *(lo perdido);* **—se a,** to look like, to resemble.

parecido, da, (pâ·re·sē´tho, thâ) *adj.* similar, like; **—,** *m.* resemblance.

pared, (pâ·reth´) *f.* wall.

pareja, (pa·re´ha) *f.* pair, couple.

parentela, (pâ·ren·te´lâ) *f.* relatives, kin.

parentesco, (pâ·ren·tes´ko) *m.* relationship.

paréntesis, (pâ·ren´te·sēs) *m.* parenthesis.

paridad, (pâ·rē·thâth´) *f.* comparison *(comparación);* parity, equality.

pariente, ta, (pâ·ryen´te, tâ) *n.* relative; (coll.) mate.

parihuela, (pâ·rē·we´lâ) *f.* barrow; stretcher *(camilla).*

parir, (pâ·rēr´) *va.* to give birth to; (fig.) to bring forth, to cause; **—,** *vn.* to give birth.

parisiense, (pâ·rē·syen´se) *m.* and *f.* and *adj.* Parisian.

parlamentario, ria, (pâr·lâ·men·tâ´ryo, ryâ) *adj.* parliamentary; **—,** *m.* member of Parliament.

parlamento, (pâr·lâ·men´to) *m.* harangue *(arenga);* oration; (pol.) parliament.

parlanchín, ina, (pâr·lân·chēn´, ē´na) *n.* chatterer, blabbermouth; **—,** *adj.* chattering.

parlero, ra, (pâr·le´ro, râ) *adj.* talkative, gossiping *(que lleva cuentos);* (fig.) expressive *(expresivo);* (fig.) babbling *(arroyo).*

parlotear, (pâr·lo·te·âr´) *vn.* to babble, to prattle.

parmesano, na, (pâr·me·sâ´no, nâ) *adj.* Parmesan; **queso —,** Parmesan cheese.

paro, (pâ´ro) *m.* lockout *(cierre patronal);* work stoppage; **— forzoso,** unemployment, layoff.

parodia, (pâ·ro´thyâ) *f.* parody.

paroxismo, (pâ·rok·sēz´mo) *m.* paroxysm, fit.

parpadear, (pâr·pâ·the·âr´) *vn.* to blink.

párpado, (pâr´pâ·tho) *m.* eyelid.

parque, (pâr´ke) *m.* park; (auto.) parking lot;**— de diversiones,** theme park.

parquedad, (pâr·ke·thâth´) *f.* frugality.

parra, (pâ´rrâ) *f.* grapevine; **subirse a la —,** (coll.) to lose one´s temper.

párrafo, (pâ´rrâ·fo) *m.* paragraph; paragraph mark *(punto y aparte).*

parral, (pâ·rrâl´) *m.* vine arbor; wild vineyard *(viña);* earthen jar *(vaso).*

parranda, (pâ·rrân´dâ) *f.* carousal, spree; **ir de —,** to go out on the town, to

make the rounds.

parrandear, (pâ·rrân·de·âr´) *vn.* to go on a spree, to go out on the town.

parricida, (pâ·rrē·sē´thâ) *m.* and *f.* parricide.

parrilla, (pâ·rrē´yâ) *f.* grill; grillroom *(comedor).*

párroco, (pâ´rro·ko) *m.* parson.

parroquia, (pâ·rro´kyâ) *f.* (eccl.) parish; parish priest *(cura);* trade, clientele, customers *(clientela).*

parroquiano, na, (pâ·rro·kyâ´no, nâ) *n.* parishioner; (com.) customer; **—,** *adj.* parochial.

parte, (pâr´te) *f.* part; side *(lado);* party *(persona);* **de ocho días a esta —,** within the last week; **por otra —,** on the other hand, besides; **en —,** partly, in part; **en alguna —,** somewhere; **en alguna otra —,** somewhere else; **en ninguna —,** no place; **en todas —s,** everywhere; **de — de,** from, by order of; **¿de — de quién?** who is calling?; **tomar —,** to take part; **por una —,** on the one hand; **por mi —,** as concerns me; **de mi —,** from me; **— superior,** upper side. top; **— inferior,** lower side, bottom.

partera, (pâr·te´râ) *f.* midwife.

partero, (pâr·te´ro) *m.* obstetrician.

partición, (pâr·tē·syon´) *f.* partition; (math.) division.

participación, (pâr·tē·sē·pâ·syon´) *f.* participation; communication *(aviso).*

participante, (pâr·tē·sē·pân´te) *m.* and *f.* participant; notifier *(que avisa).*

participar, (pâr·tē·sē·pâr´) *vn.* to participate; **—,** *va.* to inform of, to communicate.

partícipe, (pâr·tē´sē·pe) *adj.* participating; **—,** *m.* and *f.* participant.

participio, (pâr·tē·sē´pyo) *m.* participle.

partícula, (pâr·tē´kū·lâ) *f.* particle; **— beta,** beta particle.

particular, (pâr·tē·kū·lâr´) *adj.* particular; special *(especial);* private *(no público);* **— m.** private citizen; point, matter *(asunto).*

particularidad, (pâr·tē·kū·lâ·rē·thâth´) *f.* particularity; detail *(pormenor);* characteristic; trait *(distintivo).*

partida, (pâr·tē´thâ) *f.* departure; (mil.) party of soldiers; game, round *(juego);* shipment, consignment *(cantidad);* item, entry *(asiento);* copy *(copia);* **doble,** double entry.

partidario, ria, (pâr·tē·thâ´ryo, ryâ) partisan, adherent; **—,** *n.* parti advocate.

partido, (pâr·tē´tho) *m.* (pol.) party; advantage *(ventaja);* help *(amparo);* match *(deportivo);* agreement *(convenio);* measures, means *(medio);* district *(región);* **sacarle — a,** to take advantage of.

partir, (pâr·tēr´) *va.* to divide; to split, to break *(hender);* to separate *(separar);* —, *vn.* to depart; to make up one´s mind *(resolverse);* **a — de,** beginning with, starting with, as of.

partitura, (pâr·tē·tū´râ) *f.* (mus.) score.

parto, (pâr´to) *m.* childbirth; infant *(niño);* (fig.) production *(producción);* (fig.) creation *(creación);* expectation *(expectación).*

parvada, (pâr·vâ´thâ) *f.* flock, covey.

párvulo, la, (pâr´vū·lo, lâ) *adj.* very small; gullible *(inocente);* humble *(humilde);* —, *n.* child; **escuela de —los,** kindergarten.

pasa, (pâ´sâ) *f.* raisin; **ciruela —,** prune.

pasada, (pâ·sâ´thâ) *f.* passage, passing; (coll.) misbehavior; **de —,** on the way, in passing.

pasadero, ra, (pâ·sâ·the´ro, râ) *adj.* passable; —, *m.* steppingstone.

pasadizo, (pâ·sâ·thē´so) *m.* narrow passage, alley, lane.

pasado, (pâ·sâ´tho) *m.* past; (mil.) traitor; (gram.) past tense; —**s,** *pl.* ancestors; —, *adj.* past; **— mañana,** day after tomorrow; **en tiempos —s,** in former times.

pasador, (pâ·sâ·thor´) *m.* contrabandist *(contrabandista);* door bolt *(puerta);* pin; barrette *(cabello);* tie pin *(sortija);* colander *(para colar);* sieve *(manga);* **— de charnela** or **pivote,** kingpin.

pasaje, (pâ·sâ´he) *m.* passage; fare *(precio).*

pasajero, ra, (pâ·sâ·he´ro, râ) *adj.* fleeting, transitory; well-traveled *(sitio);* —, *n.* passenger.

pasamano, (pâ·sâ·mâ´no) *m.* railing, handrail, banister; lace, braid, cord *(guarnición).*

pasante, (pâ·sân´te) *m.* or *f.* assistant; tutor *(profesor).*

pasaporte, (pâ·sâ·por´te) *m.* passport; (mil.) travel allowance; (fig.) carte blanche.

pasar, (pâ·sâr´) *vt.* to transport *(conducir);* to pass; to send *(enviar);* to cross, to cross over *(atravesar);* to smuggle *(meter de contrabando);* to strain *(colar);* to swallow *(tragar);* to surpass *(exceder);* to overlook *(tolerar);* to undergo, to suffer *(sufrir);* to tutor *(explicar);* to assist *(asistir); to* review *(repasar);* to dry *(desecar);* —, *vn.* to pass; to happen *(suceder);* to last *(durar);* to get along *(tener lo necesario);* to spend *(tiempo);* to pass away *(morir);* to value, to cost *(valer);* to blow over *(cesar);* to happen; **— por alto,** to overlook, to omit; **— de largo,** to go right by; —**se,** to defect *(partido);* to end, to cease *(acabarse);* to forget *(olvidarse);* to spoil *(pudrir);* to overscore *(tener demasiados puntos);* to proctor *(ejercitar un examen);* **— unos días,** to spend a few days; **¿qué pasa?** what´s going on? what´s the matter? **¿qué le pasa?** what´s the matter with him?

pasatiempo, (pâ·sâ·tyem´po) *m.* pastime, amusement, diversion.

Pascua, (pâs´kwâ) *f.* Passover; Easter *(de flores);* —**s,** Christmastide; **dar las —s,** to wish someone a Merry Christmas.

pase, (pâ´se) *m.* permit; pass *(en el juego).*

paseador, ra, (pâ·se·â·thor´ râ) *n.* great walker.

paseante, (pâ·se·ân´te) *m.* and *f.* stroller, walker.

pasear, (pâ·se·âr´) *vn.* to take a walk, *to* walk; to go for a ride, to take a ride *(en vehículo);* walk; —, *vt.* to walk *(un caballo);* to show around *(hacer ver);* —**se,** (fig.) to ramble on; to loaf, to loiter *(estar ocioso).*

paseo, (pâ·se´o) *m.* walk, stroll *(a pie);* ride *(en vehículo);* promenade; **— en el campo,** hiking; **ir de —** or **dar un —,** to go out walking or driving; **echar de —,** to get rid of.

pasillo (pâ·sē´yo) *m.* corridor, hallway; stitch *(puntada);* short step *(paso).*

pasión, (pâ·syon´) *f.* passion; suffering *(sufrimiento).*

pasionaria, (pâ·syo·nâ´ryâ) *f.* passion flower.

pasivo, va, (pâ·sē´vo, vâ) *adj.* passive; inactive *(inactivo);* pensionary *(de un pensión);* —, *m.* liabilities.

pasmar, (pâz·mâr´) *va.* to cause a spasm; to stun, to stupefy *(entumecer);* to chill *(enfriar);* to freeze *(helar);* to astonish, to astound *(asombrar);* —**se,** to suffer spasms *(enfermedad);* to be astonished; to dull *(una pintura).*

pasmo, (pâz´mo) *m.* cold; tetanus, lockjaw *(tétanos);* amazement *(asombro);* wonder *(causa).*

paso, (pâ´so) *m.* step (espacio); pace (movimiento); passing (acto de pasar); passage (lugar); footprint, track (huella); pass (licencia); stitch (puntada); migration (de las aves); strait (estrecho); event, happening (suceso); dramatic sketch (pieza dramática); **— a nivel,** railroad crossing; **al —,** on the way, in passing; **abrirse el —,** to force one's way; **apretar el —,** to hasten one's steps; **marcar el —,** to mark time; **acortar el —,** to slow one's pace, to walk slowly.

paso doble, (pá´so tho´vle) *m.* paso doble.

pasta, (pâs´tä) *f.* pasta; dough; unworked metal *(metal);* cardboard *(cartón);* pulp *(para papel);* bookbinding *(encuadernación);* **de buena —,** good-natured; **— de dientes,** toothpaste.

pastar, (pâs·târ´) *vn.* to pasture, to graze; **—,** *va.* to lead to graze.

pastel, (pâs·tel´) *m.* pastry, cake; pastel *(lápiz);* dealing from the bottom *(en los naipes);* (fig.) plot, scheme *(convenio);* (fig.) butterball *(persona gorda);* (print.) pi.

pastelería, (pâs·te·le·rē´ä) *f.* pastry shop; pastry *(conjunto);* pastry making *(fabricación).*

pastelero, ra, (pâs·te·le´ro, râ) *n.* pastry cook.

pasterizar, (pâs·te·rē·sâr´) *va.* to pasteurize.

pastilla, (pâs·tē´yä) *f.* tablet, lozenge *(medicina);* drop; **— de limón,** lemon drop; **—de levadura,** yeast cake; **— de jabón,** cake of soap.

pasto, (pâs´to) *m.* pasture, grazing *(acción de pastar);* fodder *(alimento);* grass;(fig.) fuel, food.

pastor, (pâs·tor´) *m.* shepherd; (eccl.) pastor; **— protestante,** minister; **— alemán,** German shepherd dog.

pastoso, sa, (pâs·to´so, sâ) *adj.* mellow *(agradable);* doughy; pastose *(de la pintura).*

pata, (pâ´tä) *f.* foot, leg, paw; foot *(base);* duck *(ave);* (coll.) leg; pocket flap *(cartera);* **—s arriba,** topsy-turvy, upside down.

patada, (pâ·tä´thä) *f.* kick; (coll.) step; (fig.) footprint *(huella).*

pataleo, (pâ·tä·le´o) *m.* foot stamping.

pataleta, (pâ·tä·le´tä) *f.* (coll.) fake fit or convulsion.

patán, (pâ·tän´) *m.* yokel, hick; rustic, peasant *(rústico).*

patata, (pâ·tä´tä) *f.* potato.

patear, (pâ·te·âr´) *va.* to kick; (coll.) to light into *(maltratar);* **—,** *vn.* to stamp the feet *(dar patadas);* (coll.) to run from pillar to post *(andar mucho);* (fig.)

to be furious *(estar enfadado).*

patente, (pâ·ten´te) *adj.* patent, manifest, evident; **—,** *f.* permit, warrant, certificate; **medicina de —,** patent medicine; **— de invención,** patent.

paternal, (pâ·ter·nâl´) *adj.* paternal, fatherly.

paternalismo, (pâ·ter·nä·lēz´mo) *m.* paternalism.

paternidad, (pâ·ter·nē·thâth´) *f.* paternity *(lazo juridico);* fatherhood.

paterno, na, (pâ·ter´no, nâ) *adj.* paternal, fatherly.

patético, ca, (pâ·te´tē·ko, kâ) *adj.* pathetic.

patíbulo, (pâ·tē´vü·lo) *m.* gallows, gibbet.

patillas, (pâ·tē´yâs) *f. pl.* sidewhiskers.

patín, (pâ·tēn´) *m.* skate; **— de hielo,** ice skate; **— de ruedas,** roller skate.

pátina, (pâ´tē·nä) *f.* patina.

patinador, ra, (pâ·tē·na·thor´, râ) *n.* skater.

patinaje, (pâ·tē·nâ´he) *m.* skidding; skating *(en patines).*

patinar, (pâ·tē·nâr´) *vn.* to skate *(en patines);* to skid.

patinazo, (pâ·tē·nâ´so) *m.* skidding; (fig.) slip, false step, blunder.

patio, (pâ´tyo) *m.* patio; (theat.) pit; (Sp. Am.) yard *(corral).*

pato, ta, (pâ´to, tâ) *n.* duck.

patochada, (pâ·to·châ´thä) *f.* faux pas; foolish remark *(dicho).*

patología, (pâ·to·lo·hē´ä) *f.* pathology.

patológico, ca, (pâ·to·lo´hē·ko, kâ) *adj.* pathological.

patólogo, (pâ·to´lo·go) *m.* pathologist.

patraña, (pâ·trä´nyä) *f.* lie, story, bunk.

patria, (pâ´tryä) *f.* native country, fatherland.

patriarca, (pâ·tryâr´kä) *m.* patriarch.

patriarcal, (pâ·tryâr·kâl´) *adj.* patriarchal.

patricio, (pâ·trē´syo) *m.* patrician.

patrimonio, (pâ·trē·mo´nyo) *m.* patrimony, inheritance.

patrio, tria, (pâ´tryo, tryâ) *adj.* native; paternal *(del padre).*

patriota, (pâ·tryo´tâ) *m. and f.* patriot.

patriótico, ca, (pâ·tryo´tē·ko, kâ) *adj.* patriotic.

patriotismo, (pâ·tryo·tēz´mo) *m.* patriotism.

patrocinar, (pâ·tro·sē·nâr´) *va.* to patronize, to favor; to protect *(proteger).*

patrocinio, (pâ·tro·sē´nyo) *m.* protection *(protección);* patronage.

patrón, (pâ·tron´) *m.* patron; captain *(de un buque);* landlord *(dueño);* boss, employer *(amo);* patron saint *(santo);*

pattern *(dechado)*; standard *(metal)*; stock *(planta)*; — **oro**, gold standard.

patrona, (pâ·tro′nâ) *f.* patroness; landlady *(dueña)*; patron saint *(santa)*.

patronímico, (pâ·tro·nē′mē·ko) *m.* surname.

patrulla, (pâ·trū′yâ) *f.* (mil.) patrol, squad; gang *(pandilla)*.

patuá, (pâ·twä′) *m.* patois.

paupérrimo, ma, (pâü·pe′rrē·mo, mâ) *adj.* exceedingly poor, poverty-stricken.

pausa, (pâ′ü·sâ) *f.* pause; slowness, deliberation *(lentitud)*; (mus.) rest.

pausado, da, (pâü·sâ′tho, thâ) *adj.* slow, deliberate.

pausar, (pâü·sâr′) *vn.* to pause.

pauta, (pâ′ü·tâ) *f.* ruler; ruled lines *(rayas)*; standard, model *(dechado)*; (mus.) staff.

pava, (pâ′vâ) *f.* turkey hen; peahen *(real)*; (coll.) old maid *(mujer)*; **pelar la —**, (coll.) to flirt.

pavesa, (pâ·ve′sâ) *f.* spark, ember.

pavimentar, (pâ·vē·men·târ′) *va.* to pave.

pavimento, (pâ·vē·men′to) *m.* pavement.

pavo, (pâ′vo) *m.* turkey; (fig.) dimwit; — **real**, peacock.

pavonear, (pâ·vo·ne·âr′) *vn.* and *vr.* to strut, to parade, to show off; (coll.) to get someone's hopes up.

pavor, (pâ·vor′) *m.* terror, horror.

pavoroso, sa, (pâ·vo·ro′so, sâ) *adj.* terrible, horrible.

payasada, (pa·yâ·sâ′thâ) *f.* antic, prank.

payaso, (pâ·yâ′so) *m.* clown.

payo, ya, (pâ′yo, yâ) *n.* yokel, hick.

paz, (pâs) *f.* peace; tranquillity *(tranquilidad)*; (eccl.) kiss of peace.

pazguato, ta, (pâz·gwâ′to, tâ) *n.* nincompoop, simpleton.

p/cta.: por cuenta, (com.) on account, for account.

P.D.: posdata, P.S. postscript.

pdo. or p.do**: pasado**, pt. past.

peaje, (pe·â′he) *m.* toll.

peatón, (pe·â·ton′) *m.* pedestrian; route mailman *(cartero)*.

peca, (pe′kâ) *f.* freckle, spot.

pecado, (pe·kâ′tho) *m.* sin; (coll.) devil.

pecador, ra, (pe·kâ·thor′, râ) *n.* sinner; —, *f.* (coll.) prostitute.

pecaminoso, sa, (pe·kâ·mē·no′so, sâ) *adj.* sinful.

pecar, (pe·kâr′) *vn.* to sin; to go wrong, to make a mistake *(errar)*.

pécora, (pe′ko·râ) *f.* sheep; **buena** or **mala —**, (coll.) vixen, fox.

pecoso, sa, (pe·ko′so, sâ) *adj.* freckled.

pectina, (pek·tē′nâ) *f.* (chem.) pectin.

peculiar, (pe·kū·lyâr′) *adj.* peculiar, individual.

pecuniario, ria, (pe·kū·nyâ′ryo, ryâ) *adj.* pecuniary.

pechera, (pe·che′râ) *f.* shirt bosom; (coll.) bosom; dickey *(paño)*.

pecho, (pe′cho) *m.* breast; chest; teat *(mama)*; hillock *(cuesta)*; bosom, heart *(interior)*; courage, valor *(valor)*; voice *(voz)*; tax, tribute *(tributo)*; **dar el —**, to suckle; **tomar a —**, to take to heart.

pechuga, (pe·chū′gâ) *f.* breast; (fig.) bosom.

pedagogía, (pe·thâ·go·hē′â) *f.* pedagogy.

pedagogo, (pe·thâ·go′go) *m.* pedagogue, teacher; mentor, vergil *(mentor)*.

pedal, (pe·thâl′) *m.* (mus.) pedal; (mech.) treadle, pedal.

pedante, (pe·thân′te) *adj.* pedantic; —, *m.* and *f.* pedant.

pedantería, (pe·thân·te·rē′â) *f.* pedantry.

pedazo, (pe·thâ′so) *m.* piece, bit; **hacer —s**, to break to pieces, to shatter.

pedernal, (pe·ther·nâl′) *m.* flint; (fig.) flintiness.

pedestal, (pe·thes·tâl′) *m.* pedestal; (fig.) basis.

pediatra, (pe·thyâ′trâ) *m.* pediatrician.

pediatría, (pe·thyâ·trē′â) *f.* pediatrics.

pedicuro, (pe·thē·kū′ro) *m.* chiropodist.

pedido, (pe·thē′tho) *m.* request; (com.) order; **— de ensayo**, trial order.

pedigüeño, ña, (pe·thē·gwe′nyo, nyâ) *adj.* nagging, insistent, demanding.

pedir*, (pe·thēr′) *va.* to ask, to ask for; to solicit, to petition *(solicitar)*; to demand *(reclamar)*; to crave, to desire *(anhelar)*; to ask someone's hand in marriage *(para casarse)*; — **cuenta**, to bring a person to account; — **prestado**, to borrow.

pedo, (pe′tho) *m.* wind, flatulence.

pedrada, (pe·thrâ′thâ) *f.* stoning; mark, bruise *(señal)*; hairbow *(lazo)*; (fig.) taunt, gibe.

pedregal, (pe·thre·gâl′) *m.* rocky terrain.

pedregoso, sa, (pe·thre·go′so, sâ) *adj.* stony, rocky; afflicted by gallstones *(mal de piedra)*.

pedrería, (pe·thre·rē′â) *f.* precious stones.

pegadizo, za, (pe·gâ·thē′so, sâ) *adj.* sticky, gluey; contagious *(contagioso)*; mooching, parasitic *(parásito)*; false, artificial *(falso)*.

pegado, (pe·gâ′tho) *m.* sticking plaster, poultice, patch.

pegadura, (pe·gâ·thū′râ) *f.* sticking

---

m met, **n** not, **p** pot, **r** very, **rr** (none), **s** so, **t** toy, **th** with, **v** eve, **w** we, **y** yes, **z** zero

(acción); patch.

pegajoso, sa, (pe·gâ·ho´so, sâ) *adj.* sticky; attractive, alluring *(atractivo);* contagious *(contagioso);* (fig.) soft, smooth *(suave);* (coll.) familiar *(familiar);* (fig.) habit-forming *(difícil de deshacer);* tonada —, catchy tune.

pegar, (pe·gâr´) *va.* to cement, to stick, to paste, to glue; to join, to attach *(juntar);* to strike, to beat *(golpear);* to communicate *(comunicar);* —, *vn.* to take root *(arraigar);* (fig.) to click, to be received well; to be near *(estar cerca);* to be opportune, to be to the point *(venir al caso);* to bump *(tropezar);* to stick together *(unirse);* —se, to intrude, to steal in; to adhere *(adherirse).*

peinado, (peē·nâ´tho) *m.* coiffure, hairdo.

peinador, (peē·nâ·thor´) *m.* hairdresser; dressing gown *(bata).*

peinadora, (peē·nâ·tho´râ) *f.* hairdresser.

peinar, (peē·nâr´) *va.* to comb; —se, to comb one's hair.

peine, (pe´ē·ne) *m.* comb; card *(carda);* instep *(empeine);* (fig.) sly devil, sly one *(púa).*

peineta, (peē·ne´tâ) *f.* dress comb.

pelado, da, (pe·lâ´tho, thâ) *n.* (Mex.) peasant; —, *adj.* bald *(calvo);* peeled, pared *(sin piel);* bare *(desnudo);* poor *(pobre);* shameless *(desvergonzado);* even *(número).*

pelar, (pe·lâr´) *va.* to pull out one's hair; to pluck *(desplumar);* to peel, to pare *(mondar);* (fig.) to snatch, to grab *(despojar);* to clean out *(ganar).*

peldaño, (pel·dâ´nyo) *m.* step.

pelea, (pe·le´â) *f.* battle, fight; quarrel *(disputa);* (fig.) diligence *(diligencia).*

pelear, (pe·le·âr´) *vn.* to fight, to battle; to quarrel *(reñir);* —se, to scuffle, to fight; (fig.) to split up, to break up *(separarse).*

pelele, (pe·le´le) *m.* man of straw; Dr. Dentons´ *(traje);* (fig.) laughingstock.

peletero, (pe·le·te´ro) *m.* furrier.

pelícano, (pe·lē´kâ·no) *m.* pelican; pincers *(gatillo).*

pelicano, na, (pe·lē·kâ´no, nâ) *adj.* grayhaired.

película, (pe·lē´kū·lâ) *f.* film; (anat.) skin layer; **rollo de** —s, film roll; **tira de** —s, filmstrip.

peliculero, ra, (pe·lē·kū·le´ro, râ) *adj.* film; —, *n.* (coll.) movie actor.

peligrar, (pe·lē·grâr´) *vn.* to be in danger.

peligro, (pe·lē´gro) *m.* danger, risk, peril.

peligroso, sa, (pe·lē·gro´so, sâ) *adj.* dangerous, perilous.

pelinegro, gra, (pe·lē·ne´gro, grâ) *adj.* black-haired.

pelirrojo, ja, (pe·lē·rro´ho, hâ) *adj.* and *n.* redhead.

pelo, (pe´lo) *m.* hair *(cabello);* pile *(de un tejido);* flaw *(en una joya);* hairspring *(muelle);* fuzz, down *(vello);* raw silk *(seda);* vein *(grieta);* grain *(de madera);* (fig.) trifle; **a** —, to the purpose, timely; **tomar el** —, to tease, to kid.

pelota, (pe·lo´tâ) *f.* ball; ball game *(juego);* cowhide boat *(batea);* (fig.) prostitute *(ramera);* pile of debts *(deudas);* **en** —, stark naked.

pelotari, (pe·lo·tâ´rē) *m.* pelota player.

pelotazo, (pe·lo·tâ´so) *m.* blow with a ball.

pelotera, (pe·lo·te´râ) *f.* (coll.) row, fracas.

pelotón, (pe·lo·ton´) *m.* large ball; snarl *(enredo);* crowd *(gentío);* (mil.) platoon.

peltre, (pel´tre) *m.* pewter.

peluca, (pe·lū´kâ) *f.* wig; (coll.) bawling out, dressing down.

peludo, da, (pe·lū´tho, thâ) *adj.* hairy.

peluquería, (pe·lū·ke·rē´â) *f.* barbershop *(de hombres);* beauty parlor.

peluquero, (pe·lū·ke´ro) *m.* barber; hairdresser *(de mujeres);* wigmaker *(que hace pelucas).*

pelusa, (pe·lū´sâ) *f.* fuzz, down *(vello);* nap; (fig.) childish envy.

pelvis, (pel´vēs) *f.* pelvis.

pellejo, (pe·ye´ho) *m.* skin; hide; pelt *(de animal);* wineskin *(odre);* (coll.) drunk, lush.

pellizcar, (pe·yēs·kâr´) *va.* to pinch; to graze, to nip *(herir);* to take a speck of *(tomar pequeña cantidad);* —se, (fig.) to yearn, to pine.

pellizco, (pe·yēs´ko) *m.* pinch; graze, nip *(herida);* smidgen, pinch *(corta cantidad).*

pena, (pe´nâ) *f.* pain; sadness, shame; punishment *(castigo);* trouble, difficulty *(dificultad);* pendant *(pendiente);* (orn.) penna; **a duras** —s, with difficulty; **merecer** or **valer la** —, to be worthwhile; **so** — **de,** under penalty of.

penable, (pe·nâ´vle) *adj.* punishable.

penacho, (pe·nâ´cho) *m.* (orn.) crest; plumes *(adorno);* (fig.) pride, haughtiness.

penal, (pe·nâl´) *adj.* penal; —, *m.* penitentiary.

penalidad, (pe·nâ·lē·thâth´) *f.* trouble, hardship; culpability, punishability *(calidad de penable).*

penar, (pe·nâr´) *vn.* to suffer; (eccl.) to

suffer in Purgatory; —, va. to penalize, to punish.

pendencia, (pen·den´syâ) f. quarrel, dispute; litigation *(litispendencia).*

pendenciero, ra, (pen·den·sye´ro, râ) adj. quarrelsome.

pender, (pen·der´) vn. to hang; to depend *(depender);* to be awaiting a decision, to be pending *(estar pendiente).*

pendiente, (pen·dyen´te) adj. hanging; pending *(que está por resolverse);* — **de pago,** pending payment, unpaid; —, m. pendant; earring, eardrop *(arete);* —, f. slope, grade, incline; — **arriba,** uphill slope.

péndola, (pen´do·lâ) f. pendulum; pendulum clock *(reloj);* suspension *(varilla).*

pendón, (pen·don´) m. standard, banner, pennon; shoot *(vástago);* (coll.) frump *(mujer desaliñada);* (coll.) rake, libertine *(libertino).*

péndulo, la, (pen´dū·lo, lâ) adj. pendent, hanging; —, m. pendulum.

pene, (pe´ne) m. (anat.) penis.

penetrable, (pe·ne·trâ´vle) adj. penetrable; comprehensible *(comprensible).*

penetración, (pe·ne·trâ·syon´) f. penetration.

penetrante, (pe·ne·trân´te) adj. penetrating.

penetrar, (pe·ne·trâr´) va. to penetrate; (fig.) to fathom, to comprehend.

penicilina, (pe·nē·sē·lē´nâ) f. penicillin.

península, (pe·nēn´sū·lâ) f. peninsula.

peninsular, (pe·nēn·sū·lâr´) adj. peninsular; —, m. (Sp. Am.) Spaniard.

penitencia, (pe·nē·ten´syâ) f. penitence, repentance; penance *(sacramento).*

penitenciaría, (pe·nē ten·syâ·rē´â) f. penitentiary.

penitente, (pe·nē·ten´te) adj. penitent, repentant; —, m. penitent.

penoso, sa, (pe·no´so sâ) adj. hard, difficult *(trabajoso);* suffering, afflicted *(afligido);* (coll.) conceited, vain *(presumido).*

pensado, da, (pen·sâ´tho, thâ) adj. deliberate, intentional; **mal —,** evilminded.

pensador, ra, (pen·sâ·thor´, râ) n. thinker.

pensamiento, (pen·sâ·myen´to) m. thought; suspicion *(sospecha);* (bot.) pansy.

pensar*, (pen·sâr´) vn. to think; to intend *(proponerse).*

pensativo; va, (pen·sâ·tē´vo, vâ) adj. pensive, thoughtful.

pensión, (pen·syon´) f. pension, annuity; allowance *(asignación);* board *(pupila-*

je); grant *(para estudios);* boardinghouse, pension *(casa).*

pensionado, da, (pen·syo·nâ´tho, thâ) adj. pensioned; —, n. pensioner; —, m. boarding school.

pensionar, (pen·syo·nâr´) va. to award a pension to.

pensionista, (pen·syo·nēs´tâ) m. and f. pensioner, pensionary; boarder *(interno).*

pentágono, (pen·tâ´go·no) m. pentagon.

pentagrama, (pen·tâ·grâ´mâ) m. (mus.) staff

penumbra, (pe·nūm´brâ) f. penumbra.

penuria, (pe·nū´ryâ) f. penury, poverty, indigence, need, want.

peña, (pe´nyâ) f. rock, boulder; rocky peak *(monte);* friends, comrades *(amigos).*

peñasco, (pē·nyâs´ko) m. crag, peak; (zool.) murex.

peñón, (pē·nyon´) m. rocky peak *(monte);* boulder; **P— de Gibraltar,** Rock of Gibraltar.

peón, (pe·ôn´) f. pedestrian; laborer *(jornalero);* foot soldier *(soldado);* top *(juguete);* pawn *(del ajedrez);* checker *(del juego de damas);* axle *(árbol);* beehive *(colmena).*

peonía, (pe·o·nē´â) f. (bot.) peony.

peor, (pe·or´) adj. and adv. worse; **tanto —,** so much the worse; **de mal en —,** from bad to worse.

pepino, (pe·pē´no) m. cucumber.

pepita, (pe·pē´tâ) f. seed; pip *(enfermedad);* nugget *(metal).*

pepsina, (pep·sē´nâ) f. pepsin.

péptico, ca, (pep´tē·ko, kâ) adj. peptic.

pequeñez, (pe·ke·nyes´) f. smallness; infancy *(infancia);* (fig.) meanness.

pequeño, ña, (pe·ke´nyo, nyâ) adj. little, small; young *(joven);* lowly, humble *(humilde);* (fig.) trifling.

pera, (pe´râ) f. pear; (fig.) goatee *(barba);* (fig.) plum *(destino lucrativo).*

peral, (pe·râl´) m. pear tree.

percal, (per·kâl´) m. percale.

percance, (per·kân´se) m. perquisite; bad luck, misfortune *(infortunio).*

percepción, (per·sep·syon´) f. perception; idea *(idea).*

perceptible, (per·sep·tē´vle) adj. perceptible, perceivable; receivable, collectible *(recibir).*

percibir, (per·sē·vēr´) va. to collect, to receive *(recibir);* to perceive; to comprehend *(comprender).*

percudido, da, (per·kū·thē´tho, thâ), adj. dull, tarnished; soiled *(sucio).*

m met, **n** not, **p** pot, **r** very, **rr** (none), **s** so, **t** toy, **th** with, **v** eve, **w** we, **y** yes, **z** zero

percusión, (per·kū·syon´) f. percussion; **instrumento de —,** percussion instrument.

percha, (per´châ) f. perch; clothes tree *(colgador);* snare trap *(lazo).*

perder*, (per·ther´) va. to lose; to waste *(malgastar);* to miss *(un tren);* to fail, to flunk *(no aprobar);* to spoil *(dañar);* to ruin *(arruinar);* —, vn. to lose; to fade *(desteñirse);* **echar a —,** to ruin; **—se,** to get lost, to go astray; (fig.) to be in a jam *(estar en una dificultad);* to lose one´s senses *(conturbarse);* (fig.) to become dissipated *(de los vicios);* (fig.) to lose one´s train of thought *(borrarse la especie);* (fig.) to miss *(no percibirse);* (fig.) to miss out on *(no aprovecharse);* (fig.) to risk *(arriesgar);* (fig.) to be passionately in love with *(amar);* (fig.) to lose one´s honor.

perdición, (per·thē·syon´) f. perdition, ruin; loss *(pérdida);* unbridled love *(amor);* misuse *(abuso).*

pérdida, (per´thē·thâ) f. loss; damage *(daño).*

perdido, da (per·thē´tho, thâ) adj. lost.

perdigón, (per·thē·gon´) m. baby partridge; decoy partridge *(reclamo);* — **ones,** pl. bird shot.

perdiguero, ra, (per·thē·ge´ro, râ) adj. setting, pointing.

perdiz, (per·thēs´) f. partridge.

perdón, (per·thon´) m. pardon; forgiveness, remission *(indulgencia);* (coll.) hot drop of oil or wax *(gota).*

perdonable, (per·tho·nâ´vle) adj. pardonable.

perdonar, (per·tho·nâr´) va. to pardon; to excuse *(exceptuar);* (fig.) to renounce *(renunciar).*

perdurable, (per·thū·râ´vle) adj. perpetual, everlasting; durable, long-lasting *(durable).*

perecedero, ra, (pe·re·se·the´ro, râ) adj. perishable; —, m. necessity, want.

perecer*, (pe·re·ser´) vn. to perish, to die *(morir);* to suffer *(padecer);* to be poverty-stricken *(tener pobreza);* **—se,** (fig.) to yearn, to pine; (fig.) to anguish *(padecer).*

peregrinación, (pe·re·grē´nâ·syon´) f. pilgrimage.

peregrino, na, (pe·re·grē´no, nâ) adj. traveling; foreign *(extranjero);* migratory *(de aves);* strange, rare *(raro);* elegant *(elegante);* mortal *(mortal);* —, n. pilgrim.

perejil, (pe·re·hēl´) m. parsley; (fig.) frilli-

ness, gaudiness.

perenne, (pe·ren´ne) adj. continuous, incessant; (bot.) perennial.

perentorio, da, (pe·ren·to´ryo, ryâ) adj. peremptory.

pereza, (pe·re´sâ) f. laziness; negligence, carelessness *(descuido).*

perezoso, sa, (pe·re·so´so, sâ) adj. lazy; negligent, careless *(descuidado);* —, m. sloth.

perfección, (per·fek·syon´) f. perfection.

perfeccionamiento, (per·fek·syo·nâ·myen´-to) m. perfecting.

perfeccionar, (per·fek·syo·nâr´) va. to perfect, to give the finishing touches.

perfecto, ta, (per·fek´to, tâ) adj. perfect.

perfidia, (per·fē´thyâ) f. perfidy.

pérfido, da, (per´fē·tho, thâ), adj. perfidious.

perfil, (per·fēl´) m. profile; edging *(adorno);* sketch, outline *(de la pintura).*

perfilado, da, (per·fē·lâ´tho, thâ) adj. well-formed *(de la nariz);* long and thin *(del rostro).*

perfilar, (per·fē·lâr´) va. to profile, to outline; (fig.) to perfect, to refine; **—se,** to be outlined.

perforación, (per·fo·râ·syon´) f. perforation, puncture.

perforar, (per·fo·râr´) va. to perforate, to puncture.

perfumar, (per·fū·mâr´) va. to perfume.

perfume, (per·fū´me) m. perfume.

perfumería, (per·fū·me·rē´â) f. perfumery.

pergamino, (per·gâ·mē´no) m. parchment.

pericia, (pe·rē´syâ) f. skill, ability.

perico, (pe·rē´ko) m. periwig, peruke; parakeet *(ave);* large fan *(abanico);* giant asparagus *(espárrago);* (coll.) chamber pot *(sillico);* (Mex.) chatterbox.

periferia, (pe·rē·fe´ryâ) f. periphery.

perifollo, (pe·rē·fo´yo) m. (bot.) chervil; **—s,** pl. frippery.

perifonear, (pe·rē·fo·ne·âr´) va. (rad.) to broadcast.

perigeo, (pe·rē·he´o) m. (ast.) perigee.

perilla, (pe·rē´yâ) f. small pear; pear-shaped ornament *(adorno);* pommel *(de una silla de montar);* goatee *(barba);* earlobe *(de la oreja);* **de —,** apropos.

perímetro, (pe·rē´me·tro) m. perimeter.

periódico, ca, (pe·ryo´thē·ko, kâ) adj. periodical; —, m. newspaper.

periodismo, (pe·ryo·thēz´mo) m. journalism.

periodista, (pe·ryo·thēs´tâ) m. and f. journalist.

periodístico, ca, (pe·ryo·thēs´tē·ko, kâ) *adj.* journalistic.

período, (pe·rē´o·tho) or periodo, (pē·ryo´-tho) *m.* (gram.) periodic sentence; period; cycle *(ciclo)*.

peripecia, (pe·rē·pe´syâ) *f.* peripeteia.

periscopio, (pe·rēs·ko´pyo) *m.* periscope.

perito, ta, (pe·rē´to, tâ) *adj.* expert, skilled; —, *m.* expert.

peritonitis, (pe·rē·to·nē´tēs) *f.* (med.) peritonitis.

perjudicar, (per·hū·thē·kâr´) *va.* to harm, to damage.

perjudicial, (per·hū·thē·syâl´) *adj.* damaging, harmful, injurious.

perjuicio, (per·hwē´syo) *m.* injury, harm, damage.

perjurar, (per·hū·râr´) *vn.* to commit perjury; to swear *(jurar);* —se, to commit perjury *(jurar en falso);* to perjure oneself.

perjurio, (per·hu´ryo) *m.* perjury.

perjuro, ra, (per·hū´ro, râ) *adj.* perjured; *n.* perjurer; —, *m.* perjury.

perla, (per´lâ) *f.* pearl; de —s, just right; —s cultivadas, cultured pearls.

permanecer*, (per·mâ·ne·ser´) *vn.* to remain, to stay.

permanencia, (per·mâ·nen´syâ) *f.* permanence.

permanente, (per·mâ·nen´te) *adj.* permanent; —, *m.* permanent wave.

permiso (per·mē´so) *m.* permission, authorization; deviation *(en las monedas).*

permitido, da, (per·mē·tē´tho, thâ) *adj.* allowed, permitted; no está —do, it is not allowed.

permitir, (per·mē·tēr´) *va.* to permit, to allow; —se, to take the liberty, to permit oneself; Dios lo permita, God willing.

permutar, (per·mu·târ´) *va.* to exchange; to change *(variar).*

pernicioso, sa, (per·nē·syo´so, sâ) *adj.* pernicious, destructive.

pernil, (per·nēl´) *m.* thigh; leg *(del pantalón).*

perno, (per´no) *m.* bolt; (mech.) joint pin.

pernoctar, (per·nok·târ´) *vn.* to spend the night.

pero, (pe´ro) *conj.* but; yet *(sino);* —, *m.* defect, fault; objection *(objeción);* poner —s, to find fault.

perogrullada, (pe·ro·grū·yâ´thâ) *f.* platitude.

perorar, (pe·ro·râr´) *vn.* to make a speech; (fig.) to nag, to hound *(pedir).*

perorata, (pe·ro·râ´tâ) harangue, speech.

peróxido, (pe·rok´sē·tho) *m.* peroxide.

perpendicular, (per·pen·dē·kū·lâr´) *adj.* perpendicular.

perpetrar, (per·pe·trâr´) *va.* to perpetrate, to commit.

perpetuar, (per·pe·twâr´) *va.* to perpetuate.

perpetuidad, (per·pe·twē·thâth´) *f.* perpetuity.

perpetuo, tua, (per·pe´two, twâ) *adj.* perpetual.

perplejidad, (per·ple·hē·thâth´) *f.* perplexity.

perplejo, ja, (per·ple´ho, hâ) *adj.* perplexed.

perra, (pe´rrâ) *f.* female dog, bitch; drunkenness, intoxication *(borrachera);* (coll.) childish anger.

perrillo, (pe·rrē´yo) *m.* little dog; trigger *(gatillo);* — faldero, lap dog; — de lanas, poodle.

perro, (pe´rro) *n.* m. dog.

persa, (per´sâ) *n.* and *adj.* Persian.

perseguir*, (per·se·gēr´) *va.* to pursue; (fig.) to persecute; to dun, to hound *(importunar).*

perseverancia, (per·se·ve·rân´syâ) *f.* perseverance, persistency.

perseverante, (per·se·ve·rân´te) *adj.* perseverant.

perseverar, (per·se·ve·râr´) *vn.* to persevere, to persist.

persiana, (per·syâ´nâ) *f.* window blind, Venetian blind.

persignarse, (per·sēg·nâr´se) *vr.* to make the sign of the cross, to bless oneself; (coll.) to begin the day´s selling.

persistencia, (per·sēs·ten´syâ) *f.* persistence, persistency.

persistente, (per·sēs·ten´te) *adj.* persistent, tenacious.

persistir, (per·sēs·tēr´) *vn.* to persist.

persona, (per·so´nâ) *f.* person; personage *(persona importante);* character *(de una obra literaria);* por —, per capita; — desplazada, displaced person.

personaje, (per·so·nâ´he) *m.* personage; character *(obra literaria).*

personal, (per·so·nâl´) *adj.* personal; —, *m.* personnel, staff; staff expenses *(gastos).*

personalidad, (per·so·nâ·lē·thâth´) *f.* personality.

personificar, (per·so·nē·fē·kâr´) *va.* to personify.

personilla, (per·so·nē´yâ) *f.* nothing.

perspectiva, (pers·pek·tē´vâ) *f.* perspective; false representation *(representación falsa);* prospect *(expectiva).*

perspicacia, (pers·pē·kä´syä) *f.* clear-sightedness; perspicacity *(entendimiento).*

perspicaz, (pers·pē·käs´) *adj.* perspicacious *(sagaz);* clear-sighted.

persuadir, (per·swä·thēr´) *va.* to persuade, to convince.

persuasión, (per·swä·syon´) *f.* persuasion.

persuasivo, va, (per·swä·sē´vo, vä) *adj.* persuasive.

pertenecer*, (per·te·ne·ser´) *vn.* to belong; to pertain, to concern, to have to do *(concernir).*

perteneciente, (per·te·ne·syen´te) *adj.* belonging, pertaining.

pertenencia, (per·te·nen´syä) *f.* right of property; territory, domain *(territorio);* appurtenance, adjunct *(accesorio).*

pértiga, (per´tē·gä) *f.* long pole.

pertinacia, (per·tē·nä´syä) *f.* obstinacy, stubbornness, pertinacity.

pertinaz, (per·tē·näs´) *adj.* pertinacious, obstinate.

pertinencia, (per·tē·nen´syä) *f.* relevance, pertinence.

pertrechos, (per·tre´chos) *m. pl.* ordnance *(de guerra);* tools, instruments.

perturbación, (per·tūr·vä·syon´) *f.* disturbance, perturbation.

perturbar, (per·tūr·vär´) *va.* to perturb, to disturb, to trouble; to confuse, to mix up *(un discurso).*

peruano, na, (pe·rwä´no, nä) *adj.* and *n.* Peruvian.

perversidad, (per·ver·sē·thäth´) *f.* perversity.

perversión, (per·ver·syon´) *f.* perversion, depravation, corruption.

perverso, sa, (per·ver´so, sä) *adj.* perverse.

pervertir*, (per·ver·tēr´) *va.* to pervert, to corrupt.

pesa, (pe´sä) *f.* weight; **—s y medidas,** weights and measures.

pesadez, (pe·sä·thes´) *f.* heaviness; (phy.) gravity; (fig.) boredom, tedium.

pesadilla, (pe·sä·thē´yä) *f.* nightmare.

pesado, da, (pe·sä´tho, thä) *adj.* heavy; slow *(lento);* tiresome, tedious *(molesto);* harmful, injurious *(sensible);* harsh, hard *(áspero);* **sueño —,** profound sleep.

pesadumbre, (pe·sä·thūm´bre) *f.* heaviness; injury, offense *(injuria);* gravity *(pesantez);* quarrel, dispute *(riña);* grief, sorrow *(tristeza).*

pésame, (pe´sä·me) *m.* condolence, sympathy.

pesantez, (pe·sän·tes´) *f.* gravity.

pesar, (pe·sär´) *m.* sorrow, grief; regret, repentance *(arrepentimiento);* **a — de,** in spite of, notwithstanding; **—,** *vn.* to weigh, to have weight; to be heavy *(pesar mucho);* to be valuable *(valer);* **—,** *va.* to weigh; (fig.) to weigh down, to grieve.

pesaroso, sa, (pe·sä·ro´so, sä) *adj.* sorrowful, sorry; repentant *(arrepentido).*

pesca, (pes´kä) *f.* fishing; **— con arpón,** spear fishing.

pescadería, (pes·kä·the·rē´ä) *f.* fish market.

pescado, (pes·kä´tho) *m.* fish; salted codfish *(abadejo).*

pescador, ra, (pes·kä·thor´, rä) *n.* fisherman; **—,** *m.* (ichth.) angler.

pescar, (pes·kär´) *va.* to fish; to catch *(peces);* (coll.) to get hold of, to latch onto *(coger);* to catch, to surprise *(sorprender).*

pescozón, (pes·ko·son´) *m.* slap on the neck.

pescuezo, (pes·kwe´so) *m.* neck; (fig.) haughtiness, pride.

pesebre, (pe·se´vre) *m.* manger.

peseta, (pe·se´tä) *f.* monetary unit of Spain.

pesimista, (pe·sē·mēs´tä) *m.* and *f.* pessimist; **—,** *adj.* pessimistic.

pésimo, ma, (pe´sē·mo, mä) *adj.* very bad, abominable.

peso, (pe´so) *m.* peso *(moneda);* gravity *(pesantez);* weight; balance *(balanza);* **— atómico,** atomic weight; **— bruto,** gross weight; **— fuerte,** silver dollar; **— neto,** net weight; **en —,** bodily; **— mosca,** flyweight.

pespunte, (pes·pūn´te) *m.* backstitch.

pesquisa, (pes·kē´sä) *f.* inquiry, investigation.

pestaña, (pes·tä´nyä) *f.* eyelash; edge, edging *(ceja);* (bot.) cilium.

pestañear, (pes·tä·nye·är´) *vn.* to blink, to wink; (fig.) to be alive, to be alive and kicking.

peste, (pes´te) *f.* pest, plague; stench, stink *(mal olor);* (fig.) corruption *(corrupción);* (coll.) epidemic *(abundancia).*

pestífero, ra, (pes·tē´fe·ro, rä) *adj.* pestiferous; malodorous *(de mal olor);* **—,** *n.* plague victim.

pestilencia, (pes·tē·len´syä) *f.* pestilence, plague.

pestillo, (pes·tē´yo) *m.* bolt.

petaca, (pe·tä´kä) *f.* leather chest *(arca);* cigar box *(estuche).*

â arm, **e** they, **ē** bē, **o** fore, **ū** blūe, **b** bad, **ch** chip, **d** day, **f** fat, **g** go, **h** hot, **k** kid, **1** let

pétalo, (pe·tā·lo) *m.* petal.

petardista, (pe·târ·thēs'tä) *m.* and *f.* cheat, fraud.

petardo (pe·tar'tho) *m.* petard; bomb *(bomba);* cheat, fraud *(engaño).*

petate, (pe·tä'te) *m.* mat *(esterilla);* bedding; (coll.) luggage, baggage *(equipaje);* (fig.) swindler *(embustero);* (fig.) cad *(hombre despreciable).*

petición, (pe·tē·syon') *f.* petition, request; plea.

petirrojo, (pe·tē·rro'ho) *m.* robin redbreast.

peto, (pe'to) *m.* breastplate *(armadura);* dickey.

pétreo, trea, (pe'tre·o, tre·ä) *adj.* stony.

petrificar, (pe·trē·fē·kâr') *va.* and *vr.* to petrify.

petróleo, (pe·tro'le·o) *m.* petroleum, oil.

petrolero, ra, (pe·tro·le'ro, râ) *adj.* pertaining to oil; arsonistic *(incendiario).*

petrolífero, ra, (pe·tro·lē'fe·ro, râ) *adj.* oil producing; **campos —s,** oil fields.

petulancia, (pe·tū·län'syä) *f.* petulance, insolence; pretention, pretentiousness *(pretensión).*

petunia, (pe·tū'nyâ), *f.* (bot.) petunia.

pez, (pes) *m.* fish; long pile *(montón);* (fig.) fruit of one's labors *(resultado);* **peces de colores,** goldfish; —, *f.* pitch, tar; — **griega,** rosin.

pezón, (pe·son') *m.* stalk, stem *(rabillo);* nipple; (fig.) point *(cabo).*

pezuña, (pe·sū'nyä) *f.* hoof.

piadoso, sa, (pyä·tho'so sä) *adj.* pious; merciful, benevolent *(benigno).*

piafar, (pyä·fâr') *vn.* to paw, to stamp.

pianista, (pyä·nēs'tä) *m.* and *f.* pianist.

piano, (pyä'no) *m.* piano; — **de cola,** grand piano.

pianoforte, (pyä·no·for'te) *m.* pianoforte.

piar, (pyâr), *vn.* to peep, to chirp; to clamor, to cry *(llamar).*

pica, (pe'kä) *f.* pike, spear; goad *(garrocha);* hammer *(escoda);* pique, resentment *(pique).*

picada, (pē·kä'thä) *f.* peck *(picotazo);* bite, sting *(picadura);* strike *(del pez).*

picadillo, (pē·kä·thē'yo) *m.* mincemeat; hash *(guisado).*

picado, da, (pē·kä'tho, thä) *adj.* perforated; piqued, vexed *(enojado);* —, *m.* hash; (avi.) dive.

picador, (pē·kä·thor') *m.* picador; trainer *(de caballos);* cutting board *(tajo);* lockbreaker *(ladrón).*

picadura, (pē·kä·thū'râ) *f.* prick, puncture *(picotazo);* bite; cut, slit *(cisura);* cut

tobacco *(tobaco);* cavity *(caries).*

picaflor, (pē·kä·flor') *m.* (orn.) hummingbird; flirt *(tenorio).*

picamaderos, (pē·kä·mä·the'ros) *m.* (orn.) woodpecker.

picante, (pē·kän'te) *adj.* stinging, pricking; hot, highly seasoned, piquant *(sazonado);* (fig.) spicy, racy *(escabroso).*

picapedrero, (pē·kä·pe·thre'ro) *m.* stonecutter.

picahielo, (pē·kä·ye'lo) *m.* ice pick.

picapleitos, (pē·kä·ple'ē·tos) *m.* (coll.) troublemaker; (coll.) shyster; pettifogger *(abogado).*

picaporte, (pē·kä·por'te) *m.* latchkey *(llavín);* catch, latch; door knocker *(aldaba).*

picaposte, (pē·kä·pos'te) *m.* (orn.) woodpecker.

picar, (pē·kâr') *va.* to prick, to puncture; to jab, to goad *(al toro);* to prick, to bite *(morder);* to chop up, to mince *(dividir);* to peck *(de las aves);* to take the bait *(morder el cebo);* to itch *(escozor);* to burn *(enardecer);* to spur *(espolear);* to train *(adiestrar);* to cut *(labrar);* (fig.) to goad *(excitar);* to excite *(estimular);* to pique *(enojar);* to puncture *(agujerear);* *(mil.)* to pursue; to touch up *(de la pintura);* —, *vn.* to nibble *(comer);* to burn, to beat down *(el sol);* (fig.) to pick up; (fig.) to take hold *(tener efecto);* to dabble *(conocer un poco);* —**se,** to become motheaten; to rot, to spoil *(pudrirse);* to be in heat *(de los animales);* to be choppy *(del mar);* to be offended, to be piqued *(ofenderse);* (fig.) to boast, to brag *(jactarse);* to get carried away with oneself *(dejarse llevar).*

picardía, (pē·kâr·thē'ä) *f.* knavery, roguery; deceit, trickery *(engaño);* mischievousness *(travesura);* bunch of rascals *(junta).*

picaresco, ca, (pē·kä·res'ko, kä) *adj.* roguish, knavish; picaresque *(de la literatura).*

pícaro, ra, (pe'kâ·ro, râ) *adj.* knavish, roguish; sly, rascally, tricky *(astuto);* (fig.) mischievous *(travieso);* —, *m.* rogue, knave; rascal; mischief.

picazón, (pē·kä·son') *f.* itching, itch; (fig.) displeasure *(disgusto).*

pico, (pe'ko) *m.* beak, bill; peak *(de montaña);* pickax *(herramienta);* spout *(de vasija);* corner *(de pañuelo);* loquacity *(habladuría);* **perder por el —,** to miss out by not knowing when to keep one's mouth shut; **cien dólares y —,** a little more than one hundred dollars; **la una y —,** a little after one o'clock.

picoso, sa, (pē·ko´so, sâ) *adj.* pitted with small pox; (Mex. coll.) hot, highly seasoned.

picotear, (pē·ko·te·âr´) *va.* to peck at.

picudo, da, (pē·kū´tho, thâ) *adj.* beaked; sharp-pointed *(puntiagudo); (fig.)* talkative; **—,** *m.* spit.

pichón, (pē·chon´) *m.* young pigeon; (coll.) darling.

pie, (pye) *m.* foot; base *(base);* basis *(origen);* trunk *(de árbol);* **— cuadrado,** square foot; **— de la letra,** literally; **a —,** on foot; **dar —,** to give occasion; **estar de —,** to be standing; **ponerse de —,** to stand up; **dedo del —,** toe; **— de atleta,** (med.) athlete´s foot; **de —s a cabeza,** from head to toe.

piedad, (pye·thâth´) *f.* piety; mercy, pity *(misericordia).*

piedra, (pye´thrâ) *f.* stone; gem *(preciosa);* hail *(granizo);* **— angular,** cornerstone; **—de afilar,** whetstone; **— pómez,** pumice stone.

piel, (pyel) *f.* skin; hide, pelt *(cuero curtido);* leather *(sin pelo).*

pienso, (pyen´so) *m.* cattle feed.

pierna, (pyer´nâ) *f.* leg.

pieza, (pye´sâ) *f.* piece; play *(obra dramática);* room *(habitación).*

pifia, (pē´fyâ) *f.* miscue in billiards; blunder *(desatino).*

pigmeo, mea, (pēg·me´o, me´â) *n.* and *adj.* pygmy.

pignorar, (pēg·no·râr´) *va.* to pledge.

pijama, (pē·hâ´mâ) *m.* pajamas.

pila, (pē´lâ) *f.* trough; (eccl.) font; pile *(montón);* (elec.) battery; **— de agua bendita,** holy-water font; **nombre de —,** Christian name; **— seca,** dry battery.

pilar, (pē·lâr´) *m.* basin *(de fuente);* milestone *(hito);* (arch.) pillar; **—,** *va.* to pound, to crush.

pilastra, (pē·lâs´trâ) *f.* pilaster.

píldora, (pēl´do·râ) *f.* pill.

pilón, (pē·lon´) *m.* pylon; large water basin, drinking trough *(pila);* mortar *(mortero);* loaf of sugar; (Mex. coll.) small gift added to a purchase; **de —,** thrown in, added free.

piloto, (pē·lo´to) *m.* pilot; first mate *(segundo);* **— automático,** auto pilot; **— de prueba,** test pilot.

piltrafa, (pēl·trâ´fâ) *f.* meat that is nearly all skin; **—s,** *pl.* meat scraps.

pillada, (pē·yâ´thâ) *f.* piece of villainy.

pillaje, (pē·yâ´he) *m.* pillage, plunder.

pillar, (pē·yâr´) *va.* to pillage, to plunder; to seize, to grab, to snatch *(agarrar).*

pillo, lla, (pē´yo, yâ) *adj.* roguish; **—,** *m.* rogue, rascal.

pilluelo, (pē·ywe´lo) *m.* urchin, scamp.

pimentero, (pē·men·te´ro) *m.* pepper shaker; pepper plant *(mata).*

pimentón, (pē·men·ton´) *m.* paprika; red pepper *(colorado).*

pimienta, (pē·myen´tâ) *f.* pepper.

pimiento, (pē·myen´to) *m.* pepper; red pepper *(colorado).*

pimpollo, (pēm·po´yo) *m.* sprout, bud; (coll.) charming young thing.

pináculo, (pē·nâ´kū·lo) *m.* pinnacle.

pinar, (pē·nâr´) *m.* grove of pines.

pincel, (pēn·sel´) *m.* brush.

pincelada, (pēn·se·lâ´thâ) *f.* brushstroke.

pinchar, (pēn·châr´) *va.* to prick.

pinchazo, (pēn·châ´so) *m.* prick; puncture *(en un neumático).*

pinche, (pēn´che) *m.* kitchen boy, scullion.

pingüe, (pēn´gwe) *adj.* fat, greasy; rich, fertile *(fecundo);* **negocio —,** thriving business.

pingüino, (pēn·gwē´no) *m.* penguin.

pino, na, (pē´no, nâ) *adj.* steep; **—,** *m.* (bot.) pine.

pinocle, (pē·no´kle) *m.* pinochle.

pinta, (pēn´tâ) *f.* spot, mark; sign, mark *(señal);* pint *(medida).*

pintado, da, (pēn·tâ´tho, thâ) *adj.* mottled, spotted; **venir como —do,** to be just the ticket.

pintamonas, (pēn·tâ·mo´nâs) *m.* and *f.* (coll.) bad painter, dauber.

pintar, (pēn·târ´) *va.* to paint; to picture, to describe *(describir);* to exaggerate *(exagerar);* **—,** *vn.* to begin to ripen; (coll.) to show up, to crop out *(mostrarse);* **—se,** to put on one´s make-up.

pintor, ra, (pen·tor´, râ) *n.* painter, artist.

pintoresco, ca, (pēn·to·res´ko, kâ) *adj.* picturesque.

pintorrear, (pēn·to·rre·âr´) *va.* to daub.

pintura, (pēn·tū´râ) *f.* painting, picture *(cuadro);* paint.

pinzas, (pēn´sâs) *f. pl.* pincers; (med.) forceps.

piña, (pē´nyâ) *f.* pineapple; fir cone *(del abeto).*

piñata, (pē·nyâ´tâ) *f.* piñata, decorated jar filled with candy and toys.

piñón, (pē·nyon´) *m.* pineapple seed; pine seed *(del pino);* (mech.) pinion.

pío, pía, (pē´o, pē´â) *adj.* pious, devout; compassionate *(benigno);* —, *m.* peeping, chirping.

piojo, (pyo´ho) *m.* louse.

piojoso, sa, (pyo·ho´so, sâ) *adj.* full of lice, lousy.

piorrea, (pyo·rre´â) *f.* (med.) pyorrhea.

pipa, (pē´pâ) *f.* pipe; fuse *(espoleta);* cask *(barrica).*

pipote, (pē·po´te) *m.* keg.

pique, (pē´ke) *m.* pique, offense; **echar a —,** to sink; **a —,** in danger; steep *(costa).*

piqué, (pē·ke´) *m.* piqué.

piquete, (pē·ke´te) *m.* prick, jab; picket *(estaca);* (mil.) picket; **— de salvas,** firing squad.

piragua, (pē·râ´gwâ) *f.* pirogue.

pirámide, (pē·ra´mē·the) *f.* pyramid.

pirata, (pē·râ´tâ) *m.* pirate; (fig.) cruel wretch.

piromanía, (pē·ro·mâ·nē´â) *f.* pyromania.

piropo, (pē·ro´po) *m.* compliment, flattery.

pirotecnia, (pē·ro·teg´nyâ) *f.* pyrotechnics.

pirueta, (pē·rwe´tâ) *f.* pirouette.

pisada, (pē·sâ´thâ) *f.* footstep, footfall; footprint *(huella).*

pisapapeles, (pē·sâ·pâ·pe´les) *m.* paperweight.

pisar, (pē·sâr´) *va.* to step on, to tread on; to tramp, to stamp down *(apretar);* (fig.) to mistreat; **—le a uno la información,** to wring the information out of.

pisaverde, (pē·sâ·ver´the) *m.* fop, coxcomb, jackanapes.

piscina, (pēs·sē´nâ) *f.* fishpond *(de peces);* swimming pool.

piso, (pē´so) *m.* story; floor *(suelo);* flat, apartment *(vivienda);* **— bajo,** ground floor; **casa de tres —s,** three-story house.

pisotear, (pē·so·te·âr´) *va.* to trample on, to tread under foot.

pista, (pēs´tâ) *f.* trace, footprint *(huella);* track; **— y campo,** track and field; **— de aterrizaje,** landing strip, landing field; **— de despegue,** runway.

pistacho, (pēs·tâ´cho) *m.* pistachio, pistachio nut.

pistola, (pēs·to´lâ) *f.* pistol.

pistoletazo, (pēs·to·le·tâ´so) *m.* pistol shot.

pistón, (pēs·ton´) *m.* piston *(émbolo);* percussion cap.

pita, (pē´tâ) *f.* (bot.) century plant.

pitanza, (pē·tân´sâ) *f.* dole, ration; (Sp. Am.) real bargain.

pitazo, (pē·tâ´so) *m.* whistle; (auto.) honk.

pitillo, (pē·tē´yo) *m.* cigarette.

pito, (pē´to) *m.* whistle; **no me importa un —,** I don´t give a hang.

pituitario, ria, (pē·twē·tâ´ryo, ryâ) *adj.* pituitary.

pizarra, (pē·sâ´rrâ) *f.* slate; blackboard, chalkboard *(pizarrón).*

pizarrón, (pē·sâ·rron´) *m.* blackboard, chalkboard.

pizca, (pēs´kâ) *f.* mite, pinch, bit; **ni—,** not a bit.

pl.: plural, *pl.* plural.

placa, (plâ´kâ) *f.* plaque; sheet, plate *(plancha);* (auto.) license plate.

placentero, ra, (plâ·sen·te´ro, râ) *adj.* pleasant, agreeable.

placer, (plâ·ser´) *m.* pleasure, delight; (min.) placer; —*, vn.* to please.

plaga, (plâ´gâ) *f.* plague.

plagar, (plâ·gâr´) *va.* to plague, to torment.

plagio, (plâ´hyo) *m.* plagiarism.

plácido, da, (plâ´sē·tho, thâ) *adj.* placid, quiet.

plan, (plân) *m.* plan, design, project; **— de vuelo,** (avi.) flight plan; **— quinquenal,** five-year plan.

plana, (plâ´nâ) *f.* trowel; page *(de libro);* level *(llanura);* **— mayor,** (mil.) staff office.

plancha, (plân´châ) *f.* plate, sheet; flatiron *(utensilio).*

planchado, da, (plân·châ´tho, thâ) *adj.* ironed; —*, m.* ironing.

planchadora, (plân·châ·tho´râ) *f.* mangle, ironer.

planchar, (plân·châr´) *va.* to iron, to mangle.

planeador, (plâ·ne·â·thor´) *m.* (avi.) glider.

planear, (plâ·ne·âr´) *vn.* to glide; —*, va.* to plan, to organize.

planeo, (plâ·ne´o) *m.* (avi.) gliding; free flight.

planeta, (plâ·ne´tâ) *m.* planet.

planetario, ria, (plâ·ne·tâ´ryo, ryâ) *adj.* planetary; —*, m.* planetarium.

planicie, (plâ·nē´sye) *f.* plain, prairie.

planificación, (plâ·nē·fē·kâ·syon´) *f.* city planning; **— familiar,** family planning.

planificar, (plâ·nē·fē·kâr´) *va.* to make a plan for, to plan.

plano, na, (plâ´no, nâ) *adj.* level, flat; —*, m.* plan; (math.) plane; **de —no,** right out, directly, flatly; **primer —no,** foreground.

planta, (plân´tâ) *f.* plant; sole *(del pie);* floor plan *(de edificio);* **— baja,** ground floor.

plantación, (plân·tâ·syon´) *f.* plantation;

---

m met, **n** not, **p** pot, **r** very, **rr** (none), **s** so, **t** toy, **th** with, **v** eve, **w** we, **y** yes, **z** zero

planting *(acción)*.

plantaminas, (plän·tâ·mē′näs) *m.* mine layer.

plantar, (plän·tär′) *va.* to plant; to fix upright, to stick *(hincar)*; to put, to place *(colocar)*; to found, to establish *(plantear)*; (coll.) to jilt *(burlar)*; to give *(un golpe)*; **—se,** to stand firm.

plantear, (plän·te·âr′) *va.* to lay out, to plan *(tantear)*; to found *(establecer)*; to propose, to offer *(proponer)*.

plantel, (plän·tel′) *m.* (bot.) nursery; plant, establishment *(de educación)*.

plantilla, (plän·tē′yä) *f.* insole *(suela)*; template, pattern.

plantío, tia, (plän·tē′o, tē′ä) *adj.* planted *(plantado)*; ready to be planted; **—,** *m.* planting *(acción)*; plot, bed.

plañir*, (plä·nyēr′) *vn.* to lament, to grieve, to wail.

plaqueta, (plä·ke′tä) *f.* small plate, tag; **— sanguínea,** blood platelet.

plasma, (pläz′mä) *m.* (biol.) plasma; (min.) plasm.

plástico, ca, (pläs′tē·ko, kä) *adj.* and *m.* plastic.

plata, (plä′tä) *f.* silver; (fig.) money; **en —,** briefly, to the point; **— labrada,** silverware.

plataforma, (plä·tä·for′mä) *f.* platform; **— giratoria,** (rail.) turnplate, turntable; **— de lanzamiento,** launching pad; **— de seguridad,** safety island; **— subterránea de lanzamiento,** (avi.) silo.

plátano, (plä′tä·no) *m.* plantain, banana; plane tree *(árbol)*.

platea, (plä·te′ä) *f.* (theat.) parquet, orchestra seats.

plateado, da, (plä·te·ä′tho, thä) *adj.* silvery; silver-plated.

platear, (plä·te·âr′) *va.* to coat with silver.

platería, (plä·te·rē′ä) *f.* silversmith′s shop; silversmithing *(oficio)*.

platero, (plä·te′ro) *m.* silversmith.

plática, (plä′tē·kä) *f.* conversation, chat.

platicar, (plä·tē·kär′) *vn.* to converse, to chat.

platillo, (plä·tē′yo) *m.* saucer; (mus.) cymbal; **— volador,** flying saucer.

platina, (plä·tē′nä) *f.* microscope slide.

platino, (plä·tē′no) *m.* platinum.

plato, (plä′to) *m.* dish, plate; dish *(vianda)*; **lista de —s,** bill of fare, menu.

platónico, ca, (plä·to′nē·ko, kä) *adj.* Platonic.

plausible, (pläü·sē′vle) *adj.* plausible.

playa, (plä′yä) *f.* beach, strand.

plaza, (plä′sä) *f.* square; market place

(mercado); (mil.) fortified city; place; employment *(empleo)*; sentar (mil.) to enlist; **— de toros,** bull ring.

plazo, (plä′so) *m.* term, date of payment; **a —,** on credit, on time; **a corto —,** short-term; **a — fijo,** for a fixed period.

pleamar, (ple·â·mär′) *f.* high water, flood tide.

plebe, (ple′ve) *f.* common people, populace.

plebeyo, ya, (ple·ve′yo, yä) *adj.* plebeian; **—,** *n.* commoner.

plebiscito, (ple·vēs·sē′to) *m.* plebiscite, referendum.

plegable, (ple·gä′vle) *adj.* pliable; foldable *(doblegable)*.

plegadizo, za, (ple·gä·thē′so, sä) *adj.* folding, collapsible.

plegador, (ple·gä·thor′) *m.* folding machine.

plegar*, (ple·gär′) *va.* to fold *(doblegar)*; to pleat; **—se,** to submit.

plegaria, (ple·gä′ryä) *f.* prayer.

pleitear, (pleē·te·âr′) *va.* and *vn.* to plead, to litigate.

pleitesía, (pleē·te·sē′ä) *f.* agreement, pact; (coll.) tribute, homage; **rendir —,** to pay homage.

pleito, (ple′ē·to) *m.* dispute, controversy, quarrel *(disputa)*; lawsuit, litigation.

plenamente, (ple·nä·men′te) *adv.* fully, completely.

plenario, ria, (ple·nä′ryo, ryä) *adj.* plenary.

plenilunio, (ple·nē·lü′nyo) *m.* full moon.

plenipotenciario, ria, (ple·nē·po·ten·syä′ryo, ryä) *n.* and *adj.* plenipotentiary.

plenitud, (ple·nē·tuth′) *f.* fullness, plenitude.

pleno, na, (ple′no, nä) *adj.* full; **en — invierno,** in the dead of winter.

pleonasmo, (ple·o·näz′mo) *m.* pleonasm.

pleuresía, (pleū·re·sē′ä) *f.* pleurisy.

plexo, (plek′so) *m.* plexus; **— solar,** solar plexus.

pliego, (plye′go) *m.* sheet *(de papel)*; folder *(doblado)*; sealed document.

pliegue, (plye′ge) *m.* fold; pleat.

plomero, (plo·me′ro) *m.* plumber.

plomo, (plo′mo) *m.* lead; **— derretido,** melted lead.

pluma, (plü′mä) *f.* feather; plume *(adorno)*; pen *(para escribir)*; **— estilográfica, — fuente,** fountain pen.

plumada, (plü·mä′thä) *f.* flourish, dash, stroke.

plumaje, (plü·mä′he) *m.* plumage; feathers *(adorno)*.

plumero, (plū·me´ro) *m.* feather duster.
plumífero, ra, (plū·mē´fe·ro, rä) *adj.* (poet.) feathered; —, *n.* hack writer.
plural, (plū·ral´) *adj.* (gram.) plural.
pluralidad, (plū·rä·lē·thäth´) *f.* plurality; numerousness *(multiplicidad).*
plusvalía, (plūz·vä·lē´ä) *f.* increased value, appreciation.
plutócrata, (plū·to´krä·tä) *m.* and *f.* plutocrat.
plutonio, (plū·to´nyo) *m.* plutonium.
pluvial, (plū·vyäl´) *adj.* rainy.
pluviómetro, (plū·vyo´me·tro) *m.* pluviometer.
P.M. or p.m.: pasado meridiano, P.M. afternoon.
P.N.B.: producto nacional bruto, G.N.P., gross national product.
p/o or P.O.: por orden, (com.) by order, as per your order.
población,(po·vlä·syon´) (po·vlä·syon´) *f.* population;
poblacho, (po·vlä´cho) *m.* populace, rabble.
poblado, (po·vlä´tho) *m.* town, village, hamlet.
poblar*, (po·vlär´) *va.* to populate, to people; —, *vn.* to procreate; —se, to bud.
pobre, (po´vre) *adj.* poor, indigent; wanting, deficient *(escaso).*
pobreza, (po·vre´sä) *f.* poverty, poorness; (fig.) sterility, barrenness.
pocilga, (po·sēl´gä) *f.* pigsty.
poción, (po·syon´) *f.* potion.
poco, ca, (po´ko, kä) *adj.* little; —s, *pl.* few; —o, *adv.* little; — a —, gradually, little by little; hace —, a short time ago, a little while ago; a —, shortly after, very soon; tan — como, as little as; — común, unusual; — bondadoso, unkind; por —, almost; —, *m.* small part; un —, a little.
poda, (po´thä) *f.* pruning.
podar, (po·thär´) *va.* to prune.
podenco, (po·theng´ko) *m.* hound.
poder, (po·ther´) *m.* power; possession *(posesión);* proxy *(instrumento);* — adquisitivo, purchasing power; en — de, in the hands of; por —, by proxy; a más no —, to the limit, to the utmost; —*, *vn.* to be able; to be possible *(ser contingente).*
poderío, (po·the·rē´o) *m.* power, authority; wealth, riches *(abundancia).*
poderoso, sa, (po·the·ro´so, sä) *adj.* powerful; eminent *(eminente).*
podredumbre, (po·thre·thūm´bre) *f.* putrid matter; (fig.) grief.

podrir* (po·thrēr´) = pudrir.
poema, (po·e´mä) *m.* poem.
poesía, (po·e·sē´ä) *f.* poetry.
poeta, (po·e´tä) *m.* poet.
poético, ca, (po·e´tē·ko, kä) *adj.* poetic.
poetisa, (po·e·tē´sä) *f.* poetess.
polaco, ca, (po·lä´ko, kä) *adj.* Polish; —, *n.* Pole; —, *m.* Polish language.
polaina, (po·lä´ē·nä) *f.* legging, gaiter; —s, *pl.* spats.
polar, (po·lär´) *adj.* polar.
polca, (pol´kä) *f.* polka.
polea, (po·le´ä) *f.* pulley; (naut.) tackle.
polémica, (po·le´mē·kä) *f.* polemics; polemic *(controversia).*
polen, (po´len) *m.* (bot.) pollen.
policía, (po·lē·sē´ä) *f.* police; vigilante de —, patrolman; —, *m.* policeman.
policiaco, ca, (po·lē·syä´ko, kä) *adj.* police; novela —, detective story, whodunit.
policromo, ma, (po·lē·kro´mo, mä) *adj.* multicolored.
polietileno, (po·lye·tē·le´no) *n.* (chem.) polyethylene.
polifacético, ca, (po·lē·fä·se´tē·ko, kä) *adj.* of many aspects, many-sided.
poligamia, (po·lē·gä´myä) *f.* polygamy.
polígamo, ma, (po·lē´gä·mo, mä) *n.* polygamist; —, *adj.* polygamous.
polígono, (po·lē´go·no) *m.* polygon.
polilla, (po·lē´yä) *f.* moth.
polimerización, (po·lē·me·rē·sä·syon´) *f.* polymerization.
polímero, (po·lē´me·ro) *m.* polymer.
poliomielitis, (po·lyo·mye·lē´tēs) *f.* polio, infantile paralysis.
política, (po·lē´tē·kä) *f.* politics; policy *(programa);* manners, tact *(cortesía).*
politico, ca, (po·lē´tē·ko, kä) *adj.* political; polite *(urbano);* padre —co, father-in-law; —, *m.* politician.
póliza, (po´lē·sä) *f.* policy; — de seguro, insurance policy.
polizón, (po·lē·son´) *m.* bum, loafer; (naut.) stowaway.
polo, (po´lo) *m.* (geog. and elec.) pole; polo.
polonesa, (po·lo·ne´sä) *f.* *(mus.)* polonaise.
Polonia, (po·lo´nyä) *f.* Poland.
poltrón, ona, (pol·tron´, o´nä) *adj.* idle, lazy; silla —, armchair; —, *n.* poltroon, coward.
poluto, ta, (po·lū´to, tä) *adj.* filthy, dirty.
polvareda, (pol·vä·re´thä) *f.* cloud of dust.
polvera, (pol·ve´rä) *f.* compact.
polvo, (pol´vo) *m.* powder; dust *(tierra menuda);* — dentífrico, tooth powder; — de hornear, baking powder; — de

talco, talcum powder; **en —,** powdered.

pólvora, (pol´vo·rà) *f.* gunpowder; fireworks *(fuegos artificiales).*

polvorear, (pol·vo·re·âr´) *va.* to powder.

polvoriento, ta, (pol·vo·ryen´to, tâ) *adj.* dusty.

polvorín, (pol·vo·rēn´) *m.* finely ground gunpowder; powder flask *(cebador);* powder magazine *(santabárbara);* (fig.) tinderbox.

polvoroso, sa, (pol·vo·ro´so, sâ) *adj.* dusty; **poner pies en —sa,** (coll.) to take off, to beat it.

polla, (po´yâ) *f.* pullet; kitty, pool *(en los juegos).*

pollada, (po·yâ´thâ) *f.* covey, brood.

pollera, (po·ye´râ) *f.* (Sp. Am.) skirt *(falda);* chicken yard.

pollo, (po´yo) *m.* young chick.

pomada, (po·mâ´thâ) *f.* pomade.

pomerano, na, (po·me·ra´no, nâ) *adj.* and *n.* Pomeranian.

pómez, (po´mes) *f.* pumice stone.

pomo, (po´mo) *m.* (bot.) pome; pommel.

pompa, (pom´pâ) *f.* pomp, grandeur; bubble *(esfera);* **empresario de —s fúnebres,** undertaker, mortician.

pompón, (pom·pon´) *m.* pompon.

pomposo, sa, (pom·po´so, sâ) *adj.* pompous, ostentatious; magnificent *(magnifico).*

pómulo, (po´mū·lo) *m.* cheekbone.

ponche, (pon´che) *m.* punch; eggnog *(de huevo).*

ponchera, (pon·che´râ) *f.* punchbowl.

poncho, (pon´cho) *m.* (Sp. Am.) poncho.

ponderación, (pon·de·râ·syon´) *f.* ponderation, consideration; exaggeration *(exageración).*

ponderar, (pon·de·râr´) *va.* to weigh, to consider; to extol *(encarecer).*

ponencia, (po·nen´syâ) *f.* report, paper.

poner*, (po·ner´) *va.* to put, to place; to set *(preparar);* to suppose, to assume *(suponer);* to take *(tardar);* (theat.) to put on; to instill *(causar);* to lay *(huevos);* **— al corriente,** to bring up to date, to inform; **— casa,** to set up housekeeping; **— por escrito,** to put in writing; **— precio,** to set a price; **— la mesa,** to set the table; **— reparo,** to object; **—se,** to become, to get; to set *(el sol);* to put on *(la ropa);* **—se a,** to begin to, to set about; **—se de acuerdo,** to agree; **—se en marcha,** to start, to start out; **—se de pie,** to stand up.

poniente, (po·nyen´te) *m.* west; west wind *(viento).*

pontífice, (pon·tē´fē·se) *m.* pontiff.

pontón, (pon·ton´) *m.* pontoon.

ponzoñoso, sa, (pon·so·nyo´so, sâ) *adj.* poisonous.

popa, (po´pâ) *f.* (naut.) poop, stern.

popelina, (po·pe·lē´nâ) *f.* poplin.

popof, (po·pof´) *adj.* (Mex.) elegant, aristocratic; snobbish, high-hat *(presumido).*

popote, (po·po´te), *m.*(Mex.) drinking straw.

populacho, (po·pū·lâ´cho) *m.* populace, mob, rabble.

popular, (po·pū·lâr´) *adj.* popular.

popularidad, (po·pū·lâ·rē·thâth´) *f.* popularity.

populoso, sa, (po·pū·lo´so, sâ) *adj.* populous.

popurrí, (po·pū·rre´) *m.* potpourri, medley.

póquer, (po´ker) *m.* poker.

poquito, ta, (po·kē´to, tâ) *adj.* very little; **—,** *m.* a very little; **—to a —to,** little by little, bit by bit.

por, (por) *prep.* by *(causa);* over, through *(a través de);* as *(como);* through, by means of *(manera);* for; around, about *(aproximación);* **¿— qué?** why?; **— lo tanto,** as a result.

porcelana, (por·se·lâ´nâ) *f.* porcelain.

porcentaje, (por·sen·tâ´he) *m.* percentage.

porción, (por·syon´) *f.* portion.

pordiosear, (por·thyo·se·âr´) *vn.* to beg alms, to go begging.

pordiosero, ra, (por·thyo·se´ro, râ) *n.* beggar.

porfía, (por·fē´â) *f.* stubbornness, obstinacy; **a —,** in competition.

porfiado, da, (por·fyâ´tho, thâ) *adj.* obstinate, stubborn.

porfiar, (por·fyâr´) *vn.* to dispute obstinately; to persist in, to be dogged in *(insistir).*

pormenor, (por·me·nor´) *m.* detail.

pornográfico, ca, (por·no·grâ´fē·ko, kâ) *adj.* pornographic.

poro, (po´ro) *m.* pore.

poroso, sa, (po·ro´so, sâ) *adj.* porous.

porque, (por´ke) *conj.* because; so that, in order that *(para que).*

porqué, (por·ke´) *m.* cause, reason; (coll.) amount.

porquería, (por·ke·rē´â) *f.* nastiness, foulness; trifle *(bagatela);* vile action *(acción).*

porra, (po´rrâ) *f.* club; (coll.) last *(en un juego);* bore *(sujeto pesado);* (Mex.) rooters, backers.

porrazo, (po·rrâ´so) *m.* blow with a club.

portaaviones, (por·tâ·â·vyo´nes) *m.* aircraft carrier, flattop.

portada, (por·tâ´thâ) f. title page, frontispiece; cover *(de revista)*; facade *(de edificio)*.

portador, ra, (por·tâ·thor´, râ) n. carrier, bearer; porter *(porteador)*.

portaestandarte, (por·tâ·es·tân·dâr´te) m. (mil.) standard bearer.

portal, (por·tâl´) m. vestibule *(zaguán)*; portico, porch *(pórtico)*; creche(*belén)*.

portamonedas, (por·tâ·mo·ne´thas) m. purse, pocketbook, coin purse.

portaplumas, (por·tâ·plū´mâs) m. penholder.

portar, (por·târ´) va. to carry, to bear; —se, to behave, to conduct oneself.

portátil, (por·tâ´tēl) adj. portable.

portavoz, (por·tâ·vos´) m. megaphone; (fig.) mouthpiece, spokesman.

portazgo, (por·tâz´go) m. toll.

portazo, (por·tâ´so) m. bang of a door, slam of a door.

porte, (por´te) m. portage; freight, postage *(costo)*; conduct, bearing, carriage *(presencia)*; — a cobrar, charges collect; — pagado or cobrado, charges prepaid.

portento, (por·ten´to) m. prodigy, wonder.

portentoso, sa, (por·ten·to´so, sâ) adj. prodigious, marvelous.

porteo, (por·te´o) m. portage, transport.

portería, (por·te·rē´â) f. entryway; janitoring *(empleo)*.

portero, ra, (por·te´ro, râ) n. porter, janitor; —, m. goal keeper.

pórtico, (por´tē·ko) m. portico, porch.

portón, (por·ton´) m. gate, entrance.

portuario, ria, (por·twá´ryo, ryâ) adj. port.

portugués, esa, (por·tū·ges´, e´sa) n. and adj. Portuguese; —, m. Portuguese language.

porvenir, (por·ve·nēr´) m. future.

pos, (pos) en —, after, behind.

posada, (po·sâ´thâ) f. boardinghouse, inn *(albergue)*; lodging; (Mex.) Christmas party.

posar, (po·sâr´) vn. to lodge, to put up *(hospedarse)*; to rest *(descansar)*; to perch, to alight *(las aves)*; to pose; —, va. to set down; —se, to rest; to settle *(un líquido)*.

posdata, (poz·thâ´tâ) f. postscript.

poseedor, ra, (po·se·e·thor´, râ) n. owner, possessor; —, adj. possessing, owning.

poseer*, (po·se·er´) va. to hold, to possess, to own.

poseído, da, (po·se·ē´tho, thâ) adj. possessed.

posesión, (po·se·syon´) f. possession.

posesivo, va, (po·se·sē´vo, vâ) adj. (gram.) possessive.

posgraduado, da, (poz·grâ·thwâ´tho, thâ) n. postgraduate.

posibilidad, (po·sē·vē·lē·thâth´) f. possibility.

posible, (po·sē´vle) adj. possible; hacer lo —, to do one´s best; lo más pronto —, as soon as possible.

posición, (po·sē·syon´) f. position.

positivo, va, (po·sē·tē´vo, vâ) adj. positive.

positrón, (po·sē·tron´) m. positron.

poso, (po´so) m. sediment, dregs, lees; rest *(descanso)*.

pospierna, (pos·pyer´nâ) f. thigh.

posponer*, (pos·po·ner´) va. to postpone, to defer, to put off.

posta, (pos´tâ) f. relay; post house *(casa)*; leg *(distancia)*.

postal, (pos·tâl´) adj. postal; paquete —, parcel post.

poste, (pos´te) m. post, pillar; — de amarre, mooring mast.

postema, (pos·te´mâ) f. abscess; (fig.) bore.

postergar, (pos·ter·gâr´) va. to defer, to delay.

posteridad, (pos·te·rē·thâth´) f. posterity.

posterior, (pos·te·ryor´) adj. posterior, back, rear.

posteriormente, (pos·te·ryor·men´te) adv. later, subsequently.

postigo, (pos·tē´go) m. wicket; postern *(puerta pequeña)*.

postizo, za, (pos·tē´so, sâ) adj. artificial, false; dientes —zos, false teeth.

postnatal, (post·nâ·tâl´) adj. postnatal.

postor, (pos·tor´) m. bidder.

postración, (pos·trâ·syon´) f. prostration.

postrar, (pos·trâr´) va. to humble, to humiliate; (fig.) to weaken; —se, to prostrate oneself; to kneel down *(arrodillarse)*.

postre, (pos´tre) adj. last in order; a la —, at last; —, m. dessert.

postrer, (pos·trer´) or postrero, ra, (pos·tre´ro, râ) adj. last.

postular, (pos·tū·lâr´) va. to postulate, to seek.

póstumo, ma, (pos´tū·mo, mâ) adj. posthumous.

postura, (pos·tū´râ) f. posture, position; price offered *(oferta)*; bet, wager *(apuesta)*.

potaje, (po·tâ´he) m. pottage; (fig.) hodgepodge.

potasa, (po·tâ´sâ) f. potash.

potasio, (po·tâ´syo) m. potassium.

pote, (po´te) m. pot, jar.

m met, n not, p pot, r very, rr (none), s so, t toy, th with, v eve, w we, y yes, z zero

potencia, (po·ten´syâ) *f.* power; potential (posibilidad); **las grandes —s,** the great powers.

potencial, (po·ten·syâl´) *m.* (elec.) potential.

potencialidad, (po·ten·syâ·lē·thâth´) *f.* potentiality.

potentado, (po·ten·tâ´tho) *m.* potentate.

potente, (po·ten´te) *adj.* potent, powerful.

potestad, (po·tes·tâth´) *f.* power, dominion, jurisdiction.

potro, (po´tro) *m.* colt, foal; rack *(caballete); (fig.)* cross, burden.

pozo, (po´so) *m.* well; (min.) shaft.

P.P.: porte pagado, p.p. postpaid.

p.p.: por poder, by power of attorney, by proxy.

ppdo., p. pdo or **p.º p.ᵈᵒ: próximo pasado,** ult. in the past month.

práctica, (prâk´tē·kâ) *f.* practice; skill *(destreza).*

practicable, (prâk·tē·kâ´vle) *adj.* practicable, feasible.

practicante, (prâk·tē·kân´te) *m.* and *f.* (med.) intern.

practicar, (prâk·tē·kâr´) *va.* to practice; to exercise, to make use of *(ejercer).*

práctico, ca, (prâk´tē·ko, kâ) *adj.* practical; skillful *(diestro).*

pradera, (prâ·the´râ) *f.* meadowland.

prado, (prâ´tho) *m.* meadow.

preámbulo, (pre·âm´bū·lo) *m.* preamble; dodge, evasion *(rodeo).*

preboste, (pre·vos´te) *m.* provost.

precario, ria, (pre·kâ´ryo, ryâ) *adj.* precarious.

precaución, (pre·kâū·syon´) *f.* precaution.

precaver, (pre·kâ·ver´) *va.* to prevent, to guard against.

precedente, (pre·se·then´te) *adj.* precedent, foregoing; **—,** *m.* precedent; **sin —,** unequalled, unexcelled, all-time.

preceder, (pre·se·ther´) *va.* to precede, to go before.

precepto, (pre·sep´to) *m.* precept; order *(mandato).*

preceptor, (pre·sep·tor´) *m.* teacher; preceptor *(ayo).*

preces, (pre´ses) *f. pl.* prayers, devotions.

preciado, da, (pre·syâ´tho, thâ) *adj.* valued, esteemed; proud, presumptuous *(vano).*

preciar, (pre·syâr´) *va.* to value, to appraise; **—se de,** to take pride in, to boast.

precio, (pre´syo) *m.* price; value *(valor);* **— de costo,** cost price; **— al por mayor,** wholesale price; **— al por menor,** retail

price; **— de venta,** sale price; **poner —,** to set a price; **último —,** best or lowest price; **— tope** or **— límite,** ceiling price; **control de —s,** price control.

precioso, sa, (pre·syo´so, sâ) *adj.* precious; (coll.) beautiful *(bello);* **piedra —,** gem.

precipicio, (pre·cē·pē´syo) *m.* precipice, cliff; violent fall *(caída);* (fig.) ruin, disaster.

precipitación, (pre·se·pē·tâ·syon´) *f.* precipitation.

precipitado, da, (pre·sē·pē·tâ´tho, thâ) *adj.* precipitous.

precipitar, (pre·sē·pē·târ´) *va.* to precipitate; to dash, to cast *(lanzar);* **—se,** to run headlong, to rush.

precisar, (pre·sē·sâr´) *va.* to compel, to oblige *(obligar);* to necessitate *(necesitar);* to state *(explicar);* **—,** *vn.* to be necessary.

precisión, (pre·sē·syon´) *f.* precision; necessity *(obligación);* **con toda —,** on time, very promptly.

preciso, sa, (pre·se´so, sâ) *adj.* necessary, requisite; precise, exact *(exacto).*

precoz, (pre·kos´) *adj.* precocious.

precursor, ra, (pre·kūr·sor´, râ) *n.* forerunner; **—,** *adj.* preceding.

predecesor, ra, (pre·the·se·sor´, râ) *n.* predecessor, forerunner.

predecir*, (pre·the·sēr´) *va.* to foretell, to predict.

predestinación, (pre·thes·tē·nâ·syon´) *f.* predestination.

predeterminar, (pre·the·ter·mē·nâr´) *va.* to predetermine.

predicado, (pre·thē·kâ´tho) *m.* (gram.) predicate.

predicador, (pre·thē·kâ·thor´) *m.* preacher.

predicamento, (pre·thē·kâ·men´to) *m.* predicament; reputation *(estima).*

predicar, (pre·thē·kâr´) *va.* to preach; to praise to the skies *(alabar);* to advise, to counsel *(amonestar).*

predicción, (pre·thēk·syon´) *f.* prediction.

predilección, (pre·thē·lek·syon´) *f.* predilection, preference.

predilecto, ta, (pre·thē·lek´to, tâ) *adj.* darling, favorite; preferred *(preferido).*

predio, (pre´thyo) *m.* landed property, estate; **— rústico,** farm site; **— urbano,** town property.

predisponer*, (pre·thēs·po·ner´) *va.* to predispose.

predispuesto, ta, (pre·thēs·pwes´to,tâ) *adj.* biased, predisposed.

predominante, (pre·tho·mē·nan´te) *adj.*

predominating, predominant.
predominar, (pre·tho·mē·nâr´) va. and vn. to predominate.
predominio, (pre·tho·mē´nyo) m. predominance.
preeminencia, (pre·e·mē·nen´ syâ) f. preeminence.
prefabricar, (pre·fâ·vrē·kâr´) vt. to prefabricate.
prefacio, (pre·fâ´syo) m. preface.
prefecto, (pre·fek´to) m. prefect.
preferencia, (pre·fe·ren´syâ) f. preference; de —, preferably.
preferente, (pre·fe·ren´te) adj. preferred, preferable; acciones —s, preferred stock.
preferible, (pre·fe·rē´vle) adj. preferable.
preferir*, (pre·fe·rēr´) va. to prefer.
pregón, (pre·gon´) m. proclamation.
pregonar, (pre·go·nâr´) va. to proclaim, to announce; to peddle, to hawk (una mercancía).
pregunta, (pre·gūn´tâ) f. question; hacer una —, to ask a question.
preguntar, (pre·gūn·târ´) va. to question, to ask; —se, to wonder.
preguntón, ona, (pre·gūn·ton´, o´nâ) n. inquisitive person; —, adj. inquisitive.
prehistórico, ca, (preēs·to´rē·ko, kâ) adj. prehistoric.
prejuicio, (pre·hwē´syo) m. prejudice.
prelado, (pre·lâ´tho) m. prelate.
preliminar, (pre·lē·mē·nâr´) adj. preliminary; —es, m. pl. preliminaries, preliminary steps.
preludio, (pre·lū´thyo) m. prelude.
prematuro, ra, (pre·mâ·tū´ro, râ) adj. premature.
premeditación, (pre·me·thē·tâ·syon´) f. premeditation.
premeditar, (pre·me·thē·târ´) va. to premeditate.
premiar, (pre·myâr´) va. to reward, to remunerate.
premio, (pre´myo) m. reward, prize; (com.) premium.
premisa, (pre·mē´sâ) f. premise.
premura, (pre·mū´râ) f. haste, hurry, urgency (instancia); difficult situation (apuro).
prenatal, (pre·nâ·tâl´) adj. prenatal.
prenda, (pren´dâ) f. pledge (prueba); pawn (seguridad); piece of jewelry (alhaja); trait, quality (cualidad); loved one; — de vestir, article of clothing; —s, pl. accomplishments, talents.
prendar, (pren·dâr´) va. to pledge; to ingratiate oneself (ganar la voluntad);

—se de, to take a fancy to, to be charmed by.
prender, (pren·der´) va. to seize, to catch (asir); to imprison (aprisionar); to pin on (clavar); (P.R.) to kindle (encender); —, vn. to catch fire (encenderse); to take root (arraigar); —se, to get dressed up.
prensa, (pren´sâ) f, press; dar a la —, to have published; P— Asociada, Associated Press.
prensar, (pren·sâr´) va. to press.
preñado, da, (pre·nyâ´tho, thâ) adj. pregnant; (fig.) full (lleno).
preocupación, (pre·o·kū·pâ·syon´) f. care, preoccupation; bias, prejudice (prejuicio).
preocupar, (pre·o·kū·pâr´) va. to worry, to preoccupy; —se por, to care about, to worry about.
prep.: preposición, prep. preposition.
preparación, (pre·pâ·râ·syon´) f. preparation.
preparar, (pre·pâ·râr´) va. to prepare; — se, to get ready.
preparativos, (pre·pâ·râ·tē´vos) m. pl. preparations, preliminary steps.
preparatorio, ria, (pre·pâ·râ·to´ryo, ryâ) adj. preparatory.
preponderancia, (pre·pon·de·rân´syâ) f. preponderance.
preponderar, (pre·pon·de·râr´) vn. to prevail.
preposición, (pre·po·sē·syon´) f. (gram.) preposition.
prerrogativa, (pre·rro·gâ·tē´vâ) f. prerogative.
presa, (pre´sâ) f. capture, seizure; prey, catch (cosa apresada); dam (en un río); hold (en la lucha); —s, pl. tusks (colmillos); claws (uñas).
presagio, (pre·sâ´hyo) m. presage, omen.
présbita, (prez´vē·tâ) or présbite, (prez´vē·te) adj. farsighted.
presbítero, (prez·vē´te·ro) m. priest.
prescindir, (pres·sēn·dēr´) vn. — de, to disregard, to dispense with; to do without (privarse).
prescribir*, (pres·krē·vēr´) va. to prescribe.
prescripción, (pres·krēp·syon´) f. prescription.
presencia, (pre·sen´syâ) f. presence; appearance (aspecto); — de ánimo, serenity.
presenciar, (pre·sen·syâr´) va. to witness, to see.
presentación, (pre·sen·tâ·syon´) f. presentation; introduction; a —, (com.) at

sight.

presentar, (pre·sen·târ´) va. to present, to introduce *(introducir);* — al cobro, to present for payment; —se, to appear; to introduce oneself.

presente, (pre·sen´te) *adj.* present; —, *m.* present, gift; al —, at present, at the moment; el 20 del —, the 20th of the current month; hacer —, to call attention; la —, the present writing; tener —, to keep in mind.

presentimiento, (pre·sen·tē·myen´to) *m.* presentiment, premonition.

presentir*, (pre·sen·tēr´) va. to have a premonition of.

preservación, (pre·ser·vâ·syon´) f. preservation, protection.

preservar, (pre·ser·vâr´) va. to preserve, to protect.

presidencia, (pre·sē·then´syâ) f. presidency.

presidencial, (pre·sē·then·syal´) *adj.* presidential.

presidente, (pre·sē·then´te) *m.* president; chairman *(de un comité).*

presidiario, (pre·sē·thyâ´ryo) *m.* convict.

presidio, (pre·sē´thyo) *m.* penitentiary, prison; (mil.) garrison.

presidir, (pre·sē·thēr´) va. to preside over.

presilla, (pre·sē´yä) f. loop, fastener.

presión, (pre·syon´) f. pressure; — arterial, — sanguínea, blood pressure; — de vapor, steam pressure.

preso, sa, (pre´so, sâ) *n.* prisoner; —, *adj.* imprisoned.

prestamista, (pres·tâ·mēs´tâ) *m.* and *f.* moneylender.

préstamo, (pres´tâ·mo) *m.* loan.

prestar, (pres·târ´) va. to lend, to loan; pedir prestado, to borrow.

presteza, (pres·te´sâ) f. quickness, haste, speed.

prestidigitador, ra, (pres·tē·thē·hē·tâ thor´, râ) *n.* prestidigitator.

prestigio, (pres·tē´hyo) *m.* prestige; illusion *(engaño).*

presto, ta, (pres´to, tâ) *adj.* quick, prompt, ready; —to, *adv.* quickly, in a hurry.

presumido, da, (pre·sū·mē´tho, thâ) *adj.* presumptuous, arrogant; vain, prideful *(vanidoso).*

presumir, (pre·sū·mēr´) va. to presume; —, *vn.* to boast, to have a high opinion of oneself.

presunción, (pre·sūn·syon´) f. presumption; conceit *(amor propio).*

presunto, ta, (pre·sūn´to, tâ) *adj.* presumed, presumptive; — heredero, heir apparent.

presuntuoso, sa, (pre·sūn·two´so, sâ) *adj.* presumptuous, vain.

presuponer*, (pre·sū·po·ner´) va. to presuppose; to budget *(hacer un presupuesto).*

presupuesto, (pre·sū·pwes´to) *m.* budget; reason *(motivo).*

presuroso, sa, (pre·sū·ro´so, sâ) *adj.* hasty, prompt, quick.

pretender, (pre·ten·der´) va. to pretend to, to claim; to try, to attempt *(intentar);* to maintain, to contend *(sostener).*

pretendiente, (pre·ten·dyen´te) *m.* pretender; suitor *(novio);* candidate, office seeker *(candidato).*

pretensión, (pre·ten·syon´) f. pretension; effort *(empeño).*

pretérito, ta, (pre·te´rē·to, tâ) *adj.* preterit, past; —, *m.* (gram.) past tense.

pretexto, (pre·tes´to) *m.* pretext, pretense.

pretina, (pre·tē´nâ) f. waistband; belt *(cinturón).*

prevalecer*, (pre·vâ·le·ser´) vn. to prevail; to take root *(arraigar).*

prevención, (pre·ven·syon´) f. prevention; preparation *(preparación);* —ones, *pl.* provisions.

prevenido, da, (pre·ve·nē´tho, thâ) *adj.* prepared, provided *(provisto);* well-stocked, stocked, abundant *(abundante);* provident, careful, cautious, foresighted *(providente).*

prevenir*, (pre·ve·nēr´) va. to prepare *(preparar);* to foresee, to foreknow *(prever);* to prevent *(impedir);* to advise, to warn *(advertir);* —se, to get ready.

preventivo, va, (pre·ven·tē´vo, vâ) *m.* and *adj.* preventive.

prever*, (pre·ver´) va. to foresee, to forecast.

previo, via, (pre´vyo, vyâ) *adj.* previous, former; — el depósito de, upon deposit of.

previsión, (pre·vē·syon´) f. foresight, prevision, forecast.

previsor, ra, (pre·vē·sor´, râ) *adj.* foresighted, far-sighted; —, *n.* foreseer.

prez, (pres) *m.* or *f.* glory, honor.

prieto, ta, (prye´to, tâ) *adj.* blackish, very dark; compact, tight *(apretado);* —, *n.* very dark-complexioned person.

prima, (prē´mâ) f. prime; (mus.) treble; (com.) premium.

primacía, (prē·mâ·sē´â) f. primacy; (eccl.) primateship.

primario, ria, (prē·mâ´ryo, ryâ) *adj.* primary; escuela —, elementary school.

primavera, (prē·mâ·ve´rä) *f.* spring.
primaveral, (prē·mâ·ve·râl´) *adj.* spring-like.
primer, (prē·mer´) *adj.* (apocope of primero) first; **en — lugar,** in the first place.
primeramente, (prē·me·râ·men´te) *adv.* previously.
primero, ra, (prē·me´ro, râ) *adj.* first; prior, former *(antiguo);* **—s auxilios,** first aid; **— enseñanza,** primary education; **por —ra vez,** for the first time; **— ro,** *adv.* rather, sooner.
primicia, (prē·mē´syâ) *f.* first fruits.
primitivo, va, (prē·mē·tē´vo, vâ) *adj.* primitive.
primo, ma, (prē´mo, mâ) *adj.* first; —, *n.* cousin.
primogénito, ta, (prē·mo·he´nē·to, tâ) *adj.* and *n.* first-born.
primor, (prē·mor´) *m.* beauty; dexterity, ability *(habilidad).*
primordial, (prē·mor·thyâl´) *adj.* primordial.
primoroso, sa, (prē·mo·ro´so, sâ) *adj.* elegant, fine, excellent; able, accomplished *(diestro).*
princesa, (prēn·se´sâ) *f.* princess.
principado, (prēn·sē·pâ´tho) *m.* princedom *(título);* principality.
principal, (prēn·sē·pâl´) *adj.* principal, chief, main.
principalmente, (prēn·sē·pâl·men´te) *adv.* mainly, principally, for the most part.
príncipe, (prēn´sē·pe) *m.* prince.
principiante, (prēn·sē·pyân´te) *m.* and *f.* beginner; learner.
principiar, (prēn·sē·pyâr´) *va.* to commence, to begin.
principio, (prēn·sē´pyo) *m.* beginning, commencement; principle *(fundamento);* **en —,** essentially; **al —,** at the beginning; **desde un —,** from the beginning.
prioridad, (pryo·rē·thâth´) *f.* priority.
prisa, (prē´sâ) *f.* hurry, haste; **a toda —,** at full speed; **darse —,** to hurry; **tener —,** to be in a hurry; **con —,** in a hurry.
prisión, (prē·syon´) *f.* seizure, capture; prison *(cárcel);* **—ones,** *pl.* fetters.
prisionero, ra, (prē·syo·ne´ro, râ) *n.* prisoner; (fig.) captive, slave.
prisma, (prēz´mâ) *m.* prism.
privación, (prē·vâ·syon´) *f.* privation.
privado, da, (prē·vâ´tho, thâ) *adj.* private; devoid *(careciente).*
privar, (prē·vâr´) *va.* to deprive; to prohibit *(prohibir);* **—se,** to deprive oneself.

privilegiado, da, (prē·vē·le·hyâ´tho, thâ) *adj.* privileged, favorite.
privilegio, (prē·vē·le´hyo) *m.* privilege.
pro, (pro) *m.* or *f.* profit, benefit, advantage; **en — de,** in behalf of; **el — y el contra,** the pros and cons.
proa, (pro´â) *f.* (naut.) prow.
probabilidad, (pro·vâ·vē·lē·thâth´) *f.* probability, likelihood; **ley de —es,** law of averages.
probable, (pro·vâ´vle) *adj.* probable, likely.
probado, da, (pro·vâ´tho, thâ) *adj.* proved, tried.
probar*, (pro·vâr´) *va.* to try; to prove *(comprobar);* to taste *(saborear);* to examine, to test *(examinar);* to justify *(justificar);* —, *vn.* to suit, to agree; **— se,** to try on.
probeta, (pro·ve´tâ) *f.* test tube.
probidad, (pro·vē·thâth´) *f.* probity.
problema, (pro·vle´mâ) *m.* problem.
problemático, ca, (pro·vle·mâ´tē·ko, kâ) *adj.* problematical.
probo, ba, (pro´vo, vâ) *adj.* upright, honest.
procedencia, (pro·se·then´syâ) *f.* origin, source.
procedente, (pro·se·then´te) *adj.* coming, proceeding, originating.
proceder, (pro·se·ther´) *m.* procedure, behavior; —, *vn.* to proceed; to be wise *(convenir).*
procedimiento, (pro·se·thē·myen´to) *m.* procedure.
prócer, (pro´ser) *adj.* lofty; —, *m.* leader, outstanding figure.
procesar, (pro·se·sâr´) *va.* to sue, to prosecute; to indict *(acusar).*
procesión, (pro·se·syon´) *f.* procession; parade *(desfile).*
proceso, (pro·se´so) *m.* process, lawsuit; **en — de quiebra,** in a state of bankruptcy, in the hands of the receivers.
proclama, (pro·klâ´mâ) *f.* proclamation.
proclamación, (pro·klâ·mâ·syon´) *f.* proclamation; acclamation *(alabanza pública).*
proclamar, (pro·klâ·mâr´) *va.* to proclaim.
procrear, (pro·kre·âr´) *va.* to procreate.
procurador, (pro·kū·râ·thor´) *m.* attorney; (eccl.) procurator; **— público,** attorney at law; **P— General,** Attorney General.
procurar, (pro·kū·râr´) *va.* to act as attorney for; to try, to attempt *(intentar).*
prodigalidad, (pro·thē·gâ·lē·thâth´) *f.* prodigality.
prodigar, (pro·thē·gâr´) *va.* to waste, to lavish

prodigio, (pro·thē´hyo) *m.* prodigy, marvel, wonder.

prodigioso, sa, (pro·thē·hyo´so, sâ) *adj.* prodigious; excellent, fine *(admirable)*.

pródigo, ga, (pro´thē·go, gâ) *adj.* prodigal; lavish *(dadivoso)*.

producción, (pro·thū·syon´) *f.* production; — en serie, mass production.

producir*, (pro·thū·sēr´) *va.* to produce.

productivo, va, (pro·thūk·tē´vo, vâ) *adj.* productive.

producto, (pro·thū´to) *m.* product; proceeds, receipts *(beneficio)*; — en bruto; gross receipts; — neto or líquido, net proceeds; —s, *pl.* produce; —s alimenticios, foodstuffs.

proeza, (pro·e´sâ) *f.* prowess, exploit.

prof.: profesor, prof. professor; profeta, prophet.

profanación, (pro·fâ·nâ·syon´) *f.* profanation.

profanar, (pro·fâ·nâr´) *va.* to profane, to desecrate.

profano, na, (pro·fâ´no, nâ) *adj.* profane.

profecía, (pro·fe·sē´â) *f.* prophecy.

proferir*, (pro·fe·rēr´) *va.* to utter, to exclaim.

profesar, (pro·fe·sâr´) *va.* to profess; —, *vn.* (eccl.) to take one´s vows, to enter a religious order.

profesión, (pro·fe·syon´) *f.* profession.

profesional, (pro·fe·syo·nâl´) *adj. and m. and f.* professional.

profesor, ra, (pro·fe·sor´, râ) *n.* professor *(catedrático)*; teacher.

profesorado, (pro·fe·so·râ´tho) *m.* teachers, faculty; professorship *(cargo)*.

profeta, (pro·fe´tâ) *m.* prophet.

profético, ca, (pro·fe´tē·ko, kâ) *adj.* prophetic.

profetizar, (pro·fe·tē·sâr´) *va.* to prophesy.

profiláctico, ca, (pro·fē·lâk´tē·ko, kâ) *m. and adj.* prophylactic.

prófugo, ga, (pro´fū·go, gâ) *adj.* fugitive.

profundidad, (pro·fūn·dē·thâth´) *f.* profoundness, depth; carga de —, (mil.) depth charge.

profundizar, (pro·fūn·dē·sâr´) *va.* deepen; (fig.) to penetrate into, to go into.

profundo, da, (pro·fūn´do, dâ) *adj.* profound, deep.

profusión, (pro·fū·syon´) *f.* profusion.

progenitor, (pro·he·nē·tor´) *m.* ancestor, forefather.

programa, (pro·grâ´mâ) *m.* program; — de estudios, curriculum.

programación, (pro·grâ·mâ·syon´) *f.* programming.

progresar, (pro·gre·sâr´) *vn.* to progress, to improve.

progresión, (pro·gre·syon´) *f.* progression.

progresista, (pro·gre·sēs´tâ) *adj.* progressive.

progresivo, va, (pro·gre·sē´vo, vâ) *adj.* progressive.

progreso, (pro·gre´so) *m.* progress, advancement.

prohibición, (proē·vē·syon´) *f.* prohibition.

prohibido, da, (proē·vē´tho, thâ) *adj.* forbidden.

prohibir, (proē·vēr´) *va.* to prohibit, to forbid.

prohibitivo, va, (proē·vē·tē´vo, vâ) *adj.* prohibitive.

prohijar, (proē·hâr´) *va.* to adopt.

prohombre, (pro·om´bre) *m.* top man, leader.

prójimo, (pro´hē·mo) *m.* fellow man.

prole, (pro´le) *f.* issue, offspring.

proletariado, (pro·le·tâ·ryâ´tho) *m.* proletariat.

proletario, ria, (pro·le·tâ´ryo, ryâ) *adj.* proletarian.

prolijo, ja, (pro·lē´ho, hâ) *adj.* tedious, overly long, drawn-out.

prólogo, (pro´lo·go) *m.* prologue.

prolongación, (pro·long·gâ·syon´) *f.* prolongation, continuance, extension.

prolongado, da, (pro·long·gâ´tho, thâ) *adj.* prolonged, extended.

prolongar, (pro·long·gâr´) *va.* to prolong.

promedio, (pro·me´thyo) *m.* average, median; middle *(de una cosa)*.

promesa, (pro·me´sâ) *f.* promise.

prometedor, ra, (pro·me·te·thor´, râ) *adj.* promising.

prometer, (pro·me·ter´) *va.* to promise; —, *vn.* to be promising; —se, to get engaged.

prometido, da, (pro·me·tē´tho, thâ) *adj.* engaged; —, *f.* fiancée; —, *m.* fiancé.

prominencia, (pro·mē·nen´syâ) *f.* prominence.

prominente, (pro·mē·nen´te) *adj.* prominent.

promiscuo, cua, (pro·mēs´kwo, kwâ) *adj.* promiscuous.

promoción, (pro·mo·syon´) *f.* promotion.

promontorio, (pro·mon·to´ryo) *m.* promontory.

promotor, ra, (pro·mo·tor´, râ) *n.* promoter.

promover*, (pro·mo·ver´) *va.* to promote, to further.

promulgar, (pro·mūl·gâr´) *va.* to promulgate, to proclaim.

pronombre, (pro·nom'bre) *m.* pronoun.

pronosticar, (pro·nos·tē·kâr') *va.* to prognosticate, to predict, to forecast.

pronóstico, (pro·nos'tē·ko) *m.* prognosis, forecast; almanac *(calendario)*.

prontitud, (pron·tē·tūth') *f.* promptness, speed.

pronto, ta, (pron'to, tâ) *adj.* prompt, speedy; —to, *adv.* soon, promptly; tan —to como, as soon as; de —to, all of a sudden; por lo —to, temporarily.

prontuario, (pron·twâ'ryo) *m.* memorandum book *(agenda);* handbook.

pronunciación, (pro·nūn·syâ·syon') *f.* pronunciation.

pronunciamiento, (pro·nūn·syâ·myen'to) *m.* decree, pronouncement; military uprising *(rebelión).*

pronunciar, (pro·nūn·syâr') *va.* to pronounce; — un discurso, to make a speech; —se, to rebel.

propaganda, (pro·pâ·gân'dâ) *f.* propaganda; advertising media *(comercial).*

propagandista, (pro·pâ·gân·dēs'tâ) *m.* and *f.* and *adj.* propagandist.

propagar, (pro·pâ·gâr') *va.* to propagate; (fig.) to spread, to disseminate.

propalar, (pro·pâ·lâr') *va.* to publish, to divulge.

propensión, (pro·pen·syon') *f.* propensity, inclination.

propenso, sa, (pro·pen'so, sâ) *adj.* prone, inclined; — a accidentes, accident-prone.

propicio, cia, (pro·pē'syo, syâ) *adj.* propitious, favorable.

propiedad, (pro·pye·thâth') *f.* ownership *(dominio);* property.

propietario, ria, (pro·pye·tâ'ryo, ryâ) *n.* proprietor.

propina, (pro·pē'nâ) *f.* tip, gratuity.

propio, pia, (pro'pyo, pyâ) *adj.* proper; own *(de la misma persona);* characteristic *(distintivo);* selfsame, very *(mismo);* —, *m.* messenger.

proponer*, (pro·po·ner') *va.* to propose, to suggest; —se, to intend, to plan, to be determined.

proporción, (pro·por·syon') *f.* proportion; occasion, opportunity *(coyuntura).*

proporcionado, da, (pro·por·syo·nâ'tho, thâ) *adj.* proportionate; fit *(idóneo).*

proporcionar, (pro·por·syo·nâr') *va.* to proportion; to adjust, to adapt *(arreglar);* to provide, to afford, to supply *(suministrar).*

proposición, (pro·po·sē·syon') *f.* proposition.

propósito, (pro·po'sē·to) *m.* purpose, intention; a —, apropos, to the point, by the way; de —, on purpose, purposely; fuera de —, untimely, beside the point; a — de, with regard to, apropos of.

propuesta, (pro·pwes'tâ) *f.* proposal, proposition.

propulsión, (pro·pūl·syon') *f.* propulsion; — a chorro, jet propulsion; avión de — a chorro, jet plane.

propulsor, ra, (pro·pūl·sor', râ) *adj.* propulsive.

prorrata, (pro·rrâ'tâ) *f.* quota; a —, pro rata.

prórroga, (pro'rro·gâ) *f.* extension, renewal.

prorrogar, (pro·rro·gâr') *va.* to put off, to delay, to postpone.

prorrumpir, (pro·rrūm·pēr') *vn.* to break forth, to burst forth.

prosa, (pro'sâ) *f.* prose.

prosaico, ca, (pro·sâ'ē·ko, kâ) *adj.* prosaic.

proscribir*, (pros·krē·vēr') *va.* to exile *(desterrar);* to outlaw.

proscripción, (pros·krēp·syon') *f.* ban, proscription.

proscripto, (pros·krēp'to) *m.* outlaw; exile *(desterrado).*

prosecución, (pro·se·kū·syon') *f.* prosecution; pursuit *(perseguimiento).*

proseguir*, (pro·se·gēr') *va.* to pursue, to continue, to carry on.

prospecto, (pros·pek'to) *m.* prospectus.

prosperar, (pros·pe·râr') *va.* to favor; —, *vn.* to prosper, to thrive.

prosperidad, (pros·pe·rē·thâth') *f.* prosperity.

próspero, ra, (pros'pe·ro, râ) *adj.* prosperous.

próstata, (pros'tâ·tâ) *f.* prostate gland.

prostitución, (pros·tē·tū·syon') *f.* prostitution.

prostituta, (pros·tē·tū'tâ) *f.* prostitute.

protagonista, (pro·tâ go·nēs'tâ) *m.* and *f.* protagonist.

protección, (pro·tek·syon') *f.* protection.

proteccionismo, (pro·tek·syo·nēz'mo) *m.* protectionism.

protector, ra, (pro·tek·tor', râ) *n.* protector, patron; —, *adj.* protective.

protectorado, (pro·tek·to·râ'tho) *m.* protectorate.

proteger, (pro·te·her') *va.* to protect, to defend.

protegido, da, (pro·te·hē'tho, thâ) *n.* protégé; —, *adj.* protected.

proteína, (pro·te·ē′nâ) f. protein.

protesta, (pro·tes′tâ) f. protest.

protestante, (pro·tes·tân′te) m. and f. and adj. Protestant.

protestar, (pro·tes·târ′) va. to profess, to affirm; —, vn. to protest, to oppose; — contra, to object to, to oppose.

protocolo, (pro·to·ko′lo) m. protocol.

protoplasma, (pro·to·plâz′mâ) m. protoplasm.

prototipo, (pro·to·tē′po) m. prototype.

protuberancia, (pro·tū·ve·rân′syâ) f. protuberance.

provecho, (pro·ve′cho) m. profit benefit, advantage; usefulness (utilidad).

provechoso, sa, (pro·ve·cho′so, sâ) adj. profitable, beneficial, favorable.

proveer*, (pro·ve·er′) va. to provide, to provision; —se de, to provide oneself with.

provenir*, (pro·ve·nēr′) vn. to proceed, to arise, to originate.

proverbial, (pro·ver·vyâl′) adj. proverbial.

proverbio, (pro·ver′vyo) m. proverb.

providencia, (pro·vē·then′syâ) f. providence, foresight; (eccl.) divine providence.

providencial, (pro·vē·then·syâl′) adj. providential.

providenciar, (pro·vē·then·syâr′) va. to take the steps necessary for.

provincia, (pro·vēn′syâ) f. province.

provincialismo, (pro·vēn·syâ·lēz′mo) m. provincialism.

provinciano, na, (pro·vēn·syá′no, nâ) adj. and n. provincial.

provisión, (pro·vē·syon′) f. provision, supply, stock.

provisional, (pro·vē·syo·nâl′) adj. provisional, temporary.

provisor, ra, (pro·vē·sor′, râ) n. provider, purveyor, supplier.

provocación, (pro·vo·kâ·syon′) f. provocation.

provocar, (pro·vo·kâr′) va. to provoke; to further (facilitar).

provocativo, va, (pro·vo·kâ·tē′vo, vâ) adj. provocative.

prox.: próximo, next, nearest.

próximamente, (prok·sē·mâ·men′te) adv. very soon, shortly.

proximidad, (prok·sē·mē·thâth′) f. proximity.

próximo, ma, (prok′sē·mo, mâ) adj. next, nearest, following; pariente —, close relative.

proyección, (pro·yek·syon′) f. projection.

proyectar, (pro·yek·târ′) va. to protect; to

plan (preparar).

proyectil, (pro·yek·tēl′) m. missile, projectile; — balístico, ballistic missile; — cohete, rocket missile; — de alcance intermedio, intermediate range ballistic missile; — dirigido or guiado, guided missile; — de sondeo, probe rocket; — interceptor, interceptor missile.

proyecto, (pro·yek′to) m. project, plan; — del gobierno, government project; — de ley, proposed bill.

proyector, (pro·yek·tor′) m. projector; searchlight (reflector).

prudencia, (prū·then′syâ) f. prudence, wisdom.

prudente, (prū·then′te) adj. prudent, cautious.

prueba, (prwe′vâ) f. proof; trial, test, experiment (examen); trial, attempt (tentativa); token, sample (muestra); (phot. and print.) proof; a — de agua, water-proof; a — de bala, bulletproof; a — de bomba, bombproof.

prurito, (prū·rē′to) m. itching; (fig) burning desire.

P.S.: posdata, P.S. postscript.

pseudónimo (pseū·tho′nē·mo) = seudónimo.

psicoanálisis (psē·ko·â·nâ′lē·sēs) = sicoanálisis.

psicología (psē·ko·lo·hē′â) = sicología.

psicológico (psē·ko·lo′hē·ko) = sicológico.

psicólogo (psē·ko′lo·go) = sicólogo.

psicosis (psē·ko′sēs) = sicosis.

psicosomático (psē·ko·so·mâ′tē·ko) = sicosomático.

psiquiatra (psē·kyâ′trâ) = siquiatra.

psíquico (psē′kē·ko) = síquico.

pte.: presente, pres. present.

pto.: puerto, pt. port; punto, pt. point.

púa, (pū′â) f. sharp point; graft (vástago); tooth (de peine); (zool.) barb; (mus.) plectrum; (fig.) remorse, anguish; alambre de —, barbed wire.

pubertad, (pū·ver·tâth′) f. puberty.

publicación, (pū·vlē·kâ·syon′) f. publication.

publicar, (pū·vlē·kâr′) va. to publish; to publicize (hacer público).

publicidad, (pū·vlē·sē·thâth′) f. publicity.

público, ca, (pū′vlē·ko, kâ) adj. public; —, m. attendance, audience.

puchero, (pū·che′ro) m. pot; meat stew (guisado); pout, grimace (mueca); hacer —s, to pout.

pudiente, (pū·thyen′te) adj. rich; powerful (poderoso).

pudín, (pū·thēn′) m. pudding.

pudor, (pū·thor´) *m.* bashfulness, modesty, decorum.

pudoroso, sa, (pū·tho·ro´so, sâ) *adj.* modest, shy.

pudrir*, (pū·thrēr´) *va.* to make putrid, to putrefy; (fig.) to consume, to worry; — se, to rot.

pueblo, (pwe´vlo) *m.* town, village; country, people *(nación)*; — natal, hometown, native town.

puente, (pwen´te) *m.* bridge; — aéreo, airlift, air bridge; cabeza de —, bridgehead; — colgante, suspension bridge; — levadizo, drawbridge.

puerca, (pwer´kâ) *f.* sow.

puerco, ca, (pwer´ko, kâ) *adj.* nasty, filthy, dirty; rude *(grosero)*; —, *m.* hog, pig; carne de —co, pork; —co espín, porcupine.

puericultura, (pwe·rē·kūl·tū´râ) *f.* child care.

pueril, (pwe·rēl´) *adj.* childish, puerile.

puerro, (pwe´rro) *m.* (bot.) leek.

puerta, (pwer´tâ) *f.* door; doorway *(entrada)*; (fig.) gateway; — corrediza, sliding door; — de entrada, front door; — trasera, back door.

puerto, (pwer´to) *m.* port, harbor; narrow pass, defile *(desfiladero)*; — aéreo, airport; — franco, free port.

pues, (pwes) *conj.* since, inasmuch as; —, *adv.* then, therefore; ¡—! *interj.* well then!

puesta, (pwes´tâ) *f.* (ast.) set, setting; stake *(en el juego)*; — de sol, sunset.

puesto, (pwes´to) *m.* place, particular spot; job, position, employment *(empleo)*; (mil.) encampment; booth, stand *(tiendecilla)*; blind *(de caza)*; —, ta, *adj.* put, set, placed; —to que, since.

pugilato, (pū·hē·lâ´to) *m.* pugilism, boxing; fight, boxing match *(partido)*.

pugna, (pūg´nâ) *f.* combat, battle, struggle.

pugnar, (pūg·nâr´) *vn.* to fight, to struggle; (fig.) to strive earnestly, to work doggedly.

pujante, (pū·hân´te) *adj.* powerful, strong, robust, strapping.

pujanza, (pū·hân´sâ) *f.* power, strength.

pujar, (pū·hâr´) *va.* to outbid; to push ahead, to push through *(mejorar)*; —, *vn.* to hesitate, to falter; (fig.) to pout.

pulcritud, (pūl·krē·tūth´) *f.* neatness, tidiness.

pulcro, era, (pūl´kro, krâ) *adj.* neat, tidy, clean.

pulga, (pūl´gâ) *f.* flea.

pulgada, (pūl·gâ´thâ) *f.* inch.

pulgar, (pūl·gâr´) *m.* thumb.

pulido, da, (pū·lē´tho, thâ) *adj.* neat, nice *(nítido)*; polished.

pulir, (pū·lēr´) *va.* to polish, to burnish; to put the finishing touches on *(perfeccionar)*; —se, to get all dressed up.

pulmón, (pūl·mon´) *m.* lung; — acuático, aqualung; — de acero, iron lung.

pulmonía, (pūl·mo·nē´â) *f.* pneumonia; — atípica or — a virus, virus pneumonia.

púlpito, (pūl´pē·to) *m.* pulpit.

pulpo, (pūl´po) *m.* octopus.

pulque, (pūl´ke) *m.* pulque.

pulsar, (pūl·sâr´) *va.* to touch; (med.) to take one´s pulse; to explore, to try *(tantear)*; —, *vn.* to pulse, to throb.

pulsera, (pūl·se´râ) *f.* bracelet; (med.) wrist bandage.

pulso, (pūl´so) *m.* pulse.

pulverizador, (pūl·ve·rē·sâ·thor´) *m.* atomizer, spray, sprayer.

pulverizar, (pūl·ve·rē·sâr´) *va.* to pulverize; to atomize, to spray *(un líquido)*.

pulla, (pū´yâ) *f.* smart remark, dig, taunt; obscene expression *(grosería)*.

puma, (pū´mâ) *m.* (zool.) puma, cougar.

pundonor, (pūn·do·nor´) *m.* point of honor.

pundonoroso, sa, (pūn·do·no·ro´so, sâ) *adj.* punctilious, honor-bound.

punta, (pūn´tâ) *f.* point, tip; — de combate, warhead.

puntada, (pūn·tâ´thâ) *f.* stitch.

puntal, (pūn·tâl´) *m.* prop, stay.

puntapié, (pūn·ta·pye´) *m.* kick.

puntería, (pūn·te·rē´â) *f.* aim; marksmanship *(habilidad)*.

puntiagudo, da, (pūn·tyâ·gū´tho, thâ) *adj.* sharp-pointed.

puntilla, (pūn·tē´yâ) *f.* brad, tack; narrow lace edging *(encaje)*; de —s, on tiptoe.

puntillo, (pūn·tē´yo) *m.* small point, punctilio; (mus.) dot.

punto, (pūn´to) *m.* period *(punto redondo)*; point, matter *(asunto)*; hole, notch *(de correa)*; dot *(de la i)*; point of honor *(pundonor)*; goal, point *(de tanteo)*; mesh *(malla)*; moment, time, point *(oportunidad)*; al —, instantly; estar a — de, to be about to; hasta cierto —, in some measure, to some degree; — de partida, or de arranque, starting point; — de ebullición, boiling point; — de vista, point of view; son las dos en —, it is exactly two o´clock; — y coma, semicolon.

puntuación, (pūn·twâ·syon´) *f.* punctuation; score *(tanteo).*

puntual, (pūn·twâl´) *adj.* punctual, exact; sure, certain *(seguro).*

puntualidad, (pūn·twâ·lē·thâth´) *f.* punctuality, exactness; certainty.

puntualizar, (pūn·twâ·lē·sâr´) *va.* to fix in one´s mind, to retain in one´s memory; to accomplish *(acabar).*

punzada, (pūn·sâ´thâ) *f.* prick, sting; (fig.) pain, anguish.

punzar, (pūn·sâr´) *va.* to prick, to sting, to throb; (fig.) to hurt, to wound.

punzón, (pūn·son´) *m.* punch; burin *(buril).*

puñado, (pū·nyâ´tho) *m.* handful.

puñal, (pū·nyâl´) *m.* poniard, dagger.

puñalada, (pū·nyâ·lâ´thâ) *f.* stab with a dagger.

puñetazo, (pū·nye·tâ´so) *m.* blow with the fist.

puño, (pū´nyo) *m.* fist; handful, fistful *(manojo);* wristband, cuff *(bocamanga);* handle *(mango);* hilt *(de arma blanca).*

pupila, (pū·pē´lâ) *f.* (anat.) pupil.

pupilo, la, (pū·pē´lo, lâ) *n.* boarder; day student *(mediopensionista);* orphan, ward *(huérfano).*

pupitre, (pū·pē´tre) *m.* desk, writing desk.

puramente, (pū·râ·men´te) *adv.* purely.

puré, (pū·re´) *m.* thick soup, purée; — de

papas, or **de patatas,** mashed potatoes.

pureza, (pū·re´zâ) *f.* purity, chastity.

purga, (pūr´gâ) *f.* physic; (fig.) purge.

purgante, (pūr·gân´te) *m.* purgative, physic.

purgar, (pūr·gâr´) *va.* to purge, to purify; to clear up *(sospechas);* to expiate *(un delito).*

purgatorio, (pūr·gâ·to´ryo) *m.* purgatory.

purificación, (pū·rē·fē·kâ·syon´) *f.* purification.

purificar, (pū·rē·fē·kâr´) *va.* to purify; — **se,** to be purified, to be cleansed.

purista, (pū·rēs´tâ) *m.* and *f.* purist.

puritano, na, (pū·rē·tâ´no, nâ) *adj.* puritanical; —, *n.* Puritan.

puro, ra, (pū´ro, râ) *adj.* pure; (fig.) flawless, perfect; outright, absolute *(mero);* **a** —, by dint of; —, *m.* cigar.

púrpura, (pūr´pū·râ) *f.* purple.

purpúreo, rea, (pūr·pū´re·o, re·â) *adj.* purple.

pus, (pūs) *m.* pus.

pusilánime, (pū·sē·lâ´nē·me) *adj.* pusillanimous, cowardly.

pústula, (pūs´tū·lâ) *f.* pustule.

puta, (pū´tâ) *f.* whore.

putrefacción, (pū·tre·fâk·syon´) *f.* putrefaction.

pútrido, da, (pū´trē·tho, thâ) *adj.* putrid, rotten.

puya, (pū´yâ) *f.* goad.

pza.: pieza, pc. piece.

Q

q.e.p.d.: que en paz descanse, R.I.P. may (he, she) rest in peace.

ql. or ql: quintal, cwt. hundredweight. **qq.: quintales,** cwts. hundredweights.

que, (ke) *pron.* that, which, who, whom; —, *conj.* that; and (y); since *(pues);* whether (o); without *(sin que);* **than** *(comparativo);* **a menos** —, unless; **con tal** —, provided that.

qué, (ke) *interr. pron.* which? what?; **sin** — **ni para** —, without rhyme or reason; **no hay de** —, don´t mention it.

quebrada, (ke·vrâ´thâ) *f.* gorge, defile; (Sp. Am.) brook.

quebradero, (ke·vrâ·the´ro) *m.* breaker; — **de cabeza,** worry, concern, real problem.

quebradizo, za, (ke·vrâ·thē´so, sâ) *adj.* brittle; (fig.) fragile; quavering (voz).

quebrado, (ke·vrâ´tho) *m.* (math.) fraction; —, **da,** broken; (com.) bankrupt; faded, washed out *(de colores);* (med.) ruptured.

quebrantar, (ke·vrân·târ´) *va.* to break, to crack, to burst *(hendir);* to shatter *(estrellar);* to pound, to grind *(moler);* (fig.) to violate, to break; —**se,** to break down, to crack due to strain.

quebranto, (ke·vrân´to) *m.* breakage; (fig.) great loss, reversal *(gran pérdida);* breakdown, collapse *(de fuerzas).*

quebrar*, (ke·vrâr´) *va.* to break; (fig.) to upset, to interrupt *(interrumpir);* to soften *(suavizar);* to trouble *(molestar);* to break one´s heart *(mover a lástima);* —**se,** to break down.

queda, (ke´thâ) *f.* curfew.

quedar, (ke·thâr´) *vn.* to remain; to stop, to stay *(detenerse);* to be *(estar);* to be left, to be left over *(restar);* — **bien,** to fit well; to come out well *(salir bien);* — **en,** to agree to; —**se con,** to keep; (fig.) to deceive *(engañar);* —**se a oscuras,** to be left in the dark.

quedo, da, (ke´tho, thâ) *adj.* quiet, still; —**do,** *adv.* softly, quietly.

quehacer, (ke·â·ser´) *m.* task, job, chore; —**es de la casa,** household duties.

queja, (ke´hâ) *f.* complaint, gripe; moan.

quejarse, (ke·hâr´se) *vr.* to complain, to gripe; to moan, to wail *(gemir).*

quejido, (ke·hē´tho) *m.* groan, moan.

quejoso, sa, (ke·ho´so, sâ) *adj.* complaining, whining.

quejumbroso, sa, (ke·hūm·bro´so, sâ) *adj.* complaining, grumbling.

quemadura, (ke·mâ·thū´râ) *f.* burn, burning.

quemar, (ke·mâr´) *va.* to burn; to scorch *(el sol);* to freeze *(el hielo);* —, *vn.* to be hot, to burn.

quemarropa, (ke·mâ·rro´pâ) **a** —, directly, point-blank.

quemazón, (ke·mâ·son´) *f.* burn; intense heat *(calor);* smarting, burning sensation *(comezón).*

quepis, (ke´pēs) *m.* kepi.

querella, (ke·re´yâ) *f.* complaint; quarrel, dispute *(discordia).*

querer*, (ke·rer´) *va.* to wish, to want; to like, to be fond of *(tener cariño);* to love *(amar);* to resolve, to decide *(resolver);* — **decir,** to mean, to signify; **sin —,** unintentionally, unwillingly; **como quiera,** anyhow, anyway; **cuando quiera,** at any time; **donde quiera,** anywhere; **Dios quiera,** God willing; **quiera o no quiera,** whether or not; — **más,** to prefer.

querido, da, (ke·rē´tho, thâ) *adj.* dear, beloved; —, *n.* dear, darling.

querosina, (ke·ro·sē´nâ) *f.* kerosene, coal oil.

querubín, (ke·rū·vēn´) *m.* cherub.

quesadilla, (ke·sâ·thē´yâ) *f.* cheesecake; pastry *(pastecillo);* (Mex.) fried tortilla filled with cheese.

quesero, ra, (ke·se´ro, râ) *n.* cheese maker; cheese seller *(vendedor);* —, *f.* cheese dish.

queso, (ke´so) *m.* cheese; — **Gruyére,** Swiss cheese.

quetzal, (ket·sâl´) *m.* (orn.) quetzal; monetary unit of Guatemala.

quevedos, (ke·ve´thos) *m. pl.* pincenez.

quicial, (kē·syâl´) *m.* doorjamb *(jamba);* hinge pole.

quicio, (kē´syo) *m.* pivot hole; **estar fuera de —,** to be out of order, not to be working properly.

quid, (kēth) *m.* quiddity.

quiebra, (kye´vrâ) *f.* crack, fissure *(hendedura);* loss *(pérdida);* damage *(menoscabo);* (com.) bankruptcy; decision to liquidate *(juicio);* **en —,** in bankruptcy; bankrupt; **leyes de —,** bankruptcy laws; **en proceso de —,** in the hands of receivers.

quien, (kyen) *pron.* who, whom; whoever *(la persona que).*

quién, (kyen) *interr. pron.* who? whom?

quienquiera, (kyeng·kye´râ) *pron.* whosoever, whoever, anyone, anybody.

quieto, ta, (kye´to, tâ) *adj.* quiet, still, tranquil; (fig.) clean-living *(virtuoso).*

quietud, (kye·tūth´) *f.* quietness, peace, tranquillity; (fig.) rest, repose.

quijada (kē·hâ´thâ) *f.* jaw, jawbone.

quijotada, (kē·ho·tâ´thâ) *f.* quixotism.

quijote, (kē·ho´te) *m.* quixote, quixotic person, impractical idealist.

quilatar, (kē·lâ·târ´) *va.* to assay; to purify *(purificar).*

quilate, (kē·lâ´te) *m.* carat.

quilla, (kē´yâ) *f.* keel; sternum *(de las aves).*

quím.: química, chem. chemistry.

quimbombó, (kēm·bom·bo´) *m.* (bot.) okra, gumbo.

quimera, (kē·me´râ) *f.* chimera; quarrel *(riña).*

quimérico, ca, (kē·me´rē·ko, kâ) *adj.* chimerical, imaginary.

química, (kē´mē·kâ) *f.* chemistry; — **de polímeros,** polymer chemistry.

químico, (kē´mē·ko) *m.* chemist; —, **ca,** *adj.* chemical.

quimono or **kimono,** (kē·mo´no) *m.* kimono.

quimioterapia, (kē·myo·te·râ´pyâ) *f.* chemotherapy.

quina, (kē´nâ) *f.* chinchona bark; quinine water *(líquido).*

quincalla, (kēng·kâ´yâ) *f.* hardware; junk jewelry *(joyería).*

quincallería, (kēng·kâ·ye·rē´â) *f.* hardware store; hardware factory *(fábrica);* hardware business *(comercio);* whatnot shop *(tienda de regalos).*

quince, (kēn´se) *adj.* and *m.* fifteen.

---

m met, **n** not, **p** pot, **r** very, **rr** (none), **s** so, **t** toy, **th** with, **v** eve, **w** we, **y** yes, **z** zero

quincena, (kēn·se´nâ) *f.* two weeks, fortnight; semimonthly pay *(paga).*

quincenal, (kēn·se·nâl´) *adj.* semimonthly, fortnightly.

quincuagésimo, ma, (kēng·kwâ·he´sē·mo, mâ) *m.* and *adj.* fiftieth.

quinientos, tas, (kē·nyen´tos, tâs) *adj.* and *m.* five hundred.

quinina, (kē·nē´nâ) *f.* quinine.

quinquenio, (kēng·ke´nyo) *m.* space of five years, five years´ time.

quinta, (kēn´tâ) *f.* country house; (mil.) conscription, draft; five of a kind *(en los naipes);* (mus.) fifth.

quintacolumnista, (kēn·tâ·ko·lūm·nēs´tâ) *m.* or *f.* fifth columnist.

quintaesencia, (kēn·tâ·e·sen´syâ) *f.* quintessence.

quintal, (kēn·tâl´) *m.* quintal, hundredweight.

quinteto, (kēn·te´to) *m.* quintette.

quinto, (kēn´to) *m.* fifth; (mil.) draftee; plot *(tierra);* —, **ta,** *adj.* fifth.

quintuples, (kēn´tū·ples) *m.* or *f. pl.* quintuplets.

quíntuplo, pia, (kēn´tū·plo, plâ) *adj.* quintuple, fivefold.

quinzavo, va, (kēn·sâ´vo, vâ) *m.* and *adj.* fifteenth.

quiosco, (kyos´ko) *m.* kiosk; — **de periódi**cos, newsstand.

quiromancia, (kē·ro·mân´syâ) *f.* palmistry, chiromancy.

quirúrgico, ca, (kē·rūr´hē·ko, kâ) *adj.* surgical.

quisquilloso, sa, (kēs·kē·yo´so, sâ) *adj.* trifling, hairsplitting; touchy, peevish, irritable *(cojijoso).*

quiste, (kēs´te) *m.* cyst.

quisto, ta, (kēs´to, tâ) *adj.* liked; **bien** —, well-liked, popular; **mal** —, unpopular, disliked.

quitamanchas, (kē·tâ·mân´châs) *m.* spot remover.

quitapón, (kē·tâ·pon´) *m.* headstall; **de** —, removable, detachable.

quitar, (kē·târ´) *va.* to take away; to remove *(remover);* to abrogate, to annul *(abolir);* to prevent, to hinder *(impedir);* to free, to exempt *(libertar);* to parry *(parar);* — **la mesa,** to clear the table; —**se,** to get rid of *(deshacerse de);* to take off; to leave *(irse).*

quitasol, (kē·tâ·sol´) *m.* parasol.

quita y pon, (kē´tâ ē pon´) **de** —, detachable, removable.

quizá, quizás, (kē·sâ´, kē·sâs´) *adv.* perhaps.

quórum, (ko´rūn) *m.* quorum.

R

R.: Reverendo, Rev. Reverend; **respuesta,** reply; **reprobado,** failing grade, flunk.

rabadilla, (rrâ·vâ·thē´yâ) *f.* coccyx; (orn.) uropygium.

rábano, (rrâ´vâ·no) *m.* radish; — **picante,** horseradish.

rabí, (rrâ·vē´) *m.* rabbi.

rabia, (rrâ´vyâ) *f.* rage, fury; rabies *(enfermedad).*

rabiar, (rrâ·vyâr´) *vn.* to storm, to rage; to be in agony *(padecer dolor);* to have rabies *(enfermedad);* **a** —, like the devil.

rabieta, (rrâ·vye´tâ) *f.* fit, temper tantrum.

rabino, (rrâ·vē´no) *m.* rabbi.

rabioso, sa, (rrâ·vyo´so, sâ) *adj.* rabid; furious *(airoso);* vehement, violent *(vehemente).*

rabo, (rrâ´vo) *m.* tail; stem *(pecíolo).*

rabón, ona, (rrâ·von´, o´nâ) *adj.* tailless *(sin rabo);* short-tailed, bobtailed; (Mex. coll.) short.

racimo, (rrâ·sē´mo) *m.* bunch, cluster.

raciocinar, (rrâ·syo·sē·nâr´) *vn.* to reason, to ratiocinate.

raciocinio, (rrâ·syo·sē´nyo) *m.* reason; ratiocination *(raciocinación);* argument *(argumento).*

ración, (rrâ·syon´) *f.* ration; portion *(porción);* (eccl.) prebend.

racional, (rrâ·syo·nâl´) *adj.* rational; reasonable *(razonable).*

racionamiento, (rrâ·syo·nâ·myen´to) *m.* rationing.

racionar, (rrâ·syo·nâr´) *va.* to ration.

racismo, (rrâ·sēz´mo) *m.* racism.

racista, (rrâ·sēs´tâ) *m.* and *f.* racist.

radar, (rrâ·thâr´) *m.* radar.

radiación, (rrâ·thyâ·syon´) *f.* radiation.

radiactividad, (rrâ·thyâk·tē·vē·thâth´) *f.* radioactivity; — **atmosférica,** fallout.

radiactivo, va, (rrâ·thyâk·tē´vo, vâ) *adj.* radioactive.

â arm, **e** they, **ē** bē, **o** fore, **ū** blūe, **b** bad, **ch** chip, **d** day, **f** fat, **g** go, **h** hot, **k** kid, **1** let

radiador, (rrâ·thyâ·thor´) *m.* radiator.

radiante, (rrâ·thyân´te) *adj.* radiant.

radiar, (rrâ·thyâr´) *va.* to broadcast *(al público);* to radio; —, *vn.* to radiate.

radical, (rrâ·thē·kâl´) *adj.* radical; —, *m.* radical.

radicar, (rrâ·thē·kâr´) *vn.* to take root; to be found, to be located *(estar);* —**se,** to take root *(arraigar);* to settle down, to establish oneself *(establecerse);* to reside, to dwell *(morar).*

radio, (rrâ´thyo) *m.* or *f.* radio; —, *m.* (math. and anat.) radius; (chem.) radium.

radioactividad, (rrâ·thyo·âk·tē·vē·thâth´) *f.* radioactivity; — **atmosférica,** fallout.

radioactivo, va, (rrâ·thyo·ak·tē´vo, vâ) *adj.* radioactive.

radioaficionado, (rrâ·thyo·â·fē·syo·nâ´tho) *m.* ham operator.

radioamplificador, (rrâ·thyo·âm·plē·fē kâ·thor´) *m.* radio amplifier.

radiocomunicación, (rrâ·thyo·ko·mū· nē·kâ·syon´) *f.* radio communication.

radiodifundir, (rrâ·thyo·thē·fūn·dēr´) *va.* to broadcast.

radiodifusión, (rrâ·thyo·thē·fū·syon´) *f.* broadcast, radiobroadcast.

radiodifusora, (rrâ·thyo·thē·fū·so´râ) *f.* broadcasting station.

radioemisión, (rrâ·thyo·e·mē·syon´) *f.* transmission.

radioemisor, ra, (rrâ·thyo·e·mē·sor´, râ) *adj.* broadcasting.

radioescucha, (rrâ·thyo·es·kū´châ) *m.* and *f.* radio listener.

radiografía, (rrâ·thyo·grâ·fē´â) *f.* X ray.

radiograma, (rrâ·thyo·grâ´mâ) *m.* radiogram.

radionovela, (rrâ·thyo·no·ve´lâ) *f.* serial, soap opera.

radiorreceptor, (rrâ·thyo·rre·sep·tor´) *m.* radio receiver.

radiotécnico, (rrâ·thyo·teg´nē·ko) *m.* radio technician.

radiotelefonía, (rrâ·thyo·te·le·fo·nē´â) *f.* radiotelephony.

radioteléfono, (rrâ·thyo·te·le´fo·no) *m.* radiotelephone; — **emisor-receptor portátil,** walkie-talkie.

radiotelegrafista, (rrâ·thyo·te·le·grâ·fēs´tâ) *m.* and *f.* wireless operator.

radiotelégrafo, (rrâ·thyo·te·le´grâ·fo) *m.* radiotelegraph.

radiotelegrama, (rrâ·thyo·te·le·grâ´mâ) *m.* radiotelegram.

radiotelescopio, (rrâ·thyo·te·les·ko´pyo) *m.* radio telescope.

radioterapia, (rrâ·thyo·te·râ´pyâ) *f.* radiotherapy.

radiotrasmisor, (rrâ·thyo·trâz·mē·sor´) *m.* radio transmitter.

radioyente, (rrâ·thyo·yen´te) *m.* and *f.* radio listener.

ráfaga, (rrâ´fâ·gâ) *f.* gust of wind; cloud *(nube);* (mil.) burst of gunfire; flash of light *(luz).*

raído, da, (rrâ·ē´tho, thâ) *adj.* threadbare, shabby; (fig.) shabby, base.

raigón, (rrâê·gon´) *m.* root.

raíz, (rrâ·ēs´) *f.* root; — **cuadrada,** square root; **bienes raíces,** landed property.

raja, (rrâ´hâ) *f.* splinter, chip; slice *(rebanada);* chink, fissure, crack *(hendedura).*

rajá, (rrâ·hâ´) *m.* rajah.

rajar, (rrâ·hâr´) *va.* to split, to crack *(agrietar);* to chop, to slice *(dividir);* —, *vn.* (fig, and coll.) to tell fish stories *(mentir);* to chatter, to jabber *(hablar);* —**se,** (coll.) to back out.

raleza, (rrâ·le´sâ) *f.* thinness, sparseness.

ralo, la, (rrâ´lo, lâ) *adj.* thin, sparse.

rama, (rrâ´mâ) *f.* branch.

ramaje, (rrâ·mâ´he) *m.* foliage; branches *(ramas).*

ramera, (rrâ·me´râ) *f.* whore, prostitute.

ramificación, (rrâ·mē·fē·kâ·syon´) *f.* ramification.

ramificarse, (rrâ·mē·fē·kâr´se) *vr.* to ramify, to branch out.

ramillete, (rrâ·mē·ye´te) *m.* nosegay, bouquet; (fig.) centerpiece *(adorno);* (fig.) collection *(colección);* (bot.) cluster.

ramo, (rrâ´mo) *m.* branch; bunch, bouquet *(de flores);* (fig.) touch *(enfermedad).*

rampa, (rrâm´pâ) *f.* ramp; cramp *(calambre).*

rana, (rrâ´nâ) *f.* frog; **hombre —,** frogman.

rancio, cia, (rrân´syo, syâ) *adj.* rancid, rank; (fig.) old-fashioned.

ranchero, (rrân·che´ro) *m.* rancher; cook *(que guisa).*

rancho, (rrân´cho) *m.* mess; messmates *(que comen juntos);* camp *(campamento);* (fig.) get-together; ranch *(granja);* (Sp. Am.) hut; (naut.) command.

rango, (rrân´go) *m.* class, category; (Sp. Am.) class.

ranura, (rrâ·nū´râ) *f.* groove.

rapaz, (rrâ·pâs´) *adj.* thieving; (zool.) rapacious; —, *m.* lad.

rapaza, (rrâ·pâ´sâ) *f.* lass.

rape, (rrâ´pe) *m.* quick shave; (ichth.)

---

m met, **n** not, **p** pot, **r** very, **rr** (none), **s** so, **t** toy, **th** with, **v** eve, **w** we, **y** yes, **z** zero

angler; **al —,** close.

rapé, (rrä·pe´) *m.* snuff.

rapidez, (rrä·pē·thes´) *f.* speed, swiftness.

rápido, da, (rrá´pē·tho, thä) *adj.* fast, swift, rapid, speedy.

rapiña, (rrä·pē´nyä) *f.* rapine, robbery; **ave de —,** bird of prey.

rapsodia, (rräp·so´thyä) *f.* rhapsody.

rapto, (rräp´to) *m.* abduction, carrying off; ecstasy, rapture *(éxtasis);* (med.) faint, loss of consciousness.

raqueta, (rrä·ke´tä) *f.* racket; badminton *(juego);* rake *(de la casa de juego);* **— de nieve,** snowshoe.

raquitismo, (rrä·kē·tēz´mo) *m.* (med.) rickets.

rareza, (rrä·re´sä) *f.* rarity *(cosa);* rareness; idiosyncrasy *(acción).*

raro, ra, (rrä´ro, rä) *adj.* rare; eccentric *(extravagante).*

ras, (rräs) *m.* levelness, evenness.

rascacielos, (rräs·kä·sye´los) *m.* skyscraper.

rascar, (rräs·kär´) *va.* to scratch *(arañar);* to scrape.

rasgado, da, (rräz·gá´tho, thä) *adj.* torn; wide *(grande);* —, *m.* rip, tear; **boca —,** wide mouth; **ojos —s,** wide eyes.

rasgar, (rräz·gär´) *va.* to tear, to rip; to strum *(rasguear).*

rasgo, (rräz´go) *m.* dash, stroke, flourish; (fig.) deed, action *(acción);* characteristic, feature *(característica);* —s, *pl.* (anat.) features.

rasgón, (rräz·gon´) *m.* rip, tear.

rasguear, (rräz·ge·är´) *vn.* to make flourishes; (mus.) to strum.

rasgueo, (rräz·ge´o) *m.* strumming.

rasguño, (rräz·gu´nyo) *m.* scratch; sketch *(dibujo).*

raso, (rrä´so) *m.* satin, sateen; —, **sa,** *adj.* smooth, flat *(plano);* backless; common, undistinguished *(no distinguido);* clear *(de la atmósfera);* **al —so,** in the open air.

raspadura, (rräs·pä·thü´rä) *f.* scraping; erasure *(de papel).*

raspar, (rräs·pär´) *va.* to scrape, to rasp; to burn *(picar);* to steal *(hurtar);* to graze *(rasar).*

rastra, (rräs´trä) *f.* rake *(rastro);* sign *(vestigio);* sledge *(narria);* **caminar a —s,** to crawl.

rastrear, (rräs·tre·är´) *va.* to trace, to inquire into, to investigate; to trawl *(pesca);* —, *vn.* to skim along close to the ground.

rastreo, (rräs·tre´o) *m.* trawling; tracing;

estación de —, (avi.) tracer station.

rastrero, ra, (rräs·tre´ro, rä) *adj.* creeping; (fig.) low, vile, cringing.

rastrillo, (rräs·trē´yo) *m.* hackle, flax comb *(carda);* portcullis *(de la plaza);* rake.

rastro, (rräs´tro) *m.* track *(señal);* slaughterhouse *(matadero);* rake *(instrumento);* (fig.) sign, trail.

rastrojo, (rräs·tro´ho) *m.* stubble; rough *(en el golf).*

rasurar, (rra·sū·rär´) *va.* to shave.

rata, (rrä´tä) *f.* (zool.) rat.

ratear, (rrä·te·är´) *va.* to filch, to snatch *(hurtar);* to distribute on a pro rata basis.

ratería, (rrä·te·rē´ä) *f.* petty theft; (fig.) meanness.

ratero, ra, (rrä·te´ro, rä) *adj.* mean, vile; —, *n.* pickpocket, sneak thief.

ratificar, (rrä·tē·fē·kär´) *va.* to ratify.

rato, (rrä´to) *m.* while, moment; **al poco —,** shortly, in a short while; **a —s,** occasionally; **pasar el —,** to while away the time.

ratón, (rrä·ton´) *m.* mouse; mouse *(computación).*

ratonera, (rrä·to·ne´rä) *f.* mousetrap; place where rats breed *(madriguera).*

raudal, (rräü·thäl´) *m.* torrent, stream; (fig.) abundance, flood.

raya, (rrä´yä) *f.* stripe, line; end, limit *(término);* (gram.) dash; **lista de —,** (Mex.) payroll; **a —,** within bounds; —, *m.* (ichth.) ray.

rayado, da, (rrä·yä´tho, thä) *adj.* striped.

rayar, (rrä·yär´) *va.* to draw lines on, to rule; to stripe; to underline *(subrayar);* to cross out *(borrar);* (Mex.) to pay; **— en,** to border on.

rayo, (rrä´yo) *m.* ray, beam; flash of lightning *(relámpago);* spoke *(de rueda);* **— electrónico orientador,** (avi.) guidance beam; **— visual,** field of vision; **—X,** X ray.

rayón, (rrä·yon´) *m.* rayon.

raza, (rrä´sä) *f.* race, lineage; (fig.) strain, breed.

razón, (rrä·son´) *f.* reason, cause, motive; (math.) ratio; rate *(cómputo);* **— social,** firm name; **a — de,** at the rate of; **dar —,** to inform, to give account; **dar la —,** to agree with; **perder la —,** to go insane; **tener —,** to be right; **no tener —,** to be wrong.

razonable, (rrä·so·nä´vle) *adj.* reasonable.

razonado, da, (rrä·so·nä´tho, thä) *adj.* rational, prudent.

razonamiento, (rrä·so·nä·myen´to) *m.* reasoning.

razonar, (rrȧ·so·när´) *vn.* to reason; —, *va.* to reason out.

Rda. M or R.M.: **Reverenda Madre,** Rev erend Mother.

Rdo. P. or R.P.: **Reverendo Padre,** Rever end Father.

reacción, (rre·âk·syon´) *f.* reaction; — **en cadena,** chain reaction.

reaccionar, (rre·âk·syo·när´) *vn.* to react.

reaccionario, ria, (rre·âk·syo·nä´ryo, ryâ) *adj.* reactionary.

reacio, cia, (rre·ä´syo, syâ) *adj.* obstinate, refractory.

reactivar, (rre·âk·tē·vär´) *vt.* to reactivate.

reactor, (rre·âk·tor´) *m.* reactor.

reajuste, (rre·â·hūs´te) *m.* readjustment.

real, (rre·âl´) *adj.* real, actual; royal *(del rey);* **pavo** —, peacock; —, *m.* real.

realce, (rre·âl´se) *m.* embossing, raised work; (fig.) luster, splendor, enhancement; **dar** —, to build up, to highlight, to give importance to.

realeza, (rre·â·le´sâ) *f.* royalty.

realidad, (rre·â·lē·thäth´) *f.* reality, fact; truthfulness, sincerity *(ingenuidad);* **en** —, truly, really.

realismo, (rre·â·lēz´mo) *m.* realism.

realista, (rre·â·lēs´tâ) *m.* and *f.* royalist *(de la monarquía);* realist.

realización, (rre·â·lē·sâ·syon´) *f.* realization, fulfillment; bargain sale *(venta).*

realizar, (rre·â·lē·sär´) *va.* to realize, to fulfill; to sell off, to liquidate *(mercancías).*

realmente, (rre·âl·men´te) *adv.* really.

realzar, (rre·âl·sär´) *va.* to raise, to elevate; to emboss *(labrar);* (fig.) to heighten.

reanimar, (rre·â·nē·mär´) *va.* (fig.) to cheer up, to encourage; to reanimate.

reanudar, (rre·â·nū·thär´) *va.* to renew, to resume.

reaparecer*, (rre·â·pâ·re·ser´) *vn.* to reappear.

rearme (rre·âr´me) or **rearmamento,** (rre·âr·mâ·men´to) *m.* rearmament.

reata, (rre·â´tâ) *f.* strap to keep pack animals in line; line of pack animals *(hilera).*

rebaja, (rre·vâ´hâ) *f.* reduction, rebate.

rebasar, (rre·vâ·sär´) *va.* to lessen, to diminish; (com.) to reduce, to give a rebate on; **—se** to humble oneself.

rebanada, (rre·vâ·nä´thâ) *f.* slice.

rebanar, (rre·vâ·när´) *va.* to slice, to plane.

rebaño, (rre·vâ´nyo) *m.* flock.

rebasar, (rre·vâ·sär´) *va.* to go beyond, to exceed; to pass *(un coche).*

rebelarse, (rre·ve·lär´se) *vr.* to revolt, to rebel; (fig.) to resist, to oppose.

rebelde, (rre·vel´de) *m.* rebel; —, *adj.* rebellious.

rebeldía, (rre·vel·dē´â) *f.* rebelliousness, disobedience; **en** —, in default.

rebelión, (rre·ve·lyon´) *f.* rebellion, revolt.

reborde, (rre·vor´the) *m.* edge, border, rim.

rebosar, (rre·vo·sär´) *vn.* to run over, to overflow; (fig.) to abound, to be abundant.

rebotar, (rre·vo·tär´) *va.* to repel; —, *vn.* to rebound.

rebote, (rre·vo´te) *m.* rebound; **de** —, indirectly, on the rebound.

rebozo, (rre·vo´so) *m.* shawl; (fig.) pretext; **de** —, secretly; **sin** —, frankly, openly.

rebuscado, da, (rre·vūs·kâ´tho, thâ) *adj.* affected, stilted.

rebuznar, (rre·vūz·när´) *vn.* to bray.

rebuzno, (rre·vūz´no) *m.* braying.

recabar, (rre·kâ·vär´) *va.* to manage to get; to ask for *(pedir).*

recado, (rre·kâ´tho) *m.* message; gift *(regalo);* regards *(recuerdo).*

recaer*, (rre·kâ·er´) *vn.* to fall back, to fall again; (med.) to have a relapse; to fall, to come *(parar en uno).*

recaída, (rre·kâ·ē´thâ) *f.* relapse.

recalcar, (rre·kâl·kâr´) *va.* to squeeze in to stuff in *(apretar);* to fill, to stuff *(llenar);* fig.) to dwell on, to emphasize; —, *vn.* (naut.) to list.

recalcitrante, (rre·kâl·sē·trân´te) *adj.* obstinate, stubborn.

recalentar*, (rre·kâ·len·târ´) *va.* to reheat.

recámara, (rre·kâ´mâ·râ) *f.* dressing room; (Mex.) bedroom; chamber *(del arma);* (fig.) circumspection.

recamarera, (rre·kâ·mâ·re´râ) *f.* (Sp. Am.) chambermaid.

recapacitar, (rre·kâ·pâ·sē·tar´) *va.* to recall to mind, to run over.

recapitular, (rre·kâ·pē·tū·lâr´) *va.* to recapitulate.

recargar, (rre·kâr·gâr´) *va.* to reload; to overload *(aumentar la carga);* (fig.) to overdress, to overdecorate; to increase *(agravar).*

recargo, (rre·kâr´go) *m.* extra tax *(aumento de gravamen);* increase *(aumento);* reloading; overload; new charge *(al reo).*

recatado, da, (rre·kâ·tâ´tho, thâ) *adj.* prudent, circumspect.

recato, (rre·kâ´to) *m.* caution, circumspection *(cautela);* modesty, reserve.

recaudar, (rre·kâū·thâr´) *va.* to take in, to collect *(caudales);* to take charge of, to keep under surveillance.

recelo, (rre·se´lo) *m.* dread, suspicion, mistrust.

receloso, sa, (rre·se·lo´so, sâ) *adj.* mistrustful, suspicious.

recepción, (rre·sep·syon´) *f.* reception; acceptance *(admisión).*

receptáculo, (rre·sep·tâ´kū·lo) *m.* receptacle.

receptor, (rre·sep·tor´) *m.* receiver; — de cabeza, headset.

receso, (rre·se´so) *m.* withdrawal, separation; (Mex.) recess; estar de —, to be adjourned.

receta, (rre·se´tâ) *f.* recipe; prescription *(de un medicamento).*

recetar, (rre·se·târ´) *va.* to prescribe.

recibimiento, (rre·sē·vē·myen´to) *m.* reception; waiting room *(antesala).*

recibir, (rre·sē·vēr´) *va.* to receive; to approve, to accept *(aprobar);* to let in *(admitir);* to go to meet *(salir al encuentro de);* —se, to receive one´s degree.

recib.º: recibido, recd. received.

recibo, (rre·sē´vo) *m.* receipt, voucher; acusar —, to acknowledge receipt.

recién, (rre·syen´) *adv.* recently, lately; — casado, da, newlywed.

reciente, (rre·syen´te) *adj.* late, recent.

recientemente, (rre·syen·te·men´te) *adv.* recently, lately.

recinto, (rre·sēn´to) *m.* area, space.

recio, cia, (rre´syo, syâ) *adj.* stout, strong; coarse, heavy, thick *(abultado);* rude, sharp *(áspero);* arduous, rough *(vigoroso);* —cio, *adv.* strongly, stoutly; hablar —cio, to talk loudly.

recipiente, (rre·sē·pyen´te) *m.* recipient, container.

reciprocidad, (rre·sē·pro·sē·thâth´) *f.* reciprocity.

reciproco, ca, (rre·sē´pro·ko, kâ) *adj.* reciprocal.

recitación, (rre·sē·tâ·syon´) *f.* recitation.

recitar, (rre·sē·tar´) *va.* to recite.

reclamación, (rre·klâ·mâ·syon´) *f.* claim, demand; reclaim; complaint.

reclamante, (rre·klâ·mân´te) *m.* and *f.* claimant.

reclamar, (rre·klâ·mâr´) *va.* to claim, to demand; to reclaim *(reivindicar);* to call for, to beg for *(implorar);* to lure *(las aves);* —, *vn.* to complain.

reclinar, (rre·klē·nâr´) *va.* and *vr.* to recline, to lean.

recluir*, (rre·klwēr´) *va.* to shut in, to seclude; —se, to go into seclusion.

recluta, (rre·klū´tâ) *f*. recruiting; —, *m.* recruit.

reclutamiento, (rre·klū·tâ·myen´to) *m.* recruiting.

reclutar, (rre·klū·târ´) *va.* to recruit.

recobrar, (rre·ko·vrâr´) *va.* to recover; — se, to recover.

recodo, (rre·ko´tho) *m.* bend, turn, twist.

recogedor, ra, (rre·ko·he·thor´, râ) *n.* harborer, shelterer *(que da acogida);* gatherer; —, *m.* scraper; — de basura, dustpan.

recoger, (rre·ko·her´) *va.* to take back; to gather, to collect, to pick up *(reunir);* to shelter *(abrigar);* to compile *(compilar);* —se, to take shelter, to take refuge; to retire *(a dormir);* (fig.) to withdraw from the world.

recogimiento, (rre·ko·hē·myen´to) *m.* gathering, collecting; sheltering; retiring.

recomendación, (rre·ko·men·dâ·syon´) *f.* recommendation.

recomendar*, (rre·ko·men·dâr´) *va.* to recommend.

recompensa, (rre·kom·pen´sâ) *f.* recompense, reward; en —, as a reward.

recompensar, (rre·kom·pen·sâr´) *va.* to recompense, to reward.

reconciliación, (rre·kon·sē·lyâ·syon´) *f.* reconciliation.

reconciliar, (rre·kon·sē·lyâr´) *va.* to reconcile; —se, to become reconciled.

recóndito, ta, (rre·kon´dē·to, tâ) *adj.* recondite.

reconocer*, (re·ko·no·ser´) *va.* to examine closely; to acknowledge, to be aware of *(admitir);* to confess, to admit *(confesar);* to recognize *(distinguir);* to consider *(contemplar);* (mil.) to reconnoiter; — se, to know oneself.

reconocido, da, (re·ko·no·sē´tho, thâ) *adj.* grateful.

reconocimiento, (re·ko·no·sē·myen´to) *m.* recognition; acknowledgement; gratitude *(agradecimiento);* confession; examination, inquiry *(examen);* (mil.) reconnaissance, reconnoitering; — médico, medical examination.

reconstituyente, (re·kons·tē·tū·yen´te) *m.* (med.) tonic.

reconstruir*, (re·kons·trwēr´) *va.* to reconstruct.

reconvenir*, (re·kom·be·nēr´) *va.* to retort with, to recriminate with.

recopilación, (re·ko·pē·lâ·syon´) *f.* sumary, abridgement.

recopilador, (re·ko·pē·lä·thor´) *m.* compiler.

recopilar, (re·ko·pē·lär´) *va.* to compile.

recordar*, (re·kor·thär´) *va.* to remind of *(avisar);* to remember, to recall; —, *vn.* to remember.

recorrer, (rre·ko·rrer´) *va.* to travel, to travel over *(caminar);* to repair *(reparar);* to run over, to go over *(repasar);* to peruse, to examine *(registrar).*

recorrido, (rre·ko·rrē´tho) *m.* run, path *(trayecto);* traveling over; repair; examination; **final del —,** end of the line.

recortar, (rre·kor·tär´) *va.* to cut away, to trim off; to cut out *(figuras).*

recorte, (rre·kor´te) *m.* cutting, clipping; **—de periódico,** newspaper clipping.

recostar*, (rre·kos·tär´) *va.* to lean, to recline.

recrear, (rre·kre·är´) *va.* to amuse, to recreate; to re-create *(crear de nuevo);* **—se,** to enjoy oneself, to have some recreation.

recreativo, va, (rre·kre·ä·tē´vo, vä) *adj.* recreative, diverting.

recreo, (rre·kre´o) *m.* recreation; recess; **campo** or **patio de —,** playground; **hora de —,** recess time.

recriminación, (rre·krē·mē·nä·syon´) *f.* recrimination.

recriminar, (rre·krē·mē·nar´) *va.* to recriminate.

recrudecer*, (rre·krū·the·ser´) *vn.* and *vr.* to flare up, to break out again.

rectamente, (rrek·tä·mente) *adv.* justly, rightly.

rectangular, (rrek·täng·gū·lär´) *adj.* rectangular.

rectángulo, (rrek·täng´gū·lo) *m.* rectangle.

rectificar, (rrek·tē·fē·kär´) *va.* to rectify, to correct.

rectilíneo, nea, (rrek·tē·lē´ne·o, ne·ä) *adj.* rectilinear.

rectitud, (rrek·tē·tūth´) *f.* straightness; (fig.) rectitude.

recto, ta, (rrek´to, tä) *adj.* straight; (fig.) just, upright *(justo);* literal *(sentido primitivo).*

rector, (rrek·tor´) *m.* rector.

rectoría, (rrek·to·rē´ä) *f.* rectory.

recua, (rre´kwä) *f.* pack train; (fig.) throng,

recubrir*, (rre·kū·vrēr´) *va.* to cover; to recover *(cubrir de nuevo);* to recap *(una llanta).*

recuento, (rre·kwen´to) *m.* inventory *(inventario);* count *(enumeración);*

recount *(segunda cuenta).*

recuerdo, (rre·kwer´tho) *m.* remembrance, memory, impression; souvenir, reminder *(cosa que recuerda);* souvenir, remembrance *(regalo).*

recular, (rre·kū·lär´) *vn.* to back up; to recoil *(un arma);* (fig.) to flag, to relent *(ceder).*

recuperación, (rre·kū·pe·rä·syon´) *f.* recovery; recuperation.

recuperar, (rre·kū·pe·rär´) *va.* to recover, to regain; **—se,** to recuperate.

recurrir, (rre·kū·rrēr´) *vn.* to resort, to have recourse, to turn.

recurso, (rre·kūr´so) *m.* resorting, having recourse *(acción);* request *(solicitud);* recourse, resort *(medio);* **— s humanos,** human resources; **—s naturales,** natural resources.

rechazar, (rre·chä·sär´) *va.* to repel, to repulse *(resistir);* to reject *(no aceptar);* to resist *(no ceder a).*

rechazo, (rre·chä´so) *m.* rejection *(negativa);* recoil, rebound *(rebote).*

rechinar, (rre·chē·när´) *vn.* to gnash *(los dientes);* to grind, to creak; (fig.) to do begrudgingly, to balk *(refunfuñar).*

rechoncho, cha, (rre·chon´cho, chä) *adj.* (coll.) chubby.

red, (reth) *f.* net; mesh, netting *(tejido);* (fig.) trap *(ardid);* network *(sistema).*

redacción, (rre·thäk·syon´) *f.* editing; editorial offices *(lugar);* editorial staff *(personal).*

redactar, (rre·thäk·tär´) *va.* to edit, to word, to write up.

redactor, ra, (rre·thäk·tor, rä) *n.* editor.

redecilla, (rre·the·sē´yä) *f.* hairnet.

redentor, ra, (rre·then·tor´, rä) *n.* redeemer; —, *adj.* redeeming; **el R—,** the Redeemer.

redil, (rre·thēl´) *m.* sheepfold; **volver al —,** (fig.) to get back on the straight and narrow.

redimible, (rre·thē·mē´vle) *adj.* redeemable.

redimir, (rre·thē·mēr´) *va.* to ransom *(al cautivo);* to redeem *(lo empeñado);* to exempt *(en un censo);* to buy back *(lo vendido).*

rédito, (rre´thē·to) *m.* yield, interest.

redoblar, (rre·tho·vlär´) *va.* to double; to bend back *(un clavo);* to go over, to do again *(repetir).*

redoma, (rre·tho´mä) *f.* vial.

redonda, (rre·thon´dä) *f.* (mus.) whole note; region, area *(comarca).*

redondear, (rre·thon·de·är´) *va.* to round

off; to clear *(sanear)*.

redondez, (rre·thon·des´) *f.* roundness.

redondo, da, (rre·thon´do, dâ) *adj.* round; **a la —,** roundabout, around.

reducción, (rre·thŭk·syon´) *f.* reduction; subjugation *(sometimiento);* (Sp.Am.) village of Indian converts.

reducir*, (rre·thŭ·sēr´) *va.* to reduce; to subjugate *(someter);* **— la marcha,** to slow down; **—se,** to cut down, to make ends meet; **—se a,** to resolve to, to be obliged to.

redundante, (rre·thŭn·dân´te), *adj.* redundant, superfluous.

redundar, (rre·thŭn·dâr´) *vn.* to overflow, to spill over *(rebosar);* to redound.

reelección, (rre·e·lek·syon´) *f.* reelection.

reelegir*, (rre·e·le·hēr´) *va.* to reelect.

reembolsar (rre·em·bol·sâr´) = **rembolsar.**

reembolso (rre·em·bol´so) = **rembolso.**

reemplazar (rre·em·plâ·sâr´) = **remplazar.**

reemplazo (rre·em·plâ´so) = **remplazo.**

reencarnación, (rre·eng·kâr·nâ·syon´) *f.* reincarnation.

ref.: referencia, ref. reference.

refacción, (rre·fâk·syon´) *f.* snack, light lunch *(merienda);* (Sp. Am.) repair *(reparación);* (coll.) bonus *(añadidura);* **piezas de —,** spare parts.

refajo, (rre·fâ´ho) *m.* petticoat, half slip.

referencia, (rre·fe·ren´syâ) *f.* reference.

referéndum, (rre·fe·ren´dŭn) *m.* referendum.

referente, (rre·fe·ren´te) *adj.* related, connected.

referir*, (rre·fe·rēr´) *va.* to relate *(contar);* to refer *(encaminar);* to relate *(relacionar);* **—se,** to refer *(remitirse);* to relate.

refilón, (rre·fē·lon´) **de —,** obliquely, askance.

refinado, da. (rre·fē·nâ´tho, thâ) *adj.* refined; (fig.) outstanding, distinguished *(sobresaliente);* clever, shrewd *(astuto).*

refinamiento, (rre·fē·nâ·myen´to) *m.* good taste, care, refinement.

refinar, (rre·fē·nâr´) *va.* to refine.

reflector, (rre·flek·tor´) *m.* reflector; searchlight *(luz).*

reflejar, (rre·fle·hâr´) *va.* to reflect.

reflejo, (rre·fle´ho) *m.* reflection; reflex *(movimiento reflejo);* immediate reaction *(reacción rápida);* **—. ja,** *adj.* reflected; (gram.) reflexive; reflex *(inconsciente).*

reflexión, (rre·flek·syon´) *f.* reflection.

reflexionar, (rre·flek·syo·nâr´) *vn.* to

reflect, to meditate, to consider.

reflexivo, va, (rre·flek·se´vo, vâ) *adj.* (gram.) reflexive; thoughtful, considerate *(que obra con reflexión);* reflecting.

reflujo, (rre·flŭ´ho) *m.* ebb tide; **flujo y —,** ebb and flow.

reforma, (rre·for´mâ) *f.* reform; **R—,** (eccl.) Reformation.

reformación, (rre·for·mâ·syon´) *f.* reform.

reformar, (rre·for·mâr´) *va.* to reform.

reformatorio, (rre·for·mâ·to´ryo) *m.* reformatory.

reforzado, da, (rre·for·sâ´tho, thâ) *adj.* reinforced; strengthened.

reforzar*, (rre·for·sâr´) *va.* to strengthen; to reinforce *(dar mayor solidez);* (fig.) to encourage *(animar).*

refractario, ria, (rre·frâk·tâ´ryo, ryâ) *adj.* refractory.

refrán, (rre·frân´) *m.* proverb, saying.

refrenar, (rre·fre·nâr´) *va.* to rein; (fig.) to check, to curb.

refrendar, (rre·fren·dâr´) *va.* to countersign; to validate *(un pasaporte).*

refrescante, (rre·fres·kân´te) *adj.* refreshing.

refrescar, (rre·fres·kâr´) *va.* to cool off; to renew *(renovar);* to refresh *(un recuerdo);* **—,** *vn.* to refresh oneself; to cool off *(el tiempo).*

refresco, (rre·fres´ko) *m.* refreshment.

refriega, (rre·frye´gâ) *f.* skirmish, minor engagement.

refrigerador, (rre·frē·he·râ·thor´) *m.* refrigerator.

refrigerar, (rre·frē·he·râr´) *va.* to refrigerate.

refuerzo, (rre·fwer´so) *m.* reinforcement.

refugiado, da, (ree·fū·hyâ´tho, thâ) *n.* refugee.

refugiar, (rre·fū·hyâr´) *va.* to shelter; **—se,** to take refuge.

refugio, (rre·fū´hyo) *m.* refuge; shelter *(asilo);* **— antiaéreo,** bomb shelter.

refulgente, (rre·fūl·hen´te) *adj.* radiant, shining.

refundir, (rre·fūn·dēr´) *va.* to recast *(los metales);* to revise *(una obra literaria).*

refunfuñar, (rre·fūm·fū·nyâr´) *vn.* to growl, to grumble.

refutar, (rre·fū·târ´) *va.* to refute.

regadera, (rre·gâ·the´râ) *f.* sprinkling can; irrigation canal *(reguera).*

regadío día, (rre·gâ·thē´o, thē´â) *adj.* irrigable; **—,** *m.* irrigated land.

regalar, (rre·gâ·lâr´) *va.* to make a gift of; to regale *(halagar);* **—se,** not to spare oneself anything.

regalía, (rre·gâ·lē´â) *f.* royal prerogative *(del soberano);* (fig.) privilege; bonus *(del empleado).*

regalo, (rre·gâ´lo) *m.* gift; pleasure *(gusto);* repast *(comida);* ease *(comodidad).*

regañadientes, (rre·gâ·nyâ·thyen´tes) **a —** grudgingly, grumblingly, against one´s will.

regañar, (rre·gâ·nyâr´) *va.* (coll.) to scold, to nag, to reprimand; **—,** *vn.* to snarl; to grumble *(enfadarse).*

regañón, ona, (rre·gâ·nyon´ o´nâ) *adj.* snarling; grumbling; scolding, nagging.

regar*, (rre·gâr´) *va.* to sprinkle *(esparcir agua);* to water; to flow through *(atravesar);* to spread *(derramar).*

regata, (rre·gâ´tâ) *f.* (naut.) regatta; small irrigation ditch.

regatear, (rre·gâ·te·âr´) *va.* to haggle over; **—,** *vn.* to jockey for position.

regateo, (rre·gâ·te´o) *m.* bargaining, haggling; (naut.) regatta.

regazo, (rre·gâ´so) *m.* lap; (fig.) fold, lap.

regeneración, (re·he·ne·râ·syon´) *f.* regeneration.

regenerar, (rre·he·ne·râr´) *va.* to regenerate.

regente, (rre·hen´te) *m.* regent.

regidor, (rre·hē·thor´) *m.* alderman, councilman; director *(gobernador).*

régimen, (rre´hē·men) *m.* regime; (med.) regimen, diet; period *(periodo);* (gram.) government.

regimiento, (rre·hē·myen´to) *m.* administration, direction; aldermen, councilmen, council *(conjunto de regidores);* (mil.) regiment.

regio, gia, (rre´hyo, hyâ) *adj.* royal, regal.

región, (rre·hyon´) *f.* region.

regionalismo, (rre·hyo·nâ·lēz´mo) *m.* regionalism.

regir*, (rre·hēr´) *va.* to rule, to govern; to administrate, to direct *(guiar);-, vn.* to be in force.

registrador, ra, (rre·hēs·trâ·thor´, râ) *adj.* registering; **caja —,** cash register; , *m.* registrar; inspector.

registrar, (rre·hēs·trâr´) *va.* to inspect, to examine *(examinar);* to search *(buscar);* to enter, to record, to register *(transcribir);* to mark *(anotar);* **—se,** to register.

registro, (rre·hēs´tro) *m.* register; registry office *(lugar);* bookmark *(de libro);* record, entry *(asiento);* regulator *(del reloj);* check point *(de lo empotrado).*

regla, (rre´glâ) *f.* ruler *(instrumento);* rule; order *(disciplina);* **— áurea,** golden rule;

— de cálculo, slide rule; **— fija,** standard rule.

reglamento, (rreg·lâ·men´to) *m.* bylaws.

regocijar, (rre·go·sē·hâr´) *va.* to gladden, to delight; **—se por,** to rejoice at.

regocijo, (rre·go·sē´ho) *m.* joy, rejoicing, happiness.

regordete, (rre·gor·the´te) *adj.* chubby, plump, roly-poly.

regresar, (rre·gre·sâr´) *vn.* to return, to come back.

regreso, (rre·gre´so) *m.* return; **de —,** on the way back.

regulador, ra, (rre·gū·lâ·thor´, râ) *adj.* regulating; **—,** *m.* regulator; **—dor de humedad,** humidistat.

regular, (rre·gū·lâr´) *va.* to regulate, to adjust; **—,** *adj.* regular; average *(mediano).*

regularidad, (rre·gū·lâ·rē·thâth´) *f.* regularity.

rehabilitación, (rre·â·vē·lē·tâ·syon´) *f.* rehabilitation.

rehabilitar, (rre·â·vē·lē·târ´) *va.* to rehabilitate.

rehacer*, (rre·â·ser´) *va.* to redo, to remake; to repair *(reparar);* **—se,** to rally one´s forces; to compose oneself *(serenarse).*

rehén, (rre·en´) *m.* hostage.

rehuir*, (rre·wēr´) *va.* to avert, to turn away *(apartar);* to avoid *(evitar);* **—,** *vn.* to backtrack *(el ciervo);* **—se,** to shrink back, to flee.

rehusar, (rre·ū·sâr´) *va.* to refuse, to decline.

reimpresión, (rreēm·pre·syon´) *f.* reprint.

reimprimir, (rreēm·prē·mēr´) *va.* to reprint.

reina, (rre´ē·nâ) *f.* queen.

reinado, (rreē·nâ´tho) *m.* reign.

reinar, (rreē·nâr´) *va.* to reign; to prevail *(prevalecer).*

reincidir, (rreēn·sē·thēr´) *vn.* to relapse, to fall back; **— en un error,** to repeat an error.

reino, (rre´ē·no) *m.* kingdom.

Reino Unido, (rre´ē·no ū·nē´tho) *m.* United Kingdom.

reintegración, (rreēn·te·grâ·syon´) *f.* reintegration, restoration.

reintegrar, (rreēn·te·grâr´) *va.* to reintegrate; to restore *(reconstituir);* **—se,** to recoup one´s losses.

reintegro, (rreēn·te´gro) *m.* reintegration; restoration.

reir*, (rre·ēr´) *vn.* to laugh; **—,** *vt.* to laugh at; **reírse de,** to laugh at.

m met, **n** not, **p** pot, **r** very, **rr** (none), **s** so, **t** toy, **th** with, **v** eve, **w** we, **y** yes, **z** zero

reiterar, (rreē·te·râr´) va. to reiterate, to repeat.

reja, (rre´hâ) f. plowshare (del arado); grille, grillwork.

rejilla, (rre·hē´yâ) f. grate; wicker (para sillas); (rad.) grid.

rejuvenecer*, (rre·hŭ·ve·ne·ser´) va. to rejuvenate.

relación, (rre·lâ·syon´) f. relationship (conexión); dealing (trato); account (narración); —ones, pl. courtship.

relacionado, da, (rre·lâ·syo·nâ´tho, thâ) adj. related, connected.

relacionar, (rre·lâ·syo·nâr´) va. to relate; —se, to become acquainted.

relajar, (rre·lâ·hâr´) va. to relax.

relámpago, (rre·lâm´pâ·go) m. lightning flash; — sin trueno, heat lightning; cierre —, zipper.

relampaguear, (rre·lâm·pâ·ge·âr´) vn. to lightning; (fig.) to flash, to sparkle (centellar).

relatar, (rre·lâ·târ´) va. to relate.

relatividad, (rre·lâ·tē·vē·thâth´) f. relativity.

relativo, va, (rre·lâ·tē´vo, vâ) adj. relative; —vo a, with regard to, as concerns.

relato, (rre·lâ´to) m. statement, account.

relator, ra, (rrē·lâ·tor´, râ) n. narrator, teller; —, adj. narrating, reporting.

relegar, (rre·le·gâr´) va. to banish, to exile; (fig.) to relegate (apartar).

relevante, (rre·le·vân´te) adj. eminent, outstanding.

relevar, (rre·le·vâr´) va. to put into relief; to free, to relieve (exonerar); to replace (sustituir); —, vn. to stand out; —se, to take turns.

relevo, (rre·le´vo) m. (mil.) relief; relieving, freeing; carrera de —s, relay race.

relicario, (rre·lē·kâ´ryo) m. reliquary; (Sp. Am.) locket, medallion (medallón).

relieve, (rre·lye´ve) m. relief; bajo —, bas-relief; dar —, to emphasize, to highlight.

religión, (rre·lē·hyon´) f. religion.

religioso, sa, (rre·lē·hyo´so, sâ) adj. religious; —, m. monk, brother; —, f. nun, sister.

relinchar, (rre·lēn·châr´) vn. to neigh.

relincho, (rre·lēn´cho) m. neigh, neighing.

relindo, da, (rre·lēn´do, dâ) adj. extremely pretty.

reliquia, (rre·lē´kyâ) f. relic.

reloj, (rre·lo´) m. clock; — de pulsera, wrist watch; — de arena, hourglass; — de bolsillo, pocket watch.

relojería, (rre·lo·he·rē´â) f. watchmaking

(arte); watch shop (taller).

relojero, (rre·lo·he´ro) m. watchmaker.

reluciente, (rre·lŭ·syen´te) adj. resplendent, glittering.

relucir*, (rre·lŭ·sēr´) vn. to shine.

relumbrante, (rre·lŭm·brân´te) adj. glittering, dazzling.

rellenar, (rre·ye·nâr´) va. to refill; to stuff (henchir).

relleno, (rre·ye´no) m. filling, stuffing, padding, packing; —, na, adj. chockfull, stuffed.

remachado, da, (rre·mâ·châ´tho, thâ) adj. riveted.

remachar, (rre·mâ·châr´) va. to rivet.

remache, (rre·mâ´che) m. rivet.

remanente, (rre·mâ·nen´te) m. residue, remains, remnant.

remangar, (rre·mâng·gâr´) va. to roll up.

remar, (rre·mâr´) vn. to row.

rematado, da, (rre·mâ·tâ´tho, thâ) adj. utter, absolute, hopeless, incurable; loco —, stark raving mad.

rematar, (rre·mâ·târ´) va. to auction off (subastar); to complete, to finish (acabar); to kill off, to finish off (matar); —, vn. to end; —se, to be utterly ruined.

remate, (rre·mâ´te) m. end, completion; winning bid (en una subasta); por —, finally; de —, absolutely, hopelessly, incurably.

rembolsar, (rrem·bol·sâr´) va. to reimburse.

rembolso, (rrem·bol´so) m, reimbursement.

remediable, (rre·me·thyâ´vle) adj. remediable, curable.

remediar, (rre·me·thyâr´) va. to remedy; to free from risk (librar de riesgo); to prevent, to avoid (estorbar).

remedio, (rre·me´thyo) m. remedy; recourse (recurso); sin —, helpless, unavoidable: no tener —, to be beyond help; no tiene —, it can´t be helped.

remedo, (rre·me´tho) m. poor imitation, pale copy.

remendar*, (rre·men·dâr´) va. to mend, to repair.

remero, (rre·me´ro) m. rower, oarsman.

remesa, (rre·me´sâ) f. remittance (de dinero); shipment, sending.

remiendo, (rre·myen´do) m. patch (pedazo); repair, reparation (de una cosa); (fig.) correction; a —s, piecemeal.

remilgarse, (rre·mēl·gâr´se) vr. to act affectedly, to be overly prim.

remilgo, (rre·mēl´go) m. affectation, prim

mannerism.

reminiscencia, (rre·mē·nēs·sen′syâ) f. reminiscence.

remisión, (rre·mē·syon′) f. remission *(suspensión);* shipment *(envío);* forgiveness *(perdón);* reference *(referencia);* remittance *(de dinero).*

remiso, sa, (rre·mē′so, sâ) adj. remiss.

remitente, (rre·mē·ten′te) m. and f. remitter, sender; —, adj. remittent.

remitir, (rre·mē·tēr′) va. to remit; to send *(enviar);* to refer to *(indicar);* to reduce, to slacken *(disminuir);* —, vn. to abate, to lose force; —**se a,** to refer to, to cite.

remoción, (rre·mo·syon′) f. removal; changing around; dismissal; stirring up.

remojar, (rre·mo·hâr′) va. to soak, to steep; (fig.) to celebrate.

remojo, (rre·mo′ho) m. steeping, soaking; (fig.) celebration.

remolacha, (rre·mo·lâ′châ) f. beet.

remolcador, (rre·mol·kâ·thor′) m. tug boat.

remolcar, (rre·mol·kâr′) va. to tow.

remolino, (rre·mo·lē′no) m. dust devil *(de aire);* eddy *(de agua);* (fig.) stir, whirl; swirl *(del pelo).*

remolón, ona, (rre·mo·lon′, o′nâ) adj. slow, lazy; laggard; —, m. upper tusk.

remolque, (rre·mol′ke) m. towing, tow; tow line *(cabo);* trailer *(vehículo remolcado);* **llevar a** —, to tow along.

remono, na, (rre·mo′no, nâ) adj. (coll.) very cute, cute as a bug′s ear.

remontar, (rre·mon·târ′) va. to frighten away *(la caza);* (mil.) to provide with fresh horses; to repair *(una silla);* to resole *(el calzado);* (fig.) to raise, to elevate; —**se,** to soar; —**se hasta,** to go back to.

rémora, (rre′mo·râ) f. (ichth.) remora; (fig.) hindrance, setback.

remordimiento, (rre·mor·thē·myen′to) m. remorse.

remoto, ta, (rre·mo′to, tâ) adj. remote, distant, far.

remover*, (rre·mo·ver′) va. to remove *(quitar);* to change around *(cambiar);* to dismiss *(deponer);* to stir, to stir up *(agitar);* —**se,** to get upset.

remozar, (rre·mo·sâr′) va. to rejuvenate;— **se,** to become rejuvenated.

remplazar, (rrem·plâ·sâr′) va. to replace.

remplazo, (rrem·plâ′so) m. replacement, substitute.

remuneración, (rre·mū·ne·râ·syon′) f. remuneration, recompense.

remunerar, (rre·mū·ne·râr′) va. to reward, to remunerate, to repay.

renacer*, (rre·nâ·ser′) vn. (eccl.) to be born again; to come to life again; (fig.) to feel as good as new.

renacimiento, (rre·nâ·sē·myen′to) m. renascence, rebirth; **R—,** Renaissance.

rencilla, (rren·sē′yâ) f. bitter quarrel.

rencor, (rreng·kor′) m. rancor, grudge, ill will; **guardar** —, to bear a grudge.

rendición, (rren·dē·syon′) f. surrender; profit, yield *(réditos);* rendition (interpretación).

rendido, da, (rren·dē′tho, thâ) adj. worn-out, fatigued *(cansado);* submissive *(sumiso).*

rendija, (rren·dē′hâ) f. crevice, crack.

rendimiento, (rren·dē·myen′to) m. weariness *(fatiga);* submissiveness *(sumisión);* output, yield *(utilidad).*

rendir*, (rren·dēr′) va. to overcome *(vencer);* to deliver over *(entregar);* to subdue *(sujetar);* to produce, to yield *(producir);* —**se,** to surrender *(entregarse);* to wear oneself out *(fatigarse).*

renegado, da, (rre·ne·gâ′tho, thâ) n. apostate, renegade; —, adj. (coll.) surly.

renegar*, (rre·ne·gâr′) va. to deny, to disown *(negar);* to nag; to detest, to abhor *(abominar);* —, vn. to abandon Christianity; to blaspheme, to curse *(blasfemar).*

renglón, (rreng·glon′) m. line; (fig.) item *(del gasto).*

reno, (rre′no) m. reindeer.

renombrado, da, (rre·nom·brâ′tho, thâ) adj. renowned.

renombre, (rre·nom′bre) m. renown.

renovación, (rre·no·vâ·syon′) f. renovation, renewal.

renovar*, (rre·no·vâr′) va. to renovate; to replace *(sustituir);* to repeat *(reiterar).*

renta, (rren′tâ) f. rent, income.

rentista, (rren·tēs′tâ) m. and f. financier.

renuente, (rre·nwen′te) adj. reluctant, unwilling.

renuncia, (rre·nūn′syâ) f. refusal; resignation.

renunciar, (rre·nūn·syâr′) va. to renounce; to refuse *(no aceptar);* to resign from *(un empleo).*

reñido, da, (rre·nyē′tho, thâ) adj. at loggerheads, at odds *(enemistado);* hard-fought.

reñir*, (rre·nyēr′) vn. to wrangle, to quarrel, to fight; to have a falling out, to become enemies *(enemistarse);* —, va. to fight *(un desafío);* to scold *(regañar).*

reo, (rre′o) *m.* and *f.* offender, criminal.

reojo, (rre·o′ho) **mirar de** —, to look out of the corner of one′s eye; *(coll.)* to look at contemptuously, to look askance at *(con desprecio).*

reorganización, (rre·or·gâ′·nē·sâ·syon′) *f.* reorganization

reóstato, (rre·os′tâ·to) *m.* rheostat.

Rep.: república, rep. republic.

reparable, (rre·pâ·râ′vle) *adj.* reparable, remediable; noteworthy *(notable).*

reparación, (rre·pâ·râ·syon′) *f.* reparation, repair.

reparar, (rre·pâ·râr′) *va.* to repair, to mend *(componer);* to parry *(evitar);* to note, to observe *(notar);* to make amends for *(remediar);* to dwell on *(considerar);* to get satisfaction for *(una ofensa);* —, *vn.* to stop over, to stay over, to stop; **—se,** to contain oneself, to refrain oneself.

reparo, (rre·pâ′ro) *m.* repair, reparation; remark, observation *(observación);* warning, notice *(advertencia);* defense *(defensa);* obstacle, difficulty *(dificultad);* **poner** —, to object.

repartición, (rre·pâr·tē·syon′) *f.* distribution, division.

repartir, (rre·pâr·tēr′) *va.* to distribute, to divide up.

reparto, (rre·pâr′to) *m.* distribution; allotment *(asignación);* assessment *(contribución);* (theat.) cast of characters; (Sp. Am.) subdivision.

repasar, (rre·pâ·sâr′) *va.* to review *(recorrer);* to revise *(corregir);* to look over *(examinar);* to repass, to retrace *(desandar).*

repaso, (rre·pâ′so) *m.* review; revision.

repatriación, (rre·pâ·tryâ·syon′) *f.* repatriation.

repatriado, da, (rre·pâ·tryâ′tho, thâ) *adj.* repatriated; —, *n.* repatriate.

repeler, (rre·pe·ler′) *va.* to repel, to reject.

repelón, (rre·pe·lon′) *m.* pull on one′s hair; snag *(en las medias);* tiny bit *(porción):* bolt, dash *(del caballo);* **a —ones,** little by little, bit by bit; **de —,** quickly.

repello, (rre·pe′yo) *m.* plastering.

repente, (rre·pen′te) *m.* (coll.) burst, start; **de —,** suddenly.

repentino, na, (rre·pen·tē′no, nâ) *adj.* sudden, unforeseen.

repercusión, (rre·per·kū·syon′) *f.* reverberation, repercussion: bouncing off.

repercutir, (rre·per·kū·tēr′) *vn.* to reverberate; to be deflected, to rebound, to bounce off *(un cuerpo).*

repertorio, (rre·per·to′ryo) *m.* repertory.

repetición, (rre·pe·tē·syon′) *f.* repetition; (mus.) repeat.

repetidor, ra, (rre·pe·tē·thor′, râ) *n.* repeater; —, *adj.* repeating.

repetir*, (rre·pe·tēr′) *va.* to repeat.

repicar, (rre·pē·kâr′) *va.* to chime, to peal.

repique, (rre·pē′ke) *m.* chime, peal; (fig.) tiff *(quimera).*

repiqueteo, (rre·pē·ke·te′o) *m.* pealing, chiming *(de las campanas);* pitter-patter, patter, tattoo.

repisa, (rre·pē′sâ) *f.* stand.

repleto, ta, (rre·ple′to, tâ) *adj.* replete, full, loaded.

réplica, (rre′plē·kâ) *f.* answer, retort; replica *(copia).*

replicar, (rre·plē·kâr′) *vn.* to reply, to retort; to answer back, to argue *(poner objeciones).*

repollo, (rre·po′yo) *m.* head of cabbage.

reponer*, (rre·po·ner′) *va.* to put back, to replace; to revive *(una obra dramática);* to retort, to reply *(replicar);* to reinstate, to provide *(remplazar);* **—se,** to calm down *(serenarse);* to recover.

reportar, (rre·por·târ′) *va.* to refrain, to hold back *(refrenar);* to obtain, to reach, to attain *(lograr);* to carry, to bring *(llevar).*

reportero, ra, (rre·por·te′ro, râ) *n.* reporter; —, *adj.* reporting.

reposado, da, (rre·po·sâ′tho, thâ) *adj.* quiet, peaceful; settled *(un líquido).*

reposar, (rre·po·sâr′) *vn.* to rest, to repose; **—se,** to settle.

reposo, (rre·po′so) *m.* rest, repose.

repostería, (rre·pos·te·rē′â) *f.* pastry shop *(tienda);* butler′s pantry *(despensa).*

repostero, (rre·pos·te′ro) *m.* pastry cook.

reprender, (rre·pren·der′) *va.* to reprimand, to scold, to blame.

reprensión, (rre·pren·syon′) *f.* reprimand, scolding, blame.

represa, (rre·pre′sâ) *f.* damming up, holding back.

represalia, (rre·pre·sâ′lyâ) *f.* reprisal, retaliation.

representación, (rre·pre·sen·tâ·syon′) *f.* representation; authority *(autoridad);* (theat.) performance.

representante, (rre·pre·sen·tân′te) *m.* and *f.* representative; (theat.) actor.

representar, (rre·pre·sen·târ′) *va.* to represent; (theat.) to perform, to present.

representativo, va, (rre·pre·sen·tâ·tē′vo, vâ) *adj.* representative.

represión, (rre·pre·syon′) *f.* repression.

reprimenda, (rre·prē·men'dâ) *f.* reprimand.

reprimir, (rre·prē·mēr') *va.* to repress.

reprobable, (rre·pro·vä'vle) *adj.* reprehensible.

reprobación, (rre·pro·vâ·syon') *f.* reprobation, condemnation; failing, flunking *(en una prueba).*

reprobar*, (rre·pro·vâr') *va.* to reprove; to condemn; to fail, to flunk.

réprobo, ba, (rre'pro·vo,vä) *adj. and n.* reprobate.

reprochar, (rre·pro·châr') *va.* to reproach.

reproche, (rre·pro'che) *m.* reproach.

reproducción, (rre·pro·thūk·syon') *f.* reproduction.

reproducir*, (rre·pro·thū·sēr') *va.* to reproduce.

reptil, (rrep·tēl') *m.* reptile.

república, (rre·pū'vlē·kâ) *f.* republic.

República Sudafricana, (rre·pū'vlē·kâ sū'·thâ·frē·kâ'nä) *f.* South African Republic.

republicano, na, (rre·pū·vlē·kâ'no, nä) *adj. and n.* republican.

repudiar, (rre·pū·thyâr') *va.* to repudiate.

repuesto, (rre·pwes'to) *m.* replacement; **piezas de —,** spare parts; **llanta** or **neumático de —,** spare tire.

repugnancia, (rre·pūg·nân'syä) *f.* repugnance, contradiction.

repugnante, (rre·pūg·nân'te) *adj.* repugnant, disgusting.

repugnar, (rre·pūg·nâr') *va.* to contradict *(ser opuesto);* to do with reluctance, to be against *(hacer de mala gana);* **—,** *vn.* to be repugnant.

repulgar, (rre·pūl·gâr') *va.* to hem, to border; to flute *(un pastel).*

repulsa, (rre·pūl'sä) *f.* denial, rejection.

repulsión, (rre·pūl·syon') *f.* repulsion.

reputación, (rre·pū·tâ·syon') *f.* reputation, renown.

reputar, (rre·pū·târ') *va.* to repute; to esteem *(apreciar).*

requerimiento, (rre·ke·rē·myen'to) *m.* notification; requiring; examination.

requerir*, (rre·ke·rēr') *va.* to notify *(avisar);* to require *(necesitar);* to examine *(examinar);* to persuade *(inducir);* to court *(amorosamente).*

requesón, (rre·ke·son') *m.* cottage cheese; curds *(residuos).*

requiebro, (rre·kye'vro) *m.* flattery, flattering; flattering remark, compliment *(frase).*

réquiem, (rre'kyen) *m.* requiem.

requisito, (rre·kē·sē'to) *m.* requisite, requirement.

res, (rres) *f.* head of cattle; wild animal *(salvaje);* **carne de —,** beef.

resabio, (rre·sâ'vyo) *m.* unpleasant aftertaste; bad habit, bad feature *(vicio).*

resaca, (rre·sâ'kâ) *f.* undertow; (coll.) hangover *(malestar).*

resalado, da, (rre·sâ·lâ'tho, thâ) *adj.* (coll.) charming, delightful.

resaltar, (rre·sâl·târ') *vn.* to rebound; to project *(sobresalir);* (fig.) to stand out *(destacarse).*

resarcir, (rre·sâr·sēr') *va.* to compensate, to make amends to.

resbaladizo, za, (rrez·vâ·lâ·thē'so, sâ) *adj.* slippery; (fig.) tricky, deceptive.

resbalar, (rrez·vâ·lâr') *vn. and vr.* to slip, to slide; (fig.) to trip up, to make a mistake.

resbalón, (rrez·vâ·lon') *m.* slip, sliding; (fig.) slip, error.

resbaloso, sa, (rrez·vâ·lo'so, sâ) *adj.* slippery.

rescatar, (rres·kâ·târ') *va.* to ransom *(a un cautivo);* to redeem.

rescate, (rres·kâ'te) *m.* ransom; redemption price.

rescindir, (rres·sēn·dēr') *va.* to rescind, to annul.

resecar, (rre·se·kâr') *va.* to dry out, to dry thoroughly.

resentido, da, (rre·sen·tē'tho, thâ) *adj.* resentful, angry, hurt, offended.

resentimiento, (rre·sen·tē·myen'to) *m.* resentment.

resentirse*, (rre·sen·tēr'se) *vr.* to begin to give way, to weaken *(flaquear);* to feel resentment, to be hurt *(enojarse).*

reseña, (rre·se'nyä) *f.* review; personal description *(de una persona).*

reseñar, (rre·se·nyâr') *va.* to review; to describe *(describir).*

reserva, (rre·ser'vä) *f.* reserve; reservation *(excepción);* **con** or **bajo la mayor —,** in strictest confidence; **de —,** spare, extra; **sin —,** frankly, openly.

reservado, da, (rre·ser·vä'tho, thâ) *adj.* reserved; cautious *(cauteloso);* circumspect *(discreto);* **—,** *m.* booth.

reservar, (rre·ser·vâr') *va.* to reserve; to retain, to keep back *(retener);* to conceal, to hide *(ocultar);* to postpone *(aplazar);* **—se,** to beware, to be on one's guard.

resfriado, (rres·fryâ'tho) *m.* cold.

resfriarse, (rres·fryâr'se) *vr.* to catch cold.

resfrío, (rres·frē'o) *m.* cold.

resguardar, (rrez·gwâr·thâr') *va.* to preserve, to defend; —**se,** to be on one´s guard.

resguardo, (rez·gwar´tho) *m.* defense, protection *(defensa);* voucher *(cédula).*

residencia, (rre·sē·then´syä) *f.* residence.

residencial, (rre·sē·then·syäl´) *adj.* residential.

residente, (rre·sē·then´te) *adj.* residing; —, *m.* and *f.* resident, inhabitant.

residir, (rre·sē·thēr´) *vn.* to reside, to dwell.

residuo, (rre·sē´thwo) *m.* residue.

resignación, (rre·sēg·nä·syon´) *f.* resignation.

resignado, da, (rre·sēg·nä´tho, thä) *adj.* resigned.

resignarse, (rre·sēg·när´se) *vr.* to be resigned, to resign oneself.

resina, (rre·sē´nä) *f.* resin, rosin.

resinoso, sa, (rre·sē·no´so, sä) *adj.* resinous.

resistencia, (rre·sēs·ten´syä) *f.* resistance.

resistente, (rre·sēs·ten´te) *adj.* resistant.

resistible, (rre·sēs·tē´vle) *adj.* resistible.

resistir, (rre·sēs·tēr´) *va.* to stand, to bear *(tolerar);* to resist *(rechazar);* —, *vn.* to resist; —**se,** to struggle.

resma, (rrez´mä) *f.* ream.

resolución, (rre·so·lū·syon´) *f.* resolution.

resoluto, ta, (rre·so·lū´to, tä) *adj.* resolute, resolved.

resolver*, (rre·sol·ver´) *va.* to resolve, to solve; to decide on *(determinar);* to dissolve *(disolver);* to break down, to analyze *(analizar);* —**se,** to resolve, to determine, to make up one´s mind.

resollar*, (rre·so·yär´) *vn.* to breathe deeply, to breathe hard; (coll.) to show up *(dar noticia de si).*

resonancia, (rre·so·nän´syä) *f.* resonance.

resonar*, (rre·so·när´) *vn.* to resound; (fig.) to have repercussions.

resoplar, (rre·so·plär´) *vn.* to snort, to puff.

resorte, (rre·sor´te) *m.* spring; (fig.) springboard *(medio).*

respaldar, (rres·päl·där´) *va.* (fig.) to indorse, to back; —, *m.* backrest.

respaldo, (rres·päl´do) *m.* backrest; (fig.) backing, indorsement.

respectivo, va, (rres·pek·tē´vo, vä) *adj.* respective.

respecto, (rres·pek´to) *m.* relation, respect; **al** —, in this regard; — **a** or **con** — **a,** in regard to, relative to.

respetable, (rres·pe·tä´vle) *adj.* respectable, honorable.

respetar, (rres·pe·tär´) *va.* to respect.

respeto, (rres·pe´to) *m.* respect, regard, consideration.

respetuoso, sa, (rres·pe·two´so, sä) *adj.* respectful.

respiración, (rres·pē·rä·syon´) *f.* respiration, breathing; circulation *(en un aposento).*

respirar, (rres·pē·rär´) *vn.* and *va.* to breathe.

respiro, (rres·pē´ro) *m.* breathing; respite *(descanso);* (com.) extension.

resplandecer*, (rres·plän·de·ser´) *vn.* To shine, to glitter; (fig.) to excel, to stand out.

resplandeciente, (rres·plän·de·syen´te) *adj.* resplendent, brilliant, radiant.

resplandor, (rres·plän·dor´) *m.* brilliance, radiance.

responder, (rres·pon·der´) *va.* to answer; —, *vn.* to respond; to answer back *(ser respondón);* to be answerable, to be responsible *(ser responsable).*

responsabilidad, (rres·pon·sä·vē·lē·thäth´) *f.* responsibility.

responsable, (rres·pon·sä´vle) *adj.* responsible, accountable.

responso, (rres·pon´so) *m.* (eccl.) prayer for the dead.

respuesta, (rres·pwes´tä) *f.* answer, reply.

resquebrar*, (rres´ke·vrär´) *va.* to start to break, to open cracks.

resquicio, (rres·kē´syo) *m.* crack, cleft; (fig.) opportunity, chance *(ocasión).*

resta, (rres´tä) *f.* (math.) subtraction; remainder *(residuo).*

restablecer*, (rres·tä·vle·ser´) *va.* to reestablish, to restore; —**se,** to recover.

restablecimiento, (rres·tä·vle·sē·myen´to) *m.* reestablishment; recovery *(convalecencia).*

restante, (rres·tän´te) *m.* rest, remainder; —, *adj.* remaining.

restar, (rres·tär´) *va.* to subtract; —, *vn.* to be left, to remain.

restauración, (rres·täū·rä·syon´) *f.* restoration.

restaurante, (rres·täū·rän´te) *m.* restaurant.

restaurar, (rres·täū·rar´) *va.* to restore.

restituir*, (rres·tē·twēr´) *va.* to restore; —**se,** to return, to go back.

resto, (rres´to) *m.* remainder, rest.

restregar*, (rres·tre·gär´) *va.* to scrub hard.

restricción, (rres·trēk·syon´) *f.* restriction, limitation.

restringir, (rres·trēn·hēr´) *va.* to limit, to restrict.

â arm, **e** they, **ē** bē, **o** fore, **ū** blūe, **b** bad, **ch** chip, **d** day, **f** fat, **g** go, **h** hot, **k** kid, **1** let

restriñir*, (rres·trē·nyēr´) va. to constrict,
resucitar, (rre·sū·sē·târ´) va. to resusci-
tate; to resurrect *(volver la vida).*
resuelto, ta, (rre·swel´to, tâ) adj. resolved,
determined; rapid, diligent *(pronto).*
resuello, (rre·swe´yo) m. heavy breathing,
panting.
resulta, (rre·sūl´tä) f. result, consequence;
vacancy *(de un empleo);* de —s, as a
consequence.
resultado, (rre·sūl·tä´tho) m. result, consequence, outcome.
resultar, (rre·sūl·târ´) vn. to result; to
turn out *(salir).*
resumen, (rre·sū´men) m. summary.
resumir, (rre·sū·mēr´) va. to abridge, to
summarize.
resurgir, (rre·sūr·hēr´) vn. to reappear.
resurrección, (rre·sū·rrek·syon´) f. resurrection.
retablo, (rre·tä´vlo) m. (eccl.) reredos.
retaguardia, (rre·tä·gwär´thyä) f. rear
guard.
retahíla, (rre·tä·ē´lä) f. succession, string;
de —, one after another, in a series.
retar, (rre·târ´) va. to challenge; (coll.) to
call down *(reprender.)*
retardar, (rre·târ·thâr´) va. to retard, to
delay.
retardo, (rre·tar´tho) m. delay.
retazo, (rre·tä´so) m. remnant, scrap; —s,
pl. odds and ends.
retención, (rre·ten·syon´) f. retention.
retener*, (rre·te·ner´) va. to retain.
retentiva, (rre·ten·tē´vä) f. memory, recall.
reticencia, (rre·tē·sen´syä) f. reticence.
reticente, (rre·tē·sen´te) adj. reticent.
retina, (rre·tē´nä) f. retina.
retirada, (rre·tē·rá´thä) f. withdrawal;
retreat *(lugar).*
retirado, da, (rre·tē·rä´tho, thä) adj. retired.
retirar, (rre·tē·râr´) va. to withdraw; (mil.)
to retire; to take away *(guitar);* —se, to
retire *(irse);* to go into seclusion.
retiro, (rre·tē´ro) m. retirement.
reto, (rre´to) m. challenge; threat *(amenaza).*
retocar, (rre·to·kâr´) va. to retouch; to put
the finishing touches on *(dar la última
mano).*
retoñar, (rre·to·nyâr´) vn. to sprout; (fig.)
to crop out, to show up again.
retoño, (rre·to´nyo) m. sprout, shoot.
retoque, (rre·to´ke) m. retouching; slight
touch *(de una enfermedad).*
retorcer*, (rre·tor·ser´) va. to twist.
retorcimiento, (rre·tor·sē·myen´to) m.

twisting.
retórica, (rre·to´rē·ka) f. rhetoric.
retórico, ca, (rre·to´rē·ko, kâ), adj. rhetorical.
retornar, (rre·tor·nâr´) va. to return, to
give back; —, vn. to return, to go back.
retorno, (rre·tor´no) m. return; barter, exchange (trueque).
retortijón, (rre·tor·tē·hon´) m. twisting; —
de tripas, cramp.
retozar, (rre·to·sâr´) vn. to frisk, to frolic;
to roughhouse, to engage in horseplay
(juguetear).
retozo, (rre·to´so) m. friskiness, merrymaking.
retozón, ona, (rre·to·son´, o´nä) adj. frolicsome, playful.
retractar, (rre·trâk·târ´) va. to retract.
retraer*, (rre·trâ·er´) va. to bring back; to
dissuade (disuadir); —se, to take refuge
(refugiarse); to back off, to retreat (retirarse).
retraído, da, (rre·trâ·ē´tho, thä) adj. reserved, shy.
retraimiento, (rre·trâē·myen´to) m. retreat,
asylum, seclusion; aloofness, reserve
(reserva).
retrasar, (rre·trä·sâr´) va. to defer, to put
off; —, vn. to lag, to decline; to be
slow (el reloj); —se, to be delayed.
retraso, (rre·trä´so) m. delay, slowness.
retratar, (rre·trâ·târ´) va. to portray; to
photograph (fotografiar); —se, to sit for
a portrait.
retrato (rre·trâ´to) m. portrait; photograph; vivo —, very image.
retreta, (rre·tre´tä) f. (mil.) retreat; (Sp.
Am.) open air concert.
retrete, (rre·tre´te) m. closet; water closet,
toilet (excusado).
retribución, (rre·trē·vū·syon´) f. retribution.
retribuir*, (rre·trē·vwēr´) va. to repay.
retroactivo, va, (rre·tro·âk·tē´vo, vä) adj.
retroactive.
retrocarga, (rre·tro·kâr´gä) f. de —,
breech-loading.
retroceder, (rre·tro·se·ther´) vn. to back
up, to go backward.
retroceso, (rre·tro·se´so) m. retrocession.
retrocohete, (rre·tro·ko·e´te) m. retro-roc-
ket.
retrogradación, (rre·tro·grä·thä·syon´) f.
retrogression, retrogradation.
retrógrado, da, (rre·tro´grä·tho, thä) adj.
retrograde; (fig.) backward.
retroimpulso, (rre·troēm·pūl´so) m. jet
propulsion.

m met, n not, p pot, r very, rr (none), s so, t toy, th with, v eve, w we, y yes, z zero

retropropulsión, (rre·tro·pro·pūl·syon´) f. jet propulsion; **avión de —,** jet plane.

retrospectivo, va, (rre·tros·pek tē´vo, vâ) adj. retrospective, backward; **en —a,** in retrospect.

retumbar, (rre·tūm·bâr´) vn. to resound, to thunder, to crash.

reuma, (rre´ū·mâ) f. (med.) rheumatism.

reumático, ca, (rreū·mâ´tē·ko, kâ´) adj. rheumatic.

reumatismo, (rreū·mâ·tēz´mo) m. rheumatism.

reumatoideo, dea, (rreū·mâ·toē·the´o, the´â) adj. rheumatoid; **artritis —dea,** rheumatoid arthritis.

reunión, (rreū·nyon´) f. reunion, meeting, gathering; reuniting (acción).

reunir, (rreū·nēr´) va. to bring together, to reunite; to gather together (juntar); **— se,** to meet, to rendezvous.

revalidar, (rre·vâ·lē·thâr´) va. to revalidate; **—se,** to take one´s qualifying exams for a degree.

revaluación, (rre·vâ·lwâ·syon´) f. revaluation.

revelación, (rre·ve·lâ·syon´) f. revelation, disclosure; (phot.) development.

revelar, (rre·ve·lâr´) va. to reveal, to disclose; (phot.) to develop.

revendedor, (rre·ven·de·thor´) m. reseller.

revender, (rre·ven·der´) va. to resell.

reventa, (rre·ven´tâ) m. resale.

reventar*, (rre·ven·târ´) vn. to blow out (un neumático); to break (las olas); to burst out (brotar); to explode (por impulso interior); to be dying, to be itching (con ansias); **—,** va. to smash; to annoy (molestar); (fig.) to break, to ruin.

reverberar, (rre·ver·ve·râr´) va. to reverberate.

reverdecer*, (rre·ver·the·ser´) vn. to grow green again; (fig.) to get back one´s pep.

reverencia, (rre·ve·ren´syâ) f. reverence; bow, curtsy (inclinación).

reverenciar, (rre·ve·ren·syâr´) va. to venerate, to revere.

reverendo, da, (rre·ve·ren´do, dâ) adj. reverent; (eccl.) reverend.

reverente, (rre·ve·ren´te) adj. respectful, reverent.

reversión, (rre·ver·syon´) f. reversion, return.

reverso, (rre·ver´so) m. reverse; **el — de la medalla,** the exact opposite.

revés, (rre·ves´) m. reverse, wrong side; misfortune (desgracia); **al —,** back-

wards; inside out (invertido).

revesado, da, (rre·ve·sâ´tho, thâ) adj. difficult, entangled, obscure (difícil); wayward, indomitable (travieso).

revestir*, (rre·ves·tēr´) va. to put on, to don (vestir); to cover (cubrir); to assume, to present (un aspecto); **—se,** to grow proud (engreírse); to be swayed (imbuirse); to gird oneself.

revisar, (rre·vē·sâr´) va. to revise; to check (controlar).

revisión, (rre·vē·syon´) f. revision; checking.

revisor, ra, (rre·vē·sor´, râ) n. checker, examiner; (rail.) conductor; **—,** adj. examining.

revista, (rre·vēs´tâ) f. review; magazine, review (publicación).

revistar, (rre·vēs·târ´) va. (mil.) to review.

revivir, (rre·vē·vēr´) vn. to revive.

revocable, (rre·vo·kâ´vle) adj. revocable.

revocación, (rre·vo·kâ·syon´) f. revocation.

revocar, (rre·vo·kâr´) va. to revoke; to drive back (hacer retroceder).

revolcarse*, (rre·vol·kâr´se) vr. to wallow, to roll around.

revolotear, (rre·vo·lo·te·âr´) vn. to flutter.

revoltillo, (rre·vol·tē´yo) m. disorder, mess, jumble.

revoltoso, sa, (rre·vol·to´so, sâ) adj. seditious, riotous; wild, noisy (turbulento).

revolución, (rre·vo·lū·syon´) f. revolution.

revolucionar, (rre·vo·lū·syo·nâr´) va. to revolutionize.

revolucionario, ria, (rre·vo·lū·syo·nâ´ryo, ryâ) adj. revolutionary; **—,** n. revolutionist.

revolver*, (rre·vol·ver´) va. to stir, to shake (menear); to involve (enredar); to upset (producir náuseas); to look through, to go through (registrar); to go over (discurrir); to stir up (alborotar); to rotate, to revolve (hacer dar vueltas).

revólver, (rre·vol´ver) m. revolver.

revuelo, (rre·vwe´lo) m. flight; commotion, stir (confusión).

revuelta, (rre·vwel´tâ) f. revolt, uprising; turn (cambio de dirección).

revuelto, ta, (rre·vwel´to, tâ) adj. in disorder, confused, mixed up; boisterous, restless (turbulento).

rey, (rre´ē) m. king; **los Reyes Magos,** the three Wise Men.

reyerta, (rre·yer´tâ) f. dispute.

rezagado, da, (rre·sâ·gâ´tho, thâ) adj. left behind; **cartas —s,** unclaimed letters.

rezagar, (rre·sâ·gâr´) va. to leave behind; to defer (diferir); **—se,** to remain

behind, to lag behind.
rezar, (rrē·sâr´) va. to pray.
rezo, (rrē´so) m. praying, prayers; daily
devotions (oficio religioso).
ría, (rrē´â) f. estuary.
ribera, (rrē·ve´râ) f. shore, bank, edge.
ribereño, ña, (rrē·ve·re´nyo, nyâ) adj.
shore, coastal; riverbank (de un río).
ribete, (rrē·ve´te) m. trimming, border,
edging.
ribetear, (rrē·ve·te·âr´) va. to trim, to border, to edge.
riboflavina, (rrē·vo·flâ·vē´nâ) f. riboflavin.
ricacho, cha, (rrē·kâ´cho, châ) adj. (coll.)
rolling in money.
ricino, (rrē·sē´no) m. castor oil plant; aceite de — castor oil.
rico, ca, (rrē´ko, kâ) adj. rich; delicious
(delicioso).
ridiculez, (rrē·thē·kū·les´) f. ridiculous
thing, stupid thing.
ridiculizar, (rrē·thē·kū·lē·sâr´) va. to
ridicule.
ridículo, la, (rrē·thē´kū·lo, lâ) adj. ridiculous; poner en —, to make a fool of.
riego, (rrye´go) m. watering; sprinkling
(esparcimiento); water supply (agua
disponible).
riel, (rryel) m. rail.
rienda, (rryen´dâ) f. rein; a — suelta, with
free rein.
riesgo, (rryez´go) m. danger, risk.
rifa, (rrē´fâ) f. raffle, lottery (sorteo); scuffle, dispute (disputa).
rifar, (rrē·fâr´) va. to raffle.
rigidez, (rrē·hē·thes´) f. rigidity, stiffness.
rígido, da, (rrē´hē·tho, thâ) adj. rigid.
rigor, (rrē·gor´) m. rigor.
riguroso, sa, (rrē·gū·ro´so, sâ) adj. rigorous.
rima, (rrē´mâ) f. rhyme.
rimar, (rrē·mâr´) va. and vn. to rhyme.
rimbombante, (rrēm·bom·bân´te) adj.
flashy, showy.
rincón, (rrēng·kon´) m. corner.
rinconera, (rrēng·ko·ne´râ) f. corner table;
corner cupboard (vitrina).
rinoceronte, (rrē·no·se·ron´te) m. rhinoceros.
riña, (rrē´nyâ) f. quarrel.
riñón, (rrē·nyon´) m. kidney.
río, (rrē´o) m. river.
ripio, (rrē´pyo) m. waste (residuo); rubble
(fragmentos); padding (para completar
el verso); useless padding, verbiage (en
un discurso).
riqueza, (rrē·ke´sâ) f. riches, wealth.
risa, (rrē´sâ) f. laugh, laughter.

risco, (rrēs´ko) m. cliff.
risible, (rrē·sē´vle) adj. laughable.
risotada, (rrē·so·tâ´thâ) f. outburst of
laughter, guffaw.
risueño, ña, (rrē·swe´nyo, nyâ) adj. smiling, pleasant.
rítmico, ca, (rrēth´mē·ko, kâ) adj. rhythmical.
ritmo, (rrēth´mo) m. rhythm.
rito, (rrē´to) m. rite, ceremony.
ritual, (rrē·twâl´) adj. and m. ritual.
rival, (rrē·vâl´) m. and f. rival, competitor.
rivalidad, (rrē·vâ·lē·thâth´) f. rivalry.
rivalizar, (rrē·vâ·lē·sâr´) vn. to rival, to vie.
rizado, da, (rrē·sâ´tho, thâ) adj. curly; rippled.
rizar, (rrē·sâr´) va. to curl (el pelo); to ripple (el agua); to fold into strips (el
papel).
rizo, (rrē´so) m. curl.
róbalo (rro´vâ·lo) or robalo, (rro·vâ´lo) m.
(zool.) bass.
robar, (rro·vâr´) va. to steal, to rob; to
abduct, to kidnap (raptar).
roble, (rro´vle) m. oak tree.
roblón, (rro·vlon´) m. rivet.
robo, (rro´vo) m. robbery, theft; abduction.
robustecer*, (rro·vūs·te·ser´) va. to
strengthen, to invigorate.
robustez, (rro·vūs·tes´) f. robustness, fortitude.
robusto, ta, (rro·vūs´to, tâ) adj. robust,
vigorous.
roca, (rro´kâ) f. rock.
roce, (rro´se) m. rubbing; clearing of
underbrush; (fig.) rubbing elbows
(trato).
rociar, (rro·syâr´) va. to sprinkle; (fig.) to
scatter about; —, vn. to be dew.
rocín, (rro·sēn´) m. hack; (fig.) clod, lout.
rocinante, (rro·sē·nân´te) m. nag, hack.
rocío, (rro·sē´o) m. dew.
rocoso, sa, (rro·ko´so, sâ) adj. rocky.
rodaja, (rro·thâ´hâ) f. flat disk; rowel (de
espuela); caster (ruedecilla).
rodaje, (rro·thâ´he) m. wheels, workings;
— de una película, shooting of a film.
rodapié, (rro·thâ·pye´) m. fringe; railing
(de un balcón).
rodar*, (rro·thâr´) vn. to roll; to roll down
(caer); to rotate (alrededor de un eje).
rodear, (rro·the·âr´) vn. to go around; to
go a roundabout way (dar un rodeo);
—, va. to encircle, to surround.
rodeo, (rro·the´o) m. going around; roundabout way (camino más largo); dodge
(regate); roundup (del ganado); (fig.)

hedging, beating around the bush.

rodete, (rro·the′te) m. twist, knot *(peinado);* (mech.) drum wheel.

rodilla, (rro·thē′yâ) f. knee; **de —s,** on one′s knees, kneeling down; **hincar la —,** (fig.) to bend the knee.

rodillo, (rro·thē′yo) m. roller, cylinder; rolling pin *(de cocina).*

roedor, ra, (rro·e·thor′, râ) adj. gnawing; **—,** m. rodent.

roer*, (rro·er′) va. to gnaw; (fig.) to corrode.

rogar*, (rro·gâr′) va. to entreat, to beg, to implore.

rojizo, za, (rro·hē′so, sâ) adj. reddish.

rojo, ja, (rro′ho, hâ) adj. red; **—,** n. (poi.) Red.

rol, (rrol) m. list, roll; **— de la dotación,** muster roll.

rollizo, za, (rro·yē′so, sâ) adj. plump, robust, sturdy.

rollo, (rro′yo) m. roller *(rodillo);* roll.

Roma, (rro′mâ) f. Rome.

romadizo, (rro·mâ·thē′so) m. catarrh.

romance, (rro·mân′se) adj. Romance; **—.** m. Spanish language *(idioma);* ballad *(poema);* novel of chivalry *(novela);* **hablar en —,** to speak plainly.

romancero, ra, (rro·mân·se′ro, râ) n. ballad singer; **—,** m. ballad collection.

romano, na, (rro·mâ′no, nâ) adj. and n. Roman.

romanticismo, (rro·mân·tē·sēz′mo) m. romanticism.

romántico, ca, (rro·mân′tē·ko, kâ) adj. romantic; **—,** m. romanticist.

rombo, (rrom′bo) m. rhombus.

romería, (rro·me·rē′â) f. pilgrimage *(por devoción);* excursion, outing.

romero, (rro·me′ro) m. (bot.) rosemary; **—, ra,** n. pilgrim.

romo, ma, (rro′mo, mâ) adj. blunt, dull; flatnosed *(de nariz).*

rompecabezas, (rrom·pe·kâ·ve′sâs) m. riddle, puzzle; jigsaw puzzle *(juego).*

rompehielos, (rrom·pe·ye′los) m. icebreaker.

rompehuelgas, (rrom·pe·wel′gâs) m. strikebreaker.

rompenueces, (rrom·pe·nwe′ses) m. nutcracker.

rompeolas, (rrom·pe·o′lâs) m. breakwater.

romper*, (rrom·per′) va. to tear up *(desgarrar);* to break *(quebrar);* to ruin *(destrozar);* (fig.) to shatter, to disrupt, to interrupt; **—,** vn. to break; to break out *(prorrumpir).*

rompimiento, (rrom·pē·myen′to) m. breaking; tearing; crack *(abertura);* (fig.) falling out *(riña);* disruption.

rompope, (rrom·po′pe) m. (Mex.) eggnog.

ron, (rron) m. rum.

roncar, (rron·kâr′) vn. to snore; (fig.) to roar, to howl.

ronco, ca, (rron′ko, kâ) adj. hoarse, husky.

roncha, (rron′châ) f. welt.

ronda, (rron′dâ) f. rounds, beat; group of revelers *(grupo);* (coll.) round; **hacer la —,** to make one′s rounds; to pace one′s beat.

rondar, (rron·dâr′) vn. to patrol, to make one′s rounds; to roam around *(paseando);* **—,** va. to circle around.

ronquera, (rron·ke′râ) f. hoarseness.

ronquido, (rron·kē′tho) m. snore; (fig.) roar, howl.

ronzal, (rron·sâl′) m. halter.

roña, (rro′nyâ) f. mange, scab; caked filth *(mugre);* (fig.) cancer; (coll.) stinginess *(tacañería).*

roñoso, sa, (rro·nyo′so, sâ) adj. scabby; dirty, filthy *(sucio).*

ropa, (rro′pâ) f. clothing, clothes: material *(tela);* **— blanca,** household linen; **— hecha,** ready-made clothes; **— interior** or **— íntima,** underwear, lingerie.

ropavejero, (rro·pâ·ve·he′ro) m. oldclothes man, junk man.

ropero, (rro·pe′ro) m. wardrobe; **—, ra,** n. clothier.

ropón, (rro·pon′) m. loose coverall.

roque, (rro′ke) m. rook.

rosa, (rro′sâ) f. rose; **color de —,** rose color, pink.

rosado, da, (rro·sâ′tho, thâ) adj. rosecolored, rosy.

rosal, (rro·sâl′) m. rosebush.

rosario, (rro·sâ′ryo) m. rosary; (mech.) chain pump.

rosbif, (rroz·vēf′) m. roast beef.

rosca, (rros′kâ) f. screw and nut; screw thread *(resalto).*

roseta, (rro·se′tâ) f. rosette.

rosquilla, (rros·kē′yâ) f. roll, bun.

rostro, (rros′tro) m. countenance, face; **hacer —.** to face, to resist.

rota, (rro′tâ) f. rout, defeat.

rotación, (rro·tâ·syon′) f. rotation.

rotario, ria, (rro·tâ′ryo, ryâ) adj. Rotarian, Rotary; **—,** m. Rotarian.

rotativo, va, (rro·tâ·tē′vo, vâ) adj. revolving, rotary.

rotatorio, ria, (rro·tâ·to′ryo, ryâ) adj. rotatory.

roto, ta, (rro´to, tâ) *adj.* broken, destroyed; tattered, ragged *(andrajoso);* (fig.) corrupt, debauched *(licencioso).*

rotograbado, (rro·to·grâ·vâ´tho) *m.* rotogravure.

rótula, (rro´tū·lâ) *f.* kneecap.

rotular, (rro·tū·lâr´) *va.* to label.

rótulo, (rro´tū·lo) *m.* label; poster *(letrero).*

rotundo, da, (rro·tūn´do, dâ) *adj.* (fig.) rotund, sonorous; absolute, final *(terminante);* **éxito —,** complete success.

rotura, (rro·tū´râ) *f.* breaking; crack *(abertura).*

roturar, (rro·tū·râr´) *va.* to break up, to plow for the first time.

rozadura, (rro·sâ·thū´râ) *f.* (med.) scrape; rubbing, friction.

rozar, (rro·sâr´) *va.* to clear *(el terreno);* to graze on *(las bestias);* to rub, to scrape *(raer);* —, *vn.* to graze, to touch slightly; **—se,** to be very close.

r. p. m.: revoluciones por minuto, r.p.m. revolutions per minute.

rubéola, (rrū·ve´o·lâ) *f.* German measles.

rubí, (rrū·vē´) *m.* ruby.

rubia, (rrū´vyâ) *f.* (bot.) madder.

rubicundo, da, (rrū·vē·kūn´do, dâ´) *adj.* reddish.

rubio, bia, (rrū´vyo, vyâ) *adj.* blond.

rublo, (rrū´vlo) *m.* ruble.

rubor, (rrū·vor´) *m.* blush; bashfulness *(timidez).*

ruborizarse, (rrū·vo·rē·sâr´se) *vr.* to blush, to flush.

rúbrica, (rrū´vrē·kâ) *f.* (eccl.) rubric; flourish *(después de la firma);* heading *(título);* **ser de —,** to be of long standing.

rucio, cia, (rrū´syo, syâ) *adj.* silver-gray, light gray.

rudeza, (rrū·the´sâ) *f.* roughness, crudeness; stupidity; (fig.) rudeness.

rudimentos, (rrū·thē·men´tos) *m. pl.* rudiments.

rudo, da, (rrū´tho, thâ) *adj.* rough, crude, coarse; stupid *(torpe);* (fig.) rude *(áspero).*

rueca, (rrwe´kâ) *f.* spinning wheel.

rueda, (rrwe´thâ) *f.* wheel; turn *(turno);* slice *(rebanada);* (ichth.) sunfish; **— libre,** freewheeling; **— de la fortuna,** wheel of fortune; **— del timón,** (naut.) helm, wheel.

ruedo, (rrwe´tho) *m.* rotation; rolling; round mat *(esterilla);* edge, rounded border *(circunferencia).*

ruego, (rrwe´go) *m.* request, entreaty,

plea.

rufián, (rrū·fyân´) *m.* pimp, pander; (fig.) lowlife, scoundrel.

rugido, (rrū·hē´tho) *m.* roaring; bellowing.

rugiente, (rrū·hyen´te) *adj.* roaring, bellowing.

rugir, (rrū·hēr´) *vn.* to roar; (fig.) to bellow.

ruibarbo, (rrwē·vâr´vo) *m.* rhubarb.

ruido, (rrwē´tho) *m.* noise.

ruidoso, sa, (rrwē·tho´so, sâ) *adj.* noisy, clamorous, loud.

ruin, (rrwēn´) *adj.* mean, vile, despicable; avaricious, penny-pinching *(avaro).*

ruina, (rrwē´nâ) *f.* ruin.

ruindad, (rrwēn·dâth´) *f.* meanness, baseness; avarice.

ruinoso, sa, (rrwē·no´so, sâ) *adj.* ruinous.

ruiseñor, (rrwē·se·nyor´) *m.* nightingale.

ruleta, (rrū·le´tâ) *f.* roulette.

ruma, (rrū´mâ) *f.* (Sp. Am.) pile.

rumano, na, (rrū·mâ´no, nâ) *n.* and *adj.* Romanian.

rumba, (rrūm´bâ) *f.* rumba, rhumba.

rumbo, (rrūm´bo) *m.* (naut.) bearing, course, direction; route, way *(camino);* (coll.) pomp, show; **con — a,** bound for.

rumboso, sa, (rrūm·bo´so, sâ) *adj.* (coll.) magnificent, wonderful.

rumiante, (rrū·myân´te) *m.* and *adj.* ruminant.

rumiar, (rrū·myâr´) *va.* to ruminate.

rumor, (rrū·mor´) *m.* buzzing *(de voces);* rumor, gossip *(voz);* noise, din.

runa, (rrū´nâ) *f.* rune.

rúnico, ca, (rrū´nē·ko, kâ) *adj.* runic.

runrún, (rrūn·rrūn´) *m.* (coll.) rumor, gossip.

rupestre, (rrū·pes´tre) *adj.* rock; **arte —,** cave painting.

ruptura, (rrūp·tū´râ) *f.* rupture, break.

rural, (rrū·râl´) *adj.* rural.

Rusia, (rrū´syâ) *f.* Russia.

ruso, sa, (rrū´so, sâ) *n.* and *adj.* Russian.

rusticidad, (rrūs·tē·sē·thâth´) *f.* rusticity *(sencillez);* coarseness *(grosería).*

rústico, ca, (rrūs´tē·ko, kâ) *adj.* rustic; **en —ca** or **a la —,** paperback; —, *m.* rustic, peasant.

ruta, (rrū´tâ) *f.* route.

rutina, (rrū·tē´nâ) *f.* routine.

rutinario, ria, (rrū·tē·nâ´ryo, ryâ) *adj.* routine.

rutinero , ra, (rrū·tē·ne´ro, râ) *n.* slave to routine; —, *adj.* chained to one´s routine.

---

m met, **n** not, **p** pot, **r** very, **rr** (none), **s** so, **t** toy, **th** with, **v** eve, **w** we, **y** yes, **z** zero

S

S.: San or Santo, St. Saint; sur, So. or so. south; Sobresaliente, S. superior.

s.: sustantivo, *n.* noun; segundo, *s.* second.

S. A.: Sociedad Anónima, Inc. Incorporated; Su Alteza, His or Her Highness.

sábado, (sâ'vâ·tho) *m.* Saturday; Sabbath *(de los judíos)*

sábalo, (sâ'vâ·lo) *m.* (ichth.) tarpoon.

sabana, (sâ·vâ'nâ) *f.* savanna.

sábana, (sâ'vâ·nâ) *f.* bed sheet.

sabandija, (sâ·vân·dē'hâ) *f.* insect, bug; (fig.) worm.

sabañón, (sâ·vâ·nyon') *m.* chilblain.

sabedor, ra, (sâ·ve·thor', râ) *adj.* informed, advised.

sabelotodo, (sâ·ve·lo·to'tho) *m.* know-it-all.

saber*, (sâ·ver') *va.* to know, to find out *(conocer);* to be able to, to know how to *(ser diestro);* — a, to taste of; —, *m.* learning, knowledge; a —, namely, as follows; es de —, it is to be noted; sin —lo, unwittingly; — de, to know about; to hear from *(tener noticias de).*

sabiduría, (sâ·vē·thü·rē'â) *f.* knowledge, wisdom.

sabiendas, (sâ·vyen'dâs) a —, knowingly, consciously, deliberately.

sabio, bia, (sâ'vyo, vyâ) *adj.* sage, wise; —, *n.* sage, scholar.

sablazo, (sâ·vlâ'so) *m.* saber blow; (coll.) sponging, cadging; dar un —, to touch for a loan.

sable, (sâ'vle) *m.* saber, cutlass.

sabor, (sâ·vor') *m.* taste.

saborear, (sâ·vo·re·âr') *va.* to enjoy, to relish *(paladear);* to give a taste, to give zest *(sazonar);* —se, to savor slowly, to enjoy keenly.

sabotaje, (sâ·vo·tâ'he) *m.* sabotage.

sabotear, (sâ·vo·te·âr') *va.* to sabotage.

sabroso sa, (sâ·vro'so, sâ) *adj.* savory, delicious *(gustoso);* appetizing *(apetitoso);* (coll.) salty.

sabueso, (sâ·vwe'so) *m.* bloodhound.

sacamuelas. (sâ·kâ·mwe'lâs) *m.* (coll.) dentist; (fig.) charlatan, quack.

sacapuntas, (sâ·kâ·pūn'tâs) *m.* pencil sharpener.

sacar, (sâ·kâr') *va.* to take out *(extraer);* to release *(librar);* to figure out *(averiguar);* to get *(obtener);* to force out, to wrest *(esforzar);* to win *(ganar);* to copy *(copiar);* to except *(excluir);* — en limpio, to make the final draft of *(del borrador);* to deduce *(deducir);* — a luz, to print.

sacarina, (sâ·kâ·rē'nâ) *f.* saccharine.

sacarosa, (sâ·kâ·ro'sâ) *f.* (chem.) sucrose.

sacerdote, (sâ·ser·tho'te) *m.* priest.

sacerdotisa, (sâ·ser·tho·tē'sâ) *f.* priestess.

saciar, (sâ·syâr') *va.* to satiate.

saciedad, (sâ·sye·thâth') *f.* satiety.

saco, (sâ'ko) *m.* sack, bag *(bolsa);* sackful, bagful *(contenido);* pillage *(saqueo);* coat *(chaqueta);* — de yute, gunny sack; no echar en — roto, not to forget, not to fail to keep in mind.

sacramental, (sâ·krâ·men·tal') *adj.* sacramental.

sacramento, (sâ·krâ·men'to) *m.* sacrament.

sacrificar, (sâ·krē·fē·kâr') *va.* to sacrifice: to slaughter *(las reses).*

sacrificio, (sâ·krē·fē'syo) *m.* sacrifice.

sacrilegio, (sâ·krē·le'hyo) *m.* sacrilege.

sacrílego, ga, (sâ·krē'le·go, gâ) *adj.* sacrilegious.

sacristán, (sâ·krēs·tân') *m.* sacristan, sexton.

sacristía, (sâ·krēs·tē'â) *f.* sacristy, vestry.

sacro, cra, (sâ'kro, krâ) *adj.* holy, sacred.

sacrosanto, ta, (sâ·kro·sân'to, tâ) *adj.* sacrosanct.

sacudida, (sâ·kū·thē'thâ) *f.* shake, jerk, jolt.

sacudimiento, (sâ·kū·thē·myen'to) *m.* shaking.

sacudir, (sâ·kū·thēr') *va.* to shake, to jerk; to beat *(golpear);* to shake off *(arrojar);* —se. (coll.) to cough up *(dinero):* to dismiss brusquely *(una persona).*

sadismo, (sâ·thēz'mo) *m.* sadism.

saeta, (sâ·e'tâ) *f.* arrow, dart *(flecha);* religious couplet, usually sung *(copla).*

saetazo, (sâ·e·tâ'so) *m.* arrow wound.

saga, (sâ'gâ) *f.* saga.

sagacidad, (sâ·gâ·sē·thâth') *f.* sagacity, shrewdness.

sagaz, (sâ·gâs') *adj.* sagacious, shrewd.

sagrado, da, (sâ·grâ'tho, thâ) *adj.* sacred,

consecrated.

sainete, (sẫ•ne′te) *m.* farce, comedy *(farsa);* sauce *(salsa);* (fig.) zest, gusto.

sal, (sal) *f.* salt *(condimento);* wit *(ingenio);* grace, charm *(donaire);* — **de la Higuera** or — **de Epsom,** Epsom salts.

sala, (sá′lä) *f.* hall; parlor, living room *(de la casa);* — **de clase,** classroom;— **chat,** chat room *(internet);* — **de espera,** waiting room; — **de hospital,** hospital ward; — **de muestras,** show-room; — **de recreo,** rumpus room.

salado, da, (sâ•lä′tho, thä) *adj.* salted, salty *(sabroso);* graceful *(gracioso);* witty *(chistoso).*

salar, (sä•lâr′) *va.* to salt.

salario, (sä•lä′ryo) *m.* salary.

salazón, (sä•lä•son′) *f.* seasoning, salting.

salcochar, (sâl•ko•châr′) *va.* to boil with water and salt.

salchicha, (sâl′ che′chä) *f.* small sausage; (mil.) long, narrow fuse.

salchichón, (sal•chē•chon′) *m.* salami.

saldar, (sâl•dâr′) *va.* to settle, to pay *(pagar);* to liquidate, to sell out *(liquidar).*

saldo, (sâl′do) *m.* balance; sale items, remainders *(mercancías);* — **acreedor,** credit balance; — **deudor,** debit balance; — **líquido,** net balance.

salero, (sä•le′ro) *m.* salt shaker *(vasito);* salthouse *(salín);* (coll.) gracefulness.

saleroso, sa, (sâ•le•ro′so, sä) *adj.* (coll.) graceful, charming.

salicilato, (sä•lē•sē•lä′to) *m.* (chem.) salicylate.

salicílico, ca, (sâ•lē•sē′lē•ko, kä) *adj.* (chem.) salicylic.

salida, (sâ•lē′thä) *f.* leaving, departure *(partida);* environs *(alrededores);* projection *(proyección);* outcome, result *(resultado);* exit; (fig.) recourse, pretext *(recurso);* escape *(escapatoria);* (mil.) sortie; golf tee; — **de sol,** sunrise; — **de teatro,** light wrap; (fig.) **tener buenas** —**s,** to be witty; **tencer** —, to sell well; —**de tono,** impertinence.

saliente, (sâ•lyen′te) *adj.* projecting, salient.

salina, (sâ•lē′nä) *f.* salt pit, salt works, salt mine.

salino, na, (sä•lē′no, nä) *adj.* saline.

salir*, (sâ•lēr′) *vn.* to depart, to leave, to go out *(partir);* to free oneself *(librarse);* to appear, to come out *(aparecer);* to sprout *(brotar);* to come out *(una mancha);* to stick out *(sobresalir);* to turn out *(resultar);* to proceed, to come from *(proceder);* to begin, to start *(empezar);* to get rid of *(deshacerse de);* to cost *(costar);* to resemble *(asemejarse);* to be chosen, to be selected *(ser elegido);* to be published *(publicarse);* — **con,** to come out with; — **bien en un examen,** to pass an examination; — **fiador,** to go good for, to go bail for; —**se,** to flow, to pour out, to spill; —**se de sus casillas,** to lose one′s temper; —**se con la suya,** to win out; — **al encuentro,** to go to meet; (fig.) to stand up to, to oppose *(oponerse);* to anticipate *(prevenir).*

salitre, (sâ•lē′tre) *m.* saltpeter.

salitrera, (sâ•lē•tre′rä) *f.* saltpeter deposit.

salitroso, sa, (sâ•lē•tro′so, sä) *adj.* nitrous.

saliva, (sâ•lē′vä) *f.* saliva.

salmo, (sâl′mo) *m.* psalm.

salmón, (sâl•mon′) *m.* salmon.

salmuera, (sâl•mwe′rä) *f.* brine.

salobre, (sä•lo′vre) *adj.* brackish, salty.

salón, (sä•lon′) *m.* salon; large hall *(sala grande);* — **de baile,** ballroom; — **de belleza,** beauty parlor.

salpicadura, (sal•pē•kä•thū′rä) *f.* splash, sprinkling.

salpicar, (sâl•pē•kâr′) *va.* to splash; to sprinkle; (fig.) to punctuate, to sprinkle *(esparcir);* to skip around in, to jump around in *(la lectura).*

salpullido, (sâl•pū•yē′tho) *m.* (med.) rash, prickly heat *(erupción);* flea bite *(de pulga).*

salsa, (sâl′sä) *f.* sauce, gravy, dressing; — **francesa,** French dressing; — **de tomate,** tomato sauce, ketchup, catsup; — **inglesa,** Worcestershire sauce; **estar en su** —, (fig.) to be right in one′s element.

salsera, (sâl•se′rä) *f.* gravy boat.

saltar, (sâl•tär′) *vn.* to skip *(cabriolar);* to jump *(brincar);* to bounce *(rebotar);* to fly *(volar);* to spurt *(surgir);* to break, to explode *(estallar);* to fall *(desprenderse);* (fig.) to stand out *(notarse);* to come out with *(disparar);* to flash in one′s mind *(recordar);* —, *va.* to leap, to jump *(atravesar);* to skip over *(omitir);* — **a los ojos,** to be obvious, to stand out.

saltarín, ina, (sâl•tâ•rēn′, ē′nä) *adj.* restless, itchy, hard to handle.

salteador, (sâl•te•â•thor′) *m.* highwayman.

saltear, (sâl•te•âr′) *va.* to rob, to waylay.

salterio, (sâl•te′ryo) *m.* psaltery.

salto, (sâl′to) *m.* leap, jump, spring *(cabriola);* leapfrog *(juego);* abyss, chasm *(sima);* omission *(descuido);* palpitation *(del corazón);* — **de agua,** waterfall; **dar —s,** to jump; — **de altura, high** jump; — **mortal,** somersault; **en un —,** quickly.

saltón, (sal·ton´) *m.* grasshopper; —, **ona,** *adj.* hopping, jumping; bulging *(protuberante).*

salubridad, (sä·lū·vrē·thäth´) *f.* healthfulness; **Departamento de S—,** Public Health Department.

salud, (sä·lūth´) *f.* health; salvation *(salvación);* **estar bien de —,** to be in good health; **estar mal de —,** to be in poor health; ¡—l to your health!

saludable, (sä·lū·thä´vle) *adj.* wholesome, healthful; beneficial *(provechoso).*

saludar, (sä·lū·thär´) *va.* to greet; (mil.) to salute; to hail, to acclaim *(aclamar).*

saludo, (sä·lū´tho) *m.* (mil.) salute; greeting.

salutación, (sä·lū·tä·syon´) *f.* salutation, greeting.

salva, (säl´vä) *f.* (mil.) salvo; — **de aplausos,** thunderous applause.

salvación, (säl·vä·syon´) *f.* salvation, deliverance.

salvado, (säl·vä´tho) *m.* bran.

Salvador, (säl·vä·thor´) *m.* Saviour.

salvador, ra, (säl·vä·thor´, rä) *adj.* saving; —, *n.* saver, savior.

salvadoreño, ña, (säl·vä·tho·re´nyo, nyä) *n.* and *adj.* Salvadorean.

salvaguardia, (säl·vä·gwär´thyä) *m.* guard, watchman; —, *f.* safe-conduct; (fig.) protection, safeguard *(amparo).*

salvaje, (säl·vä´he) *adj.* savage, wild.

salvajismo, (säl·va·hēz´mo) *m.* savagery.

salvamento, (säl·vä·men´to) *m.* safety, safe place *(lugar);* rescue *(libramiento);* **escalera de —,** fire escape.

salvar, (säl·vär´) *va.* to save, to rescue *(librar);* to avoid *(evitar);* to exclude *(excluir);* to jump *(saltar);* to cover, to pass over *(recorrer);* **—se,** to be saved.

salvavidas, (säl·vä·vē´thäs) *m.* life preserver.

salvo, va, (säl´vo, vä) *adj.* saved, safe *(ileso);* omitted *(omitido);* **sano y —vo,** safe and sound; **estar a —,** to be safe; **—vo,** *adv.* except; **—vo error u omisión,** errors and omissions excepted.

salvoconducto, (säl·vo·kon·dūk´to) *m.* safe-conduct.

samba, (säm´bä) *f.* samba.

san, (sän) *adj.* saint.

sanalotodo, (sä·nä·lo·to´tho) *m.* panacea, cure-all.

sanar, (sä·när´) *va.* to heal; —, *vn.* to

heal; to recover *(recobrar la salud).*

sanatorio, (sä·nä·to´ryo) *m.* sanatorium, sanitarium.

sanción, (sän·syon´) *f.* sanction.

sancionar, (sän·syo·när´) *va.* to sanction.

sancochar, (sän·ko·chär´) *va.* to parboil.

sancocho, (sän·ko´cho) *m.* parboiled meat; (Sp. Am.) meat stew.

sandalia, (sän·dä´lyä) *f.* sandal.

sándalo, (sän´dä·lo) *m.* sandalwood.

sandez, (sän·des´) *f.* folly, stupidity.

sandía, (sän·dē´ä) *f.* watermelon.

saneamiento, (sä·ne·ä·myen´to) *m.* indemnification, going good; sanitation, making sanitary.

sanear, (sä·ne·är´) *va.* to indemnify, to go good for; to sanitize *(limpiar).*

sangrante, (säng·grän´te) *adj.* bleeding.

sangrar, (säng·rär´) *va.* to bleed; (fig.) to drain *(dar salida);* (coll.) to bleed white.

sangre, (säng´gre) *f.* blood; **a — fria,** in cold blood; **banco de —,** blood bank; **donador or donante de —,** blood donor; **tener —,** to be resolute, to have spirit.

sangría, (säng·grē´ä) *f.* bleeding; tap *(en un árbol);* drain.

sangriento, ta, (säng·gryen´to, tä) *adj.* bloody; bloodthirsty *(sanguinario).*

sanguijuela, (säng·gē·hwe´lä) *f.* leech.

sanguinario, ría, (säng·gē·nä´ryo, ryä) *adj.* cruel, bloodthirsty.

sanguíneo, nea, (säng·gē´ne·o, ne·ä) *adj.* sanguine.

sanidad, (sä·nē·thäth´) *f.* healthiness; healthfulness *(salubridad);* **patente de —,** bill of health.

sanitario, ria, (sä·nē·tä´ryo, ryä) *adj.* sanitary.

sano, na, (sä´no, nä) *adj.* healthy, sound; healthful *(saludable);* intact, complete *(sin daño);* sound *(sensato).*

sánscrito, ta, (säns´krē·to, tä) *adj.* Sanskrit.

santabárbara, (sän·tä·vär´vä·rä) *f.* powder magazine.

Santiago, (sän·tyä´go) James.

santiamén, (sän·tyä·men´) *m.* (coll.) twinkling of an eye, jiffy.

santidad, (sän·tē·thäth´) *f.* sanctity, holiness.

santificación, (sän·tē·fē·kä·syon´) *f.* sanctification.

santificar, (sän·tē·fē·kär´) *va.* to sanctify; (coll.) to excuse.

santiguar, (sän·tē·gwär´) *va.* to make the sign of the cross over; (coll.) to whack *(abofetear);* **—se,** to cross oneself.

santísimo, ma, (sän·tē´sē·mo, ma) *adj.*

most holy.

santo, ta, (sân'to, tâ) *adj.* holy; —, *n.* saint; —to y seña, (mil.) password.

santuario, (sân·twä'ryo) *m.* sanctuary.

santurrón, ona, (sân·tū·rron', o'nâ) *adj.* sanctimonious; —, *n.* plaster saint, religious hypocrite.

saña, (sä'nyä) *f.* blind fury, rage.

sañoso, sa, (sä·nyo'so, sä) *adj.* furious, enraged.

sapo, (sä'po) *m.* toad.

saque, (sä'ke) *m.* serve; service line *(raya);* server *(el que saca).*

saquear, (sä·ke·âr') *va.* to sack, to pillage.

saqueo, (sä·ke'o) *m.* pillage, sacking.

S.A.R.: Su Alteza Real, His or Her Royal Highness.

sarampión, (sä·râm·pyon') *m.* measles.

sarape, (sä·râ'pe) *m.* serape.

sarcasmo, (sâr·kâz'mo) *m.* sarcasm.

sarcástico, ca, (sâr·kâs'tē·ko, kâ) *adj.* sarcastic.

sardina, (sâr·thē'nä) *f.* sardine.

sargento, (sâr·hen'to) *m.* sergeant.

sarna, (sâr'nä) *f.* mange.

sarnoso, sa, (sâr·no'so, sä) *adj.* mangy.

sarpullido (sâr·pū·yē'tho) = salpullido.

Sarre, (sä'rre) *m.* Saar; Cuenca del —, Saar Basin.

sarro, (sä'rro) *m.* incrustation; tartar *(en los dientes).*

sarta, (sâr'tâ) *f.* string; (fig.) line, series, string *(en fila).*

sartén, (sâr·ten') *f.* frying pan.

sastre, (sâs'tre) *m.* tailor.

sastrería, (sâs·tre·rē'â) *f.* tailor's shop.

Satanás, (sä·tä·nâs') *m.* Satan.

satánico, ca, (sä·tä'nē·ko, kâ) *adj.* Satanic, devilish.

satélite, (sä·te'lē·te) *m.* satellite; (coll.) bailiff, constable *(alguacil);* (fig.) satellite, follower *(partidario);* países —s, satellite countries.

sátira, (sä'tē·râ) *f.* satire.

satírico, ca, (sä·tē'rē·ko, kâ) *adj.* satirical.

sátiro, (sä'tē·ro) *m.* satyr.

satisfacción, (sä·tēs·fâk·syon') *f.* satisfaction.

satisfacer*, (sä·tēs·fä·ser') *va.* to satisfy; —se, to get satisfaction.

satisfactorio, ria, (sä·tēs·fâk·to'ryo, ryâ) *adj.* satisfactory.

satisfecho, cha, (sä·tēs·fe'cho, châ) *adj.* satisfied, content; self-satisfied *(presumido).*

saturación, (sä·tū·râ·syon') *f.* (chem.) saturation.

sauce, (sä'ū·se) *m.* (bot.) willow.

savia, (sä'vyâ) *f.* sap.

saxofón, (sâk·so·fon') *m.* saxophone.

saya, (sä'yâ) *f.* skirt.

sayo, (sä'yo) *m.* smock.

sazón, (sä·son') *f.* maturity *(madurez);* time, season *(ocasión);* taste, flavor; en —, at the right time, opportunely; a la —, then, at that time.

sazonado, da, (sä·so·nä'tho, thâ) *adj.* seasoned; (fig.) expressive, clever.

sazonar, (sä·so·nâr') *va.* to season; —se, to ripen.

Sbre.: septiembre, Sept. September.

S. C.: su casa, your home.

s.c. or s/c.: su cargo or su cuenta, (com.) your account; su casa, your home.

s/cta. or s/c.: su cuenta, (com.) your account.

SE: sudeste, SE or S.E. southeast.

se, (se) *pron.* himself (él); herself *(ella);* itself *(ello);* yourself *(usted);* themselves *(ellos, ellas);* yourselves *(ustedes);* each other *(idea recíproca);* — dice, it is said, one says, they say; — resolvió el problema, the problem was solved.

sebo, (se'vo) *m.* tallow *(de herbívoro);* fat, grease.

seboso, sa, (se·vo'so, sä) *adj.* fat, greasy.

seca, (se'kâ) *f.* drought, dry weather *(sequía);* sandbank *(secano);* (med.) swelling.

secador, ra (se·kâ·thor') *m.* o *f.* dryer; — de pelo, blow-dryer.

secante, (se·kân'te) *m.* blotter; guard *(en deportes);* —, *adj.* drying; papel —, blotting paper.

secamente, (se·kâ·men'te) *adv.* dryly, gruffly, harshly.

secar, (se·kâr') *va.* to dry; (fig.) to annoy, to bother *(fastidiar);* —se, to dry out; to dry up *(un río);* to wither *(una planta);* to grow wizened *(enflaquecerse);* (fig.) to grow hard.

sección, (sek·syon') *f.* section; cross section *(perfil).*

secesión, (se·se·syon') *f.* secession.

secesionista, (se·se·syo·nēs'tä) *m.* or *f.* secessionist.

seco, ca, (se'ko, kâ) *adj.* dry; arid, barren *(árido);* lean *(flaco);* withered dead *(muerto);* (fig.) harsh, sharp *(áspero);* indifferent *(indiferente);* en —co, high and dry.

secretaría, (se·kre·tâ·rē'â) *f.* secretaryship *(cargo);* secretariat *(oficina).*

secretario, ria, (se·kre·tâ'ryo, ryâ) *n.* secretary; scribe *(escribano);* — particular, private secretary.

secreción, (se·kre·syon´) f. secretion.
secreto, ta, (se·kre´to, tâ) adj. secret;
secretive *(callado);* —, *m.* secret; secrecy *(sigilio);* hiding place *(lugar);* **de — inviolable,** top-secret; **en —to,** in secret, in private.
secta, (sek´tâ) f. sect; doctrine *(doctrina).*
sectario, ria, (sek·tâ´ryo, ryâ) *adj.* and *n.* sectarian.
secuaz, (se·kwâs´) *m.* follower, partisan.
secuela, (se·kwe´lâ) f. sequel, result.
secuestrar, (se·kwes·trâr´) *va.* to abduct, to kidnap; to sequester *(confiscar).*
secuestro, (se·kwes´tro) *m.* kidnapping.
secular, (se·kū·lâr´) *adj.* secular; long-seated, deep-rooted *(muy viejo).*
secundario, ria, (se·kūn·dâ´ryo, ryâ) *adj.* secondary; **escuela —,** high school.
sed, (seth) f. thirst; **tener —,** to be thirsty.
seda, (se´thâ) f. silk.
sedante, (se·thân´te) *m.* sedative, tranquilizer.
sedativo, va, (se·thâ·tē´vo, vâ) *adj.* sedative.
sede, (se´the) f. seat, headquarters *(residencia);* (eccl.) see; cathedra *(silla).*
sedentario, ria, (se·then·tâ´ryo, ryâ) *adj.* sedentary.
sedeño, ña, (se·the´nyo, nyâ) *adj.* silky *(sedoso);* bristly *(cerdoso);* —, f. fiber *(fibra);* fishing line *(sedal).*
sedería, (se·the·rē´â) f. silks; silk store *(tienda);* silk industry *(comercio).*
sedición, (se·thē·syon´) f. sedition.
sedicioso, sa, (se·thē·syo´so, sâ) *adj.* seditious.
sediento, ta, (se·thyen´to, tâ) *adj.* dry, thirsty; eager, anxious *(ansioso).*
sedimento, (se·thē·men´to) *m.* sediment.
seducción, (se·thūk·syon´) f. seduction.
seducir*, (se·thū·sēr´) *va.* to seduce; to bribe *(sobornar);* to attract, to charm, to captivate *(encantar).*
seductor, ra, (se·thūk·tor´, râ) *adj.* attractive, fascinating, charming; seductive.
segador, ra, (se·gâ·thor´, râ) *n.* mower, reaper, harvester; **—ra de césped,** lawn mower.
segar*, (se·gar´) *va.* to reap, to mow, to harvest *(cosechar);* to cut *(cortar);* (fig.) to cut down, to restrict.
seglar, (se·glâr´) *adj.* secular; —, *m.* layman.
segmento, (seg·men´to) *m.* segment.
segregación, (se·gre·gâ·syon´) f. segregation; secretion.
segregar, (se·gre·gâr´) *va.* to segregate; to secrete *(secretar).*

seguida, (se·gē´thâ) f. series, succession; **en —,** immediately, at once; **de —,** consecutively, continuously.
seguidilla, (se·gē·thē´yâ) f. seguidilla.
seguido, da, (se·gē´tho, thâ) *adj.* successive, in a row; straight *(en línea recta);* **todo —do,** straight ahead.
seguir*, (se·gēr´) *va.* to follow *(ir detrás de);* to pursue *(perseguir);* to continue; to accompany *(acompañar);* to exercise, to profess *(ejercer);* to imitate *(imitar);* **—se,** to ensue, to result; (fig.) to originate, to proceed.
según, (se·gūn´) *prep.* according to; —, *adv.* depending on how; — **aviso,** per advice; — **y como,** it depends.
segundario, ria, (se·gūn·dâ´ryo, ryâ) *adj.* secondary.
segundo, da, (se·gūn´do, dâ) *adj.* second; **en —do lugar,** secondly; **de —da mano,** secondhand; —, *m.* second.
segundón, (se·gūn·don´) *m.* second son; younger son *(por extensión).*
segur, (se·gūr´) f. axe; sickle *(guadaña).*
seguridad, (se·gū·rē·thâth´) f. security; surety *(fianza);* assurance, certainty *(certeza);* safety *(fuera de peligro);* **caja de —,** safety deposit box; **fiador de —,** safety catch.
seguro, ra, (se·gū´ro, râ) *adj.* secure, safe *(salvo);* certain, sure *(cierto);* firm, constant *(constante);* unsuspecting *(desprevenido);* —, *m.* insurance *(aseguración);* leave, safe-conduct *(salvo-conducto);* certainty, assurance *(seguridad);* safety lock *(del fusil);* **de —ro,** assuredly; **compañía de —ros,** life insurance company; **corredor de —ros,** insurance broker; **póliza de —ro,** insurance policy; **—ro de vida,** life insurance; **—ro colectivo,** group insurance; **—ro de incendios,** fire insurance; **—ro contra accidentes,** accident insurance.
seis, (se´ēs) *adj.* and *m.* six.
selección, (se·lek·syon´) f. selection, choice.
selecto, ta, (se·lek´to, tâ) *adj.* select, choice.
selva, (sel´vâ) f. forest.
sellar, (se·yâr´) *va.* to seal; (fig.) to stamp *(estampar);* to finish up *(concluir).*
sello, (se´yo) *m.* seal; stamp *(timbre);* (med.) wafer; — **de correo,** postage stamp; — **de impuesto,** revenue stamp; — **de entrega inmediata,** special delivery stamp; **poner el — a,** to finish up, to put the finishing touch on.
semáforo. (se·mâ´fo·ro) *m.* semaphore;

traffic light *(de tránsito).*

semana, (se·má'nä) *f.* week.

semanal, (se·mä·näl') *adj.* weekly.

semanalmente, (se·mä·näl·men'te) *adv.* weekly, every week.

semanario, ria, (se·mä·nä'ryo, ryä) *adj.* and *m.* weekly.

semántica, (se·män'te·kä) *f.* semantics.

semblante, (sem·blän'te) *m.* face, countenance *(cara);* aspect *(apariencia).*

sembrado, (sem·brä'tho) *m.* cultivated field.

sembrador, ra, (sem·brä·thor', rä) *n.* sower, planter.

sembrar*, (sem·brär') *va.* to sow, to plant; (fig.) to scatter.

semejante, (se·me·hän'te) *adj.* similar, like; —, *m.* fellowman.

semejanza, (se·me·hän'sä) *f.* resemblance, likeness.

semejar, (se·me·här') *vn.* to resemble.

semen, (se'men) *m.* semen; (bot.) seed.

sementar*, (se·men·tär') *va.* to seed, to plant.

sementera, (se·men·te'rä) *f.* sowing; planted land *(tierra);* seeding time *(tiempo).*

semestral, (se·mes·träl') *adj.* semiyearly, semiannual.

semestre, (se·mes'tre) *m.* semester.

semianual, (se·myä·nwäl') *adj.* semiannual.

semicírculo, (se·me·ser'ku·lo) *m.* semicircle.

semidiós, (se·me·thyos') *m.* demigod.

semifinal, (se·me·fe·näl') *adj.* and *f.* semifinal.

semilla, (se·me'yä) *f.* seed.

semillero, (se·me·ye'ro) *m.* seed plot; (fig.) hotbed.

seminario, (se·me·nä'ryo) *m.* seminary.

sempiterno, na, (sem·pe·ter'no, nä) *adj.* everlasting, eternal.

senado, (se·nä'tho) *m.* senate.

senador, (se·nä·thor') *m.* senator.

sencillez, (sen·se·yes') *f.* simplicity; (fig.) candor, naiveté.

sencillo, lla, (sen·se'yo, yä) *adj.* simple; lightweight *(ligero);* (fig.) candid, simple; —, *m.* change.

senda, (sen'dä) *f.* path, footpath.

sendero, (sen·de'ro) *m.* path, trail.

sendos, das, (sen'dos, däs) *adj. pl.* one apiece, one each; **tienen — caballos,** they have a horse apiece, they each have a horse.

senil, (se·nel') *adj.* senile.

seno, (se'no) *m.* breast, bosom; womb *(matriz);* hollow, cavity *(hueco);* sinus;

(fig.) asylum, refuge *(refugio);* innermost part *(parte interna).*

sensación, (sen·sä·syon') *f.* sensation, feeling.

sensacionalismo, (sen·sä·syo·nä·lez'mo) *m.* sensationalism.

sensatez, (sen·sä·tes') *f.* reasonableness, good sense.

sensato, ta, (sen·sä'to, tä) *adj.* reasonable, sensible.

sensibilidad, (sen·se·ve·le·thäth') *f.* sensibility; sensitivity *(emotividad).*

sensible, (sen·se'vle) *adj.* sensible; sensitive *(susceptible);* marked *(perceptible);* regrettable, deep-felt.

sensitiva, (sen·se·te'vä) *f.* sensitive plant.

sensitivo, va, (sen·se·te'vo, vä) *adj.* sensitive.

sensual, (sen·swäl') *adj.* sensual.

sensualidad, (sen·swä·le·thäth') *f.* sensuality.

sensualismo, (sen·swä·lez'mo) *m.* sensualism.

sentado, da, (sen·tä'tho, thä) *adj.* seated; **- dar por —do,** to take for granted.

sentar*, (sen·tär') *va.* to seat; —, *vn.* to agree with *(un alimento);* to be becoming, to look good *(una prenda);* to be fitting *(convenir);* to please *(agradar);* — **bien,** to do good; — **mal,** to do harm; — **se,** to sit down.

sentencia, (sen·ten'syä) *f.* sentence; decision, judgment *(decisión).*

sentenciar, (sen·ten·syär') *va.* to sentence; (fig.) to pass judgment on, to give one's opinion of.

sentido, (sen·te'tho) *m.* sense; meaning *(significado);* feeling *(conocimiento);* direction *(dirección);* — **práctico,** common sense; —, **da,** *adj.* sensitive.

sentimental, (sen·te·men·täl') *adj.* sentimental.

sentimentalismo, (sen·te·men·tä·lez'mo) *m.* sentimentalism.

sentimiento, (sen·te·myen'to) *m.* sentiment; feeling *(impresión);* sorrow *(aflicción).*

sentir*, (sen·ter') *va.* to feel; to regret, to be sorry about *(lamentar);* to hear *(oir);* to read well *(el verso);* to feel about *(juzgar);* to sense *(prever);* —**se,** to feel; to feel hurt *(formar queja).*

seña, (se'nyä) *f.* sign, mark, token; (mil.) password; —**s,** *pl.* address; —**s personales,** personal description; —**s mortales,** unmistakable evidence; **por más** —**s,** as a further proof; **hacer —s,** to hail, to wave at.

señal, (se·nyâl´) f. mark; trace (vestigio); sign (de tránsito); earnest money (dinero); — de alto or de parada, stop sign.

señalar, (se·nyâ·lâr´) va. to mark; to indicate, to point out (indicar); to determine, to designate (determinar); —se, to excel.

señalización, (se·nyâ·lē·sâ·syon´) f. system of signs; road signs (en la carretera).

señalizar, (se·nyâ·lē·sâr´) va. to mark with signs.

señor, (se·nyor´) m. owner, master (dueño); lord (de un feudo); gentleman; sir (de cortesía); Mr., Mister (con el apellido); el S—, the Lord.

señora, (se·nyo´râ) f. owner, mistress (dueña); lady; madam (de cortesía); Mrs. (con el apellido); wife (esposa); Nuestra S—, Our Lady.

señoría, (se·nyo·rē´â) f. lordship.

señoril, (se·nyo·rēl´) adj. lordly.

señorío, (se·nyo·rē´o) m. self-control, dignity (gravedad); sway, dominion (dominio).

señorita, (se·nyo·rē´tâ) f. young lady; Miss (con el apellido); (coll.) mistress of the house.

señorito, (se·nyo·rē´to) m. young gentleman; Master (con el apellido); (coll.) master of the house; playboy (joven ocioso).

señuelo, (se·nywe´lo) m. lure, enticement.

separable, (se·pâ·râ´vle) adj. separable.

separación, (se·pâ·râ·syon´) f. separation.

separado, da, (se·pâ·râ´tho, thâ) adj. separate; por —do, under separate cover.

separar, (se·pâ·râr´) va. to separate; to discharge (de un empleo); —se, to separate; to retire, to withdraw (retirarse).

separatista, (se·pâ·râ·tēs´tâ) m. or f. secessionist.

sepelio, (se·pe´lyo) m. burial.

septentrión, (sep·ten·tryon´) m. north.

septentrional, (sep·ten·tryo·nâl´) adj. northern.

septicemia, (sep·tē·se´myâ) f. (med.) septicemia, blood poisoning.

septiembre, (sep·tyem´bre) m. September.

séptimo, ma, (sep´tē·mo, mâ) m. and adj. seventh.

septuagésimo, ma, (sep·twâ·he´sē·mo, mâ) adj. seventieth; S—ma, f. Septuagesima, Septuagesima Sunday.

sepulcral, (se·pūl·krâl´) adj. sepulchral.

sepulcro, (se·pūl´kro) m. sepulcher, grave, tomb; Santo S—, Holy Sepulcher.

sepultar; (se·pūl·târ´) va. to bury, to inter.

sepultura, (se·pūl·tū´râ) f. sepulture, grave; burial, interment (acción).

sepulturero, (se·pūl·tū·re´ro) m. gravedigger.

sequedad, (se·ke·thâth´) f. dryness; (fig.) curtness, sharpness.

sequía, (se·kē´â) f. drought; (Sp. Am.) thirst, dryness (sed).

séquito, (se´kē·to) m. retinue, suite, following.

ser*, (ser) vn. to be; llegar a —, to become; — de, to be from; —, m. being, life.

serenar, (se·re·nâr´) va. to calm down; to settle (los licores); —se, to calm down.

serenata, (se·re·nâ´tâ) f. serenade.

serenidad, (se·re·nē·thâth´) f. serenity, quiet.

sereno, (se·re´no) m. night air (humedad); night watchman (vigilante); —, na, adj. serene, calm, quiet; cloudless (sin nubes).

serie, (se´rye) f. series.

seriedad, (se·rye·thâth´) f. seriousness; sternness, gravity.

serio, ria, (se´ryo, ryâ) adj. serious; stern, grave (severo).

sermón, (ser·mon´) m. sermon.

sermonear, (ser·mo·ne·âr´) va. to lecture, to reprimand.

serpentina, (ser·pen·tē´nâ) f. streamer; (min.) serpentine.

serpiente, (ser·pyen´te) f. serpent, snake.

serranía, (se·rrâ·nē´â) f. mountainous region.

serrano, na, (se·rrâ´no, nâ) adj. mountain; —, n. mountaineer.

serrucho, (se·rrū´cho) m. handsaw.

servible, (ser·vē´vle) adj. serviceable.

servicial, (ser·vē·syâl´) adj. compliant, accommodating.

servicio, (ser·vē´syo) m. service; wear (utilidad); good turn (favor); worship (culto); tableware (vajilla); chamber pot (orinal); — diurno, day service; — nocturno, night service.

servidor, ra, (ser·vē·thor´, râ) n. servant; su —, your servant, at your service.

servidumbre, (ser·vē·thūm´bre) f. servitude (esclavitud); staff of servants (conjunto de criados); (fig.) compulsion, drive (de una pasión).

servil, (ser·vēl´) adj. servile.

servilleta, (ser·vē·ye´tâ) f. napkin.

servir*, (ser·vēr´) va. to serve; to wait on (al que come); —, vn. to serve; (mil.) to be on active duty; to be of use (ser útil); —se, to deign, to please; —se de, to make use of.

servomotor, (ser·vo·mo·tor') *m.* servomotor.

sesenta, (se·sen'tâ) *m.* and *adj.* sixty.

sesgado, da, (sez·gä'tho, thä) *adj.* oblique, slanting.

sesgar, (sez·gâr') *va.* to twist *(torcer);* to cut on the bias *(cortar).*

sesgo, (sez'go) *m.* twist, bias; **al —go,** obliquely, on the bias.

sesión, (se·syon') *f.* session; show, showing *(de una película).*

seso, (se'so) *m.* brain.

sestear, (ses·te·âr') *vn.* to take a siesta.

sesudo, da, (se·sü'tho, thä) *adj.* prudent, discreet, judicious.

setecientos, tas, (se·te·syen'tos, tâs) *m.* and *adj.* seven hundred.

setenta, (se·ten'tâ) *m.* and *adj.* seventy.

setiembre (se·tyem'bre) = **septiembre.**

seto, (se'to) *m.* fence, enclosure; **— vivo,** hedge.

seudónimo, (seü·tho'nē·mo) *m.* pseudonym.

severidad, (se·ve·rē·thâth') *f.* severity *(rigor);* strictness *(exactitud);* seriousness *(seriedad).*

severo, ra, (se·ve'ro, râ) *adj.* severe; strict; serious.

sevillano, na, (se·vē·yâ'no, nâ) *n.* and *adj.* Sevillian.

sexagenario, ria, (sek·sâ·he·nâ'ryo, ryâ) *adj.* and *n.* sexagenarian.

sexagésimo, ma, (sek·sâ·he'sē·mo, mâ) *m.* and *adj.* sixtieth.

sexto, ta, (ses'to, tâ) *m.* and *adj.* sixth.

s/f.: su favor, your letter.

s/g: su giro, (com.) your draft; **sin gastos,** (com.) without expense or charge.

si, (sē) *conj.* if; even though, although *(aunque);* whether *(caso dudoso);* — **acaso,** or **por — acaso,** just in case; — **no,** if not; —, *m.* (mus.) si.

si, (sē) *adv.* yes; **él — lo hizo,** he did do it; —, *m.* yes, assent; —, *pron.* himself (Al); herself *(ella);* itself *(ello);* yourself *(usted);* themselves *(ellos, ellas);* yourselves *(ustedes);* each other *(idea recíproca);* **de —,** in himself; **de por —,** on his own, alone; **para —,** to himself; **dar de —,** to extend, to stretch; **volver en —,** to come to, to recover one´s senses.

siamés, esa, (syâ·mes', e´sâ) *adj.* and *n.* Siamese.

sicoanálisis, (sē·ko·â·nâ'lē·sēs) *m.* or *f.* psychoanalysis.

sicología, (sē·ko·lo·hē'â) *f.* psychology.

sicológico, ca, (sē·ko·lo'hē·ko, kâ) *adj.*

psychological.

sicólogo, ga, (sē·ko'lo·go, gâ) *n.* psychologist.

sicosis, (sē·ko'sēs) *f.* psychosis.

sicosomático, ca, (sē·ko·so·mä'tē·ko, kâ) *adj.* psychosomatic.

S.I.D.A.: síndrome de inmunodeficiencia adquirida, A.I.D.S., acquired immunodeficiency syndrome.

sideral, (sē·the·râl') *adj.* astral, sidereal; **viajes —es,** space travel.

siderurgia, (sē·the·rür'hyâ) *f.* iron and steel industry.

siderúrgico, ca, (sē·the·rür'he·ko, kâ) *adj.* iron and steel.

sidra, (sē'thrâ) *f.* cider.

siega, (sye'gâ) *f.* harvest.

siembra, (syem'brâ) *f.* seedtime *(tiempo);* sowing, seeding *(acto);* sown field *(campo sembrado).*

siempre, (syem'pre) *adv.* always; in any event *(en todo caso);* — **jamás,** for ever and ever.

siempreviva, (syem·pre·vē'vâ) *f.* (bat.) everlasting.

sien, (syen) *f.* temple.

sierpe, (syer'pe) *f.* serpent, snake.

sierra, (sye'rrâ) *f.* saw; mountain range *(cordillera).*

siervo, va, (syer'vo, vâ) *n.* serf; slave *(esclavo);* servant *(servidor).*

siesta, (syes'tâ) *f.* siesta.

siete, (sye'te) *m.* and *adj.* seven.

sífilis, (sē'fē·lēs) *f.* syphilis.

sigilo, (sē·hē'lo) *m.* seal *(sello);* secret, reserve *(secreto).*

sigiloso, sa, (sē·hē·lo'so, sâ) *adj.* reserved, silent.

sigla, (sē'glâ) *f.* initial *(letra inicial);* abbreviation *(abreviatura).*

siglo, (sē'glo) *m.* century; **la consumación de los —s,** the end of the world.

signatario, (sēg·nâ·tâ'ryo) *m.* signatory.

significación, (sēg·nē·fē·kâ·syon') *f.* significance.

significado, (sēg·nē·fē·kâ'tho) *m.* meaning.

significar, (sēg·nē·fē·kâr') *va.* to signify, to mean; to make known *(hacer saber).*

significativo, va, (sēg·nē·fē·kâ·tē'vo, va) *adj.* significant, meaningful.

signo, (sēg'no) *m.* sign *(señal);* mark *(de escritura).*

siguiente, (sē·gyen'te) *adj.* following, successive; **al día —,** on the following day, next day.

sílaba, (sē'lâ·vâ) *f.* syllable.

silabear, (sē·lâ·ve·âr') *va.* to sound out, to syllable.

m met, **n** not, **p** pot, **r** very, **rr** (none), **s** so, **t** toy, **th** with, **v** eve, **w** we, **y** yes, **z** zero

silbar, (sēl·vâr´) va. to hiss; —, vn. to whistle.

silbato, (sēl·vá´to) m. whistle.

silbido, (sēl·vē´tho) m. whistle; hissing (burla); whistling.

silenciador, (sē·len·syâ·thor´) m. silencer; (auto.) muffler.

silencio, (sē·len´syo) m. silence; ¡—! interj. quiet! hush!

silencioso, sa, (sē·len·syo´so, sâ) adj. silent.

silo, (sē´lo) m. silo; cave (subterráneo).

silueta, (sē·lwe´tâ) f. silhouette, outline.

silvestre, (sēl·ves´tre) adj. wild.

silla, (sē´yâ) f. chair; saddle (de montar); (eccl.) see; — de cubierta, deck chair; — de ruedas, wheel chair; — giratoria, swivel chair; — poltrona, armchair, easy chair.

sillón, (sē·yon´) m. easy chair, overstuffed chair; sidesaddle (de montar).

sima, (sē´mâ) f. abyss.

simbólico, ca, (sēm·bo´lē·ko, kâ) adj. symbolical.

simbolismo, (sēm·bo·lēz´mo) m. symbolism.

simbolizar, (sēm·bo·lē·sâr´) va. to symbolize.

símbolo, (sēm´bo·lo) m. symbol; adage (dicho).

simetría, (sē·me·trē´â) f. symmetry.

simétrico, ca, (sē·me´trē·ko, kâ) adj. symmetrical.

simiente, (sē·myen´te) f. seed (semilla); semen (semen).

símil, (sē´mēl) m. resemblance; (rhet.) simile; —, adj. similar.

similar, (sē·mē·lâr´) adj. similar.

similitud, (sē·mē·lē·tūth´) f. similitude, similarity.

simpatía, (sēm·pâ·tē´â) f. sympathy, empathy; charm (encanto); liking (cariño); affinity (afinidad); tener — por, to like, to find pleasant and congenial.

simpático, ca, (sēm·pá´tē·ko, kâ) adj. sympathetic (compasivo); likable, pleasant, nice (agradable).

simpatizar, (sēm·pâ·tē·sâr´) vn. to get along well; — con, to feel at home with, to feel kindly toward.

simple, (sēm´ple) adj. simple; single (sin duplicar); pure (puro); insipid (insipido); —, m. and f. simpleton.

simpleza, (sēm·ple´sâ) f. foolishness, stupidity.

simplicidad, (sēm·plē·sē·thâth´) f. simplicity.

simplificar, (sēm·plē·fē·kâr´) va. to simplify.

simulación, (sē·mū·lâ·syon´) f. simulation.

simulacro, (sē·mū·lâ´kro) m. simulacrum, image (imagen); phantasm, apparition (aparición); simulation, pretense (simulación); (mil.) maneuvers, war games.

simulado, da, (sē·mū·lâ´tho, thâ) adj. feigned, pretended.

simular, (sē·mū·lâr´) va. to simulate, to feign, to pretend.

simultáneo, nea, (sē·mūl·tâ´ne·o, ne·â) adj. simultaneous.

sin, (sēn) prep. without; not counting (aparte de); — embargo, notwithstanding, nevertheless; — duda, doubtlessly; — reserva, without reservation; — saberlo, unawares, without knowing it; — noticia de, without news from; — valor, of no value, without value; — piedad, without pity, pitiless; — nombre, nameless, without a name; telegrafía — hilos, wireless telegraphy.

sinagoga, (sē·nâ·go´gâ) f. synagogue.

sinceridad, (sēn·se·rē·thâth´) f. sincerity.

sincero, ra, (sēn·se´ro, râ) adj. sincere.

sincopar, (sēng·ko·pâr´) va. to syncopate.

síncope, (sēng´ko·pe) m. (med.) syncope, fainting spell.

sincrónico, ca, (sēng·kro´nē·ko, kâ) adj. synchronous, synchronic.

sincronizar, (sēng·kro·nē·sâr´) va. to synchronize.

sincrotón, (sēng·kro·ton´) m. synchroton.

sindicar, (sēn·dē·kâr´) va. to accuse (acusar); to inform on (informar contra); to unionize (agremiar); to syndicate (de dinero o valores); —se, to become unionized.

sindicato, (sēn·dē·kâ´to) m. syndicate; — de obreros, labor union.

sinecura, (sē·ne·kū´râ) f. sinecure.

sinfonía, (sēm·fo·nē´â) f. symphony.

sinfonola, (sēm·fo·no´lâ) f. jukebox.

singular, (sēng·gū·lâr´) adj. singular.

singularizar, (sēng·gū·lâ·rē·sâr´) va. to distinguish; (gram.) to singularize; —se, to distinguish oneself.

siniestra, (sē·nyes´trâ) f. left hand; left side, left.

siniestro, tra, (sē·nyes´tro, trâ) adj. left; (fig.) sinister; —, m. loss.

sinnúmero, (sēn·nū´me·ro) m. endless amount, great many, no end.

sino, (sē´no) conj. but, but rather; except (menos).

sínodo, (sē´no·tho) m. synod.

sinónimo, ma, (sē·no´nē·mo, mâ) adj. synonymous; —, m. synonym.

sinopsis, (sē·nop´sēs) *f.* synopsis.

sinrazón, (sēn·rrâ·son´) *f.* injustice, wrong.

sinsabor, (sēn·sâ·vor´) *m.* tastelessness, lack of taste *(desabor);* (fig.) displeasure, uneasiness *(desazón).*

sinsonte, (sēn·son´te) *m.* mockingbird.

sintaxis, (sēn·tâk´sēs) *f.* syntax.

síntesis, (sēn´te·sēs) *f.* synthesis.

sintético, ca, (sēn·te´tē·ko, kâ) *adj.* synthetic.

síntoma, (sēn´to·mâ) *m.* symptom.

sintonización, (sēn·to·nē·sâ·syon´) *f.* (rad.) tuning in.

sintonizar, (sēn·to·nē·sâr´) *va.* (rad.) to tune in.

sinuoso, sa, (sē·nwo´so, sâ) *adj.* sinuous,winding; (fig.) evasive, devious *(evasivo).*

sinvergüenza, (sēm·ber·gwen´sâ) *adj.* roguish, rascally; —, *m.* and *f.* scoundrel.

siquiatra, (sē·kyâ´trâ) *m.* psychiatrist.

síquico, ca, (sē´kē·ko, kâ) *adj.* psychic.

siquiera, (sē·kye´râ) *conj.* even if, although; —, *adv.* at least *(al menos);* even; **ni —,** not even.

sirena, (sē·re´nâ) *f.* siren; mermaid *(ninfa marina);* (fig.) vamp, siren.

sirviente, ta, (sēr·vyen´te, tâ) *n.* servant.

sisa, (sē´sâ) *f.* dart in an underarm *(de la costura);* filching *(hurto).*

sisear, (sē·se·âr´) *va.* to hiss.

siseo, (sē·se´o) *m.* hissing.

sísmico, ca, (sēz´mē·ko, kâ) *adj.* seismic; **movimiento —,** earthquake.

sismógrafo, (sēz·mo´grâ·fo) *m.* seismograph.

sistema, (sēs·te´mâ) *m.* system; — **escolar,** school system.

sistemático, ca, (sēs·te·mâ´tē·ko, kâ) *adj.* systematic.

sitiar, (sē·tyâr´) *va.* (mil.) to besiege, to lay siege to; (fig.) to hem in, to hole up.

sitio, (sē´tyo) *m.* place; country home *(hacienda);* (mil.) siege; — **web,** web site.

situación, (sē·twâ·syon´) *f.* position, situation.

situado, da, (sē·twâ´tho, thâ) *adj.* situated, located; —, *m.* income.

situar, (sē·twâr´) *va.* to place, to situate; to assign *(fondos).*

s/l or sL: su letra (com.) your letter.

S. M.: Su Majestad, His or Her Majesty.

smoking, *m.* tuxedo, dinner jacket.

SO: sudoeste, SW or S. W. southwest.

s/o: su orden, (com.) your order.

so, (so) *prep.* under; — **pena de,** under-penalty of; — **capa de,** in the guise of; ¡—! *interj.* whoa!; —, *m.* (coll.) *you.,*¡—**bruto!** you nitwit!

sobaco, (so·vâ´ko) *m.* armpit.

sobar, (so·vâr´) *va.* to knead, to soften*(ablandar);* to handle, to paw *(manosear);* to pummel, to beat *(pegar);* to annoy *(molestar).*

soberanía, (so·ve·râ·nē´â) *f.* sovereignty.

soberano, na, (so·ve·râ´no, nâ) *adj.* and *n.* sovereign.

soberbia, (so·ver´vyâ) *f.* pride, haughtiness; magnificence, splendor *(de un edificio);* anger, wrath *(cólera).*

soberbio, bia, (so·ver´vyo, vyâ) *adj.* proud, haughty; superb, magnificent; wrathful, angry.

sobornar, (so·vor·nâr´) *va.* to suborn, to bribe.

soborno, (so·vor´no) *m.* bribe.

sobra, (so´vrâ) *f.* excess, surplus; **—s,** pl. leftovers; waste *(desechos);* **de —,** more than enough.

sobrado, da, (so·vrâ´tho, thâ) *adj.* excessive, abundant *(excesivo);* audacious, bold *(audaz);* rich *(rico).*

sobrante, (so·vrân´te) *m.* residue, surplus; *adj.* leftover, excess.

sobrar, (so·vrâr´) *vn.* to be too much, to be unnecessary *(estar de más);* to be more than enough *(haber más que lo necesario);* to remain, to be left over *(quedar);* —, *va.* to outdo.

sobre, (so´vre) *prep.* on *(encima de);* about *(acerca de);* in addition to *(además de);* **—cero,** above zero; — **todo,** above all; **—lo cual,** on which, about which; —, *m.* envelope.

sobrealimentar, (so·vre·â·lē·men·târ´) *va.*to overfeed; (mech.) to supercharge.

sobrecama, (so·vre·kâ´mâ) *f.* bedspread.

sobrecarga, (so·vre·kâr´gâ) *f.* surcharge *(cobro);* extra load, overload *(carga);*packing cord *soga);* fig.) added annoyance *(molestia).*

sobrecargar, (so·vre·kâr·gâr´) *va.* to overload; to fell *(una costura).*

sobrecargo, (so·vre·kâr´go) *m.* (naut.) supercargo.

sobrecejo, (so·vre·se´ho) or sobreceño, (so·vre·se´nyo) *m.* frown.

sobrecoger, (so·vre·ko·her´) *va.* to surprise, to take by surprise, to startle.

sobrecomprimir, (so·vre·kom·prē·mēr´) *va.* to pressurize.

sobrecubierta, (so·vre·kū·vyer´tâ) *f.* (naut.) upper deck.

---

m met, **n** not, **p** pot, **r** very, **rr** (none), **s** so, **t** toy, **th** with, **v** eve, **w** we, **y** yes, **z** zero

sobredicho, cha, (so·vre·thē´cho, châ) adj. above-mentioned.

sobreexcitar, (so·vre´ek·sē·târ´) va. to overexcite.

sobrehumano, na, (sov·reū·mâ´no, nâ) adj. superhuman.

sobrellevar, (so·vre·ye·vâr´) va. to ease, to help with; (fig.) to put up with, to tolerate *(soportar)*.

sobremanera, (so·vre·mâ·ne´râ) adv. exceedingly.

sobremesa, (so·vre·me´sâ) f. table cover *(tapete);* dessert *(postre);* after-dinner conversation *(conversación).*

sobrenatural, (so·vre·nâ·tū·râl´) adj. supernatural.

sobrenombre, (so·vre·nom´bre) m. nickname.

sobrentender*, (so·vren·ten·der´) va. to understand, to deduce; —se, to go without saying.

sobrepaga, (so·vre·pâ´gâ) f. increase in pay.

sobreparto, (so·vre·pâr´to) m. confinement after childbirth.

sobrepasar, (so·vre·pâ·sâr´) va. to surpass.

sobrepeso, (so·vre·pe´so) m. overweight.

sobreponer*, (so·vre·po·ner´) va. to superimpose, to put on top of; —se, to master the situation, to win out, to prevail.

sobreproducción, (so·vre·pro·thūk·syon´) f. overproduction.

sobresaliente, (so·vre·sâ·lyen´te) adj. projecting; (fig.) outstanding; —, m. and f. substitute, understudy; —, m. excellent.

sobresalir*, (so·vre·sâ·lēr´) vn. to project, to stick out; (fig.) to excel, to stand out.

sobresaltado, da, (so·vre·sâl·tâ´tho, thâ) adj. frightened, startled.

sobresaltar, (so·vre·sâl·târ´) va. to attack unexpectedly *(atacar);* to frighten, to startle *(asustar);* —se, to be startled, to be frightened; —, vn. to stand out.

sobresalto, (so·vre·sâl´to) m. fright, scare,start; de —, suddenly, unexpectedly.

sobrestante, (so·vres·tân´te) m. overseer, foreman.

sobresueldo, (so·vre·swel´do) m. added stipend, fringe benefits.

sobretodo, (so·vre·to´tho) m. topcoat, overcoat.

sobrevenir*, (so·vre·ve·nēr´) vn. to come immediately afterward *(después);* to happen unexpectedly *(improvisamente);* to come at the same time *(al mismo*

tiempo); — a, to come right on top of.

sobreviviente, (so·vre·vē·vyen´te) m. and f. survivor; —, adj. surviving.

sobrevivir, (so·vre·vē·vēr´) vn. to survive; — a, to outlive, to survive.

sobriedad, (so·vrye·thâth´) f. sobriety, temperance.

sobrina, (so·vrē´nâ) f. niece.

sobrino, (so·vrē´no) m. nephew.

sobrio, bria, (so´vryo, vryâ) adj. sober, temperate, moderate.

Soc.: Sociedad, Soc. Society; Co. Company.

socaliñar, (so·kâ·lē·nyâr´) va. to trick, to wheedle.

socarrón, ona, (so·kâ·rron´, o´nâ) adj. cunning, sly, crafty.

socavar, (so·kâ·vâr´) va. to undermine, to weaken.

sociabilidad, (so·syâ·vē·lē·thâth´) f. sociability.

sociable, (so·syâ´vle) adj. sociable.

social, (so·syâl´) adj. social; company *(comercial);* razón —, firm name.

socialismo, (so·syâ·lēz´mo) m. socialism.

socialista, (so·syâ·lēs´tâ) m. and f. socialist; —, adj. socialistic, socialist.

socializar, (so·syâ·lē·sâr´) va. to socialize.

sociedad, (so·sye·thâth´) f. society; (com.)company; — anónima, corporation; — benéfica, charity, welfare organization;— colectiva, general partnership; — en comandita or comanditaria, limited partnership.

socio, cia, (so´syo, syâ) n. associate, partner; member *(miembro);* (coll.) fellow, guy.

sociología, (so·syo·lo·hē´â) f. sociology.

sociólogo, (so·syo´lo·go) m. sociologist.

socorrer, (so·ko·rrer´) va. to succor, to aid, to help; to pay in part, to pay on account *(pagar).*

socorro, (so·ko´rro) m. succor, help, aid; (mil.) reinforcement.

sodio, (so´thyo) m. sodium.

soez, (so·es´) adj. mean, vile.

sofá, (so·fâ´) m. sofa, couch, lounge; — cama, sofa bed.

sofisma, (so·fēz´mâ) m. sophism.

sofistería, (so·fēs·te·rē´â) f. sophistry.

sofístico, ca, (so·fēs´tē·ko, kâ) adj. sophistical.

soflamar, (so·flâ·mâr´) va. to humbug *(engañar);* to embarrass *(avergonzar);* —se, to get scorched.

sofocación, (so·fo·kâ·syon´) f. suffocation, smothering.

sofocante, (so·fo·kân´te) adj. suffocating,

stifling.

sofocar, (so·fo·kär´) va. to suffocate *(ahogar);* to put out, to extinguish *(apagar);* to harass *(importunar);* to inflame *(inquietar);* to embarrass *(avergonzar).*

soga, (so´gä) f. rope.

soja, (so´hä) f. (bot.) soybean.

sojuzgar, (so·hūz·gär´) va. to conquer, to subdue.

sol, (sol) m. sun; sunlight *(luz);* day *(día);* monetary unit of Peru; (mus.) sol; **hace—,** it is sunny; **puesta del —,** sunset; **rayo de —,** sunbeam; **salida del —,** sunrise.

solana, (so·lä´nä) f. sun room, sun porch *(de una casa);* sunny spot.

solapa, (so·lä´pä) f. lapel *(del vestido);* pretense, cover, pretext *(ficción).*

solapado, da, (so·lä·pä´tho, thä) adj.cunning, crafty, artful.

solapar, (so·lä·pär´) va. to put lapels on *(un vestido);* to conceal, to hide; —, vn. to drape.

solar, (so·lär´) m. lot, piece of real estate; ancestral home *(casa antigua);* lineage *(linaje);* —, adj. solar; **luz —,** sunshine;*, va. to put a floor in; to sole *(el calzado).*

solariego, ga, (so·lä·rye´go, gä) adj. ancestral.

solaz, (so·läs´) m. solace, consolation, change; **a —,** gladly.

solazar, (so·lä·sär´) va. to solace, to comfort.

solazo, (so·lä´so) m. (coll.) scorching sun.

soldadesca, (sol·dä·thes´kä) f. soldiery; raw troops *(tropa indisciplinada).*

soldadesco, ca, (sol·dä·thes´ko, kä) adj. soldierly, soldier-like.

soldado, (sol·dä´tho) m. soldier; **— de a caballo,** cavalryman; **— de marina,** marine; **— de reserva,** reservist; **— raso,** (coll.) buck private.

soldadura, (sol·dä·thū´rä) f. soldering;solder *(materia);* (fig.) correction *(corrección);* **— autógena,** welding.

soldar*, (sol·där´) va. to solder; (fig.) to connect *(unir);* to right, to make amends for *(enmendar);* **—se,** to stick together.

soleado, da, (so·le·ä´tho, thä) adj. sunny.

soledad, (so·le·thäth´) f. solitude; lonely place *(sitio);* loneliness *(melancolía).*

solemne, (so·lem´ne) adj. solemn; (coll.)awful, real, absolute.

solemnidad, (so·lem·nē·thäth´) f. solemnity; formality *(formalidad).*

solemnizar, (so·lem·nē·sär´) va. to solemnize.

soler*, (so·ler´) vn. to be accustomed to, to be in the habit of; to be customary for *(ser frecuente).*

solfa, (sol´fä) f. (mus.) sol-fa; musical notes *(signos);* (fig.) music; (coll.) beating *(zurra).*

solfeo, (sol·fe´o) m. (mus.) solfeggio; flogging, beating *(zurra).*

solicitante, (so·lē·sē·tän´te) m. and f. applicant.

solicitar, (so·lē·sē·tär´) va. to try for *(pretender);* to apply for *(gestionar);* (fig.) to attract.

solícito, ta, (so·lē´sē·to, tä) adj. solicitous, careful.

solicitud, (so·lē·sē·tūth´) f. solicitude; application, request, petition *(memorial);* **a —,** on request.

solidaridad, (so·lē·thä·rē·thäth´) f. solidarity.

solidario, ria, (so·lē·thä´ryo, ryä) adj. solidary, jointly liable.

solidez, (so·lē·thes´) f. solidity; volume *(volumen).*

sólido, da, (so´lē·tho, thä) adj. solid; strong, robust *(vigoroso);* —, m. solid.

soliloquio, (so·lē·lo´kyo) m. soliloquy.

solio, (so´lyo) m. canopied throne.

solista, (so·lēs´tä) m. and f. soloist.

solitaria, (so·lē·tä´ryä) f. tapeworm.

solitario, ria, (so·lē·tä´ryo, ryä) adj. solitary, lonely; —, m. solitaire; hermit *(ermitaño).*

solo, (so´lo) m. (mus.) solo; **—, la,** adj. alone; only, sole *(único);* **a —las,** alone, unaided.

sólo, (so´lo) adv. only.

solomillo, (so·lo·mē´yo) or **solomo,** (so·lo´mō) m. sirloin.

soltar*, (sol·tär´) va. to untie, to loosen *(desatar);* to free *(dar libertad a);* to let go of *(desasir);* to release, to let out *(dar salida a);* to explain *(explicar);* to resolve *(resolver);* to come out with *(decir);* **—se,** to become adept *(adquirir agilidad);* to loosen up, to unwind *(relajar);* to begin *(empezar).*

soltero, ra, (sol·te´ro, rä) adj. unmarried, single; —, m. bachelor; —, f. bachelor girl.

solterón, ona, (sol·te·ron´, o´nä) adj. old and still single; —, f. old maid, spinster; —, m. old bachelor.

soltura, (sol·tū´rä) f. loosening; explanation; freedom, agility *(en los movimientos);* openness, frankness *(desvergüenza);* fluency *(de dicción);* release, freeing

m met, **n** not, **p** pot, **r** very, **rr** (none), **s** so, **t** toy, **th** with, **v** eve, **w** we, **y** yes, **z** zero

(de un preso).

soluble, (so·lū´vle) *adj.* soluble.

solución, (so·lū·syon´) *f.* solution.

solucionar, (so·lū·syo·nâr´) *va.* to settle, to resolve.

solvencia, (sol·ven´syâ) *f.* solvency.

solventar, (sol·ven·târ´) *va.* to settle, to liquidate.

solvente, (sol·ven´te) *adj.* solvent.

sollozar, (so·yo·sâr´) *vn.* to sob.

sollozo, (so·yo´so) *m.* sob.

sombra, (som´brâ) *f.* shade, shadow *(proyección);* darkness *(oscuridad);* shade, spirit *(fantasma);* favor *(asilo);* **hacer —,** to be shady; **tener buena —,** to be pleasant, to be nice; **esto no tiene — de verdad,** there's not a trace of truth in this.

sombrear, (som·bre·âr´) *va.* to shade.

sombrerera, (som·bre·re´râ) *f.* hatbox *(caja);* hat designer, milliner *(persona).*

sombrerería, (som·bre·re·rē´â) *f.* hat-shop.

sombrerero, (som·bre·re´ro) *m.* hatter, hatmaker, milliner.

sombrero, (som·bre´ro) *m.* hat; **— de jipijapa** or **— panamá,** Panama hat; **— de paja,** straw hat.

sombrilla, (som·brē´yâ) *f.* parasol.

sombrío, bría, (som·brē´o, brē´â) *adj.* shady, shaded; (fig.) gloomy, bleak *(tétrico).*

somero, ra, (so·me´ro, râ) *adj. (fig.)* superficial, shallow; on the surface.

someter, (so·me·ter´) *va.* to subject, to subdue *(sujetar);* to conquer, to vanquish *(conquistar);* to submit *(encomendar);* **—se,** to humble oneself, to submit.

somnolencia, (som·no·len´syâ) *f.* sleepiness, drowsiness.

son, (son) *m.* music, soft notes; news *(noticia);* pretext *(pretexto);* manner *(modo);* **a — de,** at the sound of; **en — de,** as, like, in the manner of; **en — de burla,** in the mocking way, mockingly.

sonajero, (so·nâ·he´ro) *m.* baby's rattle.

sonámbulo, la, (so·nâm´bū·lo, lâ) *n.* and *adj.* somnambulist.

sonar*, (so·nâr´) *va.* to play *(un instrumento);* to sound; to blow *(las narices);* **—,** *vn.* to sound: to sound right, to sound familiar *(ofrecerse al recuerdo);* to seem *(parecer).*

sonata, (so·nâ´tâ) *f.* (mus.) sonata.

sonda, (son´dâ) *f.* (naut.) sounder; drill *(barrena);* (med.) probe *(tienta);* catheter *(para la alimentación).*

sondar (son·dâr´) or **sondear.** (son·de·âr´) *va.* (naut.) to sound; to drill *(barrenar);* to probe *(explorar);* (fig.) to sound out *(inquirir).*

sondeo, (son·de´o) *m.* sounding; probing; **cohete de —,** probe rocket.

soneto, (so·ne´to) *m.* sonnet.

sónico, ca, (so´nē·ko, kâ) *adj.* sonic.

sonido, (so·nē´tho) *m.* sound; (fig.) news *(noticia).*

sonoro, ra, (so·no´ro, râ) *adj.* sonorous; (gram.) voiced.

sonreir, (son·rre·ēr´) *vn.* and *vr.* to smile; **— burlonamente,** to snicker, to smile sarcastically.

sonriente, (son·rryen´te) *adj.* smiling.

sonrisa, (son·rrē´sâ) smile.

sonrojar, (son·rro·hâr´) *va.* to make blush; **—se,** to blush.

sonrojo, (son·rro´ho) *m.* blush; impropriety *(improperio).*

sonrosado, da, (son·rro·sâ´tho, thâ) *adj.* pink.

sonsacar, (son·sâ·kâr´) *va.* to make off with; (fig.) to wheedle, to pump.

sonsonete, (son·so·ne´te) *m.* tapping noise; scornful, derisive tone *(de desprecio);* dull monotone *(sin expresión).*

soñador, ra, (so·nyâ·thor´, râ) *n.* dreamer; **—,** *adj.* dreamy.

soñar*, (so·nyâr´) *va.* and *vn.* to dream; **— despierto,** to daydream; **— con,** to dream of; **¡ni —lo!** I wouldn't dream of it!

soñoliento, ta, (so·nyo·lyen´to, tâ) *adj.* sleepy, drowsy; soporific *(soporífero);* (fig.) dull, lazy *(tardo).*

sopa, (so´pâ) *f.* soup; **estar hecho una —,** to be sopping wet.

sopera, (so·pe´râ) *f.* soup tureen.

sopetón, (so·pe·ton´) *m.* hard box, hard slap; **de —,** suddenly.

soplar, (so·plâr´) *vn.* to blow; **—,** *va.* to blow away: to steal *(robar);* to blow up, to inflate *(inflar);* to inspire *(inspirar);* to whisper *(apuntar);* (fig.) to squeal on *(delatar).*

soplete, (so·ple´te) *m.* blowtorch; **— oxhídrico** oxyhydrogen torch.

soplo, (so´plo) *m.* blowing; gust *(del viento);* (fig.) moment *(instante);* (coll.) piece of advice, tip *(aviso);* tale *(delación).*

soplón, ona, (so·plon´, o´nâ) *n.* talebearer.

soponcio, (so·pon´syo) *m.* (coll.) faint, passing out.

sopor, (so·por´) *m.* drowsiness, sleepiness; stupor *(estado morboso).*

soporte (so·por´te) *m.* support.

soportable, (so·por·tâ´vle) adj. tolerable, supportable.

soportar, (so·por·târ´) va. to support, to bear, to hold up (cargar); (fig.) to tolerate, to endure (tolerar).

soprano, (so·prâ´no) f. (mus.) soprano.

sor, (sor) f. (eccl.) sister.

sorber*, (sor·ver´) va. to sip, to suck; to draw in, to soak up; to absorb (atraer); to swallow up (absorber).

sorbete, (sor·ve´te) m. sherbet.

sorbo, (sor´vo) m. sipping; sip, taste (líquido); tomar a —s, to sip.

sordera, (sor·the´râ) f. deafness.

sordina, (sor·thē´nâ) f. damper; (mus.) sordine, mute.

sordo, da, (sor´tho, thâ) adj. deaf; silent, mute (callado); muffled (no claro); (gram.) voiceless.

sordomudo, da, (sor·tho·mū´tho, thâ) adj.deaf and dumb; —, n. deafmute.

sorna, (sor´nâ) f. sluggishness, laziness, slowness ; (fig.) stalling, faking (disimulo).

sorprendente, (sor·pren·den´te) adj. surprising.

sorprender, (sor·pren·der´) va. to surprise.

sorpresa, (sor·pre´sâ) f. surprise; de —, unawares.

sortear, (sor·te·âr´) va. to draw lots for; to dodge, to sidestep (evitar); to maneuver with (al toro).

sorteo, (sor·te´o) m. drawing lots; dodging.

sortija, (sor·tē´hâ) f. ring; ringlet.

sortilegio, (sor·tē·le´hyo) m. sorcery,witchcraft.

sosegado, da, (so·se·gâ´tho, thâ) adj. quiet, peaceful, composed.

sosegar*, (so·se·gâr´) va. to calm, to quiet; —, vn. to rest, to quiet down; —se, to calm down.

sosiego, (so·sye´go) m. tranquillity, serenity, calm.

soslayo, ya, (soz·lâ´yo, yâ) adj. oblique; al —yo, obliquely, on a slant; de —yo, sideways, sidelong; mirar de —yo, to look askance at.

soso, sa, (so´so, sâ) adj. insipid, tasteless.

sospecha, (sos·pe´châ) f. suspicion.

sospechar, (sos·pe·châr´) va. and vn. to suspect.

sospechoso, sa, (sos·pe·cho´so, sâ) adj. suspicious.

sostén, (sos·ten´) m. support (apoyo); brassiere (prenda); steadiness (del buque).

sostener*, (sos·te·ner´) va. to support ,to sustain, to hold up; (fig.) to back, to

uphold (apoyar); to bear, to endure (tolerar); to maintain, to provide for (mantener); —se to support oneself.

sostenido, da, (sos·te·nē´tho, thâ) adj. sustained; —, m. (mus.) sharp.

sostenimiento, (sos·te·nē·myen´to) m. sustenance, support.

sota, (so´tâ) f. jack.

sotana, (so·tâ´nâ) f. cassock; (coll.) beating, drubbing (paliza).

sótano, (so´tâ·no) m. basement, cellar.

sotavento, (so·tâ·ven´to) m. (naut.) leeward, lee.

soviet, (so·vyet´) m. soviet.

soviético, ca, (so·vye´tē·ko, kâ) adj. soviet.

soya, (so´yâ) f. soybean.

sputnik, (spūt´nēk) m. sputnik.

s/p: su pagaré, (com.) your promissory note.

Sr.: señor, Mr. Mister.

s/r: su remesa, (com.) your remittance or shipment.

Sra. or Sra: señora, Mrs. Mistress.

Sres. or Sres: señores, Messrs. Messieurs.

sria.: secretaria, sec. secretary.

srio.: secretario, sec. secretary.

Srta. or S.rta: señorita, Miss.

S. S. or s. s.: seguro servidor, devoted servant.

S. S.: Su Santidad, His Holiness.

SS.mo P.: Santísimo Padre, Most Holy Father.

S.S.S. or s.s.s.: su seguro servidor, your devoted servant.

SS. SS. SS. or ss. ss. ss.: sus seguros servidores, your devoted servants.

Sta.: Santa, St. Saint.

Sto.: Santo, St. Saint.

su, (sū) pron. his (de él); her (de ella); its; one´s (de uno).

suave, (swâ´ve) adj. smooth, soft, suave (blando); gentle, mild (tranquilo).

suavidad, (swâ·vē·thâth´) f. softness, suaveness, smoothness; gentleness.

suavizar, (swâ·vē·sâr´) va. to soften; to mollify, to pacify (apaciguar); —se, to calm down.

subalterno, na, (sū·vâl·ter´no, nâ) adj. inferior, subordinate.

subarrendar*, (sū·vâ·rren·dâr´) va. to sublet, to sublease.

subasta, (sū·vâs´tâ) f. auction; open bidding (de contrata); sacar a pública —, to sell to the highest bidder.

subastar, (sū·vâs·târ´) va. to auction off.

subconsciente, (sūv·kon·syen´te) adj. subconscious.

subdesarrollado, da, (suv·the·sâ·rro·yâ´

tho, thâ) *adj.* underdeveloped.

súbdito, ta, (sūv´thē·to, tâ) *n.* and *adj.* subject.

subdividir, (sūv·thē·vē·thēr´) *va.* to subdivide.

subdivisión, (sūv·thē·vē·syon´) *f.* subdivision.

subgerente, (sūv·he·ren´te) *m.* assistant manager.

subida, (sū·vē´thâ) *f.* climb, ascent.

subido, da, (sū·vē´tho, thâ) *adj.* intense, penetrating *(fuerte);* fine, excellent *(fino);* very high *(elevado).*

subir, (sū·vēr´) *vn.* to climb up, to go up; to come to, to amount to *(importar);* to rise, to swell *(crecer);* (fig.) to get worse *(agravarse):* to progress, to advance *(ascender);* —, *va.* to climb, to go up; to bring up, to take up *(trasladar);* to enhance *(dar más estimación);* to erect, to raise *(erguir);* — **al tren,** to get on the train; — **en empleo,** to be promoted.

súbitamente, (sū·vē·tâ·men´te) *adv.* suddenly.

súbito, ta, (sū´vē·to, tâ) *adj.* sudden, hasty; unforeseen *(imprevisto);* **de —,** suddenly.

subjuntivo, (sūv·hūn·tē´vo) *m.* (gram.) subjunctive.

sublevación, (sū·vle·vâ·syon´) *f.* revolt, rebellion.

sublevar, (sū·vle·vâr´) *va.* to excite to rebellion; —, *vn.* to revolt, to rebel.

sublime, (sū·vlē´me) *adj.* sublime, exalted.

sublimidad, (sū·vlē·mē·thâth´) *f.* sublimity, sublimeness.

submarino, (sūv·mâ·rē´no) *m.* submarine.

subnormal, (sūv·nor·mâl´) *adj.* subnormal.

suborbital, (sū·vor·vē·tâl´) *adj.* suborbital.

subordinado, da, (sū·vor·thē·nâ´tho, thâ) *n.* and *adj.* subordinate.

subordinar, (sū·vor·thē·nâr´) *va.* to subordinate.

subrayar, (sū·vrâ·yâr´) *va.* to underline, to underscore.

subrepticiamente, (sū·vrep·tē·syâ·men´te) *adv.* surreptitiously.

subsanar, (sūv·sâ·nâr´) *va.* to excuse *(disculpar);* (fig.) to mend, to repair *(reparar).*

subscribir, (sūvs·krē·vēr´) = **suscribir.**

subscripción (sūvs·krēp·syon´) = **suscripción.**

subscrito (sūvs·krē´to) = **suscrito.**

subsecretario, ria, (sūv·se·kre·tâ´ryo, ryâ) *n.* undersecretary, assistant secretary.

subsecuente, (sūv·se·kwen´te) *adj.* subsequent, following.

subsidiario, ria, (sūv·sē·thyâ´ryo, ryâ) *adj.* subsidiary.

subsidio, (sūv·sē´thyo) *m.* subsidy.

subsiguiente, (sūv·sē·gyen´te) *adj.* subsequent, following.

subsistencia, (sūv·sēs·ten´syâ) *f.* subsistence.

subsistir, (sūv·sēs·tēr´) *vn.* to subsist.

substancia (sūvs·tân´syâ) = **sustancia.**

substancial (sūvs·tân·syâl´) = **sustancial.**

substancioso (sūvs·tân·syo´so)=**sustancioso.**

substantivo (sūvs·tân·tē´vo) = **sustantivo.**

substitución (sūvs·tē·tū·syon´)=**sustitución.**

substituir (sūvs·tē·twēr´) = **sustituir.**

substituto (sūvs·tē·tū´to) = **sustituto.**

substracción (sūvs·trâk·syon´)=**sustracción.**

substraer (sūvs·trâ·er´) = **sustraer.**

subsuelo, (sūv·swe´lo) *m.* subsoil.

subteniente, (sūv·te·nyen´te) *m.* second lieutenant.

subterfugio, (sūv·ter·fū´hyo) *m.* subterfuge.

subterráneo, nea, (sūv·te·rrâ´ne·o, ne·â) *adj.* subterraneous, subterranean.

subtítulo, (sūv·tē´tū·lo) *m.* subtitle.

subtropical, (sūv·tro·pē·kâl´) *adj.* subtropical.

suburbano, na, (sū·vūr·vâ´no, nâ) *adj.* suburban; —, *n.* suburbanite.

suburbio, (sū·vūr´vyo) *m.* suburb.

subvención, (sūv·ven·syon´) *f.* subsidy, endowment.

subversión, (sūv·ver·syon´) *f.* subversion, overthrow.

subversivo, va, (sūv·ver·sē´vo, vâ) *adj.* subversive.

subyugar, (sūv·yū·gâr´) *va.* to subdue, to subjugate.

succión, (sūk·syon´) *f.* suction.

suceder, (sū·se·ther´) *vn.* to happen *(ocurrir);* to follow, to succeed *(seguir);* to inherit *(heredar).*

sucesión, (sū·se·syon´) *f.* succession; issue, offspring *(prole).*

sucesivo, va, (sū·se·sē´vo, vâ) *adj.* successive; **en lo —vo,** from now on, in the future.

suceso, (sū·se´so) *m.* event *(acontecimiento);* outcome *(resultado);* success *(buen éxito).*

sucesor, ra, (sū·se·sor´, râ) *n.* successor; heir *(heredero).*

suciedad, (sū·sye·thâth´) *f.* filth, dirt *(inmundicia);* dirtiness, filthiness *(calidad de sucio);* (fig.) dirty remark.

sucinto, ta, (sū·sēn´to, tâ) *adj.* succinct.

sucio, cia, (sū´syo, syâ) *adj.* dirty, filthy.

sucre, (sū´kre) *m.* monetary unit of Ecuador.

suculento, ta, (sū·kū·len´to, tä) *adj.* succulent.

sucumbir, (sū·kūm·bēr´) *vn.* to succumb.

sucursal, (sū·kūr·säl´) *adj.* subsidiary; —, *f.* branch, subsidiary.

sud, (sūth) *m.* south.

sudafricano, na, (sū·thä·frē·kä´no, nä) *n.* and *adj.* South African.

sudamericano, na, (sū·thä·me·rē·kä´no,nä) *n.* and *adj.* South American.

sudar, (sū·thär´) *va.* and *vn.* to sweat.

sudario, (sū·thä´ryo) *m.* shroud.

sudeste, (sū·thes´te) *m.* southeast.

sudoeste, (sū·tho·es´te) *m.* southwest.

sudor, (sū·thor´) *m.* sweat.

Suecia, (swe´syä) *f.* Sweden.

sueco, ca, (swe´ko, kä) *adj.* Swedish; — *n.* Swede.

suegra, (swe´grä) *f.* mother-in-law.

suegro, (swe´gro) *m.* father-in-law.

suela, (swe´lä) *f.* sole; **media —,** half sole.

sueldo, (swel´do) *m.* salary, pay.

suelo, (swe´lo) *m.* ground; soil *(terreno);* floor *(piso);* bottom *(superficie inferior).*

suelto, ta, (swel´to, tä) *adj.* loose; rapid,quick *(veloz);* bold *(atrevido);* loose *(disgregado);* single *(separado).*

sueño, (swe´nyo) *m.* sleep; dream *(fantasía);* **tener —,** to be sleepy; **no dormir —,** not to sleep a wink; **conciliar el —,** to manage to get to sleep; **entre —s,** dozing.

suero, (swe´ro) *m.* serum.

suerte, (swer´te) *f.* luck, fortune; fate *(destino);* kind, sort *(género);* **tener —,** to be lucky; **echar —s,** to draw lots.

suficiencia, (sū·fē·syen´syä) *f.* sufficiency, adequacy; **a —,** sufficient, enough.

suficiente, (sū·fē·syen´te) *adj.* sufficient, enough *(bastante);* fit, apt *(apto).*

sufijo, (sū·fē´ho) *m.* suffix.

sufragar, (sū·frä·gär´) *va.* to aid, to assist *(ayudar);* to defray *(costear).*

sufragio, (sū·frä´hyo) *m.* vote, suffrage *(voto);* aid, assistance *(ayuda).*

sufrido, da, (sū·frē´tho, thä) *adj.* long-suffering, patient.

sufrimiento, (sū·frē·myen´to) *m.* patience, endurance.

sufrir, (sū·frēr´) *va.* to suffer *(padecer);* to endure, to tolerate, to bear *(sostener).*

sugerencia, (sū·he·ren´syä) *f.* suggestion.

sugerir*, (sū·he·rēr´) *va.* to suggest.

sugestión, (sū·hes·tyon´) *f.* suggestion.

sugestionar, (sū·hes· tyo·när´) *va.* to influ-

ence while under hypnosis; to have in one´s spell *(dominar).*

suicida, (swē·sē´thä) *m.* and *f.* suicide.

suicidarse, (swē·sē·thär´se) *vr.* to commit suicide.

suicidio, (swē·sē·´thyo) *m.* suicide.

Suiza, (swē´sä) *f.* Switzerland.

suizo, za, (swē´so, sä) *n.* and *adj.* Swiss; *f.* dispute, row.

sujeción, (sū·he·syon´) *f.* subjection, control; fastening, holding; **con — a,** subject to.

sujetar, (sū·he·tar´) *va.* to subject *(someter);* to hold, to fasten *(afirmar).*

sujeto, ta, (sū·he´to, tä) *adj.* subject; fastened; **estar — a,** to be subject to; —, *m.* subject.

sulfanilamida, (sūl·fä·nē·lä·me´thä) *f.* sulfanilamide.

sulfato, (sūl·fä´to) *m.* (chem.) sulphate.

sulfonamida, (sūl·fo·nä·me´thä) *f.* sulfonamide.

sulfúrico, (sūl·fū´rē·ko) *adj.* sulphuric.

sultán, (sūl·tän´) *m.* sultan.

suma, (sū´mä) *f.* addition *(acción);* sum, amount *(total);* essence *(lo más importante);* summary *(compendio);* **en —,** in short.

sumamente, (sū·mä·men´te) *adv.* exceedingly.

sumar, (sū·mär´) *va.* to add; to summarize, to sum up *(compendiar);* to amount to *(componer).*

sumario, ria, (sū·mä´ryo, ryä) *adj.* summary; —, *m.* compendium, summary.

sumergible, (sū·mer·hē·´vle) *adj.* submersible; —, *m.* submarine.

sumergir, (sū·mer·hēr´) *va.* and *vr.* to submerge, to sink.

sumersión, (sū·mer·syon´) *f.* submersion.

sumidero, (sū·mē·the´ro) *m.* sewer, drain.

suministrador, ra, (sū·mē·nēs·trä·thor´, rä) *n.* provider.

suministrar, (sū·mē·nēs·trär´) *va.* to supply, to furnish.

suministro, (sū·mē·nēs´tro) *m.* provision, supply; **—s,** pl. (mil.) supplies.

sumir, (sū·mēr´) *va.* to sink, to lower; **— se,** to be sunken in; (fig.) to wallow *(abismarse).*

sumisión, (sū·mē·syon´) *f.* submission.

sumiso, sa, (sū·mē´so sä) *adj.* submissive.

sumo, ma, (sū´mo, mä) *adj.* supreme; **a lo—mo,** at most; **de —mo,** completely.

suntuoso, sa, (sūn·two´so, sä) *adj.* sumptuous.

supeditar, (sū·pe·thē·tär´) *va.* to hold down, to overpower.

---

m met, **n** not, **p** pot, **r** very, **rr** (none), **s** so, **t** toy, **th** with, **v** eve, **w** we, **y** yes, **z** zero

superable, (sū·pe·rā´vle) *adj.* surmountable, superable.

superabundancia, (sū·pe·rā·vūn·dän´syä) *f.* superabundance.

superar, (sū·pe·rär´) *va.* to surpass, to excel *(exceder)*; to overcome, to surmount *(sobrepujar)*.

superbombardero, (sū·per·vom·bär·the´ro) *m.* superbomber.

supercarretera, (sū·per·kä·rre·te´rä) *f.* superhighway.

superficial, (sū·per·fē·syäl´) *adj.* superficial; surface.

superficie, (sū·per·fē´sye) *f.* surface; (math.) area.

superfluo, flua, (sū·per´flwo, flwä) *adj.* superfluous.

superhombre, (sū·pe·rom´bre) *m.* superman.

superintendente, (sū·pe·rēn·ten·den´te) *m.* superintendent, director.

superior, (sū·pe·ryor´) *adj.* (fig.) superior; upper *(más alto)*; higher *(más elevado)*; **parte** —, topside; —, *m.* superior.

superioridad, (sū·pe·ryo·rē·thäth´) *f.* superiority; **complejo de** —, superiority complex.

superlativo, va, (sū·per·lä·tē´vo, vä) *adj.* and *m.* superlative.

supermercado, (sū·per·mer·kä´tho) *m.* supermarket.

supernumerario, ria, (sū·per·nū·me·rä´ryo, ryä) *adj.* supernumerary.

supersónico, ca, (sū·per·so´nē·ko, kä) *adj.* supersonic; **velocidad** —ca, supersonic speed.

superstición, (sū·pers·tē·syon´) *f.* superstition.

supersticioso, sa, (sū·pers·tē·syo´so, sä) *adj.* superstitious.

super.te: superintendente, supt. superintendent.

supervivencia, (sū·per·vē·ven´syä) *f.* survival; survivorship *(de una renta)*; — **del más apto.** survival of the fittest.

superviviente, (sū·per·vē·vyen´te) *m.* and *f.* survivor; —, *adj.* surviving.

supino, na, (sū·pē´no, nä) *adj.* supine; —, *m.* (gram.) supine.

suplantar, (sū·plän·tär) *va.* to falsify *(falsificar)*; to supplant *(remplazar)*.

suplemento, (sū·ple·men´to) *m.* supplement.

suplente, (sū·plen´te) *adj.* and *m.* substitute, alternate.

súplica, (sū´plē·kä) *f.* petition, request *(escrito)*; entreaty.

suplicante, (sū·plē·kän´te) *adj.* entreating, pleading; —, *m.* and *f.* supplicant, petitioner.

suplicar, (sū·plē·kär´) *va.* to entreat, to beg, to implore *(rogar)*; to petition *(ante el tribunal)*.

suplicio, (sū·plē´syo) *m.* punishment *(castigo)*; (fig.) anguish, suffering, torment; **último** —, capital punishment.

suplir, (sū·plēr´) *va.* to make up, to supply; to replace, to take the place of *(remplazar)*; to make up for *(remediar)*.

supl.te: suplente, sub. substitute.

suponer*, (sū·po·ner´) *va.* to suppose; to imply, to call for *(importar)*; —, *vn.* to carry weight.

suposición, (sū·po·sē·syon´) *f.* supposition; weight, importance *(autoridad)*; falsehood *(impostura)*.

supositorio, (sū·po·sē·to´ryo) *m.* suppository.

supremacía, (sū·pre·mä·sē´ä) *f.* supremacy.

supremo, ma, (sū·pre´mo, mä) *adj.* supreme.

supresión, (sū·pre·syon´) *f.* suppression.

suprimir, (sū·prē·mēr´) *va.* to suppress; to omit, to leave out *(omitir)*.

supuesto, (sū·pwes´to) *m.* supposition; —, **ta,** *adj.* supposed, reputed, assumed; — **to que,** in view of the fact that, inasmuch as; **por** —**to,** of course; **dar por** —, to take for granted.

supurar, (sū·pū·rär´) *vn.* to suppurate.

sur, (sūr) *m.* south; south wind *(viento)*.

surcar, (sūr·kär´) *va.* to furrow; (fig.) to plow through, to cut through.

surco, (sūr´ko) *m.* furrow.

surgir, (sūr·hēr´) *vn.* to gush out, to spurt *(surtir)*; to arise, to spring up, to emerge *(manifestarse)*; (naut.) to anchor.

suroeste (sū·ro·es´te) = **sudoeste.**

surrealismo, (sū·rre·ä·lēz´mo) *m.* surrealism.

surtido, (sūr·tē´tho) *m.* assortment, supply.

surtidor, ra, (sūr·tē·thor´, rä) *n.* purveyor, supplier; —, *m.* spout, jet.

surtir, (sūr·tēr´) *va.* to supply, to furnish, to fit out; —, *vn.* to gush out, to jet, to spout.

sus, (sūs) *pron.* their; your *(de usted)*.

susceptible, (sūs·sep·tē´vle) *adj.* susceptible; touchy *(picajoso)*.

suscitar, (sūs·sē·tär´) *va.* to excite, to stir up.

suscribir, (sūs·krē·vēr´) *va.* to subscribe;

to subscribe to *(convenir con);* —**se a,** to subscribe to.

suscripción, (sūs·krēp·syon´) *f.* subscription.

suscriptor, ra, (sūs·krēp·tor´, râ) *n.* subscriber.

suscrito, ta, (sūs·krē´to, tâ) *adj.* undersigned.

susodicho, cha, (sū·so·thē´cho, châ´) *adj.* above-mentioned, aforesaid.

suspender, (sūs·pen·der´) *va.* to suspend; to amaze *(causar admiración);* to fail *(al examinando);* to fire, to discharge *(destituir).*

suspensión, (sūs·pen·syon´) *f.* suspension; amazement.

suspenso, sa, (sūs·pen´so, sâ) *adj.* suspended; amazed, bewildered *(admirado);* —, *m.* failing grade.

suspicacia, (sūs·pē·kâ´syâ) *f.* suspiciousness, distrust.

suspicaz, (sūs·pē·kâs´) *adj.* suspicious, distrustful.

suspirar, (sūs·pē·râr´) *vn.* to sigh; — **por,** to long for.

suspiro, (sūs·pē´ro) *m.* sigh; (P.R.) meringue.

sustancia, (sūs·tân´syâ) *f.* substance.

sustancial, (sūs·tân·syâl´) *adj.* substantial.

sustancioso, sa, (sūs·tân·syo´so, sâ) *adj.* substantial; nutritious, nourishing *(nutritivo).*

sustantivo, va, (sūs·tân·tē´vo, vâ) *adj.* and *m.* (gram.) substantive, noun.

sustentar, (sūs·ten·târ´) *va.* to sustain, to support, to maintain.

sustento, (sūs·ten´to) *m.* sustenance, support.

sustitución, (sūs·tē·tū·syon´) *f.* substitution.

sustituir*, (sūs·tē·twēr´) *va.* to replace, to substitute for.

sustituto, ta, (sūs·tē·tū´to, tâ) *adj.* and *n.* substitute.

susto, (sūs´to) *m.* fright, scare; (fig.) dread *(preocupación);* **llevarse un** —, to get a good scare.

sustracción, (sūs·trâk·syon´) *f.* subtraction.

sustraendo, (sūs·trâ en´do) *m.* subtrahend.

sustraer*, (sūs·trâ·er´) *va.* to remove, to take away; (math.) to subtract; to steal *(robar);* —**se,** to withdraw, to get out.

susurrar, (sū·sū·rrâr´) *vn.* to whisper; to be whispered about *(una cosa secreta);* to rustle *(el viento);* to murmur *(el agua).*

susurro, (sū·sū´rro) *m.* whisper; murmur; rustle.

sutil, (sū·tēl´) *adj.* fine, thin *(tenue);* (fig.) subtle.

sutileza, (sū·tē le´sâ) *f.* fineness; subtlety.

sutilizar, (sū·tē·lē·sâr´) *vt.* to refine.

sutura, (sū·tū´râ) *f.* (med.) suture.

suyo, ya, (sū´yo, yâ) *pron.* his *(de él);* hers *(de ella);* theirs *(de ellos);* one's *(de uno);* yours *(de usted);* —, *adj.* his; her; their; your; **de** —**yo,** on one´s own; in itself *(propiamente).*

T

tabaco, (tâ·vâ´ko) *m.* tobacco; — **en polvo,** snuff.

tábano, (tâ´vâ·no) *m.* horsefly.

tabaquera, (tâ·vâ·ke´râ) *f.* snuffbox.

tabaquería, (tâ·vâ·ke·rē´a) *f.* cigar store *(tienda);* cigar factory *(fábrica).*

taberna, (tâ·ver´nâ) *f.* tavern, saloon.

tabernáculo, (tâ·ver·nâ´kū·lo) *m.* tabernacle.

tabique, (tâ·vē´ke) *m.* partition.

tabla, (tâ´vlâ) *f.* board *(madera);* slab *(losa);* butcher´s block *(de carnicería);* index *(índice);* (math.) table; bed of earth *(tierra);* pleat *(pliegue);* catalogue *(catálogo);* —**s,** *pl.* tie, draw; stage *(escenario);* —**s de la ley,** (eccl.) tables of the law.

tablado, (tâ·vlâ´tho) *m.* scaffold, staging *(andamio);* frame of a bedstead *(de una cama);* stage *(escenario).*

tablero, (tâ·vle´ro) *m.* board; chessboard *(de ajedrez);* checkerboard *(de damas);* stock of a crossbow *(de una ballesta);* cutting board *(de la sastrería);* counter *(mostrador);* blackboard *(pizarrón);* (orn.) petrel; — **de dibujar,** drafting board; — **de instrumentos,** instrument board.

tableta, (tâ·vle´tâ) *f.* tablet; small chocolate cake *(pastilla);* pill *(píldora).*

m met, n not, p pot, r very, rr (none), s so, t toy, th with, v eve, w we, y yes, z zero

tablilla, (tâ·vlē´yä) f. tablet, slab (tableta); bulletin board (de anuncios).

tabú, (tâ·vū´) m. taboo.

taburete, (tâ·vū·re´te) m. narrow-backed chair (silla); stool (escabel).

tacaño, ña, (tâ·kâ´nyo, nyä) adj. artful, knavish (astuto); miserly, stingy (mezquino).

tacazo, (tâ·kâ´so) m. drive.

tácito, ta, (tâ´sē·to, tä) adj. tacit, silent (callado); implied (supuesto).

taciturno, na, (tâ·sē·tūr´no, nä) adj. taciturn, silent (callado); melancholy (triste).

taco, (tâ´ko) m. stopper, stopple; wad (cilindro); rammer (baqueta); billiard cue (del billar); snack (bocado); swallow of wine (trago); oath (grosería); (Mex.) stuffed rolled tortilla.

tacón, (tâ·kon´) m. heel; — de goma or de caucho, rubber heel.

taconeo, (tâ·ko·ne´o) m. click of one´s heels.

táctico, ca, (tâk´tē·ko, kâ) adj. tactical; —, m. tactician.

tacto, (tâk´to) m. touch, feeling; tact (diplomacia); knack (tino).

tacha, (tâ´chä) f. fault, defect; large tack (clavo); sin —, perfect.

tachar, (tâ·châr´) va. to find fault with (poner falta); to reprehend (censurar); to erase, to efface (borrar); to challenge (al testigo).

tachonar, (tâ·cho·nâr´) va. to trim (adornar); to stud (clavetear).

tachuela, (tâ·chwe´lä) f. tack, nail.

tafetán, (tâ·fe·tân´) m. taffeta.

tahona, (tâ·o´nä) f. horse-drawn crushing mill (molino); bakery (panadería).

tahúr, (tâ·ūr´) m. gambler, gamester.

taimado, da, (tāē·mâ´tho, thä) adj. sly, cunning, crafty.

taja, (tâ´hä) f. cut, incision (cortadura); shield (escudo).

tajada, (tâ·hâ´thä) f. slice; (coll.) hoarseness.

tajador, ra, (tâ·hâ·thor´, râ) n. chopper, cutter; —, m. chopping block.

tajalápices, (tâ·hâ·lâ´pē·ses) m. pencil sharpener.

tajar, (tâ·hâr´) va. to cut, to chop, to slice, to carve.

tajo, (tâ´ho) m. cut, incision; task, assignment (tarea); cliff (escarpa); cutting edge (filo); cutting board (pedazo de madera); stool (tajuelo).

tal, (tál) adj. such, such a; con — que, provided that; no hay —, no such

thing; ¿qué —? how goes it? how are you getting along? — vez, perhaps.

taladrar, (tâ·lâ·thrâr´) va. to bore, to pierce, to drill; to pierce one s ears (de un ruido); to get to the root of (de un problema).

taladro, (tâ·lâ´thro) m. borer, gimlet,auger, drill; drill hole (agujero).

tálamo, (tâ´lâ·mo) m. bridal bed; (bot.) thalamus.

talante, (tâ·lân´te) m. manner of performance (manera de ejecutar); appearance, countenance (semblante); will, desire, pleasure (voluntad); de mal —, unwillingly, with bad grace; de buen —, willingly, with good grace.

talar, (tâ·lâr´) va. to fell (árboles); to desolate, to raise havoc in (arruinar).

talco, (tâl´ko) m. talc (silicato); tinsel (lámina); polvo de —, talcum powder.

talega, (tâ·le´gä) f. bag, bagful; diaper (culero); (coll.) sins (pecados).

talego, (tâ·le´go) m. bag, sack; (coll.) clumsy, heavy individual; tener —, to have money put away.

talento, (tâ·len´to) m. talent.

talentoso, sa, (tâ·len·to´so, sä) adj. talented.

talismán, (tâ·lēz·man´) m. talisman.

talón, (tâ·lon´) m. heel; check, stub, coupon (comprobante).

talonario, (tâ·lo·nâ´ryo) m. check stubs; libro —, checkbook.

talla, (tâ´yä) f. engraving (grabado); sculpture (escultura); stature (estatura); size (tamaño); height scale (instrumento); reward (premio); hand (en las cartas).

tallado, da, (tâ·yä´tho, thä) adj. cut, carved, engraved; buen —, well-formed; m. carving; engraving.

tallador, (tâ·yä·thor´) m. engraver.

tallar, (tâ·yâr´) va. to cut (una piedra); to carve (madera); to engrave; to appraise (apreciar); to measure (medir); —, vi. to discourse (discurrir); to talk of love (del amor); —, adj. ready to be cut or carved.

tallarín, (tâ·yä·rēn´) m. noodle; sopa de— ines, noodle soup.

talle, (tâ´ye) m. shape, size, proportion (proporción); waist (cintura); appearance (apariencia).

taller, (tâ·yer´) m. workshop; (fig.) laboratory; — de reparaciones, repair shop.

tallo, (tâ´yo) m. shoot, sprout (renuevo); stem; (coll.) cabbage.

tamal. (tâ·mâl´) m. tamale.

tamaño, (tâ·mâ´nyo) m. size; —, ña, adj.

â arm, e they, ē bē, o fore, ū blūe, b bad, ch chip, d day, f fat, g go, h hot, k kid, 1 let

so small *(tan pequeño);* so large *(tan grande);* very small *(muy pequeño);* very large *(muy grande).*

tamarindo, (tâ·mä·rēn´do) *m.* tamarind.

tambalear, (tâm·bä·le·âr´) *vn.* and *vr.* to stagger, to reel, to totter.

tambaleo, (tâm·bä·le´o) *m.* staggering, reeling.

también, (tâm·byen´) *adv.* also, too, likewise, as well.

tambor, (tâm·bor´) *m.* drum; drummer *(persona);* drum *(barril);* coffee roaster *(asador);* reel *(para arrollar);* tambour frame *(aro);* eardrum *(tímpano);* — **mayor,** (mil.) drum major.

tamboril, (tâm·bo·rēl´) *m.* tabor, small drum.

tamborilero (tâm·bo·rē·le´ro) or **tamboritero,** (tam·bo·rē·te´ro) *m.* tabor player, drummer.

tamborito, (tâm·bo·rē´to) *m.* national folk dance of Panama.

tamiz, (tâ·mēs´) *m.* fine sieve.

tamizar, (tâ·mē·sâr´) *vt.* to sift, to sieve.

tampoco, (tâm·po´ko) *adv.* neither, not either.

tan, (tan) *m.* boom, drum beat; —,*adv.* so; as *(equivalencia);* — **pronto como,** as soon as.

tanda, (tän´dä) *f.* turn (turno); task *(tarea);* gang *(grupo);* shift *(que turnan);* game *(partida);* number *(número);* (Sp. Am.) performance, show.

tándem, (tân´den) *m.* tandem.

tangente, (tân·hen´te) *f.* (math.) tangent; **salir por la** —, to evade the issue.

Tánger, (tân´her) *f.* Tangier.

tangible, (tân·hē´vle) *adj.* tangible.

tango, (tâng´go) *m.* tango.

tanque, (tâng´ke) *m.* tank; beeswax *(propóleos);* water tank *(de agua);* dipper *(cazo);* pool *(estanque).*

tantear, (tân·te·âr´) *vt.* to compare *(parangonar);* to keep score *(apuntar los tantos);* to consider carefully *(considerar);* to size up *(evaluar);* to estimate *(estimar);* to sketch *(dibujar).*

tanteo, (tân·te´o) *m.* comparison *(comparación);* consideration *(consideración);* evaluation *(evaluación);* estimation *(estimación);* sketch *(dibujo);* score *(tantos);* scorekeeping *(acto de apuntar los tantos).*

tanto, (tân´to) *m.* certain sum, a quantity; copy *(copia);* chip, marker *(para tantear);* —, **ta,** *adj.* so much, as much *(tan grande);* very great *(muy grande);* —**to,** *adv.* so, that way *(de tal modo);* so

much, so long *(en tal grado);* **mientras** —, meanwhile; **por lo** —, therefore; — **como,** as much as; — **más,** so much more *(cantidad);* especially, particularly *(especialmente);* —**s,** *m. pl.* score, points.

tañer*, (tâ·nyer´) *va.* to play; —, *vn.* to drum the fingers.

tañido, (tâ·nyē´tho) *m.* tune, note *(son que se toca);* sound, tone *(sonido de un instrumento).*

tapa, (tä´pä) *f.* lid, cover *(tapadera);* book cover *(de un libro);* snack served with wine *(bocado).*

tapar, (tä·pâr´) *va.* to cover, to close *(cubrir);* to bundle up *(abrigar);* to conceal, to hide *(ocultar).*

taparrabo, (tä·pä·rrä´vo) *m.* loincloth; — **de baño,** swimming trunks.

tapete, (tä·pe´te) *m.* small carpet *(alfombra);* runner *(de mesa).*

tapia, (tä´pyä) *f.* adobe wall *(pared);* enclosure *(cerca);* **sordo como una** —, stone deaf.

tapiar, (tä·pyâr´) *va.* to wall up *(cerrar con tapias);* to stop up, to close up *(cerrar un hueco).*

tapicería, (tä·pē·se·rē´ä) *f.* tapestry; upholstery.

tapicero, (tä·pē·se´ro) *m.* tapestry maker; upholsterer *(de muebles).*

tapioca, (tä·pyo´kä) *f.* tapioca.

tapiz, (tä·pēs´) *m.* tapestry; **papel** —, wallpaper.

tapizar, (tä·pē·sâr´) *va.* to cover with tapestry *(de tapiz);* to cover with rugs *(de alfombras);* to upholster *(de muebles).*

tapón, (tä·pon´) *m.* cork, plug, stopper; (med.) tampon.

taquigrafía, (tä·kē·grä·fē´ä) *f.* shorthand, stenography.

taquigráfico, ca, (tä·ke·grä´fē·ko, kä) *adj.* in shorthand; **versión** —**ca,** shorthand record.

taquígrafo, fa, (tä·kē´grä·fo, fä) *n.* stenographer.

taquilla, (tä·kē´yä) *f.* file cabinet *(armario);* box office, ticket office, ticket window *(de billetes);* box-office take, receipts *(cantidad recaudada).*

taquillero, (tä·kē·ye´ro) *m.* ticket seller; —, **ra,** *adj.* (Mex.) successful at the box office; popular.

tara, (tä´rä) *f.* tare *(de peso);* tally *(tarja);* (med.) defect.

tarántula, (tä·rân´tū·lä) *f.* tarantula.

tararear, (tä·rä·re·âr´) *va.* to hum.

tardanza, (târ·thän´sä) *f.* tardiness, delay.

---

m met, **n** not, **p** pot, **r** very, **rr** (none), **s** so, **t** toy, **th** with, **v** eve, **w** we, **y** yes, **z** zero

tardar, (târ·thâr´) *vn.* to be long, to spend time; to take one, to spend *(emplear tiempo);* **a más —,** at the latest.

tarde, (târ´the) *f.* afternoon; dusk, early evening *(anochecer);* **buenas —s,** good afternoon; **—,** *adv.* late; **más —,** later.

tardío, día, (târ·thē´o, thē´â) *adj.* late, slow, tardy; **—s,** *m. pl.* late crops.

tardo, da, (târ´tho, thâ) *adj.* sluggish *(perezoso);* late *(tardío);* slow, dense *(torpe).*

tarea, (tâ·re´â) *f.* task; trouble, worry *(penalidad);* obsession, same old thing *(afán).*

tarifa, (tâ·rē´fâ) *f.* tariff, charge, rate, fare; price list *(catálogo);* **— de impuestos,** tax rate.

tarima, (tâ·rē´mâ) *f.* platform, stand *(entablado);* low bench *(banco).*

tarjeta, (târ·he´tâ) *f.* card; imprint *(impresión);* **— de crédito,** credit card; **— postal,** postcard; **— de visita,** visiting card.

tarlatana, (târ·lâ·tâ´nâ) *f.* tarlatan.

tarro, (tâ´rro) *m.* earthen jar.

tartamudear, (târ·tâ·mū·the·âr´) *vn.* to stutter, to stammer.

tartamudo, da, (târ·tâ·mū´tho, thâ) *n.* stammerer, stutterer; **—,** *adj.* stammering, stuttering.

tártaro, (târ´tâ·ro) *m.* cream of tartar; tartar *(de los dientes).*

tarugo, (tâ·rū´go) *m.* peg *(clavija);* chunk, hunk *(zoquete);* block *(para pavimentar);* (coll.) cheat *(embustero);* dunce *(tonto).*

tasa, (tâ´sâ) *f.* rate, value, assize; fixed price *(precio fijo);* measure, rule *(medida);* regulation *(regulación).*

tasación, (tâ·sâ·syon´) *f.* valuation, appraisal.

tasado, da, (tâ·sâ´tho, thâ) *adj.* limited, scanty.

tasajo, (tâ·sâ´ho) *m.* jerked beef.

tasar, (tâ·sâr´) *va.* to appraise, to value *(valuar);* to regulate *(regular);* to restrict, to reduce *(reducir).*

tatuaje, (tâ·twâ´he) *m.* tattoo; tattooing *(acto).*

taumaturgo, (tâū·mâ·tūr´go) *m.* miracle worker.

tauromaquia, (tâū·ro·mâ´kyâ) *f.* art of bullfighting.

taxi, (tâk´sē) *m.* taxicab.

taxidermista, (tâk·sē·ther·mēs´tâ) *m.* and *f.* taxidermist.

taxímetro, (tâk·sē´me·tro) *m.* taximeter; taxicab *(coche).*

taza, (tâ´sâ) *f.* cup; cupful *(contenido);*

bowl *(tazón);* basin *(de una fuente);* cup guard *(de una espada).*

te, (te) *pron.* you; to you *(dativo)*

té, (te) *m.* tea.

tea, (te´â) *f.* candlewood *(madera);* torch *(antorcha);* anchor rope *(cable).*

teatral, (te·â·trâl´) *adj.* theatrical.

teatro, (te·â´tro) *m.* theater, playhouse; stage *(escenario);* theater *(arte).*

tecla, (te´klâ) *f.* key; (fig.) delicate matter.

teclado, (te·klâ´tho) *m.* keyboard.

tecnicalidad, (teg·nē·kâ·lē·thâth´) *f.* technicality.

tecnicismo, (teg·nē·sēz´mo) *m.* technology; technical term (voz).

técnico, ca, (teg´nē·ko, kâ) *adj.* technical; **—,** *f.* technique; **—,** *m:* technician.

tecnicolor, (teg·nē·ko·lor´) *m.* technicolor.

tecnológico, ca, (teg·no·lo´hē·ko, kâ) *adj.* technological.

tecolote, (te·ko·lo´te) *m.* (Mex.) owl.

techo, (te´cho) *m.* roof; ceiling *(parte interior);* house *(casa);* **bajo —,** indoors.

tedio, (te´thyo) *m.* tedium, boredom.

teja, (te´hâ) *f.* roof tile; linden *(árbol).*

tejado, (te·hâ´tho) *m.* tiled roof.

tejar, (te·hâr´) *m.* tileworks; **—,** *va.* to tile.

tejedor, ra, (te·he·thor´, râ) *n.* weaver; intriguer *(intrigante).*

tejer, (te·her´) *va.* to weave; to braid *(entrelazar);* to knit *(hacer puntos);* (fig.) to contrive.

tejido, (te·hē´tho) *m.* texture, web; textile, fabric *(cosa tejida);* (anat.) tissue; **— de punto,** knitted fabric.

tejo, (te´ho) *m.* quoit; metal disk *(disco de metal);* yew tree *(árbol).*

tela, (te´lâ) *f.* cloth, fabric; membrane, tissue *(membrana);* scum *(nata);* web *(de araña);* **— de hilo,** linen cloth; **— adhesiva,** adhesive tape; **— aisladora,** (elec.) insulating tape; **en — de juicio,** in doubt, under consideration.

telar, (te·lâr´) *m.* loom; proscenium *(escenario).*

telaraña, (te·lâ·râ´nyâ) *f.* cobweb, spider web; will-o´-the-wisp *(cosa sutil);* trifle (bagatela).

teledirigir, (te·le·thē·rē·hēr´) *va.* to operate by remote control.

telefonear, (te·le·fo·ne·âr´) *va.* and *vn.* to telephone.

telefonema, (te·le·fo·ne´mâ) *m.* telephone message.

telefonista, (te·le·fo·nēs´tâ) *m.* and *f.* telephone operator.

teléfono, (te·le´fo·no) *m.* telephone; **— automático,** dial telephone;**— celular,**

cell phone.

telefoto, (te·le·fo´to) *f.* wire photo.

teleg.: telegrama, tel. telegram; **telégrafo,** tel. telegraph.

telegrafía, (te·le·grä·fē´ä) *f.* telegraphy; — **sin hilos** or — **inalámbrica,** wireless telegraphy.

telegrafiar, (te·le·grä·fyär´) *va.* and *vn.* to telegraph.

telégrafo, (te·le´grä·fo) *m.* telegraph.

telegrama, (te·le·grä´mä) *m.* telegram.

teleguiado, da, (te·le·gyä´tho, thä) *adj.*remote-control.

telémetro, (te·le´me·tro) *m.* telemeter.

telenovela, (te·le·no·ve´lä) *f.* soap opera, television serial.

telepatía, (te·le·pä·tē´ä) *f.* telepathy.

telerreceptor, (te·le·rre·sep·tor´) *m.* television set.

telescopio, (te·les·ko´pyo) *m.* telescope.

teleteatro, (te·le·te·ä´tro) *m.* teleplay.

teletipo, (te·le·tē´po) *m.* teletype.

televidente, (te·le·vē·then´te) *m.* and *f.* televiewer, television viewer.

televisión, (te·le·vē·syon´) *f.* television.

televisor, (te·le·vē·sor´) *m.* television set.

telón, (te·lon´) *m.* drop, curtain; — **de boca,** front curtain.

telúrico, ca, (te·lū´rē·ko, kä) *adj.*telluric.

tema, (te´mä) *m.* theme *(proposición);* subject *(asunto);* (mus.) theme; —, *f.* obstinacy *(porfía);* contentiousness *(oposición);* mania, obsession *(idea fija).*

temblar*, (tem·blär´) *vn.* to tremble to quiver *(agitarse);* to waver *(vacilar);* (fig.) to be terrified.

temblor, (tem·blor´) *m.* trembling, tremor; earthquake *(terremoto).*

tembloroso, sa, (tem·blo·ro´so, sä) *adj.* trembling, shaky.

temer, (te·mer´) *va.* to fear; — *vi.* to be afraid.

temerario, ria, (te·me·rä´ryo, ryä) *adj.* rash, reckless, brash; —, *n.* daredevil.

temeridad, (te·me·rē·thäth´) *f.* rashness, recklessness *(calidad);* folly, foolishness *(acto);* rash judgment *(juicio).*

temeroso, sa, (te·me·ro´so, sä) *adj.*timid, timorous.

temible, (te·mē´vle) *adj.*dreadful, terrible.

temor, (te·mor´) *m.* dread, fear; suspicion *(sospecha);* misgiving *(recelo).*

témpano, (tem´pä·no) *m.* kettle drum; drumhead *(piel);* side of bacon *(tocino);* block *(pedazo);* — **de hielo,** iceberg.

temperamento, (tem·pe·rä·men´to) *m.*weather; temperament, nature, temper *(estado fisiológico);* conciliation *(arbi-*

trio).

temperatura, (tem·pe·rä·tū´rä) *f.* temperature; weather *(temperie).*

tempestad, (tem·pes·täth´) *f.* storm; rough seas *(del mar);* (fig.) agitation, upheaval.

tempestuoso, sa, (tem·pes·two´so, sä) *adj.* tempestuous, stormy.

templado, da, (tem·plä´tho, thä) *adj.* temperate, moderate; lukewarm *(tibio);* average *(del estilo).*

templanza, (tem·plän´sä) *f.* temperance; moderation, continence *(continencia);* temperateness, mildness *(clima).*

templar, (tem·plär´) *va.* to moderate; to heat *(calentar);* to temper *(metal);* to dilute *(mezclar);* to relieve *(sosegar);* (mus.) to tune; —**se,** to be moderate.

templo, (tem´plo) *m.* temple; Protestant church *(protestante).*

temporada, (tem·po·rä´thä) *f.* time, period; season *(habitual).*

temporal, (tern·po·räl´) *adj.* temporary; temporal *(secular);* —, *m.* tempest, storm *(tempestad);* weather *(temperie).*

temprano, na, (tem·prä´no, nä) *adj.* early; —**no,** *adv.* early.

tenacidad, (te·nä·sē·thäth´) *f.* tenacity.

tenacillas, (te·nä·sē´yäs) *f. pl.* small tongs, tweezers.

tenaz, (te·näs´) *adj.*tenacious.

tenazas, (te·nä´säs) *f. pl.* tongs, pincers, pliers.

tendedero, (ten·de·the´ro) *m.* clothesline.

tendencia, (ten·den´syä) *f.* tendency.

tender*, (ten·der´) *va.* to stretch out, to unfold, to spread out; to hang out *(para secar);* to extend *(extender);* —, *vn.* to tend; —**se,** to stretch out.

tendero, ra, (ten·de´ro, rä) *n.* shopkeeper.

tendido, (ten·dē´tho) *m.* extending, spreading out; lower deck seats *(galería);* wash *(ropa);* batch of bread *(pan).*

tendón, (ten·don´) *m.* tendon; — **de Aquiles,** Achilles´ tendon.

tenebroso, sa, (te·ne·vro´so, sä) *adj.* dark, shadowy, gloomy; (fig.) obscure.

tenedor, (te·ne·thor´) *m.* holder; fork *(utensilio);* — **de libros,** bookkeeper, accountant.

teneduría, (te·ne·thū´rē·ä) *f.* position of bookkeeper; — **de libros,** bookkeeping.

tener*, (te´ner´) *va.* to have, to hold, to possess; to maintain *(mantener);* to consist of, to contain *(comprender);* to dominate, to subject *(sujetar);* to finish, to stop *(parar);* to keep, to fulfill *(cumplir);* to spend, to pass *(pasar);* —

cuidado, to be careful; — derecho a, to have the right to; — empeño, to be eager; — en cuenta, to take into consideration, to realize; — inconveniente, to have an objection; — a menos, to scorn; — por, to consider as; — que, to have to.

tenería, (te·ne·rē´ä) f. tannery.

teniente, (te·nyen´te) m. deputy (substituto); lieutenant.

tenis, (te´nēs) m. tennis; tennis court (sitio); — de mesa, ping pong, table tennis.

tenista, (te·nēs´tä) m. and f. tennis player.

tenor, (te·nor´) m. condition, nature; contents (contenido); (mus.) tenor.

tensión, (ten·syon´) f. tension; — arterial, blood pressure.

tentación, (ten·tä·syon´) f. temptation.

tentáculo, (ten·tä´kū·lo) m. tentacle.

tentador, ra, (ten·tä·thor´, rä) adj. attractive, tempting; —, n. tempter; —, m. devil.

tentar* (ten·tär´) va. to touch; to test (probar); to grope through (andar a tientas); to tempt (instigar); to try, to attempt (intentar).

tentativo, va, (ten·tä·tē´vo, vä) adj. tentative; —, f. attempt, try.

ten.te: teniente, Lt. or Lieut. Lieutenant.

tentempié, (ten·tem·pye´) m. snack, bite.

tenue, (te´nwe) adj. tenuous, delicate; unimportant, trivial (de poca importancia).

teñir*, (te·nyēr´) va. to tint, to dye; to tone down (de la pintura).

teodolito, (te·o·tho·lē´to) m. theodolite.

teología, (te·o·lo·hē´ä) f. theology.

teológico, ca, (te·o·lo´hē·ko, kä) adj. theological.

teorema, (te·o·re´mä) m. theorem.

teoría, (te·o·rē´ä) or teórica, (te·o´rē·kä) f. theory.

teórico, ca, (te·o´rē·ko, kä) adj. theoretical.

teosofía, (te·o·so·fē´ä) f. theosophy.

tequila, (te·kē´lä) m. tequila.

terapéutico, ca, (te·rä·pe´ū·tē·ko, kä) adj. therapeutic; —, f. therapeutics.

tercero, ra, (ter·se´ro, rä) adj. third; —, m. third party; pander (alcahuete).

terceto, (ter·se´to) m. tercet; (mus.) trio.

tercia, (ter´syä) f. third; (eccl.) terse; tierce (cartas).

terciado, da, (ter·syä´tho, thä) adj. slanting, crosswise; —, m. cutlass; wide ribbon (cinta).

terciana, (ter·syä´nä) f. tertian fever.

terciar, (ter·syär´) va. to place crosswise,

to put on the bias; to cut in three (dividir); to balance, to steady (equilibrar); to plow the third time (dar la tercera reja); —, vn. to mediate (mediar); to fill in.

tercio, cia, (ter´syo, syä) adj. third; —, m. third; load (fardo); (mil.) corps; hacer buen —cio, to help, to do a good turn.

terciopelado, da, (ter·syo·pe·lä´tho, thä) adj.velvety.

terciopelo, (ter·syo·pe´lo) m. velvet.

terco, ca, (ter´ko, kä) adj.obstinate, stubborn; very hard, resistant (difícil de labrar).

tergiversar, (ter·hē·ver·sär´) va. to misrepresent.

termal, (ter·mäl´) adj. thermal.

termas, (ter´mäs) f. pl. hot baths, hot springs; public baths (de los romanos).

térmico, ca, (ter´mē·ko, kä) adj.thermal, thermic.

terminación, (ter·mē·nä·syon´) f. termination; (gram.) ending.

terminal, (ter·mē·näl´) adj. terminal, final; —, m. terminal.

terminante, (ter·mē·nän´te) adj. final, decisive, conclusive; orden —, strict order.

terminar, (ter·mē·när´) va. to terminate, to end, to finish; —, vn. to end; —se, to be leading, to be pointing.

término, (ter´mē·no) m. term; termination, end; boundary (línea divisoria); limit (límite); term (tiempo); object, purpose (objeto); situation (situación); demeanor (modo de portarse); — medio, compromise.

terminología, (ter·mē·no·lo·hē´ä) f. terminology.

termodinámica, (ter·mo·thē·nä´mē·kä) f. thermodynamics; — aérea, aerothermodynamics.

termómetro, (ter·mo´me·tro) m. thermometer.

termonuclear, (ter·mo·nū·kle·är´) adj. thermonuclear.

termos, (ter´mos) m. thermos bottle.

termostato, (ter·mos·tä´to) m. thermostat.

ternero, ra, (ter·ne´ro, rä) n. calf; —, f. veal.

terneza, (ter·ne´sä) f. delicacy, tenderness; flattery (requiebro).

terno, (ter´no) m. (eccl.) vestments; celebrants (sacerdotes); three-piece suit (traje); oath (voto).

ternura, (ter·nū´rä) f. tenderness, affection.

terquedad, (ter·ke·thäth´) f. stubbornness, obstinacy.

terracota, (te·rrä·ko´tä) *f.* terra cotta.
terramicina, (te·rrä·mē·sē´nä) *f.* (med.) terramycin.
terraplén, (te·rrä·plen´) *m.* fill *(para rellenar);* embankment; rampart *(defensa);* terrace, platform *(plataforma).*
terráqueo, quea, (te·rrä´ke·o, ke·ä) *adj.* terrestrial; **globo** —, earth, globe.
terraza, (te·rrä´sä) *f.* terrace, veranda; flat roof (terrado); sidewalk cafe (café); garden plot *(era);* glazed jar *(jarra).*
terremoto, (te·rre·mo´to) *m.* earthquake.
terrenal, (te·rre·näl´) *adj.* terrestrial, earthly.
terreno, na, (te·rre´no, nä) *adj.* earthly, terrestrial; —, *m.* land, ground, terrain; (fig.) proving ground.
terrestre, (te·rres´tre) *adj.* terrestrial, earthly.
terrible, (te·rrē´vle) *adj.* terrible, dreadful;surly, gruff *(áspero de genio);* extraordinary, immeasurable *(extraordinario).*
territorial, (te·rrē·to·ryäl´) *adj.* territorial.
territorio, (te·rrē·to´ryo) *m.* territory.
terrón, (te·rron´) *m.* clod *(de tierra);* lump, mound.
terror, (te·rror´) *m.* terror, dread, fear.
terrorismo, (te·rro·rēz´mo) *m.* terrorism.
terruño, (te·rrü´nyo) *m.* clod; native land *(país natal).*
terso, sa, (ter´so, sä) *adj.* smooth, glossy; terse *(del lenguaje).*
tertulia, (ter·tü´lyä) *f.* conversational gathering, party; game area *(de los cafés).*
tesis, (te´sēs) *f.* thesis.
tesón, (te·son´) *m.* firmness, inflexibility.
tesorería, (te·so·re·rē´ä) *f.* treasury.
tesorero, ra, (te·so·re´ro, rä) *n.* treasurer.
tesoro, (te·so´ro) *m.* treasure; treasury *(erario);* treasure room; treasure house *(lugar); (fig.)* thesaurus.
testa, (tes´tä) *f.* head; front, face *(frente);* (coll.) brains, wit.
testamentario, (tes·tä·men·tä´ryo) *m.* executor.
testamento, (tes·tä·men´to) *m.* will, testament; **Viejo T—,** Old Testament; **Nuevo T—,** New Testament.
testar, (tes·tär´) *vn.* to make out one´s will; —, *va.* to erase.
testarudo, da, (tes·tä·rü´tho, thä) *adj.* obstinate, bullheaded.
testículo, (tes·tē´kü·lo) *m.* testicle.
testificar, (tes·tē·fē·kär´) *vn.* to attest, to testify; —, *va.* to witness.
testigo, (tes·tē´go) *m.* witness.
testimoniar, (tes·tē·mo·nyär´) *va.* to attest

to, to bear witness to.
testimonio, (tes·tē·mo´nyo) *m.* testimony.
testuz, (tes·tūs´) *m.* forehead *(frente);* nape *(nuca).*
teta, (te´tä) *f.* teat; hillock *(montículo).*
tétano, (te´tä·no) *m.* (med.) tetanus, lockjaw.
tetera, (te·te´rä) *f.* teapot, teakettle.
tétrico, ca, (te´trē·ko, kä) *adj.* gloomy, sad, melancholy.
textil, (tes·tēl´) *adj.* and *m.* textile.
texto, (tes´to) *m.* text; passage *(pasaje);* **libro de —,** text book; **el Sagrado —,** the Bible.
textual, (tes·twäl´) *adj.* textual.
tez, (tes) *f.* surface; skin, complexion *(del rostro humano).*
ti, (tē) *pron.* you; **para —,** for you.
tía, (tē´ä) *f.* aunt; (coll.) goody; hag *(mujer grosera).*
tiamina, (tyä·mē´nä) *f.* thiamine.
tiara, (tya´rä) *f.* tiara.
tibia, (tē´vyä) *f.* shinbone.
tibio, bia, (tē´vyo, vyä) *adj.* lukewarm; careless, remiss *(descuidado).*
tiburón, (tē·vü·ron´) *m.* shark.
tictac, (tēk·täk´) *m.* ticktock.
tiempo, (tyem´po) *m.* time; season *(estación);* weather *(temperie);* (mus.) tempo; (gram.) tense; **— atrás,** some time ago; **— desocupado,** spare time; **a —,** in time; **a —s,** at times; **a su — debido,** in due time; **a un —,** at once, at the same time; **hacer buen —,** to be good weather; **más —,** longer; **tomarse —,** to take one´s time; **en un —,** formerly; **hace mucho —,** a long time ago; **en —s pasados,** in former times.
tienda, (tyen´dä) *f.* tent; (naut.) awning; (com.) store, shop;— **de conveniencia,** convenience store; **— de oxígeno,** (med.) oxygen tent.
tienta, (tyen´tä) *f.* (med.) probe; cleverness, sagacity *(sagacidad);* **andar a —s,** to grope.
tiento, (tyen´to) *m.* touch; cane *(de los ciegos);* sure hand, sure touch *(pulso);* circumspection *(consideración);* **a —,** gropingly.
tierno, na, (tyer´no, nä) *adj.* tender, delicate, soft *(delicado);* new *(recién);* childlike, young *(de la niñez);* teary, tearful *(propenso al llanto);* affectionate, loving *(cariñoso).*
tierra, (tye´rrä) *f.* earth; soil *(materia);* land *(terreno);* homeland *(patria);* ground *(suelo);* **— abrasada,** scorched earth; **— adentro,** inland; **— baja,** low-

m met, **n** not, **p** pot, **r** very, **rr** (none), **s** so, **t** toy, **th** with, **v** eve, **w** we, **y** yes, **z** zero

lands; — **de altura,** highlands; **echar por —,** to destroy, to ruin; **echar — a,** to cover up, to hide.

tieso, sa, (tye´so, sâ) *adj.* stiff, hard, firm; tense, taut *(tenso);* robust *(robusto);* valiant *(valiente);* stubborn *(terco);* pompous *(afectadamente grave).*

tiesto, (tyes´to) *m.* potsherd; flowerpot *(maceta).*

tifoideo, dea, (tē·foē·the´o, the´â) *adj.* typhoid; —, *f.* typhoid fever.

tifus, (tē´fūs) *m.* (med.) typhus.

tigre, (tē´gre) *m.* tiger; savage *(persona brutal).*

tijeras, (tē·he´râs) *f. pl.* scissors.

tijeretas, (tē·he·re´tâs) *f. pl.* (bot.) tendrils; small scissors.

tijeretear, (tē·he·re·te·âr´) *va.* to cut with scissors; (coll.) to make a snap judgment of, to decide according to one´s whim.

tildar, (tēl·dâr´) *va.* to erase; to brand, to stigmatize *(señalar);* to put a tilde over *(poner tilde).*

tilde, (tēl´de) *f.* tilde; censure, criticism *(tacha);* iota *(cosa mínima).*

tilo, (tē´lo) *m.* linden tree.

timar, (tē·mâr´) *va.* to swindle; to deceive *(engañar);* **—se,** to make eyes.

timbal, (tēm·bâl´) *m.* kettledrum.

timbrazo, (tēm·brâ´so) *n.* clang.

timbre, (tēm´bre) *m.* postage stamp *(de correo);* seal, stamp; electric bell *(aparato);* crest *(insignia);* timbre *(modo de sonar);* (fig.) glorious deed.

timidez, (tē·mē·thes´) *f.* timidity, shyness.

tímido, da, (tē´mē·tho, thâ) *adj.* timid, shy.

timo, (tē´mo) *m.* swindle; gag, joke *(broma);* **dar un —,** to swindle; to deceive *(engañar).*

timón, (tē·mon´) *m.* plow handle; (naut.) rudder; (fig.) helm; **— de dirección,** rudder.

timonera, (tē·mo·ne´râ) *f.* (naut.) pilot-house.

timonero, (tē·mo·ne´ro) *m.* helmsman, pilot.

tímpano, (tēm´pâ·no) *m.* kettledrum; (anat.) tympanum, eardrum.

tina, (tē´nâ) *f.* earthen jar *(de barro);* tub; **— de baño,** bathtub.

tinaja, (tē·nâ´hâ) *f.* large earthen jar.

tinajón, (tē·nâ·hon´) *m.* large earthen tub.

tiniebla, (tē·nye´vlâ) *f.* darkness, obscurity; **—s,** *pl.* utter darkness; gross ignorance *(ignorancia).*

tino, (tē´no) *m.* skill, deftness; marks-

manship *(para dar en el blanco);* judgment, prudence *(juicio).*

tinta, (tēn´tâ) *f.* tint; ink *(para escribir);* **— china,** India ink; **— de imprenta,** printer´s ink; **saber algo de buena —,** to know something on good authority; **—s,** *pl.* shades, hues.

tinte, (tēn´te) *m.* tint, dye; dyeing *(acto);* dyer´s shop *(tienda).*

tintero, (tēn·te´ro) *m.* inkwell, inkstand.

tintinear, (tēn·tē·ne·âr´) *vn.* to tinkle.

tinto, ta, (tēn´to, tâ) *adj.*red; **vino —,** red wine.

tintorera, (tēn·to·re´râ) *f.* dyer; female shark *(tiburón).*

tintorería, (tēn·to·re·rē´â) *f.* dry cleaning shop.

tintura, (tēn·tū´râ) *f.* tincture *(alcohol);* dye.

tiñoso, sa, (tē·nyo´so, sâ) *adj.* scabby, scurvy; stingy, miserly *(miserable).*

tío, (tē´o) *m.* uncle; (coll.) old man *(viejo);* guy *(sujeto);* **— abuelo,** great uncle.

tiovivo, (tyo·vē´vo) *m.* merry-go-round.

típico, ca, (tē´pē·ko, kâ) *adj.* characteristic, typical.

tiple, (tē´ple) *m.* (mus.) soprano (voz); treble guitar *(guitarra);* —, *m.* and *f.* soprano.

tipo, (tē´po) *m.* type, model; standard pattern *(norma);* type *(letra);* figure, build *(figura);* rate *(razón);* **— de cambio,** rate of exchange; **— de descuento,** rate of discount; **— de interés,** rate of interest.

tipografía, (tē·po·grâ·fē´â) *f.* typography, typesetting.

tipográfico, ca, (tē·po·grâ´fē·ko, kâ) *adj.*typographical.

tipógrafo, (te·po´grâ·fo) *m.* printer.

tira, (tē´râ) *f.* strip; **—s,** *pl.* rags.

tirabuzón, (tē·râ·bū·son´) *m.* corkscrew; (fig.) ringlet, corkscrew curl.

tirada, (te· râ´thâ) *f.* cast, throw; distance *(distancia);* length of time *(tiempo);* (print.) run; stroke *(en el golf);* edition, issue *(edición);* **— aparte,** reprint.

tirador, (tē·râ·thor´) *m.* (print.) pressman; stretcher *(que estira);* handle, knob *(asidero);* cord *(cordón);* —, **ra,** *n.* good shot.

tiranía, (tē·râ·nē´â) *f.* tyranny.

tiránico, ca, (tē·râ´nē·ko, kâ) *adj.* tyrannical.

tirano, na, (tē·râ´no, nâ) *adj.* tyrannical; —, *n.* tyrant.

tirante, (tē·rân´te) *m.* beam *(de un tejado);* trace *(de las caballerías);* brace; **—s,** *pl.* suspenders; —, *adj.*tense, taut, drawn;

(fig.) strained, forced.

tirantez, (tē·rän·tes´) *f.* tenseness, tightness, strain; length *(distancia).*

tirar, (tē·râr´) *va.* to throw, to toss, to cast; to tear down *(derribar);* to stretch *(estirar);* to pull; to draw *(trazar);* to fire, to shoot *(disparar);* to throw away, to waste *(malgastar);* —, *vn.* to attract *(atraer);* to pull *(llevar tras sí);* to use *(de las armas);* to take out *(sacar);* to turn *(torcer);* to hang on, to last *(durar);* to tend, to incline *(inclinarse);* **—se,** to rush *(arrojarse);* to lie down, to stretch out *(tenderse);* **a todo —,** at the most; **— al blanco,** to shoot at a target.

tiritar, (tē·rē·târ´) *vn.* to shiver.

tiro, (tē´ro) *m.* throw, cast; mark *(impresión);* charge *(carga);* shot *(disparo);* report *(estampido);* round *(cantidad);* range *(alcance);* rifle range *(lugar);* team *(de caballerías);* trace *(tirante);* prank *(burla);* theft *(hurto);* allusion *(indirecta);* flight *(de escalera);* draft *(corriente);* harm, injury *(daño);* trajectory *(dirección);* **errar el —,** to miss the mark; **— al blanco,** target practice.

tiroides, (tē·ro´ē·thes) *adj.* and *f.* (anat.) thyroid.

tirón, (tē·ron´) *m.* pull, haul, tug; apprentice, novice *(aprendiz);* **de un —,** all at once, at one stroke.

tirotear, (tē·ro·te·âr´) *vn.* to shoot at random.

tiroteo, (tē·ro·te´o) *m.* random shooting.

tirria, (tē´rryâ) *f.* antipathy, dislike, aversion.

tísico, ca, (tē´sē·ko, kâ) *adj.* tubercular, consumptive.

tisis, (tē´sēs) *f.* consumption, tuberculosis.

titánico, ca, (tē·tâ´nē·ko, kâ) *adj.* titanic, colossal.

títere, (tē´te·re) *m.* puppet; pipsqueak *(su jeto ridículo);* good-time Charlie *(sujeto casquivano);* obsession *(idea fija);* **—s,** *pl.* puppet show.

titiritero, (tē·tē·rē·te´ro) *m.* puppeteer.

titubear, (tē·tū·ve·âr´) *vn.* to stammer, to hesitate; to totter *(perder la estabilidad);* to be perplexed *(sentir perplejidad).*

titubeo, (tē·tū·ve´o) *m.* hesitation, stammering; tottering; perplexity.

titular, (tē·tū·lâr´) *va.* to title; —, *vn.* to obtain a title; —, *adj.* and *m.* titular.

título, (tē´tū·lo) *m.* title; headline *(letrero);* epithet *(renombre);* cause, motive *(causa);* document, deed *(documento);* diploma *(testimonio);* nobility *(digni-*

dad); nobleman *(persona);* section *(ley);* (com.) bond; **a — de,** on pretense of; **a — de suficiencia,** upon proven capacity.

tiza, (tē´sâ) *f.* chalk.

tiznar, (tēz·nâr´) *va.* to cover with soot; (fig.) to tarnish, to stain.

tizne, (tez´ne) *m.* soot; partly burned stick *(madera).*

T.N.T.: trinitrotolueno T.N.T., trinitrotoluene.

toalla, (to·â´yâ) *f.* towel; pillow cover *(cubierta);* **— sin fin,** roller towel.

toallero, (to·â·ye´ro) *m.* towel rack.

tobillera, (to·vē·ye´râ) *f.* anklet; (coll.) bobby-soxer.

tobillo, (to·vē´yo) *m.* ankle.

toca, (to´kâ) *f.* hood; (eccl.) wimple; **—s,** *pl.* widow's benefits.

tocadiscos, (to·kâ·thēs´kos) *m.* record player.

tocado, (to·kâ´tho) *m.* headdress *(prenda);* hairdo *(peinado);* —, **da,** *adj.*touched, crazy.

tocador, (to·kâ·thor´) *m.* dressing table; boudoir *(aposento);* —, **ra,** *n.* player.

tocante, (to·kân´te) *adj.* touching; **— a,**concerning, relating to.

tocar, (to·kâr´) *va.* to touch, to feel; (mus.) to play; to call *(avisar);* to strike; to bump *(tropezar);* to strike *(herir);* to learn, to experience *(conocer);* to be time to *(momento oportuno);* to touch on *(tratar de);* to touch up *(pintar);* to comb *(el pelo);* —, *vn.* to belong, to pertain *(pertenecer);* to touch at *(llegar);* to be one's duty *(ser de la obligación);* to matter, to be of interest *(importar);* to touch *(estar cerca);* **—se,** (coll.) to put on one's hat, to cover one's head.

tocayo, ya, (to·kâ´yo, yâ) *n.* namesake.

tocino, (to·sē´no) *m.* bacon *(lardo);* salt pork.

tocón, (to·kon´) *m.* stump.

todavía, (to·thâ·vē´â) *adv.* yet, still; even *(aun).*

todo, da, (to´tho, thâ) *adj.* all; every *(cada);* whole *(entero);* **— el año,** all year around; **—dos los días,** every day; **—das las noches,** every night; **en —das partes,** everywhere; **— el mundo,** everybody; **de —s modos,** anyhow, anyway; —, *m.* whole, entirety; **—do,** *adv.* entirely, completely; **ante —do,** first of all; **con —do,** still, nevertheless; **sobre —do,** above all, especially.

todopoderoso, (to·tho·po·the·ro´so) *adj.* almighty.

toga, (to´gâ) *f.* toga.

togado, da, (to·gä´tho, thä) *adj.* gowned.

toldo, (tôl´do) *m.* awning; tarpaulin *(entalamadura);* (fig.) pride, vanity; (Sp. Am.) Indian hut.

tolerable, (to·le·rä´vle) *adj.* tolerable, bearable.

tolerancia, (to·le·rân´syä) *f.* tolerance;consent, permission *(permiso).*

tolerante, (to·le·rân´te) *adj.* tolerant.

tolerar, (to·le·râr´) *va.* to tolerate; to endure, to bear *(soportar).*

tolvanera, (tol·vä·ne´rä) *f.* dust storm.

toma, (to´mä) *f.* taking; capture, seizure *(conquista);* portion *(porción);* water faucet *(grifo);* — **de posesión,** inauguration.

tomaína, (to·mä·e̅´nä) *f.* ptomaine.

tomar, (to·mar´) *va.* to take *(coger);* to seize, to grasp; to receive, to accept *(recibir);* to understand, to interpret, to perceive *(entender);* to eat *(comer);* to drink *(beber);* to rent *(alquilar);* to acquire *(adquirir);* to contract, to hire *(contratar);* — **a cuestas,** to take upon oneself; — **el pelo,** to tease; — **la revancha,** to turn the tables; — **a sorbos,** to sip; — **prestado,** to borrow, to take as a loan; —**se,** to get rusty, to rust.

tomate, (to·mä´te) *m.* tomato.

tomillo, (to·me̅´yo) *m.* (bot.) thyme.

tomo, (to´mo) *m.* bulk *(grueso);* tome, volume; (fig.) importance, value.

ton, (ton) *m.* tone; **sin — ni son,** without rhyme or reason.

tonada, (to·nä´thä) *f.* tune, melody, air.

tonadilla, (to·nä·the̅´yä) *f.* musical interlude *(zarzuela);* short tune.

tonel, (to·nel´) *m.* cask, barrel.

tonelada, (to·ne·lä´thä) *f.* ton; casks *(tonelería);* (naut.) tonnage duty.

tonelaje, (to·ne·lä´he) *m.* tonnage.

tonelero, (to·ne·le´ro) *m.* cooper, barrel-maker.

tónico, ca, (to´ne̅·ko, kä) *adj.* tonic, invigorating; —, *m.* tonic; —, *f. (mus.)* keynote.

tonina, (to·ne̅´nä) *f.* (zool.) dolphin; (ichth.) tuna fish.

tono, (to´no) *m.* tone.

tonsilitis, (ton·se̅·le̅´tēs) *f.* tonsillitis.

tontada, (ton·tä´thä) *f.* nonsense.

tontear, (ton·te·är´) *vn.* to talk or act foolishly.

tontería, (ton·te·re̅´ä) *f.* foolishness, nonsense.

tonto, ta, (ton´to, tä) *adj.* stupid, foolish; —, *n.* fool, dunce; — **útil,** dupe, tool.

topacio, (to·pä´syo) *m.* topaz.

topar, (to·pâr´) *va.* to bump into; to come across *(hallar);* to find *(encontrar); vn.* to butt, to bump *(topetar);* to lie, to consist *(consistir).*

tope, (to´pe) *m.* bumper; brake *(para detener);* obstacle *(tropiezo);* blow *(golpe);* (rail.) buffers; **precio —,** ceiling price.

topetar, (to·pe·târ´) *vn.* to butt; to bump *(topar).*

topetón, (to·pe·ton´) *m.* collision, impact, bump.

tópico, ca, (to´pē·ko, kä) *adj.* topical; —, *m.* topic, subject.

topo, (to´po) *m.* (zool.) mole; (coll.) lummox.

topografia, (to·po·grä·fe̅´ä) *f.* topography.

topográfico, ca, (to·po·grä´fē·ko, kä) *adj.*topographical.

toque, (to´ke) *m.* touch; ringing *(tañido);* heart of the matter *(punto esencial);* trial, test *(prueba);* (mil.) call.

tórax (to´râks) *m.* (anat.) thorax.

torbellino, (tor·ve·yē´no) *m.* whirlwind.

torcedura, (tor·se·thū´rä) *f.* twisting, wrenching; twist; weak wine *(aguapié).*

torcer*, (tor·ser´) *va.* to twist; to double, to curve *(encorvar);* to turn *(cambiar de dirección);* to screw up *(el semblante);* to distort *(tergiversar);* to pervert *(desviar);* —**se,** to go astray; to turn sour *(agriarse).*

torcido, da, (tor se̅´tho, thä) *adj.* twisted, curved; crooked, dishonest *(no honrado).*

torcimiento, (tor·se̅·myen´to) *m.* twist, bend; circumlocution, beating around the bush *(perífrasis).*

tordo, (tor´tho) *m.* thrush; — **mimo,** catbird; —, —**da,** *adj.* dappled.

torear, (to·re·är´) *vn.* to fight bulls; —, *vt.* to tease.

toreo, (to·re´o) *m.* bullfighting.

torero, (to·re´ro) *m.* bullfighter.

toril, (to·rēl´) *m.* bull pen.

torio, (to´ryo) *m.* (chem.) thorium.

tormenta, (tor·men´tä) *f.* storm, thundershower, thunderstorm; adversity, misfortune *(adversidad);* (fig.) turmoil, unrest.

tormento, (tor·men´to) *m.* torment, pain; torture *(tortura);* (fig.) anguish, torment.

tornado, (tor·nä´tho) *m.* tornado.

tornar, (tor·när´) *va.* to return, to restore; to make *(mudar);* —, *vn.* to return.

tornasol, (tor·nä·sol´) *m.* (bot.) sunflower, heliotrope; iridescence *(reflejo);* (chem.) litmus.

â arm, **e** they, ē bē, **o** fore, ū blūe, **b** bad, **ch** chip, **d** day, **f** fat, **g** go, **h** hot, **k** kid, **1** let

tornasolado, da, (tor·nâ·so·lâ´tho, thâ) *adj.* of changing colors, iridescent, watered.

tornear, (tor·ne·âr´) *va.* to turn; —, *vn.* to tilt *(en el torneo); (fig.)* to muse, to dream.

torneo, (tor·ne´o) *m.* tournament.

tornillo, (tor·nē´yo) *m.* screw *(clavo);* vise *(prensa);* bolt; *(mil.)* desertion; **— de presión** or **de retén,** setscrew.

torniquete, (tor·nē·ke´te) *m.* turnstile; *(med.)* tourniquet.

torno, (tor´no) *m.* wheel *(rueda);* lathe; winch, windlass *(armazón);* brake *(freno);* turn *(vuelta);* vise *(prensa);* **en — de,** around.

toro, (to´ro) *m.* bull; **corrida de —s,** bullfight.

toronja, (to·ron´hâ) *f.* grapefruit.

torpe, (tor´pe) *adj.* slow, heavy *(tardo);* stupid, dull *(tonto);* clumsy, awkward *(desmañado);* licentious, lewd *(lascivo);* infamous *(infame);* ugly *(feo).*

torpedero, (tor·pe·the´ro) *m.* torpedo boat.

torpedo, (tor·pe´tho) *m.* torpedo.

torpeza, (tor·pe´sâ) *f.* slowness, heaviness, torpor *(pesadez);* stupidity, dullness *(estupidez);* clumsiness *(desmaña);* lewdness *(lascivia);* infamy *(infamia);* ugliness *(fealdad).*

torre, (to´rre) *f.* tower, turret; steeple *(de una iglesia);* country house *(casa de campo);* rook *(en el ajedrez);* **— de mando,** (naut.) conning tower.

torrecilla, (to·rre·sē´yâ) *f.* (naut.) turret.

torreja, (to·rre´hâ) *f.* (Sp. Am.) fritter.

torrente, (to·rren´te) *m.* torrent; *(fig.)* crowd, mob.

torreón, (to·rre·on´) *m.* fortified tower.

tórrido, da, (to´rrē·tho, thâ) *adj.* torrid.

torso, (tor´so) *m.* trunk, torso.

torta, (tor´tâ) *f.* cake; *(coll.)* punch *(golpe);* **— compuesta,** (Mex.) stuffed bun sandwich.

tortera, (tor·te´râ) *f.* cookie sheet.

tortilla, (tor·tē´yâ) *f.* omelet; (Mex.) tortilla.

tórtola, (tor´to·lâ) *f.* turtledove.

tortuga, (tor·tū´gâ) *f.* tortoise *(de tierra);* turtle.

tortuoso, sa, (tor·two´so, sâ) *adj.* tortuous, twisting; *(fig.)* devious.

torturar, (tor·tū·râr´) *va.* to torture.

tos, (tos) *f.* cough; **— ferina,** whooping cough.

tosco, ca, (tos´ko, kâ) *adj.* coarse, ill-bred; *(fig.)* uncultured, ignorant.

toser, (to·ser´) *vn.* to cough.

tostada, (tos·tâ´thâ) *f.* slice of toast; *(fig.)*

bother, nuisance; (Mex.) meat tart *(torta de carne).*

tostado, da, (tos·tâ´tho, thâ) *adj.* tanned; sunburned *(quemado del sol);* light brown *(marrón);* toasted *(cocido).*

tostador, (tos·ta·thor´) *m.* toaster.

tostar*, (tos·târ´) *va.* to toast; to heat too much *(calentar demasiado);* **—se al sol,** to sunbathe.

total, (to·tal´) *m.* whole, totality; —, *adj.* total, entire, all-out.

totalidad, (to·tâ·lē·thâth´) *f.* totality, whole.

totalitario, ria, (to·tâ·lē·tâ´ryo, ryâ) *adj.* totalitarian.

totalmente, (to·tâl·men´te) *adv.* totally, entirely.

tóxico, ca, (tok´sē·ko, kâ) *adj.* toxic.

toxina, (tok·sē´nâ) *f.* (med.) toxin.

tr.: transitivo, tr. transitive.

traba, (trâ´vâ) *f.* obstacle, impediment; hobble *(para atar caballos);* trammel, restraint *(para sujetar).*

trabajador, ra, (trâ·vâ·hâ·thor´, râ) *n.* worker, laborer; —, *adj.* hard-working, industrious.

trabajar, (trâ·vâ·hâr´) *vn.* to work; *(fig.)* to bend *(torcerse);* to strain *(afanarse);* —, *va.* to work.

trabajo, (trâ·vâ´ho) *m.* work; workmanship *(destreza);* difficulty, trouble *(dificultad);* **—s forzados,** hard labor; **costar —,** to be difficult; **—s,** *pl.* straits, misery.

trabajoso, sa, (trâ·vâ·ho´so, sâ) *adj.* laborious; painful *(que padece miseria);* labored *(falto de espontaneidad).*

trabalenguas, (tra·vâ·leng´gwâs) *m.* tongue twister.

trabar, (trâ·vâr´) *va.* to join, to unite; to take hold, of, to grasp *(asir);* to fetter, to shackle *(poner trabas a);* to set *(triscar);* to begin, to start *(comenzar);* to bind *(enlazar);* **— amistad,** to make friends; **—se,** to quarrel, to dispute; to stammer, to stutter *(tartamudear).*

trabilla, (trâ·vē´yâ) *f.* gaiter strap; small strap *(tira de tela);* loose stitch *(punto suelto).*

trácala, (trâ´kâ·lâ) *f.* deceit, trick.

tracción, (trâk·syon´) *f.* traction.

tracoma, (trâ·ko´mâ) *m.* (med.) trachoma.

tractor, (trâk·tor´) *m.* tractor; **— de orugas,** caterpillar tractor.

tradición, (trâ·thē·syon´) *f.* tradition; delivery *(entrega).*

tradicional, (trâ·thē·syo·nâl´) *adj.* traditional.

traducción, (trâ·thūk·syon´) *f.* translation;

trad   330   **tran**

traducir*, (trä·thü·sēr´) *va.* to translate.
traductor, ra, (trä·thük·tor´, rä) *n.* translator.
traer*, (trä·er´) *va.* to bring, to carry; to attract *(atraer);* to cause *(causar);* to have *(tener);* to wear *(llevar);* to cite, to adduce *(citar);* to make, to oblige *(obligar);* to persuade *(persuadir);* **—se,** to dress.
traficante, (trä·fē·kän´te) *m.* merchant, dealer.
traficar, (trä·fē·kär´) *vn.* to do business, to deal; to travel *(correr).*
tráfico, (trä´fē·ko) *m.* traffic, trade; traffic *(tránsito).*
tragaluz, (trä·gä·lūs´) *m.* skylight.
tragar, (trä·gär´) *va.* to swallow; to glut *(comer mucho);* to swallow up *(abismar);* **—se,** to play dumb *(disimular);* to swallow; to stand, to put up with *(soportar).*
tragedia, (trä·he´thyä) *f.* tragedy.
trágico, ca, (trä´hē·ko, kä) *adj.* tragic.
trago, (trä´go) *m.* swallow; adversity, misfortune *(adversidad);* **a —s,** by degrees, little by little.
tragón, ona, (trä·gon´, o´nä) *adj.* hoggish, piggish.
traición, (träē·syon´) *f.* treason; **a —,** deceitfully.
traicionar, (träē·syo·när´) *va.* to betray.
traidor, ra, (träē·thor´, rä) *n.* traitor; **—,** *adj.* treacherous.
traje, (trä´he) *m.* dress *(vestido);* suit; native dress *(vestido peculiar);* (Sp. Am.) mask *(máscara);* **— a la medida,** suit made to order; **— de a caballo,** riding habit; **— de etiqueta,** evening clothes, dress suit; **— hecho,** ready-made suit or dress; **— para vuelos espaciales,** space suit; **— sastre,** tailored suit.
trajín, (trä·hēn´) *m.* transporting *(acción de acarrear);* bustling.
trajinar, (trä·hē·när´) *va.* to transport; **—,** *vn.* to bustle about.
trama, (trä´mä) *f.* weave; plot, scheme *(artificio);* plot *(de una obra literaria);* blossom *(de los árboles).*
tramar, (trä·mär´) *va.* to weave; to plot, to scheme *(maquinar);* **—,** *vn.* to blossom.
tramitación, (trä·mē·tä·syon´) *f.* transaction; steps *(serie de trámites).*
trámite, (trä´mē·te) *m.* passage *(paso);* step, requirement.
tramo, (trä´mo) *m.* tract, lot *(de tierra);* flight *(de escalones);* span *(de un puen-*

te); passage *(pasaje);* length *(de piscina).*
tramoya, (trä·mo´yä) *f.* stage machinery *(máquinas);* scheme, trick *(enredo).*
tramoyista, (trä·mo·yēs´tä) *m.* scene-shifter; trickster, cheat.
trampa, (träm´pä) *f.* trap, snare; trapdoor *(puerta);* sliding door *(de un mostrador);* trick *(ardid);* fly *(portañuela);* bad debt *(deuda);* bunker *(en el golf);* **hacer —,** to cheat.
trampolín, (träm·po·lēn´) *m.* springboard.
tramposo, sa. (träm·po´so, sä) *adj.* deceitful, swindling; cheating *(en el juego).*
tranca, (träng´kä) *f.* beam; crossbar, crossbeam *(para seguridad).*
trancar, (träng·kär´) *va.* to bar.
trancazo.(träng·kä´so) *m.* clubbing; (coll.) cold, flu.
trance, (trän´se) *m.* critical moment *(apuro);* writ of payment *(judicial);* last stage *(de la vida);* **a todo —,** at all costs.
tranquilidad, (träng·kē·lē·thäth´) *f.* tranquility, quiet.
tranquilizar, (träng·kē·lē·sär´) *va.* to soothe, to quiet.
tranquilo, la, (träng·kē´lo, lä) *adj.* tranquil, calm, quiet.
transacción, (trän·säk·syon´) *f.* compromise, concession *(componenda);* adjustment *(ajustamiento);* transaction *(negocio).*
transatlántico, (trän·säth·län´tē·ko) = **trasatlántico.**
transbordar (tränz·vor·thär´) = **trasbordar.**
transcendencia. (träns·sen·den´syä) = **trascendencia.**
transcendental (träns·sen·den·täl´) = **trascendental.**
transcender (träns·sen·der´) = **trascender.**
transcribir (träns·krē·vēr´) = **trascribir.**
transcurrir (träns·kū·rrēr´) = **trascurrir.**
transcurso (träns·kūr´so) = **trascurso.**
transeúnte, (trän·se·ūn´te) *adj.* transitory; **—,** *m.* and *f.* passer-by; transient *(que reside poco).*
transferir (träns·fe·rēr´) = **trasferir.**
transfigurarse (träns·fē·gū·rär´se) = **trasfigurarse.**
transformación (träns·for·mä·syon´) = **trasformación.**
transformador (träns·for·mä·thor´) = **trasformador.**
transformar (träns·for·mär´) = **trasformar.**
transfusión (träns·fū·syon´) = **trasfusión.**
transgresor (tränz·gre·sor´) = **trasgresor.**
transición (trän·sē·syon´) *f.* transition.
transido, da, (trän·sē´tho, thä) *adj.* afflict-

â arm, **e** they, **ē** bē, **o** fore, **ū** blūe, **b** bad, **ch** chip, **d** day, **f** fat, **g** go, **h** hot, **k** kid, **1** let

ed, overcome; (fig.) stingy; — **de dolor**, brokenhearted; mournful *(lúgubre)*.

transigir, (trân·sē·hēr´) *vi.* to compromise; to adjust *(ajustar)*.

transistor, (trân·sēs·tor´) *m.* transistor.

transitar, (trân·sē·târ´) *vn.* to pass by, to pass through; to travel *(viajar)*.

tránsito, (trân´sē·to) *m.* transit; transition *(transición)*; stop *(parada)*; passage *(paso)*; death *(de un santo)*; traffic *(tráfico)*; **señal de** —, traffic sign.

transitorio, ria, (trân·sē·to´ryo, ryâ) *adj.* transitory.

transmisión (trânz·mē·syon´) = **trasmisión.**

transmitir (trânz·mē·tēr´) = **trasmitir.**

transónico, ca, (trân·so´nē·ko, kâ) *adj.* transonic.

transparente (trâns·pâ·ren´te) = **trasparente.**

transpirar (trâns·pē·râr´) = **traspirar.**

transplantar (trâns·plân·târ´) = **trasplantar.**

transponer (trâns·po·ner´) = **trasponer.**

transportar (trâns·por·târ´) = **trasportar.**

transporte (trâns·por´te) = **trasporte.**

transposición (trans·po·sē·syon´) = **trasposición**

transversal (trânz·ver·sâl´) = **trasversal.**

tranvía, (trâm·bē´â) *m.* streetcar.

trapiche, (trâ·pē´che) *m.* olive press *(paraaceitunas)*; sugar mill *(para azúcar)*.

trapisonda, (trâ·pē·son´dâ) *f.* racket, commotion *(ruido)*; scheming, hanky-panky *(embrollo)*.

trapo, (trâ´po) *m.* rag, tatter; cape *(de torero)*; (theat.) curtain; — **de limpiar**, cleaning rag; —**s**, *pl.* (coll.) duds, clothes.

tráquea, (trâ´ke·â) *f.* (med.) trachea, windpipe.

traqueo, (trâ·ke´o))*m.* popping, crack; shaking *(agitación)*; jolt *(sacudida)*.

tras, (trâs) *prep.* after, behind; after *(en busca de)*; behind, in back of *(detrás de)*; —, besides, in addition to; —, *m.* behind; —, — bang, bang.

trasanteayer, (trâ·sân·te·â·yer´) **trasantier**, (trâ·sân·tyer´) *adv.* three days ago.

trasatlántico, ca, (trâ·sâth·lân´tē·ko, kâ) *adj.* transatlantic; —, *m.* transatlantic liner.

trasbordar, (trâz·vor·thâr´) *va.* to transfer.

trascendencia, (trâs·sen·den´syâ) *f.* penetration *(penetración)*; importance, consequence *(consequencia)*; transcendence *(filosofía)*.

trascendental, (trâs·sen·den·tâl´) *adj.* extensive, important, serious *(importante)*; transcendental *(filosofía)*.

trascender*, (trâs·sen·der´) *vn.* to come to light *(empezar a ser conocido)*; to transmit, to spread *(comunicarse)*; to be fragrant *(exhalar olor)*; to transcend *(filosofía)*; —, *vt.* to dig into.

trascribir*, (trâs·krē·vēr´) *va.* to transcribe; to copy *(copiar)*.

trascurrir, (trâs·kū·rrēr´) *vn.* to pass, to go by.

trascurso, (trâs·kūr´so) *m.* course, passing.

trasero, ra, (trâ·se´ro, râ) *adj.* back, rear, hind; **asiento** —, back seat; —, *m.* buttock.

trasferir*, (trâs·fe·rēr´) *va.* to transfer; to postpone, to put off *(diferir)*.

trasfigurarse, (trâs·fē·gū·râr´se) *vr.* to be transfigured.

trasformación, (trâs·for·mâ·syon´) *f.* transformation.

trasformador, (trâs·for·mâ·thor´) *m.* transformer, converter.

trasformar, (trâs·for·mâr´) *va. and vr.* to transform, to change.

trasfusión, (trâs·fū·syon´) *f.* transfusion.

trasgresor, (trâz·gre·sor´) *m.* transgressor, lawbreaker.

trasladar, (trâz·lâ·thâr´) *va.* to move, to change; to transfer *(a un funcionario)*; to translate *(traducir)*; to postpone *(diferir)*; to copy, to transcribe *(copiar)*.

traslado, (trâz·lâ´tho) *m.* copy, transcript *(copia)*; transfer; notification *(jurídico)*.

traslapado, da, (trâz·lâ·pâ´tho, thâ) *adj.* overlapping.

traslucirse*, (trâz·lū·sēr´se) *vr.* to be transparent; to be inferred *(deducirse)*.

trasmisión, (trâz·mē·syon´) *f.* transmission.

trasmisor, (trâz·mē·sor´) *m.* transmitter.

trasmitir, (trâz·mē·tēr´) *va.* to transmit, to transfer.

trasnochar, (trâz·no·châr´) *vn.* to stay up all night; —, *vt.* to sleep on.

trasojado, da, (trâ·so·hâ´tho, thâ) *adj.* having circles under the eyes; emaciated, wan *(flaco)*.

traspapelar, (trâs·pâ·pe·lâr´) *va.* to misplace, to mislay.

trasparente, (trâs·pâ·ren´te) *adj.* transparent.

traspasar, (trâs·pâ·sâr´) *va.* to transport *(llevar)*; to cross, to cross over *(pasar)*; to transfix *(espetar)*; to transfer *(trasferir)*; to pass through again *(repasar)*; to transgress *(transgredir)*; to trespass *(exceder)*; (fig.) to distress, to grieve.

traspaso, (trâs·pá´so) *m.* transport; transfer *(traslado)*; crossing *(cruzamiento)*; trespass *(violación)*; cargo *(cargamento)*; (fig.) grief, anguish.

traspié, (trâs·pye´) *m.* slip, stumble; trip *(zancadilla)*.

traspirar, (trâs·pē·râr´) *vn.* to transpire; to perspire *(sudar)*.

trasplantar, (trâs·plân·târ´) *va.* to transplant; **—se,** to emigrate.

trasponer*, (trâs·po·ner´) *va.* to transpose, to transfer, to transport; **—se,** to detour; to be half asleep *(quedarse algo dormido)*.

trasportar, (trâs·por·târ´) *va.* to transport, to convey; (mus.) to transpose; **—se,** to get carried away.

trasporte, (trâs·por´te) *m.* transportation, transport, conveyance; transport ship *(buque)*; rapture, ecstasy *(efusión)*.

trasposición, (trâs·po·sē·syon´) *f.* transposition, transposal.

traste, (trâs´te) *m.* (mus.) fret; **dar al — con,** to ruin, to spoil.

trasteado, (trâs·te·â´tho) *m.* set of frets.

trastear, (trâs·te·âr´) *va.* to fret; to finger *(pisar las cuerdas)*; to manipulate *(manejar)*; **—,** *vn.* to move around; to talk vivaciously *(charlar)*.

trastería, (trâs·te·rē´â) *f.* pile of trash; nonsense, foolishness *(barbaridad)*.

trastienda, (tras·tyen´dâ) *f.* back room *(de una tienda)*; shrewdness, astuteness *(astucia)*.

trasto, (trâs´to) *m.* piece of junk *(mueble inútil)*; piece of furniture *(mueble)*; kitchen utensil *(utensilio)*; good-for-nothing *(persona inútil)*; (theat.) set piece.

trastornado, da, (trâs·tor·nâ´tho, thâ) *adj.* unbalanced, crazy.

trastornar, (trâs·tor·nâr´) *va.* to tip, to upset; to overturn, to turn upside-down *(volcar)*; to mix up *(invertir el orden)*; to disquiet, to disturb *(inquietar)*; to go to one's head *(perturbar el sentido)*; to persuade *(persuadir)*.

trastorno, (trâs·tor´no) *m.* confusion, upset, mix-up.

trasversal, (trâz·ver·sal´) *adj.* transverse; collateral *(de parientes)*; **calle —,** cross-road.

trata, (trâ´tâ) *f.* slave trade; **— de blancas,** white slavery.

tratable, (trâ·tâ´vle) *adj.* tractable, com-

pliant; courteous, sociable *(cortés)*.

tratado, (trâ·tâ´tho) *m.* treaty, agreement; treatise *(escrito)*; discourse *(discurso)*.

tratamiento, (trâ·tâ·myen´to) *m.* treatment; title *(título)*; procedure *(procedimiento)*.

tratar, (trâ·târ´) *va.* to manage, to handle *(manejar)*; to treat *(obrar con)*; **— con,** to deal with; to have an affair with *(relaciones amorosas)*; **— de,** to try to, to attempt to; to classify as *(calificar de)*; to dispute *(disputar)*; to discuss *(discurrir)*; **— en,** to deal in; **—se,** to behave, to conduct oneself; **—se de,** to be a question of *(ser cuestión de)*; to treat of, to deal with.

trato, (trâ´to) *m.* treatment; title *(título)*; contract *(contrato)*; business dealings *(negocio)*; agreement, deal *(tratado)*.

trauma, (trâ´ū·mâ) *m.* (med.) trauma.

través, (trâ·ves´) *m.* bent, inclination *(inclinación)*; misfortune, setback *(desgracia)*; **a — de,** across.

travesaño, (trâ·ve·sâ´nyo) *m.* cross timber, crossbar, crossbeam, transom; bolster *(almohada)*.

travesía. (trâ·ve·sē´â) *f.* side street *(callejuela)*; crossing, voyage *(viaje)*; distance *(distancia)*; (naut.) side wind; through street *(carretera)*; win *(cantidad de ganancia)*; loss *(cantidad de pérdida)*; pay *(de un marinero)*; plain *(llanura)*.

travesura, (trâ·ve·sū´râ) *f.* mischief *(acción traviesa)*; ingeniousness *(viveza de genio)*; prank, smart trick *(acción culpable)*.

traviesa, (trâ·vye´sâ) *f.* railroad tie.

travieso, sa, (trâ·vye´so, sâ) *adj.* cross; mischievous *(pícaro)*; ingenious, clever *(sagaz)*; restless, uneasy, fidgety *(inquieto)*; turbulent, rolling *(en movimiento continuo)*; debauched *(distraído en vicios)*.

trayectoria, (trâ·yek·to´ryâ) *f.* trajectory.

traza, (trâ´sâ) *f.* design *(diseño)*; plan *(plan)*; invention, scheme; *(invención)*: appearance, looks *(apariencia)*; **—s,** *pl.* (fig.) wits.

trazar, (trâ·sâr´) *va.* to design *(diseñar)*; to plan, to make plans for *(planear)*; to draw, to trace *(delinear)*; to outline, to sketch, to summarize *(bosquejar)*.

trazo, (trâ´so) *m.* plan, design; line *(línea)*; stroke *(de la letra de mano)*.

trébol, (tre´vol) *m.* (bot.) clover, trefoil; cloverleaf *(de una carretera)*.

trece, (tre´se) *m.* and *adj.* thirteen; **estarse en sus —,** to be persistent, to stick to one's guns.

trecientos (tre·syen'tos) = **trescientos.**

trecho, (tre'cho) *m.* stretch; well, while *(de tiempo);* **a —s,** at intervals.

tregua, (tre'gwâ) *f.* truce, armistice; rest, respite *(descanso);* **sin —,** unceasingly.

treinta, (tre'ēn·tâ) *m.* and *adj.* thirty.

tremedal, (tre·me·thâl') *m.* quagmire.

tremendo, da, (tre·men'do, dâ) *adj.* tremendous; terrible, terrifying *(espantoso);* awesome, imposing *(digno de respeto).*

trémulo, la, (tre'mū·lo, lâ) *adj.* tremulous, trembling.

tren, (tren) *m.* train, retinue; show, ostentation *(ostentación);* (rail.) train; **— de aterrizaje,** landing gear; **— de ruedas,** running gear; **— elevado,** elevated train.

trencilla, (tren·sē'yâ) *f.* braid, braiding.

trenza, (tren'sâ) *f.* braid *(del pelo);* braiding.

trenzar, (tren·sâr') *va.* to braid.

treo, (tre'o) *m.* (naut.) storm sail.

trepador, ra, (tre·pâ·thor', râ) *adj.* climbing.

trepar, (tre·pâr') *vn.* to climb; **—,** *vt.* to drill *(taladrar);* to put braiding on.

trepidación, (tre·pē·thâ·syon') *f.* vibration, trembling; trepidation *(miedo).*

tres, (tres) *adj.* and *m.* three; **— veces,** thrice; three times.

trescientos, tas, (tres·syen'tos, tâs) *m.* and *adj.* three hundred.

treta, (tre'tâ) *f.* feint; trick, wile *(artificio).*

triangular, (tryâng·gū·lâr') *adj.* triangular; **—,** *va.* to triangulate.

triángulo, (tryâng'gū·lo) *m.* triangle.

tribu, (trē'vū) *f.* tribe.

tribulación, (trē·vū·lâ·syon') *f.* tribulation, affliction.

tribuna, (trē·vū·nâ) *f.* tribune, platform, rostrum; (eccl.) gallery; grandstand *(galería).*

tribunal, (trē·vū·nâl') *m.* tribunal, courthouse; court *(ministro o ministros de la justicia);* **T — supremo** Supreme Court.

tribuno, (trē·vū'no) *m.* tribune; orator *(orador).*

tributar, (trē·vū·târ') *va.* to pay tribute.

tributario, ria, (trē·vū·tâ'ryo, ryâ) *adj.* tributary.

tributo, (trē·vū'to) *m.* tribute; tax *(impuesto);* retribution *(retribución).*

triceps, (trē'seps) *m.* (anat.) triceps.

triciclo, (trē·sē'klo) *m.* tricycle.

tricolor, (trē·ko·lor') *adj.* tricolored.

tridente, (trē·then'te) *adj.* three-pronged; **—,** *m.* trident.

trienio, (trye'nyo) *m.* space of three years.

trigésimo, ma, (trē·he'sē·mo, mâ) *m.* and *adj.* thirtieth.

trigo, (trē'go) *m.* wheat; money *(dinero).*

trigonometría, (trē·go·no·me·trē'â) *f.* trigonometry.

trigueño, ña, (trē·ge'nyo, nyâ) *adj.* brunet, brunette.

trilogía, (trē·lo·hē'â) *f.* trilogy.

trillado, da, (trē·yâ'tho, thâ) *adj.* beaten, well-travelled; trite, stale, hackneyed *(muy común);* **camino —,** same old routine.

trillador, ra, (trē·yâ·thor', râ) *n.* thresher; threshing machine; **—,** *adj.* threshing; **máquina —,** threshing machine.

trillar, (trē·yâr') *va.* to thresh; (coll.) to hang around; to mistreat *(maltratar).*

trimestre, (trē·mes'tre) *m.* space of three months.

trimotor, (trē·mo·tor') *m.* three-engined airplane.

trinar, (trē·nâr') *vn.* to trill, to warble; (coll.) to get impatient.

trinchante, (trēn·chân'te) *m.* carver; carving knife *(cuchillo);* carving fork *(tenedor);* carving table *(mueble).*

trinchar, (trēn·châr') *va.* to carve, to cut; (coll.) to settle.

trinchera, (trēn·che'râ) *f.* trench, entrenchment.

trinchero, (trēn·che'ro) *m.* trencher; side table, carving table *(mueble).*

trineo, (trē·ne'o) *m.* sleigh, sled.

trino, (trē'no) *m.* trill.

trio, (trē'o) *m.* (mus.) trio.

tripa, (trē'pâ) *f.* gut, entrails, tripe, intestine; belly *(panza);* filling *(del cigarro);* **—s,** *pl.* insides; **hacer de —s corazón,** to pluck up courage.

triplano, (trē·plâ'no) *m.* triplane.

triple, (trē'ple) *adj.* triple.

triplicar, (trē·plē·kâr') *va.* to triple, to treble.

trípode, (trē'po·the) *m.* or *f.* tripod.

tripulación, (trē·pū·lâ·syon') *f.* crew.

tripulado, da, (trē·pū·lâ'tho, thâ) *adj.* manned.

tripular, (trē·pū·lâr') *va.* to man; to go on board *(ir a bordo).*

triquina, (trē·kē'nâ) *f.* trichina.

triquitraque, (trē·kē·trâ'ke) *m.* clack, clatter, rat-a-tat; noisemaker *(cohete).*

tris, (trēs) *m.* tinkle; trice, instant *(instante);* **estar en un — que,** to be on the point of.

trisílabo ba, (trē·sē'lâ·vo, vâ) *adj.* trisyllabic; **—,** *m.* trisyllable.

---

m met, **n** not, **p** pot, **r** very, **rr** (none), **s** so, **t** toy, **th** with, **v** eve, **w** we, **y** yes, **z** zero

triste, (trēs´te) *adj.* sad, mournful, melancholy.

tristeza, (trēs·te´sâ) *f.* melancholy, sadness, gloom.

triturador, ra, (trē·tū·râ·thor´, râ) *adj.* crushing; —, *m.* crusher, crushing machine.

triturar, (trē·tū·râr´) *va.* to crush, to grind, to pound; to chew, to crunch *(mascar);* (fig.) to abuse, to mistreat *(maltratar).*

triunfal, (tryūm·fâl´) *adj.* triumphal.

triunfante, (tryūm·fân´te) *adj.* triumphant, exultant.

triunfar, (tryūm·fâr´) *vn.* to triumph; to trump *(en los naipes);* (fig.) to throw money around *(gastar).*

triunfo, (tryūm´fo) *m.* triumph, victory; trump *(en los naipes)* heavy spending *(acto de gastar mucho).*

triunvirato, (tryūm·bē·râ´to) *m.* triumvirate.

trivial, (trē·vyâl´) *adj.* trivial, commonplace, trite.

trivialidad, (trē·vyâ·lē·thâth´) *f.* trifle, triviality.

triza, (trē´sâ) *f.* piece, bit, shred; cord, rope *(driza).*

trocar*, (tro·kâr´) *va.* to exchange; to change, to vary *(cambiar);* to vomit *(vomitar);* to confuse, to mix up *(equivocar);* —**se,** to change; to change seats *(permutar el asiento).*

trochemoche, (tro·che·mo´che) **a —,** helter-skelter.

trofeo, (tro·fe´o) *m.* trophy; booty, plunder *(despojo);* (fig.) victory *(victoria).*

troglodita, (tro·glo·thē´tâ) *adj.* trogloditic; —, *m.* troglodite.

trolebús, (tro·le·vūs´) *m.* trolley bus.

tromba, (trom´bâ) *f.* waterspout; tornado *(terrestre).*

trombón, (trom·bon´) *m.* (mus.) trombone.

trombosis, (trom·bo´sēs) *f.* (med.) thrombosis.

trompa, (trom´bâ) *f.* trumpet, horn; trunk *(de los elefantes);* proboscis *(de insectos).*

trompeta, (trom·pe´tâ) *f.* trumpet, horn; —, *m.* trumpeter; (fig.) jerk, clunk.

trompetero, (trom·pe·te´ro) *m.* trumpeter; trumpet maker *(fabricante).*

trompetilla, (trom·pe·tē´yâ) *f.* small trumpet; ear trumpet *(para oir).*

trompo, (trom´po) *m.* top; trochid *(molusco);* (fig.) oaf *(bolo).*

tronar*, (tro·nâr´) *vn.* to thunder; (fig.) to go bankrupt *(arruinarse);* to harangue, to thunder *(hablar o escribir).*

troncar (trong·kâr´) = **truncar.**

tronco, (trong´ko) *m.* trunk; team *(de caballos);* log *(leño);* stock, lineage *(linaje);* (fig.) thickhead *(persona).*

tronchar, (tron·châr´) *va.* to break off; (fig.) to break in two.

trono, (tro´no) *m.* throne; (eccl.) shrine; —**s,** *pl.* thrones.

tronzar, (tron·sâr´) *va.* to shatter, to break; to pleat *(hacer pliegues);* (fig.) to tire out, to wear out.

tropa, (tro´pâ) *f.* troop; plebeians *(gentecilla);* mob, crowd *(muchedumbre);* —**s de asalto,** storm troops; — **de línea,** regular army.

tropel, (tro·pel´) *m.* stampede; hurry, bustle, confusion *(prisa);* heap, pile *(conjunto de cosas);* crowd *(muchedumbre);* **de —,** tumultuously.

tropezar*, (tro·pe·sâr´) *vn.* to stumble, to trip; to be detained, to be obstructed, to be held up *(detenerse);* to go wrong, to slip up *(deslizarse en un error);* (fig.) to oppose, to dispute *(oponerse);* to quarrel *(reñir);* (fig.) to bump into *(hallar).*

tropezón, ona, (tro·pe·son´, o´nâ) *adj.* stumbling; —, *m.* tripping; piece of meat *(vianda);* **a —ones,** haltingly, the hard way.

tropical, (tro·pē·kâl´) *adj.* tropical.

trópico, (tro´pē·ko) *m.* tropic; —, **ca,** *adj.* tropical.

tropiezo, (tro·pye´so) *m.* obstacle; stumble, trip *(tropezón);* slip, fault, mistake *(yerro);* quarrel, argument, *(riña).*

tropo, (tro´po) *m.* figure of speech.

troquelar, (tro·ke·lâr´) *va.* to stamp; to coin, to mint *(fabricar moneda).*

trotador, ra, (tro·tâ·thor´, râ) *n.* trotter; —, *adj.* trotting.

trotamundos, (tro·tâ·mūn´dos) *m. and f.* globetrotter.

trotar, (tro·târ´) *vn.* to trot.

trote, (tro´te) *m.* trot; fix, jam *(apuro);* **a —,** hastily, hurriedly.

trovador, ra, (tro·vâ·thor´, râ) *n.* minstrel, troubadour.

trozo, (tro´so) *m.* piece, bit, part, fragment; selection *(selección);* (rail.) section of a line.

truculento, ta, (trū·kū·len´to, tâ) *adj.* savage, truculent.

trucha, (trū´châ) *f.* trout; crane *(cabria).*

trueno, (trwe´no) *m.* thunderclap; shot, report *(del tiro);* (coll.) swinger *(persona).*

trueque, (trwe´ke) *m.* exchange; —**s,** *pl.* change.

truhán, ana, (trū·ân´, â´nâ) *n.* buffoon, clown; cheat, crook *(sinverguenza);* —, *adj.* cheating, thieving; clownish *(bufonesco).*

truhanería, (trwâ·ne·rē´â) *f.* buffoonery.

truhanesco, ca, (trwâ·nes´ko, kâ) *adj.* cheating; clownish *(bufonesco).*

truncar, (trūng·kâr´) *va.* to cut off; to behead, to decapitate *(cortar la cabeza);* to leave out *(omitir);* to weaken, to emasculate *(dejar incompleto);* — **la carrera,** to ruin one´s hopes for a career.

tu, (tū) *adj.* your.

tú, (tū) *pron.* you.

tuba, (tū´vä) *f.* tuba.

tuberculina, (tū·ver·kū·lē´nâ) *f.* tuberculin vaccine.

tuberosa, (tū·ve·ro´sâ) *f.* (bot.) tuberose.

tuberculosis, (tū·ver·kū·lo´sēs) *f.* (med.) tuberculosis.

tubería, (tū·ve·rē´â) *f.* pipeline; tubing, piping *(conjunto de tubos).*

tubo, (tū´vo) *m.* tube, pipe, duct; — **de escape,** exhaust pipe; — **de radio,** radio tube; — **lanzatorpedos,** torpedo tube; — **snorkel,** snorkel.

tuerca, (twer´kâ) *f.* screw.

tuerto, ta, (twer´to, tâ) *adj.* twisted, crooked; one-eyed *(de un ojo).*

tuétano, (twe´tâ·no) *m.* marrow.

tul, (tūl) *m.* tulle.

tulipán, (tū·lē·pân´) *m.* tulip.

tullido, da, (tū·yē´tho, thâ) *adj.* crippled, maimed.

tumba, (tūm´bâ) *f.* tomb, grave; tumble, fall *(caída).*

tumbar, (tūm·bâr´) *va.* to tip over, to knock down; (coll.) to stun; —, *vn.* to fall down, to take a fall.

tumefacerse, (tū·me·fâ·ser´se) *vr.* to tumefy, to swell.

tumefacto, ta, (tū·me·fak´to, tâ) *adj.* tumescent.

tumor, (tū·mor´) *m.* tumor.

tumulto, (tū·mūl´to) *m.* tumult, uproar.

tumultuoso, sa, (tū·mūl·two´so, sâ) *adj.* tumultuous.

tuna, (tū´nâ) *f.* prickly pear; wandering, loafing *(vida vagabunda).*

tunante, (tū·nân´te) *adj.* astute, cunning *(taimado);* vagabond; —, *m.* vagabond; rascal, hooligan *(bribón).*

tundir, (tūn·dēr´) *va.* to shear; to beat, to cudgel, to flog *(castigar).*

túnel, (tū´nel) *m.* tunnel.

tungsteno, (tūns·te´no) *m.* tungsten, wolfram.

túnica, (tū´nē·kâ) *f.* tunic; membrane *(membrana).*

tuno, na, (tū´no, nâ) *adj.* tricky, cunning; —, *n.* rascal, scamp.

tupa, (tū´pä) *f.* stuffing, packing.

tupé, (tū·pe´) *m.* toupee; (coll.) audacity, gall, crust.

tupir, (tū·pēr´) *va.* to pack tight, to make compact; —**se,** to stuff oneself.

turba, (tūr´vâ) *f.* crowd, mob *(gentío);* turf, sod, peat.

turbación, (tūr·vâ·syon´) *f.* confusion, disorder.

turbador, ra, (tūr·vâ·thor´, râ) *adj.* up-setting, disturbing.

turbante, (tūr·vân´te) *m.* turban.

turbar, (tūr·vâr´) *va.* to disturb, to upset; to stir up *(enturbiar).*

turbina, (tūr·vē´nâ) *f.* turbine.

turbio, bia, (tūr´vyo, vyâ) *adj.* muddy, turbid; (fig.) confused *(confuso);* turbulent, upset *(agitado).*

turbión, (tūr·vyon´) *m.* cloudburst, downpour; (fig.) deluge, epidemic.

turbohélice, (tūr·vo·e´lē·se) *m.* turboprop.

turborreactor, (tūr·vo·rre·âk·tor´) *m.* turbojet.

turborretropropulsión, (tūr·vo·rre·tro·pro·pūl´syon´) *f.* turbojet propulsion.

turbulencia, (tūr·vū·len´syâ) *f.* turbulence; confusion, disorder *(confusión).*

turbulento, ta, (tūr·vū·len´to, tâ) *adj.* turbulent.

turco, ca, (tūr´ko, kâ) *adj.* Turkish; —, *n.* Turk.

turismo, (tū·rēz´mo) *m.* tourism.

turista, (tū·rēs´tâ) *m.* and *f.* tourist.

turnar, (tūr·nâr´) *vn.* to alternate.

turno, (tūr´no) *m.* turn, shift; **por** —, in turn; — **diurno,** day shift.

turquesa, (tūr·ke´sâ) *f.* turquoise.

turquí, (tūr·kē´) *adj.* turquoise blue.

Turquía, (tūr·kē´â) *f.* Turkey.

turrar, (tū·rrâr´) *vt.* to toast.

turrón, (tū·rron´) *m.* nougat; public office *(destino público).*

tusa, (tū´sâ) *f.* corncob.

tutear, (tū·te·âr´) *va.* to address as tú instead of usted.

tutela, (tū·te´lâ) *f.* guardianship, tutelage.

tutelar, (tū·te·lâr´) *adj.* protective, guardian.

tutiplén, (tū·tē·plen´) **a** —, to excess, too much, a great deal.

tutor, ra, (tū·tor´, râ) *n.* guardian.

tutoría, (tū·to´ryâ) *f.* guardianship.

tuyo, ya, (tū´yo, yâ) *adj.* your; —, *pron.* yours.

U

u, (ū) *conj.* or.
ubicación, (ū·vē·kâ·syon´) *f.* location, situation.
ubicar, (ū·vē·kâr´) *vn.* and *vr.* to be located, to be situated; — *va.* (Sp. Am.) to locate, to find.
ubicuidad (ū·vē·kwē·thath´) *f.* ubiquity, presence everywhere at once.
ubre, (u´vre) *f.* teat; udder *(conjunto).*
Ud.: usted, you.
Uds.: ustedes, you.
U.E.: Unión Europea, E.U. European Union.
¡ufl (ūf) *inter.* whew! ugh!
ufanarse, (ū·fâ·nâr´se) *vr.* to boast.
ufano, na, (ū·fâ´no, nâ) *adj.* haughty, arrogant; (fig.) satisfied, content *(satisfecho).*
ujier, (ū·hyer´) *m.* usher, doorman.
úlcera, (ūl´se·râ) *f.* ulcer; — duodenal or del duodeno, duodenal ulcer.
ulceroso, sa, (ūl·se·ro´so, sâ) *adj.* ulcerous.
ulterior, (ūl·te·ryor´) *adj.* ulterior; later *(posterior).*
últimamente, (ūl·tē·mâ·men´te) *adv.* lately; finally *(finalmente).*
ultimátum, (ūl·tē·mâ´tūn) *m.* ultimatum.
último, ma, (ūl´tē·mo, ma) *adj.* last, latest, farthest *(más remoto);* best, superior *(superior);* last, final *(final);* a —mos del mes, de la semana, at the end of the month, week; por — mo, lastly, finally.
últ.°: último, ult. last.
ultra, (ūl´trâ) *adv.* besides.
ultrajar, (ūl·trâ·hâr´) *va.* to outrage, to insult; to abuse, to mistreat *(maltratar).*
ultraje, (ūl·trâ´he) *m.* abuse, outrage.
ultramar, (ūl·trâ·mâr´) *m.* country overseas; en —, overseas.
ultramarino, na, (ūl·trâ·mâ·rē´no, nâ) *adj.* overseas; azul —no, ultramarine blue; —, *m.* ultramarine; —s, *m. pl.* fancy imported groceries.
ultramoderno, na, (ūl·trâ·mo·ther´no, nâ) *adj.* ultramodern.
ultrasónico, ca, (ūl·trâ·so´nē·ko, kâ) *adj.* ultrasonic.
ultravioleta, (ūl·trâ·vyo·le´tâ) *adj.* ultraviolet.
umbilical, (ūm·bē·lē·kâl´) *adj.* umbilical.

umbral, (ūm·brâl´) *m.* threshold, doorstep; (fig.) threshold.
umbría, (ūm·brē´â) *f.* shady place.
un, una, (ūn, ū´nâ) *adj.* one; —, *art.* a, an; una vez, once.
unánime, (ū·nâ´nē·me) *adj.* unanimous.
unanimidad, (ū·nâ·nē·mē·thâth´) *f.* unanimity.
unción, (ūn·syon´) *f.* unction.
uncir, (ūn·sēr´) *va.* to yoke.
undécimo, ma, (ūn·de´sē·mo, mâ) *adj.* eleventh.
ungir, (ūn·hēr´) *va.* to anoint.
ungüento, (ūn·gwen´to) *m.* unguent, ointment; (fig.) balm.
único, ca, (ū´nē·ko, kâ) *adj.* sole, only; (fig.) unique, unusual.
unidad, (ū·nē·thâth´) *f.* unity *(cualidad);* unit; — termal británica, BTU, British thermal unit.
unificación, (ū·nē·fē·kâ·syon´) *f.* unification.
uniformar, (ū·nē·for·mâr´) *va.* to make uniform.
uniforme, (ū·nē·for´me) *adj.* and *m.* uniform.
uniformidad, (ū·nē·for·mē·thâth´) *f.* uniformity.
unigénito, ta, (ū·nē·he´nē·to, tâ) *adj.* only-begotten; hijo —, only son.
unilateral, (ū·nē·lâ·te·râl´) *adj.* unilateral.
unión, (ū·nyon´) *f.* union;
unionismo, (ū·nyo·nēz´mo) *m.* unionism.
unir, (ū·nēr´) *va.* to join, to unite.
unísono, na, (ū·nē´so·no, nâ) *adj.* unison.
universal, (ū·nē·ver·sâl´) *adj.* universal.
universidad, (ū·nē·ver·sē·thâth´) *f.* universality; university *(instituto).*
universo, (ū·nē·ver´so) *m.* universe.
uno, (ū´no) *m.* one; —, na, *pron.* one; —, *adj.* sole, the same; — a otro, one another; cada —, each one; everyone; — a —, one by one.
unos, nas, (ū´nos, nâs) *pron.* and *adj. pl.* some.
untar, (ūn·târ´) *va.* to oil, to grease; (fig.) to grease one´s palm, to bribe.
unto, (ūn´to) *m.*grease; fat *(del animal).*
untura, (ūn·tū´râ) *f.* greasing *(acción);* grease.

â arm, e they, ē bē, o fore, ū blūe, b bad, ch chip, d day, f fat, g go, h hot, k kid, 1 let

uña, (ū´nyâ) *f.* nail; hoof *(casco);* claw, talon *(garra);* stinger *(del alacrán);* thorn *(espina);* scab *(costra);* hook *(garfio);* **ser — y carne,** to be very close friends.

¡upa! (ū´pâ) *interj.* get up! up we go!

Urania (u·râ´nya) *f.* Urania, the muse of astronomy.

uranio, (ū·râ´nyo) *m.* uranium.

urbanidad, (ūr·vâ·nē·thâth´) *f.* urbanity, good manners, politeness.

urbanización, (ūr·vâ·nē·sâ·syon´) *f.* urbanization.

urbanizar, (ūr·vâ·nē·sâr´) *va* to urbanize.

urbano, na, (ūr·vâ´no, nâ) *adj.* polite, well-bred *(cortesano);* urban.

urbe, (ūr´ve) *f.* metropolis, city.

urdimbre (ūr·thēm´bre) or **urdiembre,** (ūr·thyem´bre) *f.* warp; (fig.) plot, scheme.

urdir, (ūr·thēr´) *va.* to warp; to contrive, to scheme *(maquinar).*

urea, (ū·rē´â) *f.* (chem.) urea.

urgencia, (ūr·hen´syâ) *f.* urgency; emergency *(necesidad).*

urgente, (ūr·hen´te) *adj.* pressing, urgent.

urgir, (ūr·hēr´) *vn.* to be urgent.

urinario, ria, (ū·rē·nâ´ryo, ryâ) *adj.* urinary.

urna, (ūr´nâ) *f.* urn; **— electoral,** ballot box.

urólogo, (ū·ro´lo·go) *m.* (med.) urologist.

urraca, (ū·rrâ´kâ) *f.* magpie.

urticaria, (ūr·tē·kâ´ryâ) *f.* (med.) hives.

uruguayo, ya, (ū·rū·gwâ´yo, yâ) *n.* and *adj.* Uruguayan.

usado, da, (ū·sâ´tho, thâ) *adj.* used, worn; used, accustomed *(habituado).*

usanza, (ū·sân´sâ) *f.* usage, custom *(costumbre);* use.

usar, (ū·sâr´) *va.* to use, to make use of; to practice, to follow *(un empleo);* **—,** *vn.* to be used to.

uso, (ū´so) *m.* use; style, custom *(modo).*

usted, (ūs·teth´) *pron.* you; **— mismo,** you yourself.

ustedes, (ūs·te´thes) *pron pl.* you.

ustorio, ria, (ūs·to´ryo, ryâ) *adj.* burning.

usual, (ū·swâl´) *adj.* usual, customary.

usufructo, (ū·sū·frūk´to) *m.* profit, benefit; usufruct *(derecho)*

usura, (ū·sū´râ) *f.* usury.

usurero, ra, (ū·sū·re´ro, râ) *n.* usurer.

usurpación, (ū·sūr·pâ·syon´) *f.* usurpation, seizure.

usurpar, (ū·sūr·pâr´) *va.* to usurp, to seize.

utensilio, (ū·ten·sē´lyo) *m.* utensil.

uterino, na, (ū·te·rē´no, nâ) *adj.* uterine.

útero, (ū´te·ro) *m.* uterus, womb.

útil, (ū´tēl) *adj.* useful; **—es,** *m.pl.* utensils, tools; **—es de escritorio,** stationery.

utilidad, (ū·tē·lē·thâth´) *f.* utility; profit *(provecho).*

utilitario, ria, (ū·tē·lē·tâ´ryo, ryâ) *adj.* utilitarian.

utilizable, (ū·tē·lē·sâ´vle) *adj.* usable.

utilizar, (ū·tē·lē·sâr´) *va.* to make use of, to utilize.

utopia, (ū·to·pē´â) *f.* Utopia or utopia.

uva, (ū´vâ) *f.* grape; barberry *(berberí).*

V

v: véase, vid.see, refer to; **verbo,** verb.

V: valor, val. value; amt. amount.

V.A.: Vuestra Alteza, Your Highness; **Versión Autorizada,** A.V. Authorized Version.

vaca, (bâ´kâ) *f.* cow; pool *(dinero).*

vacaciones, (bâ·kâ·syo´nes) *f. pl.* holidays, vacation.

vacante, (bâ·kân´te) *adj.* vacant; **—,** *f.* vacancy.

vaciar, (bâ·syâr´) *va.* to empty; to drain *(beber);* to cast *(metales);* to hollow out, to scoop out *(ahuecar);* to sharpen, to hone *(sacar filo);* **—,** *vn.* to empty, to drain, to discharge *(desaguar);* to dwindle, to ebb *(menguar);* **—se,** (coll.) to spill the beans.

vacilación, (bâ·sē·lâ·syon´) *f.* vacillation; wobbling, shaking.

vacilante, (bâ·sē·lân´te) *adj.* vacillating; unsteady, wobbling.

vacilar, (bâ·sē·1âr´) *vn.* to be unsteady, to

totter, to wobble *(tambalearse);* to waver, to flicker *(temblar);* (fig.) to vacillate, to hesitate, to doubt *(titubear).*

vacío, cía, (bâ·sē´o, sē´â) *adj.* empty; (fig.) void, devoid *(falto);* (fig.) vain *(presuntuoso);* —, *m.* (phy.) vacuum; hole *(hueco);* (fig.) void.

vacuna, (bâ·kū´nä) *f.* vaccine.

vacunar, (bâ·kū·när´) *va.* to vaccinate.

vacuno, na, (bâ·kū´no, nä) *adj.* bovine; **ganado** —, cattle.

vadear, (bâ·the·âr´) *va.* to wade, to ford; (fig.) to overcome.

vado, (bâ´tho) *m.* ford.

vagabundo, da, (bâ·gä·vūn´do, dä) *adj.* vagabond.

vagancia, (bâ·gân´syä) *f.* vagrancy.

vagar, (bâ·gär´) *vn.* to rove, to wander; —, *m.* leisure *(tiempo libre);* slowness.

vagina, (bâ·hē´nä) *f.* (anat.) vagina.

vago, ga, (bâ´go, gä) *adj.* vagrant, wandering; vague *(indeciso);* —, *n.* vagrant; **en —go,** unsteadily; in vain *(en vano).*

vagón, (bâ·gon´) *m.* railroad car; — **cama,** sleeping car.

vahído, (bâ·ē´tho) *m.* vertigo, dizziness.

vaho, (bâ´o) *m.* steam, vapor.

vaina, (bâ´ē·nä) *f.* scabbard, sheath; pod, husk *(cáscara).*

vainilla, (bâē·nē´yä) *f.* vanilla.

vaivén, (bâē·ven´) *m.* movement to and fro; (fig.) fluctuation; risk, danger *(riesgo).*

vajilla, (bâ·hē´yä) *f.* table service, set of dishes; — **de plata,** silverware.

vale, (bâ´le) *m.* promissory note, I·O·U. *(pagaré);* voucher.

valedero, ra, (bâ·le·the´ro, râ) *adj.* valid, binding.

valenciano, na, (bâ·len·syä´no, nä) *adj.* and *n.* Valencian.

valentía, (bâ·len·tē´â) *f.* valor, courage; bragging, boasting *(jactancia).*

valentón, (bâ·len·ton´) *m.* braggart, boaster.

valentonada, (bâ·len·to·nä´thä) *f.* great show, swaggering.

valer*, (bâ·ler´) *vn.* to be valuable; to be important *(tener autoridad);* to be valid *(de monedas);* to prevail *(prevalecer);* to avail *(servir);* (fig.) to have influence, to have pull; —, *va.* to protect, to favor *(amparar);* to result in *(redituar);* to be worth *(equivaler);* — **la pena,** to be worthwhile; —**se,** to use; to resort to *(recurrir);* —**se por sí mismo,** to be self-reliant.

valeroso, sa, (bâ·le·ro´so, sä) *adj.* valiant

brave *(valiente);* strong, powerful *(fuerte).*

valía, (bâ·lē´â) *f.* value, worth; favor *(valimiento);* faction, party *(facción).*

validar, (bâ·lē·thär´) *va.* to validate.

validez, (bâ·lē·thes´) *f.* validity; strength *(fuerza).*

válido, da, (bá´lē·tho, thä) *adj.* valid; sound, strong.

valiente, (bâ·lyen´te) *adj.* valiant, brave, courageous; vigorous *(activo);* first-rate *(excelente);* (fig.) extreme.

valija, (bâ·lē´hä) *f.* valise; mail bag *(saco);* mail *(correo);* — **diplomática,** diplomatic pouch.

valioso, sa, (bâ·lyo´so, sä) *adj.* valuable; rich, wealthy *(rico).*

valor, (bâ·lor´) *m.* value, worth; force, power *(fuerza);* equivalence *(equivalencia);* courage, valor *(calidad del alma);* cheek *(osadía);* —**es,** *pl.* (com.) securities; **por dicho —,** for the above amount; — **nominal** or **aparente,** face value; **sin —,** worthless.

valorar (bâ·lo·rär´) or **valorear,** (bâ·lo·re·âr´) *va.* to value; to use *(utilizar);* to increase the value of *(aumentar).*

vals, (bâls) *m.* waltz.

valuación, (bâ·lwä·syon´) *f.* evaluation, appraisal, estimate.

valuar, (bâ·lwär´) *va.* to evaluate, to estimate.

válvula, (bâl´vū·lä) *f.* valve; — **de seguridad,** safety valve; — **corrediza,** slide valve; — **de aire,** air valve; — **de radio,** radio tube; — **de rayos catódicos,** cathode-ray tube.

valla, (bâ´yä) *f.* barricade, fence; (fig.) obstacle, impediment.

valle, (bâ´ye) *m.* valley, vale.

¡vamos! (bâ´mos) *interj.* well then! come on now!

vanagloria, (bâ·nä·glo´ryä) *f.* conceit, vainglory.

vanagloriarse, (bâ·nä·glo·ryär´se) *vr.* to boast, to brag.

vandalismo, (bân·dä·lēz´mo) *m.* vandalism.

vándalo, la, (bân´dä·lo, lä) *m.* and *adj.* vandal.

vanguardia, (bâng·gwär´dyä) *f.* vanguard, van.

vanidad, (bâ·nē·thäth´) *f.* vanity.

vanidoso, sa, (bâ·nē·tho´so, sä) *adj.* vain.

vano, na, (bâ´no, nä) *adj.* vain; —, *m.* hollow; **en —no,** in vain.

vapor, (bâ·por´) *m.* vapor, steam; (naut.)

steamer, steamship.
vaporoso, sa, (bâ·po·ro´so, sâ) *adj.* vaporous; (fig.) ethereal.
vaquero, (bâ·ke´ro) *m.* cowboy; —, ra, *adj.* cowboy, ranch.
vaqueta, (bâ·ke´tâ) *f.* leather.
V.A.R.: **Vuestra Alteza Real,** Your Royal Highness.
vara, (bâ´râ) *f.* twig, branch *(rama);* rod, pole *(palo);* staff *(de mando);* — **alta,** upper hand.
varadero, (bâ·râ·the´ro) *m.* shipyard.
varadura, (bâ·râ·thû´râ) *f.* (naut.) grounding.
varar, (bâ·râr´) *va.* to beach; —, *vn.* and *vr.* to ground to be stranded.
variable, (bâ·rya´vle) *adj.* and *f.* variable.
variación, (bâ·ryâ·syon´) *f.* variation.
variado, da, (bâ·ryâ´tho, thâ) *adj.* variegated *(colores);* varied, diverse.
variante, (bâ·ryân´te) *adj.* and *f.* variant; —, *adj.* varying.
variar, (bâ·ryâr´) *va.* to vary, to change; —, *vn.* to vary.
varicela, (bâ·rē·se´lâ) *f.* (med.) chicken pox.
varicoso, sa, (bâ·rē·ko´so, sâ) *adj.* varicose.
variedad, (bâ·rye·thâth´) *f.* variety, diversity *(diversidad);* inconstancy, instability; change, alteration *(mudanza);* variation *(variación).*
variedades, (bâ·rye·thâ´thes) *f. pl.* vaudeville performance.
varilla, (bâ·rē´yâ) *f.* long narrow rod; rib *(de armazón).*
vario, (bâ´ryo, ryâ) *adj.* varied, various; (fig.) fickle, inconstant.
varón, (bâ·ron´) *m.* male; man *(adulto);* man of standing *(hombre respetable).*
varonil, (bâ·ro·nēl´) *adj.* male; (fig.) manly, virile.
vasallo, (bâ·sâ´yo) *m.* vassal.
vaselina, (bâ·se·lē´nâ) *f.* vaseline, petroleum jelly.
vasija, (bâ·sē´hâ) *f.* vessel, dish.
vaso, (bâ´so) *m.* glass *(para beber);* vase.
vástago, (bâs´tâ·go) *m.* bud, shoot; (fig.) offshoot, descendant; rod, bar *(barra).*
vasto, ta, (bâs´to, tâ) *adj.* vast, huge.
vate, (bâ´te) *m.* poet, bard; diviner, seer *(adivino).*
Vaticano, (bâ·tē·kâ´no) *m.* Vatican.
vaticinar, (bâ·tē·sē·nâr´) *va.* to divine, to foretell.
vaticinio, (bâ·tē·sē´nyo) *m.* foretelling, prediction, forecast.
vatio, (bâ´tyo) *m.* watt; — **hora,** watt hour.

¡**vaya!** (bâ´yâ) *interj.* well now!
Vd.: **usted,** you.
vda.: **viuda** widow.
Vds. or **VV.**: **ustedes,** you.
V.E.: **Vuestra Excelencia,** Your Excellency.
véase, (be´â·se) see, refer to.
vecindad, (be·sēn·dâth´) *f.* neighborhood; **en la** —, nearby, in the area.
vecindario, (be·sēn·dâ´ryo) *m.* neighborhood, district.
vecino, na, (be·sē´no, nâ) *adj.* neighboring, near; —, *n.* neighbor; inhabitant *(habitante).*
vector, (bek·tor´) *m.* (avi.) vector.
veda, (be´thâ) *f.* prohibition; closed season *(tiempo).*
vedado, (be·thâ´tho) *m.* park, inclosure
vedar, (be·thâr´) *va.* to prohibit, to forbid *(prohibir);* to impede *(impedir).*
veedor, (be·e·thor´) *m.* overseer, inspector; —, ra, *adj.* prying, nosy.
vega, (be´gâ) *f.* plain.
vegetación, (be·he·tâ·syon´) *f.* vegetation.
vegetal, (be·he·tâl´) *adj.* and *m.* vegetable.
vegetar, (be·he·târ´) *vn.* to vegetate.
vegetariano, na, (be·he·tâ·ryâ´no, nâ) *adj.* and *m.* vegetarian.
vehemencia, (be·e·men´syâ) *f.* vehemence.
vehemente, (be·e·men´te) *adj.* vehement.
vehículo, (be·ē´kü·lo) *m.* vehicle.
veinte, (be´ēn·te) *adj.* and *m.* twenty.
veintena, (beēn·te´nâ) *f.* score, twenty.
veinteno, na, (beēn·te´no, nâ) *adj.* twentieth.
veintiuno, na, (beēn·tyū´no, nâ) *adj.* twenty-one.
vejamen, (be·hâ´men) *m.* taunt; vexation *(molestia).*
vejar, (be·hâr´) *va.* to vex, to annoy.
vejez, (be·hes´) *f.* old age; (fig.) old story.
vejiga, (be·hē´gâ) *f.* bladder; blister *(ampolla).*
vela, (be´lâ) *f.* watch, vigil; night work *(trabajo);* pilgrimage *(romería);* guard *(centinela);* candle *(para alumbrar).*
velación, (be·lâ·syon´) *f.* watch, watching; —**ones,** *pl.* nuptial benedictions.
velada, (be·lâ´thâ) *f.* watch *(velación);* evening entertainment, soiree.
velador, (be·lâ·thor´) *m.* watchman, caretaker *(guardia);* wooden candlestick *(candelero);* lamp stand *(mesita).*
velar, (be·lâr´) *vn.* to stay awake; to work nights *(trabajar);* (fig.) to take care, to watch; —, *va.* to look after *(asistir);* (fig.) to observe closely.
veleidad, (be·leē·thâth´) *f.* caprice, whim

(capricho); inconstancy, flightiness *(inconstancia).*

veleidoso, sa, (be·leē·tho´so, sâ) *adj.* inconstant, fickle.

velero, ra, (be·le´ro, râ) *adj.* swift-sailing; —, *m.* sailboat.

veleta, (be·le´tâ) *f.* weathercock; (fig.) fickle person.

velo, (be´lo) *m.* veil; (fig.) pretext.

velocidad, (be·lo·sē·thâth´) *f.* velocity, speed; **a toda —,** at full speed; **cambio de —,** gear shift; **— aérea,** air speed; **— máxima,** speed limit.

velorio, (be·lo´ryo) *m.* wake; (eccl.) taking the veil *(una religiosa).*

veloz, (be·los´) *adj.* swift, quick.

vello, (be´yo) *m.* down, fuzz.

vellocino, (be·yo·sē´no) *m.* fleece.

vellón, (be·yon´) *m.* fleece.

velloso, sa, (be·yo´so, sâ) *adj.* downy, fuzzy.

velludo, da, (be·yū´tho, thâ) *adj.* shaggy, woolly, hairy; —, *m.* velvet.

vena, (be´nâ) *f.* vein; (fig.) inspiration; **estar en —,** to feel in the mood.

venado, (be·nâ´tho) *m.* deer.

venal, (be·nâl´) *adj.* venous; salable *(vendible);* (fig.) mercenary.

vencedor, ra, (ben·se·thor´, râ) *n.* conqueror, victor; —, *adj.* victorious.

vencer, (ben·ser´) *va.* to conquer; to exceed, to surpass *(exceder);* to prevail over *(prevalecer);* to suffer *(sufrir);* to twist, to bend *(torcer);* —, *vn.* to fall due; to expire, to run out *(terminar);* **se,** to control oneself.

vencido, da, (ben·sē´tho, thâ) *adj.* conquered; due *(debido);* **darse por —,** to give up, to yield; **letra —,** overdue draft, —, *f.* vanquishment; (com.) maturity, expiration.

vencimiento, (ben·sē·myen´to) *m.* victory; (com.) expiration.

venda, (ben´dâ) *f.* bandage; blindfold *(sobre los ojos).*

vendaje, (ben·dâ´he) *m.* bandage, dressing.

vendar, (ben·dâr´) *va.* to bandage; to blindfold; (fig.) to blind *(cegar).*

vendaval, (ben·dâ·vâl´) *m.* strong wind from the sea; **— de polvo,** dust storm.

vendedor, ra, (ben·de·thor´, râ) *n.* seller; —, *m.* salesman; —, *f.* saleswoman.

vender, (ben·der´) *va.* to sell; to sell out, to betray *(traicionar);* **— al por menor,** to sell retail; **— al por mayor,** to sell wholesale.

vendible, (ben·dē´vle) *adj.* salable, marke-

table.

vendimia, (ben·dē´myâ) *f.* vintage; (fig.) profits.

veneciano, na, (be·ne·syâ´no, nâ) *adj.* and *n.* Venetian.

veneno, (be·ne´no) *m.* poison, venom.

venenoso, sa, (be·ne·no´so, sâ) *adj.* venomous, poisonous.

venerable, (be·ne·râ´vle) *adj.* venerable.

veneración, (be·ne·râ·syon´) *f.* veneration, worship.

venerar, (be·ne·râr´) *va.* to venerate, to worship.

venéreo, rea, (be·ne´re·o, re·â) *adj.* venereal.

venezolano, na, (be·ne·so·lâ´no, nâ) *n.* and *adj.* Venezuelan.

vengador, ra, (ben·gâ·thor´, râ) *n.* avenger.

venganza, (beng·gân´sâ) *f.* revenge, vengeance.

vengar, (beng·gâr´) *va.* to revenge, to avenge; **—se de,** to take revenge for.

vengativo, va, (beng·ga·tē´vo, vâ) *adj.* revengeful, vindictive.

venia, (be´nyâ) *f.* pardon, forgiveness; leave, permission *(permiso);* bow, curtsy *(saludo).*

venial, (be·nyâl´) *adj.* venial.

venida, (be·nē´thâ) *f.* arrival; return *(regreso);* (fig.) impetuosity.

venidero, ra, (be·nē·the´ro, râ) *adj.* coming, next, approaching; **el próximo —,** the coming month; **—s,** *m. pl.* posterity.

venir*, (be·nēr´) *vn.* to come, to arrive; to agree to *(conformarse);* to fit, to suit *(ajustarse);* **— a menos,** to decay, to decline; **¿a qué viene eso?** to what purpose is that? **el mes que viene,** next month; **—de,** to come from: **ir y —,** to go back asid forth; **— de perillas, — como anillo al dedo,** to be very opportune, to be in the nick of time.

venta, (ben´tâ) *f.* sale; roadside inn *(mesón).*

ventaja, (ben·tâ´hâ) *f.* advantage; **con — recíproca,** to mutual advantage; **llevar —,** to have the advantage over.

ventajoso, sa, (ben·tâ·ho´so, sâ) *adj.* advantageous.

ventana, (ben·tâ´nâ) *f.* window; **repisa de —,** windowsill; **vidrio de —,** windowpane.

ventanal, (ben·tâ·nâl´) *m.* large window.

ventanilla, (ben·tâ·nē´yâ) *f.* small window; peephole *(abertura).*

ventarrón, (ben·tâ·rron´) *m.* violent wind.

ventero, a, (ben·te´ro, râ) *n.* innkeeper.

â arm, **e** they, **ē** bē, **o** fore, **ū** blūe, **b** bad, **ch** chip, **d** day, **f** fat, **g** go, **h** hot, **k** kid, **1** let

ventilación, (ben·tē·lä·syon´) f. ventilation; discussion (discusión).

ventilador, (ben·tē·lä·thor´) m. ventilator, fan.

ventilar, (ben·tē·lär´) va. and vr. to ventilate, to air; to discuss (discutir).

ventisca, (ben·tēs´kä) f. snowstorm.

ventisquero, (ben·tēs·ke´ro) m. snowdrift; **—s,** pl. glaciers.

ventolera, (ben·to·le´rä) f. gust; pride, loftiness (vanidad).

ventor, ra, (ben·tor´, rä) n. pointer.

ventosear, (ben·to·se·är´) vn. and vr. to break wind.

ventosidad, (ben·to·sē·thäth´) f. flatulency.

ventoso, sa, (bēn·to´so, sä) adj. windy; flatulent (flatulento).

ventrículo, (ben·trē´kū·lo) m. (anat.) ventricle.

ventrílocuo, (ben·trē´lo·kwo) m. ventriloquist.

ventura, (ben·tū´rä) f. luck, chance, fortune; risk, danger (riesgo); **por —,** perhaps.

venturoso, sa, (ben·tū·ro´so, sä) adj. lucky, fortunate, happy.

ver*, (ber) va. to see; to look at; to note, to observe (observar); to understand (comprender); to consider, to reflect (considerar); to predict (prevenir); **vamos a —,** let´s see; **veremos,** we´ll see, maybe; **hacer —,** to claim, to make believe; **ser de —,** to be worthy of attention; **—se,** to find oneself; **—se en apuros,** to be in trouble; **—se bien,** to look well; **—,** m. sight, appearance, aspect; **a mi —,** in my opinion, to my way of thinking.

vera, (be´rä) f. edge, border.

veracidad, (be·rä·sē·thäth´) f. veracity.

veranear, (be·rä·ne·är´) vn. to spend the summer, to vacation.

veraneo, (be·rä·ne´o) m. summering; **lugar de —,** summer resort.

verano. (be·rä´no) m. summer.

veras, (be´räs) f. pl. truth, sincerity; **de —,** in truth, really.

veraz, (be·räs´) adj. veracious, truthful, sincere.

verbal, (ber·väl´) adj. verbal, oral.

verbena, (ber·ve´nä) f. (bot.) verbena; (eccl.) festival on the eve of a saint´s day.

verbigracia, (ber·vē·grä´syä) adv. for example, namely.

verbo, (ber´vo) m. word, term; (gram.) verb.

verborrea, (ber·vo·rre´ä) f. wordiness.

verbosidad, (ber·vo·sē·thäth´) f. verbosity.

verboso, sa, (ber·vo´so, sä) adj. verbose.

verdad, (ber·thäth´) f. truth; **en —,** really, indeed; **ser hombre de —,** to be a man of his word; **decir a un cuatro —es,** to tell someone off.

verdaderamente, (ber·thä·the·rä·men´te) adv. truly, in fact.

verdadero, ra, (ber·thä·the´ro, rä) adj. true, real; sincere (sincero).

verde, (ber´the) adj. green; fresh, vigorous (vigoroso); (fig.) young, inexperienced (joven); off-color (desvergonzado); **—,** m. fodder; bitterness (del vino).

verdor, (ber·thor´) m. verdure, greenness; (fig.) youth, vigor.

verdoso, sa, (ber·tho´so, sä) adj. greenish.

verdugo, (ber·thū´go) m. young shoot; whip (azote); welt (roncha); (orn.) shrike; hangman (ejecutor); (fig.) savage, brute; (fig.) torment, plague (azote).

verdulero, (ber·thū·le´ro) m. greengrocer.

verdura, (ber·thū´rä) f. verdure; vegetables, greens (hortaliza).

vereda, (be·re´thä) f. path, trail.

veredicto, (be·re·thēk´to) m. verdict.

verga, (ber´gä) f. (anat.) penis; steel bow (de la ballesta); **— de garra,** topsail mast.

vergel, (ber·hel´) m. flower garden.

vergonzante, (ber·gon·sän´te) adj. shameful, shamefaced.

vergonzoso, sa, (ber·gon·so´so, sä) adj. bashful, shy; shameful (bochornoso).

vergüenza, (ber·gwen´sä) f. shame; bashfulness (timidez); confusion (confusión); **tener —,** to be ashamed; to have dignity, to be honorable (tener pundonor).

verídico, ca, (be·rē´thē·ko, kä) adj. truthful.

verificación, (be·rē·fē·kä·syon´) f. verification.

verificar, (be·rē·fē·kär´) va. to verify, to prove; to check (examinar); **—se,** to be verified, to turn out true; to take place (realizarse).

verisímil (be·rē·sē´mēl) = **verosímil.**

verja, (ber´hä) f. grate, lattice; iron fence (cerca).

vermut, (ber·mūt´) m. vermouth.

verónica, (be·ro´nē·kä) f. (bot.) speedwell; veronica (del torero).

verosímil, (be·ro·sē´mēl) adj. plausible, credible.

verraco, (be·rrä´ko) m. boar.

verruga, (be·rrū´gä) f. wart; (coll.) nuisance; (coll.) defect (tacha).

verrugoso, sa, (be·rrū·go´so, sä) adj.

---

m met, **n** not, **p** pot, **r** very, **rr** (none), **s** so, **t** toy, **th** with, **v** eve, **w** we, **y** yes, **z** zero

warty.

versado, da, (ber·sä´tho, thä) *adj.* well-versed, conversant, skilled.

versar, (ber·sâr´) *vn.* to turn, to go around; (Cuba) to versify; — **sobre,** to deal with; —**se** to become skillful.

versátil, (ber·sä´tēl) *adj.* versatile; (fig.) fickle.

versículo, (ber·sē´kū·lo) *m.* versicle; verse *(de la Biblia).*

versificar, (ber·sē·fē·kâr´) *va.* and *vn.* to versify.

versión, (ber·syon´) *f.* translation *(traducción);* version, interpretation.

verso, (ber´so) *m.* verse, stanza; — **blanco,** —**suelto,** blank verse; — **libre,** free verse.

vértebra, (ber´te·vrâ) *f.* vertebra.

vertebrado, da, (ber·te·vrä´tho, thä) *m.* and *adj.* vertebrate.

vertedero, (ber·te·the´ro) *m.* drain, sewer.

vertedor, ra, (ber·te·thor´, râ) *n.* emptier; —, *m.* conduit, sewer; (naut.) bailing scoop.

verter*, (ber·ter´) *va* and *vr.* to spill, to empty, to pour *(derramar);* to translate *(traducir);* —, *vn.* to flow.

vertical, (ber·tē·kâl´) *adj.* vertical, upright.

vértice, (ber´tē·se) *m.* vertex; (fig.) crown *(de la cabeza).*

vertiente, (ber·tyen´te) *adj.* sloping; —, *m.* or *f.* slope.

vertiginoso, sa, (ber·tē·hē·no´so, sä) *adj.* vertiginous, dizzy, giddy.

vértigo, (ber´tē·go) *m.* dizziness, vertigo; (fig.) giddiness.

vesícula, (be·sē´kū·lâ) *f.* (anat.) vesicle; — **biliar,** gall bladder

vespertino, na, (bes·per·tē´no, nä) *adj.* evening.

vestibular, (bes·tē·vū·lâr´) *adj.* (anat.) vestibular.

vestíbulo, (bes·tē´vū·lo) *m.* vestibule; (theat.) lobby.

vestido, (bes·tē´tho) *m.* suit; dress *(de mujer).*

vestidura. (bes·tē thū´râ) *f.* dress, wearing apparel; —, *pl.* (eccl.) vestments.

vestigio, (bes·tē´hyo) *m.* vestige, trace; footprint *(huella).*

vestir*, (bes·tēr´) *va.* to clothe, to dress; to furnish *(guarnecer);* (fig.) to decorate; (fig.) to cloak, to disguise *(disfrazar);* **de** —, dressy, elegant; —**se,** to get dressed.

vestuario, (bes·twä´ryo) *m.* apparel, wardrobe; (mil.) uniform; (theat.) dressing room; (eccl.) vestry.

veta, (be´tâ) *f.* vein; ribbon *(faja).*

veterano, na, (be·te·râ´no, nä) *adj.* experienced, practiced; —, *m.* veteran.

veterinario, (be·te·rē·nä´ryo) *m.*veterinary.

vetusto, ta, (be·tūs´to, tä) *adj.* old, antiquated, aged.

vez, (bes) *f.* time; turn *(turno);* **a la** —, at the same time; **a la** — **que,** while; **a veces, algunas veces,** sometimes; **en** — **de,** instead of; **otra** —, again; **varias veces,** several times; **tal** —, ´perhaps; **una** —, once; **dos veces,** twice; **a su** —, in turn; **cada** —, each time, every time; **rara** —, seldom; **por primera** —, for the first time; **algunas veces,** sometimes; **de** — **en cuando,** from time to time; **toda** — **que,** whenever; **cada** — **más,** more and more.

vg. v.g. or **v.gr.: verbigracia,** e.g. for example.

vía, (bē´â) *f.* way, road, route; mode, manner, method *(modo);* track *(carril);* — **férrea,** railway; — **aérea,** airway; — **marítima,** waterway; — **crucis,** way of the cross; — **láctea,** Milky Way; —**s respiratorias,** respiratory tract.

viaducto, (byâ·thūk´to) *m.* viaduct, underpass.

viajar, (byâ·hâr´) *vn.* to travel.

viaje, (byâ´he) *m.* journey, voyage, trip; water main *(de agua);* — **sencillo,** one-way trip; — **redondo** or **de ida y vuelta,** round trip; **gastos de** —, traveling expenses; **ir de** —, to go on a trip.

viajero, ra, (byâ·he´ro, râ) *n.* traveler.

vialidad, (byâ·lē·thâth´) *f.* road system, highway service, communication.

vianda, (byân´dâ) *f.* food.

viáticos, (byâ´tē·kos) *m. pl.* travel expenses.

víbora, (bē´vo·râ) *f.* viper.

vibración, (bē·vrâ·syon´) *f.* vibration.

vibrador, (bē·vrâ·thor´) *m.* vibrator.

vibrante, (bē·vrân´te) *adj.* vibrating, vibrant.

vibrar, (bē·vrâr´) *va.* to vibrate, to quiver; to throw, to hurl *(arrojar);* —, *vn.* to vibrate.

vicario, (bē·kâ´ryo) *m.* vicar; —, **ria,** *adj.* vicarious.

vicecónsul, (bē·se·kon´sūl) *m.* vice-consul.

vicepresidente, (bē·se·pre·sē·then´te) *m.* vice-president; vice-chairman *(de un comité).*

viceversa, (bē·se·ver´sâ) *adv.* vice versa.

viciar, (bē·syâr´) *vn.* to vitiate, to mar, to spoil; to falsify *(falsificar);* to adulterate, to corrupt *(adulterar);* to annul *(anu-*

vici 343 viol

lar); —**se,** to give oneself over to vice; to become overly fond *(aficionarse).*

vicio, (bē´syo) *m.* vice; overgrowth *(de árboles);* **de** —, without reason.

vicioso, sa, (bē·syo´so, sâ) *adj.* vicious; defective *(defectuoso);* excessive *(excesivo).*

vicisitud, (bē·sē·sē·tūth´) *f.* vicissitude.

víctima, (bēk´tē·mä) *f.* victim.

victorear (bēk·to·re·âr´) = **vitorear.**

victoria, (bēk·to´ryä) *f.* victory.

victorioso, sa, (bēk·to·ryo´so, sä) *adj.* victorious.

vid, (bēth) *f.* (bot.) vine.

vida, (bē´thä) *f.* life; — **media,** (chem.) half-life; **ganarse la** —, to earn a living.

vidalita, (bē·thä·lē´tä) *f.* Argentine popular song of woe.

video, (bē´the·o), *m.* video; — **cámara,** video camera.

vidriado, da, (bē·thryä´tho, thä) *adj.* glazed; —, *m.* glazed earthenware.

vidriera, (bē·thrye´rä) *f.* show case *(vitrina);* shop window *(escaparate);* leaded window *(ventana).*

vidriero, (bē·thrye´ro) *m.* glazier.

vidrio, (bē´thryo) *m.* glass; pane of glass *(de ventana);* piece of glassware; — **inastillable,** shatter-proof glass; — **soplado,** blown glass.

vidrioso, sa, (bē´thryo´so, sä) *adj.* glassy; brittle *(quebradizo);* (fig.) slippery *(resbaloso);* frail, fragile *(frágil).*

viejo, ja, (bye´ho, hä) *adj.* old, aged; wornout *(usado);* — **amigo,** former friend

vienés, esa, (bye·nes´, e´sä) *adj.* and *n.* Viennese.

viento, (byen´to) *m.* wind; air *(aire);* scent *(olor);* (fig.) vanity; **hace** —, it is windy; **molino de** —, windmill.

vientre, (byen´tre) *m.* stomach; belly *(panza).*

viernes, (byer´nes) *m.* Friday; **V— Santo,** Good Friday.

viga, (bē´gä) *f.* beam.

vigente, (bē·hen´te) *adj.* in force.

vigésimo, ma, (bē·he´sē·mo, mä) *m.* and *adj.* twentieth.

vigía, (bē·hē´ä) *f.* watchtower; (naut.) shoal, rock; —, *m.* lookout, watch.

vigilancia, (bē·hē·län´syä) *f.* vigilance, watchfulness; care *(cuidado).*

vigilante, (bē·hē·län´te) *adj.* vigilant, alert; —, *m.* guard, caretaker; policeman *(de policía).*

vigilar, (bē·hē·lâr´) *va.* to watch over, to look after; to observe *(observar).*

vigilia, (bē·hē´lyä) *f.* vigil, watch; watchfulness, alertness *(vela);* eve *(víspera).*

vigor, (bē·gor´) *m.* vigor; **entrar en** —, to go into effect.

vigorizar, (bē·go·rē·sâr´) *va.* to strengthen, to invigorate.

vigoroso, sa, (bē·go·ro´so, sä) *adj.* vigorous, hardy.

V.I.H.: virus de la inmunodeficiencia humana, H.I.V., human immunodeficiency virus.

vil, (bēl) *adj.* mean, sordid, low *(bajo);* worthless *(sin valor);* ungrateful *(ingrato).*

vileza, (bē·le´sä) *f.* meanness, lowness *(bajeza);* abjectness *(miseria).*

villa, (bē´yä) *f.* village, small town; villa *(casa).*

Villadiego, (bē·yä·thye´go) *m.* **tomar las de** —, to run away, to sneak out, to take off.

villancico, (bē·yän·sē´ko) *m.* Christmas carol.

villanía, (bē·yä·nē´ä) *f.* lowness of birth; villainy *(infamia);* (fig.) nasty remark.

villano, na, (bē·yä´no, nä) *adj.* rustic, boorish; —, *m.* rustic, peasant.

vinagre, (bē·nä´gre) *m.* vinegar.

vinagrera, (bē·nä·gre´rä) *f.* vinegar cruet.

vincular, (bēng·kū·lâr´) *va.* to entail *(los bienes);* (fig.) to link, to secure, to fasten.

vínculo, (bēng´kū·lo) *m.* tie, bond; entail.

vindicación, (bēn·dē·kâ·syon´) *f.* vindication.

vindicar, (bēn·dē·kâr´) *va.* to vindicate, to avenge.

vindicativo, va, (bēn·dē·kâ·tē´vo, vä) *adj.* vindictive, vengeful.

vinílico, ca, (bē·nē´lē·ko, kä) *adj.* vinyl.

vinilo, (bē·nē´lo) *m.* vinyl.

vino, (bē´no) *m.* wine; — **añejo,** aged wine; — **tinto,** red wine.

viña, (bē´nyä) *f.* vineyard.

viñedo, (bē·nye´tho) *m.* vineyard.

viola, (byo´lä) *f.* viola.

violáceo, cea, (byo·lä´se·o, se·ä) *adj.* violet-colored.

violación, (byo·lâ·syon´) *f.* violation.

violado, da, (byo·lä´tho, thä) *adj.* violet-colored *(color);* violated.

violar, (byo·lâr´) *va.* to violate, to infringe, to break; to ravish *(forzar);* to profane, to desecrate *(profanar).*

violencia, (byo·len´syä) *f.* violence.

violentar, (byo·len·târ´) *va.* to enforce by violent means; to force *(forzar);* (fig.) to distort, to do violence to.

m met, **n** not, **p** pot, **r** very, **rr** (none), **s** so, **t** toy, **th** with, **v** eve, **w** we, **y** yes, **z** zero

violento, ta, (byo·len´to, tâ) *adj.* violent.

violeta, (byo·le´tâ) *f.* (bot.) violet; —, *adj.* violet.

violin, (byo·lēn´) *m.* violin.

violinista, (byo·lē·nēs´tâ) *m.* and *f.* violinist.

violón, (byo·lon´) *m.* bass viol.

violonchelo, (byo·lon·che´lo) *m.* violoncello.

viperino, na, (bē·pē·rē´no, nâ) *adj.* viperous; lengua —, venomous tongue.

virada, (bē·râ´thâ) *f.* (naut.) tacking.

virar, (bē·râr´) *va.* (naut.) to veer, to tack; —, *vn.* to turn.

virgen, (bēr´hen) *adj.* and *f.* virgin.

virginal, (bēr·hē·nâl´) *arj.* virginal.

virginidad, (bēr·hē·nē·thath´) *f.* virginity; (fig.) purity, candor.

viril, (bē·rēl´) *adj.* virile, manly.

virilidad, (bē·rē·lē·thâth´) *f.* virility.

virología, (be·ro·lo·hē´â) *f.* virology.

virreinato, (bē·rreē·nâ´to) *m.* viceroyship.

virrey, (bē·rre´ē) *m.* viceroy.

virtud, (bēr·tūth´) *f.* virtue; efficacy *(eficacia);* vigor, courage *(vigor).*

virtuoso, sa, (bēr·two´so, sâ) *adj.* virtuous.

viruela, (bē·rwe´lâ) *f.* smallpox; —s locas, chicken pox.

virulento, ta, (bē·rū·len´to, tâ) *adj.* virulent.

virus, (bē´rūs) *m.* (med.) virus.

viruta, (bē·rū´tâ) *f.* cutting, shaving.

visa, (bē´sâ) *f.* visa.

visar, (bē·sâr´) *va.* to countersign; to visa *(un pasaporte);* to sight *(dirigir).*

visceras, (bēs´se·râs) *f. pl.* viscera.

viscosidad, (bēs·ko·sē·thâth´) *f.* viscosity.

viscoso, sa, (bēs·ko´so, sâ) *adj.* viscous.

visera, (bē·se´râ) *f.* visor, eyeshade.

visible, (bē·sē´vle) *adj.* visible; (fig.) apparent, conspicuous.

visión, (bē·syon´) *f.* vision; sight *(persona ridícula).*

visionario, ria, (bē·syo·nâ´ryo, ryâ) *adj.* visionary.

visir, (bē·sēr´) *m.* vizier.

visita, (bē·sē´tâ) *f.* visit; visitor, guest *(huésped);* hacer —s, to pay visits; — de cumplimiento, courtesy call.

visitador, ra, (bē·sē·tâ·thor´, râ) *n.* visiting inspector; frequent visitor *(huésped);* —, *adj.* visiting.

visitante, (bē·sē tân´te) *m.* and *f.* visitor.

visitar, (bē·sē·târ´) *va.* to visit; —se, to be on visiting terms.

vislumbrar, (bēz·lūm·brâr´) *va.* to catch a glimpse of, to perceive indistinctly; (fig) to have an inkling of, to conjecture

(conjeturar).

viso, (bē´so) *m.* sheen, shimmer *(reflejo);* gleam *(destello);* —s, *pl.* appearance.

visón, (bē·son´) *m.* mink; abrigo de —, mink coat.

víspera, (bēs´pe·râ) *f.* eve, day before; — de Año Nuevo, New Year´s Eve; —s, *pl.* vespers.

vista, (bēs´tâ) *f.* sight, eyesight; appearance, aspect *(aspecto);* view, vista *(paisaje);* glance *(vistazo);* purpose, intent *(intento);* trial *(ante el tribunal);* —s, windows *(ventanas);* collar and cuffs; —, *m.* customs officer; — de pájaro, bird´s-eye view; — de un pleito, day of trial; a la —, on sight; a primera —, at first sight; corto de —, nearsighted; echar una — a, to glance at; en — de, in view of, considering; hasta la —, good-bye, so long; punto de —, viewpoint; hacer la — gorda, to overlook; perder de —, to lose sight of; saltar a la —, to be obvious.

vistazo, (bēs·tâ´so) *m.* glance.

visto, (bēs´to) *adj.* obvious; — que, considering that; por lo —, apparently; — bueno, O.K.; dar el — bueno, to give one´s approval.

vistoso, sa, (bēs·to´so, sâ) *adj.* showy, flashy.

visual, (bē·swâl´) *adj.* visual.

vital, (bē·tâl´) *adj.* vital, essential.

vitalicio, cia, (bē·tâ·lē´syo, syâ) *adj.* lifelong; —, *m.* life insurance policy; life pension *(pensión).*

vitalidad, (bē·tâ·lē·thâth´)*f.* vitality.

vitamina, (bē·tâ·mē´nâ) *f.* vitamin.

vitorear, (bē·to·re·âr´) *va.* to cheer, to applaud.

vitrina, (bē·trē´nâ) *f.* showcase.

vituperar, (bē·tū·pe·râr´) *va.* to blame.

vituperio, (bē·tū·pe´ryo) *m.* vituperation.

viuda, (byū´thâ) *f.* widow.

viudez, (byū·thes´) *f.* widowhood.

viudo, (byū´tho) *m.* widower.

¡viva! (bē´vâ) *interj.* hurrah! hail!

vivacidad, (bē·vâ·sē·thâth´) *f.* vivacity, liveliness.

vivaracho, cha, (bē·vâ·râ´cho, châ) *adj.* lively, smart, sprightly.

víveres, (bē´ve·res) *m. pl.* provisions.

vivero, (bē·ve´ro) *m.* (bot.) nursery; fish hatchery *(de peces).*

viveza, (bē·ve´sâ) *f.* liveliness; keenness *(ardor);* quickness *(agudeza).*

vividor, ra, (bē·vē·thor´, râ) *adj.* lively; industrious *(trabajador);* —, *n.* sponger.

vivienda, (bē·vyen´dâ) *f.* dwelling, house;

___

â arm, e they, ē bē, o fore, ū blūe, b bad, ch chip, d day, f fat, g go, h hot, k kid, 1 let

manner of living *(modo de vivir)*.

viviente, (bē·vyen´te) *adj.* alive, living.

vivificar, (bē·vē·fē·kâr´) *va.* to vivify, to enliven.

vivir, (bē·vēr´) *vn.* to live; to last *(durar);* — **de,** to live on.

vivisección, (bē·vē·sek·syon´) *f.* vivisection.

vivo, va, (bē´vo, vâ) *adj.* living, alive; intense, sharp *(intenso);* lively *(que concibe pronto);* ingenious, sharp *(sutil);* bright *(brillante);* active, lively *(activo).*

vizconde, (bēs·kon´de) *m.* viscount.

vizcondesa, (bēs·kon·de´sâ) *f.* viscountess.

V.M.: Vuestra Majestad, Your Majesty.

V.o B.o: visto bueno, O.K.

vocablo, (bo·kâ´vlo) *m.* word.

vocabulario, (bo·kâ·vū·lâ´ryo) *m.* vocabulary; dictionary *(diccionario).*

vocación, (bo·kâ·syon´) *f.* vocation, calling.

vocacional, (bo·kâ·syo·nâl´) *adj.* vocational; **escuela —,** vocational school.

vocal, (bo·kâl´) *f.* vowel; —, *m.* member of board of directors; —, *adj.* vocal, oral.

vocalización, (bo·kâ·lē·sâ·syon´) *f. (mus.)* vocalization.

vocear, (bo·se·âr´) *vn.* to cry, to shout;to proclaim *(publicar a voces);* to calf *(llamar);* to acclaim *(aclamar).*

vociferación, (bo·sē·fe·râ·syon´) *f.* vociferation.

vociferar, (bo·sē·fe·râr´) *vn.* to shout, to proclaim.

vocinglería, (bo·sēng·gle·rē´â) *f.* clamor, shouting, hullabaloo.

vocinglero, ra, (bo·sēng·gle´ro, râ) *adj.* noisy, shouting; — *n.* loudmouth.

vol.: volumen, vol. volume; **voluntad,** will; (com.) good will.

volador, ra, (bo·lâ·thor´, râ) *adj.* flying; hanging *(pendiente);* speedy, fast *(que corre con ligereza);* —, *m.* (ichth.) flying fish; rocket.

volante, (bo·lân´te) *adj.* flying; unsettled *(que no tiene asiento fijo);* portable *(de quita y pon);* —, *m.* shuttlecock; steering wheel *(rueda);* minting press *(prensa);* note, memorandum *(papel);* ruffle *(guarnición);* lackey *(criado).*

volantín, (bo·lân·tēn´) *m.* fishing tackle.

volar, (bo·lâr´) *vn.* to fly; to project; to stick out *(sobresalir);* to do right away *(hacer);* to disappear *(desaparecer);* to spread *(propagarse);* —, *va.* to blow up, to detonate; to irritate, to anger *(irritar);* to rouse *(de la caza);* **—se,** to get angry.

volátil, (bo·lâ´tēl) *adj.* volatile; flying *(que* vuela).

volcán, (bol·kân´) *m.* volcano.

volcar*, (bol·kâr´) *va.* to tip, to tip over, to upset; to make dizzy *(turbar la cabeza);* to change one's mind *(hacer mudar de parecer);* to exasperate *(irritar);* —, *vn.* to turn over.

voleo, (bo·le´o) *m.* volley; Sunday punch *(bofetón).*

volframio, (bol·frâ´myo) *m.* wolfram, tungsten.

voltaje, (bol·tâ´he) *m.* (elec.) voltage, tension.

voltear, (bol·te·âr´) *va.* to turn over; to reverse *(poner al revés);* to move *(trastrocar);* to build *(construir);* —, *vn.* to tumble.

volteo, (bol·te´o) *m.* reversal *(inversión);* overturning; tumbling *(acción de voltearse);* **caja de —,** body of a dump truck.

voltereta, (bol·te·re´tâ) *f.* handspring.

voltio, (bol´tyo) *m.* (elec.) volt.

voluble, (bo·lū´vle) *adj.* voluble; (fig.) inconstant, fickle.

volumen, (bo·lū´men) *m.* volume.

voluminoso, sa, (bo·lū·mē·no´so, sâ) *adj.* voluminous.

voluntad, (bo·lūn·tâth´) *f.* will; free will *(libre albedrío);* good will *(benevolencia);* **a —,** at will; **de buena —,** willingly, with pleasure.

voluntario, ria, (bo·lūn·tâ´ryo, ryâ) *adj.* voluntary; —, *n.* volunteer.

voluntarioso, sa, (bo·lūn·tâ·ryo´so, sâ) *adj.* willful.

voluptuoso, sa, (bo·lūp·two´so, sâ) *adj.* voluptuous; voluptuary *(dado a los placeres).*

volver*, (bol·ver´) *vt.* to turn; to translate *(traducir);* to return, to restore *(devolver);* to change, to transform *(mudar);* to vomit *(vomitar);* to change one's mind *(hacer mudar de dictamen);* to give *(la vuelta);* to push, to pull *(de las puertas);* to plow a second time *(dar la segunda reja);* to send back, to return *(enviar);* **—se,** to become; to turn sour *(agriarse).*

vomitar, (bo·mē·târ´) *va.* to vomit.

vomitivo, va (bo·mē·tē´vo, vâ) *adj. and m.* emetic.

vómito, (bo´mē·to) *m.* vomiting, vomit.

voracidad, (bo·râ·sē·thâth´) *f.* voracity.

vorágine, (bo·râ´hē·ne) *f.* whirlpool, vortex.

voraz, (bo·râs´) *adj.* voracious.

vórtice, (bor´tē·se) *m.* vortex, whirlpool;

eye *(de un ciclón).*
vos, (bos) *pron.* you.
vosotros, tras, (bo·so'tros, trâs) *pron. pl.* you.
votación, (bo·tâ·syon') *f.* voting.
votante, (bo·tân'te) *m.* and *f.* voter.
votar, (bo·târ') *va.* and *vn.* to vow *(echar votos);* to swear; to vote.
votivo, va, (bo·tē'vo, vâ) *adj.* votive.
voto, (bo'to) *m.* vow; vote *(parecer);* wish *(deseo);* votive offering *(ruego);* voter *(persona);* curse *(juramento);* **hacer —s,** to wish well.
voz, (bos) *f.* voice; sound *(sonido);* noise *(ruido);* shout *(grito);* word.
V.P.: Vicepresidente, Vice Pres. Vice-President.
V.R.: Vuestra Reverencia, Your Reverence.
vuelco, (bwel'ko) *m.* overturning, upsetting.
vuelo, (bwe'lo) *m.* flight; wing *(ala);* width, fullness *(amplitud);* ruffle, frill *(adorno);* woodland *(arbolado);* **— a ciegas,** blind flying; **— en formación,** formation flying; **— tripulado,** manned flight; **a —, al —,** immediately, right away.

vuelta, (bwel'tâ) *f.* turn, revolution; curve *(curvatura);* return *(regreso, devolución);* beating *(zurra);* harshness *(aspereza);* repetition *(repetición);* reverse, other side *(otro lado);* ruffle *(adorno);* **a — de correo,** by return mail; **viaje de —,** return trip; **dar la —,** to turn around; to take a walk *(a pie);* to take a ride *(en vehículo).*
vuelto, (bwel'to) *m.* (Sp. Am.) change; **dar el —,** to give back one's change.
vuestro, tra, (bwes'tro, trâ) *pron.* yours; *adj.* your.
vulcanización, (būl·kâ·nē·sâ·syon') *f.* vulcanization.
vulcanizar, (būl·kâ·nē·sâr') *va.* to vulcanize.
vulgar, (būl·gâr') *adj.* vulgar, common, ordinary; vernacular *(de las lenguas).*
vulgaridad, (būl·gâ·rē·thâth') *f.* vulgarity.
vulgarismo, (būl·gâ·rēz'mo) *m.* colloquialism.
vulgo, (būl'go) *m.* common people; **—,** *adv.* commonly, vulgarly.
vulnerar, (būl·ne·râr') *va.* to injure, to damage.
VV or V.V.: ustedes, you.

W

whisky, (wēs'kē) *m.* whisky.

whist, (wēst) *m.* whist

X

xenón, (kse·non') *m.* xenon.
xerófila, (kse·ro'fē·lâ) *m.* (bot.) xerophyte.

xilófono, (ksē·lo'fo·no) *m.* (mus.) xylophone.

Y

y, (ē) *conj.* and.
ya, (yâ) *adv.* already; now *(ahora);* presently, soon *(más adelante);* immediately, right now *(en seguida);* finally *(finalmente);* **— no,** no longer; **— que,** since, seeing that; **¡—! interj.** enough *(basta)!* I see! that's right!

yacer*, (yâ·ser') *vn.* to lie, to lie down; to be buried *(estar enterrado);* to be located, to lie *(estar).*
yacimiento, (yâ·sē·myen'to) *m.* (geol.) bed, deposit.
yaguar (yâ·gwâr') = **jaguar.**
yanqui, (yâng'kē) *adj.* and *m.* Yankee.

â arm, **e** they, **ē** bē, **o** fore, **ū** blūe, **b** bad, **ch** chip, **d** day, **f** fat, **g** go, **h** hot, **k** kid, **l** let

yarda, (yär'thâ) *f.* yard.
yate, (yä'te) *m.* yacht.
ye, (ye) *f.* name of the letter y.
yedra (ye'thrâ) = **hiedra.**
yegua, (ye'gwâ) *f.* mare.
yelmo, (yel'mo) *m.* helmet.
yema, (ye'mâ) *f.* bud; yolk *(de los huevos);* (fig.) best, cream; — **del dedo,** tip of the finger.
yerba, (yer'vâ) *f.* grass; **mala** —, marijuana (Coll.); — **buena,** mint; — **mate,** Paraguay tea; —**s,** *pl.* grass, pasture.
yermo, (yer'mo) *m.* desert, wasteland; —, **ma,** *adj.* uncultivated; uninhabited, deserted *(inhabitado).*
yerno, (yer'no) *m.* son-in-law.
yerro, (ye'rro) *m.* error, mistake.
yerto, ta, (yer'to, tâ) *adj.* stiff, inflexible; rigid.
yesca, (yes'kâ) *f.* tinder, spunk; (fig.) stim-

ulus.
yeso, (ye'so) *m.* gypsum; plaster *(mezclado con agua);* plaster cast *(obra de escultura).*
yetar, (ye·târ') *vt.* (Arg.) to hex.
yo, (yo) *pron.* I; — **mismo,** I myself.
yodo, (yo'tho) *m.* iodine.
yodoformo, (yo·tho·for'mo) *m.* (chem.) iodoform.
yuca, (yū'kâ) *f.* (bot.) yucca.
yugo, (yū'go) *m.* yoke; (naut.) transom.
yugoslavo, va, (yū·goz·lâ'vo, vâ) *n.* and *adj.* Yugoslavian.
yugular, (yū·gū·lâr') *adj.* jugular; **vena** —, jugular vein.
yunque, (yūng'ke) *m.* anvil; (fig.) long-suffering person; tool *(que trabaja mucho).*
yunta, (yūn'tâ) *f.* team, yoke.
yute, (yū'te) *m.* jute (fiber). skin jacket *(chaqueta).*

Z

zacate, (sâ·kâ'te) *m.* (Mex.) hay, grass.
zafar, (sâ·fâr') *va.* (naut.) to untie, to loosen; to adorn, to garnish; —**se,** to evade *(escaparse);* (fig.) to get out of *(librarse).*
zafarrancho, (sâ·fâ·rrân'cho) *m.* (naut.) clearing for action; (coll.) destruction, devastation *(destrozo);* (coll.) wrangle, scuffle *(riña).*
zafir (sâ·fēr') or **zafiro,** (sâ·fē'ro) *m.* sapphire.
zafra, (sâ'frâ) *f.* sugar crop; sugar making *(fabricación).*
zaga, (sâ'gâ) *f.* rear load *(carga);* rear, back; —, *m.* last player in a game; **no quedarse en** —, not to be left behind.
zagal, (sâ·gâl') *m.* outrider; young man *(mozo);* boy *(muchacho);* shepherd *(pastor);* skirt *(falda).*
zagala, (sâ·gâ'lâ) *f.* shepherdess *(pastora);* lass, girl.
zaguán, (sâ·gwân') *m.* hall, vestibule.
zahúrda, (sâ·ūr'thâ) *f.* hogsty, pigpen.
zaino, na, (sâ'ē·no, nâ) *adj.* chestnut; vicious *(de los animales);* treacherous, false, traitorous *(traidor);* black *(negro);* **mirar de** or **a lo** —**no,** to look sideways.
zalamería, (sâ·lâ·me·rē'â) *f.* flattery.
zalamero, ra, (sâ·lâ·me'ro, râ) *n.* wheedler, flatterer; —, *adj.* wheedling.
zamarra, (sâ·mâ'rrâ) *f.* sheepskin; sheep-

skin jacket *(chaqueta).*
zambo, ba, (sâm'bo, bâ) *adj.* knock-kneed.
zambullida, (sâm·bū·yē'thâ) *f.* dipping, dunking.
zambullirse*, (sâm·bū·yēr'se) *vr.* to plunge, to dive, to jump; to hide *(esconderse).*
zanahoria, (sâ·nâ·o'ryâ) *f.* carrot.
zanca, (sâng'kâ) *f.* shank.
zancada, (sâng·kâ'thâ) *f.* stride, long step.
zancadilla, (sâng·kâ·thē'yâ) *f.* trip; (fig.) trick, deceit.
zanco, (sâng'ko) *m.* stilt.
zancudo, da, (sâng·kū'tho, thâ) *adj.* long-legged; (orn.) wading; —, *m.* (Sp. Am.) mosquito.
zángano, (sâng'gâ·no) *m.* drone; sponger *(que vive de gorra);* lazy lout *(ocioso).*
zanja, (sân'hâ) *f.* ditch, trench.
zanjar, (sân·hâr') *va.* to dig ditches in; (fig.) to clear the ground for.
zapa, (sâ'pâ) *f.* spade.
zapallo, (sâ·pâ'yo) *m.* (Sp. Am.) squash.
zapapico, (sâ·pâ·pē'ko) *m.* pickax.
zapar, (sâ·pâr') *vn.* to dig, to excavate.
zapatazo, (sâ·pâ·tâ'so) *m.* blow with a shoe.
zapatear, (sâ·pâ·te·âr') *va.* to strike with a shoe; —, *vn.* to tap one's foot *(dar golpes en el suelo);* to beat time *(acom-*

m met, **n** not, **p** pot, **r** very, **rr** (none), **s** so, **t** toy, **th** with, **v** eve, **w** we, **y** yes, **z** zero

pañar al tañido); **—se,** to hold one's own.

zapatería, (sâ·pâ·te·rē'â) *f.* shoe store.

zapatero, (sâ·pâ·te'ro) *m.* shoemaker; shoe seller *(vendedor).*

zapatilla, (sâ·pâ·tē'yâ) *f.* pump; slipper *(de comodidad).*

zapato, (sâ·pâ'to) *m.* shoe; **—s de goma** or **de hule,** rubbers.

¡zape! *interj.* scat!

zapote, (sâ·po'te) *m.* (bot.) sapota.

zar, (sr) *m.* czar.

zaragata, (sâ·râ·gâ'tâ) *f.* (coll.) turmoil, todo; mixup; quarrel *(riña).*

zarandearse, (sâ·rân·de·âr'se) *vr.* to run from pillar to post.

zaraza, (sâ·râ'sâ) *f.* chintz, printed cotton, gingham.

zarcillo, (sâr·sē'yo) *m.* earring; tendril *(tallito);* hoe *(azada).*

zarigüeya, (sâ·rē·gwe'yâ) *f.* opossum.

zarpa, (sâr'pâ) *f.* claw; (naut.) weighing anchor.

zarpar, (sâr·pâr') *vn.* to weigh anchor, to set sail.

zarpazo, (sâr·pâ'so) *m.* thud, thump *(batacazo);* clawing.

zarza, (sâr'sâ) *f.* bramblebush, blackberry bush.

zarzal, (sâr·sâl') *m.* brambles, blackberry patch.

zarzamora, (sâr·sâ·mo'râ) *f.* brambleberry, blackberry.

zarzo, (sâr'so) *m.* wattle, trellis.

zarzuela, (sâr·swe'lâ) *f.* zarzuela, operetta; **— cómica,** comic operetta.

¡zas, zas! (sâs sâs) *interj.* slap, slap!

zepelín, (se·pe·lēn') *m.* (avi.) blimp, zeppelin, dirigible.

zeta, (se'tâ) *f.* name of the letter z.

zigzag, (sēg·sâg') *m.* zigzag.

zirconio, (sēr·ko'nyo) *m.* zircon.

zócalo, (so'kâ·lo) *m.* (arch.) socle; (Mex.) plaza, square.

zoclo, (so'klo) *m.* wooden shoe; galosh *(de goma).*

zodiaco (so·thyâ'ko) or **zodíaco,** (so·the'â·ko) *m.* zodiac.

zona, (so'nâ) *f.* zone; belt *(faja);* **— de marcha lenta,** slow-driving zone; **— de peligro,** danger zone; **— de tránsito,**

traffic lane.

zoología, (so·o·lo·hē'â) *f.* zoology.

zoológico, ca, (so·o·lo'hē·ko, kâ) *adj.* zoological.

zoonosis, (so·o·no'sēs) *m.* zoonosis.

zoquete, (so·ke'te) *m.* block, chunk; (coll.) blockhead, numbskull.

zorra, (so'rrâ) *f.* fox; (coll.) prostitute, whore *(ramera);* drunkenness *(borrachera).*

zorrería, (so·rre·rē'â) *f.* cunning, craft.

zorrillo, (so·rrē'yo) *m.* skunk.

zorro, (so'rro) *m.* fox.

zorruno, na, (so·rrū'no, nâ) *adj.* foxy.

zorzal, (sor·sâl') *m.* (orn.) thrush.

zote, (so'te) *m.* dolt, lout, lug.

zozobra, (so·so'vrâ) *f.* foundering; (fig.) uneasiness, anxiety.

zozobrar, (so·so·vrâr') *vn.* to fail *(perderse);* to be in danger *(estar en riesgo);* to be torn *(acongojarse);* (naut.) to founder.

zuavo, (swâ'vo) *m.* (mil.) zouave.

zueco, (swe'ko) *m.* wooden shoe; galosh *(de goma).*

zumba, (sūm'bâ) *f.* cow bell *(cencerro);* whistle *(bramadera);* (fig.) joke, trick *(raya);* flogging, whipping.

zumbador, (sūm·bâ·thor') *m.* buzzer.

zumbar, (sūm·bâr') *vn.* to hum; to buzz; to ring *(los oídos);* to jest, to joke *(dar chasco).*

zumbido, (sūm·bē'tho) *m.* humming; buzzing; **— telefónico,** busy signal.

zumo, (sū'mo) *m.* juice; (fig.) advantage; **— de limón,** lemon juice.

zurcir, (sūr·sēr') *va.* to darn, to mend; to join, to unite *(unir);* (coll.) to weave, to hatch *(mentiras).*

zurdo, da, (sūr'tho, thâ) *adj.* left; left-handed *(de la mano izquierda).*

zurrador, (sū·rrâ·thor') *m.* leather dresser, currier.

zurrapa, (sū·rrâ'pâ) *f.* lees, dregs; (coll.) scum, garbage.

zurrar, (sū·rrâr') *va.* to curry, to dress; to whip, to lash *(castigar);* to bawl out *(censurar);* to get the best of *(vencer).*

zutano, na, (sū'tâ·no, nâ) *n.* so and so, what's his (her) name.

PART II

INGLÉS – ESPAÑOL

ENGLISH – SPANISH

ABREVIATURAS

adv.	adverb, adverbio
avi.	aviation, aviación
agr.	agriculture, agricultura
anat.	anatomy, anatomía
arch,	architecture, arquitectura
Arg.	Argentina, Argentina
art.	article, artículo
ast.	astronomy, astronomía
auto.	automobile, automóvil
biol.	biology, biología
Bol.	Bolivia, Bolivia
bot.	botany, botánica
chem.	chemistry, química
Col.	Columbia, Colombia
coll.	colloquial, familiar
com.	commerce, comercio
conj.	conjunction, conjunción
dent.	dentistry, dentistería
eccl.	ecclesiastic, eclesiástico
Ecu.	Ecuador, Ecuador
elec.	electricity, electricidad
ent.	entomology, entomología
f.	feminine, femenino
fig.	figurative(ly), figurado
geog.	geography, geografía
geol.	geology, geología
gram.	grammar, gramática
Guat.	Guatemala, Guatemala
ichth.	ichthyology, ictiología
interj.	interjection, interjección
interr.	interrogative, interrogativo
m.	masculine, masculino
math.	mathematics, matemáticas
mech.	mechanics, mecánica
med.	medicine, medicina
Mex.	Mexico, Méjico
mil.	military art, milicia
min.	mining, minería
mus.	music, música
n.	noun, sustantivo
naut.	nautical, náutico or marino
orn.	ornithology, ornitología
phot.	photography, fotografía
phy.	physics, física
pl.	plural, plural
poet.	poetry, poética
pol.	politics, política
p.p.	past participle, participio pasado
P.R.	Puerto Rico, Puerto Rico
prep.	preposition, preposición
print,	printing, imprenta
pron.	pronoun, pronombre
rad.	radio, radiocomunicación
rail.	railway, ferrocarril
rhet.	rhetoric, retórica
sing.	singular, singular
Sp.Am.	Spanish America, Hispanoamérica
theat.	theater, teatro
TV.	television, televisión
Urug.	Uruguay, Uruguay
v.	verb, verbo
va.	transitive verb, verbo activo
Ven.	Venezuela, Venezuela
vet.	veterinary, veterinaria
vi., vn.	intransitive verb, verbo neutro
vr.	reflexive verb, verbo reflexivo
vt.	transitive verb, verbo activo
zool.	zoology, zoología

English-Spanish

A

a, *art.* un, uno, una; —, *prep.* a, al, en, por ej. **abed,** en cama, **aloud,** en voz alta.

A.B.: Bachelor of Arts, Br. en A. Bachiller en Artes.

aback, *adv.* detrás, atrás; (naut.) en facha; **to be taken —,** quedar desconcertado.

abacus, *n.* ábaco, *m.*

abandon, *vt.* abandonar, dejar.

abase, *vt.* rebajar (en rango, puesto, estimación, etc.); degradar.

abash, *vt.* avergonzar, causar confusión, sonrojar.

abate, *vt.* minorar, disminuir, rebajar; —, *vi.* disminuirse.

abbey, *n.* abadía, *f.;* monasterio, *m.*

abbot, *n.* abad, *m.*

abbreviate, *vt.* abreviar, acortar, compendiar.

abbreviation, *n.* abreviación, abreviatura, *f.*

ABC's, *n. pl.* abecé, abecedario, *m.*

abdicate, *vt.* abdicar, renunciar.

abdication, *n.* abdicación, renuncia, *f.;* dimisión, f.

abdomen, *n.* abdomen, vientre, *m.;* barriga, *f*

abduct, *vt.* secuestrar.

aberration, *n.* desvío, extravío, *m.*, aberración, *f.*

abet, *vt.* favorecer, patrocinar, sostener; excitar, animar.

abeyance, n., **in —,** (leyes) en suspenso.

abhor, *vt.* aborrecer, detestar.

abide, *vi.* habitar, morar; permanecer; —, *vt.* soportar, sufrir; defender, sostener; **to — by,** cumplir con, sostenerse en.

ability, *n.* potencia, habilidad, capacidad, aptitud *f.;* facilidad, *f.*

abject, *adj.* vil, despreciable, bajo; desanimado; **—ly,** *adv.* abyectamente.

abjure, *vt.* abjurar; renunciar; —, *vi.* retractarse.

ablaze, *adj.* en llamas.

able, *adj.* fuerte, capaz, hábil; **to be — to,** saber; poder.

able-bodied, *adj.* robusto, vigoroso.

ably, *adv.* con habilidad.

abnormal, *adj.* anormal; deforme.

aboard, *adv.* a bordo; **to go —,** embarcarse; **all —!** señores viajeros al tren!

abode, *n.* domicilio, *m.*, habitación, *f.*

abolish, *vt.* abolir, anular, suprimir; destruir o dar fin a alguna cosa; revocar.

abolition, *n.* abolición, *f.*

A-bomb, *n.* bomba atómica.

abominable, *adj.* abominable, detestable.

aboriginal, *adj.* aborigen, primitivo, originario.

abort, *vi.* (med.) abortar; —, *n.* fracaso (en el lanzamiento de un cohete).

abortion, *n.* aborto, malparto, *m.*

abound, *vi.* abundar.

about, *prep.* cerca de, por ahí, hacia; sobre; acerca; tocante a; —, *adv.* en contorno, aquí y allá; aproximadamente, cerca de; **to go —,** andar acá y acullá; **it is — twelve,** son aproximadamente las doce; **all —,** en todo lugar; en todas partes; **to be —,** tratar de.

about-face, *n.* media vuelta; —, *vi.* dar media vuelta.

above, *prep.* encima, sobre, superior, más alto (en cuanto a situación, dignidad, etc.); —, *adv.* arriba; **— all,** sobre todo, principalmente; — **mentioned,** ya mencionado, susodicho, sobredicho.

aboveboard, adj. y adv. sincero, al descubierto.

abrasion, n. raspadura, f.; rozamiento, m.; fricción, f.; desgaste por rozamiento o fricción.

abrasive, adj. raspante, abrasivo; **—s,** n. pl. abrasivos, m. pl.

abreast, adv. de costado; **to be — of the** news, estar al corriente.

abridge, vt. abreviar, compendiar; acortar.

abroad, adv. fuera de casa o del país; **to go —,** salir, ir al extranjero.

abrupt, adj. quebrado, desigual; precipitado, repentino; bronco, rudo.

abscess, n. absceso, m., postema, f.

abscond, vi. esconderse; huirse.

absence, n. ausencia, f.; falta, f.; abstracción, f.; **leave of —,** licencia, f.

absent, adj. ausente; fuera de sí; distraído.

absentee, n. el que está ausente de su empleo, etc.

absenteeism, n. ausentismo, m.

absent-minded, adj. distraído, inatento.

absolute, adj. absoluto; categórico; positivo; arbitrario; completo; puro.

absolution, n. absolución, f.

absolve, vt. absolver, dispensar, exentar.

absorb, vt. absorber.

absorbent, n. y adj. (med.) absorbente, m.

absorption, n. absorción, f.

abstain, vi. abstenerse, privarse.

abstinence, n. abstinencia, f.; templanza, f.

abstract, vt. abstraer; compendiar; —, adj. abstracto; —, n. extracto, m.; sumario, compendio, m.

abstraction, n. abstracción, f.; distracción, f.

absurd, adj. absurdo.

absurdity, n. absurdo, m.; ridiculez, f.

abundance. n. abundancia, copia, plenitud, f.; raudal, m.; **in —,** a rodo.

abundant, adj. abundante; sobrado.

abuse, vt. abusar; engañar; maltratar, violar; —, n. abuso, engaño, m.; corruptela, seducción, f.; injuria, afrenta, f.

abusive, adj. abusivo, injurioso.

A.C., a.c.: alternating current, C.A. corriente alterna.

ac: account, c., cta. cuenta.

acacia, n. (bot.) acacia, f.

academic, academical, adj. académico.

academy, n. academia, f., colegio, m.

accede, vi. acceder, convenir en alguna cosa, asentir.

accelerate, vt. acelerar.

acceleration, n. aceleración, prisa, f., apremio, m.

accelerator, n. acelerador, m.

accelerometer, n. acelerómetro, m.

accent, n. acento, m., modulación, f., tono, m.; —, vt. acentuar, colocar los acentos; intensificar.

accentuate, vt. acentuar; intensificar.

accept, vt. aceptar; admitir; recibir favorablemente.

acceptable, adj. aceptable, grato, digno de aceptación.

acceptance, n. aceptación, recepción, f.; recibimiento, m.

access, n. acceso, m.; entrada, f.; aumento, m.

accessory, adj. accesorio; concomitante; casual; —, n. cómplice, m. y f.

accident, n. accidente, m.; casualidad, f.; suceso imprevisto, lance (funesto), m.; **— insurance,** seguro contra accidentes.

accidental, adj. accidental, casual, contingente.

acclaim, vt. aclamar, aplaudir, vitorear.

acclamation, n. aclamación, f., aplauso, m.

acclimate, vt. aclimatar.

acclimated, adj. aclimatado.

accolade, n. elogio, m.; premio, m.; reconocimiento de méritos.

accommodate, vt. acomódar, ajustar; —, vi. adaptarse, conformarse.

accommodating, adj. servicial, complaciente; obsequioso.

accommodation, n. comodidad, f.; localidad, f.; habitación, f.; cabida, f.; cuarto, m.; **—s,** localidades, f. pl.; facilidades de alojamiento.

accompaniment, n. (mus.) acompañamiento, m.

accompany, vt. acompañar.

accomplice, n. cómplice, m. y f.

accomplish, vt. efectuar, llevar a cabo, realizar, lograr, conseguir; cumplir.

accomplished, adj. perfecto; completo; capaz, bien preparado.

accomplishment, n. realización, f., cumplimiento entero de alguna cosa; **—s,** n. pl. habilidades, f. pl.; conocimientos, m. pl.; prendas, f. pl.

accord, n. acuerdo, convenio, m.; armonía, f.; simetría, f.; **of one's own —,** espontáneamente; **with one —,** unánimemente; —, vt. acordar; —, vi. estar de acuerdo.

accordance, n. conformidad, f., acuerdo, m.

according, adj. conforme; **— to,** según; **— ly,** adv. consecuentemente, por consiguiente.

accordion, n. acordeón, m.

accost, vt. saludar a uno yendo hacia él; acercarse (a alguien); trabar conversación.

account n. cuenta, f., cálculo, m., estimación, f. ; aprecio, m.; narración, f.; relación, f.; motivo, m.; **for my —, on my —,** a mi cuenta; **on — of,** a causa de, a cargo de, por motivo de; **on no —,** de ninguna manera; **to be of no —,** ser un cero a la izquierda; **to bring (a person) to —,** pedir cuentas (a una persona); **to charge to one's —,** adeudar en cuenta; **to keep an —,** llevar cuenta; **unsettled —,** cuenta pendiente; **to take into —,** tomar en cuenta.

accountable, adj. responsable.

accountant, n. contador, m., tenedor de libros.

accounting, n. contabilidad, f.

accredit, vt. acreditar, patrocinar.

accredited, adj. autorizado.

accrue, vi. resultar, provenir.

accumulate, vt. acumular; amontonar; —, vi. crecer, aumentarse.

accuracy, n. exactitud, precisión, f.; esmero, cuidado, m.

accurate, adj. exacto, puntual; certero (de un tiro o un tirador); atinado (en un cálculo, etc.).

accursed, adj. maldito, maldecido; execrable; excomulgado; **— be!** ¡mal haya!

accusation, n. acusación, f.; cargo, m.

accusative, n. (gram.) acusativo, m.

accuse, vt. acusar; culpar; formar causa.

accustom, vt. acostumbrar, avezar; **— oneself,** familiarizarse.

ace, n. as (de naipe), m.; aviador sobresaliente; migaja, partícula, f.

acetate, n. (chem.) acetato, m.

acetic, adj. acético.

acetone, n. (chem.) acetona, f.

acetylene, n. acetileno, m.

ache, n. dolor continuo, mal, m.; —, vi. doler.

achieve, vt. ejecutar, perfeccionar, ganar, obtener; lograr, realizar.

achievement, n. ejecución, f.; acción heroica; hazaña, f.; logro, m.

Achilles tendon, n. tendón de Aquiles.

aching, adj. doliente.

acid, adj. ácido, agrio, acedo; **—proof,** resistente a los ácidos; **— test,** ensayo por ácido; —, n. ácido, m.

acidimeter, n. acidímetro, m.

acidity, n. agrura, acedía, acidez, acritud, f.

ack-ack = antiaircraft.

acknowledge, vt. reconocer; confesar; **to — receipt,** acusar recibo.

acknowledgment, n. reconocimiento, m.; gratitud, f.; concesión, f.

acne, n. (med.) acné, f.

acorn, n. bellota, f.

acoustics, n. acústica, f.

acquaint, vt. advertir, avisar, enterar, familiarizar, informar; **to be —ed with,** conocer.

acquaintance, n. conocimiento, m.; familiaridad, f.; conocido, m., conocida, f.

acquiesce, vi. consentir, asentir.

acquiescence, n. asenso, consentimiento, m., sumisión, f.

acquire, vt. adquirir, obtener.

acquisition, n. adquisición, obtención, f.

acquit, vt. libertar, absolver; pagar.

acre, n. acre (medida de tierra que equivale a 40 áreas), m.

acreage, n. número de acres.

acrid, adj. acre mordaz.

acrobat, n. acróbata, m. y f., volatinero, m.

acrobatics, n. acrobacia, f.

across, adv. de través de una parte a otra; —, prep. a través de, por.

acrostic, n. acróstico, m.

act, vt. representar; obrar; —, vi. hacer, efectuar; —, n. acto, hecho, m.; acción, f.; efecto, m.; acto (de una comedia, etc.), m.

A.C.T.H., n. **ACTH,** hormona adrenocorticotropa.

acting, n. representación, f.; —, adj. interino, suplente.

action, n. acción, operación, f.; batalla, f.; gesticulación, f.; proceso, m.; actividad, f.; funcionamiento, m.; hecho, m.; gestión, f.; **—s,** conducta, f., comportamiento, m.

activate, vt. activar.

active, adj. activo; eficaz, ocupado; ágil.

activity, n. agilidad, actividad, f.; prontitud, f.; vivacidad, f.

actor, n. actor, ejecutante, m.; agente, m.; cómico, actor (en los teatros), m.

actress, n. actriz, cómica, f.

actual, adj. cierto, real; efectivo.

actuate, vt. excitar; mover, impulsar; poner en acción.

acute, adj. agudo; ingenioso; **—ly,** adv. con agudeza.

A.D. (in the year of our Lord), D. de J. C. (después de J.C.).

ad, n. anuncio, m.

adage, n. proverbio, m.; refrán, m.

adamant, adj. firme, tenaz, inflexible.

adapt, vt. adaptar; ajustar.

adaptability, n. adaptabilidad, f.

adaptable, adj. adaptable, ajustable.

add, vt. juntar; sumar; agregar, añadir.

addicted, adj. adicto; **— to,** apasionado por, adicto a.

adding machine, n. sumadora mecánica, máquina de sumar.

addition, n. adición, f.

additional, adj. adicional; **—ly,** adv. en o

por adición, además.

address, vt. hablar, dirigir la palabra; —, n. oración, f., discurso, m.; señas, f. pl., dirección, f.

addressee, n. destinatario, ria.

addressograph, n. máquina para imprimir sobrescritos (marca comercial registrada); adresógrafo, m.

adenoid, adj. adenoideo.

adept, adj. adepto, sabio, experto; —, n. sabio, bia, experto, ta.

adequate, adj. adecuado, proporcionado; suficiente; a propósito.

adhere, vi. adherir; aficionarse; pegarse.

adherent, adj. pegajoso; tenaz; adherente; —, n. adherente, m., partidario, ria.

adhesion, n. adhesión, f.; adherencia, f.

adhesive, adj. pegajoso; tenaz; — plaster, — tape, esparadrapo, m., cinta adhesiva.

adieu, interj. ¡adiós! —, n. despedida, f.

adjacent, adj. adyacente, contiguo; colindante.

adjective, n. adjetivo, m.

adjoin, vt. juntar; unir; —, vi. estar contiguo.

adjoining, adj. contiguo, siguiente.

adjourn, vt. y vi. diferir, aplazar; suspender, clausurar (una reunión, etc.).

adjournment, n. prórroga, f.; aplazamiento, m.; clausura (de una reunión, etc.),

adjure, vt. juramentar; conjurar.

adjust, vt. ajustar. acomodar.

adjustable, adj. ajustable, adaptable.

adjuster, n. mediador, ajustador, m.

adjustment, n. ajustamiento, ajuste, arreglo, m.

adjutant, n. (mil.) ayudante, m.

ad-lib, vt. improvisar, hablar sin atenerse a lo escrito.

Adm.: Admiral, Almte. almirante.

administer, vt. administrar, gobernar; desempeñar; dar, surtir, proveer.

administration, n. administración, f.; gobierno, m.; dirección, f.; gerencia, f.

admirable, adj. admirable.

admiral, n. almirante, m.

admiration, n. admiración, f.

admire, vt. admirar; estimar; contemplar.

admirer, n. admirador, m.; amante, pretendiente, m.

admiringly, adv. con admiración.

admission, n. admisión, recepción, entrada, f.; concesión, f ; ingreso, m.

admit, vt. admitir, dar entrada; recibir, conceder, permitir; confesar; reconocer.

admittance, n. entrada, admisión, f.; no —, se prohibe la entrada.

admonish, vt. amonestar, reprender.

ado, n. dificultad, f.; bullicio, tumulto, m.; fatiga, f.; much — about nothing, mucha importancia para tan poca cosa.

adobe, n. adobe, m.

adolescence, n. adolescencia, f.

adolescent, adj. y n. adolescente, m. y f.

adopt, vt. adoptar, prohijar.

adoption, n. adopción, f.

adoration, n. adoración, f.

adore, vt. adorar.

adorn, vt. adornar; ornar; to — oneself, prenderse, adornarse.

adornment, n. adorno, atavío, m.

adrenalin, n. adrenalina, f.

adrift, adj. y adv. flotante, a merced de las olas; al garete.

adroit, adj. diestro, hábil, mañoso.

adulation, n. adulación, lisonja, zalamería, f.

adult, adj. y n. adulto, ta.

adulterate, vt. adulterar, corromper, falsificar; —, adj. adúltero; adulterado, falsificado.

adultery, n. adulterio, m.

ad val.: ad valorem (in proportion to the value), ad val.ad valórem (en proporción al valor).

advance, vt. avanzar; promover; pagar adelantado; —, vi. hacer progresos; —, n. avance, m.; adelanto, m.; in —, con anticipación, por adelantado.

advanced, adj. adelantado, avanzado.

advancement, n. adelantamiento, m.; progreso, m.; promoción, f.

advantage, n. ventaja, superioridad, f.; provecho, beneficio, m.; delantera, f.; to take — of, aprovecharse de, sacarle partido a.

advantageous, adj. ventajoso, útil; —ly, adv. ventajosamente.

advent, n. venida, f.; advenimiento, m.; Advent, Adviento, m.

adventure, n. aventura, f.; riesgo, m.; —, vi. osar, emprender; —, vt. aventurar.

adventurer, n. aventurero, m.

adventuresome, adventurous, adj. intrépido; atrevido; aventurero; valeroso.

adventuress, n. aventurera, f.

adverb, n. adverbio, m.

adverbial, adj. adverbial.

adversary, n. adversario, ria, enemigo, ga.

adverse, adj. adverso, contrario.

adversity, n. adversidad, calamidad, f.; infortunio, m.

advertise, vt. anunciar, hacerle propaganda (a algo).

advertisement, n. aviso, m.; anuncio, m.

advertiser, n. anunciante, m.

advertising, n. propaganda, f.; publicidad, f.

advice, n. consejo, m.; parecer, m.

advisability, n. prudencia, conveniencia, propiedad, f.

advisable, adj. prudente, conveniente, aconsejable.

advise, vt. aconsejar; avisar; —, vi. consultar, aconsejarse.

adviser, advisor, n. consejero, consultor, m.

advisory, adj. consultivo.

advocate, n. abogado, m.; protector, m.; partidario, m.; —, vt. defender; apoyar.

aerial, adj. aéreo; —, n. (rad.) antena, f.

aerodynamics, n. aerodinámica, f.

aeroembolism, n. aeroembolismo, m.

aeromedicine, n. aeromedicina, f.

aeronautics, n. aeronáutica, f.

aeroplane, n. aeroplano, avión, m.

aerosol, n. aerosol, m.

aesthetics, n. estética, f.

afar, adv. lejos, distante; **from** —, de algún lugar distante, desde lejos.

affable, adj. afable, complaciente.

affair, n. asunto, m.; negocio, m.; lance, duelo, m.; **love** —, amorío, m.

affect, vt. conmover; afectar; hacer mella.

affectation, n. afectación, f.

affected, adj. afectado; remilgado, lleno de afectación; **—ly,** adv. con afectación.

affection, n. amor, afecto, m.; afección, f.

affectionate, adj. afectuoso, benévolo; cariñoso; **—ly,** adv. cariñosamente.

affianced, adj. desposado, prometido.

affidavit, n. testimonio, m., declaración jurada; atestación, f.

affiliate, vt. ahijar; afiliar.

affiliation, n. afiliación, f.

affirm, vt. afirmar, declarar, confirmar, ratificar, aprobar.

affirmation, n. afirmación, f.

affirmative, adj. afirmativo.

affix, vt. anexar, añadir, fijar; —, n. (gram.) afijo, m.

afflict, vt. afligir; atormentar.

affliction, n. aflicción, f.; dolor, m.; pena, f.

affluence, n. copia, abundancia, f.

affluent, adj. afluente, opulento, rico.

afford, vt. dar; proveer; producir; proporcionar; facilitar; tener los medios, tener los recursos.

affront, n. afrenta, injuria, f.; —, vt. afrentar, insultar, ultrajar.

afghan, n. especie de manta tejida de varios colores.

afield, adv. en el campo, afuera.

afire adj. en llamas.

A.F.L., A.F. of L.: American Federation of Labor, F.A.T. Federación Americana del Trabajo.

aflame, adj. en llamas.

afloat, adj. flotante, a flote.

afoot, adj. y adv. a pie; — adv. en pie, en vías de realización.

aforethought, adj. premeditado; **with malice** —, con alevosía y ventaja, premeditadamente.

afraid, adj. temeroso, espantado, tímido, miedoso; **to be** —, temer, tener miedo.

afresh, adv. de nuevo, otra vez.

aft, adv. (naut.) a popa.

after, prep. después de, detrás; según; tras de; **day** — **tomorrow,** pasado mañana; —, adv. después.

afterburner, n. quemador auxiliar (en la retropropulsión).

after-dinner, adj. de sobremesa, para después de comida.

aftereffect, n. resultado, m., efecto resultante.

afterlife, n. vida venidera.

aftermath, n. retoño, m., segunda cosecha; consecuencias (generalmente desastrosas), f. pl.

afternoon, n. tarde f.; pasado meridiano.

afterthought, n. reflexión posterior.

afterward, afterwards, adv. después, en seguida, luego.

again, adv. otra vez; **— and —,** muchas veces, repetidas veces.

against, prep. contra; enfrente.

agape, adj. con la boca abierta.

agate, n. ágata, f.

age, n. edad, f.; siglo, m.; vejez, f.; época, f.; **of** —, mayor de edad; —, vi. envejecer.

aged, adj. envejecido, anciano; añejo.

agency, n. agencia, f., medio, m.

agent, n. agente, m.; asistente, m.; casero, m.; (leyes) poderhabiente, m.; **insurance** —, agente de seguros.

aggravate, vt. agravar; empeorar; intensificar.

aggravating, adj. agravante; irritante.

aggravation, n. agravación, f., agravamiento, m.

aggregate, n. agregado, m.; unión, f.; —, vt. juntar, reunir.

aggregation, n. agregación, f.

aggression, n. agresión, f.; ataque, asalto, m.

aggressive, adj. agresivo, ofensivo.

aggressor, n. agresor, m.

aggrieve, vt. injuriar; afligir, apesadumbrar.

aghast, adj. horrorizado.

agile, adj. ágil; vivo, diestro.

agitate, vt. agitar; discutir con ahínco; — vi. excitar los ánimos, alborotar opiniones.

agitation, n. agitación, f.; perturbación, f.

agitator, *n.* agitador, incitador, *m.*

aglow, *adj.* fulgurante, ardiente; radiante.

ago, *adv.* atrás; hace; **long—,** hace mucho; **a few days —,** hace unos días.

agonizing, *adj.* agonizante.

agony, *n.* agonía, *f.; angustia extrema.*

agrarian, *adj.* agrario.

agree, *vi.* concordar, convenir; consentir; **to — with,** dar la razón a, estar de acuerdo con.

agreeable, *adj.* conveniente, agradable; amable; **— with,** según, conforme a.

agreed, *adj.* establecido, convenido; **—! interj.** ¡de acuerdo!

agreement, *n.* acuerdo, *m.; concordia, f.; conformidad, f.; unión, f.; pacto, m.;* **by —,** de acuerdo; **general —,** consenso, *m.;* **to reach an —,** ponerse de acuerdo.

agricultural, *adj.* agrario, agrícola.

agriculture, *n.* agricultura, *f.*

ague, *n.* calentura intermitente.

ahead, *adv.* más allá, delante de otro; en adelante; enfrente; **to go —,** continuar, seguir.

aid, *vt.* ayudar, socorrer; conllevar; —, *n.* ayuda, *f.; auxilio, socorro, m.*

aide, *n.* ayudante, *m.*

aide-de-camp, *n.* edecán, *m;* asistente, *m.*

A.I.D.S.: acquired immunodeficiency syndrome, S.I.D.A., síndrome de inmunodeficiencia adquirida.

ail, *vt.* afligir, molestar; **what —s you?** ¿qué le duele a Ud.?

aileron, *n.* (avi.) alerón, *m.*

ailing, *adj.* doliente, enfermizo, achacoso.

ailment, *n.* dolencia, indisposición, *f.*

aim, *vt.* apuntar, dirigir el tiro con el ojo; aspirar a; intentar; —, *n.* designio, intento, punto, *m.;* mira, *f.;* puntería, *f.;* blanco, *m.*

aimless, *adj.* sin designio, sin dirección, sin objeto.

ain't, *contracción familiar* de **am not, is not, are not,** no estar, no ser.

air, *n.* aire, *m.;* (mus.) tonada, *f.;* semblante, *m.;* —, *adj.* de aire; aéreo; **— blast,** chorro de aire; **base,** base aérea; **— brake,** freno neumático, freno de aire; **— chamber,** cámara de aire; **—conditioned,** con aire acondicionado; **— cooling,** enfriamiento o refrigeración por aire; **— force,** fuerza aérea; **— line,** línea aérea; **— liner,** avión de pasajeros; **— lock,** cámara de presión intermedia; **— mail,** correo aéreo, correspondencia aérea, vía aérea; **— pump,** máquina neumática; **— raid,** incursión aérea; — **shaft,** respiradero de mina; **— valve,** válvula de aire; —, *vt.* airear; secar; ventilar.

airborne, *adj.* aéreo, trasportado por aire.

airbrush, *n.* pulverizador neumático, brocha de aire.

air-condition, *vt.* acondicionar el clima interior.

air conditioning, *n.* acondicionamiento del aire, aire acondicionado; ventilación, *f.*

air-cooled, *adj.* enfriado por aire.

aircraft, *n.* aeronave, *f.,* avión, *m.;* — **carrier,** portaaviones, *m.*

airing, *n.* caminata, *f.,* paseo para tomar aire; ventilación, *f.*

airlift, *n.* puente aéreo; ayuda aérea

airmail, *adj.* aeropostal; **— letter,** carta aérea, carta por avión; —, *vt.* enviar por correo aéreo.

air meet, *n.* concurso aéreo; congreso de aeronáutica.

airplane, *n.* aeroplano, avión, *m.;* — **carrier,** portaaviones, *m.*

air pocket, *n.* bache aéreo, bolsa de aire.

airport, *n.* aeropuerto, aeródromo, *m.*

airproof, *adj.* hermético.

air-raid, *n.* bombardeo aéreo; **— shelter,** refugio contra bombardeos aéreos; — **warden,** el encargado de hacer cumplir las disposiciones contra bombardeos aéreos.

airship, *n.* aeronave, *f.;* dirigible, *m.;* aeroplano, *m.*

airsickness, *n.* mareo en un viaje aéreo.

airstrip, *n.* pista de aterrizaje.

airtight, *adj.* herméticamente cerrado, hermético, a prueba de aire.

airway, *n.* vía aérea.

airy, *adj.* aéreo; etéreo; alegre; lleno de aire.

aisle, *n.* nave de una iglesia; pasillo, *m.,* crujía, *f.;* pasadizo, *m.*

ajar, *adj.* entreabierto.

akin, *adj.* consanguíneo, emparentado; análogo, semejante.

alacrity, *n.* alacridad, presteza, *f.*

à la king, *adj.* en salsa blanca con hongos, pimientos, etc.

alamode o à la mode, *adj.* con helados; **pie —, cake —,** pastel o bizcocho servido con helados.

alarm, *n.* alarma, *f.;* rebato, *m.;* **— clock,** despertador, reloj despertador; **burglar —,** alarma contra ladrones; **fire —,** alarma contra incendios, **to sound the —,** dar la alarma; —, *vt.* alarmar, inquietar.

alarming, *adj.* alarmante; sorprendente.

alarmist, *n.* alarmista, *m. y f.*

alas, *interj.* ¡ay! ¡ay de mí!

albino, *n.* y *adj.* albino, na.

album, *n.* álbum, *m.*

albumen o albumin, *n.* (bot.) albumen, *m.;* (chem.) albúmina, *f.*

alcohol, *n.* alcohol, *m.*
alcoholic, *adj.* alcohólico.
alderman, *n.* regidor, concejal, *m.*
ale, *n.* variedad de cerveza.
alert, *adj.* alerto, vivo.
alertness, *n.* cuidado, *m.;* vigilancia, *f.;* viveza, actividad, *f.*
alga, *n.* alga (planta del mar), *f.*
algebra, *n.* álgebra, *f.*
alias, *adv.* alias, de otra manera.
alibi, *n.* (leyes) coartada, *f.*
alien, *adj.* extraño; — , *n.* forastero, ra; extranjero, ra; extraterrestre, *m.*
alienate, *vt.* enajenar; malquistar, indisponer.
alight, *vi.* descender; apearse; — , *adj.* encendido; ardiente.
align, *vt.* alinear.
alignment, *n.* alineación, *f.*
alike, *adj.* semejante, igual; — , *adv.* igualmente.
alimentary, *adj.* alimenticio; alimentario; — canal, tubo digestivo.
alive, *adj.* vivo, viviente; activo.
alkali, *n.* álcali, *m.*
alkaline, *adj.* alcalino.
all, *adj.* todo; — , *adv.* enteramente; — at once, — of a sudden, de repente, de un tirón; — the better, tanto mejor; not at — , de ninguna manera; no hay de qué; once and for — , una vez por todas; — right, bueno; satisfactorio; — year round, todo el año; — , *n.* todo, *m.*
all-American, *adj.* de todos los Estados Unidos (aplícase a los deportistas).
allay, *vt.* aliviar, apaciguar.
allege, *vt.* alegar; declarar.
allegiance, *n.* lealtad, fidelidad, *f.;* pledge of — , jura a la bandera.
allegorical, *adj.* alegórico.
allegory, *n.* alegoría, *f.*
allergic, *adj.* alérgico.
allergist, *n.* alergista, alergólogo, *m.*
allergy, *n.* alergia, *f.*
alleviate, *vt.* aliviar, aligerar.
alley, *n.* paseo arbolado; callejuela, *f.,* pasadizo, *m.,* callejón, *m.*
alliance, *n.* alianza, *f.;* parentela, *f.*
allied, *adj.* aliado, confederado.
alligator, *n.* lagarto, caimán, *m.*
alligator pear, *n.* aguacate, *m.*
allocate, *vt.* asignar, distribuir.
allocation, *n.* distribución, colocación, asignación, fijación, *f.*
allot, *vt.* distribuir por suerte; asignar, repartir.
allotment, *n.* asignación, *f.;* repartimiento, *m.;* lote, *m.,* parte, porción, *f.*
all-out, *adj.* supremo, total, completo; to go — , dar el todo.

allover, *adj.* de diseño repetido.
allow, *vt.* conceder, aprobar; permitir; dar, pagar; — ing that, supuesto que.
allowable, *adj.* admisible, permitido, justo.
allowance, *n.* concesión, *f.;* licencia, *f.;* bonificación, *f.;* (naut.) ración, *f.,* alimentos, *m. pl.;* mesada, *f.*
alloy, *vt.* ligar, mezclar un metal con otro; aquilatar oro;— ,*n.* liga, aleación, mezcla, *f.*
all-round, *adj.* completo; por todas partes, en todas formas.
allspice, *n.* especerías, *f. pl.*
all-time, *adj.* inigualado hasta ahora; — high, lo más alto de todos los tiempos.
allude, *vi.* aludir.
allure, *vt.* alucinar; cebar; fascinar; — *n.* seducción, *f.*
alluring, *adj.* seductor.
allusion, *n.* alusión, *f.*
ally, *n.* aliado, da; asociado, da; — , *vt.* hacer alianza; vincular.
almanac, *n.* almanaque, *m.*
almighty, *adj.* omnipotente, todopoderoso.
almond, *n.* almendra, *f.;* — tree, almendro, *m.*
almost, *adv.* casi, cerca de.
alms, *n.* limosna, *f.*
aloft, *prep.* arriba, sobre.
alone, *adj.* solo; — , *adv.* solamente, sólo; a solas; to let — , dejar en paz.
along, *adv.* a lo largo; adelante; junto con; to get — with, llevarse bien (con alguien).
alongside, *adv. y prep.* al lado.
aloof, *adv.* lejos, de lejos, a lo largo; — , *adj.* reservado, apartado.
aloud, *adv.* en voz alta.
alpaca, *n.* alpaca, *f.*
alphabet, *n.* alfabeto, *m.*
alphabetical, *adj.* alfabético.
alphabetically, *adv.* alfabéticamente, por orden alfabético.
Alps, Alpes, *m. pl.*
already, *adv.* ya.
also, *adv.* también, igualmente, además.
alter, *vt.* alterar, mudar, modificar.
alteration, *n.* alteración, *f.;* cambio, *m.*
alternate, *adj.* alternativo, recíproco; — , *vt.* alternar, variar; — , *n.* suplente, *m.*
alternating, *adj.* alterno, alternativo; — current, corriente alterna.
alternative, *n.* alternativa, disyuntiva, *f.;* — , *adj.* alternativo.
although, *conj.* aunque, no obstante, bien que; si.
altimeter, *n.* altímetro, *m.*
altitude, *n.* altitud, altura, *f.;* (avi.) elevación, *f.*
alto, *n. y adj.* contralto, *f.*

altogether, *adv.* del todo, enteramente.

altruism, *n.* altruismo, *m.*

alum, *n.* alumbre, *m.*

aluminum, *n.* (chem.) aluminio, *m.*

alumnus, *n. (pl. alumni)* ex alumno, persona graduada de una escuela o universidad.

always, *adv.* siempre, constantemente, en todo tiempo, sin cesar.

A.M.: Master of Arts, Maestro o Licenciado en Artes.

A.M., a.m.: before noon, A.M. antemeridiano.

am (1ª persona del singular de indicativo del verbo to be), soy; estoy.

amalgamate, *vt.* y *vi.* amalgamar.

amass, *vt.* acumular, amontonar.

amateur, *n.* aficionado, da, novato, ta principiante.

amateurish, *adj.* novato; superficial, como un aficionado o principiante.

amaze, *vt.* sorprender, asombrar.

amazement, *n.* asombro, pasmo, *m.*

amazing, *adj.* extraño, pasmoso, asombroso.

Amazon, Amazonas, *m.*

ambassador, *n.* embajador, *m.*

ambassador at large, *n.* embajador acreditado ante varios países.

amber, *n.* ámbar, *m.;* — , *adj.* ambarino.

ambidextrous, *adj.* ambidextro.

ambiguity, *n.* ambigüedad, duda, *f.;* equívoco, *m.*

ambiguous, *adj.* ambiguo.

ambition, *n.* ambición, *f.*

ambitious, *adj.* ambicioso.

amble, *n.* paso de andadura del caballo; — , *vi.* amblar.

ambulance, *n.* ambulancia, *f.*

ambulant, *adj.* ambulante.

ambulatory, *adj.* ambulante.

ambush, *n.* emboscada, celada, *f.;* sorpresa, *f.;* — , *vt.* emboscar.

ameba, *n.* amiba, *f.*

ameliorate, *vt.* mejorar.

amen, *interj.* amén.

amenable, *adj.* responsable; sujeto a.

amend, *vt.* enmendar; — , *vi.* enmendarse, reformarse, restablecerse.

amendment, *n.* enmienda, reforma, *f.;* remedio, *m.*

amends, *n. sing.* y *pl.* recompensa, compensación, *f.;* satisfacción, *f.;* **to make** — , reparar.

American, *n.* y *adj.* americano, na.

Americanized, *adj.* americanizado.

amethyst, *n.* amatista, *f.*

amiable, *adj.* amable, amigable.

amicable, *adj.* amigable, amistoso.

amid, amidst, *prep.* entre, en medio de.

amino acid, *n.* aminoácido, *m.*

amiss, *adj.* importuno, impropio; — , *adv.* fuera de lugar.

ammeter, *n.* amperímetro, *m.*

ammonia, *n.* amoniaco, *m.*

ammunition, *n.* munición, *f.;* pertrechos, *m. pl.*

amnesty, *n.* amnistía, *f.,* indulto, *m.*

amoeba = ameba.

among, amongst, *prep.* entre, mezclado con, en medio de.

amorous, *adj.* amoroso.

amount, *n.* importe, *m.;* cantidad, *f.;* suma, *f.;* monto, *m.;* producto, *m.;* (com.) montante, *m.;* — , *vi.* montar, importar, subir, ascender; **to** — **to,** arrojar; llegar a ser.

ampere, *n.* (elec.) amperio, *m.*

amphibious, *adj.* anfibio.

amphitheater, *n.* anfiteatro, *m.*

ample, *adj.* amplio, vasto.

amplification, *n.* amplificación, *f.;* extensión, *f.*

amplifier, *n.* amplificador, *m.*

amplify, *vt.* ampliar, extender; — , *vi.* extenderse.

amplitude, *n.* amplitud, extensión, *f.;* abundancia, *f.;* — **modulation,** (radio) modulación de amplitud.

amply, *adv.* ampliamente, copiosamente.

amputate, *vt.* amputar.

amputation, *n.* amputación, *f.;* corte, *m.*

amputee, *n.* persona que ha sufrido una amputación.

amt.: amount, v valor.

amulet, *n.* amuleto, *m.*

amuse, *vt.* entretener, divertir.

amusement, *n.* diversión, *f.,* pasatiempo, entretenimiento, *m.;* — **park,** parque de diversiones.

amusing, *adj.* divertido; **to be** — , tener gracia; ser divertido; — **ly,** *adv.* entretenidamente.

an, *art.* un, uno, una.

analogy, *n.* analogía, conformidad, *f.*

analysis, *n.* análisis, *m.* y *f.*

analytical, *adj.* analítico.

analyze, *vt.* analizar.

anarchy, *n.* anarquía, *f.*

anatomical, *adj.* anatómico.

anatomy, *n.* anatomía, *f.*

ancestor, *n.* abuelo, *m.;* — **s,** *pl.* antepasados, *m. pl.*

ancestry, *n.* linaje de antepasados; raza, estirpe, alcurnia, prosapia, *f.*

anchor, *n.* ancla, áncora, *f.;* — , *vi.* ancorar, echar las anclas; surgir; **to cast** — , dar fondo; — , *vt.* (naut.) sujetar con el ancla.

anchorage, *n.* anclaje, *m.;* rada, *f.;* surgidero, *m.*

anchovy, n. anchoa, f.
ancient, adj. antiguo, anciano.
and, conj. y; e (antes de palabras que empiezan con i o hi, con excepción de hie); — so on, y así sucesivamente.
Andalusian, n. y adj. andaluz, za.
anecdote, n. anécdota, f.
anemia, n. anemia, f.
anemic, adj. anémico.
anemometer, n. anemómetro, m.
anesthesia, n. anestesia, f.
anesthetic, adj. anestésico.
anew, adv. de nuevo, nuevamente, otra vez.
angel, n. ángel m.
angelic, angelical, adj. angélico, angelical.
anger, n. ira, cólera, f.; — , vt. enojar, irritar, encolerizar.
angle, n. ángulo, m.; punto de vista; — , vt. pescar con caña; halagar.
angler, n. pescador de caña, cañero, m.
angling n. pesca, f.
Anglo-Saxon, n. y adj. anglosajón, ona.
Angora, n. Angora; — cat, gato de Angora.
angry, adj. colérico, irritado, enojado, indignado, resentido.
anguish n. ansia, pena, angustia, f.
angular, adj. angular.
animal, n. y adj. animal, m.
animate, vt. animar; alentar; — , adj. viviente, animado.
animated, adj. animado, lleno de vida; — cartoon, caricatura animada.
animation, n. animación, f.
animosity, n. animosidad, f.
anise, n. anis, m.
ankle, n. tobillo, m.
annals, n. pl. anales, m. pl.
annex, vt. anexar; apropiarse piarse de — , n. anexo, m.; sucursal,
annexation, n. anexión, f.
annihilate, vt. aniquilar.
anniversary, n. aniversario, m.
annotation, n. anotación, f.
announce, vt. anunciar, publicar; notificar, avisar.
announcement, n. advertencia, f.; aviso, anuncio, m.; notificación, f.
announcer, n. anunciador, ra; locutor, ra; notificador, ra.
annoy, vt. molestar; fastidiar.
annoyance, n. molestia, f.; fastidio, m.; (coll.) lata, f.
annoying, adj. enfadoso, molestoso, fastidioso, importuno.
annual, adj. anual.
annuity, n. renta anual; pensión, anualidad, f.; life — , pensión vitalicia, pensión, f.; anualidad, f.
annul, vt. anular.

annulment, n. anulación, f.
annum, n. año, m.
anode, n. (elec.) ánodo, m.
anonymous, adj. anónimo.
another, adj. otro, diferente; one — , uno a otro.
anoxia, n. anoxia, f., falta de oxígeno (en algunos tejidos).
answer, vi. responder, contestar, replicar; corresponder; — , vt. refutar; contestar; satisfacer; surtir efecto; — n. respuesta, contestación, réplica, f.
answerable, adj. responsable; conforme; discutible.
ant, n. hormiga, f.
antagonism, n. antagonismo, m.; rivalidad, f.
antagonist, n. antagonista, m. y f.; contrario, ria.
antagonistic, adj. antagónico.
antagonize, vt. contrariar, oponerse a.
antarctic, adj. antártico.
anteater, n. oso hormiguero.
antecedent, adj. antecedente; — s, n. pl. antecedentes, m. pl.
antelope, n. antílope, m.
antenna, n. (zool. y rad.) antena, f.
anteroom, n. antecámara, antesala, f.
anthem, n. himno, m.; national — , himno nacional.
anthology, n. antología, f.
anthracite, n. antracita, f., carbón de piedra, m.
anthropology, n. antropología, f.
antiaircraft, adj. antiaéreo; — , n. antiaéreos, m. pl.
antibiotic, n. y adj. antibiótico, m.
antibody, n. anticuerpo, m.
antics, n. pl. travesuras, gracias, f. pl.
anticipate, vt. anticipar, prevenir.
anticipation, n. anticipación, f.
anticlimax, n. (rhet.) anticlímax, m., suceso final mucho menos importante que los precedentes.
antidote, n. antídoto, contraveneno, m.
antifreeze, n. solución incongelable.
antihistamine, n. antihistamina, f.
antiknock, n. y adj. antidetonante, m.
antimycin, n. antimicina, f.
antipathy, n. antipatía, f.
antipersonnel, adj. (mil.) que se destina a destruir tropas terrestres.
antiquated, adj. anticuado.
antique, adj. antiguo; — , n. antigüedad, f.
antiquity, n. antigüedad, f.; ancianidad, f.
anti-Semitic, adj. antisemítico.
antiseptic, adj. antiséptico.
antisocial, adj. antisocial.
antitank, adj. (mil.) antitanque.
antithesis, n. antítesis, f.

antitoxin, *n.* antitoxina, *f.*
antitrust, *adj.* contra monopolios.
antler, *n.* asta, cuerna, *f.,* mogote, *m.*
antonym, *n.* antónimo, *m.*
Antwerp, *n.* Amberes, *f.*
anvil, *n.* yunque, *m.;* bigornia, *f.*
anxiety, *n.* ansiedad, ansia, *f.;* afán, *m.;* cuidado, *m.*
anxious, *adj.* ansioso; inquieto.
any, *adj.* y *pron.* cualquier, cualquiera, alguno, alguna, todo; — **more,** más.
anybody, *pron.* alguno, alguien; cualquiera.
anyhow, *adv.* de cualquier modo; de todos modos.
anyone, *pron.* alguno, cualquiera.
anything, *pron.* algo.
anyway, *adv.* como quiera; de todos modos.
anywhere, *adv.* en cualquier lugar, dondequiera.
A.P: Associated Press, P. A. Prensa Asociada.
apace, *adv.* aprisa, con presteza o prontitud.
apart, *adv.* aparte; separadamente; — , *adj.* separado.
apartment, *n.* departamento, apartamiento, piso, *m.;* — **house,** edificio de departamentos.
apathy, *n.* apatía, *f.*
ape, *n.* mono, *m.;* simio, *m.;* —,*vt.* remedar, imitar.
aperture, *n.* abertura, *f.*
apex, *n.* ápice, *m.,* cúspide, *f.;* colmo, *m.;* cima, *f.*
apiary, *n.* colmena *f.;* colmenar, *m.*
apiece, *adv.* por cabeza, por persona.
Apocalypse, *n.* Apocalipsis, *m.*
apogee, *n.* apogeo, *m.*
apologetic, apologetical, *adj.* apologético; que se disculpa.
apologize, *vi.* disculparse, pedir excusas.
apology, *n.* apología, defensa, *f.;* satisfacción, disculpa, *f.*
apoplexy, *n.* apoplejía, *f.*
apostle, *n.* apóstol, *m.*
apostrophe, *n.* apóstrofe, *f.,* dicterio, *m.;* (gram.) apóstrofo, *m.*
apothecary, *n.* apotecario, boticario, *m.*
appall, appal, *vt.* espantar, aterrar; deprimir, abatir.
appalling, *adj.* aterrador, espantoso.
apparatus, *n.* aparato, aparejo, *m.*
apparel, *n.* traje, vestido, *m.;* ropa, *f.;* **wearing** — , vestuario, *m.;* — , *vt.* vestir, trajear; adornar.
apparent, *adj.* evidente, aparente; —**ly,** *adv.* claramente, al parecer, por lo visto.
apparition, *n.* aparición, visión, *f.*

appeal, *vi.* apelar; recurrir; interesar; atraer; suplicar; — , *n.* súplica, *f.;* exhortación, *f.;* (leyes) apelación, *f.;* incentivo, estímulo, *m.;* simpatía, atracción, *f.*
appear, *vi.* aparecer, manifestar; ser evidente; salir, parecer; tener cara de.
appearance, *n.* apariencia, *f.,* aspecto, *m.;* vista, *f.;* aparición, *f.*
appease, *vt.* apaciguar, aplacar, reconciliar.
appeasement, *n.* apaciguamiento, *m.*
append, *vt.* añadir, anexar.
appendage, *n.* cosa accesoria; apéndice, *m;* dependencia, *f.*
appendectomy, *n.* operación del apéndice.
appendicitis, *n.* apendicitis, *f.*
appendix, *n.* apéndice, *m.*
appetite, *n.* apetito, *m.*
appetizer, *n.* aperitivo, *m.*
appetizing, *adj.* apetitoso.
applaud, *vt.* aplaudir; alabar, palmear; aclamar, palmotear.
applause, *n.* aplauso, *m.*
apple, *n.* manzana, *f.;* — **orchard,** manazanal, manzanar, *m.;* — **pie,** — **tart,** pastel o pastelillo de manzanas; — **tree,** manzano, *m.*
applesauce, *n.* puré de manzana.
appliance, *n.* utensilio, instrumento, aparato, *m.;* herramienta, *f.*
applicable, *adj.* aplicable, apto; conforme.
applicant, *n.* aspirante, solicitante, *m.* y *f.* candidato, ta.
application, *n.* solicitud *f.;* aplicación, *f.*
applied, *adj.* aplicado, adaptado.
apply, *vt.* aplicar, acomodar; **to** — **for,** solicitar; — , *vi.* dirigirse a, recurrir a.
appoint, *vt.* señalar, determinar, decretar; nombrar, designar.
appointment, *n.* estipulación, *f ;* decreto, mandato, *m.,* orden, *f.;* nombramiento, *m.;* cita, *f.,* compromiso, *m.;* designación, *f .*
apportion, *vt.* repartir, prorratear.
apposition, *n.* aposición, *f.*
appraisal, *n.* avalúo, *m.;* tasación, *f.;* valuación, *f.*
appraise, *vt.* apreciar; tasar; valuar; estimar.
appreciable, *adj.* apreciable; sensible, perceptible.
appreciate, *vt.* apreciar; estimar; valuar.
appreciation, *n.* aprecio, *m.;* tasa, *f.*
appreciative, *adj.* apreciativo; agradecido.
apprehend, *vt.* aprehender, prender; concebir, comprender; temer.
apprehension, *n.* aprehensión, *f.;* recelo, *m;* presa, captura, *f.*
apprehensive, *adj.* aprehensivo, tímido;

perspicaz; **to become** — , sobrecogerse.

apprentice, n. aprendiz, m.; — , vt. poner a alguno de aprendiz.

approach, vt. y vi. abordar, aproximar, acercar, aproximarse; — , n. acceso, m.; acercamiento, m.; proximidad, f.

approbation, n. aprobación, f.

appropriate, vt. apropiar, adaptar; (com.) asignar (una partida); — , adj. apropiado; particular, peculiar.

appropriation, n. apropiación, f.; partida asignada para algún propósito.

approval, n. aprobación, f.; on — , a prueba, a vistas.

approve, vt. aprobar; dar la razón.

approximate, vt. y vi. acercar, acercarse; — , adj. aproximado.

apricot, n. albaricoque, m.; (Mex.) chabacano, m.

April, n. abril, m.

apron, n. delantal, mandil, m.

apropos, adv. a propósito, oportunamente; — , adj. oportuno.

apt, adj. apto, idóneo.

aptitude, aptness, n. aptitud, f.; disposición natural.

aquacade, n. espectáculo acuático, natación y saltos ornamentales con acompañamiento musical.

aquamarine, n. aguamarina, f.

aquaplane, n. acuaplano, m.

aquarium, n. acuario, m.; pecera, f.

aquatic, adj. acuático.

aqueduct, n. acueducto, m.

aqueous, adj. acuoso.

aquiline, adj. aguileño.

Arab, Arabian, n. y adj. árabe, m. y f., arábigo ga.

Arabian Nights, n. pl. Las Mil y una Noches.

Arabic, adj. árabe, arábigo, arábico.

arable, adj. labrantío, cultivable.

arbitrary, adj. arbitrario, despótico.

arbitrate, vt. y vi. arbitrar, juzgar como árbitro.

arbitration, n. arbitrio, arbitraje, m.

arbitrator, n. arbitrador, árbitro, m.

arbor, n. emparrado, m., enramada, f.

arc, n. arco, m.; — lamp, — light, lámpara de arco; — weld, — welding, soldadura eléctrica o de arco.

arcade, n. arcada, bóveda, f.

arch, n. arco (de círculo, de puente, etc.), m.; straight —, arco adintelado; — , vt. cubrir con arcos; — , adj. principal, insigne; grande; infame; artero, bellaco (se usa en composición como aumentativo) .

arch.: architect, arq. arquitecto.

archaeological o archeological, adj. arqueo-lógico.

archaic, adj. arcaico.

archbishop, n. arzobispo, m.

archdiocese, n. arzobispado, m.

archduke, n. archiduque, m.

arched, adj. arqueado, abovedado.

archer, n. arquero, m.

archery, n. ballestería, f.

archipelago, n. archipiélago, m.

architect, n. arquitecto, m.

architectural, adj. arquitectónico.

architecture, n. arquitectura, f.

archives, n. pl. archivos, m. pl.

archway, n. arcada, bóveda, f.

arctic, adj. ártico.

ardent, adj. ardiente; apasionado.

ardor, n. ardor, m.; vehemencia, f.; pasión, f.

arduous, adj. arduo; laborioso; difícil.

are, plural y 2° persona del singular de indicativo del verbo **to be.**

area, n. área, f.; espacio, m.; superficie, f.

arena, n. palenque, m.; arena, pista, f.

argue, vi. disputar, discutir, argüir; replicar; discurrir; — , vt. probar con argumentos.

argument, n. argumento, m., controversia, f.

arid, adj. árido, seco, estéril.

arise, vi. levantarse; nacer, provenir.

aristocracy, n. aristocracia, f.

aristocrat, n. aristócrata, m. y f.

aristocratic, adj. aristocrático.

arithmetic, n. aritmética, f.

arithmetical, adj. aritmético.

ark, n. arca, f.

arm, n. brazo, m.; rama de árbol; poder, m.; arma, f.; — in — , de bracete.

armadillo, n. armadillo, m.

armament, n. (naut.) armamento de navíos; (mil.) armamento, m.

armchair, n. silla de brazos, poltrona, butaca, f.

armful, n. brazada, f.

armhole, n. sisa, f.

armistice, n. armisticio, m.

armor, n. armadura, f.; (mil.) fuerzas y vehículos blindados; — plate, coraza, f.

armored, adj. blindado, acorazado.

armory, n. armería, f.; arsenal, m.

armpit, n. axila, f., sobaco, m.

army, n. ejército, m.; tropas, f. pl.

aroma, n. aroma, m.

aromatic, adj. aromático, oloroso.

around, prep. alrededor de; — , adv. alrededor; en o al derredor; en torno.

arouse, vt. despertar; excitar; sublevar.

arraign, vt. citar, delatar en justicia; acusar.

arrange, vt. colocar, poner en orden,

arreglar.

arrangement, n. colocación, f.; orden, arreglo, m.; **flower** —, arreglo floral.

array, n. adorno, vestido, atavío, m.; orden de batalla; serie imponente de cosas; —, vt. colocar; vestir, adornar.

arrears, n. pl. deuda atrasada; to be in —, estar atrasado en un pago.

arrest, n. arresto, m.; detención, f.; —, vt. arrestar, prender; atraer (la atención).

arrival, n. arribo, m.; llegada, venida, f.

arrive, vi. arribar; llegar; venir.

arrogance, n. arrogancia, presunción, f.

arrogant, adj. arrogante, presuntuoso.

arrow, n. flecha, saeta, f., dardo, m.

arrowhead, n. casquillo, m.; punta de flecha.

arrowroot, n. (bot.) arrurruz, m.

arsenal, n. (mil.) arsenal, m.; (naut.) atarazana, armería, f.

arsenic, n. arsénico, m.

arson, n. incendio provocado intencionalmente.

art, n. arte, m. y f.; industria, f.; ciencia, f.; **the fine** — s, las bellas artes.

artery, n. arteria, f.

artful, adj. artificioso; diestro.

arthritic, adj. artrítico.

arthritis, n. (med.) artritis, f.; **rheumatoid** —, artritis reumatoidea.

article, n. artículo, m.

articulate, adj. articulado; claro, distinto; —, vt. articular, pronunciar distintamente.

articulation, n. articulación, f.; pronunciación, f.

artichoke, n. (bot.) alcachofa, f.

artifact, n. artefacto, m.

artifice, n. artificio, fraude, m.

artificial, adj. artificial; artificioso; sintético.

artillery, n. artillería, f.

artisan, n. mecánico, artesano, m.

artist, n. artista, m. y f., pintor, ra.

artistic, adj. artístico.

artless, adj. sencillo, simple.

as, conj. y adv. como; mientras; también; pues; en son de; visto que, pues que; — **much,** tanto; — **far** —, hasta; — **it were,** por decirlo así; — **for,** — **to,** en cuanto a.

asbestos, n. asbesto, amianto, m.

ascend, vi. ascender, subir.

ascendancy, n. ascendiente, influjo, poder, m.

ascension, n. ascensión, f.

ascent, n. subida, f.; eminencia, f.; altura, f.

ascertain, vt. indagar, averiguar.

ascetic, adj. ascético; —, n. asceta, m.

ascribe, vt. adscribir; atribuir; adjudicar.

ash, n. (bot.) fresno, m.; — es, pl. ceniza, f.; reliquias de un cadáver; — tray, cenicero, m.; **Ash Wednesday,** Miércoles de Ceniza.

ashamed, adj. avergonzado; to be —, tener vergüenza.

ashcan, n. cenicero, m.; recipiente para las cenizas de carbón.

ashen, adj. ceniciento, pálido.

ashore, adv. en tierra, a tierra.

Asiatic, n. y adj. asiático, ca.

aside, adv. al lado, aparte.

asinine, adj. estúpido, como un asno.

ask, vt. y vi. preguntar; pedir, rogar; to — a question, hacer una pregunta; to — for, pedir.

askance, adv. al sesgo, oblicuamente; de refilón; sospechosamente.

aslant, adv. oblicuamente.

asleep, adj. dormido; to fall —, dormirse.

asp, n. áspid, m.

asparagus, n. espárrago, m.

aspect, n. aspecto, m.; vista, f.; aire, m.; semblante, m.

aspersion, n. aspersión, f.; difamación, calumnia, f.

asphalt, n. asfalto, m.

asphyxiate, vt. asfixiar.

asphyxiation, n. asfixia, f.

aspirant, n. aspirante, m. y f.; candidato, ta.

aspiration, n. aspiración, f.

aspire, vi. aspirar, desear.

aspirin, n. aspirina, f.

ass, n. borrico, asno, m.

assail, vt. asaltar, atacar, acometer.

assassin, n. asesino, na.

assassinate, vt. asesinar, matar.

assassination, n. asesinato, m.

assault, n. asalto, m.; insulto, m.; —, vt. acometer, asaltar.

assay, n. ensayo, análisis, m., contraste (de monedas, etc.), m.; —, vt. ensayar, copelar.

assemblage, n. multitud, f.; ensambladura, f., empalme, m.

assemble, vt. congregar, convocar; afluir; ensamblar, armar; —, vi. juntarse.

assembling, adj. de ensamble.

assembly, n. asamblea, junta, f.; congreso, m.; montaje, m.; concurso, m.; concurrencia, f.; — line, línea de montaje.

assent, n, asenso, m.; aprobación, f., consentimiento, m.; —, vi. asentir, aprobar.

assert, vt. sostener, mantener; afirmar.

assertion, n. aserción, f.

assess, vt. amillarar, imponer (contribuciones) .

assessment, *n.* amillaramiento, impuesto, *m.;* catastro, *m.*

assessor, *n.* asesor, *m.;* — of taxes, tasador de impuestos.

asset, *n.* algo de valor; ventaja, *f.;* — s, *pl.* (com.) haber, activo, capital, *m.*

assiduous, *adj.* asiduo, aplicado, constante; — ly, *adv.* constantemente; diligentemente.

assign, *vt.* asignar, destinar, fijar.

assignment, *n.* asignación, *f.;* cesión, *f.;* señalamiento, *m;* tarea escolar.

assimilate, *vt.* asimilar; asemejar.

assimilation, *n.* asimilación, *f.*

assist, *vt.* asistir, ayudar, socorrer.

assistance, *n.* asistencia, *f.;* socorro, *m.;* colaboración, *f.*

assistant, *n.* asistente, ayudante, *m.*

assn.: association, asn. asociación.

associate, *vt.* asociar; to — with, acompañar, frecuentar; — , *adj.* asociado; — , *n.* socio, compañero, *m.*

association, *n.* asociación, unión, sociedad, agrupación, *f.;* club, *m.*

assorted, *adj.* clasificado; — goods, artículos variados.

assortment, *n.* surtido, *m.;* variedad, *f.*

asst.: assistant, asistente; ayte., ayudante.

assuage, *vt.* mitigar, suavizar.

assume, *vt.* arrogar, apropiar, presumir; — , *vi.* arrogarse.

assumed, *adj.* supuesto; falso, fingido.

assumption, *n.* presunción, suposición, *f.;* A— , Asunción, *f.*

assurance, *n.* seguridad, certeza, convicción, *f.;* fianza, *f.;* confianza, *f.;* seguro, *m.*

assure, *vt.* asegurar, afirmar; prometer.

assuredly, *adv.* ciertamente, sin duda, de seguro.

asterisk, *n.* asterisco, *m.*

astern, *adv.* (naut.) por la popa.

asthma, *n.* asma, *f.*

asthmatic, *adj.* asmático.

astigmatism, *n.* (med.) astigmatismo, *m.*

astir, *adj.* agitado; activo; levantado de la cama.

astonish, *vt.* pasmar, sorprender.

astonishing, *adj.* asombroso.

astonishment, *n.* pasmo, asombro, *m.;* sorpresa, *f.*

astound, *vt.* consternar, aterrar, pasmar.

astounding, *adj.* asombroso.

astray, *adj.* y *adv.* extraviado, descaminado; en forma descaminada; to lead — , desviar, seducir; to go — , ir por mal camino.

astride, *adj.* sentado a horcajadas.

astringent, *n.* y *adj.* astringente, *m.*

astrobiology, *n.* astrobiología, *f.*

astrology, *n.* astrología, *f.*

astronaut, *n.* astronauta, *m.*

astronavigation, *n.* astronavegación, *f.,* navegación sideral.

astronomer, *n.* astrónomo, *m.*

astronomy, *n.* astronomía, *f.*

astrophysics, *n.* astrofísica, *f.*

astute, *adj.* astuto; aleve.

asunder, *adv.* separadamente, en pedazos.

asylum, *n.* asilo, refugio, *m.;* seno, *m.;* insane — , casa de locos, manicomio, *m.*

at, *prep.* a, en; — once, al instante; en seguida; — all, nada; siempre; — first, al principio; — large, en libertad; — last, al fin, por último; — your service, su servidor o servidora, a sus órdenes.

ate, *pretérito* del verbo eat.

atheist, *n.* ateo, atea.

athlete, *n.* atleta, *m.* y *f.;* —' s foot, (med.) pie de atleta; infección entre los dedos de los pies (generalmente contraída por los atletas en los gimnasios).

athletic, *adj.* atlético, deportista; robusto, vigoroso.

athletics, *n. pl.* deportes, *m. pl.*

at-home, *n.* recepción en casa de carácter sencillo.

athwart, *prep.* contra; al través; — , *adv.* oblicuamente, en contra.

Atlantic, *n.* y *adj.* Atlántico, *m.*

atlas, *n.* atlas, *m.*

A.T.M.: automatic teller machine, cajero automático.

atmosphere, *n.* atmósfera, *f.,* ambiente, *m.*

atom, *n.* átomo, *m.;* — bomb, bomba atómica; — smasher, desintegrador de átomos.

atomic, *adj.* atómico; — energy, energía atómica.

atomize, *vt.* pulverizar; reducir a átomos.

atomizer, *n.* pulverizador, aromatizador, *m.*

atone, *vt.* expiar, aplacar, pagar.

atonement, *n.* expiación, propiciación, *f.*

atop, *prep.* encima de; sobre.

atrocious, *adj.* atroz; enorme; odioso.

atrocity, *n.* atrocidad, enormidad, *f.*

atrophy, *n.* (med.) atrofia, *f.*

att.: attention, atención.

attach, *vt.* pegar, sujetar, fijar; atar, ligar; (leyes) embargar.

attaché, *n.* adjunto o agregado (a alguna legación), *m.*

attachment, *n.* adherencia, *f.;* afecto, *m.;* (leyes) embargo, secuestro, *m.;* aditamento, anexo, *m;* adjunto *(en una comunicación), m.*

attack, *vt.* atacar; acometer; — , *n.* ataque, *m.*

attain, vt. ganar, conseguir, obtener, alcanzar.

attainable, adj. asequible.

attainment, n. logro, m.; realización, f.; consecución de lo que se pretende; — **s,** pl. conocimientos, m. pl; logros, m. pl.

attempt, vt. intentar, probar, experimentar; procurar; — , n. empresa, f.; experimento infructuoso; tentativa, f.; prueba, f.

attend, vt. servir, asistir; acompañar; — , vi. prestar atención.

attendance, n. concurrencia, asistencia, f.; tren, séquito, m.; servicio, m.; cuidado, m.

attendant, n. sirviente, m.; cortejo, m.

attention, n. atención, f.; cuidado, m.; **to attract** — , llamar la atención; **to call** — , hacer presente; **to give** — **to,** ocuparse en o de; **to pay** — , hacer caso, prestar o poner atención; **to pay no** — , no hacer caso.

attentive, adj. atento; cuidadoso; — **ly,** adv. con atención.

attest, vt. atestiguar; dar fe.

attic, n. desván, m.; guardilla, f.

attire, n. atavío, m.; — , vt. adornar, ataviar.

attitude, n. actitud, f., manera de ser; postura, f.

attorney, n. procurador, abogado, m.; (leyes) mandatario, m.

attract, vt. atraer, persuadir; seducir; **to** — **attention,** llamar la atención.

attraction, n. atracción, f.; atractivo, m.

attractive, adj. atractivo, simpático; seductor.

attribute, vt. atribuir, imputar; — , n. atributo, m.

attune, vt. acordar; armonizar.

atty.: attorney, abogado; pror. procurador.

auburn, n. y adj. castaño rojizo.

auction, n. venta pública, subasta, f., remate, m.

auctioneer, n. rematador, subastador, martillero, m.

audacious, adj. audaz, temerario; — **ly,** adv. atrevidamente.

audacity, n. audacia, osadía f.

audible, adj. perceptible al oído; — **bly,** adv. alto, de modo que se pueda oír.

audience, n. audiencia, f.; auditorio, m.; concurrencia, f. oyentes, m. pl.; circunstantes, m. pl.

audiophile, n. audiófilo, m.

audio-visual, adj. audiovisual.

audit, n. remate de una cuenta; auditoría contable; — , vt. rematar una cuenta, examinar; pelotear.

audition, n. audición, f.; — , vt. conceder audición; — , vi. presentar audición.

ᵘᵗor, n. contador, m.; oidor, m.

auditorium, n. anfiteatro, m.; teatro, m.; auditorio, m.; sala de conferencias o diversiones; salón de actos.

auger, n. barrena, f.

aught, n. alguna cosa; cero, m.

augment, vt. aumentar, acrecentar; — , vi. crecer.

August, n. agosto (mes) , m.

august, adj. augusto; majestuoso.

aunt, n. tía, f.

aura, n. aureola, f.; (med.) aura, f.

Aureomycin, n. (trademark) aureomicina, f. (marca registrada).

auricle, n. oreja, f.; aurícula, f

aurora, n. aurora, f.; — **borealis,** aurora boreal.

auspices, n. pl. auspicios, m. pl.; protección, f.

auspicious, adj. próspero, favorable; propicio; — **ly,** adv. prósperamente.

austere, adj. austero, severo, rígido.

austerity, n. austeridad, f.; mortificación, f.; severidad, f.

authentic, adj. auténtico; (leyes) fehaciente.

authenticity, n. autenticidad, f .

author, n. autor, escritor, m.

authoress, n. autora, escritora, f.

authoritative, adj. autoritativo.

authority, n. autoridad f.; férula, f.

authorization, n. autorización, f., permiso, m.

authorize, vt. autorizar; — **d,** adj. autorizado, facultado.

autobiography, n. autobiografía, f.

auto, n. coche, carro, automóvil, m.; — **court,** autohotel, m.

autocracy, n. autocracia, f.

autocrat, n. autócrata, m.

autocratic, autocratical, adj. autocrático.

autogiro, autogyro, n. autogiro, m.

autograph, n. y adj. autógrafo, m.; — , vt. autografiar.

automat, n. restaurante de servicio automático.

automatic, adj. automático.

automation, n. automatización, f.

automaton, n. autómata, m.

automobile, n. automóvil, m.

automotive, adj. automotor, automotriz.

autonomous, adj. autónomo.

autonomy, n. autonomía, f.

autopilot, n. piloto automático.

autopsy, n. autopsia, necroscopia, f.

autumn, n. otoño, m.

autumnal, adj. otoñal.

auxiliary, adj. auxiliar, asistente.

avail, n. aprovechar; — , vi. servir, ser ventajoso; — , n. provecho, m.; ventaja, f.; **to no** — , en vano, sin éxito; — **oneself of,** aprovecharse de.

available, *adj.* accesible; disponible.

avalanche, *n.* avalancha, *f.;* alud, lurte, *m.;* torrente, *m.*

avarice, *n.* avaricia, *f.*

avaricious, *adj.* avaro.

ave.: **avenue,** ay. avenida.

avenge, *vt.* y *vi.* vengarse, castigar; vindicar.

avenger, *n.* vengador, ra.

avenue, *n.* avenida, *f.*

average, *vt.* tomar un término medio; promediar; — , *n.* término medio, promedio, *m.;* **law of — s,** ley de probabilidades, *f.;*(naut.) avería, *f.;* — , *adj.* medio.

aversion, *n.* aversión, *f.,* disgusto, *m.*

avert, *vt.* desviar, apartar; evitar.

aviary, *n.* avería, pajarera, *f.*

aviation, *n.* aviación, *f.*

aviator, *n.* aviador, *m.*

aviatrix, *n.* aviadora, *f.*

avid, *adj.* ávido, codicioso, voraz.

avidity, *n.* codicia, avidez, *f.*

avocado, *n.* aguacate, *m.*

avocation, *n.* ocupación accesoria; diversión, chifladura, *f.;* pasatiempo, *m.;* afición, *f.*

avoid, *vt.* evitar, escapar, huir; (leyes) anular.

avoidable, *adj.* evitable.

avoidance, *n.* evitación, *f.;* anulación, *f.*

avoirdupois, *n.* sistema de pesos vigente en E.U.A. e Inglaterra; (coll.) gordura, obesidad, *f.*

avow, *vt.* confesar, declarar.

await, *vt.* aguardar; **— ing your reply,** en espera de sus noticias.

awake, *vt.* y *vi.* despertar; — , *adj.* despierto; **wide — ,** alerta; completamente despierto.

award, *vt.* juzgar; otorgar, adjudicar; conceder; — , *n.* sentencia, decisión, *f.;* premio, *m.,* adjudicación, *f.*

aware, *adj.* cauto, vigilante; sabedor; enterado; consciente.

away, *adv.* ausente, fuera; *interj.* ¡fuera! ¡quita de ahí! **far and — ,** de mucho, con mucho.

awe, *n.* miedo, pavor, *m.,* temor reverencial; — , *vt.* infundir miedo o temor reverencial, pasmar.

awe-inspiring, *adj.* imponente.

awe-struck, *adj.* aterrado, espantado; embargado por el respeto.

awful, *adj.* tremendo; funesto; horroroso; **— ly,** *adv.* con respeto y veneración; (coll.) muy, excesivamente.

awhile, *adv.* por un rato, por algún tiempo.

awkward, *adj.* tosco, inculto, rudo, desmañado; torpe, poco diestro.

awl, *n.* lesna, *f.*

awning, *n.* (naut.) toldo (para resguardarse del sol), *m.*

ax, axe, *n.* hacha, *f.;* — , *vt.* cortar con hacha; (fig.) eliminar.

axiom, *n.* axioma, *m.*

axis, *n.* eje, *m.;* alianza, *f.*

axle, *n.* eje de una rueda; **— box,** buje, *m.*

axolotl, *n.* (zool.) ajolote, *m.*

aye, ay, *adv.* sí; — , *n.* voto afirmativo.

azalea, *n.* (bot.) azalea, *f.*

Aztec, *n.* y *adj.* azteca, *m.* y *f.*

azure, *adj.* azulado; — , *n.* color cerúleo.

B

b.: **book,** 1. libro; **born,** *n.* nacido.

B.A.: **Bachelor of Arts,** Br. en A. Bachiller en Artes.

babble, *vi.* charlar, parlotear; **— o babbling,** *n.* charla, *f.;* murmullo (de un arroyo), *m.*

babe, *n.* niño pequeño, nene, infante, bebé, *m.*

babel, *n.* babel, *m.* o *f.,* confusión, *f.*

babushka, *n.* pañoleta, *f.*

baby, *n.* niño pequeño, nene, infante, *m.;* **— boy,** nene, *m.;* **— girl,** nena, *f.*

babyhood, *n.* niñez, infancia, *f.*

babyish, *adj.* pueril, infantil, como niño chiquito.

baby-sit, *vi.* cuidar niños ocasionalmente, servir de niñera.

baby-sitter, *n.* cuidaniños, *m.* o *f.,* persona que cuida niños ajenos mientras los padres van de visita, al cine, etc.

baccalaureate, *n.* bachillerato, *m.*

bachelor, *n.* soltero, *m.;* bachiller, *m.*

bacillus, *n.* bacilo, microbio, *m.*

back, *n.* dorso, *m.;* espalda, *f.;* lomo, *m.;* revés (de la mano), *m.;* **— of a book,** lomo, *m.;* **to turn one's — ,** dar la espalda; — , adj. posterior; — **seat,** asiento trasero; — , vt. sostener, apoyar, favorecer; **to** — **up,** recular; apoyar; — , adv. atrás, detrás; **to come** — , regresar; **a few years** — , hace algunos años; **to fall** — , hacerse atrás; **to go** — **to,** remontar a; — **of,** detrás, tras de.

backbone, n. hueso dorsal, espinazo, m., espina, f.; (fig.) firmeza, decisión, f.

backdoor, n. puerta trasera.

backer, n. partidario, sostenedor, m.

backfield, n. los jugadores detrás de la línea en el juego de fútbol.

backfire, vi. abrir claros mediante fuego para contener un incendio; (mech.) producirse explosiones prematuras en cilindros o tubos de escape.

backgammon, n. juego de chaquete o tablas.

background, n. fondo, m.; ambiente, m.; antecedentes, m. pl., educación, f.

backlog, n. tronco trasero en una hoguera; (com.) reserva de pedidos pendientes.

backspin, n. retruque, m.

backstage, n. (theat.) parte detrás del telón o detrás de bastidores.

back stairs, n. pl. escalera trasera, escalera secreta.

backstop, n. reja para detener la pelota en el juego de béisbol; receptor, catcher, m.

backstroke, n. reculada, f.; revés, m.; movimiento propulsor nadando de espalda.

backward, adj. opuesto; retrógrado; retrospectivo; tardo, lento; **to be** — , ser tímido; — **s,** adv. de espaldas, hacia atrás.

bacon, n. tocino, m.

bacteria, n. pl. bacterias, f. pl.

bacteriology, n. bacteriología, f.

bad, adj. mal, malo; perverso; infeliz; dañoso; indispuesto; vicioso; **to look** — , tener mala cara.

badge, n. señal, f.; símbolo, m.; divisa, f.

badger, n. tejón, m.; — , vt. fatigar; cansar, atormentar; **to** — **with questions,** importunar con preguntas.

bad-tempered, adj. de mal humor, de mal carácter.

baffle, vt. eludir; confundir, hundir.

bag, n. saco, m.; bolsa, f.; talego, m.

baggage, n. equipaje, m.; — **car,** furgón, m., coche o carro de equipajes, vagón, m.; — **check,** talón, m.; — **master,** jefe de equipajes; — **room,** sala de equipajes.

bagpipe, n. (mus.) gaita, f.

bail, n. fianza, caución (juratoria) , f.; fiador, m.; recaudo, m.; **to go** — **for,** salir fiador; — , vt. caucionar, fiar; salir fiador, dar fianza; **to give** — , sanear; **on**

—, bajo fianza; **to** — **out,** vaciar; (avi.) descender en paracaídas.

bailiff, n. alguacil, m.; mayordomo, m.

bait, vt. cebar; azuzar; atraer; — , n. cebo, m.; anzuelo, m.; carnada, f.

bake, vt. cocer en horno.

bakelite, n. baquelita, f.

baker, n. hornero, panadero, m.

bakery, n. panadería, f.

baking, n. hornada, f.; — **powder,** polvo de hornear; — **soda,** bicarbonato de sosa.

bal.: **balance,** saldo.

balance, n. balanza, f.; equilibrio, m.; resto, m.; balance, m.; saldo de una cuenta; — **sheet,** balance, m.; **credit** — , saldo acreedor; **debit** — , saldo deudor; **net** — , saldo líquido; **to lose one's** — , caerse, perder el equilibrio; — **of power,** equilibrio político; — **of trade,** balanza comercial; — , vt. pesar en balanza; contrapesar; saldar; considerar; examinar; **to** — **an account,** cubrir una cuenta.

balcony, n. balcón, m.; galería, f.; anfiteatro, m.

bald, adj. calvo; simple, desabrido.

baldness, n. calvicie, f.

bale, n. bala, f.; fardo de mercaderías; paca, f.; — , vt. embalar; tirar el agua del bote.

baling, n. embalaje, m.; — , adj. relativo al embalaje; — **machine,** empaquetadora, f.

balk, vi. rebelarse (un caballo, etc.); resistirse.

ball, n. bola, f.; pelota, f.; bala, f.; baile, m.; — **bearing,** cojinete de bolas; — **point pen,** pluma atómica, bolígrafo, m.

ballad, n. balada, f.; romance m.

ballast, n. lastre, m.; (rail.) balasto, m.; — , vt. lastrar.

ballerina, n. bailarina, f.

ballet, n. ballet, m.

ballistic, adj. balístico; — **missile,** proyectil balístico.

ballistics, n. balística, f.

balloon, n. globo, m.; máquina aerostática; — **tire,** neumático o llanta balón.

ballot, n. cédula para votar; boleto electoral; escrutinio, m.; papeleta, balota, f.; — vi. votar con balotas; — **box,** urna electoral.

ballplayer, n. jugador de pelota.

ballroom, n. salón de baile.

ballyhoo, n. alharaca, f., aspaviento, m.; bombo, m., exagerada publicidad (a un espectáculo).

balm, n. bálsamo, m.

balmy, adj. balsámico; fragante; suave, agradable.

balsam, n. bálsamo, m.

balustrade, n. balaustrada, f.

bamboo, n. bambú, m.

bamboozle, vt. (coll.) engañar, embaucar.

ban, n. bando, anuncio, m.; excomunión, f.; proclama, f.; prohibición, f.; — , vt. prohibir, vedar; excomulgar; maldecir.

banal, adj. trivial.

banality, n. trivialidad, f.

banana, n. plátano, m., banana, f., banano, guineo, cambur, m.

band, n. venda, faja, f.; unión, f.; cuadrilla, f.; charanga, banda (de soldados), f.; orquesta, f.; — , vt. unir, juntar; vendar.

bandage, n. venda, faja, f.; vendaje, m.; — , vt. vendar, fajar.

bandanna, n. pañoleta, f., pañuelo grande de colores.

bandit, n. bandido, da.

bandstand, n. plataforma de banda, quiosco de música.

bandwagon, n. vehículo para banda de música; to get on the — , (pol.) adherirse a una candidatura probablemente triunfante; unirse a un grupo.

bane, n. destrucción, f.; azote, m.

bang, n. puñada, f.; puñetazo, m.; ruido de un golpe; — s, flequillo (del cabello), m.; — , vt. dar puñadas, sacudir; cerrar con violencia; — ! interj. ¡ pum!

bangle, n. brazalete, m., ajorca, f.

banish, vt. desterrar, echar fuera, proscribir, expatriar.

banishment, n. destierro, m.

banister, n. pasamano, m., baranda, f.

banjo, n. banjo (variedad de guitarrilla), m.

bank, n. orilla (de río), ribera, f.; montón de tierra; banco, cambio, m.; dique, m.; escollo, m.; — balance, saldo bancario; — book, libreta de banco o de depósitos; blood — , banco de sangre; savings— , banco de ahorros; — , vt. poner dinero en un banco; detener el agua con diques; (avi.) banquear; escorar.

banker, n. banquero, cambista, m.

banking, n. banca, f.; — , adj. bancario; — house, casa de banca.

bankrupt, adj. insolvente; quebrado, en bancarrota; — , n. fallido, m., persona en bancarrota.

bankruptcy, n. bancarrota, quiebra, f.

banner, n. bandera, f.; estandarte, m.

banquet, n. banquete, m., comida suntuosa; — , vt. y vi. banquetear.

bantamweight, n. peso gallo (en el boxeo) .

banter, vt. zumbar; divertirse a costa de alguno; — , n. zumba, burla, f.

baptism, n. bautismo, bautizo, m.

baptize, vt. bautizar.

bar, n. barra, f.; tranca, f.; obstáculo, m.;

(leyes) estrados, m. pl.; aparador, m.; cantina, f.; barrera, f.; palanca, f.; — s, pl. rejas, f. pl.; in — s, en barra o en barras; — , vt. barrear; cerrar con barras; impedir; prohibir; excluir; — , prep. excepto; — none, sin excluir a nadie.

barb, n. púa, f.

barbarian, n. hombre bárbaro; — , adj. bárbaro, cruel.

barbarism, n. (gram.) barbarismo, m.; crueldad, f.; barbaridad, f.

barbarous, adj. bárbaro, cruel.

barbecue, n. barbacoa, f.; — pit, asador, m.

barbed, adj. barbado; — wire, alambre de púas.

barber, n. barbero, peluquero, m.

barbershop, n. peluquería, barbería, f.

barbital, n. barbital, m.

barbiturate, n. barbitúrico, m.

bare, adj. desnudo, descubierto; simple; pobre; puro; — , vt. desnudar;descubrir.

bareback (horseback riding), adj. en cerro o en pelo (al montar a caballo).

barefoot, barefooted, adj. descalzo, sin zapatos.

bareheaded, adj. descubierto, con la cabeza al aire.

barelegged, adj. con las piernas desnudas, sin medias.

barely, adv. apenas, solamente; pobremente.

bargain, n. contrato, pacto, m.; ganga, f.; — , vi. pactar, negociar; regatear.

barge, n. chalupa, f.; barcaza, f.

baritone, n. (mus.) barítono, m.

barium, n. (chem.) bario, m.

bark, n. corteza, f.; ladrido (del perro), m.; — , vt. descortezar; — , vi. ladrar.

barkeeper, n. tabernero, cantinero, m.

barker, m. charlatán de feria, m.

barley, n. cebada, f.

barmaid, n. moza de taberna.

barn, n. granero, pajar, m.; establo, m.

barnyard, n. patio de granja, corral, m.

barometer, n. barómetro, m.

baron, n. barón, m.; (coll.) poderoso industrial.

baroness, n. baronesa, f.

baronet, n. título de honor inferior al de barón y superior al de caballero.

baroque, adj. (arch.) barroco.

barrack, n. cuartel, m.; barraca, f.

barrage, n. cortina de fuego; presa de contención; — balloon, globo de barrera.

barrel, n. barril, m.; cañón de escopeta;cilindro, m.; — , vt. embarrilar.

barren, adj. estéril, infructuoso; seco.

barricade, n. barricada, f.; estacada, f.; barrera, f.; — , vt. cerrar con barreras, empalizar; atrincherar.

barrier, n. barrera, f.; obstáculo, m.; **sound** — , barrera sónica.

barring, prep. excepto, fuera de.

barrister, n. abogado, m.

barroom, n. taberna, cantina, f.

bartender, n. tabernero, cantinero, m.

barter, vi. permutar, traficar; — , vt. cambiar, trocar; — , n. cambio, trueque, m.

basal, adj. básico, fundamental; — **metabolism,** metabolismo basal.

base, n. fondo, m.; basa, base, f.; pedestal, m.; contrabajo, m.; pie, m.; — , vt.apoyar; basar; — , adj. bajo, vil.

baseball, n. béisbol, m.; pelota de béisbol; juego de béisbol.

baseboard, n. tabla que sirve de base; friso, m.

baseless, adj. sin fondo o base.

basement, n. sótano, m.

baseness, n. bajeza, vileza, f.; ilegitimidad de nacimiento; mezquindad, f.

bashful, adj. vergonzoso, modesto, tímido.

bashfulness, n. vergüenza, modestia, timidez, cortedad, esquivez, f.

basic, adj. fundamental, básico.

basin, n. palangana, vasija, f.; cuenca (de un río), f.

basis, n. base, f.; fundamento, m., suposición, f.; pie, m.

bask, vi. exponerse (al sol); **to — in the sunshine,** ponerse a tomar el sol.

basket, n. cesta, canasta .

basketball, n. básquetbol , baloncesto, m.

Basque, n. y adj. vasco, ca.

bass, n. estera, f.; esparto, m.; (ichth.) lobina, f., róbalo o robalo, m.

bass n. (mus.) bajo, m.; tono bajo y profundo; — , adj. (mus.) bajo; — **drum,** bombo, m.; — **horn,** tuba, f.; — **viol,** violón, contrabajo, m.

bassinet, n. cesta cuna, cuna, f.; (Mex.) moisés, m.

basso, n. (mus.) bajo, m.

bassoon, n. (mus.) bajón, m.

bastard, n. y adj. bastardo, da.

baste, vt. pringar la carne en el asador; hilvanar; bastear.

basting, n. hilván, m.

bat, n. bate, garrote, palo, m.; murciélago, m.; — , vt. batear, golpear a la pelota.

bat.: battalion, bat. batallón; **battery,** bat. batería.

batch, n. hornada, f.; cantidad de cosas producidas a un tiempo; pilada, f.; carga, f.; colada, f.; (Arg.) past n, m.; (Cuba) templa, f.; (Mex.) turno de colada.

bath, n. baño, m.

bathe, vt. y vi. bañar, bañarse.

bathhouse, n. balneario, m.

bathing, n. baño, m.; — **beach,** playa para baño, balneario, m.; — **resort,** balneario, m.

bathrobe, n. peinador, m., bata, f.

bathroom, n. cuarto de baño, m.

bathtub, n. bañera, tina de baño, f.

bathyscaphe, n. batiscafo, m.

baton, n. batuta, f.

battalion, n. (mil.) batallón, m.

batter, n. batido, m.; pasta culinaria; bateador, voleador (de la pelota), m.; — , vt. apalear; batir; cañonear; demoler.

battery, n. acumulador, m.; batería, f.; pila, f.; — **box,** caja de batería; — **cell,** elemento de batería; **dry** — , batería o pila seca; **storage** — , batería de acumuladores.

battle, n. batalla, f.; combate, m.; — **front,** frente de combate; **sham** — , simulacro, m.; — , vi. batallar, combatir; — **cry,** grito de batalla; — **ground,** campo de batalla; — **royal,** pelotera, f.

battlefield, n. campo de batalla.

battleship, n. acorazado, m.

bauble, n. chuchería, f.

bawl, vi. gritar, vocear; ladrar.

bay, n. bahía, f.; laurel, lauro, m.; — **rum,** agua olorosa que sirve de cosmético; — **window,** mirador, m.; ventana salediza; — , vi. ladrar; balar; — , adj. bayo; **to keep at — ,** tener a raya.

bayonet, n. bayoneta, f.; — , vt. traspasar con la bayoneta.

bazaar, n. bazar, m.

bazooka, n. cañón portátil contra tanques.

bbl.: barrel, brl. barril.

B.C.: **Before Christ,** A. de J.C. antes de Jesucristo.

bdl.: **bundle,** bto. bulto o f/ fardo.

be, vi. ser; estar; quedar; **to — ill,** estar malo, estar enfermo; **to — in a hurry,** estar de prisa; **to — right,** tener razón; **to — well,** estar bien o bueno.

beach, n. costa, ribera, orilla, playa, f.; — **comber,** vagabundo de las playas, m.; — , vt. y vi. (naut.) encallar.

beachhead, n. (mil.) cabeza de playa.

beacon, n. fanal, faro, m.

bead, n. cuenta, chaquira, f.; — **s,** n. pl. rosario, m.

beaded, adj. adornado con cuentas o chaquiras.

beagle, n. sabueso, m.

beak, n. pico, m.; espolón de navío.

beam, n. viga, f.; rayo de luz; volante, m.; brazos de balanza; **to fly on the — ,** volar siguiendo la línea de radiación; —

of timber, madero, *m.;* —, *vi.* emitir rayos, brillar.
beaming, *adj.* radiante.
bean, *n.* (bot.) haba, habichuela, *f.;* frijol, *m.;* **kidney** — **s,** frijoles rojos o colorados; **navy** — **s,** frijoles blancos.
bear, *n.* oso, *m.;* bajista (en la bolsa), *m.;* **she** —, osa, *f.;* —, *vt.* llevar alguna cosa como carga; sostener; apoyar; soportar; producir; parir; conllevar, portar; —, *vi.* sufrir (algún dolor); tolerar; —, *vt. y vi.* resistir; **to** — **a grudge,** guardar rencor; **to** — **in mind,** tener presente, tener en cuenta.
beard, *n.* barba, *f.;* arista de espiga; —, *vt.* desafiar.
bearded, *adj.* barbado; barbudo.
beardless, *adj.* desbarbado, joven, imberbe.
bearer, *n.* portador, ra; árbol fructífero.
bearing, *n.* situación, *f.* ; comportamiento, *m.;* relación, *f.;* sufrimiento, *m.,* paciencia, *f.;* (mech.) cojinete, *m.*
beast, *n.* bestia, *f.;* bruto, *m.;* res, *f.;* hombre brutal; — **of burden,** acémila, *f.*
beastly, *adj.* bestial, brutal; —, *adv.* brutalmente.
beat, *vt.* golpear; batir; tocar (un tambor); pisar; abatir; ganar (en un juego) ; —, *vi.* pulsar, palpitar; —, *n.* golpe, *m.;* pulsación, *f.;* ronda, *f.*
beater, *n.* batidor, *m.,* batidora, *f.*
beating, *n.* paliza, zurra, *f.;* pulsación, *f.*
beatnik, *n.* bohemio estrafalario de los E.U.A.
beau, *n.* petimetre, currutaco, *m.;* novio, pretendiente, *m.*
beauteous, *adj.* bello, hermoso.
beautiful, *adj.* hermoso, bello; precioso; — **ly,** *adv.* con belleza o perfección.
beautify, *vt.* hermosear, embellecer; adornar; —, *vi.* hermosearse.
beauty, *n.* hermosura, belleza, *f.;* preciosidad, *f.;* — **parlor,** — **salon,** salón de belleza; — **spot,** lunar (que embellece), *m.*
beaver, *n.* castor, *m.;* sombrero de pelo de castor; — **board,** cartón de fibras para techos interiores y tabiques.
becalm, *vt.* serenar, sosegar.
because, *conj.* porque; pues; que; — **of,** a causa de.
beck, *n.* seña, *f.,* indicación muda; **at one's** — **and call,** a la mano, a la disposición.
beckon, *vi.* hacer seña con la cabeza o la mano, llamar con señas.
become, *vt.* sentar, quedar bien; —, *vi.* hacerse, convertirse; ponerse; llegar a ser.
becoming, *adj.* conveniente; que le queda

bien a uno.
bed, *n.* cama, *f.;* (geol.) yacimiento, *m.;* — **sheet,** sábana, *f.;* **folding** —, cama plegadiza; **river** —, cauce, *m.;* **to make the** —, hacer la cama; **to stay in** —, guardar cama; —, *vt.* acostar, meter en la cama.
bedbug, *n.* chinche, *f.*
bedclothes, *n. pl.* cobertores, *m. pl.,* mantas, colchas, f. pl.
bedding, *n.* ropa de cama; accesorios de cama.
bedeck, *vt.* adornar.
bedlam, *n.* belén, *m.,* algarabía, *f.;* confusión, *f.*
bedpan, *n.* silleta para enfermos.
bedpost, *n.* pilar de cama.
bedraggle, *vt.* ensuciar arrastrando por el suelo.
bedridden, *adj.* postrado en cama (sea por vejez o enfermedad).
bedroom, *n.* alcoba, *f.,* cuarto de dormir, dormitorio, *m.,* recámara, *f.*
bedside, *n.* lado de la cama; cabecera, *f.*
bedspread, *n.* colcha, sobrecama, *f.*
bedspring, *n.* colchón de muelles.
bedtime, *n.* hora de acostarse.
bee, *n.* abeja, *f.*
beech, *n.* (bot.) haya, *f.*
beechnut, *n.* hayuco, *m.*
beef, *n.* buey, toro, *m.;* vaca, *f.;* carne de res o de vaca.
beefsteak, *n.* bistec, *m.*
beehive, *n.* colmena, *f.*
beeline, *n.* línea recta; **to make a** — **for,** apresurarse a llegar a algún lugar (por la línea más recta).
been, *p.p.* del verbo **be.**
beer, *n.* cerveza, *f.*
beeswax, *n.* cera de abejas.
beet, *n.* remolacha, betarraga, *f.;* (Mex.) betabel, *m.;* — **root,** betarraga, *f.;* — **sugar,** azúcar de remolacha.
beetle, *n.* escarabajo, *m.;* pisón, *m.*
befall, *vi.* suceder, acontecer, sobrevenir.
befit, *vt.* convenir, acomodarse a, cuadrar.
before, *adv.* más adelante; delante, enfrente; ante, antes de; —, *prep.* antes de, ante; delante de, enfrente de; —, *conj.* antes que.
beforehand, *adv.* de antemano, con anterioridad, anticipadamente.
befriend, *vt.* favorecer, proteger, amparar.
beg, *vt.* mendigar, rogar; suplicar; pedir; —, *vi.* vivir de limosna.
began, *pretérito* del verbo **begin.**
beget, *vt.* engendrar.
beggar, *n.* mendigo, ga; limosnero, ra.
beggarly, *adj.* pobre, miserable; despreciable.

begin, vt. y vi. comenzar, principiar.

beginner, n. principiante, m. y f., novicio, cia.

beginning, n. principio, comienzo, m.; origen, m.; — s, pl. rudimentos, m. pl.; **at the** — , al principio; — **with,** a partir de.

begrudge, vt. envidiar.

beguile, vt. engañar.

begun, p.p. del verbo **begin.**

behalf, n. favor, patrocinio, m.; consideración, f.; **on** — **of,** en pro de.

behave, vi. comportarse, portarse (bien o mal), manejarse.

behavior, n. conducta, f.; proceder, m.; comportamiento, m.

behead, vt. decapitar; descabezar.

behind, prep. detrás de, tras; en zaga a, inferior a; **from** — , por detrás; — , adv. detrás, atrás; atrasadamente.

behold, vt. ver, contemplar, observar; — !interj. ¡he aquí! ¡mira!

beige, n. color entre rojo y amarillo o entre gris y pardo, color arena.

being, n. existencia, f.; estado, m.; ente, m.; persona, f.

belated, adj. demorado, atrasado.

belch, vi. eructar, vomitar; — , n. eructo, m., eructación, f.

belfry, n. campanario, m.

Belgian, n. y adj. belga, m. y f.

Belgium, Bélgica, f.

belie, vt. desmentir; desdecir, contrastar con.

belief, n. fe, creencia, f.; opinión, f.; credo, m.

believable, adj. creíble.

believe, vt. creer; — , vi. pensar, imaginar.

believer, n. creyente, fiel, cristiano, m.

belittle, vt. dar poca importancia (a algo).

bell, n. campana, f.; bronce, m.; — **ringer,** campanero, m.; **call** — , timbre, m.

bellboy, n. botones, m., mozo de hotel.

belle, n. beldad, f.

bellhop = **bellboy.**

belligerent, adj. beligerante.

bellow, vi. bramar; rugir; vociferar; — , n. bramido, m.

bellowing, adj. rugiente.

bellows, n. fuelle, m.

belly, n. vientre, m.; panza, barriga, f.

belong, vi. pertenecer, tocar a, concernir.

belongings, n. pl. propiedad, f.; efectos, anexos, m. pl.

beloved, adj. querido, amado.

below, adv. y prep. debajo, inferior; abajo.

belt, n. cinturón, cinto, m.; correa, f.; cintura, f.; **to hit below the** — , (boxeo) dar un golpe bajo; (fig.) herir con saña; **to**

tighten one's — , tomar aliento, soportar.

bemoan, vt. deplorar, lamentar.

bench, n. banco, m.; tribunal, m.

bend, vt. encorvar, inclinar, plegar; combar; hacer una reverencia; — , vi. encorvarse; combarse; cimbrarse; inclinarse; — , n. comba, encorvadura, f.; codo, m.; giro, m.

beneath, adv. y prep. debajo, abajo; de lo más hondo.

benediction, n. bendición, f.

benefactor, n. bienhechor, ra.

beneficent, adj. benéfico.

beneficial, adj. beneficioso, provechoso, útil.

beneficiary, n. beneficiario, ria.

benefit, n. beneficio, m.; utilidad, f.; provecho, m.; bien, m.; **for the** — **of,** a beneficio de; — **of clergy,** sanción de la iglesia; — , vt. beneficiar; — , vi. beneficiarse; prevalerse.

benevolence, n. benevolencia, gracia, f.

benevolent, adj. benévolo; — **society,** sociedad benéfica.

benign, adj. benigno; afable; liberal.

bent, n. inclinación, tendencia, f.

benumb, vt. entorpecer, dejar sin movimiento.

benzene, n. (chem.) bencina, f.

bequeath, vt. legar en testamento.

bequest, n. legado, m.

berate, vt. regañar con vehemencia.

bereave, vt. despojar, privar.

bereavement, n. despojo, m.; luto, duelo, m.

bereft, adj. despojado, privado.

beret, n. boina, f.

berkelium, n. elemento radiactivo artificial.

berry, n. baya, f.

berth, n. litera, f.; camarote, m.

beseech, vt. suplicar, implorar, conjurar, rogar.

beset, vt. sitiar; cercar; perseguir; acosar; aturdir, confundir.

besetting, adj. habitual (aplícase al peligro o al pecado).

beside, prep. al lado de; cerca de, junto a; en comparación con; — **oneself,** fuera de sí, trastornado.

besides, adv. por otra parte, además; — , prep. además de.

besiege, vt. sitiar, bloquear; acosar.

besmirch, vt. manchar, ensuciar.

bespeak, vt. ordenar, apalabrar alguna cosa.

best, adj. mejor; — **man,** padrino de boda; — **seller,** éxito de librería; — , n. lo mejor; **to do one's** — , hacer todo lo posible.

bestial, adj. bestial, brutal.
bestow, vt. dar, conferir; otorgar; dar en matrimonio; regalar; dedicar; — upon, deparar.
bet, n. apuesta, f.; — , vt. apostar.
beta ray, n. rayo beta, m.
betatron, n. betatrón, m.
betray, vt. hacer traición, traicionar; divulgar algún secreto.
betrayal, n. traición, f.
betroth, vt. contraer esponsales; desposarse; to become — ed, prometerse.
betrothal, n. esponsales, m. pl.
betrothed, adj. comprometido, prometido; — , n. prometido, da.
better, adj. y adv. mejor; más bien; — half, cara mitad; so much the — , tanto mejor; — s, n. pl. superiores, m. pl.; — , vt. mejorar, reformar.
bettor, better, n. apostador, ra.
between, betwixt, prep. entre, en medio de.
bevatron, n. bevatrón, m.
bevel, n. cartabón, m.; sesgadura, f.; bisel, m.; — , vt. cortar un ángulo al sesgo, biselar.
beverage, n. bebida, f.
bevy, n. bandada (de aves), f.; grupo (de mujeres), m.
bewail, vt. y vi. lamentar, deplorar.
beware, vi. tener cuidado, guardarse; — ! interj. ¡cuidado! ¡mira!
bewilder, vt. descaminar; pasmar; — , vi. extraviarse; confundirse.
bewilderment, n. extravío, m.; confusión, f.
bewitch, vt. encantar, hechizar.
bewitching, adj. encantador, cautivador.
beyond, prep. más allá, más adelante, fuera de.
bf.: bold face, (print.) letra negrilla.
biannual, adj. semestral, semianual.
bias, n. propensión, inclinación, parcialidad, f.; preocupación, f.; sesgo, m.; objeto, fin, m.; on the — , al sesgo; to cut on the — , sesear; — , vt. inclinar; preocupar; predisponer.
biased, adj. predispuesto.
bib, n. babero m.
Bible, n. Biblia (la sagrada escritura), f.
Biblical, adj. bíblico.
bibliography, n. bibliografía, f.
bicarbonate, n. bicarbonato, m.
biceps, n. bíceps, m.
bicker, vi. reñir, disputar.
bicycle, n. bicicleta, f.; to ride a — , montar en bicicleta.
bicycling, n. ciclismo, m.
bid, vt. convidar; mandar; envidar; ofrecer; — adieu to, despedirse; — , n. licitación, oferta, f.; envite, m.

bidder, n. licitador, postor, m.
bidding, n. orden, f., mandato, m.; ofrecimiento, m.
bide, vi. esperar, aguardar; permanecer; — , vt. sufrir, aguantar.
biennial, adj. bienal.
bier, n. féretro, ataúd, m.
big, adj. grande, lleno; inflado; B— Dipper, (ast.) Osa Mayor, f.
bigamist, n. bígamo, ma.
bigamy, n. bigamia, f.
big-headed, adj. cabezón, cabezudo.
bighearted, adj. generoso, liberal, espléndido, magnánimo.
bigness, n. grandeza, f.
bigot, n. persona fanática; hipócrita, m. y f.
bigoted, adj. santurrón, intolerante.
bigotry, n. fanatismo, m.; intolerancia, f.
bile, n. bilis, f.; cólera, f.
bilingual, adj. bilingüe.
bill, n. pico de ave; cédula, f.; cuenta, factura, f.; — of exchange, cédula o letra de cambio; — of fare, menú, m., lista de platos, f.; — of health, patente de sanidad; — of lading, carta de porte, declaración, f.; conocimiento, m.; — of sale, acta o contrato o escritura de venta; — s payable, documentos o efectos por pagar; — s receivable, documentos por cobrar, letras o efectos por cobrar; post no — s, no fijar carteles; show — , cartelón, m.; — , vt. enviar una cuenta, facturar.
billboard, n. cartelera, f.
billet, n. billete, m.; esquela, f.; (mil.) orden de alojamiento; — , vt. alojar soldados.
billfold, n. billetera, f., cartera de bolsillo.
billiards, n. billar, m.
billion, n. billón, m., millón de millones (en España, Inglaterra, y Alemania); mil millones (en Francia y los Estados Unidos) .
billionaire, n. billonario, ria.
billow, n. ola grande.
billowy, adj. hinchado como las olas, ondulado.
bimonthly, adj. bimestral.
bin, n. artesón, m.; armario, m., despensa, f.
bind, vt. atar; unir; encuadernar; obligar, constreñir; impedir; poner a uno a servir; — , vi. ser obligatorio.
binder, n. encuadernador, m.
binding, n. venda, faja, f.; encuadernación, f.; pasta (para libros), f.; cardboard — , encuadernación de cartón; cloth — , encuadernación en tela.
bingo, n. variedad de lotería de cartones.

binocular, *adj.* binocular; **— s,** *n. pl.* gemelos, lentes, binóculos, *m. pl.*

biochemistry, *n.* bioquímica, *f.*

biographical, *adj.* biográfico.

biography, *n.* biografía, *f.*

biological, *adj.* biológico; **— warfare,** guerra biológica.

biology, *n.* biología, *f.*

bipartisan, *adj.* representativo de dos partidos políticos.

birch, *n.* (bot.) abedul, *m.*

bird, *n.* ave, *f.;* pájaro, *m.;* **— of prey,** ave de rapiña; **— shot,** perdigones, *m. pl.*

birdie, *n.* tanto de un golpe menos de par en un agujero (en el juego de golf).

bird's-eye view, *n.* vista a vuelo de pájaro.

birth, *n.* nacimiento, *m.;* origen, *m.;* parto, *m.;* linaje, *m.;* **— certificate,** certificado o acta de nacimiento; **— control,** control de la natalidad; **— rate,** natalidad, *f.;* **to give —** , dar a luz, parir.

birthday, *n.* cumpleaños, natalicio, *m.;* **to have a —** , cumplir años.

birthmark, *n.* lunar, *m.,* marca de nacimiento.

birthplace, *n.* suelo nativo, lugar de nacimiento.

birthright, *n.* derechos de nacimiento; primogenitura, *f.*

birthstone, *n.* piedra preciosa correspondiente al mes en que uno ha nacido.

Biscay, Vizcaya, *f.*

biscuit, *n.* bizcocho, bollo, *m.;* galleta, *f.*

bisect, *vt.* bisecar, dividir en dos partes; **—** , *vi.* bifurcarse.

bishop, *n.* obispo, *m.;* alfil (en el ajedrez), *m.*

bison, *n.* bisonte, búfalo, *m.*

bit, *n.* bocado, *m.;* pedacito, *m.;* pizca, *f.;* triza, *f.;* brote, *m.;* trozo, *m.;* **two — s** (coll. E.U.A.) 25â (moneda de E.U.A.) ; **—** , *vt.* refrenar; **—** , *pretérito* del verbo **bite.**

bitch, *n.* perra, *f.;* (coll.) zorra, ramera, *f.*

bite, *vt.* morder; punzar, picar; satirizar; engañar; **— the dust,** caer muerto; (fig.) quedar totalmente derrotado; **—** , *n.* tentempié, *m.*

biting, *adj.* mordaz, acre, picante.

bitten, *p.p.* del verbo **bite.**

bitter, *adj.* amargo, áspero; mordaz, satírico.

bitterness, *n.* amargor, *m.;* amargura, *f.;* rencor, *m.;* pena, *f.;* dolor, *m.*

bituminous, *adj.* bituminoso; **— coal,** carbón bituminoso.

bivouac, *n.* (mil.) vivac, vivaque, *m.*

biweekly, *adj.* quincenal, que sucede cada dos semanas; **—** , *adv.* quincenalmente.

bizarre, *adj.* raro, extravagante.

bk.: bank, Bco. banco; **block,** manzana, cuadra (de una ciudad) ; bloque; **book,** 1. libro.

bkg.: banking, banca.

bkt.: basket, cesta.

B.L.: Bachelor of Laws, Br. en L. Bachiller en Leyes.

B/L, b.l: bill of lading, contó, conocimiento de embarque.

bl.: bale, B/bala, f/fardo; **barrel,** brl. barril.

blab, *vt.* parlar, charlar, divulgar; **—** , *vi.* chismear; **—** , *n.* chismoso, sa.

black, *adj.* negro, oscuro; tétrico, malvado; funesto; **— art,** nigromancia, *f.;* **— lead,** lápiz de plomo; **— letter,** letra gótica; **— list,** lista negra, lista de personas que merecen censura; **— magic,** magia que aspira a producir muerte o daño; **— market,** mercado negro; **— sheep,** hijo malo, oveja negra; **— widow,** araña americana, capulina; **—** , *n.* color negro; **—** , *vt.* teñir de negro, negrecer; limpiar (las botas).

blackball, *vt.* excluir a uno votando con una bolita negra; jugar la suerte con una bola negra; votar en contra.

blackberry, *n.* zarzamora, mora, *f .*

blackbird, *n.* mirlo, *m.*

blackboard, *n.* pizarra, *f.,* encerado, pizarrón, tablero, *m.*

blacken, *vt.* teñir de negro; ennegrecer.

blackhead, *n.* espinilla, *f.*

blackmail, *n.* chantaje, *m.;* **—** , *vt.* chantajear, amenazar con chantaje.

blackness, *n.* negrura, *f.*

blackout, *n.* oscurecimiento, *m.*

blacksmith, *n.* herrero, *m.*

bladder, *n.* vejiga, *f.*

blade, *n.* brizna, hoja, *f.;* pala (de remo), *f.;* valentón, *m.;* **— of a propeller,** aleta, *f.*

blame, *vt.* vituperar; culpar; achacar; **—** , *n.* culpa, vituperación, imputación, *f.*

blameless, *adj.* inocente, irreprensible, intachable, puro.

blameworthy, *adj.* culpable.

blanch, *vt.* blanquear; mondar, pelar; hacer pálido.

bland, *adj.* blando, suave, dulce, apacible, gentil, agradable, sutil.

blank, *adj.* blanco; pálido; confuso, vacío, sin interés; **— cartridge,** cartucho en blanco; **— check,** cheque en blanco; **— credit,** carta en blanco; **— form,** blanco, esqueleto, *m.;* **— verse,** verso sin rima; **—** , *n.* blanco, *m.,* espacio en blanco.

blanket, *n.* cubierta de cama, frazada, manta, *f.,* cobertor, *m;* **—** , *adj.* general; **— instructions,** instrucciones generales.

blare, *vt.* proclamar ruidosamente.

blarney, *n.* lenguaje adulador; zalamería,

blasé, *adj.* insensible al placer; hastiado, aburrido.

blaspheme, *vt. y vi.* blasfemar; jurar.

blasphemy, *n.* blasfemia, *f.,* reniego, *m.*

blast, *n.* ráfaga, *f.;* — **furnace,** horno alto; — , *vt.* marchitar, secar; arruinar; volar con pólvora.

blasting, *n.* voladura, *f.*

blast-off, *n.* despegue, *m.*

blatant, *adj.* vocinglero.

blaze, *n.* llama, *f.;* hoguera, *f.;* mancha blanca en la frente de los animales; señal de guía hecha en los troncos de los árboles; — , *vi.* encenderse en llama; brillar, resplandecer; — , *vt.* inflamar; flamear; llamear; — **s!** *interj.* ¡chispas! ¡caracoles!

blazon, *vt.* blasonar; decorar; publicar.

bldg.: building, ed. edificio.

bleach, *vt. y vi.* blanquear al sol; blanquear.

bleachers, *n. pl.* gradas al aire libre.

bleak, *adj.* pálido, descolorido; frío, helado; sombrío.

blear, bleared, blear-eyed, bleary, *adj.* legañoso o lagañoso.

bleat, *n.* balido, *m.;* — , *vi.* balar.

bled, *pretérito y p.p.* del verbo **bleed.**

bleed, *vt.* sacar sangre; (print.) sangrar; *n.* página en que se sangran grabados o texto.

bleeding, *n.* sangría, *f.;* — , *adj.* sangrante.

blemish, *vt.* manchar, ensuciar; infamar; — , *n.* tacha, *f.;* deshonra, infamia, *f.;* lunar, *m.*

blend, *vt.* mezclar, combinar; — , *vi.* armonizar; — , *n.* mezcla, *f.;* armonía, *f.*

blender, *n.* mezclador, *m.;* licuadora, *f.*

bless, *vt.* bendecir, alabar; (coll.) santiguar.

blessed, *adj.* bendito; afortunado.

blessing, *n.* bendición, *f.*

blight, *n.* tizón, *m.;* pulgón, *m.;* plaga, *f.;* daño, *m.;* — , *vi.* agostarse, perjudicarse.

blind, *adj.* ciego; oculto; oscuro; — **alley,** callejón sin salida; — **flying,** (avi.) vuelo con instrumentos, vuelo a ciegas; — **person,** ciego, ga; — , *vt.* cegar; deslumbrar; — , *n.* velo, *m.;* subterfugio, *m.;* emboscada, *f.;* **Venetian** — **s,** persianas, *f. pl.*

blindfold, *vt.* vendar los ojos; — , *adj.* con los ojos vendados.

blindly, *adv.* ciegamente, a ciegas.

blindness, *n.* ceguera, *f.*

blink, *vi.* guiñar, parpadear; cerrar los ojos; echar llama; — , *n.* guiñada, *f.,*

pestañeo, *m.;* destello, *m.;* **to be on the,** (coll.) estar descompuesto.

blinker, *n.* anteojera, *f.*

bliss, *n.* felicidad, *f.,* embeleso, *m.*

blissful, *adj.* feliz en sumo grado; beato, bienaventurado; — **ly,** *adv.* embelesadamente.

blister, *n.* vejiga, ampolla, *f.;* — , *vi.* ampollarse.

blithe, *adj.* alegre, contento, gozoso.

blitzkrieg, *n.* guerra relámpago.

blizzard, *n.* tormenta de nieve.

bloat, *vt.* hinchar; — , *vi.* entumecerse; abotagarse.

bloc, *n.* bloc, *m.,* grupo político.

block, *n.* zoquete, *m.;* horma (de sombrero), *f.;* bloque, *m.;* cuadernal, *m.;* témpano, *m.;* obstáculo, *m.;* manzana, cuadra (de una calle), *f.;* — **system,** (rail.) sistema de cobertura de una vía; — **and tackle,** polea con aparejo; — , *vt.* bloquear.

blockade, *n.* bloqueo, *m.;* 'cerco, *m.;* **to run a** — , romper el bloqueo; — , *vt.* bloquear.

blockhead, *n.* bruto, necio, zopenco, *m.*

blond, blonde, *n. y adj.* rubio, bia, (Mex.) güero, ra.

blood, *n.* sangre, *f.;* linaje, parentesco, *m.;* ira, cólera, *f.;* apetito animal; — **bank,** banco de sangre; — **clot,** embolia, *f.;* — **donor,** donante o donador de sangre; — **poisoning,** septicemia, *f.;* — **pressure,** presión arterial; — **vessel,** vena, *f.;* — **plasma,** plasma, *m.;* — **count,** cuenta de los glóbulos de la sangre; **in cold** — , en sangre fría; — **test,** análisis de la sangre; — **transfusion,** trasfusión de sangre.

bloodhound, *n.* sabueso, *m.*

bloodshed, *n.* matanza, *f.,* derramamiento de sangre.

bloodshot, *adj.* ensangrentado (aplícase a los ojos).

bloodsucker, *n.* sanguijuela, *f.;* (fig.) desollador, ra.

bloodthirsty, *adj.* sanguinario, cruel.

bloody, *adj.* sangriento, ensangrentado; cruel.

bloom, *n.* flor, *f.;* florecimiento, *m.;* — , *vi.* florecer.

bloomers, *n. pl.* calzones o pantalones de mujer (cortos y bombachos).

blossom, *n.* flor, *f.;* capullo, botón, *m.;* — , *vi.* florecer.

blot, *vt.* manchar (lo escrito); cancelar; denigrar; — , *n.* mancha, *f.*

blotch, *n.* roncha, *f.;* mancha, *f.*

blotter, *n.* papel secante, *m.*

blouse, *n.* blusa (de mujer), *f.*

blow, n. golpe, m.; pedrada, f.; —, vi. soplar, sonar; **to — (one's nose)**, sonarse (las narices); **to — up,** volar o volarse por medio de pólvora; ventear; (print.) ampliar mediante proyección; —, vt. soplar; inflar.

blow-dryer, n. secador de pelo, m, secadora de pelo, f.

blower, n. fuelle, soplador, m.

blowgun, n. bodoquera, f.

blown, adj. soplado; —, p.p. del verbo **blow.**

blowout, n. reventazón, f.; ruptura de neumático o llanta.

blowpipe, n. soplete, m.; cerbatana, f.

blowtorch, n. soplete para soldar.

blubber, n. grasa de ballena; —, vi. llorar hasta hincharse los carrillos; gimotear.

blue, adj. azul, cerúleo.

blueberry, n. baya comestible de color azul.

bluebird, n. (orn.) azulejo, m; pájaro azul; pájaro cantor.

bluegrass, n. variedad de hierba con tallos azulados.

bluejay, n. variedad de pájaro azul con copete.

blueprint, n. heliografía, f., heliógrafo, m.

blues, n. pl. (coll.) melancolía, f.; hipocondria, f.; tipo de jazz melancólico.

bluff, n. risco escarpado, morro, m.; fanfarronada, f.; —, adj. rústico, rudo, francote; —, vt. impedir con pretextos de valentía o de recursos; —, vi. baladronear; engañar, hacer alarde.

bluing, blueing, n. añil, m.

bluish, adj. azulado.

blunder, n. desatino, m.; error craso; atolondramiento, m.; pifia, f.; disparate, m.; —, vt. y vi. confundir; desatinar.

blunt, adj. obtuso, romo, boto; lerdo; bronco; grosero; —, vt. embotar; enervar; calmar (un dolor).

blur, n. mancha, f.; —, vt. manchar; infamar.

blurt (out), vt. hablar a tontas y a locas.

blush, n. rubor, m.; sonrojo, m.; —, vi. ruborizarse; sonrojarse.

bluster, n. ruido, tumulto, m.; jactancia, f.; —, vi. hacer ruido tempestuoso.

blvd.: boulevard, bulevar.

boa, n. boa (serpiente), f.; boa (cuello de pieles), f.

boar, n. verraco, m.; **wild —**, jabalí, m.

board, n. tabla, f.; mesa, f.; tribunal, consejo, m.; junta, f.; (naut.) bordo, m.; **— of directors**, consejo directivo, directorio, m., junta directiva; **— of trustees**, junta directiva; **Bristol —**, cartulina, f.; **free on —**, franco a bordo; **on —**, (naut.) a

bordo; —, vt. abordar; hospedar, alojar; subir a; —, vi. hospedarse; **to — up,** entablar.

boarder, n. pensionista, m. y f., pupilo, m.

boarding school, n. colegio para internos.

boardinghouse, n. casa de pupilos; casa de huéspedes; posada, pensión, f.

boardwalk, n. paseo entablado a la orilla del mar, malecón, m.

boast, n. jactancia, ostentación, f.; —, vi. presumir; jactarse, hacer alarde, hacer gala; preciarse de; —, vt. blasonar; **to — about,** jactarse de.

boastful, adj. jactancioso.

boat, n. bote, m.; barca, chalupa, f.; buque, barco, m.; **tug —**, remolcador, m.; **in the same —**, en una misma situación, en un mismo caso.

boatman, n. barquero, m.

boatswain, n. contramaestre, m.

bob, n. meneo, vaivén, m.; melena (corte de pelo corto de las mujeres), f.; —, vt. y vi. menear o mover la cabeza, bambolear; cortar corto el cabello.

bobbin, n. canilla, broca, bobina, f.; carrete, m.; carretel (de una máquina de coser), m.

bobby pin, n. pasador, m., horquilla corrugada para el pelo.

bobby socks, n. pl. tobilleras, f. pl.

bobby-soxer, n. tobillera, f., muchacha adolescente.

bobcat, n. variedad de lince.

bobolink, n. chambergo, m.

bobsled, n. trineo de dos rastras.

bode, vt. y vi. presagiar, pronosticar; **to — ill,** ser de mal agüero; **to — well,** prometer bien.

bodice, n. talle (de un vestido), m., cotilla, f.; corpiño, m.

bodily, adj. corpóreo, físico; —, adv. en peso; conjuntamente.

body, n. cuerpo, m.; caja o carrocería de un coche; individuo, m.; gremio, m.; consistencia, f.; **any—**, cualquiera; **every—**, cada uno, todos.

bodyguard, n. (mil.) guardaespaldas, m.

bog, n. pantano, m.; —, vt. y vi. (a veces con down), hundir, hundirse.

bogus, adj. fingido, falso.

boil, vi. hervir, bullir, hervirle a uno la sangre; —, vt. cocer; —, n. (med.) furúnculo, divieso, nacido, m.

boiler, n. caldera, f.; hervidor, m.

boiling, adj. hirviendo, hirviente; **— point,** punto de ebullición.

boisterous, adj. borrascoso, tempestuoso; violento; ruidoso.

bold, adj. atrevido; valiente; audaz; temerario; imprudente; **— face,** (print.) letra

negrilla; — **ly,** adv. descaradamente; atrevidamente.

boldness, n. intrepidez, f.; valentía, f.; osadía, f.; confianza, f.

bolero, n. bolero (baile andaluz), m.; bolero, m., chaqueta corta.

boll, n. cápsula (de lino o cáñamo), f.; — **weevil,** picudo, m., gorgojo del algodón.

bolo (knife), n. bolo (machete filipino), m.

bolster, n. travesero, m.; cabezal, cojín, m.; cabecera, f.; — , vt. apoyar, auxiliar;— **up,** sostener, apoyar; alentar.

bolt, n. dardo, m.; flecha, f; cerrojo, m.; chaveta, f.; tornillo, m.; **door** — , pasador, m.; — , vt. cerrar con cerrojo; — , vi. desbocarse (un caballo).

bomb, n. (mil.) bomba, f.; **atomic** — , bomba atómica; **hydrogen** — , bomba de hidrógeno; — **release,** — **thrower,** lanzabombas, m.

bombard, vt. bombardear.

bombardment, n. bombardeo, m.

bomber, n. bombardero, m., avión de bombardeo.

bombproof, adj. a prueba de bombas.

bombshell, n. bomba, granada, f.

bombsight, n. mira de bombardero aéreo.

bona fide, adj. de buena fe.

bonbon, n. confite, bombón, m.

bond, n. ligadura, f.; vínculo, lazo, m.; vale, m.; obligación, f.; (com.) bono, m.; **in** — , bajo fianza; — , vt. poner en depósito.

bondage, n. esclavitud, servidumbre, f.

bondholder, n. tenedor de bonos.

bondsman, bondman, n. esclavo, siervo, m.; (leyes) fiador, m.

bone, n. hueso, m.; — , vt. desosar.

boneless, adj. sin huesos, desosado.

bonfire, n. hoguera, fogata, f.

bonnet, n. gorra, f.; bonete, m.; sombrero, m.

bonny, adj. bonito, galán, gentil.

bonus, n. prima, f.; bonificación, gratificación, f.

bony, adj. huesudo.

boob, booby, n. zote, m., persona boba; **booby trap,** (mil.) granada o mina disimulada que estalla al moverse el objeto que la oculta.

boogie woogie, n. una forma popular de baile (en E.U.A.).

book, n. libro, m.; — , vt. asentar en un libro; inscribir; contratar (a un artista, etc.); fichar (al acusado).

bookbinder, n. encuadernador de libros.

bookcase, n. armario para libros, estante, m.; (Mex.) librero, m.

bookie, n. (coll.) persona cuyo negocio es

apostar a las carreras de caballos.

booking, n. registro, m.; — **office,** oficina de reservaciones (de pasajes).

bookkeeper, n. tenedor de libros.

bookkeeping, n. teneduría de libros, contabilidad, f.; **double-entry** — , contabilidad por partida doble; **single-entry** — , contabilidad por partida simple o sencilla.

booklet, n. folleto, m.

bookmaker, n. persona cuyo negocio es apostar a las carreras de caballos.

bookmark, n. marcador de libro.

bookseller, n. librero, m., vendedor de libros.

bookstand, n. puesto de libros.

bookstore, n. librería, f.

bookworm, n. polilla que roe los libros; (fig.) ratón de biblioteca.

boom, n. (naut.) botalón, m.; bonanza, f.,repentina prosperidad; rugido seco, estampido, m.; — , vi. zumbar.

boomerang, n. bumerang, m.

boon, n. presente, regalo, m.; favor, m., gracia, f.; — , adj. alegre, festivo; generoso.

boondoggle, n. obra inútil o poco práctica en que se malgastan tiempo y dinero; — , vn. (despectivo) entregarse a ocupaciones frívolas e inútiles.

boorish, adj. rústico, agreste; villano, zafio.

boost, vt. levantar o empujar hacia arriba; asistir; — , vi. aprobar con entusiasmo; — , n. ayuda, f., aumento, m.

booster, n. fomentador, secuaz, m.

booster rocket, n. cohete impulsor.

boot, n. bota, f.; **riding** — , bota de montar; **to** — , además, por añadidura.

bootblack, n. limpiabotas, m.

bootee, n. calzado tejido para niños; bota corta.

booth, n. barraca, cabaña, f.; puesto, m.; reservado (en una heladería, etc.), m.; casilla, f.; caseta, f.

bootleg, vt. y vi. contrabandear (usualmente en licores).

bootlegger, n. contrabandista (usualmente de licores), m.

bootlegging, n. tráfico ilegal de licores.

booty, n. botín, m.; presa, f.; saqueo, despojo, m.

booze, vi. (coll.) emborracharse; — , n. (coll.) bebida alcohólica.

borax, n. bórax, m.

border, n. orilla, f.; borde, m.; repulgo, m.; vera, f., margen, m.; frontera, f.; reborde, m.; cenefa, f.; — , vi. confinar; bordear; — , vt. ribetear, limitar; **to** — **on,** rayar en.

bordering, adj. contiguo, colindante; — **on,** rayano en.

borderland, *n.* frontera, *f.*, confín, *m.*

borderline, *n.* límite, *m.*, orilla, *f.*; — , *adj.* incierto; — case, caso en los límites de lo anormal.

bore, *vt.* taladrar, horadar, perforar, barrenar; fastidiar; — , *pretérito* del verbo bear; — , *n.* taladro, *m.*; calibre, *m.*;perforación, *f.*; latoso, sa, majadero, ra.

boredom, *n.* tedio, fastidio, *m.*

boric, *adj.* bórico; — acid, ácido bórico.

boring, *adj.* fastidioso, aburridor, aburrido.

born, *adj.* nacido; destinado; to be —, nacer.

borne, *p.p.* del verbo bear.

borough, *n.* villa, *f.*; burgo, *m.*, distrito administrativo de una ciudad.

borrow, *vt.* pedir prestado.

borrower, *n.* prestatario, ia.

bosom, *n.* seno, pecho, *m.*

boss, *n.* clavo *m.*; protuberancia, *f.*; (coll.) cacique, jefe, *m.*

botanical, *adj.* botánico.

botany, *n.* botánica, *f.*

botch, *n.* remiendo chapucero; roncha, *f.*; — , *vt.* remendar, chapucear.

botchy, *adj.* con ronchas; chapucero, hecho toscamente.

both, *pron.* y *adj.* ambos, ambas, los dos, las dos; — , *conj.* tanto como.

bother, *vt.* aturrullar; confundir, molestar; incomodar; — , *n.* estorbo, *m.*; mortificación, *f.*

bottle, *n.* botella, *f.*; — , *vt.* embotellar; — up, embotellar; (fig.) ahogar, reprimir.

bottleneck, *n.* cuello de botella; (fig.) obstáculo, impedimento, *m.*; cuello de estrangulación.

bottom, *n.* fondo, *m.*; fundamento, *m.*; valle, *m.*; buque, *m.*; false —, fondo doble; at —, en el fondo, realmente; — , *adj.* fundamental; mínimo.

bottomless, *adj.* insondable; sin fondo.

boudoir, *n.* tocador, *m.*, recámara, *f.*

bougainvillea, *n.* (bot.) buganvilia, *f.*

bough, *n.* rama (de un árbol), *f.*

bought, *pretérito* y *p.p.* del verbo buy.

bouillon, *n.* caldo, *m.*

boulder, *n.* canto rodado; china, peña, *f.*; guijarro, *m.*; peña desprendida de una masa de roca.

boulevard, *n.* avenida, *f.*, paseo, bulevar, *m.*

bounce, *vi.* arremeter, brincar; saltar; — , *n.* golpazo brinco, *m.*; bravata, *f.*

bouncing, *adj.* fuerte, bien formado, robusto.

bound, *n.* límite, *m.*; salto, *m.*; repercusión, *f.*; within — s, a raya; — , *vt.* confinar, limitar; destinar; obligar; reprimir; — , *vi.* resaltar, brincar; — , *pretérito* y

p.p. del verbo bind; — , *adj.* destinado; — for, con rumbo a, con destino a.

boundary, *n.* límite, *m.*; frontera, *f.*; meta, línea, *f.*; aledaño, *m.*

boundless, *adj.* ilimitado, infinito.

bounteous, bountiful, *adj.* liberal, generoso, bienhechor.

bounty, *n.* liberalidad, bondad, *f.*

bouquet, *n.* ramillete de flores, ramo, *m.*; aroma, olor, *m.*

bourgeois, *adj.* burgués.

bout, *n.* turno, *m.*; encuentro, combate, *m.*

bow, *vt.* encorvar, doblar, oprimir; — , *vi.* encorvarse; saludar; hacer reverencia; — , *n.* reverencia, inclinación, *f.*; (naut.) proa, *f.*

bow, *n.* arco, *m.*; lazo (de cinta, etc.), *m.*

bowels, *n. pl.* intestinos, *m. pl.*; entrañas, *f. pl.*

bower, *n.* enramada de jardín; bóveda, *f.*; aposento retirado.

bowl, *n.* taza, *f.*; wash —, jofaina, *f.*, lavamanos, *m.*; — , *vi.* jugar boliche o bolos, jugar a las bochas.

bowlegged, *adj.* patizambo, patiestevado.

bowling, *n.* juego de bolos, juego de boliche; — alley, bolera, *f.*, mesa de boliche; — pin, birla, *f.*, bolo, *m.*

box, *n.* caja, cajita, *f.*; cofre, *m.*; axle —, buje, *m.*; — office, taquilla, *f.*; — on the ear, bofetada, *f.*; — seat, asiento en palco; — , *vt.* meter alguna cosa en una caja; apuñetear; — , *vi.* combatir a puñadas, boxear.

boxcar, *n.* vagón cubierto, furgón cerrado.

boxer, *n.* púgil, boxeador, pugilista, *m.*

boxing, *n.* boxeo, pugilismo, pugilato, *m.*

boy, *n.* muchacho; niño, *m.*; criado, lacayo, *m.*; zagal, *m.*; — friend, amigo predilecto, novio potencial; — scout, muchacho explorador.

boycott, *vt.* boicotear; — , *n.* boicoteo, boicot, *m.*

boyhood, *n.* niñez, puericia (varones), *f.*

boyish, *adj.* pueril, propio de un niño varón; frívolo.

bra, *n.* brassiere, sostén, corpiño, soporte (para senos), *m.*

brace, *n.* abrazadera, *f.*; manija, *f.*; — , *vt.* apoyar, reforzar.

bracelet, *n.* brazalete, *m.*, pulsera, *f.*

bracing, *n.* refuerzo, *m.*; — , *adj.* fortificante, tónico.

bracket, *n.* puntal, *m.*; rinconera, *f.*; consola, *f.*; ménsula, *f.*; —s, *pl.* (print.) corchetes, *m. pl.*

brag, *n.* jactancia, *f.*; —, *vi.* jactarse, fanfarronear.

braggart, *adj.* y *n.* jactancioso, sa, fanfarrón, ona; valentón, ona, fachenda, *m.* y *f.*

braid, *n.* trenza, *f.;* pasamano, *m.,* trencilla, *f.; —, vt.* trenzar.

braille, *n.* escritura en relieve para uso de los ciegos.

brain, *n.* cerebro, *m.;* seso, juicio, *m.*

brainless, *adj.* insensato, estúpido.

brainwashing, *n.* lavado cerebral.

brake, *n.* freno, *m.;* to apply the —s, frenar; to release the —s, quitar el freno.

brakeman, *n.* (rail.) guardafrenos, *m.*

bramble, *n.* zarza, espina, *f.*

bran, *n.* salvado, afrecho, *m.*

branch, *n.* rama (de árbol), *f.;* brazo, *m.;* ramal, *m.;* sucursal, *f.;* ramo (de la ciencia, el arte, etc.), *m.; —, vt.* y *vi.* ramificar, ramificarse; — out, ramificarse.

brand, *n.* tizón, *m.;* hierro, *m.;* marca, *f.;* nota de infamia; marca de fábrica; —, *vt.* herrar (ganado); infamar.

brandish, *vt.* blandir, ondear.

brand-new, *adj.* flamante, enteramente nuevo.

brandy, *n.* aguardiente, *m.;* coñac, *m.*

brass, *n.* bronce, *m.;* desvergüenza, *f.;* — band, charanga, *f.*

brassie, *n.* mazo empleado en el juego de golf.

brassiere, *n.* brassiere, soporte (para senos), *m.;* corpiño, sostén, *m.*

brat, *n.* rapaz, chiquillo, *m.* (se usa en forma despectiva).

bravado, *n.* baladronada, *f.*

brave, *adj.* bravo, valiente, atrevido; —, *vt.* combatir, desafiar.

bravery, *n.* valor, *m.;* braveza, *f.*

brawl, *n.* quimera, disputa, camorra, pelotera, *f.; —, vi.* alborotar; vocinglear.

brawn, *n.* pulpa, *f.;* fuerza muscular.

brawny, *adj.* carnoso, musculoso.

bray, *vi.* rebuznar; —, *n.* rebuzno (del asno), *m.;* ruido bronco.

brazen, *adj.* de bronce; caradura, desvergonzado; imprudente; —, *vi.* encararse con desfachatez.

brazier, *n.* latonero, *m.;* brasero, *m.*

Brazil, Brasil, *m.*

Brazilian, *n.* y *adj.* brasileño, ña.

breach, *n.* rotura, *f.;* brecha, *f.;* violación, *f.;* — of trust, — of faith, abuso de confianza; — of promise, falta de palabra.

bread, *n.* pan, *m.;* (fig.) sustento, *m.;* — line, fila de los que esperan la gratuita distribución de pan; brown —, whole-wheat —, pan moreno, pan negro o de centeno.

breadth, *n.* anchura, *f.*

break, *vt.* y *vi.* quebrar; vencer; quebrantar; violar; domar; arruinar; partir; inte-

rrumpir, romperse; reventarse algún tumor; separarse; (com.) quebrar; to — out, abrirse salida; estallar; to — to pieces, hacer pedazos; —, *n.* rotura, *f.;* rompimiento, *m.;* ruptura, *f.;* interrupción, *f.;* — of day, aurora, *f.*

breakable, *adj.* frágil, rompible.

breakdown, *n.* descalabro, *m.;* avería repentina; decadencia, *f.,* decaimiento (de salud, de ánimo), *m.;* desarreglo, *m.;* interrupción, *f.;* postración, *f.*

break-even point, *n.* punto en que un negocio empieza a cubrir los gastos que ocasiona.

breakfast, *n.* desayuno, *m.;* — room, desayunador, *m.; —, vi.* desayunarse.

breaking, *n.* rompimiento, *m.;* fractura, *f.*

breakneck, *adj.* desenfrenado, vertiginoso; at — speed, a todo correr, a todo escape.

breakthrough, *n.* (mil.) embestida que perfora una zona de defensa.

breakwater, *n.* muelle, *m.;* dique, *m.;* escollera, *f.*

breast, *n.* pecho, seno, *m.;* corazón, *m.;* — stroke (natación), braza, *f.; —, vt.* acometer; resistir; arrostrar valerosamente.

breastwork, *n.* parapeto, *m.;* defensa, *f.*

breath, *n.* aliento, *m.,* respiración, *f.;* soplo de aire; momento, *m.;* out of —, jadeante, sin aliento.

breathe, *vt.* y *vi.* respirar; exhalar; resollar.

breathing, *n.* aspiración, *f.;* respiración, *f.;* respiro, *m.;* — spell, desahogo, descanso, *m.;* aliento, *m.*

breathless, *adj.* falto de aliento; desalentado.

breath-taking, *adj.* conmovedor, excitante.

bred, *pretérito* y *p.p.* del verbo breed; ill—, malcriado; well—, bien educado.

breech, *n.* trasero, *m.*

breeches, *n. pl.* calzones, *m. pl.*

breed, *n.* casta, raza, *f.; —, vt.* procrear, engendrar; criar; educar; —, *vi.* parir; multiplicarse.

breeding, *n.* crianza, *f.;* buena educación; modales, *m. pl.*

breeze, *n.* brisa, *f.,* céfiro, *m.*

breezy, *adj.* refrescado con brisas.

brethren, *n. pl.* de brother, hermanos, *m. pl.* (aplícase a los fieles en una iglesia, etc.).

brevity, *n.* brevedad, concisión, *f.*

brew, *vt.* tramar, maquinar, mezclar; —, *vi.* hacer cerveza; —, *n.* calderada de cerveza.

brewer, *n.* cervecero, *m.*

brewery, *n.* cervecería, *f.*

briar, brier, *n.* zarza, *f.,* espino, *m.;* —s, *pl.*

maleza, f.

bribe, n. cohecho, soborno, m.; —, vt. cohechar, corromper, sobornar.

bribery, n. cohecho, soborno, m.

brick, n. ladrillo, m.; (coll.) hombre alegre y popular.

bricklayer, n. albañil, m.

brickyard, n. adobería, f., ladrillar, m.

bridal, adj. nupcial.

bride, n. novia, desposada, f.

bridegroom, n. novio, desposado, m.

bridesmaid, n. dama, f., madrina de boda.

bridge, n. puente, m.; **suspension** —, puente colgante; —, vt. construir un puente; salvar un obstáculo.

bridgehead, n. cabeza de puente.

bridgework, n. puente dental; construcción de puentes.

bridle, n. brida, f., freno, m.; —, vt. embridar; reprimir, refrenar.

brief, adj. breve, conciso, sucinto; —, n. compendio, m.; breve, m.; (leyes) escrito, m.; — **case,** cartera, f.; portadocumentos, portapapeles, m.; **in** —, en pocas palabras, en breve; —, vt. hacer un resumen; (mil.) dar instrucciones finales para una misión.

briefing, n. instrucciones (a aviadores militares, etc.), f. pl.

brig, n. (naut.) bergantín, m.

brigade, n. (mil.) brigada, f.

brigadier, n. (mil.) general de brigada.

bright, adj. claro, luciente, brillante; luminoso; vivo.

brighten, vt. pulir, dar lustre; ilustrar; —, vi. aclarar.

brightness, n. esplendor, m., brillantez, f.; agudeza, f.; claridad, f.; lucimiento, m.

brilliance, brilliancy, n. brillantez, f., resplandor, brillo, esplendor, fulgor, m.

brilliant, adj. brillante; luminoso; resplandeciente; —, n. brillante (diamante abrillantado), m.

brilliantine, n. brillantina, f., grasa para el cabello.

brim, n. borde, extremo, m.; orilla, f.; ala (de sombrero), f.; —, vt. llenar hasta el borde; —, vi. estar lleno.

brimful, adj. lleno hasta el borde.

brimstone, n. azufre, m.

brine, n. salmuera, f.

bring, vt. llevar, traer; conducir; inducir; persuadir; **to — about,** efectuar; **to — forth,** producir; parir; **to — up,** educar; **to — to pass,** efectuar, realizar.

brink, n. orilla, f.; margen, m. y f., borde, m.

brisk, adj. vivo, alegre, jovial; fresco.

bristle, n. cerda, seta, f.; —, vi. erizarse.

bristly, adj. cerdoso, lleno de cerdas.

British Columbia, Colombia Británica.

British East Africa, Africa Oriental Inglesa.

British Guiana, Guayana Inglesa.

British Honduras, Belice, Honduras Británica.

brittle, adj. quebradizo, frágil.

broach, vt. iniciar, entablar.

broad, adj. ancho; abierto; extenso; — **jump,** salto de longitud.

broadcast, n. radiodifusión, f.; —, vt. radiodifundir, perifonear.

broadcasting, n. radiodifusión, f.; audición, f.; perifonía, f.; — **station,** emisora, radiodifusora, f.; —, adj. radioemisor.

broadcloth, n. paño fino.

broaden, vt. y vi. ensanchar, ensancharse.

broad-minded, adj. tolerante, de ideas liberales.

broadmindedness, n. amplitud de miras.

broadside, n. andanada, f.; costado de un barco; anchura, f.

brocade, n. brocado, m.

broccoli, n. (bot.) bróculi, brécol, m.

brochure, n. folleto, m.

brogue, n. abarca, f.; pronunciación regional de un idioma, en especial la pronunciación irlandesa del inglés.

broil, vt. asar a la parrilla.

broiler, n. parrilla, f.

broke, pretérito del verbo **break.**

broken, adj. roto, quebrado; interrumpido; — **English,** inglés mal articulado; —, p.p. del verbo **break.**

broken-down, adj. afligido, abatido; descompuesto.

broken-hearted, adj. triste, abatido, acongojado, con el corazón hecho trizas.

broker, n. corredor, m.; agente de bolsa; **exchange** —, corredor de cambio, **insurance** —, corredor de seguros, **money** —, cambista, m.

brokerage, n. corretaje, m.

bromide, n. bromuro, m.

bronchial, adj. bronquial; — **tube,** bronquio, m.

bronchitis, n. bronquitis, f.

bronchoscope, n. broncoscopio, m.

bronze, n. bronce, m.; —, vt. broncear.

brooch, n. broche, m.

brood, vi. cobijar; pensar alguna cosa con cuidado, madurar; —, n. raza, f.; nidada, f.

brook, n. arroyo, m.; (Sp. Am.) quebrada, f.; —, vt. sufrir, tolerar.

broom, n. escoba, f.

broomstick, n. palo de escoba.

broth, n. caldo, m.

brother, n. hermano, m.

brotherhood, n. hermandad, fraternidad, f.

brother-in-law, n. cuñado, m., hermano

político.
brotherly, *adj.* fraternal.
brought, *pretérito* y *p.p.* del verbo bring.
brow, *n.* ceja, *f.;* frente, *f.;* cima, *f.*
browbeat, *vt.* mirar con ceño; intimidar.
brown, *adj.* bruno, moreno; castaño; pardo; **dark —**, bruno, castaño oscuro; **—paper,** papel de estraza, *m.;* — **sugar,** azúcar morena; —, *vt.* dorar, tostar.
brownies, *n. pl.* duendes de los cuentos de hadas; pastelitos de chocolate y nueces.
browse, *vt.* y *vi.* ramonear, pacer; **to — over a book,** hojear, leer un libro.
bruise, *vt.* magullar, machacar, abollar, majar; pulverizar; —, *n.* magulladura, contusión, *f.*
brunet, *n.* y *adj.* moreno, trigueño, *m.*
brunette, *n.* y *adj.* morena, trigueña, *f.*
brunt, *n.* choque, *m.;* esfuerzo, *m.*
brush, *n.* bruza, *f.;* escobilla, *f.;* brocha, *f.;* cepillo, *m.;* encuentro, *m.,* escaramuza, *f.;* **artist's —,** pincel, *m.;* —, *vt.* cepillar; **to — off,** despedir con brusquedad; —, *vi.* mover apresuradamente; pasar ligeramente.
brushwood, *n.* breñal, zarzal, *m.*
brusque, *adj.* brusco, rudo, descortés.
Brussels sprouts, *n. pl.* (bot.) colecitas de Bruselas.
brutal, *adj.* brutal, bruto.
brute, *n.* bruto, *m.;* —, *adj.* feroz, bestial; irracional.
B.S.: **Bachelor of Science,** Br. en C. Bachiller en Ciencias.
b.s.: **bill of sale,** C/Vta, C / V; Cuenta de Ventas; **balance sheet,** balance.
BTU (British Thermal Unit), unidad termal británica.
bu.: **bushel,** medida de áridos (Ingl. 36,37 litros; E.U. 35,28 litros) .
bubble, *n.* burbuja, *f.;* bagatela, *f.;* —, *vi.* burbujear, bullir; **— over,** estar en efervescencia; borbotar; hervir.
buck, *n.* gamo, *m.;* macho (de algunos animales), *m.*
bucket, *n.* cubo, pozal, *m.;* cangilón, *m.;* cucharón, *m.*
buckle, *n.* hebilla, *f.;* —, *vt.* abrochar con hebilla; afianzar; **— down to,** dedicarse (a algo) con empeño; —, *vi.* encorvarse.
bucksaw, *n.* sierra de bastidor.
buckshot, *n.* perdigón grande.
buckwheat, *n.* trigo sarraceno.
bud, *n.* pimpollo, botón, *m.;* capullo, *m.;* —, *vi.* florecer, brotar; —, *vt.* injertar.
buddy, *n.* hermano, camarada, compañero, *m.*

budge, *vi.* moverse, menearse.
budget, *n.* presupuesto, *m.*
buff, *n.* pulidor, *m.;* aficionado, da; color amarillo rojizo; —, *adj.* de color amarillo rojizo; —, *vt.* lustrar, dar lustre; pulir.
buffalo, *n.* búfalo, *m.*
buffer, *n.* parachoques, *m.;* topes, *m. pl.;* pulidor (para las uñas), *m.*
buffet, *n.* puñetazo, *m.,* puñada, *f.;* —, *vi.* combatir a puñetazos.
buffet, *n.* aparador, *m.;* **— supper,** ambigú, *m.,* cena en que uno mismo se sirve.
buffoon, *n.* bufón, gracioso, *m.*
bug, *n.* chinche, *f.;* insecto, bicho, *m.*
bugbear, *n.* espantajo, coco, *m.*
buggy, *n.* calesa, *f.;* **baby —,** cochecito de niño; —, *adj.* chinchoso; con bichos.
bugle, *n.* clarín, *m.;* corneta, *f.*
bugler, *n.* corneta, trompetero, *m.*
build, *vt.* edificar; construir.
builder, *n.* arquitecto, *m.;* constructor, *m.*
building, *n.* edificio, *m.;* construcción, *f.*
bulb, *n.* bulbo, *m.;* cebolla, *f.;* **electric light —,** foco de luz eléctrica.
bulge, *vi.* combarse.
bulk, *n.* masa, *f.;* volumen, *m.;* grosura, *f.;* mayor parte; capacidad de un buque; **in —,** a granel.
bulky, *adj.* macizo, grueso, grande.
bull, *n.* toro, *m.;* disparate, *m.;* bula *f.,* breve pontificio; dicho absurdo; **— ring,** plaza de toros; **—'s eye,** centro de blanco; (naut.) claraboya, *f.*
bulldog, *n.* perro de presa.
bulldoze, *vt.* (coll.) coercer o reprimir por intimidación.
bulldozer, *n.* niveladora, *f.,* abrebrechas, *m.;* (coll.) persona que intimida.
bullet, *n.* bala, *f.*
bulletin, *n.* boletín, *m.;* **— board,** tablero para avisos.
bulletproof, *adj.* a prueba de bala.
bullfight, *n.* corrida de toros.
bullfighter, *n.* torero, *m.*
bullfrog, *n.* rana grande.
bullion, *n.* oro o plata en barras.
bully, *n.* espadachín, *m.;* valentón, *m.;* rufián, *m.;* (coll.) gallito, *m.;* —, *vi.* fanfarronear.
bulwark, *n.* baluarte, *m.;* —, *vt.* fortificar con baluartes.
bum, *n.* holgazán, bribón, *m.*
bumblebee, *n.* abejón, abejorro, zángano, *m.*
bump, *n.* hinchazón, *f.;* giba, *f.;* golpe, *m.;* —, *vt.* y *vi.* chocar contra.
bumper, *n.* parachoques o paragolpes de un auto, defensa, *f;* —, *adj.* (coll.) exce-

lente; abundante; — **crop,** cosecha abundante.

bun, n. bollo (de pan, etc.), m.

bunch, n. montón, m.; manojo, m.; ramo, racimo, m.; —, vt. y vi. agrupar, amontonar; poner en racimo.

bundle, n. atado, haz (de leña, etc.), m.; paquete, m.; rollo, m.; bulto, m.; lío, m.; —vt. atar, hacer un lío o un bulto; — **up,** envolver; abrigarse.

bungalow, n. casa de un piso.

bungle, vt. y vi. chapucear, chafallar; hacer algo chabacanamente; —, n. chabacanería, f.

bunion, n. juanete, m.

bunk, n. patraña, f., mentira fabulosa; camarote, m.; — **beds,** literas, f. pl.

bunker, n. (golf) trampa, f.

Bunsen burner, n. mechero Bunsen, m.

bunting, n. lanilla para banderas; (orn.) calandria, f.

buoy, n. (naut.) boya, f.; —, vt. boyar; — **up,** apoyar, sostener.

buoyant, adj. boyante.

bur, n. carda, f.; bardana, f.; (mech.) arandela, f.

burden, n. carga, f., cargo, m.; —, vt. cargar; gravar.

bureau, n. armario,. m.; tocador, m., cómoda, f.; escritorio, m.; oficina, f.; departamento, m., división, f.

bureaucracy, n. burocracia, f.

burette, n. (chem.) bureta f.

burglar, n. salteador, ladrón, m.; — **alarm,** alarma contra ladrones; — **insurance,** seguro contra robo.

burglary, n. asalto, robo, m.

burial, n. entierro, enterramiento, m.

burlap, n. arpillera, o harpillera, f.

burlesque, adj. burlesco; —, n.función teatral de género festivo y picaresco; —, vt. y vi. burlarse; parodiar.

burly, adj. voluminoso; vigoroso; turbulento.

burn, vt. quemar, abrasar o herir, incendiar; —, vi. arder; —, n. quemadura, f.

burner, n. quemador, m.; mechero, m.

burning, n. quemadura, f.; incendio, m.

burnish, vt. bruñir, dar lustre.

burrow, n. conejera, f.; — vi. esconderse en la conejera; excavar un hoyo en la tierra.

burst, vi. reventar; abrirse; **to — into tears,** prorrumpir en lágrimas; **to — out laughing,** soltar una carcajada; —, n. reventón, m.; rebosadura, f.

bury, vt. enterrar, sepultar; esconder.

bus, n. autobús, ómnibus, camión, m.

bush, n. arbusto, m.; cola de zorra; **to beat around the —,** acercarse indirec-

tamente a una cosa, andar con rodeos.

bushel, n. medida de áridos (Ingl., 36,37 litros; E.U., 35,28 litros).

bushing, n. buje, cojinete, m.; (mech.) encastre, encaje, m.; casquillo, m.; collera (en maquinaria), f.

bushy, adj. espeso, lleno de arbustos; lanudo.

busily, adv. solícitamente, diligentemente.

business, n. empleo, m., ocupación, f.; negocio, m.; quehacer, m.; — **house,** casa de comercio; — **man,** hombre de negocios; — **transaction.** negociación, operación, f.; **to do — with,** tratar con.

businessman. m. comerciante, m.

bust, n. busto, m.

bustle, n. confusión, f., ruido, m.; polisón, m.; —, vi. apurarse con estrépito; menearse.

busy, adj. ocupado; atareado; entremetido; —, vt. ocupar.

busybody, n. entremetido, da; (coll.) camasquince, m. y f.

but, prep. excepto; —, conj. y adv. menos; pero; solamente.

butcher, n. carnicero, m.; —'s shop, carnicería, f.; —, vt. matar atrozmente.

butler, n. mayordomo, m.

butt, n. culata, f.; blanco, hito, m.; bota, f., cuba para guardar vino, etc.; persona a quien se ridiculiza; cabezada (golpe de la cabeza), f.; —, vt. topar.

butter, n. mantequilla, manteca, f.; — **dish,** mantequillera, f.

buttercup, n. (bot.) ranúnculo, m.

butterfly, n. mariposa, f.

buttermilk. n. suero de mantequilla; (Mex.) jocoqui, m.

butterscotch, n. variedad de dulce hecho de azúcar y mantequilla.

buttock, n. nalga, f.; anca, grupa, f.

button, n. botón, m.; call —, botón de llamada; **push —,** botón de contacto; —, vt. abotonar.

buttonhole, n. ojal, m.

buttress, n. contrafuerte, m.; sostén, apoyo, m.; —, vt. suministrar un sostén; afianzar.

buxom, adj. robusto y rollizo.

buy, vt. comprar; **to — at retail,** comprar al por menor; **to — at wholesale,** comprar al por mayor; **to — for cash,** comprar al contado; **to — on credit,** comprar al crédito o fiado.

buyer, n. comprador, m., compradora, f.

buzz, n. susurro, soplo, m.; —, vi. zumbar; cuchichear; (avi.) descender en picada y volar bajo y velozmente.

buzzard, n. (orn.) gallinazo, m.

buzzer, n. zumbador, m.

bx.: box, c/ caja.
by, *prep.* por; a, en; de; con; al lado de, cerca de; —, *adv.* cerca; a un lado; — **all means,** de todos modos, cueste lo que cueste; — **and** —, dentro de poco, luego; — **much,** con mucho;— **the way,** de paso, a propósito.
bygone, *adj.* pasado; —, *n.* lo pasado.

bylaws, *n. pl.* estatutos, *m. pl.*, reglamento, *m.*
by-pass, *n.* desvío, *m.;* —, *vt.* desviar.
by-product, *n.* derivado, subproducto, *m.*
bystander, *n.* circunstante, *m.* y *f.,* espectador, ra.
byword, *n.* apodo, mote, *m.*
Byzantine, *n.* y *adj.* bizantino, na.

C

C.: centigrade, C. centígrado; **current,** corrte. cte. corriente.
C.A.: Central America, C.A. Centro América.
cab, *n.* coche de alquiler, taxi, *m.*
cabana, *n.* cabaña, caseta, *f.*
cabaret, *n.* cabaret, *m.*
cabbage, *n.* repollo, *m.;* berza, col. *f.*
cabin, *n.* cabaña, cabina, barraca, *f ;* choza, *f.;* camarote, *m.;* — **steward,** mayordomo, *m.*
cabinet, *n.* gabinete, *m.;* escritorio, *m.;* ministerio, *m.;* — **council,** consejo de ministros.
cabinetmaker, *n.* ebanista, *m.*
cable, *n.* cable, cablegrama, *m.;* (naut.) cable, *m.;* — **address,** dirección cablegráfica; — **car,** ferrocarril funicular; vehículo manejado por un cable; —, *adj.* cablegráfico; — **television,** televisión por cable, cablevisión, *f.*
cablegram, *n.* cablegrama, *m.*
cabman, *n.* chofer de taxi.
caboose, *n.* (naut.) cocina, *f.,* fogón, *m.*
cackle, *vi.* cacarear, graznar; —, *n.* cacareo, *m.;* charla, *f.*
cactus, *n.* (bot.) cacto, *m.*
cad, *n.* persona vil o despreciable.
cadaver, *n.* cadáver, cuerpo, *m.*
caddie, caddy, *n.* ayudante, paje (en el golf), *m.;* —, *vi.* servir de ayudante o paje (en el golf).
cadence, *n.* (mus.) cadencia, *f.*
cadet, *n.* cadete, *m.*
Caesarean, *adj.* cesáreo; — **section,** operación cesárea.
café, *n.* café, restaurante, *m.,* cantina, *f.*
cafeteria, *n.* cafetería, *f.,* restaurante en donde se sirve uno mismo.
cage, *n.* jaula, *f ;* alambrera, *f.;* prisión, *f.;* —, *vt.* enjaular.
cajole, *vt.* lisonjear, adular.
cake, *n.* torta, *f.;* bizcocho, pastel, *m.;*—, *vi.* endurecerse, coagularse.
calamity, *n.* calamidad, miseria, *f.*

calcimine, *n.* lechada, *f.*
calcium, *n.* calcio, *m.*
calculate, *vt.* calcular, contar.
calculating, *adj.* calculador; de calcular; — **machine,** máquina de calcular.
calculation, *n.* calculación, cuenta, *f.;* cálculo, *m.*
calculator, *n.* calculadora, *f.*
calculus, *n.* cálculo, *m.*
calendar, *n.* calendario, almanaque, *m.*
calf, *n.* ternero, ra; cuero de ternero; (anat.) pantorrilla, *f.*
calfskin, *n.* piel de ternera; becerro, *m.*
caliber, *n.* calibre, *m.*
calibration, *n.* calibración, *f.*
calico, *n.* percal, *m.,* zaraza, *f.*
californium, *n.* californio, (elemento radiactivo artificial), *m.*
calipers, *n. pl.* compás de calibres; compás de espesores.
calisthenics, *n. pl.* calisténica, gimnasia, *f.*
call, *vt.* llamar, nombrar; convocar, citar; apelar; denominar; **to — for,** ir por (algo o alguien) ; **to — names,** injuriar; **to — the roll,** pasar lista; **to — to order,** llamar al orden, abrir la sesión; **to — on,** visitar; —, *n.* llamada, *f.;* instancia, *f ;* invitación, *f ;* urgencia, *f.;* vocación, profesión, *f.;* empleo, *m.;* grito, *m.;* (naut.) pito, *m.;* (mil.) toque, *m.;* **to have a close** —, salvarse en una tablita.
calla lily, *n.* lirio, *m.;* (Mex.) alcatraz, *f*
caller, *n.* visitador, *m.,* visitadora, *f.;* visitante, *m.* y *f.;* persona que llama.
calling, *n.* profesión, vocación, *f.*
callous, *adj.* calloso, endurecido; insensible.
calm, *n.* calma, tranquilidad, *f.;* —, *adj.* quieto, tranquilo; —, *vt.* calmar, aplacar, aquietar; **to — down,** serenarse.
calorie, *n.* caloría, *f.*
calve, *vi.* parir, producir la vaca.
calves, *n. pl.* de **calf.**
calyx, *n.* (bot.) cáliz, *m.*
cam, *n.* (mech.) leva, *f.*

cambric, n. cambray, m., batista, f.
came, *pretérito* del verbo **come.**
camel, n. camello, m.
cameo, n. camafeo, m.
camera, n. cámara, f.; — **man,** camarógrara, f.; **digital—,** cámara digital;
camouflage, n. (mil.) camuflaje, m., simulación, f., fingimiento, engaño, m.; disfraz, m.
camp, n. (mil.) campo, m.; **army —,** campamento del ejército; **to break —,** levantar el campo; — adj. campal; —, vi. acampar.
campaign, n. campaña, f.; —, vi. hacer campaña; hacerle propaganda (a algún candidato) .
campfire, n. hoguera en el campo.
camphor, n. alcanfor, m.
campus, n. patio o terrenos de una universidad, un colegio, un instituto, etc.
camshaft, n. eje de levas.
can, vi. poder, saber; —, vt. envasar en latas; —, n. lata, f., bote, m.; —**opener,** abrelatas, m., abridor de latas.
Canada, Canadá, m.
Canadian, n. y adj. canadiense, m. y f.
canal, n. canal, m.
Canal Zone, Zona del Canal, f.
Canaries, Canary Islands, Las Canarias, Islas Canarias.
canary, n. canario, m.
canasta, n. canasta (juego de naipes), f.
cancel, vt. cancelar, borrar; anular, invalidar; barrear.
cancellation, n. cancelación, f.
cancer, n. (med.) cáncer, m.
cancerous, adj. canceroso.
candid, adj. cándido, sencillo, ingenuo, sincero; — **camera,** cámara para tomar fotografías sin que lo advierta el sujeto.
candidate, n. candidato, ta, aspirante (a un puesto, cargo, etc.), m. y f.
candied, adj. garapiñado, en almíbar.
candle, n. candela, vela, bujía, f.; —**power,** (elec.) potencia luminosa (en bujías) .
candlelight. n. luz artificial; luz de vela; crepúsculo, anochecer, m.
candlestick, n. candelero, m.
candor, n. candor, m.; sinceridad, ingenuidad, f.
candy, vt. confitar; garapiñar; —, n. confite, bombón, dulce, m.; — **box,** caja de dulces, confitera, f.
cane, n. caña, f.; bastón, m.; —**plantation,** cañal, cañaveral, m.
canine, adj. canino, perruno,
canker, n. llaga ulcerosa; —, vt. roer, corromper; —, vi. corromperse, roerse.
canned goods, n. pl. productos en lata o en conserva.

cannibal, n. caníbal, m., antropófago, ga.
cannon, n. cañón, m.
canny, adj. cuerdo, discreto, sagaz.
canoe, n. canoa, f.; bote, m.; (Mex.) chalupa, f.; piragua, f.
canon, n. canon, m., regla, f.; (eccl.) canónigo, m.; — **law,** derecho canónico.
canonize, vt. canonizar.
canopy, n. dosel, pabellón, m.; (avi.) cabina cerrada transparente; capota del paracaídas.
cant, n. jerigonza, f.; canto o esquina de un edificio; —, vi. hablar en jerigonza.
cantaloupe, cantaloup, n. melón de verano.
canteen, n. (mil.) cantina, f., tienda de provisiones para soldados; vasija en que los soldados, viajeros, etc. llevan agua.
canter, n. medio galope, m.
canton, n. cantón, m.; —, vt. acantonar.
canvas, n. cañamazo, m.; lona, f.
canvass, vt. escudriñar, examinar, controvertir; —, vi. solicitar votos, etc.
canyon, n. desfiladero, cañón, m.
cap, n. gorra, f.; birrete, m.; cachucha, f.; — **and gown,** traje académico o toga y birrete; —. vt. poner remate a; **to — the climax,** llegar al colmo; **percussion —,** cápsula fulminante.
cap.: **capital letter,** may. letra mayúscula.
capability, n. capacidad, aptitud, habilidad, f.
capable, adj. capaz, idóneo.
capacity, n. capacidad, f.; inteligencia, habilidad, f.; calidad, f.; **seating —,** cabida, f
cape, n. cabo, promontorio, m.; capa, f.; capota, f.; capote, m.
Cape Horn, Cabo de Hornos.
Cape of Good Hope, Cabo de Buena Esperanza.
caper, n. cabriola, f.; travesura, f.; alcaparra, f.; **to cut a —,** cabriolar; —, vi. hacer travesuras.
capillary, adj. capilar.
capital, adj. capital, excelente; principal;— **punishment,** pena de muerte; —, n. (arch.) capitel, m.; capital (la ciudad principal), f.; capital, m.; mayúscula, f.; **to invest —.** colocar un capital.
capitalist, n. capitalista, m. y f.
capitalize, vt. capitalizar.
Capitol, n. Capitolio, m.
capitulate, vi. (mil.) capitular.
capricious, adj. caprichoso.
capsize, vt. y vr. (naut.) volcar, volcarse.
capsule, n. cápsula, f.
Capt.: **Captain,** cap. capitán.
captain, n. capitán, m.
caption, n. presa, captura, f.; (print.) títu-

lo, subtítulos pie de grabado.

captivate, vt. cautivar; esclavizar.

captive, n. cautivo, va; esclavo, va.

captivity, n. cautividad, esclavitud, f.; cautiverio, m.

captor, n. apresador, m.

capture, n. captura, f.; presa, f.; toma, f.; —, vt. apresar; capturar.

car, n. carreta, f.; carro, m.; coche, automóvil, m.; **baggage, freight o express** —, furgón, vagón, m.; **dining** —, (rail.) coche comedor; **funeral** —, carroza, f.; **sleeping** —, (rail.) coche dormitorio.

caramel, n. caramelo, m.

carat, n. quilate, m.

caravan, n. caravana, f.

caraway, n. (bot.) alcaravea, f.

carbohydrate, n. carbohidrato, m.

carbolic, adj. fénico; — **acid,** ácido carbólico, ácido fénico, fenol, m.

carbon, n. carbón, m.; — **copy,** copia al carbón, copia en papel carbón; réplica, f.; — **paper,** papel carbón.

carbonic, adj. carbónico; — **acid,** ácido carbónico.

carbuncle, n. carbúnculo, carbunclo, m.

carburetor, n. carburador, m.

carcass n. animal muerto; casco, m.; armazón, f.

card, n. naipe, m., carta, f.; tarjeta, f.; carda (para cardar lana), f.; — **catalogue,** catálogo de fichas; — **index,** fichero, m.; —, vt. cardar (lana).

cardboard, n. cartón, m.

cardigan, n. suéter o chaqueta tejida con botonadura al frente.

cardinal, adj. cardinal, principal; rojo, purpurado; — **points,** puntos cardinales; —, n. cardenal, m.; (orn.) cardenal, m.

cardiogram, n. (med.) cardiograma, n.

care, n. cuidado, esmero, m.; solicitud, f.; cargo, m.; vigilancia, f.; **to take — of,** cuidar de; —, vi. cuidar, tener cuidado; inquietarse; estimar, apreciar; — **about,** preocuparse de; **what do I** —? ¿a mí qué me importa? **I don't — a fig,** no me importa un bledo; **to — for,** guardar; vigilar; cuidar.

career, n. carrera, profesión, f.; curso, m.

carefree, adj. libre, sin cuidados.

careful, adj. cuidadoso, ansioso, prudente, solícito; **to be** —, tener cuidado.

careless, adj. descuidado, negligente; indolente; —**ly,** adv. descuidadamente.

carelessness, n. descuido, m., negligencia, f.

caress, n. caricia, f.; —, vt. acariciar, halagar.

caretaker, n. velador, m.

careworn, adj. cansado, fatigado.

carfare, n. pasaje (de tranvía, etc.), m.

cargo, n. cargamento de navío; carga, f.; consignación, f.

caricature, n. caricatura, f.; —, vt. hacer caricaturas; ridiculizar.

carload, n. furgón entero, carro entero; vagonada, f.

carnal, adj. carnal; sensual.

carnation, n. (bot.) clavel, m.

carnival, n. carnaval, m.

carnivorous, adj. carnívoro.

carol, n. villancico, m.; **Christmas** —, villancico o canción de Navidad.

carouse, vi. beber excesivamente; tomar parte en una juerga.

carp, n. carpa, f.; —, vi. censurar, criticar, reprobar.

carpenter, n. carpintero, m.

carpet, n. alfombra, f.; tapete, m.; tapiz, m.; — **sweeper,** barredor de alfombra; —, vt. cubrir con alfombras, tapizar.

carpeting, n. material para tapices; tapicería, f.

carpool, n. cooperación para compartir los gastos de trasporte en automóvil.

carriage, n. porte, talante, m.; coche, m., carroza, f.; carruaje, m. vehículo, m.; carga, f.; cureña de cañón.

carrier, n. portador, carretero, m.; trasportador, m.; **aircraft** —, (naut.) portaaviones, m.; — **pigeon,** paloma mensajera.

carrion, n. carroña, f.

carrot, n. zanahoria, f.

carry, vt. llevar, conducir; portar; lograr; cargar; **to — on,** continuar; **to — out,** cumplir; llevar a cabo, realizar.

cart, n. carro, m.; carreta, f.; carretón, m.; —, vt. acarrear.

cartel, n. cartel, m.

cartilage, n. cartílago, m.

cartload, n. carretada, f.

carton, n. caja de cartón.

cartoon, n. caricatura, f.; boceto, m.; **animated** —, caricatura animada; —, vt. y vi. caricaturizar; bosquejar.

cartoonist, n. caricaturista, m. y f.

cartridge, n. cartucho, m.; **blank** —, cartucho en blanco; — **shell,** cápsula, f.

carve, vt. cincelar; trinchar; tajar; grabar.

carver, n. escultor, m.; persona que taja; trinchante, m.

carving, n. escultura, entalladura, f.; — **knife,** tajador, m., cuchillo de tajar.

cascade, n. cascada, f.; salto de agua.

case, n. estado, m.; situación, f.; causa, f.; bolsa, f.; caso, m.; estuche, m.; vaina, f.; caja, f.; (gram.) caso, m.; **in** —, si acaso, caso que; **in the — of,** en caso de.

casement, n. puertaventana, f.

cash, n. dinero contante o efectivo, caja, f.; — and carry, compra al contado en que el comprador se lleva él mismo la mercancía; — on delivery, cóbrese al entregar, contra rembolso; — on hand, efectivo en caja; — payment, pago al contado; — register, registrador, m., caja registradora; to buy for —, comprar al contado; —, vt. cobrar o hacer efectivo (un cheque, etc.).

cashbook, n. libro de caja.

cashbox, n. caja de hierro.

cashew, n. anacardo, m.; — nut, nuez de la India.

cashier, n. cajero, ra; —'s check, cheque de caja.

cashmere, n. casimir (tela) m.

casing, n. forro, m., cubierta, envoltura, f.; caja (de engranaje, etc.), f.

cask, n. barril, tonel, m., cuba, f.

casket, n ataúd, m.

casserole, n. cacerola, f.; — dish, guiso al horno de una combinación de ingredientes en una cacerola.

cast, vt. tirar, lanzar; echar; modelar; to—lots, echar suertes; —, vi. amoldarse; —, n. tiro, golpe, m.; forma, f ; matiz, m.; (theat.) reparto, elenco artístico; —, adj. fundido; — iron, hierro colado; — steel, acero, fundido.

castanets, n. pl. castañuelas, f. pl.

castaway, n. réprobo, m.; náufrago, ga.

cast-down, adj. humillado.

caste, n. casta, f., clase social; to lose —, perder la posición social.

caster, n. calculador, m.; vinagrera, aceitera , f., angarillas f. pl.; tirador, m.; adivino, m.; ruedecita (para rodar los muebles) f.

Castile, Castilla, f.

Castilian, n. y adj. castellano, na.

casting, n. tiro, m.; vaciado, m.; (theat.) distribución de papeles a los actores.

castle, n. castillo, m.; fortaleza, f.; —, vt. encastillar; to — one's king, enrocar (en el juego de ajedrez).

castoff, adj. descartado; — clothes, ropa de desecho; — iron, hierro de desecho.

castor, n. castor, m.; sombrero castor;— oil, aceite de ricino, de castor o de palmacristi.

castrate, vt. castrar, capar.

casual, adj. casual, fortuito; — clothing, ropa sencilla, ropa de calle o para deportes.

casualty, n. accidente, m.; caso, m.; — ties, n. pl. víctimas de accidentes o de guerra, etc.

cat, n. gato, m., gata, f.; to let the — out

of the bag, revelar un secreto.

cat : catalog, catálogo.

catechism, catecismo.

cataclysm, n. cataclismo, diluvio, m.

catalogue, n. catálogo, m.; rol, elenco, m., lista, f.

Catalonia, Cataluña, f.

Catalonian, n. y adj. catalán, ana.

catapult, n. catapulta, f.

cataract, n. cascada, catarata, f.; (med.) catarata, f.

catarrh, n. catarro, m.; reuma, f.

catastrophe, n. catástrofe, f.

catbird, n. tordo mimo.

catch, vt. coger, agarrar, asir; atrapar; pillar; sorprender; —, vi. pegarse, ser contagioso; prender; to — cold, resfriarse; to — fire, encenderse; —, n. botín, m., presa, f.; captura, f.; trampa, f.; buen partido; acto de parar la pelota; — bolt, picaporte, m.

catcher, n. cogedor, ra; parador de la pelota (en el béisbol).

catching, adj. contagioso.

catchup, n. salsa de tomate embotellada.

catchword, n. (print.) reclamo, m.; contraseña, f.

catchy, adj. atrayente, agradable; engañoso.

catechism, n. catecismo, m.

categorical, adj. categórico.

category, n. categoría, f.

cater, vi. abastecer, proveer; halagar, complacer.

cater-cornered, adj. diagonal.

caterer, n. proveedor, ra, abastecedor, ra; persona que proporciona lo que se ha de comer en una cena, banquete, etc.

caterpillar, n. oruga, f., — tractor, tractor de oruga.

catfish, n. (ichth.) barbo, m.

catgut, n. cuerda de violín o de guitarra.

cathartic, adj. (med.) catártico; —, n. purgante, laxante, m.

cathedral, n. catedral, f.

cathode, cathodic, adj. catódico; — ray tube, tubo de rayos catódicos.

catholic, n. y adj. católico, ca.

catholicism, n. catolicismo, m.

catnip, n. (bot.) calamento, m.

cat's-paw, n. persona que sirve de instrumento a otra; (naut.) soplo, m.

catsup = catchup.

cattle, n. ganado, m., ganado vacuno.

cattleman, n. ganadero, m., criador de ganado.

caucus, n. junta electoral.

caught, pretérito y p.p. del verbo catch.

cauliflower, n. coliflor, f.

cause, n. causa, f.; razón, f.; motivo,

lugar, *m.;* proceso, *m.;* —, *vt.* motivar, causar.

caustic, *n.* y *adj.* cáustico, *m.*

caution, *n.* prudencia, precaución, *f.;* aviso *m.;* —, *vt.* avisar, amonestar, advertir.

cautionary, *adj.* de índole preventiva; dado a tomar precauciones.

cautious, *adj.* cauteloso, prudente, circunspecto, cauto; **to be** —, estar sobre sí, ser cauteloso.

cavalcade, *n.* cabalgata, cabalgada, *f.*

cavalier, *n.* jinete, *m.;* caballero, *m.*

cavalry, *n.* caballería, *f.*

cavalryman, *n.* soldado de a caballo; soldado de caballería.

cave, *n.* cueva, caverna, *f.;* — **man,** troglodita, *m.*

cavern, *n.* caverna, *f.;* antro, *m.*

caviar, *n.* caviar, *m.*

cavity, *n.* hueco, *m.,* cavidad, *f.;* seno, *m.*

caw, *vi.* graznar.

cc., c.c.: cubic centimeter, c.c. centímetro cúbico.

C.D.: compact disc, disco compacto, *m;* — **player,** reproductor de CD, *m.*

C.E.: Civil Engineer, Ing. Civil, Ingeniero Civil.

cease, *vt.* parar suspender, cesar, dejar de; —, *vi.* desistir.

ceaseless, *adj.* incesante, continuo.

cedar, *n.* cedro, *m.*

cede, *vt.* ceder, trasferir.

ceiling, *n.* techo o cielo raso de una habitación; (avi.) cielo máximo; —, *adj.* máximo.

celebrate, *vt.* celebrar; elogiar.

celebration, *n.* celebración, *f.;* alabanza, *f.*

celebrity, *n.* celebridad, fama, *f.;* persona célebre.

celery, *n.* apio, *m.*

celestial, *adj.* celeste, divino, celestial.

celibate, *n.* y *adj.* soltero, ra, célibe, *m.* y *f.*

cell, *n.* celda, *f.;* cueva, *f.;* célula, *f.*

cellar, *n.* sótano, *m.,* bodega, *f.*

cello, *n.* violonchelo, *m.*

cellophane, *n.* celofán, *m.*

cellular, *adj.* celular;— **phone,** teléfono celular, *m.*

celluloid, *n.* celuloide, *m.*

cellulose, *n.* (chem.) celulosa, *f.*

cement, *n.* argamasa, *f.;* cemento, *m.;* —, *vt.* pesar con cemento, conglutinar; —, *vi.* unirse.

cemetery, *n.* cementerio, camposanto, *m.*

cen., cent.: central, cent. central.

censor, *n.* censor, *m.;* crítico, *m.*

censorship, *n.* censura, *f.*

censure, *n.* censura, reprensión, *f.;* vt. censurar, reprender; criticar.

census, *n.* censo, encabezamiento, empadronamiento, *m.*

cent, *n.* centavo, *m.;* céntimo, *m.;* **per** —, por ciento.

cent.: **centigrade,** C. centígrado; century, siglo.

centennial, *n.* y *adj.* centenario, *m.*

center, *n.* centro, *m.;* (fútbol) centro, *m.;* —, *vt.* colocar en un centro; reconcentrar; —, *vi.* colocarse en el centro, reconcentrarse.

centigrade, *n.* y *adj.* centígrado, *m.*

centigram, *n.* centigramo, *m.*

centimeter, *n.* centímetro, *m.*

centipede, *n.* ciempiés, *m.*

central, *adj.* central; céntrico.

Central America, América Central, *f.*

centralization, *n.* centralización, *f,*

centralize, *vt.* centralizar.

centrifugal, *adj.* centrífugo.

century, *n.* centuria, *f.,* siglo, *m.*

C.E.O.: chief executive officer, director ejecutivo, *m;* presidente ejecutivo, *m.*

ceramics, *n.* cerámica, *f.*

cereal, *n.* cereal, *m.*

cerebellum, *n.* (anat.) cerebelo, *m.*

cerebral, *adj.* cerebral; — **palsy,** parálisis cerebral, diplegia espástica.

cerebrum, *n.* cerebro, *m.*

ceremonial, *adj.* ceremonial; —, *n.* ceremonial, *m.,* rito externo.

ceremonious, *adj.* ceremonioso.

ceremony, *n.* ceremonia, *f.*

cerise, *adj.* de color cereza.

certain, *adj.* cierto, evidente; **seguro,** certero, indudable; efectivo; — **sum,** —**quantity,** un tanto.

certainty, certitude, *n.* certeza, *f.;* seguridad, *f.;* certidumbre, *f.;* **with** —, a ciencia cierta.

certificate, *n.* certificado; testimonio, *m.;* (com.) bono, *m.;* certificación, *f.;* **birth** —, acta de nacimiento.

certified, *adj.* certificado; — **public accountant,** contador público titulado.

certify, *vt.* certificar, afirmar; dar fe.

cessation, *n.* cesación *f.*

cesspool, *n.* cloaca, *f.;* sumidero, *m.*

cg.: centigram, cg. centigramo.

chafe, *vt.* frotar, irritar.

chaff, *n.* burla, fisga, *f.;* paja menuda; cosa frívola e inútil; —, *vt.* y *vi.* dar bromas, chotear.

chagrin, *n.* mortificación, *f.;* disgusto, *m.*

chain, *n.* cadena, *f.;* serie, sucesión, *f.;* — **gang,** gavilla de malhechores encadenados juntos, collera, *f.;* — **reaction,** reacción en cadena; — **store,** tienda de una serie que pertenece a una misma empresa; —**s,** *n.* *pl.* esclavitud, *f.;* —, *vt.*

encadenar, atar con cadena.

chair, *n.* silla, *f.;* **easy —,** silla poltrona; **folding —,** silla plegadiza; **swivel —,** silla giratoria; **wheel —,** silla de ruedas; **—,** *vt.* entronizar; colocar en un cargo público.

chairman, *n.* presidente (de una reunión o junta), *m.*

chaise longue, *n.* canapé, sofá, *m.*

chalice, *n.* cáliz, *m.*

chalk, *n.* tiza, *f.;* gis, *m.;* yeso, *m.;* **—,** *vt.* dibujar con yeso o tiza; bosquejar, lapizar; **to — up,** aumentar un precio; ganar puntos.

chalky, *adj.* gredoso; yesoso; calcáreo.

challenge, *n.* desafío, cartel, *m.;* pretensión, *f.;* recusación, *f.;* **—,** *vt.* desafiar; retar; provocar, reclamar.

challenger, *n.* desafiador, ra, retador, ra.

chamber, *n.* cámara, *f.;* aposento, *m.;* (mil.) cámara de mina; **air —,** cámara de aire; **— music,** música de cámara;— **of commerce,** cámara de comercio, *f.*

chamberlain, *n.* camarero, *m.;* chambelán, *m.*

chamber maid, *n.* moza de cámara, camarera, *f.*

chambray, *n.* cambray, *m.*

chameleon, *n.* camaleón, *m.*

chamois, *n.* gamuza, *f.*

champ, *vt.* morder, mascar; **—,** *n.* (coll.) campeón, ona.

champagne, *n.* champaña, *m.,* (coll.) champán, *m.*

champion, *n.* campeón, ona; paladín, *m.;* **—,** *vt.* defender, respaldar, apoyar.

championship, *n.* campeonato, *m.*

chance, *n.* ventura, suerte, ocasión, oportunidad, casualidad, *f.,* acaso, *m.;* riesgo, *m.;* **by —,** por casualidad, por carambola; **—,** *vi.* acaecer, acontecer; **—,** *adj.* fortuito, casual.

chancellor, *n.* canciller, *m.;* rector, *m.*

chandelier, *n.* araña de luces.

change, *vt.* cambiar; trasmutar; variar; **to — cars,** trasbordar; **to — one's clothes,** mudar de ropa; **— vi.** variar, alterarse; revolverse (el tiempo); **—,** *n.* mudanza, variedad, *f.;* vicisitud, *f.;* cambio, *m.;* variación, *f.;* suelto (moneda), *m.;* **to make —,** cambiar (moneda).

changeable, *adj.* variable, inconstante; mudable, cambiante.

changeless, *adj.* inmutable.

change-over, *n.* cambio de ocupación o posición.

channel, *n.* canal, *m.;* conducto, *m.;* **TV —,** canal de televisión; **—,** *vt.* acanalar, estriar.

chant, *n.* sonsonete, *m.;* **—,** *vt.* cantar; repetir algo monótonamente.

chaos, *n.* caos, *m.,* confusión, *f.*

chaotic, *adj.* confuso, caótico.

chap, *vi.* rajarse, henderse, agrietarse; **—,** *n.* rendija, *f.;* mandíbula (de animal, etc.), *f.;* (coll.) mozo, chico, *m.;* tipo, *m.*

chapel, *n.* capilla, *f.*

chaperon, *n.* señora o señor de compañía; escolta, *f.;* **—,** *vt.* acompañar; escoltar.

chaplain, *n.* capellán, *m.*

chaps, *n. pl.* zahones, *m. pl.* chaparreras, *f. pl.*

chapter, *n.* capítulo, *m.;* cabildo, *m.;* filial de una confraternidad.

char, *vt.* hacer carbón de leña; carbonizar.

character, *n.* carácter, *m.;* señal, *f.;* distintivo, *m.;* letra, *f.;* calidad, *f.;* (theat.) parte, *f.;* papel, *m.;* personaje, *m.;* modalidad, *f.;* (coll.) persona rara o excéntrica.

characteristic, *adj.* característico; típico;—, *n.* rasgo, *m.,* peculiaridad, *f.*

characterize, *vt.* caracterizar, imprimir, calificar.

charade, *n.* charada, *f.*

charcoal, *n.* carbón, *m.;* carbón vegetal; carbón de leña.

charge, *vt.* encargar, comisionar; cobrar; cargar; acusar, imputar; **to — to account,** adeudar en cuenta, cargar en cuenta; **—,** *n.* cargo, cuidado, *m.;* mandato, *m.;* acusación, *f.;* tarifa, *f ;* (mil.) ataque, *m.;* carga, *f.;* **— collect,** porte debido, porte por cobrar; **— prepaid,** porte pagado o cobrado; **extra —,** gasto adicional; **— account,** cuenta abierta; **in — of,** a cargo de.

charger, *n.* caballo de guerra; (elec.) cargador, alimentador, *m.*

chariot, *n.* faetón, carruaje, *m.*

charitable, *adj.* caritativo, limosnero, benévolo; benigno, clemente.

charity, *n.* caridad, benevolencia, *f.;* limosna, *f.;* beneficencia, *f.*

charlatan, *n.* charlatán, curandero, *m.*

charm, *n.* encanto, *m.;* atractivo, *m.;* simpatía, *f.;* **—,** *vt.* encantar, embelesar, atraer; seducir.

charming, *adj.* seductor; simpático; encantador.

chart. *n.* carta de navegar; (avi.) carta, *f.;* hoja de información gráfica; cuadro, *m.;* **—,** *vt.* marcar en un cuadro; **to — a course,** marcar un derrotero.

charter, *n.* carta constitucional: letra patente; fletamento, *m.;* privilegio, *m.;* carta, *f.;* cédula, *f.;* **—,** *vt.* fletar (un barco, etc.); estatuir; **— member,** miembro o socio fundador.

chase, *vt.* cazar; perseguir; acosar; cincelar; **—,** *n.* caza, *f.;* **to give —,** corretear, perseguir.

chaser, n. (coll.) bebida alcohólica tomada después del café, tabaco, etc.; porción pequeña de agua, cerveza u otra bebida suave que se toma después de algún licor.

chasm, n. hendidura, f.; vacío, m.; abismo, m.

chassis, n. bastidor, m., armazón, f.; (auto.) chasis, m.

chaste, adj. casto; puro; honesto; púdico.

chasten, vt. corregir, castigar.

chastise, vt. castigar, reformar, corregir.

chastity, n. castidad, pureza, f.

chat, vi. charlar, platicar; —, n. plática, charla, conversación, f; — room, (internet) sala de chat, f.

chattel, n. bienes muebles, m. pl.

chatter, vi. cotorrear; charlar; castañetear; —, n. chirrido, m.; charla, f.

chatterbox, chatterer, n. parlanchín, ina, charlatán, ana.

chattering, adj. parlanchín, locuaz; —, n. charla, f.; rechinamiento, m.

chatty, adj. locuaz, parlanchín.

chauffeur, n. chófer, m.

cheap, adj. barato; —ly, adv. barato.

cheapen, vt. abaratar; denigrar.

cheat, vt. engañar, defraudar; hacer trampa; —, n. trampa, f.; fraude, engaño, m.; trampista, trápala, m. y f.

check, vt. reprimir, refrenar; verificar, comprobar; examinar; mitigar; regañar; registrar, facturar; to —, tener a raya; to — (baggage), documentar, facturar (el equipaje) ; to — in, llegar (a un hotel); to — out, salirse (de un hotel) ; to — off, eliminar; —, n. restricción, f ; freno, m.; represión, f.; jaque, m.; libranza, f.; póliza, f.; cheque, m.; cashier's —, cheque de caja; traveler's —, cheque de viajero.

checkbook, n. libro de cheques, libro talonario.

checker, n. verificador, ra.

checkerboard, n. tablero de damas.

checkers, n. juego de damas.

checking account, n. cuenta corriente, cuenta de cheques.

checkpoint, n. punto de referencia o comprobación.

checkroom, n. consigna, guardarropía, f., guardarropa, m.

cheek, n. cachete, carrillo, m., mejilla, f.; (coll.) desvergüenza, f., atrevimiento, m.

cheekbone, n. pómulo, m.

cheer, n. alegría, f.; buen humor; —, vt. animar, alentar; vitorear; —, vi. alegrarse, regocijarse; to — up, tomar ánimo; — up! ¡valor! ¡anímese!

cheerful, adj. alegre, vivo, jovial; campechano, genial; — mien, buena cara.

cheerfulness, n. alegría, f.; buen humor, júbilo, m.

cheering, adj. consolador.

cheerless, adj. melancólico, triste.

cheese, n. queso, m.; cottage —, requesón, m.

cheeseburger, n. hamburguesa con queso.

cheesecake, n. pastel de queso; (coll.) fotografías que exhiben desnudeces femeninas.

cheesecloth, n. estopilla, f., manta de cielo.

chef, n. cocinero, m., jefe de cocina.

chemical, adj. químico; —, n. sustancia química; — engineering, ingeniería química; — warfare, guerra química.

chemist, n. químico, ca.

chemistry, n. química, f.

chenille, n. felpilla, f.

cherish, vt. mantener, fomentar, proteger; acariciar; estimar; to — the hope, abrigar la esperanza.

cherry, n. cereza, f.; —, adj. bermejo.

cherub, n. querubín, m.

chess, n. ajedrez, m.

chessboard, n. tablero de ajedrez.

chest, n. pecho, m.; arca, f ; baúl, m.; cofre, m.; — of drawers, cómoda, f.

chestnut, n. castaña, f.; color de castaña; — tree, castaño, m.; —, adj. castaño.

chew, vt. y vi. mascar, masticar; rumiar; meditar, reflexionar.

chewing gum, n. chicle, m., goma de mascar.

chic, n. chic, m.; gracia, elegancia, f.; —, adj. elegante, muy de moda.

chick, n. pollito, polluelo, m.

chicken, n. pollo, m.; (fig.) joven, m. y f.; —pox, viruelas locas; varicela, f.; young —, pollo, lla.

chicken-hearted, adj. cobarde, tímido; — person, (coll.) gallina, m. y f.

chide, vt. reprobar, regañar; —, vi. reñir, alborotar.

chief, adj. principal, capital; — clerk, oficial mayor; commander in —, generalísimo, m., comandante en jefe; — justice, presidente de la corte suprema; — of staff, jefe de estado mayor. chieftain, n. jefe, comandante, m.

chiffon, n. chifón, m., gasa, f.

chilblain, n. sabañón, m.

child, n. infante, m.; hijo, ja; niño, ña; párvulo, m.; with —, embarazada, encinta.

childbirth, n. parto, alumbramiento, m.

childhood, n. infancia, niñez, f.

childish, adj. frívolo, pueril; —ly, adv. puerilmente.

childless, *adj.* sin hijos.

childlike, *adj.* pueril, infantil.

children, *n. pl.* niños, *m. pl.;* hijos, *m. pl.*

Chilean, *n. y adj.* chileno, na.

chili, *n.* chile, *m.; —* sauce, salsa de chile o de ají.

chill, *adj.* frío; —, *n.* frío, *m.;* escalofrío, *m.;* —, *vt.* enfriar; helar.

chilly, *adj.* algo frío.

chime, *n.* armonía, *f.;* repique, *m.;* —s, *pl.* juego de campanas; —, *vi.* sonar con armonía; concordar; —, *vt.* repicar.

chimney, *n.* chimenea, *f.;* — sweep, limpiachimeneas, *m.*

chimpanzee, *n.* chimpancé, *m.*

chin, *n.* barba, *f.,* mentón, *m.*

china, chinaware, *n.* porcelana, loza, *f.*

chinchilla, *n.* chinchilla, *f.*

chink, *n.* grieta, hendidura, *f.;—* , *vi.* henderse; resonar.

chintz, *n.* zaraza satinada.

chip, *vt.* desmenuzar, picar; —, *vi.* astillarse; —, *n.* brizna, astilla, *f.*

chipper, *adj.* (coll.) jovial, alegre.

chipmunk, *n.* variedad de ardilla.

chiropodist, *n.* pedicuro, *m.,* callista, *m.*

chiropractor, *n.* quiropráctico, *m.*

chirp, *vi.* chirriar, gorjear; —, *n.* gorjeo, chirrido, *m.*

chisel, *n.* escoplo, cincel, *m.;* —, *vt.* escoplear, cincelar, grabar; (coll.) estafar, engañar.

chiseler, *n.* oportunista, *m. y f.,* estafador, ra.

chivalrous, chivalric, *adj.* caballeroso.

chivalry, *n.* caballería, *f.;* hazaña, *f.;* caballerosidad, *f.*

chives, *n.* cebollino, *m.*

chloremia, *n.* cloremia, *f.*

chloride, *n.* cloruro, *m.*

chlorine, *n.* cloro, *m.*

chloroamphenicol, *n.* cloramfenicol, *m.*

chloroform, *n.* cloroformo, *m.*

Chloromycetin, *n.* (trademark) cloromicetina, *f.* (marca registrada).

chlorophyll, *n.* clorofila, *f.*

chock-full, *adj.* completamente lleno.

chocolate, *n.* chocolate, *m.*

choice, *n.* elección, selección, *f.;* preferencia, *f.;* opción, *f.;* —, *adj.* selecto, exquisito, excelente; escogido.

choir, *n.* coro, *m.*

choke, *vt.* sofocar; oprimir; tapar; —, *vi.* estrangularse; —, *n.* (auto.) regulador de aire, *m.*

choker, *n.* collar apretado.

cholera, *n.* cólera, *m.*

cholesterol, *n.* colesterol, *m.*

choose, *vt.* escoger, elegir, seleccionar.

chop, *vt.* tajar, cortar; picar; —, *n.* chuleta, *f.;* lamb —, chuleta de cordero; pork —, chuleta de puerco; veal —, chuleta de ternera; — suey, olla china; —s, *n. pl.* quijadas, *f. pl.*

chopsticks, *n. pl.* palillos (con que comen los chinos), *m. pl.*

choral, *adj.* coral.

chord, *n.* (mus.) acorde, *m.;* cuerda, *f.;* —, *vt.* encordar.

chore, *n.* tarea, *f.;* quehacer, *m.;* —s, *n. pl.* quehaceres de la casa.

choreography, *n.* coreografía, *f.*

chorister, *n.* corista, *m. y f.*

chorus, *n.* coro, *m.*

chose, *pretérito* del verbo choose.

chosen, *p.p.* del verbo choose.

chowder, *n.* sancocho (de pescado o almejas), *m.*

Christ, *n.* Jesucristo, Cristo, *m.*

christen, *vt.* cristianar, bautizar.

christening, *n.* bautismo, bautizo, *m.*

Christian, *n. y adj.* cristiano, na; — name, nombre de pila.

Christianity, *n.* cristianismo, *m.,* cristiandad, *f.*

Christmas, *n.* Navidad, Pascua, *f.;* — gift, aguinaldo, *m.;* — carol, villancico de Navidad; — Eve, víspera de Navidad, Nochebuena, *f.;* to wish a Merry —, desear felices Pascuas; — tree, árbol de Navidad; — Day, pascua de Navidad.

chrome, *n.* cromo, *m.*

chromium, *n.* cromo, *m.*

chromosome, *n.* cromosoma, *m.*

chronic, *adj.* crónico.

chronicle, *n.* crónica, *f.;* informe, *m.;* —, *vt.* hacer una crónica.

chronological, *adj.* cronológico.

chronology, *n.* cronología, *f.*

chrysalis, *n.* crisálida, .*f.*

chrysanthemum, *n.* crisantemo, *m.*

chubby, *adj.* gordo, cariancho, rechoncho.

chuck, *vi.* cloquear; —, *vt.* hacer a uno la mamola.

chuckle, *vi.* cloquear; reírse entre dientes.

chum, *n.* camarada, *m. y f.,* compañero, ra, amigo íntimo, amiga íntima.

chump, *n.* tajo, tronco, *m.;* (coll.) zopenco, ca, tonto, tonta.

chunk, *n.* (coll.) tajo, tronco, *m.;* (fig.) cantidad suficiente.

chunky, *adj.* rechoncho, macizo.

church, *n.* iglesia, *f.;* templo, *m.;* — music, música sagrada.

churchgoer, *n.* devoto, ta, persona que asiste fielmente a la iglesia.

churchman, *n.* sacerdote, eclesiástico, *m.*

churchyard, *n.* cementerio, *m.;* patio de la iglesia.

churl, *n.* patán, rústico, *m.*

churn, *n.* mantequera, mantequillera, *f.;* —, *vt.* mazar, batir la leche para hacer manteca o mantequilla.

chute, *n.* vertedor, *m.*

cider, *n.* sidra, *f.*

C.I.F., c.i.f.: cost, insurance and freight, c.s.f. costo, seguro y flete.

cigar, *n.* cigarro, puro, *m.;* — **butt,** colilla, *f.;* — **box,** cigarrera, *f.*

cigarette, *n.* cigarrillo cigaro, *m.,* pitillo, *m.;* —**butt,** colilla, *f.;* —**case,** portacigarros, *m.,* pitillera, cigarrera, *f.;* — **holder,** boquilla, *f.;* — **lighter,** encendedor de cigarros, mechero, *m.*

cinch, *n.* cincha, *f.;* (coll.) algo muy fácil.

cinder, *n.* ceniza gruesa y caliente.

cinema, *n.* cinematógrafo, cine, *m.*

cinnamon, *n.* canela, *f.*

CIO, C.I.O.: Congress of Industrial Organizations, C.I.O. Congreso de Organizaciones Industriales (de E.U.A.).

cipher, *n.* cifra, *f.,* número, *m.;* cero, *m.;* —, *vi.* numerar, calcular.

circle, *n.* círculo, *m.;* corrillo, *m.;* asamblea, *f.;* rueda, *f.;* —, *vt.* circundar; cercar, ceñir; —, *vi.* circular.

circuit, *n.* ámbito, circuito, *m.;* vuelta, *f.*

circular, *adj.* circular, redondo; —, *n.* carta circular.

circularize, *vt.* hacer circular (algún anuncio, etc.).

circulate, *vi.* circular; moverse alrededor.

circulating, *adj.* circulante.

circulation, *n.* circulación, *f.*

circumcise, *vt.* circuncidar.

circumcision, *n.* circuncisión, *f.*

circumference, *n.* circunferencia, *f.;* circuito, *m.*

circumflex, *n.* acento circunflejo.

circumnavigate, *vt.* circumnavegar.

circumspect, *adj.* circunspecto, prudente, reservado.

circumstance, *n.* circunstancia, condición, *f.;* incidente, *m.;* —**s,** situación económica.

circumstantial, *adj.* accidental; indirecto; circunstancial; accesorio; — **evidence,** evidencia circunstancial.

circumvent, *vt.* embaucar, engañar con estratagema.

circus, *n.* circo, *m.;* arena, *f.;* hipódromo, *m.*

cistern, *n.* cisterna, *f.*

citadel, *n.* ciudadela, fortaleza, *f.*

citation, *n.* citación, mención, *f.*

cite, *vt.* citar (a juicio); alegar; citar, referirse a.

citizen, *n.* ciudadano na; **fellow —,** conciudadano, *m.*

citizenry, *n.* masa de ciudadanos.

citizenship, *n.* ciudadanía, *f.;* nacionalidad, *f.;* — **papers,** carta de ciudadanía.

citric, *adj.* cítrico.

citron, *n.* cidra, *f.*

citrus, *adj.* (bot.) cítrico.

city, *n.* ciudad, *f.;* — **hall,** ayuntamiento, *m.;* palacio municipal.

city planning, *n.* urbanización, planificación,.

civic, *adj.* cívico; —**s,** *n.* instrucción cívica.

civil, *adj.* civil, cortés; — **engineer,** ingeniero civil; — **service,** servicio civil.

civilian, *n.* paisano, na (persona no militar), particular, *m.;* jurisconsulto, *m.*

civilization, *n.* civilización, *f.*

civilize, *vt.* civilizar.

clack, *n.* ruido continuo, golpeo, *m.*

clad, *adj.* vestido, cubierto.

claim, *vt.* pedir en juicio, reclamar, pretender como cosa debida; —, *n.* pretensión, *f ;* derecho, *m.;* reclamo, *m.;* reclamación, *f.;* **to enter a —,** demandar.

claimant, *n.* reclamante, *m. y f.;* demandador, ra.

clam, *n.* almeja, *f.;* — **chowder,** sopa de almejas.

clamber, *vi.* gatear, trepar.

clammy, *adj.* viscoso; tenaz.

clamor, *n.* clamor, grito, *m.;* vocería, *f.;* —, *vi.* vociferar, gritar.

clamorous, *adj.* clamoroso, tumultuoso, estrepitoso; —**ly,** *adv.* clamorosamente.

clamp, *n.* barrilete, *m.;* collar, *m.;* abrazadera, *f.;* manija, *f.;* collera, *f.;* tenazas, pinzas, *f. pl.;* grapa, laña, *f.;* sujetador, *m.;* —, *vt.* sujetar, afianzar; empalmar.

clan, *n.* clan, *m.,* familia, tribu, raza, *f.*

clandestine, *adj.* clandestino, oculto.

clang, *n.* rechino, sonido desapacible; —, *vi.* rechinar; sonar.

clank, *vi.* rechinar; chillar; —, *n.* sonido estridente; retintín, *m.*

clannish, *adj.* estrechamente unido, gregario.

clansman, *n.* miembro de un clan.

clap, *vt.* batir; aplicar; palmear; —, *vi.* palmear, palmotear, aplaudir; **to — hands,** batir palmas; —, *n.* estrépito, *m.;* golpe, *m.;* trueno, *m.;* palmoteo, *m.*

clapboard, *n.* tejamanil, *m.;* chilla, *f.*

clapper, *n.* palmoteador, ra; badajo de campana; llamador (de una puerta), *m.*

clapping, *n.* palmada, *f.;* aplauso, palmoteo, *m.*

clarify, *vt.* clarificar, aclarar; —, *vi.* aclararse.

clarinet, *n.* clarinete, *m.*

clarity, *n.* claridad, *f.*

clash, *vi.* encontrarse; chocar; contradecir; —, *vt.* batir, golpear; —, *n.* crujido, *m.;*

estrépito, m.; disputa, f; choque, m.

clasp, n. broche, m.; hebilla, f.; sujetador, m.; manija, f.; abrazo, m.; —, vt. abrochar; abrazar.

class, n. clase, f.; género, m.; categoría, f.; —, vt. clasificar.

classic, n. y adj. clásico, m.

classical, adj. clásico.

classification, n. clasificación, f.

classify, vt. clasificar, graduar.

classmate, n. condiscípulo, la.

classroom, n. aula, f., sala de clase.

clatter, vi. resonar; hacer ruido; —, n. ruido, alboroto, m.

clause, n. cláusula, f.; artículo, m.; estipulación, f.; condición, f.

claustrophobia, n. claustrofobia, f.

claw, n. garra, f.; garfa, f.; —, vt. desgarrar, arañar.

clay, n. barro, m.; arcilla, f.

clean, adj. limpio; casto; —, adv. enteramente; —, vt. limpiar.

clean-cut, adj. bien tallado; bien parecido; de buen carácter.

cleaner, n. limpiador, ra; sacamanchas, quitamanchas, m.

cleaning, n. limpieza, f.

cleanliness, n. limpieza, f.; aseo, m.

cleanly, adj. limpio; puro, delicado; —, adv. primorosamente, aseadamente.

cleanse, vt. limpiar, purificar; purgar.

clear, adj. claro, lucido; diáfano; neto; límpido; sereno; evidente; inocente; —, vt. clarificar, aclarar; justificar; absolver; **to — the table,** quitar la mesa; **to—up,** aclararse, despejarse (por ej. el cielo); —, vi. aclararse.

clearance, n. despejo, m.; (com.) despacho de aduana; utilidad líquida; (avi.) espacio, m.; (mech.) juego limpio (de una pieza, etc.) ; **— sale,** liquidación, f.

clear-cut, adj. claro, bien definido.

clear-headed, adj. listo, inteligente.

clearing, n. espacio libre; aclaración, f. **— house,** casa de compensación.

clear-sighted, adj. perspicaz, juicioso; clarividente.

cleat, n. listón de refuerzo; abrazadera, manija, f.; (naut.) cornamusa, f.

cleave, vt. y vi. hender; partir; dividir; pegarse.

cleaver, n. cuchillo de carnicero.

clef, n. (mus.) clave, f.

cleft, n. hendidura, abertura, f.

clemency, n. clemencia, f.

clench, vt. cerrar, agarrar, asegurar.

clergy, n. clero, m.

clergyman, n. eclesiástico, clérigo, m.

cleric, n. clérigo, m.

clerical, adj. clerical, eclesiástico; —, **work,**

trabajo de oficina.

clerk, n. eclesiástico, clérigo; m.; amanuense, escribiente, m.; dependiente, m.; **chief —,** oficial mayor.

clever, adj. diestro, hábil, mañoso; inteligente.

cleverness, n. destreza, habilidad, f.; inteligencia, f.

clew, n. ovillo de hilo; pista, f.; indicio, m.; —, vt. (naut.) cargar las velas.

click, vi. sonar; (coll.) pegar, prosperar, gustar al público; —, n. ruidito (como de un reloj).

client, n. cliente, m. y f.

clientele, n. clientela, f.

cliff, n. peñasco, asco, m.; precipicio, m., barranca, f.

climate, n. clima, m.; temperatura, f.

climax, n. colmo, m., culminación, f.; clímax, m.

climb, vt. escalar, trepar; —, vi. subir.

climber, n. trepador, ra; arribista, m. y f., persona que aspira a escalas sociales más altas.

clinch, vt. empuñar, cerrar el puño; remachar un clavo; —, vi. agarrarse; —, n. agarro, agarrón, m.

cling, vi. colgar, adherirse, pegarse.

clinic, adj. clínico; —, n. clínica, f.; consultorio, m.; clínica médica.

clinical, adj. clínico.

clink, vt. hacer resonar; —, vi. resonar; —, n. retintín, m.

clip, vt. recortar; cortar a raíz; escatimar; —, n. tijeretada, f.; grapa, f.; gancho, m.

clipper, n. (naut.) navío velero; (avi.) clíper, m.; trasquilador, m.; hidroavión, m.; **—s,** n. pl. tijeras podadoras.

clipping, n. recorte, m.

clique, n. camarilla, pandilla, f.

cloak, n. capa, f.; capote, m.; pretexto, m.; —, vt. encapotar, paliar, encubrir.

cloakroom, n. guardarropa, m., guardarropía, f.

clock, n. reloj, m. **alarm —,** despertador, m.

clockmaker, n. relojero, m.

clockwise, adj. con movimiento circular a la derecha.

clockwork, n. mecanismo de un reloj; **like—,** sumamente exacto y puntual.

clod, n. terrón, m.; tierra, f.; suelo, m.; césped, m.; zoquete, m.; hombre estúpido.

clog, n. obstáculo, m.; galocha, f.; —, vt. obstruir; —, vi. coagularse.

cloister, n. claustro, monasterio, m.

close, vt. cerrar, tapar; concluir, terminar; —, vi. cerrarse, unirse, convenirse; **to —** **(an account),** finiquitar (una cuenta); —, *n.* cercado, *m.;* fin, *m.;* conclusión, *f.;* cierre, *m.;* —, *adj.* cerrado; preso; estrecho, angosto; ajustado; avaro; — **fight,** combate reñido; — **quarters,** lugar estrecho, espacio limitado; —, *adv.* de cerca; junto; estrechamente; secretamente; — **by,** muy cerca.

closed, *adj.* cerrado; — **shop,** contrato colectivo.

closed-circuit, *adj.* en circuito cerrado.

close-fitting, *adj.* entallado, ajustado, estrecho; ceñido al cuerpo.

closemouthed, *adj.* callado, discreto, reservado.

closeness, *n.* estrechez, espesura, reclusión, *f.*

closet, *n.* ropero, *m.;* gabinete, *m.;* **water** —, retrete, *m.;* —, *vt.* encerrar en un gabinete o en un ropero.

close-up, *n.* fotografía de cerca; algo visto muy de cerca.

closing, *n.* cierre, *m.;* conclusión, *f.;* clausura, *f.*

clot, *n.* grumo, *m.,* coagulación, *f.;* **blood** —, embolia, *f.;* —, *vi.* cuajarse, coagularse.

cloth, *n.* paño, *m.;* mantel, *m.;* lienzo, *m.;* material, *m.;* — **binding,** encuadernación en tela.

clothe, *vt.* vestir, cubrir.

clothes, *n. pl.* vestidura, *f.;* ropa, *f.;* — **closet,** ropero, *m.;* — **hanger,** percha, *f.;* colgador o gancho de ropa; **bed** —, ropa de cama.

clothesbasket, *n.* cesta para ropa.

clothesbrush, *n.* cepillo para ropa.

clothesline, *n.* cuerda para tender la ropa, tendedero, *m.*

clothespin, *n.* gancho de tendedero, pinza para tender la ropa.

clothier, *n.* pañero, *m.;* persona que vende ropa.

clothing, *n.* vestidos, *m. pl.;* ropa, *f.*

cloud, *n.* nube, *f.;* nublado, *m.;* (fig.) adversidad, *f.;* —, *vt.* anublar; oscurecer; —, *vi.* anublarse, nublarse; oscurecerse.

cloudburst, *n.* chaparrón, *m.,* tormenta de lluvia.

cloudy, *adj.* nublado, nubloso; oscuro; sombrío, melancólico; pardo.

clove, *n.* (bot.) clavo, *m.*

cloven, *adj.* partido, hendido.

clover, *n.* trébol, *m.*

cloverleaf, *n.* hoja de trébol; trébol (en una carretera), *m.*

clown, *n.* payaso, sa.

clownish, *adj.* bufón, truhán.

cloy, *vt.* empalagar; saciar; hartar.

club, *n.* círculo, club, *m.;* garrote, *m.;* **—s,**

pl. bastos (en la baraja), *m. pl.;* —, *vi.* unirse, formar un club; —, *vt.* golpear con un garrote; congregar; contribuir.

clubhouse, *n.* casino, club, *m.*

cluck, clucking, *n.* cloqueo, *m.*

cluck, *vi.* cacarear.

clue = **clew.**

clump, *n.* trozo sin forma; bosquecillo, *m.*

clumsiness, *n.* torpeza, desmaña, *f.*

clumsy, *adj.* torpe, sin arte; desmañado.

clung, *pretérito y p.p.* del verbo **cling.**

cluster, *n.* racimo, *m.;* manada, *f.;* pelotón, *m.;* —, *vt.* agrupar; —, *vi.* arracimarse; agruparse.

clutch, *n.* (auto.) embrague, *m.;* garra, *f.;* acoplamiento, *m.;* — **pedal,** pedal del embrague; —, *vt.* embragar; empuñar, agarrar.

clutter, *vt.* poner en desorden; **to** — **up,** alborotar; —, *n.* confusión, *f.*

Co., co.: Company, Cía., Comp. Compañía; **county,** condado.

C.O.: Commanding Officer, Comandante en Jefe.

c/o, c.o.: carried over, sigue; **in care of,** a/c a cargo de.

coach, *n.* coche, *m.;* carroza, *f ;* vagón, *m.;* entrenador (en un deporte), *m.;* —, *vt.* entrenar, preparar.

coachman, *n.* cochero, *m.*

coagulate, *vt.* coagular, cuajar; —, *vi.* coagularse, cuajarse, espesarse.

coal, *n.* carbón, *m.;* **bituminous** —, carbón bituminoso; — **dealer,** — **miner,** carbonero, *m.;* — **mine,** — **pit,** mina de carbón, carbonería, *f.;* — **oil,** querosina, *f.;* —**tar,** alquitrán de hulla, brea, *f.;* **anthracite** o **hard** —, antracita, *f.;* **soft** —, hulla, *f.;* —, *adj.* carbonero; carbonífero.

coalesce, *vi.* juntarse, incorporarse.

coalition, *n.* coalición, confederación, *f.*

coarse, *adj.* basto; ordinario; rústico; grueso.

coarsen, *vt.* hacer basto, burdo o vulgar; —, *vi.* hacerse basto.

coarseness, *n.* tosquedad, grosería, *f.*

coast, *n.* costa, *f.;* litoral, *m.;* —, *adj.* litoral; — **guard,** guardacostas, *m.;* — **line,** litoral, *m.;* costa, *f.;* línea costanera; —, *vi.* costear; ir de bajada (en un vehículo) por impulso propio.

coastal, *adj.* costero, costanero.

coaster, *n.* piloto, *m.;* buque costanero; — **brake,** freno de bicicleta.

coasting, *n.* cabotaje, *m.;* acción de rodar cuesta abajo.

coastwise, *adj.* costanero, a lo largo de la costa.

coat, *n.* saco, *m.;* chaqueta, americana, *f.;* abrigo, gabán, *m.;* capote, *m.;* — **of**

arms, escudo de armas; — **of paint,** mano de pintura; —, vt. cubrir, vestir; bañar.

coating, n. revestimiento, m.; capa, f.; mano (de pintura, etc.), f.

coatroom, n. guardarropa, m.

coax, vt. instar, rogar con lisonja.

coaxial, adj. coaxial; — **cable,** cable coaxial.

cob, n. cisne macho; mazorca de maíz; jaca, f.

cobalt, n. cobalto, m.

cobbler, n. zapatero remendón; zapatero, m.

cobblestone, n. guijarro, m.

cobweb, n. telaraña, f.; (fig.) trama, f.

cocaine, n. cocaína, f.

cock, n. gallo, m.; macho, m.; veleta, giraldilla, f.; grifo, m.; llave, f.; —, vt. montar (una escopeta); **to — the head,** erguir la cabeza.

cockfight, cockfighting, n. pelea de gallos.

cockpit, n. reñidero de gallos; (avi.) casilla o cámara de piloto; cabina, f.; (naut.) casilla, f.

cockroach, n. cucaracha, f.

cockscomb, n. cresta de gallo; (fig.) fachendoso, farolero, m.

cocktail, n. coctel, m.

cocky, adj. (coll.) engreído; arrogante.

cocoa, n. cacao, m.; chocolate, m.

coconut, n. coco, m.; — **palm,** cocotero, m.

cocoon, n. capullo del gusano de seda.

cod, n. bacalao, m.; merluza, f.

C.O.D., c.o.d.: cash on delivery, collect on delivery, C.A.E., cóbrese al entregar.

coddle, vt. sancochar (huevos, etc.); acariciar; consentir; mimar, (Max.) papachar.

code, n. código, m.; clave, f.

codfish, n. bacalao, m.

cod-liver oil, n. aceite de hígado de bacalao.

coeducational, adj. coeducativo.

coefficient, n. coeficiente, m.

coerce, vt. obligar, forzar.

coercion, n. coerción, f.

coexistence, n. coexistencia, f.

coffee, n. café, m.; — **break,** pausa en el trabajo para tomar café; — **plantation,** cafetal, m.; — **free,** cafeto, café, m.

coffeepot, n. cafetera, f.

coffer, n. cofre, m.; caja, f.

coffin, n. féretro, ataúd, m.; caja, f.

cog, n. diente (de rueda), m.

cogent, adj. convincente, urgente.

cogitate, vi. pensar, meditar.

cognac, n. coñac, m.

cognate, adj. consanguíneo; cognado, de origen similar.

cognizance, n. conocimiento, m.; divisa, f.; competencia, jurisdicción, f.

cognizant, adj. informado, sabedor; (leyes) competente.

cogwheel, n. rueda dentada; rodezno, m.

cohabit, vi. cohabitar.

coherence, n. coherencia, conexión, f.

coherent, adj. coherente, consistente, lógico.

cohesion, n. coherencia, f.; cohesión, f.

cohesive, adj. cohesivo.

cohort, n. cohorte, f.; secuaz, partidario, m.

coiffure, n. peinado, tocado, m.

coil, vt. recoger; enrollar; —, n. (elec.) carrete, m.; bobina, f.; espiral, f.; rollo, m.

coin, n. cuña, f.; moneda, f; dinero, m.; —, vt. acuñar moneda; falsificar; inventar (palabras, etc.).

coincide, vi. coincidir, concurrir, convenir.

coincidence, n. coincidencia, f.; casualidad, f.

coke, n. coque, m.; (coll.) coca cola, f.

Col.: Colonel, Cnel. Coronel.

colander, n. coladera, f.; colador, m.

cold, adj. frío; indiferente, insensible; reservado; yerto; — **cream,** crema para la cara; — **storage,** conservación en cámara frigorífica; — **war,** guerra fría; **to be —,** hacer frío; tener frío; —, n. frío, m.; frialdad, f.; (med.) catarro, resfriado; m.; **to catch —,** constiparse, resfriarse.

cold-blooded, adj. impasible; cruel; en sangre fría.

coldness, n. frialdad, f.; indiferencia, insensibilidad, apatía, f.

coleslaw, n. ensalada de col.

colic, n. cólico, m.

coliseum, n. coliseo, anfiteatro, m.

colitis, n. (med.) colitis, f.

collaborate, vt. cooperar; colaborar.

collaboration, n. colaboración, f.; cooperación, f.

collaborator, n. colaborador, ra.

collapse, vi. desplomarse; —, n. hundimiento, m.; (med.) colapso, f.; derrumbe, desplome, m.

collapsible, adj. plegadizo.

collar, n. collar, m.; collera, f.; —, vt. agarrar a uno por el cuello.

collarbone, n. clavícula, f.

collateral, adj. colateral; indirecto; —, n. aval, m., garantía (en un préstamo),

colleague, n. colega, m. y f., compañero, ra.

collect, vt. recoger, colegir; cobrar; **to —** (taxes, etc.) recaudar (impuestos, etc.).

collection, n. colecta, f.; colección, f.; compilación, f.; cobro, m.

collective, adj. colectivo, congregado; — **bargaining,** trato colectivo.

collectivism, n. colectivismo, m.

collector, n. colector, m.; agente de cobros; — **of customs,** administrador de aduana.

college, n. universidad, f., colegio universitario.

collegiate, adj. colegial.

collide, vi. chocar, estrellarse.

collie n. perro pastor, m.

collision, n. colisión, f.; choque, m., atropello (de automóvil), m.

cologne, n. agua colonia, agua de Colonia.

coll. : colloquial, fam. familiar.

colloquial, adj. familiar, aceptable en conversación familiar.

colloquialism, n. expresión familiar.

collusion, n. colusión, f.

colon, n. (anat.) colon, m.; dos puntos (signo de puntuación).

colonel, n. (mil.) coronel, m.

colonial, adj. colonial.

colonist, n. colono, m.; colonizador, ra.

colonize, vt. colonizar.

colony, n. colonia, f.

color, n. color m.; pretexto, m.; — **blindness,** daltonismo, m.; —**s,** n. pl. bandera, f.; —, vt. colorar; paliar; —, vi. enrojecerse, ponerse colorado.

color-blind adj. daltoniano.

colored, adj. colorado, pintado, teñido; de raza negra; con prejuicio.

colorful, adj. pintoresco, lleno de colorido.

coloring, n. colorido, m.; colorante, m.

colorless, adj. descolorido, incoloro.

colossal, adj. colosal.

colt, n. potro, m.; muchacho sin juicio.

Columbus, Colón.

column, n. columna, f.

columnist, n. periodista encargado de una sección especial.

Com.: Commander, jefe; **Commission,** Com. comisión; **Committee,** Com. comité, comisión; **Commodore,** Com. comodoro.

coma, n. (med.) coma, f., letargo, m.

comb, n. peine, m.; almohaza, f.; —, vt. peinar; almohazar; cardar (la lana) ; **to— one's hair,** peinarse.

combat, n. combate, m.; batalla, f.; —, vt. y vi. combatir; resistir.

combatant, n. combatiente, m. y f.

combination, n. combinación, f.

combine, vt. combinar; —, vi. unirse; —, n. (agr.) máquina segadora, máquina trilladora; (coll.) combinación de personas u organizaciones para provecho comercial o político.

combustible, adj. combustible, inflamable.

combustion, n. combustión, f.; incendio, m.; agitación violenta; — **chamber,** cámara de combustión.

Comdr.: Commander, jefe.

Comdt.: Commandant, Com. comandante.

come, vi. venir, acontecer; originar; **to — back,** volver; **to — forward,** avanzar; **to — upon,** encontrarse con; **to — to,** volver en sí.

comeback, n. vuelta, f.; recobro, m.; rehabilitación, f.; recobranza, f.; réplica mordaz.

comedian, n. comediante, m. y f., cómico, ca.

comedienne, n. actriz cómica.

comedown, n. cambio desfavorable de circunstancias; descenso en posición social.

comedy, n. comedia, f.; sainete, m.

comeliness, n. gracia, f.; garbo, m.

comely, adj. garboso, gracioso.

comet, n. cometa, m.

comfort, n. consuelo, m.; comodidad, f.; bienestar, m.; —, vt. confortar; alentar; consolar.

comfortable, adj. cómodo; consolatorio.

comforter, n. colcha, f.; consolador, ra.

comforting, adj. confortante, consolador.

comic, adj. cómico, burlesco; chistoso; — **opera,** ópera bufa; — **strip,** historieta cómica; —**s,** n. pl. historietas cómicas, (Mex.) montos, m. pl.

comical, adj. chistoso, gracioso, bufo, burlesco.

coming, n. venida, llegada, f.; —, adj. venidero, entrante; — **from,** procedente de.

comma, n. (gram.) coma, f.

command, vt. ordenar; mandar; —, vi. gobernar; imperar; mandar; —, n. orden, f., comando, m.; señorío, m.

commandant, n. comandante, m.

commandeer, vt. (mil.) decomisar, confiscar; obligar el reclutamiento.

commander, n. jefe, m.; comandante, m.; capitán, m.; capitán de fragata; — **in chief,** capitán general, generalísimo, m.; **lieutenant —,** capitán de corbeta.

commandment, n. mandato, precepto, m.; mandamiento, m.

commando, n. comando, m., incursión o expedición militar.

commemorate, vt. conmemorar; celebrar.

commemoration, n. conmemoración, f.

commence, vt. y vi. comenzar.

commencement, n. principio, m.; ejercicios de graduación.

commend, vt. encomendar, encargar; alabar.

commendable, adj. recomendable; digno

de encomio.

commendation, n. recomendación, f.; encomio, m.

commensurate, adj. conmensurativo, en proporción.

comment, n. glosa, f.; comentario, m.; —, vt. comentar, glosar.

commentary, n. comentario, m.; interpretación, f.; glosa, f.

commentator, n. comentador, ra; (rad. y TV.) locutor, ra.

commerce, n. comercio, tráfico, trato, negocio, m.; **chamber of —,** cámara de comercio.

commercial, adj. comercial; —, n. comercial, anuncio, m.

commercialize, vt. comerciar, explotar un negocio, poner un producto en el mercado.

commissar, n. jefe de gobierno en la Rusia soviética.

commiserate, vt. compadecer, tener compasión; —, vi. compadecerse.

commissary, n. comisario, m.; comisariato, m.

commission, n. comisión, f.; patente, f.; corretaje, m.; **— agent,** agente comisionista; **out of —,** inutilizado, gastado; **— merchant,** comisionista, m.; —, vt. comisionar; encargar; apoderar. **commissioned officer,** n. (mil.) oficial, m.

commissioner, n. comisionado, delegado, m.

commit, vt. cometer; depositar; encargar; **to — to memory,** aprender de memoria.

commitment, commital, n. compromiso, m.; comisión, f.; (leyes) auto de prisión.

committee, n. comité, m.; comisión, junta, f.

commodious, adj. cómodo, conveniente; **— ly,** adv. cómodamente.

commodity, n. artículo de consumo; mercadería, f.

commodore, n. (naut.) jefe de escuadra, comodoro, m.

common, adj. común, público, general; ordinario; **— carrier,** portador, m.; **— law,** ley a fuerza de costumbre; **— people,** pueblo, m.; **— pleas,** (leyes) causas ajenas; **— sense,** sentido práctico; **— stock,** acciones comunes u ordinarias; —, n. lo usual; **in —,** en común.

commoner, n. plebeyo, ya; miembro de la cámara baja (en Inglaterra) .

commonplace, n. lugar común; —, adj. trivial, banal.

commonwealth, n. república, f.; estado, m.; nación, f.

commotion, n. tumulto, m.; perturbación del ánimo.

commune, vi. conversar; tener confidencias; comulgar; —, n. comuna, f., menor división política de Francia, Italia, etc.; distrito municipal.

communicable, adj. comunicable.

communicate, vt. comunicar, participar; —, vi. comunicarse.

communication, n. comunicación, f.; participación, f.; escrito, m.

communicative, adj. comunicativo.

communion, n. comunidad, f.; comunión, f.; **to take —,** comulgar.

communiqué, n. comunicación oficial.

communism, n. comunismo, m.

communist, n. comunista, m. y f.

community, n. comunidad, f.; república, f.; común, m.; colectividad, f.; —, adj. comunal; **— chest,** caja de la comunidad, fondos benéficos de la comunidad.

commutation, n. mudanza, f.; conmutación, f.; **— ticket,** billete o boleto de abono.

commutator, n. (elec.) conmutador, colector, m.

commute, vt. conmutar; —, vi. viajar diariamente.

commuter, n. persona que viaja diariamente de una localidad a otra.

compact, adj. compacto, sólido, denso; **— car,** automóvil pequeño; —, n. pacto, convenio, m.; neceser, m.; polvera, f.; **— ly,** adv. estrechamente; en pocas palabras.

companion, n. compañero, ra; acompañante, m. y f.

companionable, adj. sociable.

companionship, n. camaradería, f.; compañerismo, m.; sociedad, compañía, f.

company, n. compañía, sociedad, f.; compañía comercial; **to keep —,** hacer compañía a; tener relaciones con; **to part —** (with), separarse; **— union,** unión de los obreros de una empresa sin otras conexiones.

comparable, adj. comparable.

comparative, adj. comparativo.

compare, vt. comparar, colacionar; confrontar; —, n. comparación, f.; **beyond —,** sin igual, sin comparación.

comparison, n. comparación, f.; símil, m.; **in — with,** comparado con; **beyond —,** sin comparación, sin igual.

compartment, n. compartimiento, compartimento, m.

compass, n. alcance, m.; circunferencia, f.; compás, m.; brújula, f.; —, vt. circundar.

compassion, n. compasión, piedad, f.

compatibility, n. compatibilidad, f.

compatible, adj. compatible.

compatriot, *n.* compatriota, *m.* y *f.*

compel, *vt.* compeler, obligar, constreñir.

compensate, *vt.* y *vi.* compensar.

compensation, *n.* compensación, *f.;* resarcimiento, *m.*

compete, *vi.* competir.

competence, *n.* competencia, *f.;* suficiencia, *f.*

competent, *adj.* competente, capaz; adecuado; caracterizado.

competition, *n.* competencia, *f.;* concurso, *m.*

competitive, *adj.* competidor.

competitor, *n.* competidor, ra; rival, *m.*

compilation, *n.* compilación, *f.*

compile, *vt.* compilar.

complacence, complacency, *n.* complacencia, *f.;* propia satisfacción.

complacent, *adj.* complaciente, deseoso de servir; satisfecho de sí mismo.

complain, *vi.* quejarse, lamentarse; dolerse.

complainant, *n.* (leyes) querellante, demandante, *m.*

complaining, *adj.* quejoso.

complaint, *n.* queja, pena; *f.;* lamento, llanto, quejido, *m.;* reclamación, *f.; to file a —,* (leyes) quejarse, poner una queja.

complaisant, *adj.* complaciente, cortés.

complement, *n.* complemento, *m.; —, vt.* completar, complementar.

complementary, *adj.* complementario.

complete, *adj.* completo, cumplido, perfecto; *—, vt.* completar, acabar; llevar a cabo; rematar; *—ly, adv.* completamente, a fondo.

completion, *n.* complemento, colmo, *m.,* terminación, *f.;* perfeccionamiento, *m.*

complex, *adj.* complejo, compuesto; *—, n.* complejo, *m.;* **inferiority —,** complejo de inferioridad.

complexion, *n.* cutis, *m.,* tez, *f.;* aspecto general.

compliance, *n.* sumisión, condescendencia, *f.;* consentimiento, *m.;* **in — with,** de acuerdo con, accediendo (a sus deseos, etc.).

complicate, *vt.* complicar.

complicated, *adj.* complicado, embrollado.

complication, *n.* complicación, *f.*

complicity, *n.* complicidad, *f.*

compliment, *n.* cumplido, *m.;* lisonja, *f.;* (coll.) piropo, requiebro, *m.; —, vt.* echar flores; ensalzar, alabar.

complimentary, *adj.* ceremonioso; piropero; gratis, de cortesía.

comply, *vi.* cumplir; condescender, conformarse.

component, *adj.* componente.

compose, *vt.* componer; sosegar; concertar, reglar, ordenar; **to — oneself,** serenarse.

composed, *adj.* sosegado, moderado; **to be — of,** componerse de.

composer, *n.* autor, ra; compositor, ra; cajista, *m.* y *f.*

composite, *n.* compuesto, *m.;* mezcla, *f.;* combinación de varias partes.

composition, *n.* composición, *f.;* compuesto, *m.*

compositor, *n.* cajista, *m.* y *f.; (mus.)* compositor, ra.

composure, *n.* calma, *f.;* tranquilidad, *f.;* sangre fría; **to lose one's —,** perder la calma, perder la serenidad.

compound, *vt.* componer, combinar; *—, adj.* compuesto; *—, n.* compuesto, *m.;* (med.) confección, *f* .

comprehend, *vt.* comprender, contener; entender, penetrar.

comprehensible, *adj.* comprensible, fácil de comprender, concebible.

comprehension, *n.* comprensión, *f.;* inteligencia, *f.*

comprehensive, *adj.* comprensivo, que contiene o incluye.

compress, *vt.* comprimir, estrechar; *—, n.* cabezal, fomento, *m.*

compression, *n.* compresión, *f.*

comprise, *vt.* comprender; incluir.

compromise, *n.* transacción, *f.,* convenio, *m.; —, vi.* transigir.

comptometer, *n.* contómetro, *m.*

comptroller, *n.* sobrestante, interventor, *m.*

compulsion, *n.* compulsión, *f.;* apremio, *m.*

compulsive, *adj.* coactivo; obligatorio, compulsivo; *—ly, adv.* por fuerza.

compulsory, *adj.* obligatorio, compulsivo.

compunction, *n.* compunción, contrición, *f.*

computation, *n.* computación, cuenta, *f.;* cómputo, cálculo, *m.*

compute, *vt.* computar, calcular.

computer, *n.* computadora, *f.;* ordenador, *m.*

comrade, *n.* camarada, *m.* y *f.;* compañero, ra.

comradeship, *n.* camaradería, *f.;* compañerismo íntimo.

con: **against,** contra; **conclusion,** conclusión.

concave, *adj.* cóncavo.

conceal, *vt.* ocultar, esconder; *—ed, adj.* escondido, oculto; disimulado; secreto.

concealment, *n.* ocultación, *f.;* encubrimiento, *m.*

concede, *vt.* conceder, admitir; *—, vi.* asentir, acceder.

conceit, n. vanidad, presunción, f.; vanagloria, f.

conceited, adj. afectado, vano, presumido.

conceivable, adj. concebible.

conceive, vt. concebir, comprender.

concentrate, vt. y vi. concentrar, concentrarse.

concentration, n. concentración, f. — camp, campo de concentración.'

concentric, concentrical, adj. concéntrico.

concept, n. concepto, m.

conception, n. concepción, f.; concepto, m.

concern, vt. concernir, importar; pertenecer; —, n. negocio, m.; interés, m.; importancia, consecuencia, f.

concerned, adj. interesado; inquieto, apesarado, mortificado.

concerning, prep. tocante a, respecto a.

concert, n. concierto, m.; convenio, m.; — performer, concertista, m. y f.; —, vt. y vi. concertar, concertarse.

concerted, adj. concertado, acordado, ajustado.

concerto, n. (mus.) concierto, m.; trozo hecho para un instrumento con acompañamiento de orquesta.

concession, n. concesión, cesión, f.; privilegio, m.

conciliate, vt. conciliar; atraer.

conciliation, n. conciliación, f.

concise, adj. conciso, sucinto.

conclude, vt. concluir; decidir; finalizar, terminar; epilogar.

conclusion, n. conclusión, terminación, f.; fin, m.; clausura, f.; consecuencia, f.

conclusive, adj. decisivo, concluyente.

concoct, vt. confeccionar; maquinar; mezclar.

concoction, n. maquinación, f.; mezcla, f.

concomitant, adj. concomitante.

concord, n. concordia, armonía f.

concordance, n. concordancia, f.

concourse, n. concurso, m.; reunión, f.; multitud, f.; gentío, m.

concrete, n. concreto, m.; hormigón, cemento, m.; — mixer, mezcladora, f.; reinforced —, hormigón armado; —, adj. concreto; —, vt. y vi. concretar.

concubine, n. concubina, f.

concur, vi. convenir, coincidir; acceder.

concurrence, n. coincidencia, f.; acuerdo, convenio, m.

concussion, n. concusión, f.

condemn, vt. condenar; desaprobar; vituperar.

condemnation, n. condenación, f.

condensation, n. condensación, f.

condense, vt. condensar; comprimir.

condenser, n. condensador, m.

condescend, vi. condescender; consentir.

condescending, adj. complaciente, afable.

condescension, n. condescendencia, f.

condiment, n. condimento, m.; salsa, f.

condition, n. situación, condición, f.; calidad, f.; requisito, m.; estado, m.; circunstancia, f.; on — that, con tal que.

conditional, adj. condicional, hipotético.

conditioned, adj. condicionado, acondicionado.

condolence, n. pésame, m., condolencia, f.

condom, n. condón.

condone, vt. condonar.

condor, n. (orn.) cóndor, m.

conduce, vt. conducir.

conducive, adj. conducente; útil.

conduct, n. conducta f.; manejo, proceder, m.; conducción (de tropas), f.; porte, m.; safe —, salvoconducto, m.

conduct, vt. conducir, guiar.

conductor, n. conductor, m.; guía, director, m.; conductor (de electricidad) m.

conduit, n. conducto, m.; caño, m., cañería, f.

cone, n. cono, m.; paper —, cucurucho, m.; ice-cream —, barquillo de mantecado, de nieve o de helados.

confection, n. confitura, f.; confección, f.; confite, m.

confectionery, n. dulcería, confitería, f.; confitura, f.; confites, dulces, m. pl.

confederacy, n. confederación, f.

confederate, vi. confederarse; —, adj. confederado; —, n. confederado, m.

confederation, n. federación, confederación, f.

confer, vi. conferenciar; consultarse; —, vt. otorgar, dar.

conference, n. conferencia, f.; sesión, junta, f.

confess, vt. y vi. confesar, confesarse.

confession, n. confesión, f.

confessional, n. confesionario, m.

confessor, n. confesor, m.

confetti, n. confeti, m.

confidant, confidante, n. confidente, m., confidenta, f.

confide, vt. y vi. confiar; fiarse.

confidence, n. confianza, seguridad, f.; confidencia, f.; in strictest —, con o bajo la mayor reserva.

confident, adj. cierto; fiado; seguro; confiado; —, n. confidente, m. y f.; —ly, adv. con seguridad.

confidential, adj. confidencial; —ly, adv. en confianza, confidencialmente.

confiding, adj. fiel, seguro, confiado.

configuration, n. configuración, f.

confine, n. confín, límite, m.; —, vt. limitar; aprisionar; —; vi. confinar.

confinement, n. prisión, f.; encierro, m.;

parto, m.; sobreparto, m.

confirm, vt. confirmar; ratificar.

confirmation, n. confirmación, f.; ratificación, f.; prueba, f.

confiscate, vt. confiscar, decomisar.

conflagration, n. conflagración, f.; incendio, m.

conflict, n. conflicto, m.; combate, m.; pelea, f.; —, vt. contender; combatir; chocar; estar en conflicto.

conform vt. y vi. conformar, conformarse.

conformity, n. conformidad, f.; concordia, f.

confound, vt. turbar, confundir; destruir; — it! interj. ¡caracoles!

confront, vt. afrontar; confrontar, comparar.

confuse, vt. confundir; desordenar.

confused, adj. confuso, desorientado; embrollado.

confusion, n. confusión, baraúnda, f.; desorden, m.; perturbación, f.; trápala, f.; trastorno, m.

congeal, vt. y vi. helar, congelar; congelarse.

congenial, adj. compatible; **to be** —, simpatizar.

congenital, adj. congénito.

congestion, n. congestión, f.

conglomerate, vt. conglomerar; aglomerar;—, adj. aglomerado; —, n. conglomerado, m.

conglomeration, n. aglomeración, f.

congratulate, vt. congratular, felicitar.

congratulation, n. congratulación, felicitación, f.

congregate, vt. congregar, reunir; —, vi. afluir; congregarse.

congregation, n. congregación, reunión, f.

congress, n. congreso, m.; conferencia, f.

congressional, adj. perteneciente o relativo al congreso.

congressman, n. diputado al congreso, congresista, m.

congresswoman, n. diputada al congreso, congresista, f.

congruous, adj. idóneo, congruente, congruo, apto.

conic, conical, adj. cónico.

conjecture, n. conjetura, suposición, f.; —, vt. conjeturar; pronosticar.

conjointly, adv. conjuntamente, mancomunadamente.

conjugate, vt. (gram.) conjugar.

conjugation, n. (gram.) conjugación, f.

conjunction, n. (gram.) conjunción, f.; unión, f.

conjure, vt. rogar, pedir con instancia; —, vi. conjurar, encantar; hechizar.

connect, vt. juntar, unir, enlazar; relacio-

nar.

connection, n. conexión, f.; —s, n. pl. relaciones, f. pl.

connivance, n. connivencia, f.

connive, vi. confabularse; fingir ignorancia; disimular.

connoisseur, n. perito, ta, conocedor, ra.

connotation, n. connotación, f.

connote, vt. connotar.

connubial, adj. conyugal, matrimonial.

conquer, vt. conquistar; vencer.

conqueror, n. vencedor, conquistador, m.

conquest, n. conquista, f.

conscience, n. conciencia, f.; escrúpulo. m.

conscience-stricken, adj. con remordimientos, hostigado por el remordimiento.

conscientious, adj. concienzudo, escrupuloso; meticuloso; —**ly**, adv. según conciencia, concienzudamente.

conscious, adj. sabedor, convencido; consciente; —**ly**, adv. a sabiendas.

consciousness, n. conocimiento, sentido, m.

conscript, adj. reclutado, seleccionado; —, n. conscripto, m., recluta de servicio forzoso.

conscription, n. conscripción, f., reclutamiento obligatorio.

consecrate, vt. consagrar; dedicar.

consecration, n. consagración, f.

consecutive, adj. consecutivo, consiguiente.

consensus, n. consenso, asenso, consentimiento, m.; opinión colectiva; consentimiento general.

consent, n. consentimiento, asenso, m.; aprobación, f.; —, vi. consentir; aprobar.

consequence, n. consecuencia, f.; importancia, f.; efecto, m.

consequent, adj. consiguiente.

conservation, n. conservación, f.

conservative, n. y adj. conservador, ra.

conservatory, n. conservatorio, m.

conserve, vt. conservar, cuidar; hacer conservas; —, n. conserva, f.

consider, vt. considerar, examinar; —, vi. pensar, deliberar; ponderar; reflexionar.

considerable, adj. considerable; importante; bastante; —**bly**, adv. considerablemente.

considerate, adj. considerado, prudente, discreto; deferente.

consideration, n. consideración, f.; deliberación, f.; importancia, f.; valor, mérito, m.

considering, prep. en atención a; en vista de; — **that,** en vista de que, considerando que.

consign, *vt.* consignar.

consignee, *n.* consignatario, ria; depositario, ria.

consignment, *n.* consignación, partida, *f.*

consist, *vi.* consistir.

consistence, consistency, *n.* consistencia, *f.*

consistent, *adj.* consistente; congruente; conveniente, conforme; sólido, estable.

consolation, *n.* consolación, *f.;* consuelo, *m.*

console, *vt.* consolar; —, *n.* consola, *f.*

consolidate, *vt.* y *vi.* consolidar, consolidarse.

consolidation, *n.* consolidación, *f.*

consommé, *n.* consomé, caldo, *m.*

consonant, *adj.* consonante, conforme; —, *n.* (gram.) consonante, *f.*

consort, *n.* consorte, *m.* y *f.;* esposo, sa; —, *vi.* asociarse.

conspicuous, *adj.* conspicuo, aparente; notable; llamativo, sobresaliente; to be —, destacarse; —ly, *adv.* claramente, insignemente.

conspiracy, *n.* conspiración, *f.;* trama, *f.;* complot, *m.;* lío, *m.*

conspirator, *n.* conspirador, ra.

conspire, *vi.* conspirar, maquinar.

constable, *n.* condestable, *m.;* alguacil, *m.*

constabulary, *n.* fuerza de policía.

constancy, *n.* constancia, perseverancia, persistencia, *f.*

constant, *adj.* constante; seguro, firme; fiel; perseverante.

constellation, *n.* constelación, *f.*

consternation, *n.* consternación, *f.;* terror, *m.*

constipation, *n.* estreñimiento, *m.*

constituency, *n.* junta electoral.

constituent, *n.* constitutivo, *m.;* elector, votante, *m.;* —, *adj.* constituyente.

constitute, *vt.* constituir; establecer, diputar.

constitution, *n.* constitución, *f.;* estado, *m.;* temperamento, *m.;* complexión *f.*

constitutional, *adj.* constitucional, legal.

constrain, *vt.* constreñir; forzar; restringir.

constraint, *n.* constreñimiento, *m.;* restricción, *f.*

constrict, *vt.* constreñir, estrechar.

constriction, *n.* constricción, contracción, *f.*

construct, *vt.* construir, edificar.

construction, *n.* construcción, *f.;* interpretación, *f.*

constructive, *adj.* constructivo, constructor.

construe, *vt.* construir; interpretar.

consul, *n.* cónsul, *m.*

consular, *adj.* consular; — corps, cuerpo consular.

consulate, consulship, *n.* consulado, *m.*

consult, *vt.* y *vi.* consultar, consultarse; aconsejar; aconsejarse; — together, conferenciar.

consultant, *n.* consultor, *m.*

consultation, *n.* consulta, deliberación, *f.*

consume, *vt.* consumir; disipar; destruir; desperdiciar; devorar (alimento); —, *vi.* consumirse.

consumer, *n.* consumidor, ra.

consummate, *vt.* consumar; acabar; —, *adj.* cumplido, consumado.

consumption, *n.* consunción, *f.;* tisis *f.*

contact, *n.* contacto, *m.;* — lenses, lentes de contacto, pupilentes, *m. pl.;* —, *vt.* y *vi.* tocar; poner en contacto; ponerse en contacto.

contagion, *n.* contagio, *m.;* infección, *f.*

contagious, *adj.* contagioso.

contain, *vt.* contener, comprender; reprimir, refrenar.

container, *n.* envase, *m.,* recipiente, *m.*

contaminate, *vt.* contaminar; corromper.

contemplate, *vt.* contemplar; —, *vi.* meditar, pensar.

contemplative, *adj.* contemplativo.

contemporaneous, contemporary, *adj.* contemporáneo.

contempt, *n.* desprecio, desdén, *m.*

contemptible, *adj.* despreciable, vil.

contemptuous, *adj.* desdeñoso, insolente.

contend, *vi.* contender, disputar, afirmar; lidiar; competir.

content, *adj.* contento, satisfecho; —, *vt.* contentar, satisfacer; —, *n.* contento, *m.;* satisfacción, *f.;* to one's heart's —, a pedir de boca, a satisfacción perfecta.

content, *n.* contenido, *m.;* sustancia, esencia, significación (de un discurso, etc.), *f.;* —s, *pl.* contenido *m.*

contention, *n.* contención, altercación, *f.;* tema, *f.*

contentment, *n.* contentamiento, placer, *m.*

contest, *vt.* contestar, disputar, litigar; —, *n.* concurso, *m.;* competencia, *f.;* disputa, altercación, *f.*

contestant, *adj.* contendiente, litigante; —, *n.* contendiente, litigante, *m.* y *f.;* concursante, *m.* y *f.*

context, *n.* contexto, *m.;* contextura, *f.*

contiguous, *adj.* contiguo, vecino; to be —, colindar.

continent, *adj.* continente; —ly, *adv.* castamente; —, *n.* continente, *m.*

continental, *adj.* continental.

contingency, *n.* contingencia, *f.;* acontecimiento, *m.;* eventualidad, *f.*

contingent, n. contingente, m.; cuota, f.; —, adj. contingente, casual.
continual, adj. continuo.
continuance, n. continuación, permanencia, f.; duración, f.; prolongación, f.
continuation, n. continuación, f.; serie, f.
continue, vt. continuar; —, vi. durar, perseverar, persistir.
continuity, n. continuidad, f.
continuous, adj. continuo.
contortion, n. contorsión, f.
contour, n. contorno, m.; — plowing, cultivo en contorno.
contraband, n. contrabando, m.; —, adj. prohibido, ilegal.
contraceptive, adj. que evita la concepción; —, n. contraceptivo, anticonceptivo, m.
contract, vt. contraer; abreviar; contratar; —, vi. contraerse; —, n. contrato, pacto, m.
contraction, n. contracción, f.; abreviatura, f.
contractor, n. contratante, contratista, m.
contradict, vt. contradecir.
contradiction, n. contradicción, oposición, f.
contradictory, adj. contradictorio.
contrail, n. estela de vapor.
contralto, n. contralto (voz), m.; contralto (persona), m. y f.
contraption, n. (coll.) dispositivo, artefacto, m.
contrary, adj. contrario, opuesto; —, n. contrario, ria; on the —, al contrario, antes bien; —rily, adv. contrariamente.
contrast, n. contraste, m.; oposición, f.; —, vt. contrastar, oponer.
contribute, vt. contribuir, ayudar.
contribution, n. contribución, f.
contributor, n. contribuidor, ra, contribuyente, m. y f.
contrite, adj. contrito, arrepentido.
contrition, n. penitencia, contrición, f.
contrivance, n. designio, m.; invención, f.
contrive, vt. inventar, trazar, maquinar; manejar; combinar.
control, n. control, m.; inspección, f; conducción, f.; sujeción, f.; dirección, f.; mando, m.; gobierno, m.; — tower, torre de mando; —, vt. controlar, restringir; gobernar; refutar; registrar; criticar; to — oneself, contenerse; vencerse.
controller, n. contralor, registrador, interventor, m.
controversial, adj. controvertible, discutible; sujeto a controversia.
controversy, n. controversia, f.
contusion, n. contusión, f.; magullamiento, m.
conundrum, n. adivinanza, f.; acertijo, m.

convalescence, n. convalecencia, f.
convalescent, adj. convaleciente.
convene, vt. convocar; juntar, unir; —, vi. convenir, juntarse.
convenience, n. conveniencia, comodidad, f.; conformidad, f.; at your —, cuando le sea posible, cuando quiera; — store, tienda de conveniencia, f.
convenient, adj. conveniente, apto, cómodo, propio.
convent, n. convento, claustro, monasterio, m.
convention, n. convención, f.; convencionalismo, m.
conventional, adj. convencional; estipulado; tradicional.
conventionalism, n. convencionalismo, m.
conventionality, n. uso convencional; costumbre establecida.
converge, vi. convergir.
conversant, adj. versado, familiarizado; — with, versado en.
conversation, n. conversación, plática, f.; tertulia, f.
conversational adj. de conversación.
conversationalist, n. buen conversador o buena conversadora.
converse, vi. conversar, platicar; —, adj. inverso; —ly, adv. a la inversa.
conversion, n. conversión, trasmutación, f.
convert, vt. convertir, trasmutar; reducir; —, vi. convertirse; —, n. converso, convertido, m.; catecúmeno, na.
converter, n. convertidor, m.; depurador, m.; (elec.) conversor, trasformador, m.
convertibility, n. convertibilidad, f.
convertible, adj. convertible, trasmutable; —, n. (auto.) convertible, m.
convex, adj. convexo.
convey, vt. trasportar; trasmitir, trasferir; conducir.
conveyance, n. trasporte, m.; conducción, f.; vehículo, m.
conveyer, conveyor, n. conductor, trasportador, m.
convict, vt. probar la culpabilidad; condenar.
convict, n. reo, convicto, presidiario, m.
conviction, n. convicción, f.; certidumbre, f.; condenación, f.
convince, vt. convencer, poner en evidencia; persuadir.
convincing, adj. convincente, con convicción; —ly, adv. de una manera convincente.
convocation, n. convocación, f.; sínodo, m.
convoy, vt. convoyar; —, n. convoy, m.; escolta, f.
convulse, vt. conmover, trastornar.
convulsion, n. convulsión, f.; conmoción, f.

convulsive, *adj.* convulsivo.

cony, coney, *n.* conejo, *m.;* piel de conejo.

coo, *vi.* arrullar.

cooing, *n.* arrullo de palomas; conversación amorosa.

cook, *n.* cocinero, ra; **pastry** —, repostero, ra; —, *vt.* cocinar, aderezar las viandas;—, *vi.* cocer, cocinar; guisar.

cookbook, *n.* libro de cocina.

cooker, *n.* olla para cocinar; **pressure** —, olla a presión; (Mex.) olla express.

cookie, *n.* bollo, *m.;* galleta, galletita, *f.*

cooking, *n.* cocina, *f.;* arte culinario; —, *adj.* relativo a la cocina; — **range**, cocina económica; — **stove**, estufa, *f.*, cocina económica; — **utensils**, batería de cocina.

cool, *adj.* fresco; indiferente; —, *vt.* enfriar, refrescar; **to** — **off**, aplacarse; refrescarse.

cooler, *n.* enfriadera, *f.;* enfriador, *m.;* (med.) refrigerante, *m.;* (coll.) prisión, cárcel, *f.*

cool-headed, *adj.* sereno, calmado.

cooling, *adj.* refrescante.

coolness, *n.* fresco, *m.;* frialdad, frescura, *f.;* estolidez, *f.*

coop, *n.* gallinero, *m.;* —, *vt.* enjaular, encarcelar.

cooperate, *vi.* cooperar.

cooperation, *n.* cooperación, *f.*

cooperative, *adj.* cooperativo, cooperador; — **apartment**, departamento de condominio.

coordinate *vt.* coordinar.

coordination, *n.* coordinación, *f.*

cop, *n.* (coll.) policía, gendarme, *m.*

cope, *n.* (eccl.) capa pluvial; arco, *m.,* bóveda, *f.;* albardilla, *f.;* —, *vi.* competir, lidiar con.

copious, *adj.* copioso, abundante;— **ly**, *adv.* en abundancia.

copper, *n.* cobre, *m.;* cobre (color), *m.;* moneda de cobre; — **sulphate**, sulfato de cobre.

copperplate, *n.* lámina o plancha de cobre.

coppersmith, *n.* trabajador en cobre.

copy, *n.* copia, *f.;* original, *m.;* ejemplar, *m.;* —, *vt.* copiar; imitar.

copybook, *n.* cuaderno para escribir; copiador de cartas (libro).

copyist, *n.* copista, *m. y f.;* plagiario, ria.

copyright, *n.* propiedad, derechos (de una obra literaria).

coquette, *n.* coqueta, *f.*

coquettish, *adj.* coquetona, coqueta.

coral, *n.* coral, *m.;* —, *adj.* coralino, de coral; — **reef**, banco de coral.

cord, *n.* cuerda, *f.;* cordel, *m.;* cuerda (medida para leña), *f.;* cordón, pasa-

mano, *m.;* —, *vt.* encordelar.

cordage, *n.* cordaje, *m.*

cordial, *adj.* cordial, de corazón, amistoso; —, *n.* cordial (licor), *m.*

corduroy, *n.* pana, *f.*

core, *n.* cuesco, *m.;* interior, centro, corazón, *m.;* cogollo, *m.;* núcleo, *m.*

cork, *n.* corcho, *m.;* —, *vt.* tapar con corchos.

corkscrew, *n.* tirabuzón, *m.*

corn, *n.* grano, *m.;* callo, *m.;* maíz, *m.;* — **meal**, harina de maíz; **sweet** —, maíz tierno; (Mex.) elote, *m.;* — **popper**, tostador de maíz; —, *vt.* salpresar; salar; granular.

corncob, *n.* tusa, *f.;* (Mex.) olote, *m.*

cornea, *n.* (anat.) córnea, *f.*

corned beef, *n.* cecina, *f.,* carne de vaca preparada en salmuera.

corner, *n.* ángulo, *m.;* rincón, *m.;* esquina, *f.;* extremidad, *f.;* **to turn the** —, doblar la esquina; —, *vt.* acaparar.

cornered, *adj.* anguloso; en aprieto.

cornerstone, *n.* piedra angular.

cornet, *n.* corneta, *f.*

cornfield, *n.* maizal, *m.*

cornflower, *n.* aciano, *m.*

cornice, *n.* cornisa, *f.*

cornstalk, *n.* tallo de maíz.

cornstarch, *n.* maicena, *f.*

cornucopia, *n.* cornucopia, *f.*

corny, *adj.* (coll.) cursi.

corollary, *n.* corolario, *m.*

corona, *n.* (arch.) corona, *f.;* (astr.) halo, meteoro luminoso; (biol.) coronilla, *f.*

coronation, *n.* coronación, *f.*

coroner, *n.* oficial que hace la inspección jurídica de los cadáveres.

coronet, *n.* corona que corresponde a algún título de noble; diadema, *f.*

Corp., corp.: corporal, cabo; **corporation**, S.A. sociedad anónima.

corporal, *n.* (mil.) cabo, *m.;* —, *adj.* corpóreo, corporal; material, físico.

corporate, *adj.* formado en cuerpo o en comunidad; colectivo.

corporation, *n.* corporación, *f.;* gremio, *m.;* sociedad anónima.

corps, *n.* cuerpo de ejército; regimiento, *m.;* cuerpo, *m.;* **air** —, cuerpo de aviación.

corpse, *n.* cadáver, *m.*

corpuscle, *n.* corpúsculo, *m.*

corpuscular, *adj.* corpuscular.

corral, *n.* corral, *m.;* —, *vt.* acorralar.

correct, *vt.* corregir, reprender, castigar; enmendar, amonestar; rectificar; —, *adj.* correcto, cierto; —**ly**, *adv.* correctamente.

correction, *n.* corrección, *f.;* castigo, *m.;*

enmienda, f.; censura, f.; remedio, m.

corrective, n. y adj. correctivo, m.

correlate, vt. poner en correlación.

correlation, n. correlación, f.

correspond, vi. corresponder.

correspondence, n. correspondencia, f.; reciprocidad, f.; **to carry on the —,**llevar la correspondencia.

correspondent, adj. correspondiente; conforme; —, n. corresponsal, m.

corresponding, adj. correspondiente; similar; congruente; **— secretary,** secretario encargado de la correspondencia.

corridor, n. crujía, f.; pasillo, corredor, m.

corroborate, vt. corroborar.

corrode, vt. corroer.

corrosive, adj. corrosivo.

corrugate, vt. corrugar, arrugar.

corrugated, adj. corrugado, acanalado, ondulado.

corrupt, vt. corromper; sobornar; infectar; —, vi. corromperse, pudrirse; —, adj. corrompido; depravado.

corruptible, adj. corruptible.

corruption, n. corrupción, perversión, f.; depravación, f.; impureza, f.

corsage, n. ramillete para el vestido.

corset, n. corsé, m.

cortex, n. corteza, f.

cortisone, n. (med.) cortisona, f.

cosmetic, n. y adj. cosmético, m.; **— kit,** neceser, m.

cosmic, adj. cósmico; **— ray,** rayo cósmico.

cosmology, n. cosmología, f.

cosmonaut, n. cosmonauta, m.

cosmopolitan, cosmopolite, n. y adj. cosmopolita, m. y f.

Cossack, n. y adj. cosaco, ca.

cost, n. coste, costo, precio, m.; expensas, f. pl.; **at all —s,** a toda costa, a todo trance; —, vi. costar.

costly, adj. costoso, suntuoso caro.

costume, n. traje, m.; ropa, f.; disfraz, m.

costumer, n. sastre, m.; persona que vende o alquila vestuario para el teatro.

cot, n. catre, m.

cottage, n. cabaña, casucha, f.; choza, f.; **— cheese,** requesón, m.

cotton, n. algodón, m.; **— flannel,** franela de algodón; **— goods,** tela de algodón; **spun —,** algodón hilado.

cottonseed, n. semilla de algodón; **— oil,** aceite de semilla de algodón.

cottonwood, n. variedad de álamo americano.

couch, vi. echarse; acostarse; —, vt. acostar; extender; esconder; expresar, manifestar; —, n. cama, f.; lecho, m.; canapé; sofa, m.

cough, n. tos, f.; —, vi. toser; **— drop,** pastilla para la tos.

could, pretérito del verbo **can.**

council, n. concilio, concejo, m.; junta, f.; sínodo, m.; **town —,** cabildo, ayuntamiento, m.

councilor, councillor, n. concejal, miembro del concejo.

counsel, n. consejo, aviso, m.; abogado, m.

counselor, counsellor, n. consejero, abogado, m.

count, vt. contar, numerar; calcular; **to — on,** confiar, depender de; —, n. cuenta, f.; cálculo, m.; conde (título), m.

countdown, n. conteo regresivo.

countenance, n. rostro, m.; fisonomía, f.; aspecto, m.; semblante, m.; apoyo, m.; talante, m.; —, vt. proteger, ayudar, favorecer.

counter, n. contador, m.; ficha, f.; mostrador, tablero, m.; **Geiger —,** contador Geiger, m.; —,adv. al revés; —, adj. contrario, adverso.

counteract, vt. contrariar, impedir, estorbar; frustrar.

counterattack, n. contraataque, m.

counterbalance, vt. contrapesar; igualar; compensar; —, n. contrapeso, m.

counterclockwise, adj. con movimiento circular a la izquierda.

counterfeit, vt. contrahacer, imitar, falsear; —, adj. falsificado; fingido; **— note,** billete de banco falsificado.

counterfeiter, n. falsificador, ra (de moneda, etc.).

counterintelligence, n. contraespionaje, m.

counteroffensive, n. contraofensiva, f.

counterpart, n. complemento, m.; réplica, f.; persona que semeja mucho a otra.

counterplot, n. contratreta, f.

counterpoint, n. contrapunto, m.

countersign, vt. refrendar; firmar (un decreto); visar; —, n. (mil.) consigna, f.

countess, n. condesa, f.

countless, adj. innumerable.

country, n. país, m.; campo, m.; campiña, f.; región, f.; patria, f.; —, adj. rústico; campestre, rural; **— club,** club campestre; **— house,** casa de campo, granja, f.

countryman, n. paisano, compatriota, m.

countryside, n. campo, m., región rural.

countrywoman, n. paisana, compatriota, f.; campesina, f.

county, n. condado, m.

coup, n. golpe maestro, golpe repentino; acción brillante; **— de grace,** golpe de gracia; **— d'état,** golpe de Estado.

coupé, n. cupé, m.

couple, n. par, m.; pareja, f.; vínculo, m.; —, vt. unir, parear, casar; —, vi. juntarse, unirse en un par.

coupling, n. acoplamiento, m.; unión, junta, f.; empalme, m.; **—s**, n. pl. (rail.) locomotoras acopladas.

coupon, n. cupón, talón, m.

courage, n. coraje, valor, m.; **to lose —**, intimidarse; **to take —**, cobrar ánimo.

courageous, adj. valeroso, valiente. courier, n. correo, mensajero, m.; expreso, m.

course, n. curso, m.; carrera, f.; camino, m.; ruta, f.; rumbo, m.; plato, m.; método, m.; entrada, f ; servicio, m.; asignatura, f.; **— (of time)**, trascurso (del tiempo), m.; **of —**, naturalmente, por supuesto, desde luego; **in due —**, a su debido tiempo.

court, n. corte, f.; palacio, m.; patio, m.; cortejo, m.; frontón, m.; **— of justice**, juzgado, m.; tribunal de justicia; **—**, vt. cortejar; solicitar; adular; requerir, requebrar (una mujer).

courteous, adj. cortés; benévolo; caballeresco.

courtesy, n. cortesía f.; benignidad, f.; (Mex.) caravana, f .

courthouse, n. foro, tribunal, m.; palacio de justicia.

courtier, n. cortesano, palaciego, m.

courtly, adj. cortesano, elegante.

court-martial, n. (mil.) consejo militar, consejo de guerra.

courtroom, n. sala de justicia; tribunal, m.

courtship, n. cortejo, m.; galantería, f.

courtyard, n. patio, m.

cousin, n. primo, ma; **first —**, primo hermano, prima hermana.

cove, n. (naut.) ensenada, cala, caleta, f.

covenant, n. contrato, pacto, convenio, m.; **—**, vi. pactar, estipular.

cover, n. cubierta, f.; abrigo, m.; pretexto, m.; **under separate —**, por separado; **— charge**, precio del cubierto (en un restaurante); **—**, vt. cubrir; tapar; ocultar; proteger; paliar.

covering, n. ropa, f.; vestido, m.; cubierta, f.

coverlet, coverlid, n. colcha, f.

covet, vt. codiciar, desear con ansia.

covetous, adj. avariento, sórdido.

cow, n. vaca, f.; **—**, vt. acobardar, intimidar.

coward, n. cobarde, m. y f.

cowardice, n. cobardía, timidez, f.

cowardly, adj. cobarde; pusilánime.

cowboy, n. vaquero, gaucho, m.

cower, vi. agacharse, intimidarse.

cowherd, n. vaquero, m.

cowhide, n. cuero, m.; látigo, m.

cowl, n. capucho, m.

co-worker, n. colaborador, ra, compañero o compañera de trabajo.

cowpuncher, n. vaquero, gaucho, m.

coy, adj. recatado, modesto; tímido; **—ly**, adv. con timidez.

coyote, n. coyote, m.

cozy, adj. cómodo y agradable.

C.P.A.: Certified Public Accountant, C.P.T. Contador Público Titulado.

crab, n. cangrejo, m.; jaiba, f.; persona de mal carácter; **— apple**, manzana silvestre.

crabbed, crabby, adj. áspero, austero, bronco, tosco.

crack, n. crujido, m.; raja, f.; quebraja, f.; **—**, vt. hender, rajar; romper; craquear (el petróleo); **to—down**, (coll.) compeler, obligar a obedecer; **—**, vi. reventar; jactarse; agrietarse; **—**, adj. raro, fino, de superior calidad.

crackdown, n. (coll.) acción de aumentar la severidad de regulaciones o restricciones.

cracked, adj. quebrado, rajado; (coll.) demente; estúpido.

cracker, n. galleta, f.; cohete, m.

cracking, n. craqueo (del petróleo), m.

crackle, vi. crujir, chillar.

crackling, n. estallido, crujido, m.

crack-up, n. (med.) colapso; colisión, f., choque, m.

cradle, n. cuna, f.; **—**, vt. acunar.

craft, n. arte, m.; artificio, m.; astucia, f.

craftiness, n. astucia, estratagema, f.

craftsman, n. artífice, artesano, m.

crafty, adj. astuto, artificioso.

crag, n. despeñadero, m.

craggy, adj. escabroso, áspero.

cram, vt. embutir; engordar; empujar; engullir; recargar; estudiar intensamente a la última hora (para un examen); **—**, vi. atracarse de comida.

cramp, n. calambre, retortijón de tripas; vt. constreñir, apretar.

cranberry, n. arándano, m.

crane, n. (orn.) grulla, f.; (mech.) grúa, f.; pescante, m.

cranium, n. cráneo, m.

crank, n. manivela, f.; manija, f.; (coll.) maniático, ca; **—**, vt. poner en marcha un motor.

crankcase, n. (auto.) cárter, m.; caja del cigüeñal.

crankshaft, n. cigüeñal, m.; manivela, f.

cranky, adj. malhumorado, excéntrico.

cranny, n. grieta, hendidura, f.

crash, vt. y vi. estallar, rechinar; estrellar, estrellarse; chocar;

to — **a party,** (coll.) concurrir a una fiesta sin invitación; —, *n.* estallido, fracaso, *m.;* choque, *m.;* —, *adj.* de socorro; — **landing,** aterrizaje accidentado o de emergencia.

crash-dive, *vi.* sumergirse repentinamente como un submarino.

crate, *n.* caja para embalar loza, etc.

crater, *n.* cráter, *m.*

crave, *vt.* y *vi.* rogar, suplicar; apetecer; pedir; anhelar.

craving, *adj.* insaciable, pedigüeño; —, *n.* deseo ardiente; antojo, *m.*

crawl, *vi.* arrastrarse; caminar a rastras; —, *n.* crawl (en natación), *m.*

crayfish, *n.* cangrejo de río.

crayon, *n.* lápiz, pastel, *m.*

craze, *n.* locura, demencia, *f.;* antojo, capricho, *m.;* —, *vt.* enloquecer; —, *vi.* enloquecerse.

crazy, *adj.* fatuo, simple; trastornado, loco.

creak, *vi.* crujir, chirriar.

creaky, *adj.* crujiente.

cream, *n.* crema, *f.;* nata, *f.;* — **of tartar,** crémor tártaro; — **puff,** bollo de crema; **whipped** —, crema batida.

creamery, *n.* lechería, *f.*

creamy, *adj.* cremoso; lleno de nata o crema; parecido a la nata o la crema.

crease, *n.* doblez, pliegue, *m.;* arruga, *f.;* — **resistant,** inarrugable; —, *vt.* arrugar, ajar, doblar.

create, *vt.* crear; causar.

creation, *n.* creación, *f.;* obra creada.

creative, *adj.* creador, con habilidad o facultad para crear.

creator, *n.* criador, ra; **the C**—, el Criador.

creature, *n.* criatura, *f.*

crèche, *n.* nacimiento de Navidad.

credentials, *n. pl.* credenciales, *f. pl.*

credibility, *n.* credibilidad, *f.*

credible, *adj.* creíble, verosímil.

credit, *n.* crédito, *m.;* reputación, *f.;* — **balance,** saldo acreedor; **blank** —, carta en blanco; **letter of** —, carta credencial o de crédito; **on** —, a crédito o fiado; —, *vt.* creer; fiar, acreditar; **to buy on** —, comprar a crédito; **to** — **with,** abonar en cuenta.

creditable, *adj.* estimable, digno de encomio; —**bly,** *adv.* honorablemente; de manera encomiable.

credit card, *n.* tarjeta de crédito.

creditor, *n.* acreedor, ra.

credulous, *adj.* crédulo; —**ly,** *adv.* con credulidad.

creed, *n.* credo, *m.;* profesión de fe.

creek, *n.* riachuelo, arroyo, *m.*

creep, *vi.* arrastrar, serpentear; gatear.

creepy, *adj.* pavoroso; que hormiguea.

creeper, *n.* reptil, *m.;* (bot.) enredadera, *f.;* pájaro trepador; vestido de una sola pieza para niños muy pequeños.

cremate, *vt.* incinerar cadáveres.

cremation, *n.* cremación, incineración (de cadáveres), *f.*

crepe, *n.* crepé, crespón, *m.*

crescent, *adj.* creciente; —, *n.* creciente (fase de la luna), *f.*

cress, *n.* (bot.) mastuerzo, *m.;* **water** —, berro, *m.*

crest, *n.* cresta, *f.;* copete, *m.;* orgullo, *m.*

crestfallen, *adj.* acobardado, abatido de espíritu, decaído.

cretonne, *n.* cretona, *f.*

crevice, *n.* raja, hendidura, *f.*

crew, *n.* (naut.) tripulación, *f.;* cuadrilla, *f.*

crib, *n.* pesebre, *m.;* cuna *f.;* casucha, *f.;* (coll.) chuleta, *f.;* —, *vi.* plagiar, hacer chuletas.

cribbage, *n.* variedad de juego de naipes.

cricket, *n.* (zool.) grillo, *m.;* vilorta (juego), *f.;* **field** —, saltamontes, *m.;* caballeta, *f.*

crier, *n.* pregonero, *m.*

crime, *n.* crimen, delito, *m.*

criminal, *adj.* criminal, reo; —, *n.* reo convicto, criminal, *m.* y *f.*

criminology, *n.* criminología, *f.*

crimp, *n.* rizado (de cabello), *m.;* **to put a** — **in,** (coll.) poner un impedimento; —, *vt.* rizar, encrespar.

crimson, *n.* carmesí, *m.;* —, *adj.* carmesí, bermejo.

cringe, *n.* bajeza, *f.;* servilismo, *m.;* —, *vi.* adular servilmente; encogerse, sobresaltarse.

crinkle, *n.* arruga, *f.;* —, *vt.* serpentear; arrugar.

crinoline, *n.* crinolina, *f.*

cripple, *n.* y *adj.* lisiado, da; —, *vt.* estropear, derrengar, tullir, lisiar.

crisis, *n.* crisis, *f.*

crisp, *adj.* crespo; frágil, quebradizo; fresco, terso, lozano (aplícase a la lechuga, el apio, etc.); claro, definido; —, *vt.* y *vi.* encrespar; ponerse crespo, rizarse.

crisscross, *adj.* entrelazado; —, *vt.* entrelazar, cruzar.

criterion, *n.* criterio, *m.*

critic, *n.* crítico, *m.*

critical, *adj.* crítico; exacto; delicado; —**ly,** *adv.* en forma crítica.

criticism, *n.* crítica, *f.;* censura, *f.*

criticize, *vt.* criticar, censurar; **to give cause to** —, dar que decir.

critique, *n.* crítica, *f.;* juicio crítico.

croak, *vi.* graznar, crascitar; croar.

crochet, *n.* tejido de gancho; —, *vt.* tejer con aguja de gancho.

crock, n. cazuela, olla, f.

crockery, n. loza, f.; vasijas de barro.

crocodile, n. cocodrilo, m.; — **tears,** lágrimas de cocodrilo, dolor fingido.

crone, n. anciana, vieja, f.

crony, n. amigo (o conocido) antiguo; (coll.) compinche, m.

crook, n. gancho, m.; curva, f.; petardista, m. y f.; ladrón, ona; —, vt. encorvar, torcer; — vi. encorvarse.

crooked, adj. torcido, corvo; perverso; deshonesto, avieso; tortuoso; **to go** —, torcerse, desviarse del camino recto de la virtud.

croon, vt. y vi. canturrear, cantar con melancolía exagerada.

crop, n. cosecha, f.; mieses, f. pl.; producción, f.; buche de ave; cabello cortado corto; —, vt. segar, cosechar; cortar, desmochar.

croquet, n. croquet (juego), m.

croquette, n. croqueta, f.

cross, n. cruz, f.; carga, f.; trabajo, m.; pena, aflicción, f.; tormento, m.; —, adj. contrario, opuesto, atravesado; enojado; mal humorado; — **reference,** contrarreferencia, comprobación, verificación, f.; — **section,** sección trasversal; sección representativa (de una población, etc.); —, vt. atravesar, cruzar; **to — off,** barrear; **to — over,** traspasar; — **ly,** adv. enojadamente, malhumoradamente.

crossbar, crossbeam, n. tranca, f.; travesaño, m.

crossbeam, n. viga trasversal.

crossbreed, n. raza cruzada.

cross-country, adj. a campo traviesa; a través del país.

crosscut, adj. de corte trasversal; —, n. atajo, m.; corte trasversal.

crossed, adj. cruzado.

cross-examine, vt. repreguntar; (fig.) acribillar a preguntas.

cross-eyed, adj. bizco, bisojo.

crossing, n. (rail.) cruzamiento de dos vías, cruce, m.; travesía, f.; **street** —, cruce de calle; **grade** —, paso o cruce a nivel.

crossroad, n. paso, cruce, m.; encrucijada, f.

cross-stitch, n. punto de cruz; —, vt. y vi. hacer puntos de cruz.

crossways, adv. terciadamente; atravesadamente.

crosswise, adj. atravesado; —, adv. atravesadamente.

crossword puzzle, n. crucigrama, rompecabezas, m.

crotch, n. gancho, corchete, m.; bragadura, f.; bifurcación, f.

crotchet, n. (mus.) semínima, f.; capricho, m.; corchete, m.

crouch, vi. agacharse, bajarse.

croup, n. grupa (de caballo), f.; (med.) garrotillo, m.

crow, n. (orn.) cuervo, m.; barra, f.; canto del gallo; —, vi. cantar el gallo; alardearse.

crowbar, n. palanca de hierro; barreta, f.; pie de cabra.

crowd, n. tropel, m.; turba, muchedumbre, f.; multitud, f.; pelotón, m.; — **of people,** gentío, m.; —, vt. amontonar; —, vi. agruparse, amontonarse.

crowded, adj. concurrido, lleno de gente.

crown, n. corona, f.; diadema, guirnalda, f.; rueda, f.; moneda de plata que vale cinco chelines; complemento, colmo, m.; —, vt. coronar, recompensar; dar cima; cubrir el peón que ha llegado a ser dama (en el juego de damas).

crown prince, n. príncipe heredero.

crucial, adj. crucial, decisivo, crítico.

crucible, n. crisol, m.

crucifix, n. crucifijo, m.

crucify, vt. crucificar; atormentar.

crude, adj. crudo; inculto; tosco; — **(ore, oil, etc.),** (mineral, petróleo, etc.) bruto.

cruel, adj. cruel, inhumano.

cruelty, n. crueldad, f.; barbarie, f.

cruise, n. crucero, m.; viaje, m.; travesía, f.; excursión, f.; —, vi. navegar; viajar.

cruiser, n. crucero, m.; navegante, m.; acorazado, m.

crumb, n. miga, f.; brote, m.; migaja (de pan, etc.), f.

crumble, vt. desmigajar, desmenuzar; — **away,** derrumbarse; —, vi. desmigajarse; desmoronarse.

crumple, vt. arrugar, ajar; rabosear.

crunch, vi. crujir; —, vt. cascar con los dientes, mascar haciendo ruido.

crusade, n. cruzada, f.

crush, vt. apretar, oprimir; aplastar, machacar; —, n. choque, m.; estrujamiento, m.

crusher, n. triturador, ra; máquina trituradora, f.

crushing, n. trituración, f.; —, adj. triturador; — **machine,** trituradora, f.

crust, n. costra, f.; corteza, f.; —, vt. encostrar; vi. encostrarse.

crustaceous, adj. crustáceo.

crusty, adj. costroso; bronco, áspero.

crutch, n. muleta, f.

cry, vt. y vi. gritar; pregonar; exclamar; llorar; —, n. grito, m.; llanto, m.; clamor, m.; **to — out,** dar gritos.

crybaby, n. niño llorón.

crying, adj. lloroso; —, n. lloro, grito, m.

crypt, n. cripta, f., bóveda subterránea.

cryptic, adj. escondido, secreto.

cryptography, n. criptografía, f.

crystal, n. cristal, m.

crystalline, adj. cristalino; transparente.

crystallize, vt. cristalizar; —, vi. cristalizarse.

C.S.T.: Central Standard Time, hora normal del centro (de E.U.A.).

cub, n. cachorro, m.; — **reporter,** aprendiz de reportero; — **scout,** cachorro, m.

Cuban, n. y adj. cubano, na.

cubbyhole, n. casilla, f., casillero, m.; cualquier lugar pequeño y encerrado en forma de caverna.

cube, n. cubo, m.; **in —s,** cubicado.

cubic, cubical, adj. cúbico.

cuckold, n. cornudo, m.

cuckoo, n. cuclillo, cuco, m.

cucumber, n. pepino, m.

cud, n. panza, f.; primer estómago de los rumiantes; pasto contenido en la panza; **to chew the —,** rumiar; (fig.) reflexionar.

cuddle, vt. y vi. abrazar; acariciarse.

cudgel, n. garrote, palo, m.; —, vt. apalear; **take up the —s for,** salir en defensa de.

cue, n. cola, f.; apunte de comedia; indirecta, f.; taco (de billar), m.

cuff, n. puño de camisa o de vestido; — **links,** gemelos, m. pl., mancuernillas, f. pl.

cul-de-sac, n. callejón sin salida.

culinary, adj. culinario, de la cocina.

culminate, vi. culminar.

culmination, n. culminación, f.

culprit, n. reo, delincuente, m.; criminal, m.

cult, n. culto, m., devoción, f.

cultivate, vi. cultivar; mejorar; perfeccionar.

cultivated, adj. cultivado, labrado; culto.

cultivation, n. cultivación, f.; cultivo, m.

cultivator, n. (agr.) cultivador, ra, agricultor, ra; arado de cultivo.

cultural, adj. cultural.

culture, n. cultura, f.; cultivo (de bacterias), m.; civilización, f.

cumbersome, adj. engorroso, pesado, confuso.

cumulative, adj. cumulativo.

cunning, adj. hábil; artificioso, astuto; intrigante; —, n. astucia, sutileza, .

cup, n. taza, f.; (bot.) cáliz, m.; —, vt. aplicar ventosas; ahuecar en forma de taza.

cupboard, n. armario, aparador, m., alacena, f.; rinconera, f.

cupcake, n. pastelito, bizcocho pequeño.

cupful, n. taza (medida), f.

cupola, n. cúpula, f.

cur, n. perro de la calle; villano, canalla, m.

curate, n. ayudante de un párroco.

curative, adj. curativo; terapéutico.

curator, n. curador, m.; guardián, m.; curador (de un museo, etc.), m.

curb, n. barbada, f.; freno, m.; restricción, f.; orilla de la acera; —, vt. refrenar, contener, moderar.

curbstone, n. brocal, m.; contrafuerte de una acera.

curd, n. cuajada, f.; requesón, m.; —, vt. cuajar, coagular.

curdle, vt. cuajar, coagular; —, vi. cuajarse, coagularse.

cure, n. remedio, m.; curato, m.; —, vt. curar, sanar; **to — skins,** curar las pieles.

cure-all, n. panacea, f.

curfew, n. toque de queda.

curio, n. chuchería, f., objeto curioso; — **shop,** tienda de curiosidades.

curiosity, n. curiosidad, f.; rareza, f.

curious, adj. curioso; raro, extraño.

curl, n. rizo de cabello; rizado, m.; —, vt. rizar, encrespar; enrizar, enchinar; —, vi. rizarse, encresparse.

curling, n. ensortijamiento, m.; — **iron,** — **tongs,** encrespador, m.

curly, adj. rizado.

currant, n. grosella, f.

currency, n. circulación, f.; moneda corriente; dinero, m.; **national —,** moneda nacional.

current, adj. corriente; del día; — **events,** sucesos del día; —, n. tendencia, f., curso, m.; corriente, f.; corriente (eléctrica), f.; **—ly,** adv. actualmente.

curricular, adj. perteneciente al curso de estudios en una escuela.

curriculum, n. programa de estudios.

curse, vt. maldecir; —, vi. imprecar; blasfemar; —, n. maldición, f.; imprecación, f.; reniego, m.

cursed, adj. maldito; enfadoso.

cursory, adj. precipitado, inconsiderado.

curt, adj. sucinto; brusco.

curtail, vt. cortar; mutilar; rebajar, reducir.

curtain, n. cortina, f.; telón (en los teatros), m.; — **raiser,** pieza breve con que empieza una función de teatro; —, vt. proveer con cortinas.

curtsy, n. reverencia, f., saludo (de una mujer), m., (Mex.) caravana, f.; —, vt. y vi. hacer una reverencia o caravana.

curvature, n. curvatura, f.

curve, vt. encorvar; —, adj. corvo, torcido; —, n. curva, combadura, f.

cushion, n. cojín, m., almohada, f.

custard, *n.* natillas, *f. pl.;* flan, *m.,* crema, *f.*

custodian, *n.* custodio, *m.*

custody, *n.* custodia, *f.;* prisión, *f.;* cuidado, *m.*

custom, *n.* costumbre, *f.;* uso, *m.;* —s collector, administrador de aduana; — duties, derechos de aduana o arancelarios.

customary, *adj.* usual, acostumbrado, ordinario.

custom-built, *adj.* hecho a la orden o a la medida.

customer, *n.* parroquiano, *m.;* cliente, *m.* y *f.;* comprador, ra.

custom-free, *adj.* exento de derechos.

customhouse, *n.* aduana, *f.;* — declaration, manifiesto, *m.*

custom-made, *adj.* hecho a la medida.

cut, *vt.* cortar; separar; herir; dividir; alzar (los naipes); to — short, interrumpir; to — teeth, nacerle los dientes (a un niño); —, *adj.* cortado; — glass, cristal tallado o cortado; — tobacco, picadura, *f.;* —, *n.* cortadura, *f.;* herida, *f.;* (print.) grabado, *m.;* clisé, *m.*

cutback, *n.* reducción, de la producción; (coll.) reintegro ilegal de fondos públicos.

cute, *adj.* agradable, atractivo, gracioso; chistoso; (coll.) listo, inteligente.

cuticle, *n.* epidermis, *f.;* lapa, *f.;* cutícula, *f.*

cutlery, *n.* cuchillería, *f.*

cutlet, *n.* costilla o chuleta para asar.

cutout, *n.* (elec.) desconectador, interruptor, *m.;* (auto.) silenciador, *m.;* recortado, recorte, *m.;* figura para recortar.

cutter, *n.* cortador, ra; (naut.) cúter, *m.*

cutthroat, *n.* asesino, degollador; (fig.) garrotero.

cutting, *adj.* cortante; sarcástico; —, *n.* cortadura, *f.;* incisión, *f.;* alce (de naipes), *m.;* trinchado, *m.;* wood —s, metal —s, virutas, *f. pl.*

cutworm, *n.* larva destructora.

cwt.: hundredweight, ql. quintal.

cybernetics, *n.* cibernética, *f.*

cyclamen, *n.* (bot.) pamporcino, *m.*

cycle, *n.* ciclo, *m.*

cyclist, *n.* ciclista, *m.* y *f.*

cyclone, *n.* ciclón, huracán, *m.*

cyclotron, *n.* ciclotrón, *m.*

cylinder, *n.* cilindro, *m.;* rollo, *m.;* rodillo, *ni.;* — head, culata de cilindro.

cylindric, cylindrical, *adj.* cilíndrico.

cymbal, *n.* címbalo, platillo, *m.*

cynic, cynical, *adj.* cínico.

cynic, *n.* cínico, *m.*

cynicism, *n.* cinismo, *m.*

cypher = cipher.

cypress, *n.* ciprés, *m.;* — nut, piñuela, *f.*

cyst, *n.* quiste, *m.;* lobanillo, *m.*

C.Z.: Canal Zone, Z. del C. Zona del Canal.

czar, *n.* zar, *m.*

Czechoslovakian, *n.* y *adj.* checoslovaco, ca.

D

d.: date, fha, fecha; daughter, hija; day, día; diameter, diámetro; died, murió.

D.A.: District Attorney, procurador, fiscal.

d/a: days after acceptance, d/v días vista.

dab, *vt.* frotar suavemente con algo blando o mojado; golpear suavemente; —, *n.* pedazo pequeño; salpicadura, *f.;* golpe blando; (ichth.) barbada, *f.*

dabble, *vt.* rociar, salpicar; —, *vi.* chapotear; to — in politics, meterse en política (en forma superficial).

dachshund, *n.* perro de origen alemán, de cuerpo largo y patas muy cortas.

dacron, *n.* dacrón, *m.*

dad, daddy, *n.* papá, *m.*

daffodil, *n.* (bot.) narciso, *m.*

dagger, *n.* puñal, *m.*

dahlia, *n.* (bot.) dalia, *f.*

daily, *adj.* diario, cotidiano; — *adv.* diaria-

mente, cada día.

daintiness, *n.* elegancia, *f.;* delicadeza, *f.*

dainty, *adj.* delicado; meticuloso, refinado; —, *n.* bocado exquisito.

dairy, *n.* lechería, quesería, *f.;* — cattle, vacas lecheras, vacas de leche.

daisy, *n.* (bot.) margarita, maya, *f.*

dally, *vi.* juguetear, divertirse; tardar, dilatar; pasar el tiempo con gusto.

dam, *n.* madre, *f.* (aplícase especialmente a los animales cuadrúpedos); dique, *m.;* azud, *m.,* presa, *f.;* represa, *f.;* —, *vt.* represar; tapar.

damage, *n.* daño, detrimento, *m.;* perjuicio, *m.;* —s, *n. pl.* daños y perjuicios, *m. pl.;* — *vt.* dañar.

damask, *n.* damasco, *m.;* —, *adj.* de damasco; —, *vt.* adornar a manera de damasco.

dame, *n.* dama, señora, *f.;* matrona, *f.*

damn, *vt.* condenar; maldecir; —!, — it! *inter j.* ¡maldito sea!

damnable, *adj.* condenable; —bly, *adv.* de un modo condenable; horriblemente.

damnation, *n.* condenación, maldición, *f.*

damned, *adj.* condenado.

damp, *adj.* húmedo; —, *n.* humedad, *f.*

dampen, *vt.* humedecer; desanimar, abatir.

damper, *n.* sordina, *f.;* apagador, *m.;* registro (de una chimenea), *m.;* persona o cosa que desalienta.

dampness, *n.* humedad, *f.*

damsel, *n.* damisela, señorita, *f.*

dance, *n.* danza, *f.;* baile *m.;* — hall, salón de baile; —, *vi.* bailar.

dancer, *n.* danzarín, ina, bailarín, ina.

dandelion, *n.* (bot.) diente de león, amargón, *m.*

dandruff, *n.* caspa, *f.*

dandy, *n.* petimetre, currutaco, *m.*

Dane, *n.* danés, esa.

danger, *n.* peligro, riesgo, escollo, *m.;* — zone, zona de peligro.

dangerous, *adj.* peligroso.

dangle, *vi.* fluctuar; estar colgado en el aire; colgar, columpiarse.

Danish, *adj.* danés, dinamarqués.

dank, *adj.* húmedo y desagradable.

dapper, *adj.* activo, vivaz, despierto; apuesto.

dapple, *vt.* abigarrar; —, *adj.* vareteado; rayado; — gray horse, caballo rucio rodado.

D.A.R.: Daughters of the American Revolution, Organización "Hijas de la Revolución Norteamericana".

dare, *vi.* osar, atreverse, arriesgarse; —, *vt.* desafiar, provocar; —, *n.* reto, *m.*

daredevil, *n.* temerario, ria; calavera, *m.;* atrevido, da, valeroso, sa, valiente, *m. y f.;* persona que no teme a la muerte, que arriesga su vida.

daring, *n.* osadía, *f.;* — *adj.* osado, temerario; emprendedor.

dark, *adj.* oscuro, opaco; ciego; ignorante, hosco, tétrico; moreno, trigueño; — horse, candidato incógnito que se postula en el momento más propicio; —, *n.* oscuridad, *f.;* ignorancia, *f.;* in the —, a oscuras.

darken, *vt.* oscurecer; —, *vi.* oscurecerse.

darkness, *n.* oscuridad, *f.;* tinieblas, *f. pl.*

darkroom, *n.* (phot.) cámara oscura, cuarto oscuro.

darling, *n.* predilecto, ta, favorito, ta; —, *adj.* querido, amado.

darn, *vt.* zurcir.

dart, *n.* dardo, *m.;* (costura) sisa, cuchilla,

pinza. *f.;* —, *vt.* lanzar, tirar; echar; —, *vi.* volar como un dardo.

dash, *n.* arranque, *m.;* acometida, *f.;* raya, *f.;* donaire, *m.;* — *vt.* arrojar, tirar; chocar, estrellar, batir; to — off, bosquejar, escribir apresuradamente; to — out, salir precipitadamente.

dashboard, *n.* guardafango, paralodo, *m.;* tablero de instrumentos.

dashing, *adj.* vistoso, brillante.

dastardly, *adj.* cobarde, vil.

data, *n. pl.* datos, *m. pl;*— base, base de datos, *f.*

date, *n.* data, fecha, *f.;* duración, *f.;* cita, *f.;* (bot.) dátil, *m.;*— line, límite fijado en el mapa para el cambio de fecha; newspaper — line, fecha en que se publica un periódico, una revista, etc.; to —, hasta la fecha; out of —, anticuado, fuera de moda; under —, con fecha; up-to— muy de moda, en boga; what is the —? ¿a cómo estamos? —, *vt.* datar; (coll.) to — (some one), salir de paseo (con un pretendiente o con una novia).

dated, *adj.* fechado.

dateless, *adj.* sin fecha.

daub, *vt.* pintorrear; untar; manchar; ensuciar.

daughter, *n.* hija, *f.;* — -in-law, nuera, *f.*

daunt, *vt.* intimidar, espantar.

dauntless, *adj.* intrépido, arrojado.

davenport, *n.* sofá tapizado.

dawdle, *vt. y vi.* desperdiciar (el tiempo) ; haraganear.

dawn, *n.* alba, *f.;* albor, *m.;* madrugada, *f.;* —, *vi.* amanecer.

day, *n.* día, *m.;* periodo, *m.;* by —, de día; — after tomorrow, pasado mañana; — before, víspera, *f.;* — by —, día por día; — laborer, jornalero, *m.;* — letter, telegrama diurno; — nursery, guardería infantil; — school, escuela diurna; — shift, turno diurno; — work, trabajo diurno; every —, todos los días; on the following —, al otro día; —s, *n. pl.* tiempo, *m.;* vida, *f.;* these —s, hoy día; thirty —s' sight, treinta días vista o fecha.

daybreak, *n.* alba, *f.*

daydream, *n.* ilusión, fantasía, *f.;* ensueño, *m.;* quimera, *f.;* castillos en el aire; —, *vi.* soñar despierto, hacerse ilusiones; estar en la luna.

daylight, *n.* día, *m.,* luz del día, luz natural; — saving time, hora oficial de verano.

daytime, *n.* tiempo del día.

daze, *vt.* deslumbrar; ofuscar con luz demasiado viva.

dazed, *adj.* aturdido, ofuscado.

dazzle, vt. deslumbrar, ofuscar.

D.C.: District of Columbia, D.C. Distrito de Columbia, E.U.A.

d.c.: direct current, C.D. corriente directa; C.C. corriente continua.

DDT, DDT (insecticida), m.

deacon, n. diácono, m.

deaconess, n. diaconisa, f.

deactivate, vt. desactivar.

dead, adj. muerto, flojo, entorpecido; vacío; inútil; triste; apagado, sin espíritu; despoblado; evaporado; marchito; finado; — center, punto muerto; — end, callejón sin salida; — heat, corrida indecisa; — letter, carta no reclamada; — silence, silencio profundo; — weight, carga onerosa; peso propio de una máquina o vehículo; the —, los finados, los muertos; — reckoning, estima, f., derrotero estimado.

deaden, vt. amortecer, amortiguar.

deadline, n. fecha fijada para la realización de una cosa, como la fecha de tirada de una revista, periódico, etc.

deadlock, n. estancamiento, m.; paro, m.; interrupción, f.; desacuerdo, m.

deadly, adj. mortal; terrible, implacable.

deaf, adj. sordo; — ears, orejas de mercader; to fall on — ears, caer en saco roto.

deafen, vt. ensordecer.

deaf-mute, n. sordomudo, da.

deafness, n. sordera, f.; desinclinación a oír.

deal, n. negocio, convenio, m.; partida, porción, parte, f.; (com.) trato, m.; negociación, f.; mano (en el juego de naipes), f.; square —, trato equitativo; —, vt. distribuir; dar (las cartas); traficar; to — in, comerciar en; to — with, tratar de.

dealer, n. negociante, distribuidor, m.; el que da las cartas en el juego de naipes.

dealing, n. conducta, f.; trato, m.; tráfico, comercio, m.; —s, n. pl. transacciones, f. pl.; relaciones, f. pl.

dean, n. deán, decano, m.

dear, adj. predilecto, amado; caro, costoso; querido; —ly, adv. caramente.

dearth, n. carestía, f.; hambre, f.; — of news, escasez de noticias.

death, n. muerte, f.; — penalty, pena de muerte, pena capital; — rate, mortalidad, f.; — warrant, sentencia de muerte.

deathbed, n. lecho de muerte.

deathless, adj. inmortal, imperecedero.

deathlike, adj. cadavérico; inmóvil.

deathly, adj. cadavérico; mortal.

debark, vt. y vi. desembarcar.

debase, vt. humillar, envilecer; rebajar, deteriorar.

debate, n. debate, m.; riña, disputa, f.; —, vt. discutir; ponderar; —, vi. deliberar; disputar.

debauch, n. vida disoluta; exceso, libertinaje, m.; —, vt. depravar; corromper; —, vi. depravarse.

debit, n. debe, cargo, m.; — balance, saldo deudor; —, vt. (com.) adeudar, cargar en una cuenta, debitar.

debonair, adj. afable y cortés; alegre y agraciado.

debris, n. despojos, escombros, m. pl.

debt, n. deuda, f.; débito, m.; obligación, f.; floating —, deuda flotante; public —, deuda pública; to run into —, adeudar, adeudarse, (Mex.) endrogarse.

debtor, n. deudor, ra.

debut, n. estreno, debut, m.; to make one's —, debutar.

debutante, n. debutante, f., señorita presentada por primera vez en sociedad.

Dec.: December, dic., dic. diciembre.

dec.: deceased, M., m. murió o muerto; decimeter, dm. decímetro.

decade, n. década, f.

decadence, n. decadencia, f.

decadent, adj. decadente.

decalcomania, n. calcomanía, f

decapitate, vt. decapitar, degollar.

decay, vi. decaer, descaecer, declinar; degenerar; venir a menos; —, n. descaecimiento, m.; decadencia, declinación, diminución, f.; (dent.) caries, f.

deceased, n. y adj. finado, da, fallecido, da, muerto, ta, difunto, ta, extinto, ta.

deceit, n. engaño, fraude, m.; impostura, f.; zancadilla, f.; (coll.) trápala, f.

deceitful, adj. fraudulento, engañoso; falaz.

deceive, vt. engañar, defraudar, embaucar.

December, n. diciembre, m.

decency, n. decencia, f.; modestia, f.

decent, adj. decente, razonable; propio, conveniente; —ly, adv. decentemente.

deception, n. decepción, impostura, f.; engaño, m.; trapisonda, f.

deceptive, adj. falso, engañoso.

decibel, n. decibel, decibelio, m.

decide, vt. y vi. decidir, determinar, resolver, juzgar; decretar.

decidedly, adv. decididamente.

deciduous, adj. caedizo; temporáneo.

decimal, adj. decimal; — point, punto decimal; — fraction, fracción decimal.

decipher, vt. descifrar.

decision, n. decisión, determinación, resolución, f.

decisive, adj. decisivo, terminante; —ly, adv. decisivamente.

deck, n. (naut.) bordo, m., cubierta, f.;

baraja de naipes; — **chair,** silla de cubierta; — **hand,** marinero, estibador, m.; —, vt. adornar.

declaration, n. declaración, manifestación, f.; explicación, f.

declare, vt. declarar, manifestar.

declension, n. (gram.) declinación, f.; declive, m.; inclinación, f.

decline, vt. (gram.) declinar; rehusar; —, vi. decaer, desmejorar, venir a menos; inclinarse; —, n. declinación, f.; decadencia, f.; declive, m.; ocaso, m.

decode, vt. descifrar (un cable, un escrito, etc.).

décolleté, adj. escotado.

decompose, vt. descomponer; —, vi. pudrirse, descomponerse.

decorate, vt. decorar, adornar; condecorar.

decorator, n. decorador, ra.

decorous, adj. decente, decoroso.

decorum, n. decoro, garbo, m.; decencia, f.; conveniencia, f.; pudor, m.

decoy, vt. atraer (algún pájaro); embaucar, engañar; —, n. seducción, f.; reclamo, m.; lazo, ardid, m.

decrease, vt. disminuir, reducir, minorar; —, vi. menguar; —, n. disminución, f.

decree, n. decreto, edicto, m.; —, vt. decretar, ordenar.

decrepit, adj. decrépito.

dedicate, vt. dedicar; consagrar.

dedication, n. dedicación, f.; dedicatoria, f.

deduce, vt. deducir; derivar; inferir.

deduct, vt. deducir, sustraer.

deduction, n. deducción, rebaja, f.; descuento, m.

deed, n. acción, f.; hecho, m.; hazaña, f.; (law) escritura, f.

deem, vi. juzgar, pensar, estimar.

deep, adj. profundo; sagaz; grave; oscuro; taciturno; subido (aplícase al color); intenso; — **seated,** arraigado, profundo; **the** —, n. el piélago, la mar.

deepen, vt. y vi. profundizar; oscurecer; intensificar.

deep-freeze, n. congelador, m., congeladora, f.

deer, n. sing. y pl. ciervo(s), venado(s), m.

deface, vt. borrar, destruir; desfigurar, afear.

defame, vt. difamar; calumniar.

default, n. delito de omisión; morosidad en el pago de cuentas; defecto, m., falta, f.; **to lose by** —, perder por ausencia, por no presentarse (a un torneo, a un juzgado, etc.); —, vt. y vi. faltar, delinquir.

defeat, n. derrota, f.; vencimiento, m.; —, vt. derrotar; frustrar.

defeatist, n. pesimista, m. y f.; derrotista,

abandonista, m. y f.

defect, n. defecto, m.; falta, f.

defection, n. defección, f.; fracaso, malogro, m.

defective, adj. defectuoso, imperfecto.

defend, vt. defender; proteger.

defendant, adj. defensivo; —, n. demandado, da, acusado, da.

defender, n. defensor, abogado, m.

defense, n. defensa, f.; protección, f.; amparo, apoyo, sostén, m.

defenseless, adj. indefenso; impotente.

defensive, adj. defensivo; —**ly,** adv. de un modo defensivo; —, n. defensiva, f.

defer, vt. diferir, retardar; posponer; postergar; —, vi. deferir.

deference, n. deferencia, f.; respeto, m.; consideración, f.; **in** — **to,** por consideración a.

deferential, adj. respetuoso.

defiance, n. desafío, m.; **in** — **of,** a despecho de.

defiant, adj. atrevido; porfiado.

deficiency, n. defecto, m.; imperfección, f.; falta, f.; insolvencia, f.; deficiencia, f.

deficient, adj. deficiente, pobre.

deficit, n. déficit, m.

defile, n. desfiladero, m.; —, vt. corromper; deshonrar; ensuciar; —, vi. desfilar.

define, vt. definir; limitar; determinar.

definite, adj. definido, exacto, preciso, limitado; cierto; concreto.

definition, n. definición, f.

definitive, adj. definitivo; —**ly,** adv. definitivamente.

deflatable, adj. desinflable.

deflate, vt. desinflar.

deflation, n. desinflación, f.

deflect, vi. desviarse; ladearse.

deform, vt. deformar, desfigurar.

deformed, adj. deformado, desfigurado.

deformity, n. deformidad, f.

defraud, vt. defraudar frustrar.

defray, vt. costear; sufragar; subvenir.

defrost, vt. descongelar, deshelar.

defroster, n. descongelador, desescarchador, m.

deft, adj. despierto, despejado, diestro; —**ly,** adv. con ingenio y viveza.

defunct, adj. difunto, muerto; —, n. difunto, ta.

defy, vt. desafiar, retar; despreciar; desdeñar.

degenerate, vi. degenerar; —, adj. degenerado.

degeneration, n. degeneración, f.

degrade, vt. degradar; deshonrar, envilecer.

degree, n. grado, m.; rango, m.; condición, f.; título universitario; **by** —**s,** gradualmente.

dehumidify, *vt.* deshumedecer.

dehydrate, *vt.* deshidratar.

deicer, *n.* descongelador, deshelador, *m.*

deify, *vt.* deificar; divinizar.

deign, *vi.* dignarse; condescender.

deity, *n.* deidad, divinidad, *f.*

deject, *vt.* abatir, desanimar.

dejected, *adj.* abatido.

dejection, *n.* decaimiento, *m.;* tristeza, aflicción, *f.;* (med.) evacuación, *f.*

del.: delegate, delegado; **delete,** suprímase.

delay, *vt.* diferir; retardar; postergar; — *vi.* demorar; —, *n.* dilación, demora, *f.;* retardo, *m.;* retraso, *m.*

delectable, *adj.* deleitoso, deleitable.

delegate, *vt.* delegar, diputar; —, *n.* delegado, da, diputado, da.

delegation, *n.* delegación, diputación, comisión, *f.*

delete, *vt.* suprimir, tachar.

deliberate, *vt.* deliberar, considerar; —, *adj.* cauto; avisado, pensado, premeditado; —**ly,** *adv.* con premeditación, deliberadamente.

deliberation, *n.* deliberación, circunspección, *f.;* reflexión, *f.;* consulta, *f.*

delicacy, *n.* delicadeza, *f.;* fragilidad, *f.;* escrupulosidad, *f.;* manjar, *m.*

delicate, *adj.* delicado; exquisito; tierno; escrupuloso; —**ly,** *adv.* delicadamente.

delicatessen, *n.* salchichonería, *f.,* tienda donde se venden fiambres, queso, etc.

delicious, *adj.* delicioso; sabroso, exquisito.

delight, *n.* delicia, *f.;* deleite, *m.;* placer, gozo, encanto, *m.;* **to take — in,** tener gusto en, estar encantado de; —, *vt.* deleitar; regocijar; —, *vi.* deleitarse.

delighted, *adj.* complacido, gozoso.

delightful, *adj.* delicioso; deleitable.

delineate, *vt.* delinear, diseñar.

delinquency, *n.* delito, *m.;* culpa, *f.;* delincuencia, *f.;* **juvenile —,** delincuencia juvenil.

delinquent, *n.* delincuente, *m.* y *f.*

delirious, *adj.* delirante, desvariado; **to be —,** delirar.

delirium, *n.* delirio, *m.;* — **tremens,** delirium tremens, *m.*

deliver, *vt.* entregar; dar; rendir; libertar; recitar, relatar; partear.

deliverance, *n.* libramiento, *m.;* liberación, salvación, *f.*

delivery, *n.* entrega, *f.;* liberación *f.;* alumbramiento, parto, *m.;* **general —** lista de correos, entrega general; **special —,** entrega inmediata.

dell, *n.* valle hondo, *m.;* hondonada, cañada, *f.*

delouse, *vt.* despiojar.

delta, *n.* delta, *f.*

delude, *vt.* engañar, alucinar.

deluge, *n.* inundación, *f.;* diluvio, *m.;* —, *vt.* inundar.

delusion, *n.* engaño, *m.;* ilusión, *f.*

de luxe, *adj.* lujoso, ostentoso; — **edition,** edición de lujo.

delve, *vt.* cavar; penetrar; sondear en busca de información.

demagogue, *n.* demagogo, *m.*

demand, *n.* demanda, *f.;* petición jurídica (de una deuda); venta continuada; — **(for merchandise),** consumo (de mercancías), *m.;* —, *vt.* demandar, reclamar, pedir, requerir, exigir.

demarcation, *n.* demarcación, *f.;* límite, *m.*

demeanor, *n.* porte, *m.;* conducta, *f.;* comportamiento, *m.;* **proper —,** corrección, *f.*

demented, *adj.* demente, loco.

demerit, *vt.* desmerecer.

demigod, *n.* semidiós, *m.*

demise, *vt.* legar, dejar en testamento; ceder, arrendar; —, *n.* muerte, *f.;* óbito, *m.;* trasmisión de la corona por abdicación o muerte.

demitasse, *n.* taza pequeña (de café).

demobilize, *vt.* desmovilizar.

democracy, *n.* democracia, *f.*

democrat, *n.* demócrata, *m.* y *f.*

democratic, *adj.* democrático, demócrata.

demolish, *vt.* demoler, arruinar; arrasar; batir.

demolition, *n.* demolición, *f ;* derribo, *m.;* — **bomb,** bomba de demolición.

demon, *n.* demonio, diablo, *m .*

demonstrate, *vt.* demostrar, probar.

demonstration, *n.* demostración, *f.;* manifestación, *f.*

demonstrative, *adj.* demostrativo; expresivo; —**ly,** *adv.* demostrativamente.

demonstrator, *n.* demostrador, ra.

demoralize, *vt.* desmoralizar.

demote, *vt.* degradar, rebajar en clase o en grado.

demotion, *n.* (mil.) degradación, *f.;* descenso de rango, categoría o empleo.

demur, *vi.* objetar; demorar; vacilar, fluctuar; —, *n.* demora, *f.;* objeción, *f.*

demure, *adj.* reservado; decoroso; grave, serio; —**ly,** *adv.* modestamente.

den, *n.* caverna, *f.;* antro, *m.;* estudio, *m.,* habitación para lectura o descanso.

denature, *vt.* desnaturalizar; —**d alcohol,** alcohol desnaturalizado, *m.*

deniable, *adj.* negable.

denial, *n.* denegación, repulsa, *f.*

denim, *n.* mezclilla, *f .,* tela de algodón basta y fuerte.

Denmark, Dinamarca, *f.*

denomination, *n.* denominación, *f.; título,* nombre, apelativo, *m.*

denominational, *adj.* sectario.

denominator, *n.* (math.) denominador, *m.*

denote, *vt.* denotar, indicar.

denounce *vt.* denunciar.

dense, *adj.* denso, espeso; cerrado, estúpido; impenetrable.

density, *n.* densidad, solidez, *f.*

dent, *n.* abolladura, *f.;* mella, *f.;* —, *vt.* abollar.

dental, *adj.* dental; — **clinic,** clínica dental; *n.* dental, *f.*

dentifrice, *n.* dentífrico, *m.*

dentist, *n.* dentista, *m.* y *f.;* (coll.) sacamuelas, *m.*

dentistry, *n.* dentistería, *f.*

dentition, *n.* dentición, *f.;* dentadura (de un animal), *f.*

denture, *n.* dentadura postiza.

denunciation, *n.* denunciación, *f.*

deny, *vt.* negar, rehusar; renunciar; abjurar.

deodorant, *n.* y *adj.* desodorante, *m.*

deodorize, *vt.* quitar o disipar el mal olor (de algo).

depart, *vi.* depender; irse, salir; morir; desistir.

department, *n.* departamento, *m.;* — **store,** bazar, *m.;* tienda dividida en secciones o departamentos.

departure, *n.* partida, salida, *f.;* desviación, *f.*

depend, *vi.* depender; **it —s,** según y conforme, depende; **to — on, to — upon,** confiar en, contar con.

dependable, *adj.* digno de confianza.

dependence, *n.* dependencia, confianza, *f.*

dependency, *n.* dependencia, *f.*

dependent, *n.* dependiente, *m.* y *f.,* persona que depende de otra para su manutención; —, *adj.* dependiente, cifrado; — **upon,** cifrado en.

depict, *vt.* pintar, retratar; describir.

depilatory, *n.* y *adj.* depilatorio, *m.*

deplete, *vt.* agotar, vaciar.

deplorable, *adj.* deplorable, lamentable.

deplore, *vt.* deplorar, lamentar.

depopulate, *vt.* despoblar, devastar.

deport, *vt.* deportar.

deportment, *n.* comportamiento, *m.,* conducta, *f.;* porte, manejo, *m.*

depose, *vt.* deponer; destronar; testificar; **to — upon oath,** declarar bajo juramento.

deposit, *vt.* depositar; —, *n.* depósito, *m.*

deposition, *n.* deposición, *f.,* testimonio, *m.;* destitución, *f.*

depositor, *n.* depositante, *m.* y *f.*

depository, *n.* depositario, ria; almacén, depósito, *m.*

depot, *n.* depósito, almacén, *m.;* (rail.) estación, *f.,* paradero, *m.*

deprave, *vt.* depravar, corromper.

depravity, *n.* depravación, *f.*

deprecate, *vt.* deprecar.

depreciate, *vt.* depreciar.

depreciation, *n.* descrédito, *m.;* desestimación, *f.;* depreciación, *f.*

depredation, *n.* depredación, *f.;* pillaje, *m.*

depress, *vt.* deprimir, humillar.

depressed, *adj.* desgraciado, deprimido; — (in spirit), descorazonado.

depression, *n.* depresión, *f.;* abatimiento, *m.;* contracción económica.

deprive, *vt.* privar, despojar, **to — of,** quitar.

dept.: department, dep., depto. departamento.

depth, *n.* profundidad, *f.;* abismo, *m.;* (fig.) seriedad, *f.;* oscuridad, *f.;* — **bomb,** bomba de profundidad; — **charge,** carga de profundidad.

deputy, *n.* diputado, delegado, *m.;* lugarteniente, *m.;* comisario, *m.*

derail, *vt.* descarrilar.

derange, *vt.* desarreglar, desordenar; trastornar, volver loco.

derby, *n.* sombrero hongo; carrera especial de caballos celebrada anualmente; (coll.) bombín, *m.*

derelict, *adj.* abandonado; infiel; descuidado; —, *n.* (naut.) derrelicto, *m.;* paria, *m.* y *f.*

dereliction, *n.* desamparo, abandono, *m.*

deride, *vt.* burlar, mofar.

derision, *n.* irrisión, mofa, *f.;* escarnio, *m.*

derisive, *adj.* irrisorio.

derivation, *n.* derivación, *f.*

derivative, *n.* (gram.) derivado, *m.*

derive, *vt.* derivar; sacar; —, *vi.* derivarse, proceder.

dermatologist, *n.* dermatólogo, *m.*

dermatology, *n.* dermatología, *f.*

dermis, *n.* (anat.) dermis, *f.,* cutis, *m.*

derogatory, *adj.* derogatorio; despectivo.

derrick, *n.* grúa, *f.*

descend, *vi.* descender.

descendant, *n.* vástago, *m.,* descendiente, *m.* y *f.*

descent, *n.* descenso, *m.;* pendiente, *f.;* invasión, *f.;* descendencia, posteridad, *f.*

describe, *vt.* describir, delinear; calificar; explicar.

description, *n.* descripción, *f.;* **brief —,** reseña, *f.*

descriptive, *adj.* descriptivo.

desecrate, *vt.* profanar.

desegregate, *vt.* integrar, suprimir la

segregación (de razas).

desensitize, vt. insensibilizar; (phot.) hacer insensible a la luz.

desert, n. desierto, m.

desert, n. mérito, m.; merecimiento, m.; —, vt. abandonar; —, vi. (mil.) desertar.

deserter, n. desertor, m.

desertion, n. deserción, f.

deserve, vt. merecer; ser digno.

deserving, adj. meritorio; merecedor; **to be** —, valer, merecer.

design, vt. designar, proyectar; tramar; diseñar; —, n. designio, intento, m.; diseño, plan, m.; dibujo, m.

designate, vt. designar; apuntar, señalar; distinguir.

designation, n. designación, f.

designer, n. dibujante, proyectista, m. y f.; diseñador, ra; intrigante, m. y f.

designing, adj. insidioso, astuto.

desirability, n. ansia, f.; conveniencia, f.

desirable, adj. deseable.

desire, n. deseo, m.; apetencia, f.; —, vt. desear, apetecer, querer, pedir.

desirous, adj. deseoso, ansioso.

desist, vi. desistir.

desk, n. escritorio, m.; papelera, f.; pupitre, m.; bufete, m.

desolate, vt. desolar, devastar; —, adj. desolado; solitario.

desolation, n. desolación, ruina, destrucción, f.

despair, n. desesperación, f.; —, vi. desesperar.

despairing, adj. desesperado, sin esperanza.

desperate, adj. desesperado; furioso.

desperation, n. desesperación, f.

despicable, adj. vil, despreciable.

despise, vt. despreciar; desdeñar. despite, n. despecho, m.;

despique, m.; malicia, f.; —, prep. a pesar de, a despecho de.

despoil, vt. despojar; privar.

despond, vi. desanimarse, abatirse; desesperarse.

despondent, adj. abatido, desalentado, desesperado, desanimado.

despot, n. déspota, m. y f.

despotic, despotical, adj. despótico, absoluto, arbitrario.

despotism, n. despotismo, m.

dessert, n. postre, m.

destination, n. destino, paradero, m.

destine, vt. destinar, dedicar.

destiny, n. destino, hado, sino, m.; suerte, f.

destitute, adj. carente; en extrema necesidad.

destitution, n. destitución, privación, f.;

abandono, m.

destroy, vt. destruir, arruinar; hacer pedazos.

destroyer, n. destructor, ra; (naut.) destructor, m., barco de guerra.

destruction, n. destrucción, ruina, f.

destructive, adj. destructivo, ruinoso.

desultory, adj. irregular, inconstante, sin método.

detach, vt. separar, desprender; (mil.) destacar.

detachable, adj. desmontable.

detail, n. detalle, m.; particularidad, f.; circunstancia, f.; (mil.) destacamento, m.; **in** —, al por menor; detalladamente; **to go into** —, menudear; —, vt. detallar; referir con pormenores.

detain, vt. retener, detener; impedir.

detect, vt. descubrir; discernir.

detective, n. detective, m.; — **story,** novela policiaca.

detector, n. descubridor, ra; detector, ra; indicador, m.

detention, n. detención, retención, f.; cautividad, f.; cautiverio, m.

deter, vt. desanimar; disuadir.

detergent, n. y adj. detergente, m. deteriorate, vt. deteriorar.

deterioration, n. deterioración, f., deterioro, m.

determination, n. determinación, f.; decisión, resolución, f.

determine, vt. determinar, decidir; —, vi. decidir, resolver; **to be** —**d,** proponerse.

deterrence, n. disuasión, f.

deterrent, adj. disuasivo, desanimador; —, n. lo que desanima o disuade.

detest, vt. detestar, aborrecer.

detestable, adj. detestable, abominable.

dethrone, vt. destronar.

detonation, n. detonación, fulminación, f.

detour, n. rodeo, m.; desvío, m.; desviación, f.; vuelta, f.; —, vt. desviar (el tránsito).

detract, vt. detractar, retirar; disminuir; —, vi. denigrar.

detriment, n. detrimento, daño, perjuicio, m.

detrimental, adj. perjudicial.

deuce, n. dos (en los juegos de naipes), m.; diantre, m.; **the** —**l** interj. ¡demonios!

devaluate, vt. depreciar, rebajar el valor.

devastate, vt. devastar; robar.

devastation, n. devastación, ruina, f.

develop, vt. desenvolver; desarrollar; revelar (una fotografía); —, vi. desarrollarse.

development, n. desarrollo, m.

deviate, vi. desviarse.

deviation, n. desvío, m.; desviación, f.

device, n. invento, m.; aparato, mecanismo, artefacto, m.; plan, ardid, m.; lema, m.; proyecto, m.; artificio, m.

devil, n. diablo, demonio, m.

deviled eggs, n. pl. huevos rellenos y condimentados.

deviltry, n. diablura, f.

devious, adj. desviado; tortuoso.

devise, vt. trazar; inventar; idear; legar; —, n. legado, m.; donación testamentaria.

devitalize, vt. restar vitalidad.

devoid, adj. vacío; carente.

devote, vt. dedicar; consagrar; destinar; — **oneself,** consagrarse.

devotion, n. devoción, f.; oración, f.; rezo, m.; afición, f.; dedicación, f.

devour, vt. devorar.

devout, adj. devoto, piadoso.

dew, n. rocío, m.

dewdrop, n. gota de rocío.

dewy, adj. rociado, con rocío.

dexterity, n. destreza, f.

dexterous, adj. diestro, hábil.

dextrose, n. glucosa, dextrosa, f.

dextrous, adj. diestro, experto.

diabetes, n. diabetes, f.

diabetic, adj. diabético.

diabolic, diabolical, adj. diabólico.

diagnose, vt. diagnosticar.

diagnosis, n. (med.) diagnosis, f.

diagonal, n. y adj. diagonal, f.

diagram, n. esquema, m.; diagrama, m.; gráfico, m.

dial, n. esfera de reloj; cuadrante, reloj de sol; — **telephone,** teléfono automático **to** — **the number,** marcar el número.

dialing, n. acción de llamar por teléfono automático; sintonización, f.

dialect, n. dialecto, m.

dialectics, n. dialéctica, f.

dialogue, n. diálogo, m.

diameter, n. diámetro, m.

diamond, n. diamante, m.; brillante, m.; oro (de baraja), m.; — **cutter,** diamantista, m.

diapason, n. (mus.) diapasón, m.

diaper, n. pañal, m.; —, vt. proveer con pañales.

diaphragm, n. diafragma, m.

diarrhea, n. diarrea, f.

diary, n. diario, m.

diathermy, n. (med.) diatermia, f.

dice, n. pl. dados, m. pl.

dicker, vi. regatear.

dickey, n. peto, m., pechera, f.; (auto.) asiento del conductor.

dictaphone, n. dictáfono, m., aparato para dictar cartas.

dictate, vt. dictar; —, n. dictamen, m.

dictation, n. dictado, m.

dictator, n. caudillo, m.; dictador, m.

dictatorial, adj. autoritativo, dictatorial, dictatorio, imperioso.

dictatorship, n. dictadura, f.

diction, n. dicción, f.; estilo, m.

dictionary, n. diccionario, léxico, m.

did, pretérito del verbo **do.**

die, vi. morir, expirar; evaporarse; desvanecerse; marchitarse; —, n. dado, m.; cuño, molde, troquel, m.; matriz, f.

die-hard, n. persona intransigente y conservadora.

diesel, adj. diesel; — **engine,** motor diesel.

diet, n. dieta, f.; régimen, m.; —, vi. estar a dieta.

dietetics, n. dietética, f.

dietician, n. dietista, m. y f.

differ, vi. diferenciarse; contradecir.

difference, n. diferencia, disparidad, f.; variante, f.

different, adj. diferente; desemejante.

differential, n. y adj. diferencial, f.; — **calculus,** (math.) cálculo diferencial.

differentiate, vt. diferenciar.

difficult, adj. difícil; áspero; enrevesado.

difficulty, n. dificultad, f.; obstáculo, escollo, m.; trabajo, m.; **with** —, a duras penas, trabajosamente.

diffident, adj. tímido, modesto; falto de confianza en sí mismo.

diffuse, vt. difundir, esparcir; —, adj. difundido, esparcido; prolijo.

dig, vt. cavar, excavar; — **up,** desenterrar, desarraigar; —, n. (coll.) pulla, indirecta, f.

digest, vt. digerir; clasificar; asimilar mentalmente; —, vi. digerir; —, n. extracto, compendio, m.

digestible, adj. digerible.

digestion, n. digestión, f.

digestive, adj. digestivo.

digger, n. cavador, ra.

digging, n. excavación, f.; —**s,** n. pl. lo excavado; lavaderos de arenas auríferas.

digit, n. dígito, m.

dignified, adj. altivo; serio, grave, con dignidad.

dignify, vt. exaltar, elevar.

dignitary, n. dignatario, m.

dignity, n. dignidad, f.; rango, m.; mesura, f.

digression, n. digresión, f.; divagación, f.; desvío, m.

dike, n. dique, canal, m.

dilapidate, vt. dilapidar.

dilapidated, adj. arruinado; desvencijado.

dilate, vt. dilatar, extender; —, vi. dilatarse, extenderse.

dilated, adj. dilatado, extendido; explayado, prolijo, difuso.

dilation, *n.* dilatación, *f.*

dilemma, *n.* dilema, *m.*

dilettante, *n.* aficionado, da (de las bellas artes) .

diligence, *n.* diligencia, *f.;* asiduidad, *f.*

diligent, *adj.* diligente, asiduo; aplicado, hacendoso; **—ly,** *adv.* diligentemente.

dill, *n.* eneldo, *m.;* **— pickle,** encurtido con eneldo.

dilute, *vt.* diluir.

dim, *adj.* turbio de vista, oscuro; confuso; **—,** *vt.* ofuscar, oscurecer; eclipsar.

dime, *n.* moneda de diez centavos en E.U.A.

dimension, *n.* dimensión, medida, extensión, *f.*

diminish, *vt.* decrecer, disminuir; **—,** *vi.* ceder; menguar, disminuirse.

diminishing, *adj.* menguante.

diminutive, *n.* y *adj.* diminutivo, *m.*

dimity, *n.* cotonía, *f.*

dimmer, *n.* (auto.) amortiguador de intensidad de luz.

dimness, *n.* oscuridad, *f.;* opacidad, *f.*

dimple, *n.* hoyuelo, *m.*

din, *n.* ruido violento, alboroto, *m.;* **—,** *vt.* atolondrar.

dine, *vt.* dar de comer o de cenar; **—,** *vi.* comer, cenar.

diner, *n.* (rail.) coche comedor.

dingy, *adj.* sucio; empañado.

dining, *adj.* comedor; **— car,** coche comedor; **— room,** comedor, *m.;* refectorio, *m.*

dinner, *n.* comida, cena, *f.*

dinosaur, *n.* dinosaurio, *m.*

dint, *n.* golpe, *m.;* **by — of,** a fuerza de, a puro.

diocese, *n.* diócesis, *f.*

diorama, *n.* diorama, *m.*

dip, *vt.* remojar, sumergir; **—,** *vi.* sumergirse; penetrar; inclinarse; **—,** *n.* inmersión, *f.;* inclinación, *f.*

diphtheria, *n.* difteria, *f.*

diphthong, *n.* diptongo, *m.*

diploma, *n.* diploma, *m.*

diplomacy, *n.* diplomacia, *f.;* tacto, *m.*

diplomat, *n.* diplomático, *m.*

diplomatic, *adj.* diplomático; **— corps,** cuerpo diplomático.

dipper, *n.* cucharón, cangilón, cazo, *m.;* **Big D—,** Osa Mayor.

dire, *adj.* horrendo, cruel; deplorable.

direct, *adj.* directo, derecho, recto; claro; **— current,** (elec.) corriente continua; **— hit,** blanco directo; **—,** *vt.* dirigir, enderezar; ordenar.

direction, *n.* dirección, *f.;* instrucción, *f.;* manejo, *m.;* rumbo, curso, *m.*

director, *n.* director, *m.;* guía, *m.;* superintendente, *m.;* **board of —s,** directorio, *m.,* junta directiva.

directory, *n.* directorio, *m.;* guía, *f.*

dirge, *n.* canción lúgubre.

dirt, *n.* suciedad, porquería, mugre, *f.*

dirty, *adj.* puerco, sucio; vil; bajo; **— trick,** mala partida, mala broma; **—,** *vt.* ensuciar, emporcar.

disability, *n.* impotencia, *f.;* inhabilidad, incapacidad, *f.*

disable, *vt.* hacer incapaz, incapacitar; (naut.) desaparejar (un navío).

disablement, *n.* (leyes) impedimento, *m.;* (naut.) desaparejo de una nave como resultado de algún combate.

disadvantage, *n.* desventaja, *f.;* daño, *m.*

disagree, *vi.* desconvenir, discordar, no estar de acuerdo.

disagreeable, *adj.* desagradable.

disagreement, *n.* desacuerdo, *m.,* discordia, desavenencia, *f.;* diferencia, *f.;* desconformidad, *f.*

disappear, *vi.* desaparecer; salir; esfumarse; ausentarse.

disappearance, *n.* desaparición, *f.*

disappoint, *vt.* frustrar, faltar a la palabra; decepcionar, engañar; **to be —ed,** llevarse chasco; estar decepcionado.

disappointment, *n.* chasco, *m.;* contratiempo, *m.;* decepción, *f.*

disapproval, *n.* desaprobación, censura, *f.*

disapprove, *vt.* desaprobar.

disarm, *vt.* desarmar, privar de armas.

disarmament, *n.* desarme, *m.*

disarray, *n.* desarreglo, *m.;* **—,** *vt.* desnudar; desarreglar.

disassociate, *vt.* desasociar.

disaster, *n.* desastre, *m.;* infortunio, *m.;* catástrofe, *f.*

disastrous, *adj.* desastroso, infeliz; funesto.

disband, *vt.* dividir, desunir; **—,** *vi.* dispersarse.

disbelief, *n.* incredulidad, desconfianza, *f.*

disbelieve, *vt.* descreer, desconfiar.

disburse, *vt.* desembolsar, pagar.

disbursement, *n.* desembolso, *m.*

disc = disk.

discard, *vt.* descartar; **—,** *n.* descarte (en el juego de naipes), *m.*

discern, *vt.* y *vi.* discernir, percibir, distinguir.

discernible, *adj.* perceptible.

discerning, *adj.* juicioso, perspicaz.

discernment, *n.* discernimiento, *m.*

discharge, *vt.* descargar, pagar (una deuda, etc.); (mil.) licenciar; ejecutar, cumplir; descartar; despedir; **—,** *vi.* descargarse; **—,** *n.* descarga, *f ;* descargo, *m.;* finiquito, *m.;* dimisión, *f.;* absolución, *f.*

disciple, *n.* discípulo, secuaz, *m.*

disciplinary, *adj.* disciplinario.

discipline, *n.* disciplina, *f.;* enseñanza, *f.;* rigor, *m;* —, *vt.* disciplinar, instruir.

disclaim, *vt.* negar, renunciar; repudiar, rechazar.

disclose, *vt.* descubrir, revelar.

disclosure, *n.* descubrimiento, *m.;* revelación, *f.*

discolor, *vt.* descolorar.

discoloration, *n.* descoloramiento, *m.;* mancha, *f.*

discomfort, *n.* incomodidad, *f.;* aflicción, *f.;* molestia, *f.*

disconcert, *vt.* desconcertar, confundir, turbar.

disconnect, *vt.* desconectar.

disconsolate, *adj.* inconsolable; desconsolador; **—ly,** *adv.* desconsoladamente.

discontent, *n.* descontento, *m.;* —, *adj.* descontento, disgustado; —, *vt.* descontentar.

discontented, *adj.* descontento.

discontinue, *vi.* descontinuar, interrumpir; cesar.

discord, discordance, *n.* discordia, *f.;* discordancia, disensión, *f.*

discordant, *adj.* discorde; incongruo; **—ly,** *adv.* con discordancia.

discount, *n.* descuento, *m.;* rebaja, *f.;* **rate of** —, tipo de descuento; —, *vt.* descontar.

discourage, *vt.* desalentar, desanimar.

discouragement, *n.* desaliento, *m.*

discourse, *n.* discurso, *m.;* tratado, *m.;* —, *vi.* conversar, discurrir, tratar (de).

discourteous, *adj.* descortés, grosero.

discourtesy, *n.* descortesia, grosería, *f.*

discover, *vt.* descubrir; revelar; manifestar.

discovery, *n.* descubrimiento, *m.;* revelación, *f.*

discredit, *n.* descrédito, deshonor, *m.;* —, *vt.* desacreditar, deshonrar.

discreet, *adj.* discreto; circunspecto; callado.

discrepancy, *n.* discrepancia, diferencia, *f.;* variante, *f.*

discretion, *n.* discreción, *f.*

discriminate, *vt.* discriminar.

discriminating, *adj.* parcial, discerniente.

discrimination, *n.* discriminación, *f.*

discuss, *vt.* discutir.

discussion, *n.* discusión, *f.*

disdain, *vt.* desdeñar, despreciar; —, *n.* desdén, desprecio, *m.*

disdainful, *adj.* desdeñoso.

disease, *n.* mal, *m.;* enfermedad, *f.;* **conta-**

gious —, enfermedad contagiosa.

diseased, *adj.* enfermo.

disembark, *vt.* y *vi.* desembarcar.

disengage, *vt.* desenredar, librar; —, *vi.* libertarse de.

disfavor, *vt.* desfavorecer; —, *n.* disfavor, *m.;* desaprobación, *f.*

disfigure, *vt.* desfigurar, afear.

disfigurement, *n.* deformidad, *f.;* desfiguración, *f.*

disgrace, *n.* deshonra, *f.;* desgracia, *f.;* —, *vt.* deshonrar; hacer caer en desgracia.

disgraceful, *adj.* deshonroso, ignominioso; **—ly,** *adv.* vergonzosamente.

disguise, *vt.* disfrazar, enmascarar; simular; —, *n.* disfraz, *m.;* máscara, *f.*

disgust, *n.* disgusto, *m.;* aversión, *f.;* fastidio, *m.;* **to cause** —, repugnar; —, *vt.* disgustar, inspirar aversión.

dish, *n.* fuente, *f.,* plato, *m.;* taza, *f.;* **set of —es,** vajilla, *f.;* —, *vt.* servir en un plato.

dishcloth, *n.* paño para lavar platos.

dishearten, *vt.* desalentar, descorazonar.

dishevel, *vt.* desgreñar.

dishonest, *adj.* deshonesto; ignominioso.

dishonesty, *n.* falta de honradez; deshonestidad, impureza, *f.*

dishonor, *n.* deshonra, ignominia, *f.;* —, *vt.* deshonrar, infamar.

dishonorable, *adj.* deshonroso, afrentoso, indecoroso; **—bly,** *adv.* ignominiosamente.

dishpan, *n.* vasija para fregar platos.

dishrag = **dishcloth.**

dishwasher, *n.* lavadora eléctrica de platos; lavaplatos, *m.* o *f.*

dishwater, *n.* agua para lavar platos.

disillusion, *n.* desengaño, *m.,* desilusión, *f.;* —, *vt.* desengañar, desilusionar.

disinfect, *vt.* desinfectar.

disinfectant, *n.* desinfectante, *m.*

disinherit, *vt.* desheredar.

disintegrate, *vt.* desintegrar; despedazar.

disintegration, *n.* desintegración, *f.*

disinterested, *adj.* desinteresado.

disjointed, *adj.* dislocado; **—ly,** *adv.* separadamente.

disk, *n.* disco, *m.;* — **jockey,** (radio o TV.) anunciador de programa con base en discos; D.J., tocadiscos,.

diskette, *n.* disquete, *m.*

dislike, *n.* aversión, repugnancia, *f.;* disgusto, *m.;* —, *vt.* disgustar; desagradar.

dislocate, *vt.* dislocar, descoyuntar.

dislodge, *vt.* y *vi.* desalojar.

disloyal, *adj.* desleal; infiel.

disloyalty, *n.* deslealtad, infidelidad, perfidia,

dismal, *adj.* triste, funesto; horrendo.

dismantle, *vt.* (mil.) desmantelar (una plaza) ; desamueblar; (naut.) desaparejar.

dismay, *n.* consternación, *f.;* terror, *m.;* —, *vt. y vi.* consternar, consternarse, abatirse.

dismember, *vt.* desmembrar.

dismiss, *vt.* despedir; echar; descartar.

dismissal, dismission, *n.* despedida, *f.;* dimisión, *f.;* destitución, *f.*

dismount, *vt.* desmontar, apearse (del caballo); —, *vi.* desmontar, descender.

disobedience, *n.* desobediencia, *f.*

disobedient, *adj.* desobediente.

disobey, *vt.* desobedecer.

disorder, *n.* desorden, *m.;* confusión, *f.;* indisposición, *f.;* desequilibrio, *m.;* —, *vt.* desordenar; perturbar.

disorderly, *adj.* desarreglado, confuso.

disorganization, *n.* desorganización, *f.*

disorganize, *vt.* desorganizar.

disown, *vt.* negar, desconocer; repudiar.

disparage, *vt.* envilecer; mofar, menospreciar.

disparagement, *n.* menosprecio, desprecio, *m.;* insulto, *m.*

disparity, *n.* disparidad, *f.*

dispassionate, *adj.* sereno, desapasionado; templado.

dispatch, *n.* despacho, *m.;* embarque, *m.;* corn.) envío, *m.;* remisión, *f.;* —, *vt.* despachar; embarcar; remitir, enviar.

dispel, *vt.* disipar, dispersar.

dispensary, *n.* dispensario, *m.*

dispensation, *n.* dispensación, *f.;* dispensa,

dispense, *vt.* dispensar; distribuir; eximir.

disperse, *vt.* esparcir, disipar; dispersar.

displace, *vt.* desplazar; dislocar, desordenar.

displaced, *adj.* desplazado, dislocado; — **person,** persona desplazada.

displacement, *n.* cambio de situación, mudanza, *f.;* desalojamiento *m.;* (chem.) coladura, *f* ; (naut.) desplazamiento, *m.*

display, *vt.* desplegar; explicar; exponer; ostentar; —, *n.* ostentación, *f.;* despliegue, *m.;* exhibición, *f.*

displease, *vt.* disgustar; ofender; desagradar; chocar.

displeasure, *n.* disgusto, desagrado, *m.;* indignación, *f.*

disposable, *adj.* desechable.

disposal, *n.* disposición, *f.*

dispose, *vt.* disponer; dar; arreglar; **to — of,** deshacerse de.

disposed, *adj.* dispuesto, inclinado; **well —,** bien dispuesto; **ill —,** mal dispuesto.

disposition, *n.* disposición, *f.;* índole, *f.;* inclinación, *f.;* carácter, *m.;* humor, *m.;*

good —, buen humor, buen carácter.

dispossess, *vt.* desposeer; desalojar.

disproportion, *n.* desproporción, *f.*

disproportionate, *adj.* desproporcionado.

disprove, *vt.* confutar, refutar.

disputable, *adj.* disputable, contestable.

dispute, *n.* disputa, controversia, *f.;* —, *vt. y vi.* disputar, controvertir, argüir.

disqualify, *vt.* descalificar; inhabilitar.

disquiet, *n.* inquietud, perturbación, *f.;* —, *vt.* inquietar, turbar.

disregard, *vt.* desatender, desdeñar; —, *n.* desatención, *f.;* desdén, *m.*

disreputable, *adj.* deshonroso; despreciable.

disrepute, *n.* descrédito, *m.;* mala fama; **to bring into —,** desacreditar, difamar, desprestigiar.

disrespect, *n.* irreverencia, falta de respeto.

disrespectful, *adj.* irreverente, descortés.

disrobe, *vt. y vi.* desnudar, desnudarse.

disrupt, *vt.* desbaratar, hacer pedazos; desorganizar, enredar.

disruption, *n.* rompimiento, *m.;* fractura, *f.*

dissatisfaction, *n.* descontento, disgusto, *m.*

dissatisfied, *adj.* descontento, no satisfecho.

dissatisfy, *vt.* descontentar, desagradar.

dissect, *vt.* disecar.

dissection, *n.* disección, *f.*

dissemble, *vt. y vi.* disimular, fingir.

disseminate, *vt.* diseminar, sembrar, esparcir, propagar.

dissension, *n.* disensión, discordia, *f.*

dissent, *vi.* disentir, estar en desacuerdo; —, *n.* disensión, *f.*

dissertation, *n.* disertación, tesis, *f.*

dissimilar, *adj.* disímil.

dissipate, *vt.* disipar.

dissipation, *n.* disipación, *f.;* libertinaje, *m.*

dissociate, *vt.* disociar.

dissolute, *adj.* disoluto, libertino.

dissolution, *n.* disolución, *f.;* muerte, *f.*

dissolve, *vt.* disolver; —, *vi.* disolverse, derretirse.

dissonant, *adj.* disonante; discordante; diferente.

dissuade, *vt.* disuadir.

distance, *n.* distancia, *f.;* lejanía, *f.;* lontananza, *f.;* respeto, *m.;* esquivez, *f.;* **at a —,** de lejos; **in the —,** a lo lejos; —, *vt.* apartar; sobrepasar; espaciar.

distant, *adj.* distante, lejano; esquivo; reservado; **very —,** a leguas, muy distante; muy esquivo.

distaste, *n.* hastío, disgusto, tedio, *m.*

distasteful, *adj.* desabrido, desagradable; chocante; maligno.

distemper, *n.* indisposición, *f.;* desasosiego, *m.;* moquillo, *m.;* desorden tumultuoso; morbo, *m.*

distension, *n.* distensión, *f.;* dilatación, anchura, *f.*

distill, *vt.* y *vi.* destilar; gotear.

distiller, *n.* destilador, *m.*

distillery, *n.* destilería, *f.;* destilatorio, *m.*

distinct, *adj.* distinto, diferente; claro, sin confusión; —**ly,** *adv.* con claridad.

distinction, *n.* distinción, diferencia, *f.;* **person of —,** persona distinguida o eminente.

distinctive, *adj.* característico.

distinctness, *n.* claridad, *f.*

distinguish, *vt.* distinguir; discernir; —**ed,** *adj.* distinguido, caracterizado, señalado; eminente; notable, famoso, ilustre, considerado.

distort, *vt.* tergiversar, pervertir, torcer; disfrazar, falsear.

distortion, *n.* contorsión, *f.;* torcimiento, *m.;* perversión, *f.*

distract, *vt.* distraer; perturbar; —**ed,** *adj.* distraído; aturdido; perturbado.

distraction, *n.* distracción, *f.;* confusión, *f.;* frenesí, *m,* locura, *f.*

distress, *n.* aflicción, *f.;* calamidad, miseria, *f.;* —, *vt.* angustiar, acongojar; (leyes) secuestrar, embargar.

distribute, *vt.* distribuir, dividir, repartir.

distribution, *n.* distribución, *f.;* reparto, *m.*

distributor, *n.* distribuidor, ra.

district, *n.* distrito, *m.;* región, *f.;* jurisdicción, *f.;* zona, *f.;* vecindario, *m.;* barrio (de una ciudad), *m.*

distrust, *vt.* desconfiar; —, *n.* desconfianza, sospecha, *f.;* suspicacia, *f.*

distrustful, *adj.* desconfiado; sospechoso; suspicaz; —**ly,** *adv.* desconfiadamente.

disturb, *vt.* perturbar, estorbar.

disturbance, *n.* disturbio, *m.;* confusión, *f.;* tumulto, *m.;* perturbación, *f.*

disuse, *n.* desuso, *m.;* —, *vt.* desusar.

ditch, *n.* zanja, *f.;* foso, *m.;* cauce, *m.;* —, *vt.* abrir zanjas o fosos; (coll.) desembarazarse, dar calabazas.

ditto, *n.* ídem, marca (") o abreviatura (id.) que se usa en lugar de ídem; copia, *f.,* duplicado, *m.;* —, *vt.* copiar, duplicar; —, *adv.* también, asimismo.

ditty, *n.* cancioncita, *f.* aire, *m.*

diuretic, *n.* y *adj.* diurético, *m.*

divan, *n.* diván, *m.*

dive, *vi.* sumergirse, zambullirse; bucear; (Mex.) echarse un clavado; —, *n.* zambullidura, *f.;* (Mex.) clavado, *m.;* (coll.)

garito, *m.,* leonera, *f.;* — **bomber,** bombardero en picada.

diver, *n.* buzo, *m.;* (orn.) somorgujo, *m.*

diverge, *vi.* divergir; divergirse; discrepar.

divergence, *n.* divergencia, *f.*

divergent, *adj.* divergente.

divers, *adj.* varios, diversos, muchos.

diverse, *adj.* diverso, diferente, variado.

diversify, *vt.* diversificar.

diversion, *n.* diversión, *f.;* pasatiempo, *m.*

diversity, *n.* diversidad, *f.;* variedad, *f.*

divert, *vt.* desviar; divertir; recrear.

divest, *vt.* desnudar; privar, despojar.

divide, *vt.* dividir, distribuir; repartir; partir; desunir; —, *vi.* desunirse, dividirse.

dividend, *n.* dividendo, *m.*

divider, *n.* (math.) divisor, *m.;* distribuidor, *m.;* compás de puntas.

divine, *adj.* divino, sublime, excelente; —, *n.* teólogo, *m.;* —, *vt.* conjeturar; —, *vi.* presentir; profetizar; adivinar.

diving, *n.* buceo, *m.;* —, *adj.* buceador; relativo al buceo; — **bell,** campana de bucear; — **suit,** escafandra, *f.*

divinity, *n.* divinidad, *f.;* deidad, *f.;* teología, *f.*

divisibility, *n.* divisibilidad, *f.*

divisible, *adj.* divisible.

division, *n.* (math.) división, *f.;* desunión, *f.;* separación *f.*

divisor, *n.* (math) divisor, *m.*

divorce, *n.* divorcio, *m.;* —, *vt.* divorciar; divorciarse de.

divulge, *vt.* divulgar, publicar.

dizziness, *n.* vértigo, *m.;* ligereza, *f.;* vahído, *m.;* vaivén, *m.;* mareo, *m.*

dizzy, *adj.* vertiginoso; mareado; (coll.) tonto, estúpido.

D.N.A.: deoxyribonucleic acid, A.D.N., ácido desoxirribonucleico.

do, *vt.* hacer, ejecutar, finalizar; despachar; —, *vi.* obrar; comportarse; prosperar; **to — away with,** suprimir, quitar; **how — you —?** ¿cómo está usted? **to — without,** pasarse sin, prescindir de.

docile, *adj.* dócil, apacible.

dock, *n.* (naut.) muelle, desembarcadero, *m.;* **dry —,** astillero, *f.;* —, *vt.* descolar; entrar en muelle; cortar; descontar (parte del sueldo de alguien).

docket, *n.* extracto, sumario, *m.;* minuta, *f.;* rótulo, marbete, *m.;* —, *vt.* rotular; inscribir en el orden del día.

doctor, *n.* doctor, médico, *m.;* **D— of Law,** Doctor en Derecho; **D— of Philosophy,** Doctor en Filosofía; —**'s office,** consultorio de médico, gabinete, *m.;* —, *vt.* medicinar.

doctrine, *n.* doctrina, *f.;* erudición, *f.;* ciencia, *f.*

document, n. documento, m.; precepto, m.
documentary, n. y adj. documental, m.
dodge, vt. evadir, esquivar.
doe, n. (zool.) gama, f.
doer, n. hacedor, actor, ejecutante, m.
does, 3ª persona del singular del verbo **do**.
doeskin, n. piel de ante.
doff, vt. quitarse; desposeerse de.
dog. n. perro, m.; — **days,** caniculares, m.
  pl.; — **fight,** pelea de perros, refriega, f.;
  (avi.) combate aéreo a muerte; — **ken-**
  nel, perrera, f.; D— **Star,** Sirio,
  Canícula; —, vt. espiar, perseguir.
dogcart n. variedad de coche de dos ruedas; carruaje tirado por perros.
dogged, adj. tenaz, persistente; ceñudo,
  intratable, áspero, brutal; —**ly,** adv.
  adustamente; con persistencia, tenaz-
  mente.
doghouse, n. perrera, casa de perro, f.; **to**
  be in the —, (coll.) estar castigado, estar
  en desgracia.
dogma, n. dogma, m.
dogmatic, dogmatical, adj. dogmático.
dogwood, n. (bot.) cornejo, m.
doily, n. carpetita, f., pañito de adorno.
doings, n. pl. hechos, m. pl.; acciones, f.
  pl.; eventos, m. pl.
doldrums, n. pl. fastidio, m.; abatimiento, m.
dole, n. distribución, f.; porción, f.; limosna, f.; —, vt. repartir, distribuir.
doleful, adj. doloroso, lúgubre, triste.
doll, n. muñeca, f.; **boy** —, muñeco, m.
dollar, n. dólar, peso (moneda de E.U.A.),
  m.; **silver** —, peso fuerte.
dolly, n. muñequita, f.; remachador, m.;
  (rail.) plataforma de tracción.
dolphin, n. delfín, m.
dolt, n. hombre bobo.
domain, n. dominio, m.
dome, n. cúpula, f.; domo, m.
domestic, adj. doméstico; interno; casero;
  —, n. criado, da, sirviente, ta.
domesticate, vt. domesticar.
domicile, n. domicilio, m.
dominance, n. predominio, m., ascendencia, autoridad, f.
dominant, adj. dominante.
dominate, vt. y vi. dominar, predominar.
domination, n. dominación, f.
domineer, vi. dominar, señorear.
domineering, adj. tiránico, arrogante.
Dominican Republic, República
  Dominicana.
dominion, n. dominio, territorio, m.; señorío, m.; soberanía, f.
domino, n. dominó, m.; traje de máscara;
  —**es,** n. pl. dominó (juego), m.
don, vt. ponerse (un vestido, etc.).

donate, vt. donar, contribuir; obsequiar.
donation, n. donación, dádiva, contribución, f.
done, adj. hecho; cocido, asado; **well** —,
  bien hecho; bien cocido, bien asado; —,
  p.p. del verbo **do.**
donkey, n. burro, asno, borrico, m.
donor, n. donador, ra.
doodle, n. garrapato, m.; garabatos, m.
  pl.; —, vt. y vi. garrapatear, hacer garabatos.
doom, n. sentencia, f.; condena, f.; suerte,
  f.; —, vt. sentenciar, juzgar, condenar.
doomsday, n. día del juicio final; **until** —,
  (coll.) hasta quién sabe cuándo.
door, n. puerta, f.; — **bolt,** pasador, m.; —
  knocker, picaporte, llamador, m., aldaba, f.; **front** —, puerta de entrada;
  within —**s,** en casa, bajo techo; **sliding**
  —, puerta corrediza.
doorbell, n. timbre de llamada.
doorhandle, n. tirador para puertas.
doorkeeper, n. portero, ujier, m.
doorknob, n. perilla, f.
doorman, n. portero, m.
doorstep, n. umbral, m.
doorway, n. portada, f.; portal, m.; puerta
  de entrada.
dope, n. narcótico, m., droga heroica;
  (coll.) información, f.; (coll.) persona
  muy estúpida; — **fiend,** morfinómano,
  na, persona adicta a las drogas heroicas.
dormant, adj. durmiente; secreto; latente.
dormitory, n. dormitorio, m.
dorsal, adj. dorsal.
dose, n. dosis, porción, f.; —, vt. disponer
  la dosis de un remedio.
dot, n. punto, m.; (mus.) puntillo, m.; —,
  vt. poner punto (a una letra).
dote, vi. chochear.
doting, adj. senil, chocho, excesivamente
  aficionado o enamorado.
double, adj. doble, duplicado, duplo; falso,
  insincero; — **chin,** papada, f.; — **entry,**
  (com.) partida doble; — **play,** (béisbol)
  maniobra que pone fuera de juego a dos
  de los jugadores rivales; — **talk** (coll.)
  charla vacía de sentido aunque seria en
  apariencia; — **time,** paso doble o rápido; — **cross,** engañar; —, n. duplicado,
  m.; doble, m.; engaño, m.; artificio, m.;
  —, vt. doblar; duplicar; plegar.
double boiler, n. baño de María.
double-breasted, adj. con dos filas de
  botones (chaqueta o abrigo) .
double-feature, n. función con dos películas de largo metraje.
double-quick, adj. a paso muy rápido.
doubles, n. pl. (tenis) juego de dobles.

doubt, n. duda, sospecha, f.; **there is no —,** no cabe duda; **without —,** sin duda; **—,** vt. y vi. dudar; sospechar.

doubter, n. incrédulo, la.

doubtful, adj. dudoso, dudable; incierto.

doubtless, adj. indudable; **—ly,** adv. sin duda, indudablemente.

douche, n. ducha, f.

dough, n. masa, pasta, f.; (coll.) dinero, m.

doughnut, n. rosquilla, f., variedad de buñuelo.

dour, adj. torvo, austero.

douse, vt. zambullir; empapar; **—,** vi. zambullirse; empaparse.

dove, n. paloma, f.; **ring —,** paloma torcaz.

dowager, n. viuda respetable con viudedad; (coll.) matrona respetable.

dowdy, adj. desaliñado; **—,** n. mujer desaliñada.

dowel, n. tarugo, zoquete, m., clavija de madera.

dower, n. viudedad, f.

down, n. plumón, flojel, m.; bozo, vello, m.; revés de fortuna; **ups and —s,** vaivenes, m. pl., altas y bajas; **—,** adj. pendiente; **—,** adv. abajo; **so much —,** tanto al contado; **—,** vt. derribar; **— with!** ¡abajo!

downcast, adj. apesadumbrado, cabizbajo.

downfall, n. ruina, decadencia, f.; desplome, m.

downgrade, n. cuesta abajo, bajada, f.; **—,** vt. rebajar en calidad; (mil.) degradar.

downhearted, adj. abatido, desanimado.

downhill, adj. pendiente, hacia abajo; **—,** adv. cuesta abajo.

down payment, n. pago inicial; (Mex.) enganche, m.

downpour, n. aguacero, m.; chubasco, chaparrón, m.

downright, adv. sin ceremonias; de manera patente; por completo.

downstairs, adv. abajo de las escaleras; abajo; **—,** n. piso inferior.

downstream, adv. aguas abajo.

downtown, n. centro, m., parte céntrica de una ciudad.

downward, adj. inclinado; **—s,** adv. hacia abajo.

downy, adj. velloso; suave.

dowry, n. dote, m. o f.

doze, n. sueño ligero, siesta, m.; **—,** vi. dormitar.

dozen, n. docena, f.

D.P.: displaced person, persona desplazada.

Dr.: Doctor, Dr. Doctor.

drab, n. paño castaño; mujer desaliñada; prostituta, f.; color entre gris y café; **—,** adj. opaco; murrio; monótono.

draft, n. dibujo, m.; (com.) giro, m., letra de cambio, libranza, f.; corriente de aire; (mil.) leva, conscripción, f.; (naut.) calado, m.; **— board,** junta de conscripción; **—ing board,** tablero de dibujar, tabla para dibujo; **rough —,** borrador, m.; **sight —,** giro a la vista; **time —,** letra a plazo; **to honor a —,** dar acogida a una letra o un giro; **—,** vt. dibujar; redactar; reclutar forzosamente (en un ejército).

draftee, n. quinto, recluta, m.

draftsman, n. dibujante, m.; diseñador, m.

drag, vt. arrastrar; tirar con fuerza; **—,** vi. arrastrarse por el suelo; **—,** n. rastro, m.; rémora, f.; (coll.) influencia, f.

drag chute, n. (avi.) paracaídas de frenado.

dragon, n. dragón, m.

dragonfly, n. libélula, f.

drain, vt. desaguar; secar; sanear; **—,** n. desaguadero, m.; (naut.) colador, m.; cauce, m.; cuneta, f.; sangradera, f.

drainage, n. desagüe, m.; saneamiento, m.

drainpipe, n. tubo de desagüe.

drake, n. ánade macho.

dram, n. dracma, f.; porción de licor que se bebe de una vez.

drama, n. drama, m.

dramatic, dramatical, adj. dramático.

dramatics, n. pl. arte dramático; declamación, f.

dramatist, n. dramaturgo, m.

dramatization, n. versión dramatizada; representación o descripción dramática.

dramatize, vt. dramatizar.

drank, pretérito del verbo **drink.**

drape, n. cortina, colgadura, f.; **—,** vt. vestir, colgar decorativamente.

drapery, n. ropaje, m.; cortinaje, m.

drastic, adj. drástico.

draught, n. trago, m., poción, f.; corriente de aire.

draw, vt. tirar, traer; atraer; arrastrar; dibujar; librar una letra de cambio; **to — lots,** echar suertes; **to — nigh,** acercarse; **to — on,** librar a cargo de una persona; **to — out,** sacar; **to — up,** redactar, formular; **—,** vi. tirar, encogerse; moverse.

drawback, n. desventaja, f., inconveniente, m.

drawer, n. cajón (de un mueble), m., gaveta, f.; girador de una letra; **—s,** n. pl. calzones, m. pl.; calzoncillos, m. pl.

drawing, n. dibujo, m.; rifa, f.; **— room,** sala de recibo.

drawl, vi. hablar con pesadez; **—,** n. enunciación penosa y lenta.

drawn, adj. movido; halado; dibujado; desenvainado; estirado; **—,** p.p. del verbo draw.

dray (cart), n. carro, carretón, m.

drayman, n. carretero, m.

dread, n. miedo, terror, espanto, m.; —, adj. terrible; —, vt. y vi. temer.

dreadful, adj. terrible, espantoso; —ly, adv. terriblemente.

dream, n. sueño, m.; fantasía, f.; ensueño, m.; —, vi. soñar; imaginarse.

dreamer, n. soñador, ra; visionario, ria.

dreamland, n. reino de los sueños.

dreamy, adj. quimérico, soñador; soñoliento.

dreary, adj. lúgubre, triste.

dredge, vt. (naut.) rastrear con el rezón; excavar.

dredger, n. draga, f.; pescador de ostras.

dredging, n. dragado, m.; — **machine**, draga, f.

dregs, n. pl. heces, f. pl.; escoria, f.; morralla, f.

drench, vt. empapar, mojar, humedecer; —, n. bebida purgante; empapada, f.

dress, n. vestido, m.; atavío, tocado, m.; traje, m.; — **ball**, baile de etiqueta; — **goods**, tela para vestidos; — **rehearsal**, último ensayo (de una comedia, etc.); — **suit**, traje de etiqueta; **ready-made** —, traje hecho; —, vt. vestir, ataviar; revestir; curar las heridas; cocinar; —, vi. vestirse.

dresser, n. el que viste o adereza; tocador, m.

dressing, n. curación, f.; adorno, m.; salsa, f.; aderezo, m.; — **case**, neceser, m.; — **gown**, peinador, m., bata, f.; — **table**, tocador, m.; **French** —, salsa francesa, (para ensaladas), f.

dressmaker, n. modista, costurera, f.

dressmaking, n. modistería, confección de vestidos.

dressy, adj. vistoso; elegante.

drew, pretérito del verbo draw.

dribble, vt. hacer caer gota a gota; —, vi. gotear.

drift, n. impulso, m.; tempestad, f.; montón, m.; tendencia, f., propósito, designio, m.; significado, m.; (naut.) deriva, f.; —, vt. impeler; amontonar; —, vi. formar en montones.

driftwood, n. leña acarreada por el agua.

drill, n. taladro, m., barrena, f.; (mil.) instrucción de reclutas; —, vt. taladrar; (mil.) disciplinar reclutas; —, vi. hacer el ejercicio.

drilling, n. perforación, f.

drink, vt. y vi. beber, embeber, absorber; embriagarse; —, n. bebida, f.

drinker, n. bebedor, ra; borracho, cha.

drinking fountain, n. fuente pública para beber agua.

drip, vt. despedir algún líquido a gotas; —, vi. gotear, destilar; —, n. gotera, f.

dripping, n. pringue, m. o f.; chorreo, m.; —s, n. pl. pringue, m.; **bacon** —s, pringue, m. o f., grasa de tocino.

drive, n. accionamiento, m.; paseo, m.; (golf) tacazo, m.; **to go out for a** —, ir de paseo, dar un paseo; —, vt. y vi. impeler; guiar, manejar, conducir; llevar; (mech.) impulsar; andar en coche; — **into**, hincar, forzar a; reducir a.

drive-in, n. restaurante en que el cliente es servido en su automóvil.

drive-in theatre, n. autocinema, m.

driven, p.p. del verbo **drive**.

driver, n. empujador, m.; cochero, m.; carretero, m.; conductor, m.; chófer m.; maquinista, m.

driveway, n. calzada o entrada para coches.

driving, adj. motor; conductor; impulsor; —**license**, matrícula para conducir vehículos, licencia de conductor o de chófer; — **permit**, tarjeta de circulación; **to go out** —, ir de paseo, dar un paseo (en coche, etc.)

drizzle, vi. lloviznar; —, n. llovizna, f.

drogue, n. artefacto aerodinámico remolcado para sostener mangueras de alimentación de combustible o frenar el descenso de asientos expulsores, aviones o cápsulas espaciales.

droll, adj. jocoso, gracioso; —, n. bufón, m.

drone, n. zángano de colmena, m.; haragán, m.; avión radioguiado; —, vi. zanganear; dar un sonido sordo.

drool, vi. babear.

droop, vi. inclinarse, colgar; desanimarse, desfallecer; —, vt. dejar caer.

drop, n. gota, f.; pastilla, f.; pendiente, arete, m.; — **curtain**, telón de boca; **by** —s, gota a gota; **lemon** —, pastilla de limón; **letter** —, buzón, m.; —, vt. destilar, soltar; cesar; dejar; dejar caer; —, vi. gotear; desvanecerse; sobrevenir; languidecer; salirse; **to** — **dead**, caerse muerto.

dropsy, n. hidropesía, f.

dross, n. escoria de metales; hez, f.

drought, n. seca, sequía, f.; sequedad, f.; sed, f.

drouth = **drought**.

drove, n. manada, f.; hato, m.; muchedumbre, f.; rebaño, m.; —, pretérito del verbo **drive**.

drown, vt. sumergir; anegar; —, vi. anegarse; ahogarse.

drowse, vt. y vi. adormecer, adormecerse.

drowsily, *adv.* soñolientamente; lentamente.

drowsiness, *n.* somnolencia, pereza, *f.*

drowsy, *adj.* soñoliento.

drudge, *vi.* trabajar ardua y monótonamente; —, *n.* ganapán, *m.;* yunque, esclavo, *m.*

drudgery, *n.* trabajo arduo y monótono.

drug, *n.* droga, *f.,* medicamento, *m.;* **—s,** *pl.* drogas, *f. pl.;* narcóticos, estupefacientes, *m. pl.;* —, *vt.* narcotizar.

druggist, *n.* farmacéutico, boticario, *m.*

drugstore, *n.* botica, farmacia, *f.*

drum, *n.* tambor, *m.;* tímpano (del oído), *m.;* **— major,** tambor mayor.

drummer, *n.* tambor, tamborilero, tamboritero, *m.;* (com.) viajante, *m.*

drumstick, *n.* palillo de tambor; pata (de ave cocida), *f.*

drunk, *adj.* borracho, ebrio, embriagado; —, *pp.* del verbo drink.

drunkard, *n.* borrachín, ina.

drunken, *adj.* ebrio; **— revel,** orgía, *f.*

drunkenness, *n.* embriaguez, borrachera, *f.*

dry, *adj.* árido, seco; sediento; insípido; severo; **— battery,** pila seca, batería seca; **— cell,** pila seca; **— cleaning,** lavado en seco; **—cleaning shop,** tintorería, *f.;* **— dock,** dique de carena; **— goods,** mercancías generales (como ropas, telas, menudencias, etc.); **— goods store,** mercería, *f.;* **— ice,** hielo seco, anhídrido carbónico solidificado; —, *vt.* secar; enjugar; **to — clean,** limpiar en seco; **to make too —,** resecar; —, *vi.* secarse.

dryness, *n.* sequedad, *f.;* aridez de estilo.

D.S.C.: Distinguished Service Cross, Cruz de Servicios Distinguidos.

D.S.M.: Distinguished Service Medal, Medalla de Servicios Distinguidos.

D.S.O.: Distinguished Service Order, Orden de Servicios Distinguidos.

D.S.T.: Daylight Saving Time, hora oficial de verano (aprovechamiento de la luz del día).

dual, *adj.* binario; **— control,** mando doble; mandos gemelos; **— personality,** doble personalidad.

dub, *vt.* armar a alguno caballero; apellidar, poner apodo; doblar (películas).

dubious, *adj.* dudoso.

duchess, *n.* duquesa, *f.*

duchy, *n.* ducado, *m.*

duck, *n.* ánade, *m.* y *f.;* pato, ta; tela fuerte más delgada que la lona; sumergida, *f.;* agachada, *f.;* (mil.) camión anfibio para descargar buques de carga; —, *vt.* y *vi.* zambullir, zambullirse, agacharse.

duct, *n.* canal, tubo, *m.;* conducto, *m.*

ductless, *adj.* sin canales o tubos.

dud, *n.* bomba que no estalla; (coll.) persona o cosa que resulta un fracaso; **—s,** *pl.* (coll.) ropa vieja.

dude, *n.* petimetre, *m.*

due, *adj.* debido, adecuado; **— bill,** abonaré, pagaré, *m.;* **in — time,** oportunamente; —, *n.* derecho, *m.;* tributo, impuesto, *m.;* **to become —,** (com.) vencerse (una deuda, un plazo, etc.); **— to,** debido a.

duel, *n.* duelo, desafío, *m.;* —, *vi.* batirse en duelo.

duelist, *n.* duelista, *m.*

duet, *n.* (mus.) dúo, dueto, *m.*

dug, *n.* teta, *f.;* —, *pretérito* y *p.p.* del verbo dig.

dugout, *n.* refugio subterráneo usado en casos de bombardeo; piragua, *f.*

duke, *n.* duque, *m.*

dull, *adj.* lerdo, estúpido; insípido; obtuso; tosco; triste, murrio; opaco; romo; **— of hearing,** algo sordo; —, *vt.* entontecer; obstruir; ofuscar.

dullness, *n.* estupidez, torpeza; *f.;* somnolencia, *f.;* pereza, *f.;* pesadez, *f.*

duly, *adv.* debidamente; puntualmente.

dumb, *adj.* mudo; (coll.) estúpido; **—ly,** *adv.* sin chistar, silenciosamente.

dumbbell, *n.* (coll.) pesa, haltera, *f.;* persona estúpida.

dumb-waiter, *n.* ascensor para comidas, basura, etc.

dumfound, *vt.* y *vi.* confundir; enmudecer.

dummy, *n.* mudo, da; estúpido, da; maniquí, *m.;* (print.) maqueta, *f.*

dump, *n.* tristeza, *f* vaciadero, depósito, basurero, *m.;* **—s,** *n. pl.* abatimiento, *m.,* murria, *f.;* **— truck,** carro de volteo; **to be in the —s,** tener melancolía.

dumping, *n.* vertimiento, *m.;* acto de arrojar, verter, descargar o volcar (basura, escombros, materiales de construcción, etc.); **— place, — ground,** lugar de descarga, vertedero, *m.*

dumpling, *n.* pastelito relleno con fruta o carne.

dumpy, *adj.* gordo, rollizo.

dun, *adj.* bruno; sombrío; —, *n* acreedor inoportuno; —, *vt.* y *vi.* pedir un acreedor a su deudor con importunidad; importunar.

dunce, *n.* zote, zopenco, *m.;* tonto, ta, bobo, ba, zonzo, za.

dune, *n.* médano, *m.,* duna, *f.*

dung, *n.* estiércol, *m.;* —, *vt.* estercolar.

dungeon, *n.* calabozo, *m.*

duodenal, *adj.* duodenal, del duodeno; **— ulcer,** úlcera duodenal o del duodeno.

dupe, n. bobo, ba; víctima, f.; tonto, ta; —, vt. engañar, embaucar.

duplex, adj. duplo, gemelo, doble; — (apartment), departamento de dos pisos.

duplicate, n. duplicado, m.; copia, f.; —, vt. duplicar.

duplicity, n. duplicidad, f.; doblez, m. y f.

durability, n. duración, f.; estabilidad, f.

durable, adj. durable, duradero.

duration, n. duración, f.

duress, n. compulsión, f.; prisión, f.

during, prep. durante.

dusk, n. crepúsculo, m.; —, vi. hacerse noche.

dusky, adj. oscuro.

dust, n. polvo, m.; — **storm**, vendaval de polvo; polvareda, f.; —, vt. limpiar de polvo, desempolvar.

duster, n. plumero, m.; persona o cosa que quita el polvo; guardapolvo, m.

dustpan, n. recogedor de basura, basurero, m.

dusty, adj. polvoriento; empolvado.

Dutch, n. y adj. holandés, esa.

dutiable, adj. sujeto a derechos de aduana.

dutiful, adj. obediente, sumiso; respetuoso.

duty, n. deber, m.; obligación, f.; quehacer, m.; respeto, homenaje, m.; (mil.) facción, f.; derechos de aduana; **off** —, libre; **on** —, de servicio, de guardia.

dwarf, n. enano, na; —, vt. impedir que alguna cosa llegue a su tamaño natural; —, vi. empequeñecerse.

dwell, vi. habitar, morar; dilatarse; — **upon**, explayarse.

dweller, n. habitante, m. y f.; morador, ra.

dwelling, n. habitación, residencia, f.; domicilio, m.; posada, f.

dwindle, vi. mermar, disminuirse; degenerar; consumirse.

dye, vt. teñir, colorar; —, n. tinte, colorante, m.

dyed-in-the-wool, adj. fanático, ferviente, convencido.

dyeing, n. tintorería, f.; arte o proceso de teñir.

dyer, n. tintorero, ra.

dying, adj. agonizante, moribundo.

dynamic, adj. dinámico, enérgico; **—s**, n. pl. dinámica, f.; **—ally**, adv. con energía.

dynamite, n. dinamita, f.

dynamo, n. dínamo o dinamo, m. o f.

dynasty, n. dinastía, f.

dysentery, n. disentería, f.

dyspepsia, n. (med.) dispepsia, f.

dystrophy, n. distrofia, f.

E

E.: east, E. este, oriente.

ea.: each, c/u. cada uno.

each, adj. cada; —, pron. cada uno, cada una, cada cual; — **other**, unos a otros, mutuamente.

eager, adj. deseoso; fogoso; ardiente, vehemente; celoso, fervoroso.

eagerness, n. ansia, f.; anhelo, m.; vehemencia, f.; ardor, m.

eagle, n. águila, f.

eagle-eyed, adj. de vista de lince, perspicaz.

ear, n. oreja, f.; oído, m.; asa, f.; (bot.) espiga, f.; **by** —, de oído; — **of corn**, mazorca; f.; — **specialist**, otólogo, m.; — **trumpet**, trompetilla, f.

earache, n. dolor de oído.

eardrum, n. tímpano, m.

earl, n. conde, m.

early, adj. temprano; primero; —, adv. temprano; — **bird**, madrugador, ra.

earmark, n. marca de identificación.

earmuff, n. orejera, f.

earn, vt. ganar, obtener, conseguir.

earnest, adj. ardiente, fervoroso, serio, importante; —, n. seriedad, f.; señal, f.; prueba, f.; **in good** —, de buena fe; **—ly**, adv. con ahínco.

earnestness, n. ansia, f.; ardor, celo, m.; seriedad, vehemencia, f.; **with** —, con ahínco.

earnings, n. pl. ingresos, m. pl., ganancias, f. pl.

earphone, n. audífono, auricular, m.

earring, n. arete, pendiente, m.

earshot, n. distancia a que se puede oír algo; **within** —, al alcance del oído.

earth, n. tierra, f., globo terráqueo; suelo, m.

earthen, adj. terreno; hecho de tierra; de barro.

earthenware, n. loza de barro.

earthly, adj. terrestre, mundano.

earthquake, n. terremoto, m.; temblor de

tierra.

earthworm, *n.* lombriz de tierra.

earthy, *adj.* mundano, terrestre, terreno.

earwax, *n.* cerumen, *m.*

ease, *n.* quietud, *f.;* reposo, ocio, *m.;* comodidad *f.;* facilidad, *f.;* **at —,** con desahogo; con soltura; —, *vt.* aliviar; mitigar.

easel, *n.* caballete, *m.*

easily, *adv.* fácilmente.

east, *n.* oriente, este, *m.*

Easter, *n.* Pascua de Resurrección; **— egg,** huevo real o de dulce dado como regalo para la Pascua florida.

easterly, eastern, *adj.* oriental, del este.

eastward, *adv.* hacia el oriente, hacia el este.

easy, *adj.* fácil; cortés, sociable; cómodo, pronto; libre; tranquilo; aliviado; **— chair,** silla poltrona; **on — street,** próspero; **— mark,** blanco, *m.,* víctima, *f.*

easygoing, *adj.* lento, tranquilo, bonazo; sereno; inalterable.

eat, *vt.* comer; roer; —, *vi.* alimentarse.

eatable, *adj.* comestible.

eaves, *n. pl.* socarrén *m.;* alero, *m.*

eavesdropper, *n.* espía, *m.* y *f.,* persona que escucha a escondidas lo que no debe oír.

ebb, *n.* menguante, *m.;* disminución, *f.;* decadencia, *f.;* **— tide,** marea menguante; —, *vi.* menguar; decaer, disminuir; **— and flow,** flujo y reflujo.

ebony, *n.* ébano, *m.*

eccentric, *adj.* excéntrico.

eccentricity, *n.* excentricidad, *f.*

ecclesiastic, *n.* y *adj.* eclesiástico, *m.*

echelon, *n.* (mil.) escalón, *m.,* tropas o barcos de guerra en formación.

echo, *n.* eco, *m.;* —, *vi.* resonar, repercutir (la voz) ; —, *vt.* hacer eco.

éclair, *n.* pastelito relleno con crema.

eclipse, *n.* eclipse, *m.;* —, *vt.* eclipsar.

economic, economical, *adj.* económico, frugal, parco, moderado.

economics, *n.* economía, *f.*

economist, *n.* economista, *m.*

economize, *vt.* y *vi.* economizar; ser económico.

economy, *n.* economía, *f.;* frugalidad, *f.*

ecotourism, *n.* ecoturismo, *m.*

ecstasy, *n.* éxtasis, *m.*

ecstatic, *adj.* extático; **—ally,** *adv.* en éxtasis.

eczema, *n.* eccema, *f.*

eddy, *n.* reflujo de agua; remolino, *m.;* —, *vi.* remolinar.

edge, *n.* filo, borde, *m.;* orilla, *f.;* vera, *f.;* punta, *f.;* esquina, *f.;* margen, *in.* y *f.;* **on —,** impaciente, nervioso; —, *vt.* afilar, ribetear; introducir; — *vi.* avanzar poco a poco escurriéndose; **— away,** alejarse.

edgewise, *adv.* de canto, de lado.

edging, *n.* orla, orilla, *f.*

edible, *adj.* comedero, comestible.

edict, *n.* edicto, mandato, *m.*

edifice, *n.* edificio, *m.;* fábrica, *f.*

edify, *vt.* edificar.

edit, *vt.* redactar; dirigir (una publicación); revisar o corregir (un artículo, etc.).

edition, *n.* edición, *f.;* publicación, *f.;* impresión, *f.;* tirada, *f.*

editor, *n.* director, redactor, editor (de una publicación), *m.;* persona que corrige o revisa (un artículo, etc.).

editorial, *n.* editorial, *m.;* artículo de fondo; **— staff,** redacción, *f.,* cuerpo de redacción.

educate, *vt.* educar; enseñar.

educated, *adj.* educado, instruido.

education, *n.* educación, *f.;* crianza, *f.*

educational, *adj.* educativo.

educator, *n.* pedagogo educador, maestro, *m.*

eel, *n.* anguila, *f.*

eerie, *adj.* que infunde terror, como un fantasma; asustado; horripilante.

efface, *vt.* borrar, destruir.

effect, *n.* efecto, *m.;* realidad, *f.;* **to take —,** entrar en vigor; **—s,** *n. pl.* efectos, bienes, *m. pl.;* —, *vt.* efectuar, ejecutar.

effective, *adj.* eficaz; efectivo; real; —, *n.* soldado disponible para la guerra.

effeminate, *vt.* afeminar, debilitar; —, *vi.* afeminarse, enervarse; —, *adj.* afeminado; **— man,** marica, maricón, hombre afeminado.

effervescent, *adj.* efervescente.

efficacious, *adj.* eficaz.

efficacy, *n.* eficacia, *f.*

efficiency, *n.* eficiencia, virtud, *f.,* rendimiento (de una máquina), *m.*

efficient, *adj.* eficaz; eficiente.

effigy, *n.* efigie, imagen, *f.;* retrato, *m.*

effort, *n.* esfuerzo, empeño, *m.,* gestión, *f.*

effusion, *n.* efusión, *f.*

effusive, *adj.* expansivo, efusivo.

eft, *n.* tritón, *m.*

e.g.: for example, p.ej. por ejemplo, vg. verbigracia.

egg, *n.* huevo, *m.;* **— beater,** batidor de huevos; **— cell,** célula embrionaria; **— white,** clara de huevo; **deviled —,** huevo relleno; **fried —,** huevo frito o estrellado; **hard-boiled —,** huevo cocido o duro; **poached —,** huevo escalfado; **scrambled —,** huevo revuelto; **soft-boiled —,** huevo tibio o pasado por agua; —, *vt.* mezclar con huevos; **to — on,** incitar, hurgar, azuzar.

eggnog, *n.* yema mejida, ponche de huevo, (Mex.) rompope, *m.*

eggplant, *n.* (bot.) berenjena, *f.*

eggshell, *n.* cascarón de huevo.

egg yolk, *n.* yema de huevo.

ego, *n.* ego, yo, *m.*

egoism, egotism, *n.* egoísmo, *m.*

egoistical, egotistical, *adj.* egoísta.

Egypt, Egipto, *m.*

Egyptian, *n.* y *adj.* egipcio, cia.

eiderdown, *n.* edredón, plumón, *m.*

eight, *n.* y *adj.* ocho, *m.*

eight ball *n.* (billar) bola No. 8; **behind the —,** (coll.) en situación desventajosa o desconcertante en extremo.

eighteen, *n.* y *adj.* dieciocho o diez y ocho, *m.*

eighteenth, *n.* y *adj.* decimoctavo, dieciocheno, *m.*

eighth, *n.* y *adj.* octavo, *m.*

eightieth, *n.* y *adj.* octogésimo, *m.*

eighty, *n.* y *adj.* ochenta, *m.*

either, *pron.* y *adj.* cualquiera, uno de dos; **—,** *conj.* o, sea, ya, ora.

ejaculation, *n.* jaculatoria, *f.*

eject, *vt.* expeler, desechar.

ejection, *n.* expulsión, *f.;* (med.) evacuación, *f.;* **— seat,** asiento expulsor.

elaborate, *vt.* elaborar; **—,** *adj.* trabajado, primoroso.

elapse, *vi.* pasar, correr, trascurrir (el tiempo) .

elastic, *n.* goma, *f.;* **—,** *adj.* elástico; repercusivo.

elate, *vt.* exaltar, elevar; **—d,** *adj.* exaltado, animoso.

elation, *n.* júbilo, *m.*

elbow, *n.* codo, *m.;* **—,** *vt.* y *vi.* dar codazos, empujar con el codo; codearse.

elbowroom, *n.* anchura, *f.;* espacio suficiente; (fig.) libertad, latitud, *f.*

elder, *adj.* que tiene más edad, mayor; **—,** *n.* anciano, antepasado, *m.;* eclesiástico, *m.;* jefe de una tribu; (bot.) saúco, *m.*

elderly, *adj.* de edad madura, anciano.

eldest, *adj.* mayor, más anciano.

elect, *vt.* elegir; **—,** *adj.* elegido, electo, escogido.

election, *n.* elección, *f.;* **—s,** comicios, *m. pl.*

electioneering, *n.* propaganda electoral.

elective, *adj.* electivo.

elector, *n.* elector, ra.

electoral, *adj.* electoral; **— college,** colegio electoral.

electorate, *n.* electorado, *m.*

electric, *adj.* eléctrico; **— bulb,** bombilla eléctrica, foco; **— cable,** cable conductor; **— chair,** silla eléctrica; **— eye,** célula fotoeléctrica; **— fixtures,** instalación eléctrica; **— lamp,** lámpara eléctrica; **— meter,** contador electrómetro; **— motor,** electromotor, *m.;* **— plant,** planta eléctrica; **— railroad,** ferrocarril eléctrico; **— switch,** conmutador, *m.;* **—wire,** hilo o alambre conductor; **— welding,** soldadura eléctrica.

electrical, *adj.* eléctrico; **— engineering,** electrotecnia, ingeniería eléctrica; **— transcripción,** (radio y TV.) trascripción mediante cinta magnética.

electrician, *n.* electricista, *m.*

electricity, *n.* electricidad, *f.*

electrify, *vt.* electrizar.

electrocardiogram, *n.* electrocardiograma, *m.*

electrochemistry, *n.* electroquímica, *f.*

electrocute, *vt.* electrocutar.

electrocution, *n.* electrocución, *f.*

electrolysis, *n.* electrólisis, *f.*

electrolyte, *n.* electrólito, *m.*

electrolytic, *adj.* electrolítico.

electromagnet, *n.* electroimán, *m.*

electromagnetic, *adj.* electromagnético; **— field,** campo electromagnético.

electromotive, *adj.* electromotor, electromotriz; **— force,** fuerza electromotriz.

electron, *n.* electrón, *m.*

electronics, *n.* electrónica, *f.*

electrotherapy, *n.* electroterapia, *f.*

electrotype, *n.* electrotipo, *m.*

elegance, *n.* elegancia, *f.*

elegant, *adj.* elegante, delicado; lujoso.

elegy, *n.* elegía, *f.*

element, *n.* elemento, *m.;* fundamento, *m.;* **—s,** *n. pl.* elementos, *m. pl.;* principios, *m. pl.;* bases, *f. pl.;* elementos atmosféricos.

elemental, *adj.* elemental, simple, inicial.

elementary, *adj.* elemental, simple, inicial; **—school,** escuela primaria.

elephant, *n.* elefante, *m.*

elevate, *vt.* elevar, alzar, exaltar.

elevated, *adj.* elevado; **— railroad,** ferrocarril elevado; **— train,** tren elevado.

elevation, *n.* elevación, *f.;* altura, *f.;* alteza (de pensamientos), *f.*

elevator, *n.* ascensor, elevador, *m.*

eleven, *n.* y *adj.* once, *m.;* oncena, *f.*

eleventh, *n.* y *adj.* onceno, undécimo, *m.*

elf, *n.* duende, *m.;* persona traviesa.

elicit, *vt.* incitar; educir; sacar; atraer.

eligible, *adj.* elegible; deseable.

eliminate, *vt.* eliminar, descartar.

elk, *n.* alce, *m.*, anta, *f.*

elliptic, elliptical, *adj.* elíptico.

elm, *n.* olmo, *m.*

elocution, *n.* elocución, *f.;* declamación, *f.*

elongate, *vt.* y *vi.* alargar, extender.

elope, *vi.* escapar, huir; fugarse con un amante.

elopement, *n.* fuga con un amante; huida, *f.*

eloquence, *n.* elocuencia, *f.;* facundia, *f.*

eloquent, *adj.* elocuente.

else, *adj.* otro; más; —, *adv.* si no; de otro modo; **nothing** —, nada más; **somewhere** —, en alguna otra parte.

elsewhere, *adv.* en otra parte.

elucidate, *vt.* dilucidar, explicar.

elude, *vt.* eludir, evadir.

elusive, elusory, *adj.* artificioso, falaz; evasivo.

emaciate, *vt.* extenuar, adelgazar.

emaciated, *adj.* demacrado; chupado; **to become** —, demacrarse.

e-mail, *n.* correo electrónico, *m.*

emanate, *vi.* emanar.

emanation, *n.* emanación, *f.;* origen, *m.*

emancipate, *vt.* emancipar; dar libertad.

emancipation, *n.* emancipación, *f.*

emancipator, *n.* libertador, *m.*

embalm, *vt.* embalsamar.

embank, *vt.* terraplenar; represar.

embankment, *n.* encajonamiento, *m.;* malecón, dique, *m.,* presa, *f.;* terraplén, *m.*

embargo, *n.* embargo, *m.;* detención, *f.;* comiso, *m.;* —, *vt.* embargar.

embark, *vt.* y *vi.* embarcar; embarcarse.

embarkation, *n.* embarcación, *f.*

embarrass, *vt.* avergonzar, desconcertar, turbar.

embarrassed, *adj.* avergonzado, cortado.

embarrassing, *adj.* penoso, vergonzoso.

embarrassment, *n.* turbación, *f.;* bochorno, *m.;* vergüenza, pena, *f.*

embassy, *n.* embajada, *f.*

embellish, *vt.* hermosear, adornar.

ember, *n.* ascua, pavesa, *f.*

embezzle, *vt.* desfalcar.

embezzlement, *n.* hurto, *m.;* desfalco, *m.*

embezzler, *n.* desfalcador, ra.

embitter, *vt.* amargar, agriar.

emblazon, *vt.* blasonar.

emblem, *n.* emblema, *m.*

embody, *vt.* encarnar, incluir.

embolism, *n.* embolismo, *m.*

emboss, *vt.* realzar, imprimir en relieve.

embrace, *vt.* abrazar; contener; —, *n.* abrazo, *m.*

embroider, *vt.* bordar.

embroidery, *n.* bordado, *m.*

embroil, *vt.* embrollar; confundir.

embryo, *n.* embrión, *m.*

emerald, *n.* esmeralda, *f.*

emerge, *vi.* surgir; emerger.

emergence, *n.* emergencia, aparición, *f.*

emergency, *n.* aprieto, *m.;* emergencia, *f ;* necesidad urgente; — **landing field,** (avi.) campo de aterrizaje de emergencia; **in case of** —, en caso de necesidad o de emergencia; — **room,** sala de emergencia, *f.*

emeritus, *adj.* emérito, retirado.

emery, *n.* esmeril, *m.*

emigrant, *n.* y *adj.* emigrante, *m.* y *f.*

emigrate, *vi.* emigrar.

emigration, *n.* emigración, *f.*

eminence, *n.* altura, sumidad, *f.;* eminencia, excelencia, *f.*

eminent, *adj.* eminente, elevado; distinguido; relevante.

emissary, *n.* emisario, *m.;* espía, *m.* y *f.*

emit, *vt.* emitir, echar de sí; arrojar, despedir.

emolument, *n.* emolumento, provecho, *m.*

emotion, *n.* emoción, *f.;* conmoción, *f.*

emotional, *adj.* emocional; sensible, impresionable.

emperor, *n.* emperador, *m.*

emphasis, *n.* énfasis, *m.* y *f.*

emphasize, *vt.* hablar con énfasis; acentuar; hacer hincapié; recalcar.

emphatic, *adj.* enfático.

empire, *n.* imperio, *m.*

employ, *vt.* emplear, ocupar; —, *n.* empleo, *m.;* ocupación, *f.*

employee, *n.* empleado, da.

employer, *n.* amo, dueño, patrón, *m.*

employment, *n.* empleo, *m.;* ocupación, *f.;* cargo, *m.;* **to give** — **to,** colocar, emplear.

emporium, *n.* emporio, *m.*

empower, *vt.* autorizar, dar poder, facultar.

empress, *n.* emperatriz *f*

emptiness, *n.* vacuidad, *f.,* vacío, *m.;* futilidad, *f.*

empty, *adj.* vacío; vano; ignorante; —, *vt.* vaciar, evacuar, verter.

empty-handed, *adj.* manivacío, con las manos vacías.

empty-headed, *adj.* vano, hueco, frívolo, tonto.

emulate, *vt.* emular, competir con; imitar.

emulsify, *vt.* emulsionar.

emulsion, *n.* emulsión, *f.*

enable, *vt.* habilitar; poner en estado de.

enact, *vt.* establecer, decretar; efectuar; estatuir.

enamel, *n.* esmalte, *m.;* —, *vt.* esmaltar.

enamelware, *n.* vasijas esmaltadas.

enamored, *adj.* enamorado.

encampment, *n.* campamento, *m.*

encase, *vt.* encajar, encajonar, incluir.

enchant, *vt.* encantar.

enchanting, *adj.* encantador.

enchantment, *n.* encanto, *m.*

enchantress, *n.* encantadora, *f.; mujer seductora.

encircle, *vt.* cercar, circundar, circunvalar.

enclose, *vt.* cercar, circunvalar, circundar; incluir; encerrar.

enclosure, *n.* cercamiento, *m.; cercado, *m.; caja (de engranaje, etc.), *f.; anexo (en una carta), *m.

encompass, *vt.* circundar; cercar; circuir.

encore, *n.* (theat.) bis, *m.*, repetición, *f.; inter]. ¡bis! ¡otra vez! ¡que se repita! —, *vt.* pedir que un actor repita lo que ha ejecutado.

encounter, *n.* encuentro, *m.; duelo, *m.; pelea, *f.; —, *vt.* encontrar; —, *vi.* encontrarse.

encourage, *vt.* animar, alentar; envalentonar; dar aliento.

encouragement, *n.* estímulo, aliento, *m.*, animación, *f.*

encouraging, *adj.* alentador.

encroach, *vt.* usurpar, avanzar gradualmente.

encumber, *vt.* embarazar, cargar; estorbar.

encumbrance, *n.* impedimento, *m.; estorbo, *m.*, carga, *f.*

encyclopedia, *n.* enciclopedia, *f.*

end, *n.* fin, *m.; extremidad, *f.; cabo, *m.; término, *m.; propósito, intento, *m.; punto, *m.; no —, sinnúmero, *m.; to accomplish one's —, salirse con la suya; to no —, en vano; —, *vt.* matar, concluir, fenecer; terminar; —, *vi.* acabarse, terminarse.

endanger, *vt.* poner en peligro, arriesgar.

endear, *vt.* hacer querer.

endearment, *n.* terneza, *f.; encarecimiento, afecto, *m.*

endeavor, *vi.* esforzarse; intentar; —, *n.* esfuerzo, *m.*

ending, *n.* terminación, conclusión, cesación, *f.; muerte, *f.*

endless, *adj.* infinito, perpetuo, sin fin.

endorse, *vt.* endosar (una letra de cambio); apoyar, sancionar.

endorsee, *n.* endosatario, ria; cesionario, ria.

endorsement, *n.* endorso, endoso, endose, *m.*

endorser (of a draft), *n.* cedente (de un giro o letra), *m.*

endow, *vt.* dotar.

endowment, *n.* dotación, *f.; — insurance, seguro dotal.

endurable, *adj.* soportable.

endurance, *n.* duración, *f.; paciencia, *f.; sufrimiento, *m.*

endure, *vt.* sufrir, soportar; —, *vi.* durar; conllevar; sufrir.

endways, endwise, *adv.* de punta, derecho; a lo largo.

ENE, E.N.E.: east-northeast, ENE estenordeste.

enema, *n.* lavativa, enema, *f.*

enemy, *n.* enemigo, ga; antagonista, *m.* y *f.*

energetic, *adj.* enérgico, vigoroso.

energy, *n.* energía, fuerza, *f.*

enervate, *vt.* enervar, debilitar, quitar las fuerzas.

enfeeble, *vt.* debilitar, enervar.

enfold, *vt.* envolver, arrollar; rodear.

enforce, *vt.* compeler; hacer cumplir (una ley), poner en vigor.

enforcement, *n.* compulsión, coacción, *f.; cumplimiento (de una ley), *m.*

enfranchise, *vt.* franquear, conceder franquicia; naturalizar.

engage, *vt.* empeñar, obligar; contratar; —, *vi.* comprometerse.

engaged, *adj.* comprometido, prometido.

engagement, *n.* noviazgo, compromiso, *m.; cita, *f.; (theat.) contrato, *m.; (mil.) combate, *m.*

engaging, *adj.* simpático, atractivo.

engender, *vt.* y *vi.* engendrar, procrear.

engine, *n.* máquina, *f.; locomotora, *f.; instrumento, *m.; — house, casa de máquinas; internal-combustion —, motor de explosión, motor de combustión interna.

engineer, *n.* ingeniero, *m.; maquinista, *m.*

engineering, *n.* ingeniería, *f.*

England, Inglaterra, *f.*

English, *n.* y *adj.* inglés, sa; — language, inglés, *m.; — Channel, Canal de la Mancha.

Englishman, *n.* inglés, *m.*

Englishwoman, *n.* inglesa, *f.*

engrave, *vt.* grabar; esculpir; tallar.

engraver, *n.* grabador, *m.*

engraving, *n.* grabado, *m.; estampa, *f.*

engrossing, *adj.* absorbente.

engulf, *vt.* engolfar, tragar, sumir.

enhance, *vt.* realzar, elevar, intensificar.

enigma, *n.* enigma, *m.*

enigmatic, *adj.* enigmático.

enjoin, *vt.* ordenar, mandar; advertir; prohibir.

enjoy, *vt.* gozar; poseer; saborear; disfrutar de.

enjoyable, *adj.* agradable.

enjoyment *n.* goce, disfrute, *m.; placer, *m.; fruición, *f.; usufructo, *m.*

enlarge, *vt.* engrandecer, dilatar, extende ampliar; —, *vi.* extenderse, dilatarse; upon, explayarse.

enlargement, *n.* aumento, *m.; ampliac

(de una fotografía, etc.), *f.*

enlighten, *vt.* aclarar; iluminar; instruir.

enlightenment, *n.* ilustración, *f.;* aclaración, *f.*

enlist, *vt.* alistar, reclutar; —, *vi.* inscribirse como recluta, engancharse.

enlistment, *n.* alistamiento, *m.*

enliven, *vt.* animar; avivar; alegrar.

enmity, *n.* enemistad, *f.;* odio, *m.*

ennoble, *vt.* ennoblecer.

enormity, *n.* enormidad, *f.;* atrocidad, *f.*

enormous, *adj.* enorme.

enough, *adj.* bastante, suficiente; —, *adv.* suficientemente; —, *n.* suficiencia, *f.;* —! *interj.* ¡basta! ¡suficiente! ¡ya!

enquire = **inquire.**

enrage, *vt.* enfurecer, irritar.

enraged, *adj.* colérico, sañoso.

enrapture, *vt.* arrebatar, entusiasmar; encantar.

enrich, *vt.* enriquecer; adornar.

enroll, *vt.* registrar, inscribir; arrollar.

enrollment, *n.* inscripción, *f.;* matriculación, *f.*

ensemble, *n.* conjunto, *m.;* traje de mujer compuesto de más de una pieza.

enshrine, *vt.* guardar como reliquia; estimar como cosa sagrada.

ensign, *n.* bandera, *f.;* enseña, *f.;* **naval** —, alférez, *m.;* subteniente, *m.*

enslave, *vt.* esclavizar, cautivar.

ensue, *vi.* seguirse; suceder.

ensure, *vt.* asegurar.

entail, *n.* vínculo, mayorazgo, *m.;* —, *vt.* vincular; ocasionar.

entangle, *vt.* enmarañar, embrollar.

enter, *vt.* entrar, meter; admitir; registrar; penetrar; —, *vi.* entrar, empeñarse en algo; emprender; aventurar.

enteritis, *n.* (med.) enteritis, *f.*

enterprise, *n.* empresa, *f.*

enterprising, *adj.* emprendedor.

entertain, *vt.* entretener; obsequiar, agasajar; divertir.

entertainer, *n.* festejador, ra; persona que divierte a otra; cantante, bailarín, etc., que entretiene en una fiesta.

entertaining, *adj.* divertido, chistoso.

entertainment, *n.* festejo, *m.;* diversión, *f.,* entretenimiento, pasatiempo, *m.*

enthrone, *vt.* entronizar.

enthusiasm, *n.* entusiasmo, *m.*

enthusiast, *n.* entusiasta, *m.* y *f.*

enthusiastic, *adj.* entusiasmado, entusiasta.

entice, *vt.* halagar; acariciar, excitar, inducir.

enticing, *adj.* atractivo, incitante.

entire, *adj.* entero, cumplido, completo, perfecto, todo.

entirety, *n.* entereza, integridad, totalidad, *f.;* todo, *m.*

entitle, *vt.* intitular; conferir algún derecho; autorizar.

entity, *n.* entidad, existencia, *f.*

entrails, *n. pl.* entrañas, *f. pl.;* tripa, *f.*

entrance, *n.* entrada, *f.;* admisión, *f.;* principio, *m.;* boca, *f.;* ingreso, *m.*

entrance, *vt.* extasiar.

entreat, *vt.* rogar, suplicar.

entreaty, *n.* petición, súplica, instancia, *f.*

entree o entrée, *n.* principio (en una comida), *m.,* entrada, *f.,* plato principal.

entrench, *vt.* atrincherar; — **on,** usurpar.

entrust, intrust, *vt.* confiar.

entry, *n.* entrada, *f.;* (com.) partida, *f.*

entwine, *vt.* entrelazar, enroscar, torcer.

enumerate, *vt.* enumerar, numerar.

enunciate, *vt.* enunciar, declarar.

envelop, *vt.* envolver, cubrir.

envelope, *n.* sobre, *m.,* cubierta, *f.*

enviable, *adj.* envidiable.

envious, *adj.* envidioso.

environment, *n.* medio ambiente, *m.*

environmental, *adj.* ambiental.

environmentalism, *n.* ambientalismo, *m.*

environs, *n. pl.* vecindad, *f.;* alrededores, contornos, *m. pl.*

envoy, *n.* enviado, *m.;* mensajero, *m.*

envy, *n.* envidia, *f.;* malicia, *f.;* —, *vt.* envidiar.

enzyme, *n.* (biol.) enzima, *f.*

epaulet, *n.* (mil.) charretera, *f.*

epic, *adj.* épico; —, *n.* epopeya, *f.*

epicenter, *n.* epicentro, *m.*

epicure, *n.* gastrónomo, ma.

epicurean, *adj.* epicúreo.

epidemic, *adj.* epidémico; —, *n.* epidemia,

epidermis, *n.* epidermis, *f.*

epigram, *n.* epigrama, *m.*

epilepsy, *n.* epilepsia, *f.*

epileptic, *n.* y *adj.* epiléptico, ca.

Episcopalian, *n.* episcopal, *m.* y *f.*

episode, *n.* episodio, *m.*

epistle, *n.* epístola, *f.*

epitaph, *n.* epitafio, *m.*

epithet, *n.* epíteto, *m.*

epitome, *n.* epítome, compendio, *m.;* sinopsis, *f.*

epoch, *n.* época, edad, era, *f.*

equable, *adj.* uniforme, parejo, tranquilo.

equal, *adj.* igual; justo; semejante; imparcial; —, *n.* par, *m.,* cantidad igual; persona igual; —, *vt.* igualar; compensar.

equality, *n.* igualdad, uniformidad, *f.*

equalize, *vt.* igualar.

equanimity, *n.* ecuanimidad, *f.*

equation, *n.* equilibrio, *m.;* (math.) ecuación, *f.*

equator, *n.* ecuador, *m.*

equatorial, *adj.* ecuatorial.
equestrian, *adj.* ecuestre; —, *n.* jinete, *m.*
equidistant, *adj.* equidistante.
equilateral, *n.* y *adj.* equilátero, *m.*
equilibrium, *n.* equilibrio, *m.*
equinox, *n.* equinoccio, *m.*
equip, *vt.* equipar, pertrechar; aprestar (un navío).
equipment, *n.* equipo, *m.;* avíos, *m. pl.*
equitable, *adj.* equitativo, imparcial.
equity, *n.* equidad, justicia, imparcialidad, *f.*
equivalent, *n.* y *adj.* equivalente, *m.*
equivocal, *adj.* equívoco, ambiguo.
equivocate, *vt.* equivocar, usar equívocos.
era, *n.* edad, época, era, *f.*
eradicate, *vt.* erradicar, desarraigar, extirpar.
eradicator, *n.* erradicador, *m.*
erase, *vt.* borrar; cancelar, rayar, tachar.
eraser, *n.* goma de borrar, borrador, *m.*
erasure, *n.* borradura, *f.*
ere, *conj.* antes que.
erect, *vt.* erigir; establecer; —, *adj.* derecho, erguido.
erection, *n.* erección, *f.;* estructura, construcción, *f.*
erelong, *adv.* dentro de poco.
ermine, *n.* armiño, *m.*
erode, *vt.* y *vi.* roer, corroer, comer, gastarse.
erosion, *n.* erosión, *f.*
err, *vi.* equivocarse, errar; desviarse.
errand, *n.* recado, mensaje, *m.;* encargo, *m.;* — **boy,** mensajero, mandadero, *m.*
erratic, *adj.* errático, errante; irregular, excéntrico.
erroneous, *adj.* erróneo; falso.
error, *n.* error, yerro, *m.,* equivocación, *f.*
erstwhile, *adv.* antiguamente, en tiempos pasados.
erudite, *adj.* erudito.
erudition, *n.* erudición, *f.*
erupt, *vi.* hacer erupción.
eruption, *n.* erupción, *f.;* sarpullido, *m.*
escalator, *n.* escalera mecánica; — **clause,** cláusula que permite fluctuaciones en los salarios.
escallop = **scallop**
escapade, *n.* fuga, escapada, *f.;* travesura, *f.;* calaverada, *f.*
escape, *vt.* evitar; escapar; —, *vi.* evadirse, salvarse; **to — from danger,** salvarse; —, *n.* escapada, huida, fuga, *f.;* inadvertencia, *f.;* salvamento, *m.;* — **capsule,** cápsula de escape, cápsula de emergencia; **to have a narrow —,** salvarse en una tablita; — **literature,** escapismo, *m.,* literatura huidiza que trata de escapar de la realidad.

escapism, *n.* escapismo, *m.,* estilo literario mediante el cual se trata de escapar o huir de la realidad.
escapist, *n.* soñador, ra, fantaseador, ra.
escort, *n.* escolta; *f.;* acompañante, *m.;* —, *vt.* escoltar, convoyar; acompañar.
Eskimo, *n.* y *adj.* esquimal, *m.* y *f.*
esophagus, *n.* esófago, *m.*
esoteric, *adj.* esotérico.
especial, *adj.* especial, excepcional; —**ly,** *adv.* particularmente; sobre todo.
espionage, *n.* espionaje, *m.*
espouse, *vt.* desposar.
esquire, *n.* señor (en Inglaterra, título que sigue al apellido), *m.,* noble inglés (inferior al título de caballero).
essay, *vt.* ensayar, intentar, probar; —, *n.* ensayo literario; tentativa, *f.*
essence, *n.* esencia, *f.;* perfume, *m.;* quid, *m.;* médula, *f.*
essential, *adj.* esencial, sustancial, principal; imprescindible; vital; —, *n.* lo esencial.
E.S.T.: Eastern Standard Time, hora normal de la región oriental de E.U.A.
establish, *vt.* establecer, estatuir, fundar, fijar; confirmar; **to — oneself,** radicarse; establecerse.
establishment, *n.* establecimiento, *m.;* fundación, *f ;* institución, *f.*
estate, *n.* estado, *m.;* patrimonio, *m.;* hacienda, *f.;* bienes, *m. pl.*
esteem, *vt.* estimar, apreciar; —, *n.* estima, *f.;* consideración, *f.*
esteemed, *adj.* estimado, considerado.
esthetic, *adj.* estético; —**s,** *n. pl.* estética, *f.*
estimate, *vt.* estimar, apreciar, tasar; —, *n.* presupuesto, *m.;* cálculo, *m.*
estimation, *n.* estimación, *f.;* cálculo, *m.;* opinión, *f.;* juicio, *m.*
estrange, *vt.* apartar, enajenar, malquistar.
estuary, *n.* estuario, estero, *m.;* desembocadura de lago o río.
etch, *vt.* grabar al agua fuerte.
etcher, *n.* acuafortista, *m.* y *f.*
etching, *n.* aguafuerte, *m.* o *f.;* grabado al agua fuerte.
eternal, *adj.* eterno, perpetuo, inmortal.
eternity, *n.* eternidad, *f.*
ether, *n.* éter, *m.*
ethereal, *adj.* etéreo; vaporoso.
ethical, *adj.* ético; —**ly,** *adv.* moralmente.
ethics, *n. pl.* ética, moralidad, *f.*
Ethiopian, *n.* y *adj.* etíope, *m.* y *f.*
ethnographer, *n.* etnógrafo, *m.*
ethnologist, *n.* etnólogo, *m.*
ethyl, *n.* etilo, *m.*
etiquette, *n.* etiqueta, *f.*

etymology, n. etimología, f.
E.U.: European Union, Unión Europea, f.
eucalyptus, n. eucalipto, m.
Eucharist, n. Eucaristía, f.
eucharistic, adj. eucarístico.
eugenics, n. eugenesia, f.
eulogize, vt. elogiar.
eulogy, n. elogio, encomio, m., alabanza, f.
euphonious, adj. eufónico.
Europe, Europa, f.
European, n. y adj. europeo, pea.
euthanasia, n. (med.) eutanasia, f.
evacuate, vt. evacuar.
evacuation, n. evacuación, f.
evacuee, n. evacuado, da, persona desalojada de una plaza militar.
evade, vt. evadir, escapar, evitar.
evaluate, vt. evaluar.
evaluation, n. evaluación, valuación, f.
evanescent, adj. fugitivo; imperceptible.
evangelical, adj. evangélico.
evangelist, n. evangelista, m. y f.
evaporate, vt. evaporar, vaporizar; —, vi. evaporarse; disiparse; —d milk, leche evaporada, f.
evaporation, n. evaporación, f.
evasion, n. evasión, f.; escape, refugio, m.; tergiversación, f.
evasive, adj. evasivo; sofístico.
eve, n. tardecita, f.; vigilia, víspera, f.; Christmas —, Nochebuena, f.
even, adj. llano, igual; par; semejante; —, adv. aun, supuesto que; no obstante; — as, como; — now, aun ahora; ahora mismo; —so aun así; — or odd, pares o nones; — though, aun cuando; not —, ni siquiera; —, vt. igualar, allanar.
evening, adj. vespertino; — clothes, traje de etiqueta; —, n. tarde, noche, f.
evenness, n. igualdad, uniformidad, f.
event, n. evento, acontecimiento, m.; circunstancia, f.; caso, m.; ocurrencia, f., suceso, m.; in any —, en todo caso.
eventful, adj. lleno de acontecimientos; memorable.
eventual, adj. eventual, fortuito; —ly, adv. finalmente, con el tiempo.
ever, adj. siempre; for — and —, por siempre jamás, eternamente; — since, desde que.
evergreen, adj. siempre verde; —, n. (bot.) siempreviva., f.
everlasting, adj. eterno; —, n. eternidad, f.
evermore, adj. eternamente, para siempre jamás.
every, adj. todo, cada; — day, todos los días; — time, cada vez.
everybody, pron. cada uno, cada una; todo el mundo.
everyday, adj. ordinario, rutinario, de todos los días.
everyone, pron. cada cual, cada uno.
everything, n. todo, m.
everywhere, adv. en todas partes, por todas partes, por doquier.
evict, vt. despojar jurídicamente; desalojar, expulsar.
eviction, n. evicción, expulsión, f.; despojo jurídico.
evidence, n. evidencia, f.; testimonio, m., prueba, f.; —, vt. evidenciar.
evident, adj. evidente; patente, manifiesto; indudable.
evil, adj. malo, depravado, pernicioso; dañoso; —, n. maldad, f.; daño, m.; calamidad, f.; mal, m.
evildoer, n. malhechor, ra.
evil-minded, adj. malicioso, mal intencionado.
evince, vt. probar, justificar, demostrar.
evoke, vt. evocar.
evolution, n. evolución, f.; desarrollo, m.
evolve, vt. y vi. desenvolver; desplegarse; emitir.
ewe, n. oveja (hembra del carnero), f.
exact, adj. exacto, puntual; riguroso; cuidadoso; —, vt. exigir.
exacting, adj. severo, exigente.
exactness, exactitude, n. exactitud, f.
exaggerate, vt. exagerar; extremar.
exaggeration, n. exageración, f.
exalt, vt. exaltar, elevar; alabar; realzar; enaltecer.
exalted, adj. sublime.
examination, n. examen, m.; medical —, reconocimiento médico.
examine, vt. examinar; escudriñar; ver, revisar.
examiner, n. examinador, ra; comprobador, ra.
examining, adj. revisor; examinador.
example, n. ejemplo, m.; to set an —, dar el ejemplo.
exasperate, vt. exasperar, irritar, enojar, provocar; agravar, amargar.
exasperation, n. exasperación, irritación, f.
excavate, vt. excavar, cavar, ahondar.
excavation, n. excavación, f.; cavidad, f.
exceed, vt. exceder; sobrepujar; rebasar; —, vi. excederse.
exceeding, adj. excesivo; —ly, adv. extremadamente, en sumo grado; sobremanera.
excel, vt. sobresalir, exceder; descollar; superar.
excellence, n. excelencia, f.
excellent, adj. excelente; sobresaliente.
excelsior, n. trizas rizadas de madera para entapizar, empacar, etc.
except, vt. exceptuar, excluir; sacar; —, vi.

recusar.

excepting, *prep.* menos, salvo, excepto, a excepción de.

exception, *n.* excepción, exclusión, *f.*

exceptional, *adj.* excepcional.

excerpt, *vt.* extraer; extractar; —, *n.* extracto, *m.*

excess, *n.* exceso, *m.;* intemperancia, *f.;* desmesura, *f.;* sobra, *f.;* — **baggage,** exceso de equipaje.

excessive, *adj.* excesivo.

exchange, *vt.* cambiar; trocar, permutar; —, *n.* cambio, *m.;* bolsa, lonja, *f.;* — **office,** casa de cambio; **bill of** —, letra de cambio, cédula de cambio; **domestic** —, cambio interior; **foreign** —, cambio exterior o cambio extranjero; **in — for,** a cambio de; **rate of** —, tipo de cambio; **stock** —, bolsa, *f.;* **telephone** —, central telefónica.

excise, *n.* sisa, *f.,* impuesto, *m.*

excitable, *adj.* excitable; nervioso.

excite, *vt.* excitar; estimular; agitar.

excitement, *n.* estímulo, *m.;* agitación, *f.;* excitación, conmoción, *f.*

exciting, *adj.* excitante; conmovedor.

exclaim, *vi.* exclamar; —, *vt.* proferir.

exclamation, *n.* exclamación, *f.;* clamor, *m.;* — **mark,** — **point,** punto de admiración.

exclude, *vt.* excluir; exceptuar.

exclusion, *n.* exclusión, exclusiva, *f.;* excepción *f.*

exclusive, *adj.* exclusivo.

excommunicate, *vt.* excomulgar, descomulgar.

excrement, *n.* excremento, *m.*

excretion, *n.* excremento, *m.;* excreción, *f.*

excruciating, *adj.* atroz, enorme, grave; muy agudo.

excursion, *n.* excursión, expedición, *f.;* digresión, *f.;* romería, *f.;* correría, *f.;* jira, *f.*

excusable, *adj.* excusable, perdonable.

excuse, *vt.* excusar; perdonar; —, *n.* excusa, *f.*

execute, *vt.* ejecutar; ajusticiar; llevar a cabo, cumplir.

execution, *n.* ejecución, *f.*

executioner, *n.* ejecutor, *m.;* verdugo, *m.*

executive, *adj.* y *n.* ejecutivo, *m.*

executor, *n.* testamentario, *m.;* albacea, *m.*

exemplary, *adj.* ejemplar.

exemplify, *vt.* ejemplificar.

exempt, *adj.* exento, libre por privilegio; —, *vt.* eximir, exentar.

exemption, *n.* exención, franquicia, *f.*

exercise, *n.* ejercicio, *m.;* ensayo, *m.;* tarea, *f.;* práctica, *f.;* —, *vi.* hacer ejerci-

cio; —, *vt.* ejercitar; atarear; practicar; profesar.

exert, *vt.* ejercer; **to — oneself,** esforzarse.

exertion, *n.* esfuerzo, *m.*

exhalation, *n.* exhalación, *f.;* vapor, *m.*

exhale, *vt.* exhalar.

exhaust, *n.* cámara de escape; (auto., avi.) escape, *m.;* — **fan,** expulsor de aire; — **pipe,** tubo de salida de gases; —, *vt.* agotar, consumir.

exhausting, *adj.* enervante, agotador.

exhaustion, *n.* agotamiento, *m.;* extenuación, *f.*

exhaustive, *adj.* agotador; completo, minucioso.

exhibit, *vt.* exhibir; mostrar; —, *n.* memorial, *m.;* exposición, *f.*

exhibition, *n.* exhibición, presentación, exposición, *f.;* espectáculo, *m.*

exhibitionism, *n.* exhibicionismo, *m.*

exhibitor, *n.* expositor, ra.

exhilarate, *vt.* alegrar, causar alegría.

exhilaration, *n.* alegría, *f.;* buen humor, regocijo, *in.*

exhort, *vt.* exhortar, excitar.

exhortation, *n.* exhortación, *f.*

exhume, *vt.* exhumar, desenterrar.

exigency, *n.* exigencia, necesidad, urgencia, *f.*

exile, *n.* destierro, exilio, *m.;* desterrado, da, exiliado, da; —, *vt.* desterrar, exiliar.

exist, *vi.* existir.

existence, *n.* existencia, *f.*

existent, *adj.* existente.

existentialism, *n.* existencialismo, *m.*

existing, *adj.* actual, presente; existente.

exit, *n.* partida, salida, *f.*

exodus, *n.* éxodo, *m.,* salida, *f.*

exonerate, *vt.* exonerar, disculpar.

exorbitant, *adj.* exorbitante, excesivo.

exotic, *adj.* exótico, extranjero; —, *n.* cosa exótica (como una planta o una palabra).

expand, *vt.* extender, dilatar, expandir.

expanse, *n.* extensión de lugar.

expansion, *n.* expansión, *f.;* desarrollo, *m.*

expansive, *adj.* expansivo.

expatriation, *n.* expatriación, extrañación,

expect, *vt.* esperar, aguardar.

expectant, *adj.* expectante, que espera; preñada, encinta, embarazada; — **mother,** mujer embarazada o encinta.

expectation, *n.* expectativa, *f.;* esperanza,

expediency, *n.* conveniencia, oportunidad,

expedient, *adj.* oportuno, conveniente; —, *n.* expediente, medio, *m.*

expedite, *vt.* acelerar; expedir.

expedition, *n.* expedición, excursión, *f.;* cruzada, *f.;* campaña, *f.*

expeditionary, *adj.* expedicionario.

expel, vt. expeler, expulsar; desterrar.

expend, vt. expender; desembolsar.

expendable, adj. (mil.) sacrificable, no indispensable.

expenditure, n. gasto, desembolso, m.

expense, n. gasto, m.

expensive, adj. caro, costoso.

experience, n. experiencia, f.; práctica, f.; —, vt. experimentar; saber.

experienced, adj. experimentado; versado, perito.

experiment, n. experimento, m.; prueba, f. —, vt. experimentar, hacer la prueba.

experimental, adj. experimental.

expert, adj. experto, práctico, diestro; perito; —, n. maestro, tra; conocedor, ra; perito, ta; — in, conocedor de.

expiate, vt. expiar; reparar un daño.

expiration, n. expiración, f.; muerte, f.; vapor, vaho, m.; vencimiento (plazo de una letra o un pagaré, etc.), m.

expire, vi. expirar, morir; vencerse (una suscripción, etc.).

explain, vt. explicar.

explanation, n. explicación, aclaración, f.

explanatory, adj. explicativo.

explicit, adj. explícito.

explode, vt. y vi. disparar con estallido; volar, estallar; refutar; explotar.

exploit, n. hazaña, proeza, f.; hecho heroico; —, vt. explotar; aprovecharse (de alguien).

exploitation, n. explotación, f.

exploration, n. exploración, f ; examen, m.

explore, vt. explorar, examinar; sondear.

explorer, n. explorador, ra.

explosion, n. explosión, f.

explosive, adj. explosivo, fulminante; —, n. explosivo, detonante, m.

exponent, n. exponente, m. y f.; (math.) exponente, m.

export, vt. exportar; —, n. exportación, f.; —house, casa exportadora.

exportation, n. exportación, f.

exporter, n. exportador, ra.

expose, vt. exponer; mostrar; descubrir; poner en peligro.

exposé, n. desenmascaramiento, m.

exposition, n. exposición, exhibición, f.

expostulate, vi. debatir seriamente (con alguien).

expostulation, n. debate, m.; disputa, f.; protesta, f.; reconvención, f.

exposure, n. exposición, f.

expound, vt. exponer, explicar; interpretar.

express, vt. expresar, exteriorizar; representar; —, adj. expreso, claro, a propósito; — car, furgón, furgón del expreso, vagón expreso; — company, compa-

ñía de porteo; — train, tren rápido o expreso; —, n. expreso, correo expreso.

expression, n. expresión, f.; locución, f.; animación del rostro.

expressionless, adj. sin expresión.

expressive, adj. expresivo.

expressly, adv. expresamente.

expressman, n. empleado de empresa de trasporte rápido.

expropriate, vt. expropiar, confiscar.

expulsion, n. expulsión, f.

expurgate, vt. expurgar.

exquisite, adj. exquisito, perfecto, excelente.

extemporaneous, extemporary, adj., improviso, al improviso, a la improvista.

extemporize, vt. y vi. improvisar.

extend, vt. extender; amplificar; to — (time), prorrogar (un plazo); —, vi. extenderse; cundir.

extended, adj. prolongado; extendido.

extension, n. extensión, f.; prórroga, f.

extensive, adj. extenso; amplio; general.

extent, n. extensión, f.; grado, m.; to such an —, a tal grado.

extenuate, vt. extenuar, disminuir, atenuar.

exterior, n. y adj. exterior, m.

exterminate, vt. exterminar; extirpar.

exterminator, n. exterminador, m.

external, adj. externo, exterior.

extinct, adj. extinto; abolido.

extinction, n. extinción, f.; abolición, f.

extinguish, vt. extinguir; suprimir.

extinguisher, n. apagador, extinguidor, m.; fire —, apagador de incendios.

extol, vt. alabar, magnificar, exaltar.

extort, vt. sacar por fuerza; adquirir por violencia; arrebatar.

extortion, n. extorsión, f.

extra, adj. extraordinario, adicional; de reserva, de repuesto; —, n. suplemento extraordinario de un periódico; algo de calidad extraordinaria; (coll.) actor de cine que desempeña papeles insignificantes; — mileage, más millas por unidad de combustible.

extract, vt. extraer; extractar; —, n. extracto, m.; compendio, m.

extraction, n. extracción, f.; descendencia, f.

extracurricular, adj. que no forma parte de un plan de estudios.

extradition, n. extradición, f.

extraordinary, adj. extraordinario.

extrasensory, adj. extrasensorio.

extravagance, n. extravagancia, f.; derroche, m., profusión de lujo.

extravagant, adj. extravagante, singular, exorbitante; excesivo; pródigo; gastador, derrochador.

extreme, *adj.* extremo, supremo; último; —, *n.* extremo, *m.;* **to go to —s,** tomar medidas extremas.

extremist, *n.* extremista, radical, *m.*

extremity, *n.* extremidad, *f.*

extricate, *vt.* sacar (de un apuro, etc.); desenredar.

extrovert, *n.* extrovertido, da.

exuberance, *n.* exuberancia, *f.*

exuberant, *adj.* exuberante, abundantísimo; **—ly,** *adv.* abundantemente.

exude, *vi.* exudar, traspirar.

exult, *vi.* regocijarse, alegrarse de un triunfo.

exultant, *adj.* regocijado; triunfante, victorioso.

exultation, *n.* exultación, *f.;* regocijo, *m.*

eye, *n.* ojo, *m.;* vista, *f.;* (bot.) yema, *f.,* botón, *m.;* **in the twinkling of an —,** en un abrir y cerrar de ojos; —, *vt.* ojear, contemplar, observar.

eyeball, *n.* niña del ojo.

eyebrow, *n.* ceja, *f.*

eyeful, *n.* completa visión de algo; (coll.) muchacha atractiva.

eyeglasses, *n. pl.* anteojos, lentes, *m. pl.*

eyelash, *n.* pestaña, *f.*

eyeless, *adj.* sin ojos, ciego.

eyelet, *n.* ojete, *m.*

eyelid, *n.* párpado, *m.*

eyeshade, *n.* visera, *f.,* guardavista, *m.*

eyesight, *n.* vista, *f.,* potencia visiva.

eye socket, *n.* cuenca del ojo.

eyesore, *n.* adefesio, *m.,* cosa ofensiva a la vista.

eyestrain, *n.* cansancio o tensión de los ojos.

eyetooth, *n.* colmillo, *m.*

eyewash, *n.* colirio, *m.,* loción para los ojos; (coll.) lisonja hipócrita.

eyewitness, *n.* testigo ocular.

F

F.: Fellow, miembro de una sociedad científica o académica; **Fahrenheit,** Fahrenheit; **Friday,** vier. viernes.

f.: following, sig.^te siguiente; **feminine,** *f.* femenino; folio, fol, folio.

fable, *n.* fábula, *f.;* ficción, *f.*

fabled, *adj.* celebrado o puesto en fábulas.

fabric, *n.* tejido, *m.,* tela, *f.*

fabricate, *vt.* fabricar, edificar; inventar (un cuento, una mentira, etc.).

fabulous, *adj.* fabuloso.

facade, *n.* fachada, *f.,* frontispicio de un edificio.

face, *n.* cara, faz, *f.;* superficie, *f.;* fachada, *f.;* rostro, *m.;* frente, *f.;* aspecto, *m.;* apariencia, *f.;* atrevimiento, *m.;* esfera (de un reloj), *f.;* **to lose —,** sufrir pérdida de prestigio; **to make —s,** hacer gestos o muecas; **— down,** boca abajo; **— to —,** cara a cara; **— value,** valor nominal o aparente; —, *vt.* encararse; hacer frente; **to — about,** dar media vuelta; **to — the street,** dar a la calle.

facet, *n.* faceta, *f.*

facetious, *adj.* chistoso, jocoso; gracioso.

facial, *adj.* facial.

facile, *adj.* fácil; afable, complaciente.

facilitate, *vt.* facilitar.

facility, *n.* facilidad, ligereza, *f.;* afabilidad, *f.;* destreza, *f.*

facing, *n.* paramento, *m.;* cara, *f.;* guarnición *f.;* forro, *m.*

facsimile, *n.* facsímil, *m.*

fact, *n.* hecho, *m.;* realidad, *f.;* **in —,** en efecto, verdaderamente; **matter of —,** hecho positivo o cierto.

faction, *n.* facción, *f.;* disensión, *f.*

factious, *adj.* faccioso.

factitious, *adj.* facticio, artificial.

factor, *n.* factor, *m.;* agente, *m.;* (math.) factor, *m.*

factory, *n.* fábrica, *f.,* taller, *m.;* factoría, *f.*

factual, *adj.* actual, relacionado a hechos.

faculty, *n.* facultad, *f.;* poder, privilegio, *m.;* profesorado, *m.*

fad, *n.* fruslería, niñería, *f.;* boga, *f.;* novedad, *f.*

fade, *vi.* desteñirse; decaer, marchitarse.

fade-out, *n.* desaparecimiento gradual (en una película) .

fag, *vt.* cansar, fatigar; hacer trabajar como a un esclavo; —, *vi.* trabajar has-ta agotarse; fatigarse; trabajar como un esclavo; **— end,** cadillos, *m. pl.,* retazo, *m.*

fagot, faggot, *n.* haz, *m.,* gavilla de leña.

fail, *vt.* abandonar; descuidar; faltar; decepcionar; —, *vi.* fallar, fracasar; menguar; debilitarse; perecer; **without —,** sin falta.

failing, *n.* falta, *f.;* defecto, *m.*

failure, *n.* falta, *f.;* culpa, *f.;* quiebra, bancarrota, *f.;* fiasco, *m.;* **to be a —,** quedar o salir deslucido; ser un fracaso.

faint, vi. desmayarse; —, adj. tímido, lánguido; fatigoso, desfallecido; borroso, sin claridad; —, n. desmayo, m.

faint-hearted, adj. cobarde, medroso, pusilánime; **—ly,** adv. medrosamente.

faintness, n. languidez, flaqueza, f.; timidez, f.

fair, adj. hermoso, bello; blanco; rubio; claro, sereno; favorable; recto, justo, franco; **— ball,** (béisbol) pelota que cae dentro de los límites permitidos en el juego; **— weather,** (naut.) bonanza, f.; buen tiempo; —, n. feria, exposición, f.

fair-haired, adj. de cabellos rubios.

fairly, adv. positivamente; favorablemente; justamente, honradamente; claramente; bastante, tolerablemente; **— well,** bastante bien.

fair-minded, adj. razonable, imparcial.

fairness, n. hermosura, f.; honradez, f.; justicia, f

fair -trade, adj. relativo al comercio equitativo; **— agreement,** convenio de reciprocidad comercial.

fairway, n. paso libre o despejado; (golf) pista, f.

fairy, n. hada, f.; duende, m.; —, adj. de hadas, relativo a las hadas; **— tale,** cuento de hadas.

fairyland, n. tierra de las hadas; sitio maravilloso, lugar encantador.

faith, n. fe, f.; fidelidad, sinceridad, f.; fervor, m.

faithful, adj. fiel, leal; **—ly,** adv. fielmente.

faithless, adj. infiel, pérfido, desleal.

fake, n. (naut.) aduja, f.; (coll.) imitación fraudulenta; —, adj. (coll.) falsos fraudulento; —, vt. (coll.) engañar; imitar.

faker, n. farsante, m. y f.

falcon, n. halcón, m.

fall, vi. caer, caerse; perder el poder; disminuir, decrecer en precio; **to — asleep,** dormirse; **to — back,** recular; **to — back again,** recaer; **to — due,** cumplir, vencer; **to — headlong,** caer de bruces; **to — short,** no corresponder a lo esperado; **to — sick,** enfermar; **to — in love,** enamorarse; **to — off,** menguar, disminuir; caerse; **to — out,** reñir, disputar; **to — upon,** atacar, asaltar; —, n. caída, f.; declive, m.; catarata, f.; otoño, m.; **— in prices,** baja, f.

fallacious, adj. falaz, fraudulento; delusorio.

fallacy, n. falacia, sofistería, f., engaño, m.

fallen, adj. caído; arruinado; **—** p.p. del verbo **fall.**

fallout, n. lluvia nuclear, radiactividad atmosférica.

fallow, adj. sin cultivar (aplícase a la tierra) ; **— deer,** corzo, za; —, n. barbecho, m., tierra que se deja sin cultivar por un tiempo; —, vt. barbechar.

false, adj. falso, pérfido; postizo; supuesto; **— bottom,** fondo doble; **— colors,** bandera falsa; **— teeth,** dientes postizos.

falsehood, n. falsedad, f.; perfidia, f.; mentira, f.

falsetto, n. falsete, m.; **— voice,** falsete, m.

falsification, n. falsificación, f.

falsify, vt. falsificar.

falter, vi. tartamudear; vacilar, titubear.

faltering, adj. balbuciente, titubeante.

fame, n. fama, f.; renombre, m.

famed, adj. celebrado, famoso.

familiar, adj. familiar, casero; conocido; **— with,** acostumbrado a, versado en, conocedor de.

familiarity, n. familiaridad, f.

familiarize, vt. familiarizar.

family, n. familia, f.; linaje, m.; clase, especie, f.; **— name,** apellido, m.; **— tree,** árbol genealógico.

famine, n. hambre, f.; carestía, f.

famish, vt. hambrear.

famous, adj. famoso, afamado, célebre.

fan, n. abanico, m.; aventador, ventilador, m.; aficionado, da; —, vt. abanicar; aventar; soplar.

fanatic, n. y adj. fanático, ca; mojigato, ta.

fancied, adj. imaginario.

fancier, n. aficionado, da.

fanciful, adj. imaginativo, caprichoso; fantástico; **—ly,** adv. caprichosamente.

fancy, n. fantasía, imaginación, imaginativa, f.; capricho, m.; **— goods,** novedades, modas, f. pl.; **foolish —,** quimera, f.; —, vt. imaginar; gustar de; suponer.

fancywork, n. labores manuales; trabajo de costura.

falsification, n. falsificación, f.

fang, n. colmillo, m.; garra, uña, f.; raíz de un diente.

fantastic, adj. fantástico; caprichoso.

fantasy, n. fantasía, f.

far, adv. lejos, a una gran distancia; **— be it from me!** ¡ni lo permita Dios! —, adj. lejano, distante, remoto; **— off,** lejano, distante.

faraway, adj. lejano; abstraído.

farce, n. farsa, f.

fare, n. alimento, m., comida, f.; viajero, ra; pasaje, m.; tarifa, f.; —, vi. viajar; **to — well (or ill),** irle a uno bien (o mal).

farewell, n. despedida, f; **—!** interj. ¡ adiós! ¡que le vaya bien!

farfetched, adj. forzado, traído de los cabellos.

far-flung, adj. extendido, de gran alcance.

farm, n. tierra arrendada; alquería, f.;

hacienda, granja, f.; —, vt. arrendar; tomar en arriendo; cultivar.

farmer, n. labrador, hacendado; agricultor; **small** —, estanciero, ranchero.

farmhand, n. peón de granja.

farmhouse, n. hacienda, f.; cortijo, m.

farming n. agricultura, f., cultivo, m.

farmyard, n. corral, m.

far-off, adj. remoto, distante.

far-reaching, adj. de gran alcance, trascendental.

farseeing, adj. perspicaz, previsor, precavido.

farsighted, adj. présbita, présbite; (fig.) precavido; astuto, sagaz, agudo.

farther, adv. más lejos; más adelante; —, adj. más remoto, ulterior.

farthermost, adj. que está a mayor distancia.

farthest, adj. más distante, más remoto; más largo; más extendido; —, adv. a la mayor distancia.

fascinate, vt. fascinar, encantar.

fascinating, adj. fascinador, seductor.

fascination, n. fascinación, f.; encanto, m.

fascism, n. fascismo, m.

fashion, n. forma, figura, f.; moda, f., estilo, m.; uso, m., costumbre, f.; condición, f.; guisa, f.; **latest** —, última moda; —, vt. formar, amoldar; confeccionar.

fashionable, adj. hecho a la moda; en boga, de moda; elegante; **the — world**, el gran mundo; **—bly**, adv. según la moda, de acuerdo con la última moda.

fast, vi. ayunar; —, n. ayuno, m.; —, adj. firme, estable, veloz, pronto; disipado, disoluto; **— clock**, reloj adelantado; **— day**, día de ayuno; —, adv. de prisa;— **food**, comida rápida, f.

fasten, vt. afirmar, asegurar, atar, fiar; —, vi. fijarse.

fastener, n. asegurador, sujetador, m.

fastening, n. atadura, ligazón, f.; nudo, m.

fastidious, adj. delicado, melindroso; desdeñoso.

fasting, n. ayuno, m.

fastness, n. prontitud, f.; ligereza, f.; firmeza, f.; fortaleza, f.

fat, adj. gordo, pingüe; **to get** —, echar carnes, engordar; —, n. gordo, m., gordura, f.; grasa, manteca, f.; sebo, m.

fatal, adj. fatal; funesto.

fatalist, n. fatalista m. y f.

fatality, n. fatalidad, predestinación, f.; muerte por accidente.

fate, n. hado, destino, m.; fatalidad, f., sino, m.; suerte, f.

fateful, adj. fatídico, ominoso, funesto.

father, n. padre, m.

father-in-law, n. suegro, m.

fatherland, n. patria, f.

fatherless, adj. huérfano de padre.

fatherly, adj. paternal.

fathom, n. braza (medida), f.; —, vt. sondar; penetrar; **to — a mystery**, desentrañar un misterio.

fathomless, adj. insondable.

fatigue, n. fatiga, f., cansancio, m.; —, vt. y vi. fatigar, cansar, rendirse.

fatness, n. gordura, f.

fatten, vt. cebar, engordar; —, vi. engrosarse, engordarse.

fatty, adj. grasoso, untoso, craso, pingüe.

fatuous, adj. fatuo, vanidoso.

faucet, n. grifo, m.; **water** —, toma, llave, f., caño de agua.

fault, n. falta, culpa, f.; delito, m.; defecto, m.; **to find** —, tachar, criticar, poner faltas.

faultfinder, n. criticón, ona, censurador, ra.

faultfinding, adj. cavilloso; criticón.

faultless, adj. perfecto, cumplido, sin tacha.

faulty, adj. culpable, defectuoso.

faun, n. fauno, m.

fauna, n. (zool.) fauna, f.

faux pas, n. paso en falso; (coll.) metida de pata.

favor, n. favor, beneficio, m.; gracia, f.; patrocinio, m.; **in — of**, a favor de; **in his** —, en su provecho; **your** —, su apreciable, su grata (carta); —, vt. favorecer, proteger, apoyar.

favorable, adj. favorable, propicio; provechoso; **—bly**, adv. favorablemente.

favorite, n. y adj. favorito, ta, favorecido, da.

favoritism, n. favoritismo, m.

fawn, n. cervato, m.; —, vi. parir la cierva; adular servilmente.

FBI: Federal Bureau of Investigation, Departamento Federal de Investigación.

fear, vt. y vi. temer, tener miedo; —, n. miedo, terror, pavor, m.

fearful, adj. medroso, temeroso; tímido.

fearless, adj. intrépido, atrevido; **—ly**, adv. sin miedo.

fearsome, adj. espantoso, horroroso.

feasible, adj. factible, práctico.

feast, n. banquete, festín, m.; fiesta, f.; —, vt. festejar, regalar; —, vi. comer opíparamente.

feat, n. hecho, m.; acción, hazaña, f.

feather, n. pluma, f.; **— bed**, colchón de plumas; **— duster**, plumero, m.; —, vt. emplumar; enriquecer.

featherbed, vt. crear sinecuras.

featherbedding, n. sinecura, f.

featherbrained, adj. casquivano, tonto,

frívolo.

feathered, adj. plumado, alado; veloz.

featherweight, n. peso pluma, m.

feathery, adj. cubierto de plumas; ligero como una pluma.

feature, n. facción del rostro; forma, f.; rasgo, m.; atracción principal; —s, n. pl. facciones, f. pl., fisonomía, f.

Feb.: February, feb. febrero.

February, febrero, m.

federal, adj. federal.

federate, adj. confederado; —, vt. y vi. confederar, confederarse.

federation, n. confederación, federación, f.

fedora, n. fieltro, m.; sombrero de fieltro.

fee, n. feudo, m.; paga, gratificación, f.; emolumento, m.; honorarios, m. pl.; derecho, m.; cuota, f.

feeble, adj. flaco, débil.

feeble-minded, adj. imbécil, escaso de entendimiento.

feed, vt. pacer; nutrir; alimentar, dar de comer; —, vi. alimentarse, nutrirse; —, n. alimento, m.; pasto, m.

feeder, n. persona que da de comer; alimentador, m.

feeding, n. nutrición, f., alimento, m.; cebadura (para animales), f.

feel, vt. sentir; palpar; **to — like,** tener ganas de; apetecer; —, vi. tener sensibilidad; —, n. tacto, sentido, m.

feeler, n. antena, f.; (fig.) tentativa, f.

feeling, n. tacto, m.; sensibilidad, f.; sentimiento, m.; presentimiento m.

feet, n. pl. de **foot,** pies, m. pl.

feign, vt. inventar, fingir; simular; —, vi. fingirse, disimular.

feint, n. ficción, f.; finta, treta, f.

felicitation, n. felicitación, congratulación, f.

felicity, n. felicidad, dicha, f.

feline, adj. felino, gatuno; —, n. gato, animal felino.

fell, adj. cruel, bárbaro; —, n. cuero, m.; piel, f.; pellejo, m.; —, vt. matar las reses; cortar árboles; sobrecargar (en costura); —, pretérito del verbo **fall.**

fellow, n. compañero, camarada, m.; sujeto, m.; socio de algún colegio; **— citizen,** conciudadano, na; **— creature,** semejante, m.; **— member,** consocio, m.; **— student,** condiscípulo, la; **— traveler,** compañero o compañera de viaje; comunistoide, filocomunista, m. o f.

fellowship, n. compañía, sociedad, f.; beca (en una universidad), f.; camaradería, f.

felon, n. reo de un delito gravísimo.

felony, n. delito gravísimo.

felt, n. fieltro, m.; —, pret. y p.p. del verbo **feel.**

female, n. hembra, f.; —, adj. femenino.

feminine, adj. femenino; tierno; afeminado, amujerado.

fence, n. cerca, palizada, valla, f.; perista, m.; —, vt. cercar; preservar; —, vi. esgrimir.

fencer, n. esgrimidor, m.

fencing, n. esgrima, f.

fend, vt. parar; rechazar, —, vi. defenderse.

fender, n. guardabarros, guardalodo, guardafango, m.; guardafuegos, m.

ferment, n. fermento, m., levadura, f.; —, vt. y vi. hacer fermentar, fermentarse.

fern, n. (bot.) helecho, m.

ferocious, adj. feroz; fiero.

ferocity, n. ferocidad, fiereza, f.

ferrous, adj. férreo.

ferry, n. barca de trasporte, barca de trasbordo; —, vt. llevar en barca.

ferryboat, n. barco para cruzar ríos, etc.

ferryman, n. barquero, m.

fertile, adj. fértil, fecundo, productivo.

fertilization, n. fertilización, f.

fertilize, vt. fertilizar.

fertilizer, n. abono, fertilizante, m.

ferule, n. férula, palmeta, f.

fervent, adj. ferviente; fervoroso; —ly, adv. fervientemente, con fervor.

fervid, adj. ardiente, vehemente, férvido.

fervor, n. fervor, ardor, m.

fester, vi. enconarse, inflamarse.

festival, n. fiesta, f., festival, m.

festive, adj. festivo, alegre.

festivity, n. festividad, f.

fetch, vt. buscar; producir; llevar; arrebatar; —, n. estratagema, f.; artificio, ardid, m.

fete, fête, n. fiesta, f.; —, vt. festejar, honrar, agasajar con una fiesta.

fetish, n. fetiche, m., adoración ciega de algo.

fetter, vt. atar con cadenas.

fetters, n. pl. manija, f., grillos, hierros, m. pl., esposas, f. pl.

feud, n. riña, contienda, f.; feudo, m.

feudal, adj. feudal.

feudalism, n. feudalismo, m.

fever, n. fiebre, f.; **typhoid —,** tifoidea, fiebre tifoidea.

feverish, adj. febril.

few, adj. pocos; **a —,** algunos; **— and far between** poquísimos.

fewer, adj. menos.

fiancé, n. novio, m.

fiancée, n. novia, f.

fib, n. mentirilla, f.

fiber, fibre, n. fibra, hebra, f.

fibroid, adj. fibroso; **— tumor,** fibroma, m.

fibrous adj. fibroso.

fickle, adj. voluble, inconstante, mudable, frívolo; caprichoso.

fiction, n. ficción, f.; invención, f.

fictitious, adj. ficticio; fingido.

fiddle, n. violín, m.; —, vi. tocar el violín; jugar nerviosamente con los dedos.

fiddler, n. violinista, m. y f.

fidelity, n. fidelidad, lealtad, f.

fidget, vi. (coll.) contonearse, moverse inquieta y nerviosamente; —, n. agitación nerviosa; persona nerviosa e inquieta.

field, n. campo, m.; campaña, f.; espacio, m.; **sown** —, sembrado, m.; —, adj. campal; — **cricket**, caballeta, f.; saltamontes, m.; — **artillery**, artillería de campaña, m.; — **day**, día de revista; día cuando las tropas hacen ejercicios en sus evoluciones campales; día de concursos gimnásticos al aire libre; — **glasses**, gemelos de campo; — **hospital**, hospital de sangre, hospital de campaña; — **marshal**, mariscal de campo; — **officer**, (mil.) oficial del estado mayor.

fielder, n. jardinero (en el béisbol), m.

fiend, n. demonio, m.; persona malvada; **dope** —, morfinómano, na.

fiendish, adj. diabólico, demoniaco.

fierce, adj. fiero, feroz; cruel, furioso.

fiery, adj. ardiente, fogoso, colérico; brioso.

fife, n. pífano, flautín, pito, m.

fifteen, n. y adj. quince, m.

fifteenth, n. y adj. decimoquinto, m.

fifth, n. y adj. quinto, m.; quinto de galón (medida de vinos y licores); — **column**, quinta columna; — **columnist**, quintacolumnista, m. y f.; — **wheel**, rodete, m.; estorbo, m., persona superflua; —**ly**, adv. en quinto lugar.

fiftieth, n. y adj. quincuagésimo, m.

fifty, n. y adj. cincuenta, m.

fifty-fifty, adj. y adv. mitad y mitad, por partes iguales.

fig, n. higo, m.; (coll.) bagatela, f.; **I don't care a** —, no me importa un bledo; — **tree**, higuera, f.

fight, vt. y vi. reñir; batallar; combatir; luchar con; —, vi. lidiar; —, n. batalla, f.; combate, m., pelea, f.; conflicto, m.

fighter, n. batallador, ra; peleador, ra; — **plane**, aeroplano de combate.

fighting, n. combate, m.; riña, f.; —, adj. pugnante; combatiente.

figment, n. invención, f., algo imaginado.

figurative, adj. figurativo, figurado; —**ly**, adv. figuradamente.

figure, n. figura, forma, hechura, f.; imagen, f.; cifra, f.; **good** —, buen cuerpo; — **of speech**, tropo, m., frase en sentido figurado; —, vt. figurar; calcular.

figurehead, n. (naut.) roda, f.; figurón de proa; pelele, jefe nominal.

filament, n. filamento, m.; fibra, f.

filch, vt. ratear.

file, n. archivo, m.; lista, f.; (mil.) fila, hilera, f.; lima, f.; — **case**, fichero, m.; — **clerk**, archivero, ra; —, vt. archivar; limar; pulir.

filial, adj. filial.

filibuster, n. pirata, filibustero, m.; (E.U.A.) prolongadísimo discurso en el congreso para aplazar una ley.

filing, n. clasificación, f.; archivo, m.; —**s**, pl. limaduras, f. pl.

fill, vt. llenar, henchir; hartar; **to** — **out**, llenar (un formulario, cuestionario, etc.); **to** — **up**, colmar; —, vi. hartarse; —, n. hartura, abundancia, f.

filler, n. llenador, m.; relleno, m.

fillet, n. faja, tira, banda, f.; filete (de pescado), m.; (arch.) filete, m.

filling, n. tapadura, f., relleno, m.; orificación (de un diente); tripa, f.; — **station**, estación de gasolina.

filly, n. potranca, f.

film, n. filme, m., película, f.; membrana, f.; — **festival**, reseña cinematográfica; — **strip**, película auxiliar en clases o conferencias; —, vt. filmar.

filter, n. filtro, m.; —, vt. filtrar.

filth, filthiness, n. inmundicia, porquería, f.; fango, lodo, m.

filthy, adj. sucio, puerco.

filtrate, vt. filtrar.

fin, n. aleta (de un pez), f.

final, adj. final, último; definitivo; terminal; —**ly**, adv. finalmente, por último, al cabo; —**s**, n. pl. final, f.

finalist, n. finalista, m. o f.

finality, n. finalidad, f.

finance, n. renta, f.; economía, f.; hacienda pública; finanzas, f. pl.; —, vt. financiar; costear, sufragar los gastos (de).

financial, adj. financiero, pecuniario, económico.

financier, n. rentista, hacendista, m.; financista, m.

financing, n. financiamiento, m.

find, vt. hallar, descubrir; proveer; dar con; **to** — **oneself**, hallarse, estar; verse; **to** — **out**, descubrir, enterarse (de); —, n. hallazgo, descubrimiento, m.

finder, n. descubridor, m.; (phot.) visor, m.

fine, adj. fino; agudo, cortante; claro; trasparente, delicado; elegante; bello; bien criado; bueno; **the** — **arts**, las bellas artes; —, n. multa, f.; —, vt. multar; —! interj. ¡bien! ¡magnífico!

fineness, n. fineza, sutileza, perfección, f.

finery, n. perifollos, m. pl.; ropa vistosa.

finespun, adj. sutil, atenuado; insustancial; ilusorio.

finesse, n. sutileza, astucia, pericia, f.

finger, n. dedo, m.; — **bowl,** lavadedos, m.; —, vt. tocar, manosear; manejar.

fingering, n. tecleo, m.; manoseo, m.; (mus.) pulsación, f.

fingernail, n. uña, f.; — **polish,** esmalte para uñas.

fingerprints, n. pl. huellas digitales.

finicky, adj. melindroso.

finish, vt. acabar, terminar, concluir, llevar a cabo; —, n. conclusión, f., final, m.; pulimento, m.; acabado, m.

finished, adj. concluido; perfeccionado, refinado; retocado; (coll.) arruinado.

finishing, n. última mano; —, adj. de retoque; — **school,** colegio de cursos culturales para niñas.

finite, adj. limitado, finito.

fiord, n. fiordo, m.

fir, n. (bot.) abeto, oyamel, m.

fire, n. fuego, m.; candela, f.; incendio, m.; quemazón, f.; — **alarm,** alarma o llamada de incendios; — **department,** cuerpo de bomberos; — **engine,** bomba de apagar incendios; — **escape,** escalera de salvamento para incendios; **on** —, en llamas; — **extinguisher,** apagador de incendios, matafuegos, m.; — **insurance,** seguro contra incendio; — **screen,** guardafuegos, m., pantalla, mampara, f.; — **truck,** autobomba, f.; **to catch** —, inflamarse, encenderse; **to open** —, (mil.) hacer una descarga; —, vt. quemar, inflamar; —, vi. encenderse; (mil.) tirar, hacer fuego.

firearms, n. pl. armas de fuego.

firebox, n. caja del fogón.

firebrand, n. tizón, m.; incendiario, ria; persona sediciosa.

firebug, n. incendiario, ria.

firecracker, n. petardo, m.; buscapiés, cohete, m.

firefly, n. luciérnaga, f., cocuyo, cucuyo, m.

fireman, n. bombero, m.; (rail.) fogonero, m.

fireplace, n. hogar, m., chimenea, f.

fireplug, n. boca de incendios, toma de agua.

firepower, n. (mil.) potencia efectiva de disparo.

fireproof, adj. a prueba de incendio, incombustible; refractario.

fireside, n. sitio cerca a la chimenea u hogar; vida de hogar.

firetrap, n. lugar susceptible de incendiarse.

firewarden, n. guardia encargado de prevenir incendios.

firewater, n. aguardiente, m.

firewood, n. leña para la lumbre.

fireworks, n. pl. fuegos artificiales.

firing, n. encendimiento, m.; leña, f.; (mil.) descarga, f.; — **line,** línea de fuego; — **squad,** pelotón de fusilamiento; piquete de salvas.

firm, adj. firme, estable, constante; seguro; —, n. (com.) razón social, casa de comercio; — **name,** razón social.

firmament, n. firmamento, m.

firmness, n. firmeza, f.; constancia, f.; fijeza, f.

first, adj. primero; primario; delantero; — **aid,** primeros auxilios; — **mate,** piloto, m.; —, adv. primeramente; — **of all,** ante todo; —**ly,** adv. en primer lugar.

first-aid, adj. de primer auxilio; — **kit,** botiquín, m.

first-born, n. y adj. primogénito, ta.

first-class, adj. de primera clase; **private** —, (mil.) soldado de primera.

first cousin, n. primo hermano, prima hermana.

firsthand, adj. directo, de primera mano.

first-rate, adj. primordial; admirable, de primera clase.

fiscal, adj. fiscal.

fish, n. pez, m.; pescado, m.; — **cured** —, pescado salado; — **globe,** pecera, f.; — **market,** pescadería, f.; — **pole,** caña de pescar; — **story,** (coll.) cuento increíble, relato fabuloso; —, vt. y vi. pescar.

fishbone, n. espina de pescado.

fisherman, n. pescador, m.

fishery, n. pesca, f.

fishhook, n. anzuelo, m.

fishing, n. pesca, f.; — **bait,** cebo para pescar; — **line,** sedal, m.; — **reel,** carretel, m.; — **rod,** caña de pescar; — **tackle,** avíos de pescar.

fishworm, n. gusano que sirve de carnada.

fission, n. desintegración, f.

fissionable, adj. desintegrable (en química atómica).

fissure, n. grieta, hendedura, f.; —, vt. y vi. agrietar, agrietarse.

fist, n. puño, m.; —, vt. empuñar.

fit, adj. apto, idóneo, capaz, cómodo; justo; —, n. paroxismo, m.; convulsión, f.; capricho, m.; ataque repentino de algún mal; —, vt. ajustar, acomodar, adaptar; sentar, quedar bien; **to** — **out,** proveer; —, vi. convenir, venir; caber.

fitful, adj. alternado con paroxismos; caprichoso; inquieto.

fitness, n. aptitud, conveniencia, f.; proporción, f.; oportunidad, f.

fitter, n. ajustador, m.; arreglador, ra;

(naut.) armador, equipador, m.; instalador, m.; costurera, entalladora, f.

fitting, adj. conveniente, idóneo, justo; a propósito; adecuado; —, n. instalación, f.; ajuste, m.; —s, n. pl. guarniciones, f. pl.; accesorios, avíos, m. pl.

five, n. y adj. cinco, m.

fix, vt. fijar, establecer; componer; to — up, concertar; arreglar, arreglarse; —, vi. fijarse, determinarse.

fixation, n. fijación, firmeza, estabilidad, f.; (chem.) fijación, f.

fixed, adj. firme, fijo.

fixing, n. fijación, f.; ensambladura, f.

fixings, n. pl. equipajes, accesorios, m. pl.; pertrechos, m. pl.; ajuar, m.

fixture, n. mueble fijo de una casa; —s, pl. instalación, f.; enseres, m. pl.

fizz, vi. sisear; —, n. siseo, m.

fizzle, n. fiasco, fracaso, m.; —, vi. sisear; (coll.) fallar.

Fla.: Florida, Florida (E.U.A.).

flabbergasted, adj. (coll.) atónito, pasmado.

flabby, adj. blando, flojo, lacio; fofo, débil.

flag, n. bandera, f.; (naut.) pabellón, m.; — officer, (naut.) jefe de una escuadra; — of truce, bandera de parlamento; —, vt. hacer señales con una bandera; to — (a train), hacer parar (a un tren) ; —, vi. pender; flaquear, debilitarse.

flagging, adj. lánguido, flojo; —, n. enlosado, m.

flagman, n. (rail.) guardavía, vigilante, m.

flagpole, n. asta de bandera.

flagrant, adj. flagrante; notorio.

flagship, n. navío almirante, nave capitana.

flagstaff, n. asta de pabellón o de bandera.

flagstone, n. losa, f.

flail, n. (agr.) mayal, m.; —, vt. y vi. batir, sacudir.

flair, n. afición, inclinación, f.

flake, n. copo, m.; lámina, f.; soap —s, jabón en escamas; —, vt. y vi. desmenuzar, desmenuzarse.

flamboyant, adj. flamante, suntuoso; (arch.) de líneas ondulantes.

flame, n. llama, f.; fuego (del amor), m.; — thrower, arrojallamas, m.; —, vi. arder; brillar; flamear, llamear.

flaming, adj. llameante; flamante, llamativo.

flamingo, n. (orn.) flamenco, m.

flange, n. ribete, dobladillo, m.; (arch.) repisa, f.; (mech.) pestaña, f.; reborde, m.; herramienta para hacer rebordes; —, vt. hacer un reborde.

flank, n. ijada, f.; (mil.) flanco, m.; —, vt. atacar el flanco; flanquear.

flannel, n. franela, f.; thick —, bayeta, f.

flannelette, n. franela de algodón.

flap, n. ala (de sombrero), f.; bragueta, f.; solapa, f.; aleta, f.; —, vt. y vi. aletear; sacudir.

flapjack = griddlecake.

flare, vi. lucir, brillar; —, n. llama, f.; (avi.) cohete de señales.

flare-up, n. fulguración, f.; recrudecimiento (de una enfermedad, etc.), m.

flash, n. relámpago, m.; llamarada, f.; borbollón, m.; destello, m.; — of lightning, rayo, relámpago, m.; —, vt. enviar (un mensaje) por telégrafo; dar a conocer (noticias) rápidamente; —, vi. relampaguear, brillar.

flashback, n. interrupción de la continuidad de un relato para introducir acontecimientos previos (como en un filme), m.

flasher, n. (elec.) destellador, generador instantáneo; — sign, anuncio intermitente.

flashing, n. centelleo, m.; tapajuntas (en la construcción de edificios), m.

flash lamp, n. (phot.) lámpara especial para tomar fotografías.

flashlight, n. linterna, f.; linterna eléctrica de bolsillo; lámpara de intermitencia; — photography, fotografía instantánea de relámpago.

flashy, adj. resplandeciente; chillón, charro; superficial; vistoso, alegre.

flask, n. frasco, m.; botella, f.

flat, adj. llano, plano; insípido; — back, lomo plano; — tire, llanta reventada o desinflada, neumático desinflado; —, n. llanura, f.; piano, m.; (naut.) bajío, m.; (mus.) bemol, m.; apartamiento, departamento, m.; —ly, adv. horizontalmente; de plano, francamente.

flatboat, n. buque de fondo plano para flete.

flat-bottomed, adj. de fondo plano.

flat-footed, adj. de pies achatados; (coll.) resuelto, firme.

flatiron, n. plancha (para ropa), f.

flatness, n. llanura, f.; insipidez, f.

flatten, vt. allanar; abatir; chafar; —, vi. aplanarse.

flatter, vt. adular, lisonjear, echar flores.

flatterer, n. galanteador, ra; zalamero, ra.

flattering, adj. adulador, lisonjero.

flattery, n. adulación, lisonja, f.; requiebro, m.; (coll.) piropo, m.

flatware, n. vajilla, f.; cubiertos de plata.

flaunt, vi. pavonearse; —, vt. exhibir con ostentación; —, n. alarde, m.

flavor, n. sabor, gusto, m.; —, vt. sazonar, condimentar.

flavoring, n. condimento, m.; sabor, m.

flaw, *n.* resquebradura, hendidura, *f.;* falta, tacha, *f.;* ráfaga, *f.;* —, *vt.* rajar, hender; —, *vi.* agrietarse, rajarse.

flawless, *adj.* sin defecto, sin tacha.

flax, *n.* lino, *m.;* **to dress** —, rastrillar lino.

flaxen, *adj.* de lino, de hilo; blondo, rubio.

flaxseed, *n.* semilla de lino.

flay, *vt.* desollar, descortezar; censurar severamente.

flea, *n.* pulga, *f.*

flea-bitten, *adj.* picado de pulgas.

fleck, *n.* mancha, raya, *f.;* —, *vt.* manchar, rayar.

flecked, *adj.* abigarrado, vareteado.

flee, *vi.* escapar; huir; tramontarse.

fleece, *n.* vellón, vellocino, *m.,* lana, *f.;* —, *vt.* esquilar; tonsurar; desnudar, despojar.

fleecy, *adj.* lanudo.

fleet, *n.* flota, *f.;* —, *adj.* veloz, acelerado, ligero.

fleeting, *adj.* pasajero, fugitivo.

flesh, *n.* carne, *f.;* — **color,** color de carne; — **wound,** herida superficial o ligera.

flesh-colored, *adj.* encarnado, de color de carne.

fleshy, *adj.* carnoso, pulposo.

flew, *pretérito* del verbo fly.

flexibility, *n.* flexibilidad, *f.*

flexible, *adj.* flexible, adaptable, movible.

flick, *vt.* dar ligeramente con un látigo; —, *n.* golpe como de un látigo; movimiento rápido.

flicker, *vi.* aletear, fluctuar; —, *n.* aleteo, *m.;* — **of an eyelash,** pestañeo, *m.*

flier, *n.* fugitivo, *m.;* volante, *m.;* aviador, ra; tren muy rápido; hoja de anuncios (de una tienda, etc.).

flight, *n.* huida, fuga, *f.;* vuelo, *m.;* bandada (de pájaros); (fig.) elevación, *f.;* — **pattern,** *n.* (avi.) forma de vuelo; — **strip,** (avi.) pita al borde de una carretera para el aterrizaje de emergencia; — **of stairs,** tramo de una escalera.

flighty, *adj.* veloz; inconstante, voluble, frívolo; casquivano; travieso.

flimsy, *adj.* débil; fútil.

flinch, *vi.* respingar; desistir, faltar; retirarse; vacilar.

fling, *vt.* lanzar, echar; —, *vi.* lanzarse con violencia; —, *n.* tiro, *m.;* burla, chufleta, *f.;* tentativa, *f.*

flint, *n.* pedernal, *m.;* — **glass,** cristal de piedra.

flip, *vt.* arrojar, lanzar.

flippant, *adj.* ligero, veloz; petulante, locuaz.

flirt, *vt.* arrojar, lanzar; —, *vi.* flirtear, coquetear; —, *n.* coqueta, *f.,* persona coqueta.

flirtation, *n.* coquetería, *f.,* flirteo, *m.*

flit, *vi.* volar, huir; aletear.

float, *vt.* inundar; —, *vi.* flotar; fluctuar; —, *n.* carro alegórico.

floating, *adj.* flotante.

flock, *n.* manada, *f.;* rebaño, *m.;* gentío, *m.;* vedija de lana; —, *vi.* congregarse.

flog, *vt.* azotar.

flogging, *n.* tunda, zurra, *f.*

flood, *n.* diluvio, *m.;* inundación, *f.;* flujo, *m.;* —, *vt.* y *vi.* inundar, inundarse; — **tide,** pleamar, *f.*

floodgate, *n.* compuerta, *f.*

floodlight, *n.* reflector o lámpara que despide un rayo concentrado de luz.

floor, *n.* pavimento, suelo, piso, *m.;* piso de una casa; — **brush,** escobeta, *f.;* **ground** —, piso bajo; — **show,** espectáculo de variedad en un cabaret; —, *vt.* solar; echar al suelo; (fig.) enmudecer; derrotar.

flooring, *n.* suelo, pavimento, *m.;* ensamblaje de madera para suelos.

floorwalker, *n.* superintendente de cada departamento de una tienda.

flop, *vi.* malograrse, fracasar; caerse; —, *n.* fracaso, *m.,* persona fracasada.

florid, *adj.* florido.

Florida Keys, Cayos de la Florida.

florist, *n.* florista, *m.* y *f.*

floss, floss silk, *n.* seda floja (para bordar).

flounce, *n.* volante, adorno plegado (de un vestido); (Mex.) olán, *m.;* —, *vt.* adornar con volantes u olanes.

flounder, *n.* (ichth.) rodaballo, *m.;* —, *vi.* forcejar, debatirse.

flour, *n.* harina, *f.;* — **mill,** molino de harina.

flourish, *vt.* blandir; agitar; —, *vi.* gozar de prosperidad; crecer lozanamente; jactarse; rasguear; (mus.) preludiar, florear; —, *n.* floreo de palabras; (mus.) floreo, preludio, *m.;* rasgo (de una pluma), *m.;* lozanía, *f.*

flout, *vt.* y *vi.* mofar, burlarse; —, *n.* mofa, burla, *f.*

flow, *vi.* fluir, manar; crecer (la marea); ondear, verter; correr; —, *n.* creciente de la marea; abundancia, *f.;* **flujo,** *m.,* corriente, *f.;* caudal, *m.*

flower, *n.* flor, *f.; (fig.)* lo mejor; — **garden,** jardín de flores, vergel, *m.;* —, *vi.* florear; florecer.

flowered, *adj.* floreado; abierto en forma de flor; adornado con dibujos florales.

flowerpot, *n.* tiesto de flores, tiesto, *m.,* maceta, *f.*

flowery, *adj.* florido.

flown, *p.p.* del verbo fly.

flu, *n.* (coll.) influenza, gripe, *f.,* trancazo, m.

fluctuate, vi. fluctuar.

flue, n. humero, m.; cañón de organo.

fluency, n. fluidez, facundia, f.

fluent, adj. fluido; fluente, fácil, corriente; **—ly,** adv. con fluidez; **to speak (a language) —ly,** hablar (un idioma) a la perfección.

fluff, vt. mullir; **—,** n. pelusa, f., tamo, m.

fluffy, adj. blando y velloso; fofo.

fluid, n. y adj. fluido, m.

flume, n. canal de esclusa, saetín, m.

flunk, vt. y vi. (coll.) reprobar; **—,** n. reprobación.

flunkey, n. lacayo, m.; persona adulona.

flunk-out, n. (coll.) persona fracasada.

fluorescent, adj. fluorescente.

fluoridation, n. fluoruración, f.

fluoroscope, n. fluoroscopio, m.

flurry, n. ráfaga, f.; agitación nerviosa, conmoción, f.; **—,** vt. confundir; alarmar; agitar.

flush, vt. sacar agua de algún lugar; echar agua, limpiar con un chorro de agua (por ej., un inodoro); animar, alentar; **—,** vi. sonrojarse, ruborizarse; fluir repentinamente; **—,** n. rubor, m.; conmoción, f.; calor intenso (como de fiebre) ; chorro de agua que limpia; flor, f., flux, m. (de naipes), una mano de naipes todos del mismo palo; (print.) composición pareja en el margen izquierdo, composición sin sangrías; **—,** adj. bien provisto; vigoroso, lozano; pródigo; parejo.

fluster, vt. confundir, atropellar; **—,** vi. confundirse; **—,** n. agitación, confusión, f.

flute, n. flauta, f.; (arch.) estría, f.; **—,** vt. estriar.

fluted, adj. acanalado.

fluting, n. estriadura, acanaladura, f.

flutist, n. flautista, m. y f.

flutter, vt. turbar, desordenar; **—,** vi. revolotear; flamear; estar en agitación; **—,** n. confusión, f.; agitación, f.

flux, n. flujo, m.

fly, vt. y vi. volar; pasar ligeramente; huir; escapar; **to — on the beam,** (rad.) volar por la banda radiofónica; **—,** n. mosca, f.; pliegue, volante, m.; (béisbol) pelota que al ser golpeada se eleva.

flycatcher, n. (orn.) papamoscas, m.

flying, n. vuelo, m.; aviación, f.; **—,** adj. volante, volador; temporal, de pasada; repentino; **— colors,** bandera desplegada; **to come off with — colors,** salir victorioso (en una prueba, examen, etc.); **— field,** campo de aviación; **— fish,** pez volador; **blind —,** vuelo a ciegas, vuelo

con instrumentos; **— fortress,** (avi.) fortaleza aérea; **— saucer,** platillo volante o volador.

flypaper, n. papel pegajoso para atrapar moscas.

fly swatter, n. matamoscas, m.

flytrap, n. mosquero, m.

flyweight, n. peso mosca (boxeador), m.

flywheel, n. (mech.) volante, m.

F.M., f.m.: frequency modulation, (rad.) modulación de frecuencia.

foal, n. potro, m., potra, f.; **—,** vt. y vi. parir una yegua.

foam, n. espuma, f.; **— rubber,** hule espuma, m.; **—,** vi. hacer espuma.

foamy, adj. espumoso.

fob, n. faltriquera pequeña; leopoldina, cadena de reloj; **to — off,** colar.

f.o.b., F.O.B.: free on board, L.A.B. libre a bordo o f.a.b. franco a bordo.

focal, adj. focal.

focus, n. foco, m., punto céntrico; enfoque, m.; **—,** vt. enfocar.

fodder, n. forraje, m., pastura, f.

foe, n. adversario, ria, enemigo, ga.

fog, n. niebla, neblina, f.

foggy, adj. nebuloso, brumoso.

foghorn, n. (naut.) sirena, f.; pito de los buques.

foible, n. debilidad, f., lado flaco.

foil, vt. vencer; frustrar; **—,** n. fracaso, m.; hoja (de estaño), f.; florete, m.

foist, vt. insertar (subrepticiamente); vender con engaño, colar.

fold, n. redil, aprisco, m.; plegadura, f., doblez, m.; **—,** vt. apriscar el ganado; plegar, doblar.

folder, n. plegador, m., plegadera, f.; carpeta, f.

folding, n. plegadura, f.; **— bed,** catre de tijera o de campaña; cama plegadiza; **— chair,** silla de tijera, silla plegadiza.

foliage, n. follaje, ramaje, m.

folio, n. folio, infolio, m., libro en folio.

folk, n. grupo de personas que forman una nación; gente, f.; **common —,** gente común y corriente; **— music,** música folklórica o tradicional; **— song,** canto folklórico; **— tale,** cuento tradicional o folklórico.

folklore, n. folklore, m.

follow, vt. seguir; acompañar; imitar; **—,** vi. seguirse, resultar, provenir.

follower, n. seguidor, ra; imitador, ra; secuaz, m. y f.; partidario, ria; adherente, m. y f.; discípulo, la; compañero, ra.

following, n. séquito, cortejo, m.; profesión, f.; **—,** adj. próximo, siguiente.

follow-up, adj. que sigue; **— letter,** carta recordatoria, carta que confirma una anterior.

folly, *n.* extravagancia, *f.;* bobería, *f.;* temeridad, *f.;* vicio, *m.*

foment, *vt.* fomentar; proteger.

fond, *adj.* afectuoso; aficionado; demasiado indulgente; **to be — of,** aficionarse, tener simpatía por; **—ly,** *adv.* cariñosamente.

fondant, *n.* pasta de azúcar que sirve de base a muchos confites.

fondle, *vt.* mimar, hacer caricias.

fondness, *n.* afecto, *m.;* afición, *f.;* indulgencia, *f.;* bienquerencia, *f.*

font, *n.* pila bautismal; fundición, *f.*

food, *n.* alimento, *m.;* comida, *f.;* **—s,** comestibles, *m. pl.,* viandas, *f. pl .*

foodstuffs, *n. pl.* productos alimenticios.

fool, *n.* loco, ca, tonto, ta, bobo, ba; bufón, ona; mentecato, ta; **—,** *vt.* engañar; infatuar; **—,** *vi.* tontear.

foolhardy, *adj.* temerario, atrevido.

foolish, *adj.* bobo, tonto, majadero; **—ly,** *adv.* bobamente, sin juicio.

foolishness, *n.* tontería, *f.*

foolproof, *adj.* muy evidente, seguro, fácil hasta para un tonto.

foot, *n.* pie, *m.;* pezuña (de vacas, cabras, etc.), *f ;* base, *f.;* extremo, final, *m.;* pie (medida), *m.;* paso, *m.;* **— soldier,** soldado de infantería; **on —, by —,** a pie; **square —,** pie cuadrado; **—,** *vi.* bailar, saltar, brincar; ir a pie; **—,** *vt.* pasar, caminar por encima; **to — the bill,** (coll.) pagar la cuenta.

foot-and-mouth disease, *n.* fiebre aftosa.

football, *n.* fútbol, *m.*

footbridge, *n.* puente para peatones.

footfall, *n.* pisada, *f.;* ruido de pasos.

footgear, *n.* calzado, *m.*

foothill, *n.* cerro al pie de una sierra.

foothold, *n.* espacio en que cabe el pie; apoyo, *m.;* afianzamiento, *m.*

footing, *n.* base, *f ;* pisada, *f ;* paso, *m.;* estado, *m.;* condición, *f.;* fundamento, *m.;* afianzamiento *m.*

footlights, *n. pl.* luces del proscenio; (fig.) el teatro, *m.,* las tablas, *f. pl.*

footman, *n.* lacayo, *m.;* volante, *m.;* criado de librea.

footmark, *n.* huella, *f.*

footnote, *n.* anotación, *f.;* glosa, *f.;* nota, *f.;*

footpath, *n.* senda para peatones.

footprint, *n.* huella, pisada, *f.;* vestigio, *m.*

footrace, *n.* corrida, carrera, *f.*

footrest, *n.* apoyo para los pies, escabel, *m.*

footsore, *adj.* despeado, con los pies lastimados.

footstep, *n.* vestigio, *m.;* huella, *f.;* paso, *m.;* pisada, *f.*

footstool, *n.* escabel, *m.,* banquillo para los pies.

footwear, *n.* calzado, *m.*

footwork, *n.* manejo de los pies en boxeo, en el fútbol, etc.; trabajo de periodista recogiendo noticias.

for, *prep.* para; por; **—,** *conj.* porque, pues; **as — me,** en cuanto a mí; **what —?** ¿para qué?

forage, *n.* forraje, *m.;* **—,** *vt.* forrajear; saquear.

foray, *n.* correría, *f.;* saqueo, *m.;* **—,** *vt.* saquear.

forbear, *vt.* y *vi.* cesar, detenerse; abstenerse; reprimirse.

forbearance, *n.* paciencia, *f.;* indulgencia, *f.;* longanimidad, *f.*

forbid, *vt.* prohibir, vedar; impedir; **God —!** ¡ni lo quiera Dios!

forbidden, *adj.* prohibido.

forbidding, *adj.* que prohibe; **repugnante;** formidable, que infunde respeto.

force, *n.* fuerza, *f.;* poder, vigor, *m.;* valor, *m.;* **—s,** tropas, *f. pl.;* **to be in —,** regir; **with full —,** de plano, en pleno vigor; **—,** *vt.* forzar, violentar; esforzar; obligar; constreñir; **to — one's way,** abrirse el paso.

forced, *adj.* forzoso; forzado, estirado; **— landing,** (avi.) aterrizaje forzoso.

forceful, *adj.* fuerte, poderoso; dominante.

forceps, *n. pl.* fórceps, *m. pl.;* pinzas, *f. pl.*

forcible, *adj.* fuerte, eficaz, poderoso, enérgico; **—bly,** *adv.* con energía.

ford, *n.* vado, *m.;* **—,** *vt.* vadear.

fore, *adj.* anterior; (naut.) de proa; **—,** prefijo que denota anterioridad, por ej., **forerunner,** precursor, *m.*

forearm, *n.* antebrazo, *m.;* **—,** *vt.* armar con anticipación.

forebears, *n. pl.* antepasados, *m. pl.*

forebode, *vt.* y *vi.* pronosticar, presagiar.

foreboding, *n.* corazonada, *f.;* pronóstico, *m.*

forecast, *vt.* y *vi.* proyectar, prever; conjeturar de antemano; **—,** *n.* previsión, *f.;* profecía, *f.;* **weather —,** pronóstico del tiempo.

forecastle, *n.* (naut.) castillo de proa.

foreclose, *vt.* entablar, decidir un juicio hipotecario.

foreclosure, *n.* exclusión, *f.;* juicio hipotecario.

forefather, *n.* abuelo, antecesor, antepasado, *m.*

forefinger, *n.* dedo índice.

forefoot, *n.* pata delantera de un animal.

forefront, *n.* primera fila; parte delantera.

forego, *vt.* ceder, abandonar, renunciar a;

preceder.

foregoing, adj. anterior, precedente.

foregone, adj. pasado; anticipado, prede-
terminado; previo.

foreground, n. delantera, f.; primer plano.

forehanded, adj. temprano; oportuno; prudente, frugal.

forehead, n. frente, f.

foreign, adj. extranjero; extraño.

foreign-born, adj. nacido en el extranjero.

foreigner, n. extranjero, ra, forastero, ra.

foreleg, n. pata o pierna delantera.

forelock, n. mechón de cabello que cae
sobre la frente.

foreman, n. presidente del jurado; jefe,
capataz, m.

foremost, adj. delantero, primero; —, adv.
en primer lugar.

forenoon, n. la mañana, f., las horas antes
del mediodía.

forensic, adj. forense.

foreordain, vt. predestinar, preordinar.

forepaw, n. pata delantera.

forequarter, n. cuarto delantero (de un
animal).

forerunner, n. precursor, ra; predecesor,
ra.

foresail, n. (naut.) trinquete, m.

foresee, vt. prever.

foreshadow, vt. pronosticar, prefigurar.

foreshorten, vt. escorzar (en dibujo).

foresight, n. previsión, f.; presciencia, f.

foresighted, adj. perspicaz, previsor, precavido.

forest, n. bosque, m.; selva, f.

forestall, vt. anticipar; obstruir, impedir;
monopolizar.

forestation, n. silvicultura, forestación, f.

forester, n. guardabosque, m.

forestry, n. silvicultura, f.

foretaste, vt. probar con anticipación; —,
n. prueba de antemano; goce anticipado.

foretell, vt. predecir, profetizar.

forethought, n. providencia, f.; premeditación, f.

forever, adv. por siempre, para siempre.

forevermore, adv. por siempre jamás.

forewarn, vt. prevenir de antemano.

foreword, n. advertencia, f.; prefacio, prólogo, preámbulo, m.

forfeit, n. multa, f.; confiscación, f.; prenda, f.; —, vt. confiscar, decomisar; perder; pagar una multa.

forge, n. fragua, f.; fábrica de metales; —,
vt. forjar; contrahacer; inventar; falsear;
falsificar.

forger, n. forjador, m.; falsario, ria; falsificador, ra.

forgery, n. falsificación, f.; forjadura, f.

forget, vt. olvidar; descuidar.

forgetful, adj. olvidadizo; descuidado.

forgetfulness, n. olvido, m.; negligencia, f.

forget-me-not, n. (bot.) nomeolvides,
miosota, f.

forgive, vt. perdonar.

forgiveness, n. perdón, m.

forgiving, adj. misericordioso, clemente,
que perdona.

forgot, pretérito del verbo **forget.**

forgotten, p.p. del verbo **forget.**

fork, n. tenedor, m.; horca, f.; —, vi. bifurcarse; —, vt. ahorquillar; **to — out,**
(coll.) dar, entregar.

forked, adj. bifurcado.

fork-lift truck, n. carretilla elevadora.

forlorn, adj. abandonado, perdido; desdichado, triste.

form, n. forma, f.; esqueleto, modelo, m.;
modo, m.; formalidad, f.; método, m.;
molde, m.; patrón, m.; **— letter,** carta
circular, carta general; **in proper —,** en
forma debida; —, vt. formar, configurar;
idear, concebir; —, vi. formarse.

formal, adj. formal, metódico; ceremonioso; **— dance,** baile de etiqueta.

formality, n. formalidad, f.; ceremonia, f.
format, n. formato, m.

formation, n. formación, f.; **— flying,** vuelo
en formación.

formative, adj. formativo.

former, adj. precedente; anterior, pasado;
previo; **the —,** aquél; **—ly,** adv. antiguamente, en tiempos pasados, en otro
tiempo.

formidable, adj. formidable, temible.

formless, adj. informe, disforme.

formula, n. fórmula, f.

formulate, vt. formular, articular.

formulation, n. formulación, f.

forsake, vt. dejar, abandonar.

forsaken, adj. desamparado, abandonado.

fort, n. castillo, m.; fortaleza, f.; fuerte, m.;
small —, fortín, m.

forth, adv. en adelante; afuera; **and so —,**
y así sucesivamente, etcétera.

forthcoming, adj. próximo, pronto a comparecer.

forthright, adj. directo; franco; —, adv.
directamente adelante; con franqueza;
inmediatamente.

forthwith, adv. inmediatamente, sin tardanza.

fortieth, n. y adj. cuadragésimo, m.

fortification, n. fortificación, f.

fortify, vt. fortificar; corroborar.

fortissimo, adj. y adv. (mus.) fortísimo.

fortitude, n. fortaleza, f.; valor, m., fortitud, f.

fortnight, *n.* quincena, *f.*, quince días, dos semanas; —**ly,** *adj.* quincenal; —**ly,** *adv.* cada quince días.

fortress, *n.* (mil.) fortaleza, *f.*; castillo, *m.*

fortunate, *adj.* afortunado, dichoso; —**ly,** *adv.* felizmente, por fortuna.

fortune, *n.* fortuna, *f.*; suerte, *f.*; condición, *f.*; bienes de fortuna.

fortuneteller, *n.* sortílego, ga, adivino, na.

forty, *n.* y *adj.* cuarenta, *m.*

forum, *n.* foro, tribunal, *m.*

forward, *adj.* anterior, delantero; precoz; atrevido; pronto, activo, dispuesto; — **pass** (fútbol) lance de la pelota en dirección del equipo contrario; —, *n.* delantero (en Rugby, básquetbol); —, *adv.* adelante, más allá; hacia adelante; —, *vt.* expedir, trasmitir, enviar más adelante.

forwards, *adv.* adelante.

fossil, *adj.* y *n.* fósil, *m.*

foster, *vt.* criar, nutrir; alentar; —, *adj.* allegado; — **brother,** hermano de leche; — **child,** hijo de leche, hijo adoptivo; — **father,** padre adoptivo, el que cría y enseña a un hijo ajeno; — **mother,** madre adoptiva.

foul, *adj.* sucio, puerco; impuro, detestable; — **ball,** pelota que cae fuera del primer o tercer ángulo del diamante de béisbol; — **play,** conducta falsa y pérfida; —, *n.* violación de reglas.

found, *vt.* fundar, establecer; edificar; fundir; basar; —, *pretérito* y *p.p.* del verbo **find.**

foundation, *n.* fundación, *f.*; cimiento, fundamento, *m.*; pie, *m.*; fondo, *m.*

founder, *n.* fundador, ra; fundidor, *m.*; —, *vi.* (naut.) irse a pique; caerse; tropezar.

founding, *n.* establecimiento, *m.*

foundling, *n.* niño expósito.

foundry, *n.* fundición, *f.*

fountain, *n.* fuente, *f.*; manantial, *m.*; — **pen,** plumafuente, estilográfica, *f.*, pluma estilográfica.

fountainhead, *n.* origen, *m.*; fuente, *f.*

four, *n.* y *adj.* cuatro, *m.*; — **o'clock,** las cuatro; **on all —s,** a gatas.

four-footed, *adj.* cuadrúpedo.

fourteen, *n.* y *adj.* catorce, *m.*

fourteenth, *n.* y *adj.* decimocuarto, *m.*

fourth, *n.* y *adj.* cuarto, *m.*; —**ly,** *adv.* en cuarto lugar.

fowl, *n.* ave., *f.*

fox, *n.* zorra, *f.*, zorro, *m.*

foxglove, *n.* (bot.) dedalera, digital, *f.*

foxhole, *n.* hoyo protector para uno o dos soldados.

foxhound, *n.* perro zorrero.

foxy, *adj.* zorruno; astuto.

foyer, *n.* salón de descanso o espera (en un teatro, hotel, etc.).

fraction, *n.* fracción, *f.*

fractional, *adj.* fraccionario.

fracture, *n.* fractura, confracción, rotura, *f.*; —, *vt.* fracturar, romper.

fragile, *adj.* frágil; débil, deleznable.

fragment, *n.* fragmento, trozo, *m.*

fragrance, *n.* fragancia, *f.*

fragrant, *adj.* fragante, oloroso; —**ly,** *adv.* con fragancia.

frail, *adj.* frágil, débil.

frailty, *n.* fragilidad, *f.*; debilidad, *f.*

frame, *n.* marco, cerco, *m.*; bastidor, *m.*; armazón, *f.*; telar, *m.*; cuadro de vidriera; estructura, *f.*; figura, forma, *f.*, cuerpo, *m.*; forjadura, *f.*; — **of mind,** estado de ánimo; **embroidery —,** bastidor, *m.*; **structural —,** armazón, *f.*; —, *vt.* fabricar, componer; construir, formar; ajustar; idear; poner en bastidor; enmarcar, encuadrar; (coll.) incriminar fraudulentamente; prefijar el resultado (de un concurso, etc.).

framework, *n.* labor hecha en el bastidor o telar; armazón, *f.*

France, Francia, *f.*

franchise, *n.* franquicia, inmunidad, *f.*; privilegio, *m.*

frank, *adj.* franco, liberal, campechano; — **ly,** *adv.* francamente, abiertamente.

frankfurter, *n.* salchicha, *f.*

frankness, *n.* franqueza, ingenuidad, *f.*, candor, *m.*

frantic, *adj.* frenético, furioso.

frappé, *n.* bebida a base de hielo triturado.

fraternal, *adj.* fraternal.

fraternity, *n.* fraternidad, *f.*

fraternize, *vt.* y *vi.* fraternizar, confraternar.

fraud, *n.* fraude, engaño, *m.*

fraudulent, *adj.* fraudulento.

fraught, *adj.* cargado, lleno.

fray, *n.* riña, disputa, querella, *f.*; —, *vt.* y *vi.* estregar; romper, romperse; desgastar, desgastarse.

freak, *n.* fantasía, *f.*; capricho, *m.*; monstruosidad, *f.*

freakish, *adj.* extravagante, estrambótico.

freckle, *n.* peca, *f.*

freckled, *adj.* pecoso.

free, *adj.* libre; liberal; franco, ingenuo; exento, dispensado, privilegiado; gratuito, gratis; — **enterprise,** empresa libre, iniciativa privada; — **lance,** aventurero, ra; persona que escribe para alguna publicación o trabaja para alguna empresa sin contrato u obligación especial; — **on rail,** franco sobre vagón; —

port, puerto franco o libre; **— thought,** libre pensamiento (esp. en religión); **— trade,** libre cambio; **— trader,** libre cambista; **— verse** verso suelto o libre; **— will,** libre albedrío; voluntariedad, *f.;* **—,** *vt.* libertar; librar; eximir.

freeborn, *adj.* nacido libre; adecuado para el que ha nacido libre.

freedom, *n.* libertad, *f.;* soltura, *f.;* inmunidad, *f.;* **— of speech,** libertad de palabra; **— of the press,** libertad de prensa.

free fall, *n.* caída incontrolada.

free-for-all, *n.* (coll.) contienda general; pelotera, *f.;* certamen en que todos pueden participar.

freehand, *adj.* hecho a pulso, sin instrumentos.

freehanded, *adj.* liberal, generoso.

freeman, *n.* hombre libre; ciudadano, *m.*

free-spoken, *adj.* dicho sin reserva.

freethinker, *n.* librepensador, ra.

freeway, *n.* autopista de acceso limitado.

freewill, *adj.* espontáneo, voluntario.

freeze, *vi.* helar, helarse; **—,** *vt.* helar, congelar.

freezer, *n.* congelador, *m.,* congeladora, *f.*

freezing, *n.* congelación, *f.;* **— point,** punto de congelación.

freight, *n.* carga, *f.;* flete, *m.;* conducción, *f.;* porte, *m.;* **— car,** furgón, *m.,* vagón de mercancías o de carga; **— house,** embarcadero de mercancías; **—,** *vt.* (naut.) fletar; cargar.

freighter, *n.* fletador, cargador, *m.*

French, *adj.* francés, esa; **— doors,** puertas vidrieras dobles; **— language,** francés, *m.;* **— leave,** despedida a la francesa, despedida precipitada o secreta; **— dressing,** salsa francesa (para ensaladas); **— horn,** (mus.) corno francés, *m.;* **the —,** *n. pl.* los franceses, *m. pl.*

Frenchman, *n.* francés, *m.*

frenzied, *adj.* loco, delirante.

frenzy, *n.* frenesí, *m.;* locura, *f.*

frequency, *n.* frecuencia, *f.;* **— modulation,** modulación de frecuencia; **high —,** alta frecuencia.

frequent, *adj.* frecuente; **—ly,** *adv.* con frecuencia, frecuentemente; **—,** *vt.* frecuentar.

fresco, *n.* pintura al fresco.

fresh, *adj.* fresco; nuevo, reciente; **— water,** agua dulce.

freshen, *vt.* refrescar.

freshman, *n.* estudiante de primer año en la escuela superior o universidad; novicio, cia, novato, ta.

freshness, *n.* frescura, *f.,* frescor, *m.;* (fig.) descaro, *m.*

fresh-water, *adj.* de agua dulce.

fret, *n.* enojo, *m.;* irritación, *f.;* **—,** *vt.* frotar; corroer; cincelar; irritar; enojar; **—,** *vi.* quejarse; enojarse.

fretful, *adj.* enojadizo, colérico; **—ly,** *adv.* de mala gana.

friar, *n.* fraile, fray, *m.*

fricassee, *n.* fricasé, *m.*

friction, *n.* fricción, rozadura, *f.*

Friday, *n.* viernes, *m.;* **Good F—,** Viernes Santo.

fried, *adj.* frito; **— potato,** patata o papa frita.

friend, *n.* amigo, ga; **to be close —s,** ser uña y carne; **to make —s,** trabar amistad, hacerse amigos.

friendless, *adj.* sin amigos.

friendliness, *n.* amistad, benevolencia, bondad, *f.*

friendly, *adj.* amigable, amistoso.

friendship, *n.* amistad, *f.*

frier = **fryer.**

fright, *n.* susto, espanto, pánico, terror, *m.*

frighten, *vt.* espantar; **to — away,** remontar, ahuyentar; espantar.

frightful, *adj.* espantoso, horrible.

frigid, *adj.* frío, frígido; **— zone,** zona glacial; **—ly,** *adv.* fríamente.

frill, *n.* faralá, volante, vuelo *m.;* (coll.) adorno excesivo; ostentación en el vestir, en los modales, etc.

fringe, *n.* fleco, *m.;* franja, *f.;* **—s,** cenefas, *f. pl.;* borde, *m.;* **—,** *vt.* guarnecer con franjas; adornar con flecos.

frisk, *vi.* saltar, cabriolar; **—,** *n.* brinco, *m.*

frisky, *adj.* retozón; alegre.

fritter, *n.* fritura, *f.;* trozo, fragmento, *m.;* **—,** *vt.* desmenuzar; desperdiciar.

frivolity, *n.* frivolidad, *f.;* pamplinada, *f.*

frivolous, *adj.* frívolo, vano.

frizzle, *vt.* rizar, encrespar.

fro, *adv.* atrás; **to go to and —,** ir *y* venir.

frock, *n.* toga, túnica, *f.,* sayo, *m.;* vestido, *m.;* **— coat,** casaca, *f.,* levitón, *m.*

frog, *n.* rana, *f.*

frogman, *n.* hombre rana, *m.*

frolic, *n.* alegría, *f.;* travesura, *f.;* fiesta, *f.;* **—,** *vi.* retozar, juguetear.

frolicsome, *adj.* juguetón, travieso.

from, *prep.* de; después; desde; **— now on,** en lo sucesivo, desde ahora en adelante.

front, *n.* frente, *f.;* frontispicio, *m.;* portada, *f.;* faz, *f.;* cara, *f.;* **labor —,** frente obrero; **— door,** puerta de entrada; **— seat,** asiento delantero; **in —,** enfrente; **in — of,** delante de; **—,** *vt.* hacer frente; **—,** *vi.* dar cara.

frontage, *n.* extensión frontera; prolongación lineal de frente.

frontal, *n.* banda en la frente; frontal, *m.;* —, *adj.* frontal.

frontier, *n.* frontera, *f.*

frontispiece, *n.* frontispicio, *m.;* portada,

frost, *n.* helada, *f.;* hielo, *m.;* escarcha, *f.;* frialdad de temperamento, austeridad, *f.; (coll.)* indiferencia, *f.;* —, *vt.* congelar; cubrir (un pastel o torta) con una capa azucarada.

frostbitten, *adj.* helado, quemado del hielo.

frosted, *adj.* garapiñado.

frosting, *n.* capa azucarada (para adornar pasteles o tortas), (Mex.) betún, *m.*

frosty, *adj.* helado, frío como el hielo.

froth, *n.* espuma (de algún líquido), *f.;* —, *vt.* y *vi.* espumar.

frown, *vt.* mirar con ceño; —, *vi.* fruncir el entrecejo; —, *n.* ceño; enojo, *m.;* mala cara.

froze, *pretérito* del verbo **freeze.**

frozen, *adj.* helado; congelado; — **foods,** alimentos congelados; —, *p.p.* del verbo **freeze.**

frugal, *adj.* frugal; económico; sobrio.

fruit, *n.* fruto, ta; producto, *m.;* **candied** —, fruta azucarada; — **stand,** puesto de frutas; — **store,** frutería, *f.;* — **sugar,** fructosa, *f.;* — **tree,** frutal, *m.*

fruitcake, *n.* pastel de frutas.

fruitful, *adj.* fructífero, fértil; provechoso; útil; —**ly,** *adv.* fructuosamente.

fruition, *n.* fruición, *f.,* goce, *m.*

fruitless, *adj.* estéril; inútil; infructuoso.

frump, *n.* mujer desaliñada y regañona.

frumpy, *adj.* desaliñado, descuidado en el vestir; malhumorado, regañón.

frustrate, *vt.* frustrar; anular.

frustration, *n.* contratiempo, chasco, malogro, *m.*

fry, *vt.* freír.

fryer, *n.* pollo para freír.

frying pan, *n.* sartén: *f.*

ft.: **foot, feet, pie,** pies (medida).

fuchsia, *n.* (bot.) fucsia, *f.;* color fucsia.

fudge, *n.* variedad de dulce de chocolate; cuento, embuste, *m.;* —! *interj.* ¡que va! (exclamación que indica desdén o menosprecio) .

fuel, *n.* combustible, *m.;* — **gauge,** indicador de combustible; — **tank,** depósito de combustible; — **oil,** aceite combustible.

fugitive, *n.* y *adj.* fugitivo, va, prófugo, ga.

fulfill, *vt.* colmar; cumplir, realizar.

fulfillment, *n.* cumplimiento, *m.,* realización, *f.*

full, *adj.* lleno, repleto, completo; cumplido; pleno; todo; perfecto; cargado; — **dress,** traje de etiqueta; — **moon,** luna llena, plenilunio, *m.;* **in** — **swing,** en plena actividad; — **scale,** tamaño natural; —, *n.* total, *m.;* —, *adv.* enteramente, del todo.

full-fashioned, *adj.* entallado con amplitud.

full-fledged, *adj.* maduro, con todos los derechos.

full-grown, *adj.* desarrollado, crecido, maduro.

full-length, *adj.* a todo el largo natural; de cuerpo entero; de largo metraje.

fullness, *n.* plenitud, llenura, abundancia, *f.*

fully, *adv.* enteramente; a fondo.

fumble, *vt.* y *vi.* tartamudear; chapucear; andar a tientas.

fume, *n.* humo, vapor, *m.;* cólera, *f* ; —, *vt.* ahumar; —, *vi.* humear, exhalar; encolerizarse.

fumigate, *vt.* fumigar.

fuming, *adj.* humeante.

fun, *n.* chanza, burla, *f.;* chasco *m.;* diversión, *f.;* **to make** — **of,** burlarse de; **to have** —, divertirse.

function, *n.* función, *f.;* empleo, *m.;* —. vi. funcionar.

functional, *adj.* funcional.

functionary, *n.* empleado, *m.;* oficial, funcionario, *m.*

functioning, *n.* funcionamiento, *m.*

fund, *n.* fondo (de dinero), *m.;* —, *vt..* colocar en un fondo.

fundamental, *adj.* fundamental, básico, cardinal; —**ly,** *adv.* fundamentalmente.

funeral, *n.* y *adj.* funeral, *m.;* — **car,** carroza, *f* ; — **director,** director de pompas fúnebres; — **parlor,** casa mortuoria, agencia de inhumaciones o funeraria.

fungus, *n.* hongo, *m.;* seta, *f.;* fungosidad,

funnel, *n.* embudo, *m.;* cañón (de chimenea), *m.;* (naut.) chimenea, *f.*

funny, *adj.* burlesco, bufón; cómico; — **papers** o **funnies,** historietas cómicas, (Mex.) monitos, *m. pl.;* **to strike as** —, hacer gracia.

fur, *n.* piel (para abrigos), *f.;* —, *adj.* hecho de pieles; — **coat,** abrigo de pieles.

furious, *adj.* furioso, frenético, sañoso; —**ly,** *adv.* con furia.

furl, *vt.* enrollar (una bandera, etc.) ; (naut.) aferrar (las velas).

furlong, *n.* estadio (octava parte de una milla), *m.*

furlough, *n.* (mil.) licencia, *f.;* permiso, *m.;* —, *vt.* conceder un permiso o licencia (a un soldado, etc.).

furnace, *n.* horno, *m.;* hornaza, *f.;* **blast** —, alto horno o de cuba; **open-hearth** — horno Siemens Martin; **hot-air** —, calorífero de aire caliente.

furnish, vt. suplir, proporcionar, surtir, proveer; deparar; equipar; **to — a house,** amueblar una casa.

furnished, adj. amueblado.

furnishings, n. pl. mobiliario, m.; accesorios, avíos, m. pl.

furniture, n. ajuar, mueblaje, mobiliario, m., muebles m. pl.; **— set,** juego de muebles; **piece of —,** mueble, m.

furor, n. rabia, f.; —, entusiasmo, m.

furred, adj. forrado o cubierto de piel.

furrier, n. peletero, m.

furrow, n. surco, m.; —, vt. y vi. surcar; estriar.

furry, adj. parecido a la piel; hecho o guarnecido de pieles.

further, adj. ulterior, más distante; —, adv. más lejos, más allá; aún; además de eso; —, vt. adelantar, promover, ayudar, impulsar, fomentar.

furthermore, adv. además.

furthest, adj. y adv. más lejos, más remoto.

furtive, adj. furtivo; secreto; **to look at — ly,** mirar de reojo.

fury, n. furor, m.; furia, f.; ira, f.

fuse, n. cohete, m.; (elec.) fusible, m.; detonador, m.; mecha f.; espoleta, f.; **— box,** caja de fusibles; —, vt. y vi. fundir; derretirse.

fuselage, n. fuselaje, m.

fusion, n. fusión, licuación, f.

fuss, n. (coll.) alboroto, tumulto, m.; —, vi. preocuparse por pequeñeces; —, vt. (coll.) molestar con pequeñeces.

fussbudget, n. persona molestosa y exigente.

fussy, adj. melindroso; exigente.

futile, adj. fútil, vano; frívolo.

futility, n. futilidad, vanidad, f.

future, adj. futuro, venidero; —, n. lo futuro, el tiempo venidero, porvenir; **in the —,** en adelante, en lo sucesivo.

fuzz, n. tamo, m., pelusa, f.

fuzzy, adj. velloso.

G

Ga.: Georgia, Georgia (E.U.A.)

gab, n. (coll.) locuacidad, f.; —, vi. (coll.) charlar locuazmente.

gabardine, n. gabardina, f.; **— coat,** gabán, m., gabardina, f.

gabble, vi. charlar, parlotear; —, n. algarabía, f.

gable, n. socarrén, alero, m.

gad, vi. tunar, corretear, callejear; —, n. aguijón, m.; cuña, f.

gadfly, n. tábano, m.

gadget, n. baratija, chuchería, f.; utensilio, aparato, m.; pieza (de máquina), f;

gag, n. mordaza, f.; (coll.) expresión aguda y jocosa; —, vt. tapar la boca con mordaza.

gaiety, n. alegría, f.

gaily, adv. alegremente.

gain, n. ganancia, f.; interés, provecho, beneficio, m.; —, vt. ganar; conseguir; —, vi. enriquecerse; avanzar.

gainful, adj. ventajoso, lucrativo.

gainsay, vt. contradecir; prohibir.

gait, n. marcha; f.; porte, m.

gaiter, n. polaina, f.; borceguí, m.

gala, adj. de gala, de fiesta.

galaxy, n. galaxia, f., vía láctea; **— of stars,** congregación de artistas prominentes.

gale, n. (naut.) ventarrón, m.; **—s of laughter,** risotadas, f. pl.

gall, n. hiel, f.; rencor, odio, m.; **— bladder,** vesícula biliar; —, vt. rozar, ludir; irritar, atosigar.

gallant, adj. galante, elegante; gallardo; valeroso; —, n. galán, m.; cortejo, m.

gallantry, n. galantería, gallardía, f.; bravura, f.

gallery, n. galería, f.; corredor, m.

galley, n. (naut.) galera, f.; **— proof,** (print.) galerada, f.; primera prueba.

gallon, n. galón (medida), m.

gallop, n. galope, m.; —, vi. galopar.

gallows, n. horca, f.

gallstone, n. cálculo biliario.

galosh, n. galocha (generalmente de goma o caucho), f., bota de hule, etc. (para la nieve).

galvanize, vt. galvanizar.

gamble, vi. jugar por dinero; —, vt. aventurar.

gambler, n. tahúr, ra, jugador, ra.

gambling, n. juego por dinero; —, adj. de juego; **— house,** garito, m., casa de juego, casino, m.

gambol, n. cabriola, f.; —, vi. brincar, saltar.

game, n. juego, m.; pasatiempo, m.; partida de juego; burla, f.; caza, f.; **— warden,** guardabosque, m.; —, vi. jugar.

gamecock, n. gallo de pelea.
gamekeeper, n. guardabosque, m.
gamma, n. gama; — **globulin,** globulina gamma; — **rays,** rayos gamma.
gamut, n. escala, gama, serie, f.
gander, n. ánsar, ganso, m.; simplón, papanatas, m.
gang, n. cuadrilla, banda, pandilla, patrulla f.; — **plow,** arado de reja múltiple.
ganglion, n. ganglio m.
gangplank, n. plancha, f.
gangrene, n. gangrena, f.; —, vt. y vi. gangrenar, gangrenarse.
gangster, n. rufián, m.
gangway, n. portalón, m.; pasamano de un navío; plancha, f.; andamio, m.; —! interj. ¡háganse a un lado! ¡abran paso!
gantry, n. caballete, portalón, m.
gap, n. boquete, m., brecha, f.; laguna, f.
gape, vi. bostezar, boquear; ansiar, hendirse; estar con la boca abierta.
garage, n. garaje, garage, m., cochera, f.
garb, n. atavío, m.; vestidura, f.; traje, m.; apariencia exterior.
garbage, n. basura, f., desperdicios, m. pl.
garble, vt. entresacar, mutilar engañosamente (una cuenta, etc.).
garden, n. huerto, m.; jardín, m.; **vegetable** —, huerto de hortalizas; —, vi. cultivar un jardín o un huerto.
gardener, n. jardinero, ra.
gardenia, n. (bot.) gardenia, f.
gardening, n. jardinería, f.
gargle, vt. y vi. gargarizar, hacer gárgaras; —, n. gárgara, f., gargarismo, m.
garish, adj. ostentoso y de mal gusto.
garland, n. guirnalda, f.
garlic, n. (bot.) ajo, m.
garment, n. traje, vestido, m.; vestidura, f.
garner, n. granero, m.; —, vt. almacenar (grano, etc.); acopiar.
garnet, n. granate, piropo, m.; (naut.) trinquete, m., cargadera, f.
garnish, vt. guarnecer, adornar, aderezar; —, n. guarnición, f.; adorno, m.
garnishee, n. persona a quien se le embarga el crédito o el sueldo; —, vt. ordenar la retención o embargo de crédito o sueldo.
garret, n. guardilla, f.; desván m.
garrison, n. (mil.) guarnición, f.; fortaleza, f.; —, vt. (mil.) guarnecer.
garrulous, adj. gárrulo, locuaz, charlador.
garter, n. liga, f., cenojil, m.; jarretera, f.
gas, n. gas, m.; **carbonic acid** —, gas carbónico; **chlorine** —, cloro, m.; — **burner,** — **jet,** mechero de gas; — **main,** cañería, f.; alimentadora de gas; — **mask,** mascarilla o careta contra gases asfixiantes; — **meter,** medidor de gas;

— **pedal,** acelerador (de un auto); — **stove,** estufa o cocina de gas.
gaseous, adj. gaseoso.
gash, n. cuchillada, f.; —, vt. dar una cuchillada.
gasket, n. relleno, m., empaquetadura, f.
gasoline, n. gasolina, nafta, f.; — **tank,** depósito o tanque de gasolina.
gasp, vi. boquear; anhelar; —, n. respiración difícil; **last** —, última boqueada.
gaspipe, n. tubería de gas.
gastric, adj. gástrico.
gate, n. puerta, f., portón, m.
gatekeeper, n. portero, ra.
gateway, n. entrada, f., paso, m.; puerta cochera.
gather, vt. recoger, amontonar, **reunir;** fruncir; inferir; arrugar, plegar; —, vi. juntarse; supurar.
gathering, n. reunión, f.; acumulación, f.; colecta, f.
gaudy, adj. brillante, fastuoso.
gauge, gage, n. aforo, m.; graduador, m.; indicador, m.; calibrador, m.; manómetro, m.; calibre, m.; **tire** —, medidor de presión de aire de neumático; —, vt. aforar; calar; calibrar; graduar, medir.
gaunt, adj. flaco, delgado.
gauntlet, n. guantelete, m.; manopla, f.
gauze, pretérito del verbo **give.**
gavel, n. mazo, m., gavilla, f.
gawk, n. majadero, ra; chabacano, na, tonto, ta; —, vi. obrar como un majadero; mirar fijamente como un tonto.
gawky, adj. bobo, tonto, rudo, desgarbado, deslucido.
gay, adj. alegre, festivo; pajarero; **to be** —, estar de buen humor; ser alegre; homosexual.
gaze, vi. contemplar, considerar; —, n. mirada, f.
gazelle, n. gacela, f.
gazette, n. gaceta, f.
G.B.: Great Britain, Gran Bretaña.
gear, n. atavío, m.; aparato, m.; engranaje, encaje, m., trasmisión, f.; — **case,** caja de engranajes; **changing** —**s,** cambio de velocidad, cambio de marcha; **landing** —, tren de aterrizaje; — **wheel,** rueda dentada; **in** —, embragado, en juego; **out of** — desembragado, fuera de juego; **to throw out of** —, desencajar, desmontar, desembragar.
gearshift, n. cambio de velocidad, cambio de marcha; — **lever,** palanca de cambios.
geese, n. pl. de **goose,** gansos, m. pl.
Geiger counter, n. contador Geiger, m.
gelatin, gelatine, n. gelatina, jaletina, f.
gelding, n. caballo capón.
gem, n. joya, f.; piedra, piedra preciosa,

presea, f.
gender, n. (gram.) género, m.
gene, n. (biol.) gen, m.
genealogy, n. genealogía, f.
general, adj. general, común, usual; — delivery, lista de correos; — partnership, sociedad colectiva; —, n. general, m.; in —, por lo común.
generality, n. generalidad, f.
generalization; n. generalización, f.
generalize, vt. generalizar.
generate, vt. engendrar; producir; causar.
generation, n. generación, f.
generator, n. engendrador, dinamo o dínamo, generador, m.
generic, adj. genérico.
generosity, n. generosidad, liberalidad, f.
generous, adj. generoso.
genesis, n. génesis, f., origen, m.
genetics, n. genética, f.
genial, adj. genial, natural; cordial; alegre.
geniality, n. ingenuidad, f.; alegría, f.
genitals, n. pl. órganos genitales.
genitive, n. (gram.) genitivo, m.
genius, n. genio, m.
genocide, n. genocidio, m.
genteel, adj. gentil, elegante.
gentian, n. (bot.) genciana, f.
gentile, n. pagano, na, gentil, m. y f.
Gentile, n. persona no judía.
gentility, n. gentileza, f.; nobleza de sangre.
gentle, adj. suave, dócil, manso, moderado; benigno.
gentleman, n. caballero, gentilhombre, m.; —'s agreement, obligación moral.
gentleness, n. gentileza, f.; dulzura, f., suavidad de carácter; nobleza, f.
gently, adv. suavemente, con dulzura.
genuflection, n. genuflexión, f.
genuine, adj. genuino, puro.
genuineness, n. pureza, f.; sinceridad, f.
genus, n. género, m., clase, especie, f.
geodetic, adj. geodésico.
geographer, n. geógrafo, m.
geographic, geographical, adj. geográfico.
geography, n. geografía, f.
geological, adj. geológico.
geologist, n. geólogo, m.
geology, n. geología, f.
geometric, geometrical, adj. geométrico.
geometry, n. geometría, f.; solid —, geometría del espacio; plane —, geometría plana.
georgette, n. crespón de seda de tejido fino.
geranium, n. (bot.) geranio, m.
geriatrics, n. geriatría, f.
germ, n. germen, m.; microbio, m.; — cell, célula embrional; — plasm, germen

plasma.
German, n. y adj. alemán, ana; — measles, rubéola, f., sarampión benigno.
Germany, Alemania, f.; Germania, f.
germicide, n. bactericida, germicida, m.
germinate, vi. brotar, germinar.
germination, n. germinación, f.
gerund, n. (gram.) gerundio, m.
gestation, n. gestación, preñez, f.
gesticulate, vi. gesticular; to — with the hands, manotear; hacer ademanes.
gesticulation, n. gesticulación, f.
gesture, n. gesto, movimiento, ademán, m.
get, vt. obtener, conseguir, alcanzar, coger; agarrar, robar; persuadir; to go and —, ir a buscar; —, vi. alcanzar; llegar; venir; hacerse, ponerse; prevalecer; introducirse; to — along, ir pasándola; to — away, irse, fugarse, escaparse; to — together, reunirse; to — up, levantarse.
getaway, n. escapada, huida, f.
getup, n. atavío, m.; estructura, f.
geyser, n. géiser, m., surtidor de agua termal.
G-force, n. y adj. grado de aceleración producido por la gravedad.
ghastly, adj. pálido, cadavérico; espantoso.
ghetto, n. ghetto, barrio judío
ghost, n. espectro, m.; espíritu, m.; fantasma, m.; — writer, escritor o escritora cuyos artículos aparecen bajo el nombre de otra persona.
ghostly, adj. espectral, como un espectro.
ghoul, n. vampiro, m.
GI, n. militar, soldado, m.; —, vt. limpiar, frotar.
giant, n. gigante, m.
giantess, n. giganta, f.
gibe, vt. escarnecer; —, vi. burlarse, mofarse; —, n. mofa, burla, f.
giblets, n. pl. despojos y menudillos (de ave), m. pl.
giddiness, n. vértigo, m.; inconstancia, f.
giddy, adj. vertiginoso; inconstante.
gift, n. don, m.; regalo, m.; dádiva, f.; talento, m.; habilidad, f.; presente, obsequio, m.
gifted, adj. hábil, talentoso.
gigantic, adj. gigantesco.
giggle, vi. reírse disimuladamente; reírse nerviosamente y sin motivo; —, n. risilla disimulada o nerviosa.
gigolo, n. gigoló, m.
gild, vt. dorar.
gilding, n. doradura, f.; dorado, m.
gill, n. cuarta parte de una pinta; papada, f.; —s, pl. barbas del gallo; agallas de los peces.
gilt, n. y adj. dorado, m.

gilt-edged, *adj.* con el borde dorado; (coll.) de la mejor calidad.

gin, *n.* desmotadora (de algodón), *f.;* ginebra (bebida alcohólica), *f.;* — **rummy,** cierto juego de naipes; —, *vt.* despepitar (algodón, etc.).

ginger, *n.* jengibre, *m.;* — **ale,** cerveza de jengibre.

gingerbread, *n.* pan de jengibre.

gingerly, *adv.* timidamente, cautelosamente; —, *adj.* cauteloso, cuidadoso.

gingersnap, *n.* galletita de jengibre.

gingham, *n.* zaraza, guinga, *f.*

gingivitis, *n.* (med.) gingivitis, *f.*

gipsy = **gypsy.**

giraffe, *n.* jirafa, *f.*

gird, *vt.* ceñir; cercar; —, *vi.* mofarse.

girder, *n.* viga, *f.*

girdle, *n.* faja, *f.;* cinturón, *m.;* —, *vt.* ceñir.

girl, *n.* muchacha, doncella, niña, *f.;* — **friend,** amiga predilecta, novia potencial; — **guide,** guía, niña guía, *f.;* — **scout,** muchacha exploradora; **young** —, joven, jovencita, *f.*

girlhood, *n.* niñez, doncellez, *f.,* juventud femenina.

girlish, *adj.* juvenil, propio de una joven o de una niña.

girth, *n.* cincha, *f.;* circunferencia, *f.*

gist, *n.* quid, *m.;* punto principal de una acusación.

give, *vt. y vi.* dar, donar, conceder; abandonar; aplicarse; **to** — **account,** dar razón; **to** — **away,** regalar; divulgar; **to** — **back,** retornar; devolver; **to** — **birth,** dar a luz; **to** — **in,** rendirse, ceder; **to** — **up,** renunciar; rendirse; ceder; transigir; darse por vencido; **to** — **leave,** permitir; **to** — **off,** emitir; **to** — **out,** anunciar públicamente; agotarse, **to** — **security,** dar fianza.

give-and-take, *n.* toma y daca; concesiones mutuas; intercambio (de ideas, etc.), *m.*

given, *p.p.* del verbo **give;** — **name,** nombre de pila.

giver, *n.* dador, ra, donador, ra.

gizzard, *n.* molleja, *f.,* papo (de ave), *m.*

glacé, *adj.* garapiñado.

glacier, *n.* glaciar, *m.*

glad, *adj.* alegre, contento; **I am** — **to see,** me alegro de ver; —**ly,** *adv.* con gusto.

gladden, *vt.* alegrar, recrear; regocijar.

gladiator, *n.* gladiador, *m.*

gladiolus, *n.* (bot.) gladiolo, *m.;* gladiola, *f.*

gladness, *n.* alegría, *f.,* regocijo, placer, *m.*

glamor, glamour, *n.* encanto, hechizo, *m.;* elegancia, *f.*

glamorous, *adj.* fascinador, encantador,
seductor, tentador.

glance, *n.* vislumbre, *f.;* vistazo, *m.;* ojeada, *f.;* vista, *f.;* **at first** —, a primera vista; —, *vi.* lanzar miradas; pasar ligeramente.

gland, *n.* glándula, *f.*

glandular, *adj.* glandular, glanduloso.

glare, *n.* deslumbramiento, *m.;* reflejo, *m.;* mirada feroz y penetrante; —, *vi.* relumbrar, brillar; echar miradas de indignación.

glaring, *adj.* deslumbrante; manifiesto; penetrante.

glass, *n.* vidrio, *m.;* vaso para beber; espejo, *m.;* — **blower,** soplador de vidrio; — **case,** vidriera, *f.;* **plate** —, vidrio cilindrado; **water** —, vidrio soluble; —**es,** *n. pl.* anteojos, *m. pl.,* gafas, *f. pl.;* —, *adj.* vítreo, de vidrio.

glassful, *n.* vaso, *m.,* vaso lleno.

glassware, *n.* cristalería, *f.*

glassy, *adj.* vítreo, cristalino, vidrioso.

glaucoma, *n.* (med.) glaucoma, *m.*

glaze, *vt.* vidriar, embarnizar.

glazed, *adj.* vidriado, satinado.

glazing, *n.* vidriado, *m.*

gleam, *n.* claridad, *f.;* brillo, destello, centelleo, *m.*

glean, *vt.* espigar; recoger.

glee, *n.* alegría, *f.;* gozo, *m.;* jovialidad, *f.;* canción sin acompañamiento para tres o más voces; — **club,** coro, *m.*

gleeful, *adj.* alegre, gozoso.

glen, *n.* valle, *m.;* llanura, *f.*

glib, *adj.* de lengua fácil, fluido; —**ly,** *adv.* corrientemente, volublemente; fácilmente.

glide, *vi.* resbalar; pasar ligeramente.

glider, *n.* (aer.) deslizador, planeador, *m.;* hidroplano, hidrodeslizador, *m.*

gliding, *n.* deslizamiento, *m.;* (avi.) planeo, planeamiento, *m.*

glimmer, *n.* vislumbre, *f.;* —, *vi.* vislumbrarse.

glimpse, *n.* vislumbre, *f.;* ojeada, *f.;*—, *vt.* descubrir, percibir.

glint, *n.* reflejo, brillo, *m.*

glisten, *vi.* relucir, brillar; —, *n.* brillo, *m.*

glitter, *vi.* resplandecer, brillar; —, *n.* brillantez, *f.,* brillo, *m.;* ostentación, *f.*

gloat, *vi.* ojear con admiración; deleitarse.

global, *adj.* global.

globalization, *n.* globalización, *f.*

globe, *n.* globo, *m.;* esfera, *f.;* orbe, *m.*

globe-trotter, *n.* trotamundos, *m. y f.,* persona que viaja extensamente.

gloom, *n.* oscuridad, *f.;* melancolía, tristeza, *f.*

gloomy, *adj.* sombrío, oscuro; nublado; triste, melancólico; hosco, tenebroso.

glorify, *vt.* glorificar, celebrar.

glorious, *adj.* glorioso, ilustre.

glory, *n.* gloria, fama, celebridad, *f.;* lauro, *m.;* aureola o auréola, *f.;* —, *vi.* gloriarse, jactarse.

gloss, *n.* glosa, *f.,* escolio, *m.;* lustre, *m.;* —, *vt.* glosar, interpretar; lustrar, barnizar.

glossary, *n.* glosario, *m.*

glossy, *adj.* lustroso, brillante.

glove, *n.* guante, *m.*

glow, *vi.* arder; inflamarse; relucir; —, *n.* fulgor, *m.;* color vivo; viveza de color; vehemencia de una pasión.

glower, *vi.* mirar con ceño o con ira.

glowworm, *n.* luciérnaga, *f.*

glucose, *n.* glucosa, *f.*

glue, *n.* cola, *f.,* sustancia glutinosa; —, *vt.* encolar, pegar.

glum, *adj.* tétrico; de mal humor.

glut, *vt.* hartar, saciar; —, *n.* hartura, sobreabundancia, *f.*

glutinous, *adj.* glutinoso, viscoso.

glutton, *n.* glotón, ona, tragón, ona.

gluttony, *n.* glotonería, *f.*

glycerine, *n.* glicerina, *f.*

gm.: gram, g. gramo.

G-man, *n. (E.U.A.)* miembro de la policía secreta.

gnarled, *adj.* nudoso; enredado.

gnash, *vt.* hacer crujir, hacer rechinar.

gnat, *n.* jején, *m.*

gnaw, *vt.* roer, mordicar.

G.N.P.: gross national product, P.N.B. producto nacional bruto, *m.*

go, *vi.* ir, irse, andar, caminar; partir; correr; pasar; **to — away,** marcharse, salir; **to — astray,** extraviarse; **to — forward,** ir adelante; **to — back,** regresar; remontar a; **to — beyond,** rebasar; trascender, ir más allá; **to— out,** salir; **to — without,** pasarse sin; **— to it!** ¡ vamos! ¡a ello! —, *n.* (coll.) energía, *f.;* actividad, *f.;* espíritu, *m.;* **on the —,** en plena actividad, sin parar, siempre moviéndose.

goad, *n.* aguijada, *f.,* aguijón, *m.;* garrocha, *f.;* —, *vt.* aguijar; estimular, incitar.

goal, *n.* meta, *f ;* fin, *m.;* tanto, gol, *m.;* — **line,** raya de la meta; **— post,** poste de la meta.

goat, *n.* cabra, chiva, *f.;* **he —,** cabrón, *m.*

goatskin, *n.* piel de cabra.

gobble, *vt.* engullir, tragar; —, *vt.* gorgorear como los gallipavos.

gobbledygook, *n.* (coll.) galimatías, *m.,* lenguaje incomprensible y oscuro.

gobbler, *n.* pavo, *m.;* glotón, ona.

go-between, *n.* mediador, ra; entremetido, da.

goblet, *n.* copa, *f.;* cáliz, *m.*

goblin, *n.* duende, *m.*

gocart, *n.* andaderas, *f. pl.,* carretilla, *f.;* cochecito para niños.

God, *n.* Dios, *m.;* **act of —,** fuerza mayor; **— willing,** Dios mediante.

god, *n.* dios, *m.*

godchild, *n.* ahijado, da.

goddaughter, *n.* ahijada, *f.*

goddess, *n.* diosa, *f.*

godfather, *n.* padrino, *m.*

godless, *adj.* infiel, impío, ateo.

godlike, *adj.* divino.

godliness, *n.* piedad, devoción, santidad, *f.*

godly, *adj.* piadoso, devoto, religioso; recto, justificado.

godmother, *n.* madrina, *f.*

godsend, *n.* bendición, *f.,* cosa llovida del cielo.

godson, *n.* ahijado, *m.*

Godspeed, *n.* bienandanza, *f.,* buen viaje.

goes, 3ª *persona del singular* del verbo **go.**

goggle, *vi.* volver los ojos, mirar fijamente.

goggles, *n. pl.* gafas, *f. pl.*

going, *n.* paso, *m.,* andadura, *f.;* partida, *f.;* progreso, *m.;* **—s-on,** (coll.) sucesos, acontecimientos, *m. pl.*

goiter, goitre, *n.* papera, *f.,* coto, bocio, *m.*

gold, *n.* oro, *m.;* **— leaf,** hoja de oro batido; **— mine,** mina de oro; fuente abundante de riqueza; **— standard,** patrón de oro.

goldbrick, *vi.* eludir la responsabilidad o el deber; —, *n.* persona haragana.

golden, *adj.* áureo, de oro; excelente; **— mean,** moderación, *f.,* justo medio; **— rule,** regla áurea; **— wedding,** bodas de oro.

goldenrod, (bot.) solidago, *m.*

gold-filled, *adj.* enchapado en oro.

goldfinch, *n.* (orn.) cardelina, *f.,* jilguero, *m.*

goldfish, *n.* carpa pequeña dorada.

goldsmith, *n.* orífice, orfebre, *m.*

golf, *n.* golf, *m.;* **— club,** palo o bastón o mazo de golf; **— links,** campo de golf, *m.*

golfer, *n.* jugador o jugadora de golf.

golosh = **galosh.**

gone, *adj.* ido; perdido; pasado; gastado; muerto; —, *p.p.* del verbo **go.**

gong, *n.* campana chinesca.

good, *adj.* bueno, buen, benévolo, bondadoso, cariñoso; conveniente, apto; **— cheer,** jovialidad, *f.,* regocijo, *m.;* **— day,** buenos días; **— evening,** buenas tardes, buenas noches; **— humor,** buen humor; **— luck,** buena suerte; **— morning,** buenos días; **— nature,** temperamento agradable, buen carácter; **G—Neighbor Policy,** política de buena vecindad, política del buen vecino; — **night**, buenas noches; — **sense**, sensatez, f.; sentido común, m.; — **turn**, favor, m.; — **will**, buena voluntad, benevolencia, bondad, f.; bienquerencia, f.; (com.) buena reputación; crédito mercantil; **to say — day**, dar los buenos días; —, adv. bien; —, n. bien, m., prosperidad, ventaja, f.; —, interj. ¡bien! ¡está bien! — **news!** ¡ albricias!

good-by, good-bye, n. adiós, m.; —, interj. ¡adiós! ¡hasta luego! ¡hasta después! ¡hasta la vista! ¡vaya con Dios!

good-for-nothing, adj. despreciable, sin valor; —, n. haragán, ana.

goodhearted, adj. bondadoso, de buen corazón.

good-looking, adj. bien parecido, guapo.

goodly, adj. considerable, algo numeroso; agradable.

good-natured, adj. bondadoso; de buen carácter.

goodness, n. bondad, f.

goods, n. pl. bienes muebles, m. pl.; mercaderías, f. pl.; efectos, m. pl.; **household —**, enseres, m. pl.; **straight of —**, hilo (en costura), m.

good-sized, adj. de buen tamaño.

goon, n. rufián al servicio de bandidos o sindicatos con propósitos terroristas.

goose, n. ganso, m.; oca, f.; tonto, ta; — **flesh**, — **pimples**, (fig.) carne de gallina (producida por el frío o miedo).

gooseberry, n. uva espina, grosella, f.

G.O.P.: Grand Old Party (Republican Party), Partido Republicano (E.U.A.).

gopher, n. variedad de mamífero roedor.

gore, n. sangre cuajada; sesga, f.; —, vt. acornar, dar cornadas, cornear.

gorge, n. gorja, gola, garganta, f.; barranco, m.; desfiladero, cañón, m.; —, vt. engullir, tragar.

gorgeous, adj. primoroso, brillante, vistoso; —**ly**, adv. con esplendor y magnificencia.

gorilla, n. (zool.) gorila, f.

gory, adj. cubierto de sangre grumosa; sangriento.

gospel, n. evangelio, m.

gossamer, n. telaraña, f.; tejido muy fino como gasa.

gossip, n. charla, f.; caramillo, m.; chisme, m.; murmuración, comadrería, f.; runrún, m.; —, vi. charlar, murmurar, decir chismes.

got, pretérito y p.p. del verbo **get**.

Gothic, adj. gótico; — **type**, letra gótica.

gouge, n. gubia, gurbia, f.; (coll.) ranura o estría hecha con gubia; (coll.) imposición, f.; impostor, ra; —, vt. escoplear;

sacarle (los ojos a alguien); (coll.) defraudar, engañar.

goulash, n. carne guisada al estilo húngaro.

gourd, n. (bot.) calabaza, f.; calabacera, f.

gout, n. (med.) gota, f.; podagra, f.

govern, vt. y vi. gobernar, dirigir, regir; mandar.

governess, n. aya, institutriz, f.

government, n. gobierno, m.; administración pública; — **bonds**, bonos de gobierno; **municipal —**, ayuntamiento, m.

governmental, adj. gubernativo, gubernamental.

governor, n. gobernador, m.; gobernante, m.; (mech.) regulador, m.; —**'s office**, —**'s mansion**, gobernación, f.

gown, n. toga, f.; vestido de mujer; bata, f.; túnica, f.

G.P.A.: grade point average, promedio de notas, m.

grab, vt. agarrar, arrebatar; —, n. arrebato, m.; cosa arrebatada, gancho para arrancar.

grace, n. gracia, f.; favor, m.; gentileza, f.; merced, f.; perdón, m.; **to say —**, bendecir la mesa; —, vt. adornar; agraciar.

graceful, adj. que tiene gracia; —**ly**, adv. con gracia, elegantemente.

graceless, adj. sin gracia, desagraciado; réprobo, malvado.

gracious, adj. gentil, afable, cortés; —! interj. ¡válgame Dios! —**ly**, adv. con gentileza.

gradation, n. gradación, f.

grade, n. grado, m.; pendiente, f; nivel, m.; categoría, f.; calidad, f.; calificación, f.; — **school**, escuela primaria, **passing —**, aprobado, m.; —, vt. graduar, clasificar.

grader, n. nivelador, ra, explanadora, f.

gradient, n. (rail.) pendiente, contrapendiente, f.; **falling —**, declive, m.

grading, n. nivelación, f.

gradual, adj. gradual.

graduate, vt. graduar; **to be —d**, recibirse, diplomarse; —, n. diplomado, da, graduado, da; recibido, da; (chem.) probeta, f.

graduation, n. graduación, f.

graft, n. injerto, m.; soborno público; —, vt. injertar, ingerir.

graham bread, n. acemita, f.

grain, n. grano, m.; semilla, f.; disposición, índole, f.; cereal, m.; **against the —**, a contrapelo; con repugnancia; — **alcohol**, alcohol de granos.

grained, adj. granulado; áspero; teñido en crudo.

gram, n. gramo (peso), m.

grammar, n. gramática, f.; — school, escuela de primera enseñanza, escuela primaria o elemental.

grammatical, adj. gramatical.

gramophone, n. gramófono, m.

granary, n. granero, m.

grand, adj. grande, ilustre; magnífico, espléndido; — piano, piano de cola, m.; —slam, bola, f.

grandchild, n. nieto, ta.

granddaughter, n. nieta, f.

grandee, n. grande (título de nobleza de España).

grandeur, n. grandeza, f.; pompa, f.

grandfather, n. abuelo, m.

grandiose, adj. grandioso.

grandmother, n. abuela, f.

grandparents, n. pl. abuelos, m. pl.

grandson, n. nieto, m.

grandstand, n. andanada, tribuna, f.

grange, n. granja, f., cortijo, m., casa de labranza.

granger, n. granjero, ra, labriego, ga.

granite, n. granito, m.

grant, vt. conceder; conferir; dar; otorgar; —ing that, supuesto que; to take for — ed, presuponer, dar por sentado; —, n. concesión, f.; subvención, f.

granular, adj. granular, granoso.

granulate, vt. granular.

granulated, adj. granulado.

granule, n. gránulo, m.

grape, n. uva, f.; bunch of —s, racimo de uvas.

grapefruit, n. toronja, f.

grapevine, n. parra, vid, viña, f.; through the —, por vía secreta (aplícase a rumores, etc.).

graph, n. diagrama, m.; gráfico, m.

graphic, adj. gráfico; pintoresco; — arts, artes gráficas; —ally, adv. gráficamente.

graphite, n. grafito, m.

grapple, vt. y vi. agarrar, agarrarse; luchar.

grasp, vt. empuñar, asir, agarrar; comprender; —, vi. esforzarse a agarrar; —, n. puño, puñado, m.; poder, m.

grasping, adj. codicioso.

grass, n. hierba, f.; herbaje, m.; yerba, f., césped, m.; — seed, semilla de césped; — widow, mujer divorciada o separada del marido; mujer cuyo marido está ausente; — widower, hombre divorciado o separado de su esposa.

grasshopper, n. saltamontes, chapulín, m.

grassy, adj. herboso.

grate, n. reja, verja, rejilla, f.; —, vt. rallar; hacer rechinar; enrejar; ofender; irritar.

grateful, adj. grato, agradecido.

grater, n. rallo, raspador, m.

gratification, n. gratificación, f.

gratify, vt. contentar; gratificar; satisfacer.

grating, n. rejado, m.; reja, f.; rejilla, f.; —, adj. áspero; ofensivo.

gratis, adj. gratuito, gratis; —, adv. gratis, de balde.

gratitude, n. gratitud, f., agradecimiento, m.

gratuity, n. propina, f.

grave, n. sepultura, f.; tumba, fosa, f.; —, adj. grave, serio; —ly, adv. con gravedad, seriamente.

gravedigger, n. sepulturero, m.

gravel, n. cascajo, m.; (med.) piedra, f.; mal de piedra; —, vt. cubrir con cascajo; (coll.) desconcertar.

graven, adj. grabado, esculpido.

graver, n. grabador, m.; buril, m.

gravestone, n. piedra sepulcral.

graveyard, n. cementerio, panteón, m.

gravitate, vi. gravitar.

gravitation, n. gravitación, f.

gravity, n. gravedad, f.; seriedad, f

gravy, n. jugo de la carne; salsa, f.; — dish, salsera, f.

gray, adj. gris; cano; —, n. gris, m.

grayish, adj. pardusco; entrecano.

graze, vt. pastorear; tocar ligeramente; to lead (cattle) to —, pastar (el ganado); —, vi. rozar; pacer.

grease, n. grasa, f.; pringue, m.; to remove —, desgrasar; —, vt. untar, engrasar, lubricar.

greasy, adj. grasiento, craso, gordo, mantecoso.

great, adj. gran, grande; principal; ilustre; noble, magnánimo; colosal; revelante; G— Bear, (ast.) Osa Mayor, f.; —ly, adv. muy, mucho; grandemente.

Great Britain, Gran Bretaña, f.

great-grandchild, n. bisnieto, ta.

great-grandparent, n. bisabuelo, la.

greatness, n. grandeza, f.; dignidad, f.; poder, m.; magnanimidad, f.

Grecian, n. y adj. griego, ga.

Greece, Grecia, f.

greed, greediness, n. voracidad, f.; gula, f.; codicia, f.

greedy, adj. voraz, goloso; hambriento; ansioso, deseoso; insaciable.

Greek, n. y adj. griego, ga.

green, adj. verde, fresco, reciente; no maduro; —, n. verde, m.; verdor, m.; llanura verde; —s, n. pl. verduras, f. pl.

greenback, n. papel moneda, m.

green-eyed, adj. ojiverde.

greenhorn, n. joven sin experiencia; neófito, ta; novato, ta.

greenhouse, n. invernáculo, invernadero, m.

greenish, adj. verdoso.

Greenland, Groenlandia, f.

Greenlander, n. y adj. groenlandés, esa.

greens, n. pl. verduras, hortalizas, f. pl.

greet, vt. saludar; —, vi. encontrarse y saludarse.

greeting, n. salutación, f., saludo, m.

gregarious, adj. gregario.

grenade, n. (mil.) granada, f.

grew, pretérito del verbo grow.

grey = gray

greyhound, n. galgo, lebrel, m.

grid, n. parrilla, rejilla, f.; (elec.) soporte de plomo de las placas de acumuladores.

griddle, n. plancha, tartera, parrilla, f.

griddlecake, n. tortilla de harina cocida en una tartera, torta frita.

gridiron, n. parrilla, f.; campo marcado para el juego de fútbol.

grief, n. dolor, m., aflicción, pena, f.; quebranto, m.; congoja, f.

grievance, n. pesar, m.; molestia, f.; agravio, m.; injusticia, f.; perjuicio, m.

grieve, vt. agraviar, afligir; —, vi. afligirse, llorar.

grievous, adj. doloroso; enorme; cargoso; —ly, adv. penosamente; cruelmente.

grill, vt. asar en parrillas; —, n. parrilla, f.

grille, n. enrejado, m., reja, f.

grillroom, n. parrilla, f., comedor que especializa en alimentos a la parrilla.

grim, adj. feo; horrendo; ceñudo; austero.

grimace, n. visaje, m.; mueca, f., mohín, m.

grime, n. mugre, f.; —, vt. ensuciar.

grimness, n. austeridad, severidad, f.

grimy, adj. sucio, manchado.

grin, n. sonrisa franca; —, vi. sonreir abiertamente, sonreírse francamente.

grind, vt. moler; pulverizar; afilar; estregar; mascar.

grinder, n. molinero, ra; molinillo, m.; amolador, m.; muela, f.; piedra molar, piedra de afilar.

grindstone, n. piedra amoladera.

grip, vt. agarrar, empuñar, asir; —, n. maleta, f.

gripe, vt. asir, empuñar; —, vi. padecer cólico; (coll.) lamentarse, quejarse; —s, n. pl. cólico, m.

grippe, n. (med.) gripe, f.; (Mex.) gripa, f.

gripping, adj. emocionante.

grisly, adj. espantoso, horroroso.

grist, n. molienda, f.; provisión, f.

gristle, n. tendón, nervio, cartílago, m.

grit, n. moyuelo, m.; —s, n. pl. maíz, avena o trigo descascarado y molido.

gritty, adj. arenoso.

grizzled, grizzly, adj. mezclado con gris, pardusco.

grizzly bear, n. oso pardo.

groan, vi. gemir, suspirar; dar gemidos; —, n. gemido, suspiro, m.; quejido, m.

grocer, n. especiero, bodeguero, abarrotero, m.

grocery, n. especiería, abacería, f.; bodega, f.; — store, tienda de comestibles, tienda de abarrotes; —ries, comestibles, m. pl.

groggy, adj. mareado o atontado por un golpe (aplícase generalmente a los pugilistas); (coll.) medio borracho.

groom, n. establero, m.; criado, m.; mozo de caballos; novio, m.; —, vt. cuidar; aliñar, asear.

groove, n. muesca, ranura, f.; rutina, f.; —, vt. acanalar.

grooved, adj. acanalado, estriado.

grope, vt. y vi. tentar, buscar a oscuras; andar a tientas.

grosgrain, n. gro, m.

gross, adj. grueso, corpulento, espeso; grosero; estúpido; — profits, beneficio bruto; — weight, peso bruto; —ly, adv. groseramente; en bruto; —, n. gruesa, f.; todo, m.

grotesque, adj. grotesco.

grouch, n. descontento, mal humor, m.; persona malhumorada; —, vi. gruñir, refunfuñar.

grouchy, adj. mal humorado, de mal humor.

ground, n. tierra, f.; terreno, suelo, pavimento, m.; fundamento, m.; razón fundamental, f.; (elec.) tierra, f.; campo (de batalla), m.; fondo, m.; — control approach, acceso de control terrestre; — floor, piso bajo, planta baja; — hog, marmota, f.; — wire, alambre de tierra; —s, heces, f. pl.; poso, sedimento, m.; —, vt. establecer; traer a tierra; —, vi. varar.

groundless, adj. infundado; —ly, adv. sin fundamento, sin razón o motivo.

groundwork, n. plan, fundamento, m.

group, n. grupo, m.; —, vt. agrupar.

grouse, n. gallina silvestre.

grove, n. arboleda, f.; boscaje, m.; pine — pinar, m.

grovel, vi. serpear; arrastrarse; envilecerse.

grow, vt. cultivar; —, vi. crecer, aumentarse; nacer, brotar; vegetar; adelantar; hacerse, ponerse, volverse; to — soft, to —tender, relentecer; enternecerse; to — up, crecer; to — young again, rejuvenecer.

grower, n. cultivador, m.

growing, n. crecimiento, m.; cultivo, m.; —, adj. creciente.

growl, *vi.* regañar, gruñir, rezongar, refunfuñar; —, *n.* gruñido, *m.*

growling, *n.* refunfuño, *m.*

grown, *p.p.* del verbo **grow.**

grown-up, *adj.* mayor de edad, maduro; —, *n.* persona mayor de edad, adulto, ta.

growth, *n.* vegetación, *f.;* crecimiento, *m.;* producto, *m.;* aumento, *m.;* progreso, adelanto, *m.;* nacencia, *f.,* tumor, *m.*

grub, *n.* gorgojo, *m.;* (coll.) alimento, *m.;* (coll.) persona desaliñada que trabaja muy fuerte; —, *vt.* desarraigar; desmontar, rozar; (coll.) dar de comer; —, *vi.* (coll.) comer; trabajar muy fuerte en la tierra.

grubby, *adj.* gusarapiento; sucio; desaliñado.

grudge, *n.* rencor, odio, *m.;* envidia, *f.;* **to bear a** —, guardar rencor; —, *vt.* y *vi.* envidiar; repugnar; malquerer.

grudgingly, *adv.* con repugnancia, de mala gana.

gruel, *n.* harina de avena mondada; (Mex.) atole, *m.*

grueling, *adj.* muy severo, agotador.

gruesome, *adj.* horrible, espantoso.

gruff, *adj.* ceñudo, grosero, brusco; **—ly,** *adv.* ásperamente.

grumble, *vi.* gruñir; murmurar.

grumpy, *adj.* regañón, quejoso, ceñudo.

grunt, *vi.* gruñir; gemir.

guarantee, *n.* garante, *m.* y *f.,* fiador, ra; garantía, fianza, *f.;* —, *vt.* garantir, garantizar.

guarantor, *n.* garante, *m.* y *f.,* fiador, ra; **to be a** —, salir fiador, salir garante.

guaranty, *n.* garante, *m.;* garantía, *f.*

guard, *n.* guarda, *m.* o *f.,* guardia, *f.,* centinela, *m.* y *f.;* rondador, *m.;* vigilante, *m.;* guardafrenos, *m.;* (fútbol) defensa, *m.;* **to be on** —, estar de centinela; estar alerta; —, *vt.* guardar; defender; custodiar; —, *vi.* guardarse; prevenirse; velar; **to — against,** cautelar; precaverse.

guarded, *adj.* mesurado, circunspecto.

guardhouse, *n.* (mil.) cuartel de guardia.

guardian, *n.* tutor, *m.;* curador, *m.;* guardián (prelado), *m.;* **— saint,** patrón, *m.;* —, *adj.* tutelar; **— angel,** ángel de la guarda.

guardianship, *n.* tutela, *f.*

guerrilla, *n.* guerrillero, *m.*

guess, *vt.* y *vi.* conjeturar; adivinar; —, *n.* conjetura, *f.*

guesswork, *n.* conjetura, *f.*

guest *n.* huésped, da, invitado, da, convidado, da.

guffaw, *n.* carcajada, risotada, *f.*

guidance, *n.* gobierno, *m.;* dirección, *f.;* —

beam, (avi.) rayo electrónico orientador.

guide, *vt.* guiar, dirigir; —, *n.* guía, *m.* y *f.;* conductor, *m.;* **girl** —, guía, niña guía.

guidebook, *n.* manual (para viajeros), *m.,* guía, *f.*

guidepost, *n.* poste indicador, hito, *m.*

guild, *n.* gremio, *m.;* comunidad, corporación, *f.*

guile, *n.* engaño, fraude, *m.*

guileless, *adj.* cándido, sincero.

guilt, *n.* delito, *m.;* culpa, delincuencia, *f.*

guiltless, *adj.* inocente, libre de culpa.

guilty, *adj.* reo, culpable, culpado.

guinea, *n.* guinea (moneda), *f.; —* **pig,** conejillo de Indias, cobayo, *m.*

guise, *n.* modo, *m.;* manera, *f.;* práctica, *f.*

guitar, *n.* guitarra, *f.*

gulch, *n.* barranca, quebrada, cañada, *f.*

gulf, *n.* golfo, *m.;* abismo, *m.,* sima, *f.;* torbellino, *m.*

Gulf Stream, *n.* corriente del Golfo (de México).

gull, *n.* (orn.) gaviota, *f.;* persona fácil de engañar o defraudar; —, *vi.* engañar, defraudar.

gullet, *n.* tragadero, gaznate, *m.*

gullible, *adj.* crédulo, fácil de engañar.

gully, *n.* barranca, *f.;* —, *vi.* formar canal.

gulp, *n.* trago, *m.;* —, *vt.* engullir, tragar.

gum, *n.* goma, *f.;* encía, *f.;* **chewing** —, chicle, *m.,* goma de mascar; **— tree,** árbol gomífero; —, *vt.* engomar.

gumbo, *n.* (bot.) quimbombó, *m.;* sopa de quimbombó.

gumdrop, *n.* pastilla de goma.

gummy, *adj.* gomoso.

gumption, *n.* (coll.) inteligencia, *f.;* juicio, *m.;* astucia, *f.;* iniciativa, *f.*

gumwood, *n.* madera del árbol de goma.

gun, *n.* arma de fuego; cañón, *m.;* fusil, *m.;* escopeta, *f* pistola, *f ;* revólver, *m.;* **— barrel,** cañón de fusil; **— carriage,** cureña de cañón; **— metal,** bronce de cañones; imitación de cobre.

gunboat, *n.* cañonero, ra.

gunfire, *n.* cañoneo, *m.*

gunner, *n.* artillero, *m.*

gunny, *n.* tejido basto para sacos; **— sack,** saco de yute.

gunpowder, *n.* pólvora, *f.*

gunshot, *n.* tiro de escopeta; herida de arma; alcance de un tiro.

gunwale, *n.* (naut.) borda, *f.*

gurgle, *vi.* gorjear; —, *n.* gorjeo, *m.*

gush, *vi.* brotar; chorrear; demostrar afecto exageradamente; —, *n.* chorro, *m.;* efusión, *f.*

gusher, *n.* pozo surgente (de petróleo).

gust, *n.* soplo de aire; ráfaga, *f.*

gusto, n. gusto, placer, m.
gut, n. intestino, m., cuerda de tripa; barriga, f.; —s, n. pl. (coll.) valor, m., valentía, fuerza, f.; —, vt. desventrar, destripar.
gutter, n. gotera, canal, f.; zanja, f.; cuneta, f.; caño, m.; arroyo de la calle; —, vt. y vi. acanalar; caer en gotas.
guttural, adj. gutural.
guy, n. (naut.) retenida, f.; tipo, sujeto, m.

guzzle, vt. y vi. beber o comer con glotonería.
gymnasium, n. gimnasio, m.
gymnastic, adj. gimnástico; —s, n. pl. gimnástica, gimnasia, f.
gynecology, n. (med.) ginecología, f.
gypsum, n. yeso, m.
gypsy, n. y adj. gitano, na; bohemio, mia.
gyroscope, n. giroscopio, m.

H

haberdasher, n. tendero, camisero, m.
haberdashery, n. mercería, camisería, f.; tienda de ropa para hombres.
habilitate, vt. habilitar.
habit, n. hábito, vestido, m.; uso, m.; costumbre, f.
habitable, adj. habitable.
habitat, n. habitación, morada, f.
habitation, n. habitación, f.; domicilio, m.
habitual, adj. habitual.
hack, n. caballo de alquiler, rocín, cuártago, m.; —, vt. tajar, cortar; usar (algo) demasiado hasta vulgarizarlo, (Mex.) chotear.
hackney, n. caballo de alquiler; —, adj. alquilable; vulgar; —ed, adj. trillado, trivial, manoseado.
had, pretérito y p.p. del verbo have.
haddock, n. (ichth.) merluza, f.
Hades, n. pl. los infiernos, m. pl.
hag, n. bruja, hechicera, f.
haggard, adj. macilento, ojeroso, trasnochado.
haggle, vt. cortar en tajadas; —, vi. regatear.
hail, n. granizo, m.; saludo, m.; —, vt. saludar; —, vi. granizar; —! interj. ¡viva! ¡salve! ¡salud! Hail Mary, Ave María.
hailstone, n. piedra de granizo.
hailstorm, n. granizada, f.
hair, n. cabello, pelo, m.; bobbed —, melena, f., pelo corto; — ribbon, cinta para el cabello; — trigger, disparador muy sensible (con gatillo que descansa en un pelo); to comb one's —, peinarse; to cut one's -, cortarse el pelo.
hairbrush, n. cepillo para el cabello.
haircut, n. corte de pelo; to have a —, cortarse el pelo.
hairdo, n. peinado, m.
hairdresser, n. peluquero, m.; peinador, ra; —'s shop, peluquería, f.; salón de

belleza.
hairdressing, n. peinado, m.
hairless, adj. calvo, sin pelo.
hairpin, n. horquilla (para el cabello), f.
hair-raising, adj. espantoso, aterrador.
hairy, adj. peludo, velludo, cabelludo.
hale, adj. sano, vigoroso; ileso.
half, n. mitad, f.; —, adj. medio; — blood, parentesco que existe entre hermanos de padre o de madre; medio hermano, media hermana; — brother, hermanastro, m.; — pay, media paga, medio sueldo; — sister, hermanastra, f.; — sole, media suela; — tone, (mus.) semitono, m.; fotograbado a media tinta.
halfback, n. (fútbol) medio, m.
half-blooded, adj. mestizo; encastado (animales); de padre o de madre (hermanos).
half-breed, n. y adj. mestizo, za.
half-caste, n. casta cruzada; (coll.) cholo, la; mestizo, za.
halfhearted, adj. indiferente, sin entusiasmo.
half-hour, n. media hora.
half-mast, n. media asta; —, adj. a media asta.
half-moon, n. semilunio, m.
halfway, adv. a medio camino; —, adj. medio; parcial.
half-witted, adj. imbécil.
halibut, n. (ichth.) hipogloso, m.
halitosis, n. halitosis, f., mal aliento.
hall, n. vestíbulo, m., sala, f.; salón, colegio, m.; sala, f.; cámara, f.
hallow, vt. consagrar, santificar.
Halloween, n. víspera de Todos los Santos.
hallucination, n. alucinación, f.
hallway, n. pasillo corredor, m.
halo, n. halo, nimbo, m., corona, f.
halt, vi. cojear, parar, hacer alto; dudar;

—, n. cojera, f.; parada, f.; alto, m.; —!
interj. ¡alto!

halter, n. soga, f.; cuerda, f.; cabestro,
ronzal, camal, m.; pechera, f., blusa sin
mangas que se amarra al cuello y deja
la espalda descubierta.

halve, vt. partir en dos mitades.

halves, n. pl. de **half,** mitades, f. pl.; **by —,**
a medias.

ham, n. jamón, m., (anat.) corva, f.

hamburger, n. hamburguesa, f., carne
picada de res.

hamlet, n. villorrio, m., aldea, f.

hammer, n. martillo, m.; — **of a gun,** ser-
pentín (de fusil), m.; —, vt. martillar;
forjar; —, vi. trabajar; reiterar esfuerzos.

hammock, n. hamaca, f.

hamper, n. cuévano, m., cesto grande
(para ropa, etc.); —, vt. restringir; estorbar, impedir; entrampar.

hand, n. mano, f.; palmo (medida), m.;
carácter de escritura; (coll.) salva de
aplausos; poder, m.; habilidad, destreza, f.; (naut.) marinero, m.; obrero, m.;
mano o manecilla (de un reloj), f.; **at —,**
a la mano, al lado; — **baggage,** equipaje
o bulto de mano; — **grenade,** granada
de mano; — **organ,** n. organillo, m.; —
to —, cuerpo a cuerpo; **in the —s of,** en
poder de; **on the other —,** en cambio,
por otra parte; **with bare —s,** a brazo
partido; **with one's own —,** de propia
mano; **to clap —s,** batir palmas, aplaudir; —, vt. dar, entregar; alargar; guiar
por la mano; **to — down,** trasmitir,
bajar; pasar más abajo.

handbag, n. bolsa, f., saquillo de mano,
maletilla, f.

handball, n. pelota, f.; **juego de pelota.**

handbill, n. cartel, m.

handbook, n. manual, prontuario, m.

handcart, n. carretilla de mano.

handcuffs, n. pl. manillas, esposas, f. pl.

handful, n. manojo, puñado, m.

handicap, n. carrera ciega con caballos de
peso igualado; obstáculo, m.; ventaja, f.
(en juegos); lastre (en el golf), m.

handicraft, n. arte mecánica; destreza
manual; mano de obra.

handiwork, n. obra manual.

handkerchief, n. pañuelo, m.

handle, n. mango, puño, m., asa, manija,
manigueta, f.; palanca, f.; — **bar,**
manubrio, m.; —, vt. manejar; tratar.

handling, n. manejo, m.; toque, m.

handmade, adj. hecho a mano.

handout, n. (coll.) alimento o ropa que se
regala a un limosnero.

hand-picked, adj. escogido, selecto, favorecido.

handrail, n. barandilla, f.; pasamano, m.

handsaw, n. serrucho, m.

handset, n. trasmisor y receptor telefónico.

handshake, n. apretón de manos, m.

handsome, adj. hermoso, bello, gentil,
guapo; **—ly,** adv. primorosamente; con
generosidad.

hand-to-mouth, adj. precario, imprόvido,
escaso.

handwork, n. obra hecha a mano, trabajo
a mano.

handwriting, n. escritura a mano; caligrafía, f.; letra, f.

handy, adj. manual; diestro, mafioso; —
man, factótum, m.; hombre hábil para
trabajos de la casa, reparaciones, etc.

hang, vt. colgar, suspender; ahorcar; entapizar; guindar; —, vi. colgar; ser ahor-
cado; pegarse; quedarse suspenso;
depender.

hangar, n. (avi.) hangar, m.; cobertizo, m.

hangdog, adj. avergonzado, corrido, degra-
dante; —, n. persona vil y despreciable.

hanger, n. alfanje, m.; espada ancha; colgador, gancho (para ropa), m.

hanger-on, n. gorrista, m. y f., gorrón,
ona, parásito, m.

hanging, adj. pendiente.

hangings, n. pl. tapicería, f.; cortinaje, m.

hangman, n. verdugo, m.

hangnail, n. respigón, uñero, padrastro, m.

hangover, n. resaca, f.; (Mex.) cruda, f.

hank, n. madeja de hilo.

hanker, vi. ansiar, apetecer.

hankering, n. anhelo, m.

hansom, n. cabriolé, m.

haphazard, n. accidente, lance, m.; —,
adj. casual, descuidado.

hapless, adj. desgraciado, desventurado.

happen, vi. acontecer, acaecer, suceder,
sobrevenir, caer; **to — to,** acertar, suceder por casualidad.

happening, n. suceso, acontecimiento, m.

happily, adv. felizmente.

happiness, n. felicidad, dicha, f.

happy, adj. feliz, bienaventurado; jubiloso.

happy-go-lucky, adj. calmado, sereno, filosófico, sin preocupaciones.

harangue, n. arenga, f.; —, vi. arengar.

harass, vt. cansar, fatigar, sofocar, acosar.

harbinger, n. precursor, ra.

harbor, n. albergue, m.; puerto, m.; bahía,
f.; asilo, m.; —, vt. albergar; hospedar;
—, vi. tomar albergue.

hard, adj. duro, firme; difícil; penoso;
cruel, severo, rígido; — **and fast,** rígido;
sin excepción; — **cash,** numerario efec-

tivo; — **cider,** sidra fermentada; — **coal,** antracita, f.; — **of hearing,** medio sordo, duro de oído; —, adv. cerca, a la mano, difícilmente.

hard-boiled, adj. cocido hasta endurecerse; — **eggs,** huevos duros.

hard-earned, adj. ganado con mucho trabajo.

harden, vt. y vi. endurecer, endurecerse.

hardening, n. endurecimiento, m.

hardhearted, adj. duro de corazón, insensible.

hardly, adv. apenas; severamente.

hardness, n. dureza, f.; dificultad, f.; inhumanidad, f.; severidad, f.

hard-pressed, adj. apurado, falto de recursos.

hardship, n. injuria, opresión, f.; injusticia, f.; penalidad, f.; trabajo, m.; molestia, fatiga, f.

hardware, n. ferretería, quincallería, f.; — **store,** quincallería, ferretería, f.

hardwood, n. madera dura.

hard-working, adj. trabajador.

hardy, adj. atrevido, bravo, intrépido; fuerte, robusto, vigoroso.

hare, n. liebre, f.

harebrained, adj. aturdido, atolondrado.

hare-lipped, adj. labihendido.

harem, n. harén, m.

hark, vi. escuchar; —! interj. ¡ oye! ¡mira!

harlot, n. puta, meretriz, prostituta, f.

harm, n. mal, daño, m.; desgracia, f.; perjuicio, m.; —, vt. dañar, injuriar, ofender.

harmful, adj. dañoso, dañino, perjudicial.

harmless, adj. inocente, inofensivo.

harmonic, adj. armónico; —s, n. pl. armonía, teoría musical.

harmonica, n. armónica, f.

harmonious, adj. armonioso.

harmonize, vt. armonizar, concertar, ajustar; concretar; —, vi. convenir, corresponder.

harmony, n. armonía, f.

harness, n. arreos de un caballo; —, vt. enjaezar.

harp, n. arpa, f.; —, vt. y vi. tocar el arpa; **to — upon,** machacar, porfiar, importunar con insistencia (sobre algo).

harpist, n. arpista, m. y f.

harpoon, n. arpón, m.

harpsichord, n. clavicordio, clave, m.

harpy, n. arpía, f.

harrow, n. grada, f.; rastro, m.; —, vt. gradar.

harrowing, adj. conmovedor; horripilante.

harry, vt. atormentar, acosar, molestar.

harsh, adj. áspero, agrio, rígido, duro, austero.

harshness, n. aspereza, dureza, rudeza, austeridad, severidad, f.

hart, n. (zool.) ciervo, m.

harvest, n. cosecha, f.; agosto, m.; —, vt. cosechar, recoger las mieses.

harvester, n. agostero, m., segador, ra; (máquina) segadora, f.

has, 3ra persona del singular del verbo **have.**

has-been, n. (coll.) persona que fue importante y ya no lo es, (Mex. coll.) cartucho quemado.

hash, n. jigote, picadillo, m.; —, vt. **picar** (carne, etc.).

hassock, n. cojín para los pies.

haste, n. prisa, f.; presteza, f.; **to be in —,** estar de prisa.

hasten, vt. acelerar, apresurar; —, vi. estar de prisa, apresurarse.

hastily, adv. pecipitadamente; airadamente.

hasty, adj. pronto, apresurado; colérico.

hat, n. sombrero, m.; —**s off!** ¡quítense el sombrero! **straw —,** sombrero de paja.

hatband, n. cintillo de sombrero.

hatch, vt. criar pollos; empollar; tramar; —, n. pollada, nidada, f.; media puerta; (naut.) cuartel, m.; compuerta de esclusa; trampa, f.

hatchet, n. destral, m., hacha pequeña.

hatching, n. incubación, cloquera, f.

hatchway, n. escotilla, f.

hate, n. odio, aborrecimiento, m.; —, vt. odiar, detestar.

hateful, adj. odioso, detestable; —**ly,** adv. detestablemente, con tirria.

hatpin, n. alfiler de sombrero.

hatrack, n. cuelgasombreros, m., percha para sombreros.

hatred, n. odio, aborrecimiento, m.

hatter, n. sombrerero, ra.

haughty, adj. altanero, altivo, orgulloso.

haul, vt. tirar, halar o jalar; acarrear; —, n. estirón, tirón, m.; botín, m., presa, f.

haunch, n. anca, f.

haunt, vt. frecuentar, rondar; —, n. guarida, f.; lugar frecuentado.

haunted, adj. encantado, frecuentado por espantos.

Havana, Habana, f.

have, vt. haber, tener; poseer.

haven, n. puerto, m.; abrigo, asilo, m.

havoc, n. estrago, m.; ruina, f.

Hawaiian Islands, Islas Hawaianas, f. pl.

hawk, n. (orn.) halcón, gavilán, m.; —, vi. cazar con halcón; pregonar, llevar y vender mercaderías por las calles.

hawker, n. vendedor ambulante, buhonero, chalán, m.

hawk-eyed, adj. lince, agudo; con vista de

lince.

hawser, n. (naut.) guindaleza, amarra, f.

hawthorn, n. (bot.) espino blanco, acerolo, m.

hay, n. heno, m.; — **fever,** romadizo, m., catarro de origen alérgico.

hayfield, n. henar, m.

hayfork, n. horca, laya (para el heno), f.

hayloft, n. henil, m.

haymaker, n. guadañil, m.; golpe tremendo.

haystack n. almiar, m.

hazard, n. acaso, accidente, m.; riesgo, m.; juego de azar a los dados; —, vt. arriesgar; aventurar.

hazardous, adj. arriesgado, peligroso.

haze, n. niebla, bruma, f.; aturdimiento, m.

hazel, n. avellano, m.; —, adj. castaño.

hazelnut, n. avellana, f.

hazy, adj. anieblado, oscuro, brumoso; aturdido.

hdkf.: handkerchief, pañuelo.

hdqrs.: headquarters, cuartel general.

he, pron. él.

H.E.: His Excellency, Su Excelencia.

head, n. cabeza, f.; jefe, m.; juicio, m.; talento, m.; puño (de bastón), m.; fuente, f.; nacimiento (de un río), m.; **bald** —, calva, f.; **from** — **to foot,** de arriba abajo; — **of hair,** cabellera, f.; —**s or tails,** cara o cruz, cara o sello; —, vt. gobernar, dirigir; degollar; podar los árboles; encabezar; **to** — **off,** alcanzar, prevenir.

headache, n. dolor de cabeza; hemicránea, jaqueca, f.

headcheese, n. queso de cerdo.

headdress, n. cofia, f.; tocado, m.

headfirst, adv. de cabeza.

headgear, n. tocado, m.

heading, n. título, membrete, m.

headland, n. promontorio, cabo, m.

headless, adj. descabezado; estúpido.

headlight, n. linterna delantera; farol delantero.

headline, n. encabezamiento, título (de un periódico, etc.), m.

headlong, adj. temerario, precipitoso, inconsiderado.

headmaster, n. director de una escuela.

headmost, adj. primero, más adelantado.

head-on, adj. de cabeza.

headphone, n. auricular para la cabeza.

headpiece, n. casco, yelmo, m.; cabeza, f., intelecto, m.; entendimiento, m.; (print.) viñeta, f.; auricular telefónico con soporte para la cabeza.

headquarters, n. (mil.) cuartel general; jefatura, administración, f.; **police** —,

jefatura de policía.

headset, n. (radio y TV.) casco con auricular.

headstone, n. lápida, f.

headstrong, adj. testarudo, cabezudo.

headwaiter, n. primer mozo, jefe de los mozos de un restaurante.

headwaters, n. fuente, cabecera, f., lugar donde nace un río.

headway, n. (naut.) salida, marcha, f.; avance, progreso, m.; intervalo entre dos trenes en una misma ruta.

headwork, n. trabajo mental.

heal, vt. y vi. curar, sanar, cicatrizar; —, vi. recobrar la salud.

health, n. salud, sanidad, salubridad, f.; **bill of** —, patente de sanidad; — **officer,** oficial de sanidad o de cuarentena; sanitario, m.; — **resort,** centro de salud; **to be in good** —, estar bien de salud; **to be in poor** —, estar mal de salud.

healthful, adj. saludable.

healthy, adj. sano; salubre, saludable, lozano.

heap, n. montón, m.; mojón, m.; rima, f., rimero, m.; **ash** —, cenicero, m.; —, vt. amontonar, acumular.

hear, vt. oir; entender; acceder; —, vi. oir; escuchar.

hearing, n. oído, m., oreja, f.; audiencia, f.

hearken, vi. escuchar, atender.

hearsay, n. rumor, m.; fama, f.; voz pública; **by** —, de oídas, por oídas.

hearse, n. carroza fúnebre.

heart, n. corazón, m.; alma, f.; interior, centro, m.; ánimo, valor, m.; emoción, f.; **by** —, de memoria; — **trouble,** enfermedad del corazón; **to one's** —**'s content,** a pedir de boca; **with all my** —, con toda mi alma.

heartache, n. angustia, congoja, f.

heartbeat, n. latido del corazón.

heartbreak, n. decepción amorosa; pesar, m., aflicción, f.; disgusto, m.

heartbreaking, adj. doloroso, conmovedor.

heartbroken, adj. transido de dolor.

heartburn, n. acedía, f.

heartfelt, adj. expresivo, muy sentido, muy sincero.

hearth, n. hogar, m., chimenea, f.

hearthstone, n. hogar, m., casa, f.

heartiness, n. cordialidad, f.

heartless, adj. sin corazón, inhumano, cruel.

heart-rending, adj. agudo, penetrante, desgarrador.

heartsick, adj. dolorido, afligido.

heart-to-heart, adj. íntimo, sincero, abierto; confidencial.

hearty, adj. sincero; sano; vigoroso; campechano; — **meal,** comida sana y abundante.

heat, *n.* calor, *m.;* calefacción, *f.;* ardor, *m.;* vehemencia, *f.;* animosidad, *f.;* (coll.) extremada presión en investigaciones judiciales; carrera, *f.;* — **shield,** cubierta o protector contra el calor; — **wave,** onda cálida; **in** —, en celo (aplícase a los animales) ; **prickly** —, salpullido, *m.;* —, *vt.* calentar; encender.

heater, *n.* escalfador, *m.;* calentador, *m.,* estufa, *f.*

heath, *n.* (bot.) brezo, *m.;* brezal, matorral, *m.*

heathen, *n.* gentil, *m.* y *f.,* pagano, na.

heather, *n.* (bot.) brezo, *m.*

heating, *n.* calefacción, *f.;* **central** —, calefacción central.

heatstroke, *n.* insolación, *f.*

heave, *vt.* alzar; elevar; arrojar; (naut.) virar para proa; —, *vi.* palpitar; respirar trabajosamente; —, *n.* esfuerzo para levantarse; suspiro de congoja.

heaven, *n.* cielo, *m.;* firmamento, *m.;* —**s!** *interj.* ¡cielos! ¡caramba!

heavenly, *adj.* celestial, divino.

heavily, *adv.* pesadamente.

heaviness, *n.* pesadez, *f.;* peso, *m.; (fig.)* carga, *f.;* aflicción, *f.;* opresión, *f.*

heavy, *adj.* grave, pesado; opresivo, penoso, molesto; triste; tardo, soñoliento; oneroso; **to be** —, pesar.

heavyweight, *adj.* (boxeo) de peso completo; —, *n.* peso completo; (coll.) persona obesa.

heckle, *vt.* importunar con preguntas.

heckler, *n.* preguntón importuno.

hectic, *adj.* inquieto, agitado.

hectograph, *n.* hectógrafo, *m.*

hedge, *n.* seto, *m.;* barrera, *f.;* —, *vt.* cercar con un seto.

hedgehog, *n.* erizo, *m.*

hedgerow, *n.* serie de árboles en los cercados.

heed, *vt.* atender, observar; —, *n.* cuidado, *m.;* atención, precaución, *f.;* **to give** —, reparar, atender.

heedless, *adj.* descuidado, negligente, impróvido; —**ly,** *adv.* negligentemente.

heel, *n.* talón, carcañal, calcañar, *m.;* (coll.) canalla, bribón, bellaco, *m.,* pérfido villano; **rubber** —, tacón de goma o de caucho; **to take to one's** —**s,** apretar los talones, huir; —, *vt.* poner tacón (a un zapato); (naut.) escorar.

heifer, *n.* becerra, vaquilla, ternera, *f.*

height, *n.* altura, elevación, *f.;* sublimidad, *f.*

heighten, *vt.* realzar; adelantar; mejorar; exaltar.

heinous, *adj.* atroz, odioso.

heir, *n.* heredero, *m.;* — **apparent,** heredero forzoso; — **presumptive,** presunto heredero.

heiress, *n.* heredera, *f.*

heirloom, *n.* mueble heredado; reliquia de familia.

helibus, *n.* helicóptero grande (hasta para diez personas).

helicopter, *n.* helicóptero, *m.*

heliotrope, *n.* (bot.) heliotropo, *m.*

helium, *n.* (chem.) helio, *m.*

hell, *n.* infierno *m.*

hellish, *adj.* infernal, malvado; —**ly,** *adv.* diabólicamente.

hello, *interj.* ¡hola! ¡qué hay! ¡qué hubo! (expresión de saludo).

helm, *n.* (naut.) timón, gobierno, *m.*

helmet, *n.* yelmo, casco, *m.*

help, *vt.* y *vi.* ayudar, asistir, socorrer; aliviar, remediar, reparar; evitar; **to** — **oneself to,** servirse (algún alimento); **I cannot** — **it,** no puedo remediarlo; —, *n.* ayuda, *f.;* socorro, remedio, *m.*

helper, *n.* auxiliador, ra, socorredor, ra. helpful, *adj.* útil, provechoso; saludable.

helpless, *adj.* inútil; imposibilitado.

helpmate, *n.* compañero, ra; ayudante, *m.* y *f.;* esposa, *f.*

helter-skelter, *adv.* (coll.) a trochemoche, en desorden.

hem, *n.* ribete, *m.;* bastilla, *f.;* —**!** *interj.* ¡ejem! —, *vt.* bastillar; repulgar; ribetear; —, *vi.* vacilar; fingir tos; — **in,** circundar, rodear, ceñir.

hemisphere, *n.* hemisferio, *m.*

hemlock, *n.* (bot.) abeto, *m.;* (bot.) cicuta, *f.*

hemoglobin, *n.* (med.) hemoglobina, *f.*

hemophilia, *n.* (med.) hemofilia, *f.*

hemorrhage, *n.* hemorragia, *f.*

hemorrhoids, *n. pl.* hemorroides, almorranas, *f. pl.*

hemp, *n.* cáñamo, *m.*

hemstitch, *n.* (costura) vainica, *f.,* ojito, deshilado, *m.;* —, *vt.* (costura) hacer una vainica; hacer ojito, deshilar.

hen, *n.* gallina, *f.*

hence, *adv.* de aquí; por esto.

henceforth, *adv.* de aquí en adelante; en lo sucesivo.

henchman, *n.* secuaz, servil, *m.*

hencoop, *n.* gallinero, *m.*

henhouse, *n.* gallinero, *m.*

henna, *n.* (bot.) alheña, *f.*

henpeck, *vt.* encocorar una mujer a su marido tratando de mandarlo; —**ed husband,** marido dominado por su mujer.

hepatitis, *n.* (med.) hepatitis, *f.*

hepcat, n. miembro de una banda de jazz; experto en música de jazz.

her, pron. le; la; a ella; —, adj. su, de ella.

herald, n. heraldo, m.

herb, n. yerba, hierba, f.; **—s,** pl. hierbas medicinales.

herbaceous, adj. herbáceo.

herbage, n. herbaje, m., hierba, f.

herbivorous, adj. herbívoro.

herculean, adj. hercúleo.

herd, n. hato, rebaño, m.; manada, f.; grey, f.; —, vi. ir en hatos; asociarse; —, vt. guiar (el ganado) en rebaño.

herder, n. pastor de ganado.

herdsman, n. pastor, m.

here, adv. aquí, acá.

hereabout, hereabouts, adv. por aquí, por los alrededores.

hereafter, adv. en lo futuro; —, n. estado venidero, el futuro, m.

hereby, adv. por esto.

hereditary, adj. hereditario.

heredity, n. derecho de sucesión.

herein, adv. en esto, aquí dentro.

hereinafter, adv. después, más adelante.

heresy, n. herejía, f.

heretic, n. hereje, m. y f.; —, adj. herético.

heretical, adj. herético.

heretofore, adv. antes, en tiempos pasados; hasta ahora.

hereupon, adv. sobre esto.

herewith, adv. con esto.

heritage, n. herencia, f.

hermetic, adj. hermético.

hermit, n. ermitaño, eremita, m.

hermitage, n. ermita, f.

hernia, n. hernia, rotura, ruptura, f.

hero, n. héroe, m.

heroic, adj. heroico; **—s,** n. pl. expresión o acto extravagantes.

heroine, n. heroína, f.

heroism, n. heroísmo, m.

heron, n. garza, f.

herring, n. arenque, m.

herringbone, n. punto espigado, punto de ojal.

hers, pron. el suyo (de ella).

herself, pron. sí, ella misma.

hesitant, adj. indeciso, vacilante.

hesitate, vi. vacilar, titubear.

hesitation, n. duda, irresolución, vacilación, f., titubeo, m.

heterogeneous, adj. heterogéneo.

hew, vt. leñar; tajar; cortar; picar.

hexagon, n. hexágono, m.

hexameter, n. hexámetro, m.

hey, interj. ¡he! ¡oye!

heyday, n. apogeo, auge, m., sumo vigor, suma vitalidad.

H.H.: His Holiness (the Pope), S.S. Su

Santidad (el papa); **His or Her Highness,** Su Alteza.

hiatus, n. abertura, hendidura, f.; laguna, f.; (gram.) hiato, m.

hibernate, vi. invernar.

hibernation, n. invernada, f.

hiccough, n. hipo, m.;—, vi. tener hipo.

hickory, n. nogal americano.

hid, pretérito del verbo **hide.**

hidden, adj. escondido; secreto; —, p.p. del verbo **hide.**

hide, vt. esconder; apalear; -, vi. esconderse; —, n. cuero, m.; piel, f.

hide-and-seek, n. juego de escondite, escondite, m.

hideous, adj. horrible, macabro.

hiding, n. encubrimiento, m.; — **place,** escondite, escondrijo, m., madriguera, f.

hie, vi. apresurarse.

hierarchy, n. jerarquía, f.

hi-fi = high fidelity.

high, adj. alto, elevado; arduo; altivo; noble, ilustre; sublime; caro; — **fidelity,** alta fidelidad; — **frequency,** frecuencia elevada; — **jump,** salto de altura; — **light,** parte subida de una fotografía o pintura; acontecimiento de primordial interés; — **school,** escuela secundaria; **—seas,** alta mar; — **spirits,** alegría, jovialidad, f.; — **tide,** pleamar, f.; — **time,** buena hora; jarana, f.; — **treason,** alta traición; delito de lesa majestad; — **voltage,** alta tensión; — **water,** marea alta, mar llena.

highball, n. jaibol, m.

high-fidelity, adj. de alta fidelidad (fonógrafo).

high-frequency, adj. de alta frecuencia, de frecuencia elevada.

high-grade, adj. de alta calidad, excelente.

highhanded, adj. tiránico, arbitrario.

high-hat, adj. aristócrata, presuntuoso; (Mex. coll.) popof.

highland, n. tierra montañosa.

highlight, vt. alumbrar con reflectores eléctricos; destacar, dar realce, dar relieve.

highly, adv. altamente; en sumo grado; arrogantemente; ambiciosamente; sumamente.

high-minded, adj. orgulloso, arrogante; magnánimo.

Highness, n. Alteza, f.

highness, n. altura, f.

high-octane, adj. de alto octanaje.

high-pitched, adj. agudo; sensitivo.

high-powered, adj. de alta potencia.

high-pressure, adj. de alta presión; intenso, urgente; — **salesman,** vendedor persistente y tenaz.

high-priced, adj. caro, de precio elevado.
highroad, n. camino, m., carretera, f.
high school, n. escuela secundaria.
high-sounding, adj. pomposo, retumbante.
high-speed, adj. de gran velocidad.
high-spirited, adj. bizarro, gallardo,
valiente.
high-strung, adj. nervioso, excitable.
high-test, adj. que pasa cierta prueba
(aplícase a la gasolina).
high-water mark, n. colmo, pináculo, m.
highway, n. carretera, f.
highwayman, n. salteador de caminos.
hike, n. caminata, f., paseo a pie (generalmente en el campo).
hilarious, adj. alegre y bullicioso.
hill, n. collado, cerro, otero, m., colina, f.
hilly, adj. montañoso.
hilt, n. puño de espada.
him, pron. le, lo, a él.
himself, pron. sí, él mismo.
hind, adj. trasero, posterior; —, n. cierva
(hembra del ciervo), f.
hinder, vt. impedir, embarazar, estorbar.
hindmost, adj. postrero; último.
hindquarter, n. cuarto trasero de algunos
animales.
hindrance, n. impedimento, obstáculo, m.;
rémora, f.
hindsight, n. mira posterior de una arma
de fuego; percepción de la naturaleza y
exigencias de un suceso pasado.
hinge, n. charnela, bisagra, f., gozne, m.;
punto principal, centro, m.; —, vt.
engoznar.
hint, n. seña, f.; sugestión, insinuación, f.;
luz, f.; aviso, m.; buscapié, m.; —, vt.
apuntar, insinuar; sugerir; hacer señas.
hip, n. cadera, f.
hipbone, n. hueso de la cadera.
hippopotamus, n. hipopótamo, m.
hire, vt. alquilar; arrendar; contratar;—, n.
alquiler, m.; salario, m.
hireling, n. jornalero, m.; hombre mercenario; —, adj. mercenario, venal.
his, adj. su, de él; —, pron. el suyo (de él).
His Holiness, (the Pope), Su Santidad (el
papa).
Hispaniola, Isla Española, f.
hiss, vt. y vi. silbar.
hissing, n. chifla, f.; siseo, m.
historian, n. historiador, m.
historic, historical, adj. histórico.
history, n. historia, f.; narración, f.
hit, vt. golpear, dar, atinar; —, vi. salir
bien; encontrar, encontrarse; to — the
target, dar en el blanco; —, n. golpe,
m.; suerte feliz; alcance, m.; (coll.) éxito,
m.; (béisbol) golpe, m.
hitch, vt. enganchar, atar, amarrar; —, n.

impedimento, m.; (naut.) nudo o lazo
fácil de soltar.
hitchhike, vi. hacer auto-stop, ir por auto-
stop.
hither, adv. acá; hacia acá; —, adj. cite-
rior.
hitherto, adv. hasta ahora, hasta aquí.
H.I.V.: human immunodeficiency virus,
V.I.H., virus de la inmunodeficiencia
humana.
hive, n. colmena f.; —, vi. vivir muchos en
un mismo lugar.
hives, n. pl. (med.) urticaria, f., ronchas, f.
pl.
H.M.: His Majesty, Her Majesty, S.M. Su
Majestad.
hoard, n. montón, m.; tesoro escondido;
—, vt. atesorar, acumular.
hoarding, n. acaparamiento, atesoramien-
to, m.; acumulación de mercancías ante
posible escasez.
hoarfrost, n. escarcha, f.
hoarse, adj. ronco; —ly adv. roncamente.
hoarseness, n. ronquera, carraspera, f.
hoary, adj. blanquecino, cano.
hoax, n. burla, f.; petardo, m.; trufa, f.; —,
vt. engañar, burlar.
hobble, vi. cojear; —, vt. enredar; —, n.
dificultad, f.; cojera, f.; maniota f.
hobby, n. caballico, m.; manía, afición, f.
hobbyhorse, n. caballito de madera en que
corren los niños.
hobnail, n. clavo de herradura.
hobnob, vi. codearse, rozarse.
hobo, n. vagabundo, m.
hock, n. vino añejo del Rin; corvejón,
jarrete, m.; —, vt. desjarretar; (coll.) dar
en prenda, empeñar.
hockey, n. hockey, m.
hocus-pocus, n. pasapasa, m.; engaño,
m.; treta, f.
hodgepodge, n. almodrote, baturrillo, m.;
morralla, f.
hoe, n. azada, f., azadón, m.; —, vt. cavar
la tierra con azada, azadonar.
hog, n. cerdo, puerco, m.
hoggish, adj. porcuno; egoísta; glotón.
hogshead, n. tonel, m.; barrica, f.;
bocoy, m.
hoist, vt. alzar; (naut.) izar; —, n.
monta-cargas, m.; cric, m.; elevador, m.; grúa, f.
hoisting, n. izamiento, m.; — crane, montacargas, m.; — engine, malacate, m.
hold, vt. tener, asir, detener; sostener;
mantener; juzgar, reputar; poseer; continuar, proseguir; contener; celebrar;
sujetar; to — one's own, mantenerse
firme, no ceder; —, vi. valer; mantenerse; durar, abstenerse; adherirse; pos-

poner; **to lay —**, echar mano; **— on!**, *interj.* ¡espera! **—**, *n.* presa, *f.;* mango, *m.;* asa, *f.;* prisión, *f.;* custodia, *f.;* (naut.) bodega, *f.;* apoyo, *m.;* poder, *m.*

holder, *n.* tenedor, posesor; mango, *m.,* asa, *f.;* **cigar —, cigarette —**, boquilla, *f.*

holding, *n.* tenencia, posesión, *f.;* **— company**, compañía tenedora.

holdup, *n.* asalto, salteamiento, *m.*

hole, *n.* agujero, *m.;* cueva, *f.;* **hoyo**, *m.;* seno, *m.;* hueco, *m.*

holiday, *n.* día de fiesta, día festivo; **—s**, *n. pl.* vacaciones, *f. pl.;* días de fiesta.

holiness, *n.* santidad, *f.*

Holland, Holanda, *f.*

Hollander, *n.* y *adj.* holandés, esa.

hollow, *adj.* hueco; falso, engañoso, insincero; **—**, *n.* cavidad, caverna, *f.;* **—**, *vt.* excavar, ahuecar.

hollow-eyed, *adj.* con los ojos hundidos.

holly, *n.* (bot.) acebo, agrifolio, *m.*

hollyhock, *n.* (bot.) malva hortense.

holocaust, *n.* holocausto, *m.*

holster, *n.* funda de pistola.

holy, *adj.* santo, pío; consagrado; **— water**, agua bendita; **Holy Week**, Semana Santa; **most —**, santísimo.

homage, *n.* homenaje, culto, *m.*

home, *n.* casa, casa propia, morada, *f.;* patria, *f.;* domicilio, hogar *m.;* **at —**, en casa; **—**, *adj.* doméstico; **— page**, página inicial, *f.*

homeland, *n.* patria, *f.,* tierra natal.

homeless, *adj.* sin casa, sin hogar.

homelike, *adj.* como de casa, cómodo.

homeliness, *n.* simpleza, *f.;* fealdad, *f.*

homely, *adj.* feo; casero.

homemade, *adj.* hecho en casa; casero.

homemaker, *n.* ama de casa.

homeopath, *n.* homeópata, *m.* y *f.*

homerun, *n.* (béisbol) jonrón, cuadrangular, *m.*

homesick, *adj.* nostálgico.

homesickness, *n.* nostalgia por el hogar o el país natal.

homespun, *adj.* casero; tosco, basto.

homestead, *n.* heredad, *f.;* casa solariega; hogar, solar, *m.*

homestretch, *n.* último trecho de una carrera.

homeward, homewards, *adv.* hacia casa, hacia su país.

homeward-bound, *adj.* con rumbo al hogar, de regreso.

homework, *n.* tarea, *f.;* trabajo hecho en casa, estudio fuera de la clase.

homicidal, *adj.* homicida.

homicide, *n.* homicidio, *m.;* homicida, *m.* y *f.*

homily, *n.* homilía, *f.*

homing, *n.* (avi.) rumbo automático; orientación automática hacia un trasmisor.

homing pigeon, *n.* paloma mensajera.

hominy, *n.* maíz de grano, maíz machacado o molido.

homogeneous, *adj.* homogéneo.

homogenize, *vt.* homogenizar.

homograph, *n.* homógrafo, *m.*

homosexual, *n.* y *adj.* homosexual, *m.*

Honduran, *n.* y *adj.* hondureño, ña.

honest, *adj.* honesto, probo; honrado; justo.

honesty, *n.* honestidad, justicia, probidad, *f.;* hombría de bien; *f.;* honradez, *f.*

honey, *n.* miel, *f.;* dulzura, *f.;* (coll.) querido, ta; **like —**, meloso.

honeybee, *n.* abeja obrera.

honeycomb, *n.* panal, *m.,* bresca, *f.,* ceras, *f. pl.*

honeydew melon, *n.* melón de Valencia, rocío de miel.

honeyed, *adj.* dulce, meloso, enmelado.

honeymoon, *n.* luna de miel.

honeysuckle, *n.* (bot.) madreselva, *f.*

honk, *n.* graznido de ganso; pitazo de bocina de automóvil.

honor, *n.* honra, *f.,* honor, lauro, *m.;* **on my —**, a fe mía; **point of —**, pundonor, *m.;* **—**, *vt.* honrar; **to — (a draft)**, (com.) aceptar (un giro o letra de cambio).

honorable, *adj.* honorable; ilustre; respetable; **— behavior**, caballerosidad, *f.*

honorably, *adv.* honorablemente.

honorarium, *n.* honorarios, *m. pl.*

honorary, *adj.* honorario.

hood, *n.* caperuza, *f.;* capirote (de graduados), *m.;* capucha (de religioso), *f.;* gorro, *m.;* (auto.) cofre, cubierta del motor; **—**, *vt.* proveer de caperuza; cubrir con caperuza.

hoodlum, *n.* (coll.) pillo, tunante, *m.*

hoodoo, *n.* (coll.) mal de ojo, persona o cosa que trae mala suerte; **—**, *vt.* causar mala suerte.

hoodwink, *vt.* vendar a uno los ojos; engañar, burlar.

hoof, *n.* pezuña, *f.,* casco de las bestias caballares; **— and-mouth disease**, fiebre aftosa.

hoofbeat, *n.* ruido de los cascos.

hook, *n.* gancho, *m.;* anzuelo, *m.;* **by — or crook**, de un modo u otro; **— and eye**, corchete macho y hembra; **—**, *vt.* enganchar.

hooked, *adj.* enganchado, encorvado; **— rug**, tapete tejido a mano.

hookup, *n.* empalme, sistema de conexión, *m.;* (rad. y TV.) circuito, *m.,* red de radiodifusoras.

hookworm, *n.* lombriz intestinal, *f.*

hoop, n. cerco, m.; cerco de barril; — **skirt,** miriñaque, m.; —, vt. cercar.

hoot, vi. gritar; —, n. grito, m.

hop, n. salto, m.; —s, (bot.) lúpulo, m.; —, vi. saltar, brincar.

hope, n. esperanza, f.; — **chest,** caja en que una mujer guarda trajes, ropa blanca, etc., en anticipación de casamiento; —, vi. esperar, tener esperanzas.

hopeful, adj. lleno de esperanzas, esperanzado; optimista; —**ly,** adv. con esperanza; —, n. joven prometedor por sus buenas cualidades.

hopeless, adj. desesperado; sin remedio; —**ly,** adv. sin esperanza.

hopper, n. saltador, m.; tolva (en los molinos), f.

hopscotch, n. coxcojilla (juego), f.

horde, n. horda, f.; enjambre, m.; manada, f.

horehound, n. (bot.) marrubio, m.

horizon, n. horizonte, m.

horizontal, adj. horizontal.

hormone, n. hormona, f.

horn, n. cuerno, m.; corneta, f.; trompeta, f.; cacho, m.; bocina, f.; clarín, m.

horned, adj. cornudo.

hornet, n. abejón, m.

hornpipe, n. gaita, f.

horny, adj. hecho de cuerno; calloso.

horoscope, n. horóscopo, m.

horrible, adj. horrible, terrible.

horrid, adj. horroroso, horrible.

horrify, vt. horrorizar.

horror, n. horror, terror, m.

horror-stricken, adj. horrorizado.

hors d'oeuvre, n. pl. entremés, m.; (Mex.) botana, f.

horse, n. caballo, m.; (mil.) caballería, f.; caballete, m.; — **race,** carrera de caballos; —, vi. cabalgar; —, vt. suministrar caballos.

horseback, n. espinazo del caballo; **on** —, a caballo.

horsefly, n. tábano, moscardón, m., moscarda, f.

horsehair, n. crin de caballo; tela de crin.

horsehide, n. corambre de caballo.

horselaugh, n. carcajada, risotada, f.

horseman, n. jinete, m.

horsemanship, n. equitación, f.

horseplay, n. retozo vigoroso; (Sp. Am.) relajo, m.

horsepower, n. caballo de fuerza.

horseradish, n. rábano silvestre, rábano picante.

horseshoe, n. herradura de caballo.

horsewhip, n. látigo, m.; fusta, f.; fuete, m.; —, vt. azotar.

horticulture, n. horticultura, jardinería, f.

hose, n. medias, f.pl.; manguera, f.; tubo flexible.

hosiery, n. medias, f.pl.; calcetines, m.pl.

hospitable, adj. hospitalario; — **bly,** adv. con hospitalidad.

hospital, n. hospital, m.; — **ward,** sala o crujía de hospital; **maternity** —, casa de maternidad.

hospitality, n. hospitalidad, f.

hospitalization, n. hospitalización, f.

host, n. anfitrión, m.; huésped, m.; mesonero, m.; ejército, m.; hostia, f.

hostage, n. rehén, m.

hostel, n. posada, hostería, f., hotel, m.; **youth** —, posada para jóvenes (movimiento educativo de excursiones de jóvenes).

hostess, n. anfitriona, f.; posadera, mesonera, patrona, f.

hostile, adj. hostil; contrario.

hostility, n. hostilidad, f.

hot, adj. caliente, cálido; ardiente; picante, picoso, muy condimentado; (coll.) agitado, violento (aplícase a música, bailes, etc.); (coll.) recién robado.

hot-air, adj. de aire caliente.

hotbed, n. era, f.; invernadero (con estufas), m.; semillero, m.; (fig.) foco, m.

hot-blooded, adj. excitable, de sangre ardiente.

hotbox, n. cojinete calentado excesivamente por fricción.

hot dog, n. perro caliente.

hotel, n. hotel, m., posada, fonda, f.

hotheaded, adj. sañoso, fogoso, exaltado.

hothouse, n. estufa, f.; invernadero, m.

hot rod, n. automóvil reforzado para alcanzar grandes velocidades.

hot-tempered, adj. fogoso, exaltado.

hound, n. sabueso, podenco, m.; hombre vil y despreciable.

hour, n. hora, f.; — **hand,** horario (de un reloj).

hourglass, n. reloj de arena; (naut.) ampolleta, f.

hourly, adv. a cada hora; frecuentemente; —, adj. que sucede a cada hora, frecuente.

house, n. casa, f.; familia, f.; linaje, m.; cámara (del parlamento), f.; **banking** —, casa de banco; **business** —, casa de comercio; **clearing** —, casa de compensación; **commission** —, casa de comisiones; **country** —, casa de campo; **gambling** —, casino, m.; — **of correction,** casa de corrección, reformatorio, m.; — **party,** fiesta en que los invitados permanecen más de un día, tertulia generalmente en una casa de campo; **H— of Representatives,** Cámara de

Representantes; **lodging** —, casa de
posada o de huéspedes; **publishing** —,
casa editora; **to keep** —, poner casa; ser
ama de casa; **whosesale** —, casa mayorista; —, vt. y vi. albergar; residir.

houseboat, n. barco-habitación, m.

housebreaker, n. ladrón que fuerza las
puertas de una casa para robarla.

housecoat, n. bata de casa.

housefly, n. mosca, f.

household, n. familia, f.; casa, f.; establecimiento, m.; — **goods**, enseres, m.pl.; —
management, manejo doméstico.

householder, n. jefe de una casa, padre de
familia.

housekeeper, n. ama de casa, ama de llaves.

housekeeping, n. gobierno doméstico;
manejo casero.

housemaid, n. criada de casa.

housetop, n. tejado, m.

housewarming, n. tertulia para el estreno
de una casa.

housewife, n. ama de casa.

housework, n. quehaceres domésticos, trabajo de casa.

housing, n. edificación de casas, alojamiento, m.; almacenaje, m.; (mech.) cárter, m.; cubierta, f.; **—s**, gualdrapa, f.

hovel, n. choza, cabaña, f.

hover, vi. colgar; dudar; rondar.

how, adv. cómo, cuán; cuánto; — **do you
do?** ¿cómo le va a usted? — **goes it?**
¿qué tal? — **are you getting along?** ¿qué
tal? — **so?** ¿por qué? ¿cómo así?

however, conj. como quiera que; —, adv.
sin embargo, no obstante.

howitzer, n. (mil.) obús, bombero, m.

howl, vi. aullar; reir a carcajadas; —, n.
aúllo, aullido, m.

howsoever, adv. como quiera, como quiera
que sea.

hub, n. cubo, m.; centro, m.; cubo de una
rueda.

hubbub, n. grito, ruido, m.; alboroto, tumulto, m.

hubcap, n. tapacubo, m.

huckleberry, n. variedad de gayuba.

huckster, n. revendedor, vendedor ambulante.

huddle, vt. amontonar en desorden; —, vi.
amontonarse en confusión; agruparse
para recibir señas (en el juego de fútbol);
—, n. confusión, f.; (coll.) conferencia
secreta.

hue, n. color, m.; tez del rostro; matiz, m.,
tinta, f.; — **and cry**, alarma que se da
contra un criminal.

huff, n. arrebato, m.; cólera, f.; —, vt. ofender; tratar con arrogancia; —, vi. eno-

jarse, patear de enfado.

huffy, adj. malhumorado, irascible; arrogante.

hug, vt. abrazar, acariciar; —, n. abrazo
apretado.

huge, adj. vasto, enorme; gigantesco.

hulk, n. (naut.) casco de una embarcación,
armatoste, m.

hull, n. cáscara, f.; (naut.) casco (de un
buque), m.; —, vt. descortezar.

hullabaloo, n. tumulto, alboroto, m.

hum, vi. zumbar, susurrar, murmurar; —,
vt. tararear (una canción, etc.); —, n.
zumbido, m.

human, n. y adj. humano, na; — **being**, ser
humano, m; — **resources**, recursos
humanos, m.pl.; — **rights**, derechos
humanos, m.pl.

humane, adj. humano, compasivo.

humanist, n. humanista, m.y f.

humanitarian, n. filántropo, pa; —, adj.
humanitario.

humanity, n. humanidad, f.

humanize, vt. hacer humano; civilizar; —,
vi. humanizarse.

humankind, n. el género humano.

humble, adj. humilde, modesto; —, vt.
humillar; postrar; **to — oneself**, humillarse; doblar o bajar la cerviz.

humbleness, n. humildad, f.

humbly, adv. humildemente.

humbug, n. engaño, m., farsa, f.; —, vt.
engañar, embaucar.

humdrum, adj. lerdo, estúpido; monótono;
—, n. monotonía, f., tedio, m.

humid, adj. húmedo.

humidify, vt. humedecer.

humidity, n. humedad, f.

humidor, n. caja humedecida para puros,
bote para tabaco de fumar.

humiliate, vt. humillar.

humiliation, n. humillación, mortificación,
f., bochorno, m.

humility, n. humildad, f.

hummingbird, n. (orn.) colibrí, m.

humor, n. humor, m.; comicidad, f.; humorada, fantasía, f.; capricho, m.; **bad —**,
berrinche, m., mal humor; —, vt. complacer, dar gusto; matar un antojo.

humorist, n. humorista, m.y f.

humorous, adj. humorista, chistoso, jocoso; **—ly**, adv. de buen humor; en forma
jocosa.

hump, n. giba, joroba, f.

humpbacked, adj. jorobado, giboso.

humph! interj. ¡uf!

humus, n. humus, mantillo, m., tierra
vegetal.

hunch, n. giba, f.; (coll.) idea, corazonada,
f., presentimiento, m.

hunchback, *n*. joroba, *f.*; jorobado, da.
hunchbacked = **humpbacked**.
hundred, *adj*. cien, ciento; —, *n*. centenar, *m.*; un ciento, *m*.
hundredth, *n*. y *adj*. centésimo, *m*.
hundredweight, *n*. quintal, *m*.
hung, *pretérito* y p.p. del verbo **hang**.
Hungary, Hungría, *f*.
hunger, *n*. hambre, *f.*; — **strike**, huelga de hambre; —, *vi*. hambrear; anhelar, ansiar.
hungry, *adj*. hambriento; voraz; **to be** —, tener hambre.
hunk, *n*. pedazo grande, trozo, *m*.
hunt, *vt*. cazar; perseguir; buscar; —, *vi*. andar a caza; —, *n*. caza, *f*.
hunter, *n*. cazador, *m.*; caballo de caza; perro de monte, perro braco.
hunting, *n*. montería, caza, *f.*; —, *adj*. de caza.
hurdle, *n*. zarzo, *m.*; valla, *f.*, obstáculo, *m.*; —**s**, carrera de obstáculos.
hurdy-gurdy, *n*. organillo, *m*.
hurl, *vt*. tirar con violencia; arrojar.
hurrah! *interj*. ¡viva!
hurricane, *n*. huracán, *m*.
hurried, *adj*. apresurado, hecho de prisa.
hurry, *vt*. acelerar, apresurar, precipitar; —, *vi*. atropellarse, apresurarse; —, *n*. precipitación, *f.*; confusión, *f.*; urgencia, *f.*; **in a** —, a prisa; **to be in a** —, tener prisa, estar de prisa, darse prisa.
hurt, *vt*. dañar, hacer daño, herir; ofender; —, *n*. mal, daño, perjuicio, *m.*; golpe, *m.*; herida, *f.*; —, *adj*. sentido; lastimado; perjudicado.
husband, *n*. marido, esposo, *m.*; —, *vt*. administrar con frugalidad.
husbandman, *n*. labrador, granjero, *m*.
husbandry, *n*. agricultura, *f.*; economía, *f*.
hush, *n*. silencio, *m.*; —! *interj*. ¡chitón! ¡silencio! ¡paz! ¡calla! —, *vt*. aquietar; acallar; —, *vi*. hacer silencio.
husk, *n*. cáscara, *f.*; pellejo, *m.*; —, *vt*. descascarar, mondar.
huskiness, *n*. ronquedad, ronquera, *f*.
husky, *adj*. cascarudo; ronco; (coll.) fornido, fuerte; —, *n*. persona robusta.
hussy, *n*. tunanta, *f.*, mujer descarada.
hustle, *vt*. y *vi*. bullir; apurar (un trabajo); apurarse, andar de prisa.

hut, *n*. cabaña, barraca, choza, *f*.
hyacinth, *n*. (bot.) jacinto, *m*.
hybrid, *n*. y *adj*. híbrido, *m*.
hydrant, hydrangea boca de agua (para incendios) .
hydraulic, *adj*. hidráulico; — **engineering**, hidrotecnia, *f*.
hydraulics, *n*. hidráulica, *f*.
hydrochloric, *adj*. hidroclórico, clorhídrico.
hydrodynamics, *n*. hidrodinámica, *f*.
hydroelectric, *adj*. hidroeléctrico.
hydrogen, *n*. (chem.) hidrógeno, *m.*; — **bomb**, bomba de hidrógeno; **carbureted** —, hidrocarburo, *m.*; — **peroxide**, agua oxigenada, peróxido hidrogenado; — **sulphide**, sulfhídrico, *m*.
hydromatic, *adj*. hidromático.
hydrophobia, *n*. hidrofobia, *f*.
hydroplane, *n*. hidroplano, hidroavión, *m*.
hydroponics, *n*. hidropónica, *f*.
hydrostatic, *adj*. hidrostático; —**s**, *n. pl.* hidrostática, *f*.
hyena, *n*. hiena, *f*.
hygiene, *n*. higiene *f*.
hygienic, *adj*. higiénico.
hymn, *n*. himno, *m*.
hymnal, *n*. himnario, *m*.
hyperbole, *n*. hipérbole, *f.*; exageración, *f*.
hypersensitive, *adj*. excesivamente impresionable.
hypersonic, *adj*. hipersónico.
hypertension, *n*. hipertensión, *f*.
hyphen, *n*. (gram.) guión, *m*.
hyphenate, *vt*. separar con guión.
hypnosis, *n*. hipnosis, *f*.
hypnotic, *adj*. hipnótico.
hypnotism, *n*. hipnotismo, *m*.
hypnotize, *vt*. hipnotizar.
hypochondria, *n*. hipocondría, *f*.
hypocrisy, *n*. hipocresía, *f*.
hypocrite, *n*. hipócrita, *m.* y *f.*; mojigato, ta.
hypocritical, *adj*. hipócrita, disimulado.
hypodermic, *adj*. hipodérmico; —, *n*. inyección hipodérmica.
hypotenuse, *n*. hipotenusa, *f*.
hypothesis, *n*. hipótesis, .
hypothetical, *adj*. hipotético .
hysterectomy, *n*. (med.) histerectomía, *f*.
hysteria, *n*. histeria, *f.*, histerismo, *m*.
hysteric, hysterical, *adj*. histérico .
hysterics, *n. pl.* paroxismo histérico.

I

I, *pron*. yo.
iambic, *adj*. yámbico.
Iberian, *n*. y *adj*. íbero, ra.

ibex , *n*. íbice, *m*.
ibid.: **in the same place**, ib. íbidem, en el mismo lugar.

I.C.C.: Interstate Commerce Commission, Comisión de Comercio entre Estados (E.U.A.).

ice, n. hielo, m.; granizado, m.; — **age,** época glacial,f.; **dry** —, hielo seco; — **hockey,** hockey sobre hielo; — **pack,** bolsa de hielo para aplicaciones frías; — **pick,** picahielo, m.; — **sheet,** manto de hielo; — **skate,** patín de hielo; — **water,** agua helada; —, vt. helar; **to** — **a cake,** garapiñar o ponerle betún a un pastel.

iceberg, n. témpano de hielo.

iceboat, n. embarcación con patines para deslizarse sobre el hielo; barco rompehielos.

icebound, adj. rodeado de hielo.

icebox, n. refrigerador, m., nevera, f.

icebreaker, n. rompehielos, m.

ice cream, n. helado, mantecado, m., nieve, f.

ice-cream, adj. de helado o de mantecado; —**cone,** barquillo de helado o de mantecado.

icehouse, n. nevería, nevera, refrigeradora, f.; empacadora de hielo f.

Iceland, Islandia, f.

Icelander, n. islandés, esa.

Icelandic, adj. islándico, islandés.

iceman, n. repartidor de hielo.

Icicle, n. cerrión, carámbano, canelón, m.

icing, n. capa dulce para pasteles; (Mex.) betún, m.

iconoclast, n. iconoclasta, m.y f.

iconoscope, n. (TV.) iconoscopio, m. **icy,** adj. helado; frío; (fig.) indiferente.

idea, n. idea, f.; imagen mental; concepto, m.; **clever** —, feliz idea.

ideal, n. y adj. ideal, m.

idealism, n. idealismo, m.

idealist, n. idealista, m.y f.

idealistic, adj. idealista.

idealize, vt. y vi. idealizar.

identical, adj. idéntico.

identification, n. identificación, f.; — **card,** — **papers,** cédula personal o de vecindad.

identify, vt. identificar; **to** — **oneself,** identificarse.

identity, n. identidad, f.

ideology, n. ideología, f., ideario, m.

idiocy, n. idiotismo, m.

idiom, n. idioma, m.; dialecto, m.; modismo, m., frase idiomática.

idiomatic, idiomatical, adj. idiomático, peculiar a alguna lengua.

idiosyncrasy, n. idiosincrasia, f.

idiot, n. idiota, m. y f., necio, cia.

idiotic, adj. tonto, bobo.

idle, adj. ocioso, perezoso, desocupado, holgazán; inútil, vano, frívolo; —, vi.

holgazanear, estar ocioso.

idleness, n. ociosidad, pereza, f.; negligencia, f.; frivolidad, f.

idler, n. holgazán, ana; (coll.) gandul, gandula; (mech.) rueda intermedia.

idol, n. idolo, m.; imagen, f.

idolatry, n. idolatría, f.

idolize, vt. idolatrar.

idyl, n. idilio, m.

idyllic, adj. idílico, como un idilio.

i.e.: that is, es decir, esto es.

if, conj. si; aunque, supuesto que; — **not,** si no.

igloo, n. iglú, m., choza esquimal.

ignite, vt. y vi. encender, abrasar, encenderse.

ignition, n. (chem.) ignición, f.; (auto.) ignición, f.; encendido, m.; — **switch,** contacto del magneto.

ignoble, adj. innoble; bajo.

ignominious, adj. ignominioso.

ignominy, n. ignominia, infamia, f.

ignoramus, n. ignorante, m.y f.; tonto, ta.

ignorance, n. ignorancia, f.

ignorant, adj. ignorante, inculto.

ignore, vt. pasar por alto, desconocer.

ill, adj. malo, enfermo, doliente; — **turn,** mala jugada; —, n. mal, infortunio; —, adv. mal, malamente.

Ill.: Illinois, Illinois (E.U.A.)

ill-bred, adj. malcriado, descortés.

ill-disposed, adj. malintencionado, contrario.

illegal, adj. ilegal; —**ly,** adv. ilegalmente.

illegible, adj. ilegible; —**bly,** adv. de un modo ilegible.

illegitimate, adj. ilegítimo.

ill-fated, adj. desgraciado, desdichado.

ill-gotten, adj. mal habido.

ill-humored, adj. malhumorado.

illicit, adj. ilícito; —**ly,** adv. ilícitamente.

illimitable, adj. ilimitado.

illiteracy, n. analfabetismo, m.

illiterate, adj. indocto, iliterato, analfabeto; —, n. analfabeto, ta.

ill-mannered, adj. malcriado, descortés.

ill-natured, adj. irascible, de mal carácter.

illness, n. enfermedad, f.; maldad, f.; mal, m.

illogical, adj. ilógico.

ill-starred, adj. desdichado.

ill-suited, adj. inadecuado, inapropiado.

ill-tempered, adj. malhumorado, de mal carácter.

ill-treat, vt. maltratar.

illuminate, vt. iluminar.

illumination, n. iluminación, f.; alumbrado, m.

illumine, vt. iluminar.

illusion, n. ilusión, f.; ensueño, m.

illusory, *adj.* ilusorio.

illustrate, *vt.* ilustrar; explicar.

illustrated, *adj.* ilustrado, de grabados.

illustration, *n.* ilustración, *f.;* elucidación, *f.;* ejemplo, *m.;* grabado, *m.*

illustrative, *adj.* explicativo.

illustrator, *n.* ilustrador, ra.

illustrious, *adj.* ilustre, insigne, célebre.

ill-will, *n.* malevolencia, mala voluntad.

image, *n.* imagen, estatua, *f.;* —, *vt.* imaginar.

imagery, *n.* imagen, pintura, *f.;* vuelos de la fantasía.

imaginable, *adj.* imaginable, concebible.

imaginary, *adj.* imaginario.

imagination, *n.* imaginación, imaginativa, *f.;* idea fantástica.

imaginative, *adj.* imaginativo.

imagine, *vt.* imaginar; idear, inventar.

imbecile, *n. y adj.* imbécil, *m.y f.*

imbecility, *n.* imbecilidad, *f.;* idiotismo, *m.*

imbibe, *vt.* embeber; chupar.

imbue, *vt.* imbuir, infundir.

imitate, *vt.* imitar, copiar.

imitation, *n.* imitación, copia, *f.*

imitative, *adj.* imitativo, imitado.

imitator, *n.* imitador, ra.

immaculate, *adj.* inmaculado, puro.

immanent, *adj.* inmanente.

immaterial, *adj.* inmaterial; de poca importancia.

immature, *adj.* inmaduro, inmaturo.

immeasurable, *adj.* inmensurable, inmenso.

immediate, *adj.* inmediato; —ly, *adv.* inmediatamente, en seguida, en el acto, acto continuo.

immemorial, *adj.* inmemorial.

immense, *adj.* inmenso; vasto.

immensity, *n.* inmensidad, *f.*

immerse, *vt.* sumir, sumergir.

immersion, *n.* inmersión, *f.*

immigrant, *n.* inmigrante, *m.y f.*

immigrate, *vi.* inmigrar.

immigration, *n.* inmigración, *f.*

imminent, *adj.* inminente.

immobile, *adj.* inmóvil.

immoderate, *adj.* inmoderado, excesivo.

immodest, *adj.* inmodesto.

immoral, *adj.* inmoral, depravado.

immorality, *n.* inmoralidad, *f.,* corrupción de costumbres.

immortal, *adj.* inmortal.

immortality, *n.* inmortalidad, *f.*

immortalize, *vt.* inmortalizar, eternizar.

immovable, *adj.* inmóvil, inmoble; inmovible; —s, *n. pl.* bienes raíces.

immune, *adj.* inmune, exento.

immunity, *n.* inmunidad, franquicia, *f.,* privilegio, *m.*

immunize, *vt.* inmunizar.

immutable, *adj.* inmutable.

imp, *n.* niño travieso; diablillo, *m.;* duende, *m.*

impact, *n.* impulso, *m.;* choque, *m.*

impair, *vt.* empeorar, deteriorar; disminuir.

impale, *vt.* empalar (a un reo).

impanel, *vt.* formar la lista de personas que han de integrar un jurado, etc.

impart, *vt.* comunicar, dar parte.

impartial, *adj.* imparcial.

impartiality, *n.* imparcialidad, *f.*

impassable, *adj.* intransitable.

impasse, *n.* camino intransitable; callejón sin salida; obstáculo insuperable.

impassioned, *adj.* apasionado, ardiente.

impassive, *adj.* impasible.

impatience, *n.* impaciencia, *f.*

impatient, *adj.* impaciente.

impeach, *vt.* acusar, denunciar, delatar (aplícase especialmente a funcionarios públicos).

impede, *vt.* impedir; paralizar.

impediment, *n.* impedimento, obstáculo, *m.*

impel, *vt.* impeler, impulsar.

impend, *vi.* amenazar, aproximar.

impenetrable, *adj.* impenetrable.

impenitent, *adj.* impenitente; —ly, *adv.* sin penitencia.

imperative, *adj.* imperativo, imprescindible; — mood, (gram.) modo imperativo.

imperceptible, *adj.* imperceptible.

imperfect, *adj.* imperfecto, defectuoso; —, *n.* (gram.) pretérito imperfecto.

imperfection, *n.* imperfección, *f.,* defecto, *m.*

imperial, *adj.* imperial, supremo, soberano.

imperialism, *n.* imperialismo, *m.*

imperialist, *n. y adj.* imperialista, *m.y f.*

imperil, *vt.* arriesgar, poner en peligro.

imperious, *adj.* imperioso; arrogante.

imperishable, *adj.* indestructible; eterno; imperecedero.

impersonal, *adj.* impersonal.

impersonate, *vt.* imitar, personificar; representar.

impersonation, *n.* personificación, *f.;* (theat.) imitación, *f.*

impertinence, *n.* impertinencia, *f.;* descaro, *m.*

impertinent, *adj.* impertinente; inadecuado, inaplicable; —ly, *adv.* impertinentemente; fuera de propósito.

imperturbable, *adj.* imperturbable; —bly, *adv.* sin perturbación.

impervious, *adj.* impenetrable.

impetuosity, *n.* impetuosidad, *f.,* ímpetu, *m.*

impetuous, adj. impetuoso; —ly, adv. a borbotones.

impetus, n. ímpetu, m.

impinge, vt. chocar, tropezar; — upon, invadir, usurpar, abusar de.

impious, adj. impío, irreligioso; desapiadado.

impish, adj. travieso.

implacable, adj. implacable, irreconciliable.

implant, vt. plantar; injertar; imprimir.

implement, n. herramienta, f.; utensilio, m.; mueble, m.; —s, n. pl. aperos, m.pl.; enseres, m.pl.; —, vt. poner en ejecución, ejecutar, completar, cumplir.

implicate, vt. implicar, envolver.

implication, n. implicación, f.

implicit, adj. implícito.

implied, adj. implícito.

implore, vt. implorar, suplicar.

imply, vt. implicar.

impolite, adj. descortés, mal educado.

import, vt. importar; —, n. importancia, f.; artículo importado; sentido, m.; significación, f.; — duties, derechos de importación.

importance, n. importancia, f.; trascendencia, f.

important, adj. importante.

importation, n. importación, f.

importer, n. importador, ra.

importing, adj. importador; — house, empresa importadora.

importunate, adj. importuno, insistente.

importune, vt. importunar.

impose, vt. imponer (obligaciones, etc.); to — upon, imponerse, abusar de.

imposing, adj. imponente, que infunde respeto; tremendo.

imposition, n. imposición, carga, f.; impostura, f.

impossibility, n. imposibilidad, f.

impossible, adj. imposible; to seem —, parecer mentira.

impost, n. impuesto, tributo, m., carga, f.

impostor, n. impostor, ra.

imposture, n. impostura, f.; engaño, m.

impotence, n. impotencia, f.; incapacidad, f.

impotent, adj. impotente; incapaz; —ly, adv. sin poder, impotentemente.

impound, vt. encerrar, acorralar; depositar o embargar, poner en custodia (de algún tribunal).

impoverish, vt. empobrecer.

impracticable, adj. impracticable, imposible.

impractical, adj. impracticable, irrealizable.

imprecation, n. imprecación, maldición, f.

impregnable, adj. impregnable; inexpugnable.

impregnate, vt. impregnar; empreñar.

impresario, n. empresario, m.

impress, vt. imprimir, estampar; —, n.

impresión, f.; empresa, divisa, f.

impression, n. impresión, f.; edición, f.

impressionable, adj. impresionable.

impressionism, n. impresionismo, m.

impressive, adj. penetrante; impresionable; imponente; —ly, adv. de un modo impresionante.

imprint, vt. imprimir, estampar; —, n. florón, m., impresión, f.; huella, f.; pie de imprenta.

imprison, vt. aprisionar; prender.

imprisonment, n. prisión, f., encierro, m.

improbable, adj. improbable; inverosímil.

impromptu, adj. extemporáneo, improvisado.

improper, adj. impropio, indecente.

impropriety, n. impropiedad, incongruencia, f.

improve, vt. y vi. mejorar, perfeccionar; —, vi. progresar.

improved, adj. mejorado, perfeccionado.

improvement, n. progreso, mejoramiento, perfeccionamiento, m.

improvident, adj. impróvido.

improvisation, n. improvisación, f.

improvise, vt. improvisar.

imprudence, n. imprudencia, f.

imprudent, adj. imprudente.

impudence, n. impudencia, f., cinismo, descaro, m.

impudent, adj. atrevido, insolente.

impulse, n. impulsión, f., impulso, m.; ímpetu, m.

impulsive, adj. impulsivo.

impunity, n. impunidad, f.

impure, adj. impuro; impúdico, sucio.

impurity, n. impureza, f.

impute, vt. imputar.

in, prep. en; por; a; de; durante; bajo; dentro de; —. adv. dentro, adentro.

in.: inch, pl. pulgada; inches, plgs. pulgadas.

inability, n. inhabilidad, incapacidad, f.

inaccessible, adj. inaccesible.

inaccuracy, n. inexactitud, incorrección, f.

inaccurate, adj. inexacto.

inactive, adj. inactivo; flojo, perezoso, negligente; pasivo.

inactivity, n. ociosidad, desidia, inactividad, f.

inadequacy, n. insuficiencia, f.

inadequate, adj. inadecuado, defectuoso; imperfecto, insuficiente.

inadvertent, adj. inadvertido.

inalienable, adj. inajenable, inalienable.

inane, *adj.* vacío, sin sentido, tonto.

inanimate, *adj.* inanimado; exánime.

inarticulate, *adj.* inarticulado.

inasmuch as, visto o puesto que.

inaudible, *adj.* que no se puede oír; imperceptible.

inaugural, *adj.* inaugural.

inaugurate, *vt.* inaugurar.

inauguration, *n.* inauguración, *f.*

inborn, *adj.* innato, ingénito.

in-box, *n.* bandeja de entrada, *f.*

inbred, *adj.* innato; sin mezcla (de razas, etc.).

Inc.: Incorporated, Inc. Incorporado.

incalculable, *adj.* incalculable.

incandescent, *adj.* incandescente; — **light,** luz eléctrica incandescente.

incapable, *adj.* incapaz, inhábil.

incapacitate, *vt.* incapacitar; inhabilitar, imposibilitar.

incapacity, *n.* incapacidad, insuficiencia, *f.;* estolidez, *f.*

incarcerate, *vt.* encarcelar, aprisionar.

incarnate, *adj.* encarnado; —, *vt.* encarnar.

incarnation, *n.* encarnación, encarnadura, *f.*

incase, *vt.* encajar, incluir.

incendiary, *n.* y *adj.* incendiario; — **bomb,** bomba incendiaria.

incense, *n.* incienso, *m.;* — **stick,** pebete, *m.;* —, *vt.* exasperar, irritar, provocar; incensar.

incentive, *n.* incentivo, estímulo, *m.*

inception, *n.* principio, *m.*

incessant, *adj.* incesante, constante.

incest, *n.* incesto, *m.*

inch, *n.* pulgada, *f.;* — **by** —, palmo a palmo; —, *vi.* avanzar o moverse por pulgadas o a pasos muy pequeños.

incidence, *n.* incidencia, *f.;* — **wires,** (avi.) tirantes o alambres de incidencia.

incident, *adj.* incidente; dependiente; —, *n.* incidente, *m.;* circunstancia, ocurrencia, *f.*

incidental, *adj.* accidental, casual; contingente; -ly, *adv.* incidentalmente.

incinerate, *vt.* incinerar.

incinerator, *n.* incinerador, *m.*

incipient, *adj.* incipiente.

incision, *n.* incisión, *f.*

incisive, *adj.* incisivo, incisorio.

incisor, *n.* diente incisivo, *m.*

incite, *vt.* incitar, estimular.

incivility, *n.* incivilidad, descortesía, *f.*

inclemency, *n.* inclemencia, severidad, *f.*

inclement, *adj.* inclemente.

inclination, *n.* inclinación, propensión, *f.;* declive, *m.*

incline, *vt.* inclinar; —, *vi.* inclinarse; —, *n.* pendiente, *f.*

inclined, *adj.* inclinado.

inclose, *vt.* encerrar, incluir.

inclosure, *n.* cercamiento, *m.;* cercado, *m.*

include, *vt.* incluir, comprender.

inclusion, *n.* inclusión, *f.*

inclusive, *adj.* inclusivo.

incognito, *adj.* y *adv.* de incógnito.

incoherence, *n.* incoherencia, *f.*

incoherent, *adj.* incoherente.

income, *n.* renta, *f.,* entradas, *f.pl.;* rendimiento, *m.;* — **tax,** impuesto sobre la renta.

incoming, *adj.* entrante, que acaba de llegar; — **mail,** correspondencia que acaba de recibirse; — **president,** presidente entrante.

incommode, *vt.* incomodar.

incommunicado, *adj.* incomunicado.

incomparable, *adj.* incomparable, excelente; —**bly,** *adv.* incomparablemente.

incompatible, *adj.* incompatible; opuesto.

incompetence, *n.* incompetencia, *f.*

incompetent, *adj.* incompetente.

incomplete, *adj.* incompleto, falto, imperfecto.

incomprehensible, *adj.* incomprensible.

inconceivable, *adj.* incomprensible, inconcebible.

inconclusive, *adj.* ineficaz, que no presenta razones concluyentes.

incongruous, *adj.* incongruo.

inconsequential, *adj.* inconsecuente.

inconsiderate, *adj.* inconsiderado.

inconsistent, *adj.* inconsistente.

inconspicuous, *adj.* no conspicuo, que pasa desapercibido.

incontestable, *adj.* incontestable, incontrastable.

incontinence, *n.* incontinencia, *f.*

inconvenience, *n.* inconveniencia, incomodidad, *f.;* —, *vt.* incomodar.

inconvenient, *adj.* incómodo, inconveniente.

incorporate, *vt.* incorporar; —, *vi.* incorporarse; —, *adj.* incorporado.

incorporation, *n.* incorporación, *f.*

incorrect, *adj.* incorrecto; —**ly,** *adv.* de un modo incorrecto, incorrectamente.

incorrigible, *adj.* incorregible.

increase, *vt.* acrecentar, aumentar; —, *vi.* crecer, aumentarse; —, *n.* aumento, acrecentamiento, *m.*

increasing, *adj.* creciente.

incredible, *adj.* increíble.

incredulity, *n.* incredulidad, *f.*

incredulous, *adj.* incrédulo.

increment, *n.* incremento, *m.*

incriminate, *vt.* acriminar, acusar de algún crimen.

incubation, n. incubación, empolladura, f.
incubator, n. incubadora, f.; empolladror, m.
inculcate, vt. inculcar.
incumbent, adj. echado; obligatorio; to be — on, competer, incumbir; —, n. beneficiado, da; titular m. y f.
incur, vt. incurrir; ocurrir.
incurable, adj. incurable; —bly, adv. de un modo incurable.
indebted, adj. endeudado, empeñado, obligado.
indebtedness, n. deuda, obligación, f.; pasivo, m.
indecency, n. indecencia, f.
indecent, adj. indecente.
indecision, n. irresolución, indecisión, f.
indecisive, adj. indeciso.
indeed, adv. verdaderamente, de veras; sí; —no! ¡de ninguna manera!
indefatigable, adj. infatigable.
indefinite, adj. indefinido, indeterminado.
indelible, adj. indeleble.
indemnification, n. indemnización, f.
indemnity, n. indemnidad, f.; — bond, contrafianza, f.
indent, vt. mellar; dar mayor margen.
indentation, n. mella, muesca, f.; mayor margen.
indenture, n. escritura, f.; contrato de un aprendiz.
independence, n. independencia, f.
independent, adj. independiente.
indescribable, adj. indescriptible.
indestructible, adj. indestructible.
index, n. indicador, m.; índice, m.; (math.) exponente, m.; — finger, dedo índice; —, vt. arreglar en un índice.
India, n. India, f.; — rubber, goma elástica, caucho, m.
Indian, n. y adj. indiano, na; indio, dia; — summer, veranillo de San Martín, veranillo de San Miguel.
indicate, vt. indicar.
indication, n. indicación, f.; indicio, m.; señal, f.
indicative, n. (gram.) indicativo, m.; —, adj. indicativo.
indicator, n. indicador, apuntador, m.
indict, vt. procesar.
indictment, n. acusación ante el jurado, denuncia, f.
indifference, n. indiferencia, apatía, f.
indigenous, adj. indígena.
indigent, adj. indigente, pobre.
indigestible, adj. indigesto, indigestible.
indigestion, n. indigestión, f.
indignant, adj. airado, indignado.
indignation, n. indignación, f.; despecho, m.

indignity, n. indignidad, f.
indigo, n. añil, m.
indirect, adj. indirecto.
indiscreet, adj. indiscreto, inconsiderado.
indiscretion, n. indiscreción, imprudencia, inconsideración, f.
indiscriminate, adj. indistinto; —ly, adv. sin distinción, sin discriminación.
indispensable, adj. indispensable, imprescindible; —bly, adv. indispensablemente.
indispose, vt. indisponer.
indisposed, adj. indispuesto, achacoso.
indisposition, n. indisposición, f., malestar, m.; mala gana.
indisputable, adj. indisputable.
indistinct, adj. indistinto, confuso; borroso.
indistinguishable, adj. indistinguible.
individual, adj. individual, —, n. individuo, m.
individualism, n. individualismo, m.
individuality, n. individualidad, f.
indivisible, adj. indivisible.
indoctrinate, vt. doctrinar, adoctrinar; inculcar.
indolence, n. indolencia, pereza, f.
indolent, adj. indolente; desidioso; —ly, adv. indolentemente, con negligencia.
indomitable, adj. indomable; invencible.
indoor, adj. interior, de puertas adentro; —s, adv. bajo techo, adentro.
indorse, vt. endosar (una letra, un vale u otro documento).
indorsee, n. endosatario, ria.
indorsement, n. endorso, endoso, m.
indorser, n. (com.) endosante (de un giro), m. y f.
indubitable, adj. indubitable, indudable.
induce, vt. inducir, persuadir; causar.
inducement, n. motivo, móvil, aliciente, m.
induct, vt. instalar, iniciar.
induction, n. iniciación, instalación, f.; inducción, deducción, f.; ilación, f.; — coil, carrete de inducción, bobina de inducción.
inductive, adj. inductivo; persuasivo; tentador.
indulge, vt. y vi. favorecer; conceder; ser indulgente; to — in, entregarse a.
indulgence, n. indulgencia, f., mimo, m.
indulgent, adj. indulgente; —ly, adv. de un modo indulgente.
industrial, adj. industrial.
industrialism, n. industrialismo, m.
industrious, adj. industrioso, hacendoso; trabajador, laborioso.
industry, n. industria, f.
inebriate, vt. embriagar.
ineffable, adj. inefable.

ineffective, *adj.* ineficaz.

inefficiency, *n.* ineficacia, *f.*

inefficient, *adj.* ineficiente; ineficaz.

ineligibility, *n.* ineligibilidad, *f.,* calidad que excluye elección.

ineligible, *adj.* no eligible, que no llena los requisitos para algún puesto.

inept, *adj.* inepto.

ineptitude, *n.* ineptitud, *f.*

inequality, *n.* desigualdad, disparidad, diferencia, *f.*

inert, *adj.* inerte, perezoso; —ly, *adv.* indolentemente.

inertia, *n.* inercia, *f.*

inescapable, *adj.* ineludible.

inevitable, *adj.* inevitable, fatal, sin remedio; —bly, *adv.* inevitablemente.

inexcusable, *adj.* inexcusable.

inexhaustible, *adj.* inexhausto, inagotable.

inexorable, *adj.* inexorable, inflexible, duro; incommovible.

inexpedient, *adj.* impropio, impracticable.

inexpensive, *adj.* de poco costo, barato.

inexperience, *n.* inexperiencia, impericia, *f.*

inexperienced, *adj.* inexperto, bisoño, sin experiencia, novel.

inexplicable, *adj.* inexplicable.

inextricable, *adj.* intrincado; enmarañado.

infallible, *adj.* infalible.

infamous, *adj.* vil, infame.

infamy, *n.* infamia, *f.,* oprobio, *m.*

infancy, *n.* infancia, *f.*

infant, *n.* infante, *m.; niño, ña.*

infanticide, *n.* infanticidio, *m.;* infanticida, *m.y f.*

infantile, *adj.* pueril, infantil; — paralysis, (med.) parálisis infantil, poliomielitis, *f.*

infantry, *n.* infantería, *f.*

infatuate, *vt.* infatuar, embobar; fascinar.

infatuation, *n.* infatuación, *f.*

infect, *vt.* infectar.

infection, *n.* infección, *f.*

infectious, *adj.* infeccioso; contagioso; —ly, *adv.* por infección.

infer, *vt.* inferir, deducir, colegir.

inference, *n.* inferencia, ilación, *f.;* conclusión lógica, deducción, *f.*

inferior, *adj.* inferior; of — quality, (coll.) de pacotilla, de calidad inferior; —, *n.* inferior, *m.* o *f.;* oficial subordinado.

inferiority, *n.* inferioridad, *f.; —* complex, complejo de inferioridad.

infernal, *adj.* infernal.

infest, *vt.* infestar.

infidel, *n.* y *adj.* infiel, pagano, desleal.

infidelity, *n.* infidelidad, *f.;* perfidia, *f.*

infield, *n.* (béisbol) diamante y jugadores que actúan en él.

infiltrate, *vi.* infiltrarse, penetrar.

infinite, *adj.* infinito, innumerable; —ly, *adv.* infinitamente.

infinitesimal, *adj.* infinitesimal.

infinitive, *n.* infinitivo, *m.*

infinity, *n.* infinidad, eternidad, *f.;* inmensidad, *f.;* infinito, *m.*

infirm, *adj.* enfermo, débil.

infirmary, *n.* enfermería, *f.*

infirmity, *n.* fragilidad, enfermedad, *f.*

inflame, *vt.* inflamar; —, *vi.* inflamarse.

inflamed, *adj.* encendido.

inflammable, *adj.* inflamable.

inflammation, *n.* inflamación, *f.,* encendimiento, *m.*

inflammatory, *adj.* inflamatorio.

inflate, *vt.* inflar, hinchar.

inflation, *n.* inflación, *f.;* hinchazón, *f.*

inflection, *n.* inflexión, modulación de la voz.

inflexible, *adj.* inflexible.

inflict, *vt.* castigar; infligir (penas corporales, etc.).

infliction, *n.* imposición, *f.;* castigo, *m.*

inflow, *n.* flujo, *m.,* afluencia, *f.;* entrada, *f.*

influence, *n.* influencia, *f.; —, vt.* influir; to — by suggestion, sugestionar.

influential, *adj.* influyente.

influenza, *n.* (med.) influenza, gripe, *f.,* trancazo, *m.*

influx, *n.* influjo, *m.;* afluencia, *f.;* desembocadura, *f.*

infold, *vt.* envolver, abrazar.,

inform, *vt.* informar, poner en conocimiento; hacer saber, enseñar, poner al corriente, dar razón de; to — oneself, enterarse.

informal, *adj.* íntimo, sin formulismos.

informality, *n.* sencillez, intimidad, *f.,* ausencia de formulismos.

informant, *n.* denunciador, ra; informante, *m.* y *f.,* informador, ra.

information, *n.* información, instrucción, *f.;* informe, *m.;* aviso, *m.;* luz, *f.; —* bureau, oficina de información.

informed, *adj.* sabedor, bien informado.

informer, *n.* informante, delator, *m.*

infraction, *n.* infracción, violación, *f.*

infrared, *adj.* infrarrojo.

infrequent, *adj.* raro, insólito.

infringe, *vt.* violar (una ley o pacto); contravenir, infringir.

infringement, *n.* violación, infracción, *f.*

infuriate, *vt.* irritar, provocar, enfurecer; sacar de sus casillas.

infusion, *n.* infusión, *f.*

ingenious, *adj.* ingenioso; vivo.

ingenuity, *n.* ingeniosidad, inventiva, *f.;* ingenuidad *f.;* destreza, *f.*

ingenuous, *adj.* ingenuo, sincero; —ly,

adv. ingenuamente.

ingot, *n.* lingote, *m.*, barra de metal (sin labrar).

ingrained, *adj.* teñido en rama; impregnado.

ingrate, *n.* ingrato, ta.

ingratiate, *vt.* hacer aceptar; **to — oneself,** congraciarse.

ingratitude, *n.* ingratitud, *f.*

ingredient, *n.* ingrediente, *m.*

ingrown, *adj.* crecido hacia dentro; **— nail,** uñero, *m.*, uña enterrada.

inhabit, *vt.* habitar, ocupar.

inhabitable, *adj.* habitable.

inhabitant, *n.* habitante, residente, *m.* y *f.*

inhalation, *n.* inhalación, *f.*

inhale, *vt.* aspirar, inhalar.

inhaler, *n.* inhalador, *m.*

inherent, *adj.* inherente.

inherit, *vt.* heredar.

inheritance, *n.* herencia, *f.*; patrimonio, *m.*; **— tax,** impuesto sobre herencia.

inhibit, *vt.* inhibir, prohibir.

inhibition, *n.* inhibición, prohibición *f.*

inhospitable, *adj.* inhospitalario, inhospitable.

inhuman, *adj.* inhumano, cruel.

inhumanity, *n.* inhumanidad, crueldad, *f.*

inimitable, *adj.* inimitable.

iniquitous, *adj.* inicuo, injusto.

iniquity, *n.* iniquidad, injusticia, *f.*

initial, *adj.* inicial; **—,** *n.* letra inicial.

initiate, *vt.* principian iniciar.

initiation, *n.* principio, *m.*; iniciación, *f.*

initiative, *adj.* iniciativo; **—,** *n.* iniciativa, *f.*

inject, *vt.* inyectar.

injection, *n.* inyección, *f.*; **— pump,** bomba de inyección.

injunction, *n.* mandato, entredicho, *m.*

injure, *vt.* injuriar, ofender; hacer daño; lastimar.

injured, *adj.* lesionado.

injurious, *adj.* injurioso, injusto; perjudicial, nocivo; **—ly,** *adv.* injuriosamente.

injury, *n.* injuria, afrenta, sinrazón, ofensa, *f.*; mal, *m.*; perjuicio, *m.*; daño, *m.*

injustice, *n.* injusticia, *f.*; agravio, *m.*

ink, *n.* tinta, *f.*; **India —,** tinta china.

inkling, *n.* insinuación, noción vaga.

inkpad, *n.* almohadilla, *f.*

inkstand, *n.* tintero, *m.*

inkwell, *n.* tintero, *m.*

inky, *adj.* de tinta; semejante a la tinta.

inlaid, *adj.* ataraceado; **— work,** embutido, encaje, *m.*, taracea, *f.*

inland, *n.* parte interior de un país; **—,** *adj.* interior; **—,** *adv.* dentro de un país.

in-law, *n.* (coll.) pariente político.

inlay, *vt.* ataracear; **—,** *n.* ataracea, *f.*; **relleno** (en un diente), *m.*; **gold —,** orifi-

cación (en un diente), *f.*

inlet, *n.* entrada, *f.*; cala, ensenada, *f.*

inmate, *n.* inquilino, na; ocupante; preso, sa.

inmost, *adj.* íntimo, muy interior.

inn, *n.* posada, *f.*; mesón, *m.*

innate, *adj.* innato, natural, ínsito.

inner, *adj.* interior; **— tube,** cámara de aire.

innermost, *adj.* íntimo, muy interior.

inning, *n.* (en juegos) mano, *f.*; (béisbol) entrada, *f.*

innkeeper, *n.* posadero, mesonero, *m.*

innocence, *n.* inocencia, *f.*

innocent, *adj.* inocente.

innocuous, *adj.* inocuo, inofensivo.

innovation, *n.* innovación, *f.*

innuendo, *n.* indirecta, insinuación, *f.*

innumerable, *adj.* innumerable.

inoculate, *vt.* inocular; injertar.

inoculation, *n.* inoculación, *f.*

inoffensive, *adj.* pacífico; inofensivo.

inordinate, *adj.* desordenado; excesivo.

inorganic, *adj.* inorgánico.

inquest, *n.* pesquisa, indagación, *f.*

inquire, *vt.* preguntar (alguna cosa); **—,** *vi.* inquirir, examinar.

inquirer, *n.* averiguador, ra, investigador, ra, preguntador, ra.

inquiry, *n.* interrogación, pregunta, *f.*; investigación, *f.*; pesquisa, *f.*

inquisition, *n.* inquisición, *f.*; escudriñamiento, *m.*

inquisitive, *adj.* curioso, preguntón; **—ly,** *adv.* en forma inquiridora.

inquisitiveness, *n.* curiosidad, *f.*

inquisitor, *n.* juez pesquisidor; inquisidor, *m.*

inroad, *n.* incursión, invasión, *f.*

insane, *adj.* insano, loco, demente; **— asylum,** casa de locos, manicomio, *m.*; **to go —,** perder la razón.

insanity, *n.* insania, locura, *f.*

insatiable, *adj.* insaciable.

inscribe, *vt.* inscribir; dedicar; grabar.

inscription, *n.* inscripción, letra, leyenda, *f.*; letrero, *m.*; dedicatoria, *f.*

inscrutable, *adj.* inescrutable.

insect, *n.* insecto, bicho, *m.*; **— killer, — poison,** insecticida, *m.*

insecticide, *n.* insecticida, *m.*

insecure, *adj.* inseguro.

insecurity, *n.* inseguridad, *f.*; incertidumbre, *f.*

insensibility, *n.* insensibilidad, *f.*; estupidez, *f.*

insensible, *adj.* insensible; imperceptible.

inseparable, *adj.* inseparable.

insert, *vt.* insertar, ingerir una cosa en otra, meter.

insertion, n. inserción, f.

inset, vt. injertar, plantar, fijar; grabar; —, n. hoja intercalada en un libro; carta geográfica o lámina dentro de una más grande; intercalación f.

inside, n. y adj. interior, m.; f. (coll.) entrañas, f. pl. ; **on the** —, por dentro; **toward the** —, hacia dentro; —, adv. adentro, dentro; — **of,** dentro de; — **out,** al revés.

insider, n. persona que posee información de primera mano.

insidious, adj. insidioso.

insight, n. conocimiento profundo; perspicacia, f.

insignia, n. pl. insignias, f. pl. ; estandartes, m. pl.

insignificance, n. insignificancia, f.; nulidad, f.

insignificant, adj. insignificante; trivial; **to be** —, ser un cero a la izquierda.

insincere, adj. poco sincero, hipócrita.

insincerity, n. insinceridad, f.

insinuate, vt. insinuar.

insinuation, n. insinuación, f.

insipid, adj. insípido; insulso.

insist, vi. insistir, persistir, hacer hincapié.

insistence, n. insistencia, f.

insistent, adj. insistente, persistente.

insole, n. plantilla, f.

insolence, n. insolencia, f.

insolent, adj. insolente.

insoluble, adj. insoluble, indisoluble.

insolvent, adj. insolvente.

insomnia, n. insomnio, m.

insomuch as, ya que.

inspect, vt. reconocer, examinar, inspeccionar.

inspection, n. inspección, f.; registro, m.; **tour of** —, jira de inspección.

inspector, n. inspector, superintendente, m., registrador, ra.

inspiration, n. inspiración, f.; numen, m.

inspirar, servir de inspiración.

inspire, vt. inspirar (el aire); —, vt. y vi.

instability, n. instabilidad, inconstancia, f.

install, vt. instalar.

installation, n. instalación, f.

installment, instalment, n. instalación, f.; pago parcial, plazo, m.; entrega, f ; **monthly** —, mensualidad, f.; **on the — plan,** a crédito, en pagos parciales, (Mex.) en abonos.

instance, n. instancia, f.; ejemplo, caso, m.; instigación, f.; sugestión, f.; **for** —, por ejemplo; —, vt. citar ejemplos.

instant, adj. instante, urgente; presente; **the 20th** —, el 20 del presente; —**ly,** adv. en un instante; al punto; —, n.

instante, momento, m.

instantaneous, adj. instantáneo.

instead of, en lugar de, en vez de.

instep, n. empeine del pie, m.

instigate, vt. instigar, mover.

instigation, n. instigación, sugestión, f.; provocación a hacer daño.

instigator, n. instigador, ra.

instill, instil, vt. inculcar, **infundir,** insinuar.

instinct, n. instinto, m.; —, adj. animado, impulsado; lleno, cargado.

instinctive, adj. instintivo; —**ly,** adv. por instinto.

institute, vt. instituir, establecer; —, n. instituto, m.

institution, n. institución, f.

institutional, adj. institucional.

instruct, vt. instruir, enseñar.

instruction, n. instrucción, enseñanza, f.

instructive, adj. instructivo.

instructor, n. instructor, m.

instrument, n. instrumento, m.; contrato, m., escritura, f.; — **approach,** (avi.) aproximación a ciegas o mediante instrumentos; — **board,** tablero de instrumentos; — **flying,** vuelo con instrumentos, vuelo a ciegas; — **landing,** aterrizaje mediante instrumentos.

instrumental, adj. instrumental.

insubordinate, adj. insubordinado.

insubordination, n. insubordinación, f.

insufferable, adj. insufrible, insoportable; —**ly,** adv. inaguantablemente, de un modo insoportable.

insufficient, adj. insuficiente; —**ly,** adv. insuficientemente.

insular, adj. insular, isleño.

insulate, vt. aislar (las corrientes eléctricas) .

insulating, adj. (elec.) aislante; — **tape,** cinta aisladora.

insulation, n. (elec.) aislamiento, m.

insulator, n. (elec.) aislador, m.

insulin, n. insulina, f.

insult, vt. insultar; —, n. insulto, m.

insulting, adj. insultante; —**ly,** adv. con insultos, con insolencia.

insurance, n. (com.) seguro, m., seguridad, f.; **accident** —, seguro contra accidente; **burglary** —, seguro contra robo; **fire** —, seguro contra fuego o incendio; — **agent,** agente de seguros; — **broker,** corredor de seguros; — **policy,** póliza de seguro; — **premium,** prima de seguro; **life** —, seguro de vida.

insure, vt. asegurar.

insurgent, n. y adj. insurgente, insurrecto, rebelde, m.

insurrection, n. insurrección, sedición, f.

intact, *adj.* intacto, entero.

intake, *n.* acceso de aire; orificio de entrada o acceso de agua; canal de alimentación; (min.) aereación, *f.;* — **manifold,** válvula múltiple de admisión.

intangible, *adj.* intangible.

integral, *adj.* integro; (chem.) integrante; —**ly,** *adv.* integralmente; —, *n.* todo, *m.*

integrate, *vt.* integrar.

integration, *n.* integración, *f.*

integrity, *n.* integridad, *f.;* pureza, *f.*

intellect, *n.* entendimiento, intelecto, *m.*

intellectual, *n.* intelectual, *m.* y *f.;* —, *adj.* intelectual, mental.

intelligence, *n.* inteligencia, *f.;* conocimiento, *m.;* correspondencia, *f.;* — **test,** prueba de inteligencia.

intelligent, *adj.* inteligente.

intelligentsia, *n.* clase culta, clase intelectual.

intelligible, *adj.* inteligible.

intemperate, *adj.* destemplado; inmoderado.

intend, *vt.* intentar; —, *vi.* proponerse; **to** — **(to go, to do, etc.),** pensar (ir, hacer, etc.).

intense. *adj.* intenso; vehemente.

intensify, *vt.* intensificar, hacer más intenso.

intensity, *n.* intensidad, *f.*

intensive, *adj.* completo, concentrado; — **study,** estudio completo.

intent, *adj.* atento, cuidadoso; —**ly,** *adv.* con aplicación; —, *n.* intento, designio, *m.*

intention, *n.* intención, *f.;* designio, *m.;* (fig.) mira, *f.*

intentional, *adj.* intencional; —**ly,** *adv.* de intento, intencionalmente.

inter, *vt.* enterrar, soterrar.

intercede, *vi.* interceder, mediar.

intercept, *vt.* interceptar; impedir.

interceptor, *n.* interceptor, *m.;* — **missile,** proyectil interceptor; — **plane,** interceptor, *m.*

intercession, *n.* intercesión, mediación, *f.*

interchange, *vt.* alternar, trocar; —, *n.* comercio, *m.;* canje, intercambio, *m.*

interchangeable, *adj.* intercambiable.

intercollegiate, *adj.* interescolar, interuniversitario.

intercommunicate, *vi.* comunicarse mutuamente.

intercourse, *n.* comercio, *m.;* comunicación, *f.;* coito, *m.;* contacto carnal.

interdenominational, *adj.* intersectario.

interdepartmental, *adj.* entre departamentos.

interdependence, *n.* dependencia mutua.

interdict, *n.* entredicho, *m.;* —, *vt.* interdecir, prohibir.

interest, *vt.* interesar; empeñar; —, *n.* interés, provecho, *m.;* influjo, empeño, *m.;* **compound** —, interés compuesto; **rate of** —, tipo de interés.

interested, *adj.* interesado.

interesting, *adj.* interesante, atractivo.

interfere, *vi.* entremeterse, ingerirse, mezclarse, intervenir.

interference, *n.* interposición, mediación, ingerencia, *f.;* (rad.) interferencia estática.

interim, *n.* intermedio, *m.;* **ad** —, entre tanto; en el ínterin.

interior, *adj.* interior, interno.

interject, *vt.* interponer.

interjection, *n.* (gram.) interjección, *f.*

interlining, *n.* entretela, *f.*

interlock, *vt.* y *vi.* trabar, trabarse, engranar.

interloper, *n.* entremetido, da, intruso, sa.

interlude, *n.* intermedio, *m.*

intermarriage, *n.* casamiento entre los miembros de dos familias, razas, etc.

intermediary, *adj.* intermediario; —, *n.* intermediario, ria.

intermediate, *adj.* intermedio; — **range ballistic missile (IRBM),** proyectil balístico de alcance intermedio; —, *n.* intermediario, ria.

interment, *n.* entierro, *m.;* sepultura, *f.*

intermezzo, *n.* intermedio, *m.*

interminable, *adj.* interminable, ilimitado.

intermingle, *vt.* y *vi.* entremezclar; mezclarse.

intermission, *n.* intermedio, *m.*

intermittent, *adj.* intermitente.

intermix, *vt.* entremezclar, mezclar.

intern, *vt.* internar; encerrar; —, *n.* (med.) practicante, *m.;* médico interno (en un hospital).

internal, *adj.* interno; — **medicine,** medicina interna.

international, *adj.* internacional; — **law,** derecho internacional; — **date line,** línea internacional de cambio de fecha.

internet, *n.* internet, *m.*

internment, *n.* encerramiento, *m.,* concentración, *f.*

intermittent, *adj.* intermitente.

internship, *n.* práctica que como médicos residentes hacen los posgraduados en un hospital.

interplanetary, *adj.* interplanetario.

interpolate, *vt.* interpolar.

interpose, *vt.* interponer, entreponer; —, *vi.* interponerse.

interpret, *vt.* interpretar.

interpretation, *n.* interpretación, *f.;* versión, *f.*

interpreter, *n.* intérprete, *m.* y *f.*

interracial, *adj.* entre razas.

interrelated, *adj.* con relación recíproca.

interrogate, *vt.* interrogar, examinar.

interrogation, *n.* interrogación, pregunta, *f.*

interrogator, *n.* interrogante, *m.* y *f.*

interrupt, *vt.* interrumpir, romper.

interruption, *n.* interrupción, *f.*

interscholastic, *adj.* interescolar.

intersect, *vt.* entrecortar; cortar; cruzar.

intersection, *n.* intersección, *f.;* bocacalle *f.*

intersperse, *vt.* intercalar, esparcir una cosa entre otras.

interstate, *adj.* entre estados.

intertwine, *vt.* entretejer.

interurban, *n.* y *adj.* interurbano, *m.*

interval, *n.* intervalo, *m.;* at —s, a ratos.

intervene, *vi.* intervenir; ocurrir.

intervention, *n.* intervención, interposición, *f.*

interview, *n.* entrevista, *f.;* —, *vt.* entrevistar.

interviewer, *n.* persona que celebra entrevistas.

interwoven, *adj.* entretejido, entrelazado.

intestate, *adj.* intestado, abintestato.

intestinal, *adj.* intestinal.

intestine, *adj.* intestino, doméstico; —s, *n. pl.* intestinos, *m. pl.*

intimacy, *n.* intimidad, confianza, *f.;* familiaridad, *f.*

intimate, *n.* amigo íntimo; —, *adj.* íntimo, familiar; —, *vt.* insinuar, dar a entender.

intimation, *n.* insinuación, indirecta, *f.*

intimidate, *vt.* intimidar.

intimidation, *n.* intimidación, *f.*

into, *prep.* en, dentro.

intolerable, *adj.* intolerable.

intolerance, *n.* intolerancia, *f.*

intolerant, *adj.* intolerante.

intonation, *n.* entonación, *f.*

intoxicant, *n.* bebida alcohólica.

intoxicate, *vt.* embriagar.

intoxicated, *adj.* bebido, ebrio, borracho.

intoxicating, *adj.* embriagante; — liquor, bebida embriagante.

intoxication, *n.* embriaguez, *f.;* intoxicación, *f.*

intramural, *adj.* situado intramuros, que tiene lugar dentro de un pueblo o un colegio.

intransitive, *adj.* (gram.) intransitivo.

intravenous, *adj.* intravenoso; — shot, inyección intravenosa.

intrench = entrench.

intrepid, *adj.* arrojado, intrépido.

intricacy, *n.* embrollo, embarazo, *m.;* dificultad, *f.*

intricate, *adj.* intrincado, complicado; complejo.

intrigue, *n.* intriga, *f.;* trama, *f.;* —, *vi.* intrigar.

intrinsic, *adj.* intrínseco, inherente.

introduce, *vt.* introducir, meter; to — (a person), presentar (a una persona).

introduction, *n.* introducción, *f.;* presentación, *f.;* prólogo, preámbulo, *m.*

introductory, *adj.* previo, preliminar, introductorio.

introvert, *n.* introvertido, da.

intrude, *vi.* entremeterse, introducirse, ingerirse.

intruder, *n.* intruso, sa, entremetido, da.

intrusion, *n.* intrusión, *f.*

intrust, *vt.* confiar.

intuition, *n.* intuición, *f.*

intuitive, *adj.* intuitivo.

inundate, *vt.* inundar.

inundation, *n.* inundación, *f.*

inured, *adj.* endurecido; to become —, connaturalizarse.

invade, *vt.* invadir, asaltar.

invader, *n.* usurpador, ra, invasor, ra.

invalid, *adj.* inválido; nulo; — diet, dieta para inválidos; —, *n.* inválido, da.

invalidate, *vt.* invalidar, anular.

invaluable, *adj.* inapreciable.

invariable, *adj.* invariable.

invasion, *n.* invasión, *f.*

invective, *n.* invectiva, *f.*

inveigle, *vt.* seducir, persuadir.

invent, *vt.* inventar.

invention, *n.* invención, *f.;* invento, *m.*

inventive, *adj.* inventivo.

inventor, *n.* inventor, *m.;* forjador, *m.*

inventory, *n.* inventario, *m.*

inverse, *adj.* inverso, trastornado.

invert, *vt.* invertir, trastrocar.

invertebrate, *n.* y *adj.* invertebrado, *m.*

inverted, *adj.* invertido, permutado.

invest, *vt.* investir; emplear dinero en; (com.) invertir; to — money, colocar o invertir dinero.

investigate, *vt.* investigar.

investigation, *n.* investigación, pesquisa, *f.*

investigator, *n.* pesquisidor, ra, investigador, ra.

investiture, *n.* investidura, *f.*

investment, *n.* inversión, *f.*

investor, *n.* inversionista, *m.* y *f.*

inveterate, *adj.* inveterado.

invigorate, *vt.* vigorizar, dar vigor, fortificar, confortar, robustecer.

invigorating, *adj.* vigorizante.

invincible, *adj.* invencible.

inviolate, *adj.* ileso, inviolado.

invisible, *adj.* invisible.

invitation, n. convite, m., invitación, f.
invite, vt. convidar, invitar.
inviting, adj. incitante, atractivo, seductor.
invocation, n. invocación, f.
invoice, n. factura, f.; —, vt. facturar.
invoke, vt. invocar.
involuntary, adj. involuntario.
involve, vt. envolver, implicar.
involved, adj. complejo, complexo; implicado, envuelto.
invulnerable, adj. invulnerable.
inward, adj. interior; interno; —s, adv. interiormente; internamente, hacia adentro.
iodine, n. (chem.) yodo, m.
ion, n. ion, m.
ionization, n. ionización, f.
ionosphere, n. ionosfera, f.
iota, n. iota (letra griega), f.; ápice, m., jota, f.
I.O.U., IOU: I owe you, pagaré, vale.
IQ., IQ: intelligence quotient, cuociente intelectual.
irate, adj. iracundo, colérico.
IRBM (intermediate range ballistic missile), n. proyectil balistico de alcance intermedio.
ire, n. ira, iracundia, f.
Ireland, Irlanda, f.
iridescent, adj. iridiscente, tornasolado.
iris, n. arco iris; (anat.) iris, m.; (bot.) flor de lis.
irish, n. y adj. irlandés, esa.
irk, vt. fastidiar, cansar.
irksome, adj. tedioso, fastidioso.
iron, n. hierro, m.; cast —, hierro fundido o de fundición; galvanized —, hierro galvanizado; — curtain, cortina de hierro; — lung, pulmón de acero; — rust, herrumbre, f.; pig —, fundición, f.; sheet —, hierro laminado; wrought —, hierro forjado o de fragua; —, vt. aplanchar, planchar; poner en grillos.
ironclad, adj. blindado, acorazado, o armado de hierro.
ironic, adj. irónico.
ironical, adj. irónico; —ly, adv. con ironía, irónicamente.
ironing, n. planchado, m.; — board, tabla de planchar.
ironware, n. ferretería, f.; quincallería, f.
ironwork, n. herraje, m.; —s, n. pl. herrería, f.
irony, n. ironía, f.
irradiate, vt. y vi. irradiar, brillar.
irradiated, adj. irradiado.
irrational, adj. irracional.
irrefutable, adj. irrefutable.
irregular. adj. irregular.
irregularity, n. irregularidad, f.

irrelevance, n. calidad de inaplicable.
irrelevant, adj. no aplicable; que no prueba nada; no concluyente, desatinado.
irremediable, adj. irremediable.
irremovable, adj. irremovible.
irreparable, adj. irreparable.
irrepressible, adj. irrefrenable.
irreproachable, adj. irreprochable; intachable.
irresistible, adj. irresistible.
irresolute, adj. irresoluto, vacilante.
irrespective, adj. independiente; — of, sin consideración a, sin tomar en cuenta.
irresponsible, adj. no responsable, irresponsable.
irreverent, adj. irreverente.
irrevocable, adj. irrevocable.
irrigate, vt. regar, mojar.
irrigation, n. riego, m.; irrigación, f.
irritable, adj. irritable; colérico.
irritant, n. (med.) estimulante, m.
irritate, vt. irritar, exasperar, azuzar.
irritation, n. irritación, f.
is, 3ra persona del singular del verbo be.
isinglass, n. colapez, f., cola de pescado; mica, f.
island, n. isla, f.
islander, n. isleño, ña; insular, m. y f.
isle, n. islote, m., isleta, f.
isobaric, adj. isobárico.
isolate, vt. aislar, apartar.
isolation, n. aislamiento, m.
isolationism, n. aislacionismo, m.
isolationist, n. aislacionista, m. y f.
isosceles, adj. isósceles.
isothermal, adj. isotermo.
isotope, n. isótopo, m.
issuance, n. emisión, f.
issue, n. salida, f.; evento, m.; fin, término, m.; flujo, m.; sucesión, f.; producto, m.; consecuencia, f.; punto en debate; (med.) exutorio, m.; prole, progenie, f.; tirada, edición, f.; número (de una publicación); —, vi. salir, nacer, prorrumpir, brotar; venir, proceder; provenir; terminarse; —, vt. echar; brotar; expedir, despachar; publicar; emitir.
isthmus, n. istmo, m.
it, pron. él, ella, ello, lo, la, le.
italic, n. letra cursiva, bastardilla, f.
Italy, Italia, f.
itch, n. sarna, picazón, f.; prurito, m.; —, vi. picar, tener comezón.
item, adv. ítem, otrosí, aun más; —, n. artículo, suelto, m.; (com.) renglón, m.
itemize, vt. particularizar, detallar, estipular.
itinerant, adj. ambulante, errante.
itinerary, n. itinerario, m.

its, *pron.* el suyo, suyo; —, *adj.* su, de él, de ella.
itself, *pron.* el mismo, la misma, lo mismo; sí; **by —,** de por sí.
ivory, *n.* marfil, *m.*

ivory black, *n.* negro de marfil.
Ivory Coast, Costa de Marfil, *f.*
ivory nut, *n.* nuez de marfil.
ivory tower, *n.* torre de marfil.
ivy, *n.* hiedra, *f.*

J

jab, *n.* pinchazo, *m.;* (boxeo) golpe inverso, *m.;* —, *vt.* pinchar.
jabber, *vi.* charlar, farfullar.
jack, *n.* gato, sacabotas, *m.;* martinete, *m.;* cric, *m.,* clavija, *f.;* (coll.) dinero, *m.;* boliche, *m.;* macho, *m.;* burro, *m.;* sota (de la baraja) *f.;* **—pot,** (póquer) jugada que no puede abrirse mientras un jugador no tenga un par de sotas o algo mejor; **to hit the —pot,** sacarse el premio gordo (en la lotería, etc.).
jackal, *n.* adiva, *f.,* adive, chacal, *m.*
jackass, *n.* garañón, burro, asno, *m.*
jacket, *n.* chaqueta, *f.,* saco, *m.;* envoltura, *f.;* forro de papel (de un libro).
jackknife, *n.* navaja de bolsillo.
jack-o'-lantern, *n.* linterna hecha de una calabaza; fuego fatuo.
jackrabbit, *n.* liebre, *f.*
jade, *n.* jade, *m.;* rocín, *m.;* mujer desacreditada; —, *vt.* cansar.
jag, *n.* diente de sierra; mella, *f.;* diente, *m.;* —, *vt.* dentar.
jagged, *adj.* desigual, dentado.
jaguar, *n.* jaguar, *m.*
jail, *n.* cárcel, *f.*
jailbird, *n.* preso, *m.;* criminal, *m.*
jailer, *n.* carcelero, bastonero, *m.*
jalopy, *n.* automóvil destartalado; (Mex.) carcacha, *f.*
jam, *n.* compota, conserva, *f.;* mermelada de frutas; apretadura, *f.;* aprieto, *m.;* **to be in a —,** estar en un aprieto; **— session,** reunión de músicos para improvisar música popular; —, *vt.* apiñar, apretar, estrechar.
jamboree, *n.* reunión nacional o internacional de muchachos exploradores; (coll.) juerga, *f.,* jolgorio, *m.*
jangle, *vi.* reñir, altercar; sonar en discordancia; —, *vt.* hacer sonar; —, *n.* sonido discordante; altercado, *m.*
janitor, *n.* ujier, portero, conserje, *m.*
January, *n.* enero, *m.*
Japan, Japón, *m.*
Japanese, *n.* y *adj.* japonés, esa, nipón, ona.
jar, *vi.* chocar; (mus.) discordar; reñir; —,

n. jarro, *m.;* tinaja, *f.;* riña, *f.;* sonido desapacible; tarro, *m.*
jardiniere, *n.* jardinera, *f.;* florero, *m.*
jargon, *n.* jerga, jerigonza, *f.*
jasmine, *n.* (bot.) jazmín, *m.*
jasper, *n.* (min.) jaspe, *m.*
jato (jet-assisted takeoff), *n.* (avi.) propulsión auxiliar para el despegue de aviones.
jaundice, *n.* ictericia, *f.*
jaunt, *n.* excursión, *f.*
jauntiness, *n.* viveza, *f.,* garbo, *m.*
jaunty, *adj.* alegre, festivo.
javelin, *n.* venablo, *m.,* jabalina, *f.*
jaw, *n.* quijada, *f.;* boca, *f.*
jawbone, *n.* quijada, mandíbula, *f.*
jay, *n.* picaza, urraca, marica, *f.*
jaywalker, *n.* peatón que cruza la calle con las luces en contra.
jazz, *n.* jazz, *m.*
jealous, *adj.* celoso; envidioso; **to be — of,** tener celos de.
jealousy, *n.* celos, *m.* pl.
jean, *n.* mezclilla, *f.,* dril, *m.,* tela burda de algodón.
jeans, *n.* pl. pantalones ajustados de dril, generalmente azules, que usa la juventud.
jeep, *n.* (mil.) pequeño automóvil de trasporte.
jeer, *vi.* ridiculizar, mofar, escarnecer; —, *n.* befa, mofa, burla, *f.*
jelly, *n.* jalea, *f.;* gelatina, *f.*
jellyfish, *n.* aguamar, *m.;* medusa, *f.*
jeopardize, *vt.* arriesgar, poner en riesgo.
jeopardy, *n.* peligro, riesgo, *m.*
jerk, *n.* sacudida, sobarbada, *f.,* respingo, *m.;* (coll.) tonto, ta; —, *vt.* y *vi.* sacudir.
jerky, *adj.* espasmódico, a tirones.
jersey, *n.* jersey, *m.,* tejido de punto; ganado vacuno de la isla de Jersey.
jest, *n.* chanza, burla, *f.;* zumba, *f.;* chasco, *m.;* —, *vi.* chancear; —, *vt.* ridiculizar.
jester, *n.* mofador, ra, bufón, ona.
Jesuit, *n.* jesuita, *m.*
Jesus Christ, Jesucristo, *m.*
jet, *n.* azabache, *m.;* surtidor, *m.;* —

plane, avión de retropropulsión; — **propelled,** impulsado por motor de retropropulsión; — **propulsion,** retropropulsión, *f.,* retroimpulso, *m.;* — **stream,** corriente de vientos occidentales veloces estratosféricos; manga por chorro de aire.

jetty, *n.* muelle, *m.;* rompeolas, *m.*

Jew, *n.* judío, día.

jewel, *n.* joya, alhaja, *f.;* —**s,** *n. pl.* rubíes (de un reloj), *m. pl.*

jeweler, *n.* joyero, *m.*

jewelry, *n.* joyería, pedrería, *f.;* — **store,** joyería, *f.;* **novelty** —, bisutería, joyería de imitación.

Jewish, *adj.* judaico, ca, judío, día.

jibe, *vt.* (naut.) mudar un botavante; —, *vi.* (coll.) concordar, convenir, estar de acuerdo.

jiffy, *n.* (coll.) momentito, *m.*

jig, *n.* baile alegre; — **saw,** sierra, sierra de vaivén.

jigger, *n.* dispositivo, artefacto, *m.;* medida de licor que contiene onza y media.

jiggle, *vt.* mover a tirones; —, *vi.* moverse a tirones.

jigsaw puzzle, *n.* rompecabezas, *m.*

jilt, *n.* coqueta, *f.;* —, *vt.* dar calabazas, despedir a un galán; (coll.) plantar.

jingle, *vi.* retiñir, resonar; —, *n.* retintín, resonido, *m.;* sonaja, *f.*

jingoist, *n.* y *adj.* jingoísta, *m.,* patriotero exaltado.

jitterbug, *n.* (coll.) amante de cierta música popular norteamericana y del baile violento y movido a que ha dado origen.

job, *n.* empleo, *m.;* (Mex. coll.) chamba, *f.;* destajo, *m.;* — **lot,** colección, miscelánea de géneros; *vt.* comprar en calidad de corredor.

jobber, *n.* agiotista, *m.;* destajero, *m.*

jobbing, *n.* oficio de comprar y revender.

jobless, *adj.* cesante, sin trabajo.

jockey, *n.* jockey, *m.,* jinete profesional; **disc** o **disk** —, anunciador de programa con base en discos; —, *vt.* y *vi.* engañar, estafar.

jocose, *adj.* jocoso, burlesco.

jocular, *adj.* jocoso, alegre.

jocund, *adj.* jovial; alegre.

jog, *vt.* empujar; dar un golpe suave; —, *vi.* bambolearse; andar a saltos; —, *n.* empellón, *m.;* traqueo, *m.*

joggle, *vt.* mover a sacudidas.

John Doe, *n.* Fulano de Tal, *m.*

johnnycake, *n.* variedad de pan de maíz.

join, *vt.* juntar, unir; —, *vi.* unirse, juntarse, asociarse; confluir.

joint, *n.* coyuntura, articulación, *f.;* charnela, *f.;* (coll.) lugar de reunión; (bot.)

nudo, *m.;* **out of** —, desunido; —, *adj.* unido; participante; — **account,** cuenta en participación; — **heir,** coheredero, ra; —**ly,** *adv.* juntamente, conjuntamente, en común; —**ly liable,** solidario; —, *vt.* juntar, ensamblar; descuartizar.

joke, *n.* chanza, burla, zumba, *f.;* chasco, *m.;* **to play a** —, hacer una burla; **to play a** — **on,** dar broma a; —, *vi.* chancear, bromear.

joker, *n.* bromista, *m.* y *f.;* comodín (en la baraja), *m.*

jollity, *n.* alegría, *f.,* regocijo, *m.*

jolly, *adj.* alegre, jovial.

jolt, *vt.* y *vi.* traquear, sacudir; —, *n.* traqueo, *m.,* sacudida, *f.*

jonquil, *n.* (bot.) junquillo, *m.*

jostle, *vt.* rempujar, empellar.

jot, *n.* jota, *f.,* cosa mínima; ápice, *m.;* — **(down),** *vt.* apuntar, tomar apuntes, anotar.

jounce, *vt.* sacudir.

journal, *n.* diario, periódico, *m.;* libro diario.

journalism, *n.* periodismo, *m.*

journalist, *n.* periodista, *m.* y *f.*

journey, *n.* jornada, *f.;* viaje, *m.;* —, *vi.* viajar.

jovial, *adj.* jovial, alegre.

jowl, *n.* quijada, *f.*

joy, *n.* alegría, *f.;* júbilo, *m.;* **to give** —, alegrar, causar regocijo; **to wish** —, congratular.

joyful, joyous, *adj.* alegre, gozoso.

J.P.: Justice of the Peace, Juez de Paz.

jubilee, *n.* jubileo, *m.*

Judaism, *n.* judaísmo, *m.*

judge, *n.* juez, *m.;* —, *vi.* juzgar; inferir.

judgment, *n.* juicio, *m.;* sentir, *m.;* meollo, concepto, *m.;* opinión, *f.;* decisión, *f.;* **to pass** —, pronunciar la sentencia; juzgar.

judicial, *adj.* judicial.

judiciary, *n.* magistratura, administración de justicia.

judicious, *adj.* juicioso, prudente.

jug, *n.* jarro, *m.*

juggle, *n.* juego de manos; —, *vi.* hacer juegos de manos, escamotear.

juggler, *n.* prestidigitador, *m.;* impostor, estafador, *m.*

jugular, *adj.* yugular; — **vein,** vena yugular.

juice, *n.* zumo, jugo, *m.*

juicy, *adj.* jugoso.

jujitsu, *n.* jiu-jitsu, *m.*

juke box, *n.* (coll.) tragaperras, tragamonedas, *m.*

July, *n.* (mes) julio, *m.*

jumble, *vt.* mezclar confusamente; —, *n.*

mezcla, confusión, f.

jumbled, adj. destartalado.

jumbo, n. persona o cosa excesivamente voluminosa; —, adj. colosal, excesivamente voluminoso.

jump, vi. saltar, brincar; convenir, concordar; dar saltos; —, n. salto, m.

jumper, n. brincador, ra; vestido sin mangas que se usa encima de una blusa con mangas.

jumping, n. salto, brinco, m.; —. adj. saltante.

jumping jack, n. títere, m.

junction, n. junta, unión, f., empalme, contacto, m.; bifurcación, f.

June, n. (mes) junio, m.; — **bug,** escarabajo americano.

jungle, n. matorral, m.

junior, adj. más joven; —, n. estudiante de tercer año; — **college,** los dos primeros años universitarios; — **high school,** los dos primeros años de escuela secundaria.

juniper, n. (bot.) junípero, enebro, m., sabina, f

junk, n. chatarra, f., hierro viejo; cosa despreciable; (naut.) junco, m.; — **food,** comida chatarra, f.

junket, n. variedad de flan; convite familiar; —, vt. y vi. dar un convite; asistir a un convite costeado con fondos públicos.

junkman, n. comprador de hierro viejo, de papeles, trapos, etc.

jurisdiction, n. jurisdicción f.

jurisprudence, n. jurisprudencia, f.

jurist, n. jurista, m. y f., jurisconsulto, m.

juror, n. jurado, m.

jury, n. junta de jurados; jurado, m.

juryman, n. jurado, miembro de un jurado.

just, adj. justo, honrado, virtuoso, derecho; — **as,** como, así como; — **now,** ahora mismo; —**ly,** adv. justamente.

justice, n. justicia, f., derecho, m.; juez, m.

justification, n. justificación, f.; defensa, f.

justify, vt. justificar.

jut, vi. sobresalir.

jute, n. yute, m.

juvenile, adj. juvenil.

juxtapose, vt. yuxtaponer.

K

kangaroo, n. canguro, m.

katydid, n. cigarra, f.

kc.: kilocycle, kc. kilociclo.

keel, n. (naut.) quilla, f.

keen, adj. afilado, agudo; penetrante, sutil, vivo; vehemente; satírico, picante; —**ly,** adv. con viveza.

keenness, n. agudeza, sutileza, perspicacia, f.; aspereza, f.

keep, vt. tener, mantener, retener; preservar, guardar; proteger; detener; conservar; reservar; sostener; observar; solemnizar; **to — accounts,** llevar cuentas; **to — aloof,** apartarse; **to — books,** llevar los libros; **to — house,** poner casa, ser ama de casa; —, vi. perseverar; soler; mantenerse; —, n. sustentación, manutención, f., sustento, m.

keeper, n. guardián, tenedor, m.; — **of a prison,** carcelero, m.

keeping, n. custodia, f.; guarda, f.

keepsake, n. dádiva, f., recuerdo, regalo, m.

keg, n. barrilito, m.

kennel, n. perrera, f.; jauría, f.; zorrera, f.

kerchief, n. pañuelo, m.

kernel, n. almendra, pepita, f.; meollo, grano, m.

kerosene, n. querosina, f.

ketchup = **catchup.**

kettle, n. caldera, marmita, olla, f.

key, n. llave, f.; (mus.) clave, f.; clavija, f.; chaveta, f.; tecla, f.; — **ring,** llavero, m.; — **word,** palabra clave; **master —,** llave maestra.

keyboard, n. teclado de órgano o piano; teclado de máquina de escribir.

keyhole, n. agujero de la llave.

keynote, n. (mus.) tónica, f.; idea básica o fundamental, m. y f.; — **speech,** discurso principal (en una convención, etc.).

Key West, Cayohueso, Cayo Hueso, m.

kg.: kilogram, kg. kilogramo.

khaki, n. y adj. kaki, caqui, m.

kibitzer, n. (coll.) espectador en un juego de naipes; camasquince, m. y f.; mirón, ona, entremetido, da; (coll.) metiche, m. y f.

kick, vt. acocear; —, vi. patear; (coll.) reclamar, objetar; —, n. puntapié, m.; patada, f.; culatada de armas de fuego; (coll.) efecto estimulador, placer, m.

kickoff, n. saque (en el fútbol), m.

kid, n. cabrito m.; (coll.) chaval, la; —, vt. y vi. (coll.) bromear; chotear; chancearse.

kidnap, vt. secuestrar.

kidnapper, n. secuestrador, ra.

kidnapping, n. secuestro, m.

kidney, n. riñón, m.; (fig.) clase, índole, especie, f.; temperamento, m.; — **bean,** judía.

kidskin, n. cuero de cabritilla.

kill, vt. matar, asesinar.

killer, n. matador, asesino, na, criminal, m. y f.

killing, n. matanza, f.

kiln, n. horno, m.; **brick** —, horno de ladrillo.

kilocycle, n. kilociclo, m.

kilogram, n. kilogramo, m.

kilometer, n. kilómetro, m.

kilometric, adj. kilométrico.

kiloton, n. kilotonelada, f., kilotón, m.

kilowatt, n. kilovatio, m.; — **hour,** kilovatio-hora, m.

kimono, n. quimono, m., bata japonesa.

kin, n. parentesco, m.; afinidad, f.; **next of** —, pariente más cercano.

kind, adj. benévolo, benigno, bondadoso, afable, cariñoso; —, n. género, m.; clase, f.; especie, naturaleza, f.; manera, f.; tenor, m.; calidad, f.

kindergarten, n. escuela de párvulos; jardín de la infancia.

kindhearted, adj. bondadoso.

kindle, vt. y vi. encender; arder.

kindliness, n. benevolencia, benignidad, f.

kindling wood, n. leña, f.

kindly, adj. blando, suave, tratable; —, adv. benignamente; bondadosamente.

kindness, n. benevolencia, f.; favor, beneficio, m.; **have the** — **to,** tenga la bondad de.

kindred, n. parentesco, m.; parentela, casta, f.; —, adj. emparentado; parecido.

kinescope, n. (TV.) cinescopio, m.

kinetics, n. cinética, f.

king, n. rey, m.; rey o doble dama (en el juego de damas); —**ly,** adv. regiamente; —**ly,** adj. real, suntuoso.

kingdom, n. reino, m.

kingfisher, n. (orn.) martín pescador.

kingpin, n. bolo central en un juego de bolos; pasador de charnela o pivote; persona principal en un grupo o empresa.

king-size, adj. de tamaño regio.

kink, n. retorcimiento o ensortijamiento de pelo, alambre, hilo, etc.; peculiaridad, f.

kinky, adj. grifo; ensortijado; — **hair,** cabello duro o demasiado crespo.

kinsfolk, n. parientes, m. pl.

kinship, n. parentela, f.

kinsman, n. pariente, m.

kinswoman, n. parienta, f.

kipper, n. salmón o arenque ahumado; —, vt. ahumar (pescado), etc.

kiss, n. beso, ósculo, m.; —, vt. besar.

kissing, n. acción de besar, besuqueo, m.

kit, n. estuche, m.; **first-aid** —, botiquín, m.; **sewing** —, costurero, m., estuche de costura.

kitchen, n. cocina, f.; — **police,** soldados que asisten en el trabajo de cocina; trabajo de cocina en un campamento militar; — **range,** estufa, f., cocina económica; — **utensils,** trastos, m. pl. , batería de cocina.

kitchenette, n. cocina pequeña; — **apartment,** pequeño departamento en que la cocina forma parte del resto de la habitación.

kite, n. (orn.) milano, m.; cometa, birlocha, pandorga, f.; (Mex.) papalote, m.

kitten, n. gatito, ta; —, vi. parir (la gata).

kitty, n. gatito, m.; polla, puesta (en los juegos de naipes), f.

kleptomaniac, n. cleptómano, na.

km.: kilometer, km. kilómetro.

knack, n. maña, destreza, f.

knapsack, n. mochila, f.

knave, n. bribón, pícaro, bellaco, m.; (en naipes) sota, f.

knavery, n. picardía, bribonada, f.

knavish, adj. fraudulento; pícaro; truhán.

knead, vt. amasar.

knee, n. rodilla, f.; — **bone,** rótula, f.

kneecap, n. rótula, f.

knee-deep, adj. hasta las rodillas; (fig.) muy comprometido, metido muy profundamente.

kneel, vi. arrodillarse, hincar la rodilla, postrarse.

kneepad, n. cojincillo para las rodillas.

knell, n. clamoreo, m.; tañido fúnebre.

knew, pretérito del verbo **know.**

knickerbockers, knickers, n. pl. calzones cortos, pantalones, m. pl. ; bragas, f. pl.

knife, n. cuchillo, m.

knight, n. caballero, paladín, m.; — **(in chess),** caballo (en el ajedrez), m.; —, vt. crear a uno caballero.

knighthood, n. caballería, dignidad de caballero.

knit, vt. y vi. enlazar; atar, unir; trabajar a punto de aguja, tejer.

knitting, n. trabajo de punto, tejido con agujas.

knives, n. pl. de **knife,** cuchillos, m. pl.

knob, *n.* protuberancia, *f.;* perilla, *f.;* nudo en la madera.

knock, *vt.* y *vi.* chocar; golpear, tocar; pegar; **to — down,** derribar, tumbar; **to — on the door,** llamar a la puerta; —, *n.* golpe, *m.;* llamada, *f.*

knocker, *n.* llamador, picaporte, *m.,* aldaba, *f.*

knock-kneed, *adj.* patituerto, patizambo.

knockout, *n.* (boxeo) nocaut, puñetazo que pone fuera de combate, golpe decisivo; (coll.) persona o cosa sumamente atractiva.

knoll, *n.* otero, *m.;* cima de una colina.

knot, *n.* nudo, *m.;* lazo, *m.;* maraña, *f.;* atadura, *f.;* dificultad, *f.;* —, *vt.* enredar, juntar, anudar.

knothole, *n.* agujero que deja un nudo en la madera.

knotted, *adj.* nudoso.

knout, *n.* látigo para azotar.

know, *vt.* y *vi.* conocer, saber; tener noticia de; **I — positively,** me consta; **to — a thing perfectly,** saber una cosa al dedillo.

know-how, *n.* experiencia y habilidad técnicas.

knowing, *adj.* instruido, inteligente, entendido, sabedor; **—ly,** *adv.* hábilmente; a sabiendas.

know-it-all, *n.* sabelotodo, *m.*

knowledge, *n.* conocimiento, saber, *m.;* ciencia, *f.;* inteligencia, habilidad, *f.*

known, *adj.* conocido, sabido.

knuckle, *n.* coyuntura, *f.,* nudillo, *m.;* jarrete de ternera.

kodak, *n.* (marca de fábrica)

kodak, *f.,* cámara fotográfica.

Korean, *n.* y *adj.* coreano, na.

kosher, *n.* alimento judío; —, *adj.* autorizado por la ley judía; (fig.) regular, natural.

L

£ pound, £ libra esterlina.

label, *n.* esquela, *f.;* marbete, billete, *m.;* etiqueta, *f.;* rótulo, *m.;* —, *vt.* rotular o señalar alguna cosa con un rótulo.

labor, *n.* trabajo, *m.;* labor, *f.;* fatiga, *f.;* mano de obra; **hard —,** trabajos forzados; **L— Day,** Día del Trabajo; **— union,** gremio o sindicato obrero; **to be in —,** estar de parto; —, *vt.* y *vi.* trabajar; afanarse, estar con dolores de parto.

laboratory, *n.* laboratorio, *m.;* gabinete, *m.*

laborer, *n.* labrador, trabajador, obrero, *m.;* **day —,** jornalero, *m.*

laborious, *adj.* laborioso; difícil.

laborsaving, *adj.* ahorrador o economizador de trabajo; **— device,** dispositivo que ahorra trabajo.

labyrinth, *n.* laberinto, dédalo, *m.*

lace, *n.* lazo, cordón, *m.;* encaje, *m.;* galón, pasamano, *m.;* **shoe —,** agujeta, *f.,* cordón de zapato; **— trimming,** adorno de encaje, randa, *f.;* —, *vt.* abrochar, encordonar; amarrar (los cordones de los zapatos, etc.).

lacerate, *vt.* lacerar, rasgar.

lacework, *n.* obra de encaje o parecida al encaje.

lacing, *n.* cordón, *m.;* acción de atar o amarrar (con un cordón, etc.).

lack, *vt.* y *vi.* carecer, necesitar; faltar algo; —, *n.* falta, carencia, *f.;* necesidad, *f.*

lackey, *n.* lacayo, *m.*

lacking, *adj.* falto; **to be —,** hacer falta.

laconic, *adj.* lacónico.

lacquer, *n.* laca, *f.;* charol, barniz, *m.;* —, *vt.* charolar.

lactic, *adj.* lácteo; **— acid,** ácido lácteo.

lad, *n.* mozo, muchacho, mozalbete, *m.*

ladder, *n.* escalera portátil.

laden, *adj.* cargado; oprimido.

lading, *n.* carga, *f.;* cargamento, *m.;* **bill of —,** conocimiento de embarque; (rail.) carta de porte.

ladle, *n.* cucharón, cazo, *m.;* achicador, *m.*

lady, *n.* señora, señorita, dama, *f.*

ladybird, ladybug, *n.* (ent.) mariquita, *f.*

ladyfinger, *n.* melindre, *m.,* variedad de bizcocho, (Mex.) soleta, *f.*

lady-killer, *n.* (coll.) donjuán, tenorio, *m.;* favorito de las mujeres.

ladylike, *adj.* que se comporta como una dama; afeminado.

ladylove, *n.* querida, *f.*

lag, *vi.* moverse lentamente; quedarse atrás, rezagarse.

laggard, lagger, *n.* haragán, ana, holgazán, ana.

lagoon, *n.* laguna, *f.*

laid, *pretérito* y *p.p.* del verbo **lay.**

lain, *p.p.* del verbo **lie** (yacer, acostarse).

lair, *n.* cubil, *m.*

laity, *n.* estado seglar.

lake, *n.* lago, *m.;* laguna, *f.*

lamb, n. cordero, m.; carne de cordero.
lame, adj. lisiado, estropeado; cojo; imperfecto; —, vt. lisiar, estropear.
lameness, n. cojera, f.; imperfección, f.
lament, vt. lamentar; —, vi. lamentarse; —, n. lamento, m.
lamentable, adj. lamentable, deplorable, desconsolador.
lamp, n. lámpara, f.; **electric —,** lámpara eléctrica; — **shade,** pantalla, f.
lamplight, n. luz de lámpara.
lampoon, n. sátira, f.; libelo, m.; —, vt. escribir sátiras.
lamppost, n. pie de farol, poste de farola.
lamprey, n. (ichth.) lamprea, f.
lance, n. lanza, f.; lanceta, f.; —, vt. dar un lancetazo; abrir, cortar, perforar; hacer una operación quirúrgica con lanceta.
land, n. país, m.; región, f.; territorio, m.; tierra, f.; — **forces,** tropas de tierra; — **mine,** mina terrestre; —, vt. y vi. desembarcar; saltar en tierra, aterrizar.
landholder, n. hacendado, m.
landing, n. desembarco, m.; aterrizaje, m.; **emergency — field,** (avi.) campo de emergencia; — **field,** campo de aterrizaje; — **gear,** tren de aterrizaje.
landlady, n. propietaria, arrendadora, f.; mesonera, f.; posadera, f.; casera, f.
landlord, n. propietario, m.; posadero, m.; casero, m.
landlubber, n. marinero bisoño.
landmark, n. mojón, linde, m.; señal, marca, f.; hecho o acontecimiento importante.
landowner, n. hacendado, m.
landscape, n. paisaje, m.; — **gardener,** persona que proyecta y construye jardines o parques; — **gardening,** jardinería, f.
landslide, n. derrumbe, desprendimiento de tierra; (pol.) mayoría de votos abrumadora.
landsman, n. persona que vive en la tierra; marinero de poca experiencia.
lane, n. callejuela, calle, f.; vereda, f.; **traffic —,** zona de tránsito.
language, n. lengua, f.; lenguaje, idioma, m.
languid, adj. lánguido, débil.
languish, vi. entristecerse, afligirse, languidecer.
languishing, adj. lánguido.
languor, n. languidez, f.
lank, lanky, adj. alto y delgado.
lanolin, lanoline, n. lanolina, f.
lantern, n. linterna, f.; farol, m.; — **slide,** diapositiva, f.; fotografía positiva.
lap, n. falda, f; seno, m.; regazo, m.;

(deportes) vuelta, etapa, f —, vt. arrollar, envolver; traslapar, sobreponer; lamer.
lapel, n. solapa, f.
Laplander, n. lapón, ona.
lapse, n. lapso, m.; caída, f.; falta ligera; traslación de derecho o dominio; —, vi. escurrir, manar; deslizarse; caer; caducar; vencerse (un plazo, etc.).
laptop, n. laptop, m.
larceny, n. ratería, f.; hurto, m.
larch, n. (bot.) alerce, lárice, m.
lard, n. manteca, f.; lardo, m.; gordo, m.; —, vt. mechar.
larder, n. despensa, f.
large, adj. grande, amplio, vasto; liberal; **at —,** en libertad, suelto; — **type,** tipo de cartel; —**ly,** adv. en gran parte.
large-scale, adj. en gran escala.
lariat, n. lazo, m., reata, f.
lark, n. (orn.) alondra, f.
larkspur, n. (bot.) espuela de caballero.
larva, n. larva, oruga, f.
laryngitis, n. laringitis, f.
larynx, n. laringe, f.
lash, n. latigazo, m.; sarcasmo, m.; —, vt. dar latigazos, azotar; atar; satirizar.
lass, n. doncella, moza, f.
lassitude, n. lasitud, fatiga, f.
lasso, n. lazo, m., reata, f.
last, adj. último, postrero, pasado; — **night,** anoche; — **word,** decisión final; última moda; la última palabra; lo mejor; algo que no se puede mejorar; —**ly,** adv. al fin, por último; —, n. horma de zapatero; (naut.) carga de un navío; **at —,** al fin, al cabo, por último; —, vi. durar, subsistir.
lastex, n. hilo elástico hecho de látex y algodón seda, lana o seda artificial.
lasting, adj. duradero, permanente; —**ly,** adv. perpetuamente.
latch, n. aldaba (de puerta), f.; cerrojo, m.; —, vt. cerrar con aldaba.
latchkey, n, picaporte, m.; llave de la puerta principal.
late, adj. tardío; tardo, lento; difunto; último; —, adv. tarde; **of —,** de poco tiempo acá; —**ly,** adv. poco ha, recientemente.
lateness, n. retraso, m., tardanza, f.
latent, adj. escondido, oculto, latente.
later, adj. posterior; —, adv. más tarde.
lateral, adj. lateral; —**ly,** adv. lateralmente.
latest, adj. último; más reciente; — **fashion,** última moda; **at the —,** a más tardar.
latex, n. (bot.) látex, m.
lath, n. lata, f.; listón, m.; —, vt. enlistonar.
lathe, n. torno, m.

lather, n. espuma de jabón, jabonaduras, f. pl. ; —, vt. y vi. lavar con espuma de jabón; espumar.

Latin, n. latín (lenguaje), m.; —, n. y adj. latino, na.

Latin-American, n. latinoamericano, na.

latitude, n. latitud, f.

latrine, n. letrina, f.

latter, adj. posterior, último; **the** —, éste, el último.

lattice, n. celosía, f.; reja, f.; enrejado, m.; —, vt. enrejar.

laud, n. alabanza, f.; (eccl.) laudes, f. pl. ; —, vt. alabar, ensalzar.

laudable, adj. laudable, loable; meritorio.

laudatory, adj. laudatorio.

laugh, vi. reir; — **at,** reírse de, burlarse de; —, n. risa, risotada, f.

laughable, adj. risible.

laughing, adj. risueño; — **gas,** óxido nitroso; —, n. risa, f.; **to burst out** —, soltar una carcajada; —**ly,** adv. con risa.

laughing-stock, n. hazmerreir, m.

laughter, n. risa, risotada, f.; **hearty** —, carcajada, f.; **outburst of** —, risotada, f.

launch, vt. lanzar; —, vi. lanzarse; —, n. (naut.) lancha, f.

launching, n. (avi.) lanzamiento, m.; —, **pad,** plataforma de lanzamiento.

launder, vt. lavar (la ropa).

laundromat, n. lavandería de auto servicio.

laundry, n. lavadero, m.; lavandería, f.; ropa lavada o para lavar.

laundryman, n. lavandero, m.

laundrywoman, n. lavandera, f.

laurel, n. (bot.) lauro, laurel, m.; honor, m., fama, f.

lava, n. lava, f.

lavatory, n. lavabo, lavatorio, m.

lavender, n. (bot.) espliego, m.; lavándula, f.; cantueso, m.; —, adj. lila.

lavish, adj. pródigo; gastador; —, vt. disipar, prodigar.

law, n. ley, f.; derecho, m.; litigio judicial; jurisprudencia, f.; regla, f.; **according to** —, procedente, de acuerdo con la ley.

law-abiding, adj. obediente de las leyes.

lawbreaker, n. delincuente, m. y f.; trasgresor, ra, persona que infringe la ley.

lawful, adj. legal; legítimo.

lawgiver, n. legislador, m.

lawless, adj. ilegal; anárquico, sin ley.

lawlessness, n. desobediencia o trasgresión de la ley; ilegalidad, f.; desorden, m.

lawmaker, n. legislador ra.

lawn, n. prado, m.; linón, m.; césped, m.; — **mower,** segadora de césped, cortacésped, f.

lawsuit, n. proceso, pleito, m.; demanda, f.

lawyer, n. abogado, licenciado, m.; jurisconsulto, m.; —**'s office,** bufete de abogado.

lax, adj. laxo, flojo.

laxative, n. y adj. purgante, laxante, m.

laxity, n. laxitud, flojedad, f.; relajación, f.

lay, vt. poner, colocar, extender; calmar, sosegar; imputar; apostar; exhibir; poner (un huevo); **to** — **claim,** reclamar; pretender; —, vi. aovar, poner huevos las aves; —, pret. del verbo **lie** (echarse, recostarse).

lay, adj. laico, secular, seglar; — **brother,** lego, m.; —, n. canción, melodía, f.; — **of the land,** forma del tendido del terreno o suelo; consideración de la disposición o circunstancia; estado de asuntos.

layer, n. gallina que pone; estrato, m.; capa, f.

layette, n. canastilla, f.

layman, n. lego, seglar, m.

layoff, n. despedida del trabajo; —, vt. despedir del trabajo.

layout, n. plan, trazado, esquema, arreglo, m.; disposición, distribución, f.

lazily, adv. perezosamente; lentamente.

laziness, n. pereza, f.

lazy, adj. perezoso, tardo, pesado.

lb.: pound, lb. libra.

l.c.: letter of credit, carta de crédito; **lower case,** min. minúscula.

l.c.l.: less than carload, (rail.) menos de carro entero, menos de vagonada.

lead, vt. conducir, guiar; gobernar; emplomar; llevar la batuta; —, vi. mandar, tener el mando; ser mano (en el juego de naipes); sobresalir, ser el primero; —, n. delantera, f.; mano (en los naipes); **to take the** —, tomar la delantera.

lead, n. plomo, m.; — **pencil,** lápiz, m.; **molten** —, plomo derretido.

leaden, adj. hecho de plomo; pesado, estúpido.

leader, n. líder, guía, conductor, m.; jefe general; caudillo, m.; **political** —, cacique, m.

leadership, n. capacidad dirigente.

leading, adj. principal; capital; — **article,** artículo de fondo de una publicación; — **man,** — **lady** (theat.) primer actor, primera actriz.

leaf, n. folio, m.; hoja (de una planta); hoja (de un libro); hoja (de puerta), f.; (bot.) fronda, f.

leafless, adj. deshojado, sin hojas.

leaflet, n. hojilla, f.; folleto, volante, m.

leafy, adj. frondoso.

league, n. liga, alianza, f.; legua, f.; —, vi. confederarse.

leak, *n.* fuga, *f*; salida o escape (de gas, líquido, etc.); goteo, *m.*; gotera, *f.*; (naut.) vía de agua; —, *vi.* (naut.) hacer agua; gotear, salirse o escaparse (el agua, gas, etc.).

leakage, *n.* derrame, escape, goteo, *m.*; merma, *f.*; filtración, *f.*; gotera, fuga, *f.*

leakproof, *adj.* libre de goteo; a prueba de escape.

leaky, *adj.* agujereado, que se gotea.

lean, *vt. y vi.* ladear, inclinar, apoyarse; **to — back,** recostarse; —, *adj.* magro, seco, chupado.

leaning, *n.* ladeo, *m.*; inclinación, tendencia, *f.*

leap, *vi.* saltar, brincar; salir con ímpetu; palpitar; dar brincos; —, *n.* salto, *m.*; **— year,** año bisiesto o intercalar.

learn, *vt. y vi.* aprender, conocer.

learned, *adj.* docto, instruido; **the —,** literatos, *m. pl.*

learning, *n.* literatura, ciencia, erudición, *f.*; saber, *m.*; letras, *f. pl.*

lease, *n.* arriendo, arrendamiento, *m.*; contrato de arrendamiento; —, *vt.* arrendar.

leash, *n.* correa, traílla, *f.*; —, *vt.* atar con correa.

least, *adj.* mínimo; —, *adv.* en el grado mínimo; **at —,** a lo menos; **not in the —,** ni en lo más mínimo; **the — posible,** lo menos posible.

leastwise, *adv.* (coll.) al menos, a lo menos.

leather, *n.* cuero, pellejo, *m.*

leatherette, *n.* cuero artificial, imitación de piel.

leathery, *adj.* correoso.

leave, *n.* licencia, *f.*; permiso, *m.*; despedida, *f.*; **— of absence,** licencia, *f.*; permiso para ausentarse; **by your —,** con su permiso; **to give —,** permitir; **to take —,** despedirse; —, *vt. y vi.* dejar, abandonar; ceder; cesar; salir.

leaven, *n.* levadura, *f.*; fermento, *m.*; —, *vt.* fermentar.

leaves, *n. pl.* de **leaf,** hojas, *f. pl.*

leave-taking, *n.* despedida, *f.*

leavings, *n. pl.* sobras, *f. pl.*, residuos, desechos, desperdicios, *m. pl.*

lecture, *n.* conferencia, *f.*; corrección, *f.*; represión, *f.*; —, *vt.* enseñar; censurar; reprender.

lecturer, *n.* conferenciante, *m. y f.*; lector, instructor, *m.*

ledge, *n.* capa, tonga, *f.*; borde, *m.*; reborde, *m.*; anaquel, *m.*

ledger, *n.* (com.) libro mayor.

lee, *n.* (naut.) sotavento, *m.*; —, *adj.* sotaventado.

leech, *n.* sanguijuela, *f.*

leek, *n.* (bot.) puerro, *m.*

leer, *n.* ojeada de soslayo y maliciosa; **to — at,** ojear al soslayo y con malicia.

lees, *n. pl.* heces, *f. pl.*; sedimento, foso, *m.*

leeside, *n.* (naut.) banda de sotavento.

leeward, *adv.* (naut.) hacia el sotavento; —, *adj.* relativo al sotavento; —, *n.* sotavento, *m.*

leeway, *n.* desviación, *f.*; libertad, *f.*; margen, *m.*; (naut.) deriva, *f.*

left, *adj.* siniestro, izquierdo; **— winger,** izquierdista, *m. y f.*; **— behind,** rezagado; —, *n.* izquierda, *f.*; (pol.) izquierda, *f.*; **on the —,** a la izquierda.

left-handed, *adj.* zurdo; desmañado; insincero, malicioso.

leftist, *n. y adj.* (pol.) izquierdista, *m. y f.*

leftover, *n.* sobrante, *m.*; lo que queda por hacer; sobras, *f. pl.*, restos, *m. pl.*

leg, *n.* pierna, *f.*; pie, *m.*; (math.) cateto, *m.*

legacy, *n.* legado, *m.*, manda, *f.*

legal, *adj.* legal, legítimo; **— tender,** moneda legal; curso legal.

legality, *n.* legalidad, legitimidad, *f.*

legalize, *vt.* legalizar, autorizar.

legation, *n.* legación, embajada, *f.*

legend, *n.* leyenda, *f.*

legendary, *adj.* fabuloso, quijotesco, legendario.

legging, *n.* polaina, *f.*; botín, *m.*

legibility, *n.* legibilidad, *f.*

legible, *adj.* legible, que puede leerse.

legion, *n.* legión, *f.*

legislate, *vt.* legislar.

legislation, *n.* legislación, *f.*

legislative, *adj.* legislativo.

legislator, *n.* legislador, *m.*

legislature, *n.* legislatura, *f.*; cuerpo legislativo.

legitimate, *adj.* legítimo; —, *vt.* legitimar.

legume, *n.* legumbre, *f.*

leisure, *n.* desocupación, *f.*; ocio, *m.*; comodidad, *f.*; **at —,** cómodamente, con sosiego; **— hours,** horas o ratos libres.

lemon, *n.* limón, *m.*; **— drop,** pastilla de limón; **— squeezer,** exprimidor de limones.

lemonade, *n.* limonada, *f.*

lend, *vt.* prestar, dar prestado.

lender, *n.* prestamista, *m. y f.*, prestador, ra.

lend-lease, *adj.* de préstamos y arrendamientos; —, *vt.* otorgar préstamos y arrendamientos.

length, *n.* longitud, *f.*; largo, *m.*; duración, *f.*; distancia, *f.*; **at —,** finalmente; largamente.

lengthen, vt. alargar; —, vi. alargarse, dilatarse.

lengthwise, adv. longitudinalmente, a lo largo; —, adj. colocado a lo largo.

lengthy, adj. largo; fastidioso.

leniency, n. benignidad, lenidad, f.

lenient, adj. lenitivo, indulgente.

lens, n. lente (vidrio convexo), m. y f.

lent, n. cuaresma, f.

lentil, n. (bot.) lenteja, f.

leopard, n. (zool.) leopardo, pardal, m.

leper, n. leproso, sa.

leprous, adj. leproso.

leprosy, n. lepra, f.

lesion, n. lesión, f.

less, adj. inferior, menos; —, adv. menos.

lessee, n. arrendatario, ria.

lessen, vt. minorar, disminuir; —, vi. disminuirse.

lesser, adj. más pequeño; inferior.

lesson, n. lección, f.

lessor, n. arrendador, casero, m.

lest, conj. para que no, por temor de que.

let, vt. dejar, permitir; arrendar; —'s see, a ver; —'s go, vámonos.

letdown, n. aflojamiento, m.; relajación, f.; (coll.) decepción, f.; desanimación, f.

lethal, adj. letal.

lethargy, n. letargo, estupor, m.

letter, n. letra, f.; carta, f.; **air mail** —, carta aérea; **capital** —, mayúscula, f.; **circular** —, carta circular; **form** —, carta general, carta circular; **general delivery** —, carta en lista; — **box,** buzón para las cartas; — **case,** cartera, f.; — **drop,** buzón, m.; — **file,** archivo para cartas; — **of credit,** carta credencial o de crédito; — **of introduction,** carta de presentación; — **opener,** plegadera, f.; **love** —, carta amorosa, carta de amor; **registered** —, carta certificada; **lower case** —, letra minúscula.

letterhead, n. membrete, m.

lettering, n. inscripción, leyenda, f.; rótulo, m.

letter-perfect, adj. que se sabe a la perfección.

lettuce, n. lechuga, f.

leucocyte, n. (anat.) leucocito, m.

levee, n. dique, m.; recepción, f.

level, adj. llano, igual; nivelado, plano; allanado; —, n. llanura, f.; plano, m.; nivel, m.; —, vt. allanar; nivelar.

levelheaded, adj. discreto, sensato.

leveling, n. igualación, nivelación, f.; —, adj. nivelador.

lever, n. palanca, f.; **clutch** —, palanca, f.; **firing** —, palanca de desenganche; **operating** —, **driving** —, palanca de impulsión; **reverse** —, palanca de cambio de marcha.

leverage, n. acción de palanca.

levity, n. levedad, ligereza, f.; inconstancia, veleidad, f.

levy, n. leva (de tropas), f.; —, vt. embargar una propiedad; imponer (una multa, tributos, etc.).

lewd, adj. lascivo, disoluto, libidinoso.

lexicon, n. léxico, diccionario, m.

liability, n. responsabilidad, f.; —**les,** (com.) pasivo, m., créditos pasivos.

liable, adj. sujeto, expuesto a; responsable; capaz.

liaison, n. vinculación, coordinación, f.

liar, n. embustero, ra, mentiroso, sa.

libel, n. libelo, m.; —, vt. difamar.

libeler, libeller, n. libelista, m. y f.; difamador, ra.

libelous, libellous, adj. difamatorio.

liberal, adj. liberal, generoso; franco; —, n. persona de ideas liberales; miembro del Partido Liberal; — **arts,** artes liberales; —**ly,** adv. a manos llenas.

liberalism, n. liberalismo, m.

liberality, n. liberalidad, generosidad, f.

liberal-minded, adj. tolerante, de ideas liberales.

liberate, vt. libertar.

liberation, n. liberación, f.

liberator, n. libertador, m.

libertine, n. libertino, na; —, adj. libertino, disoluto.

liberty, n. libertad, f.; privilegio, m.; **to take the** — **to,** permitirse, tomarse la libertad.

librarian, n. bibliotecario, ria.

library, n. biblioteca, f.

libretto, n. (mus.) libreto, m.

lice, n. pl. de louse, piojos.

license, licence, n. licencia, f.; permiso, m.; **driver's** —, licencia para manejar; — **plate,** placa, f.

licentious, adj. licencioso, disoluto.

lichen, n. (bot.) liquen, m.

licit, adj. lícito.

lick, vt. lamer, chupar; (coll.) golpear, tundir; derrotar (en una pelea, etc.).

licking, n. paliza, f.

licorice, n. orozuz, m.

lid, n. tapa, f.; tapadera, f.; — **(of the eye),** párpado, m.

lie, n. mentira, f.; (coll.) trápala, f.; —, vi. mentir; echarse; reposar, acostarse; yacer.

lied, pret. del verbo **lie** (mentir).

lief, adv. de buena gana.

lien, n. (leyes) derecho de retención.

lieu, n. lugar, m.; **in** — **of,** en vez de.

lieutenant, n. lugarteniente, teniente, m.; alférez, m.; — **commander,** capitán de corbeta; — **colonel,** teniente coronel; — **general,** teniente general; **second** —, subteniente, m.

life, n. vida, f.; ser, m.; vivacidad, f.; **for** —, por toda la vida; **from** —, del natural; **high** —, el gran mundo; — **belt,** cinturón salvavidas; — **buoy,** boya, f.; — **insurance,** seguro de vida; — **preserver,** salvavidas, m.; — **raft,** balsa salvavidas.

lifeboat, n. bote salvavidas; lancha salvavidas.

lifeguard, n. salvavidas, guardavidas (nadador), m.

lifeless, adj. muerto, inanimado; sin vivacidad.

lifelike, adj. natural, que parece vivo.

lifelong, adj. de toda la vida, que dura toda la vida.

lifesaver, n. salvavidas, m., miembro del servicio de salvavidas.

life-size, adj. de tamaño natural.

lifetime, n. duración de la vida; —, adj. de por vida, que dura toda la vida.

lifework, n. obra total o principal de la vida de uno.

lift, vt. alzar, elevar, levantar; hurtar, robar; —, n. acción de levantar, alza, f.; ayuda, f.; ascensor (hidráulico), m.

lifting, n. izamiento, m., acción de levantar.

ligament, n. ligamento, m.

ligature, n. ligadura, f.

light, n. luz, f.; claridad, f.; conocimiento, m.; día, m.; reflejo, m.; candela, f.; resplandor, m.; — **bulb,** foco, m., bombilla, f.; —, adj. ligero, leve, fácil; frívolo; superficial; ágil; inconstante; claro; blondo; —, vt. encender; alumbrar; —, vi. hallar, encontrar; desmontarse; desembarcar.

lighten, vi. centellear como relámpago, brillar; aclarar; —, vt. iluminar; aligerar; aclarar.

lighter, n. (naut.) alijador, m.; (naut.) chalana, barcaza, gabarra, f.; encendedor, m.; **cigarette** —, encendedor de cigarrillos, mechero, m.

lighthearted, adj. despreocupado; alegre.

lighthouse, n. (naut.) faro, fanal, m.

lighting, n. iluminación, f.

lightly, adv. levemente; alegremente; ágilmente.

lightness, n. ligereza, f.; agilidad, velocidad, f.

lightning, n. relámpago, m.; **heat** —, relámpago sin trueno; — **bug,** luciérnaga, f.; — **rod,** pararrayos, m.; —, vi. relampaguear.

lightweight, adj. de peso ligero.

likable, adj. simpático, agradable.

like, adj. semejante; igual; verosímil; —, n. semejante, m., parecido, m.; **to look** —, parecerse a; —, prep. como; —, vt. y vi. querer, amar; gustar, agradar alguna cosa; **as you** — **it,** como quiera usted; **to be** —**d,** caer en gracia; **to** — **someone,** tener simpatía por.

likelihood, n. probabilidad, f.; indicación, f.

likely, adj. probable, verosímil; —, adv. con toda probabilidad.

liken, vt. asemejar; comparar.

likeness, n. semejanza, f.; igualdad, f.; retrato fiel.

likewise, adv. igualmente, asimismo.

liking, n. gusto, agrado, m.

lilac, n. (bot.) lila, f.; —, adj. de color lila.

lilt, vt. cantar alegremente; —, n. canción alegre; movimiento rápido.

lily, n. lirio, m.; — **of the valley,** lirio de los valles, muguete, m.

limb, n. miembro (del cuerpo), m.; pierna, f.; rama (de un árbol), f.

limber, adj. manejable, flexible; —, vt. y vi. poner manejable, hacer flexible.

lime, n. cal, f.; variedad de limón; tilo, m., tila, f.

limelight, n. centro de atención pública.

limerick, n. verso jocoso.

limestone, n. piedra de cal, caliza, f.

limewater, n. agua de cal.

limit, n. límite, término, m.; línea, f.; **to the** —, hasta no más; —, vt. restringir; concretar, confinar.

limitation, n. limitación, f.; restricción, f.; coartación, f.

limited, adj. tasado, limitado.

limitless, adj. inmenso, ilimitado, sin límite.

limousine, n. limosina, f.

limp, vi. cojear; —, n. cojera, f.; —, adj. fláccido, flojo, blando.

limpid, adj. limpio, claro, trasparente; límpido.

linden, n. tilo, m.; — **tea,** tila, f.

line, n. línea, f.; (mil.) línea de batalla; raya, f.; contorno, m.; cola, f.; ferrocarril, m.; vía, f.; renglón, m.; verso, m.; linaje, m.; cordón (muy delgado), m.; **pipe** —, cañería, f.; —, vt. forrar; revestir; rayar, trazar líneas; —, vi. alinearse.

lineage, n. linaje, m.; descendencia, f.; prosapia, f.; generación, f.

lineal, linear, adj. lineal.

lineman, n. (rail.) guardavía, guardabarreras, m.; reparador de líneas telefónicas; (fútbol) atajador o guarda en la línea de embestida.

linen, n. lienzo, lino, m.; tela de hilo; ropa blanca; —, adj. de lino, de tela de hilo.

liner, *n.* avión o vapor de travesía.

linesman, *n.* juez de línea en el fútbol.

line-up, *n.* formación, *f.;* (fútbol) formación de los jugadores antes de principiar el juego.

linger, *vi.* demorarse, tardar, permanecer por un tiempo.

lingerie, *n.* ropa interior femenina, ropa íntima, *f.*

lingering, *n.* tardanza, dilación, *f.; —, adj.* moroso, lento.

linguist, *n.* lingüista, *m.* y *f.*

liniment, *n.* linimento, *m.*

lining, *n.* forro, *m.*

link, *n.* eslabón, *m.;* vínculo, *m.;* anillo de cadena; (mech.) articulación, *f.,* gozne, *m.; —, vt.* y *vi.* unir, vincular.

linnet, *n.* (orn.) pardillo, pardal, *m.*

linoleum, *n.* linóleo, *m.*

linotype, *n.* linotipo, *m.;* máquina linotipista.

linseed, *n.* linaza, *f.; —* **oil,** aceite de linaza.

lint, *n.* hilas, *f. pl.;* hilacha, *f.*

lintel, *n.* lintel o dintel de puerta o ventana.

lion, *n.* león, *m.*

lioness, *n.* leona, *f.*

lip, *n.* labio, *m.;* borde, *m.; —* **reading,** lectura por el movimiento de los labios.

lipstick, *n.* lápiz para los labios, lápiz labial.

liquefy, *vt.* y *vi.* licuar, liquidar; derretir.

liqueur, *n.* licor, aguardiente, *m.*

liquid, *adj.* líquido; — **air,** aire fluido o líquido; — **fire,** fuego líquido; — **measure,** cántara, *f.,* medida para líquidos; —, *n.* licor, líquido, *m.*

liquidate, *vt.* liquidar, saldar (cuentas).

liquidation, *n.* (com.) liquidación, *f.*

liquidizer, *n.* licuadora, *f.*

liquor, *n.* licor, *m.; —* **case,** licorera, *f.*

Lisbon, Lisboa, *f.*

lisp, *vi.* balbucear; cecear; —, *n.* ceceo, *m.;* balbuceo, *m.*

list, *n.* lista, *f.;* elenco, *m.;* catálogo, *m.; —* **price,** precio de catálogo; —, *vt.* poner en lista; registrar; —, *vi.* (mil.) alistarse; (naut.) recalcar.

listen, *vi.* escuchar; atender.

listener, *n.* escuchador, ra, oyente, *m.* y *f.*

listless, *adj.* indiferente, descuidado.

litany, *n.* letanía, *f.*

liter, *n.* litro, *m.*

literacy, *n.* capacidad para leer y escribir.

literal, *adj.* literal, al pie de la letra, a la letra; **—ly,** *adv.* literalmente.

literary, *adj.* literario.

literature, *n.* literatura, *f.*

lithe, *adj.* ágil, flexible.

lithograph, *n.* litografía, *f.; —, vt.* litografiar.

lithography, *n.* litografía, *f.*

lithosphere, *n.* litosfera, *f.*

litigation, *n.* litigio, pleito, *m.;* litigación, *f.*

litmus, *n.* (chem.) tornasol, *m.*

litter, *n.* litera, cama, *f.;* cama portátil; lechigada, ventregada, *f.; —, vt.* y *vi.* parir los animales; —, *vt.* desordenar.

little, *adj.* pequeño; poco; chico; **a —,** poquito; — **boy,** chico, chiquito, *m.; —* **girl,** chica, chiquita, *f.;* **very —,** muy chico; muy poquito; —, *n.* poco, *m.;* parte pequeña.

liturgy, *n.* liturgia, *f.*

live, *vi.* vivir; manifestarse; habitar.

live, *adj.* vivo; — **wire,** persona lista o muy activa; alambre cargado.

livelihood, *n.* vida, *f.;* subsistencia, *f.*

liveliness, *n.* vivacidad, *f.*

livelong, *adj.* todo; **the — day,** el día entero.

lively, *adj.* vivo, brioso; gallardo; animado, alegre.

liver, *n.* hígado, *m.*

liverwurst, *n.* salchicha de hígado.

livery, *n.* librea, *f.*

lives, *n.* pl. de **life.**

livestock, *n.* ganadería, *f.;* ganado en pie. livid, *adj.* lívido; amoratado.

living, *n.* modo de vivir; subsistencia, *f.;* —, *adj.* vivo; viviente; — **room,** sala de recibo; salón, *m.; —* **wage,** salario adecuado para vivir.

lizard, *n.* lagarto, *m.;* lagartija, *f.*

llama, *n.* (zool.) llama *f.*

L.L.D.: Doctor of Laws, Doctor en Derecho.

load, *vt.* cargar; llenar; embarcar; —, *n.* carga, *f.;* cargamento, *m.;* peso, *m.; —* **of a firearm,** carga (de una arma de fuego), *f.*

loading, *n.* cargo, *m.;* acción de cargar.

loaf, *n.* pan, bollo de pan, *m.;* **meat —,** pan de carne; —, *vi.* haraganear, holgazanear.

loafer, *n.* holgazán, ana, gandul, la.

loam, *n.* marga, *f.*

loan, *n.* préstamo, empréstito, *m.; —* **office,** casa de préstamos; —, *vt.* prestar.

loath, loth, *adj.* con aversión, poco dispuesto (a hacer algo).

loathe, *vt.* aborrecer, detestar.

loathing, *n.* repugnancia, aversión, *f.*

loathsome, *adj.* detestable, repugnante.

loathly, *adj.* repugnante; —, *adv.* de mala gana.

loaves, *n.* pl. de **loaf.**

lobby, *n.* vestíbulo, *m.; —, vi.* cabildear.

lobbying, *n.* cabildeo, *m.*

lobe, *n.* lóbulo, *m.*

lobster, *n.* langosta, *f.*

local, *adj.* local; —, *n.* (rail.) tren local.

locale, *n.* local, *m.*

locality, *n.* localidad, *f.*

localize, *vt.* localizar.

locally, *adv.* localmente.

locate, *vt.* ubicar, colocar, situar; localizar.

located, *adj.* situado, ubicado.

location, *n.* ubicación, *f.;* localización, colocación, *f.*

lock, *n.* cerradura, cerraja, *f.;* llave (de arma de fuego), *f.;* vedija (de lana), *f.;* mechón (de cabello), *m.;* compuerta, *f.;* **spring —,** cerradura de golpe o de muelle; —, *vt.* cerrar, cerrar con llave; **to — out,** cerrar la puerta a uno para que no entre; —, *vi.* cerrarse con llave.

locked, *adj.* cerrado (bajo llave); encerrado; enganchado; trabado, entrelazado.

locker, *n.* armario, *m.;* cofre, *m.;* gaveta, *f.*

locket, *n.* medallón, guardapelo, *m.*

lockjaw, *n.* (med.) tétano, *m.*

lockout, *n.* cesación del trabajo; paro forzoso.

locksmith, *n.* cerrajero, llavero, *m*

locomotion, *n.* locomoción, *f.*

locomotive, *n.* locomotora, *f.*

locust, *n.* langosta, *f.;* saltamontes, *m.*

lode, *n.* filón, *m.,* vena, veta, *f.*

lodge, *n.* casa de guarda en el bosque; casita pequeña; sucursal o casa de una sociedad; —, *vt.* alojar; depositar; presentar; —, *vi.* residir, habitar.

lodger, *n.* huésped, *m.* y *f.,* inquilino, na.

lodging, *n.* posada, casa, habitación, *f.;* hospedaje, *m.*

loft, *n.* desván, *m.;* pajar, *m.*

loftiness, *n.* altura, *f.;* sublimidad, *f.;* soberbia, *f.*

lofty, *adj.* alto; sublime; altivo; elevado.

log, *n.* leño, trozo de árbol; (naut.) barquilla, *f.;* cuaderno de bitácora; **— cabin,** cabaña rústica.

loganberry, *n.* planta híbrida de zarzamora y frambuesa roja.

logarithm, *n.* logaritmo, *m.*

logbook, *n.* (naut.) diario de navegación.

logger, *n.* persona que corta árboles; máquina para el corte y trasporte de trozas.

logging, *n.* corte y trasporte de trozas.

logic, *n.* lógica, *f.*

logical, *adj.* lógico, consecuente.

logistics, *n.* (mil.) logística, *f.*

logrolling, *n.* acuerdo entre los políticos para ayudarse recíprocamente.

logwood, *n.* palo de Campeche, campeche, *m.*

loin, *n.* ijada, *f.;* ijar, *m.;* **—s,** *n. pl.* lomos,

m. pl.

loiter, *vi.* haraganear, holgazanear.

loiterer, *n.* haragán, ana, holgazán, ana.

loll, *vt.* dejar colgar; —, *vi.* apoyarse, recostarse; dejar colgar la lengua (aplícase a los animales).

lollipop, *n.* paleta, *f.*

London, Londres, *m.*

lone, *adj.* solitario, soltero.

loneliness, *n.* soledad, *f.*

lonely = **lonesome.**

lonesome, *adj.* solitario, solo; triste, abatido por la soledad.

long, *adj.* largo, prolongado; **a — time,** mucho tiempo, un largo rato; —, *adv.* durante mucho tiempo.

long-distance, *adj.* de larga distancia; **— call,** llamada de larga distancia.

longer, *adj.* más largo; —, *adv.* más tiempo; **no —,** ya no, no más.

longevity, *n.* longevidad, *f.*

longhand, *n.* escritura a mano.

longhorn, *n.* buey español con cuernos muy largos.

longing, *n.* deseo vehemente, anhelo, *m.*

longitude, *n.* longitud, *f.*

long-lived, *adj.* longevo, muy anciano.

long-playing, *adj.* de larga duración (aplícase a discos fonográficos).

long-range, *adj.* de gran alcance.

longshoreman, *n.* estibador, *m.*

long-standing, *adj.* de larga duración.

long-winded, *adj.* locuaz.

look, *vt.* y *vi.* mirar; ver; considerar, pensar, contemplar, esperar; parecer; tener cara de; **as it —s to me,** a mi ver; **— out!** ¡cuidado! **to — after,** echar una vista, cuidar de; **to — bad,** tener mala cara; verse mal; **to — for,** buscar; **to — well,** verse bien; **to — over,** repasar; —, *n.* aspecto, *m.;* mirada, *f.;* ojeada, *f.*

looking glass, *n.* espejo, *m.*

lookout, *n.* (mil.) centinela, *m.* y *f.;* (naut.) vigía, *m.*

loom, *n.* telar, *m.;* —, *vi.* destacarse, descollar; perfilarse; (fig.) amenazar.

loony, *adj.* (coll.) loco.

loop, *n.* ojal, *m.;* presilla, *f.;* aro, anillo, *m.;* lazo, *m.;* vuelta, *f.*

loophole, *n.* tronera, buhedera, *f.;* evasiva, escapatoria, *f.*

loose, *adj.* suelto, desatado, holgado, flojo; suelto de vientre; vago, relajado; disoluto; desenredado; **—ly,** *adv.* sueltamente; **—ly speaking,** en términos generales.

loose-jointed, *adj.* con las coyunturas al parecer flojas; capaz de mover las coyunturas con gran facilidad.

loose-leaf, *adj.* de hojas sueltas (insertables en forma de libro).

loosen, *vt.* aflojar, laxar; desliar, desatar.

looseness, *n.* flojedad, *f.;* relajación, *f.;* flujo de vientre.

loot, *n.* pillaje, botín, *m.;* —, *vt.* pillar, saquear.

lop, *vt.* desmochar.

loquacious, *adj.* locuaz, charlador, palabrero.

lord, *n.* señor, *m.;* amo, dueño, *m.;* lord (título de nobleza inglés), *m.;* —, *vi.* señorear, dominar.

lordly, *adj.* señoril, orgulloso, imperioso.

lordship, *n.* excelencia, señoría, *f.;* dominio, *m.;* autoridad, *f.*

lore, *n.* saber, *m.;* erudición, *f.;* conocimiento de hechos y costumbres tradicionales.

lose, *vt.* perder; disipar, malgastar; —, *vi.* perderse, decaer; **to — face,** perder prestigio; **to — one's senses,** perder la chaveta; **to — one's temper, to — one's composure,** salirse de sus casillas; **to — one's way,** extraviarse, perder el camino; **to — out,** ser derrotado.

loser, *n.* perdedor, ra; **good —,** buen perdedor, buena perdedora.

loss, *n.* pérdida, *f.;* daño, *m.;* **to be at a —,** estar perplejo, estar en duda.

lot, *n.* suerte, *f ;* lote, *m.;* cuota, *f.;* porción, *f.;* **building —,** solar, *m.;* **to draw —s,** decidir por suerte, echar a suerte.

lotion, *n.* loción, *f.*

lottery, *n.* lotería, rifa, *f.*

lotus, *n.* (bot.) loto, *m.*

loud, *adj.* ruidoso, alto; clamoroso; (coll.) charro, vulgar; **—ly,** *adv.* en voz alta.

loudness, *n.* ruido, *m.;* (coll.) vulgaridad, *f.,* falta de delicadeza; mal gusto.

loudspeaker, *n.* altoparlante, *m.*

lounge, *n.* sofá, canapé, *m.;* **— room,** sala de esparcimiento social, *f.;* salón social, *m.;* —, *vi.* holgazanear.

louse, *n. (pl. lice),* piojo, *m.*

lousy, *adj.* piojoso; miserable; vil; (coll.) horrible, detestable.

lout, *n.* patán, rústico, zafio, *m.*

lovable, *adj.* amable, digno de ser querido.

love, *n.* amor, cariño, *m.;* galanteo, *m.;* **— game,** (tenis) juego a cero; **to fall in —,** enamorarse; **to make —,** cortejar, galantear, enamorar; —, *vt.* amar; gustar de; querer.

lovebird, *n.* (orn.) periquito, *m.*

loveliness, *n.* amabilidad, *f.;* agrado, *m.;* belleza, *f.*

lovely, *adj.* amable, hermoso, bello.

love-making, *n.* enamoramiento, *m.*

lover, *n.* amante, galán, *m.*

lovesick, *adj.* enamorado; herido de amor.

loving, *adj.* amoroso, afectuoso.

low, *adj.* bajo, pequeño; hondo; abatido; vil; —, *vi.* mugir; —, *adv.* a precio bajo; en posición baja.

lower, *adj.* más bajo; **— berth,** litera o cama baja; **— case,** (print.) caja baja, caja de minúsculas; —, *vt.* bajar, humillar; disminuir; **to — (price),** rebajar (el precio); —, *vi.* disminuirse.

lowermost, lowest, *adj.* más bajo, ínfimo.

lowland, *n.* tierra baja.

lowliness, *n.* bajeza, *f.;* humildad, *f.*

lowly, *adj.* humilde; —, *adv.* modestamente.

low-minded, *adj.* bajo, ruin.

low-pressure, *adj.* de baja presión.

low-priced, *adj.* barato.

low water, *n.* bajamar, *f.*

low-water mark, *n.* línea de bajamar; (fig.) nivel más bajo.

lox, *n.* oxígeno líquido.

loyal, *adj.* leal, fiel; **—ly,** *adv.* lealmente.

loyalist, *n.* (pol.) realista, *m.* y *f.*

loyalty, *n.* lealtad, fidelidad, *f.*

L.P.: long playing, *adj.* de larga duración (discos fonográficos).

lube, *n.* (mech.) aceite lubricante.

lubricant, *n.* y *adj.* lubricante, *m.*

lubricate, *vt.* lubricar, engrasar.

lubricating, *adj.* lubricante, lubricador.

lubrication, *n.* lubricación, *f.*

lucid, *adj.* luciente, luminoso; claro.

luck, *n.* acaso, *m.;* suerte, fortuna, *f.*

luckily, *adv.* por fortuna, afortunadamente.

luckless, *adj.* infeliz, desventurado.

lucky, *adj.* afortunado, feliz, venturoso, dichoso; **to be —,** tener suerte.

lucrative, *adj.* lucrativo.

ludicrous, *adj.* burlesco; ridículo.

lug, *vt.* tirar; arrastrar; (naut.) tirar de un cabo; —, *n.* esfuerzo, *m.;* agarradera, asa, *f.*

luggage, *n.* equipaje, *m.;* **carry-on—,** equipaje de mano, *m.;* **— rack,** porta-equipajes, *m.*

lukewarm, *adj.* tibio; templado.

lull, *vt.* arrullar; adormecer; aquietar; —, *n.* pausa, *f.;* momento de calma.

lullaby, *n.* arrullo, *m.;* canción de cuna.

lumber, *n.* madera de construcción; **— dealer,** maderero, comerciante en maderas.

lumberjack, *n.* leñador, hachero, *m.*

lumberman, *n.* maderero, *m.*

lumberyard, *n.* depósito de maderas de construcción.

luminous, *adj.* luminoso, resplandeciente.

lump, *n.* protuberancia, *f.;* chichón, *m.;* **— of sugar,** terrón de azúcar; —, *vt.* amontonar; —, *vi.* agrumarse.

lunacy, n. locura, f.; frenesi, m.
lunatic, adj. lunático, loco, frenético; fantástico; —, n. loco, ca.
lunch, n. merienda, colación, f.; almuerzo, m.; —, vi. almorzar, merendar.
luncheon, n. almuerzo, m.; merienda, colación, f.
lung, n. pulmón, m.; **iron** —, pulmón de acero.
lunge, n. embestida, estocada, f.; —, vi. embestir.
lurch, n. abandono, m.; vaivén, m.; (naut.) bandazo, m.; sacudida, f.; —, vi. dar bandazos; caminar con vaivén.
lure, n. señuelo, cebo, m.; —, vt. atraer, inducir.
lurid, adj. fantástico, lívido, descolorido.
lurk, vi. espiar, ponerse en acecho.
luscious, adj. delicioso, sabroso; atractivo, apetitoso.
lush, adj. jugoso; suculento.
lust, n. lujuria, sensualidad, f.; libídine,

codicia, f.; concupiscencia, f.; —, vi. lujuriar.
luster, lustre, n. lustre, m.; brillantez, f.; lucimiento, m.; realce, m.; viso, m.
lustrum, n. lustro, quinquenio, m.
lusty, adj. fuerte, vigoroso.
Lutheran, n. y adj. luterano, na.
luxuriant, adj. exuberante, superabundante.
luxurious, adj. lujoso; exuberante.
luxury, n. voluptuosidad, f.; exuberancia, f.; lujo, m.
lyceum, n. liceo, m.
lye, n. lejía, f.
lying, n. mentir, m., mentira, f.; —, adj. mentiroso; tendido, recostado.
lying-in, n. parto, m.
lymph, n. linfa, f.
lymphatic, adj. linfático.
lynch, vt. linchar.
lynx, n. lince, m.
lyric, lyrical, adj. lírico.

M

macadam, n. macádam, m.
macaroni, n. macarrones, m. pl.
macaroon, n. almendrado, macarrón de almendras.
Mach, Mach number, n. (aeronáutica) número Mach, m. (relación de la velocidad de un cuerpo con la del sonido).
machination, n. maquinación, trama, f.
machine, n. máquina, f.; — **gun,** ametralladora, f.; — **tool,** herramienta de máquina.
machinery, n. maquinaria, mecánica, f.
machinist, n. maquinista, mecánico, m.
mackerel, n. (ichth.) escombro, m., caballa, f.; (Sp. Am.) macarela, f.
mackinaw, n. chamarra, f.
mackintosh, n. abrigo impermeable.
mad, adj. loco, furioso, rabioso, insensato; **stark** —, loco rematado; **to go** —, volverse loco.
madam, madame, n. madama, señora, f.
madden, vt. enloquecer, trastornar; enfurecer.
made, adj. hecho, fabricado, producido; —, pret. y p.p. del verbo **make.**
made-to-order, adj. hecho a la medida o a la orden; — **clothing,** ropa hecha a la medida.
made-up, adj. ficticio; artificial; pintado.
madhouse, n. casa de locos, manicomio, m.

madman, n. loco, maniático, m.
madness, n. locura, manía, f.; furor, m.
madras, n. madras, m.
magazine, n. revista, f; almacén, depósito, m.; (naut.) santabárbara, f.
maggot, n. gusano, m.; noción fantástica.
magic, n. magia, nigromancia, f.; —, adj. mágico.
magician, n. mago, nigromante, m. **magistrate,** n. magistrado, m.
magnanimity, n. magnanimidad, f.
magnanimous, adj. magnánimo.
magnate, n. magnate, m.
magnesia, n. magnesia, f.
magnesium, n. magnesio, m.
magnet, n. imán, m., piedra imán.
magnetic, adj. magnético; — **needle,** calamita, brújula, f.
magnetism, n. magnetismo, m.
magnificence, n. magnificencia, f.
magnificent, adj. magnífico; pomposo, rumboso.
magnify, vt. amplificar, magnificar; exaltar, exagerar.
magnifying glass, n. vidrio de aumento.
magnitude, n. magnitud, grandeza, f.
magnolia, n. magnolia, f.
magpie, n. urraca, picaza, f.
mahogany, n. caoba, f.
maid, n. doncella, joven, f.; moza, criada, f.

maiden, *adj.* virgen, virginal; nuevo; — **name,** nombre de soltera; — **voyage,** primer viaje (de un barco); —, *n.* doncella, joven, *f.*

maidservant, *n.* criada, sirvienta, *f.*

mail, *n.* correo, *m.; malla, armadura, f.;* correspondencia, *f.;* cota de malla; **by registered** —, bajo sobre certificado, por correo certificado; **by return** —, a vuelta de correo.

mailbag, *n.* portacartas, *m.,* valija de correo.

mailbox, *n.* buzón, *m.*

mailman, *n.* cartero, *m.*

mail order, *n.* pedido postal; compra de artículos por correo.

mail-order house, *n.* casa de ventas por correo.

maim, *vt.* mutilar; estropear; tullir.

main, *adj.* principal; esencial; — **office,** casa matriz; —, *n.* océano, *m.;* alta mar; fuerza, *f.;* **in the** —, en general; —**ly,** *adv.* principalmente, sobre todo.

mainland, *n.* continente, *m.*

mainmast, *n.* palo mayor de un navío.

mainsail, *n.* vela mayor.

mainspring, *n.* muelle (de reloj, etc.), *m.*

mainstay, *n.* (naut.) apoyo principal del mastelero; sostén principal; motivo principal.

maintain, *vt.* y *vi.* mantener, sostener; conservar.

maintenance, *n.* mantenimiento, *m.;* protección, *f.;* sustento, *m.;* conservación (de carreteras, caminos, etc.), *f.*

maize, *n.* maíz, *m.*

majestic, majestical, *adj.* majestuoso; grande; —**ally,** *adv.* majestuosamente.

majesty, *n.* majestad, *f.*

major, *adj.* mayor; —, *n.* (mil.) mayor, *m.,* sargento mayor; (mil.) comandante, *m.;* primera proposición de un silogismo; — **general,** mariscal de campo.

majority, *n.* mayoría, *f.;* pluralidad, *f.;* — **(of votes in an election),** mayoría absoluta (en una elección).

make, *vt.* hacer, crear, producir, fabricar; ejecutar; obligar; forzar; confeccionar; **to** — **for,** ir hacia, encaminarse a; **to** — **believe,** hacer ver, hacer de cuenta; **to** — **a fool of,** engañar; **to** — **a point of,** dar importancia a; **to** — **over,** hacer de nuevo; **to** — **ready,** preparar; **to** — **room,** hacer lugar; **to** — **use of,** servirse de, utilizar; **to** — **a show of,** ostentar; **to** — **fun of,** burlarse de; **to** — **known,** dar a conocer; **to** — **no difference,** no importar; **to** — **out,** divisar, columbrar; **to** — **up,** constituirse, componerse; inventar; contentarse, hacer las paces; maquillar;

—, *n.* hechura, *f.;* forma, figura, *f.*

make-believe, *n.* disimulo, *m.;* pretexto, *m.*

makeshift, *n.* expediente, medio, *m.;* —, *adj.* temporal; mal confeccionado, mal hecho.

makeup, *n.* maquillaje, tocado, *m.*

making, *n.* composición, *f.;* estructura, hechura, *f.*

maladjustment, *n.* mal ajuste; discordancia, *f.;* desequilibrio, *m.*

malady, *n.* enfermedad, *f.*

malaria, *n.* malaria, *f.;* paludismo, *m.*

male, *adj.* masculino; —, *n.* macho, *m.*

malefactor, *n.* malhechor, *m.*

malevolent, *adj.* malévolo.

malformed, *adj.* malhecho, contrahecho.

malice, *n.* malicia, *f.*

malicious, *adj.* malicioso.

malign, *adj.* maligno; malandrín; —, *vt.* difamar.

malignant, *adj.* maligno.

malignity, *n.* malignidad, *f.*

mall, *n.* plaza comercial, *f.;* centro comercial, *m.*

mallard, *n.* anadón, *m.*

mallet, *n.* mazo, *m.*

malnutrition, *n.* desnutrición, *f.*

malt, *n.* malta, *f.,* cebada fermentada.

maltose, *n.* (chem.) maltosa, *f.,* azúcar de almidón y malta.

maltreat, *vt.* maltratar.

mamma, mama, *n.* mamá, *f.*

mammal, *n.* mamífero, *m.*

mammoth, *adj.* enorme, gigantesco; —, *n.* mamut, *m.*

man, *n.* hombre, *m.;* marido, *m.;* criado, peón, *m.;* — **overboard,** hombre al agua; **mechanical** —, autómata, *m.;* **young** —, joven, *m.;* —, *vt.* (naut.) tripular, armar.

manage, *vt.* y *vi.* manejar, manipular, gobernar, administrar; dirigir; gestionar.

manageable, *adj.* manejable, dócil, tratable; dirigible.

management, *n.* manejo, *m.;* administración, dirección, *f.;* conducta, *f.;* gestión, *f.;* (com.) gerencia, *f.*

manager, *n.* administrador, director, *m.;* gestor, *m.;* gerente, *m.;* **assistant** —, subgerente, *m.*

managing, *adj.* dirigente; gestor.

mandate, *n.* mandato, *m.,* comisión, *f.*

mandatory, *adj.* obligatorio.

mandolin, *n.* mandolín, bandolín, *m.;* mandolina, bandolina, *f.*

mane, *n.* melena, *f.;* crines del caballo.

man-eater, *n.* caníbal, antropófago, *m.*

maneuver, *n.* maniobra, *f.;* —, *vt.* y *vi.* maniobrar.

manful, adj. bravo, valiente.

manganese, n. manganeso, m.

mange, n. roña, f.; sarna perruna.

manger, n. pesebre, m.; nacimiento (de Navidad).

mangle, n. planchadora, f.; planchadora mecánica; —, vt. mutilar; planchar con planchadora mecánica.

manhandle, vt. maltratar.

manhole, n. registro, m.; abertura para la inspección de alcantarillas, calderas, etc.

manhood, n. virilidad, f.; edad viril; hombría, f.; valentía, f.; valor, m.

mania, n. manía, f.; tema, m.

maniac, n. y adj. maniático, ca.

manicure, n. arreglo de las uñas; —, vt. arreglar las uñas.

manicurist, n. manicurista, f.

manifest, adj. manifiesto, patente; —, n. manifiesto, m.; —, vt. manifestar.

manifestation, n. manifestación, f.

manifesto, n. manifiesto, m.; declaración pública, proclamación, f.

manifold, adj. muchos, varios, múltiple.

manikin, n. maniquí, m.

manila, n. (bot.) abacá; — **paper,** papel de Manila.

manipulate, vt. manejar, manipular.

mankind, n. género humano, humanidad, f.

manliness, n. valentía, f., valor, m.

manly, adj. varonil, valeroso.

man-made, adj. hecho por el hombre; — **satellite,** satélite artificial.

mannequin, n. maniquí, m.

manner, n. manera, f.; modo, m.; forma, f.; método, m.; maña, f.; hábito, m.; moda, f.; especie, f.; guisa, f.; vía, f.; —s, n. pl. modales, m. pl., urbanidad, crianza, f.; in such a —, de tal modo; in the — of, a fuer de, en son de, a guisa de.

mannerism, n. amaneramiento, m.

mannerly, adj. cortés, atento; — adv. cortésmente.

manor, n. señorío, m.; feudo, m.

manpower, n. fuerza de trabajo, mano de obra; brazos, m. pl.; (mil.) elemento humano.

mansion, n. casa grande, casa de gran lujo; solar, m.

manslaughter, n. homicidio (sin premeditación), m.

mantel, mantelpiece, n. repisa de chimenea.

mantle, n. manto, m.; capa, f.

manual, n. manual, m.; —, adj. manual; — **training,** instrucción en artes y oficios.

manufacture, n. manufactura, fabricación, f.; artefacto, m.; —, vt. fabricar, manufacturar, hacer.

manufacturer, n. fabricante, manufacturero, m.

manufacturing, n. fabricación, manufactura, f.

manure, n. abono, estiércol, m.; —, vt. abonar, estercolar, cultivar.

manuscript, n. manuscrito, escrito, m.; original, m.

many, adj. muchos, muchas; — **a time,** muchas veces; how —? ¿cuántos? as — as, tantos como.

map, n. mapa, m.; carta geográfica; — **maker,** cartógrafo, m.; —, vt. delinear mapas; trazar, hacer planes.

maple, n. arce, m.; — **syrup,** jarabe de arce.

mapping, n. cartografía, f.

mar, vt. dañar, corromper; desfigurar.

marauder, n. merodeador, ra.

marble, n. mármol, m.; canica, bolilla de mármol, bola, f.; —, adj. marmóreo, de mármol; —, vt. jaspear.

March, n. marzo, m.

march, n. marcha, f.; pasodoble, m.; —, vi. marchar, caminar.

mare, n. yegua, f.

margarine, n. margarina, f.

margin, n. margen, m. y f.; borde, m.; orilla, f.; —, vt. marginar.

marigold, n. (bot.) caléndula, f.

marijuana, marihuana, n. marijuana, marihuana, f.

marimba, n. marimba, f.

marina, n. dársena para yates.

marine, n. marina, f.; soldado de marina; —, adj. marino.

mariner, n. marinero, m.

marionette, n. (theat.) títere, muñeco, m.

marital, adj. marital.

maritime, adj. marítimo, naval.

mark, n. marca, f.; señal, nota, f.; seña, f.; blanco, m.; calificación (en escuela o examen), f.; — **down,** reducción de precio; **printer's** —, pie de imprenta; —, vt. marcar; advertir; **to** — **down,** bajar (el precio); **to** — **time,** marcar el paso, llevar el compás; quedar inactivo u ocioso.

marker, n. marca, ficha, f.; marcador, m.

market, n. mercado, m.; plaza, f.; **meat** —, carnicería, f.; — **report,** revista del mercado.

marketable, adj. vendible, comercial.

marketing, n. mercadotecnia, f.

marking, adj. marcador.

marksman, n. tirador, m.

marksmanship, n. puntería, f.

marmalade, n. mermelada, f.

marmoset, *n.* mono tití.

marmot, *n.* marmota, *f.*

maroon, *n.* esclavo fugitivo; negro descendiente de esclavo fugitivo; color rojo oscuro; —, *vt.* abandonar a uno en una costa desierta.

marquis, *n.* marqués, *m.*

marquisette, *n.* tejido fino de malla.

marriage, *n.* matrimonio, casamiento, *m.*

marriageable, *adj.* casadero, núbil.

married, *adj.* casado, conyugal; to get —, casarse.

marrow, *n.* tuétano, meollo, *m.;* médula, *f.*

marry, *vt.* casar; casarse con; —, *vi.* casarse.

marsh, *n.* pantano, *m.*

marshal, *n.* mariscal, *m.;* field —, capitán general.

marshmallow, *n.* malvavisco, *m.,* altea, *f.*

marshy, *adj.* pantanoso.

mart, *n.* emporio, *m.;* comercio, *m.;* feria, *f.*

marten, *n.* (zool.) garduña, marta, *f.*

martial, *adj.* marcial, guerrero; — law, ley marcial.

martin, *n.* (orn.) vencejo, *m.*

martyr, *n.* mártir, *m.* y *f.*

martyrdom, *n.* martirio, *m.*

marvel, *n.* maravilla, *f.;* prodigio, *m.;* —, *vi.* maravillarse.

marvelous, *adj.* maravilloso.

Marxist, *n.* marxista, *m.* y *f.*

mascara, *n.* preparación para teñir las pestañas.

mascot, *n.* mascota, *f.*

masculine, *adj.* masculino, varonil.

mash, *n.* masa, *f.;* —, *vt.* amasar; mezclar; majar.

mask, *n.* máscara, *f.;* pretexto, *m.;* —, *vt.* enmascarar; disimular, ocultar.

mason, *n.* albañil, *m.;* masón, *m.*

masonry, *n.* albañilería, mampostería, *f.;*

masonería, *f.;* stone —, calicanto, *m.*

masquerade, *n.* mascarada, *f.;* — ball, — dance, baile de máscaras o de disfraz.

masquerader, *n.* máscara, *m.* y *f.,* disfrazado, da.

mass, *n.* misa, *f.;* midnight —, misa de gallo; to say —, cantar o celebrar misa.

mass, *n.* masa, *f.;* montón, *m.;* bulto, *m.;* —es, *n. pl.* vulgo, *m.,* las masas, el pueblo en general; — meeting, mitin popular, reunión del pueblo en masa; — production, fabricación en serie o en gran escala.

massacre, *n.* carnicería, matanza, *f.;* —, *vt.* matar atrozmente, hacer una carnicería.

massage, *n.* masaje, *m.;* soba, *f.;* —, *vt.* sobar, dar masaje.

masseur, masseuse, *n.* masajista, *m.* y *f.*

massive, *adj.* macizo, sólido.

mast, *n.* árbol de navio, palo, *m.;* fabuco, *m.;* topsail —, verga de garra; —, *vt.* (naut.) arbolar.

master, *n.* amo, dueño, *m.;* maestro, *m.;* señor, *m.;* señorito, *m.;* (naut.) maestre, *m.;* patrón, *m.;* — of ceremonies, maestro de ceremonias; — hand, mano maestra, maestría, *f.;* — stroke, — touch, golpe de maestro o diestro, golpe magistral; —, *vt.* domar, gobernar; dominar; sobreponerse.

masterly, *adj.* imperioso, despótico; magistral; —, *adv.* con maestría.

masterpiece, *n.* obra o pieza maestra.

mastery, *n.* superioridad, maestría, *f.*

masthead, *n.* (periodismo) cabeza fija.

masticate, *vt.* mascar, masticar.

mastoid, *n.* mastoides, *f.*

mat, *n.* estera, esterilla, *f.;* —, *vt.* esterar.

match, *n.* mecha, pajuela, *f.;* fósforo, *m.;* cerilla, *f.,* cerillo, *m.;* torneo, partido, *m.;* contrincante, *m.;* pareja, *f.;* casamiento, *m.;* combate, *m.;* —, *vt.* igualar, aparear; casar; —, *vi.* hermanarse.

matchbox, *n.* cajita de fósforos o cerillos.

matching, *n.* igualación, *f.;* aparejamiento, *m.*

matchless, *adj.* incomparable, sin par.

matchmaker, *n.* casamentero, ra; organizador de juegos o certámenes.

mate, *n.* consorte, *m.* o *f.;* compañero, ra; (naut.) piloto, *m.;* first —, (naut.) piloto, *m.;* —, *vt.* desposar; igualar.

material, *adj.* material, físico; —, *n.* tela, género, *m.*

materialism, *n.* materialismo, *m.*

materialistic, *adj.* materialista.

materialize, *vt.* consumar, realizar; llevar a efecto.

maternal, *adj.* maternal, materno.

maternity, *n.* maternidad, *f.*

mathematical, *adj.* matemático.

mathematician, *n.* matemático, ca.

mathematics, *n. pl.* matemáticas, *f. pl.*

matinee, *n.* matiné, *f.*

mating, *n.* apareamiento, *m.;* — time (of animals), brama (de los animales), *f.*

matriarch, *n.* matriarca, *f.,* mujer que encabeza una familia, grupo o estado.

matriculate, *vt.* matricular.

matriculation, *n.* matrícula, matriculación, *f.*

matrimonial, *adj.* matrimonial, marital.

matrimony, *n.* matrimonio, casamiento, *m.*

matrix, *n.* matriz, *f.;* molde, *m.*

matron, *n.* matrona, *f.*

matted, *adj.* enredado; desgreñado.

matter, *n.* materia, sustancia, *f.;* asunto,

objeto, _m._; cuestión, importancia, _f_; **it
is no** —, no importa; **what is the** —?
¿de qué se trata? **a** — **of fact,** hecho
positivo o cierto, _m._; — **of form,** cuestión de fórmula, _f.;_ —, _vi._ importar.
matter-of-fact, _adj._ positivo, trivial, rutinario.

mattress, _n._ colchón, _m._; **spring** —, colchón de muelle.

mature, _adj._ maduro; juicioso; —, _vt._
madurar; —, _vi._ vencerse (una letra, un
documento, etc.).

maturity, _n._ madurez, _f._

maudlin, _adj._ lloroso, sentimental en
extremo.

maul, _vt._ apalear, maltratar a golpes.

mausoleum, _n._ mausoleo, _m._

mauve, _adj._ color malva.

maverick, _n._ animal sin marca de hierro.

maw, _n._ cuajar, _m.;_ molleja de las aves.

maxim, _n._ máxima, _f.;_ axioma, _m._

maximum, _adj._ máximo.

May, _n._ mayo, _m._

may, _vi._ poder; ser posible.

maybe, _adv._ quizás, tal vez.

May Day, _n._ día primero de mayo.

mayonnaise, _n._ mayonesa, _f.,_ salsa mayonesa.

mayor, _n._ corregidor, alcalde, _m._

maze, _n._ laberinto, _m.;_ perplejidad, _f._

M.C.: Master of Ceremonies, Maestro de
Ceremonias.

M.D.: Doctor of Medicine, Doctor en
Medicina.

me, _pron._ mí; me.

meadow, _n._ pradera, _f.;_ prado, _m.;_ vega, _f._

meager, meagre, _adj._ magro; flaco; momio;
seco.

meal, _n._ comida, _f.;_ harina, _f._

mealy, _adj._ harinoso.

mean, _adj._ bajo, vil, despreciable; abatido;
mediocre; mezquino; de término medio;
— **temperature,** promedio de temperatura, _m.;_ **in the** —**time,** — **while,** en el
ínterin, mientras tanto; —, _n._ medio,
_m.;_ —**s,** _pl._ medios, recursos, _m. pl.;_
person of —**s,** persona acaudalada; **by
all** —**s,** sin falta; **by no** —**s,** de ningún
modo; —, _vt._ y _vi._ significar; querer
decir; intentar; **you don't** — **it!** ¡calla!
¿de veras?

meander, _n._ laberinto, _m.;_ camino tortuoso; —, _vt._ y _vi._ serpear, seguir un camino tortuoso; caminar sin rumbo.

meaning, _n._ intención, _f.;_ inteligencia, _f.;_
sentido, significado, _m.;_ significación, _f._

meanness, _n._ bajeza, _f.;_ pobreza, _f.;_ mezquindad, _f.;_ mediocridad, _f.;_ pequeñez,
_f._

meantime, _adv._ mientras tanto, en el
entretanto; al mismo tiempo.

meanwhile, _adv._ entretanto, mientras
tanto; —, _n._ ínterin, _m._

measles, _n. pl._ sarampión, _m.;_ rubéola, _f._

measure, _n._ medida, _f.;_ regla, _f.;_ (mus.)
compás, _m.;_ **in some** —, hasta cierto
punto; **liquid** —, medida para líquidos;
—, _vt._ medir; ajustar; calibrar; calar.

measurement, _n._ medición, _f.;_ medida, _f._

meat, _n._ carne, _f.;_ **baked** —, carne asada
en horno; **broiled** —, carne asada en
parrilla.

meatless, _adj._ sin carne; — **day,** día de
vigilia.

meaty, _adj._ carnoso, sustancioso.

mechanic, _n._ mecánico, _m._

mechanical, _adj._ mecánico; rutinario; —**ly,**
adv. mecánicamente.

mechanics, _n. pl._ mecánica, _f._

mechanism, _n._ mecanismo, _m._

mechanize, _vt._ mecanizar.

medal, _n._ medalla, _f._

medallion, _n._ medallón, _m._

meddle, _vi._ entremeterse.

meddler, _n._ entremetido, da, camasquince, _m._

meddlesome, _adj._ entremetido, da.

mediate, _vi._ mediar; promediar.

mediation, _n._ mediación, interposición, _f._

mediator, _n._ mediador, ra.

medical, _adj._ médico; — **examination,**
reconocimiento o examen médico.

medicinal, _adj._ medicinal.

medicine, _n._ medicina, _f.;_ medicamento, _m._

medieval, _adj._ medieval.

mediocre, _adj._ mediocre.

mediocrity, _n._ mediocridad, _f._

meditate, _vt._ y _vi._ meditar, idear.

meditation, _n._ meditación, _f._

medium, _n._ medio, _m.;_ expediente, _m.;_ —,
adj. mediano.

medium-sized, _adj._ de tamaño regular o
mediano.

medley, _n._ mezcla, _f.;_ baturrillo, _m.;_ (mus.)
popurrí, _m._

meek, _adj._ paciente y tímido, corto de
ánimo; —**ly,** _adv._ tímida y humildemente.

meekness, _n._ mansedumbre, _f.;_ modestia,
timidez, _f.;_ humildad, _f._

meet, _vt._ encontrar; convocar; reunir, dar
con; —, _vi._ encontrarse, juntarse; **till we
— **again, hasta la vista; **to go to** —, ir al
encuentro; —, _adj._ idóneo, propio; —, _n._
reunión, _f._

meeting, _n._ asamblea, _f.;_ congreso, _m.;_
entrevista, _f.;_ sesión, reunión, _f.;_ mitin,
_m.;_ **to call a** —, llamar a junta, convocar a una junta.

megaphone, _n._ megáfono, portavoz, _m._

melancholy, *n.* melancolía, *f.*

meld, *n.* mezcla en que se confunden los elementos; —, *vt.* mezclar; acusar (en juegos de naipes).

mellow, *adj.* maduro, meloso; tierno, suave, blando; —, *vt.* y *vi.* madurar, madurarse.

melodious, *adj.* melodioso.

melodrama, *n.* melodrama, *m.*

melody, *n.* melodía, *f.*

melon, *n.* melón, *m.*

melt, *vt.* derretir, fundir; enternecer; —, *vi.* derretirse, enternecerse.

melting, *n.* fusión, *f.;* — **point,** punto o temperatura de fusión; — **pot,** crisol, *m.*

member, *n.* miembro, *m.;* parte, *f.;* individuo, socio, *m.*

membership, *n.* número de socios, personal de socios.

membrane, *n.* membrana, *f.*

memento, *n.* memento, *m.*

memo: memorandum, memorándum, *m.*

memoir, *n.* memoria, relación, narrativa, *f.*

memorable, *adj.* memorable.

memorandum, *n.* memorándum, *m.;* — **book,** libreta, *f.;* carnet, *m.,* libro de apuntes.

memorial, *n.* memoria, *f.;* memorial, *m.;* —, *adj.* conmemorativo.

Memorial Day, *n.* Día de los Soldados Difuntos.

memorize, *vt.* memorizar; aprender de memoria.

memory, *n.* memoria, *f.;* recuerdo, *m.;* retentiva, *f.*

men, *n. pl.* de **man,** hombres, *m. pl.*

menace, *n.* amenaza, *f.;* —, *vt.* amenazar.

menagerie, *n.* colección de animales; casa de fieras.

mend, *vt.* reparar, remendar, retocar; mejorar, corregir; —, *vi.* enmendarse, corregirse.

mendicant, *adj.* mendicante; —, *n.* mendicante, *m.* y *f.,* mendigo, ga.

menial, *adj.* servil, doméstico.

menstruation, *n.* menstruación, regla, *f.*

mensuration, *n.* medición, *f.*

mental, *adj.* mental, intelectual.

mentality, *n.* mentalidad, *f.*

mention, *n.* mención, *f.;* —, *vt.* mencionar; **don't** — **it,** no hay de qué.

mentor, *n.* mentor, guía, *m.*

menu, *n.* menú, *m.,* lista de platos, comida, *f.*

mercantile, *adj.* mercantil.

mercenary, *adj.* mercenario, venal; —, *n.* mercenario, ria.

mercerize, *vt.* mercerizar, abrillantar, dar lustre.

merchandise, *n.* mercancía, *f.;* efectos comerciales.

merchant, *n.* comerciante, *m.;* mercader, *m.;* negociante, *m.* y *f.;* —, *adj.* mercante.

merciful, *adj.* misericordioso, compasivo, piadoso; —**ly,** *adv.* misericordiosamente.

merciless, *adj.* duro de corazón, inhumano; —**ly,** *adv.* cruelmente, sin misericordia.

mercurochrome, *n.* mercurocromo, *m.*

mercury, *n.* mercurio, *m.*

mercy, *n.* misericordia, piedad, clemencia, *f.;* perdón, *m.;* — **killing,** eutanasia, *f.*

mere, *adj.* mero, puro.

merge, *vt.* unir, juntar, combinar; —, *vi.* absorberse, fusionarse.

merger, *n.* consolidación, combinación, *f.;* fusión, *f.*

meridian, *n.* mediodía, *m.;* meridiano, *m.*

meringue, *n.* merengue, *m.*

merit, *n.* mérito, *m.;* merecimiento, *m.;* —, *vt.* merecer.

merited, *adj.* meritorio, digno, merecido.

meritorious, *adj.* meritorio.

mermaid, *n.* sirena, *f.*

merrily, *adv.* alegremente.

merriment, *n.* diversión, *f.;* regocijo, *m.*

merry, *adj.* alegre, jovial, festivo.

merry-go-round, *n.* caballitos, *m. pl.,* tiovivo, carrusel, *m.*

merrymaking, *n.* retozo, bullicio, jolgorio, holgorio, *m.*

mesa, *n.* mesa, meseta, altiplanicie, *f.*

mesh, *n.* malla, *f.*

meson, *n.* (chem. y phy.) mesón, *m.*

mess, *n.* plato de comida; vianda, *f.;* ración o porción (de comida); grupo de personas que comen juntas; comida para un grupo; (coll.) confusión, *f.,* lío, *m.*

message, *n.* mensaje, *m.*

messenger, *n.* mensajero, ra.

metabolism, *n.* metabolismo, *m.*

metal, *n.* metal, *m.;* (fig.) coraje, espíritu, *m.*

metallic, *adj.* metálico.

metallurgy, *n.* metalurgia, *f.*

metamorphosis, *n.* metamorfosis, *f.*

metaphor, *n.* metáfora, *f.*

metaphysical, *adj.* metafísico.

metaphysics, *n. pl.* metafísica, *f.*

metatarsal, *adj.* metatarsiano.

mete, *vt.* asignar; repartir.

meteor, *n.* meteoro, *m.*

meteorite, *n.* meteorito, *m.*

meteorology, *n.* meteorología, *f.*

meter, *n.* medidor, *m.;* metro, *m.*

method, *n.* método, *m.;* vía, *f.;* medio, *m.*

methodic, methodical, *adj.* metódico.

Methodist, *n.* metodista, *m.* y *f.*

methylene, *n.* metileno, *m.*

meticulous, *adj.* meticuloso.

metric, *adj.* métrico; — **system**, sistema métrico.

metropolis, *n.* metrópoli, capital. *f.*

metropolitan, *n.* (eccl.) metropolitano, *m.*, ciudadano o ciudadana de una metrópoli; —, *adj.* metropolitano.

Mex.: **Mexico, Mex. o Mej.** México o Méjico.

Mexican, *n.* y *adj.* mexicano, na o mejicano, na.

mezzanine, *n.* (theat.) entresuelo, *m.*, mezanina, *f.*

mfg.: **manufacturing,** manuf. manufactura.

mfr.: **manufacturer,** fab. fabricante.

mica, mg. miligramo.

mica, *n.* (min.) mica, *f.*

mice, *n. pl.* de **mouse,** ratones, *m. pl.*

microbe, *n.* microbio, bacilo, *m.*

microfilm, *n.* microfilme, *m.*

microgroove, *n.* microsurco, *m.;* —, *adj.* de microsurco.

micron, *n.* micra, *f.*

microphone, *n.* micrófono, *m.*

microscope, *n.* microscopio, *m.;* — **slide** platina, *f.*

microscopic, microscopical, *adj.* microscópico.

microwave, *n.* microonda, *f.*

midday, *n.* mediodía, *m.*

middle, *adj.* medio, intermedio; mediocre;—, *n.* medio, centro, *m.;* mitad, *f.;* — **ear,** tímpano del oído.

middle-aged, *adj.* entrado en años, de edad madura.

Middle Ages, *n. pl.* Edad Media.

middle class, *n.* clase media.

middleman, *n.* revendedor, intermediario, *m.*

middleweight, *n.* peso medio; —, *adj.* de peso medio.

middy (blouse), *n.* blusa holgada para mujeres y niñas; chaqueta semejante a la que usan los marinos.

midget, *n.* enano, na.

midnight, *n.* medianoche, *f.*

midriff, *n.* diafragma, *m.;* parte de un vestido que ciñe el diafragma.

midshipman, *n.* cadete, *m.*, aspirante a oficial de marina.

midst, *n.* medio, centro, *m.*

midstream, *n.* centro de la corriente.

midsummer, *n.* solsticio estival; pleno verano.

midway, *n.* avenida central de una exposición en que suelen instalarse diversiones; —, *adj.* medio; —, *adv.* a medio camino.

Midwest, Middle West, *n.* Medio Oeste (de los E.U.A.).

midwife, *n.* comadre, partera, comadrona, *f.*

midwinter, *n.* pleno invierno, solsticio invernal.

midyear, *adj.* a mediados de año; — **exam,** examen de medio año.

might, *n.* poder, *m.*, fuerza, *f.;* — **and main,** fuerza máxima; —, *pretérito* del verbo **may.**

mightily, *adv.* poderosamente, sumamente.

mighty, *adj.* fuerte, potente.

migraine, *n.* hemicránea, jaqueca, *f.*

migrant, *adj.* migratorio, de paso, nómade, nómada; —, *n.* planta o ave migratoria.

migrate, *vi.* emigrar.

migration, *n.* emigración, *f.*

migratory, *adj.* migratorio.

mild, *adj.* indulgente, blando, dulce, apacible, suave, moderado; —**ly,** *adv.* suavemente, moderadamente.

mildew, *n.* moho, tizón, tizoncillo, *m.;* roya, *f.;* añublo, *m.;* —, *vi.* enmohecerse.

mile, *n.* milla, *f.*

mileage, *n.* longitud en millas; kilometraje, *m.*

milestone, *n.* piedra miliaria.

militant, *adj.* militante.

militarism, *n.* militarismo, *m.*

military, *adj.* militar; **compulsory** — **service,** servicio militar obligatorio; — **police,** policía militar.

militia, *n.* milicia, *f.*

milk, *n.* leche, *f.;* — **of magnesia,** leche de magnesia; —, *vt.* ordeñar.

milking machine, *n.* máquina ordeñadora.

milkmaid, *n.* lechera, *f.*

milkman, *n.* lechero, *m.*

milkweed, *n.* titímalo, *m.*, cardo lechero.

milky, *adj.* lácteo, lechoso.

Milky Way, *n.* Vía Láctea, Galaxia *f.*

mill, *n.* molino, *m.;* —, *vt.* moler, triturar; batir con el molinillo.

millenium, *n.* milenio, *m.*

miller, *n.* molinero, *m.*

milligram, *n.* miligramo, *m.*

millimeter, *n.* milímetro, *m.*

milliner, *n.* persona que vende o confecciona sombreros de mujer.

millinery, *n.* artículos para sombreros de señora; confección de sombreros para señora.

million, *n.* millón, *m.*

millionaire, *n.* y *adj.* millonario, ria.

mimeograph, *n.* mimeógrafo, *m.*

mimic, *vt.* imitar, contrahacer; —, *adj.* burlesco, mímico; —, *n.* mimo, *m.*

mimicry, *n.* mímica, *f.;* bufonería, *f.*

mince, *vt.* picar (carne) ; —, *vi.* hablar o pasearse con afectación; andar con pasos muy cortos o muy afectadamente.

mincemeat, *n.* picadillo de carne; picadillo de manzana, pasas, etc. con o sin carne.

mind, *n.* mente, *f.;* entendimiento, *m.;* gusto, afecto, *m.;* voluntad, intención, *f.;* pensamiento, *m.;* opinión, *f.;* ánimo, *m.;* **of sound** —, consciente; —, *vt.* notar, observar, considerar; pensar; obedecer; tener cuidado; importar; **not to** —, no importar; —, *vi.* tener cuidado o cautela; preocuparse; obedecer.

mindful, *adj.* atento, diligente.

mindreader, *n.* adivinador o adivinadora del pensamiento; persona intuitiva y perspicaz.

mine, *pron.* el mío, los míos; —, *n.* mina, *f.;* — **field,** (mil., naut.) campo de minas; cuenca minera; zona donde se han colocado minas explosivas; — **layer,** (naut.) plantaminas o lanzaminas, *m.;* **land** —, mina terrestre; — **sweeper,** (naut.) dragaminas o recogedor de minas explosivas; —, *vt.* y *vi.* minar, cavar.

miner, *n.* minero, minador, *m.*

mineral, *adj.* mineral; — **oil,** aceite mineral, petróleo, *m.;* — **water,** agua mineral; — **wool,** lana de escoria; —, *n,* mineral, *m.*

mingle, *vt.* y *vi.* mezclar, mezclarse.

mingled, *adj.* revuelto, mezclado.

miniature, *n.* miniatura, *f.*

minimize, *vt.* reducir a un mínimo, menospreciar.

minimum, *n.* mínimum, mínimo, *m.;* —, *adj.* mínimo; — **wage,** jornal mínimo.

mining, *n.* minería, explotación de minas; —, *adj.* minero; — **engineer,** ingeniero de minas.

minister, *n.* ministro, pastor, capellán, *m.;* —, *vt.* ministrar; servir; suministrar; proveer; socorrer.

ministry, *n.* ministerio, *m.*

mink, *n.* visón, *m.;* — **coat,** abrigo de visón.

minnow, *n.* (ichth.) gobio pequeño.

minor, *adj.* menor, pequeño; inferior; (mus.) menor; —, *n.* menor (de edad), *m.* y *f.;* asignatura secundaria en las escuelas.

minority, *n.* minoridad, *f.;* minoría, *f.*

minstrel, *n.* juglar, trovador, *m.*

mint, *n.* (bot.) menta, *f.;* ceca, *f.,* casa de moneda; —, *vt.* acuñar.

minuet, *n.* minué, *m.*

minus, *prep.* menos; **seven** — **four,** siete menos cuatro; —, *adj.* negativo; —

quantity, cantidad negativa; (coll.) despojado; —, *n.* (math.) el signo menos.

minute, *adj.* menudo, pequeño, nimio; minucioso; —**ly,** *adv.* minuciosamente.

minute, *n.* minuto, *m.;* momento, instante, *m.;* minuta, *f.;* — **book,** libro de minutas.

miracle, *n.* milagro, *m.;* maravilla, *f.*

miraculous, *adj.* milagroso.

mirage, *n.* espejismo, *m.*

mire, *n.* fango, limo, *m.*

mirror, *n.* espejo, *m.*

mirth, *n.* alegría, *f.;* regocijo, *m.*

mirthful, *adj.* alegre, jovial.

misadventure, *n.* desventura, *f.;* infortunio, *m.*

misalliance, *n.* boda con persona de posición social inferior.

misanthrope, *n.* misántropo, *m.*

misapprehend, *vt.* entender mal.

misapprehension, *n.* error, yerro, *m.;* interpretación errónea.

misappropriate, *vt.* malversar.

misbehave, *vi.* portarse mal.

misbehavior, *n.* mal comportamiento.

miscalculate, *vt.* calcular mal.

miscarriage, *n.* aborto, malparto, *m.;* fracaso, *m.*

miscarry, *vi.* frustrarse, malograrse; abortar, malparir.

miscellaneous, *adj.* misceláneo, mezclado.

miscellany, *n.* miscelánea, *f.*

mischance, *n.* desventura, *f.;* infortunio, *m.,* mal suceso.

mischief, *n.* travesura, *f.;* daño, infortunio, *m.*

mischievous, *adj.* travieso, pícaro; dañoso, malicioso, malévolo.

misconception, *n.* equivocación, *f.;* falso concepto.

misconduct, *n.* mala conducta; —, *vt.* conducir o manejar mal.

misconstrue, *vt.* interpretar mal.

misdeal, *vt.* dar mal las cartas (en el juego de naipes); —, *n.* distribución equivocada.

misdeed, *n.* delito, *m.*

misdemeanor, *n.* mala conducta; culpa, falta, *f.*

misdirect, *vt.* dirigir erradamente.

miser, *n.* avaro, ra.

miserable, *adj.* miserable, infeliz; pobre; mísero; mezquino.

miserly, *adj.* mezquino, tacaño.

misery, *n.* miseria, *f.;* infortunio, *m.*

misfit, *vt.* y *vi.* quedar mal (un vestido, etc.); —, *n.* mal ajuste; vestimenta que no ajusta o cae bien; desadaptado, da, persona que no se adapta al ambiente.

misfortune, *n.* infortunio, revés, *m.;* per-

cance, m.; calamidad, f.; contratiempo, m.

misgiving, n. recelo, m.; duda, f.; presentimiento, m.; rescoldo, m.

misguide, vt. guiar mal.

mishap, n. desventura, f.; desastre, contratiempo, m.

misinform, vt. informar mal.

misinterpret, vt. interpretar mal.

misjudge, vt. y vi. juzgar mal.

mislay, vt. colocar mal, traspapelar.

mislead, vt. extraviar, descaminar; engañar.

misleading, adj. engañoso, desorientador.

mismanagement, n. mala administración,
f.; desarreglo, m.

misnomer, n. nombre o título falso.

misplace, vt. colocar mal, traspapelar;
sacar algo de su quicio; extraviar.

misprint, vt. imprimir mal; —, n. errata, f.

mispronounce, vt. pronunciar mal.

misquote, vt. citar falsa o erróneamente.

misrepresent, vt. representar mal; tergiversar.

misrepresentation, n. representación falsa;
tergiversación, f.

misrule, n. tumulto, m.; confusión, f.; —,
vt. gobernar mal.

miss, n. señorita, f.; pérdida, falta, f.; —,
vt. errar, perder; omitir; echar de
menos; **to — one's mark,** errar el blanco; **to — (in shooting),** errar el tiro; —
vi. frustrarse, malograrse.

missal, n. misal, m.

misshape, vt. deformar, desfigurar.

misshapen, adj. deformado, desfigurado.

missile, n. proyectil, m.

missing, adj. que falta; perdido; **to be —,**
hacer falta, faltar.

mission, n. misión, comisión, f.;
cometido, m.

missionary, n. misionero, m.

missive, n. carta, misiva, f.; —, adj. misi-
vo.

misspell, vt. deletrear mal, escribir con
mala ortografía.

misstatement, n. aserción equivocada o
falsa.

misstep, n. paso en falso.

mist, n. niebla, bruma, f.

mistake, n. equivocación, f.; yerro, error,
m.; —, vt. equivocar; —, vi. equivocarse,
engañarse; **to be —n,** estar equivocado,
estar errado.

Mister, n. Señor (título), m.

mistletoe, n. (bot.) muérdago, m., liga, f.

mistreat, vt. maltratar, injuriar.

mistreatment, n. maltrato, maltratamien-
to, m.

mistress, n. ama, f.; señora, f.; con-

cubina, f.

mistrial, n. anulación de un juicio.

mistrust, vt. desconfiar; sospechar; —, n.
desconfianza, sospecha, f.

misty, adj. nebuloso, brumoso.

misunderstand, vt. entender mal.

misunderstanding, n. mal entendimiento,
m.; disensión, f.; error, m.

misuse, vt. maltratar; abusar de algo.

mite, n. pizca, mota, f.; ápice, m.

mitigate, vt. mitigar, calmar.

mitt, mitten, n. mitón, m.

mix, vt. mezclar.

mixed, adj. mezclado; **— up,** revuelto; confuso, indeciso.

mixer, n. mezclador, ra; **concrete —,** mezcladora, hormigonera, mezcladora de
hormigón.

mixmaster, n. batidora eléctrica.

mixture, n. mixtura, mezcla, f.

mix-up, n. (coll.) confusión, f.; conflicto,
m.

mm.: millimeter, mm. milímetro.

Mo.: Missouri, Misuri (E.U.A.)

moan, n. lamento, gemido, m.; —, vt.
lamentar, gemir; —, vi. afligirse, quejarse.

mob, n. populacho, m.; canalla, f.; chusma, gentuza, f.; gente baja; —, vt. atropellar desordenadamente, formar un
tropel.

mobile, adj. movedizo, móvil.

mobility, n. movilidad, f.

mobilization, n. movilización, f.

mobilize, vt. (mil.) movilizar.

moccasin, n. mocasín, m., abarca, f.

mock, vt. mofar, burlar, chiflar; —, n.
mofa, burla, f.; —, adj. ficticio, falso.

mockery, n. mofa, burla, zumba, f.

mockingbird, n. (orn.) arrendajo, m.

mockingly, adv. burlonamente, en son de
burla.

mock-up, n. maqueta, f.

mode, n. modo, m.; forma, f.; manera,
f.; costumbre, f.; vía, f.; (mus.) modalidad, f.

model, n. modelo, m.; pauta, f.; muestra,
f.; patrón, m.; tipo, m.; —, vt. modelar.

modeling, n. modelado, m.

moderate, adj. moderado; mediocre; módico; **—ly,** adv. bastante; moderadamente;
—, vt. moderar.

moderation, n. moderación, f.; sobriedad, f.

moderator, n. moderador, apaciguador, m.

modern, adj. moderno, reciente.

modernism, n. modernismo, m.

modernistic, adj. modernista.

modernize, vt. modernizar.

modest, adj. modesto.

modesty, n. modestia, decencia, f.; pudor, m.
modification, n. modificación, f.
modifier, n. modificador, modificante, m.
modify, vt. modificar.
modulate, vt. modular.
modulating, adj. modulante.
modulation, n. modulación, f.
modulator, n. modulador, ra.
mohair, n. tela hecha de pelo de camello.
moist, adj. húmedo, mojado.
moisten, vt. humedecer.
moisture, n. humedad, f.; jugosidad, f.
molar, adj. molar; — **tooth,** muela, f., diente molar; — **teeth,** muelas, f. pl.
molasses, n. melaza, f.
mold, n. moho, m.; tierra, f.; suelo, m.; **molde,** m.; matriz, f.; —, vt. enmohecer, moldar; formar; —, vi. enmohecerse.
molding, n. molduras, f. pl., cornisamiento, m.
moldy, adj. mohoso, lleno de moho.
mole, n. topo, m.; lunar, m.; muelle, dique, m.
molecule, n. molécula, f.
molest, vt. acometer; acosar.
mollify, vt. ablandar.
mollusk, n. molusco, m.
molt, vt. y vi. mudar, estar de muda las aves.
molten, adj. derretido.
moment, n. momento, rato, m.; importancia, f.
momentarily, adv. a cada momento, momentáneamente.
momentary, adj. momentáneo.
momentous, adj. importante.
momentum, n. ímpetu, m.; fuerza de impulsión de un cuerpo.
monarch, n. monarca, m.
monarchist, n. monarquista, m. y f.
monarchy, n. monarquía, f.
monastery, n. monasterio, m.
Monday, n. lunes, m.
monetary, adj. monetario.
money, n. moneda, f.; dinero, m.; plata, f.; oro, m.; — **changer,** cambista, m.; — **chest,** caja, f.; — **exchange,** bolsa, f.; cambio de moneda; — **order,** libranza o giro postal; **paper** —, papel moneda.
moneyed, monied, adj. adinerado, rico.
mongrel, adj. mixto, mestizo; —, n. mestizo, za.
monitor, n. admonitor, m.; (naut.) monitor, m.
monk, n. monje, m.; cenobita, m. y f.
monkey, n. mono, na; simio, mia; — **wrench,** llave inglesa, llave de tuercas.
monocle, n. monóculo, m.
monogamy, n. monogamia, m.

monogram, n. monograma, m.
monolith, n. monolito, m.
monologue, n. monólogo, m.
monomial, n. monomio, m.
monoplane, n. monoplano, m.
monopolist, n. monopolista, m. y f.
monopolize, vt. monopolizar, acaparar.
monopoly, n. monopolio, m.
monorail, n. monorriel, m.
monosyllabic, adj. monosilábico; —, n. monosílabo, m.
monotonous, adj. monótono.
monotony, n. monotonía, f.
monotype, monotyping, n. monotipia, f.
monoxide, n. (chem.) monóxido, m.
monsoon, n. (naut.) monzón, m.
monster, n. monstruo, m.
monstrosity, n. monstruosidad, f.
monstrous, adj. monstruoso.
month, n. mes, m.; —**'s pay,** —**'s allowance,** mensualidad, f.; **next** —, el mes entrante, el mes que viene.
monthly, adj. mensual; —, adv. mensualmente.
monument, n. monumento, m.
monumental, adj. monumental.
mood, n. (gram.) modo, m.; humor, talante, m.
moody, adj. caprichoso; taciturno.
moon, n. luna, f.; **full** —, plenilunio, m., luna llena.
moonbeam, n. rayo lunar.
moonlight, n. luz de la luna.
moonshine, n. claridad de la luna; (coll.) licor fabricado ilícitamente.
moor, n. pantano, marjal, m.; —, vt. (naut.) amarrar.
mooring, n. (naut.) amarra, f.
moose, n. (zool.) alce, m.
moot, vt. debatir en pro y en contra; —, adj. sujeto a discusión; ficticio.
mop, n. trapeador, m.; —, vt. trapear, fregar.
mope, vi. ir cabizbajo, estar melancólico.
moppet, n. (coll.) chiquillo, lla.
moral, adj. moral, ético; — **support,** apoyo moral; —, n. moraleja, f.; —**s,** n. pl. moralidad, conducta, f.; conducta moral, costumbres, f. pl.
morale, n. moralidad, f.; animación, f.; buen espíritu, entusiasmo entre tropas.
moralist, n. moralista, m. y f.; moralizador, ra.
morality, n. ética, moralidad, f.
moralize, vt. y vi. moralizar.
morass, n. pantano, m.
moratorium, n. moratoria, f.
morbid, adj. enfermo, morboso, mórbido.
more, adj. más, adicional; —, adv. más, en mayor grado; — **or less,** más o menos;

—, n. mayor cantidad; **once** —, una vez más; **there's** — **than enough**, hay de sobra.

moreover, adv. además.

morgue, n. depósito de cadáveres.

morning, n. mañana, f.; **good** —, buenos días; —, adj. matutino; — **gown**, bata, f.

morning-glory, n. (bot.) dondiego de día.

morocco, morocco leather, n. marroquí, m.

moron, n. idiota, m. y f.; retrasado o retrasada mental.

morose, adj. hosco, sombrío, adusto.

morphine, n. morfina, f.

Morse code, n. clave telegráfica de Morse.

morsel, n. bocado, m.

mortal, adj. mortal; humano; —**ly**, adv. mortalmente; —, n. mortal, m.

mortality, n. mortalidad, f.

mortar, n. mortero, almirez, m.; (mil.) obús, m.; argamasa, f.; — **and pestle**, almirez y mano, mortero y majador.

mortarboard, n. gorro académico; esparavel o tabla que usan los albañiles.

mortgage, n. hipoteca, f.; —, vt. hipotecar.

mortgagor, mortgager, n. deudor hipotecario.

mortician, n. sepulturero, enterrador, m.; agente funerario.

mortification, n. mortificación, f.; (med.) gangrena, f.

mortify, vt. y vi. mortificar, mortificarse.

mortise, n. mortaja, f.

mortuary, adj. funeral.

mosaic, n. y adj. mosaico, m.

Moscow, Moscú, f.

mosquito, n. mosquito, zancudo, m.

moss, n. (bot.) musgo, m.

mossy, adj. musgoso.

most, adj. más; —, adv. sumamente, en sumo grado; —, n. los más; mayor número; mayor valor; **at** —, a lo más, cuando más; —**ly**, adv. por lo común; principalmente.

motel, n. (contracción de motor y hotel) autohotel, hotel para automovilistas.

moth, n. polilla, f.; — **ball**, bola de naftalina para la polilla.

mother, n. madre, f.; — **tongue**, lengua materna.

motherhood, n. maternidad, f.

mother-in-law, n. suegra, f.

motherless, adj. sin madre, huérfana de madre.

motherly, adj. maternal, materno.

mother-of-pearl, n. madreperla, f.

motif, n. motivo, tema, m.

motion, n. movimiento, m., moción, f.; vaivén, m.; proposición, f.; — **picture**, película, f., filme, m.; — **pictures**, cinematografía, f., cinematógrafo, m.; —, vt.

hacer señas (para indicar algo).

motionless, adj. inmoble, inmóvil.

motivate, vt. motivar, proveer con un motivo; incitar, inducir, estimular interés activo por medio de intereses relacionados o recursos especiales.

motive, adj. motivo, motor; — **power**, fuerza motriz; —, n. motivo, móvil, m.; razón, f.

motley, adj. abigarrado, gayado, variado.

motor, n. motor, m.; — **truck**, autocamión, m.

motorboat, n. lancha de motor.

motorbus, n. autobús, m.

motorcade, n. desfile de automóviles.

motorcar, n. automóvil, m.

motorcycle, n. motocicleta, f.

motorist, n. automovilista, motorista, m. y f.

motorize, vt. motorizar.

motorman, n. motorista de un tranvía o tren.

mottled, adj. moteado; veteado.

motto, n. lema, m.; mote, m.; divisa, f.

mound, n. terraplén, baluarte, dique, terrón, m.

mount, n. monte, m.; montaña, f.; montaje, m.; —, vt. y vi. ascender, subir; montar.

mountain, n. montaña, sierra, f.; monte, m.; **range of** —**s**, cadena de montañas.

mountaineer, n. montañés, esa.

mountainous, adj. montañoso.

mounted, adj. montado.

mounting, n. montaje, m.

mourn, vt. deplorar; —, vi. lamentar; llevar luto.

mourner, n. lamentador, ra; llorón, ona; doliente, m. y f.

mournful, adj. triste; fúnebre.

mourning, n. luto, m.; **in** —, de luto.

mouse, n. (pl. mice) ratón, m.; — **trap**, ratonera, f.

moustache = **mustache**.

mouth, n. boca, f.; entrada, f.; embocadura, f.; **by word of** —, boca a boca, de palabra; — **organ**, armónica, f.; **to make the** — **water**, hacerse agua la boca; —, vi. hablar a gritos; —, vt. poner en la boca; pronunciar.

mouthful, n. bocado, m.

mouthpiece, n. vocero, m.; boquilla de un instrumento de música.

movable, adj. movible, movedizo; —**s**, n. pl. bienes muebles, m.

move, vt. mover; proponer; excitar; persuadir; emocionar; bullir; mover a piedad; —, vi. moverse, menearse; andar; marchar un ejército; **to** — **to and fro**, moverse de un lado para otro; zarandearse; revolverse; —, n. movimiento, m.

movement, n. movimiento, m.; moción, f. movies, n. pl. (coll.) cine, cinematógrafo, m.

moving, n. movimiento, m.; —, adj. patético, persuasivo; conmovedor; — **pictures**, cine, cinematógrafo, m.; **—ly**, adv. patéticamente.

mow, vt. guadañar, segar.

mower, n. guadañero, m.; cortadora, f.; segador, ra.

mowing, n. siega, f.; — **machine**, guadañadora, f.

mph, m.p.h.: miles per hour, m.p.h. millas por hora.

Mr.: Mister, Sr. Señor.

Mrs.: Mistress, Sra. Señora.

Ms. MS., ms.; manuscript, M.S. manuscrito, original.

much, adj. mucho; —, adv. mucho, con mucho; **so —, as —**, tanto; **too —**, demasiado.

mucilage, n. mucílago, m.; goma para pegar.

muck, n. abono, estiércol, m.; basura, f.

mucous, adj. mocoso, viscoso.

mucus, n. moco, m., mucosidad, f.

mud, n. fango, limo, légamo, lodo, m.

muddle, vt. enturbiar; embriagar; enredar; confundir; —, n. confusión, f.; enredo, m.

muddy, adj. cenagoso; turbio; lodoso.

muff, n. manguito, m.

muffin, n. variedad de bizcochuelo o panecillo suave.

muffle, vt. embozar; envolver.

muffler, n. (auto.) silenciador, m.; sordina, f.; desconectador, m.

mufti, n. (mil.) ropa civil en contraste con uniformes militares.

mug, n. cubilete, m.; (coll.) cara, f.

muggy, adj. húmedo y caluroso.

mulberry, n. mora, f.; — **tree**, morera, f.

mule, n. mulo, m., mula, f.

mull, vt. entibiar; calentar cualquier licor; —, vt. y vi. (coll.) cavilar.

multimillionaire, n. multimillonario, ria.

multiple, adj. multíplice; múltiple; —, n. múltiplo, m.

multiplication, n. multiplicación, f.; — **table**, tabla de multiplicar.

multiplier, n. multiplicador, m.

multiplex, adj. múltiplex, múltiple.

multiply, vt. multiplicar; —, vi. propagarse, multiplicarse.

multistage rocket, n. cohete de ignición múltiple.

multitude, n. multitud, f.; vulgo, m.

multitudinous, adj. numeroso, múltiple.

mum, interj. ¡chitón! ¡silencio! —, adj.

silencioso, callado; **to keep —**, callarse.

mumble, vt. barbotar, mascullar; —, vi. hablar o decir entre dientes; gruñir; murmurar.

mummy, n. momia, f

mumps, n. pl. (med.) papera, parótida, f.

munch, vt. masticar a bocados grandes.

mundane, adj. mundano.

municipal, adj. municipal; — **government**, ayuntamiento, gobierno municipal.

municipality, n. municipalidad, f.

munificence, n. munificencia, liberalidad, f.

munition, n. municiones, f. pl.

mural, n. y adj. mural, m.

murder, n. asesinato, homicidio, m.; —, vt. asesinar, cometer homicidio.

murderer, n. asesino, na.

murderess, n. asesina, matadora, f.

murderous, adj. sanguinario, cruel.

murky, adj. oscuro, lóbrego; sombrío; turbio; empañado.

murmur, n. murmullo, m.; cuchicheo, m.; —, vi. murmurar.

muscle, n. músculo, m.

muscle-bound, adj. con los músculos rígidos por el trabajo muscular excesivo.

muscular, adj. muscular; — **distrophy**, distrofia muscular.

muse, n. musa, f.; meditación profunda; —, vi. meditar, pensar profundamente.

museum, n. museo, m.

mush, n. gachas, papas, f. pl.; (coll.) sentimentalismo barato.

mushroom, n. (bot.) seta, f., hongo, m.

music, n. música, f.; — **hall**, sala de concierto; — **staff**, pentagrama, m.

musical, adj. musical; melodioso; — **comedy**, zarzuela, f., comedia musical; **—ly**, adv. con armonía.

musician, n. músico, m.

musing, n. meditación, f.

musk, n. almizcle, m.

musket, n. mosquete, fusil, m.; (coll.) chopo, m.

muskrat, n. rata almizclera.

muslin, n. muselina, f.; percal, m.

muss, vt. manosear.

mussel, n. marisco, m.

must, vi. estar obligado; ser menester, ser necesario; convenir.

mustache, n. bigote, mostacho, m.

mustard, n. mostaza, f.

muster, vt. pasar revista de tropa; agregar; —, n. (mil.) revista, f.; — **roll**, rol, m., lista de dotación; rol de la tripulación.

musty, adj. mohoso, añejo.

mutate, vt. trasformar, alterar.

mutation, n. mudanza, f.; mutación, f.

mute, adj. mudo, silencioso; —, n. sordi-

na, *f.;* —**ly**, *adv.* sin chistar.
mutilate, *vt.* mutilar.
mutineer, *n.* amotinador, sedicioso, *m.*
mutinous, *adj.* sedicioso; —**ly**, *adv.* amoti-
nadamente.
mutiny, *n.* motín, tumulto, *m.;* —, *vi.*
amotinarse, rebelarse.
mutter, *vt.* y *vi.* murmurar, musitar,
hablar entre dientes; —, *n.* murmuración, *f.*
mutton, *n.* carnero, *m.*
mutual, *adj.* mutuo, recíproco; **by** — **con
sent**, de común acuerdo; — **aid association**, asociación de apoyo mutuo, sociedad de beneficencia.
muzzle, *n.* bozal, frenillo, *m.;* hocico, *m.;*

—, *vt.* amordazar.
my, *adj.* mi.
myocardium, *n.* miocardio, *m.*
myriad, *n.* miríada, *f.;* gran número.
myrtle, *n.* mirto, arrayán, *m.*
myself, *pron.* yo mismo, mí mismo.
mysterious, *adj.* misterioso.
mystery, *n.* misterio, *m.*
mystery play, *n.* auto, *m.*
mystic, mystical, *adj.* místico.
mysticism, *n.* misticismo, *m.*
mystify, *vt.* desconcertar, ofuscar.
myth, *n.* fábula mitológica; mito, *m.*
mythical, *adj.* mítico, fabuloso.
mythological, *adj.* mitológico.
mythology, *n.* mitología, *f.*

N

n.: noun, s. sustantivo, nombre.
N.: North, *n.* Norte.
N.A.: North America, N.A. Norte América,
América del Norte.
nab, *vt.* atrapar, prender.
nacelle, *n.* (avi.) nacela, *f.*
nag, *n.* rocín, matalón, caballejo, *m.;* —,
vt. y *vi.* regañar continuamente, molestar, sermonear.
nail, *n.* uña, *f.;* garra, *f.;* clavo, *m.;* — **cleaner**, limpiaúñas, *m.;* — **file**, lima para
las uñas; —, *vt.* clavar.
naive, *adj.* ingenuo.
naked, *adj.* desnudo; evidente; puro, simple; **stark** —, en pelota.
nakedness, *n.* desnudez, *f.*
name, *n.* nombre, *m.;* fama, reputación, *f.*
nameless, *adj.* anónimo; sin nombre.
namely, *adv.* particularmente; a saber.
namesake, *n.* tocayo, ya.
nap, *n.* siesta, *f.,* sueño ligero; lanilla, *f.,*
flojel, *m.*
nape, *n.* nuca, cerviz, *f.;* testuz, *m.*
naphtha, *n.* nafta, *f.*
napkin, *n.* servilleta, *f.;* **sanitary** —, servilleta higiénica.
Naples, Nápoles, *f.*
narcissus, *n.* (bot.) narciso, *m.*
narcosis, *n.* narcosis, *f.*
narcotic, *adj.* narcótico; —**s**, *n.* pl. drogas
heroicas, estupefacientes, *m.* pl.
narrate, *vt.* narrar, relatar.
narration, *n.* narración, *f.;* relación de
alguna cosa.
narrative, *n.* cuento, relato, *m.;* —, *adj.*
narrativo.
narrator, *n.* narrador, ra.

narrow, *adj.* angosto, estrecho; avariento;
próximo; escrupuloso; —**ly**, *adv.* estrechamente; —, *vt.* estrechar; limitar.
narrowminded, *adj.* mezquino, fanático,
intolerante.
narrowness, *n.* angostura, estrechez, *f.;*
pobreza, *f.*
nasal, *adj.* nasal.
nastily, *adv.* suciamente; desagradable-
mente.
nasturtium, *n.* (bot.) nasturcio, *m.,* capuchina, *f.*
nasty, *adj.* sucio, puerco; obsceno; sórdido; desagradable.
natal, *adj.* nativo; natal.
nation, *n.* nación, *f.,* país, *m.*
national, *adj.* nacional.
nationalism, *n.* nacionalismo, *m.*
nationalist, *n.* nacionalista, *m.* y *f.*
nationality, *n.* nacionalidad, *f.*
nationalize, *vt.* nacionalizar.
nation-wide, *adj.* y *adv.* nacional, por toda
la nación; a través del país.
native, *adj.* nativo; — **land**, terruño, *m.;* —
of, oriundo de; —, *n.* natural, *m.* y *f.*
native-born, *adj.* natural (de un país o
lugar indicado).
nativity, *n.* nacimiento, *m.;* natividad, *f.;*
horóscopo, *m.*
natl.: national, nac. nacional.
**N.A.T.O.: North Atlantic Treaty
Organization,** O.T.A.N. Organización del
Tratado del Altántico Norte.
natural, *adj.* natural; sencillo; ilegítimo;
ingénito; —**ly**, *adv.* naturalmente; —, *n.*
(mus.) becuadro, *m.*
naturalist, *n.* naturalista, *m.* y *f.*

naturalization, n. naturalización, f.; obtención de la ciudadanía de un país.
naturalize, vt. y vi. naturalizar, naturalizarse.
naturalness, n. sencillez, naturalidad, f.
nature, n. naturaleza, f.; índole, f.; modalidad, f.; carácter, m.; tenor, m.; humor, m.; genio, m.; temperamento, m.; **good** —, buen humor.
naught, n. nada, f.; cero, m.; —, adj. nulo.
naughtiness, n. picardía, travesura, f.
naughty, adj. travieso, pícaro; desobediente.
nausea, n. náusea, basca, f.
nauseate, vt. dar disgusto; nausear.
nautical, adj. náutico.
naval, adj. naval.
navel, n. ombligo, m.
navigable, adj. navegable.
navigate, vt. y vi. navegar.
navigation, n. navegación, f.
navigator, n. navegante, m.
navy, n. marina, f.; armada, f.; — **yard**, arsenal de la marina de guerra.
nay, adv. y aun, más aún; —, n. no, m., voto negativo; contestación negativa.
Nazi, n. y adj. nazi, m. y f.
N.B.: nota bene, Ojo, nótese bien.
NE, N.E.: northeast, N.E. nordeste.
near, prep. cerca de, junto a; —, adv. casi; cerca, cerca de; —, adj. cercano, próximo, inmediato; allegado.
nearby, adj. cercano, próximo; —, adv. cerca, a la mano.
Near East, Cercano Oriente.
nearly, adv. casi; por poco.
nearness, n. proximidad, f.; mezquindad, f.
near-sighted, adj. miope, corto de vista; — **person,** miope, m. y f.
neat, adj. hermoso, pulido; puro; neto; pulcro; ordenado; —**ly,** adv. elegantemente; con nitidez; —, n. ganado vacuno.
nebulous, adj. nebuloso.
necessaries, n. pl. cosas necesarias; requisitos, m. pl
necessarily, adv. necesariamente.
necessary, adj. necesario; **to be —,** hacer falta, ser preciso, ser menester.
necessitate, vt. necesitar.
necessity, n. necesidad, f.; **of —,** forzosamente.
neck, n. cuello, m.; **back of the —,** nuca, f.
neckerchief, n. pañoleta, f.
necklace, n. collar, m.
necktie, n. corbata, f.
neckwear, n. cuellos, m. pl.; corbatas, f. pl.
nectar, n. néctar, m.
need, n. necesidad, f.; pobreza, f.; —, vt. y

vi. necesitar; requerir.
needle, n. aguja, f.; **darning —,** aguja de zurcir; **hypodermic —,** aguja hipodérmica; **magnetic —,** calamita, brújula f.
needless, adj. superfluo, inútil, innecesario.
needlework, n. costura, f.; bordado de aguja.
needy, adj. indigente, necesitado, pobre.
negation, n. negación, f.
negative, adj. negativo; —, n. negativa, f.
neglect, vt. descuidar, desatender; —, n. negligencia, f.
negligee, n. bata de casa.
negligence, n. negligencia, f.; descuido, m.
negligent, adj. negligente, descuidado.
negligible, adj. insignificante.
negotiable, adj. negociable.
negotiate, vt. gestionar; —, vi. negociar, comerciar.
negotiation, n. negociación, f.; negocio, m.
negro, n. y adj. negro, negra.
neigh, vi. relinchar; —, n. relincho, m.
neighbor, n. vecino, na; —, vt. estar contiguo; colindar con; —, vi. tratarse como vecinos.
neighborhood, n. vecindad, f.; vecindario, m.; inmediación, cercanía, f.
neighboring, adj. cercano, vecino.
neighborly, adj. sociable, amigable.
neither, conj. ni; —, adj. ninguno; —, pron. ninguno, ni uno ni otro.
neomycin, n. (med.) neomicina, f.
neon, n. neón, m.; — **light,** lámpara neón.
neophyte, n. neófito, ta, novicio, cia.
nephew, n. sobrino, m.
nepotism, n. nepotismo, m.
neptunium, n. neptunio, m.
nerve, n. nervio, m.; vigor, m.; (coll.) audacia, f.; descaro, m.
nerveless, adj. enervado, débil.
nerve-racking, nerve-wracking, adj. exasperante, que pone los nervios de punta.
nervous, adj. nervioso; excitable; nervudo.
nervousness, n. nerviosidad, f.
nest, n. nido, m.; nidada, f.; — **egg,** nidal, m.; (fig.) ahorros, m. pl.
nestle, vi. acurrucarse; —, vt. abrigar; acomodar (como en un nido).
net, n. red, f.; malla, f.; —, adj. neto, líquido; — **balance,** saldo líquido; — **cost,** costo neto; — **proceeds,** producto líquido; — **weight,** peso neto.
nether, adj. inferior, más bajo.
Netherlands, Países Bajos, m. pl.
netting, n. elaboración de redes; pesca con redes; pedazo de red.
nettle, n. ortiga, f.; —, vt. picar como ortiga; irritar.
network, n. (rad. y TV.) red radiodifusora,

red televisora.

neuralgia, n. neuralgia, f.

neurasthenia, n. (med.) neurastenia, f.

neuritis, n. neuritis, f., inflamación de los nervios.

neurosis, n. (med.) neurosis, f.

neurotic, adj. neurótico.

neuter, n. y adj. (grain.) neutro, m.

neutral, adj. neutral.

neutrality, n. neutralidad, f.

neutralize, vt. neutralizar.

neutrino, n. (chem. y phy.) neutrino, m.

neutron, n. neutrón, m.; — **bomb,** bomba de neutrones.

never, adv. nunca, jamás; — **mind,** no importa; — **a whit,** ni una pizca.

nevermore, adv. jamás, nunca.

nevertheless, adv. a pesar de todo, no obstante, así y todo, con todo, sin embargo.

new, adj. nuevo, fresco, reciente, original.

newborn, adj. recién nacido.

newcomer, n. recién llegado, da.

Newfoundland, Terranova, f.

newlywed, n. recién casado, da.

newness, n. novedad, f., calidad de nuevo.

news n. pl. noticias, nuevas, f. pl.

newsboy, n. vendedor de periódicos.

newscast, n. radiodifusión de noticias; noticiero, noticiario, m.

newscaster, n. (radio y TV.) comentarista, m.y f.

newsdealer, n. vendedor de periódicos.

newspaper, n. gaceta, f.; periódico, m.; diario, m.; — **clipping,** recorte de periódico.

newsprint, n. papel para periódicos.

newsreel, n. noticiero, m., película que ilustra las noticias del día.

newsstand, n. puesto de periódicos.

new-world, adj. del Nuevo Mundo, relacionado con el Hemisferio Occiden-tal.

New Zealand, Nueva Zelanda o Nueva Zelandia, f.

next, adj. próximo; entrante, venidero; **the — day,** el día siguiente; —, adv. luego, inmediatamente después.

N.G.O.: nongovernmental organization, **O.N.G.:** organización no gubernamental, f.

niacin, n. niacina, f.

nib, n. pico, m., punta, f.

nibble, vt. y vi. mordiscar, picar.

nice, adj. delicado, exacto, solícito; circunspecto; tierno; fino; elegante; escrupuloso; —**ly,** adv. bastante bien.

nicety, n. exactitud, f.; esmero, m.; delicadeza, f.;

niceties, n. pl. delicadezas, f. pl.; sutilezas, f. pl.

niche, n. nicho, m.

nick, n. muesca, f.; punto crítico; ocasión

oportuna; — **of time,** momento oportuno.

nickel, n. níquel, m.

nickel-plated, adj. niquelado.

nickname, n. mote, apodo, m.; —, vt. poner apodos.

nicotine, n. nicotina, f.

niece, n. sobrina, f.

niggardly, adj. avaro, sórdido; —, adv. tacañamente, miserablemente.

nigh, adv. casi.

night, n. noche, f.; **by —,** de noche; **good —,** buenas noches; — **club,** cabaret, club nocturno; — **letter,** telegrama nocturno; — **owl,** trasnochador, ra; — **school,** escuela de noche o nocturna; — **watch,** sereno, m., vela, f.

nightcap, n. gorro de dormir; bebida que se toma antes de acostarse.

nightfall, n. anochecer, m.; caída de la tarde.

nightgown, n. camisón, m., camisa de dormir.

nighthawk, n. pájaro nocturno; trasnochador, ra.

nightingale, n. ruiseñor, m.

nightly, adv. por las noches, todas las noches; —, adj. nocturno.

nightmare, n. pesadilla, f.

nightshirt, n. camisa de dormir (de hombre).

nimble, adj. ligero, activo, listo, ágil.

nine, n. y adj. nueve, m.

nineteen, n. y adj. diez y nueve, diecinueve, m

nineteenth, n. y adj. decimonono, m.

ninety, n. y adj. noventa, m.

ninny, n. badulaque, m., bobo, ba, tonto, ta.

ninth, n. y adj. nono, **noveno,** m.; —**ly,** adv. en noveno lugar.

nip, vt. arañar, rasguñar; morder; **to go — and tuck,** regatear.

nipping, adj. mordaz, picante; sensible (frío).

nipple, n. pezón, m.

nisei, n. japonés nacido en los E.U.A.

nitrate, n. nitrato m.

nitrogen, n. nitrógeno, m.; — **peroxide,** peróxido de nitrógeno.

no, adv. no; —, adj. ningún, ninguno; **by —means, in — way,** de ningún modo; — **end,** sinnúmero; — **longer,** no más; **there is — such thing,** no hay tal cosa.

No.: north, n. norte; **number,** No., núm. número.

nobility, n. nobleza, f.

noble, adj. noble; insigne; generoso; solariego; —, n. noble, m.

nobleman, n. noble, m.

nobleness, n. nobleza, caballerosidad, f.

nobody, pron. nadie, ninguno, na; —, n. persona insignificante.

nocturnal, adj. nocturnal.

nocturno. nod, n. cabeceo, m.; señal, f.; —, vt. inclinar (la cabeza) en señal de asentimiento; —, vi. cabecear.

noise, n. ruido, estruendo, m.; baraúnda, f.; bulla, f.; rumor, m.; **to make** —, hacer ruido, meter bulla.

noiseless, adj. silencioso, sin ruido.

noisy, adj. ruidoso, turbulento, fragoso, vocinglero.

nomad, n. y adj. nómada, m. y f.

nomadic, adj. nómada.

no-man's-land, n. tierra de nadie; faja de terreno no reclamada o en disputa; terreno que separa dos ejércitos enemigos.

nomenclature, n. nomenclatura, f.

nominal, adj. nominal.

nominate, vt. nombrar; proponer (a alguna persona para un puesto, cargo, etc.).

nomination, n. nominación, f.; propuesta, f.

nominative, n. (gram.) nominativo, m.

nominator, n. nominador, ra.

nonacceptance, n. falta de aceptación.

nonaggression, n. no agresión, f.

nonchalance, n. indiferencia, f.

nonchalant, adj. indiferente, calmado.

noncombatant, n. no combatiente, m.

noncommissioned, adj. (mil.) subordinado, sin comisión; — **officer,** sargento, cabo, m., oficial nombrado por el jefe de un cuerpo.

noncommittal, adj. evasivo, esquivo, reservado.

nonconformist, n. y adj. disidente, m. y f.

nondescript, adj. de difícil descripción o clasificación; —, n. persona o cosa que no pertenece a determinada clase o categoría; persona o cosa indescriptible.

none, pron. nadie, ninguno.

nonentity, n. nada, nulidad, f.

nonintervention, n. no intervención, f.

nonpartisan, adj. independiente, sin afiliación política; —, n. miembro o grupo sin afiliación política.

nonpayment, n. falta de pago.

nonproductive, adj. no productivo.

nonsectarian, adj. no sectario, que no pertenece a denominación alguna.

nonsense, n. tontería, f.; disparate, absurdo, m.; (coll.) pamplinada, f.

nonsensical, adj. absurdo; tonto.

nonskid, adj. antideslizante.

nonstop, adj. directo, sin parar o sin etapas; — **flight,** vuelo directo.

non support, n. incumplimiento respecto al mantenimiento (de alguien).

noodle, n. tallarín fideo, m.; (coll.) cabeza, f.; simplón, mentecato, m.; — **soup,** sopa de tallarines o de fideos.

nook, n. rincón, ángulo, m.

noon, n. mediodía, m.

noonday, n. mediodía, m.

noontide, n. mediodía, m.

noose, n. lazo corredizo; —, vt. enlazar.

nor, conj. ni.

norm, n. norma, f.; tipo, m.

normal, adj. normal; — **school,** escuela normal.

north, n. norte, m.; —, adj. septentrional, del norte.

northeast, n. nordeste, m.

northeastern, adj. del nordeste.

northerly, northern, adj. septentrional, del norte.

northern lights, n. pl. aurora boreal.

North Pole, n. Polo Norte, m.

northward, northwards, adv. hacia el norte.

northwest, n. noroeste, m.

northwestern, adj. del noroeste.

Norway, Noruega, f.

nose, n. nariz, f.; olfato, m.; sagacidad, f.

nosebag, n. morral, m.

nosebleed, n. epistaxis, f., hemorragia nasal.

nose dive, n. clavado de proa; descenso repentino de un aeroplano.

nostalgia, n. nostalgia, f.

nostril, n. ventana de la nariz.

not, adv. no; **if** —, si no; — **any,** ningún; ninguno; — **at all,** de ninguna manera; —**even,** ni siquiera.

notable, adj. notable; memorable.

notarize, vt. autorizar ante notario.

notary, n. notario, m.

notation, n. notación, f.

notch, n. muesca, f.; —, vt. hacer muescas.

note, n. nota, marca, f.; señal, f.; aprecio, m.; billete, m.; esquela, f.; consecuencia, f.; noticia, f.; explicación, f.; comentario, m.; (mus.) nota, f.; **bank** — billete de banco; **counterfeit** —, billete falso; —, vt. notar, marcar; observar.

notebook, n. cuaderno, librito de apuntes.

noted, adj. afamado, célebre.

noteworthy, adj. notable, digno de encomio, digno de atención.

nothing, n. nada, f., ninguna cosa; **good for** —, inútil, que no sirve para nada.

notice, n. noticia, f.; aviso, m.; nota, f.; —, vt. observar, reparar, fijarse en.

noticeable, adj. notable, reparable.

notification, n. notificación, f., aviso, m.

notify, vt. notificar; requerir.

notion, n. noción, f.; opinión, f ; idea, f.; — **s**, n. pl. novedades, f. pl.; mercería, f.
notoriety, n. notoriedad, f.
notorious, adj. notorio.
notwithstanding, prep. a pesar de; —, adv. sin embargo; —, conj. aunque.
nougat, n. nogada, f.
noun, n. (gram.) sustantivo, nombre, m.
nourish, vt. nutrir, alimentar.
nourishing, adj. sustancioso, nutritivo.
Nov.: November, Nov. noviembre.
novel, n. novela, f.; —, adj. novedoso, original.
novelist, n. novelista, m. y f.
novelty, n. novedad, f.; — **jewelry**, bisutería, f., joyas de fantasía; —**ties**, n. pl. artículos de fantasía.
November, n. noviembre, m.
novice, n. novicio, cia; novato, ta; bisoño, ña.
novitiate, n. noviciado, m.
novocaine, n. novocaína, f.
now, adv. ahora, en el tiempo presente; — **and then**, de cuando en cuando; **till** —, hasta ahora, hasta aquí; —! interj. ¡vaya!
nowadays, adv. hoy día, en estos días.
nowhere, adv. en ninguna parte.
nowise, adv. de ningún modo.
nozzle, n. boquilla (de una manguera, etc.), f.; gollete, m.; nariz de un animal; (coll.) hocico, m.
nuclear, adj. nuclear, nucleario; — **fission**, desintegración nuclearia; — **reactor**, reactor nuclear.
nucleus, n. núcleo, m.
nude, adj. desnudo, en carnes, en cuero, sin vestido; nulo.
nudge, vt. dar a uno un codazo disimuladamente.
nudism, n. desnudismo, m.
nudist, n. desnudista, m. y f.
nudity, n. desnudez, f.
nugget, n. pepita, f.; **gold** —, pepita de oro.
nuisance, n. daño, perjuicio, m.; incomodidad, f., estorbo, m.; (coll.) lata, f., fastidio, m.

null, adj. nulo, inválido.
nullify, vt. anular, invalidar.
numb, adj. entumecido, entorpecido; —, vt. entorpecer, entumecer.
number, n. número, m.; cantidad, f.; cifra, f.; **back** —, número atrasado; **round** —, número redondo; —, vt. numerar.
numbering, n. numeración, f.
numberless, adj. innumerable, sin número.
numeral, adj. numeral; —, n. número, m., cifra,
numerator, n. (math.) numerador, m.
numerical, adj. numérico.
numerous, adj. numeroso.
numbskull, n. zote, m., estúpido, da.
nun, n. monja, religiosa, f.
nunnery, n. convento de monjas.
nuptial, adj. nupcial; —**s**, n. pl. nupcias, f. pl., boda, f.
nurse, n. ama de cría; enfermera, f.; **wet** —, nodriza, nutriz, f.; —, vt. criar, alimentar, amamantar; cuidar (un enfermo) .
nursery, n. cuarto dedicado a los niños; guardería infantil; plantel, criadero, m.; almáciga, f.
nursemaid, n. niñera, aya, f.; (Mex.) nana, f.
nursing, n. crianza, f.; — **bottle**, mamadera, f., biberón, m.
nurture, vt. criar, educar.
nut, n. nuez, f.; (mech.) tuerca, f.; **lock** —, contratuerca, f.
nutcracker, n. cascanueces, m.
nuthatch, n. (orn.) trepatroncos, m.
nutmeg, n. nuez moscada.
nutriment, n. nutrimento, alimento, m.
nutrition, n. nutrición, f., nutrimento, m.
nutritious, nutritive, adj. nutritivo, alimenticio; sustancioso.
nutshell, n. cáscara de nuez.
NW, N.W., n.w.: northwest, NO, noroeste.
N.Y.C.: New York City, Ciudad de Nueva York.
nylon, n. nylon, m.
nymph, n. ninfa, f.
N.Z.: New Zealand, N.Z. Nueva Zelanda.

O

O.: Ohio, Ohio (E.U.A.)
oaf, n. idiota, zote, zoquete, m.
oak, n. roble, m., encina, f.
oakum, n. estopa, f.
oar, n. remo, m.
oarsman, n. remero, m.

O.A.S.: Organization of American States, O.E.A, Organización de los Estados Americanos.
oasis, n. oasis, m.
oat, n. avena, f.
oath, n. juramento, m.; jura, f.; blasfemia,

f.; **to take —,** prestar juramento.

oatmeal, n. harina de avena, avena, f.

obdurate, adj. endurecido, duro; **—ly,** adv. ásperamente.

obedience, n. obediencia, f.

obedient, adj. obediente.

obeisance, n. cortesía, reverencia, f.; deferencia, f.; homenaje, m.

obese, adj. obeso, gordo.

obesity, n. obesidad, crasitud, gordura, f.

obey, vt. obedecer.

obituary, n. necrología, f.; obituario, m.

object, n. objeto, m.; punto, m.; (gram.) complemento, m.; **— lesson,** lección objetiva o práctica, enseñanza objetiva; **—,** vt. objetar, poner reparo; oponer.

objection, n. oposición, objeción, réplica, f.; **to raise an —,** objetar, poner objeción.

objectionable, adj. censurable, reprensible.

objective, adj. objetivo; **—,** n. meta, f.; fin, objetivo, m.

obligate, vt. obligar; comprometer.

obligation, n. obligación, f.; compromiso, m.; cargo, m.; **to be under —,** verse obligado.

oblige, vt. obligar; complacer, favorecer.

obliging, adj. servicial; condescendiente; **—ly,** adv. cortésmente; gustosamente.

oblique, adj. oblicuo; indirecto, de refilón.

obliterate, vt. borrar; destruir; (med.) obliterar.

oblivion, n. olvido, m.

oblivious, adj. abstraído; **— of,** inconsciente de.

oblong, adj. oblongo.

obnoxious, adj. odioso, aborrecible.

oboe, n. (mus.) oboe, obué, m.

obscene, adj. obsceno, impúdico.

obscenity, n. obscenidad, f.

obscure, adj. oscuro; **—,** vt. oscurecer.

obscurity, n. oscuridad, f.

obsequious, adj. obsequioso; servicial.

observance, n. observancia, f.; costumbre, f.; rito, m.; ceremonia, f.

observant, adj. observador, atento.

observation, n. observación, f.

observatory, n. observatorio, m.

observe, vt. observar, mirar; reparar; ver; notar, guardar (una fiesta, etc.); **—,** vi. comentar.

observer, n. observador, ra.

observing, adj. observador.

obsess, vt. obsesionar, causar obsesión.

obsession, n. obsesión, f.

obsolete, adj. anticuado, obsoleto.

obstacle, n. obstáculo, m.; valla, f.

obstetrician, n. partero, m.

obstetrics, n. obstetricia, f.

obstinacy, n. obstinación, terquedad, f.

obstinate, adj. terco, porfiado.

obstruct, vt. obstruir; impedir; estorbar.

obstruction, n. obstrucción, f.; impedimento, m.

obstructionism, n. obstruccionismo, m.

obtain, vt. obtener, adquirir, lograr; **—,** vi. estar en uso, prevalecer.

obtainable, adj. asequible.

obtrude, vt. introducir con violencia; **—,** vi. entrometerse.

obtrusive, adj. intruso, importuno.

obtuse, adj. obtuso, romo, sin punta; sordo, apagado.

obviate, vt. obviar, evitar.

obvious, adj. obvio, evidente, visto.

occasion, n. ocasión, ocurrencia, f.; caso, m.; tiempo oportuno; acontecimiento, m.; **to give —,** dar pie; **—,** vt. ocasionar, causar.

occasional, adj. ocasional, casual; **—ly,** adv. ocasionalmente, a veces, a ratos.

Occident, n. occidente, m.

Occidental, adj. occidental.

occult, adj. oculto, escondido.

occupancy, n. toma de posesión.

occupant, occupier, n. ocupador, ra; poseedor, ra; inquilino, na.

occupation, n. ocupación, f.; empleo, m.; quehacer, m.

occupied, adj. ocupado.

occupy, vt. ocupar, emplear.

occur, vi. ocurrir; suceder; **to — frequently,** acontecer a menudo.

occurrence, n. ocurrencia, f.; incidente, m.; caso, m.

ocean, n. océano, m., alta mar, m. o f.

oceanic, adj. oceánico.

oceanography, n. oceanografía, f.

o'clock, del reloj; por el reloj; **two —,** las dos.

Oct.: October, Oct. octubre.

octagon, n. octágono, m.

octane, n. (chem.) octano, m.; **— rating,** número empleado para medir las propiedades antidetonantes de combustibles líquidos.

octave, n. (mus.) octava, f.

October, n. octubre, m.

octogenarian, n. y adj. octogenario, ria.

octopus, n. (zool.) pulpo, pólipo, m.

oculist, n. oculista, oftalmólogo, m.

odd, adj. impar; raro; particular; extravagante; extraño; **—ly,** adv. raramente.

oddity, n. rareza, f.

odds, n. pl. diferencia, disparidad f.; ventaja, f.; **— and ends,** trozos o fragmentos sobrantes.

ode, n. oda, f.

odious, adj. odioso; **—ly,** adv. odiosamente.

odontologist, n. odontólogo, dentista, m.
odor, odour, n. olor, m.; fragancia, f.
of, prep. de; tocante; acerca de.
off, adj. y adv. lejos, a distancia; **hands —,** no tocar; **— and on,** de quitaipón; **— flavor,** desabrido; que no tiene el verdadero sabor.
off-color, adj. descolorido; impropio, inapropiado.
offend, vt. ofender, irritar; injuriar; —, vi. pecar.
offender, n. delincuente, m. y f.; ofensor, ra, trasgresor, ra.
offending, adj. ofensor.
offense, n. ofensa, f.; injuria, f.; delincuencia, f., crimen, delito, m.
offensive, adj. ofensivo, injurioso; —, n. (mil.) ofensiva, f.
offer, vt. ofrecer; inmolar; atentar; brindar; **to — one's services,** brindarse; —, vi. ofrecerse; —, n. oferta, proposición, propuesta, f.
offering, n. sacrificio, m.; oferta, f.; propuesta, f.
offertory, n. ofertorio, m.
office, n. oficina, f.; oficio, empleo, m.; servicio, m.; cargo, m.; lugar, m.; **doctor's —,** consultorio, m.; **main —,** casa matriz; **— seeker,** pretendiente a un puesto, aspirante; **— supplies,** artículos para escritorio; **secretary's —,** secretaría, f.
officeholder, n. empleado público, funcionario, m.
officer, n. oficial, m.; funcionario, m.; agente de policía.
official, adj. oficial; —, n. oficial, m.; funcionario, m.; **public —,** funcionario público; **—ly,** adv. oficialmente.
officiate, vi. oficiar; ejercer un cargo.
officious, adj. oficioso.
offset, n. (print.) offset, m.; —, vt. balancear, compensar; neutralizar.
offshoot, n. retoño, vástago, m.; ramal, m.
offshore, adv. en la cercanía de la costa.
off side, adv. en el lado contrario (en ciertos juegos de pelota); (fútbol) en posición fuera de juego.
offspring, n. prole, f.; linaje, m.; descendencia, f.; vástago, m.
off-stage, adj. (theat.) fuera del escenario.
oft, often, oftentimes, adv. muchas veces, frecuentemente, a menudo.
ogle, vt. mirar al soslayo; echar ojeadas contemplativas.
ogre, n. ogro, m.
oil, n. aceite, m.; óleo, m.; petróleo, m.; **crude —,** aceite crudo; **mineral —,** aceite mineral; **— color,** color preparado con aceite; **— field,** campo de petróleo;

cuenca petrolífera; **— painting,** pintura al óleo; **— pipe line,** oleoducto, m.; **— silk,** encerado, hule, m.; **vegetable —,** aceite vegetal; —, vt. aceitar, engrasar.
oilcan, n. aceitera, alcuza, f., lata de aceite.
oilcloth, n. encerado, hule, m.
oilpaper, n. papel encerado.
oilskin, n. encerado, hule, m.
oily, adj. aceitoso, oleaginoso.
ointment, n. ungüento, m.
O.K.: all correct, correcto, V.° B.° visto bueno; **approval,** aprobación.
okay, adj. y adv. bueno, está bien; —, vt. aprobar; dar el visto bueno; —, n. aprobación, f.; visto bueno, m.
okra, n. (bot.) quimbombó, m.
old, adj. viejo; antiguo; rancio; **— age,** vejez, ancianidad, f.; **of —,** antiguamente; **— hand,** experto, ta, persona experimentada; **— line,** conservador, de ideas antiguas; **— maid,** soltera, solterona, f.; persona remilgada; **to become —,** envejecerse, gastarse.
old-age, adj. relativo a la vejez; **— pension,** pensión para la vejez.
old-fashioned, adj. anticuado, fuera de moda.
old-time, adj. antiguo, anciano.
old-timer, n. antiguo residente, miembro o trabajador; persona anticuada.
oleomargarine, n. oleomargarina, f.
olfactory, adj. olfatorio.
oligarchy, n. oligarquía, f.
olive, n. olivo, m.; oliva, aceituna, f.; **— branch,** ramo de olivo, emblema de paz; **— drab,** color verde amarillo oscuro (de los uniformes del ejército de los Estados Unidos) ; **— oil,** aceite de oliva; **— press,** trapiche, m.; **— tree,** olivo, m.; **pickled —s,** aceitunas en salmuera.
Olympics, n. pl. Olimpiada, f., juegos olímpicos.
omelet, omelette, n. tortilla de huevos.
omen, n. agüero, presagio, m.
ominous, adj. ominoso, de mal agüero.
omission, n. omisión, f.; descuido, m.; salto, m.; olvido, m.
omit, vt. omitir.
omnibus, n. ómnibus, m.
omnipotent, adj. omnipotente, todopoderoso.
omnirange, adj. (rad.) de alcance en todas direcciones; **— stations,** estaciones de alcance general.
omnivorous, adj. omnívoro.
on, prep. sobre, encima, en; de; a; —, adv. adelante, sin cesar.
once, adv. una vez; **— for all,** una vez por todas; **at —,** en seguida, cuanto antes,

a un tiempo; **all at —,** de una vez, de un tirón; **— more,** una vez más; **— upon a time,** érase una vez.

oncoming, *adj.* próximo, cercano, venidero.

one, *adj.* un, uno; **at — stroke,** de un tirón; **— by —,** uno a uno, uno por uno; **— o'clock,** la una.

one-horse, *adj.* tirado por un caballo; inferior, de poca importancia.

oneness, *n.* unidad, *f.*

oneself, *pron.* sí mismo; **with —,** consigo.

one-sided, *adj.* unilateral, parcial.

onetime, *adj.* anterior, de antes.

one-track, *adj.* (rail.) de una sola vía; estrecho; que entiende o hace una sola cosa a la vez.

one-way, *adj.* en una sola dirección; **— trip,** viaje sencillo o en un solo sentido; **— ticket,** boleto sencillo.

onion, *n.* cebolla, *f.*

onionskin, *n.* papel trasparente o de seda.

onlooker, *n.* espectador, ra.

only, *adj.* único, solo; mero; **—,** *adv.* solamente, únicamente.

only-begotten, *adj.* unigénito, *m.*

onrush, *n.* arranque, *m.,* embestida, *f.*

onset, onslaught, *n.* primer ímpetu; ataque, *m.*

onshore, *adj.* que se mueve o se dirige hacia las orillas.

onto, *prep.* encima de, sobre, en.

onward, onwards, *adv.* adelante.

onyx, *n.* ónice, ónix, *m.*

ooze, *n.* fango, cieno; **—,** *vi.* escurrir o fluir (algún líquido), manar o correr (algún líquido) suavemente; exudar.

opal, *n.* ópalo, *m.*

opaque, *adj.* opaco.

open, *adj.* abierto; patente, evidente; sincero, franco; cándido; rasgado; **— air,** aire libre; **— house,** fiesta para todos los que quieran concurrir; **— letter,** carta abierta (de protesta o súplica); **— question,** cuestión dudosa o sujeta a duda; **— secret,** secreto que todo el mundo sabe; **— shop,** taller que emplea obreros que pertenezcan o no a un gremio; **—ly,** *adv.* con franqueza, claramente, sin rebozo; **—,** *vt.* abrir; descubrir; **—,** *vi.* abrirse, descubrirse.

open-eyed, *adj.* vigilante, alerta; pasmado, asombrado.

openhanded, *adj.* dadivoso, liberal.

openhearted, *adj.* franco, sincero, sencillo.

opening, *n.* abertura, grieta, *f ;* (com.) salida, *f.;* principio, *m.;* boca *f ;* orificio, *m.;* apertura, inauguración, *f.*

open-minded, *adj.* liberal; imparcial; receptivo.

openmouthed, *adj.* boquiabierto, ávido, voraz, rapaz, bocón, bocudo.

openwork, *n.* obra a claros, calado, *m.*

opera, *n.* ópera, *f.*

opera glasses, *n. pl.* gemelos de teatro.

opera hat, *n.* clac, *m.,* sombrero de copa alta.

operate, *vi.* obrar; operar; **—,** *vt.* explotar.

operatic, *adj.* de ópera, relativo a la ópera.

operation, *n.* operación, *f.;* funcionamiento, *m.;* **to have an —,** operarse.

operator, *n.* operario, ria; operador, ra.

operetta, *n.* opereta, *f.*

opiate, *n.* opiato, *m.,* opiata, *f.;* **—,** *adj.* opiato.

opine, *vi.* opinar, juzgar.

opinion, *n.* opinión, *f.;* juicio, *m.;* parecer, *m.;* sentencia, *f.;* concepto, *m.;* **in my —,** a mi ver; **to give an —,** opinar.

opinionated, *adj.* obstinado, pertinaz; doctrinal.

opium, *n.* opio, *m.*

opossum, *n.* (zool.) zarigüeya, *f.*

opponent, *n.* antagonista, *m.* y *f.;* contrario, ria; contendiente, *m.* y *f.*

opportune, *adj.* oportuno, tempestivo, favorable, apropiado.

opportunity, *n.* oportunidad, sazón, *f.*

oppose, *vi.* oponer, oponerse.

opposite, *adj.* fronterizo, opuesto; contrario; frente; de cara; **to take the — side,** llevar la contraria; **—,** *n.* antagonista, *m.* y *f.,* adversario, ria.

opposition, *n.* oposición, *f.;* resistencia, *f.;* impedimento, *m.*

oppress, *vt.* oprimir.

oppression, *n.* opresión, vejación, *f.*

oppressor, *n.* opresor, ra.

opprobrious, *adj.* oprobioso, ignominioso.

optic, *adj.* óptico; **—s,** *n. pl.* óptica, *f.*

optical, *adj.* óptico; **— illusion,** ilusión de óptica.

optician, *n.* óptico, *m.*

optimism, *n.* optimismo, *m.*

optimist, *n.* optimista, *m.* y *f.*

optimistic, *adj.* optimista.

option, *n.* opción, *f.;* deseo, *m.*

optional, *adj.* facultativo, opcional.

optometrist, *n.* optómetra, *m.*

optometry, *n.* optometría, *f.*

opulence, *n.* opulencia, riqueza, *f.*

opulent, *adj.* opulento.

or, *conj.* o; ó (entre números); u (antes de o y ho).

oracle, *n.* oráculo, *m.*

oral, *adj.* oral, vocal; **—ly,** *adv.* de palabra.

orange, *n.* naranja, *f.;* **— juice,** jugo de naranja; **— tree,** naranjo, *m.*

orangeade, *n.* naranjada, *f.*

oration, *n.* oración, arenga, *f.*

orator, n. orador, ra, tribuno, m.

oratory, n. oratoria, f.; oratorio, m.; elocuencia, f., arte oratoria.

orb, n. orbe, m., esfera, f.; (poet.) ojo, m.

orbit, n. órbita, f.

orbital, adj. orbital; — **flight,** vuelo orbital.

orchard, n. vergel, huerto, m., huerta, f.

orchestra, n. orquesta, f.; — **seat,** luneta, platea, f.

orchestration, n. orquestación, f.

orchid, n. orquídea, f.

ordain, vt. (eccl.) ordenar; establecer.

ordeal, n. ordalías, f. pl.; prueba severa.

order, n. orden, m. y f.; regla, f.; mandato, m.; serie, clase, f.; encargo, m.; (com.) pedido, m.; **in — that,** para que; **out of** —, descompuesto; **rush** —, pedido urgente; **trial** —, pedido de ensayo; **unfilled** —, pedido pendiente; —, vt. ordenar, arreglar; mandar; pedir, hacer un pedido.

orderly, adj. ordenado, regular; —, n. asistente o criado de hospital.

ordinance, n. ordenanza, f.

ordinarily, adv. ordinariamente.

ordinary, adj. ordinario; burdo, vulgar; —, n. ordinario, m.; **out of the** —, fuera de lo común.

ordnance, n. artillería, f.; cañones, m. pl., pertrechos de guerra.

ore, n. mineral, m., mena, f.; — **deposit,** yacimiento, m.

organ, n. órgano, m.; **internal** —**s,** vísceras, f. pl.; — **pipe,** cañón de órgano; — **stop,** registro de un órgano.

organdy, n. organdí, m.

organgrinder, n. organillero, m.

organic, adj. orgánico.

organism, n. organismo, m.

organist, n. organista, m. y f.

organization, n. organización n, f.; organismo, m.

organize, vt. organizar.

orgy, n. orgía, f.

Orient, n. oriente, m.

orient, vt. orientar.

Oriental, adj. oriental.

orientation, n. orientación, posición, f.

orifice, n. orificio, m.

origin, n. origen, principio, m.; procedencia, f.; tronco, m.

original, adj. original, primitivo; ingenioso; —, n. original, m.

originality, n. originalidad, f.

originate, vt. originar; —, vi. originar, provenir, originarse.

oriole, n. (orn.) oriol, m., oropéndola, f.; (Sp. Am.) turpial, m.

orlon, n. orlón (fibra sintética), m.

ornament, n. ornamento, m., decoración, f.; —, vt. ornamentar, adornar.

ornamental, adj. decorativo.

ornamentation, n. ornamentación, f.

ornate, adj. muy adornado, historiado.

ornery, adj. de mal carácter, difícil de manejar.

ornithologist, n. ornitólogo, m.

ornithology, n. ornitología, f.

orphan, n. y adj. huérfano, na.

orphanage, n. orfandad, f.; orfanato, asilo de huérfanos.

orthodox, adj. ortodoxo.

orthopedic, adj. ortopédico.

oscillate, vi. oscilar, vibrar.

oscillation, n. oscilación, vibración, f.

oscillator, n. oscilador, m.

osculation, n. osculación, f., beso, m.

osmosis, n. osmosis, f.

ostensible, adj. ostensible, aparente.

ostentation, n. ostentación, f.

ostentatious, adj. ostentoso, fastuoso; — **ly,** adv. pomposamente, con ostentación.

osteopath, n. osteópata, m.

osteopathy, n. osteopatía, f.

ostracize, vt. desterrar, excluir.

ostrich, n. avestruz, m.

other, pron. y adj. otro.

otherwise, adv. de otra manera, por otra parte.

otter, n. nutria, f.

ought, vi. deber, ser menester.

ounce, n. onza, f.

our, adj. nuestro.

ours, pron. el nuestro.

ourselves, pron. pl. nosotros mismos.

oust, vt. quitar; desposeer, desalojar.

ouster, n. desposeimiento (de una propiedad, etc.), m.

out, adv. fuera, afuera; —, adj. de fuera; —**! interj.** ¡fuera!; —, n. acción de sacar o dejar fuera a un jugador (en el juego de béisbol); —, vt. expeler, desposeer.

out-and-out, adj. sin reserva, completo.

outbid, vt. pujar, ofrecer más dinero (en subasta, etc.).

out-box, n. bandeja de salida, f.

outbreak, n. erupción, f.; estallido, m.; principio, m.

outburst, n. explosión, f.

outcast, adj. desechado; desterrado, expulso; —, n. desterrado, da.

outclass, vt. aventajar, ser superior a.

outcome, n. conclusión, f.; consecuencia, f., resultado, m.

outcry, n. clamor, m.; gritería, f.; venta en subasta pública.

outdated, adj. anticuado, atrasado.

outdistance, vt. dejar detrás, sobrepasar.

outdo, *vt.* exceder a otro, sobrepujar.

outdoor, *adj.* al aire libre, fuera de casa, al raso; — **exercise,** ejercicio al aire libre.

outdoors, *adv.* al aire libre, a la intemperie, fuera de la casa; —, *adj.* relativo al aire libre o a la intemperie.

outer, *adj.* exterior; — **space,** espacio extraterrestre.

outermost, *adj.* extremo; lo más exterior.

outfit, *n.* vestido, *m.*, vestimenta, *f.*; ropa, *f.*; —, *vt.* equipar, ataviar.

outgoing, *n.* salida *f.*; gasto, *m.*; —, *adj.* saliente; — **mail,** correspondencia de salida.

outgrow, *vt.* quedar chico, no servirle a uno por quedar ya chico (vestido, calzado, etc.).

outgrowth, *n.* resultado, *m.*; consecuencia, *f.*

outing, *n.* excursión o salida al campo, jira campestre.

outlandish, *adj.* de apariencia exótica; ridículo, grotesco.

outlast, *vt.* exceder en duración.

outlaw, *n.* forajido, da; bandido, *m.*; —, *vt.* proscribir.

outlay, *n.* gastos, *m. pl.*

outlet, *n.* salida, *f.*; sangrador, tomadero, *m.*

outline, *n.* contorno, *m.*; bosquejo, *m.*; esbozo, *m.*; silueta, *f.*; —, *vt.* esbozar.

outlined, *adj.* perfilado; delineado.

outlive, *vt.* sobrevivir.

outlook, *n.* perspectiva, *f.*

outlying, *adj.* lejos de la parte central; remoto.

outmatch, *vt.* prevalecer, mostrarse superior, distinguirse, sobresalir.

outmoded = **out-of-date.**

outnumber, *vt.* exceder en número.

out-of-date, *adj.* anticuado, pasado o fuera de moda.

out-of-door, out-of-doors, *adj.* fuera de casa, al aire libre.

out-of-print, *adj.* (print.) agotado; — **edition,** edición agotada.

out-of-stock, *adj.* (com.) agotado; sin existencia.

out-of-the-way, *adj.* y *adv.* remoto, distante; fuera del camino; poco usual, raro.

outpatient, *n.* enfermo o paciente externo de un hospital.

outpost, *n.* puesto avanzado.

outpouring, *n.* efusión, *f.*

output, *n.* capacidad, *f.*, rendimiento, *m.*, producción total; cantidad producida.

outrage, *n.* ultraje, *m.*, infamia, *f.*; —, *vt.* ultrajar.

outrageous, *adj.* ultrajoso; atroz; —**ly,** *adv.* injuriosamente; enormemente.

outrank, *vt.* sobresalir, exceder en rango, grado o posición.

outright, *adv.* cumplidamente, luego, al momento.

outshine, *vt.* exceder en brillantez, eclipsar.

outside, *n.* superficie, *f.*; exterior, *m.*; apariencia, *f.*; —, *adv.* afuera.

outsider, *n.* forastero, ra, extranjero, ra; persona no perteneciente a determinada institución, partido, etc.

outskirts, *n. pl.* suburbio, *m.*, parte exterior (de una población, etc.).

outspoken, *adj.* franco; que habla en forma atrevida.

outspread, *adj.* esparcido; —, *vt.* y *vi.* extender, extenderse.

outstanding, *adj.* sobresaliente, notable, extraordinario.

outstretch, *vt.* extender, alargar.

outward, *adj.* exterior, externo; —**ly,** *adv.* por fuera, exteriormente.

outweigh, *vt.* pesar más (que otra cosa); compensar.

outwit, *vt.* engañar a uno a fuerza de tretas.

outworn, *adj.* usado, gastado, anticuado, ajado.

oval, *n.* óvalo, *m.*; —, *adj.* ovalado.

ovary, *n.* ovario, *m.*

ovation, *n.* ovación, *f.*

oven, *n.* horno, *m.*

over, *prep.* sobre, por encima de; **all —,** por todos lados; —, *adv.* demás; — **again,** otra vez; — **and above,** de sobra; — **and —,** repetidas veces.

overabundance, *n.* plétora, superabundancia, *f.*, exceso, *m.*

overact, *vt.* (theat.) exagerar la actuación.

overage, *adj.* demasiado viejo desde el punto de vista de la eficacia de su servicio.

over-all, *adj.* que incluye todo.

overalls, *n. pl.* pantalón de trabajo con pechera.

overbearing, *adj.* ultrajoso, despótico.

overboard, *adv.* (naut.) al agua, al mar.

overcast, *vt.* anublar, oscurecer; repulgar; **to be —,** nublarse, estar (el cielo) encapotado.

overcharge, *vt.* sobrecargar; poner alguna cosa a precio muy subido.

overcoat, *n.* gabán, abrigo, sobretodo, *m.*

overcome, *vt.* vencer; superar; salvar (obstáculos).

overconfident, *adj.* demasiado confiado, demasiado atrevido.

overcooked, *adj.* recocido.

overcrowd, vt. atestar, llenar demasiado.

overdo, vt. exagerar; cocer demasiado (la carne, etc.) ; —, vi. hacer más de lo necesario.

overdose, n. dosis excesiva.

overdue, adj. (com.) atrasado, vencido; —, **draft,** letra vencida.

overeat, vi. hartarse, comer demasiado.

overestimate, vt. estimar o avaluar en exceso.

overexposure, n. (phot.) exceso de exposición.

overflow, vt. inundar; —, vi. salir de madre; rebosar desbordar; redundar; —, n. inundación, f.; superabundancia, f.

overflowing, n. desbordamiento, m.

overgrown, adj. grandulón, que ha crecido demasiado.

overhang, vt. estar colgando sobre alguna cosa; salir algo fuera del nivel (de un edificio, etc.).

overhaul, vt. remendar por completo, reacondicionar; componer; alcanzar.

overhead, adv. sobre la cabeza, en lo alto; —, n. (com.) gastos de administración.

overhear, vt. oir por casualidad.

overheat, vt. acalorar, calentar demasiado.

overindulge, vt. consentir o mimar demasiado; darse uno gusto en exceso.

overjoyed, adj. encantado, muy contento.

overland, adv. por tierra.

overlap, vt. sobreponer; sobrepasar; montar; traslapar.

overlapping, n. acción de traslapar; —, adj. traslapado.

overlay, vt. cubrir, extender sobre; abrumar.

overload, vt. sobrecargar; —, n. sobrecarga, f., recargo, m.

overlook, vt. mirar desde lo alto; examinar; repasar; pasar por alto; tolerar; descuidar; desdeñar.

overnight, adv. de noche, durante o toda la noche; —, adj. de una noche.

overpass, vt. y vi. atravesar, cruzar; vencer; trasgredir; exceder, sobrepasar; pasar por alto; —, n. puente o camino por encima de un ferrocarril, canal u otra vía.

overpower, vt. predominar, oprimir.

overproduction, n. exceso de producción, sobreproducción, f.

overrate, vt. apreciar o valuar alguna cosa en más de lo que vale.

override, vt. atropellar; fatigar (un caballo) con exceso; prevalecer; anular, no hacer caso de.

overrule, vt. predominar, dominar.

overrun, vt. hacer correrías; cubrir enteramente; inundar; infestar; repasar; —, vi. rebosar.

oversea, overseas, adv. ultramar; —, adj. de ultramar.

oversee, vt. inspeccionar; examinar.

overseer, n. superintendente, m.; capataz, m.

overshadow, vt. asombrar, oscurecer; predominar.

overshoe, n. galocha, f.

oversight, n. yerro, m.; equivocación, f.; olvido, m.

oversize, adj. grande en exceso.

oversleep, vi. dormir demasiado.

overstatement, n. declaración exagerada.

overstay, vt. permanecer demasiado tiempo.

overstep, vt. y vi. pasar más allá; extralimitarse, excederse.

overstuffed, adj. relleno o rellenado (aplicase a muebles).

oversupply, n. provisión, cantidad excesiva.

overt, adj. abierto, público.

overtake, vt. alcanzar; coger en el hecho.

overthrow, vt. trastornar; demoler; destruir; derribar, derrocar; —, n. trastorno, m.; ruina, derrota, f.; derrocamiento, m.

overtime, n. trabajo en exceso de las horas regulares.

overtone, n. armónico, m., entonación más baja o alta oida con el sonido principal o fundamental.

overture, n. abertura, f.; (mus.) obertura, f.; proposición formal (de paz, etc.).

overturn, vt. volcar; subvertir, trastornar.

overweight, n. exceso de peso; —, adj. demasiado pesado, muy obeso.

overwhelm, vt. abrumar; oprimir; sumergir.

overwhelming, adj. abrumador, arrollador, dominante.

overwork, vt. hacer trabajar demasiado; —, vi. trabajar demasiado; —, n. exceso de trabajo.

overwrought, adj. sobreexcitado.

ovule, n. óvulo, m.

ovum, n. (biol.) huevo, m.

owe, vt. deber; tener deudas; estar obligado.

owing, adj. que es debido; — **to,** a causa de.

owl, owlet, n. lechuza, f., búho, m., (Mex.) tecolote, m.

own, adj. propio; **my** —, mío, mia; —, vt. reconocer; poseer; **to — up,** confesar.

owner, n. dueño, ña, propietario, ria;

poseedor, ra.
ownership, *n.* dominio, *m.;* propiedad, *f.*
ox, *n.* buey, *m.*
oxbow, *n.* horcate de yugo.
oxen, *n. pl.* de **ox,** bueyes, *m. pl.*
Oxford grey, *n.* gris muy oscuro tirando a negro.
oxidation, *n.* oxidación, *f.*

oxidize, *vt.* oxidar.
oxygen, *n.* oxígeno, *m.;* — **tent,** tienda de oxígeno.
oxygenize, *vt.* oxigenar.
oyster, *n.* ostra, *f.,* ostión, *m.*
oyster cracker, *n.* galletita salada.
oz.: ounce, ounces, onz. onza, onzas.
ozone, *n.* (chem.) ozona, *f.,* ozono, *m.*

P

pace, *n.* paso, *m.,* marcha, *f.;* —, *vt.* medir a pasos; —, *vi.* pasear; **to — one's beat,** hacer la ronda.
Pacific, *n.* Pacífico, *m.,* Océano Pacífico.
pacific, *adj.* pacífico.
pacifist, *n.* pacifista, *m.* y *f.*
pacify, *vt.* pacificar; asosegar, apaciguar.
pack, *n.* lío, fardo, *m.;* baraja de naipes; muta, perrada, *f.;* cuadrilla, *f.;* carga, *f.;* — **animal,** acémila, *f.,* animal de carga; — **horse,** caballo de carga; — **of cigarettes,** cajetilla de cigarros; — **of wolves,** manada de lobos; — **saddle,** albarda, *f.;* — **train,** reata, recua, *f.;* —, *vt.* empaquetar; empacar; enfardelar, embalar.
package, *n.* fardo, bulto, *m.;* embalaje, *m.;* paquete, *m.*
packer, *n.* empaquetador, embalador, *m.*
packet, *n.* paquete, *m.*
packing, *n.* embalaje, *m.;* envase, *m.;* empaque, *m.;* relleno, *m.;* empaquetadura, *f.;* — **house,** empresa empacadora, frigorífico, *m.*
pact, *n.* pacto, convenio, acuerdo, arreglo, contrato, *m.*
pad, *n.* cojincillo, *m.,* almohadilla, *f.,* relleno, *m.;* — **(of paper),** bloc (de papel), *m.;* —, *vt.* rellenar.
padded, *adj.* acojinado, relleno, rellenado (de algodón, paja, papel, etc.).
padding, *n.* relleno, *m.*
paddle, *vi.* remar; chapotear; — *n.* remo, canalete, *m.;* — **wheel,** rueda de paletas.
paddock, *n.* dehesa, *f.*
padlock, *n.* candado, *m.*
pagan, *n.* y *adj.* pagano, na.
paganism, *n.* paganismo, *m.*
page, *n.* página, *f.;* paje, *m.;* —, *vt.* foliar; llamar (a alguien en un hotel, etc.).
pageant, *n.* espectáculo público; procesión, *f.*
pageantry, *n.* fausto, *m.,* pompa, *f.*
paid-up, *adj.* pagado, terminado de

pagar.
pail, *n.* balde, cubo, *m.,* cubeta, *f.*
pain, *n.* pena, *f ;* castigo, *m.;* dolor, *m.;* —, *vt.* afligir; doler; —, *vi.* causar dolor.
painful, *adj.* dolorido; penoso.
painless, *adj.* sin pena; sin dolor.
painstaking, *adj.* laborioso afanoso; esmerado; —**ly,** *adv.* detenidamente.
paint, *vt.* y *vi.* pintar; —, *n.* pintura, *f.*
paintbrush, *n.* brocha, *f.,* pincel, *m.*
painter, *n.* pintor, ra.
painting, *n.* pintura, *f.*
pair, *n.* par, *m.;* —, *vt.* parear; —, *vi.* aparearse.
paisley, *adj.* parecido a un chal de Paisley.
pajamas, *n. pl.* pijamas, *m. pl.*
pal, *n.* camarada, compañero, ra, compinche, *m.* y *f.,* amigo, ga; cómplice, confederado, *m.*
palace, *n.* palacio, *m.*
palatable, *adj.* sabroso.
palate, *n.* paladar, *m.;* gusto, *m.*
palatial, *adj.* propio de palacios, palaciego.
pale, *adj.* pálido; claro; **to turn —,** palidecer; —, *n.* palizada, *f.;* estaca, *f.;* límite, *m.;* —, *vt.* empalizar, cercar, rodear.
paleface, *n.* caripálido, da.
paleness, *n.* palidez, *f.*
palette, *n.* paleta (de pintor), *f.*
paling, *n.* estacada, palizada, *f.*
palisade, *n.* palizada, *f.,* palenque, *m.*
pall, *n.* palio de arzobispo; palia, *f.;* —, *vi.* desvanecerse; —, *vt.* y *vi.* saciar.
pallbearer, *n.* el que acompaña a un cadáver.
pallet, *n.* camilla, *f.;* cama pequeña y pobre.
palliate, *vt.* paliar.
pallid, *adj.* pálido.
pallor, *n.* palidez, *f.*
palm, *n.* (bot.) palma, *f.;* victoria, *f.;* palma (de la mano), *f.;* — **oil,** aceite de palma o palmera; —, *vt.* escamotear;

tocar con la palma de la mano.
palmetto, n. (bot.) palmito, m.
palmistry, n. quiromancia, f.
Palm Sunday, n. domingo de Ramos.
palpable, adj. palpable; evidente.
palpitate, vi. palpitar.
palpitation, n. palpitación, f.
palsied, adj. paralítico.
palsy, n. parálisis, perlesía, f.
paltry, adj. vil; mezquino.
pampas, n. pl. pampas, f. pl.
pamper, vt. mimar.
pamphlet, n. folleto, libreto, m.
pan, n. cazuela, cacerola, sartén, f.
panacea, n. panacea, f.
Panama hat, n. sombrero de jipijapa,
   sombrero panamá.
Panamanian, n. y adj. panameño, ña.
pancake, n. pancake, hotcake, m.
pancreas, n. (anat.) páncreas, m.
panda, n. panda, m.
pane, n. cuadro de vidrio.
panel, n. entrepaño, m.; bastidor, m.;
   lista de jurados; — discussion, discusión de asuntos de interés general,
   como problemas públicos, a cargo de
   oradores previamente seleccionados.
pang, n. angustia, congoja, f.
panhandler, n. pordiosero, ra, mendigo,
   ga; callejero, ra.
panic, n. y adj. pánico, m.
panicky, adj. consternado, aterrorizado.
panic-stricken, adj. aterrorizado, pasmado, espantado.
panorama, n. panorama, m.
pansy, n. (bot.) pensamiento, m., trinita-
   ria, f.; (coll.) hombre afeminado.
pant, vi. palpitar; jadear; to — for, to —
   after, suspirar por; —, n. jadeo, m.
pantaloon, n. bufón, m.; —s, n. pl. pantalones, m. pl.
panther, n. pantera, f.
panties, n. pl. calzones de mujer.
panting, adj. jadeante, anhelante, sin respiración, sin aliento.
pantomime, n. pantomima, f.
pantry, n. despensa, f.
pants, n. pl. pantalones, m. pl.
pap, n. papa, papilla, gacha, f.
papacy, n. papado, m.
papal, adj. papal.
papaw, n. papaya, f.
paper, n. papel, m.; periódico, m.; —s, n.
   pl.; escrituras, f. pl.; documento, m.;
   blotting —, papel secante; brown —,
   papel de estraza; carbon —, papel carbón; glazed —, papel satinado; in a —
   cover, a la rústica (encuadernación) ;
   litmus —, (chem.) papel reactivo; tissue
   —, papel de seda; toilet — papel de

excusado; vellum —, papel avitelado;
   wrapping —, papel de envolver; writing
   —, papel de escribir; marbled —, papel
   jaspeado; — clip, sujetapapeles, m.; —
   cone, cucurucho, m.; — cutter, —
   knife, cortapapel, m.; — money, papel
   moneda; stamped —, papel sellado; —,
   adj. de papel; —, vt. entapizar con
   papel.
paperweight, n. sujetapapeles, pisapapeles, prensapapeles, m.
paprika, n. pimentón, m.
par, n. equivalencia, f.; igualdad, f.; (golf)
   número de jugadas para un agujero; at
   —, (com.) a la par; exchange at —,
   cambio a la par; exchange under —,
   cambio con quebrado; — value, valor a
   la par.
parable, n. parábola, f.
parachute, n. paracaídas, m.; — troops,
   cuerpo de paracaidistas.
parachutist, n. paracaidista, m.
parade, n. ostentación, pompa, f.; desfile,
   m.; (mil.) parada, f.; —, vt. y vi. formar
   parada; tomar parte en un desfile;
   pasear; hacer gala.
paradise, n. paraíso, m.
paradox, n. paradoja, f.
paraffin, n. parafina, f.
paragon, n. modelo perfecto; (print.)
   parangona, f.; —, vt. comparar, comparar con.
paragraph, n. párrafo, m.
parakeet, n. periquito, m.
parallel, n. línea paralela; —, adj. paralelo; —, vt. parangonar.
parallelogram, n. paralelogramo, m.
paralysis, n. parálisis, f.
paralytic, adj. paralítico.
paralyze, vt. paralizar.
paramount, adj. supremo, superior.
paramour, n. amante (generalmente ilícito), m. y f.
paranoia, n. paranoia, f.
parapet, n. parapeto, m.; pretil, m.
paraphernalia, n. equipo, m., atavíos,
   adornos, m. pl.
paraphrase, n. paráfrasis, f.; —, vt. parafrasear.
paraplegic, n. y adj. parapléjico, ca.
parasite, n. parásito, m.
parasol, n. parasol, quitasol, m.
paratroops, n. pl. tropas de paracaídas;
   paracaidistas, m. pl.
parboil, vt. medio cocer; sancochar.
parcel, n. paquete, m.; porción, cantidad,
   f.; bulto, m.; lío, m.; — post, paquete
   postal; —, vt. partir, dividir.
parch, vt. tostar.
parchment, n. pergamino, m.

pardon, n. perdón, m., gracia, f.; —, vt. perdonar.

pardonable, adj. perdonable.

pare, vt. recortar; pelar, quitar la corteza.

parent, n. padre, m.; madre, f.; —s, n. pl. padres, m. pl.

parentage, n. ascendencia, extracción, f., origen, m.

parental, adj. paternal; maternal.

parenthesis, n. paréntesis, m.

parenthood, n. paternidad o maternidad, f.

parfait, n. variedad de postre congelado.

paring knife, n. cuchillo para pelar verdura, etc.

parings, n. pl. peladuras, mondaduras, f. pl.

Paris green, n. cardenillo, m., verde de París.

parish, n. parroquia, f.; —, adj. parroquial.

parishioner, n. parroquiano, na.

parity, n. paridad, igualdad, f.

park, n. parque, m.; —, vt. estacionar (vehículos).

parking, n. estacionamiento (de automóviles), m.; — place, lugar de estacionamiento; no —, se prohíbe estacionarse.

parkway, n. calzada arbolada.

parley, n. conferencia, plática, f.

parliament, n. parlamento, m.; member of —, parlamentario, m.

parliamentary, adj. parlamentario.

parlor, n. sala, sala de recibo, f.; funeral —, casa mortuoria; beauty —, salón de belleza.

parochial, adj. parroquial.

parody, n. parodia, f.; —, vt. parodiar.

parole, n. libertad que se da a un prisionero; —, vt. y vi. libertar bajo palabra.

paroxysm, n. paroxismo, m.

parrot, n. papagayo, loro, m.

parry, vi. evadir; rechazar; —, n. rechazo, m.

parse, vt. (gram.) construir.

parsimonious, adj. económico, moderado en sus gastos; —ly, adv. con parsimonia, con economía.

parsley, n. (bot.) perejil, m.

parsnip, n. (bot.) chirivía, f.

parson, n. párroco, m.

parsonage, n. beneficio, curado, m.; rectoría, f., casa cural.

part, n. parte, f.; oficio, m.; papel, m.; raya, f., partido, m.; obligación, f.; in—, parcialmente; — of speech, parte de la oración; — time, trabajo de unas cuantas horas por día, trabajo temporal por semana; rear —, zaga, f.; —s, n. pl. partes, f. pl., paraje, distrito, m.; —, vt.

partir, separar, desunir; —, vi. partirse, separarse; — from, despedirse; — with, deshacerse de.

partake, vt. y vi. participar, tomar parte.

partial, adj. parcial.

partiality, n. parcialidad, f.

participant, adj. participante; —, n. partícipe, participante, m. y f.

participate, vt. participar.

participation, n. participación, f.

participle, n. (gram.) participio, m.

particle, n. partícula, f.

particular, adj. particular, singular; —, n. particular, m.; particularidad, f.

parting, n. separación, partida,. f.

partisan, n. y adj. partidario, ra.

partisanship, n. partidarismo, m.

partition, n. partición, separación, f.; tabique, m.; —, vt. partir, dividir en varias partes.

partly, adv. en parte.

partner, n. socio, cia, compañero, ra; active —, managing —, socio gerente o gestor; silent —, socio comanditario.

partnership, n. compañía, sociedad, f., sociedad de comercio, sociedad mercantil, asociación comercial; consorcio, m.; general —, sociedad regular colectiva; limited —, sociedad limitada; silent —, sociedad en comandita o comanditaria.

partridge, n. perdiz, f.

part-time, adj. parcial; — work, trabajo de medio tiempo.

party, n. partido, m.; parte, f.; función, f.; tertulia, f.; (mil.) partida, f.; — line, línea telefónica usada por dos o más abonados.

parvenu, n. arribista, advenedizo, m.

pass, vt. pasar; traspasar; trasferir; —, vi. pasar, ocurrir; trascurrir; —, n. pasillo, m.; paso, camino, m.; pase, m.; estado, m.; condición, f.; estocada, f.; (fútbol) pase m.; narrow —, callejón, m.

passable, adj. pasadero, transitable.

passage, n. pasaje, m.; travesía, f.; pasadizo, m.

passageway, n. pasadizo, pasaje, callejón, m.; paso, m.

passbook, n. libreta de banco.

passé, adj. pasado, anticuado.

passenger, n. pasajero, ra.

passer-by, n. transeúnte, m. y f.

passing, adj. pasajero, transitorio, momentáneo; casual; que pasa; — grade, calificación que permite pasar (el examen, etc.); — bell, toque de difuntos; —, n. paso, m.; in —, al paso, al pasar.

passion, n. pasión, f.; amor, m.; celo,

ardor, *m.*; **to fly into a —**, montar en cólera.

passionate, *adj.* apasionado; colérico.

passionflower, *n.* pasionaria, *f.*

passive, *adj.* pasivo.

passkey, *n.* llave maestra.

Passover, *n.* Pascua (de los judíos), *f.*

passport, *n.* pasaporte, salvoconducto, *m.*

password, *n.* (mil.) seña, contraseña, *f.*

past, *adj.* pasado; gastado; **— tense,** (gram.) pretérito, *m.*; **— master,** experto, *m.; autoridad, f.;* ex funcionario de una logia o sociedad; **— participle,** participio pasado; **— perfect,** *n.* y *adj.* pretérito perfecto; **—,** *n.* pasado, *m.;* (gram.) pretérito, *m.;* **—,** *prep.* más allá de, fuera de.

paste, *n.* pasta, *f.;* engrudo, *m.;* **—,** *vt.* engrudar, pegar.

pasteboard, *n.* cartón fuerte.

pastel, *n.* (arte) pastel, *m.;* pintura al pastel.

pasteurization, *n.* pasterización, *f.*

pasteurize, *vt.* pasterizar.

pastime, *n.* pasatiempo, *m.;* diversión, *f.;* recreo, *m.;* distracción, *f.*

past master, *n.* ex maestro (de una logia masónica); experto, ta, conocedor, ra.

pastor, *n.* pastor, *m.*

pastoral, *adj.* pastoril; pastoral, bucólico; **— poetry,** bucólica, *f.*

pastorate, *n.* curato, *m.*

pastry, *n.* pastelería, *f.;* **— cook,** repostero, *m.;* **— shop,** repostería, *f.*

pasture, *n.* pastura, dehesa, *f.;* **—,** *vt.* pastar, apacentar; **—,** *vi.* pastar, pacer.

pasty, *adj.* pastoso.

pat, *adj.* apto, conveniente, propio; (coll.) firme, fijo; imposible de olvidar; **to stand —,** mantenerse firme; **—,** *n.* golpecillo, *m.;* **—,** *vt.* dar golpecillos; acariciar con la mano.

patch, *n.* remiendo, *m.;* lunar, *m.;* parche, *m.;* **—,** *vt.* remendar; **to — up,** remendar; ajustar, solucionar; **to — up a quarrel,** hacer las paces.

patchwork, *n.* obra de retacitos; chapucería, *f.*

pate, *n.* (coll.) cabeza, *f.*

patent, *adj.* patente, manifiesto; **— leather,** charol, *m.;* **— medicine,** remedio de patente, medicina patentada; **—,** *n.* patente, *f.,* privilegio de invención; cédula, *f.;* **—,** *vt.* patentar.

paternal, *adj.* paternal.

paternity, *n.* paternidad, *f.*

path, *n.* senda, *f.,* sendero, *m.*

pathetic, *adj.* patético.

pathfinder, *n.* explorador, *m.;* descubridor de senderos.

pathless, *adj.* sin senda, intransitable.

pathological, *adj.* patológico.

pathology, *n.* patología, *f.*

pathos, *n.* sentimiento, *m.*

pathway, *n.* vereda, senda, *f.*

patience, *n.* paciencia, *f.*

patient, *adj.* paciente, sufrido; **—ly,** *adv.* con paciencia; **—,** *n.* enfermo, ma; paciente, doliente, *m.* y *f.*

patina, *n.* pátina, *f.*

patio, *n.* patio, *m.*

patriarch, *n.* patriarca, *m.*

patrician, *n.* y *adj.* patricio, *m.*

patriot, *n.* patriota, *m.*

patriotic, *adj.* patriótico.

patriotism, *n.* patriotismo, *m.*

patrol, *n.* patrulla, *f.;* **—,** *vi.* y *vt.* patrullar; **— wagon,** camión de policía.

patrolman, *n.* rondador, *m.,* guardia municipal, vigilante de policía.

patron, *n.* patrón, protector, *m.;* **— saint,** santo patrón.

patronage, *n.* patrocinio, *m.;* patronato, patronazgo, *m.;* clientela, *f.*

patroness, *n.* patrona, *f.*

patronize, *vt.* patrocinar, proteger.

patter, *vi.* patalear, patear; charlar; **—,** *n.* charlatanería, *f.;* serie de golpecitos; pataleo, *m.;* pisadas (de niño), *f. pl.*

pattern, *n.* modelo, *m.;* ejemplar, *m.;* patrón, *m.;* muestra, *f.;* molde, *m.;* tipo, *m.*

patty, *n.* pastelillo, *m.*

paunch, *n.* panza, *f.;* vientre, *m.*

pauper, *n.* pobre, *m.* y *f.;* limosnero, ra.

pause, *n.* pausa, *f.;* **—,** *vi.* pausar; deliberar.

pave, *vt.* empedrar; enlosar, embaldosar; pavimentar.

pavement, *n.* pavimento, piso, empedrado de calle.

pavilion, *n.* (naut.) pabellón, *m.;* quiosco, *m.;* (anat.) pabellón (de la oreja), *m.*

paving, *n.* pavimento, piso, *m.;* pavimentación, *f.*

paw, *n.* garra, *f.;* **—,** *vt.* y *vi.* piafar (el caballo); manosear alguna cosa con poca maña.

pawn, *n.* prenda, *f.;* peón (de ajedrez), *m.;* **—,** *vt.* empeñar.

pawnbroker, *n.* prendero, *m.;* prestamista, *m.* y *f.*

pawnshop, *n.* casa de préstamos o empeños.

pawpaw = **papaw.**

pay, *vt.* pagar; saldar; sufrir (por); **to — back,** devolver; pagar (una deuda); vengarse de; **to — no attention,** no hacer caso; **to — off,** despedir; castigar; recompensar; **to — up,** pagar por com-

paya

517

pend

pleto; —, *n.* paga, *f.*, pago, *m.;* sueldo, salario, *m.;* **monthly** —, mensualidad, mesada, *f.;* — **roll**, nómina, nómina de sueldos.

payable, *adj.* pagadero.

payday, *n.* día de paga.

payee, *n.* portador de una libranza o giro.

paying teller, *n.* pagador, ra.

payload, *n.* carga útil.

paymaster, *n.* pagador, *m.*

payment, *n.* pago, *m.;* paga, *f.;* recompensa, *f.;* premio, *m.;* pagamento, *m.;* **cash** —, pago al contado; **down** —, pago inicial; (Mex.) enganche, *m.;* **on** — **of,** mediante el pago de; — **in advance,** pago adelantado, anticipo, *m.;* — **in full,** saldo de cuenta; **terms of** —, condiciones de pago; **to delay** —, **to defer** —, diferir o aplazar el pago; **to make** —, efectuar un pago; **to present for** —, presentar al cobro; **to stop** —, suspender el pago.

pd.: paid, pagd.º, pagd.ª, pagado, pagada.

P.D.A.: personal digital assistant, asistente personal digital.

pea, *n.* guisante, chícharo, *m.;* — **green,** verde claro.

peace, *n.* paz, *f.*

peaceable, *adj.* tranquilo, pacífico.

peaceful, *adj.* pacífico, apacible, tranquilo; silencioso.

peacemaker, *n.* pacificador, ra.

peace offering, *n.* sacrificio propiciatorio.

peach, *n.* melocotón, durazno, *m.;* — **tree,** melocotonero, duraznero, *m.*

peacock, *n.* pavo real, pavón, *m.*

peak, *n.* cima, *f.;* cúspide, *f.*

peaked, *adj.* puntiagudo; endeble.

peal, *n.* campaneo, *m.;* estruendo, *m.;* repique, *m.;* —, *vt.* y *vi.* hacer resonar; repicar.

peanut, *n.* cacahuate, cacahuete, maní, *m.;* — **brittle,** crocante, *m.,* (Mex.) palanqueta, *f.;* — **butter,** mantequilla de cacahuate o maní; — **vendor,** manicero, *m.*

pear, *n.* pera, *f.;* — **orchard,** peral, *m.;* — **tree,** peral, *m.*

pearl, *n.* perla, *f.*

pearly, *adj.* perlino.

peasant, *n.* labriego, ga, campesino, na.

peat, *n.* turba, *f.*

pebble, *n.* guijarro, *m.,* piedrecilla, *f.*

pecan, *n.* pacana, *f.,* nuez encarcelada.

peck, *n.* picotazo, *m.;* celemín (medida de granos), *m.;* —, *vt.* picotear; picar.

peculiar, *adj.* peculiar, particular, singular.

peculiarity, *n.* particularidad, singularidad, *f.*

pecuniary, *adj.* pecuniario.

pedagogue, *n.* pedagogo, *m.*

pedal, *n.* pedal, *m.;* **gas** —, acelerador (de un auto); —, *adj.* relativo a los pies; —, *vt.* y *vi.* pedalear.

pedant, *n.* y *adj.* pedante, *m.*

peddle, *vt.* y *vi.* vender menudencias de casa en casa.

peddler, *n.* buhonero, vendedor ambulante.

pedestal, *n.* pedestal, *m.,* basa, *f.*

pedestrian, *n.* andador, ra, peatón, ona; —, *adj.* pedestre.

pediatrician, *n.* (med.) pediatra, *m.* y *f.*

pediatrics, *n.* (med.) pediatría, *f.*

pedigree, *n.* genealogía, *f.,* linaje, *m.*

pedigreed, *adj.* de casta escogida; — **dog,** perro de raza fina.

peek, *vi.* atisbar; —, *n.* atisbo, *m.,* atisbadura, *f.*

peel, *vt.* descortezar, pelar; —, corteza, *f.,* pellejo (de frutas), *m.*

peeling, *n.* peladura, mondadura, *f.*

peep, *vi.* asomar; atisbar; piar, pipiar; clavar la mirada; —, *n.* asomo, *m.;* ojeada, *f.*

peephole, *n.* atisbadero, *m.*

peer, *n.* compañero, *m.;* par (grande de Inglaterra), *m.;* —, *vi.* mirar fijamente; fisgar.

peerage, *n.* dignidad de par, nobleza, *f.*

peerless, *adj.* incomparable, sin par.

peevish, *adj.* regañón, bronco; enojadizo; —**ly,** *adv.* con impertinencia.

peg, *n.* clavija, espita, estaquilla, *f.,* gancho, *m.;* —, *vt.* clavar.

pelican, *n.* pelícano, *m.*

pellagra, *n.* (med.) pelagra, *f.*

pellet, *n.* pelotilla, *f.;* píldora, *f.;* bodoque, *m.*

pell-mell, *adv.* a trochemoche.

pelt, *n.* pellejo, cuero, *m.;* —, *vt.* golpear; **to** — **with stones,** apedrear.

pelvic, *adj.* pélvico.

pelvis, *n.* pelvis, *f.*

pen, *n.* pluma, *f.;* corral, *m.;* caponera, *f.;* — **name,** seudónimo, *m.;* **ball point** —, pluma atómica, bolígrafo, *m.;* —, *vt.* enjaular, encerrar; escribir.

penal, *adj.* penal.

penalize, *vt.* penar, imponer pena a.

penalty, *n.* pena, *f.,* castigo, *m.;* multa, *f.*

penance, *n.* penitencia, *f.;* **to do** —, penar.

penchant, *n.* tendencia, inclinación, *f.*

pencil, *n.* pincel, *m.;* lápiz, *m.;* **mechanical** —, lapicero, *m.;* — **case,** estuche para lápices; — **holder,** lapicero, *m.;* — **sharpener,** tajalápices, sacapuntas, *m.;* —, *vt.* pintar; escribir con lápiz.

pendant, *n.* pendiente, *m.*

pending, *adj.* pendiente; indeciso; — **payment**, pendiente de pago; **to be** —, pender.

pendulum, *n.* péndulo, *m.*

penetrate, *vt.* y *vi.* penetrar.

penetration, *n.* penetración, *f.;* sagacidad, *f.*

penguin, *n.* pingüino, pájaro bobo, *m.*

penholder, *n.* portaplumas, *m.*

penicillin, *n.* (med.) penicilina, *f.*

peninsula, *n.* península, *f*

penitence, *n.* penitencia, *f.*

penitent, *adj.* y *n.* penitente, *m.* y *f.;* —**ly**, *adv.* con arrepentimiento.

penitentiary, *n.* penitenciaría, *f.;* penitenciario, *m.*

penknife, *n.* cortaplumas, *m.*

penmanship, *n.* caligrafía, *f.*

pennant, pennon, *n.* (naut.) flámula, banderola, *f.;* jirón, gallardete, *m.*

penniless, *adj.* falto de dinero, indigente.

penny, *n.* centavo, *m.;* penique, *m.;* dinero, *m.*

penology, *n.* penología, *f.*

pension, *n.* pensión, *f.;* **widow's** —, viudedad, *f.;* —, *vt.* dar alguna pensión.

pensioner, *n.* pensionista, *m.* y *f.,* pensionado, da.

pensive, *adj.* pensativo; reflexivo.

pentagon, *n.* pentágono, *m.*

pentameter, *n.* pentámetro, verso de cinco pies.

penthouse, *n.* cobertizo, tejadillo, *m.;* habitación construida en un techo.

pent-up, *adj.* acorralado, encerrado, reprimido.

penultimate, *adj.* penúltimo.

penurious, *adj.* tacaño, avaro.

penury, *n.* penuria, carestía, *f.*

peon, *n.* peón, criado, *m.*

peony, *n.* peonía, *f.*

people, *n.* gente, *f.;* pueblo, *m.;* nación, *f.;* vulgo, *m.;* —, *vt.* poblar.

pep, *n.* (coll.) energía, *f.,* vigor, entusiasmo, espíritu, *m.*

pepper, *n.* pimienta, *f.;* — **pot,** sopa de carne y legumbres condimentada con pimientos, ají, etc.; **red** —, pimiento, chile, *m.;* —, *vt.* sazonar con pimienta; golpear, azotar.

pepper-and-salt, *adj.* mezclado de negro y blanco, grisáceo; — **hair,** cabello entre gris y cano.

peppermint, *n.* menta, hierbabuena, *f.;* — **drop,** pastilla de menta.

peppery, *adj.* picante; de mal humor; mordaz.

pepsin, *n.* pepsina, *f.*

peptic, *adj.* péptico, digestivo.

peptone, *n.* peptona, *f.*

per, *prep,* por; — **annum,** al año; — **capita,** por persona, por cabeza; — **cent,** por ciento (%); — **diem,** por día.

perambulator, *n.* cochecito para niños.

percale, *n.* percal, *m.*

perceive, *vt.* percibir, comprender.

percentage, *n.* porcentaje, *m.,* tanto por ciento.

perceptible, *adj.* perceptible.

perception, *n.* percepción, idea, noción, *f.*

perch, *n.* (ichth.) perca, *f.;* (medida) pértica, *f.;* percha, *f.;* —, *vt.* emperchar; —, *vi.* posarse, encaramarse.

perchance, *adv.* (poet.) posiblemente, quizá.

percolator, *n.* cafetera filtradora, percolador, colador de café.

percussion, *n.* percusión, *f.;* golpe, *m.;* — **cap,** *n.* pistón, fulminante, *m.;* — **instrument,** instrumento de percusión.

perdition, *n.* perdición, ruina, *f.*

peremptory, *adj.* perentorio; decisivo, rotundo.

perennial, *adj.* perenne, perpetuo.

perfect, *adj.* perfecto, acabado; puro; derecho; —**ly,** *adv.* a fondo; —, *vt.* perfeccionar, acabar.

perfection, *n.* perfección, *f.*

perfectionist, *n.* persona amante de la perfección.

perfidious, *adj.* pérfido, desleal.

perforate, *vt.* horadar, perforar.

perforation, *n.* perforación, *f.*

perforce, *adv.* forzosamente.

perform, *vt.* ejecutar; efectuar; ejercer; hacer; realizar; —, *vi.* representar, hacer papel.

performance, *n.* ejecución, *f.;* cumplimiento, *m.;* actuación, *f.;* obra, *f.;* representación teatral, función, *f.;* funcionamiento, *m.;* **first** —, estreno, *m.*

performer, *n.* ejecutor, ra, ejecutante, *m.* y *f.,* actor, *m.,* actriz, *f.*

perfume, *n.* perfume, *m.;* fragancia, *f.;* — **bottle,** frasco de perfume; —, *vt.* perfumar.

perfumery, *n.* perfumería, *f.*

perfunctory, *adj.* descuidado, superficial, negligente.

perhaps, *adv.* quizá, quizás, tal vez.

perigee, *n.* perigeo, *m.*

peril, *n.* peligro, riesgo, *m.*

perilous, *adj.* peligroso.

perimeter, *n.* perímetro, *m.*

period, *n.* periodo o período, *m.;* época, *f.;* punto, *m.;* **for a fixed** —, a plazo fijo.

periodic, *adj.* periódico.

periodical, *n.* y *adj.* periódico, *m.*

periodically, *adv.* periódicamente.

periphery, *n.* periferia, *f.*

periscope, n. periscopio, m.
perish, vi. perecer; sucumbir.
perishable, adj. perecedero.
peritonitis, n. (med.) peritonitis, f.
periwinkle, n. caracol marino; (bot.) vincapervinca, f.
perjure, vt. y vi. perjurar.
perk, vi. levantar la cabeza, pavonearse; to — up, reanimarse.
perky, adj. garboso, gallardo.
permanence, n. permanencia, f.
permanent, adj. permanente, perenne; — wave, permanente, m.
permeate, vt. penetrar, atravesar.
permissible, adj. lícito, permitido.
permission, n. permiso, m., licencia, f.
permit, vt. permitir; —, n. permiso, m., cédula, f.
pernicious, adj. pernicioso; perjudicial; — anemia, (med.) anemia perniciosa.
peroxide, n. peróxido, m.; hydrogen —, peróxido hidrogenado; — blonde, rubia oxigenada.
perpendicular, adj. perpendicular; —, n. línea perpendicular.
perpetrate, vt. perpetrar, cometer (algún delito).
perpetual, adj. perpetuo.
perpetuate, vt. perpetuar, eternizar.
perplex, vt. confundir, embrollar.
perplexity, n. perplejidad, f.
persecute, vt. perseguir; importunar.
persecution, n. persecución, f.
perseverance, n. perseverancia, f.
persevere, vi. perseverar; obstinarse.
persimmon, n. variedad de níspero (árbol); níspola (fruto), f.
persist, vi. persistir.
persistency, n. persistencia, f.
persistent, adj. persistente.
person, n. persona, f.
personable, adj. bien parecido, donoso.
personage, n. personaje, m.
personal, adj. personal; — effects, efectos de uso personal.
personality, n. personalidad, f.
personification, n. personificación, f.
personify, vt. personificar.
personnel, n. personal, cuerpo de empleados; tripulación, f.
perspective, n. perspectiva, f.; —, adj. en perspectiva.
perspicacious, adj. perspicaz, penetrante.
perspiration, n. traspiración, f., sudor, m.
perspire, vi. traspirar, sudar.
perspiring, adj. que suda.
persuade, vt. persuadir.
persuasion, n. persuasión, f.
persuasive, adj. persuasivo; —ly, adv. de un modo persuasivo.

pert, adj. listo, vivo; petulante.
pertain, vi. pertenecer; relacionar, tocar.
pertaining, adj. perteneciente; — to, relativo a.
pertinacious, adj. pertinaz, obstinado.
pertinence, n. conexión, f., relación de una cosa con otra.
pertinent, adj. pertinente; perteneciente; —ly, adv. oportunamente.
perturb, vt. perturbar.
perusal, n. examen, m., ojeada, lectura, f.
peruse, vt. leer; examinar o estudiar (algo) atentamente.
Peruvian, n. y adj. peruano, na.
pervade, vt. penetrar.
pervasive, adj. penetrante.
perverse, adj. perverso, depravado.
perversion, n. perversión, f.
perversity, n. perversidad, protervia, f.
pervert, vt. pervertir, corromper.
pessimism, n. pesimismo, m.
pessimist, n. pesimista, m. y f.
pessimistic, adj. pesimista.
pest, n. peste, pestilencia, f.; plaga, f., persona fastidiosa.
pesthouse, n. lazareto, m.; hospital de contagiosos.
pestilence, n. pestilencia, f.
pestle, n. majador, m., mano de almirez; mortar and —, mortero y majador.
pet, n. favorito, ta; animal doméstico, mascota, f.; —, vt. mimar; acariciar.
petal, n. (bot.) pétalo, m.
petition, n. memorial, m.; solicitud, f.; petición, súplica, f.; to make a —, elevar una instancia o solicitud; —, vt. suplicar, demandar, pedir; requerir en justicia.
petrel, n. (orn.) petrel, m.
petrify, vt. y vi. petrificar.
petrol, n. gasolina, f., petróleo, m.
petroleum, n. petróleo, m.; — jelly, ungüento de petróleo, vaselina, f.
petticoat, n. enagua, f., zagalejo, m.; crinolina, f.
pettiness, n. pequeñez, f.; mezquindad, f.
petting, n. mimo, m.; acción de acariciar.
petty, adj. pequeño, corto; mezquino; — cash, efectivo para el pago de gastos menores; — larceny, hurto, m., ratería, f.; — officer, oficial de marina entre alférez y teniente.
petulant, adj. petulante; —ly, adv. con petulancia.
petunia, n. (bot.) petunia, f.
pew, n. banco de iglesia.
pewter, n. peltre, m.
phantasy, n. fantasía, f.
phantom, n. espectro, fantasma, m.; —, adj. espectral.

pharmaceutic, pharmaceutical, *adj.* farmacéutico.

pharmacist, *n.* boticario, farmacéutico, *m.*

pharmacy, *n.* farmacia, botica, *f.*

pharyngitis, *n.* faringitis, *f.*

pharynx, *n.* faringe, *f.*

phase, *n.* fase, *f.* aspecto, *m.*

PhD., doctorado, *m.*

pheasant, *n.* faisán, *m.*

phenol, *n.* fenol, *m.*

phenomenal, *adj.* prominente, fenomenal.

phenomenon, *n.* fenómeno, *m.*

phial, *n.* redomilla, *f.*, frasco, *m.*

philander, *vi.* galantear, coquetear.

philanthropic, philanthropical, *adj.* filantrópico.

philanthropist, *n.* filántropo, pa.

philanthropy, *n.* filantropía, *f.*

philatelist, *n.* filatelista, *m.* y *f.*

philately, *n.* filatelia, *f.*

philharmonic, *adj.* filarmónico.

Philippines, Filipinas, *f. pl.*

philosopher, *n.* filósofo, *m.*

philosophic, philosophical, *adj.* filosófico.

philosophize, *vi.* filosofar.

philosophy, *n.* filosofía, *f.*

phlegm, *n.* flema, *f.*

phlegmatic, phlegmatical, *adj.* flemático, lento, apático.

phobia, *n.* fobia, obsesión, *f.*

phone, *n.* teléfono, *m.;* — **call,** telefonema, *m.*, llamada telefónica; —, *vt.* telefonear.

phonetic, *adj.* fonético.

phonetics, *n. pl.* fonética, *f.*

phonic, *adj.* fónico; —**s,** fonología, *f.*

phonograph, *n.* fonógrafo, gramófono, *m.;* — **record,** disco de fonógrafo.

phosphate, *n.* fosfato, *m.*

phosphorescence, *n.* fosforescencia, *f.*

phosphorescent, *adj.* fosforescente.

phosphoric, *adj.* fosfórico; — **acid,** ácido fosfórico.

phosphorus, *n.* fósforo, *m.*

photo = **photograph.**

photoengraving, *n.* fotograbado, *m.*

photo finish, *n.* llegada de corredores a la meta con tan poca diferencia que el triunfador se determina al examinar la fotografía tomada al concluir la carrera.

photogenic, *adj.* fotogénico.

photograph, *n.* fotografía, *f.;* retrato, *m.;* —, *vt.* fotografiar, retratar; to be —ed, retratarse.

photographer, *n.* fotógrafo, *m.*

photographic, *adj.* fotográfico.

photography, *n.* fotografía, *f.*

photogravure, *n.* fotograbado, *m.*

photoplay, *n.* representación cinematográfica.

photostat, *n.* fotostato, *m.*

phrase, *n.* frase, *f.;* estilo, *m.;* (mus.) frase musical; —, *vt.* expresar; (mus.) dividir en frases musicales.

phraseology, *n.* fraseología, dicción, *f.*

physic, *n.* medicina, *f.;* medicamento, *m.;* purgante, *m.*, purga, *f.;* —**s,** *n. pl.* física, *f ;* —, *vt.* purgar, dar un purgante; aliviar sanar.

physical, *adj.* físico; — **education,** educación física, gimnasia, *f.*

physician, *n.* médico, *m.;* **attending** —, médico de cabecera.

physicist, *n.* físico, *m.*

physics, *n.* física, *f.*

physiognomy, *n.* fisonomía, *f.;* facciones, *f. pl.*

physiological, *adj.* fisiológico.

physiologist, *n.* fisiólogo, *m.*

physiology, *n.* fisiología, *f.*

physiotherapy, *n.* fisioterapia, *f.*

physique, *n.* físico, *m.*

P.I.: Philippine Islands, Islas Filipinas.

pi, *n.* (math.) pi (letra griega).

pi, pie, *n.* (print.) pastel, *m.*, letras de imprenta en confusión o desorden; —, *vt.* (print.) empastelar, mezclar desordenadamente las letras de imprenta.

pianist, *n.* pianista, *m.* y *f.*

piano, *n.* piano, pianoforte, *m.;* **grand** —, piano, pianola, **player** —, piano mecánico, pianola.

piazza, *n.* corredor cubierto, galería, *f.*, pórtico, *m.*

pica, *n.* cícero, *m.;* — **type,** tipo cícero.

picayune, *n.* bagatela, chuchería, pequeñez, *f.;* —, *adj.* de poco valor, mezquino.

piccalilli, *n.* encurtidos picados.

piccolo, *n.* flautín, *m.*

pick, *vt.* escoger, elegir; recoger, mondar, limpiar; to — **a pocket,** ratear el bolsillo; —, *vi.* picar; to — **out,** escoger, señalar; to — **over,** escoger, examinar; —, *n.* pico (herramienta), *m.;* lo escogido, lo mejor.

pickaback, *adv.* sobre los hombros, a modo de fardo.

pickax, *n.* pico, zapapico, *m.*

pickerel, *n.* (ichth.) sollo, *m.*

picket, *n.* estaca, *f.;* piquete, *m.;* (mil.) piquete, guardia de huelguistas; —, *vt.* cercar con estacas o piquetes; hacer guardia o colocar guardias de huelguistas; —, *adj.* de estaca; — **fence,** cerca hecha de estacas puntiagudas.

pickings, *n. pl.* desperdicios, residuos, *m. pl.;* beneficios pequeños o de poco valor.

pickle, *n.* salmuera, *f.;* encurtido, *m.;* (coll.) dificultad, *f.;* **to be in a —,** (coll.) estar en un lío; — *vt.* escabechar.

pickpocket, *n.* ratero, ra, ladrón, ona.

pickup, *n.* (auto.) aceleración, *f.*

picnic, *n.* comida, merienda, *f.;* romería, *f.;* jira o paseo campestre; día de campo.

picnicker, *n.* participante en una fiesta campestre.

pictorial, *adj.* pictórico.

picture, *n.* pintura, *f.;* retrato, *m.;* fotografía, *f.;* cuadro, *m.;* — **frame,** marco, *m.;* **motion —,** película, *f.,* filme, *m.;* — **gallery,** pinacoteca, *f.,* salón de pinturas, museo de cuadros.

picturesque, *adj.* pintoresco.

pie, *n.* pastel, *m.;* empanada, *f.;* (orn.) urraca, *f.;* — **a la mode,** pastel servido con helados.

piebald, *adj.* pío, pintado; manchado de varios colores; —, *n.* animal pío (caballo, asno, etc.).

piece, *n.* pedazo, *m.;* pieza, obra, *f;* cañón o fusil, *m.;* **to tear to —s,** hacer pedazos; —, *vt.* remendar; unir los pedazos.

pièce de résistance, *n.* lo principal, lo más aplaudido (en una función, etc.).

piecemeal, *adv.* en pedazos; a remiendos.

piecework, *n.* trabajo a destajo, obra que se paga por pieza.

pier, *n.* estribo de puente; muelle, *m.*

pierce, *vt.* penetrar, agujerear, taladrar; excitar; internar; traspasar.

piercing, *adj.* penetrante, conmovedor.

piety, *n.* piedad, devoción, *f.;* **affected —,** beatería, *f.*

pig, *n.* cochinillo, lechón, *m.;* cerdo; *m.,* puerco, ca; lingote, *m.;* — **iron,** hierro en lingotes; — **latin,** jerigonza, *f.;* —, *vi.* parir la puerca.

pigeon, *n.* palomo, *m.,* paloma, *f.;* **homing —,** paloma viajera o mensajera; **wood —,** paloma zorita.

pigeonhole, *n.* casilla, *f.*

pigeon-toed, *adj.* patituerto.

piggish, *adj.* voraz; puerco; cochino.

piggyback, *adj.* sobre los hombros; —, *n.* trasporte en plataformas de ferrocarril de remolques cargados.

piggy bank, *n.* alcancía (generalmente en forma de cochino), *f.*

pigheaded, *adj.* terco.

pigment, *n.* pigmento, *m.;* solución para pinturas.

pigmy, *n.* y *adj.* pigmeo, mea.

pigpen, *n.* zahúrda, *f.*

pigskin, *n.* piel de cerdo.

pigsty, *n.* zahúrda, pocilga, *f.*

pigtail, *n.* cola de cochino, *f.;* trenza de cabello; tabaco torcido.

pike, *n.* (ichth.) lucio, *m.;* pica, *f*

pile, *n.* estaca *f.;* pila, *f.;* montón, *m.;* pira, *f.;* edificio grande y macizo; pelo, *m.;* pelillo (en las telas de lana), *m.;* rimero, *m.;* **—s,** *pl.* (med.) hemorroides, almorranas, *f. pl.;* —, *vt.* amontonar, apilar.

pilfer, *vt.* ratear, hurtar.

pilgrim, *n.* peregrino, na, romero, ra.

pilgrimage, *n.* peregrinación, romería, *f.*

pill, *n.* píldora, *f.*

pillage, *n.* pillaje, botín, saqueo, *m.;* —, *vt.* pillar, hurtar.

pillar, *n.* pilar, poste, *m.,* columna, *f.;* fig.) sostén, *m.*

pillory, *n.* argolla, picota, *f.;* cepo, *m.;* —, *vt.* empicotar, poner a un malhechor en alguna picota o argolla; poner públicamente en ridículo.

pillow, *n.* almohada, *f.,* cojín, *m.;* cabezal, *m.*

pillowcase, pillowslip, *n.* funda de almohada.

pilot, *n.* piloto, *m.;* — **house,** timonera, *f.,* sitio del timonel; — **light,** lámpara de comprobación o piloto; luz pequeña y permanente que se usa para encender el mechero de gas; —, *vt.* pilotear, pilotar.

pimento, pimiento, *n.* pimiento, *m.*

pimple, *n.* barro, grano, *m.*

pin, *n.* alfiler, *m.;* prendedor, *m.;* clavija, *f.;* chaveta, *f.;* — **money,** alfileres, *m. pl.,* dinero para alfileres; **safety —,** imperdible, *m.,* alfiler de gancho; —, *vt.* prender, asegurar con alfileres; fijar con clavija; **to — (some one) down,** obligar (a alguien) a resolver.

P.I.N.: personal identification number, N.I.P., número de identificación personal.

pinafore, *n.* delantal, *m.*

pince-nez, *n.* quevedos, *m. pl.*

pincers, pinchers, *n. pl.* pinzas, tenazuelas, *f. pl.;*

pincer movement, (mil.) movimiento de pinzas, *m.*

pinch, *vt.* pellizcar, apretar con pinzas; —, *vi.* ser frugal, escatimar gastos; —, *n.* pellizco, *m.;* pulgarada, *f.;* aprieto, *m.*

pinch-hit, *vi.* (béisbol) batear en lugar de otro; tomar el lugar de otro en un aprieto.

pincushion, *n.* alfiletero, *m.*

pine, *n.* (bot.) pino, *m.;* — **needle,** pinocha, *f.;* —, *vi.* languidecer; **to — for,** anhelar, ansiar (alguna cosa).

pineapple, *n.* piña, *f.*, ananá, ananás, *m.*

pinfeather, *n.* cañón, *m.*, pluma del ave cuando empieza a nacer.

pingpong, *n.* tenis de mesa.

pinhead, *n.* cabeza de alfiler; algo muy pequeño o sin valor.

pinhole, *n.* agujero que hace un alfiler; agujero muy pequeño.

pinion, *n.* piñón, *m.;* ala, *f.;* —, *vt.* atar las alas; maniatar.

pink, *n.* (bot.) clavel, *m.;* —, *adj.* rosa, rosado, sonrosado.

pinnacle, *n.* pináculo, chapitel, *m.;* cima, cumbre, *f.*

pinochle, *n.* pinocle (juego de naipes), *m.*

pint, *n.* pinta (medida de líquidos), *f.*

pioneer, *n.* (mil.) zapador, *m.;* descubridor, explorador, precursor, *m.*

pious, *adj.* pío, devoto, piadoso.

pipe, *n.* tubo, cañón, conducto, caño, *m.;* pipa para fumar; (Sp. Am.) cachimbo, a (de fumar); (mus.) churumbela, *f.;* **oil** — **line,** oleoducto, *m.;* **organ** —, cañón de órgano; — **clay,** arcilla refractaria; — **line,** cañería, tubería, *f.;* — **organ,** órgano de cañones; —, *vt.* y *vi.* tocar (la flauta) ; cantar con voz aguda; —, *vt.* proveer de cañerías; conducir por medio de cañerías; (costura) adornar con vivos.

piper, *n.* flautista, *m.* y *f.*

piping, *n.* tubería, *f.;* (costura) vivo, cordoncillo, *m.;* —, *adj.* agudo; — **hot,** hirviente.

piquant, *adj.* punzante, picante; mordaz; —**ly,** *adv.* con picardía.

pique, *n.* pique, *m.;* desazón, *f.;* ojeriza; pundonor, *m.;* —, *vt.* picar; irritar.

piqué, *n.* piqué, *m.*

piracy, *n.* piratería, *f.*

pirate, *n.* pirata, *m.;* —, *vt.* y *vi.* piratear, robar, plagiar.

pirating, *n.* piratería, reproducción ilícita de obras literarias.

pistachio, *n.* (bot.) alfóncigo, pistacho, *m.*

pistil, *n.* (bot.) pistilo, *m.*

pistol, *n.* pistola, *f.*, revólver, *m.;* pistolete, *m.;* — **shot,** pistoletazo, *m.*

piston, *n.* pistón, émbolo, *m.;* — **ring,** anillo de empaquetadura del émbolo o pistón; — **rod,** vástago del émbolo.

pit, *n.* hoyo, *m.;* sepultura, *f.;* patio, *m.;* (min.) pozo, *m.;* **ash** —, cenicero, *m.;* **engine** —, (rail.) cenicero, *m.;* —, *vt.* oponer, poner en juego; marcar, picar.

pitapat, *adv.* con una serie rápida de palpitaciones; agitadamente; —, *vi.* moverse o palpitar agitadamente.

pitch, *n.* pez, brea, *f.*, alquitrán, *m.;* cima,

f.; grado de elevación; (mus.) tono, *m.;* (en béisbol) lanzamiento, *m.;* — **pine,** pino de tea, pino rizado; — **pipe,** diapasón vocal; —, *vt.* fijar, plantar; colocar; ordenar; tirar; arrojar; embrear; oscurecer; —, *vi.* caerse alguna cosa hacia abajo; caer de cabeza.

pitch-dark, *adj.* negro como la pez, perfectamente negro.

pitched battle, *n.* batalla campal.

pitcher, *n.* cántaro, *m.;* (béisbol) lanzador, *m.*

pitchfork, *n.* horca, horquilla, *f.*

pitching, *n.* (avi., naut.) cabeceo, *m.*

piteous, *adj.* lastimoso; compasivo, tierno.

pitfall, *n.* trampa, *f.*, armadijo, *m.;* peligro insospechado.

pith, *n.* meollo, *m.;* médula, *f.;* energía, *f.*

pithy, *adj.* enérgico; meduloso.

pitiful, *adj.* lastimoso, compasivo.

pitiless, *adj.* desapiadado, cruel.

pittance, *n.* pitanza, ración, porcioncilla, *f.*

pitted, *adj.* cavado, picado.

pitter-patter, *n.* repiqueteo, *m.;* parloteo, *m.*

pituitary, *adj.* pituitario; — **gland,** glándula pituitaria.

pity, *n.* piedad, compasión, *f.;* misericordia, *f.;* —, *vt.* compadecer, apiadarse de; —, *vi.* tener piedad.

pivot, *n.* espigón, *m.;* quicio, *m.;* chaveta, *f.;* eje de rotación.

pizza, *n.* torta muy condimentada de la cocina italiana, hecha de harina con salsa de tomate y que generalmente contiene también anchoas, queso, etc.

pkg.: package, paquete, bulto.

pl.: plural, *pl.* plural.

placard, *n.* cartel, letrero, anuncio, *m.*

place, *n.* lugar, sitio, *m.;* local, *m.;* colocación, *f.;* posición, *f.;* recinto, *m.;* rango, empleo, *m.;* (mil.) plaza, fortaleza, *f.;* — **kick,** (fútbol) acción de patear la pelota después de colocarla en tierra; **stopping** —, paradero, *m.;* **to take** —, verificarse, tener lugar; —, *vt.* colocar; poner; poner (dinero a ganancias).

placement, *n.* empleo, *m.;* colocación, *f.*

placid, *adj.* plácido, quieto; —**ly,** *adv.* apaciblemente.

plagiarism, *n.* plagio, *m.*

plagiarize, *vt.* plagiar.

plague, *n.* peste, plaga, *f.;* —, *vt.* atormentar; infestar, apestar.

plaid, *n.* capa suelta de sarga listada que usan los montañeses de Escocia; tela listada a cuadros.

plain, *adj.* liso, llano, abierto, sencillo; sincero; puro, simple; común; claro, evidente; — **sailing,** (fig.) camino fácil; — **dealing,** buena fe; llaneza, f.; —, n. llano, m., llanada, vega, f.

plainness, n. llaneza, igualdad, f.; sinceridad, f.; claridad, f.

plainsman, n. llanero, m.

plaint, n. queja, f.; lamento, m.

plaintiff, n. demandador, ra, demandante, m.y f.

plaintive, adj. lamentoso, lastimoso; —ly, adv. de manera lastimosa.

plait, n. pliegue, m.; trenza, f.; —, vt. plegar; trenzar; rizar; tejer.

plan, n. plano, m.; sistema, m.; proyecto, plan, m.; planificación, f.; delineación (de un edificio, etc.), f.; —, vt. proyectar; planear; plantear; planificar; —, vi. proponerse; pensar.

plane, n. plano, m.; cepillo de carpintería; aeroplano, m.; — **geometry,** geometría plana; **reconnaisance** —, aeroplano de reconocimiento; —, vt. allanar; acepillar.

planet, n. planeta, m.

planetarium, n. planetario, m.

plank, n. tablón, m.; (naut.) tablaje, m.; —, vt. entablar, asegurar con tablas.

planned, adj. planeado; — **economy,** economía dirigida.

plant, n. mata, planta, f.; planta (del pie), f.; — **louse,** pulgón, m.; —, vt. plantar, sembrar.

plantain, n. (bot.) llantén, m.; plátano, m.

plantation, n. plantación, planta, f., plantío, m.; **coffee** —, cafetal, m.; **rubber** —, cauchal, m.

planter, n. plantador, m.; colono, m.; hacendado, m.; sembrador, ra.

planting, n. plantación, f.

plaque, n. placa, f.

plasma, n. (biol.) plasma, m.; (min.) plasma, f., prasma, m.

plaster, n. yeso, m.; emplasto, m.; enlucido, estuco, revoque, m.; repello, m.; **corn** —, emplasto para los callos; — **cast,** vendaje enyesado, yeso, m.; — **coating,** enlucido, enyesado, m.; — **of Paris,** yeso, m. , yeso mate; —, vt. enyesar; emplastar.

plasterer, n. albañil que enyesa, yesero,m.

plastering, n. revoque, m., revocadura, f.

plastic, adj. plástico, formativo; — **surgery,** anaplastia, cirugía plástica; —s, n. pl. plásticos, m. pl.

plat, n. parcela, f., solar, m.; plano o mapa de una ciudad; —, vt. entretejer, trenzar; trazar el plano (de una ciudad).

plate, n. plancha o lámina de metal; placa, f.; clisé, m.; plata labrada; plato,

m.; — **glass,** vidrio cilindrado o en planchas; —, vt. planchear; batir hoja.

plateau, n. mesa, meseta, f.

platform, n. plataforma, tarima, f.; tribunal, m.; — **scale,** báscula, f.

platinum, n. platino, m.; — **ore,** platina, f.

platitude, n. perogrullada, f., la verdad de Perogrullo, trivialidad, f.

platonic, adj. platónico.

platoon, n. (mil.) pelotón, m.

platter, n. fuente, f., plato grande.

plausible, adj. plausible, verosímil; —bly, adv. plausiblemente.

play, n. juego, m.; recreo, m.; representación dramática, comedia, f.; — **on words,** juego de palabras; —, vt. y vi. jugar; juguetear; burlarse; representar, jugar (un papel); (mus.) tocar, sonar; **to — a joke,** hacer una burla; —ed out, exhausto, agotado, postrado; to — up to, adular.

playboy, n. hombre disoluto amante de los placeres.

player, n. jugador, ra; comediante, ta, actor, m., actriz, f.; (mus.) tocador, ra; ejecutante, m. y f.; **pelota** —, pelotari, m.; **ball** —, jugador o jugadora de pelota; — **piano,** pianola, f., piano mecánico o automático.

playfellow, n. camarada, m. y f., compañero o compañera de juego.

playful, adj. juguetón, travieso; —ly, adv. juguetonamente, en forma retozona.

playground, n. campo de deportes o de juegos.

playhouse, n. teatro, m.

playing card, n. naipe, m., carta (de baraja), f.

playmate, n. compañero o compañera de juego.

plaything, n. juguete, m.

playtime, n. hora de recreo.

playwright, n. dramaturgo, ga.

plea, n. defensa, f.; excusa, f.; pretexto, efugio, m.; ruego, argumento, m.; súplica, f.; petición, f.

plead, vt. defender en juicio; alegar; suplicar.

pleading, n. acto de abogar por; alegación, f.; —s, n. pl. debates, litigios, m. pl.

pleasant, adj. agradable; placentero, alegre; risueño, genial.

pleasantry, n. chocarrería, chanza, f.

please, vt. agradar, complacer; placer, gustar; **do as you** —, haga usted lo que guste; **if you** —, con permiso de usted; — **be seated,** favor de tomar asiento.

pleasing, adj. agradable, placentero, grato; **to be** —, caer bien.

pleasure, n. gusto, placer, m.; arbitrio, m.;

recreo, m.; — **trip,** viaje de recreo.

pleat, vt. plegar; rizar; —, n. pliegue, m.

pleating, n. plegado, m., plegadura, f.

plebeian, adj. plebeyo, vulgar, bajo; —, n. plebeyo, ya.

plebiscite, n. plebiscito, m.

pledge, n. prenda, f.; fianza, f.; compromiso, m.; garantía, f.; empeño, m.; —, vt. empeñar, pignorar; dar fianza.

plentiful, adj. copioso, abundante; —**ly,** adv. con abundancia.

plenty, n. copia, abundancia, f.; plenitud, f.; —, adj. abundante.

pleurisy, n. pleuresía, f.

pliable, pliant, adj. flexible, dócil, blando; tratable.

pliers, n. pl. tenacillas, f. pl.

plight, n. estado, m.; condición, f.; apuro, aprieto, m.; —, vt. empeñar; prometer.

plod, vi. afanarse mucho, ajetrearse.

plodder, n. persona laboriosa y asidua.

plot, n. pedazo pequeño de terreno; plano, m.; conspiración, trama, f.; complot, m.; estratagema, f.; —, vt. y vi. trazar; conspirar, tramar.

plotter, n. conspirador, ra.

plough = **plow.**

plover, n. (orn.) ave fría, frailecillo, m.

plow, n. arado, m.; **disc** —, arado de discos; **gang** —, arado múltiple; **rotary** —, arado giratorio; —, vt. arar, labrar la tierra; **to** — **through,** surcar.

plowboy, n. arador, m.

plowing, n. rompimiento, m.; aradura, f.

pluck, vt. tirar con fuerza; arrancar; desplumar; —, n. asadura, f., hígado y bofes; arranque, tirón, m.; valor, m., valentía, f.

plucky, adj. valiente.

plug, n. tapón, tarugo, m.; obturador, m.; clavija, f.; (elec.) tapón, m., clavija eléctrica o de contacto; (radio y TV.) anuncio improvisado; **to** — **in,** enchufar; **to pull the** — **of,** desenchufar.

plum, n. ciruela, f.; — **pudding,** variedad de pudín; — **tree,** ciruelo, m.

plumage, n. plumaje, m.

plumb, n. plomada, f.; — **line,** cuerda de plomada; nivel, m.; —, adj. a plomo, vertical; —, adv. verticalmente, a plomo; —, vt. aplomar.

plumber, n. plomero, emplomador, m.; fontanero, m.

plumbing, n. plomería, instalación de cañerías.

plume, n. pluma, f.; plumaje, penacho, m.; —, vt. desplumar; adornar con plumas.

plump, adj. gordo, rollizo; — adv. de repente; —, vt. y vi. engordar; caer a

plomo.

plunder, vt. saquear, pillar, robar; —, n. pillaje, botín, m., despojos, m. pl.

plunge, vt. y vi. sumergir, sumergirse, precipitarse.

plunger, n. buzo, somorgujador, m.; émbolo de bomba.

plural, adj. y n. plural, m.

plurality, n. pluralidad, f.; mayoría relativa.

plus, prep. más; —, adj. adicional.

plush, n. tripe (tela felpada), m.

plutocrat, n. plutócrata, m. y f.

plutonium, n. plutonio, m.

ply, vt. trabajar con ahínco; importunar, solicitar; —, vi. afanarse; aplicarse; viajar con rutinario fijo.

plywood, n. madera enchapada.

p.m.: afternoon, p.m. tarde, pasado meridiano.

pneumatic, adj. neumático.

pneumonia, n. neumonía, pulmonía, f.

poach, vt. medio cocer (huevos); —, vi. cazar en vedado.

poacher, n. cazador furtivo.

pock, n. viruela, pústula, f.

pocket, n. bolsillo, m., faltriquera, f.; — **money,** dinero para los gastos menudos; — **veto,** retención por parte del presidente de los Estados Unidos de un proyecto de ley; —, vt. embolsar.

pocketbook, n. portamonedas, m., cartera, f.; (fig.) dinero, m., recursos económicos.

pocketful, n. bolsillo lleno.

pocketknife, n. cortaplumas, m.

pock-marked, adj. picado de viruelas.

pod, n. vaina, f.

podium, n. (arch.) podio, m.

poem, n. poema, m.

poet, n. poeta, m.; vate, m.; bardo, m.

poetic, poetical, adj. poético; — **license,** licencia poética.

poetry, n. poesía, f.; **pastoral** —, bucólica, f.; **to write** —, poetizar; trovar.

pogrom, n. pogrom (especie de genocidio), m.

poignant, adj. picante; punzante; satírico; conmovedor.

poinsettia, n. (bot.) nochebuena, f., flor de la Pascua.

point, n. punta, f.; punto, m.; promontorio, m.; puntillo, m.; estado, m.; pico, m.; —**s,** n. pl. tantos, m. pl.; **main** —, quid, m.; **make a** — **of,** tener presente; **stretch a** —, exagerar; — **of honor,** pundonor, m.; — **of order,** cuestión de orden o reglamento; — **of view,** punto de vista; **to get to the** —, ir al grano; **to the** —, al grano, en plata; —, vt. apuntar; aguzar; **to — out,** señalar.

point-blank, *adv.* directamente, a boca de jarro; —, *adj.* directo, sin rodeos.

pointed, *adj.* puntiagudo; epigramático; conspicuo; satírico; **—ly,** *adv.* sutilmente, explícitamente.

pointer, *n.* apuntador, *m.;* ventor, perro ventor.

pointless, *adj.* obtuso, sin punta; insustancial, insípido, tonto.

poise, *n.* peso, *m.;* equilibrio, *m.;* aplomo, *m.;* reposo, *m.;* —, *vt.* pesar, equilibrar.

poison, *n.* veneno, *m.;* **— ivy,** variedad de hiedra venenosa; —, *vt.* envenenar; pervertir.

poisoning, *n.* envenenamiento, *m.*

poisonous, *adj.* venenoso.

poke, *n.* empujón, codazo, *m.;* hurgonazo, *m.;* **— bonnet,** gorra de mujer con ala abovedada al frente; —, *vt.* aguijonear, hurgar; asomar; **to — fun at,** burlarse de; —, *vi.* andar asomándose.

poker, *n.* hurgón, *m.;* póquer (juego de naipes), *m.*

poky, *adj.* despacioso, lento, flojo.

Poland, Polonia, *f.*

polar, *adj.* polar; **— bear,** oso blanco o polar; **— cap,** casquete polar.

Pole, *n.* polaco, ca.

pole, *n.* polo, *m.;* (naut.) palo, *m.;* pértiga, *f.;* percha, *f.;* **— vault,** salto de garrocha.

polecat, *n.* gato montés.

polestar, *n.* estrella polar.

police, *n.* policía, *f.;* **— court,** tribunal de policía; **— dog,** perro de policía; **— headquarters,** jefatura de policía; **— state,** (pol.) estado policía.

policeman, *n.* policía, *m.,* agente de policía, gendarme, *m.*

policewoman, *n.* agente femenino de policía.

policy, *n.* política de estado, póliza, *f.;* astucia, *f.;* sistema, *m.;* **insurance —,** póliza de seguro.

policyholder, *n.* asegurado, da, persona que tiene póliza de seguro.

poliomyelitis, *n.* (med.) poliomielitis, *f.,* parálisis infantil.

polish, *vt.* pulir, alisar; limar; charolar; —, *vi.* recibir pulimento; —, *n.* pulimento, *m.;* barniz, lustre, *m.*

Polish, *n.* y *adj.* polaco, ca.

polished, *adj.* elegante, pulido; bruñido.

polite, *adj.* pulido, cortés; **—ly,** *adv.* urbanamente, cortésmente.

politeness, *n.* cortesía, *f.*

political, *adj.* político; **— economy,** economía política; **— group,** bloque, *m.;* **— leader,** cacique, *m.;* **— science,** ciencia política; **—ly,** *adv.* según reglas de política.

politician, *n.* político, *m.*

politics, *n. pl.* política, *f.*

polka, *n.* polca, *f.;* **— dot,** diseño de puntos regularmente distribuidos en una tela; **— dot goods,** tela de bolitas.

poll, *n.* cabeza, *f.;* votación, *f.;* voto, *m.;* **— s,** *n. pl.* comicios, *m. pl.;* **— tax,** capitación, *f.;* —, *vt.* descabezar; desmochar; hacer una encuesta; —, *vi.* dar voto en las elecciones.

pollen, *n.* (bot.) polen, *m.*

pollination, *n.* polinización, *f.*

polling, *n.* votación, *f.;* **— booth,** casilla electoral.

pollute, *vi.* ensuciar; corromper.

pollution, *n.* corrupción, contaminación, *f.*

polo, *n.* juego de polo.

polyester, *n.* poliéster, *m.*

polygamist, *n.* polígamo, ma.

polygamy, *n.* poligamia, *f.*

polymerization, *n.* polimerización, *f.*

polysyllable, *n.* polisílabo, *m.*

pomade, *n.* pomada, *f.*

pomegranate, *n.* (bot.) granado, *m.;* granada, *f.*

pommel, *n.* perilla de una silla de caballería; pomo de una espada; —, *vt.* golpear.

pomp, *n.* pompa, *f.;* esplendor, *m.;* solemnidad, *f.*

pompadour, *n.* copete, *m.*

pompano, *n.* (ichth.) pámpano, *m.*

pompous, *adj.* pomposo.

pond, *n.* charca, *f.,* estanque de agua.

ponder, *vt.* y *vi.* ponderar, considerar, deliberar, meditar.

ponderous, *adj.* ponderoso, pesado.

pongee, *n.* variedad de tela de seda.

pontiff, *n.* pontífice, papa, *m.*

pontoon, *n.* pontón, *m.;* **— bridge,** puente de pontones.

pony, *n.* haca, *f.,* jaco, *m.;* caballito, *m.*

poodle, *n.* perro de lanas.

pooh-pooh, *vt.* rechazar con desprecio; burlarse de; **—!** *interj.* ¡bah!

pool, *n.* charco, *m.;* lago, *m.;* tanque, *m.;* billar, *m.;* vaca, *f.,* dinero o cosas reunidas por varias personas; **swimming —,** alberca, piscina, *f.;* —, *vt.* reunir.

poolroom, *n.* salón de billares.

poor, *adj.* pobre; humilde; de poco valor; deficiente; estéril; mísero; **— farm,** casa de caridad, casa del pobre; **the —,** los pobres, *m. pl.;* **to become —,** venir a menos, empobrecer.

poorhouse, *n.* asilo, *m.,* casa de caridad.

pop, *n.* chasquido, *m.;* bebida gaseosa; —, *vt.* y *vi.* entrar o salir de sopetón; meter alguna cosa repentinamente.

popcorn, n. palomitas de maíz, maíz tostado y reventado.

Pope, n. papa, m.

poplar, n. álamo temblón.

poplin, n. (tela) popelina, f.

popover, n. panecillo ligero y hueco.

popper, n. vasija para tostar maíz.

poppy, n. (bot.) adormidera, amapola, f.

populace, n. populacho, m.; pueblo, m.

popular, adj. popular.

popularity, n. popularidad, boga, f.

popularize, vt. popularizar.

populate, vt. poblar.

population, n. población, f., número de habitantes (en una ciudad, país, etc.).

populous, adj. populoso.

porcelain, n. porcelana, china, f., loza fina.

porch, n. pórtico, vestíbulo, m.

porcupine, n. puerco espín.

pore, n. poro, m.

pork, n. carne de puerco; — sausage, longaniza, f., salchicha de puerco.

porous, adj. poroso.

porpoise, n. puerco marino.

porridge, n. potaje, m., sopa, f.

port, n. puerto, m.; (naut.) babor, m., escala, f.; vino de Oporto.

portable, adj. portátil; — typewriter, máquina de escribir portátil.

portage, n. porte, acarreo, m.; portaje, m.

portal, n. portal, m.; portada, f.; — to —, desde el momento de entrar hasta el de salir (en la fábrica).

portend, vt. pronosticar, augurar.

portent, n. portento, prodigio, m.; presagio, m.

porter, n. portero, m.; mozo, mozo de cuerda.

porterhouse steak, n. bistec de solomillo, filete, m.

portfolio, n. cartera, f., cartera portapapeles; — (of a minister of state) cartera (de un ministro de estado).

porthole, n. claraboya, f., ojo de buey.

portiere, n. portier, m., cortinaje de puerta.

portion, n. porción, parte, f.; ración, f.; dote, m. y f.; —, vt. partir, dividir; dotar.

portliness, n. porte majestuoso; corpulencia, f.

portly, adj. majestuoso; rollizo, corpulento.

portrait, n. retrato, m.; to make a — of, retratar; to sit for a —, retratarse.

portray, vt. retratar.

Portuguese, n. y adj. portugués, esa; — language, portugués, m.

pose, vt. colocar en determinada posición (para retratar, etc.); proponer; —, vi. asumir cierta actitud o postura; —, n. postura, actitud, f.

position, n. posición, situación, f.; estación, f.; orientación, f.

positive, adj. positivo, real, verdadero; definitivo; —ly, adv. ciertamente.

positron, n. positrón, m.

posse, n. fuerza armada; fuerza con autoridad legal.

possess, vt. poseer.

possession, n. posesión, f.; to take — of, hacerse dueño de; posesionarse de.

possessive, adj. posesivo.

possessor, n. poseedor, ra.

possibility, n. posibilidad, f.

possible, adj. posible; as soon as —, cuanto antes; —bly, adv. quizá, quizás.

post, n. correo, m.; puesto, m.; empleo, m.; poste, m.; palo, m.; — card, tarjeta postal; — office, oficina de correos, administración de correos;

post-office box, apartado de correos, casilla de correos; —, vt. fijar; enviar por correo; —no bills, se prohibe fijar carteles.

postage, n. porte de carta, franqueo, m.; — stamp, timbre, sello, m., estampilla, f., sello de correo o de franqueo, m.

postal, adj. postal; — card, tarjeta postal.

poster, n. cartel, cartelón, letrero, m.

posterior, adj. posterior, trasero.

posterity, n. posteridad, f.; venideros, m. pl.

postgraduate, n. y adj. posgraduado, da.

posthaste, adv. a rienda suelta, con gran celeridad.

posthumous, adj. póstumo.

postman, n. cartero, m.; correo, m.

postmark, n. sello o marca de la oficina de correos.

postmaster, n. administrador de correos.

postmeridian, adj. postmeridiano.

post-mortem, adj. que sucede después de la muerte; —, n. autopsia, f.

post office, n. correo, m., oficina postal, casa de correos.

postpaid, adj. franco; porte pagado; franco de porte.

postpone, vt. diferir, suspender; posponer; trasladar.

postponement, n. aplazamiento, m.

postscript, n. posdata, f.

postulate, n. postulado, m.; —, vt. postular.

posture, n. postura, f.

postwar, adj. de la posguerra; — period, posguerra, f.

posy, n. mote, m.; flor, f.; ramillete de flores.

pot, n. marmita, f.; olla, f.; tarro, m.; — **roast,** carne asada en marmita.

potash, n. potasa, f

potassium, n. potasio, m.

potato, n. patata, papa, f.; **fried —es,** patatas o papas fritas; **mashed —es,** puré de patata o de papa; **sweet —,** camote, m.; batata, f ; boniato, m.

potbellied, adj. panzudo.

potboiler, n. obra hecha de prisa para ganar dinero.

potency, n. potencia, energía, fuerza, f.; influjo, m.

potent, adj. potente, poderoso, eficaz.

potential, adj. potencial, poderoso.

potentiality, n. potencialidad, f.

potholder, n. portaollas, m.

pothole, n. agujero grande.

potion, n. poción, bebida medicinal.

potluck, n. comida ordinaria; **to take —,** comer varias personas juntas sin formalidad.

potpie, n. pastel o fricasé de carne.

potpourri, n. popurrí, m.

potter, n. alfarero, m.; **—'s ware,** alfarería, f., cacharros, m. pl.

pottery, n. alfarería, f.

pouch, n. buche, m.; bolsillo, m., faltriquera, f.; bolsa, f.

poultice, n. cataplasma, f., pegado, m.

poultry, n. aves caseras, aves de corral, f.; **— yard,** corral de aves caseras.

pounce, n. garra, f., grasilla, f.; —, vt. apomazar; —, vi. entrar repentinamente; **— upon,** precipitarse sobre.

pound n. libra, f.; libra esterlina; corral púbico; **— sterling,** libra esterlina; —, vt. machacar; golpear, martillar.

pour, vt. verter, vaciar; servir (el té); —, vi. fluir con rapidez; llover a cántaros.

pout, vi. hacer pucheros, ponerse ceñudo; n. puchero, m., mueca fingida.

poverty, n. pobreza f.

poverty-stricken, adj. muy pobre, desamparado.

POW (prisoner of war), n. prisionero de guerra.

powder, n. polvo, m.; pólvora, f.; **— case,** polvera, f.; **— magazine,** polvorín, m., santabárbara, f., pañol de pólvora; **— puff,** borla o mota de empolvarse; —, vt. pulverizar; empolvar.

powdered, adj. en polvo, pulverizado.

power, n. poder, m.; potestad, f ; imperio, m.; potencia, f.; autoridad, f.; valor, m.; **— dive,** (avi.) picada a todo motor; **in —,** en el poder; **— of attorney,** carta poder; **— plant,** casa de máquinas, de calderas, de fuerza motriz; motor, m.; **the —s that be,** los superiores, los que dominan.

powerful, adj. poderoso; **—ly,** adv. poderosamente, con mucha fuerza.

powerhouse, n. central, f.; casa de máquinas, de calderas o de fuerza motriz.

powerless, adj. impotente.

powwow, n. conjuración, f.; reunión de jefes de partidos; —, vi. conjurar; reunirse.

pox, n. viruelas, f. pl.; **chicken —,** viruelas locas; **cow —,** vacuna, f.

pp.: **pages,** págs. páginas;

past participle, p. pdo. participio pasado.

p.p.: **parcel post,** paquete postal.

practicability, n. factibilidad, f.

practicable, adj. practicable, factible.

practical, adj. práctico; **— joke,** chasco, m., burla, f., broma pesada; **— nurse,** enfermera práctica (sin título).

practice, n. práctica, f.; uso, m., costumbre, f.; ejercicio, m.; **—s,** n. pl. costumbres, f. pl.; —, vt. y vi. practicar, ejercer; ensayar.

practitioner, n. persona que ejerce una profesión; en la Ciencia Cristiana, persona autorizada para curar.

pragmatic, pragmatical, adj. pragmático; entremetido.

prairie, n. prado, m., pampa, f.

praise, n. fama, f.; renombre, m.; alabanza, loa, f.; —, vt. celebrar, alabar, enaltecer, ensalzar, elogiar.

praiseworthy, adj. digno de alabanza.

praline, n. almendra confitada.

prance, vi. cabriolar.

prank, n. travesura, extravagancia, f.

prate, vt. y vi. charlar, parlotear; —, n. parlería, charla.

prattle, vi. charlar, parlotear; murmurar; —, n. charla frívola; murmullo (de un arroyo).

pray, vt. y vi. suplicar, rezar, rogar, orar.

prayer, n. oración, súplica, f.; **the Lord's P—,** el Padre Nuestro, m.; **— book,** devocionario, m.; capitulario, m.; **— meeting,** reunión para orar en común.

preach, vt. y vi. predicar.

preacher, n. predicador, m.

preaching, n. predicación, f.; prédica, f.

preamble, n. preámbulo, m.

prearrange, vt. preparar de antemano.

precarious, adj. precario, incierto.

precaution, n. precaución, f.

precautionary, adj. preventivo.

precede, vt. anteceder, preceder.

precedence, n. precedencia, f.

precedent, n. y adj. precedente, m.

preceding, adj. precursor.

precept, n. precepto, m.

precinct, n. lindero, m.; barriada, f.; distrito electoral.

precious, *adj.* precioso; valioso; **— stone,** piedra preciosa.

precipice, *n.* precipicio, *m.*

precipitate, *vt.* precipitar; **—,** *vi.* precipitarse; **—,** *adj.* precipitado; **—,** *n.* (chem.) precipitado, *m.*

precipitation, *n.* precipitación, impetuosidad, *f.*

precise, *adj.* preciso, exacto.

precision, *n.* precisión, *f.*

preclude, *vt.* prevenir, impedir, excluir.

precocious, *adj.* precoz, temprano, prematuro.

predatory, *adj.* rapaz, voraz.

predecessor, *n.* predecesor, ra, antecesor, ra.

predestination, *n.* predestinación, *f.*

predetermine, *vt.* predeterminar.

predicament, *n.* predicamento, *m.;* aprieto, *m.,* situación desagradable.

predicate, *vt.* predicar; afirmar; **—,** *n.* (gram.) atributo, predicado, *m.*

predication, *n.* predicación, *f.;* afirmación, *f.*

predict. *vt.* predecir.

prediction, *n.* predicción, *f.*

predilection, *n.* predilección, *f.*

predisposed, *adj.* predispuesto.

predominate, *vt.* predominar.

pre-eminence, *n.* preeminencia, *f.*

pre-eminent, *adj.* preeminente.

preen, *vt.* limpiar, concertar y componer sus plumas las aves; arreglarse, acicalarse.

pre-existence, *n.* preexistencia, *f.*

prefabricate, *vt.* prefabricar.

preface, *n.* prefacio, preámbulo, prólogo, *m.;* **—,** *vt.* hacer un prólogo (a un libro, etc.); ser preliminar a.

prefect, *n.* prefecto, *m.*

prefer, *vt.* preferir, proponer, presentar.

preferable, *adj.* preferible, preferente.

preference, *n.* preferencia, *f.*

preferential, *adj.* privilegiado; de preferencia.

preferred, *adj.* preferente; predilecto; **— stock,** acciones preferidas o preferentes.

prefix, *vt.* prefijar; **—,** *n.* (gram.) prefijo, *m.*

pregnancy, *n.* preñez, gravidez, *f.*

pregnant, *adj.* preñada, encinta; fértil.

preheat, *vt.* calentar previamente.

prehistoric, *adj.* prehistórico.

prejudice, *n.* prejuicio, daño, *m.;* preocupación, *f.;* **—,** *vt.* perjudicar, hacer daño; preocupar.

prelate, *n.* prelado, *m.*

preliminary, *adj.* preliminar.

prelude, *n.* preludio, *m.;* **—,** *vt.* preludiar.

premature, *adj.* prematuro.

premedical, *adj.* preparatorio para el estudio de medicina.

premeditate, *vi.* premeditar.

premier, *n.* primer ministro, *m.*

premiere, *n.* estreno, debut, *m.*

premise, *n.* premisa, *f.;* **—s,** *n. pl.* predio, *m.,* propiedad, *f.*

premium, *n.* premio, *m.;* remuneración, *f.;* prima, *f.;* **at a —,** a premio; muy valioso debido a su escasez.

premonition, *n.* presentimiento, *m.*

prenatal, *adj.* antenatal, prenatal.

preoccupation, *n.* preocupación, *f*

prep.: preposition, prep. preposición.

prepaid, *adj.* franco de porte, porte pagado, prepagado.

preparation, *n.* preparación, *f.;* preparativo, *m.*

preparatory, *adj.* preparatorio.

prepare, *vt.* preparar; **—,** *vi.* prepararse.

prepay, *vt.* franquear (una carta); pagar anticipadamente, prepagar.

prepayment, *n.* franqueo o pago adelantado.

preponderance, *n.* preponderancia, *f.*

preposition, *n.* preposición, *f.*

preposterous, *adj.* absurdo; **—ly,** *adv.* absurdamente; sin razón.

prerequisite, *n.* condición o requisito necesario; **—,** *adj.* exigido anticipadamente; necesario para el fin que uno se propone.

prerogative, *n.* prerrogativa, *f.*

preschool, *adj.* preescolar.

prescribe, *vt.* y *vi.* prescribir, ordenar; (med.) recetar.

prescription, *n.* receta medicinal.

presence, *n.* presencia, *f.;* porte, aspecto, *m.;* **— of mind,** serenidad de ánimo.

present. *n.* presente, regalo, *m.;* **to make a — of,** regalar; **—,** *adj.* presente; **at —,** en la actualidad; **—ly,** *adv.* al presente; luego; **—,** *vt.* ofrecer, presentar; regalar; **to — itself,** surgir; **to — charges against,** acusar, denunciar.

presentable, *adj.* presentable, decente, decoroso.

presentation, *n.* presentación, *f.*

present-day, *adj.* corriente, de hoy, del presente.

preserve, *vt.* preservar, conservar; hacer conservas (de frutas, etc.); **—,** *n.* conserva, confitura, *f.;* **—s,** *n. pl.* compota, *f.*

preside, *vi.* presidir; dirigir; llevar la batuta.

presidency, *n.* presidencia, *f.*

president, *n.* presidente, *m.;* rector, *m.;* rector de una escuela.

presidential, *adj.* presidencial.

press, *vt.* planchar, aprensar, apretar; oprimir, angustiar; compeler; importunar; estrechar; —, *vi.* apresurarse; agolparse la gente alrededor de una persona o cosa; —, *n.* prensa, *f.;* imprenta, *f.;* **Associated P—,** Prensa Asociada; — **agent,** agente de publicidad.

pressing, *adj.* urgente, apremiante.

pressure, *n.* presión, *f.;* opresión, *f.;* — **cooker,** olla de cocer a presión, (Mex.) olla express, *f.;* — **gauge,** manómetro, *m.;* — **group,** minoría que en cuerpos legisladores ejerce presión por medios extraoficiales.

pressurize, *vt.* (avi.) sobrecomprimir; —d **cabin,** cabina a presión.

presswork, *n.* impresión, tirada, *f.*

prestige, *n.* prestigio, *m.,* reputación, fama, *f.*

presume, *vi.* presumir, suponer.

presumption, *n.* presunción, *f.*

presumptuous, *adj.* presuntuoso.

presuppose, *vt.* presuponer.

pretend, *vt.* y *vi.* hacer ver, simular; pretender.

pretender, *n.* pretendiente, *m.*

pretense, pretence, *n.* pretexto, *m.;* pretensión, *f.*

pretentious, *adj.* pretencioso, presuntuoso, vanidoso.

pretext, *n.* pretexto, socolor, viso, *m.*

prettily, *adv.* bonitamente; agradablemente.

prettiness, *n.* belleza, *f.*

pretty, *adj.* hermoso, lindo, bien parecido, bonito; —, *adv.* algo, un poco, bastante.

pretzel, *n.* galleta dura y salada generalmente en forma de nudo.

prevail, *vi.* prevalecer, predominar, imperar.

prevailing, *adj.* dominante, prevaleciente (uso, costumbre, etc.).

prevalent, *adj.* prevaleciente, que existe extensamente.

prevaricate, *vi.* prevaricar, mentir.

prevent, *vt.* prevenir; impedir; remediar.

preventable, *adj.* prevenible, evitable.

prevention, *n.* prevención, *f.*

preventive, *adj.* preventivo; —, *n.* preventivo, preservativo, *m.*

preview, *n.* exhibición preliminar.

previous, *adj.* previo; antecedente; —ly, *adv.* de antemano.

prewar, *adj.* de la preguerra.

prey, *n.* botín, *m.;* rapiña, *f.;* presa, *f.;* —, *vi.* pillar, robar.

price, *n.* precio, premio, valor, *m.;* best —, lowest —, último precio; cost —, precio de costo; fixed —, precio fijo; high —s, carestía, *f.;* — ceiling, límite máximo de precios; — fixing, fijación de precios; — list, lista de precios, tarifa, *f.;* sale —, precio de venta, precio rebajado; to set a —, poner precio; —, *vt.* apreciar, valuar.

priceless, *adj.* inapreciable.

prick, *vt.* punzar, picar; apuntar; hincar; clavar; —, *n.* puntura, *f.;* picadura, *f.;* punzada, *f.;* púa, *f.;* pinchazo, *m.*

pricking, *n.* picadura, *f.;* punzada, *f.;* picada, *f.;* —, *adj.* picante.

prickly, *adj.* espinoso; — **heat,** salpullido, *m.;* — **pear,** higo chumbo o de pala.

pride, *n.* orgullo, *m.;* vanidad, *f.;* jactancia, *f.;* to — **oneself on,** enorgullecerse de; jactarse de; to take — in, preciarse de.

priest, *n.* sacerdote, presbítero, cura, *m.*

priestess, *n.* sacerdotisa, *f.*

priesthood, *n.* sacerdocio, *m.*

prig, *n.* persona pedante y remilgada.

priggish, *adj.* afectado.

prim, *adj.* peripuesto, afectado, remilgado.

primacy, *n.* primacía, *f.*

primarily, *adv.* primariamente, sobre todo.

primary, *adj.* primario, principal; primero; — **colors,** colores primitivos; — **education,** primera enseñanza; — **election,** elección primaria; — **school,** escuela primaria.

primate, *n.* primado, *m.*

prime, *n.* madrugada, alba, *f.;* (fig.) flor, nata, *f.;* primavera, *f.;* principio, *m.;* —, *adj.* primero; primoroso, excelente; —, *vt.* cebar; preparar, prevenir.

primer, *n.* cartilla de lectura.

primeval, *adj.* primitivo.

priming, *n.* cebo, *m.;* preparación, *f.;* cebadura (de una bomba), *f.*

primitive, *adj.* primitivo.

primrose, *n.* (bot.) primavera, *f.;* color amarillo rojizo; —, *adj.* alegre; — **path,** sendero de placeres.

prince, *n.* príncipe, soberano, *m.*

princely, *adj.* principesco; —, *adv.* como un príncipe.

princess, *n.* princesa, *f.*

principal, *adj.* principal; —, *n.* principal, jefe, *m.;* rector, director (de un colegio), *m.;* capital (dinero empleado), *m.*

principality, *n.* principado, *m.*

principally, *adv.* principalmente, máxime.

principle, *n.* principio, *m.;* causa primitiva; fundamento, motivo, *m.*

print, *vt.* estampar, imprimir; —, *n.* impresión, estampa, *f.;* copia, *f.;* impreso, *m.;* out of —, vendido, agotado (libros, etc.).

printed, *adj.* impreso; — **goods,** estampados, *m. pl.;* — **matter,** impresos, *m. pl.*

printer, *n.* impresor, *m.;* —'s devil, aprendiz de impresor; —'s mark, pie de imprenta.

printing, *n.* tipografía, imprenta, *f.;* impresión, *f.;* — **office,** imprenta, *f.;* — **press,** prensa tipográfica.

printshop, *n.* imprenta, *f.*

prior, *adj.* anterior, precedente; —, *n.* prior (prelado), *m.*

priority, *n.* prioridad, prelación, antelación, *f.*

prism, *n.* prisma, *m.*

prison, *n.* prisión, cárcel, *f.;* presidio, *m.*

prisoner, *n.* preso, sa, prisionero, ra, cautivo, va.

pristine, *adj.* prístino, primitivo.

privacy, *n.* retiro, *m.,* posibilidad de aislamiento, independencia, *f.*

private, *adj.* secreto, privado; particular; —, *n.* (mil.) soldado raso; **in —,** secreto; **—ly,** *adv.* en secreto, en particular.

privation, *n.* privación, *f.*

privilege, *n.* privilegio, *m.;* **—d,** *adj.* privilegiado.

privy, *adj.* privado, secreto; confidente; —, *n.* secreta, letrina, *f.,* retrete, *m.*

prize, *n.* premio, precio, *m.;* — **fight,** pugilato, *m.;* — **story,** relato interesante digno de premiarse; —, *vt.* apreciar, valuar.

prizefighter, *n.* boxeador profesional.

pro, *prep.* para, pro; —, *adj.* en el lado afirmativo (de un debate, etc.); —, *n.* persona que toma el afirmativo (en algún debate, votación, etc.); **the —s and cons,** el pro y el contra.

P.R.O.: Public Relations Officer, Encargado de Relaciones Públicas.

probability, *n.* probabilidad, *f.*

probable, *adj.* probable, verosímil; **—bly,** *adv.* probablemente.

probation, *n.* prueba, *f.;* examen, *m.;* libertad condicional; noviciado, *m.*

probationer, *n.* novicio, *m.;* delincuente que disfruta de libertad condicional.

probe, *n.* (med.) tienta, *f.;* sonda espacial; **—rocket,** cohete de sondeo, proyectil-sonda, *m.;* —, *vt.* tentar (alguna herida); sondar.

problem, *n.* problema, *m.*

problematic, problematical, *adj.* problemático.

procedure, *n.* procedimiento, *m.;* progreso, proceso, *m.*

proceed, *vi.* proceder; provenir; portarse; originarse; ponerse en marcha; **—s,** *n. pl.* producto, rédito, *m.;* resultado, *m.;* **gross —s,** producto íntegro; **net —s,** producto neto o líquido.

proceeding, *n.* procedimiento, *m.;* proceso, *m.;* conducta, *f.;* **—s,** *n. pl.* actas, *f. pl.;* expediente, *m.;* memoria, *f.,* o informe,

m., (de una conferencia, etc.).

process, *n.* proceso, *m.;* procedimiento, *m.;* progreso, *m.;* —, *vt.* procesar; fabricar, tratar o preparar con un método especial.

procession, *n.* procesión, *f.*

proclaim, *vt.* proclamar; publicar.

proclamation, *n.* proclamación, *f.;* decreto, bando, *m.;* cedulón, *m.*

procrastinate, *vt.* diferir, retardar.

procreation, *n.* procreación, producción, *f.*

proctor, *n.* procurador, *m.;* juez escolástico.

procurable, *adj.* asequible.

procure, *vt.* adquirir, conseguir.

prod, *n.* pinchazo, aguijón, *m.;* —, *vt.* aguijonear, pinchar; aguzar, instar.

prodigal, *adj.* pródigo; derrochador; —, *n.* disipador, ra; derrochador, ra.

prodigious, *adj.* prodigioso.

prodigy, *n.* prodigio, *m.;* **infant —,** niño prodigio.

produce, *vt.* producir, criar; rendir; causar; —, *n.* producto, *m.*

producer, *n.* productor, ra.

product, *n.* producto, *m.;* obra, *f.;* efecto, *m.*

production, *n.* producción, *f.;* producto, *m.;* — **cost,** costo de fabricación o de producción.

productive, *adj.* productivo.

Prof.: professor, Prof. profesor.

profane, *adj.* profano; —, *vt.* profanar.

profanity, *n.* blasfemia, impiedad, *f.;* lenguaje profano.

profess, *vt.* profesar; ejercer; declarar.

professedly, *adv.* declaradamente; públicamente.

profession, *n.* profesión, *f.*

professional, *adj.* profesional; —, *n.* profesional, *m.;* actor o actriz profesional.

professor, *n.* profesor, ra, catedrático, *m.*

proffer, *vt.* proponer, ofrecer; —, *n.* oferta, *f.*

proficient, *adj.* proficiente, adelantado.

profile, *n.* perfil, *m.;* bosquejo biográfico.

profit, *n.* ganancia, *f.;* provecho, *m.;* ventaja, *f.;* utilidad, *f.;* **net —,** ganancia líquida; — **and loss,** ganancias y pérdidas, *f. pl.;* lucros y daños, *m. pl.;* — **sharing,** distribución de la ganancia entre los empleados; —, *vt. y vi.* aprovechar, servir; ser útil; adelantar; beneficiar; aprovecharse; **to — by,** beneficiarse con.

profitable, *adj.* provechoso, ventajoso; productivo; **—bly,** *ad.* provechosamente.

profiteer, *vi.* usurear, explotar; —, *n.* usurero, ra, explotador, ra.

profound, *adj.* profundo.

profuse, *adj.* profuso, pródigo.

profusion, n. prodigalidad, f.; abundancia, profusión, f.
progenitor, n. progenitor, ra.
prognostication, n. pronóstico, m.
program, programme, n. programa, m.
programming, n. programación, f.
progress, n. progreso, m.; adelanto, m.; viaje, curso, m.; —, vi. progresar.
progressive, adj. progresivo.
prohibit, vt. prohibir, vedar; impedir.
prohibition, n. prohibición, f.; auto prohibitorio.
project, vt. proyectar, trazar; —, n. proyecto, m.
projectile, n. proyectil, m.
projection, n. proyección, f.; proyectura, f.
projector, n. proyectista, proyector, m.; movie —, proyector de cine, cinematógrafo, m.
proletarian, n. y adj. proletario, ria.
proletariat, n. proletariado, m.
prolific, adj. prolífico, fecundo.
prologue, n. prólogo, m.
prolong, vt. prolongar; diferir; prorrogar.
prom, n. baile de graduación (de un colegio).
promenade, vi. pasearse; —, n. paseo, m.
prominence, n. prominencia, eminencia, f.
prominent, adj. prominente; saledizo; conspicuo; to be —, sobresalir; ser eminente.
promiscuous, adj. promiscuo.
promise, n. promesa, f.; prometido, m.; —, vt. prometer.
promising, adj. prometedor.
promissory, adj. promisorio; — note, pagaré, m.
promontory, n. promontorio, m.
promote, vt. promover.
promoter, n. promotor, promovedor, m.
promotion, n. promoción, f.
prompt, adj. pronto, listo, expedito; —ly, adv. con toda precisión; pronto; —, vt. sugerir, insinuar; apuntar (en el teatro).
promulgate, vt. promulgar, publicar.
prone, adj. prono, inclinado; dispuesto.
prong, n. púa, punta, f.; —, vt. perforar, traspasar con una púa.
pronoun, n. pronombre, m.
pronounce, vt. pronunciar; recitar.
pronouncement, n. declaración formal; anuncio oficial.
pronunciation, n. pronunciación, f.
proof, n. prueba, f.; bomb—, a prueba de bomba; water—, impermeable; fool—, fácil (hasta para un tonto).
proofread, vt. corregir pruebas.
proofreader, n. corrector o correctora de pruebas.
prop, vt. sostener, apuntalar; —, n. apoyo,

puntal, m.; sostén, m.
propaganda, n. propaganda, f.; anuncios, m. pl.
propagandist, n. y adj. propagandista, propagador, ra.
propagate, vt. propagar; —, vi. propagarse.
propel, vt. impeler.
propeller, n. propulsor, m.; hélice, f.; — blade, segmento o paleta de hélice.
propensity, n. propensión, tendencia, f.
proper, adj. propio; conveniente; exacto; decente; debido; in — form, en forma debida; —ly, adv. justamente; adecuadamente.
property, n. propiedad, f.; bien, m.; peculiaridad, cualidad, f.
prophecy, n. profecía, f.
prophesy, vt. profetizar; predicar.
prophet, n. profeta, m.
prophetic, adj. profético.
prophylactic, n. y adj. profiláctico, m.
propitious, adj. propicio, favorable.
proponent, n. proponente, m. y f.
proportion, n. proporción, f.; simetría, f.; in —, a prorrata; —, vt. proporcionar.
proportional, adj. proporcional.
proportionate, adj. proporcionado; en proporciones; —ly, adv. proporcionalmente.
proportioned, adj. proporcionado.
proposal, n. propuesta, proposición, f.; oferta, f.
propose, vt. proponer.
proposition, n. proposición, propuesta, f.
propound, vt. proponer; sentar una proposición.
proprietor, n. propietario, ria, dueño, ña.
propriety, n. propiedad, f.
prorate, vt. prorratear.
prosaic, adj. prosaico, en prosa; insulso.
proscription, n. proscripción, f.
prose, n. prosa, f.
prosecute, vt. proseguir, acusar.
prosecution, n. prosecución, f.
prosecutor, n. acusador, m.
prospect, n. perspectiva, f.; esperanza, f.
prospective, adj. en perspectiva; anticipado.
prospector, n. buscador de minas.
prospectus, n. prospecto, m.
prosper, vi. prosperar.
prosperity, n. prosperidad, bonanza, f.
prosperous, adj. próspero, feliz.
prostitute, vt. prostituir; —, n. prostituta, f.
prostitution, n. prostitución, f.
prostrate, adj. postrado, prosternado; —, vt. postrar; —, vi. prosternarse, postrarse.
prostrated, adj. postrado; decaído.

prostration, *n.* postración, adinamia, *f.;* colapso, *m.*
protect, *vt.* proteger, amparar.
protection, *n.* protección, *f.*
protective, *adj.* protector.
protector, *n.* protector, ra; patron, na; defensor, ra.
protégé, protégée, *n.* protegido, da; paniaguado, da.
protein, *n.* proteína, *f.*
protest, *vt.* y *vi.* protestar; —, *n.* protesta, *f.; (corn.)* protesto (de una libranza).
Protestant, *n.* y *adj.* protestante, *m.* y *f.*
protocol, *n.* protocolo, *m.*
proton, *n.* (elec.) protón, *m.*
protoplasm, *n.* protoplasma, *m.*
prototype, *n.* prototipo, *m.*
protract, *vt.* prolongar, dilatar, diferir.
protrude, *vt.* empujar, impeler; —, *vi.* sobresalir.
protuberance, *n.* protuberancia, *f.*
protuberant, *adj.* prominente, saliente.
proud, *adj.* soberbio, orgulloso.
prove, *vt.* probar, justificar; experimentar; —, *vi.* resultar; salir (bien o mal).
proverb, *n.* proverbio, *m.*
proverbial, *adj.* proverbial.
provide, *vt.* proveer, surtir; proporcionar; **to — oneself with,** proveerse de.
provided, *adj.* provisto; **— that,** con tal que, a condición de que, siempre que, dado que.
providence, *n.* providencia, *f.;* economía, *f.*
provident, *adj.* próvido; providente.
provider, *n.* proveedor, ra.
province, *n.* provincia, *f.;* obligación particular; jurisdicción, *f.*
provincial, *adj.* provincial; —, *n.* provinciano, na.
provision, *n.* provisión, *f.;* precaución, *f.;* **—s,** *n. pl.* comestibles, *m. pl.*
provisional, *adj.* provisional.
provocation, *n.* provocación, *f.*
provocative, *adj.* provocativo; estimulante; —, *n.* excitante, *m.*
provoke, *vt.* provocar, incitar.
provoking, *adj.* provocativo; **—ly,** *adv.* de un modo provocativo.
prow, *n.* (naut.) proa, *f.*
prowess, *n.* proeza, valentía, *f.*
prowl, *vi.* andar en busca de pillaje; rondar, vagar; rastrear.
prowler, *n.* ladrón, vago, *m.*
proximity, *n.* proximidad, cercanía, *f.*
proxy, *n.* procuración, *f.;* procurador, *m.;* apoderado, da; **by —,** por poder.
prude, *n.* mojigato, ta.
prudence, *n.* prudencia, *f.;* precaución, *f.*
prudent, *adj.* prudente, circunspecto, cauteloso, cauto; **—ly,** *adv.* con juicio.

prudery, *n.* mojigatez, *f.,* afectación de modestia.
prudish, *adj.* mojigato, modesto en extremo.
prune, *vt.* podar; escamondar (los árboles); —, *n.* ciruela seca, ciruela pasa, *f.*
pruning, *n.* poda, *f.*
pry, *vi.* espiar, acechar; curiosear.
P.S.: postscript, P.D. o P.S. posdata.
psalm, *n.* salmo, *m.*
pseudonym, *n.* seudónimo o pseudónimo, *m.*
psychiatrist, *n.* psiquiatra o siquiatra, *m.y f.*
psychiatry, *n.* psiquiatría o siquiatría, *f.*
psychic, *adj.* psíquico o síquico.
psychoanalysis, *n.* psicoanálisis o sicoanálisis, *f.*
psychologic, psychological, *adj.* psicológico o sicológico.
psychologist, *n.* psicólogo, ga o sicólogo, ga.
psychology, *n.* psicología o sicología, *f.*
psychopathic, *adj.* psicopático o sicopático.
pt.: pint, pinta (medida de líquidos), *f.*
P.T.A.: Parent-Teacher Association, Asociación de Padres y Maestros.
p.t.o.: please turn over, véase a la vuelta.
ptomaine, ptomain, *n.* tomaína, *f.;* **— poison,** envenenamiento por tomaínas.
puberty, *n.* pubertad, *f.*
public, *adj.* público; común; notorio; **— official,** funcionario público; **— relations,** relaciones con el público; **—spirited,** de espíritu cívico; **— utility,** empresa pública, empresa de servicios públicos; **— works,** obras públicas; **—ly,** *adv.* públicamente; —, *n.* público, *m.*
publication, *n.* publicación, *f*
publicist, *n.* publicista, *m.* y *f.*
publicity, *n.* publicidad, *f.*
publicize, *vt.* publicar.
publish, *vt.* publicar, dar a la prensa.
publisher, *n.* publicador, editor, *m.*
publishing, *n.* publicación, *f.;* —, *adj.* editor, editorial; **— house,** casa editorial; casa editora.
puck, *n.* duende travieso.
pucker, *vt.* arrugar, hacer pliegues.
pudding, *n.* pudin, *m.;* morcilla, *f.*
puddle, *n.* lodazal, cenagal, *m.;* —, *vt.* enlodar; enturbiar el agua con lodo.
pudgy, *adj.* regordete.
puff, *n.* bufido, soplo, *m.;* bocanada, *f.;* **powder —,** mota para polvos, mota para empolvarse; —, *vt.* hinchar; soplar; ensoberbecer; —, *vi.* inflarse; bufar; resoplar.
puffy, *adj.* hinchado, entumecido.
pug, *n.* variedad de perro muy pequeño de

pelo corto; — **nose,** nariz respingona

pugilism, n. pugilato, boxeo, m.

pugilist, n. púgil, boxeador, m.

pugnacious, adj. belicoso, pugnaz.

pulchritude, n. belleza, f.

pull, vt. tirar, halar o jalar; coger; rasgar; desgarrar; **to — off,** arrancar; **to — out,** sacar; — ,n. tirón, m.; sacudida, f.; (coll.) influencia, f.

pullet, n. polla, f.

pulley, n. polea, garrucha, f., cuadernal, m.; (naut.) motón, m.

pulmonary, adj. pulmonar.

pulmotor, n. pulmotor, m.

pulp, n. pulpa, f.; carne (de fruta), f.

pulpit, n. púlpito, m.

pulpwood, n. madera de pulpa.

pulsate, vi. pulsar, latir.

pulse, n. pulso, m.; legumbres, f. pl.

pulverize, vt. pulverizar.

puma, n. (zool.) puma, f.

pumice, n. piedra pómez.

pump, n. bomba, f.; zapatilla, f.; **air —,** máquina neumática; **feed —,** bomba de alimentación; **tire —,** bomba para neumáticos; **vacuum —,** bomba de vacío; —, vt. dar a la bomba; sondear; sonsacar.

pumpkin, n. calabaza, f.

pun, n. equívoco, chiste, m.; juego de palabras; —, vi. jugar del vocablo, hacer juego de palabras.

punch, n. punzón, m.; puñetazo, m.; sacabocados, m.; ponche, m.; —, vt. punzar, horadar, taladrar; dar puñetazos.

punctilious, adj. puntilloso.

punctual, adj. puntual, exacto.

punctuality, n. exactitud, puntualidad, f.

punctuate, vi. puntuar.

punctuation, n. puntuación, f.

puncture, n. puntura, f.; pinchazo, m., pinchadura, f.; perforación, f.; —, vt. perforar.

pungent, adj. picante, acre, mordaz.

punish, vt. castigar, penar.

punishable, adj. punible, castigable.

punishment, n. castigo, m.; pena, f.

punk, n. yesca, f.; —, adj. (coll.) muy malo.

punt, n. (naut.) pontón, m.

puny, adj. insignificante, pequeño; débil.

pup, n. cachorrillo, m.; —, vi. parir la perra.

pupa, n. crisálida, f.

pupil, n. (anat.) pupila, f.; pupilo, m.; discípulo, la; **— of the eye,** niña del ojo.

puppet, n. títere, muñeco, m.; **— show,** representación de títeres.

puppy, n. perrillo, cachorro, m.

purchase, vt. comprar; mercar.

purchaser, n. comprador, ra.

purchasing, adj. comprador; **— power,** poder adquisitivo.

pure, adj. puro; simple, mero; **—ly,** adv. puramente.

purée, n. puré, m.

purgatory, n. purgatorio, m.

purge, vt. purgar; —, n. purga, purgación, f.; catártico, purgante, m.

purify, vt. purificar; —, vi. purificarse.

puritan, n. puritano, na.

purity, n. pureza, f.

purple, adj. purpúreo, morado; cárdeno; —, n. púrpura, f.; —, vi. ponerse morado; —, vt. teñir de color morado.

purport, n. designio, m.; contenido, m.; — vt. significar, designar, implicar, dar a entender.

purpose, n. intención, f.; designio, proyecto, m.; objetivo, m.; vista, f.; mira, f.; efecto, m.; **on —,** de propósito, adrede; **to no —,** inútilmente; **to the —,** al propósito, de perilla; —, vt. y vi. proponerse, resolver, intentar.

purr, vi. ronronear (aplicase a los gatos).

purse, n. bolsa, f.; portamonedas, m.; —, vt. embolsar.

purser, n. sobrecargo de un navío, sobrecargo, m.

pursuance, n. prosecución, f.

pursue, vt. y vi. perseguir; seguir; acosar; continuar.

pursuit, n. perseguimiento, m.; ocupación, f.; persecución, f.

purvey, vt. y vi. proveer, suministrar.

purveyor, n. provisor, ra, abastecedor, ra, surtidor, ra.

push, vt. empujar; empellar; apretar; —, vi. hacer esfuerzos; **to — ahead, to — through,** pujar, avanzar; —, n. impulso, m.; **— button,** botón de contacto, botón automático.

pushing, adj. emprendedor, agresivo.

pusillanimous, adj. pusilánime, cobarde.

puss, pussy, n. micho, gato, m.

put, vt. poner, colocar; proponer; imponer, obligar; **to — in order,** poner en orden; **to — in writing,** poner por escrito; **to — on shoes,** calzar; **to — out (a light, etc.),** apagar (una luz, etc.); **to — through,** ejecutar, llevar a cabo; **to — together,** confeccionar, armar.

putrefy, vi. pudrirse.

putrid, adj. podrido, pútrido, putrefacto, corrompido.

putt, n. (golf) tirada que hace rodar la pelota al agujero o cerca de él.

putter, n. uno de los palos de golf; —, vi. hacer un poquito de cada cosa, malgastar el tiempo en trivialidades.

putty, *n.* almáciga, masilla, *f.;* cemento, *m.;* —, *vt.* enmasillar.

puzzle, *n.* acertijo, enigma, rompecabezas, *m.;* perplejidad, *f.;* **jigsaw** —, rompecabezas, *m.;* —, *vt.* embrollar, confundir; —, *vi.* confundirse.

puzzling, *adj.* enigmático; engañador.

pygmy, *n. y adj.* pigmeo, mea.

pyramid, *n.* pirámide, *f.*

pyre, *n.* pira, hoguera, *f.*

pyrex, *n.* vidrio resistente al calor; —, *adj.* refractario.

pyrometer, *n.* pirómetro, *m.*

python, *n.* pitón, *m.*

Q

qt.: quantity, cantidad;

quart, cuarto de galón.

quack, *vi.* graznar (como un pato); —, *n.* charlatán, curandero, *m.*

quadrangle, *n.* cuadrángulo, *m.*

quadrant, *n.* cuadrante, *m.;* (naut.) octante, *m.*

quadrilateral, *adj.* cuadrilátero.

quadruple, *adj.* cuádruplo.

quaff, *vt.* beber a grandes tragos; —, *vi.* beber demasiado.

quagmire, *n.* tremedal, *m.;* (fig.) situación difícil y escabrosa.

quail, *n.* codorniz, *f.*

quaint, *adj.* extraño pero agradable por su sabor de antaño; **—ly,** *adv.* en forma extraña pero agradable.

quake, *vi.* temblar, tiritar; —, *n.* temblor, *m.*

Quaker, *n. y adj.* cuáquero, ra.

qualification, *n.* calificación, *f.;* requisito, *m.;* cualidad, *f.*

qualify, *vt.* calificar; modificar; templar; —, *vi.* habilitarse, llenar los requisitos.

qualitative, *adj.* cualitativo.

quality, *n.* calidad, *f.;* don, *m.;* condición, *f.;* prenda, *f.;* **average** —, calidad media.

qualm, *n.* deliquio, desmayo, *m.;* escrúpulo, *m.;* duda, *f.*

quandary, *n.* incertidumbre, duda, *f.;* dilema, *m.*

quantity, *n.* cantidad, *f.*

quarantine, *n.* cuarentena, *f.;* —, *vt.* poner en cuarentena; **to — a nation,** declarar cuarentena contra una nación.

quarrel, *n.* quimera, riña, pelea, contienda, *f.;* —, *vi.* reñir, disputar.

quarrelsome, *adj.* pendenciero, quimerista, peleador.

quarry, *n.* cantera, *f.*

quart, *n.* un cuarto de galón.

quarter, *n.* cuarto, *m.,* cuarta parte, *f.;* cuartel, *m.;* barriada, *f.;* barrio, *m.;* moneda de E.U.A. que equivale a 25 centavos de dólar; **— of an hour,** cuarto de hora; —, *vt.* cuartear; acuartelar; dividir en cuatro.

quarterly, *adj.* trimestral.

quartermaster, *n.* (mil.) comisario u oficial que provee alojamiento, ropa, combustible y trasporte; (naut.) cabo de brigada; **— general,** intendente del ejército.

quartet, *n.* (mus.) cuarteto, *m.*

quartz, *n.* (min.) cuarzo, *m.*

quash, *vt.* reprimir, aplastar.

quaver, *n.* estremecimiento, *m.;* (mus.) corchea, *f.;* —, *vi.* gorgoritear, trinar; temblar.

quay, *n.* muelle, *m.*

queasy, *adj.* nauseabundo; fastidioso.

queen, *n.* reina, *f.;* dama (en el juego de ajedrez), *f.*

queenly, *adj.* majestuoso, como una reina.

queer, *adj.* extraño; ridículo; enrevesado; raro; **—ly,** *adv.* en forma rara.

quell, *vt.* subyugar, postrar, avasallar; mitigar.

quench, *vt.* apagar; extinguir, saciar.

querulous, *adj.* quejoso.

query, *n.* pregunta, *f.;* duda, *f.;* —, *vt.* preguntar.

quest, *n.* pesquisa, inquisición, *f.;* busca, *f.*

question, *n.* cuestión, *f.,* asunto, *m.;* duda, *f.;* pregunta, *f.;* **to ask a —,** hacer una pregunta; **to be a — of,** tratarse de; —, *vi.* preguntar; —, *vt.* dudar, desconfiar; poner en duda.

questionable, *adj.* cuestionable, dudoso.

questionnaire, *n.* cuestionario, *m.*

quibble, *n.* subterfugio, *m.;* evasiva, *f.;* —, *vi.* sutilizar; hacer uso de subterfugios.

quick, *adj.* listo; rápido; veloz; ligero; pronto; ágil, ardiente, penetrante; **—ly,** *adv.* rápidamente, con presteza; —, *n.* carne viva; parte vital.

quicken, *vt.* vivificar; acelerar; animar.

quick-freeze, *vt.* congelar rápidamente.

quick-freezing, n. congelación rápida.
quickie, n. (coll.) algo hecho de prisa y mal.
quicklime, n. cal viva.
quickness, n. ligereza, presteza, f.; actividad, f.; viveza, penetración.
quicksand, n. arena movediza.
quicksilver, n. azogue, mercurio, m.
quick-tempered, adj. irascible, irritable, colérico.
quick-witted, adj. agudo, perspicaz.
quiescent, adj. quieto, inmóvil.
quiet, adj. quedo, quieto, tranquilo, llado; —, n. calma, serenidad, f.; vt. tranquilizar.
quietness, quietude, n. quietud, tranquilidad, f.
quill, n. pluma de ave; cañón, m., pluma, f., (para escribir); púa del puerco espín.
quilt, n. colcha, f.; **crazy** —, centón, m.
quince, n. (bot.) membrillo, m.; — **jelly**, jalea de membrillo.
quinine, n. quinina, f.
quinsy, n. (med.) angina, esquinencia, f.
quintessence, n. quintaesencia, f.
quintet, n. (mus.) quinteto, m.
quintuplets, n. pl. quíntuples, m. o f. pl.

quip, n. pulla, f.; humorada, agudeza, f.; —, vt. echar pullas; decir humoradas.
quirk, n. desviación, f.; pulla, f.; sutileza, f.; rasgo (como en la escritura).
quit, vt. descargar; desempeñar; absolver; **to** — **work**, dejar de trabajar; —, vi. desistir, dejar (de hacer algo).
quite, adv. totalmente, enteramente, absolutamente, bastante.
quitter, n. el que abandona una obra, un trabajo, etc.; desertor, cobarde, m.
quiver, n. temblor, tiritón, m.; —, vi. temblar, retemblar, blandir.
quixotic, adj. quijotesco; — **person**, quijote, m.
quiz, vt. examinar; —, n. examen por medio de preguntas.
quorum, n. quórum, m.
quota, n. cuota, f.; prorrata, f.
quotable, adj. citable.
quotation, n. citación, cotización, cita, f.; **list of** —**s**, boletín de cotizaciones; — **marks**, comillas, f. pl.
quote, vt. citar; **to** — **(a price)**, cotizar (precio).
quotient, n. cociente o cuociente, m.; **intelligence** —, cociente intelectual.

R

rabbi, n. rabí, rabino, m.
rabbit, n. conejo, m.
rabble, n. chusma, gentuza, f.; gente baja.
rabid, adj. rabioso, furioso.
rabies, n. rabia, hidrofobia, f.
raccoon, n. (zool.) mapache, m.
race, n. raza, casta, f.; carrera, corrida, f.; — **track**, corredera, pista, f.; —, vi. competir en un carrera; correr con mucha ligereza; —, vt. (auto.) acelerar con carga disminuida.
racer, n. caballo de carrera; corredor, ra.
racial, adj. racial, de raza.
rack, n. tormento, m.; rueca, f.; cremallera, f.; percha, f.; destrucción, f.; —, vt. atormentar; trasegar.
racket, n. baraúnda, confusión, f.; raqueta, f.; explotación, f.; cualquier ardid fraudulento.
racketeer, n. individuo que recurre a amenazas o a la violencia para robar dinero; —, vi. robar dinero recurriendo a amenazas o violencia.
racoon = **raccoon**.

racy, adj. fresco, con su aroma natural (vino); picante, espiritoso.
radar, n. radar, m.
radiance, n. brillo, esplendor, m.
radiant, adj. radiante, brillante.
radiate, vi. echar rayos, centellear; irradiar.
radiation, n. irradiación, f.; radiación, f.
radiator, n. calorífero, calentador, m., estufa, f.; (auto.) radiador, m.; **steam** —, calorífero de vapor.
radical, adj. radical; —, n. (math.) radical, m.; —**ly**, adv. radicalmente.
radicalism, n. radicalismo, m.
radio, n. radio, m. o f., radiocomunicación, f.; — **amplifier**, radioamplificador, m.; — **announcer**, anunciador de radio; — **beam**, faro radioeléctrico; — **broad-casting station**, estación radiodifusora; — **hookup**, circuito, m.; — **listener**, radioescucha, radioyente, m. y f.; — **message**, comunicación radioeléctrica; — **receiver**, radiorreceptor, m.; — **technician**, radiotécnico, m.; — **tube**, válvula de radio.

radioactive, adj. radiactivo.
radioactivity, n. radiactividad, f.
radiobroadcast, vt. y vi. difundir por radiotrasmisión.
radiobroadcasting, n. radiodifusión, f.
radiogram, n. radiograma, m.
radiophoto, n. radiofoto, f.
radiotelegram, n. radiotelegrama, m.
radio telescope, n. radiotelescopio, m.
radiotherapy, n. radioterapia, f.
radish, n. rábano, m.
radium, n. (chem.) radio, m.
radius, n. (math., anat.) radio, m.
raffle, n. rifa, f., sorteo, m.; —, vt. rifar, sortear.
raft, n. balsa, f.; armadía, f.; (coll.) gran cantidad; **a — of people,** un gentio, m.
rafter, n. cabrio, m., viga, f.
rag, n. trapo, andrajo, jirón, m..; —**s,** n. pl. andrajos, m. pl.
ragamuffin, n. mendigo, ga, pordiosero, ra; bribón, ona.
rage, n. rabia, f.; furor, m.; cólera, f.; **to fly into a —,** montar en cólera; —, vi. rabiar, encolerizarse.
ragged, adj. andrajoso.
raging, n. furia, rabia, f.; —**ly,** adv. furiosamente.
raglan, n. raglán, abrigo holgado; — **sleeves,** mangas raglán (muy holgadas).
ragtime, n. ritmo popular norteamericano.
ragweed, n. (bot.) ambrosia, f.
raid, n. invasión, f.; —, vt. invadir, hacer una incursión.
raider, n. corsario, m.
rail, n. baranda, barrera, f.; balaustrada, f.; (rail.) carril, riel, m.; **by —,** por ferrocarril; —, vt. cercar con balaustradas; —, vi., injuriar de palabra.
railing, n. baranda, f., barandal, pretil, m.
railroad, n. ferrocarril, m.; vía férrea; **electric —**ferrocarril eléctrico; **elevated —,** ferrocarril elevado; **narrow gauge —,** ferrocarril de vía angosta; **— crossing,** paso a nivel; **— station,** estación de ferrocarril; **— stock,** acciones ferrocarrileras; **— track,** vía férrea.
railway, n. ferrocarril, m.; **cable —,** funicular —, ferrocarril de cable; **— express,** servicio rápido de carga por ferrocarril; **street —,** ferrocarril urbano.
raiment, n. ropa, f.; vestido, m.
rain, n. lluvia, f.; **— water,** agua lluvia, agua llovediza; —, vi. llover; **to — heavily,** llover a cántaros; **to stop — ing,** escampar.
rainbow, n. arco iris.

raincheck, n. contraseña en espectáculos al aire libre para casos de suspensión de función por mal tiempo; (coll.) **to take a —,** postergar la aceptación de una invitación.
raincoat, n. impermeable, m.; capote, m.
raindrop, n. gota de lluvia.
rainfall, n. aguacero, m., lluvia, f.; precipitación pluvial.
rainproof, adj. impermeable, a prueba de lluvia.
rainy, adj. lluvioso.
raise, vt. levantar, alzar; fabricar, edificar; izar (la bandera); engrandecer, elevar, excitar, causar; **to — an objection,** poner objeción, objetar; **to — up,** suspender, alzar.
raisin, n. pasa (uva seca), f.
raising, n. izamiento, m.
rake, n. rastro, rastrillo, m.; tunante, m.; —, vt. rastrillar; raer; rebuscar.
rally, vt. (mil.) reunir; ridiculizar; —, vi. reunirse; burlarse de alguno.
ram, n. ariete, m.; **battering —,** brigola, f.; —, vt. impeler con violencia; pegar contra; atestar, henchir.
ramble, vi. vagar; callejear; —, n. correría, f.
rambler, n. vagabundo, da, callejero. ra.
ramification, n. ramificación, f.; ramal, m.
ramjet engine, n. (avi.) motor de retropropulsión.
ramp, n. rampa, f.
rampage, n. conducta violenta o desenfrenada.
rampant, adj. desenfrenado; rampante (en heráldica).
rampart, n. baluarte, m.; terraplén, m.; (mil.) muralla, f.
ramrod, n. baqueta, f.; atacador, m.; (mil.) roquete, m.
ramshackle, adj. en ruina, ruinoso.
ran, pretérito del verbo **run.**
ranch, n. finca rústica de ganado.
rancher, n. hacendado, da; ranchero, ra.
rancid, adj. rancio.
rancor, n. rencor, m.
random, n. ventura, casualidad, f.; **at —,** a trochemoche, al azar.
rang, pretérito del verbo **ring.**
range, vr. colocar, ordenar; clasificar; —, vi. fluctuar; vagar; —, n. clase, f.; orden, m.; hilera, f.; correria, f.; alcance, m.; línea de un tiro de artillería; cocina económica, estufa, f.; **— finder,** telémetro, m.; **— of mountains,** sierra, f. cadena de montañas.
ranger, n. guardabosque, m.; (mil.) comando (de E.U.A.), m.

rank, *adj.* exuberante; rancio; fétido; vulgar; indecente; —, *n.* fila, hilera, *f.;* clase, *f.;* grado, *m.;* — and file, (mil.) individuos de tropa; las masas, *f. pl.*

rankle, *vi.* enconarse; inflamarse.

ransack, *vt.* saquear, pillar.

ransom, *vt.* rescatar; —, *n.* rescate, *m.*

rant, *vi.* decir disparates; regañar con vehemencia.

rap, *vt. y vi.* dar un golpe vivo y repentino; to — at the door, tocar a la puerta; —, *n.* golpe ligero y seco.

rapacious, *adj.* rapaz; —ly, *adv.* con rapacidad.

rape, *n.* violación, *f.*, estupro, *m.;* —, *vt.* estuprar.

rapid, *adj.* rápido.

rapid-fire, *adj.* de tiro rápido.

rapidity, *n.* rapidez, *f.*

rapine, *n.* rapiña, *f.*

rapt, *adj.* encantado, enajenado.

rapture, *n.* rapto, éxtasis, *m.*

rapturous, *adj.* embelesado.

rare, *adj.* raro, extraordinario.

rarebit, *n.* tostada hecha con queso y cerveza.

rarity, *n.* raridad, rareza, *f.*

rascal, *n.* pícaro, ra, bribón, ona, pillo, lla.

rascally, *adj.* truhán, truhanesco, tuno; —, *adv.* en forma truhanesca.

rash, *adj.* precipitado, temerario; —ly, *adv.* precipitadamente; —, *n.* brote, *m.;* urticaria, *f.;* erupción, *f.;* sarpullido, *m.*

rashness, *n.* temeridad, *f.;* arrojo, *m.*

rasp, *n.* escofina, *f.;* raspador, *m.;* —, *vt.* raspar; escofinar.

raspberry, *n.* frambuesa, *f.;* — bush, frambueso, *m.*

rat, *n.* rata, *f.*

ratchet, *n.* rueda o diente de engranaje; trinquete, *m.*

rate, *n.* tipo, *m.*, tasa, *f.*, precio, valor, *m.;* grado, *m.;* manera, *f.;* tarifa, *f.;* razón, *f.;* velocidad, *f.;* at the — of, a razón de; at the — of exchange, al cambio de; at what — of exchange? ¿a qué cambio? — of interest, tipo de interés; —, *vt.* tasar, apreciar; calcular, calificar; reñir a uno; —, *vi.* ser considerado favorablemente; (coll.) tener influencia.

rather, *adv.* de mejor gana; más bien; antes; antes bien; bastante; mejor dicho.

ratification, *n.* ratificación, *f.*

ratify, *vt.* ratificar.

rating, *n.* valuación, *f.*

ratio, *n.* proporción, *f.;* razón, *f.;* direct —

razón directa; inverse —, razón inversa.

ration, *n.* (mil.) ración, *f.;* —, *vt.* racionar.

rational, *adj.* racional; razonable.

rationing, *n.* racionamiento, *m.*

rattle, *vt. y vi.* hacer ruido; confundir; zumbar; rechinar; to become —d, perder la chaveta; confundirse; —, *n.* ruido (como el de matracas), *m.;* sonajero, *m.;* matraca, *f.*

rattlesnake, *n.* culebra de cascabel.

raucous, *adj.* ronco, áspero, bronco; — voice, voz ronca y desagradable.

ravage, *vi.* saquear, pillar; asolar; —, *n.* saqueo, *m.*

rave, *vi.* delirar; enfurecerse; echar chispas.

ravel, *vt.* embrollar; enredar; deshebrar; —, *vi.* deshilarse, destorcerse.

raven, *n.* cuervo, *m.*

ravenous, *adj.* voraz, famélico.

ravine, *n.* barranca, cañada, *f.*

raving, *adj.* furioso, frenético; —ly, *adv.* como un loco furioso.

ravish, *vt.* estuprar; arrebatar.

ravishing, *adj.* encantador.

raw, *adj.* crudo; puro; nuevo; in a — state, en bruto; — materials, primeras materias, materias primas.

rawhide, *n.* cuero sin curtir, *m.;* látigo hecho de este cuero.

ray, *n.* rayo (de luz), *m.;* (ichth.) raya, *f.*

rayon, *n.* rayón, *m.*

raze, *vt.* arrasar, extirpar; borrar.

razor, *n.* navaja de afeitar; — blade, hoja de afeitar; electric —, afeitadora o rasuradora eléctrica; — strop, asentador, *m.;* safety —, navaja de seguridad.

rd.: road, camino; rod, pértica.

reach, *vt.* alcanzar; llegar hasta; —, *vi.* extenderse, llegar; alcanzar, penetrar; esforzarse; —, *n.* alcance, poder, *m.;* capacidad, *f.*

react, *vi.* reaccionar; resistir; obrar recíprocamente.

reaction, *n.* reacción, *f.*

reactionary, *n.* reaccionario, ria; (pol.) derechista, *m. y f.;* —, *adj.* reaccionario.

reactivate, *vt.* reactivar.

reactor, *n.* reactor, *m.*

read, *vt.* leer; interpretar; adivinar, predecir; —, *vi.* leer; estudiar.

read, *adj.* leído, erudito; well — man, hombre letrado.

readable, *adj.* legible.

reader, *n.* lector, ra.

readily, *adv.* prontamente; de buena gana.

readiness, *n.* facilidad, *f.;* vivacidad del

ingenio; voluntad, gana, f.; prontitud, f.

reading, n. lectura, f.; — **room,** salón de lectura.

readjust, vt. recomponer; reajustar.

readjustment. n. reajuste, m.

ready, adj. listo, pronto; inclinado; fácil; ligero.

ready-made, adj. hecho, confeccionado, ya hecho; — **clothes,** ropa hecha.

real, adj. real, verdadero, efectivo; inmueble; — **estate,** bienes raíces o inmuebles.

realism, n. realismo, m.

realist. n. realista, m. y f.

realistic, adj. realista; natural.

reality, n. realidad, f.; efectividad, f.

realization, n. comprensión, f.; realización, f.

realize, vt. hacerse cargo de, darse cuenta de; realizar.

really, adv. realmente, verdaderamente.

realm, n. reino, m.; dominio, m.

ream, n. resma, f.

reap, vt. segar.

reaper, n. segador, ra.

reappear. vi. reaparecer.

reapportion, vt. asignar o repartir de nuevo.

rear, n. retaguardia, f.; parte posterior; —, adj. posterior; — **admiral,** contraalmirante, m.; — **part,** zaga, f.; —, vi. encabritarse el caballo: —, vt. criar, educar; levantar; construir.

rearmament, n. rearme, rearmamento, m.

rearrange, vt. refundir, dar nueva forma (a una comedia, discurso, etc.); volver a arreglar.

rear-view mirror, n. (auto.) espejo de retrovisión.

reason. n. razón, f.; causa, f.; motivo, m.; juicio, m.; quid, m.; by — of, con motivo de, a causa de; for this —, por esto; without —, sin qué ni para qué, sin razón; —, vt. razonar, raciocinar.

reasonable, adj. razonable, módico, lógico.

reasoning, n. raciocinio, m.

reassurance, n. confirmación, f.; reiteración de confianza; restauración de ánimo.

reassure, vt. tranquilizar, calmar; asegurar de nuevo.

rebate, n, rebaja, deducción, f., descuento, m.; —, vt. descontar, rebajar.

rebel, n. rebelde, m. y f., insurrecto, ta; —, adj. insurrecto; —, vi. rebelarse; insubordinarse.

rebellion, n. rebelión, insubordinación, f.

rebellious, adj. rebelde.

rebirth, n. renacimiento, m.

rebound, vt. y vi. repercutir; —, n. rebote (de una pelota); repercusión, f.

rebroadcast, n. retrasmisión radiofónica.

rebuff, vt. rechazar; —, n. desaire, m.

rebuild, vt. reedificar, reconstruir.

rebuke, vt. reprender, regañar; —, n. reprensión, f., regaño, m.

rebut, vt. refutar, contradecir.

recalcitrant, adj. recalcitrante.

recall, vt. llamar, hacer volver; revocar; — **to mind,** recapacitar; —, n. revocación, f.

recant, vt. retractarse, desdecirse.

recapitulate, vt. recapitular.

recapping (of tires), n. revestimiento (de neumáticos o llantas).

recapture, n. represa (de un navío, etc.); —, vt. volver a tomar; represar.

recede, vi. retroceder; desistir.

receipt, n. recibo, m.; receta, f., ingreso, m.; to acknowledge —, acusar recibo.

receivable, adj. admisible; bills —, cuentas por cobrar.

receive, vt. recibir; aceptar, admitir; cobrar.

receiver, n. receptor, m.; recipiente, m.; audífono, m.; depositario, m.; — **in bankruptcy,** síndico, m.

receivership, n. sindicatura, f.

receiving set, n. (rad.) radiorreceptor, m.

recent, adj. reciente, nuevo; fresco.

receptacle, n. receptáculo, m.

reception. n. acogida, f.; recepción, f.

receptionist, n. recepcionista, f., persona encargada de recibir a los visitantes en una oficina.

receptive, adj. receptivo.

recess, n. recreo, m.; retiro, m.; nicho, m.; lugar apartado; grieta, f.; tregua, f.; receso, m.

recession, n. retirada, f.; receso, m. recipe, n. receta de cocina.

recipient, n. receptor, ra.

reciprocal, adj. recíproco.

reciprocate, vi. corresponder; —, vt. reciprocar, compensar.

reciprocity, n. reciprocidad, f.

recital, n. recitación, f.; concierto musical.

recitation, n. recitación f.

recite, vt. recitar; referir, relatar; declamar; to — a lesson, dar una lección.

reckless, adj. descuidado; audaz; —ly, adv. audazmente; descuidadamente.

reckon, vt. contar, numerar; —, vi. computar, calcular.

reckoning, n. cuenta, f.; cálculo, m.

reclaim, vt. reformar, corregir; recobrar; hacer utilizable; reclamar.

reclamation, n. aprovechamiento, m., utilización, f.; reclamación, f.

recline, vt. y vi. reclinar; reposar.

recluse, adj. recluso, retirado; —, n. recluso, sa.

recognition, n. reconocimiento, m.; agradecimiento, m.

recognize , vt. reconocer.

recoil, vi. recular, retirarse; —, n. rechazo, m.; reculada, f.

recollect, vt. y vi. recordar; acordarse.

recollect, vt. recobrar.

recollection, n. recuerdo, m.; reminiscencia, f.

recommend, vt. recomendar.

recommendation, n. recomendación, f.

recompense, n. recompensa, f.; —, vt. recompensar.

reconcile, vt. reconciliar.

reconciliation, n. reconciliación, f.

recondition, vt. reacondicionar.

reconnaissance, n. reconocimiento, m., exploración, f.

reconnoiter, vt. (mil.) reconocer.

reconsider, vt. considerar de nuevo.

reconstruct, vt. reedificar, reconstruir.

record, vt. registrar; protocolar; grabar.

record, n. registro, archivo, m.; disco, m.; — **player,** tocadiscos, fonógrafo, m.; **off the —,** confidencialmente, extraoficialmente (tratándose de una declaración que no debe publicarse) ; **—s,** n. pl. anales, m. pl.; —, adj. sin precedente.

record-breaking, adj. que supera precedentes.

recorder, n. registrador, archivero, m.; grabadora, f.

recount, vt. referir, contar de nuevo; —, n. recuento, m.

recourse, n. recurso, retorno, m.

recover, vt. recobrar; cobrar; reparar; restablecer; **to — (property),** recobrar (propiedad); **to — one's senses,** volver en sí; —, vi. convalecer, restablecerse; **to — (health),** sanar, recobrar (la salud), reponerse.

recovery, n. convalecencia, f.; recobro, m.; recuperación, f., restablecimiento, m.

recreant, adj. cobarde; —, n. cobarde, m. y f.; apóstata, m. y f.

recreate, vt. recrear, deleitar, divertir.

recreation, n. recreación, f.; recreo, m.

recrimination, n. recriminación, f.

recruit, vt. reclutar; —, n. (mil.) recluta, m.

recruiting, n. recluta, f., reclutamiento, m.

rectangle, n. rectángulo, m.

rectangular, adj. rectangular.

rectify, vt. rectificar.

rector, n. rector, m.; párroco, m.; jefe, m.

rectory, n. rectoría, f.

recuperate, vi. restablecerse, recuperarse; —, vt. recobrar, recuperar.

recur, vi. recurrir.

recurrence, n. retorno, m.; vuelta, f.; repetición, f.

recurrent, adj. periódico, que reaparece de cuando en cuando.

red, adj. rojo; rubio; colorado; — **herring,** arenque ahumado; acción para distraer la atención del asunto principal; — **lead,** minio, bermellón, m.; — **man,** piel roja, m., indio norteamericano; — **pepper,** pimiento, pimentón, m.; — **tape,** balduque, m.; expedienteo, m., (Mex.) papeleo, m.; **R— (communist),** n. y adj. rojo (comunista), m.

redbird, n. (orn.) cardenal, m.

red-blooded, adj. valiente, denodado; vigoroso.

redbreast, n. petirrojo, pechirrojo, m.

redcap, n. (orn.) cardelina, f.; mozo de cordel, cargador, m.

redden, vt. teñir de color rojo; —, vi. ponerse colorado, sonrojarse.

reddish, adj. rojizo, bermejizo.

redeem, vt. redimir, rescatar.

redeemer, n. redentor, ra, salvador, ra; the **R—,** el Redentor, m.

redeeming, adj. redentor.

redemption, n. redención, f.

red-haired, adj. pelirrojo.

redhead, n. pelirrojo, ja.

red-hot, adj. candente, ardiente.

red-letter, adj. notable, extraordinario, fuera de lo común; — **day,** día de fiesta, día especial, día extraordinario.

redness, n. rojez, bermejura, f.

redolent, adj. fragante, oloroso.

redound, vi. resaltar, rebotar; redundar.

redress. vt. enderezar; corregir; reformar; rectificar; —, n. reforma, corrección, f.

redskin, n. piel roja, m., indio norteamericano.

redtop, n. variedad de hierba forrajera.

reduce, vt. reducir; perder peso; disminuir; sujetar; —, vi. reducirse.

reducing agent, n. agente reductor.

reduction, n. reducción, rebaja, f.

redundant, adj. redundante, superfluo; **to be —,** redundar.

redwing, n. malvís, m.

redwood, n. (bot.) pino de California.

reed, n. caña, f.; flecha, f.

reef, vt. (naut.) tomar rizos a las velas; —, n. arrecife, escollo, m.

reek, n. humo, vapor, m.; —, vi. humear; vahear; oler a.

reel, *n.* aspa, devanadera, *f.;* variedad de baile; carrete, *m.;* película de cine; **fishing —,** carretel, *m.;* **—,** *vt.* aspar; *vi.* vacilar al andar, tambalearse.

re-elect, *vt.* reelegir.

re-election, *n.* reelección, *f.*

re-enforce, *vt.* reforzar.

re-enter, *vt.* volver a entrar.

re-establish, *vt.* restablecer, volver a establecer una cosa.

refer, *vt. y vi.* referir, remitir; dirigir; referirse; **— to,** véase.

referee, *n.* arbitrador, árbitro, *m.;* **—,** *vt. y vi.* servir de árbitro o de juez.

reference, *n.* referencia, relación, *f.*

referendum, *n.* plebiscito, *m.*

refill, *vt.* rellenar; **—,** *n.* relleno, *m.;* repuesto, *m.*

refine, *vt. y vi.* refinar, purificar, purificarse.

refinement, *n.* refinación, *f.;* refinamiento, *m.;* refinadura, *f.;* elegancia afectada.

refinery, *n.* refinería, *f.*

reflect, *vt. y vi.* reflejar, repercutir; reflexionar; recaer; meditar.

reflection, *n.* reflexión, meditación, *f.;* reflejo, *m.*

reflector, *n.* reflector, *m.*

reflex, *n. y adj.* reflejo, *m.*

reforest, *vt.* repoblar de árboles.

reform, *vt.* reformar; **—,** *vi.* reformarse; **—,** *n.* reforma, *f.*

reformation, *n.* reformación, *f.;* reforma, *f.*

reformatory, *n.* reformatorio, *m.*

reformer, *n.* reformador, ra.

refract, *vt.* refractar, refringir.

refractor, *n.* refractor, telescopio de refracción.

refrain, *vi.* reprimirse, abstenerse; mesurarse; **—,** *n.* estribillo, *m.*

refresh, *vt.* refrigerar, refrescar.

refresher, *n.* repaso, *m.;* **— course,** curso de repaso.

refreshing, *adj.* refrescante.

refreshment, *n.* refresco, refrigerio, *m.*

refrigerate, *vt.* refrigerar.

refrigeration, *n.* refrigeración, *f.*

refrigerator, *n.* refrigerador, frigorífero, *m.*

refuel, *vt.* poner nuevo combustible.

refuge, *n.* refugio, asilo, *m.;* seno, *m.;* recurso, *m.*

refugee, *n.* refugiado, da.

refund, *vt.* restituir; devolver, rembolsar.

refurbish, *vt.* renovar, retocar.

refusal, *n.* repulsa, denegación, *f.;* negativa, *f.*

refuse, *vt.* rehusar, repulsar, negarse a;

—, *n.* desecho, *m.,* sobra, *f.;* limpiaduras, *f. pl.;* basura, *f.*

refute, *vt.* refutar; confutar.

regain, *vt.* recobrar, recuperar.

regal, *adj.* real.

regale, *vt. y vi.* agasajar, festejarse.

regalia, *n.* insignias, *f. pl.*

regard, *vt.* estimar; considerar; **—,** *n.* consideración, *f.;* respeto, *m.;* **—s,** *n. pl* recuerdos, *m. pl.,* memorias, *f. pl.;* **in — to,** en cuanto a, respecto a, con respecto a; **in this —,** a este respecto; **to give —s,** dar saludos; **with — to,** a propósito de, relativo a.

regarding, *prep.* concerniente a.

regardless, *adj.* descuidado, negligente; indiferente; **— of,** a pesar de.

regency, *n.* regencia, *f.;* gobierno, *m.*

regeneration, *n.* regeneración, *f.;* renacimiento, *m.*

regent, *n.* regente, *m.*

regime, *n.* régimen, *m.;* administración, *f.*

regiment, *n.* regimiento, *m.;* **—,** *vt.* regimentar; asignar a un regimiento o grupo; regimentar (en el sentido del estado totalitario).

regimentation, *n.* regimentación, *f.*

region, *n.* región, *f.;* distrito, *m.;* país, *m.*

regional, *adj.* regional.

register, *n.* registro, *m.;* **cash —,** caja registradora; **—,** *vt.* inscribir; registrar; certificar (una carta); **—,** *vi.* matricularse, registrarse.

registered, *adj.* registrado, matriculado; **— letter,** carta certificada.

registrar, *n.* registrador, ra.

registration, *n.* registro, *m.;* inscripción, *f.;* empadronamiento, *m.*

registry, *n.* asiento, registro, *m.*

regress, *n.* retroceso, *m.;* **—,** *vi.* retrogradar, retroceder.

regret, *n.* arrepentimiento, *m.;* pesar, *m.;* **—** *vt.* sentir (pena o dolor), lamentar, deplorar.

regretful, *adj.* pesaroso, arrepentido.

regrettable, *adj.* sensible, lamentable, deplorable.

regular, *adj.* regular; ordinario; **— army,** tropas de línea; **—,** *n.* regular, *m.*

regularity, *n.* regularidad, *f.*

regulate, *vt.* regular, ordenar.

regulation, *n.* reglamentación, *f.,* reglas, *f. pl.;* arreglo, *m.*

rehabilitate, *vt.* rehabilitar.

rehabilitation, *n.* rehabilitación, *f.*

rehash, *vt.* refundir, recomponer; **—,** *n.* refundición, *f.*

rehearsal, *n.* repetición, *f.;* (theat.) ensayo, *m.;* **dress —,** último ensayo (con vestuario y demás detalles).

rehearse, *vt.* ensayar.

reign, *n.* reinado, reino, *m.;* —, *vi.* reinar, prevalecer, imperar.

reimburse, *vt.* rembolsar.

reimbursement, *n.* rembolso, reintegro, *m.*

rein, *n.* rienda, *f.;* —, *vt.* refrenar.

reincarnation, *n.* reencarnación, *f.*

reindeer, *n. sing.* y *pl.* reno (s), rangífero (s), *m.*

reinforced, *adj.* reforzado, armado; — concrete, hormigón armado.

reinforcement, *n.* refuerzo, *m.*

reinstate, *vt.* instalar de nuevo; restablecer.

reinsure, *vt.* volver a asegurar (a alguien).

reissue, *n.* reimpresión, *f.;* nueva edición; —, *vt.* reimprimir.

reiterate, *vt.* reiterar.

reject, *vt.* rechazar, rebatir; despreciar.

rejection, *n.* rechazamiento, rechazo, *m.,* repudiación, *f.*

rejoice, *vt.* y *vi.* regocijar, regocijarse.

rejoicing, *n.* regocijo, *m.*

rejoin, *vi.* volver a juntarse; —, *vt.* replicar.

rejoinder, *n.* contrarréplica, *f.*

rejoinder, *vt.* y *vi.* rejuvenecer, rejuvenecerse.

relapse, *vi.* recaer; —, *n.* reincidencia, recidiva, *f.;* recaída, *f.*

relate, *vt.* y *vi.* relatar, contar; referirse.

related, *adj.* emparentado, relacionado.

relation, *n.* relación, *f.;* parentesco, *m.;* pariente, *m.* y *f.*

relationship, *n.* parentesco, *m.;* relación, *f.*

relative, *adj.* relativo; —ly, *adv.* relativamente; —, *n.* pariente, *m.* y *f.*

relativity, *n.* relatividad, *f.*

relax, *vt.* relajar, aflojar; —, *vi.* descansar, reposar.

relaxation, *n.* reposo, descanso, *m.;* relajación, *f.*

relay, *n.* parada, posta, *f.;* — race, carrera de relevos; —, *vt.* trasmitir.

release, *vt.* soltar, libertar; relevar; dar al público; —, *n.* soltura, *f.;* descargo, *m.;* permiso para publicar o exhibir (una noticia, película, etc.).

relegate, *vt.* desterrar, relegar.

relent, *vi.* relentecer, ablandarse.

relentless, *adj.* empedernido, inflexible, implacable.

relevant, *adj.* pertinente; concerniente.

reliability, *n.* responsabilidad, *f.;* calidad de digno de confianza.

reliable, *adj.* digno de confianza, responsable.

reliance, *n.* confianza, *f.*

reliant, *adj.* de confianza; self—, responsable, capaz, con confianza en sí mismo.

relic, *n.* reliquia, *f.*

relict, *n.* viuda, *f.*

relief, *n.* relieve (escultura), *m.;* alivio, consuelo, *m.;* to be on —, recibir ayuda económica del gobierno; — map, mapa de relieve.

relieve, *vt.* relevar; aliviar, consolar; socorrer.

religion, *n.* religión, *f.;* culto, *m.*

religious, *adj.* religioso; — instruction, catequismo, *m.;* —ly, *adv.* religiosamente.

relinquish, *vt.* abandonar, dejar.

relish, *n.* sabor, *m.;* gusto, deleite, *m.;* condimento, *m.;* —, *vt.* agradar; saborear; —, *vi.* saber, tener sabor.

reload, *vt.* volver a cargar.

reluctance, *n.* repugnancia, *f.,* disgusto, *m.*

reluctant, *adj.* renuente, con disgusto.

rely, *vi.* confiar en; contar con.

remain, *vi.* quedar, restar, permanecer, durar.

remainder, *n.* resto, residuo, *m.;* restante, *m.;* sobra, *f.*

remains, *n. pl.* restos, residuos, *m. pl.,* sobras, *f. pl.*

remark, *n.* observación, nota, *f.,* comentario, *m.;* —, *vt.* notar, observar, comentar.

remarkable, *adj.* notable, interesante.

remedy, *n.* remedio, medicamento, *m.;* cura, *f.;* —, *vt.* remediar.

remember, *vt.* recordar, tener presente; dar memorias; —, *vi.* acordarse.

remembrance, *n.* memoria, *f.;* recuerdo, *m.*

remind, *vt.* acordar, recordar.

reminder, *n.* recuerdo, recordatorio, *m.*

reminisce, *vi.* recordar, contar recuerdos.

reminiscence, *n.* reminiscencia, *f.*

reminiscent, *adj.* recordativo, que recuerda acontecimientos pasados.

remiss, *adj.* remiso, flojo, perezoso.

remit, *vt.* remitir, enviar; restituir.

remittance, *n.* remesa, *f.;* remisión, *f.*

remitter, *n.* remitente, *m.* y *f.*

remnant, *n.* resto, residuo, *m.;* retazo, *m.*

remodel, *vt.* reformar.

remonstrance, *n.* súplica motivada, protesta, reconvención, *f.*

remonstrate, *vi.* protestar, reconvenir.

remorse, *n.* remordimiento, *m.;* compunción, *f.;* cargo de conciencia.

remorseful, *adj.* con remordimiento.

remorseless, *adj.* insensible a los remordimientos.

remote, *adj.* remoto, lejano; **—ly,** *adv.* remotamente, a lo lejos.

remoteness, *n.* alejamiento, *m.;* distancia, *f.;* lejanía, *f.*

removable, *adj.* amovible; de quita y pon.

removal, *n.* remoción, deposición, *f.;* alejamiento, *m.;* acción de quitar.

remove, *vt.* remover, alejar; privar (del empleo); quitar; sacar; —, *vi.* mudarse.

remover, *n.* detergente, *m.;* **spot** —, sacamanchas, *m.;* **nail polish** —, quita esmalte.

remunerate, *vt.* remunerar.

remuneration, *n.* remuneración, *f.*

rend, *vt.* lacerar, hacer pedazos, rasgar.

render, *vt.* volver, restituir; traducir; rendir.

rendezvous, *n.* cita (particularmente amorosa), *f.;* lugar señalado para una cita amorosa.

rendition, *n.* rendición, *f.;* rendimiento, *m.;* ejecución, *f.*

renegade, *n.* renegado da, apóstata, *m.* y *f.*

renew, *vt.* renovar, restablecer, reanudar, instaurar.

renewal, *n.* renovación, *f.;* renuevo, *m.;* prórroga, *f.*

rennet, *n.* cuajo, *m.*

renounce, *vt.* renunciar.

renovate, *vt.* renovar, instaurar.

renown, *n.* renombre, *m.;* celebridad, *f.*

renowned, *adj.* célebre.

rent, *n.* renta, *f.;* arrendamiento, *m.;* rendimiento, *m.;* alquiler, *m.;* rasgón, *m.;* —, *vt.* arrendar, alquilar.

rental, *n.* renta, *f.,* arriendo, alquiler, *m.;* —, *adj.* relativo a renta o alquiler.

renter, *n.* inquilino, na, arrendatario, ria.

renunciation, *n.* renuncia, renunciación, *f.*

reopen, *vt.* abrir de nuevo; reiniciar.

reorder, *vt.* hacer un nuevo pedido; ordenar, arreglar.

reorganization, *n.* reorganización, *f.*

reorganize, *vt.* reorganizar.

repair, *vt.* reparar, resarcir, restaurar; —, *vi.* ir; regresar; —, *n.* reparo, remiendo, *m.;* reparación, compostura, *f.;* — **ship,** buque taller; — **shop,** maestranza, *f.,* taller de reparaciones; **beyond** —, sin posible reparación.

repaired, *adj.* compuesto, remendado.

reparable, *adj.* reparable.

reparation, *n.* reparación, *f.,* remedio, *m.*

repartee, *n.* réplica aguda o picante.

repast, *n.* comida, colación, *f.*

repatriate, *vt.* repatriar.

repay, *vt.* volver a pagar, restituir, devol-

ver.

repeal, *vt.* abrogar, revocar; —, *n.* revocación, anulación, cesación, *f.*

repeat, *vt.* repetir.

repeated, *adj.* repetido, reiterado.

repeatedly, *adv.* repetidamente, repetidas veces.

repeater, *n.* repetidor, ra; arma de repetición.

repel, *vt.* repeler, rechazar.

repellent, *adj.* repelente, repulsivo.

repent, *vi.* arrepentirse.

repentance, *n.* arrepentimiento, *m.*

repentant *adj.* arrepentido.

repercussion, *n.* repercusión, *f.*

repertoire, *n.* repertorio, *m.*

repetition, *n.* repetición, reiteración, *f.*

repetitious, *adj.* redundante, que contiene repeticiones.

replace, *vt.* remplazar; reponer; sustituir.

replacement, *n.* remplazo, *m.,* sustitución, *f.;* pieza de repuesto.

replenish, *vt.* llenar, surtir.

replete, *adj.* repleto, lleno.

replica, *n.* réplica, *f.*

reply, *vt.* replicar, contestar, responder; —, *n.* réplica, respuesta, contestación, *f.;* **awaiting your** —, en espera de su respuesta, en espera de sus noticias.

report, *vt.* referir, contar; informar; dar cuenta; —, *n.* voz, *f.;* rumor, *m.;* fama, *f.;* relación, *f.;* informe, *m.;* memoria, *f.*

reporter, *n.* relator, ra; reportero, *m.;* periodista, *m.* y *f.,* cronista, *m.* y *f.*

repose, *vi.* reposar, descansar; —, *vt.* abrigar, tener; —, *n.* reposo, *m.*

repository, *n.* depósito, *m.*

represent, *vt.* representar.

representation, *n.* representación, *f.*

representative, *adj.* representativo; —, *n.* representante, *m.* y *f.;* **House of R—s,** Cámara de Representantes.

repress, *vt.* reprimir, domar.

reprieve, *vt.* suspender una ejecución; demorar un castigo; —, *n.* dilación (de algún castigo), *f.;* suspensión, *f.*

reprimand, *vt.* reprender, corregir; regañar; —, *n.* reprensión, *f.;* reprimenda, *f.*

reprint, *n.* tirada aparte; reimpresión, *f.;* —, *vt.* reimprimir.

reprisal, *n.* represalia, *f.*

reproach, *n.* reproche, *m.;* censura, *f.;* —, *vt.* culpar, reprochar; vituperar; improperar.

reprobate, *adj.* corrompido, depravado; —, *n.* malvado, réprobo, *m.;* —, *vt.* rechazar, reprobar.

reproduce, *vt.* reproducir.

reproduction, *n.* reproducción, *f.*

reproof, n. reprensión, censura, f.

reprove, vt. censurar; improperar; regañar.

reptile, n. reptil, m.

republic, n. república, f.

republican, n. y adj. republicano, na.

repudiate, vt. repudiar.

repudiation, n. repudio, m., repudiación, f.

repugnant, adj. repugnante; —ly, adv. de muy mala gana, con repugnancia.

repulse, vt. repulsar, desechar; —, n. repulsa, f.; rechazo, m.

repulsion, n. repulsión, repulsa, f.

repulsive, adj. repulsivo.

reputable, adj. honroso, estimable.

reputation, n. reputación, f.

repute, vt. reputar.

request, n. solicitud, petición, súplica, f.; pedido, m.; encargo, m.; on —, a solicitud; —, vt. rogar, suplicar; pedir, solicitar.

require, vt. requerir, demandar.

required, adj. obligatorio.

requirement, n. requisito, m.; exigencia, f.

requisite, adj. necesario, indispensable; —, n. requisito, m.

requisition, n. requisición, f.; petición, demanda, f.

rerun, n. nueva exhibición, (de una película); —, vt. volver a exhibir (una película o filme).

resale, n. reventa, f., venta de segunda mano.

rescind, vt. rescindir, abrogar.

rescue, n. rescate, libramiento, recobro, m.; —, vt. librar, rescatar; socorrer; salvar.

research, n. investigación, f.

resell, vt. revender, volver a vender.

resemblance, n. semejanza, f.

resemble, vt. asemejarse a, parecerse a.

resent, vt. resentir.

resentful, adj. resentido; vengativo; —ly, adv. con resentimiento.

resentment, n. resentimiento, m.; (fig.) escama, f.

reservation, n. reservación, f.; reserva, f.; restricción mental.

reserve, vt. reservar; —, n. reserva, f.; sigilo, m.

reserved, adj. reservado; callado; —ly, adv. con reserva.

reservoir, n. depósito, m.; tanque, m.

reset, vt. reengastar; montar de nuevo; to — a bone, reducir un hueso (roto o dislocado); to — type, (print.) volver a componer el tipo.

reshipment, n. reembarque, m.

reside, vi. residir, morar.

residence, n. residencia, morada, f.

resident, n. y adj. residente, m. y f.

residential, adj. residencial.

residual, adj. residual; —, n. residuo, m.

residue, n. residuo, resto, m.

resign, vt. y vi. resignar, renunciar, ceder; resignarse, rendirse, conformarse.

resignation, n. resignación, f.; renuncia, f.

resigned, adj. resignado.

resignedly, adv. con resignación, resignadamente.

resilient, adj. elástico, flexible.

resin, n. resina, colofonia, f., pez griega.

resinous, adj. resinoso.

resist, vt. y vi. resistir; oponerse.

resistance, n. resistencia, f.; — coil, bobina de resistencia.

resistant, adj. resistente.

resole, vt. remontar, solar de nuevo, echar suela nueva.

resolute, adj. resuelto.

resolution, n. resolución, f.

resolve, vt. resolver; decretar; —, vi. resolverse.

resolved, adj. resuelto.

resonance, n. resonancia, f.

resonant, adj. resonante.

resort, vi. recurrir, frecuentar; —, n. centro de recreo; summer —, lugar de veraneo; bathing —, balneario, m.

resound, vi. resonar.

resource, n. recurso, m.; expediente, m.

resourceful, adj. ingenioso, hábil; fértil en recursos o expedientes; —ness, n. ingeniosidad, habilidad, expedición, f.

respect, n. respecto, m.; respeto, m.; motivo, m.; —s, n. pl. saludos, m. pl., enhorabuena, f.; —, vt. apreciar; respetar; venerar.

respectability, n. respetabilidad, f.

respectable, adj. respetable; decente; considerable.

respected, adj. considerado, apreciado.

respectful, adj. respetuoso; —ly, adv. respetuosamente.

respecting, prep. con respecto a.

respective, adj. respectivo, relativo.

respiration, n. respiración, f.

respirator, n. respirador, aparato para respiración artificial.

respiratory, adj. respiratorio; — ailment, enfermedad del aparato respiratorio.

respite, n. suspensión, f.; respiro, m.; tregua, f.; —, vt. suspender, diferir.

resplendent, adj. resplandeciente, fulgurante, reluciente.

respond, vt. responder; corresponder.

response, n. respuesta, réplica, f.

responsibility, n. responsabilidad, f.; encargo, m.; **to assume** —, tomar por su cuenta, asumir responsabilidad.

responsible, adj. responsable.

responsive, adj. sensible, de simpatía.

rest, n. reposo, m.; sueño, m.; quietud, f.; (mus.) pausa, f.; resto, residuo, restante, m., sobra, f.; **the** —, los demás; **— room,** excusado, retrete, m.; (Chile) descanso, m.; —, vt. poner a descansar; apoyar; —, vi. dormir, reposar, recostarse; **to — upon,** basarse en.

restaurant, n. restaurante, m., fonda, f.

restful, adj. sosegado, tranquilo.

restitution, n. restitución, f.

restless, adj. inquieto, intranquilo, revuelto.

restlessness, n. impaciencia, inquietud, f.

restoration, n. restauración, f.

restore, vt. restaurar, restituir, restablecer, devolver, instaurar.

restrain, vt. restringir, refrenar; **to — oneself,** reprimirse.

restraint, n. refrenamiento, m., coerción, f.; **without** —, a rienda suelta.

restrict, vt. restringir, limitar.

restriction, n. restricción, coartación, f.

result, n. resultado, m.; consecuencia, f.; éxito, m.; —, vi. resultar; redundar en.

resume, vt. resumir, reanudar; empezar de nuevo.

resurrect, vt. resucitar.

resurrection, n. resurrección, f.

retail, vt. revender, vender al por menor; —, n. venta al por menor, menudeo, m.; **at** —, al menudeo, al por menor.

retailer, n. comerciante al por menor, detallista, m.

retain, vt. retener, guardar.

retainer, n. retenedor, ra; adherente, partidario, m.; honorario, m.; **— fee,** iguala, f.

retaliate, vi., vengarse, desquitarse.

retaliation, n. venganza, f., desquite, m.

retard, vt. retardar.

retention, n. retención, f.

reticence, n. reticencia, f.

reticent, adj. reticente.

retina, n. retina (del ojo), f.

retire, vt. retirar; —, vi. retirarse, sustraerse; jubilarse.

retired, adj. apartado, retirado.

retirement, n. retiro, retiramiento, m.; jubilación, f.; receso, m.

retiring, adj. recatado, callado.

retort, vt. redargüir, retorcer (un argumento); —, n. contrarréplica, redargución, f.; réplica, f.; (chem.) retorta, f.

retouch, vt. retocar (fotografías, etc.).

retrace, vt. volver a trazar; **to — one's steps,** volver sobre sus huellas.

retract, vt. retractar, retirar; retraer.

retread, vt. reponer la superficie rodante de un neumático; reandar (un camino, etc.); —, n. recubierta (de un neumático o llanta), f.

retreat, n. retirada, f.; (mil.) retreta, f.; (eccl.) retiro, m.; —, vi. retirarse.

retrench, vt. cercenar; (mil.) atrincherar; —, vi. economizar.

retribution, n. retribución, recompensa, f.; refacción, f.

retrieve, vt. recuperar, recobrar.

retroactive, adj. retroactivo.

retrogression, n. retrogradación, f.

retrorocket, n. retrocohete, m.

retrospect, retrospection, n. reflexión de las cosas pasadas.

return, vt. retribuir; restituir; volver; devolver; —, vi. regresar; —, n. retorno, regreso, m.; vuelta, f.; recompensa, retribución, f.; recaída, f.

returnable, adj. que puede devolverse.

reunion, n. reunión, f.

reunite, vt. reunir, volver a unir; —, vi. reunirse, reconciliarse.

Rev.: Reverend, R. Reverendo.

revaluation, n. revaluación, f.

revalue, vt. valorizar de nuevo.

revamp, vt. meter capellada nueva; remendar, renovar.

reveal, vt. revelar; publicar.

revel, vi. andar en borracheras; —, n. borrachera, f.; **drunken** —, orgía, f.

revelation, n. revelación, f.

reveler, reveller, n. fiestero, ra, parrandero, ra.

revelry, n. borrachera, f.; jarana, f.

revenge, vt. vengar; —, n. venganza, f.

revengeful, adj. vengativo; **—ly,** adv. con venganza.

revenue, n. renta, f.; rédito, m.; ingreso, m.; **— cutter,** guardacostas, m.; **— stamp,** sello de impuesto.

reverberate, vt. y vi. reverberar; resonar, retumbar.

revere, vt. reverenciar, venerar.

reverence, n. reverencia, f.; —, vt. reverenciar.

reverend, adj. reverendo; venerable; —, n. clérigo, abad, m.; pastor, m.

reverent, reverential, adj. reverencial, respetuoso.

reverie, n. ensueño, m.; embelesamiento, m.; ilusión, f.

reversal, n. revocación (de una sentencia), f.; reversión, f.

reverse, n. vicisitud, f.; contrario, m.; reverso (de una moneda), m.; revés, *m.;* través, *m.;* contramarcha, *f.;* —, *adj.* inverso; contrario; —, *vt.* invertir, poner al revés; **to — the charges (on a phone call),** cobrar (una llamada telefónica) al número llamado, pedir (una llamada telefónica) por cobrar; **to put in —,** dar marcha atrás.

reversible, *adj.* revocable, reversible.

revert, *vt.* y *vi.* revertir, trastrocar; volverse atrás.

revery = **reverie.**

review, *n.* revista, *f.;* reseña, *f.;* repaso, *m.;* **to make a —,** reseñar; —, *vt.* rever; repasar; (mil.) revistar.

reviewer, *n.* revisor, ra; crítico profesional (de libros, etc.).

revile, *vt.* ultrajar; difamar.

revise, *vt.* revisar, rever; —, *n.* revista, revisión, *f.;* (print.) segunda prueba.

revision, *n.* revisión, *f.*

revival, *n.* restauración, *f.;* renacimiento, *m.;* (theat.) nueva representación de una obra antigua.

revive, *vt.* avivar; restablecer; (theat.) volver a presentar (una comedia antigua, etc.); —, *vi.* revivir.

revocable, *adj.* revocable.

revoke, *vt.* revocar, anular.

revolt, *vi.* rebelarse; alzarse en armas; —, *n.* rebelión, *f.*

revolting, *adj.* repugnante.

revolution, *n.* revolución, *f.*

revolutionary, *n.* y *adj.* revolucionario, ria.

revolutionist, *n.* revolucionario, ria.

revolutionize, *vt.* revolucionar.

revolve, *vt.* revolver; meditar; —, *vi.* girar.

revolver, *n.* revólver, *m.,* pistola, *f.*

revolving, *adj.* giratorio.

revue, *n.* revista teatral.

revulsion, *n.* reacción repentina; (med.) revulsión, *f.*

reward, *n.* recompensa, *f.;* fruto, *m.;* pago, *m.;* —, *vt.* recompensar.

rewrite, *vt.* volver a escribir, escribir de nuevo.

R.F., r. f.: radio frequency, radiofrecuencia.

R.F.D., r.f.d.: rural free delivery, distribución gratuita del correo en regiones rurales.

Rh factor, (med.) factor Rh, *m.*

R.H.: Royal Highness, Alteza Real.

rhapsody, *n.* rapsodia, *f.*

rhetoric, *n.* retórica, *f.*

rhetorical, *adj.* retórico.

rheumatic, *adj.* reumático.

rheumatism, *n.* reumatismo, *m.*

rhinoceros, *n.* rinoceronte, *m.*

rhubarb, *n.* ruibarbo, *m.*

rhumba, *n.* rumba, *f.*

rhyme, *n.* rima, *f.;* poema, *m.;* —, *vi.* rimar.

rhythm, *n.* ritmo, *m.*

rhythmic, rhythmical, *adj.* rítmico.

rib, *n.* costilla, *f.;* nervio, *m.,* nervadura, (de un puente, barco, etc.), *f.;* varilla (de un paraguas), *f.;* —, *vt.* (coll.) chotear, burlarse de.

ribald, *adj.* obsceno, ribaldo.

ribbon, *n.* listón, *m.,* cinta, *f.;* —s, *n. pl.* perifollos, *m. pl.*

riboflavin, *n.* riboflavina *f.*

rice, *n.* arroz, *m.;* — **field,** arrozal, *m.;* — **paper,** papel de paja de arroz.

rich, *adj.* rico; opulento; abundante; empalagoso.

riches, *n. pl.* riqueza, *f.;* bienes, *m. pl.*

richness, *n.* riqueza, suntuosidad, *f.* **rickets,** *n.* raquitismo, *m.*

rickety, *adj.* raquítico, desvencijado.

rid, *vt.* librar, desembarazar.

riddance, *n.* libramiento, *m.;* zafada, *f.*

ridden, *p.p.* del verbo **ride.**

riddle, *n.* enigma, rompecabezas, acertijo, *m.;* criba, *f.;* (min.) garbillo, *m.;* —, *vt.* acribillar; cribar.

ride, *vi.* cabalgar; andar en coche; **to — a bicycle,** montar en bicicleta; —, *n.* paseo a caballo o en coche.

rider, *n.* cabalgador, *m.;* pasajero (en un auto, autobús, tren, *etc.),* *m.*

ridge, *n.* espinazo, lomo, *m.;* cordillera, *f.;* arruga, *f.;* —, *vt.* formar lomos o surcos.

ridgepole, *n.* (arch.) parhilera, *f.*

ridicule, *n.* ridiculez, *f.;* ridículo, *m.;* —, *vt.* ridiculizar.

ridiculous, *adj.* ridículo.

riding, *n.* paseo a caballo o en auto; —, *adj.* relativo a la equitación; — **boot,** bota de montar; — **breeches,** pantalones de equitación o de montar a caballo; — **habit,** — **outfit,** traje de montar; — **master,** profesor de equitación.

rife, *adj.* común, frecuente; — **with,** lleno de; abundante en.

riffraff, *n.* desecho, desperdicio, *m.;* gentuza, *f.*

rifle, *vt.* robar, pillar; estriar, rayar; —, *n.* fusil, *m.,* carabina rayada; — **case,** carcaj, *m.;* — **corps,** fusilería, *f.;* — **range,** alcance de proyectil de rifle; lugar para tirar al blanco.

rifleman, *n.* escopetero, fusilero, *m.*

rift, *n.* hendidura, *f.;* división, *f.;* disensión, *f.*

rig, *vt.* ataviar; (naut.) aparejar; —, *n.* aparejo, *m.;* traje ridículo o de mal gusto.

rigging, n. (naut.) aparejo, m.

right, adj. derecho, recto; justo; honesto; —! interj. ¡bueno! ¡bien! **all** —! ¡bien! —, adv. derechamente, rectamente; ¡justamente; bien; — **away,** en seguida, luego; — **now,** ahora mismo; **to be** —, tener razón; **to set** —, poner en claro; —, n. justicia, f.; razón, f.; derecho, m.; mano derecha; (pol.) derecha, f.; **all** —**s reserved,** derechos reservados; — **of way,** derecho de vía; —, vt. hacer justicia.

rightabout, n. vuelta a la derecha, vuelta atrás, media vuelta.

right angle, n. ángulo recto.

righteous, adj. justo, honrado.

right-hand, adj. a la derecha; **to the — side,** a la derecha.

rightist, n. (pol.) derechista, m. y f.

right-wing, adj. derechista (en política).

rigid, adj. rígido; austero, severo; —**ly,** adv. con rigidez.

rigidity, n. rigidez, austeridad, f.

rigmarole, n. (coll.) jerigonza, f., galimatías, m.

rigor, n. rigor, m.; severidad, f.

rigorous, adj. riguroso.

rill, n. riachuelo, m.

rim, n. margen, m. y f., orilla, f., borde, m.

rime, n. escarcha, f.; rima, f.

rind, n. corteza, f.; hollejo, m.

ring, n. círculo, cerco, m.; anillo, m.; campaneo, m.;(boxeo) cuadrilátero m.; (mech.) manija, f.; — **finger,** dedo anular; —, vt. sonar; **to — the bell,** tocar la campana, tocar el timbre; —, vi. retiñir, retumbar; resonar.

ringing, adj. sonoro, resonante; —, n. repique, m.

ringleader, n. cabecilla, m., cabeza de partido o bando.

ringlet. n. anillejo, m.; rizo, m.

ringside, n. lugar donde se puede ver bien (un espectáculo); — **seat,** asiento cerca al escenario (con magnífica vista al espectáculo).

ringworm, n. (med.) empeine, m., tiña, f.

rink, n. patinadero, m.

rinse, vt. lavar, limpiar, enjuagar.

riot, n. tumulto, bullicio, m.; peletera, f.; orgía, f.; borrachera, f.; motín, m.; —, vi. andar en orgías; causar alborotos; armar motines.

rioter, n. amotinador, ra; revoltoso, sa;(coll.) bullanguero, ra, alborotador, ra.

riotous, adj. bullicioso, sedicioso; disoluto; —**ly,** adv. disolutamente.

rip, vt. rasgar, lacerar; descoser; —, n.

rasgadura, f.; — **cord,** (avi.) cuerda que al tirar de ella abre el paracaídas.

R.I.P.: rest in peace, RIP., requiescat in pace, Q.E.P.D., que en paz descanse.

ripe, adj. maduro, sazonado.

ripen, vt. y vi. madurar.

ripping, adj. (coll.) admirable, espléndido.

ripple, vi. susurrar; ondular; rizar, ondear; —, n. susurro, m.

rise, vi. levantarse; nacer, salir (los astros); rebelarse; ascender; hincharse; elevarse; resucitar; surgir; **to — above,** trascender; —, n. levantamiento, m.; elevación, f.; subida, f.; salida (del sol), f.; causa, f.

risen, p.p. del verbo **rise.**

riser, n. persona o cosa que se levanta; (arch.) contrahuella, f.; **early —,** madrugador, ra.

risk, n. riesgo, peligro, m.; **without —,** sobre seguro; —, vt. arriesgar.

risky, adj. peligroso.

rite, n. rito, m.

ritual, adj. y n. ritual, m.

rival, adj. competidor, —, n. rival, m. y f.; —, vt. competir, emular.

rivalry, n. rivalidad, f.

river, n. río, m.; — **basin,** cuenca de un río; — **bed,** cauce, m.

riverside, n. ribera, f.; —, adj. situado a la orilla de un río.

rivet, n. remache, roblón, m.; — **plate,** roseta, f., plancha de contrarremache; —, vt. remachar, roblar.

rivulet, n. riachuelo, m.

R.N.: registered nurse, enfermera titulada.

roach, n. (ichth.) escarcho, rubio, m.; cucaracha, f.

road, n. camino, m.; camino real; vía, f.; ruta, f.; carretera, f.; **main —,** carretera, f.; **paved —,** carretera pavimentada.

roadblock, n. (mil.) bloqueo de caminos.

roadhouse, n. posada o venta a la vera de un camino.

roadside, adj. al lado de un camino.

roadster, n. automóvil pequeño de turismo.

roadway, n. camino afirmado; firme del camino; calzada, f.

roam, vt. y vi. corretear; tunar, vagar.

roan, adj. roano, ruano.

roar, vi. rugir; aullar; bramar; —, n. rugido, m.; bramido, estruendo, m.; mugido, m.

roaring, n. bramido, m.; —, adj. rugiente.

roast, vt. asar; tostar; — **beef,** rosbif, m.

roaster, n. asador, m.

rob, vt. robar, hurtar.

robber, n. ladrón, ona.

robbery, *n.* robo, *m.*

robe, *n.* manto, *m.;* toga, *f.;* bata, *f.;* peinador, *m.;* —, *vt.* y *vi.* vestir, vestirse, ataviarse.

robin, *n.* (orn.) petirrojo, pechirrojo, pechicolorado, *m.*

robot, *n.* autómata, *m.,* hombre mecánico; (avi.) piloto mecánico.

robust, *adj.* robusto.

rock, *n.* roca, *f.;* escollo, *m.;* (naut.) vigía, *m.;* — **bottom,** el fondo, lo más profundo; — **crystal,** cuarzo, *m.;* — **garden,** jardín entre rocas; — **salt,** sal gema; —, *vt.* mecer; arrullar; conmover; —, *vi.* bambolear, balancearse, oscilar.

rock-bound, *adj.* rodeado de rocas.

rocker, *n.* mecedora, *f.;* cunera, *f.*

rocket, *n.* cohete, volador, *m.;* **space** —, cohete espacial; **probe** —, cohete de sondeo, proyectil-sonda, *m.*

rocking, *n.* balanceo, *m.;* —, *adj.* mecedor; —**chair,** mecedora, *f.*

rocky, *adj.* peñascoso, pedregoso, rocoso, roqueño; **R— Mountains,** Montañas Rocallosas o Rocosas, *f. pl.*

rod, *n.* varilla, caña, *f.;* **connecting** —, (mech.) biela, *f.*

rode, *pretérito* del verbo **ride.**

rodent, *n.* roedor, *m.*

roe, *n.* corzo, *m.;* hueva, *f.*

rogue, *n.* bribón, pícaro, pillo, villano, *m.;* (colt) granuja, *m.;* —**s' gallery,** colección de retratos de malhechores para uso de la policía.

roguish, *adj.* pícaro, pillo.

role, rôle, *n.* (theat.) papel, *m.,* parte, *f.;* papel (que desempeña una persona), *m.*

roll, *vt.* rodar; volver; arrollar, enrollar; —, *vi.* rodar; girar; —, *n.* rodadura, *f.;* rollo, *m.;* lista, *f.;* catálogo, *m.;* rasero, *m.;* panecillo, *m.;* **to call the** —, pasar lista.

roller, *n.* rodillo, cilindro, aplanador, *m.;* rodo, *m.;* aplanadora, *f.;* rueda, *f.;* — **bearing,** cojinete de rodillos; — **coaster,** montaña rusa; — **skate,** patín de ruedas, patín, *m.;* — **towel,** toalla sin fin.

rollicking, *adj.* jovial, retozón.

rolling, *adj.* rodante; ondulante; — **mill,** taller de laminar; — **pin,** rodillo de pastelero; — **stock,** (rail.) material rodante; —, *n.* rodadura, *f.;* (avi.) balanceo, *m.;* (naut.) balance, *m.*

roll-top, *adj.* de cubierta plegadiza o corrediza (aplícase a un escritorio).

roly-poly, *adj.* rechoncho; —, *n.* persona rechoncha; variedad de pudín.

Roman, *adj.* romano; romanesco; —, *n.*

romano, na; — **type,** letra redonda.

romance, *n.* romance, *m.;* ficción, *f.;* cuento, *m.;* fábula, *f.;* **R**—, *adj.* romance.

romantic, *adj.* romántico; sentimental.

romanticism, *n.* romanticismo, *m.*

Rome, Roma, *f.*

romp, *n.* muchacha retozona; juego, retozo, *m.;* —, *vi.* retozar.

rompers, *n. pl.* traje de niño de una sola pieza y en forma de pantalón.

roof, *n.* tejado, techo, *m.;* azotea, *f.;* — **of the mouth,** paladar, *m.;* — **garden,** azotea, *f.;* —, *vt.* techar.

roofing, *n.* techado, *m.;* material para techos.

rook, *n.* (orn.) corneja, *f.;* roque (en el juego de ajedrez), *m.;* trampista, *m.* y *f.;* —, *vt.* y *vi.* trampear, engañar.

rookie, *n.* bisoño, *m.*

room, *n.* cuarto, *m.* habitación, cámara, *f.;* aposento, *m.;* fugar, espacio, *m.*

roomer, *n.* inquilino, na, persona que ocupa un cuarto en una casa de huéspedes.

roomful, *n.* cuarto lleno; personas o cosas que llenan un cuarto.

roommate, *n.* compañero o compañera de cuarto.

roomy, *adj.* espacioso.

roost, *n.* pértiga del gallinero; —, *vi.* dormir las aves en una pértiga.

rooster, *n.* gallo, *m.*

root, *n.* raíz, *f.;* origen, *m.;* — **beer,** bebida de extractos de varias raíces; **to take** —, echar raíces, prender; radicarse; —, *vt.* y *vi.* arraigar; echar raíces; (coll.) gritar o aplaudir ruidosamente a los jugadores para animarlos; **to** — **out,** desarraigar.

rooted, *adj.* inveterado; arraigado.

rooter, *n.* (coll.) persona que grita y aplaude ruidosamente a los jugadores para animarlos.

rope, *n.* cuerda, *f.;* cordel, *m.;* cable, *m.;* soga, *f.,* (Mex.) mecate, *m.;* —, *vt.* atar con un cordel.

rosary, *n.* rosario, *m.*

rose, *n.* (bot.) rosa, *f.;* color de rosa; —, *pretérito* del verbo **rise.**

rosebud, *n.* capullo de rosa.

rosebush, *n.* (bot.) rosal, *m.*

rosette, *n.* roseta, *f.;* (arch.) florón, *m.*

rosewood, *n.* palo de rosa, palisandro, *m.*

rosin, *n.* resina, *f.,* pez griega.

roster, *n.* lista, *f.;* matrícula, *f.;* registro, *m.*

rostrum, *n.* tribuna, *f.;* (anat.) rostro, pico del ave.

rosy, *adj.* róseo, de color de rosa.

rot, *vi.* pudrirse; —, *n.* morriña, *f.;* putrefacción, *f.*

rotary, *adj.* giratorio; — **press,** máquina rotativa.

rotate, *vt.* y *vi.* girar; alternar; dar vueltas.

rotating, *adj.* giratorio, rotativo.

rotation, *n.* rotación, *f.*

rote, *n.* uso, *m.;* práctica, *f.*

rotogravure, *n.* rotograbado, *m.*

rotten, *adj.* podrido, corrompido.

rottenness, *n.* podredumbre, putrefacción, *f.*

rotund, *adj.* rotundo, redondo, circular, esférico.

rouge, *n.* arrebol, colorete, afeite, *m.*

rough, *adj.* áspero; bronco, brusco; bruto, tosco; tempestuoso; **in the** —, en bruto; —**draft,** borrador, *m.;* — **sea,** mar borrascoso; —, *n.* (golf) rastrojo, *m.*

roughage, *n.* alimento o forraje difícil de digerir.

rough-and-ready, *adj.* tosco pero eficaz en acción.

roughen, *vt.* y *vi.* poner áspero o ponerse áspero.

roughhouse, *vi.* (coll.) retozar.

roughness, *n.* aspereza, *f.;* rudeza, tosquedad, *f.;* tempestad, *f.*

roulette, *n.* ruleta, *f.*

round, *adj.* redondo; circular; cabal; rotundo, franco, sincero; — **number,** número redondo; — **steak,** corte especial de carne de vaca; — **trip,** viaje redondo, viaje de ida y vuelta; **to make** —, redondear; —, *n.* círculo, *m.;* redondez, *f.;* vuelta, *f.;* giro, *m.;* escalón, *m.;* (mil.) ronda, *f.;* andanada de cañones; descarga, *f.;* (boxeo) asalto, *m.;* —, *adv.* redondamente; por todos lados; —, *vt.* cercar, rodear; redondear; **to** — **up,** rodear, recoger (el ganado).

roundabout, *adj.* amplio; indirecto, a la redonda.

roundhouse, *n.* casa de máquinas; (rail.) rotunda, *f.;* (naut.) toldilla, *f.*

roundness, *n.* redondez, *f.*

round-shouldered, *adj.* cargado de espaldas.

round table, *n.* mesa redonda, reunión de un grupo para discutir problemas de interés mutuo.

roundup, *n.* rodeo (de ganado), *m.;* (coll.) reunión, congregación (de personas).

rouse, *vt.* despertar; excitar.

roustabout, *n.* peón de embarcadero, gañán.

rout, *n.* rota, derrota, *f.;* —, *vt.* derrotar.

route, *n.* ruta, vía, *f.,* camino, *m.;* **en** —, en ruta, en camino.

routine, *n.* rutina, *f.;* hábito, *m.;* —, *adj.* rutinario.

rove, *vi.* vagar.

rover, *n.* vagamundo, *m.;* pirata, *m.*

row, *n.* riña, camorra, *f.,* zipizape, *m.*

row, *n.* hilera, fila, *f.;* — **of seats,** tendido, *m.;* —, *vt.* y *vi.* (naut.) remar, bogar.

rowboat, *n.* (naut.) bote de remos.

rowdy, *n.* alborotador, ra, bullanguero, ra; —, *adj.* alborotoso, bullanguero.

royal, *adj.* real; regio; —**ly,** *adv.* regiamente.

royalist, *n.* realista, *m.* y *f.*

royalty, *n.* realeza, dignidad real; —**ties,** *n. pl.* regalías, *f. pl.,* derechos de autor.

r.p.m.: revolutions per minute, r.p.m., revoluciones por minuto.

R.R.: railroad, f.c. ferrocarril; **Right Reverend,** Reverendísimo.

R.S.V.P.: please answer, R.S.V.P. sírvase enviar respuesta.

rub, *vt.* estregar, fregar, frotar, raspar, restregar; friccionar; **to** — **against,** rozar; —, *n.* frotamiento, *m.;* roce, *m.;* (fig.) tropiezo, obstáculo, *m.;* dificultad, *f.*

rubber, *n.* goma, *f.,* goma elástica, caucho, hule, *m.;* **hard** —, caucho endurecido; —**band,** liga de caucho; — **cement,** cemento de caucho; — **heel,** tacón de goma o de caucho; — **plantation,** cauchal, *m.;* — **stamp,** sello de goma; (coll.) persona que obra de una manera rutinaria; **synthetic** —, caucho artificial; **vulcanized** —, caucho vulcanizado; —**s,** *n. pl.* chanclos, zapatos de goma o de caucho; —, *adj.* de goma, de caucho.

rubberize, *vt.* engomar.

rubber-stamp, *vt.* aprobar servilmente; estampar con un sello de goma.

rubbish, *n.* escombro, *m.;* ruinas, *f. pl.;* andrajos, *m. pl.;* cacharro, ripio, *m.*

rubble, *n.* mampostería, *f.*

rubdown, *n.* masaje, *m.*

ruby, *n.* rubí, *m.*

ruching, *n.* material para hacer lechuguillas.

rudder, *n.* timón, gobernalle, *m.,* timón de dirección.

ruddy, *adj.* colorado, rubio; lozano.

rude, *adj.* rudo, brutal, rústico, grosero, tosco.

rudeness, *n.* descortesía, *f.;* rudeza, insolencia, *f.;* barbaridad, *f.;* brusquedad, *f.*

rudiment, *n.* rudimento, *m.*

rueful, *adj.* lamentable, triste.

ruffian, *n.* malhechor, bandolero, rufián, *m.;* —, *adj.* brutal.

ruffle, *vt.* desordenar, desazonar; rizar; fruncir (un volante, una vuelta, etc.); irritar, enojar; —, *n.* volante fruncido, vuelta, *f.;* conmoción, *f.;* enojo, enfado, *m.*

rufous, *adj.* rojizo.

rug, *n.* tapete, *m.;* alfombra, *f.;* **steamer** —, manta de viaje.

rugged, *adj.* áspero, tosco; robusto, vigoroso.

rugosity, *n.* rugosidad, *f.*

ruin, *n.* ruina, *f.;* perdición, *f.;* escombros, *m. pl.;* —, *vt.* arruinar; destruir, echar a perder.

ruination, *n.* arruinamiento, *m.*

ruinous, *adj.* ruinoso.

rule, *n.* mando, *m.;* regla, *f.;* máxima, *f.;* norma, *f.;* férula, *f.;* ordenanza, *f.;* **as a** —, por lo general; **by** —, a regla, por regla; **standard** —, regla fija; **to make it a** —, tener por costumbre; —, *vt.* y *vi.* gobernar; reglar; dirigir; imperar, mandar; —, *vt.* rayar.

ruler, *n.* gobernador, gobernante, *m.;* mandatario, *m.;* regla, *f.*

ruling, *n.* rayadura, *f.;* (leyes) decisión, *f.;* —, *adj.* gobernante, dirigente.

rum, *n.* ron, *m.*

Rumanian, *n.* y *adj.* rumano, na.

rumba, *n.* rumba, *f.*

rumble, *vi.* crujir, rugir; — **seat,** (auto.) asiento trasero descubierto.

ruminant, *n.* rumiante, *m.*

ruminate, *vt.* y *vi.* rumiar.

rumination, *n.* rumiación, *f.*

rummage, *vt.* trastornar, revolver, escudriñar; —, *n.* registro, *m.;* — **sale,** venta de artículos usados, venta de remates (con fines caritativos).

rumor, *n.* rumor, runrún, *m.;* —, *vt.* divulgar alguna noticia.

rump, *n.* anca, nalga (de animal), *f.*

rumple, *n.* arruga, *f.;* —, *vt.* ajar, arrugar.

rumpus, *n.* alboroto, *m.*

run, *vt.* correr; manejar; traspasar; **to** — **down a pedestrian,** atropellar un peatón, *vi.* correr; fluir, manar; pasar rápidamente; proceder; **to** — **across,** tropezar con; **to** — **aground,** encallar; **to** — **down,** averiguar; alcanzar; pararse (un reloj); descargarse; agotarse; **to** — **into,** topar, chocar con; **to** — **off,** escaparse, escurrir; **to** — **out of,** no tener más (de algo), agotarse (un artículo); **to** — **the risk of,** arriesgar, aventurar; **to** — **through,** examinar o ensayar rápidamente; —, *n.*

corrida, carrera, *f.;* curso, *m.;* recorrido, *m.;* serie, *f.;* libertad en el uso de cosas; (mus.) escala, *f.;* **in the long** —, a la larga.

runaway, *n.* fugitivo, va, desertor, ra.

run-down, *adj.* cansado, rendido, agotado, fatigado; parado por falta de cuerda (un reloj).

rung, *n.* escalón, peldaño (de escalera de mano), *m.;* —, *p.p.* del verbo **ring.**

runic, *adj.* ruso.

run-in, *n.* riña, *f.*

runner, *n.* corredor, ra; mensajero, ra; alfombra larga y angosta (para una escalera o pasadizo).

runner-up, *n.* competidor que queda en segundo lugar.

running, *n.* carrera, corrida, *f.;* curso, *m.;* — **board,** estribo, *m.;* — **gear,** juego de ruedas y ejes de un vehículo; — **water,** agua corriente; —, *adj.* corriente, que corre o fluye.

runproof, *adj.* indesmallable.

runt, *n.* enano, *m.*

runway, *n.* cauce, *m.;* corredera, *f.;* vía, *f.;* pasadizo para ganado; pasadizo para exhibición de modelos; pista de aviones en un aeropuerto.

rupture, *n.* rotura, *f.;* hernia, quebradura, *f.;* —, *vt.* reventar, romper.

rural, *adj.* rural, campestre, rústico.

ruse, *n.* astucia, maña, *f.*

rush, *n.* (bot.) junco, *m.;* ímpetu, *m.;* prisa, *f.;* — **hour,** hora de tránsito intenso; — **order,** pedido urgente, pedido de precisión; —, *vi.* abalanzarse, tirarse; ir de prisa, apresurarse.

russet, *adj.* bermejizo.

Russia, Rusia, *f.*

Russian, *n.* y *adj.* ruso; sa; — **language,** ruso, *m.*

rust, *n.* herrumbre, *f.;* orín, moho, *m.;* (bot.) roya, *f.;* color bermejo; —, *vi.* enmohecerse.

rustic, *adj.* rústico, pardal; —, *n.* patán, rústico, *m.*

rusticate, *vi.* rusticar.

rustle, *n.* susurro, *m.;* —, *vi.* crujir, susurrar.

rustproof, *adj.* a prueba de herrumbre, inoxidable.

rusty, *adj.* mohoso, enmohecido.

rut, *vi.* estar en celo; —, *n.* brama, *f.;* cantinela, rutina, *f.*

rutabaga, *n.* (bot.) naba, *f.*

ruthless, *adj.* cruel, insensible; —**ly,** *adv.* inhumanamente.

Ry.: Railway, f.c. ferrocarril.

rye, *n.* (bot.) centeno, *m.;* — **field,** centenal, *m.*

S

S.A.: Salvation Army, Ejército de Salvación;
South America, S. A. Sud América;
South Africa, Sud Africa.
SAC (Strategic Air Command), n. Mando Aéreo Estratégico (E.U.A.).
sabbath, n. día de descanso (sábado para los judíos, domingo para los cristianos).
saber, sabre, n. sable, m.
sable, n. cebellina, marta, f.
sabotage, n. sabotaje, m.
saboteur, n. saboteador, ra.
saccharine, n. sacarina, f.; —, adj. sacarino, azucarado.
sachet, n. bolsita con polvo perfumado.
sack, n. saco, talego, m.; — **coat,** americana, f.; saco de hombre; —, vt. meter en sacos; saquear.
sackcloth, n. arpillera, f.; cilicio, m.
sacrament, n. sacramento, m.; Eucaristía, f.
sacred, adj. sagrado, sacro; inviolable.
sacrifice, n. sacrificio, m.; —, vt. sacrificar; **to — oneself,** sacrificarse.
sacrilege, n. sacrilegio, m.
sacrilegious, adj. sacrílego.
sad, adj. triste, melancólico; infausto.
sadden, vt. entristecer.
saddle, n. silla, silla de montar; — **horse,** caballo de montar; —, vt. ensillar.
saddlebag, n. alforja, f.
sadism, n. sadismo, m.
sadistic, adj. sádico.
sadness, n. tristeza, f.; aspecto tétrico.
safari, n. expedición de caza, safari, m.
safe, adj. seguro; incólume; salvo; — **and sound,** sano y salvo; —, n. caja fuerte; **—ly,** adv. a salvo.
safe-conduct, n. salvoconducto, seguro, m., carta de amparo.
safe-deposit, adj. de seguridad; — **box,** caja de seguridad.
safeguard, n. salvaguardia, f.; —, vt. proteger.
safety, n. seguridad, f.; salvamento, m.; — **belt,** cinto salvavidas; — **island,** plataforma de seguridad; refugio, m.; — **match,** fósforo de seguridad; — **pin,** alfiler de gancho, imperdible, m.; — **razor,** navaja de seguridad.
saffron, n. (bot.) azafrán, m.
sag, n. desviación, f., pandeo, seno, m.; —, vi. empandarse, combarse; doblegarse.

saga, n. saga, leyenda de los Eddas.
sagacious, adj. sagaz, sutil.
sage, n. y adj. sabio, m.
sagebrush, n. (bot.) artemisa, f.
sail, n. vela, f.; —, vi. navegar.
sailboat, n. velero, m., buque de vela.
sailcloth, n. lona, f.
sailfish, n. pez espada, m.
sailing, n. navegación, f.; partida, salida, f.; —, adj. de vela.
sailor, n. marinero, m.
saint, n. santo, ta; ángel, m.; **patron —,** santo patrón; —, vt. canonizar.
saintlike, adj. como santo.
saintly, adj. santo.
sake, n. causa, razón, f.; amor, m., consideración, f.; **for your own —,** por tu propio bien.
salad, n. ensalada, f.; — **bowl,** ensaladera, f.; — **dressing,** aderezo, m., salsa para ensalada.
salamander, n. salamandra, f.
salary, n. salario, sueldo, m., paga, f.
sale, n. venta, f.; (com.) realización, f.; **auction —,** remate, m.; **clearance —,** liquidación, f.; — **price,** precio de venta, precio reducido; **—s tax,** impuesto sobre ventas.
salesclerk, n. vendedor, ra, dependiente, m. y f.
salesman, n. vendedor, tendero, m.; **traveling —,** comisionista, agente viajero.
salesmanship, n. arte de vender.
salicylic, adj. (chem.) salicílico.
salicylate, n. (chem.) salicilato, m.
salient, adj. saliente, saledizo.
saliva, n. saliva, f.
Salk vaccine, n. vacuna Salk, vacuna contra la poliomielitis.
sallow, adj. cetrino, pálido; — **face,** cara pálida y amarillenta.
sally, n. (mil.) salida, surtida, f.; excursión, f., paseo, m.; agudeza, f.; —, vi. salir.
salmon, n. salmón, m.; —, adj. de color salmón; — **trout,** trucha salmonada.
salon, n. salón, m., sala de exhibición; **beauty —,** salón de belleza.
saloon, n. cantina, taberna, f.
salt, n. sal, f.; (fig.) sabor, m.; gracia, f.; agudeza, f.; —, adj. salado; —, vt. salar; salpresar.
saltcellar, saltshaker, n. salero, m., receptáculo para sal.
salted, adj. salado; — **fish,** pescado sala-

do; — **meat,** carne salpresa.
salty, adj. salado, salobre.
salutation, n. salutación, f.; saludo, m.
salute, vt. saludar; —, n. salutación, f., saludo, m.
salvage, n. salvamento, m.; (naut.) derecho de salvamento; —, vt. salvar.
salvation, n. salvación, f.
salve, n. emplasto, ungüento, m., pomada, f.
same, adj. mismo; idéntico; propio.
sample, n. muestra, f.; ejemplo, m.; — **book,** muestrario, m.; —, vt. catar, probar una muestra.
sampler, n. muestra, f.; dechado, modelo, m.
sanatorium, n. sanatorio, m.
sanctify, vt. santificar.
sanctimonious, adj. hipócritamente piadoso.
sanction, n. sanción, f.; —, vt. sancionar.
sanctity, n. santidad, santimonia, f.
sanctuary, n. santuario, m.; asilo, m.
sanctum, n. lugar sagrado; lugar de retiro.
sand, n. arena, f.; — **dune,** médano, m., duna, f.; — **pit,** arenal, m.; —, vt. enarenar.
sandal, n. sandalia, f.
sandalwood, n. sándalo, m.
sandbag, n. saco de arena; —, vt. resguardar con sacos de arena; golpear con sacos de arena.
sandbank, n. banco de arena.
sandblast, n. máquina sopladora de arena; chorro de arena lanzado por aire o vapor para grabar o cortar vidrio, piedra, etc.; soplete de arena; —, vt. lanzar por aire o vapor un chorro de arena para limpiar fachadas, etc.
sandbox, n. caja de arena.
sandpaper, n. papel de lija, lija, f.; —, vt. lijar.
sandstone, n. piedra arenisca.
sandstorm, n. tormenta de arena.
sandwich, n. sandwich, emparedado, m.; —, vt. emparedar; intercalar.
sandy, adj. arenoso, arenisco.
sane, adj. sano.
sang, pretérito del verbo **sing.**
sanguine, adj. sanguíneo.
sanitarium, n. sanatorio, m.
sanitary, adj. sanitario; — **napkin,** servilleta higiénica.
sanitation, n. saneamiento, m.
sanity, n. cordura, f.; juicio sano, sentido común; **to lose one's** —, volverse loco.
sank, pretérito del verbo **sink.**
sap, n. savia, f.; (mil.) zapa, f.; —, vt. zapar.

sapling, n. renuevo, vástago, m.; mozalbete, m.
sapphire, n. zafir, zafiro, m.
sarcasm, n. sarcasmo, m.
sarcastic, adj. sarcástico, mordaz, cáustico.
sardine, n. sardina, f.
S.A.R.S.: severe acute respiratory syndrome, síndrome respiratorio agudo severo.
sash, n. faja, f.; cinturón, m.; cinta, f.; bastidor de ventana o de puerta.
sassafras, n. sasafrás, m.
sat, pretérito y p.p. del verbo **sit.**
Sat.: Saturday, sáb. sábado.
Satan, n. Satanás, m.
satanic, adj. diabólico, satánico.
satchel, n. saquillo de mano, maletín, m., maleta, f.
sateen, n. rasete m., tela similar al raso pero de inferior calidad.
satellite, n. satélite, m.
satiate, vt. saciar, hartar; —, vi. saciarse, hartarse.
satin, n. raso, m.
satire, n. sátira, f.
satirical, adj. satírico.
satirist, n. autor satírico, persona que usa sátira.
satirize, vt. satirizar.
satisfaction, n. satisfacción, f.
satisfactorily, adj. satisfactoriamente.
satisfactory, adj. satisfactorio; **to be — to you,** ser de su agrado.
satisfy, vt. satisfacer.
saturate, vt. saturar.
Saturday, n. sábado, m.
saturnine, adj. saturnino, melancólico.
satyr, n. sátiro, m.
sauce, n. salsa, f.
saucepan, n. cacerola, f.
saucer, n. plato pequeño.
saucy, adj. atrevido, malcriado, respondón.
sauerkraut, n. col fermentada.
saunter, vi. callejear, vagar, andar sin rumbo.
sausage, n. salchicha, f.; **pork** —, longaniza, f.
savage, adj. salvaje, bárbaro; —, n. salvaje, m.
savagery, n. salvajismo, m., salvajez, f.
savant, n. sabio, bía, erudito, ta.
save, vt. salvar; economizar, ahorrar; conservar; —, prep. excepto.
saver, n. libertador, ra; ahorrador, ra.
saving, adj. frugal, económico; salvador; —, prep. fuera de, excepto; —, n. salvamento, m.; —**s,** n. pl. ahorros, m. pl., economías, f. pl.; —**s bank,** caja de

ahorros, banco de ahorros.
savior, saviour, *n.* salvador, ra.
Saviour, *n.* Redentor, Salvador, *m.*
savor, savour, *n.* olor, *m.; ;* sabor, *m.; ;* —, *vt. y vi.* gustar, saborear; **to — of,** oler a, saber a; tener la característica de.
savory, *adj.* sabroso.
saw, *n.* sierra, *f.; ;* —, *vt.* serrar; —, *pretérito del verbo* see.
sawdust, *n.* aserraduras, *f. pl.,* aserrín, *m.*
sawmill, *n.* molino de aserrar.
saxophone, *n.* (mus.) saxofón, *m.*
say, *vt.* decir, hablar; proferir; **that is to —,** es decir; **to — mass,** cantar misa; **to — to oneself,** decir para su capote; —, *n.* habla, *f.*
saying, *n.* dicho, proverbio, refrán *m.*
s.c.: small capitals, pequeñas mayúsculas.
scab, *n.* costra, *f.;* roña, *f.;* (coll.) hombre roñoso; bribón, *m.*
scabbard, *n.* vaina de espada; cobertura, *f.;* carcaj, *m.*
scaffold, *n.* tablado, andamio; cadalso, *m.*
scaffolding, *n.* andamiaje, *m.;* construcción de tablados o andamios.
scald, *vt.* escaldar; —, *n.* escaldadura, *f.;* quemadura, *f.*
scale, *n.* balanza, *f.;* escama, *f.;* escala, *f.;* gama, *f.;* lámina delgada; **balance —,** balanza, *f.;* **platform —,** báscula, *f.;* —, *vt. y vi.* escalar, descostrarse; desconchar (una pared, un techo, etc.) .
scaling, *n.* desconchamiento (de una pared o un techo, etc.); (mil.) escalamiento, *m.;* escamadura, *f.*
scallop, *n.* (ichth.) venera, pechina, *f.;* festón, *m.;* —, *vt.* festonear.
scalp, *n.* cuero cabelludo; —, *vt.* escalpar; comprar y revender billetes de teatro, etc., por una ganancia.
scalper, *n.* revendedor, *m.,* persona que revende billetes de teatro, etc., por una ganancia; **ticket —,** revendedor, *m.*
scamp, *n.* bribón, ona; ladrón, ona.
scamper, *vi.* escapar, huir.
scan, *vt.* escudriñar; medir las sílabas de un verso.
scandal, *n.* escándalo, *m.;* infamia, *f.*
scandalize, *vt.* escandalizar.
scandalous, *adj.* escandaloso.
Scandinavia, Escandinavia, *f.*
scanner, *n.* escudriñador, *m.; (TV.)* explorador, *m.*
scant, scanty, *adj.* escaso, parco; sórdido.
scapegoat, *n* víctima inocente; (Mex.) chivo expiatorio.
scar, *n.* cicatriz, *f.;* —, *vt.* hacer alguna cicatriz.

scarce, *adj.* raro; **—ly,** *adv.* apenas, escasamente; solamente; pobremente.
scarcity, *n.* escasez, *f.*
scare, *n.* susto, *m.;* **to get a —,** llevarse un susto; —, *vt.* espantar.
scarecrow, *n.* espantapájaros, mamarracho, *m.*
scarf, *n.* bufanda, *f.;* chal, *m.,* chalina, *f.*
scarfpin, *n.* alfiler de corbata.
scarlet, *n.* escarlata, *f.;* —, *adj.* de color escarlata o grana; **— fever,** (med.) escarlatina, *f.*
scat! *interj.* ¡zape!
scatter, *vt.* esparcir, dispersar; disipar; —, *vi.* derramarse, disiparse.
scatterbrained, *adj.* atolondrado, distraído.
scavenger, *n.* basurero, *m.;* barrendero, ra; animal que se alimenta de carroña.
scenario, *n.* guión, argumento de una película cinematográfica.
scenarist, *n.* escritor o escritora de argumentos cinematográficos.
scene, *n.* escena, perspectiva, vista, *f.;* paisaje, *m.;* (theat.) escena, *f.;* lugar de un suceso.
scenery, *n.* vista, *f.;* **paisaje,** *m.;* **(theat.)** escenografía, decoración, *f.,* bastidores, *m. pl.*
sceneshifter, *n.* tramoyista, *m.*
scenic, scenical, *adj.* escénico.
scent, *n.* olfato, *m.;* olor, *m.;* rastro, *m.;* —, *vt.* oler, olfatear; —, *vi.* olfatear.
scepter, sceptre, *n.* cetro, *m.*
sceptic, sceptical = skeptic, skeptical.
schedule, *n.* plan, programa, *m.;* catálogo, *m.;* horario, itinerario, *m.;* —, *vt.* fijar en un plan o en un programa.
schematic, *adj.* esquemático.
scheme, *n.* proyecto, designio, *m.;* esquema, plan, modelo, *m.;* —, *vt.* proyectar.
schemer, *n.* proyectista, *m. y f.;* intrigante, *m. y f.*
schism, *n.* cisma, *m.*
schist, *n.* (geol.) esquisto, *m.*
scholar, *n.* estudiante, *m. y f.;* literato, ta; erudito, ta.
scholarly, *adj.* de estudiante; erudito, muy instruido; —, *adv.* eruditamente.
scholarship, *n.* educación literaria; beca, *f.;* erudición, *f.*
scholastic, *adj.* escolástico; estudiantil.
school, *n.* escuela, *f.;* **high —,** escuela secundaria, escuela superior; **— vt.** instruir, enseñar; disciplinar.
schoolhouse, *n.* escuela (edificio), *f.*
schooling, *n.* instrucción, enseñanza, *f.*
schoolteacher, *n.* maestro o maestra de escuela.
schooner, *n.* (naut.) goleta, *f.*

sciatic, *adj.* ciático; **— nerve,** nervio ciático.
science, *n.* ciencia,
scientific, *adj.* científico.
scientist, *n.* hombre de ciencia, científico, ca.
scintillate, *vi.* chispear, centellear.
scion, *n.* vástago, *m.;* renuevo, *m.*
scissors, *n. pl.* tijeras, *f. pl.*
scoff, *vi.* mofarse, burlarse; —, *n.* mofa, burla, *f.*
scold, *vt. y vi.* regañar, reñir, refunfuñar; —, *n.* persona regañona.
scolding, *n.* regaño, *m.;* —, *adj.* regañón.
scoop, *n.* cucharón, *m.* (naut.) achicador, *m.;* cesta (en el juego de pelota); (coll. periodismo) acción de ganar una noticia; —, *vt.* cavar, socavar.
scope, *n.* alcance, *m.;* rienda suelta; libertad, *f.*
scorch, *vt.* quemar por encima; tostar; socarrar; calcinar; —, *vi.* quemarse, secarse.
scorched, *adj.* chamuscado; abrasado, agostado.
score, *n.* muesca, *f.;* consideración, *f.;* cuenta, *f;* razón, *f;* motivo, *m.;* veintena, *f.;* (deportes) tantos, *m. pl.,* puntuación, *f.;* (mus.) partitura, *f.;* —, *vt.* sentar alguna deuda; imputar; señalar con una linea; —, *vi.* hacer tantos (en un juego).
scorn, *vt. y vi.* despreciar; mofar; —, *n.* desdén, menosprecio, *m.*
scornful, *adj.* desdeñoso; **—ly,** *adv.* con desdén.
scorpion, *n.* escorpión, *m.*
Scotch, *n. y adj.* escocés, esa; —, *n.* whisky escocés.
Scotland, Escocia, *f.*
scoundrel, *n.* pícaro, ra, bribón, ona, infame, *m. y f.;* canalla, *m.*
scour, *vt.* fregar, estregar; limpiar; rebuscar, sondear.
scourge, *n.* azote, *m.;* castigo, *m.;* —, *vt.* azotar, castigar.
scout, *n.* (mil.) batidor, corredor, *m.;* escucha, *f.;* centinela avanzada; **boy —,** niño explorador, niño de la Asociación de Niños Exploradores; **girl —,** niña exploradora, niña de la Asociación de Niñas Exploradoras; —, *vi.* reconocer secretamente los movimientos del enemigo; (mil.) explorar.
scoutmaster, *n.* jefe de tropa de niños exploradores.
scowl, *n.* ceño, *m.,* semblante ceñudo; —, *vi.* mirar con ceño.
scramble, *vi.* trepar; arrebatar, disputar; esparcirse en forma irregular; —, *vt.*

mezclar confusamente; **—d eggs,** huevos revueltos; —, *n.* disputa, arrebatiña, *f.;* (avi.) despegue rápido de emergencia en operaciones de defensa.
scrap, *n.* migaja, *f.;* pedacito, *m.;* **—s,** *pl* sobras, *f. pl.,* retazos, *m. pl.;* **— heap,** montón de desechos, pila de desperdicios; **— iron, — metal,** chatarra, *f.;* —, *vt.* descartar; —, *vi.* (coll.) disputar, reñir.
scrapbook, *n.* álbum de recortes.
scrape, *vt. y vi.* raer, raspar, arañar; juntar gradualmente (dinero, etc.); —, *n.* dificultad, *f.;* lío, *m.*
scraper, *n.* raspador, *m.*
scratch, *vt.* rascar, raspar; borrar; arañar; —, *n.* rasguño, *m.*
scratch pad, *n.* bloc de papel para apuntes.
scrawl, *vt. y vi.* garrapatear; —, *n.* garabatos, *m. pl.,* garrapato, *m.*
scrawny, *adj.* flaco y huesudo.
scream, *vi.* gritar, chillar, dar alaridos; —, *n.* chillido, grito, alarido, *m.*
screech, *vi.* chillar, dar alaridos; —, *n.* chillido, grito, alarido, *m.;* **— owl,** lechuza, *f.*
screen, *n.* pantalla, *f.;* biombo, *m.;* mampara, *f.;* pantalla de cine; **fire —,** pantalla de chimenea; —, *vt.* abrigar, esconder; cribar, cerner, tamizar; seleccionar por eliminación; proyectar en la pantalla.
screw, *n.* tornillo, *m.;* clavo de rosca; rosca, *f.;* **— driver,** destornillador, *m.;* **— propeller,** hélice, *f.;* **to have a — loose,** (coll.) tener un tornillo flojo, ser alocado; —, *vt.* atornillar; forzar, apretar.
scribble, *vi.* borrajear; —, *n.* escrito de poco mérito.
scribe, *n.* escritor, *m.;* escriba, *m.;* escribiente, *m.*
scrimmage, *n.* arrebatiña, *f.*
scrimp, *vt. y vi.* escatimar, economizar, pasarse sin.
scrip, *n.* cédula, *f.;* esquela, *f.*
script, *n.* (rad. y TV.) guión, argumento, libreto, *m.;* (print.) plumilla inglesa.
scriptural, *adj.* biblico.
Scripture, *n.* Escritura Sagrada.
scroll, *n.* rollo (de papel o pergamino), *m.;* voluta, *f.;* **— saw,** sierra de cinta, sierra de marquetería; —, *vt.* decorar con volutas.
scrollwork, *n.* adornos de voluta.
scrub, *vt.* estregar con un estropajo; fregar, restregar; —, *n.* estropajo, *m.;* ganapán, *m.;* (Mex.) afanador, *m.*
scrubbing, *n.* fregadura, *f.;* **— brush,** fre-

gador, cepillo para fregar.
scruff, *n.* nuca, *f.*
scruple, *n.* escrúpulo, rescoldo, *m.;* —, *vi.* tener escrúpulos de conciencia.
scrupulous, *adj.* escrupuloso.
scrutinize, *vt.* escudriñar, examiner; escrutar.
scrutiny, *n.* escrutinio, examen, *m.*
Scuba, *n.* escafandra autónoma.
scuff, *vt.* arrastrar los pies; dañar una superficie dura; restregar; —, *n.* variedad de chinela.
scuffle, *n.* quimera, riña, *f.;* —, *vi.* reñir, pelear.
scullery, *n.* fregadero, *m.*
sculptor, *n.* escultor, *m.*
sculptress, *n.* escultora, *f.*
sculpture, *n.* escultura, *f.;* —, *vt.* esculpir.
scum, *n.* nata, *f.;* espuma, *f.;* escoria, *f.;* —, *vt.* espumar.
scurvy, *n.* escorbuto, *m.;* —, *adj.* vil, despreciable.
scuttle, *n.* banasta, *f.;* balde para carbón; paso veloz; —, *vi.* apretar a correr; —, *vt.* (naut.) echar a pique.
scuttlebutt, *n.* rumor, runrún que corre especialmente entre gente de mar.
scythe, *n.* guadaña, *f.*
S.E., SE: South East, S.E. Sureste, Sudeste.
sea, *n.* mar, *m.* y *f.;* **rough** —, mar alta; — **breeze,** viento de mar; — **food,** marisco o pescado; — **gull,** gaviota, *f.;* — **horse,** hipocampo, *m.;* — **wall,** malecón, *m.;* —, *adj.* de mar, marítimo.
seaboard, *n.* costa, playa, *f.;* —, *adj.* al lado del mar, costanero.
seacoast, *n.* costa marítima.
seafaring, *adj.* marino, de mar; —, *n.* viajes por mar.
seagoing, *adj.* capaz de navegar en el océano; navegante.
seal, *n.* sello, *m.;* (zool.) foca, *f.;* becerro marino; —, *vt.* sellar.
sea level, *n.* nivel del mar.
sealing, *n.* caza de focas; selladura, *f.;* — **wax,** lacre, *m.*
sealskin, *n.* piel de foca.
seam, *n.* costura, *f.;* cicatriz, *f.;* sutura, *f.;* —, *vt.* coser.
seaman, *n.* marinero, marino, *m.*
seamless, *adj.* sin costura; — **hosiery,** medias sin costura.
seamstress, *n.* costurera, *f.*
seaplane, *n.* hidroavión, *m.*
seaport, *n.* puerto de mar.
sear, *vt.* cauterizar; quemar; dorar o freír (la superficie de la carne, etc.); secar.
search, *vt.* examinar, registrar; escudriñar, inquirir, tentar, pesquisar; —, *n.*

pesquisa, *f.;* busca, *f.;* búsqueda, *f.;* **in — of,** en busca de; — **engine,** motor de búsqueda, *m.*
searchlight, *n.* reflector, *m.*
seashore, *n.* ribera, *f.;* litoral, *m.*
seasick, *adj.* mareado.
seaside, *n.* orilla o ribera del mar; —, *adj.* en la costa; del mar; — **resort,** lugar de recreo a la orilla del mar.
season, *n.* estación, *f.;* tiempo, *m.;* tiempo oportuno; sazón, *f.;* temporada, *f.;* — **ticket,** (theat.) abono para la temporada; (rail.) abono de pasaje; —, *vt.* sazonar; imbuir; curar; condimentar; —, *vi.* sazonarse.
seasonable, *adj.,* oportuno, tempestivo, a propósito.
seasonal, *adj.* de temporada, estacional.
seasoned, *adj.* curado; sazonado; **highly** —, picante, picoso.
seasoning, *n.* condimento, *m.*
seat, *n.* silla, *f.;* localidad, *f.;* morada, *f.;* domicilio, *m.;* situación, *f.;* **front** —, asiento delantero; **back** —, asiento trasero; — **cover,** cubreasiento, *m.;* —, *vt.* situar; colocar; asentar; sentar.
seating, *n.* acción de sentar; material para entapizar sillas; — **capacity,** cabida, *f.;* número de asientos.
seaward, *adj.* del litoral; —, —**s,** *adv.* hacia el mar.
seaweed, *n.* alga marina.
secede, *vi.* apartarse, separarse.
secession, *n.* separación, *f.;* secesión, *f.*
secessionist, *n.* secesionista, separatista, *m.*
seclude, *vt.* apartar, excluir, recluir.
seclusion, *n.* separación, *f.;* reclusión, *f.*
second, *adj.* segundo; — **childhood,** segunda infancia, chochera, *f.;* — **hand,** segundero (de un reloj); — **lieutenant,** alférez, subteniente, *m.;* — **nature,** costumbre arraigada; —**ly,** *adv.* en segundo lugar; —, *n.* padrino (en un duelo), *m.;* defensor, *m.;* segundo, *m.;* (mus.) segunda, *f.;* —, *vt.* apoyar, ayudar; **to — the motion,** apoyar la moción.
secondary, *adj.* secundario; — **school,** escuela secundaria.
second-class, *adj.* de segunda clase, mediocre.
secondhand, *adj.* de ocasión; usado; de segunda mano; — **dealer,** prendero, ropavejero, *m.;* — **shop,** baratillo, *m.,* tienda de artículos de segunda mano.
secrecy, *n.* secreto, *m.;* reserva, *f.;* reticencia, *f.*
secret, *n.* secreto, *m.;* **in** —, en secreto; —, *adj.* privado; secreto; reservado; —

service, policía secreta; **—ly,** *adv.* secretamente, a escondidas, de rebozo.

secretariat, *n.* secretaría, *f.*

secretary, *n.* secretario, ria; **private —,** secretario (o secretaria) particular; **—'s office,** secretaría, *f.*

secrete, *vt.* esconder; guardar en secreto; (med.) secretar.

secretion, *n.* secreción, *f.*

secretive, *adj.* misterioso; reservado; secretorio.

sect, *n.* secta, *f.*

sectarian, sectary, *n.* y *adj.* sectario, ria; secuaz, *m.* y *f.*

section, *n.* sección, *f.;* departamento, *m.*

sector, *n.* sector, *m.*

secular, *adj.* secular, seglar.

secure, *adj.* seguro; salvo; **—ly,** *adv.* en forma segura; **—,** *vt.* asegurar; conseguir; resguardar.

security, *n.* seguridad, *f.;* defensa, *f.;* confianza, *f.;* fianza, *f.;* **to give —,** dar o prestar fianza; **— risk,** individuo que representa un peligro para la seguridad pública.

secy., sec'y.: secretary, srio., secretario, sria., secretaria.

sedan, *n.* (auto.) sedán, *m.*

sedate, *adj.* sosegado, tranquilo.

sedative, *n.* y *adj.* sedativo, sedante, calmante, confortante, *m.*

sedentary, *adj.* sedentario.

sediment, *n.* sedimento, *m.;* hez, *f.;* poso, *m.*

sedimentary, *adj.* sedimentario.

sedition, *n.* sedición, *f.;* tumulto, alboroto, motín, *m.;* revuelta, *f.*

seditious, *adj.* sedicioso.

seduce *vt.* seducir; engañar.

seduction, *n.* seducción, *f.*

seductive, *adj.* seductivo, seductor.

see, *vt.* y *vi.* ver, observar, descubrir; advertir; conocer, juzgar, comprender; presenciar; **let's —,** vamos a ver, a ver; **to — to it that,** encargarse de; **—,** véase; **—! interj.** ¡mira! **—,** silla episcopal; **the Holy S—,** la Santa Sede.

seed, *n.* semilla, simiente, *f.;* origen, *m.;* **— corn,** semilla para maíz; **to go to —,** (coll.) degenerar, decaer, echarse a perder; **—,** *vi.* granar, sembrar.

seedless, *adj.* sin semilla; **— grapes,** uvas sin semilla.

seedy, *adj.* lleno de semillas; (coll.) andrajoso, de aspecto miserable.

seeing, *n.* vista, *f.;* acto de ver, ver, *m.;* **— that,** visto que, en consideración a; **— eye dog,** perro lazarillo, perro guía (para los ciegos).

seek, *vt.* y *vi.* buscar; pretender.

seem, *vi.* parecer, semejarse; tener cara de.

seeming, *n.* apariencia, *f.;* **—ly,** *adv.* al parecer.

seemly, *adj.* decoroso; agradable.

seen, *p.p.* del verbo **see.**

seep, *vi.* colarse, escurrirse.

seer, *n.* profeta, vidente, *m.*

seersucker, *n.* variedad de tela de algodón.

seesaw, *n.* vaivén *m.;* balancín de sube y baja; **—,** *vi.* balancear.

seethe, *vi.* hervir, bullir.

segment, *n.* segmento, *m.*

segregate, *adj.* segregado, apartado; **—,** *vt.* segregar.

segregation *n.* segregación, separación, *f.*

seismograph, *n.* sismógrafo, *m.*

seize, *vt.* asir, agarrar, prender; secuestrar bienes o efectos; decomisar.

seizure, *n.* captura, toma, *f.;* secuestro, *m.*

seldom, *adv.* raramente, rara vez.

select, *vt.* elegir, escoger; **—,** *adj.* selecto, escogido, granado.

selection, *n.* selección, *f.;* trozo, *m.*

selective, *adj.* selectivo, relativo a la selección; que escore.

self, *adj.* propio, mismo; **—,** *n.* sí mismo.

self-addressed, *adj.* rotulado.

self-centered, *adj.* egoísta, concentrado en sí mismo; independiente.

self-confident, *adj.* que tiene confianza en sí mismo.

self-conscious, *adj.* consciente de sí mismo; tímido, vergonzoso.

self-contained, *adj.* reservado; independiente; completo, que contiene todos sus elementos.

self-controlled, *adj.* dueño de sí mismo.

self-defeating, *adj.* contraproducente.

self-defense, *n.* defensa propia.

self-denial, *n.* abnegación, *f.*

self-esteem, *n.* amor propio.

self-evident, *adj.* natural, patente; **to be —,** caerse de suyo.

self-explanatory, *adj.* que se explica por sí mismo.

self-expression, *n.* expresión de personalidad; aserción de rasgos individuales.

self-governing, *adj.* autónomo, que tiene dominio sobre sí mismo.

self-help, *n.* ayuda de sí mismo.

self-improvement, *n.* mejoramiento de sí mismo.

self-indulgence, *n.* intemperancia, *f.;* entrega a la satisfacción de los propios deseos.

selfish, *adj.* interesado; egoísta.

selfishness, *n.* egoísmo, *m.*

self-made, *adj.* formado o desarrollado por sus propios esfuerzos; — **man,** hombre forjado por sus propios esfuerzos.

self-possession, *n.* sangre fría, tranquilidad de ánimo.

self-preservation, *n.* instinto de conservación.

self-propelling, *adj.* automotor.

self-reliance, *n.* confianza en sí mismo.

self-reliant, *adj.* independiente, que confía en sí mismo.

self-respect, *n.* respeto de sí mismo.

self-sacrifice, *n.* abnegación, *f.*

selfsame, *adj.* idéntico, el mismo, exactamente lo mismo.

self-satisfied, *adj.* satisfecho de sí mismo.

self-seeking, *adj.* egoísta, interesado.

self-starter, *n.* motor de arranque, arranque automático.

self-sufficient, *adj.* capaz de mantenerse; independiente; confiado en sí mismo; altanero.

self-support, *n.* sostenimiento económico propio.

self-taught, *adj.* autodidacto.

self-winding, *adj.* de cuerda automática.

sell, *vt.* y *vi.* vender; traficar; —, *n.* (coll.) patraña, *f.;* engaño, *m.*

seller, *n.* vendedor, ra.

seltzer, *n.* agua de seltzer, agua carbónica.

selvage, *n.* orilla de una tela.

selves, *n. pl.* de **self.**

semblance, *n.* semejanza, apariencia, *f.*

semester, *n.* semestre, *m.*

semiannual, *adj.* semianual, semestral.

semicircle, *n.* semicírculo, *m.*

semicolon, *n.* punto y coma.

semifinal, *adj.* semifinal; —**s,** *n. pl.* semifinales, *m. pl.*

semimonthly, *adj.* quincenal; — **pay,** quincena, paga quincenal; —, *adv.* quincenalmente.

seminar, *n.* seminario, grupo de estudiantes dirigido por un profesor que hace estudios superiores.

seminary, *n.* seminario, *m.*

semitropical, *adj.* semitropical.

semiweekly, *adj.* bisemanal; —, *adv.* bisemanalmente.

semiyearly, *adj.* semestral; —, *adv.* semestralmente.

Sen.: Senate, senado; **Senator,** senador; **senior,** padre; socio más antiguo o más caracterizado.

senate, *n.* senado, *m.*

senator, *n.* senador, *m.*

senatorial, *adj.* senatorio, senatorial.

send, *vt.* enviar, despachar, mandar; producir; trasmitir.

sender, *n.* remitente, *m.* y *f.;* (elec.) trasmisor, *m.*

sending, *n.* trasmisión, *f.,* envío, *m.*

senile, *adj.* senil.

senior, *adj.* mayor; — **high school,** años superiores de una escuela secundaria; —, *n.* estudiante de cuarto año.

seniority, *n.* antigüedad, ancianidad, *f.*

sensation, *n.* sensación, *f.;* sentimiento, *m.*

sensational, *adj.* sensacional.

sense, *n.* sentido, *m.;* entendimiento, *m.;* razón, *f.;* juicio, *m.;* sentimiento, *m.;* sensatez, *f.;* **common** —, sentido práctico, sentido común; — **of sight,** ver, *m.,* vista, *f.;* — **organ,** órgano sensorio; —, *vt.* percibir; sentir.

senseless, *adj.* insensible; insensato.

sensibility, *n.* sensibilidad, *f.*

sensible, *adj.* sensato, juicioso.

sensitive, *adj.* sensible; sensitivo.

sensitize, *vt.* sensibilizar.

sensory, *adj.* sensorio.

sensual, *adj.* sensual.

sensuality, *n.* sensualidad, *f.*

sensuous, *adj.* sensorio, sensitivo; sensual.

sent, *pretérito* y *p.p.* del verbo **send.**

sentence, *n.* sentencia, frase, oración, *f.;* (leyes) sentencia, *f.;* —, *vt.* sentenciar, condenar.

sentiment, *n.* sentimiento, *m.;* opinión, *f.*

sentimental, *adj.* sentimental.

sentimentalist, *n.* sentimentalista, *m.* y *f.*

sentinel, *n.* centinela, *m.* y *f.*

sentry, *n.* centinela, *m.* y *f.*

separable, *adj.* separable.

separate, *vt.* separar; —, *vi.* separarse; —, *adj.* separado; **under** — **cover,** por separado; —**ly,** *adv.* separadamente.

separation, *n.* separación, *f.*

separator, *n.* abaleador, *m.;* **cream** —, desnatadora.

Sept.: September, Sept. septiembre.

September, *n.* septiembre o setiembre, *m.*

septic, *adj.* séptico; — **tank,** foso séptico.

sepulchre, *n.* sepulcro, *m.*

sequel, *n.* secuela, consecuencia, *f.;* continuación, *f.*

sequence, *n.* serie, continuación, *f.*

sequin, *n.* lentejuela, *f.*

sequoia, *n.* secoya, *f.*

seraph, *n.* serafín, *m.*

serenade, *n.* serenata, *f.;* (Mex.) gallo, *m.;* —, *vt.* llevar una serenata o un gallo (a alguien).

serene, *adj.* sereno, tranquilo; —**ly,** *adv.* serenamente.

serenity, *n.* serenidad, *f.*

serf, *n.* siervo, esclavo, *m.*

serge, *n.* sarga, *f.*

sergeant, *n.* sargento, *m.; alguacil, *m.*

serial, *adj.* que se publica en series; —, *n.* publicación en cuadernos periódicos; película cinematográfica de episodios.

series, *n.* serie, cadena, *f.*

serious, *adj.* serio, grave; **—ly,** *adv.* seriamente.

sermon, *n.* sermón, *m.*

sermonize, *vt.* y *vi.* sermonear; regañar; amonestar.

serous, *adj.* seroso.

serpent, *n.* serpiente, sierpe, *f.*

serpentine, *adj.* serpentino; —, *n.* (chem.) serpentina, *f.;* —, *vi.* serpentear.

serum, *n.* suero, *m.*

servant, *n.* criado, da; servidor, ra; sirviente, ta; paniaguado, *m.*

serve, *vt.* y *vi.* servir; asistir o servir (a la mesa); ser a propósito.

service, *n.* servicio, *m.; servidumbre, *f.;* utilidad, *f.;* culto divino; **at your —,** su servidor, ra, a sus órdenes; **day —,** servicio diurno; **night —,** servicio nocturno; **— station,** estación de gasolina; estación de servicios; taller de repuestos y reparaciones; **to be of —,** ser útil.

serviceable, *adj.* servible, útil; beneficioso, ventajoso.

servile, *adj.* servil; **—ly,** *adv.* servilmente.

servitude, *n.* servidumbre, esclavitud, *f.*

servomotor, *n.* servomotor, *m.*

sesame, *n.* (bot.) sésamo, *m.; **open —,** sésamo ábrete (frase mágica de contraseña).

session, *n.* junta, *f.;* sesión, *f.;* **joint —,** sesión plena.

set, *vt.* poner, colocar, fijar; establecer, determinar; basar; —, *vi.* ponerse (el sol o los astros); tramontar (el sol o los astros); cuajarse; aplicarse; **to — a diamond,** montar un diamante; **to — aside,** poner a un lado; **to — back,** hacer retroceder; **to — forward,** hacer adelantar; **to — on fire,** pegar fuego a; **to — the table,** poner la mesa; **to — up,** erigir; sentar; —, *n.* juego, *m.,* conjunto (de cartas), *m.;* servicio (de plata), *m.;* conjunto de varias cosas; colección, *f.;* cuadrilla, bandada, *f.;* **— of dishes,** vajilla, *f.;* —, *adj.* puesto, fijo.

setback, *n.* revés, *m.;* (arch.) voladizo, *m.*

setter, *n.* perro de ajeo.

setting, *n.* establecimiento, *m.;* colocación, *f.;* asentamiento, *m.;* fraguado, *m.;* montadura, *f.;* (theat.) escenario, decorado, *m.;* marco, *m.;* **— of the sun,** puesta del sol.

settle, *vt.* colocar, fijar, afirmar; componer; arreglar; calmar; solventar (deudas); —, *vi.* reposarse; establecerse; radicarse; sosegarse; **to — an account,** finiquitar, saldar, ajustar una cuenta.

settlement, *n.* establecimiento, *m.;* domicilio, *m.;* contrato, *m.;* arreglo, *m.;* liquidación, *f.;* empleo, *m.;* colonia, *f.*

settler, *n.* colono, *m.*

set-to, *n.* combate, *m.;* contienda, *f.*

setup, *n.* disposición, *f.;* arreglo, *m.;* organización, *f.*

seven, *n.* y *adj.* siete, *m.*

seventeen, *n.* y *adj.* diez y siete, diecisiete, *m.*

seventeenth, *n.* y *adj.* decimoséptimo, *m.*

seventh, *n.* y *adj.* séptimo, *m.;* **— heaven,** séptimo cielo, éxtasis, *m.*

seventy, *n.* y *adj.* setenta, *m.*

sever, *vt.* y *vi.* separar, dividir; cortar; desligar; **to — connections,** romper las relaciones; apartarse.

several, *adj.* diversos, varios.

severance, *n.* separación, *f.;* **— pay,** compensación de despido (de un empleado, etc.).

severe, *adj.* severo, riguroso; serio; áspero; duro, cruel; **—ly,** *adv.* severamente.

severity, *n.* severidad, *f.*

sew, *vt.* y *vi.* coser.

sewage, *n.* inmundicias, *f. pl.;* **— system,** alcantarillado, *m.*

sewer, *n.* albañal, *m.;* cloaca, *f.;* caño, *m.*

sewing, *n.* costura, *f.;* **— machine,** máquina de coser.

sex, *n.* sexo, *m.*

sexton, *n.* sacristán, *m.;* sepulturero, *m.*

sexual, *adj.* sexual.

Sgt.: Sergeant, Sar. Sargento.

shabbiness, *n.* miseria, pobreza, *f.;* vileza, bajeza, *f.*

shabby, *adj.* vil, bajo; desharrapado; destartalado; miserable.

shack, *n.* choza, cabaña, *f.;* (coll.) casa en mal estado.

shackle, *vt.* encadenar; **—s,** *n. pl.* grillos, *m. pl.*

shad, *n.* (ichth.) alosa, *f.,* sábalo, *m.*

shade, *n.* sombra, oscuridad, *f.;* matiz, *m.;* sombrilla, *f.;* umbría, *f.;* —, *vt.* dar sombra; matizar; esconder.

shadow, *n.* sombra, *f.;* protección, *f.;* —, *vt.* sombrear.

shadowboxing, *n.* acto de pelear o boxear con un adversario imaginario.

shadowy, *adj.* umbroso; oscuro; quimérico.

shady, *adj.* con sombra, sombrío, umbroso; **— character,** individuo sospechoso.

shaft, *n.* flecha, saeta, *f.;* fuste de columna; pozo de una mina; cañón de chimenea.

shaggy, adj. afelpado; peludo; desaliñado; áspero.

shake, vt. sacudir; agitar; —, vi. temblar; **to — hands,** darse las manos; —, n. concusión, sacudida, f.; vibración f.

shakedown, n. cama improvisada; (coll.) demanda de dinero por compulsión.

shaker, n. agitador, m.; estremecedor, m.; **cocktail —,** coctelera, f.; **salt —,** salero, m.

shake-up, n. agitación, f.; reorganización, f.

shaking, n. sacudimiento, m.; temblor, m.

shaky, adj. titubeante, tembloroso; inestable; (coll.) dudoso, sospechoso.

shall, vi. verbo auxiliar para indicar el futuro en la primera persona del singular y del plural, o el imperativo en las demás personas, por ej., **I — eat,** comeré; **we — eat,** comeremos; **he — eat,** comerá de todos modos, tendrá que comer, etc.

shallow, adj. somero; poco profundo; —, n. bajío (banco de arena), m.

sham, vt. engañar, chasquear; —, n. socolor, m.; fingimiento, m.; impostura, f.; —, adj. fingido, disimulado; **— battle,** simulacro de batalla.

shambles, n. pl. carnicería, f.; (fig.) escena de destrucción.

shame, n. vergüenza, f.; deshonra; **what a —!** ¡qué pena! ¡qué lástima! —, vt. avergonzar, deshonrar.

shamefaced, adj. vergonzoso, pudoroso.

shameful, adj. vergonzoso; deshonroso; **— ly,** adv. ignominiosamente.

shameless, adj. desvergonzado.

shampoo, vt. dar champú, lavar la cabeza; —, n. champú, m.

shamrock, n. trébol, trifolio, m.

shank, n. pierna, f.; asta, f.; asta de ancla.

shantung, n. variedad de tela de seda en rama.

shanty, n. cabaña f.

shape, vt. y vi. formar; concebir; configurar; dar forma; adaptar; —, n. forma, figura, f.; modelo, m.

shapeless, adj. informe, sin forma.

shapely, adj. bien hecho, bien formado; **— figure,** buen cuerpo.

share, n. parte, porción, cuota, f.; (com.) acción, f.; reja del arado; participación, f.; —, vt. y vi. repartir, participar; compartir.

sharecropper, n. mediero, inquilino, m.

shareholder, n. (com.) accionista, m. y f.

shark, n. tiburón, m.; petardista, m.

sharkskin, n. tela en su mayor parte de algodón, con hilos de varias hebras finas y apariencia sedosa.

sharp, adj. agudo, aguzado; astuto; perspicaz, sagaz; penetrante; picante, acre, mordaz, severo, rígido; vivo, violento; **— bend,** curva cerrada; —, n. (mus.) sostenido, m.; **two o'clock —,** las dos en punto; **—ly,** adv. con filo; ingeniosamente; ásperamente.

sharpen, vt. afilar, aguzar.

sharpener, n. aguzador, afilador, amolador, m.; máquina de afilar; **pencil —,** tajalápices, sacapuntas, m.

sharper, n. petardista, estafador, m.

sharpness, n. agudeza, f.; sutileza, perspicacia, f.; acrimonia, f.

sharpshooter, n. buen tirador; soldado elegido por su buena puntería.

shatter, vt. destrozar, estrellar; —, vi. hacerse pedazos; —, n. pedazo, fragmento, m.

shatterproof, adj. inastillable.

shave, vt. rasurar, afeitar; raspar; rozar; (fig.) escatimar; —, n. afeitada, f.; (coll.) escape, m.

shaver, n. barbero, m.; usurero, m.; (coll.) muchacho, chico, m.; **electric —,** rasuradora eléctrica.

shaving, n. raedura, acepilladura, f.; rasurada, afeitada, f.; **— cream,** crema de afeitar; **—s,** pl. virutas, f. pl.

shawl, n. chal, mantón, m.

she, pron. ella.

sheaf, n. gavilla, f.; —, vt. agavillar.

shear, vt. atusar; tundir; tonsurar; **—s,** n. pl. tijeras grandes; cizalla, f.

sheath, n. vaina, funda, f.; vestido recto y ajustado; —, vt. envainar; (naut.) aforrar el fondo de un navío.

sheave, n. rueda de polea, roldana, f.; **—s,** n. pl. de **sheaf.**

shed, vt. verter, derramar; esparcir; —, n. sotechado, tejadillo, m.; cabaña, barraca, f.; cobertizo, m.; techo, m.; choza, f.

sheen, n. resplandor, m.; brillo, m.

sheep, n. sing. y pl. oveja(s), f., carnero, m.; criatura indefensa y tímida; (coll.) papanatas, m.

sheepish, adj. vergonzoso; tímido; cortado.

sheepskin, n. piel de carnero; (fig.) diploma, m.

sheer, adj. puro, claro, sin mezcla; delgado, trasparente; —, adv. de un solo golpe; completamente; —, vi. desviarse.

sheet, n. pliego de papel; (naut.) escota, f.; **bed —,** sábana, f.; **blank —,** hoja en blanco; **— anchor,** áncora mayor de un navío; **— glass,** vidrio en lámina; **— iron,** plancha de hierro batido; **— light-**

ning, relampagueo a manera de fucila-
zos; — **metal,** hoja metálica; metal en
hojas, palastro, *m.,* lámina, *f.;* —
music, música publicada en hojas
sueltas; — **(of paper),** — **(of metal),**
hoja, *f.;* —, *vt.* ensabanar; extender en
láminas.

sheeting, *n.* tela para sábanas; encofrado, *m.*

shelf, *n.* anaquel, estante, *m.;* (naut.)
arrecife, *m.;* escollera, *f.;* **corner** —, rinconera, *f.;* **on the** —, (coll.) desechado,
archivado.

shell, *n.* cáscara, *f.;* concha, *f.;* corteza, *f.;*
bomba, *f.;* cartucho, *m.;* granada, *f.;*
carapacho, *m.;* **cartridge** —, cápsula, *f.;*
— **room,** (naut.) pañol de granadas;
tortoise —, carey, *m.;* —, *vt.* descascarar, descortezar; bombardear; —, *vi.*
descascararse.

shellac, *n.* goma laca; —, *vt.* cubrir con
laca.

shellfire, *n.* fuego de bomba o metralla.

shellfish, *n.* marisco, *m.*

shellproof, *adj.* a prueba de bombas.

shelter, *n.* guarida, *f.;* amparo, abrigo, *m.;*
asilo, refugio, *m.;* cubierta, *f.;* —, *vt.*
guarecer, abrigar; acoger.

shelve, *vt.* echar a un lado, arrinconar;
desechar.

shelves, *n. pl.* de **shelf.**

shelving, *n.* estantería, *f.;* material para
anaqueles.

shepherd, *n.* pastor, *m.;* —, *vt.* pastorear.

shepherdess, *n.* pastora, ovejera, *f.*

sherbet, *n.* sorbete, *m.*

sheriff, *n.* alguacil, *m.,* funcionario administrativo de un condado.

sherry, *n.* jerez, vino de Jerez.

shield, *n.* escudo, *m.;* patrocinio, *m.;* —,
vt. defender; amparar.

shift, *vi.* cambiarse; moverse; trasladarse;
ingeniarse; trampear; —, *vt.* mudar;
cambiar; trasportar; —, *n.* último
recurso; (mech.) cambio de marcha;
tanda, *f.;* conmutación, *f.;* artificio, *m.;*
astucia, *f.;* efugio, *m.*

shiftless, *adj.* perezoso; negligente; descuidado.

shilling, *n.* chelín, *m.*

shimmer, *vi.* brillar tenuemente; —, *n.* luz
trémula.

shin, *n.* espinilla, *f.*

shinbone, *n.* tibia, espinilla, *f.*

shine, *vi.* lucir, brillar, resplandecer;
—, *vt.* dar lustre (a los zapatos, etc.),
embolar; —, *n.* brillo, *m.;* resplandor, *m.*

shingle, *n.* ripia, *f.;* tejamaní, tejamanil,
m.; muestra, *f.,* letrero en un bufete (de

un médico, un abogado, etc.); —, *vt.*
cubrir (un techo, etc.) con ripias; tras-
quilar; cinglar.

shingles, *n.* (med.) herpes, *m.* o *f. pl.*

shining, *adj.* resplandeciente, luciente,
reluciente.

shiny, *adj.* brillante, luciente.

ship, *n.* nave, *f.;* bajel, navio, barco, *m.;*
merchant —, buque mercante; **repair**
—, buque taller; **scouting** —, buque
explorador; —**'s captain,** capitán,
patrón, *m.;* —**'s papers,** documentación
de a bordo; —, *vt.* embarcar; expedir.

shipboard, *n.* barco, *m.;* **on** —, a bordo.

shipbuilding, *n.* arquitectura naval, construcción de buques.

shipmate, *n.* (naut.) ayudante, *m.;* compañero de camarote.

shipment, *n.* cargazón, expedición, *f.;* cargamento, *m.;* envio, despacho, embar-
que, *m.,* remesa, *f.*

shipowner, *n.* naviero, *m.*

shipper, *n.* expedidor, remitente, *m.;*
(com.) embarcador, *m.*

shipping, *n.* navegación, *f ;* marina, flota,
f.; expedición, *f.;* embarque, *m.;* —
clerk, dependiente encargado de
embarques y remisiones; — **company,**
compañía naviera; — **expenses,** gastos
de expedición; — **room,** departamento
de embarques; —, *adj.* naviero.

shipwreck, *n.* naufragio, *m.*

shipwrecked, *adj.* náufrago; — **person,**
náufrago, ga.

shipyard, *n.* varadero, astillero, *m.*

shirk, *vt.* esquivar, evitar; —, *n.* persona
que elude o se esquiva de hacer algo.

shirr, *vt.* (costura) fruncir; (cocina) escalfar; —**ed eggs,** huevos escalfados.

shirt, *n.* camisa de hombre; — **store,**
camisería, *f ;* **sport** —, camisa sport.

shiver, *n.* cacho, pedazo, fragmento, *m.;*
estremecimiento, *m.;* —, *vi.* tiritar de
miedo o frío; —, *vt.* romper, estrellar.

shivering, *n.* temblor, estremecimiento, *m.*

shoal, *n.* multitud, *f.;* bajío, *m.;* (naut.)
vigía, *f.;* — **of fish,** manada de peces;
—, *adj.* bajo, vadoso; —, *vi.* perder profundidad gradualmente.

shock, *n.* choque, encuentro, *m.;* concusión, *f.;* combate, *m.;* ofensa, *f.;* hacina,
f.; — **absorber,** amortiguador, *m.;* —
troops, tropas escogidas, tropas ofensi-
vas o de asalto; — **wave,** onda de choque; —, *vt.* sacudir, ofender.

shocking, *adj.* espantoso, horroroso,
horrible, ofensivo, chocante; — **pink,**
color rosa subido.

shockproof, *adj.* a prueba de choques.

shoddy, *adj.* cursi.

shoe, *n.* zapato, *m.;* herradura de caballo; **old —,** chancla, *f.;* **rubber —,** chanclo, *m.,* zapato de goma; **— polish,** grasa para calzado, betún, *m.;* **— store,** zapatería, *f.;* **— tree,** horma de zapatos; **to put on one's —s,** calzarse; **—,** *vt.* calzar; herrar un caballo.

shoeblack, *n.* limpiabotas, *m.*

shoehorn, *n.* calzador, *m.*

shoelace, *n.* cordón de zapato, agujeta, *f.*

shoemaker, *n.* zapatero, *m.*

shoestring = **shoelace.**

shone, *pretérito y p.p. del verbo* **shine.**

shoot, *vt.* tirar, disparar; arrojar, lanzar; fusilar; matar o herir con escopeta; **to —at a target,** tirar al blanco; **—,** *vi.* brotar, germinar; sobresalir; lanzarse; **—,** *n.* tiro, *m.;* brote, vástago, retoño, tallo, *m.*

shop, *n.* tienda, *f.;* taller, *m.;* **in the —s,** en el comercio, en las tiendas; **pastry —,** repostería, *f.;* **confectionery —,** dulcería, *f.;* **beauty —,** salón de belleza; **—,** *vi.* hacer compras, ir de compras.

shopkeeper, *n.* tendero, ra; mercader, *m.*

shoplifter, *n.* ratero, *m.*

shopper, *n.* comprador, ra.

shopping, *n.* compras, *f. pl.;* **to go —,** ir de compras.

shopwindow, *n.* vidriera, vitrina, *f.;* aparador, *m.*

shore, *n.* costa, ribera, playa, orilla, *f.;* **— leave,** (naut.) permiso para ir a tierra; **—line,** ribera, costa, *f.*

short, *adj.* corto; breve, sucinto, conciso; brusco; **in a — while,** dentro de poco, al poco rato; **— circuit,** (elec.) cortocircuito, *m.;* **— cut,** atajo, *m.,* camino corto; medio rápido; **to —circuit,** causar un cortocircuito; **— sale,** promesa de venta de valores u otros bienes que no se poseen, pero cuya adquisición se espera pronto; **— wave,** onda corta; **on — notice,** con poco tiempo de aviso; **—,** *n.* cortocircuito, *m.;* **in —,** en resumen, en concreto, en definitiva; **—ly,** *adv.* brevemente; presto; en pocas palabras; dentro de poco.

shortage, *n.* escasez, falta, *f.;* merma, *f.;* déficit, *m.*

shortcake, *n.* variedad de torta o pastel.

shorten, *vt.* acortar; abreviar.

shortening, *n.* acortamiento, *m.;* disminución, *f.;* manteca, mantequilla o grasa vegetal usada para pastelería.

shorthand, *n.* taquigrafía, estenografía, *f.*

short-lived, *adj.* de breve vida o duración.

shorts, *n. pl.* calzones cortos; calzoncillos, *m. pl.;* pantalones cortos de mujer.

shortsighted, *adj.* corto de vista, miope.

shortstop, *n.* (béisbol) campo corto.

short-term, *adj.* a corto plazo.

shot, *n.* tiro, *m.;* alcance, *m.;* (coll.) inyección hipodérmica; (coll.) trago de licor; **bird —,** perdigones, *m. pl.;* **—,** *pret. y p.p. del verbo* **shoot.**

shotgun, *n.* escopeta, *f.*

should, *condicional de* **shall** (úsase como auxiliar de otros verbos).

shoulder, *n.* hombro, *m.;* **round —ed,** cargado de espaldas; **— blade,** omóplato, *m.;* **—,** *vt.* cargar al hombro; soportar.

shout, *vi.* dar vivas, aclamar; reprobar con gritos; gritar; **—,** *n.* aclamación, *f.,* grito, *m.*

shove, *vt. y vi.* empujar; impeler; **—,** *n.* empujón, *m.*

shovel, *n.* pala, *f.;* **fire —,** paleta, *f.;* **—,** *vt.* traspalar.

show, *vt.* mostrar, enseñar, explicar, hacer ver; descubrir, manifestar; probar; **—,** *vi.* parecer; **to — off,** lucirse; **to — oneself superior to,** sobreponerse a; **—,** *n.* espectáculo, *m.;* muestra, *f.;* exposición, *f.;* (theat.) función, *f.;* **— bill,** cartelón, cartel, *m.;* **— boat,** buque-teatro, *m.;* **— card,** rótulo, cartel, letrero, *m.*

showcase, *n.* escaparate, mostrador, *m.,* vitrina, *f.*

showdown, *n.* revelación franca de hechos, recursos, etc.

shower, *n.* aguacero, chubasco, *m.;* llovizna, *f.;* fiesta de regalos (para una novia, etc.); (fig.) abundancia, *f.;* **— bath,** baño de ducha o de regadera; **—,** *vi.* llover; **—,** *vt.* derramar profusamente.

showman, *n.* empresario, director de espectáculos públicos; (fig.) buen actor.

showmanship, *n.* habilidad para presentar espectáculos.

shown, *p.p. del verbo* **show.**

showroom, *n.* sala de muestras; sala de exhibición de modelos.

showy, *adj.* ostentoso, suntuoso; vistoso, llamativo, chillón.

shrank, *pretérito del verbo* **shrink.**

shrapnel, *n.* granada de metralla.

shred, *n.* cacho, *m.,* pedazo pequeño; triza, *f.;* jirón, *m.;* **—,** *vt.* picar, hacer trizas; rallar.

shrew, *n.* mujer de mal genio; (zool.) musgaño, *m.*

shrewd, *adj.* astuto, sagaz; mordaz.

shrewdness, *n.* astucia, *f.;* sagacidad, *f.*

shriek, *vi.* chillar; **—,** *n.* chillido, *m.*

shrill, *adj.* agudo, penetrante, chillón.

shrimp, *n.* camarón, *m.;* hombrecillo, *m.*

shrine, n. relicario, m.; tumba de santo; (eccl.) trono, m.

shrink, vi. encoger (una tela); encogerse, rehuir; —, vt. contraer, encoger.

shrinkage, n. contracción, f.; encogimiento, m.

shrivel, vt. y vi. arrugar, arrugarse, encogerse.

shroud, n. cubierta, f ; mortaja, f.; sudario, m.; —s, n. pl. (naut.) obenques,m. pl.; —, vt. cubrir, esconder; amortajar.

shrub, n. arbusto, m.

shrubbery, n. arbustos, m. pl.

shrug, vi. encogerse de hombros; —, n. encogimiento de hombros.

shrunk, p.p. del verbo **shrink.**

shuck, n. cáscara, f.; —, vt. descascar, descascarar, desgranar.

shudder, vi. estremecerse, despeluzarse; —, n. despeluzamiento, temblor, estremecimiento, m.

shuffle, vt. y vi. poner en confusión, desordenar; barajar los naipes; trampear; tergiversar; arrastrar (los pies); —, n. barajadura, f.; treta, f.

shuffling, n. tramoya, f.; acción de arrastrar (los pies).

shun, vt. huir, evitar.

shut, vt. cerrar, encerrar.

shutdown, n. paro, m.; cesación de trabajo.

shut-in, n. persona confinada en su casa o en hospital por enfermedad.

shutter, n. persiana, celosia, f.; obturador de aparato fotográfico.

shuttle, n. lanzadera, f.

shy, adj. tímido; reservado; vergonzoso; contenido; pudoroso.

shyness, n. timidez, f.

Siamese, n. y adj. siamés, esa.

sick, adj. malo, enfermo; disgustado, aburrido.

sicken, vt. y vi. enfermar, enfermarse.

sickening, adj. repugnante, asqueroso, nauseabundo.

sickle, n. hoz, segadera, f.

sickly, adj. enfermizo, malsano.

sickness, n. enfermedad, f.

side, n. lado, m.; costado, m.; facción, f.; partido, m.; — **arms,** armas llevadas al cinto; — **dish,** platillo, entremés, m.; — **light,** luz lateral; información incidental; — **line,** negocio o actividad accesorios; — **show,** función o diversión secundaria; —, adj. lateral, oblicuo; — **by** —, juntos; —, vi. apoyar la opinión (de alguien), declararse a favor (de alguien o algún partido).

sideboard, n. aparador, m.

sideburns, n. patillas, f. pl.

sidecar, n. carro lateral.

sidelong, adj. lateral; —, adv. lateralmente; oblicuamente.

side-step, vt. evitar; —, vi. hacerse a un lado.

sidetrack, vt. (rail.) desviar a un apartadero; arrinconar; apartarse de.

sidewalk, n. banqueta, acera, vereda, f.

sideways, adv. de lado, al través.

siding, n. cobertura exterior de una casa de madera; (rail.) apartadero, desviadero, m.

sidle, vi. ir de lado.

siege, n. (mil.) sitio, m.

sierra, n. sierra, cadena de montañas.

siesta, n. siesta, f.

sieve, n. tamiz, cedazo; m.; colador, m.

sift, vt. cerner, cernir; cribar; examinar; investigar.

sigh, vi. suspirar, gemir; —, n. suspiro, m.

sight, n. vista, mira, f.; perspectiva, f.; mamarracho, espantajo, m.; **at first** —, a primera vista; **at** —, a presentación; **gun** —, punto (de escopeta), m.; **on** —, a la vista; **sense of** —, ver, m., sentido de la vista; — **draft,** letra o giro a la vista.

sightless, adj. ciego.

sightly, adj. vistoso, hermoso.

sight-seer, n. excursionista, m. y f.

sight-seeing, n. paseo, m.; excursión, f.

sign, n. señal, f.; indicio, m.; tablilla, f.; signo, m.; firma, f.; seña, f.; letrero, m.; marca, f.; rótulo, m.; —, vt. y vi. señalar, hacer señas; suscribir, firmar.

signal, n. señal, seña, f.; aviso, m.; —, adj. insigne, señalado; — **light,** (rail.) farol (de mano o de disco), m.; (naut.) fanal, faro, m.; — **man,** (rail.) guardavía, m.; — **mast,** semáforo, m., mástil de señales.

signature, n. firma, f.; seña, f.; signatura, f.

signboard, n. tablero de anuncios.

signet, n. sello, m.

significance, n. importancia, significación, f.

significant, adj. significativo, importante.

signify, vt. significar; —, vi. importar.

sign language, n. lenguaje de señales.

signpost, n. hito, m.; pilar de anuncios.

silence, n. silencio, m.; —, vt. imponer silencio, hacer callar.

silencer, n. silenciador, apagador, m.; (Mex.) mofle, m.

silent, adj. silencioso; callado; mudo; — **partner,** socio comanditario.

silhouette, n. silueta, f.

silica, n. (chem.) sílice, f.

silk, *n.* seda, *f.*
silken, *adj.* de seda, sedeño.
silkiness, *n.* suavidad de seda.
silkworm, *n.* gusano de seda.
silky, *adj.* hecho de seda; sedeño, sedoso.
sill, *n.* umbral de puerta; **window —,** repisa de ventana.
silliness, *n.* simpleza, bobería, tontería, necedad, *f.*
silly, *adj.* tonto, mentecato, imbécil, bobo.
silo, *n.* silo, *m.;* (mil.) plataforma de lanzamiento.
silt, *n.* cieno, limo, légamo, *m.*
silver, *n.* plata, *f.;* —, *adj.* de plata; — **dollar,** peso fuerte; — **fox,** zorro plateado; piel de zorro plateado; — **nitrate,** nitrato de plata; — **screen,** pantalla cinematográfica; — **wedding,** bodas de plata; **to — plate,** platear.
silversmith, *n.* platero, *m.*
silverware, *n.* cuchillería de plata; vajilla de plata.
silvery, *adj.* plateado.
similar, *adj.* similar; semejante; **—ly,** *adv.* en forma similar.
similarity, *n.* semejanza, *f.*
simile, *n.* semejanza, similitud, *f.;* símil, *m.*
simmer, *vi.* hervir a fuego lento.
simper, *vi.* sonreir tontamente; —, *n.* sonrisilla tonta.
simple, *adj.* simple, puro, sencillo.
simple-minded, *adj.* imbécil, idiota.
simpleton, *n.* simplón, ona, mentecato, ta, pazguato, ta, zonzo, za.
simplicity, *n.* simplicidad, *f.;* simpleza, llaneza, *f.*
simplify, *vt.* simplificar.
simply, *adv.* simplemente.
simulate, *vt.* simular, fingir.
simultaneous, *adj.* simultáneo, sincrónico.
sin, *n.* pecado, *m.;* culpa, *f.;* —, *vi.* pecar, faltar.
since, *adv.* desde entonces; —, *conj.* ya que, pues que, pues, puesto que; —, *prep.* desde, después de.
sincere, *adj.* sencillo; sincero, franco; — **ly,** *adv.* sinceramente; **—ly yours,** (despedida de una carta) su seguro servidor, de usted muy sinceramente, etc.
sincerity, *n.* sinceridad, *f.;* llaneza, *f.*
sinew, *n.* tendón, *m.;* nervio, *m.*
sinewy, *adj.* nervudo, robusto.
sinful, *adj.* pecaminoso, malvado.
sing, *vt.* y *vi.* cantar; gorjear (los pájaros).
singe, *vt.* chamuscar, socarrar.
singer, *n.* cantor, *m.;* cantora, *f.;* cantante, *m.* y *f.*
singing, *n.* canto, *m.,* acción de cantar.

single, *adj.* sencillo, simple, solo; soltero, soltera; — **file,** fila india; uno tras otro; — **man,** soltero, *m.;* — **woman,** soltera, *f.;* —, *vt.* singularizar; separar.
single-breasted, *adj.* de botonadura sencilla (chaqueta u otra prenda similar).
single-handed, *adj.* sin ayuda.
single-minded, *adj.* cándido, sencillo; con un solo propósito.
singleness, *n.* sencillez, sinceridad, *f.;* celibato, *m.,* soltería, *f.*
single-track, *adj.* de una sola vía, de un solo carril; — **mind,** mentalidad estrecha.
singly, *adv.* separadamente.
singsong, *n.* sonsonete, *m.;* tonadita, *f.*
singular, *adj.* singular, peculiar; (gram.) singular.
sinister, *adj.* siniestro; hacia la izquierda; viciado; infeliz, funesto.
sink, *vi.* hundirse; sumergirse; bajarse; penetrar; arruinarse, decaer, sucumbir; —, *vt.* hundir, echar a lo hondo; echar a pique; sumergir; deprimir, destruir; —, *n.* fregadero, *m.*
sinker, *n.* plomada, *f.*
sinking fund, *n.* caja de amortización.
sinner, *n.* pecador, ora.
sinus, *n.* seno, *m.,* cavidad, *f.;* seno frontal.
sip, *vt.* y *vi.* tomar a sorbos, sorber; —, *n.* sorbo, *m.*
siphon, *n.* sifón, *m.;* — **bottle,** sifón, *m.,* botella de sifón.
sir, *n.* señor, *m.;* **dear —,** muy señor mío, muy señor nuestro.
sire, *n.* caballero, *m.;* (poet.) padre, *m.*
siren, *n.* sirena, *f.*
sirloin, *n.* lomo de buey o vaca, solomillo, *m.*
sirup, syrup, *n.* jarabe, *m.*
sissy, *n.* marica, *m.,* varón de modales afeminados.
sister, *n.* hermana, *f.;* religiosa, *f.*
sisterhood, *n.* hermandad, *f.*
sister-in-law, *n.* cuñada, *f.*
sisterly, *adj.* como hermana.
sit, *vi.* sentarse; estar situado.
sit-down strike, *n.* huelga de brazos caídos.
site, *n.* sitio, *m.;* situación, *f.;* emplazamiento, *m.;* localización.
sitting, *n.* sesión, junta, *f.;* sentada, *f.;* postura ante un pintor para un retrato; — **room,** sala, *f.*
situate, *vt.* colocar, situar.
situation, *n.* situación, *f.;* ubicación, *f.*
six, *n.* y *adj.* seis.
sixpence, *n.* seis peniques (medio chelín).
sixshooter, *n.* revólver de seis cámaras.

sixteen, *n.* y *adj.* dieciséis, diez y seis, *m.*

sixteenth, *n.* y *adj.* decimosexto, *m.*

sixth, *n.* y *adj.* sexto, *m.;* — **sense,** sexto sentido, sentido intuitivo; —**ly,** *adv.* en sexto lugar.

sixty, *n.* y *adj.* sesenta, *m.*

size, *n.* tamaño, talle, *m.;* calibre, *m.;* dimensión, *f.;* estatura, *f.;* condición, *f.;* variedad de cola o goma; —, *vt.* encolar; ajustar, calibrar.

sized, *adj.* de tamaño especial; preparado con una especie de cola o goma.

sizzle, *vi.* chamuscar, sisear; —, *n.* siseo, *m.*

skate, *n.* patín, *m.;* **ice** —, patín de hielo; **roller** —, patín de ruedas; —, *vi.* patinar.

skater, *n.* patinador, ra.

skating, *n.* acto de patinar; — **rink,** patinadero, *m.,* pista para patinar.

skein, *n.* madeja, *f.*

skeleton, *n.* esqueleto, *m.;* — **key,** llave maestra.

skeptic, *n.* y *adj.* escéptico, ca.

skeptical, *adj.* escéptico.

sketch, *n.* esbozo, *m.;* esquicio, *m.;* bosquejo, *m.;* boceto, *m.;* esquema, *m.;* croquis, *m.;* —, *vt.* bosquejar, esbozar.

skewer, *n.* aguja de lardear; espetón, *m.;* —, *vt.* espetar.

ski, *n.* esquí, *m.;* — **jump,** salto en esquíes; pista para esquiar; —, *vi.* patinar con esquíes.

skid, *n.* patinaje (de un auto), *m.;* calza o cuña (para detener una rueda), *f.;* —, *vi.* patinar, resbalarse.

skidding, *n.* patinaje, *m.*

skiff, *n.* esquife, *m.*

skill, *n.* destreza, pericia, *f.,* ingenio, *m.;* maestría, maña, *f.*

skilled, *adj.* práctico, instruido, versado, diestro.

skillet, *n.* cazuela, sartén, *f.*

skillful, skilful, *adj.* práctico, diestro, perito; mañoso; —**ly,** *adv.* diestramente.

skim, *vt.* espumar; tratar superficialmente; —, *n.* espuma, *f.*

skimp, *vt.* y *vi.* (coll.) ser parco; escatimar.

skimpy, *adj.* tacaño, miserable; corto, escaso.

skin, *n.* cutis, *m.;* cuero, *m.;* piel, *f.;* —, *vt.* desollar; (coll.) robarle dinero (a alguien).

skin-deep, *adj.* superficial, sin sustancia.

skinned, *adj.* desollado.

skinny, *adj.* flaco, macilento.

skin-tight, *adj.* ajustado al cuerpo.

skip, *vi.* saltar, brincar; —, *vt.* pasar,

omitir; —, *n.* salto, brinco, *m.*

skipper, *n.* capitán de una embarcación pequeña.

skirmish, *n.* escaramuza, *f.;* tiroteo, *m.;* —, *vi.* escaramuzar.

skirt, *n.* falda, enagua, pollera, *f.;* —, *vt.* orillar.

skit, *n.* burla, zumba, *f.;* pasquín, *m.;* sainete, *m.,* piececita cómica o dramática.

skittish, *adj.* espantadizo, retozón; caprichoso; frívolo; —**ly,** *adv.* caprichosamente.

skulk, *vi.* espiar a hurtadillas, acechar furtivamente; esconderse.

skull, *n.* cráneo, *m.;* calavera, *f.*

skullcap, *n.* gorro, *m.;* casquete, *m.*

skunk, *n.* zorrillo, zorrino, *m.;* persona despreciable.

sky, *n.* cielo, firmamento, *m.;* — **blue,** azul celeste.

sky-high, *adj.* muy alto, por las nubes.

skylark, *n.* (zool.) alondra, *f.;* —, *vi.* bromear, retozar.

skylight, *n.* claraboya, *f.*

skyline, *n.* horizonte, *m.;* perspectiva de una ciudad.

skyrocket, *n.* cohete volador; —, *vi.* elevarse súbitamente, por ej., los precios.

skyscraper, *n.* rascacielos, *m.*

slab, *n.* losa, *f.;* plancha, *f.;* tablilla, *f.*

slabber, *vi.* babear; —, *vt.* babosear.

slack, *adj.* flojo, perezoso, negligente; lento; —**s,** *n. pl.* pantalones bombachos.

slack, slacken, *vt.* y *vi.* aflojar; ablandar; entibiarse; decaer; relajar; aliviar.

slacker, *n.* cobarde, *m.* y *f.;* hombre que elude sus deberes militares en tiempo de guerra.

slag, *n.* escoria, *f.*

slake, *vt.* extinguir, apagar.

slam, *n.* capote (en los juegos de naipes), *m.;* portazo, *m.;* —, *vt.* dar capote; empujar con violencia.

slander, *vt.* calumniar, infamar; —, *n.* calumnia, *f.*

slanderer, *n.* calumniador, ra, maldiciente, *m.* y *f.*

slang, *n.* vulgarismo, *m.;* jerga, *f.*

slant, *vi.* inclinarse, pender oblicuamente; —, *vt.* sesgar, inclinar.

slanting, *adj.* sesgado, oblicuo, terciado.

slap, *n.* manotada, *f.;* — **on the face,** bofetada, *f.;* —, *adv.* de sopetón; —, *vt.* golpear, dar una bofetada.

slapstick, *n.* farsa con actividad física rápida y violenta y en la que abundan los porrazos.

slash, *vt.* acuchillar; —, *n.* cuchillada, *f.*

slat, *n.* tablilla, *f.*

slate, *n.* pizarra, *f.;* —, *vt.* empizarrar; golpear; castigar; criticar severamente.

slaughter, *n.* carnicería, matanza, *f.;* —, *vt.* matar atrozmente; matar en la carnicería.

slaughterhouse, *n.* rastro, matadero, degolladero, *m.*

slave, *n.* esclavo, va; —, *vi.* trabajar como esclavo.

slavery, *n.* esclavitud, *f.;* **white** —, trata de blancas.

slaw, *n.* ensalada de col.

slay, *vt.* matar, quitar la vida.

slayer, *n.* asesino, na.

sled, sledge, sleigh, *n.* rastra, narria, *f.;* trineo, *m.*

sledge, *n.* rastra, *f.;* — **hammer,** macho, acotillo, *m.,* martillo pesado.

sleek, *adj.* liso, bruñido; —, *vt.* alisar, pulir.

sleep, *vi.* dormir; **to** — **soundly,** dormir profundamente, dormir como un bendito; —, *n.* sueño, *m.*

sleeper, *n.* persona que duerme, zángano, *m.;* durmiente, *m.;* (rail.) coche dormitorio; éxito inesperado de librería; película insignificante que resulta un éxito pecuniario.

sleepily, *adv.* con somnolencia o torpeza, con sueño.

sleepiness, *n.* adormecimiento, *m.;* **to cause** —, adormecer.

sleeping, *n.* sueño, *m.;* — **bag,** talego para dormir a la intemperie; — **car,** coche dormitorio, vagón cama; — **room,** dormitorio, *m.;* — **sickness,** encefalitis letárgica.

sleepless, *adj.* desvelado, sin dormir; **to spend a** — **night,** pasar la noche en blanco.

sleepwalker, *n.* sonámbulo, la.

sleepwalking, *n.* sonambulismo, *m.*

sleepy, *adj.* soñoliento; **to be** —, tener sueño.

sleepyhead, *n.* dormilón, ona.

sleet, *n.* aguanieve, *f.;* —, *vi.* caer aguanieve.

sleeve, *n.* manga, *f.*

sleeveless, *adj.* sin mangas.

sleigh, *n.* trineo, *m.;* — **bell,** cascabel, *m.*

slender, *adj.* delgado, sutil, débil, pequeño; escaso; —**ly,** *adv.* delgadamente.

sleuth, *n.* detective, *m.*

slice, *n.* rebanada, lonja, *f.;* espátula, *f.;* (golf) contragancho, *m.;* —, *vt.* rebanar.

slicing, *adj.* rebanador; — **machine,** máquina cortadora o rebanadora.

slick, *adj.* liso; lustroso; —, *vt.* hacer liso o lustroso.

slicker, *n.* impermeable, *m.;* trampista,

petardista, *m.*

slide, *vi.* resbalar, deslizarse; —, *n.* resbalón, *m.;* resbaladero, *m.;* corredera, *f.;* **lantern** —, diapositiva, *f.;* — **rule,** regla de cálculo; — **valve,** válvula corrediza.

sliding, *adj.* deslizante, corredizo, deslizable; — **door,** puerta corrediza.

slight, *adj.* ligero, leve, pequeño; —, descuido, *m.;* —, *vt.* despreciar.

slightness, *n.* debilidad, *f.;* pequeñez, *f.*

slim, *adj.* delgado, sutil.

slime, *n.* lodo, *m.;* sustancia viscosa; pecina, *f.*

slimness, *n.* delgadez, *f.;* sutileza, tenuidad, *f.*

slimy, *adj.* viscoso, pegajoso.

sling, *n.* honda, *f.;* hondazo, cabestrillo, *m.;* —, *vt.* tirar con honda; (naut.) embragar.

slingshot, *n.* tirador, *m.*

slink, *vi.* deslizarse furtivamente.

slip, *vi.* resbalar; escapar, huirse; —, *vt.* meter; correr; **to** — **on,** ponerse; —, *n.* resbalón, *m.;* tropiezo, *m.;* escapada, *f.;* patinazo, *m.;* enagua, combinación, *f.;* — **cover,** funda de mueble.

slip-on, *n.* prenda de vestir que se pone por la cabeza.

slipper, *n.* chinela, zapatilla, *f.*

slippery, *adj.* resbaladizo, deleznable, resbaloso.

slipshod, *adj.* desaliñado, negligente, descuidado.

slit, *vt.* rajar, hender; —, *n.* raja, hendidura, *f.*

sliver, *n.* astilla, tira, *f.;* —, *vt.* rasgar, cortar en tiras.

slobber, *n.* baba, *f.;* —, *vt.* babosear; —, *vi.* babear.

slogan, *n.* lema, mote, *m.;* grito de combate; frase popularizada para anunciar un producto.

sloop, *n.* (naut.) balandra, *f.*

slop, *n.* aguachirle, *f.;* agua sucia; —**s,** *pl.* ropa de pacotilla.

slope, *n.* sesgo, *m.;* escarpa, *f.;* ladera, vertiente, *f.;* declive, *m.;* cuesta, *f.;* —, *vt.* sesgar; —, *vi.* inclinarse.

sloping, *adj.* oblicuo; inclinado.

sloppy, *adj.* lodoso, fangoso; (coll.) desaliñado, descuidado.

slot, *n.* hendidura, *f.;* — **machine,** máquina automática con ranura para monedas.

sloth, *n.* pereza, *f.;* (zool.) perezoso, *m.*

slothful, *adj.* perezoso.

slouch, *vt.* y *vi.* estar cabizbajo (como un patán); bambolearse pesadamente; ponerse gacho; —, *n.* persona incompetente y perezosa; joroba, f.

slough, n. lodazal, cenagal, m.; decaimiento espiritual.

slovenly, adj. desaliñado, puerco, sucio.

slow, adj. tardío, lento, torpe, perezoso; — **motion,** velocidad reducida; —, vt. y vi. retardar, demorar; **to — down,** reducir o acortar la marcha.

slowly, adv. despacio, despaciosamente, lentamente.

slowness, n. lentitud, tardanza, pesadez, f.

slug, n. holgazán, zángano, m.; (zool.) babosa, f.; (print.) lingote, m.; —, vt. aporrear, golpear fuertemente.

sluggard, n. haragán, holgazán, m.

sluggish, adj. perezoso; lento.

sluggishness, n. pereza, lentitud, f.

sluice, n. compuerta, f.; —, vt. dejar correr abriendo la compuerta; —, vi. descorrerse.

slum, vi. visitar viviendas o barrios bajos o escuálidos; **—s,** n. pl. barrios bajos; viviendas escuálidas.

slumber, vi. dormitar; —, n. sueño ligero.

slump, n. hundimiento, m.; quiebra, f.; baja considerable de precios o actividades en los negocios.

slur, vt. ensuciar; pasar ligeramente; —, n. (mus.) ligado, m.; afrenta, estigma, calumnia, f.

slush, n. lodo, barro, cieno, m.

slut, n. mujer sucia.

sly, adj. astuto; furtivo.

small, adj. pequeño, menudo, chico; — **arms,** armas de fuego portátiles.

small-minded, adj. mezquino, despreciable.

smallness, n. pequeñez, f.

small of the back, n. parte más estrecha de la espalda.

smallpox, n. viruelas, f. pl.

smart, n. escozor, m.; —, adj. punzante, agudo, agrio; ingenioso; mordaz; doloroso; inteligente; elegante, apuesto; —, vi. escocer, arder.

smartness, n. agudeza, viveza, sutileza, f.; elegancia, f.

smash, vt. romper, quebrantar; —, n. fracaso, m.; (tenis) volea alta.

smash-up, n. choque desastroso.

smattering, n. conocimiento superficial.

smear, vt. untar; emporcar; manchar; calumniar.

smell, vt. y vi. oler; percibir; olfatear; —, n. olfato, m.; olor, m.; hediondez, f.; **sense of —,** olfato, m.

smelt, n. (ichth.) eperlano, m.; —, vt. fundir (el metal).

smile, vi. sonreír, sonreírse; —, n. sonrisa, f.

smirk, vi. sonreír burlonamente.

smite, vt. herir, golpear.

smith, n. forjador de metales; **black—,** herrero, m.

smithers, smithereens, n. pl. fragmentos, pedacitos, m. pl.

smithery, smithy, n. herrería, f.

smock, n. bata, f.

smog, n. combinación de humo y niebla.

smoke, n. humo, m.; vapor, m.; — **screen,** cortina de humo; —, vt. y vi. ahumar; humear; fumar (tabaco).

smokehouse, n. ahumadero, m.

smokeless, adj. sin humo; — **powder,** pólvora sin humo.

smoker, n. fumador, m.; (rail.) coche fumador.

smokestack, n. chimenea, f.

smoking, adj. fumífero, que despide humo; **—car,** (rail.) coche fumador; — **jacket,** batín, m.; **no —,** se prohíbe fumar.

smoky, adj. humeante; humoso.

smolder, vi. arder sin llama; existir en forma latente; —, n. humo, m.

smooth, adj. liso, pulido, llano; suave; afable; —, vt. allanar; alisar; lisonjear.

smoothly, adv. llanamente; con blandura.

smoothness, n. lisura, f.; llanura, f.; suavidad, f.

smother, vt. sofocar; apagar; —, n. humareda, f.

smoulder, vi. arder debajo de la ceniza; existir en forma latente.

smudge, vt. fumigar; ensuciar, tiznar; —, n. tiznadura, mugre, f.

smug, adj. atildado; escrupulosamente limpio o compuesto; satisfecho de sí mismo.

smuggle, vt. contrabandear.

smuggler, n. contrabandista, m. y f.

smuggling, n. contrabando, m.

smut, n. tiznón, m.; suciedad, f.; —, vt. tiznar; ensuciar.

smutty, adj. tiznado; anieblado; obsceno.

snack, n. parte, porción, f.; tentempié, refrigerio, m., colación, f.; merienda, f.; —, vi. merendar.

snag, n. protuberancia, f.; raigón de diente; diente que sobresale; rama de un árbol escondida en el fondo de un lago o río; tocón, m.; obstáculo inesperado.

snail, n. caracol, m.

snake, n. culebra, sierpe, serpiente, f.; —, vi. culebrear.

snap, vt. y vi. romper; agarrar; morder; contestar con grosería; chasquear; estallar; **to — one's fingers,** castañetear los dedos; **to — open,** abrirse de golpe;

to — a picture, tomar una instantánea;
—, n. estallido, m.; castañeteo, m.;
corchete, m.; —, adj. repentino; —
judgment, opinión a la ligera.
snapdragon, n. (bot.) antirrino, m., hierba
becerra.
snapper, n. (ichth.) pargo, m.; corchete.
snapping, n. acción de romper; acción de
agarrar.
snappy, adj. vivaz, animado; elegante.
snapshot, n. instantánea, fotografía, f.
snare, n. lazo, m.; trampa, f.; garlito, m.;
trapisonda, f.; — drum, pequeño tambor militar; to fall into a —, caer en la
ratonera; —, vt. cazar animales con
lazos; trapisondear.
snarl, vi. regañar, gruñir; —, vt. enredar;
—, n. gruñido, m.; complicación, f.
snatch, vt. arrebatar; agarrar; —, arreba-
tamiento, m.; arrebatiña, f.; pedazo,
m.; ratito, m.
sneak, vi. arrastrar; ratear; to — out,
salirse a escondidas, tomar las de
Villadiego; —, n. persona traicionera;
—thief, ratero, ra.
sneer, vi. hablar con desprecio; fisgarse;
—, n. fisga, f.
sneeze, vi. estornudar; —, n. estornudo, m.
snicker, vi. reir a menudo y socarrona-
mente; —, n. risita socarrona.
sniff, vi. resollar con fuerza; vt. olfatear; —, n. olfateo, m.
sniffle, vi. aspirar ruidosamente por la
nariz; gimotear.
snip, vt. tijeretear; —, n. tijeretada, f.;
pedazo pequeño, pedacito, m.
snipe, n. (orn.) agachadiza, f., becardón,
m.; —, vi. cazar becardones; tirar de
un apostadero.
sniper, n. tirador apostado.
snippy, adj. fragmentario; (coll.) grosero,
brusco, desdeñoso.
snivel, n. moquita, f.; —, vi. moquear;
gimotear.
snob, n. snob, m. y f., persona presuntuosa; advenedizo social o intelectual.
snobbish, adj. presuntuoso; jactancioso;
propio del snob.
snood, n. gorro tejido que sujeta el cabello de las mujeres.
snoop, vi. (coll.) espiar, fisgar, acechar;
escudriñar; —, n. (coll.) metiche,
fisgón, m.
snooze, n. sueño ligero; —, vi. dormir
ligeramente, dormitar.
snore, vi. roncar; —, n. ronquido, m.
snorkel, n. doble tubo de respiración para
submarinos; — pen, pluma fuente que
se llena mediante un tubo aspirante.

snort, vi. resoplar, bufar como un caballo
fogoso.
snout, n. hocico, m.; trompa de elefante;
(coll.) nariz, f.; boquilla (de manguera,
etc.), f.
snow, n. nieve, f.; — line, límite de las
nieves perpetuas; —, vi. nevar.
snowball, n. pelota de nieve.
snowberry, n. baya blanca americana.
snowbird, n. (orn.) variedad de pinzón.
snow-blind, snow-blinded, adj. cegado
por el brillo del sol en la nieve.
snowbound, adj. bloqueado por la nieve.
snowdrift, n. nieve acumulada por el
viento.
snowdrop, n. (bot.) campanilla blanca.
snowfall, n. nevada, f.
snowflake, n. coro de nieve.
snowplow, n. quitanieve, m.
snowshed, n. guardaaludes, m.
snowstorm, n. nevada, f., tormenta de
nieve.
snowsuit, n. traje para nieve.
snow-white, adj. níveo, blanco como la
nieve.
snowy, adj. nevoso; nevado.
snub, vt. desairar, tratar con desprecio;
—, n. altanería, f.; desaire, m.
snub-nosed, adj. de nariz respingona.
snuff, n. pabilo, m.; tabaco en polvo;
rapé, m.; —, vt. olfatear, aspirar; despabilar.
snuffbox, n. tabaquera, f.
snuffer, n. despabilador, m.; despabilade-
ras, f. pl.
snuffle, vi. ganguear; hablar gangoso; —s,
n. pl. catarro, m.
snug, adj. abrigado; conveniente, cómodo,
agradable, grato.
snuggle, vi. acurrucarse; estar como
apretado; arrimarse a otro en busca de
calor o cariño.
so, adv. así; tal; por consiguiente; tanto;
and — forth, y así sucesivamente; —,
and —, Fulano de Tal, m., Fulana de
Tal, f.; — much, tanto; — that, para
que, de modo que; — then, conque;
that is —, eso es, así es; —what? ¿y
qué?
So.: South, S. sur.
soak, vt. y vi. remojar; calarse; empapar, remojar; to — through, calarse (un
líquido, etc.); —, n. calada (de un líquido, etc.), f.; (coll.) borrachín, m.
soap, n. jabón, m.; cake of —, pastilla de
jabón; — bubble, globo de jabón; —
opera, (coll.) telenovela, f.; radio-nove-
la, f.; —, vt. jabonar, enjabonar.
soapbox, n. plataforma improvisada para
oradores de las calles.

soapstone, n. esteatita, f.
soapsuds, n. pl. jabonaduras, f. pl., espuma de jabón.
soapy, adj. jabonoso.
soar, vi. remontarse, sublimarse.
soaring, n. vuelo muy alto; acción de remontarse.
sob, n. sollozo, m.; —, vi. sollozar.
sober, adj. sobrio; serio; —ly, adv. sobriamente; juiciosamente.
sobriety, n. sobriedad, f.; seriedad, gravedad, f.
so-called, adj. así llamado.
soccer, n. fútbol inglés, m.
sociability, n. sociabilidad, f.
sociable, adj. sociable, comunicativo.
social, adj. social, sociable; — sciences, ciencias sociales; — security, seguro social; — service, — work, servicio social, servicio en pro de las clases pobres; — worker, trabajador social; —, n. tertulia, f.
socialism, n. socialismo, m.
socialist, n. y adj. socialista, m. y f.
socialistic, adj. socialista.
socialite, n. (coll.) persona prominente en sociedad.
socialize, vt. socializar.
society, n. sociedad, f.; compañía, f.
sociological, adj. sociológico.
sociologist, n. sociólogo, ga.
sociology, n. sociología, f.
sock, n. calcetín, m.; zueco, m.; (coll.) golpe fuerte; —, vt. golpear con violencia.
socket, n. cubo, encaje, casquillo, m.; alveolo de un diente; encastre, m.; eye —, órbita, f., cuenca del ojo; electric —, enchufe, m.
sod, n. césped, m.; turba, tierra, f.; —, vt. enyerbar.
soda, n. sosa, soda, f.; baking —, bicarbonato de sosa o de soda; — cracker, galleta de soda; — fountain, fuente de sodas; — water, gaseosa, f.
sodality, n. hermandad, cofradía, fraternidad, f.
sodden, adj. empapado; de aspecto pesado por la disipación; ebrio.
sodium, n. (chem.) sodio, m.; — chloride, cloruro de sodio, sal de cocina.
sofa, n. sofá, m.
soft, adj. blando, mole, suave; benigno; tierno, compasivo; jugoso; afeminado; —coal, hulla grasa, carbón bituminoso; — drink, refresco, m., bebida no alcohólica; — water, agua dulce, agua no cruda; —ly, adv. con suavidad, quedamente.
softball, n. juego parecido al béisbol que

se juega con pelota blanda.
soft-boiled, adj. cocido, pasado por agua; —eggs, huevos pasados por agua.
soften, vt. ablandar, mitigar; enternecer; reblandecer, suavizar.
softhearted, adj. compasivo; sensible, de buen corazón.
softness, n. suavidad, blandura, f.; dulzura, f
soft-pedal, vt. suavizar; contener, reprimir.
soft-spoken, adj. afable, que habla con dulzura.
softwood, n. madera blanda.
soggy, adj. empapado, mojado.
soil, vt. ensuciar, emporcar; —, n. mancha; suelo, m., tierra, f.
soiled, adj. sucio; — clothes, ropa sucia.
soiree, soirée, n. velada, f.
sojourn, vi. residir, morar; —, n. morada, f.; estadía, permanencia, f.
sol, n. (mus.) sol, m.; sol (moneda del Perú), m.
solace, vt. solazar, consolar; —, n. consuelo, solaz, m.
solar, adj. solar; — plexus, (anat.) plexo solar; — system, sistema solar; — year, año solar.
solarium, n. solana, f.; habitación para tomar el sol con propósitos terapéuticos.
sold, pret. y p.p. del verbo sell, vender; — out, agotado, vendido.
solder, vt. soldar; —, n. soldadura, f.
soldier, n. soldado, m.; —ly, adj. soldadesco; marcial; —, vi. prestar servicio militar.
sole, n. planta del pie; suela del zapato; —, adj. único, solo; —, vt. solar, poner suela al calzado.
sole, n. (ichth.) lenguado.
solemn, adj. solemne.
solemnity, n. solemnidad, f.
solemnize, vt. solemnizar.
solicit, vt. solicitar; implorar; pedir.
solicitation, n. solicitación, f.
solicitor, n. procurador, solicitador, m.
solicitous, adj. solícito, diligente.
solicitude, n. solicitud, f.; cuidado, m.
solid, adj. sólido, compacto; — color, color entero, m.; — geometry, geometría del espacio; —, n. sólido, m.
solidarity, n. solidaridad, f.
solidify, vt. congelar; solidar; solidificar.
solidity, n. solidez, f.
soliloquize, vi. soliloquiar, hablar a solas.
soliloquy, n. soliloquio, m.
solitaire, n. solitario (diamante grueso), m.; solitario (juego de una sola persona, generalmente de naipes), m.

solitary, adj. solitario, retirado; —, n. ermitaño, m.

solitude, n. soledad, f.; vida solitaria.

solo, n. y adj. solo, m.

soloist, n. solista, m. y f.

soluble, adj. soluble.

solution, n. solución, f.

solve, vt. solver, disolver; aclarar, resolver.

solvency, n. solvencia, f.

solvent, adj. solvente.

somber, adj. sombrío, nebuloso, oscuro; lúgubre, triste, tétrico, melancólico.

some, adj. algo de, un poco de; algún, alguna; —, pron. unos pocos, ciertos, algunos.

somebody, n. alguien, m., alguno, na.

somehow, adv. de algún modo, de alguna manera.

someone, pron. alguien, alguna persona.

somersault, somerset, n. voltereta, f.; salto mortal; —, vi. dar un salto mortal.

something, n. alguna cosa; algo, m.; — **else,** otra cosa, alguna otra cosa.

sometime, adv. en algún tiempo.

sometimes, adv. algunas veces, a veces.

somewhat, n. un poco, algo, algún tanto; —, adv. algún tanto. un poco; — **cold,** algo frío, un poco frío.

somewhere, adv. en alguna parte.

somnambulism, n. sonambulismo, m.

son, n. hijo, m.

sonata, n. (mus.) sonata, f.

song, n. canción, f., canto, m.; cántico, m.; **Song of Solomon,** Cantar de los Cantares; — **sparrow,** gorrión canoro; — **thrush,** tordo canoro; — **writer,** compositor de canciones.

songbook, n. cancionero, m., libro de canciones.

songster, n. cantante, m. y f.; ave canora.

sonic, adj. sónico; — **barrier,** barrera sónica.

son-in-law, n. yerno, m.

sonnet, n. soneto, m.

sonorous, adj. sonoro.

soon, adv. presto, pronto, prontamente; **as — as,** luego que, en cuanto; **as — as possible,** lo más pronto posible.

sooner, adv. más pronto, primero; más bien.

soot, n. hollín, m.

soothe, vt. sosegar, calmar, tranquilizar.

soothsayer, n. adivino, m.

sooty, adj. holliniento, fuliginoso.

sop, n. pan mojado, m.; soborno, m., adulación, f.

sophisticate, n. persona de mundo.

sophisticated, adj. artificial, afectado; re-finado y sutil.

sophistication, n. afectación, f.; artificio, m. falta de sencillez.

sophistry, n. sofistería, f.

sophomore, n. estudiante de segundo año de una escuela superior o universidad.

sopping, adj. ensopado; — **wet,** empapado.

soprano, n. (mus.) soprano, tiple, m.; — **singer,** tiple, soprano, f.

sorcerer, n. hechicero, brujo, m.

sorceress, n. hechicera, bruja, f.

sorcery, n. hechizo, encanto, m.; hechicería, f.

sordid, adj. sórdido, sucio; avariento; — **ly,** adv. sórdidamente.

sore, n. llaga, úlcera, f.; —, adj. doloroso, penoso; (coll.) enojado, resentido; — **throat,** carraspera, f., mal de garganta.

sorghum, n. (bot.) sorgo, m., zahína, f.; melaza de sorgo.

sorority, n. hermandad de mujeres.

sorrel, n. (bot.) acedera, f.; —, adj. alazán.

sorrow, n. pesar, m.; tristeza, f.; —, vi. entristecerse.

sorrowful, adj. pesaroso, afligido; sentido; triste; —**ly,** adv. con aflicción.

sorry, adj. triste; afligido; pesaroso; miserable; **to be —,** sentir; **to feel — for,** compadecerse (de alguien), tenerle lástima; **I am very —,** lo siento mucho.

sort, n. género, m., especie, f.; calidad, clase, f.; manera, f.; —, vt. separar, clasificar.

sortie, n. (mil.) salida, misión o ataque aéreos.

sot, n. zote, m.

soul, n. alma, f.; esencia, f.; persona, f.

sound, adj. sano; entero; puro; firme; (com.) solvente; — **barrier,** barrera sónica; — **track,** guía sonora (en películas cinematográficas); — **wave,** onda sonora; —**ly,** adv. vigorosamente; —, n. tienta, sonda, f.; sonido, ruido, m.; son, m.; estrecho, m.; **at the — of,** al son de; —, vt. (naut.) sondar; tocar; celebrar; sondar (intenciones) ; —, vi. sonar, resonar.

sounding, n. (naut.) sondeo, m.; —, adj. sonante; — **line,** sondaleza, f.

soundproof, adj. a prueba de sonido.

soup, n. sopa, f.; — **plate,** plato sopero; **vegetable —,** sopa de verdura.

sour, adj. agrio, ácido; áspero; — **grapes,** uvas verdes; (fig.) indiferencia hacia algo que no se puede poseer; —, vt. y vi. agriar, acedar; agriarse.

source, n. manantial, m., mina, f.; principio, origen, m.

souse, n. salmuera, f.; zambullida, f.; —,

vt. escabechar; —, vt. y vi. empapar, chapuzar.

south, n. sur, sud, mediodía, m.; **S—,** la región meridional (en Estados Unidos generalmente la región al sur del Río Ohio); —, adj. meridional, del sur.

southeast, n. y adj. sureste, sudeste, m.

southern, adj. meridional.

southerner, n. persona de la región meridional (en Estados Unidos generalmente nacido o que reside al sur del Río Ohio).

southernmost, adj. lo más al sur.

southland, n. región meridional, región del sur.

southward, adv. hacia el sur, con rumbo al sur.

southwest, n. y adj. sudoeste, m.; —, adv. del sudoeste; hacia el sudoeste.

souvenir, n. recuerdo, m.; memoria, f.

sovereign, n. y adj. soberano, na.

sovereignty, n. soberanía, f.

sow, n. puerca, marrana, f.

sow, vt. sembrar, sementar; esparcir.

sowing, n. siembra, f.

soy, n. soja, f.; semilla de soja; salsa de soja.

space, n. espacio, trecho, m.; intersticio, m.; lugar, m.; —, vt. espaciar.

space capsule, n. cápsula espacial.

spacecraft, n. nave espacial.

space medicine, n. medicina espacial.

space probe, n. cohete de sondeo; vehículo de exploración espacial.

space ship, n. nave espacial.

spacious, adj. espacioso, amplio; —ly, adv. con bastante espacio.

spade, n. laya, azada, f.; (en los naipes) espada, f.; —, vt. azadonar.

Spain, España, f.

SPAM, n. mensajes no deseados, m. pl.

span, n. palmo, m.; espacio, m.; — **of a bridge,** tramo, m.; —, vt. medir a palmos; extenderse sobre; atravesar.

spangle, n. lentejuela, f.; —, vt. Adornar con lentejuelas.

Spaniard, n. español, la.

spaniel, n. sabueso, m.

Spanish, adj. español; — **America,** Hispanoamérica, f., América española; — **American,** hispanoamericano, na; — **ballad,** romance, m.; — **language,** castellano, m.

spank, n. palmada, f.; —, vt. pegar, dar palmadas, dar nalgadas.

spanking, n. nalgada, f.

spar, n. espato, m.; —, vi. boxear.

spare, vt. y vi. ahorrar, economizar, perdonar; vivir con economía —, adj. escaso, económico; de reserva; — **time,**

tiempo desocupado; — **tire,** neumático o llanta de repuesto o de reserva; — **parts,** piezas de repuesto.

sparely, adv. escasamente.

sparerib, n. costilla de puerco.

sparing, adj. frugal; parco; económico; — **ly,** adv. parcamente.

spark, n. chispa, f.; bujía, f.; (poet.) centella, f.; (coll.) pisaverde, m.; — **plug,** bujía, f.; —, vi. echar chispas, chispear; —, vt. y vi. (coll.) enamorar, cortejar.

sparkle, n. centella, chispa, f.; —, vi. chispear; espumar.

sparkling, adj. centelleante; efervescente; vivo, animado; — **wine,** vino espumoso; — **personality,** personalidad atrayente.

sparrow, n. gorrión, pardal, m.; — **hawk,** gavilán, m.

sparse, adj. escaso; esparcido.

spasm, n. espasmo, m.

spasmodic, adj. espasmódico.

spastic, adj. (med.) espástico; espasmódico.

spat, n. riña, f.; hueva de ostras; bofetada, f.; —, vi. reñir.

spats, n. pl. polainas, f. pl.

spatter, n. salpicadura, f.; —, vt. salpicar, manchar; esparcir.

spattering, n. salpicadura, f.

spatula, n. espátula, f.

spawn, n. freza, f.; hueva, f.; —, vt. y vi. desovar; engendrar.

spawning, n. freza, f.

speak, vt. y vi. hablar; decir; conversar; pronunciar; **to — plainly,** hablar con claridad; **to — in torrents,** hablar a borbotones; **to — to,** dirigirse a.

speaker, n. el que habla; orador, ra; **S—of the House,** presidente de la Cámara de Representantes (en E.U.A.).

speaking, n. habla, f.; oratoria, f.; —, adj. que habla; — **trumpet,** portavoz, m.; — **tube,** tubo acústico.

spear, n. lanza, f.; pica, f.; arpón, m.; —, vt. herir con lanza; alancear.

spearhead, n. roquete, m.; tropas en el puesto delantero de un ataque.

spearmint, n. hierbabuena, f.

special, adj. especial, particular.

special-delivery, adj. de urgencia; de entrega inmediata; — **letter,** carta urgente, carta de entrega inmediata; — **stamp,** sello de entrega inmediata.

specialist, n. especialista, m. y f.

specialty, n. especialidad, f., rasgo característico.

specialize, vt. y vi. especializar; especializarse.

specialty, n. especialidad, f.

species, n. especie, clase, f.; género, m.
specific, adj. específico; — **gravity,** densidad específica; peso específico; —, n. específico, m.; **—ally,** adv. específicamente.
specification, n. especificación, f.; **—s,** pl. pliego de condiciones.
specify, vt. especificar.
specimen, n. espécimen, m., muestra, f.; prueba, f.
speck, speckle, n. mancha, mácula, tacha, f.; —, vt. manchar, abigarrar.
spectacle, n. espectáculo, m.; exhibición, f.; **—s,** pl. anteojos, espejuelos, m. pl., gafas, f pl.
spectacular, adj. espectacular, aparatoso; grandioso; —, n. programa extraordinario (de televisión).
spectator, n. espectador, ra.
specter, spectre, n. espectro, m.
spectral, adj. aduendado; espectrométrico; — **analysis,** análisis espectral, análisis del espectro solar.
spectroscope, n. espectroscopio, m.
spectrum, n. espectro, m.
speculate, vi. especular; reflexionar.
speculation, n. especulación, f.; especulativa, f.; meditación, f.
speculative, adj. especulativo; teórico.
speculator, n. especulador (especialmente en acciones de la bolsa), m.
speech, n. habla, f.; discurso, m., oración, arenga, f.; conversación, f.; perorata, f.; (theat.) parlamento, m.; **to make a —,** perorar, pronunciar un discurso.
speechless, adj. mudo, sin habla.
speed, n. prisa, f.; celeridad, rapidez, f.; prontitud, f.; velocidad, f.; **at full —,** a todo escape, a toda velocidad, a toda prisa, de corrida; — **limit,** límite de velocidad, velocidad máxima; —, vt. apresurar; despachar; ayudar; —, vi. darse prisa.
speedboat, n. lancha de carrera.
speedily, adv. aceleradamente, de prisa.
speedometer, n. velocímetro, celerímetro, m.
speed-up, n. aceleramiento, m., aceleración, f.
speedway, n. autopista, f.; autódromo, m.
speedy, adj. veloz, pronto, diligente.
spell, n. hechizo, encanto, m.; periodo de descanso; periodo corto; —, vt. y vi. deletrear; hechizar, encantar; (coll.) revezar.
spellbound, adj. fascinado, encantado.
speller, n. libro de deletrear; deletreador, ra.
spelling, n. ortografía, f.; deletreo, m.
spend, vt. gastar; disipar; consumir; **to —**

(time), pasar (tiempo); —, vi. hacer gastos.
spender, n. gastador, ra; derrochador, ra.
spendthrift, n. derrochador, ra, pródigo, ga.
spent, adj. alcanzado de fuerzas; gastado.
sperm, n. esperma, f.; semen, m.
spew, vt. y vi. vomitar.
S.P.F. sun protection factor, F.P.S., factor de protección solar.
sphere, n. esfera, f.
spheric, spherical, adj. esférico.
spheroid, n. esferoide, m.; —, adj. esferoidal.
sphinx, n. esfinge, f., persona de carácter misterioso e indescifrable.
spice, n. especia, f ; sal, f., picante, m.; **—s,** especiería, f., especias, f. pl.; —, vt. sazonar con especias.
spick-and-span, adj. flamante, muy limpio o muy nuevo; pulcro y ordenado.
spicy, adj. especiado; aromático; picante.
spider, n. araña, f.
spigot, n. llave, f., grifo, m.; espita, f.
spike, n. alcayata, escarpia, f.; púa metálica de algunos zapatos para deporte; (bot.) variedad de espiga.
spill, vt. derramar, verter; —, n. clavija, espiga, f.; astilla, f.; (coll.) vuelco, m.
spillway, n. vertedero lateral; canal de desagüe.
spin, vt. hilar; alargar, prolongar; —, vi. hilar; girar, dar vueltas; —, n. vuelta, f.; paseo, m.; giro, m.
spinach, n. espinaca, f.
spinal, adj. espinal; — **column,** espina dorsal.
spindle, n. huso, m.; quicio, m.; carretel, m.; — **of a lathe,** (mech.) mandril, m.
spine, n. espinazo, m., espina, f.
spinet, n. piano pequeño.
spinning, n. hilandería, f.; rotación, f.; —, adj. de hilar; — **mill,** hilandería, f.; — **top,** trompo, m.; — **wheel,** rueca, f., torno de hilar.
spinster, n. hilandera, f.; soltera, f.; soltrona, f.
spiral, adj. espiral; — **staircase,** escalera de caracol; **—ly,** adv. en forma espiral.
spire, n. espira, f ; cúspide, cima, f.; aguja (de una torre), f.
spirit, n. aliento, m.; espíritu, m.; ánimo, valor, m.; brío, m.; humor, m.; fantasma, m.; —, vt. incitar, animar; **to — away,** arrebatar, secuestrar.
spirited, adj. vivo, brioso; **—ly,** adv. con espíritu.
spiritual, adj. espiritual.
spiritualism, spiritism, n. espiritismo, m.
spiritualist, n. espiritualista, m. y f.

spit, *n.* asador, *m.;* saliva, *f.,* expectoración, *f.;* —, *vt.* y *vi.* espetar; escupir, salivar.

spite, *n.* rencor, *m.,* malevolencia, *f.;* **in** — **of,** a pesar de, a despecho de; —, *vt.* dar pesar, mortificar.

spiteful, *adj.* rencoroso, malicioso; **—ly,** *adv.* malignamente, con tirria.

spitfire, *n.* fierabrás, *m.*

spittle, *n.* saliva, *f.;* esputo, *m.*

spittoon, *n.* escupidera, *f.*

splash, *vt.* salpicar, enlodar; —, *n.* salpicadura, rociada, *f.*

splay, *vt.* exponer a la vista; extender; —, *adj.* extendido; desmañado.

spleen, *n.* bazo, *m.;* esplín, *m.*

splendid, *adj.* espléndido, magnífico.

splendor, *n.* esplendor, *m.;* pompa, —, *f.;* brillo, *m.*

splice, *vt.* (naut.) empalmar, unir; (coll.) casar; —, *n.* empalme, *m.*

splint, *n.* astilla, *f.;* cabestrillo, *m.;* —, *vt.* entablillar.

splinter, *n.* cacho, *m.;* astilla, *f.;* brizna, *f.;* —, *vt.* astillar; —, *vi.* astillarse.

split, *vt.* hender, rajar; —, *vi.* henderse; **to** — **with laughter,** desternillarse de risa; —, *n.* hendidura, raja, *f.;* **banana** —, mezcla de helados con jarabe, nueces y plátano.

split-level, *adj.* de piso escalonado; — **house,** casa de pisos con distintos niveles.

splitting, *adj.* rajador partidor, desintegrador; severo, violento; — **head-ache,** fuerte dolor de cabeza.

splotch, *vt.* manchar, salpicar; —, *n.* mancha, *f.,* borrón, *m.*

spoil, *vt.* pillar, robar; despojar; contaminar; arruinar; dañar; pudrir; mimar demasiado; echar a perder; —, *vi.* corromperse; dañarse, echarse a perder; **—s,** *n. pl.* despojo, botín, *m.*

spoiler, *n.* corruptor, robador, *m.*

spoke, *n.* rayo de la rueda; —, *pretérito* del verbo **speak.**

spoken, *p.p.* del verbo **speak.**

spokesman, *n.* interlocutor, *m.;* vocero, *m.;* portavoz, *m.*

sponge, *n.* esponja, *f.;* —, *vt.* limpiar con esponja; —, *vi.* gorronear, ser gorrón.

spongecake, *n.* variedad de bizcochuelo.

sponger, *n.* pegote, mogollón, *m.;* gorrón, ona; vividor, ra.

spongy, *adj.* esponjoso.

sponsor, *n.* fiador, *m.;* padrino, *m.;* madrina, *f;* garante, *m.* y *f.;* persona responsable.

spontaneity, *n.* espontaneidad, voluntariedad, *f.*

spontaneous, *adj.* espontáneo; — **combustion,** combustión espontánea.

spool, *n.* canilla, broca, bobina, *f.,* carrete, carretel, *m.;* — **of thread,** carrete de hilo.

spoon, *n.* cuchara, *f.*

spoonful, *n.* cucharada, *f.*

sporadic, *adj.* esporádico.

spore, *n.* espora, *f.*

sport, *n.* juego, retozo, *m.;* juguete, divertimiento, recreo, pasatiempo, *m.;* deporte, *m.;* —, *adj.* deportivo; — **shirt,** camisa para deportes, camisa sport; —, *vt.* lucir, —, *vi.* chancear, juguetear.

sporting, *adj.* deportivo.

sportive, *adj.* festivo, juguetón.

sportsman, *n.* deportista, *m.;* persona equitativa y generosa en los deportes; buen perdedor.

sportsmanship, *n.* espíritu de equidad en los deportes y en los negocios.

spot, *n.* mancha, *f.;* borrón, *m.;* sitio, lugar, *m.;* — **cash,** dinero al contado; —**remover,** quitamanchas, sacámanchas, *m.;* —, *vt.* manchar; (coll.) observar, reconocer.

spotless, *adj.* limpio, inmaculado; puro; sin mancha.

spotlight, *n.* luz concentrada; proyector, *m.;* (auto.) faro giratorio; —, *vt.* dar realce.

spotted, spotty, *adj.* lleno de manchas, sucio; moteado.

spouse, *n.* esposo, sa.

spout, *vt.* y *vi.* arrojar agua con mucho ímpetu; borbotar; chorrear; —, *n.* llave de fuente; gárgola, *f.;* bomba marina; chorro de agua; pico (de una cafetera, etc.), *m.*

sprain, *vt.* torcer; —, *n.* torcedura, *f.*

sprang, *pretérito* del verbo **spring.**

sprawl, *vi.* revolcarse; arrastrarse con las piernas extendidas; extenderse irregularmente (como las viñas).

spray, *n.* rociada, *f.;* ramita, *f;* espuma del mar; rociador, pulverizador, *m.;* vaporizador, *m.;* — **gun,** pistola pulverizadora; — **net,** loción para rociar el cabello; —, *vt.* rociar, pulverizar.

spraying, *n.* rociada, *f.;* riego, *m.;* pulverización, *f.*

spread, *vt.* extender, desplegar, tender; esparcir, divulgar; regar; untar; propagar; generalizar; —, *vi.* **extenderse,** desplegarse; — **over,** cubrir; —, *n.* extensión, dilatación, *f.;* **sobrecama,** *f.;* —, *adj.* extendido, aumentado.

speadsheet, *n.* hoja de cálculo, *f.*

spree, *n.* fiesta, *f.,* festín, *m.;* (coll.) juerga, *f.*

sprig, n. ramito, m.

sprightly, adj. alegre, despierto, vivaracho.

spring, vi. brotar, arrojar; nacer, provenir; dimanar, originarse; saltar, brincar; —, vt. soltar, hacer saltar; revelar (una sorpresa, etc.); to — back, saltar hacia atrás; to — forward, arrojarse; to — from, venir, proceder de; to — a leak, (naut.) declararse una vía de agua; —, n. primavera, f.; elasticidad, f.; muelle, resorte, m.; salto, m.; manantial, m.; hot —s, burga, f.; — of water, fuente f.

springboard, n. trampolín, m.

springer, n. brincador, ra, saltador, ra.

springlike, adj. primaveral.

springy, adj. elástico.

sprinkle, vt. rociar; salpicar; —, vi. lloviznar; —, n. rociada, f.; lluvia ligera.

sprinkler, n. rociador, m.; (Mex.) rehilete (para regar el prado, etc.), m.

sprinkling, n. rociada, aspersión, f.; — can, regadera, f.

sprint, n. carrera breve a todo correr; —, vi. correr velozmente.

sprite, n. duende, m., hada, f.

sprocket, n. diente de rueda de cadena; — wheel, (mech.) erizo, m., rueda dentada para cadena; rueda catalina, rueda de cabillas.

sprout, n. vástago, renuevo, tallo, retoño, m.; —s, n. pl. bretones, m. pl.; —, vi. brotar, pulular.

spruce, adj. pulido, gentil; —ly, adv. bellamente, lindamente; —, n. (bot.) abeto, m.; to — up, aliñar; aliñarse.

sprung, p.p. del verbo spring.

spry, adj. activo, listo, vivo, ágil, veloz, ligero.

spun glass, n. lana de vidrio.

spur, n. espuela, f.; espolón, (de gallo), m.; on the — of the moment, en un impulso repentino; —, vt. espolear; estimular.

spurge, n. (bot.) titímalo, m.

spurious, adj. espurio, falso; contrahecho; supuesto; bastardo.

spurn, vt. acocear; despreciar, desdeñar.

spurt, vt. chorrear, arrojar; —, vi. manar a borbotones, borbotar; —, n. chorro, m.; esfuerzo grande.

sputnik, n. sputnik, satélite ruso.

sputter, vi. escupir con frecuencia; babear; chisporrotear; barbotar, hablar a borbotones.

sputum, n. (med.) esputo, m.; saliva, f.

spy, n. espía, m. y f.; —, vt. y vi. espiar; columbrar.

spyglass, n. anteojo de larga vista.

sq.: square, cuadrado.

squab, adj. implume; cachigordo, regordete; —, n. pichón, m., palomita, f.; canapé, sofá, m.; cojín, m.

squabble, vi. reñir, disputar; —, n. riña, disputa, f.

squad, n. patrulla, f.; escuadra, f.; —car, automóvil de patrulla de policía.

squadron, n. (mil.) escuadrón, m.

squalid, adj. sucio, puerco, escuálido.

squall, n. grito desgarrador; chubasco, m.; — of wind, ráfaga de viento; —, vi. chillar.

squalor, n. porquería, suciedad, escualidez, f.

squander, vt. malgastar, disipar, derrochar.

square, adj. cuadrado, cuadrángulo; exacto; cabal; equitativo; — dance, contradanza, f.; baile de figuras; — root, raíz cuadrada; — deal, trato equitativo; — foot, pie cuadrado; —, n. cuadro, m.; plaza, f.; bevel —, falsarregla, f.; carpenter's —, escuadra, f.; —, vt. cuadrar; ajustar, arreglar; —, vi. ajustarse.

squared, adj. cuadrado.

squash, vt. aplastar; —, n. calabaza, f.; calabacera, f.; (Sp. Am.) zapallo, m.

squat, vi. agacharse, sentarse en cuclillas; —, adj. agachado; rechoncho.

squaw, n. mujer india de E.U.A.

squawk, vi. graznar; (coll.) quejarse; —, n. graznido, m.

squeak, vi. chillar; —, n. grito, chillido, m.

squeal, vi. plañir, gritar; delatar.

squeamish, adj. fastidioso; demasiado delicado; remilgado.

squeeze, vt. apretar, comprimir; estrechar; —, n. compresión, f., acción de apretar; abrazo, m.

squeezer, n. exprimidor, estrujador, m.

squelch, vt. aplastar; hacer callar.

squint, adj. ojizaino; bizco; —, vi. mirar de reojo; mirar con los ojos medio cerrados.

squire, n. caballero (título de cortesía), m.; (en Inglaterra) hacendado, m.; alcalde, m.; —, vt. acompañar (a una señora, etc.).

squirm, vi. retorcerse, contorcerse.

squirrel, n. ardilla, f.

squirt, vt. jeringar; —, n. jeringa, f.; chorro, m.; (coll.) joven grosero; persona insignificante y presuntuosa.

S.R.O.: Standing room only, (theat.) espacio sólo para estar de pie.

S.S.: steamship, v. vapor; Sunday School, escuela dominical.

St.: Saint, Sto., San, Santo; Sta., Santa;

Strait, Estrecho; **Street,** Calle.

stab, vt. dar de puñaladas; —, n. puñalada, f.

stability, n. estabilidad, solidez, fijeza, f.

stabilize, vt. estabilizar, hacer firme.

stable, n. establo, m.; —, vt. poner en el establo; —, adj. estable.

staccato, adj. y adv. (mus.) staccato.

stack, n. niara, f.; (coll.) gran cantidad; montón, m.; —, vt. hacinar; amontonar.

stadium, n. estadio, m.

staff, n. báculo, palo, m.; apoyo, m.; cuerpo, m.; personal, m.; **editorial** —, redacción, f., cuerpo de redacción; **music** —, pentagrama, m.; **ruled** —, (mus.) pauta, f.; — **officer,** oficial del estado mayor.

stag, n. ciervo, m.; (coll.) hombre que va a una fiesta sin compañera; — **party,** tertulia para hombres.

stage, n. tablado, m.; teatro, escenario, m.; parada, f.; escalón, m.; — **fright,** nerviosidad al presentarse en público; —**lights,** candilejas, f. pl.; — **scenery,** escenografía, f., decoración, f., decorado, m.; bastidores, m. pl.; — **setting,** decoración, f.; — **struck,** loco por ingresar a las tablas; —, vt. (theat.) poner en escena.

stagecoach, n. diligencia, f.

stagecraft, n. arte teatral.

stage whisper, n. cuchicheo de actores que pueden oir los espectadores.

stagger, vi. vacilar, titubear; estar incierto; tambalear; —, vt. escalonar, alternar; asustar; hacer vacilar.

stagnant, adj. estancado.

stagnate, vi. estancarse.

stagnation, n. estancamiento, m.

staid, adj. grave, serio.

stain, vt. manchar; empañar la reputación; —, n. mancha, tacha, f., borrón, m.; deshonra, f.

stainless, adj. limpio, inmaculado; impecable; inoxidable; — **steel,** acero inoxidable.

stair, n. escalón, m.; —**s,** n. pl. escalera, f.; **back —s,** escalera de servicio, escalera trasera.

staircase, n. escalera, f.

stairway, n. escalera, f.

stake, n. estaca, f.; posta (en el juego), f.; **to have much at** —, tener mucho que perder; **to pull up —s,** levantar el campo; —, vt. estacar; poner en el juego; apostar; arriesgar.

stale, adj. añejo, viejo, rancio; —, vi. hacerse rancio o viejo; orinar el ganado; —, n. orina de ganado.

stalemate, n. tablas (en el juego de ajedrez), f. pl.; empate, m.; —, vt. hacer tablas (en el juego de ajedrez); parar, paralizar.

staleness, n. vejez, f.; rancidez, f.

stalk, vt. acechar; —, vi. ir pavoneándose; —, n. paso majestuoso; tallo, pie, tronco, m.; troncho (de ciertas hortalizas).

stall, n. pesebre, m.; tienda portátil; tabanco, m.; barraca, f.; (avi.) desplome, m.; silla (de coro), f.; butaca en el teatro; —, vt. meter en el establo; —vi. demorarse premeditadamente; (auto.) pararse.

stallion, n. caballo padre.

stalwart, adj. robusto, vigoroso.

stamen, n. (bot.) estambre, m.

stamina, n. fuerza vital; vigor, m.; resistencia, f.

stammer, vi. tartamudear, balbucear.

stammerer, n. tartamudo, da.

stamp, vt. patear (los pies); estampar, imprimir, sellar; acuñar; —, n. cuño, m.; sello, m.; impresión, f.; estampa, f.; timbre, m.; **postage** —, sello de correo; **revenue** —, sello de impuesto.

stampede, n. huida atropellada, fuga precipitada, estampida, f.; —, vi. huir en tropel.

stance, n. posición, postura, f.

stanch, vt. estancar; —, vi. estancarse; —, adj. sano; leal; firme, seguro; hermético, a prueba de agua.

stanchion, n. puntal, m.; apoyo que se pone en tierra firme para sostener las paredes, etc.

stand, vi. estar de pie o derecho; sostenerse; resistir; permanecer; pararse; hacer alto, estar situado; hallarse; — **by,** estar cerca o listo para ayudar; —, vt. sostener; soportar; **to — aside,** apartarse; **to — in line,** hacer cola; **to — out,** resaltar, destacarse; **to — still,** estarse parado o quieto; **to — up,** ponerse de pie, pararse; —, n. puesto, sitio, m.; posición, f.; parada, f.; tarima, f.; estante, m.

standard, n. estandarte, m.; modelo, m.; norma, f.; pauta, f.; tipo, m.; regla fija; patrón, m.; **gold** —, patrón de oro; — **equipment,** equipo corriente, equipo regular; — **of living,** nivel de vida; —, adj. normal; — **measure,** medida patrón; — **time,** hora normal.

standard-gauge, adj. de vía normal.

standardization, n. uniformidad, igualación, f.

standardize, vt. normalizar, regularizar, estandardizar.

stand-by, n. cosa o persona con que se

puede contar en un momento dado; — **credit,** crédito contingente.

standing, *adj.* permanente, fijado, establecido; estancado; — **army,** ejército permanente; — **room,** espacio para estar de pie; —, *n.* duración, *f.;* posición, *f.;* puesto, *m.* ; reputación, *f.*

standpoint, *n.* punto de vista.

standstill, *n.* pausa, *f.;* alto, *m.*

stanza, *n.* verso, *m.* , estrofa, *f.*

staple, *n.* materia prima; producto principal; presilla, grapa, *f.;* —**s,** *n. pl.* artículos de primera necesidad; —, *adj.* establecido; principal; —, *vt.* engrapar.

stapler, *n.* engrapador, *m.*

star, *n.* estrella, *f.;* asterisco, *m.* ; astro, *m.* ; —, *vt.* decorar con estrellas; marcar con asteriscos; presentar en calidad de estrella; **S— Spangled Banner,** bandera tachonada de estrellas; —, *vi.* (theat.) ser estrella, tomar el papel principal.

starboard, *n.* (naut.) estribor, *m.*

starch, *n.* almidón, *m.* ; —, *vt.* almidonar.

stare, *vt.* clavar la vista; —, *n.* mirada fija.

starfish, *n.* estrella de mar.

stark, *adj.* fuerte, áspero; puro; — **mad,** loco rematadamente; —**ly,** *adv.* del todo.

starlet, *n.* estrella joven de cine.

starlight, *n.* luz de las estrellas.

starling, *n.* (orn.) estornino, *m.*

starred, starry, *adj.* estrellado, como estrellas.

start, *vi.* sobrecogerse, sobresaltarse; estremecerse; levantarse de repente; salir los caballos en las carreras; —, *vt.* empezar, comenzar; fomentar; cebar, poner en marcha; **to — off, to — out,** ponerse en marcha;. , *n.* sobresalto, *m.* ; ímpetu, *m.* ; principio, *m.* ; **to get a —,** tomar la delantera.

starter, *n.* iniciador, ra; arrancador, ra; principio, *m.* ; (auto.) arranque, *m.* ; **to step on the —,** pisar el arranque.

starting, *n.* principio, *m.* ; origen, *m.* ; comienzo, *m.* ; — **point,** punto de partida; poste de salida (en las carreras).

startle, *vi.* sobresaltarse, estremecerse de repente; —, *n.* espanto, susto repentino.

startling, *adj.* espantoso, pasmoso, alarmante.

starvation, *n.* muerte por hambre, (med.) inanición, *f.*

starve, *vi.* perecer o morirse de hambre.

state, *n.* estado, *m.* ; condición, *f.;* (pol.) Estado, *m.* ; pompa, grandeza, *f.;* situación, *f.;* estación, *f.;* circunstancia,

f.; —**'s evidence,** (leyes) testimonio en favor del estado en una audiencia; —, *vt.* plantear; fijar; declarar; precisar.

statecraft, *n.* arte de gobernar.

statehouse, *n.* sede de la legislatura de un estado (en E.U.A.).

stately, *adj.* augusto, majestuoso.

statement, *n.* relación, cuenta, *f.;* afirmación, *f.;* (com.) estado de cuenta; relato, *m.* ; manifestación, *f.;* declaración, *f.*

stateroom, *n.* (naut.) camarote, *m.* ; (rail.) compartimiento, *m.*

statesman, *n.* estadista, político, *m.* ; hombre de estado.

statesmanship, *n.* política, *f.;* arte de gobernar.

static, *n.* (rad.) estática, *f.;* —, *adj.* estático.

statics, *n.* estática, *f.*

station, *n.* estación, *f.;* empleo, puesto, *m.* ; situación, postura, *f.;* grado, *m.* ; condición, *f.;* (rail.) estación, *f.;* paradero, *m.* ; **central —, main —,** central, *f.;* — **to— phone call,** llamada telefónica a quien conteste; — **wagon,** camioneta, *f.;* —, *vt.* apostar, situar, alojar.

stationary, *adj.* estacionario, fijo.

stationery, *n.* útiles o efectos de escritorio; papelería, *f.;* — **store,** papelería, *f.*

statistic, statistical, *adj.* estadístico.

statistician, *n.* experto en estadística.

statistics, *n. pl.* estadística, *f.*

stat. mile: statute mile, milla ordinaria.

statuary, *n.* estatuario, escultor, *m.* ; escultura de estatuas; grupo de estatuas; —, *adj.* estatuario.

statue, *n.* estatua, *f.*

stature, *n.* estatura, talla, *f.*

status, *n.* posición, condición, *f.;* — **quo,** statu quo.

statute, *n.* estatuto, *m.* ; reglamento, *m.* ; regla, *f.*

statutory, *adj.* estatuido, establecido por la ley; perteneciente a un estatuto; castigable por el estatuto.

staunch = stanch

stave, *vt.* romper las duelas; quebrantar; **to — off,** impedir, alejar, evitar; —, *n.* duela de barril.

stay, *n.* estancia, permanencia, *f.;* suspensión (de una sentencia); cesación, *f.* ; apoyo, *m.* ; estribo, *m.* ; —**s,** corsé, justillo, *m.* ; —, *vi.* quedarse, permanecer, estarse; tardar, detenerse, aguardarse, esperarse; **to — in bed,** guardar cama; —, *vt.* detener, contener; apoyar.

stead, *n.* lugar, sitio, paraje, *m.*

steadfast, *adj.* firme, estable, sólido; —**ly,** *adv.* con constancia.

steadily, *adv.* firmemente; invariablemente.
steady, *adj.* firme, fijo; —, *vt.* hacer firme.
steak, *n.* bistec, *m.*
steal, *vt.* y *vi.* hurtar, robar; **to — in,** colarse; **to — away,** escabullirse.
stealth, *n.* hurto, *m.* ; **by —,** a hurtadillas.
stealthily, *adv.* a hurtadillas.
stealthy, *adj.* furtivo.
steam, *n.* vapor, *m.* ; —, *adj.* de vapor; — **bath,** baño de vapor; — **boiler,** caldera de una máquina de vapor; — **engine,** bomba de vapor, máquina de vapor; — **fitter,** montador de tubos y calderas de vapor; — **heat,** calefacción por vapor; — **radiator,** calorífero de vapor; — **roller,** aplanadora de vapor; — **shovel,** pala de vapor; — **pressure,** presión del vapor; —, *vi.* vahear; —, *vt.* limpiar con vapor; cocer al vapor.
steamboat, *n.* vapor, *m.* ; buque de vapor.
steamer, *n.* vapor, *m.* ; máquina o carro de vapor; — **rug,** manta de viaje.
steamship, *n.* vapor, *m.* ; buque de vapor; — **agency,** agencia de vapores; — **line,** línea de vapores.
steed, *n.* caballo brioso; corcel, *m.*
steel, *n.* acero, *m.* ; **alloy —,** aleación de acero; **bar —,** acero en barras; **carbon —,** acero al carbón; **chrome —,** acero al cromo; **hard —,** acero fundido; **nickel —,** acero níquel; **raw —,** acero bruto; **silver —,** acero de plata; **stain-less —,** acero inoxidable; — **wool,** lana de acero; **tempered —,** acero recocido; **vanadium —,** acero al vana-dio; —, *vt.* acerar; fortalecer, endurecer.
steelworker, *n.* obrero en una fábrica de acero.
steelworks, *n.* acería, *f.,* fábrica de acero; talleres de acero.
steep, *adj.* escarpado, pino; (coll.) exorbitante; —, *n.* precipicio, *m.* ; —, *vt.* empapar, remojar.
steeple, *n.* torre, *f.;* campanario, *m.* ; espira,
steeplechase, *n.* carrera ciega, carrera de obstáculos.
steeplejack, *n.* reparador de espiras, chimeneas, etc.
steer, *n.* novillo, *m.* ; (coll.) consejo, *m.* ; buey, *m.* ; —, *vt.* gobernar; guiar, dirigir.
steerage, *n.* gobierno, *m.* ; (naut.) antecámara de un navío; proa, *f.*
steering, *n.* dirección, *f.;* —, *adj.* de gobierno (de automóvil, etc.); — **gear,** (naut.) aparato de gobierno; — **wheel,** volante, *m.*

stein, *n.* tarro especial para cerveza.
stellar, *adj.* estelar.
stem, *n.* vástago, tallo, *m.* ; estirpe, *f.;* (naut.) branque, *m.* ; —, *vt.* cortar (la corriente) ; estancar.
stench, *n.* hedor, *m.*
stencil, *n.* patrón, dechado, *m.* ; patrón estarcidor, estarcidor, *m.* ; estarcido, *m.* ; —, *vt.* estarcir.
stenographer, *n.* taquígrafo, fa, estenógrafo, fa; mecanógrafo, fa.
stenographic, stenographical, *adj.* estenográfico.
stenography, *n.* taquigrafía, estenografía, *f.*
stenotype, *n.* estenotipia, *f.*
stenotypist, *n.* estenomecanógrafo, fa, mecanotaquígrafo, fa.
step, *n.* paso, *m.* ; peldaño, escalón, *m.* ; huella, *f.;* trámite, *m.;* gestión, *f.;* **in —,** de acuerdo; **to be in —,** llevar el paso; *vi.* dar un paso; andar; —, *vt.* escalonar; **to — in,** entrar; **to — on,** pisar; **to — out,** salir; (coll.) ir de parranda; **to — up,** acelerar, avivar.
stepbrother, *n.* medio hermano, hermanastro, *m.*
stepdaughter, *n.* hijastra, *f.*
stepfather, *n.* padrastro, *m.*
stepladder, *n.* escalera de mano; gradilla, *f.*
stepmother, *n.* madrastra, *f.*
steppingstone, *n.* pasadera, *f.;* medio para progresar o adelantar.
stepsister, *n.* media hermana, hermanastra, *f.*
stepson, *n.* hijastro, *m.*
stereophonic, *adj.* estereofónico.
stereoscope, *n.* estereoscopio, *m.*
stereotype, *n.* estereotipia, *f.;* —, *vt.* estereotipar.
sterile, *adj.* estéril.
sterility, *n.* esterilidad, *f.*
sterilization, *n.* esterilización, *f.*
sterilize, *vt.* desinfectar, esterilizar.
sterling, *adj.* genuino, verdadero; —, *n.* moneda esterlina; — **silver,** plata esterlina.
stern, *adj.* austero, rígido, severo; ceñudo; —, *n.* (naut.) popa, *f.*
sternum, (anat.) *n.* esternón, *m.*
steroid, *n.* esteroide, *m.*
stet, (print.) reténgase.
stethoscope, *n.* (med.) estetoscopio, *m.*
stevedore, *n.* (naut.) estibador, *m.*
stew, *vt.* y *vi.* estofar; guisar; (coll.) mortificarse; —, *n.* guisado, guiso, *m.* ; sancocho, *m.*
steward, *n.* mayordomo, *m.* ; (naut.) despensero, *m.* ; **cabin —,** camarero, *m.*
stewardess, *n.* camarera; **plane —,** azafa-

ta, sobrecargo, aeromoza, *f.*

stewpan, *n.* cazuela, *f.*

stick, *n.* palo, bastón, *m.* ; vara, *f.;* **incense** —, pebete, *m.* ; —, *vt.* pegar; picar; punzar; —, *vi.* pegarse; detenerse; perseverar.

sticker, *n.* etiqueta engomada.

sticking, *n.* pegadura, *f.*

stickleback, *n.* (ichth.) espino, *m.*

stickler, *n.* porfiador, ra; persona escrupulosa.

stickpin, *n.* alfiler de corbata, (Mex.) fistol, *m.*

stick-up, *n.* (coll.) asalto, robo, *m.*

sticky, *adj.* viscoso, pegajoso, pegadizo.

stiff, *adj.* tieso; duro, torpe; rígido; obstinado; — **neck**, torticolis o tortícolis, *m.*

stiffen, *vt.* atiesar, endurecer; —, *vi.* endurecerse.

stiffness, *n.* tesura, rigidez, *f.;* obstinación,

stifle, *vt.* sofocar.

stifling, *adj.* sofocante; — **heat**, calor asfixiante.

stigma, *n.* nota de infamia, estigma, *m.* ; borrón, *m.*

stile, *n.* portillo con escalones (para pasar de un cercado a otro).

still, *vt.* aquietar, aplacar; calmar; —, *adj.* silencioso, tranquilo; —, *n.* silencio, *m.* ; alambique, *m.* ; fotografía para anunciar una película; —, *adv.* todavía; siempre, hasta ahora; no obstante.

stillborn, *adj.* nacido muerto.

stillness, *n.* calma, quietud, *f.*

stilt, *n.* zanco, *m.*

stilted, *adj.* altisonante, afectado.

stimulant, *n.* estimulante, *m.*

stimulate, *vt.* estimular, aguijonear.

stimulation, *n.* estímulo, *m.* ; estimulación, *f.*

stimulus, *n.* estímulo, *m.*

sting, *vt.* picar o morder (un insecto); —, *n.* aguijón, *m.;* punzada, picadura, picada, *f.;* remordimiento de conciencia.

stinginess, *n.* tacañería, avaricia, *f.*

stinging, *adj.* picante; mordaz; punzante; —**nettle**, (bot.) ortiga, *f.*

stingy, *adj.* mezquino, tacaño, avaro.

stink, *vi.* heder; —, *n.* hedor, *m.*

stint, *vt.* limitar; ser económico; —, *n.* límite, *m.* ; restricción, *f.;* tarea asignada.

stipulate, *vt.* y *vi.* estipular.

stipulation, *n.* estipulación, *f.;* contrato mutuo.

stir, *vt.* mover; agitar; menear; conmover; incitar; —, *vi.* moverse; bullir; —, *n.* tumulto, *m.* ; turbulencia, *f.;* movi-

miento, *m.* ; (coll.) cárcel, *f.*

stirring, *adj.* emocionante, animador.

stirrup, *n.* estribo, *m.*

stitch, *vt.* coser, bastear; —, *n.* puntada, *f.;* punto, *m.*

stock, *n.* tronco, *m.* ; injerto, *m.* ; zoquete, *m.* ; mango, *m.* ; corbatín, *m.* ; estirpe, *m.* ; linaje, *m.* ; (com.) capital, principal, *m.* ; fondo, *m.* ; (com.) acción, *f.;* ganado, *m.* ; **in** —, en existencia; **preferred** —**s**, acciones preferentes; — **company**, sociedad anónima; — **exchange**, bolsa, *f.*, bolsa de comercio, bolsa financiera; — **market**, mercado de valores; —**s**, *pl.* acciones en los fondos públicos; **supply** —, provisión, *f.;* **to speculate in** —**s**, jugar a la bolsa; —, *vt.* proveer, abastecer.

stockade, *n.* palizada, *f.;* estacada, *f.*

stockbroker, *n.* agente de cambio, corredor de bolsa, bolsista, *m.*

stockholder, *n.* accionista, *m.* y *f.*

stocking, *n.* media, *f.*

stock-in-trade, *n.* existencias, *f. pl.* ; surtido, *m.* ; recursos para un negocio.

stockjobbing, *n.* juego de bolsa, agiotaje, *m.*

stockpile, *n.* acumulación de mercancías de reserva; —, *vt.* acumular mercancías de reserva.

stockroom, *n.* depósito, *m.*

stocky, *adj.* rechoncho.

stockyard, *n.* rastro, *m.* ; corral de ganado.

stodgy, *adj.* hinchado; regordete; pesado, indigesto.

stoic, *n.* y *adj.* estoico, ca.

stoical, *adj.* estoico; —**ly**, *adv.* estoicamente.

stoicism, *n.* estoicismo, *m.*

stoke, *vt.* y *vi.* atizar el fuego.

stoker, *n.* fogonero, *m.* ; cargador, *m.*

stole, *n.* estola, *f.;* —, *pretérito* del verbo **steal**.

stolen, *p.p.* del verbo **steal**.

stolid, *adj.* estólido.

stomach, *n.* estómago, *m.* ; apetito, *m.* ; **on the** —, boca abajo; —, *vt.* aguantar; soportar.

stone, *n.* piedra, *f.;* canto, *m.* ; (med.) cálculo, *m.* ; cuesco, *m.* ; pepita, *f.*, hueso de fruta; alhaja, *f.*, piedra preciosa; **hewn** —, cantería, *f.;* **of** —, pétreo; — **fruit**, fruta de hueso; **corner** —, piedra angular; **foundation** —, piedra fundamental; —, *vt.* apedrear; quitar los huesos de las frutas; empedrar; trabajar de albañilería.

stonecutter, *n.* picapedrero, *m.*

stony, *adj.* de piedra, pétreo; duro.

---

stood, *pretérito y p.p.* del verbo **stand.**

stooge, *n.* cómico, *m.* ; paniaguado, *m.* ; secuaz servil; (Mex.) palero (en el teatro), *m.*

stool, *n.* banquillo, taburete, *m.* ; silleta, ; evacuación, *f.;* **piano —,** banqueta, *f.;* **— pigeon,** señuelo, *m.* ; espía, *m.* y *f.,* delatador, ora; persona empleada para embaucar.

stoop, *n.* inclinación hacia abajo; abatimiento, *m.* ; escalinata, *f.;* **—,** *vi.* encorvarse, inclinarse; bajarse; agacharse.

stop, *vt.* detener, parar, diferir; cesar, suspender, paralizar; tapar; **—,** *vi.* pararse, hacer alto; **to — a clock,** parar un reloj; **—,** *n.* pausa, *f.;* obstáculo, *m.* ; parada, *f.;* detención, *f.;* **— signal,** señal de alto o de parada; **— light,** luz de parada; **— watch,** cronógrafo, *m.*

stopover, *n.* escala, *f.;* parada en un punto intermediario del camino.

stoppage, *n.* obstrucción, *f.;* impedimento, *m.* ; (rail.) alto, *m.*

stopping, *n.* obstrucción, *f.;* impedimento, *m.* ; (rail.) alto, *m.* ; **— place,** paradero, *m.*

storage, *n.* almacenamiento, *m.* ; almacenaje, *m.* ; **cold —,** cámara frigorífica; **— battery,** batería, *f.,* batería de acumuladores, acumulador, *m.*

store, *n.* abundancia, *f.;* provisión, *f.;* almacén, *m.* ; **department —,** bazar, *m.,* tienda de departamentos; **dry goods —,** mercería, *f.;* **—,** *vt.* surtir, proveer, abastecer; almacenar.

storehouse, *n.* almacén, *m.*

storekeeper, *n.* guardaalmacén, *m.* ; (naut.) pañolero, *m.*

storeroom, *n.* almacén, depósito, *m.* ; (naut.) pañol, *m.*

storied, *adj.* con pisos; **three — house,** casa de tres pisos.

stork, *n.* cigüeña, *f.*

storm, *n.* tormenta, tempestad, borrasca, *f.;* (mil.) asalto, *m.* ; tumulto, *m.* ; **— center,** centro tempestuoso; **— door,** guardapuerta, *f.;* **— window,** contraventana, *f.;* **—,** *vt.* tomar por asalto; **—,** *vi.* haber tormenta.

stormy, *adj.* tempestuoso; violento, turbulento.

story, *n.* cuento, *m.* ; historia, *f.;* crónica, *f.;* fábula, *f.;* (coll.) mentira, *f.;* piso de una casa.

stout, *adj.* robusto, vigoroso; corpulento; fuerte; **—ly,** *adv.* valientemente, obstinadamente; **—,** *n.* cerveza fuerte; persona corpulenta; vestido propio para personas gruesas.

stove, *n.* estufa, *f.;* fogón, *m.* ; hornillo, *m.*

stow, *vt.* meter, colocar; (coll.) dejar; (naut.) estibar.

stowaway, *n.* polizón, ona.

straddle, *vt.* montar a horcajadas; **—,** *vi.* evitar tomar un partido; **—,** *n.* el estar a horcajadas.

straggle, *vi.* vagar; extenderse.

straggler, *n.* rezagado, da.

straight, *adj.* derecho, recto; justo; **— line,** línea recta; **— razor,** navaja ordinaria de afeitar; **—,** *adv.* directamente; en línea recta.

straightaway, *n.* curso directo; **—,** *adj.* derecho, en dirección continua.

straightedge, *n.* regla (para trazar línea recta), *f.*

straighten, *vt.* enderezar.

straightforward, *adj.* derecho; franco; leal.

straightway, *adv.* inmediatamente, luego.

strain, *vt.* colar, filtrar; cerner, trascolar; apretar (a uno contra sí) ; forzar; violentar; **—,** *vi.* esforzarse; **—,** *n.* retorcimiento, *m.* ; raza, *f.;* linaje, *m.* ; estilo, *m.* ; sonido, *m.* ; armonía, *f.;* tensión, tirantez, *f.*

strainer, *n.* colador, *m.* , coladera, *f.*

strait, *adj.* rígido; exacto; escaso; **— jacket,** camisa de fuerza; **—,** *n.* (geog.) estrecho, *m.* ; aprieto, *m.* , angustia, *f.;* penuria, *f.*

straiten, *vt.* acortar, estrechar, angostar; **—ed circumstances,** circunstancias reducidas, escasos recursos.

strand, *n.* costa, playa, ribera, *f.;* cordón, *m.* ; **—,** *vi.* encallar; **—,** *vt.* embarrancar; abandonar; **to be —ed,** perderse, estar uno solo y abandonado.

strange, *adj.* extraño; curioso; raro; peculiar; **—ly,** *adv.* extraordinariamente.

stranger, *n.* extranjero, ra, desconocido, da; forastero, ra.

strangle, *vt.* ahogar, estrangular; **— hold,** (entre luchadores) presa que ahoga al antagonista.

strap, *n.* correa, *f.,* tira de cuero; correa o trabilla (de calzado); **—,** *vt.* atar con correas.

strapping, *adj.* robusto, fornido, fuerte.

stratagem, *n.* estratagema, *f.;* astucia, *f.*

strategic, *adj.* estratégico.

Strategic Air Command (S.A.C.), *n.* Mando Aéreo Estratégico.

strategy, *n.* estrategia, *f.*

stratocruiser, *n.* (avi.) estratocrucero, *m.*

stratosphere, *n.* estratosfera, *f.*

stratum, *n.* lecho, estrato, *m.*

straw, *n.* paja, *f.;* bagatela, *f.;* (Mex.)popote (para tomar líquidos), *m.;***—,** *adj.* de paja, falso; **— hat,** sombrero de paja; **— vote,** voto no oficial para determinar la opinión pública.

strawberry, n. fresa, frutilla, f.

stray, vi. extraviarse; perder el camino; —, n. persona descarriada; animal extraviado; —, adj. extraviado, perdido, aislado, sin conexión.

streak, n. raya, lista, f.; —, vt. rayar.

stream, n. arroyo, río, torrente, raudal, m.; corriente, f.; a — of children, una muchedumbre infantil; down —, agua abajo; —, vt. y vi. correr, fluir; entrar a torrentes.

streamer, n. (naut.) flámula, f., gallardete, m. ; cinta colgante.

streamline, n. línea en que corre una corriente; —, vt. dar forma aerodinámica; modernizar.

streamlined, adj. aerodinámico.

street, n. calle, f.; — crossing, cruce de calle; — intersection, bocacalle, f.

streetcar, n. tranvía, m. ; — conductor, cobrador, m. ; — line, línea de tranvía.

streetwalker, n. ramera, prostituta, mujer de la calle.

strength, n. fuerza, robustez, f., vigor, m. ; fortitud, f.; potencia, f.; fortaleza, resistencia, f.; to gain —, cobrar fuerzas; tensile —, resistencia a la tracción.

strengthen, vt. corroborar, consolidar; fortificar; reforzar; —, vi. fortalecerse.

strenuous, adj. estrenuo, fuerte; vigoroso; arduo; activo; —ly, adv. vigorosamente.

streptococcus, n. estreptococo, m.

streptomycin, n. (med.) estreptomicina, f.

stress, n. fuerza, f.; tensión, f.; acento, m.; —ed syllable, sílaba acentuada; —, vt. acentuar, dar énfasis, hacer hincapié en.

stretch, vt. y vi. extender, alargar; estirar; extenderse; esforzarse; —, n. extensión, f.; esfuerzo, m. ; estirón, m. ; trecho, m.

stretcher, n. estirador, m. ; tendedor, m. ; parihuela, camilla, f.

strew, vt. esparcir; sembrar.

strict, adj. estricto, estrecho; exacto; riguroso, severo; terminante; — order, orden terminante; —ly, adv. estrictamente, con severidad.

stride, n. tranco, m. ; adelanto, avance, m.; —, vt. cruzar, pasar a zancadas; —, vi. andar a pasos largos.

strident, adj. estridente.

strife, n. contienda, disputa, f.; rivalidad, f.

strike, vt. y vi. golpear; dar; chocar; declararse en huelga; — out, tachar; (béisbol) hacer perder el tanto al bateador que falla en golpear la pelota en tres golpes consecutivos; —, n. golpe, m.; hallazgo, m. ; huelga, f.

strikebreaker, n. rompehuelgas, m. y f., esquirol, m.

striker, n. huelguista, m. y f.; golpeador, ra.

striking, adj. impresionante, sorprendente, llamativo; —ly, adv. de un modo sorprendente.

string, n. cordón, m. ; cuerda, f ; hilo, m. ; hilera, f.; fibra, f.; — bean, habichuela verde, judía, f., (Mex.) ejote, m.

stringed, adj. encordado; — instrument, instrumento de cuerda.

stringent, adj. severo, riguroso, rígido; convincente.

strip, n. tira, faja, f.; —, vt. desnudar, despojar.

stripe, n. raya, lista, f.; roncha, f., cardenal, m. ; azote, m. ; —, vt. rayar.

striped, adj. rayado.

strive, vi. esforzarse; empeñarse; disputar; contender; oponerse.

stroboscope, n. estroboscopio, m.

stroke, n. golpe, m. ; toque (en la pintura), m. ; sonido (de reloj), m. ; (golf) tirada, f.; golpe de émbolo; caricia con la mano; (med.) apoplejía, f.; plumada, f.; palote, m. ; —, vt. acariciar.

stroll, vi. tunar, vagar, pasearse; —, n. paseo, m.

stroller, n. paseante, m. y f.

strong, adj. fuerte, vigoroso, robusto; concentrado; poderoso; violento; pujante; —ly, adv. con fuerza.

strongbox, n. caja fuerte.

stronghold, n. fortaleza, f.

strontium, n. (chem.) estroncio, m.

struck, adj. cerrado o afectado por huelga; golpeado.

structural, adj. estructural; construccional; — iron, hierro para construcciones.

structure, n. estructura, f.; edificio, m. ; fábrica, f.

struggle, n. lucha, contienda, f., conflicto, m. ; brega, f.; —, vi. esforzarse; luchar, lidiar; agitarse; contender.

strum, vt. (mus.) tocar defectuosamente (un instrumento de cuerda); rasguear (una guitarra, etc.).

strut, vi. pavonearse, zarandearse; —, n. pavonada, f.; contoneo, m. ; poste, puntal, m.

strychnine, n. estricnina, f.

stub, n. tocón, m. ; talón, m. ; colilla, f.; fragmento, m. ; —, vt. pegar, dar.

stubble, n. rastrojo, m.

stubborn, adj. obstinado, terco, testarudo; enrevesado; cabezón; to be —, ser porfiado o terco.

stubby, adj. cachigordete; gordo.

stucco, n. estuco, m. , escayola, f.

stuck-up, adj. (coll.) arrogante, presumido, presuntuoso.

stud, n. botón de camisa; tachón, m. ; yeguada, f.; — mare, yegua para cría; , *vt.* tachonar.

student, *n.* estudiante, *m.* y *f.,* alumno, na; —, *adj.* estudiantil.

studhorse, *n.* caballo padre.

studio, *n.* estudio de un artista (pintor, escultor, etc.); **moving picture** —, estudio cinematográfico.

studio couch, *n.* sofá cama, *m.*

studious, *adj.* estudioso; diligente.

study, *n.* estudio, *m.* ; aplicación, *f.*; meditación profunda; gabinete, *m.* ; —, *vt.* estudiar, cursar; observar; —, *vi.* estudiar, aplicarse.

stuff, *n.* materia, *f.*; material, *m.* ; efectos. *m. pl.* ; cosas, *f. pl.* ; materia prima; — **and nonsense!** ¡bagatela! ¡niñería! —, *vt.* henchir, llenar; cebar; rellenar; —, *vi.* atracarse; tragar; **to — oneself,** hartarse, soplarse.

stuffing, *n.* relleno, *m.* ; atestadura, *f.*

stuffy, *adj.* mal ventilado; (coll.) enojado y terco; (coll.) estirado, presuntuoso.

stumble, *vi.* tropezar; —, *n.* traspié, tropiezo, *m.*

stumbling, *n.* tropezón, *m.* ; — **block,** tropezadero, *m.* ; obstáculo, impedimento, *m.*

stump, *n.* tocón, *m.* ; colilla, *f.*; muñón, *m.*; — **speech,** discurso de política; —, *vt.* aplastar, confundir, dejar estupefacto; coger —, *vi.* (coll.) pronunciar discursos políticos.

stun, *vt.* aturdir; pasmar.

stung, *pretérito,* y *p.p.* del verbo **sting.**

stunning, *adj.* elegante, atractivo; aturdidor.

stunt, *vt.* no dejar crecer; reprimir —, *n.* hazaña, *f.*; — **flying,** acrobacia aérea.

stupefy, *vt.* atontar, atolondrar.

stupendous, *adj.* estupendo, maravilloso; — **ly,** *adv.* estupendamente.

stupid, *adj.* estúpido, tonto, bruto; **to be —,** ser duro de mollera; —, *n.* bobo, ba; tonto, ta; **—ly,** *adv.* estúpidamente.

stupidity, *n.* estupidez, *f.*

stupor, *n.* estupor, letargo, *m.*

sturdily, *adv.* robustamente, vigorosamente.

sturdy, *adj.* fuerte, tieso, robusto, rollizo; determinado, firme.

sturgeon, *n.* (ichth.) esturión, *m.*

stutter, *vi.* tartamudear; (Sp. Am.) gaguear; —, *n.* tartamudeo, *m.*

sty, *n.* zahúrda, pocilga, *f.*; (med.) orzuelo, *m.*

style, *n.* estilo, *m.* ; título, *m.* ; **gnomon,** *m.* ; modo, *m.* ; moda, *f.*; **in —,** a la moda; —, *vt.* intitular, nombrar; confeccionar según la moda.

stylish, *adj.* elegante, a la moda.

stylist, *n.* estilista, *m.* y *f.*

stylize, *vt.* estilizar.

stylograph, *n.* estilográfica, *f.,* pluma estilográfica.

stylographic, *adj.* estilográfico.

suave, *adj.* pulido y cortés; **—ly,** *adv.* pulida cortésmente.

sub, *n.* (coll.) sustituto, ta; submarino, *m.*; subordinado, da.

subcommittee, *n.* subcomisión, *f.,* subcomité, *m.*

subconscious, *adj.* subconsciente; —, *n.* subconsciencia, *f.*

subdivide, *vt.* subdividir.

subdivision, *n.* subdivisión, *f.*

subdue, *vt.* sojuzgar, rendir, sujetar; conquistar; mortificar.

subhead, *n.* subtítulo, *m.* , título o encabezamiento secundario.

subject, *n.* sujeto, tema tópico, *m.* ; asignatura, *f.*; materia, *f* ; —, *adj.* sujeto, sometido a; — **matter,** asunto, tema, *m.*; —, *vt.* sujetar, someter; supeditar; rendir, exponer.

subjection, *n.* sujeción, *f.*; supeditación, *f.*

subjective, *adj.* subjetivo; — , *adv.* subjetivamente.

subjugate, *vt.* sojuzgar, sujetar.

subjunctive, *n.* y *adj.* subjuntivo, *m.*

sublease, *vt.* subarrendar; —, *n.* subarriendo, *m.*

sublet, *vt.* subarrendar, dar en alquiler.

sublime, *adj.* sublime, excelso; **—ly,** *adv.* de un modo sublime; —, *n.* sublimidad, *f.*; —, *vt.* hacer sublime, exaltar; purificar; (chem.) sublimar.

submarine, *n.* y *adj.* submarino, sumergible, *m.*

submerge, submerse, *vt.* sumergir.

submission, *n.* sumisión, *f.,* rendimiento, *m.* ; resignación, *f.*; humildad, *f.*

submissive, *adj.* sumiso, obsequioso; **—ly,** *adv.* con sumisión.

submit, *vt.* someter, rendir; —, *vi.* someterse.

suborbital, *adj.* suborbital.

subordinate, *n.* y *adj.* subordinado, subalterno, inferior, dependiente, *m.* ; —, *vt.* subordinar; someter.

subordination, *n.* subordinación, *f.*

subpoena, subpena, *n.* orden de comparecer, comparendo, *m.* ; —, *vt.* citar para comparecencia, citar con comparendo.

subscribe, *vt.* y *vi.* suscribir, certificar con su firma; suscribirse (a una revista, periódico, etc.); consentir; abonarse (a una función de ópera, etc.).

subscriber, *n.* suscriptor, ra, abonado, da.

subscription, *n.* suscripción, *f.*, abono, *m.*

subsequent, *adj.* subsiguiente, subsecuente; **—ly,** *adv.* posteriormente.

subservient, *adj.* subordinado; útil.

subside, *vi.* apaciguarse; bajar, disminuirse.

subsidiary, *adj.* subsidiario, afiliado, auxiliar; —, *n.* auxiliar, *m.*

subsidize, *vt.* dar subsidios.

subsidy, *n.* subsidio, socorro, *m.* , subvención, *f.*

subsist, *vi.* subsistir, existir; —, *vt.* mantener.

subsistence, *n.* existencia, *f.;* subsistencia, *f.*

subsoil, *n.* subsuelo, *m.*

substance, *n.* sustancia, *f.;* entidad, *f.;* esencia, *f.*

substantial, *adj.* sustancial; real, material; sustancioso; fuerte.

substantiate, *vt.* corroborar; verificar; comprobar; sustanciar.

substantive, *n.* (gram.) sustantivo, *m.*

substitute, *vt.* sustituir, remplazar; relevar; —, *n.* sustituto, ta; remplazo, *m.* ; suplente, *m.* ; lugarteniente, *m.* ; sobresaliente, *m.* ; —, *adj.* de sustituto.

substitution, *n.* sustitución, *f.*

subterfuge, *n.* subterfugio, *m.* , evasiva, *f.*

subterranean, subterraneous, *adj.* subterráneo; oculto; secreto.

subtitle, *n.* subtítulo, *m.* , título secundario.

subtle, *adj.* sutil, delicado, tenue; agudo, penetrante; astuto.

subtlety, *n.* sutileza, *f.*

subtract, *vt.* sustraer; (math.) restar.

subtraction, *n.* sustracción, *f.;* (math.) resta, *f.*

suburb, *n.* suburbio, arrabal, *m.;* —s, *pl.* afueras, *f. pl.*

suburban, *adj.* suburbano.

suburbanite, *n.* suburbano, na, morador o moradora de suburbio.

subversive, *adj.* subversivo.

subway, *n.* túnel, *m.* ; ferrocarril subterráneo; (coll.) metro, *m.*

sucaryl, *n.* nombre comercial de un compuesto azucarado parecido a la sacarina.

succeed, *vt.* y *vi.* suceder, seguir; conseguir, lograr, tener éxito.

success, *n.* éxito, *m.* , buen éxito; lucimiento, *m.*

successful, *adj.* próspero, dichoso; to be , tener buen éxito; —ly, *adv.* con éxito.

succession, *n.* sucesión, *f.;* descendencia, *f.;* herencia, *f.*

successive, *adj.* sucesivo.

successor, *n.* sucesor, ra.

succinct, *adj.* sucinto, compendioso; —ly, *adv.* de modo compendioso.

succor, *vt.* socorrer, ayudar; subvenir; —, *n.* socorro, *m.* ; ayuda, asistencia, *f.*

succotash, *n.* combinación de habas y maíz.

succulent, *adj.* suculento, jugoso.

succumb, *vi.* sucumbir.

such, *adj.* y *pron.* tal, semejante; — as, tal

como; — as (go there, etc.), los o las que (van allí, etc.); in — a manner, de tal modo.

suck, *vt.* y *vi.* chupar, mamar; —, *n.* chupada, *f.*

sucker, *n.* chupador, ra; persona fácil de engañar; (coll.) caramelo, *m.* , (Mex.) paleta, *f.*

sucking, *n.* chupadura, *f.;* —, *adj.* mamante; chupador.

suckle, *vt.* amamantar.

sucre, *n.* sucre, (unidad monetaria del Ecuador), *m.*

suction, *n.* succión, *f.;* chupada, *f.*

sudden, *adj.* repentino, no prevenido; —ly, *adv.* de repente, súbitamente, de pronto.

suds, *n. pl.* jabonadura, *f.,* espuma de jabón.

sue, *vt.* y *vi.* poner pleito, demandar.

suede, *n.* piel de ante.

suet, *n.* sebo, *m.* , grasa, *f.*

suffer, *vt.* y *vi.* sufrir; tolerar, padecer.

suffering, *n.* sufrimiento, *m.* , pena, *f.;* dolor, *m.* ; —, *adj.* doliente.

suffice, *vt.* y *vi.* bastar, ser suficiente.

sufficient, *adj.* suficiente, bastante.

suffix, *n.* (gram.) sufijo, *m.* ; —, *vt.* añadir un sufijo.

suffocate, *vt.* sofocar, ahogar; —, *vi.* sofocarse.

suffocation, *n.* sofocación, *f.*

suffrage, *n.* sufragio, voto, *m.*

suffuse, *vt.* difundir, derramar, extender.

suffusion, *n.* (med.) sufusión, *f.;* difusión, *f.*

sugar, *n.* azúcar, *m.* y *f.* (coll.) lisonja, *f.;* beet —, azúcar de remolacha; brown —, azúcar morena; corn — (glucose), glucosa, *f.;* cube —, azúcar cubicado, da; fruit —, fructosa, *f.;* granulated —, azúcar granulado, da; loaf —, azúcar de pilón; refined —, azúcar blanco, ca; — bowl, azucarero, *m.* , azucarera, *f.;* — cane, caña de azúcar; — crop, zafra, *f.;* — loaf, pan de azúcar; — mill, trapiche, *m.* ; (Sp. Am.) central, *f.;* —, *vt.* azucarar; confitar.

sugar-cane, *adj.* de caña de azúcar; — plantation, cañaveral, *m.* ; — juice, guarapo, *m.*

sugar-coat, *vt.* azucarar, garapiñar; hermosear lo feo; ocultar la verdad.

sugary, *adj.* azucarado, dulce.

suggest, *vt.* sugerir; proponer.

suggestion, *n.* sugestión, *f.*

suggestive, *adj.* sugestivo.

suicidal, *adj.* suicida.

suicide, *n.* suicidio, *m.* ; suicida, *m.* y *f.;* to commit —, suicidarse.

suit, *n.* vestido entero; traje, *m.* ; galanteo, *m.* ; petición, *f.;* pleito, *m.* ; ready-made —, traje hecho; — made to order, traje a la medida; **to bring** —, formar causa, demandar, entablar un juicio; —, vt. y vi. adaptar; surtir; ajustarse, acomodarse; convenir; —, vt. sentar, caer bien.

suitability, n. conveniencia, f.; compatibilidad, f.

suitable, adj. conforme, conveniente, satisfactorio; idóneo; **—bly,** adv. apropiadamente, debidamente.

suitcase, n. maleta, f.

suite, n. serie, f.; tren, m. , comitiva, f.; — **of rooms,** habitación de varios cuartos (en un hotel).

suitor, n. pretendiente, galán, m. ; demandante, m.

sulfa drugs, n. pl. sulfanilamidos, m. pl.

sulfonamide, n. sulfonamida, f.

sulk, n. mal humor; —, vi. ponerse malhumorado, hacer pucheros.

sulky, adj. regañón, malhumorado, resentido.

sullen, adj. intratable; hosco; **—ly,** adv. de mal humor; tercamente.

sully, vt. manchar, ensuciar; —, vi. empañarse.

sulphate, n. sulfato, m.

sulphur, n. azufre, m. ; — **dioxide,** gas sulfuroso, bióxido sulfuroso.

sultry, adj. caluroso y húmedo; sofocante; (coll.) ardiente, sensual.

sum, n. suma, f.; monto, m. ; (com.) montante, m. ; **certain** —, tanto, m. ; — **total,** total, m. , cifra total; —, vt. sumar; recopilar; **to — up,** resumir.

summarize, vt. resumir; recopilar.

summary, n. epítome, sumario, resumen, m. ; —, adj. sumario.

summation, n. total, m. , suma, f.

summer, n. verano, estío, m. ; —, adj. estival, de verano; — **house,** cenadero, quiosco, m. ; — **resort,** lugar de veraneo; —, vi. veranear.

summersault = somersault.

summertime, n. verano, m. , época de verano.

summit, n. ápice, m. ; cima, cresta, cumbre, f.; — **conference,** conferencia en la cumbre.

summon, vt. citar; requerir por auto de juez; convocar, convidar; (mil.) intimar la rendición.

summons, n. pl. citación, f.; requerimiento, m. ; emplazamiento, m.

sumptuous, adj. suntuoso.

sun, n. sol, m. ; — **parlor,** — **porch,** solana, f.; —, vt. asolear; —, vi. asolearse; tomar el sol.

sunbeam, n. rayo de sol.

sunblock, n. bloqueador solar, m.

sunbonnet, n. papalina, cofia para el sol.

sunburn, n. quemadura de sol; —, vi. quemarse por el sol.

sunburnt, adj. tostado por el sol, asoleado.

sundae, n. helado cubierto con jarabe y fruta o nueces machacadas.

Sunday, n. domingo, m. ; — **School** doctrina dominical, escuela dominical.

sunder, vt. separar, apartar.

sundial, n. reloj de sol, cuadrante, m.

sundown = sunset.

sundries, n. pl. géneros varios.

sundry, adj. vanos, muchos, diversos.

sunfast, adj. firme, a prueba de sol.

sunfish, n. (ichth.) rueda, f.

sunflower, n. girasol, mirasol, tornasol, m.

sung, p.p. del verbo **sing.**

sunglass, n. espejo ustorio; **—es,** anteojos contra el sol, gafas para el sol.

sunk, p.p. del verbo **sink.**

sunlamp, n. lámpara de rayos ultravioletas.

sunless, adj. sin sol, sin luz.

sunlight, n. luz del sol.

sunny, adj. asoleado; brillante; alegre; **it is** —, hace sol.

sunproof, adj. a prueba de sol.

sunrise, n. salida del sol.

sunroom, n. solana, f.

sunset, n. puesta del sol, f., ocaso, m.

sunshade, n. quitasol, m. ; pantalla, f.; visera contra el sol.

sunshine, n. luz solar, luz del sol, f.

sunshiny, adj. lleno de sol; resplandeciente como el sol.

sunstroke, n. insolación, f.

sup, vt. sorber, beber a sorbos; dar de cenar; —, vi. cenar.

superb, adj. soberbio, espléndido, excelente.

supercargo, n. (naut.) sobrecargo, m.

supercharge, vt. sobrealimentar (un motor).

supercilious, adj. arrogante, altanero; **—ly,** adv. con altivez.

superficial, adj. superficial.

superfine, adj. superfino.

superfluous, adj. superfluo; prolijo; redundante; **—ly,** adv. superfluamente.

superhighway, n. autopista, f.

superhuman, adj. sobrehumano.

superimpose, vt. sobreponer.

superintend, vt. inspeccionar, vigilar, dirigir.

superintendent, n. superintendente, mayordomo, m.

superior, n. y adj. jefe, superior, m.

superiority, n. superioridad, f.; arrogancia, f.

superlative, n. y adj. superlativo, m. ; **—ly,** adv. en sumo grado.

superman, n. superhombre, m.

supermarket, n. supermercado, m.

supernatural, adj. sobrenatural.

supersede, vt. sobreseer; remplazar; invalidar.

supersonic, adj. supersónico.

superstition, n. superstición, f.

superstitious, adj. supersticioso.

superstructure, n. superestructura, f.; edificio levantado sobre otra fábrica.

supervene, vi. sobrevenir.

supervise, vt. inspeccionar, dirigir, vigilar.

supervision, n. superintendencia, f.; dirección, inspección, vigilancia, f.

supervisor, n. superintendente, m. y f.; inspector, ra.

supper, n. cena, f.; Last S—, Ultima Cena; Lord's S—, institución de la Eucaristía; to have —, cenar.

supplant, vt. suplantar.

supple, adj. flexible, manejable; blando; —, vt. hacer flexible.

supplement, n. suplemento, m. ; —, vt. suplir; adicionar.

supplemental, supplementary, adj. adicional, suplementario.

suppliant, supplicant, n. y adj. suplicante, m. y f.

supplicate, vt. suplicar.

supply, vt. suplir, completar; surtir; proporcionar; dar, proveer; abastecer; —, n. surtido, m. ; provisión, f.; — and demand, oferta y demanda.

support, vt. sostener; soportar, asistir; basar; —, n. sustento, m. ; apoyo, m.

supporter, n. apoyo, m. ; protector, ra, defensor, ra.

suppose, vt. suponer.

supposed, adj. supuesto.

supposedly, adv. según se supone, hipotéticamente.

supposing, conj. (coll.) en caso de que; — that, suponiendo que.

supposition, n. suposición, f., supuesto, m.

suppress, vt. suprimir; reprimir.

suppression, n. supresión, f.

supremacy, n. supremacía, f.

supreme, adj. supremo.

Supreme Being, n. Ser Supremo, El Creador, Dios, m.

Supt., supt.: superintendent, super.te superintendente.

surcease, n. cesación, parada, f.; final, m.

surcharge, vt. sobrecargar; —, n. sobrecarga, f., recargo, m.

sure, adj. seguro, cierto, certero; firme; estable; to be —, sin duda; seguramente; ya se ve; —ly, adv. sin duda. sure-footed, adj. seguro, de pie firme.

surety, n. seguridad, f.; fiador, m. ; to go —, salir fiador.

surf, n. (naut.) resaca, f.; oleaje, m. ; — bathing, baño de oleaje.

surface, n. superficie, cara, f.; — tension, tensión superficial; —, vt. alisar; —, vi. emerger, surgir.

surfacing, n. recubrimiento (de un camino), m. ; revestimiento, m. ; alisamiento, m.

surfboard, n. acuaplano m.

surfboat, n. embarcación para navegar a través de rompientes fuertes.

surfeit, vt. y vi. hartar, saciar; ahitarse, saciarse; —, n. ahíto, empacho, m. ; indigestión, f.

surge, n. ola, onda, f.; golpe de mar; —, vi. embravecerse (el mar); agitarse; surgir.

surgeon, n. cirujano, m.

surgery, n. cirugía, f.

surgical, adj. quirúrgico.

surly, adj. aspero de genio; insolente.

surmise, vt. sospechar; suponer; —, n. sospecha, f.; suposición, f.

surmount, vt. sobrepujar; superar.

surname, n. apellido, patronímico, m.; —, vt. apellidar, dar un apellido (a alguien).

surpass, vt. sobresalir, sobrepujar, exceder, aventajar, sobrepasar.

surplice, n. sobrepelliz, f.

surplus, n. sobrante, m. , sobra, f.

surprise, vt. sorprender; —, n. sorpresa, extrañeza, f.

surprising, adj. sorprendente, inesperado.

surrealism, n. surrealismo, m.

surrender, vt. rendir; ceder, renunciar; —, vi. rendirse; —, n. rendición, f.; sumisión, f.

surreptitious, adj. subrepticio.

surrogate, vt. subrogar; —, n. suplente, sustituto, m.

surround, vt. circundar, cercar, rodear.

surrounding, adj. circunstante; que rodea; —, n. acción de circundar; —s, pl. cercanías, f. pl. , alrededores, m. pl. ; ambiente, m.

surtax, n. impuesto especial, impuesto adicional.

surveillance, n. vigilancia, f.

survey, vt. inspeccionar, examinar; apear (tierras); —, n. inspección, f.; apeo (de tierras), m. ; estudio, m.

surveying, n. agrimensura, f.; estudio, examen, m. ; inspección, f.

surveyor, n. sobrestante, m. ; agrimensor, topógrafo, m.

survival, n. supervivencia, f.; — of the fittest, supervivencia de los más aptos.

survive, vi. sobrevivir.

surviving, adj. sobreviviente.

survivor, n. sobreviviente, m. y f.

susceptibility, n. susceptibilidad, f.

susceptible, adj. susceptible.

suspect, *vt.* y *vi.* sospechar, tener malicia; barruntar; —, *n.* persona sospechosa.

suspend, *vt.* suspender, prorrogar, aplazar.

suspenders, *n. pl.* tirantes, *m. pl.*

suspense, *n.* suspensión, *f.;* detención, *f.;* incertidumbre, duda, *f.;* — **movie,** película de misterio.

suspension, *n.* suspensión, *f.;* — **bridge,** puente colgante; — **of work,** paro, *m.*

suspicion, *n.* sospecha, *f.*

suspicious, *adj.* suspicaz; sospechoso, receloso; **to make** —, dar que pensar.

sustain, *vt.* sostener, sustentar, mantener; apoyar; sufrir.

sustaining, *adj.* que sustenta; — **program,** (rad. y TV.) programa radiofónico que perifonean por su cuenta las radiodifusoras.

sustenance, *n.* sostenimiento, sustento, *m.;* alimentos, *m. pl.*

svelte, *adj.* esbelto.

SW S.W. s.w.: southwest, SO. sudoeste.

swab, *n.* (naut.) lampazo, *m.;* (med.) esponja, *f.;* —, *vt.* fregar, limpiar; (naut.) lampacear.

swaddling, *n.* empañadura, *f.;* — **clothes,** pañales, *m. pl.,* envolturas, *f. pl.*

swagger, *vi.* baladronear; —, *n.* baladronada, *f.;* — **stick,** bastón corto y liviano.

swain, *n.* enamorado, *m.;* zagal, *m.*

swale, *n.* terreno pantanoso.

swallow, *n.* (orn.) golondrina, *f.;* bocado, *m.;* trago, *m.;* —, *vt.* tragar, engullir.

swallow-tailed, *adj.* de cola bifurcada como una golondrina; — **coat,** frac, *m.*

swam, *pretérito* del verbo **swim.**

swamp, *n.* pantano, fangal, *m.;* —, *vt.* sumergir; abrumar (de trabajo).

swan, *n.* cisne, *m.;* — **song,** canto del cisne, *m.;* última obra de un poeta o un músico; — **dive** (natación) salto del ángel.

swank, *adj.* (coll.) elegante; —, *n.* (coll.) moda, *f.;* —, *vi.* (coll.) baladronear.

swanky, *adj.* (coll.) de moda ostentosa; elegante.

swap, *vt.* y *vi.* (coll.) cambalachear, cambiar; (coll.) hacer permutas; —, *n.* (coll.) cambio, trueque, *m.*

swarm, *n.* enjambre, *m.;* gentío, *m.;* hormiguero, *m.;* —, *vi.* enjambrar; hormiguear de gente; abundar.

swarthy, *adj.* atezado, moreno.

swatch, *n.* muestrecita (de tela, etc.), *f.*

swath, *n.* rastro, *m.,* huella, *f.;* hilera, *f.;* guadañada, *f.*

swathe, *n.* faja, *f.;* rastro, *m.,* huell. *f.;* guadañada, *f ;* —, *vt.* fajar, envolver.

sway, *vt.* disuadir; cimbrar; dominar, gobernar; —, *vi.* ladearse, inclinarse; tener influjo; —, *n.* bamboleo, *m.;* poder, imperio, influjo, *m.*

sway-backed, *adj.* (coll.) pando.

swear, *vt.* y *vi.* jurar; juramentar; blasfemar.

swearing, *n.* jura, *f.,* juramento, *m.;* blasfemia, *f.*

sweat, *n.* sudor, *m.;* —, *vi.* sudar; trabajar con fatiga.

sweater, *n.* suéter, *m.,* chaqueta de punto de lana.

sweatshop, *n.* taller donde se trabaja excesivamente por paga escasa.

Swede, *n.* sueco, ca.

Sweden, Suecia, *f.*

Swedish, *adj.* sueco; — **language,** sueco, *m.*

sweep, *vt.* y *vi.* barrer; arrebatar, deshollinar; pasar o tocar ligeramente; oscilar; —, *n.* barredura, *f.;* vuelta, *f.;* giro, *m.;* alcance, *m.*

sweeper, *n.* barredor, ra; **carpet** —, barredora de alfombra.

sweeping, *adj.* rápido; barredero; vasto; —, *n.* barrido, *m.;* —s, *pl.* barreduras, *f. pl.,* desperdicios, *m. pl.*

sweet, *adj.* dulce, grato, meloso, gustoso; suave; oloroso; melodioso; hermoso; amable; — **alyssum,** alhelí dulce; — **basil,** albahaca, *f.;* — **clover,** trébol, *m.;* — **corn,** maíz tierno; — **potato,** batata, *f.,* camote, moniato, buniato, *m.;* — **william,** variedad de clavel; **to have a** — **tooth,** ser amante del dulce, ser goloso; —, *n.* dulzura, *f.;* querida, *f.;* —s, dulces, *m. pl.;* —ly, *adv.* dulcemente.

sweetbread, *n.* mollejas de ternera.

sweetbriar, sweetbrier, *n.* (bot.) escaramujo, *m.*

sweeten, *vt.* endulzar; suavizar; aplacar; perfumar.

sweetheart, *n.* querido, da, novio, via; galanteador, *m.*

sweetmeats, *n. pl.* dulces secos; compota, *f.*

sweetness, *n.* dulzura, suavidad, *f.*

swell, *vi.* hincharse; ensoberbecerse; embravecerse; —, *vt.* hinchar, inflar, agravar; — **up,** soplar; —, *n.* hinchazón, *f.;* bulto, *m.;* petimetre, *m.;* mar de leva; —, *adj.* elegante, a la moda.

swelling, *n.* hinchazón, *f.;* tumor, *m.;* bulto, *m.,* protuberancia, *f.*

swelter, *vi.* sofocarse, ahogarse de calor; sudar.

sweltering, *adj.* sofocante.

swept, *adj.* barrido; —, *pretérito* y *p.p.* del verbo **sweep.**

swerve, vi. vagar; desviarse; —, vt. desviar, torcer; —, n. desviación, f.

swift, adj. veloz, ligero, rápido; —, n. (orn.) vencejo, m.; —ly, adv. velozmente.

swig, vt. beber vorazmente; —, n. trapo, m. swim, vi. nadar; abundar en; ser vertiginoso; —, vt. pasar a nado.

swimmer, n. nadador, ra.

swimming, n. natación, f.; vértigo, m.; — pool, piscina o alberca de natación; — ly, adv. sin dificultad.

swindle, vt. petardear, estafar; —, n. estafa, f., petardo, m.

swindler, n. petardista, m., tramposo, sa.

swine, n. sing. y pl. puerco(s), cochino(s), m.; ganado de cerda.

swineherd, n. porquerizo, m.

swing, vi. balancear, columpiarse, oscilar; mecerse; agitarse; —, vt. esgrimir; mecer; manejar con éxito; to — a loan, lograr obtener un préstamo; —, n. balanceo, m.; columpio, m.; — bar, balancín, m.; — music, variedad de jazz.

swinging, n. vibración, f.; balanceo, m.; oscilación, f.; — adj. oscilante.

swipe, n. mango de bomba; (coll.) golpe fuerte; —, vt. dar golpes fuertes; coll.) hurtar, robar.

swirl, vt. y vi. hacer remolinos el agua; arremolinar; —, n. torcimiento, m.

swish, n. chasquido (como el que hace el látigo al hendir el aire), m.; crujido (como el roce de la ropa de seda), m.; —, vt. y vi. mover o moverse rápidamente; pasar velozmente.

switch, n. varilla, f.; (rail.) aguja, f.; (elec.) interruptor, conmutador, m.; ignition —, contacto de la ignición; — box, caja de interruptores; —, vt. varear; desviar; (elec.) cambiar; to — off, desviar; apagar; to — on, poner, encender.

switchboard, n. cuadro de distribución o conmutador telefónico.

switchman, n. (rail.) guardagujas, m.

Switzerland, Suiza, f.

Swiss, n. y adj. suizo, za; — cheese, queso Gruyère.

swivel, n. torniquete, m.; — chair, silla giratoria; —, vt. y vi. girar.

swollen, adj. hinchado, inflado; —, p.p. del verbo swell.

swoon, vi. desmayarse; —, n. desmayo, deliquio, pasmo, soponcio, m.

swoop, vt. coger, agarrar; —, vi. precipitarse, caer;—, n. acto de echarse un ave de rapiña sobre su presa; at one —, de un golpe.

sword, n. espada, f.

swordfish, n. pez espada, m.

swore, pretérito del verbo swear.

sworn, p.p. del verbo swear.

swum, p.p. del verbo swim.

swung, pretérito y p.p. del verbo swing.

sycamore, n. (bot.) sicómoro, m.

syllabication, syllabification, n. silabeo, m.

syllable, n. sílaba, f.

sylph, n. silfo, m.; sílfide, f.

symbol, n. símbolo, m.

symbolic, adj. simbólico.

symbolism, n. simbolismo, m.

symbolize, vt. simbolizar.

symmetrical, adj. simétrico; —ly, adv. con simetría.

symmetry, n. simetría, f.

sympathetic, adj. que congenia; inclinado a sentir compasión o a condolerse; — ally, adv. con compasión.

sympathize, vi. compadecerse, simpatizar; — with, compadecer.

sympathizer, n. compadecedor, ra, simpatizador, ra.

sympathy, n. compasión, condolencia, f.; simpatía, f.; pésame, m.

symphony, n. sinfonía, armonía, f.

symposium, n. simposia, f., festín o banquete de los antiguos griegos en donde se cruzaban ideas; simposio, m., conferencia para discutir un tema; colección de opinones sobre un mismo tema.

symptom, n. síntoma, m.

synagogue, n. sinagoga, f.

synchronize, vt. sincronizar.

synchroton, n. sincrotón, m.

syncopation, n. (gram.) (mus.) síncopa, f.

syndicate, n. sindicato, m.; —, vt. y vi. sindicar.

synod, n. sínodo, m.

synonym, n. sinónimo, m.

synonymous, adj. sinónimo; —ly, adv. en forma sinónima.

synopsis, n. sinopsis, f.; sumario, resumen, m.

syntax, n. sintaxis, f.

synthesis, n. síntesis, f.

synthetic, adj. sintético; fabricado; — rubber, caucho artificial, caucho sintético.

synthetize, vt. sintetizar.

syphilis, n. sífilis, f., gálico, m.

syringe, n. jeringa, f.; hypodermic —, jeringa hipodérmica.

syrup o sirup, n. jarabe, m.; cough —, jarabe para la tos.

system, n. sistema, m.; instalación, f.

systematic, adj. sistemático, metódico.

systematize, vt. sistematizar, sistematar.

tab 585 **talk**

T

tab, *n.* pequeña etiqueta o lengüeta saliente; (coll.) cuenta; **to pick up the** —, pagar la cuenta de varios (en un restaurante, etc.); **to keep — on,** (coll.) vigilar (a alguien), comprobar lo que hace.

tabernacle, *n.* tabernáculo, *m.;* templo, *m.*

table, *n.* mesa, *f.;* velador, *m.;* tabla, *f.;* elenco, *m.;* **on the —,** sobre la mesa; **round —,** mesa redonda; **side —,** trinchero, *m.;* **— cover,** carpeta, *f.;* **— d' hôte,** mesa redonda; comida corrida; **— linen,** mantelería, *f.;* **— service,** vajilla, *f.;* **to set the —,** poner la mesa; —, *vt.* apuntar en forma sinóptica; poner sobre la mesa.

tableau, *n.* cuadro, *m.,* cuadro plástico.

tablecloth, *n.* mantel, *m.*

tableland, *n.* meseta, altiplanicie, *f.*

tablespoon, *n.* cuchara, *f.*

tablespoonful, *n.* cucharada, *f.*

tablet, *n.* tableta, *f.;* tablilla, *f.;* pastilla, *f.;* plancha, lámina, *f.;* (med.) oblea, *f.;* — **of paper,** bloc de papel.

tableware, *n.* servicio de mesa.

tabloid, *n.* noticiero ilustrado.

taboo, tabu, *n.* tabú, *m.;* —, *adj.* prohibido; —, *vt.* interdecir, vedar, prohibir.

tabular, *adj.* en forma de tabla, tabular.

tabulate, *vt.* presentar cifras o datos en forma de tabla, tabular.

tacit, *adj.* tácito; **—ly,** *adv.* tácitamente.

taciturn, *adj.* taciturno, callado.

tack, *n.* tachuela, *f.;* —, *vt.* clavar; atar; pegar; —, *vi.* (naut.) virar.

tackle, *n.* todo género de instrumentos o aparejos; **fishing —,** arreos de pescar; (naut.) cordaje, cuadernal, *m.;* jarcia, *f.;* (fútbol norteamericano) atajador, *m.,* jugador en la primera línea de un equipo; —, *vt.* asir, forcejear; atajar; acometer, emprender, intentar.

tact, *n.* tacto, *m.*

tactful, *adj.* sensato, sigiloso; prudente, con tacto; **—ly,** *adv.* sigilosamente, prudentemente, con tacto.

tactics, *n. pl.* táctica, *f.*

tactless, *adj.* sin tacto, imprudente.

tadpole, *n.* renacuajo, *m.*

taffeta, *n.* tafetán, *m.*

taffy, *n.* melcocha, *f.;* (coll.) zalamería, *f.*

tan, *n.* marbete, *m.,* marca, *f.;* etiqueta, *f.;* juego infantil en que se persigue a un niño hasta tocarlo; (Mex.) juego de la roña; —, *vt.* poner marbete.

tail, *n.* cola, *f.,* rabo, *m.;* — **spin,** (avi.) barrena de cola.

taillight, *n.* (auto.) farol de cola, (Mex. coll.) calavera, *f.*

tailor, *n.* sastre, *m.*

tailoring, *n.* sastrería, *f.*

tailor-made, *adj.* a la medida; como hecho a mano.

taint, *vt.* tinturar, manchar; inficionar; viciar; —, *n.* mácula, mancha, *f.*

take, *vt.* tomar, coger, asir; recibir, aceptar; pillar; prender; admitir; aguantar; —, *vi.* encaminarse, dirigirse; salir bien; arraigarse; prender (el fuego); **to — a breath,** resollar; **to — apart,** desarmar, desmontar; **to — a walk,** pasear, dar un paseo; **to — away,** llevar; quitar; **to — charge of,** encargarse de; **to — for granted,** dar por sentado; **to — home,** llevar a casa; **to — off,** (avi.) despegar; **to — out,** suprimir; llevar a pasear; **to — place,** verificarse, tener lugar; **to — the liberty,** permitirse; **to — upon oneself,** encargarse de; **to — it,** (coll.) sobrellevar, soportar (algo); —, *n.* toma, *f.;* presa, *f.;* parte de una escena filmada o televisada sin interrupción.

take-home, *adj.* neto. (Dícese del salario después de descontados los impuestos, etc.)

take-in, *n.* engaño, *m.*

taken, *p.p.* del verbo **take.**

take-off, *n.* caricatura, *f.;* parodia, *f.;* (avi.) despegue, *m.*

take-out, *n.* comida para llevar.

taker, *n.* tomador, ra; persona que acepta una apuesta.

taking, *adj.* agradable, simpático, cautivador; (coll.) contagioso; —, *n.* presa, *f.;* secuestro, *m.;* **—s,** *pl.* colectas, *f. pl.,* dinero recogido.

talcum, *n.* talco, *m.;* — **powder,** polvo de talco.

tale, *n.* cuento, *m.,* fábula, *f.*

talebearer, *n.* soplón, ona, chismero, ra.

talent, *n.* talento, *m.;* ingenio, *m.;* capacidad, habilidad, *f.*

talented, *adj.* talentoso, capaz.

talisman, *n.* talismán, *m.*

talk, *vi.* hablar, conversar; charlar; —, *n.* plática, habla, *f.;* charla, *f.;* fama, *f.;* conferencia, *f.,* discurso, *m.*

talkative, *adj.* gárrulo, locuaz, palabrero,

hablador, parlero, charlatán.

talker, *n.* charlador, ra.

talkies, *n. pl.* cine sonoro, cine hablado.

talking, *adj.* hablante; — **machine,** fonógrafo, tocadiscos, *m.;* — **picture,** película sonora o hablada.

tall, *adj.* alto, elevado; (coll.) raro, increíble; — **story,** relato exagerado e increíble.

tallow, *n.* sebo, *m.;* —, *vt.* ensebar.

tally, *n.* cuenta, *f.;* — **sheet,** hoja de apuntes; —, *vt.* ajustar; tarjar.

talon, *n.* garra del ave de rapiña.

tambourine, *n.* pandero, *m.,* pandereta, *f.*

tame, *adj.* amansado, domado, domesticado; abatido; manso; sumiso; —, *vt.* domar, domesticar.

taming, *n.* domadura, *f.*

tamper, *vi.* tramar; sobornar; entremeterse en lo que no se debe.

tan, *vt.* curtir, zurrar, tostar, broncear; —, *vi.* broncearse, —, *n.* casca, *f.;* color café claro, color de arena.

tanbark, *n.* casca rica en tanino.

tandem, *adv.* uno tras otro; —, *n.* tándem. *m.,* bicicleta usada por dos ciclistas al mismo tiempo; coche con caballos uno tras otro; —, *adj.* tándem.

tang, *n.* sabor, *m.;* olor fuerte; retintín, *m.;* —, *vi.* retiñir.

tangent, *n.* y *adj.* tangente, *f.*

tangerine, *n.* naranja tangerina o mandarina.

tangible, *adj.* tangible.

tangle, *vt.* enredar, embrollar; —, *vi.* enredarse; —, *n.* enredo, embrollo, *m.;* confusión, *f.;* maraña, *f.*

tango, *n.* tango, *m.*

tank, *n.* (mil.) tanque, *m.,* carro blindado; depósito, tanque, *m.;* cisterna, *f.,* aljibe, *m.;* — car, (rail.) vagón-tanque, *m.;* — **trap,** (mil.) trampa u obstáculo para tanques; —, *vt.* almacenar.

tanned, *adj.* curtido; tostado del sol.

tanner, *n.* curtidor, *m.*

tannery, *n.* curtiduría, tenería, *f.*

tannic, *adj.* tánico.

tannin, *n.* tanino, *m.*

tanning, *n.* curtimiento, *m.*

tantalize, *vt.* atormentar a alguno mostrándole placeres que no puede alcanzar.

tantalizing, *adj.* atormentador; tentador.

tantrum, *n.* berrinche, *m.*

tap, *vt.* tocar ligeramente; barrenar; golpear ligeramente; decentar; utilizar, usufructuar; sacar; —, *n.* palmada suave; toque ligero; grifo, *m.;* espita, *f.;* tomadero, *m.;* — **dance,** baile zapateado (común en los E.U.A.).

tape, *n.* cinta, *f.;* cinta de grabar; — **measure,** cinta de medir; — **recorder,** magnetófono, *m.,* grabadora, *f.;* —, *vt.* vendar; grabar en cinta.

taper, *n.* candela, *f.;* cirio, *m.;* taladro de reducción; —, *adj.* cónico; —, *vi.* rematar en punta, ahusar; —, *vt.* dar forma ahusada.

tapestry, *n.* tapiz, *m.;* tapicería, *f.*

tapeworm, *n.* tenia, lombriz solitaria, solitaria, *f.*

tapioca, *n.* tapioca, *f.*

taproom, *n.* taberna, *f.*

taproot, *n.* raíz que penetra verticalmente.

taps, *n. pl.* (mil.) toque de queda.

tar, *n.* brea, *f.;* (coll.) marinero, *m.;* alquitrán, *m.,* pez, *f.;* —, *vt.* embrear.

tarantula, *n.* tarántula, *f.*

tardiness, *n.* tardanza, *f.*

tardy, *adj.* tardo, lento.

target, *n.* rodela, *f.;* blanco (para tirar), *m.;* **to hit the** —, dar en el blanco, acertar.

tariff, *n.* tarifa, *f.,* arancel, *m.*

tarnish, *vt.* deslustrar; manchar; —, *vi.* deslustrarse; —, *n.* borrón, *m.,* mancha, *f.*

tarpaulin, *n.* tela embreada; toldo, *m.*

tarpoon, *n.* (ichth.) sábalo, *m.*

tarry, *vi.* tardar, pararse; demorar; —, *adj.* embreado.

tart, *adj.* agrio; acedo, acre; —, *n.* torta, *f.,* pastelillo, *m.;* —**ly,** *adv.* agriamente.

tartar, *n.* tártaro, *m.;* sarro (de los dientes), *m.*

task, *n.* tarea, *f.;* cometido, quehacer, *m.;* — **force,** tropa o contingente naval a los cuales se asignan tareas de combate.

tassel, *n.* mota, borlita, *f.;* —, *vt.* decorar con borlitas.

taste, *n.* gusto, *m.;* sabor, *m.;* prueba, *f.;* saboreo, *m.;* ensayo, *m.;* —, *vt.* y *vi.* gustar; probar; experimentar; agradar; tener sabor.

tasteful, *adj.* elegante, galano, de buen gusto; —**ly,** *adv.* con buen gusto.

tasteless, *adj.* insípido, sin sabor; de mal gusto.

tasty, *adj.* sabroso, gustoso.

tat, *vt.* y *vi.* hacer encaje de hilo.

tatter, *n.* andrajo, *m.*

tattered, *adj.* andrajoso, haraposo.

tatting, *n.* encaje de hilo.

tattle, *vt.* y *vi.* charlar, parlotear; chismear; —, *n.* charla, *f.*

tattletale, *n.* chismoso, sa, chismero, ra, soplón, ona, delator, ra.

tattoo, *n.* tatuaje, *m.;* (mil.) retreta, *f.;* —, *vt.* tatuar.

taunt, *vt.* mofar; ridiculizar; dar chanza;

—, *n.* mofa, burla, chanza, *f.;* pulla, *f.*

taupe, *n.* y *adj.* gris pardo.

taut, *adj.* tieso, terco, tirante; nítido, en orden.

tavern, *n.* taberna, *f.;* posada, *f.*

tawdry, *adj.* chabacano y vistoso.

tawny, *adj.* moreno; de color tostado.

tax, *n.* impuesto, tributo, gravamen, *m.,* contribución, *f.;* carga, *f.;* **additional** —, recargo, *m.;* **income** —, impuesto sobre la renta; — **rate,** tarifa de impuestos; —, *vt.* imponer tributos o impuestos; agotar (la paciencia); abrumar.

taxable, *adj.* sujeto a impuestos.

taxation, *n.* tributación, *f.*

tax-exempt, *adj.* exento de impuestos.

taxi, *n.* taxímetro, taxi, *m.,* automóvil de plaza o de alquiler; (Mex.) libre, *m.;* —, *vi.* ir en un taxímetro o automóvil de alquiler; (avi.) moverse sobre la superficie.

taxicab, *n.* taxímetro, automóvil de alquiler; (Mex.) libre, *m.*

taxpayer, *n.* contribuyente, *m.* y *f.,* pagador o pagadora de impuestos.

tea, *n.* té, *m.;* — **ball,** bola metálica perforada para el té; — **bag,** bolsita con hojas de té.

teacart, *n.* carrito para servir el té.

teach, *vt.* enseñar, instruir; —, *vi.* ejercer el magisterio.

teacher, *n.* maestro, tra, profesor, ra, preceptor, ra, pedagogo, ga.

teaching, *n.* enseñanza, *f.;* —, *adj.* docente; — **staff,** personal docente.

teacup, *n.* taza para té.

teak, *n.* (bot.) teca, *f.*

teakettle, *n.* tetera, *f.*

teal, *n.* cerceta, zarceta, *f.,* variedad de ánade silvestre.

team, *n.* tiro de caballos; pareja, *f.;* equipo, *m.*

teamwork, *n.* trabajo de cooperación; auxilio mutuo.

teapot, *n.* tetera, *f.*

tear, *n.* lágrima, *f.;* gota, *f.;* — **bomb,** bomba lacrimógena; — **gas,** gas lacrimógeno.

tear, *vt.* despedazar, lacerar; rasgar; arrancar; —, *n.* rasgón, *m.;* raja, *f.;* jirón, *m.*

teardrop, *n.* lágrima, *f.*

tearful, *adj.* lloroso, lacrimoso; —**ly,** *adv.* con llanto.

tearoom, *n.* salón de té.

tease, *vt.* cardar (lana o lino); molestar, atormentar; dar broma; (coll.) tomar el pelo.

teaspoon, *n.* cucharita, *f.*

teaspoonful, *n.* cucharadita, *f.*

teat, *n.* ubre, *f.;* teta, *f.*

technical, *adj.* técnico; — **staff,** personal técnico.

technicality, *n.* asunto técnico; cuestión técnica.

technician, *n.* experto, técnico, *m.*

technicolor, *n.* tecnicolor, *m.*

technique, *n.* técnica, *f.,* método, *m.*

technological, *adj.* tecnológico.

technology, *n.* tecnología, *f.*

tedious, *adj.* tedioso, fastidioso.

tee, *n.* (golf) salida, *f.;* meta, *f.*

teem, *vi.* abundar; rebosar.

teen-ager, *n.* joven de 13 a 19 años.

teens, *n. pl.* números y años desde 13 hasta 19; periodo de 13 a 19 años de edad.

teeter, *vt.* y *vi.* balancearse; —, *n.* balanceo, *m.;* columpio de sube y baja.

teeth, *n. pl.* de **tooth,** dientes, *m. pl.;* **false** —, dientes postizos; **set of** —, dentadura, *f.*

teethe, *vi.* endentecer, echar los dientes.

teething, *n.* dentición, *f.;* — **ring,** chupador, *m.*

teetotaler, *n.* abstemio, mia.

telecast, *vt.* y *vi.* televisar, trasmitir por televisión; —, *n.* teledifusión, *f.*

telegram, *n.* telegrama, *m.*

telegraph, *n.* telégrafo, *m.;* — **operator,** telegrafista, *m.* y *f.;* —, *vi.*

telegrafiar, telemeter, *n.* telémetro, *m.*

telepathy, *n.* telepatía, *f.*

telephone, *n.* teléfono, *m.;* **dial** —, teléfono automático; — **booth,** cabina telefónica; — **exchange,** central telefónica; — **operator,** telefonista, *m.* y *f.;* — **receiver,** receptor, *m.;* — **directory,** directorio de teléfonos, lista de abonados al teléfono; —, *vt.* y *vi.* telefonear.

teleprompter, *n.* apuntador electrónico.

telescope, *n.* telescopio, *m.*

teletype, *n.* teletipo, *m.;* —, *vt.* enviar un mensaje por teletipo.

televiewer, *n.* televidente, *m.* y *f.*

televise, *vt.* televisar.

television, *n.* televisión, *f.;* — **set,** telerreceptor, televisor, aparato de televisión.

tell, *vt.* y *vi.* decir; informar, contar; numerar, revelar; mandar; hacer efecto.

teller, *n.* relator, ra; computista, *m.* y *f.;* **paying** —, pagador, ra; **receiving** —, recibidor, ra.

telltale, *n.* soplón, ona, delator, ra; —, *adj.* revelador.

tellurian, telluric, *adj.* telúrico, relativo al planeta Tierra.

temerity, *n.* temeridad, *f.*

temper, *vt.* templar, moderar; atemperar; —, *n.* temperamento, *m.;* humor, genio,

ill —, mal humor; **to lose one's —,**
enojarse; salirse de sus casillas.
temperament, n. temperamento, m.;
carácter, genio, m.
temperamental, adj. genial; de carácter
caprichoso.
temperance, n. templanza, moderación, f.;
sobriedad, f.
temperate, adj. templado, moderado,
sobrio; — **zone,** zona templada.
temperature, n. temperatura, f.
tempered, adj. templado, acondicionado;
ill —, de mal genio; **even —,** parejo,
apacible, de buen carácter.
tempest, n. tempestad, f.
tempestuous, adj. tempestuoso, proceloso; **—ly,** adv. tempestuosamente.
temple, n. templo, m.; sien, f.
tempo, n. tiempo, compás, m.; ritmo, m.
temporal, adj. temporal, provisional;
secular, profano; (anat., zool.) temporal.
temporarily, adv. temporalmente, provisionalmente; por lo pronto.
temporary, adj. provisional, temporario,
temporal.
temporize, vi. temporizar, contemporizar.
tempt, vt. tentar; provocar.
temptation, n. tentación, f.; prueba, f.
tempting, adj. tentador; **—ly,** adv. en
forma tentadora.
temptress, n. tentadora, mujer fascinadora.
ten, n. y adj. diez, m.; (math.) decena, f.
tenacious; adj. tenaz.
tenacity, n. tenacidad, f.; porfía, f.
tenant, n. arrendador, ra, tenedor, ra,
inquilino, na; —, vt. arrendar.
tend, vt. guardar, velar; atender; —, vi.
tirar, dirigirse; atender.
tendency, n. tendencia, f.; inclinación, f.
tender, adj. tierno, delicado; sensible; —
ly, adv. tiernamente; —, n. oferta, propuesta, f.; (naut.) patache, m.; (rail.)
ténder (de una locomotora), m.; (com.)
lo que se emplea para pagar; —, vt.
ofrecer, proponer; presentar.
tenderfoot, n. recién llegado; novato, principiante, m.
tender-hearted, adj. compasivo, impresionable.
tenderloin, n. filete, solomillo, m.
tenderness, n. terneza, delicadeza, f.
tendon, n. tendón, m.
tendril, n. (bot.) zarcillo, m.; filamento, m.
tenement, n. tenencia, habitación, f.; —
house, casa de vecindad.
tenet, n. dogma, m.; aserción, f.; credo, m.
tennis, n. tenis, m., raqueta (juego), f.; —
court, campo de tenis; — **player,** tenis-

ta, m. y f.
tenor, n. (mus.) tenor, m.; tenor, curso,
m.; contenido, m.; sustancia, f.; —, adj.
de tenor.
tense, adj. tieso; tenso; —, n. (gram.)
tiempo, m.; **past —,** pasado, m.; **present —,** presente, m.
tenseness, n. tirantez, tensión, f.
tensile, adj. extensible; — **strength,** resistencia a la tracción o tensión.
tension, n. tensión, tirantez, f.; (elec.) voltaje, m.
tent, n. (mil.) tienda de campaña; pabellón, m.; (cirugía) tienta, f.; **oxygen —,**
tienda de oxígeno; —, vi. acampar en
tienda de campaña.
tentacle, n. tentáculo, m.
tentative, adj. tentativo; de ensayo; de
prueba; **—ly,** adv. como prueba.
tenth, n. y adj. décimo, ma; **—ly,** adv. en
décimo lugar.
tenuous, adj. tenue, delgado.
tenure, n. tenencia, incumbencia, f.
tepid, adj. tibio.
term, n. término, confín, m.; plazo, m.;
tiempo, periodo, m.; estipulación, f.; **—s
of payment,** condiciones de pago; **to
come to —s,** llegar a un acuerdo; —, vt.
nombrar, llamar.
terminal, adj. terminal, final; —, n. terminal, m.; (rail.) estación terminal.
terminate, vt. y vi. terminar, limitar.
termination, n. terminación, conclusión, f.
terminology, n. terminología, f.
terminus, n. (rail.) última estación, terminal, f.
termite, n. comején, m., termita, f.
terra, n, tierra, f.; — cotta, terracota, f.,
barro, m.; — **firma,** tierra firme.
terrace, n. terraza, f., terrado, m.; terraplén, m.; —, vt. terraplenar.
terramycin, n. (med.) terramicina, f.
terrestrial, adj. terrestre, terreno.
terrible, adj. terrible, espantoso; **how —!**
¡qué barbaridad! **—ly,** adv. terriblemente.
terrier, n. zorrero, m.
terrific, adj. terrífico, terrible, espantoso;
(coll.) tremendo, maravilloso.
terrify, vt. espantar, llenar de terror.
territory, n. territorio, m.
terror, n. terror, espanto, m.
terrorist, n. terrorista, m.
terrorize, vt. aterrorizar, aterrar, espantar.
terror-stricken, adj. aterrorizado, horrorizado.
terse, adj. terso, sucinto.
terseness, n. brevedad, concisión, f.
test, n. ensayo, m., prueba, f.; examen,
m.; — **pilot,** piloto de prueba; — **tube,**

probeta, f.; —, vt. ensayar, probar; examinar.

Testament. n. Testamento, m.; New —, el Nuevo Testamento; Old —, el Viejo Testamento.

testament, n. testamento, m.

tester, n. probador, ra; cielo de cama o de púlpito.

testify, vt. testificar, atestiguar; aseverar.

testimonial, n. atestación, f.; recomendación, f., elogio, m.; —, adj. testimonial.

testimony, n. testimonio, m.

testing, n. ensayo, m., prueba, f.

testy, adj. displicente, descontentadizo; quisquilloso.

tetanus, n. tétano, m.

tête-a-tête, adj. de cara a cara; confidencial; —, n. conversación confidencial entre dos.

tether, n. correa, maniota, f.; traba, f.; —, vt. atar con una correa.

tetter, n. (med.) herpes, m. y f. pl.; serpigo, m.

Tex.: Texas, Tejas (E.U.A.).

text, n. texto, m.; tema, m.

textbook, n. texto, libro de texto.

textile, adj. hilable; textil; —, n. tejido, m.

textual, adj. textual.

texture, n. textura, f.; tejido, m.

thalamus, n. (bot.) tálamo, m.; (anat.) tálamo óptico.

thallus, n. (bot.) talo, m.

than, conj. que o de (en sentido comparativo).

thank, vt. agradecer, dar gracias; — offering, ofrecimiento en acción de gracias; —s, gracias, f. pl.; — you, gracias, f. pl.

thankful, adj. grato, agradecido; —ly, adv. con gratitud.

thankfulness, n. gratitud, f.

thankless, adj. ingrato.

Thanksgiving, Thanksgiving Day, n. día de dar gracias, día de acción de gracias (en Estados Unidos).

thanksgiving, n. acción de gracias.

that, pron. ése, ésa, eso; aquél, aquélla, aquello; que, quien, el cual, la cual, lo cual; —, conj. que, para que; —, adj. ese, esa, aquel, aquella; —, adv. así de, a tal grado; de este tamaño; not — large, no tan grande.

thatch n. paja; —, vt. techar con paja; — ed roof, techo de paja.

thaw, n. deshielo, m.; —, vi. derretirse, disolverse; deshelarse; —, vt. derretir.

the, art. el, la, lo; los, las.

theater, n. teatro, m.

theatrical, adj. teatral; fingido para impresionar; —ly, adv. en forma teatral.

thee, pron. (acusativo de thou) ti, a ti.

theft, n. hurto, robo, m.

their, adj. su, sus (de ellos o de ellas); — s, pron. el suyo, los suyos, suyo, suyos (de ellos o ellas).

them, pron. (acusativo y dativo de they) los, las, les; ellos, ellas.

theme, n. tema, asunto, m.; (mus.) motivo, m.; — park, parque de diversiones, m;— song, (rad. y TV.) música que inicia un programa o que sirve de motivo al mismo.

themselves, pron. pl. ellos mismos, ellas mismas; si mismos o mismas.

then, adv. entonces, después; en tal caso; now and —, de cuando en cuando.

thence, adv. desde allí, de ahí.

thenceforth, adv. desde entonces.

theological, adj. teológico.

theology, n. teología, f.

theorem, n. teorema, m.; binomial —, binomio de Newton.

theoretical, adj. teórico.

theorist, n. teórico, m.

theorize, vt. teorizar.

theory, n. teoría, f.

theosophy, n. teosofía, f.

therapeutic, therapeutical, adj. terapéutico.

therapeutics, n. terapéutica, f.

therapy, n. terapia, f.

there, adv. allí, allá; ahí; — is, — are, hay; —! interj. ¡mira! ¡ya lo ves! ¡te lo dije!

thereabouts, adv. por allí, cerca de allí; casi.

thereafter, adv. después; subsiguientemente.

thereby, adv. por medio de eso; con eso; por lo tanto.

therefore, adv. por lo tanto, por esto, por esa razón; a consecuencia de eso.

therefrom, adv. de allí, de allá, de eso.

therein, adv. en ese lugar; en ese particular; en esto, en eso.

thereof, adv. de eso, de ello; de allí, de ese particular.

thereon, adv. en eso, sobre eso.

thereto, thereunto, adv. a eso, a ello; además.

theretofore, adv. hasta entonces.

thereupon, adv. en eso, sobre eso; por lo tanto; inmediatamente después; en seguida.

therewith, adv. con eso; inmediatamente.

thermal, adj. termal; — waters, termas, caldas, f. pl.

thermic, adj. termal; térmico.

thermite, n. (chem.) termita, f.

thermometer, n. termómetro, m.

thermonuclear, adj. termonuclear.

thermos, thermos bottle, *n.* termos, *m.* thermostat, *n.* termostato, *m.*

thesaurus, *n.* tesauro, *m.*

these, *pron. pl.* éstos, éstas; —, *adj.* estos, estas.

thesis, *n.* tesis, *f.*

they, *pron. pl.* ellos, ellas.

thiamine, *n.* tiamina, *f.*

thick, *adj.* espeso, denso; grueso; turbio; frecuente; torpe; ronco; **through — and thin,** por toda situación difícil o penosa (expresión que demuestra la lealtad de alguien); —, *n.* la parte más gruesa; — **ly,** *adv.* espesamente; frecuentemente.

thicken, *vi.* y *vt.* espesar, condensar; condensarse, espesarse.

thickening, *n.* sustancia para espesar; acción de espesarse.

thicket, *n.* espesar, matorral, *m.;* maleza, *f.*

thickness, *n.* espesura, densidad, *f.;* grosor, espesor, grueso, *m.*

thief, *n.* ladrón, ona.

thieve, *vt.* y *vi.* hurtar, robar; **—s,** *n. pl.* de **thief.**

thigh, *n.* muslo, *m.*

thighbone, *n.* fémur, *m.*

thimble, *n.* dedal, *m.*

thimbleful, *n.* cantidad que cabe en un dedal, cantidad muy pequeña.

thin, *adj.* delgado, delicado; sutil; flaco; claro; ralo; —, *vt.* enrarecer; atenuar; adelgazar; aclarar.

thine, *pron.* tuyo, tuya, tuyos, tuyas.

thing, *n.* cosa, *f.;* asunto, *m.*

think, *vt.* y *vi.* pensar, imaginar, meditar, considerar; creer, juzgar, opinar.

thinker, *n.* pensador, ra.

thinking, *n.* pensamiento, *m.;* juicio, *m.;* opinión, *f.*

thinness, *n.* tenuidad, delgadez, *f.;* raleza, *f.;* escasez, *f.*

third, *n.* y *adj.* tercero, *m.;* **— degree,** (coll.) abuso de autoridad por parte de la policía para obtener información; — **person,** (gram.) tercera persona; tercero, *m.;* **—ly,** *adv.* en tercer lugar.

thirst, *n.* sed, *f.;* anhelo, *m.;* —, *vi.* tener sed, padecer sed.

thirstiness. *n.* sed, *f.;* anhelo, *m.*

thirsty, *adj.* sediento; **to be —,** tener sed.

thirteen, *n.* y *adj.* trece, *m.*

thirtieth, *n.* y *adj.* trigésimo, treintavo, *m.*

thirty, *n.* y *adj.* treinta, *m.*

this, *adj.* este, esta; —, *pron.* éste, ésta; esto.

thistle, *n.* cardo silvestre, abrojo, *m.;* espina, *f.*

thither, *adv.* allá, a aquel lugar; —, *adj.* más remoto.

thong, *n.* correa, correhuela, *f.*

thorax, *n.* tórax, *m.*

thorium, *n.* (chem.) torio, *m.*

thorn, *n.* espino, *m.;* espina, *f.:* — **in the side,** (coll.) molestia, mortificación, *f.;* —, *vt.* pinchar; proveer de espinas.

thorny, *adj.* espinoso; arduo.

thorough, *adj.* entero, cabal, perfecto; — **ly,** *adv.* enteramente, cabalmente, detenidamente.

thoroughbred, *adj.* de sangre, de casta (de caballos) ; —, *n.* persona bien nacida **o** de buena crianza, persona de sangre **azul;** caballo u otro animal de casta.

thoroughfare, *n.* paso, tránsito, *m.;* vía pública, vía principal; **no —,** se prohíbe el paso.

thoroughness, *n.* entereza, *f.;* perfección *f.*

those, *adj. pl.* de that; aquellos, aquellas esos, esas; —, *pron.* aquéllos, aquéllas, ésos, ésas.

thou, *pron.* tú; —, *vt.* tutear.

though, *conj.* aunque, no obstante; **as —,** como que, como si; —, *adv.* sin embargo, no obstante.

thought, *n.* pensamiento, juicio, *m.;* opinión, *f.;* cuidado, *m.;* concepto, *m.;* **to give — to,** pensar en; —, *pretérito* y *p.p.* del verbo **think.**

thoughtful, *adj.* pensativo, meditabundo; pensado; **—ly,** *adv.* de un modo muy pensativo.

thoughtfulness, *n.* meditación profunda; consideración, atención, *f.*

thoughtless, *adj.* inconsiderado, descuidado; insensato; **—ly,** *adv.* sin reflexión.

thousand, *n.* mil, *m.;* millar, *m.;* **per —,** por mil; —, *adj.* mil.

thousandth, *n.* y *adj.* milésimo, *m.*

thrash, *vt.* golpear; batir; sacudir; trillar (grano).

thrasher, *n.* trillador, *m.*

thrashing, *n.* desgranamiento, *m.;* tunda, golpiza, *f.*

thread, *n.* hilo, *m.;* fibra, *f.;* —, *vt.* enhebrar; atravesar.

threadbare, *adj.* raído, muy usado.

threat, *n.* amenaza, *f.*

threaten, *vt.* amenazar.

threatening, *n.* amenaza, *f.;* —, *adj.* amenazador; **—ly,** *adv.* con amenazas.

three, *n.* y *adj.* tres, *m.*

three-legged, *adj.* de tres patas; **— stool,** tajuela, *f.,* banquillo de tres patas.

threescore, *adj.* de tres veintenas; — **years,** sesenta años, tres veintenas.

thresh, *vt.* trillar; desgranar; golpear; batir; sacudir.

thresher, *n.* trillador, *m.*

threshing, *adj.* trillador; **— machine,** tri-

lladora, f., máquina trilladora, trillo, m.
threshold, n. umbral, m.; entrada, f.
threw, pretérito del verbo **throw.**
thrice, adv. tres veces.
thrift, n. economía, frugalidad, f.; **—ily,**
adv. económicamente.
thriftiness, n. frugalidad, parsimonia, f.
thriftless, adj. manirroto.
thrifty, adj. frugal, económico; próspero,
vigoroso.
thrill, vt. emocionar; —, vi. estremecerse;
—, n. estremecimiento, m.; emoción, f.
thrilling, adj. excitante; emocionante; conmovedor.
thrive, vi. prosperar, adelantar, aprovechar.
thriving, adj. próspero.
throat, n. garganta, f.; cuello, m.; **sore** —,
dolor de garganta.
throaty, adj. gutural.
throb, vi. palpitar; vibrar; —, n. palpitación, f.; latido, m.
throe, n. agonía, f.; angustia, f.; dolor
agudo; dolor de parto.
thrombosis, n. (med.) trombosis, f.
throne, n. trono, m.; —, vt. entronizar.
throng, n. muchedumbre, f.; tropel de
gente; —, vt. atestar; —, vi. apiñarse.
throttle, n. gaznate, garguero, m.; regulador, m.; **— of an engine,** válvula regula-
dora; —, vt. ahogar; estrangular.
through, prep. a través, por medio de; por
conducto de; —, adj. continuo; **— train**
tren directo; —, adv. del principio al
fin, de extremo a extremo; completamente; **— and —,** de un lado a otro,
por completo.
throughout, prep. por todo, en todo; **—
the country,** por todo el país; —, adv.
en todas partes; en todos sentidos.
throw, vt. echar, arrojar, tirar, lanzar;
botar; **to — down,** derribar; **to — into
gear,** engranar; **to — out of gear,** desengranar; —, n. tiro, m., tirada, f.;
derribo, m.
thrown, p.p. del verbo **throw.**
thrush, n. (orn.) tordo, m.
thrust, vt. empujar, impeler; meter; **—** vi.
entremeterse, introducirse; **to — aside,**
rechazar; **to — in,** hincar; —, n. estocada, f.; puñalada, f.; lanzada, f.
thud, n. sonido sordo; —, vi. hacer un sonido sordo.
thug, n. asesino, m.; malhechor, m.
thumb, n. pulgar, m.; **— notches,** muescas para el dedo pulgar (como índice de
libros, etc.); —, vt. manosear con poca
destreza; emporcar con los dedos; **to —
a ride,** (coll.) hacer el auto-stop.
thumbnail, n. uña del pulgar; —, adj. en

miniatura; **— sketch,** esbozo breve.
thumbscrew, n. tornillo de mano; empul-
gueras, f. pl.
thumbtack, n. chinche, tachuela, f.
thump, n. porrazo, golpe, m.; —, vt. y vi.
aporrear, apuñear.
thunder, n. trueno, m.; estrépito, m.; —,
vt. y vi. tronar; atronar; fulminar.
thunderbolt, n. rayo, m., centella, f.
thunderclap, n. trueno, m.
thundercloud, n. nube cargada de electricidad.
thundering, adj. atronador, fulminante.
thundershower, n. aguacero con truenos,
tormenta, f.
thunderstorm, n. temporal, m., tormenta,
tronada, tempestad, f.
thunderstruck, adj. atónito, estupefacto.
Thursday, n. jueves, m.; **Holy —,** Jueves
Santo.
thus, adv. así, de este modo.
thwart, vt. frustrar, desbaratar; —, n.
(naut.) banco de remero.
thy, adj. tu, tus.
thymus, n. (anat.) timo, m.
thyroid, n. (anat.) tiroides, m., glándula
tiroides; —, adj. tiroideo.
thyself, pron. ti mismo.
tiara, n. tiara, f.
tibia, n. (anat.) tibia, f.
tic, n. tic, m., contracción nerviosa de la
cara.
tick, n. garrapata, f.; (coll.) tic tac, m.; —,
vi. hacer sonido de tic tac; —, vt. marcar en lista.
ticker, n. indicador eléctrico de cotizaciones; reloj, m.; lo que produce el sonido
de tictac; **— tape,** cinta en que se
imprimen telegráficamente las cotizaciones de la bolsa.
ticket, n. boleto, m., boleta, f.; cédula, f.;
(rail.) billete, m., localidad, f.; **round
trip —,** boleto de ida y vuelta; **season
—,** billete de abono; (rail.) **— collector,**
expendedor de billetes; **— office,** (rail.)
despacho, m., taquilla, f.; **— scalper,**
revendedor, m.; **— seller,** taquillero, ra;
— window, taquilla, f.; —, vt. marcar.
ticking, n. terliz, cotí, cutí, m.; tictac, m.
tickle, vt. cosquillear, hacer cosquillas; —,
vi. tener cosquillas; —, n. cosquilla, f.
tickling, n. cosquillas, f. pl.; cosquilleo, m.
ticklish, adj. cosquilloso.
ticktock, n. tictac, m.
tidal, adj. (naut.) de la marea; **— wave,**
maremoto, m.
tidbit, n. bocadito delicado.
tide, n. tiempo, m.; estación, f.; marea, f.;
high —, marea alta, pleamar, f.; —, vt.
llevar; **to — over,** ayudar momentánea-

mente.

tidewater, n. agua de marea; litoral, m.; —, adj. a lo largo del litoral.

tidings, n. pl. noticias, f. pl.

tidy, adj. aseado, pulcro; ordenado; —, vt. arreglar, poner en orden, limpiar; —, vi. asearse.

tie, vt. anudar, atar; enlazar; empatar; amarrar; —, n. nudo, m.; corbata, f.; lazo, m.; (mus.) ligadura, f.; (rail.) traviesa, f.; empate, m.

tier, n. fila, hilera, f.; (theat.) hilera de palcos.

tie-up, n. (coll.) suspensión de tráfico, embotellamiento, m.; interrupción de trabajo (debido a huelga, etc.).

tiff, n. pique, disgusto, m.; —, vi. picarse.

tiger, n. tigre, m.; — **lily,** (bot.) tigridia, f.; — **moth,** variedad grande de polilla.

tight, adj. tirante, tieso, tenso, estrecho; apretado; escaso; (coll.) tacaño; — **squeeze,** apuro, m.

tighten, vt. tirar, estirar; apretar.

tight-lipped, adj. callado, reservado; hermético.

tightrope, n. cuerda tiesa; cuerda de volatinero.

tights, n. pl. mallas, calzas, f. pl., trajes ajustados que usan los acróbatas.

tigress, n. hembra del tigre.

tile, n. teja, f.; losa, f., azulejo, m.; —, vt. tejar.

tiling, n. tejado, m.; azulejos, m. pl.

till, prep. y conj. hasta que, hasta; — **now,** hasta ahora; —, n. cajón, m.; gaveta para dinero; —, vt. cultivar, labrar, laborar.

tiller, n. agricultor, ra; (naut.) caña del timón; — **rope,** guardín, m.

tilt, n. declive, m., inclinación, f.; cubierta, f.; justa, f.; —, vt. inclinar, empinar; apuntar la lanza; —, vi. justar.

timber, n. madera, f.; **beam of** —, madero, m.; **building** —, madera de construcciones; — **line,** límite de los bosques; — **wolf,** lobo gris; —, vt. enmaderar.

timberland, n. terreno maderable.

timberwork, n. maderamen, maderaje, m.

timbre, n. timbre (de voz), tono, m.

time, n. tiempo, m.; (mus.) compás, m.; edad, época, f.; hora, f.; vez, f.; **at any** —, cuando quiera; **a long** — **ago,** hace mucho tiempo; **at the proper** —, a su tiempo; **at the same** —, al mismo tiempo, a la vez; **at this** —, al presente; **at** —s, a veces; **behind** —, atrasado; **from** — **to** —, de cuando en cuando; **in olden** —s, antiguamente; **in** —, a tiempo, de perilla; **on** —, a plazos; **some** — **ago,** tiempo atrás; **spare** —, tiempo desocu-

pado; — **clock,** reloj que indica las horas de entrada y salida de los obreros; — **exposure,** (phot.) exposición de tiempo; **to mark** —, marcar el paso; **to take** —, tomarse tiempo; — **bomb,** bomba de explosión demorada; —, vt. medir el tiempo de; hacer a tiempos regulares; escoger el tiempo.

timecard, n. tarjeta para marcar las horas de entrada y salida de los trabajadores.

timekeeper, n. listero, m.; cronómetro, m.

timeless, adj. eterno.

timeliness, n. calidad de oportuno.

timely, adv. con tiempo; a propósito; —, adj. oportuno, tempestivo; a buen tiempo.

timepiece, n. reloj, m.

timer, n. persona o instrumento para registrar el tiempo; regulador o marcador de tiempo.

timesaving, adj. que ahorra tiempo; — **device,** dispositivo para ahorrar tiempo.

timetable, n. (rail.) horario, itinerario, m.

timeworn, adj. usado, gastado, deslustrado.

timid, adj. tímido, temeroso; —**ly,** adv. con timidez.

timidity, n. timidez, pusilanimidad, f.

timing, n. regulación de tiempo, sincronización, f.; coincidencia, f.

timorous, adj. temeroso, timorato.

timothy, n. (bot.) fleo, m.

tin, n. estaño, m.; hojalata, f.; — **can,** lata, f.; — **foil,** hoja de estaño; — **plate,** hoja de lata, hojalata, f.; —, vt. estañar; cubrir con hojalata.

tincture, n. tintura, f.; tinta, f.; —, vt. teñir, tinturar.

tine, n. diente o punta (de un tenedor, una horquilla, etc.).

tinge, n. tinte, m.; traza, f.; —, vt. tinturar, teñir.

tingle, vi. zumbar los oídos; punzar; estremecerse; —, n. retintín, m.; picazon, m.

tinker, n. latonero, m.; calderero, remendón, m.; —, vt. remendar; desabollar; tratar torpemente de componer algo.

tinkle, vt. y vi. cencerrear; —, vi. tintinear; retiñir; —, n. retintín, m.

tinkling, n. retintín, m.

tinner, n. minero de estaño; hojalatero, m.

tinsel, n. oropel, m.; —, vt. adornar con oropel.

tinsmith, n. hojalatero, m.

tint, n. tinta, f.; tinte, m.; —, vt. teñir, colorar.

tinware, n. cosas de hojalata.

tiny, adj. pequeño, chico.

tip, n. punta, extremidad, f.; cabo, m.;

graficación, propina, f.; información oportuna; —, vt. Golpear ligeramente; dar propina; inclinar, ladear; volcar.

tip-off, n. advertencia oportuna, informe oportuno (por debajo de cuerda).

tipple, vi. beber con exceso; —, n. bebida (alcohólica), f.; licor, m.; mecanismo para accionar carros de volteo.

tipsy, adj. algo borracho; inestable.

tiptoe, n. punta del pie; **on** —, de puntillas.

tiptop, n. cumbre, f.; —, adj. (coll.) excelente, de la más alta calidad.

tirade, n. invectiva, diatriba, f.

tire, n. llanta, goma, f., neumático, m.; **balloon** —, neumático balón, llanta balón; **change of** —, repuesto, m.; **flat** —, pinchazo, m., llanta desinflada; **spare** —, neumático o llanta de repuesto; — **cover**, cubrellanta, m.; — **gauge**, medidor de presión en los neumáticos; —, vt. cansar, fatigar; proveer con una llanta; —, vi. cansarse, fastidiarse; rendirse.

tired, adj. fatigado, cansado; rendido.

tireless, adj. incansable.

tiresome, adj. tedioso; molesto.

tissue, n. tisú, m.; (anat.) tejido, m.; — **paper**, papel de seda.

tit, n. jaca, haca, f.; (orn.) paro, m.; — **for tat**, dando y dando.

titanic, adj. titánico.

titbit = **tidbit**.

tithe, n. diezmo, m.; —, vi. diezmar.

title, n. título, m.; — **deed**, derecho de propiedad; — **page**, portada, carátula, f., frontispicio (de un libro), m.; — **role**, papel principal; —, vt. titular, intitular.

titmouse, n. (orn.) paro, m.

titter, vi. reírse disimuladamente; —, n. risilla disimulada.

titular, n. y adj. titular, m.

TNT, T.N.T.: TNT, trinitrotolueno.

to, prep. a, para; por; de; hasta; en; con; que; —, adv. hacia adelante.

toad, n. sapo, m.

toadstool, n. (bot.) variedad de hongo venenoso.

toady, n. adulador, ra; —**ish**, adj. adulador; —, vi. y vt. adular; ser adulador. **to-and-fro**, adj. de acá para allá; de un lado a otro.

toast, vt. tostar; brindar; —, n. tostada, f., pan tostado; brindis, m.

toasted, adj. tostado.

toaster, n. parrilla, f., tostador, m.

toastmaster, n. maestro de ceremonias.

tobacco, n. tabaco, m.; **cut** —, picadura, f.; — **box**, tabaquera, f.; — **pouch**, bolsa para tabaco; — **shop**, tabaquería, f.

toboggan, n. tobogán, trineo para deslizarse; —, vi. deslizarse en tobogán.

today, to-day, n. y adv. hoy, m.; **a week from** —, dentro de ocho días, de hoy en ocho días.

toddle, vi. andar con pasitos inciertos; tambalearse.

toddler, n. el que da pasitos inciertos; niño de uno a tres años de edad.

toddy, n. grog, m., variedad de bebida fermentada.

to-do, n. (coll.) alboroto, m., alharaca, f.

toe, n. dedo del pie; punta del calzado; —, vt. tocar con los dedos del pie; **to** — **the line**, comportarse bien, hacer lo que se le manda al pie de la letra.

toenail, n. uña del dedo del pie.

togs, n. pl. (coll.) vestimenta, ropa, f.

together, adv. juntamente, en compañía de otro; al mismo tiempo; **to get** —, unirse, juntarse.

toil, vi. fatigarse, trabajar mucho; afanarse; —, n. trabajo, m.; fatiga, f.; afán, m.

toilet, n. tocado, m.; excusado, retrete, m.; — **articles**, artículos de tocador; — **paper**, papel de excusado, papel higiénico; — **water**, agua de tocador.

token, n. señal, f.; memoria, f.; recuerdo, m.; prueba, f.; — **payment**, (com.) pago parcial como reconocimiento de un adeudo; **by the same** —, por lo mismo, por el mismo motivo.

told, pretérito y p.p. del verbo **tell**.

tolerable, adj. tolerable; mediocre; —**ly**, adv. tolerablemente, así así.

tolerance, n. tolerancia, f.

tolerant, adj. tolerante.

tolerate, vt. tolerar.

toleration, n. tolerancia, f.

toll, n. peaje, portazgo, m.; tañido lento de las campanas; — **bridge**, puente de peaje; — **call**, llamada telefónica de larga distancia; —, vt. tocar o doblar una campana; colectar peajes; —, vi. sonar las campanas.

tollgate, n. entrada de camino de cuota.

tolling, n. campaneo, m.; — **of bells**, repique o tañido de las campanas.

tomato, n. tomate, m., (Mex.) jitomate, m.; — **sauce**, salsa de tomate.

tomb, n. tumba, f.; sepulcro, m.; —, vt. poner en tumba.

tomboy, n. jovencita retozona, marimacho, m.

tombstone, n. piedra o lápida sepulcral.

tomcat, n. gato, m.

tome, n. tomo, m.

tomfoolery, n. tontería, payasada, f.

tommy gun, n. ametralladora pequeña.

tomorrow, n. y adv. mañana, f.; **day after** —, pasado mañana; — **morning**, mañana por la mañana.

tomtit, (orn.) paro, m.

tom-tom, n. tantán, m.

ton, n. tonelada, f.

tonal, adj. tonal.

tone, n. tono, m.; tono de la voz; acento, m.; (mus.) modalidad, f.; —, vt. cambiar el tono; armonizar el tono; **to — down**, suavizar; **to — up**, animar.

tongs, n. pl. tenazas, f. pl.

tongue, n. (anat.) lengua, f.; lenguaje, m.; habla, f.; lengua de tierra; **to hold one's** —, callarse; — **twister**, n. trabalenguas, m.

tongue-tied, adj. con frenillo; mudo, sin habla.

tonic, n. (med.) tónico, reconstituyente, m.; (mus.) tónica, f.; tónico, m.; —, adj. tónico.

tonight, to-night, n. y adv. esta noche.

tonnage, n. tonelaje, porte de un buque.

tonsil, n. tonsila, amígdala, agalla, f.

tonsillectomy, n. amigdalotomía, operación de las amígdalas.

tonsillitis, n. tonsilitis, amigdalitis, f.

tonsorial, adj. de barbería.

too, adv. también; — **much**, demasiado; —**many things**, demasiadas cosas.

took, pretérito del verbo **take**.

tool, n. herramienta, f.; utensilio, m.; persona usada como instrumento; — **bag**, talega de herramientas, cartera de herramientas; — **chest**, caja de herramientas; —**s**, pertrechos, m. pl.; útiles, bártulos, m. pl.; —, vt. labrar con herramientas.

toot, vt. y vi. sonar un cuerno o una bocina; —, n. sonido de cuerno o de bocina.

tooth, n. diente, m.; gusto, m.; (mach.) diente de rueda; **molar** —, diente molar; — **powder**, dentífrico, m., polvo dentífrico.

toothache, n. dolor de muelas.

toothbrush, n. cepillo de dientes.

toothless, adj. desdentado, sin dientes.

toothpaste, n. dentífrico, m., pasta dentífrica.

toothpick, n. mondadientes, escarbadientes, palillo de dientes.

top, n. cima, cumbre, cresta, f.; último grado; cabeza, f.; capota, f.; trompo, peón, m.; — **hat**, sombrero de copa, sombrero de copa alta; —, vt. y vi. elevarse por encima; sobrepujar, exceder; descabezar los árboles.

topaz, n. topacio, m.

topcoat, n. sobretodo, abrigo, gabán, m.; abrigo liviano.

toper, n. bebedor, borrachón, m.

topflight, adj. superior en aptitud o eminencia; — **artist**, artista de primera categoría.

topic, n. tópico, particular, asunto, tema, m.

topical, adj. tópico; sobre el tema o asunto.

topknot, n. copete, m.

topmost, adj. superior, más alto.

topnotch, adj. (coll.) de primera, excelente.

topographer, n. topógrafo, m.

topography, n. topografía, f.

topple, vi. volcarse.

top-secret, adj. absolutamente secreto.

topside, n. parte superior.

topsoil, n. capa arable, capa fértil del suelo.

topsy-turvy, adv. patas arriba, desordenadamente; —, adj. de patas arriba, revuelto.

torch, n. antorcha, hacha, f.

torchbearer, n. hachero, m.; portaantorcha, m.

torchlight, n. luz de antorcha; — **procession**, procesión con antorchas.

tore, pretérito del verbo **tear**.

toreador, n. torero, m.

torment, n. tormento, m.; pena, f.; —, vt. atormentar.

tormentor, tormenter, n. atormentador, ra.

torn, adj. destrozado, rasgado, descosido; —, p.p. del verbo **tear**.

tornado, n. tornado, huracán, m.

torpedo, n. torpedo, m.; (ichth.) tremielga, f.; **to fire a** —, lanzar un torpedo; — **boat**, torpedero, m.; — **tube**, lanza-torpedos, tubo lanzatorpedos; — vt. torpedear.

torpid, adj. entorpecido; inerte, apático.

torpor, n. entorpecimiento, estupor, m.

torque, n. (mech.) fuerza de torsión.

torrent, n. torrente, m.

torrential, adj. torrencial.

torrid, adj. tórrido, ardiente; — **zone**, zona tórrida.

torso. n. torso, m.

tortoise, n. tortuga, f.; carey, m.; — **shell**, concha de tortuga, carey, m.

tortoise-shell, adj. de carey.

tortuous, adj. tortuoso, sinuoso.

torture, n. tortura, f.; suplicio, m.; martirio, m.; —, vt. atormentar, torturar, martirizar.

Tory, n. tory, m., miembro del partido conservador de Inglaterra.

tory o Tory, adj. conservador en extremo.

toss, *vt.* tirar, lanzar, arrojar; agitar, sacudir; **to — up,** lanzar algo al aire; jugar a cara o cruz; —, *vi.* agitarse; mecerse; —, *n.* sacudida, *f.;* meneo, *m.,* agitación, *f.*

toss-up, *n.* incertidumbre sobre el resultado; cara o cruz.

tot, *n.* niño, ña.

total, *n.* total, *m.;* —, *adj.* entero, completo; **— war,** guerra total; **— loss,** pérdida total; **— weight,** peso total.

totalitarian, *n.* y *adj.* totalitario, *m.*

totter, *vi.* bambolear; tambalear, vacilar, titubear.

tottering, *adj.* vacilante, titubeante; **—ly,** *adv.* en forma tambaleante.

touch, *vt.* tocar, palpar; emocionar, conmover; —, *vi.* aproximarse a; —, *n.* tocamiento, toque, contacto, *m.;* **sense of —,** sentido del tacto; **in — with,** en contacto con; **to get in — with,** comunicarse con.

touchable, *adj.* tangible.

touch-and-go, *adj.* precario, incierto, arriesgado.

touchback, *n.* (fútbol) posesión de la pelota detrás de la propia meta.

touchdown, *n.* (fútbol) acción del jugador al poner la pelota detrás de la meta del contrario.

touching, *adj.* patético, conmovedor.

touch-me-not, *n.* (bot.) mercurial, *f.;* (coll.) mírame y no me toques.

touchstone, *n.* piedra de toque; ensayo, *m.,* prueba, *f.*

touchy, *adj.* quisquilloso, melindroso, susceptible.

tough, *adj.* tosco; correoso; tieso; vicioso; vigoroso; pendenciero; difícil; **— contest,** concurso reñido; **— battle,** batalla ardua.

toughen, *vi.* hacerse correoso; endurecerse; —, *vt.* hacer tosco; hacer correoso; endurecer.

toupee, *n.* tupé, *m.*

tour, *n.* viaje, *m.,* peregrinación, *f.;* vuelta, *f.;* —, *vt.* viajar.

touring, *n.* turismo, *m.;* **— agency,** agencia de turismo.

tourist, *n.* turista, *m.* y *f.;* viajero, ra; **— court,** posada para automovilistas.

tournament, *n.* torneo, combate, concurso, *m.*

tourniquet, *n.* torniquete, *m.*

tousle, *vt.* desordenar, desgreñar; despeinar.

tow, *n.* estopa, *f.;* remolque, *m.;* —, *vt.* (naut.) remolcar.

toward, towards, *prep.* hacia, con dirección a; cerca de.

towboat, *n.* bote remolcador, *m.*

towel, *n.* toalla, *f.;* **roller —,** toalla sin fin.

tower, *n.* torre, *f.;* ciudadela, *f.;* **fortified —,** torreón, *m.;* —, *vi.* remontarse; elevarse a una altura; **to — above,** sobrepasar mucho en altura.

towhead, *n.* cabellera suave y muy rubia; persona con cabello suave y muy rubio.

towline, *n.* cable, *m.,* soga o cadena de remolque.

town, *n.* ciudad, *f.;* pueblo, *m.,* población, *f.;* villa, *f.;* **home —,** ciudad natal; **— council,** ayuntamiento, cabildo, *m.;* **— crier,** pregonero, voceador, *m.;* **— hall, — house,** casa de ayuntamiento, casa consistorial, comuna; *f.;* **— planning,** urbanización, *f.*

township, *n.* ayuntamiento, *m.*

townsman, *n.* conciudadano, *m.*

toxic, *adj.* tóxico.

toxin, *n.* toxina, *f.,* veneno, *m.*

toy, *n.* juguete, *m.;* chuchería, *f.;* miriñaque, *m.;* —, *vi.* jugar, divertirse.

trace, *n.* huella, pisada, *f.;* vestigio, *m.,* señal, *f.;* —, *vt.* delinear, trazar; seguir la pista.

traceable, *adj.* que se puede trazar.

tracer, *n.* cédula de investigación; trazador, *m.;* **— station,** (avi.) estación de rastreo.

trachea, *n.* (anat.) tráquea, *f.*

trachoma, *n.* (med.) tracoma, *f.*

tracing, *n.* calco, *m.;* trazo, *m.*

track, *n.* vestigio, *m.;* huella, pista, *f.;* rodada, *f.;* **— meet,** concurso de pista y campo; **race —,** hipódromo, *m.;* **— of a wheel,** carrilera, *f.;* —, *vt.* rastrear.

trackless, *adj.* sin huella.

tract, *n.* trecho, *m.;* región, comarca, *f.;* tratado, *m.;* (anat.) sistema, *m.*

tractable, *adj.* tratable, manejable.

traction, *n.* acarreamiento, *m.,* tracción, *f.;* (med.) tracción, *f.*

tractor, *n.* tractor, *m.*

trade, *n.* comercio, tráfico, *m.;* negocio, trato, *m.,* contratación, *f.;* **board of —,** junta de comercio; **— name,** nombre de fábrica; **— price,** precio para el comerciante; **— school,** escuela de artes y oficios; **— union,** gremio, *m.;* **— winds,** vientos alisios; —, *vi.* comerciar, traficar, negociar, cambiar (una cosa por otra), (coll.) cambalachear.

trade-in, *n.* objeto dado como pago o pago parcial en la compra de otro.

trade-mark, *n.* marca de fábrica.

trader, *n.* comerciante, traficante, *m.;* navío mercante.

tradesman, *n.* tendero, mercader, *m.;* artesano, *m.*

...ple, *n. pl.* comerciantes, *m. pl.*

...ionism, *n.* sindicalismo, *m.*

..., *n.* comercio, *m.; —, adj.* comercial.

tradition, *n.* tradición, *f.*

traditional, *adj.* tradicional; **—ly,** *adv.* tra-
dicionalmente.

traduce, *vt.* vituperar; calumniar; acusar.

traffic, *n.* tráfico, *m.,* circulación, *f.;* mercaderías, *f. pl.;* tránsito, *m.;* trasporte,
m.; **heavy —,** tránsito intenso; **light —,**
tránsito ligero; **— lane,** zona de tránsito; **— light,** semáforo, *m.;* **— sign,** señal
de tránsito; **—,** *vi.* traficar, co-merciar.

tragedian, *n.* actor trágico; autor de trage-
dias.

tragedy, *n.* tragedia, *f.*

tragic, *adj.* trágico.

tragically, *adv.* trágicamente.

trail, *vt.* y *vi.* rastrear; arrastrar; **—,** *n.*
rastro, *m.;* pisada, *f.;* vereda, trocha, *f.;*
sendero, *m.*

trailer, *n.* remolque, acoplado, *m.,* carro
de remolque; persona que sigue una
pista o un rastro.

trailing, *adj.* rastrero; **— arbutus,** (bot.)
gayuba, *f.*

train, *vt.* arrastrar, amaestrar, enseñar,
criar, adiestrar; disciplinar; entrenar;
—, *n.* (rail.) tren, *m.;* séquito, tren, *m.;*
serie, *f.;* cola (de vestido), *f.;* **pack —,**
recua, *f.;* **— conductor,** motorista,
cobrador, *m.;* **— oil,** aceite de ballena.

trainee, *n.* persona que recibe entrenamiento.

trainer, *n.* enseñador, *m.;* entrenador, *m.*

training, *n.* educación, disciplina, *f.;*
entrenamiento, *m.;* **—,** *adj.* de instrucción, de entrenamiento.

trainload, *n.* carga de un tren.

trainman, *n.* empleado en un tren.

trait, *n.* rasgo de carácter; toque, *m.*

traitor, *n.* traidor, *m.*

traitorous, *adj.* pérfido, traidor, traicione-
ro.

traitress, *n.* traidora, *f.*

trajectory, *n.* trayectoria, *f.*

trammel, *n.* trasmallo, *m.;* **—s,** *pl.* obstáculos, impedimentos, *m. pl.;* **—,** *vt.*
coger, interceptar; impedir.

tramp, *n.* sonido de pasos pesados; paso
fuerte; caminata, *f.;* vagabundo, *m.;*
bigardo, *m.;* **— steamer,** vapor que
toma carga donde y cuando puede; **—,**
vi. vagabundear; **—,** *vt.* patear.

trample, *vi.* pisar muy fuerte; hollar; **—,**
n. pisoteo, *m.;* sonido de pisoteo.

trance, *n.* rapto, *m.;* éxtasis, *m.;* estado
hipnótico.

tranquil, *adj.* tranquilo.

tranquilizer, *n.* calmante, sedante, *m.*

tranquillity o **tranquility,** *n.* tranquilidad,
paz, calma, *f.*

transact, *vt.* negociar, transigir.

transaction, *n.* transacción, *f.;* negociación, *f.;* tramitación, *f.*

transatlantic, *adj.* trasatlántico; **— airplane,** avión trasatlántico; **— liner,** vapor
trasatlántico.

transcend, *vt.* trascender, pasar; exceder.

transcendent, *adj.* trascendente; sobresaliente.

transcendental, *adj.* trascendental; sobresaliente.

transcontinental, *adj.* trascontinental.

transcribe, *vt.* trascribir, copiar, trasladar.

transcript, *n.* trasunto, traslado, *m.,*
copia (de un documento, etc.), *f.*

transcription, *n.* traslado, *m.;* copia, *f.;*
electrical —, (rad. y TV.) trascripción
eléctrica.

transept, *n.* nave trasversal de una iglesia.

transistor, *n.* transistor, *m.*

transfer, *vt.* trasferir, trasportar, trasbordar, trasladar, trasponer; **—,** *n.*
cesión, trasferencia, *f.,* traspaso, *m.;*
traslado, *m.*

transferable, *adj.* trasferible.

transference, *n.* trasferencia, *f.*

transfiguration, *n.* trasfiguración, *f.*

transfigure, *vt.* trasformar, trasfigurar.

transfix, *vt.* traspasar.

transform, *vt.* trasformar; **—,** *vi.* trasfor-
mase.

transformation, *n.* trasformación, *f.*

transformer, *n.* trasformador, *m.*

transfusion, *n.* trasfusión, *f.;* **blood —,**
trasfusión de sangre.

transgress, *vt.* y *vi.* trasgredir; violar.

transgression, *n.* trasgresión, *f.*

transgressor, *n.* trasgresor, ra.

transient, *adj.* pasajero, transitorio; **—,** *n.*
transeúnte, *m.* y *f.;* **—ly,** *adv.* de un
modo transitorio.

transit, *n.* tránsito, *m.;* trámite, *m.;* teodolito, *m.;* **— theodolite,** teodolito, *m.;*
—, *vt.* pasar por.

transition, *n.* transición, *f.;* tránsito, *m.*

transitive, *adj.* transitivo; **—,** *n.* verbo
transitivo.

transitory, *adj.* transitorio.

translate, *vt.* trasladar, traducir, verter;
interpretar.

translation, *n.* traducción, *f.;* interpretación, *f.*

translator, *n.* traductor, ra.

translucent, *adj.* trasluciente, diáfano.

transmission, *n.* trasmisión, *f.;* **— belt,**

correa de trasmisión.

transmit, *vt.* trasmitir.

transmitter, *n.* trasmisor, *m.*

transmute, *vt.* trasmutar.

transom, *n.* travesaño, *m.*

transonic, *adj.* transónico.

transparency, *n.* trasparencia, *f.*

transparent, *adj.* trasparente, diáfano.

transpiration, *n.* traspiración, *f.*

transpire, *vt.* traspirar, exhalar; —, *vi.* (coll.) acontecer.

transplant, *n.* trasplante, *m.;* **corneal —,** trasplante de córnea; —, *vt.* trasplantar.

transport, *vt.* trasportar; deportar; llevar; trasponer; —, *n.* trasportación, *f.;* rapto, *m.;* (naut.) trasporte, *m.;* criminal condenado a la deportación; — **company,** empresa porteadora, compañía de transportes.

transportation, *n.* trasportación, *f.,* trasporte, acarreo, *m.*

transpose, *vt.* trasponer; (mus.) trasportar.

transposition, *n.* trasposición, *f.*

transverse, *adj.* trasverso, travesero; **—ly,** *adv.* trasversalmente.

trap, *n.* trampa, *f.;* garlito, lazo, *m.;* especie de carruaje; — **door,** puerta disimulada, escotillón, *m.;* —, *vt.* hacer caer en la trampa, atrapar.

trapeze, *n.* trapecio, *m.*

trapper, *n.* cazador de animales de piel.

trappings, *n. pl.* jaeces, *m. pl.*

trapshooter, *n.* tirador al vuelo o a blancos movibles.

trash, *n.* heces, *f. pl.,* desecho, *m.;* cachivache, cacharro, *m.;* basura, *f.*

trashy, *adj.* vil, despreciable, de ningún valor.

trauma, *n.* (med.) traumatismo, *m.,* lesión, *f.*

traumatic, *adj.* traumático.

travail, *n.* trabajo, *m.;* dolores de parto; —, *vi.* trabajar; estar de parto.

travel, *vt.* y *vi.* viajar; **to — over,** recorrer; —, *n.* viaje, *m.*

traveler, *n.* viajante, *m.* y *f.,* viajero; **—'s check,** cheque de viajero.

traveling, *adj.* de viaje; — **companion,** compañero o compañera de viaje; — **salesman,** agente viajero, viajante, *m.;* — **expenses,** viáticos, *m. pl.*

travelogue o travelog, *n.* conferencia ilustrada sobre viajes.

traverse, *vt.* atravesar, cruzar; recorrer; examinar con cuidado; —, *vi.* atravesarse; recorrer; —, *adj.* trasversal; —, *n.* traviesa, *f.;* travesaño, *m.;* (leyes) negación, objeción legal.

travesty, *n.* parodia, *f.;* —, *vt.* disfrazar.

trawl, *vi.* pescar con red rastrera; —, *n.* red larga para rastrear.

trawler, *n.* embarcación para pescar o dragar a la rastra; persona que pesca o draga a la rastra.

tray, *n.* bandeja, salvilla, *f.;* batea, *f.;* (Mex.) charola, *f.*

treacherous, *adj.* traidor, pérfido.

treachery, *n.* perfidia, deslealtad, traición, *f.*

tread, *vt.* y *vi.* pisar, hollar, apretar con el pie; pisotear; patalear; caminar con majestad; —, *n.* pisada, *f.;* galladura, *f.*

treadle, *n.* cárcola, *f.*

treason, *n.* traición, *f.*

treasure, *n.* tesoro, *m.;* riqueza, *f.;* —, *vt.* atesorar; guardar riquezas.

treasurer, *n.* tesorero, ra.

treasury, *n.* tesorería (oficina), *f.*

treat, *vt.* y *vi.* tratar; regalar; medicinar; **to — of,** versar sobre, tratar de; —, *n.* trato, *m.;* banquete, festín, *m.,* convidada, *f.*

treatise, *n.* tratado, *m.*

treatment, *n.* trato, *m.;* (med.) tratamiento, *m.*

treaty, *n.* tratado, pacto, trato, *m.*

treble, *adj.* triple, tríplice; —, *vt.* triplicar; —, *vi.* triplicarse; —, *n.* (mus.) tiple, *m.*

tree, *n.* árbol, *m.;* cepo, palo, *m.;* **family —** árbol genealógico; — **frog,** rana arbórea.

treeless, *adj.* sin árboles.

trek, *n.* prolongado viaje; jornada, *f.;* —, *vi.* hacer una jornada ardua.

trellis, *n.* enrejado, *m.*

tremble, *vi.* temblar; estremecerse; —, *n.* temblor, *m.*

trembling, *adj.* tembloroso; —, *n.* estremecimiento, *m.;* temor, *m.*

tremendous, *adj.* tremendo; inmenso; **—ly,** *adv.* de un modo tremendo. tremor, *n.* temblor, estremecimiento, *m.*

tremulous, *adj.* trémulo, tembloroso; **—ly,** *adv.* temblorosamente.

french, *n.* foso, *m.;* (mil.) trinchera, *f.;* cauce, *m.;* —, *vt.* cortar; atrincherar; hacer cauces.

trend, *n.* tendencia, *f.,* curso, *m.;* —, *vi.* tender, inclinarse.

trepidation, *n.* trepidación, *f.*

trespass, *vt.* quebrantar, traspasar, violar; —, *n.* trasgresión, violación, *f.*

trespasser, *n.* trasgresor, ra.

tress, *n.* trenza, *f;* rizo de pelo.

trestle, *n.* bastidor, caballete, *m.;* armazón, *f.*

triad, *n.* (mus.) acorde, *m.;* terno, *m.*

trial, *n.* prueba, *f.;* ensayo, *m.;* juicio, *m.;*

— **balance,** balance de prueba; — **order,** pedido de ensayo; — **run,** presentación de un espectáculo por algún tiempo como prueba o ensayo; marcha de ensayo.

triangle, n. triángulo, m.; grupo de tres personas.

triangular, adj. triangular.

tribal, adj. tribal, perteneciente a una tribu.

tribe, n. tribu, f.; raza, casta, f.

tribulation, n. tribulación, f.

tribunal, n. tribunal, m.; juzgado, m.

tribune, n. tribuno, m.; tribuna, f.

tributary, n. y adj. tributario, m.

tribute, n. tributo, m.; **to render** —, rendir pleitesía, tributar homenaje.

trick, n. engaño, fraude, m.; superchería, astucia, f.; burla, f.; maña, f.; baza (en el juego de naipes), f.; —, vt. engañar; ataviar; hacer juegos de manos; embaucar.

trickery, n. engaño, dolo, fraude, m.

trickle, vi. gotear; —, n. goteo, chorrito, m., corriente pequeña.

tricky, adj. astuto, artificioso; tramposo.

tricolor, n. bandera tricolor; —, adj. tricolor.

tricycle, n. triciclo, m.

tried, adj. ensayado; probado; fiel.

triennial, adj. trienal; —, n. tercer aniversario; acontecimiento trienal.

trifle, n. bagatela, niñería, pamplina, pequeñez, bicoca, f.; —, vi. bobear; chancear, juguetear.

trifling, adj. frívolo, inútil; —**ly,** adv. sin consecuencia.

trigger, n. gatillo (de una arma de fuego), m.

trigonometry, n. trigonometría, f.

trilingual, adj. trilingüe.

trill, n. trino, m.; —, vt. trinar, gorgoritear.

trillion, n. trillón, m., la tercera potencia de un millón, o 1,000,000,000,000,000,000 (en la América Ibera, España, Inglaterra, y Alemania); un millón de millones, o 1,000,000,000,000 (en Francia y los Estados Unidos).

trim, adj. acicalado, compuesto, bien ataviado; —**ly,** adv. lindamente; en buen estado; —, n. atavío, adorno, aderezo, m.; —, vt. preparar; acomodar; adornar, ornar; podar; recortar, cortar; recortar (el cabello); (naut.) orientar (las velas); equilibrar.

trimming, n. guarnición de vestido; galón, m.; adorno, m.

trinity, n. grupo de tres, trinidad, f.

trinket, n. joya, alhaja, f.; adorno, m.; fruslería, chuchería, f.; juguete, m. trio, n. (mus.) terceto, trío, m.

trip, vt. echar zancadilla; hacer tropezar; —, vi. tropezar; dar traspié; —, n. zancadilla, f.; traspié, m.; resbalón, m.; viaje, m.; **one-way** —, viaje sencillo; **return** —, viaje de vuelta; **round** —, viaje redondo, viaje de ida y vuelta.

tripe, n. tripas, f. pl., callos, m. pl.; menudo, m.

triple, adj. tríplice, triple, triplo; —, vt. triplicar.

triplet, n. (poet.) terceto, m.; —**s,** gemelos, trillizos, m. pl.

triplicate, vt. triplicar; hacer tres copias; —, adj. triplicado; —, n. una de tres copias idénticas.

tripod, n. trípode, m.

tripping, adj. veloz, ágil, ligero; —, n. baile ligero; tropiezo, tropezón, m.

trisyllable, n. trisílabo, m.

trite, adj. trivial, usado, banal.

triumph, n. triunfo, m.; —, vi. triunfar; vencer.

triumphant, adj. triunfante; victorioso.

trivial, adj. trivial, vulgar.

triviality, n. trivialidad, f.

troglodyte, n. troglodita, m.

trolley, n. tranvía, m.; — **bus,** — **coach,** ómnibus eléctrico.

trombone, n. (mus.) trombón, m.

troop, n. tropa, f.; cuadrilla, turba, f.; —, vi. atroparse.

trooper, n. soldado a caballo, también su caballo; policía a caballo.

troopship, n. trasporte de guerra.

trophy, n. trofeo, m.

tropic, n. y adj. trópico, m.; **the** —**s,** el trópico.

tropical, adj. trópico, tropical.

trot, n. trote, m.; —, vi. trotar.

troth, n. fe, fidelidad, f.; desposorio, m.

trotter, n. caballo trotón; trotador, m.

trotting, adj. trotador.

troubadour, n. trovador, m.

trouble, vt. perturbar; afligir; incomodar, molestar; —, vi. incomodarse; —, n. turbación, f.; disturbio, m.; inquietud, f.; aflicción, pena, f.; congoja, f.; trabajo, m.; **to be in** —, verse en apuros.

troubled, adj. afligido; agitado.

troublemaker, n. perturbador, ra, alborotador, ra.

trouble shooter, n. (coll.) persona encargada de descubrir y corregir fallas (en talleres de reparación, plantas de luz, etc.).

troublesome, adj. penoso, fatigoso; importuno; fastidioso, molesto, majadero.

trough, *n.* artesa, gamella, *f.,* dornajo, *m.*

troupe, *n.* compañía o tropa, especialmente de actores de teatro.

trouper, *n.* (theat.) miembro de una compañía que viaja; **a good —,** actor o actriz que viaja sin importarle incomodidades.

trousers, *n. pl.* calzones, pantalones, *m. pl.*

trousseau, *n.* ajuar de novia, *m.*

trout, *n.* trucha, *f.*

trowel, *n.* trulla, llana, paleta, *f.*

truant, *n.* y *adj.* holgazán, ana, haragán, ana.

truce, *n.* tregua, suspensión de armas.

truck, *vt.* y *vi.* trocar, cambiar; acarrear; trasportar; —, *n.* camión, carretón, *m.;* cambio, trueque, *m.;* **small —,** camioneta, *f.;* **— farm,** pequeña labranza en que se produce hortaliza para vender en el mercado; **— frame,** bastidor para camión.

truckage, *n.* acarreo, *m.*

trackman, *n.* carretero, camionero, *m.*

truculent, *adj.* truculento, cruel.

trudge, *vi.* caminar con pesadez y cansancio; —, *n.* paseo fatigoso.

true, *adj.* verdadero, cierto; sincero, exacto; efectivo; **— bill,** acusación de un gran jurado.

truehearted, *adj.* leal, sincero, franco, fiel.

truly, *adv.* en verdad; sinceramente.

trump, *n.* triunfo (en el juego de naipes), *m.;* (coll.) excelente persona; —, *vt.* ganar con el triunfo; **— card,** triunfo (en los juegos de naipes), *m.;* **to — up,** forjar, inventar.

trumpet, *n.* trompeta, *f.;* **— creeper,** jazmín trompeta; —, *vt.* trompetear; pregonar con trompeta.

trumpeter, *n.* trompetero, *m.*

trundle, *n.* rueda baja; carreta de ruedas bajas; rodillo, *m.;* **— bed,** carriola, *f.;* —, *vt.* y *vi.* rodar; girar.

trunk, *n.* tronco, *m.;* baúl, cofre, *m.;* **— of an elephant,** trompa, *f.;* **— (of trees and plants),** pie, tronco (de los árboles y plantas), *m.;* **auto —,** portaequipajes, maletero, *m.;* —, *adj.* troncal.

trunks, *n. pl.* calzón corto de hombre; **swimming —,** traje de baño de hombre, taparrabo, *m.*

truss, *n.* braguero, *m.;* haz, *m.;* atado, *m.;* *vt.* empaquetar; liar.

trussing, *n.* armadura, *f.*

trust, *n.* confianza, *f.;* cargo, depósito, fideicomiso, *m.;* crédito, *m.;* cometido, *m.;* cuidado, *m.;* asociación comercial para monopolizar la venta de algún género; consorcio, *m.;* **in —,** en administración; **on —,** al fiado; —, *vt.* y *vi.* confiar; encargar y fiar; dar crédito; esperar; —, *vi.* confiarse, fiarse.

trustee, *n.* fideicomisario, depositario, síndico, *m.*

trusteeship, *n.* sindicatura, *f.*

trustful, *adj.* fiel; confiado.

trustiness, *n.* probidad, integridad, *f.*

trusting, *adj.* confiado.

trustworthy, *adj.* digno de confianza.

trusty, *adj.* fiel, leal; seguro.

truth, *n.* verdad, *f.;* fidelidad, *f.;* realidad, *f.;* **in —,** en verdad.

truthful, *adj.* verídico, veraz.

truthfulness, *n.* veracidad, *f.*

try, *vt.* y *vi.* examinar, ensayar, probar; experimentar; tentar; intentar; juzgar; purificar; refinar; —, *vt.* procurar; **to — on clothes,** probarse ropa; —, *n.* prueba, *f.;* ensayo, *m.*

trying, *adj.* crítico; penoso; cruel; agravante.

tryout, *n.* prueba, *f.,* ensayo, *m.*

tryst, *n.* cita, *f.;* lugar de cita; —, *vt.* y *vi.* convenir en encontrarse; arreglar; nombrar; ponerse de acuerdo.

tub, *n.* tina, *f.;* cuba, *f.;* cubo, barreño, *m.;* barreña, *f.;* —, *vt.* y *vi.* (coll.) bañar, bañarse o lavarse en una tina.

tuba, *n.* (mus.) bombardino, *m.*

tubbing, *n.* baño, lavamiento, *m.*

tube, *n.* tubo, cañón, cañuto, caño, *m.;* (rail.) ferrocarril subterráneo, *m.;* **amplifying —,** válvula amplificadora; **electronic —,** tubo electrónico; **inner —,** cámara de aire; **test —,** probeta, *f.;* **vacuum —,** tubo al vacío; —, *vt.* poner en tubo; entubar.

tuber, *n.* tubérculo, *m.;* (anat.) protuberancia, prominencia, *f.*

tubercular, *adj.* tísico, tuberculoso.

tuberculin, *n.* tuberculina, *f.*

tuberculosis, *n.* (med.) tuberculosis, tisis, *f.*

tuberose, *n.* (bot.) tuberosa, *f.;* nardo, *m.*

tuck, *n.* alforza, *f.;* pliegue, *m.;* doblez, *m.;* —, *vt.* arremangar, recoger.

Tues.: Tuesday, Mar. martes.

Tuesday, *n.* martes, *m.*

tuft, *n.* borla, *f.;* penacho, *m.;* moño, *m.;* —, *vt.* adornar con borlas; dividir en borlas.

tufted, *adj.* empenachado.

tug, *vt.* tirar con fuerza; arrancar; —, *vi.* esforzarse; —, *n.* tirada, *f.;* esfuerzo, *m.;* tirón, *m.;* (naut.) remolcador, *m.*

tugboat, *n.* remolcador, *m.*

tuition, *n.* instrucción, enseñanza, *f.;* costo de la matrícula y la enseñanza.

tulip, *n.* tulipán, *m.*

tulle, n. tul, m.

tumble, vi. caer, hundirse, voltear; revolcarse; —, vt. revolver; rodar; volcar; —, n. caída, f.; vuelco, m.; confusión, f.

tumbler, n. volteador, m.; variedad de vaso para beber; (orn.) volteador, m.; (mech.) tambor, m.; seguro, fiador (de cerradura), m.

tumor, n. tumor, m., hinchazón, nacencia, f.

tumult, n. tumulto, m.; agitación, f.; alboroto, m.

tumultuous, adj. tumultuoso; alborotado.

tuna, n. (bot.) tuna, f.; — **fish,** atún, m.

tune, n. tono, m.; armonía, f.; aria, f.; **in** —, afinado; —, vt. afinar un instrumento musical; armonizar; (rad.) sintonizar.

tuneful, adj. armonioso, acorde, melodioso; sonoro.

tuner, n. afinador, templador, m.

tungsten, n. tungsteno, volframio, m.

tunic, n. túnica, f.

tuning, n. afinación, f.; templadura, f.; — **dial,** cuadrante de sintonización; — **fork,** horquilla tónica.

tunnel, n. túnel, m.; galería, f.; —, vi. construir un túnel.

turban, n. turbante, m.

turbid, adj. turbio, cenagoso; turbulento.

turbine, n. turbina, f.; **blast** —,turbosopladora, f.

turbojet, n. turborretropropulsión, f.

turboprop, n. avión de turbohélice.

turbulence, n. turbulencia, confusión, f.

turbulent, adj. turbulento, tumultuoso.

tureen, n. sopera, f.

turf, n. césped, m.; turba, f.; hipódromo, m.; carreras de caballos; —, vt. cubrir con césped.

Turk, n. turco, ca.

turkey, n. pavo, m.; (Mex.) guajolote, m.; — **buzzard,** gallinazo, m.; — **hen,** pava, f.

Turkey, Turquía, f.

Turkish, adj. turco; — **bath,** baño turco; — **towel,** toalla rusa.

turmoil, n. disturbio, m., baraúnda, confusión, f.

turn, vt. volver, trocar; verter, traducir; cambiar; tornear; —, vi. volver, girar, rodar; voltear; dar vueltas; volverse a, mudarse, trasformarse; dirigirse; **to** — **back,** regresar, volver atrás; (coll.) virar; **to** — **down,** poner boca abajo, voltear; rehusar, bajar (la llama de gas, etc.); **to** — **off,** cerrar; **to** — **on,** abrir, encender, poner; **to** — **over,** revolver; **to** — **pale,** palidecer; **to** — **the corner,** doblar la esquina; **to** — **to,** recurrir a; —, n. vuelta, f.; giro, m.; rodeo, recodo, m.; turno,

m.; vez, f.; habilidad, inclinación, f.; servicio, m.; forma, figura, hechura, f.; **a good** —, un favor; **sharp** —, codo, m.

turndown, adj. doblado hacia abajo; —, n. denegación, f.

turning, n. vuelta, f.; rodeo, m.; recodo, m.; —, adj. de vuelta; — **point,** punto decisivo.

turnip, n. (bot.) nabo, m.

turnout, n. coche y demás aparejos; (rail.) aguja, f.; producto limpio o neto; asamblea grande de personas; **they had a good** —, tuvieron una buena concurrencia.

turnover, n. vuelco, m.; (com.) ventas, f. pl., evolución o movimiento de mercancías; —, adj. doblado hacia abajo, volteado.

turnpike, n. entrada de camino de portazgo; camino de portazgo.

turnstile, n. torniquete, m.

turntable, n. (rail.) plataforma giratoria, tornavía, f.

turpentine, n. trementina, f.; **oil of** —, aguarrás, m.

turpitude, n. maldad, infamia, f.

turquoise, n. turquesa, f.

turret, n. torrecilla, f.

turtle, n. tortuga, f.; galápago, m.

turtledove, n. tórtola, f.

tusk, n. colmillo, m.; diente, m.

tussle, n. lucha, f.; riña, f.; agarrada, f.; pelea, f.; rebatiña, f.; —, vi. pelear; reñir; agarrarse.

tutelar, tutelary, adj. tutelar.

tutor, n. tutor, m.; preceptor, m.; —, vt. enseñar, instruir.

tuxedo, n. smoking, m.

TV., T.V.: television, T.V., TV., televisión.

twaddle, vi. charlar; —, n. charla, f. twain n. y adj. (poet.) dos, m.

twang, vt. y vi. producir un sonido agudo; restallar; hablar con tono nasal; —, n. tañido (de un instrumento), m.; tono nasal.

tweak, vt. agarrar y halar con un tirón retorcido; —, n. tirón retorcido.

tweed, n. género tejido de lana de superficie áspera y de dos colores; —**s,** pl. ropa hecha de paño de lana y de superficie áspera.

tweezers, n. pl. tenacillas, f. pl.

twelfth, n. y adj. duodécimo, m.

twelve, n. y adj. doce, m.

twelvemonth, n. año, m., doce meses.

twentieth, n. y adj. vigésimo, veintavo, m.

twenty, n. y adj. veinte, m.; — **odd,** veintitantos.

twice, adv. dos veces; al doble.

twice-told, adj. que se ha dicho dos veces;

repetido.

twiddle, vt. hacer girar; enroscar (los dedos, etc.); —, n. vuelta, f.; movimiento giratorio (de los dedos, etc.).

twig, n. varita, varilla, f.; vástago, m.

twilight, n. crepúsculo, m.; —, adj. crepuscular; — **sleep,** narcosis obstétrica parcial.

twill, n. paño tejido en forma cruzada; —, vt. tejer paño en forma cruzada.

twin, n. y adj. gemelo, la, mellizo, za.

twine, vt. torcer, enroscar; —, vi. entrelazarse; caracolear; —, n. amarradura, f.; bramante, m.

twinge, vt. punzar; —, vi. sentir comezón; sufrir dolor (de una punzada, etc.); —, n. dolor punzante; comezón, m.

twinkle, vi. centellear; parpadear; —, n. centello, m.; pestañeo, m.; movimiento rápido.

twinkling, n. guiñada, f.; pestañeo, m.; momento, m.; **in the — of an eye,** en un abrir y cerrar de ojos.

twirl, vt. voltear; hacer girar; —, n. vuelta, f.; giro, m.

twist, vt. y vi. torcer, retorcer; entretejer; retortijar; **to — one's body,** contorcerse; —, n. trenza, f.; hilo de algodón; torcedura, f.; baile y ritmo popular de los E.U.A.

twisted, adj. torcido; enredado.

twisting, adj. torcedor; —, n. torcedura, f., torcimiento, m.

twit, vt. vituperar; censurar; regañar; —, n. tonto, ta; dicterio, m.; reproche, m.

twitch, vt. tirar bruscamente, agarrar; arrancar; —, vi. crisparse, contorcerse, tener una contracción nerviosa; —, n. tirón, m., crispatura, f., contracción nerviosa.

twitter, vi. gorjear; —, n. gorjeo, m. **two,** n. y adj. dos, m.

two-by-four, adj. que mide cuatro por dos pulgadas; (coll.) pequeño, mezquino; apretado.

two-faced, adj. falso; de dos caras; disimulado.

two-fisted, adj. belicoso, denodado, viril.

twofold, adj. doble, duplicado; —, adv. al doble.

two-seater, n. vehículo de dos asientos.

twosome, n. juego en que toman parte dos personas; pareja, f.

two-step, n. paso doble (música y baile).

tycoon, n. título dado antiguamente al jefe del ejército japonés; magnate industrial.

type, n. tipo, m.; letra, f.; carácter, m.; clase, f.; género, m.; **bold-faced —,** tipo negro; **canon —,** canon, m.; **large —,** tipo de cartel; **light-faced —,** tipo delgado; **lower-case —,** letra minúscula; **Old English —,** letra gótica; **pica —,** tipo cícero; **Roman —,** letra redonda; **upper-case —,** letra mayúscula; **— bar,** línea de tipos; —, vt. y vi. escribir a máquina; —, vt. clasificar.

typesetter, n. cajista, m. y f.

typesetting, n. cajistería, f.; composición tipográfica.

typewrite, vt. escribir a máquina.

typewriter, n. máquina de escribir; dactilógrafo, m.; dactilografista, m. y f.; **portable —,** máquina de escribir portátil.

typewriting, n. acción de escribir a máquina; dactilografía, mecanografía, f.; escritura a máquina; trabajo hecho en una máquina de escribir.

typewritten, adj. escrito a máquina.

typhoid, n. tifoidea, f.; —, adj. tifoideo; — **fever,** fiebre tifoidea.

typhoon, n. tifón, huracán, m.

typhus, n. (med.) tifus, tifo, m.

typical, adj. típico; **—ly,** adv. en forma típica.

typify, vt. simbolizar, representar.

typing, n. mecanografía, dactilografía, f.

typist, n. mecanógrafo, fa.

typographer, n. tipógrafo, m.

typographical, adj. tipográfico.

typography, n. tipografía, f.

tyrannic, tyrannical, adj. tiránico.

tyrannous, adj. tiránico, tirano, arbitrario; cruel; injusto.

tyranny, n. tiranía, crueldad, opresión, f.

tyrant, n. tirano, m.

tyro, tiro, n. aprendiz, novicio, m.

Tyrolean, n. y adj. tirolés, esa.

U

U.: University, universidad.

ubiquitous, adj. ubicuo.

udder, n. ubre, f.

ugliness, n. fealdad, deformidad, f.; (coll.) rudeza, f.

ugly, adj. feo, disforme; (coll.) rudo, desagradable.

ukulele, n. guitarrita de cuatro cuerdas.

ulcer, *n.* úlcera, *f.*

ulcerate, *vt.* ulcerar.

ulster, *n.* abrigo flojo y pesado.

ulterior, *adj.* ulterior; — **motive,** motivo oculto.

ultimate, *adj.* último; —, *n.* lo último.

ultimatum, *n.* ultimatum, *m.;* última condición irrevocable.

ultimo, *adj.* y *adv.* en o del mes próximo pasado.

ultra, *adj.* extremo; excesivo; —, *n.* extremista, *m.* y *f.;* persona radical.

ultramarine, *n.* azul de ultramar; —, *adj.* ultramarino.

ultramodern, *adj.* ultramoderno.

ultrasonic, *adj.* ultrasónico.

ultraviolet, *adj.* ultravioleta, ultraviolado; — **rays,** rayos ultraviolados.

umber, *n.* tierra de sombra, tierra de Nocera, tierra de Umbría; —, *adj.* de tierra de sombra; pardo.

umbilical, *adj.* umbilical; — **cord,** ombligo, *m.*

umbrage, *n.* follaje, *m.;* umbría, *f.;* resentimiento, *m.;* **to take** —, tener sospecha o resentimiento.

umbrella, *n.* paraguas, *m.;* parasol, quitasol, *m.;* — **stand,** portaparaguas, *m.*

umlaut, *n.* diéresis, *f.*

umpire, *n.* árbitro, arbitrador, *m.;* —, *vt.* arbitrar.

umpteenth, *adj.* enésimo; **for the** — **time,** por enésima vez.

U.N.: United Nations, ONU, Organización de las Naciones Unidas.

unabashed, *adj.* desvergonzado, descocado.

unabated, *adj.* no disminuido, no agotado; cabal.

unable, *adj.* incapaz; **to be** —, no poder.

unabridged, *adj.* completo, sin abreviar.

unaccompanied, *adj.* solo, sin acompañante.

unaccountable, *adj.* inexplicable, extraño.

unaccustomed, *adj.* desacostumbrado, desusado.

unacquainted, *adj.* desconocido; **I am** — **with him,** no lo conozco.

unadulterated, *adj.* genuino, puro; sin mezcla.

unaffected, *adj.* sin afectación, sincero, natural; —**ly,** *adv.* en forma natural, sencillamente.

unaided, *adj.* sin ayuda.

unaltered, *adj.* invariado; sin ningún cambio.

un-American, *adj.* antiamericano.

unanimity, *n.* unanimidad, *f.*

unanimous, *adj.* unánime; —**ly,** *adv.* por aclamación, por unanimidad.

unapproachable, *adj.* inaccesible.

unarmed, *adj.* inerme, desarmado.

unassailable, *adj.* inatacable; inexpugnable.

unassisted, *adj.* sin ayuda, solo; sin auxilio.

unassuming, *adj.* modesto, sencillo, sin pretensiones.

unattached, *adj.* separado, independiente; disponible.

unattainable, *adj.* inasequible.

unattended, *adj.* solo, sin comitiva.

unavailing, *adj.* inútil, vano, infructuoso.

unavoidable, *adj.* inevitable; **to be** —, no tener remedio, no poder evitarse.

unaware, *adj.* incauto; de sorpresa, sin saber.

unawares, *adv.* inadvertidamente; de improviso, inesperadamente.

unbalanced, *adj.* trastornado; no equilibrado.

unbearable, *adj.* intolerable.

unbecoming, *adj.* indecoroso; que no queda bien, que no sienta (un vestido, etc.).

unbeliever, *n.* incrédulo, la; infiel, *m.* y *f.*

unbend, *vt.* aflojar; —, *vi.* condescender; descansar.

unbending, *adj.* inflexible.

unbiased, *adj.* imparcial, exento de prejuicios.

unbidden, *adj.* no invitado, no ordenado, espontáneo.

unbind, *vt.* desatar; aflojar.

unblemished, *adj.* sin mancha, sin tacha.

unborn, *adj.* sin nacer, no nacido todavía.

unbosom, *vt.* confesar; desembuchar; —, *vi.* desahogarse.

unbound, *adj.* sin encuadernar, a la rústica (aplícase a libros); desatado.

unbounded, *adj.* infinito; ilimitado.

unbreakable, *adj.* irrompible.

unbridle, *vt.* desenfrenar; —**d,** *adj.* desenfrenado, licencioso; violento.

unbroken, *adj.* indómito; entero; no interrumpido, continuado.

unbuckle, *vt.* deshebillar.

unburden, *vt.* descargar, aliviar.

unbutton, *vt.* desabotonar.

uncalled-for, *adj.* que no viene al caso, que está fuera de lugar; impertinente, grosero; inmerecido.

uncanny, *adj.* extraño, misterioso.

unceasing, *adj.* sin cesar, continuo; —**ly,** *adv.* sin tregua.

uncertain, *adj.* inseguro; incierto, dudoso; vacilante.

uncertainty, *n.* incertidumbre, *f.*

unchecked, *adj.* desenfrenado.

uncivilized, *adj.* salvaje, incivilizado.

unclaimed, adj. no reclamado, sin reclamar; sin recoger.

uncle, n. tío, m.

unclean, adj. inmundo, sucio, puerco; obsceno; inmoral.

unclouded, adj. sereno, despejado; sin nubes.

uncoil, vt. desarrollar, devanar.

uncomfortable, adj. incómodo; intranquilo; desagradable.

uncommon, adj. raro, extraordinario, fuera de lo común.

uncompromising, adj. inflexible; irreconciliable.

unconcern, n. indiferencia, f.; descuido, m.; despreocupación, f.

unconcerned, adj. indiferente; —ly, adv. sin empacho.

unconditional, adj. incondicional, absoluto; — surrender, rendición absoluta, rendición incondicional.

unconscious, adj. inconsciente; desmayado.

unconventional, adj. informal, sin ceremonia, sin formulismos.

uncouple, vt. desatraillar; desenganchar.

uncouth, adj. extraño; incivil, tosco, grosero; — word, palabrota, f.

uncover, vt. descubrir.

unction, n. unción, f.

uncultivated, adj. inculto; sin cultivar.

uncut, adj. no cortado, entero.

undamaged, adj. ileso, libre de daño.

undaunted, adj. intrépido, atrevido.

undecided, adj. indeciso.

undeniable, adj. innegable; indudable; — bly, adv. innegablemente.

under, prep. debajo de, bajo; — penalty of fine, so pena de multa; — penalty of death, so pena de muerte; —, adv. debajo, abajo, más abajo.

underage, adj. menor de edad.

underbrush, n. maleza, f.; breñal, m.

undercharge, vt. cobrar de menos.

underclothing, n. ropa interior.

undercover, adv. bajo cuerda, secretamente.

undercurrent, n. tendencia oculta; corriente submarina.

undercut, n. solomillo, m.; puñetazo hacia arriba; —, vi. vender a precios más bajos que el competidor; —, vt. socavar.

underdeveloped, adj. subdesarrollado; — countries, países subdesarrollados.

underdog, n. persona oprimida; el que lleva la peor parte.

underdone, adj. poco cocido.

underestimate, vt. menospreciar; calcular de menos; subestimar.

underexposure, n. (phot.) insuficiente exposición.

underfoot, adv. bajo los pies de uno; bajo tierra, debajo; en el camino.

undergo, vt. sufrir; sostener.

undergraduate, n. estudiante universitario no graduado.

underground, adj. subterráneo; subrepticio; —, adv. debajo de la tierra; en secreto; subrepticiamente; —, n. subterráneo, m.; ferrocarril subterráneo.

underhand, adj. secreto, clandestino; ejecutado con las manos hacia abajo; fraudulento; injusto; —, adv. con las manos hacia abajo; clandestinamente.

underhanded, adj. bajo cuerda, por debajo de cuerda, secreto, clandestino; —ly, adv. en forma clandestina.

underlie, vi. estar debajo; ser base de.

underline, vt. subrayar.

underling, n. subordinado, m.; suboficial, m.

underlying, adj. fundamental, básico; esencial; yaciente, que yace debajo.

undermine, vt. minar; desprestigiar por debajo de cuerda.

underneath, adv. debajo.

undernourished, adj. malnutrido, desnutrido, malalimentado.

underpass, n. viaducto, m.

underpay, vt. y vi. remunerar deficientemente.

underprivileged, adj. desvalido, menesteroso, necesitado; the — classes, las clases menesterosas.

underrate, vt. menoscabar; deslustrar; menospreciar.

underscore, vt. subrayar; recalcar.

undersell, vt. vender por menos (que otro).

undershirt, n. camiseta, f.

underside, n. lado inferior, fondo de una cosa.

undersigned, n. y adj. suscrito, ta.

underskirt, n. enagua, f., refajo, fondo, zagalejo, m.

understand, vt. entender, comprender; do you —? ¿entiende Ud.? we — each other, nos comprendemos.

understanding, n. entendimiento, m., comprensión, f.; inteligencia, f.; conocimiento, m.; correspondencia, f.; meollo, m.; slow in —, torpe, tardo en comprender; —, adj. comprensivo; inteligente, perito.

understatement, n. declaración o manifestación incompleta donde no se hacen constar todos los hechos.

understudy, n. (theat.) sustituto, ta, actor o actriz que se prepara para remplazar a otro en un momento dado; —, vt. y vi. (theat.) prepararse para tomar el papel de otro en un momento dado.

undertake, vt. y vi. emprender.

undertaker, n. empresario o director de pompas fúnebres.

undertaking, n. empresa, obra, f.; empeño, m.; — **establishment,** funeraria, f.

undertone, n. tono (de voz) bajo; voz baja; color tenue u opaco.

undertow, n. resaca, f.

underwater, adj. subacuático, submarino.

underwear, n. ropa interior, ropa íntima.

underweight, adj. de bajo peso, que pesa menos del término medio.

underworld, n. hampa, f., clase baja y criminal de la sociedad; morada de los muertos.

underwrite, vt. suscribir; asegurar contra riesgos.

underwriter, n. asegurador, m.

undesirable, adj. no deseable, nocivo.

undeveloped, adj. no desarrollado; — **country,** país no explotado; — **photograph,** fotografía no revelada.

undevout, adj. indevoto.

undiluted, adj. puro, sin diluir.

undiminished, adj. entero, sin disminuir.

undismayed, adj. intrépido.

undisputed, adj. incontestable.

undisturbed, adj. quieto, tranquilo, sin haber sido estorbado.

undivided, adj. indiviso, entero.

undo, vt. deshacer, desatar.

undoing, n. destrucción, ruina, f.

undone, adj. sin hacer; **to leave nothing** —, no dejar nada por hacer.

undoubted, adj. evidente; —**ly,** adv. sin duda, indudablemente.

undress, vt. desnudar; —, n. paños menores.

undue, adj. indebido; injusto.

undulant fever, n. fiebre mediterránea.

undulate, vi. ondear, ondular.

unduly, adv. excesivamente; indebidamente; ilícitamente.

undying, adj. inmortal; imperecedero.

unearned, adj. inmerecido; que no se ha ganado.

unearth, vt. desenterrar; revelar; divulgar; descubrir.

unearthly, adj. sobrenatural; espantoso.

uneasiness, n. malestar, m.; inquietud, intranquilidad, f.; desasosiego, m.

uneasy, adj. inquieto, desasosegado; incómodo; intranquilo.

uneducated, adj. sin educación.

unemployed, adj. desocupado, sin trabajo; ocioso.

unemployment, n. desempleo, m.; paro, m.

unending, adj. inacabable, sin fin; eterno, perpetuo.

unequal, adj. desigual.

unequaled, adj. incomparable.

unerring, adj. infalible.

UNESCO: United Nations' Educational, Scientific and Cultural Organization, UNESCO, Organización de las Naciones Unidas para la Educación, la Ciencia y la Cultura.

uneven, adj. desigual; barrancoso; disparejo, impar; —**ly,** adv. desigualmente.

unexpected, adj. inesperado; inopinado; —**ly,** adv. de repente.

unexplored, adj. ignorado, no descubierto, sin explorar.

unfailing, adj. infalible, seguro.

unfair, adj. injusto; —**ly,** adv. injustamente.

unfaithful, adj. infiel, pérfido.

unfaltering, adj. firme, asegurado.

unfamiliar, adj. desacostumbrado, desconocido.

unfavorable, adj. desfavorable.

unfed, adj. sin haber comido.

unfeeling, adj. insensible, duro, cruel.

unfit, adj. inepto, incapaz; inadecuado; indigno; —, vt. incapacitar; inhabilitar.

unfold, vt. desplegar; revelar; desdoblar.

unforeseen, adj. imprevisto.

unforgettable, adj. inolvidable.

unfortunate, adj. desafortunado, infeliz; malhadado; —**ly,** adv. por desgracia, infelizmente, desgraciadamente.

unfounded, adj. sin fundamento.

unfrequented, adj. poco frecuentado.

unfurl, vt. desplegar, extender.

unfurnished, adj. sin muebles, no amueblado; — **apartment,** departamento sin amueblar.

ungainly, adj. desmañado; desgarbado.

ungodly, adj. impío.

ungrounded, adj. infundado.

unhand, vt. soltar de las manos.

unhappy, adj. infeliz; descontento, triste.

unharmed, adj. ileso, sano y salvo, incólume.

unhealthy, adj. enfermizo; insalubre, malsano.

unheard-of, adj. inaudito, extraño; no imaginado.

unheeded, adj. despreciado, no atendido.

unhorse, vt. botar de la silla al jinete.

unhurt, adj. ileso, sin haber sufrido daño.

UNICEF: United Nations' International Children's Emergency Fund, UNICEF, Fondo de las Naciones Unidas para la Infancia.

unification, n. unificación, f.

uniform, *n.* uniforme, *m.;* —, *adj.* uniforme; —ly, *adv.* uniformemente.
uniformity, *n.* uniformidad, *f.*
unilateral, *adj.* unilateral.
unify, *vt.* unificar, unir.
uninformed, *adj.* sin conocimientos.
uninjured, *adj.* ileso, sin haber sufrido daño.
union, *n.* unión, *f.;* conjunción, *f.;* fusión, *f.*
unionism, *n.* unionismo, *m.,* sindicalismo obrero, agrupación obrera; formación de gremios obreros.
unionize, *vt.* sindicar; unionizar; incorporar en un gremio.
unique, *adj.* único, singular, extraordinario.
unison, *n.* unisonancia, *f.;* concordancia, unión, *f.;* in —, al unísono.
unit, *n.* unidad, *f.*
Unitarian, *n.* (eccl.) unitario, ria; u—, *adj.* unitario.
unite, *vt.* y *vi.* unir, unirse; juntarse; concretar.
united, *adj.* unido, junto.
United Kingdom, Reino Unido, *m.*
unity, *n.* unidad, concordia, conformidad, *f.*
universal, *adj.* universal; — joint, cardán, *m.;* —ly, *adv.* universalmente.
universality, *n.* universalidad, *f.*
universe, *n.* universo *m.*
university, *n.* universidad, *f.*
unjust, *adj.* injusto.
unjustified, *adj.* injustificado.
unkempt, *adj.* despeinado; descuidado en el traje; tosco.
unkind, *adj.* poco bondadoso; cruel; —ly, *adv.* desfavorablemente; ásperamente.
unknowingly, *adv.* sin saberlo; desapercibidamente.
unknown, *adj.* incógnito, ignoto; desconocido.
unlace, *vt.* desenlazar, desamarrar.
unless, *conj.* a menos que, si no.
unlike, *adj.* disímil, desemejante; —, *conj.* al contrario de.
unlikely, *adj.* improbable; inverosímil.
unlimited, *adj.* ilimitado.
unload, *vt.* descargar.
unlock, *vt.* abrir alguna cerradura.
unlucky, *adj.* desafortunado; siniestro.
unmanageable, *adj.* inmanejable, intratable.
unmanly, *adj.* pusilánime, cobarde; afeminado.
unmannerly, *adj.* malcriado, descortés, incivil.
unmarried, *adj.* soltero; soltera; — woman, soltera, *f.;* — man, soltero, *m.*

unmask, *vt.* desenmascarar, revelar; —, *vi.* desenmascararse, quitarse la máscara.
unmentionable, *adj.* que no se puede mencionar, indigno de mencionarse; —s, *n. pl.* cosas que no pueden mencionarse, por ejemplo (en forma jocosa), ropa interior, etc.
unmixed, *adj.* sin mezcla.
unnatural, *adj.* artificial; contrario a las leyes de la naturaleza.
unnecessary, *adj.* innecesario, inútil.
unnerve, *vt.* enervar.
unnoticed, *adj.* no observado.
unnumbered, *adj.* innumerable; sin número.
unobserved, *adj.* no observado; inadvertido.
unobtrusive, *adj.* modesto, recatado.
unofficial, *adj.* extraoficial; particular, privado.
unorthodox, *adj.* heterodoxo.
unpack, *vt.* desempacar; desempaquetar; desenvolver.
unpaid, *adj.* pendiente de pago.
unpalatable, *adj.* desabrido.
unpleasant, *adj.* desagradable.
unplug, *vt.* desenchufar.
unpopular, *adj.* impopular.
unprecedented, *adj.* sin precedente.
unpremeditated, *adj.* sin premeditación.
unpretending, *adj.* sin pretensiones, sencillo, modesto.
unprincipled, *adj.* sin principios morales, sin escrúpulos.
unproductive, *adj.* estéril, infructuoso.
unprofitable, *adj.* inútil, vano, que no rinde utilidad o provecho; —bly, *adv.* inútilmente, en forma infructuosa.
unprotected, *adj.* sin protección, sin defensa; desvalido.
unpunished, *adj.* impune.
unquenchable, *adj.* inextinguible.
unravel, *vt.* desenredar; resolver.
unreal, *adj.* fantástico, ilusorio, que no tiene realidad.
unrecognizable, *adj.* irreconocible.
unreliable, *adj.* informal, incumplido.
unremitting, *adj.* perseverante, constante, incansable.
unreserved, *adj.* franco, abierto.
unrest, *n.* inquietud, impaciencia, *f.;* movimiento, *m.*
unrestrained, *adj.* desenfrenado; ilimitado.
unripe, *adj.* inmaturo; precoz, prematuro; — fruit, fruta verde, fruta no madura.
unrivaled, *adj.* sin rival, sin igual.
unroll, *vt.* desenrollar, desplegar.
unruffled, *adj.* plácido, sereno, calmado.

unruly, *adj.* desenfrenado, inmanejable, refractario; desarreglado.

unsavory, *adj.* desabrido, insípido; ofensivo.

unscathed, *adj.* a salvo; sano y salvo; sin daño o perjuicio.

unschooled, *adj.* indocto; sin escuela.

unscrew, *vt.* destornillar, desatornillar, desentornillar.

unscrupulous, *adj.* sin escrúpulos, inmoral, desalmado.

unseasonable, *adj.* fuera de la estación; a destiempo, inoportuno.

unseat, *vt.* quitar del asiento; privar del derecho de formar parte de una cámara legislativa.

unseemly, *adj.* indecente, indecoroso.

unseen, *adj.* no visto; invisible.

unselfish, *adj.* desinteresado, generoso.

unsettled, *adj.* voluble, inconstante; incierto, indeciso; no establecido; — **accounts,** cuentas por pagar, cuentas no liquidadas.

unshakable, *adj.* inmutable, firme, estable, impasible, inconmovible; insacudible.

unshod, *adj.* descalzo; desherrado.

unsightly, *adj.* desagradable a la vista, feo.

unskilled, *adj.* inexperto, inhábil.

unsociable, *adj.* insociable.

unsought, *adj.* hallado sin buscarlo, no solicitado.

unsound, *adj.* falto de salud; falto de sentido; inestable; erróneo, falso.

unsparing, *adj.* generoso, liberal; incompasivo, cruel.

unspeakable, *adj.* indecible; —**ly,** *adv.* en forma indecible.

unstable, *adj.* inestable, inconstante.

unsubdued, *adj.* indomado.

unsuitable, *adj.* inadecuado, impropio.

unsullied, *adj.* inmaculado, puro, limpio.

unswerving, *adj.* indesviable; leal.

untamed, *adj.* indómito, indomado.

untangle, *vt.* desenredar.

untaught, *adj.* ignorante, sin instrucción.

unthinking, *adj.* desatento, inconsiderado, indiscreto; irreflexivo.

unthought-of, *adj.* impensado.

untidy, *adj.* desaseado, descuidado, desaliñado.

untie, *vt.* desatar, deshacer, soltar, desamarrar.

until, *prep.* hasta; —, *conj.* hasta que.

untimely, *adj.* intempestivo; prematuro.

untiring, *adj.* incansable.

unto, *prep.* (poet.) a, en, para, hasta.

untold, *adj.* no relatado, no dicho.

untouched, *adj.* intacto, no tocado.

untoward, *adj.* perverso; siniestro, adverso; refractario, testarudo.

untried, *adj.* no ensayado o probado.

untrod, untrodden, *adj.* que no ha sido pisado; no recorrido.

untroubled, *adj.* no perturbado, tranquilo, calmado.

untrustworthy, *adj.* incumplido, indigno de confianza.

untruth, *n.* falsedad, mentira, *f.*

untutored, *adj.* no instruido, sin escuela; sencillo.

unused, *adj.* inusitado; desacostumbrado.

unusual, *adj.* inusitado, raro, insólito; poco común; —**ly,** *adv.* excepcionalmente.

unutterable, *adj.* inefable, indecible, inexpresable.

unvarying, *adj.* invariable.

unveil, *vt.* y *vi.* descubrir; revelar; quitar el velo (a alguna cosa); estrenar.

unwarranted, *adj.* injustificable, inexcusable.

unwary, *adj.* incauto, desprevenido.

unwelcome, *adj.* inoportuno; mal acogido, no recibido con gusto.

unwieldy, *adj.* pesado, difícil de manejar.

unwilling, *adj.* renuente, sin deseos, sin querer; —**ly,** *adv.* de mala gana.

unwind, *vt.* desenredar, desenrollar; desenmarañar; relajar.

unwise, *adj.* imprudente; —**ly,** *adv.* sin juicio.

unwittingly, *adv.* sin saber, sin darse cuenta.

unwonted, *adj.* insólito.

unworldly, *adj.* espiritual, ajeno a las cosas mundanas.

unworthy, *adj.* indigno, vil.

unwound, *adj.* sin cuerda; desenrollado.

unwrap, *vt.* desenvolver; abrir; revelar.

unwritten, *adj.* verbal, no escrito; — **law,** ley de la costumbre, derecho consuetudinario.

unyielding, *adj.* inflexible.

up, *adv.* arriba, en lo alto; — **to,** hasta; — **to date,** hasta la fecha; hasta ahora, **to make —,** hacer las paces; inventar; compensar; maquillarse; **to bring —,** criar, educar; **to call —,** telefonear; **it is — to me,** depende de mí.

unbraid, *vt.* echar en cara, vituperar.

upbraiding, *n.* reproche, *m.,* censura, *f.,* regaño, *m.*

upbringing, *n.* educación, crianza, *f.*

upbuild, *vt.* reconstruir; vigorizar.

upcountry, *n.* (coll.) el interior de un país; —, *adj.* que reside en el interior de un país.

upgrade, *n.* cuesta arriba, pendiente arriba; —, vt. ascender en categoría (a un obrero); mejorar un producto para subirle el precio.

upheaval, n. alzamiento, levantamiento, m.; conmoción, f.

uphill, adj. difícil, penoso; —, adv. en grado ascendente.

uphold, vt. levantar en alto; sostener; apoyar, proteger; defender.

upholster, vt. entapizar, tapizar.

upholstery, n. tapicería, f., tapizado, m.

upkeep, n. conservación, f., mantenimiento, m.

upland, n. tierra montañosa; —, adj. alto, elevado.

uplift, vt. levantar en alto; mejorar.

upmost, adj. lo más alto; lo más prominente; lo más influyente; —, adv. en el lugar más alto; en primer lugar.

upon, prep. sobre, encima.

upper, adj. superior; más elevado; — berth, cama o litera alta (en un tren, un vapor, etc.); — case, (print.) caja alta, letras mayúsculas; — deck, (naut.) sobrecubierta, f.; plataforma de arriba ; — hand, dominio, m., predominancia, f.

upper-case, adj. (print.) de caja alta, mayúsculo.

upper-class, adj. aristocrático; relativo a los grados superiores de un colegio.

uppermost, adj. superior en posición, rango, poder, etc.; to be —, predominar.

uppish, adj. (coll.) engreído, altivo, orgulloso, presuntuoso.

upright, adj. derecho, recto, justo; perpendicular; —ly, adv. rectamente.

uprising, n. subida, f.; levantamiento, m., insurrección, f.

uproar, n. tumulto, alboroto, m.

uproarious, adj. tumultuoso, ruidoso.

uproot, vt. desarraigar, extirpar.

upset, vt. volcar, trastornar; perturbar; —, adj. desordenado; volcano; agitado (de ánimo); —, n. trastorno, m.; vuelco, m.

upshot, n. remate, m.; fin, m., conclusión, f.

upside-down, adj. de arriba abajo.

upstairs, adv. en el piso de arriba, arriba.

upstart, n. advenedizo, za.

upstream, adv. aguas arriba, río arriba.

up-to-date, adj. moderno, de última moda, reciente.

uptown, n. sección de la ciudad fuera del centro; parte alta de la ciudad.

upturn, vt. mejorar; volver hacia arriba; —, n. mejoramiento, m.; subida, f.

upward, upwards, adv. hacia arriba.

uranium, n. uranio, m.

urban, adj. urbano.

urbane, adj. civil, atento, cortés.

urbanity, n. urbanidad, f.

urbanization, n. urbanización, f.

urchin, n. pilluelo, m.; (coll.) granuja, m.; (zool.) erizo, m.

urea, n. urea, f.

uremia, n. uremia, f.

urethra, n. uretra, f.

urge, vt. y vi. incitar, hurgar; activar; urgir, instar.

urgency, n. urgencia, f.; premura, f.

urgent, adj. urgente; —ly, adv. urgentemente, con urgencia.

urinal, n. orinal, m.

urinary, adj. urinario.

urinate, vi. orinar, mear.

urine, n. orina, f., orines, m. pl.

urn, n. urna, f.

U.S.A.: United States of America, E.U.A. Estados Unidos de América.

usable, adj. apto, hábil; utilizable.

usage, n. uso, m.; tratamiento, m.

use, n. uso, m., utilidad, f.; servicio, m.; —, vt. y vi. usar, emplear, servirse de; acostumbrar; soler; to make — of, utilizar.

used, adj. usado; de ocasión; to get — to, acostumbrarse a.

used-up, adj. agotado; gastado; to become —, gastarse; agotarse.

useful, adj. útil; to make —, utilizar; —ly, adv. en forma útil.

usefulness, n. utilidad, f.

useless, adj. inútil.

uselessness, n. inutilidad, f.

usher, n. acomodador, m.; ujier, m.; —, vt. introducir; anunciar; acomodar (en un teatro, iglesia, etc.).

U.S.S.R.: Union of Soviet Socialist Republics, U.R.S.S. Unión de Repúblicas Socialistas Soviéticas.

usual, adj. usual, común, usado; general, ordinario; —ly, adv. de costumbre.

usurer, n. usurero, m.

usurp, vt. usurpar.

usury, n. usura, f.

Ut.: Utah, Utah (E.U.A.).

utensil, n. utensilio, m.; —s, n. pl. útiles, m. pl.; kitchen —s, trastos, m. pl., batería de cocina.

uterus, n. útero, m., matriz, f.

utilitarian, adj. utilitario.

utility, n. utilidad, f.; public —ies, servicios públicos.

utilization, n. utilización, f.

utilize, vt. utilizar; emplear.

utmost, adj. extremo, sumo; último; to the —, hasta más no poder.

Utopian, utopian, adj. utópico; imaginario; —, n. utopista, m. y f.

utter, *adj.* acabado; todo; extremo; entero; —, *vt.* proferir; expresar; publicar.

utterance, *n.* habla, expresión, manifestación, *f.*

utterly, *adv.* enteramente, del todo.

uttermost, *adj.* el más lejano; el más distante; el mayor posible; extremo, sumo; —, *n.* lo más posible.

uvula, *n.* úvula, *f.*

uvular, *adj.* uvular.

V

V., vid.: vide, V. véase.

Va.: Virginia, Virginia, E.U.A.

vacancy, *n.* vacante, *f.;* vacío, *m.*

vacant, *adj.* vacío, desocupado, vacante.

vacate, *vt.* desocupar; anular, invalidar.

vacation, *n.* vacación, *f.,* vacaciones, *f. pl.*

vaccinate, *vt.* vacunar.

vaccination, *n.* vacuna, *f.;* vacunación, *f.*

vaccine, *n.* vacuna, *f.*

vacillate, *vi.* vacilar.

vacuous, *adj.* vacío.

vacuum, *n.* vacío, *m.;* — bottle, termos, *m.;* — cleaner, aspiradora, *f.;* — pump, bomba aspirante, bomba de vacío; — tube, tubo al vacío.

vagabond, *n.* y *adj.* vagabundo, *m.*

vagary, *n.* capricho, *m.;* extravagancia, *f.*

vagina, *n.* (anat.) vagina, *f.;* (bot.) vaina, *f.*

vagrancy, *n.* vagancia, tuna, *f.*

vagrant, *adj.* vagabundo; —, *n.* bribón, *m.*

vague, *adj.* vago; —ly, *adv.* vagamente.

vain, *adj.* vano, inútil; vanidoso, presuntuoso; in —, en vano.

valance, *n.* cenefa, doselera, *f.*

valence, *n.* (chem.) valencia, *f.*

valentine, *n.* persona a quien se le tributa amor el día de San Valentín (14 de febrero); tarjeta o regalo que se envía el día de San Valentín en señal de amor.

valet, *n.* criado, camarero, *m.,* (Mex.) camarista, *m.*

valiant, *adj.* valiente, valeroso.

valid, *adj.* válido.

validity, *n.* validación, validez, *f.*

valise, *n.* maleta, valija, *f.*

valley, *n.* valle, *m.,* cuenca, *f.*

valor, *n.* valor, aliento, brío, *m.,* fortaleza, *f.*

valorous, *adj.* valeroso; —ly, *adv.* con valor.

valuable, *adj.* precioso, valioso; to be —, valer; —s, *n. pl.* objetos de valor.

valuation, *n.* tasa, valuación, *f.*

value, *n.* valor, precio, importe, *m.;* real —, valor efectivo; — stipulated, — agreed on, valor entendido, *m.;* face —, valor nominal o aparente; —, *vt.* valuar, apreciar.

valve, *n.* válvula, *f.,* regulador, *m.;* safety —, válvula de seguridad; slide —, válvula corrediza; air —, válvula de aire.

vampire, *n.* (zool.) vampiro, *m.;* (fig.) vampiro, *m.,* persona codiciosa; vampiresa, mujer coqueta y aventurera.

van, *n.* vagón, *m.;* camión de mudanza.

Van Allen radiation belt, *n.* faja de radiación Van Allen.

vandal, *n.* y *adj.* vándalo, la.

vandalism, *n.* vandalismo, *m.*

vane, *n.* veleta, *f.;* (naut.) grímpola, *f.*

vanguard, *n.* vanguardia, *f.*

vanilla, *n.* vainilla, *f.*

vanish, *vi.* desvanecerse, desaparecer.

vanishing point, *n.* punto de fuga.

vanity, *n.* vanidad, *f.;* — case, neceser, *m.,* polvera, *f.,* estuche o caja de afeites.

vanquish, *vt.* vencer, conquistar.

vantage, *n.* ventaja, superioridad, *f.;* — point, situación ventajosa.

vapid, *adj.* insípido, sin espíritu; soso.

vapor, *n.* vapor, *m.;* exhalación, *f.*

vaporous, *adj.* vaporoso.

variable, *adj.* variable.

variance, *n.* discordia, desavenencia, *f.;* diferencia, *f.;* desviación, *f.;* discrepancia, *f.*

variation, *n.* variación, mudanza, *f.*

varicose, *adj.* varicoso; — vein, várice, *f.*

varied, *adj.* variado; cambiado, alterado.

variegated, *adj.* abigarrado.

variety, *n.* variedad, *f.*

various, *adj.* varios, diversos, diferentes.

varnish, *n.* barniz, *m.;* —, *vt.* barnizar; charolar.

varsity, *n.* equipo deportivo principal seleccionado para representar a una universidad, etc.

vary, *vt.* y *vi.* variar, diferenciar; cambiar, mudarse, discrepar.

varying, *adj.* variante.

vase, *n.* vaso, jarrón, florero, *m.*

Vaseline, *n.* Vaselina (marca de fábrica), *f.,* ungüento de petróleo.

vassal, *n.* vasallo, *m.*

vast, *adj.* vasto; inmenso; —ly, *adv.* excesivamente; vastamente.

vat, *n.* tina, paila, *f.*, tacho, *m.*

vaudeville, *n.* (theat.) función de variedades.

vault, *n.* bóveda, *f.*; cueva, caverna, *f.*; salto, *m.*, voltereta, *f.*; — *vt.* abovedar; —, *vi.* saltar, dar una voltereta.

vaunt, *vi.* jactarse, vanagloriarse.

veal, *n.* ternera, *f.*, ternero, *m.*; — **cutlet,** chuleta de ternera.

vector, *n.* (math., phys.) vector, *m.*

veer, *vi.* (naut.) virar, cambiar (el viento); desviarse.

vegetable, *adj.* vegetal; — **man,** verdulero, *m.*; — **soup,** menestra, *f.*, sopa de verdura; —, *n.* vegetal, *m.*; —**s,** *n. pl.* verduras, hortalizas, *f. pl.*

vegetarian, *n.* y *adj.* vegetariano, na.

vegetate, *vi.* vegetar.

vegetation, *n.* vegetación, *f.*

vehemence, *n.* vehemencia, violencia, *f.*; viveza, *f.*

vehement, *adj.* vehemente, violento; —**ly,** *adv.* con vehemencia.

vehicle, *n.* vehículo, *m.*

veil, *n.* velo, *m.*; disfraz, *m.*; —, *vt.* encubrir, ocultar, cubrir con velo.

vein, *n.* vena, *f.*; cavidad, *f.*; inclinación del ingenio; humor, *m.*

veined, **veiny**, *adj.* venoso; vetado.

vellum, *n.* vitela, *f.*; pergamino, *m.*; cuero curtido; — **paper,** papel avitelado.

velocity, *n.* velocidad, *f.*

velour, *n.* terciopelo, *m.*

velvet, *n.* terciopelo, *m.*; —, *adj.* de terciopelo; terciopelado.

velveteen, *n.* pana, *f.*

velvety, *adj.* terciopelado, aterciopelado.

venal, *adj.* venal, mercenario.

vend, *vt.* vender, especialmente en la calle; exclamar públicamente.

vendor, *n.* vendedor, revendedor, *m.*

veneer; *vt.* taracear; —, *n.* chapa, capa, *f.*; apariencia, ostentación, *f.*, brillo, *m.*

venerable, *adj.* venerable.

venerate, *vt.* venerar, honrar.

veneration, *n.* veneración, *f.*; culto, *m.*

venereal, *adj.* venéreo.

Venetian, *n.* y *adj.* veneciano, na.

Venezuelan, *n.* y *adj.* venezolano, na.

vengeance, *n.* venganza, *f.*

vengeful, *adj.* vengativo.

venial, *adj.* venial.

Venice, Venecia, *f.*

venison, *n.* carne de venado.

venom, *n.* veneno, *m.*

venomous, *adj.* venenoso.

vent, *n.* respiradero, *m.*; salida, *f.*; apertura, *f.*; —, *vt.* dar salida; echar fuera; **to — one's anger,** desahogarse, expresar furia.

ventilate, *vt.* ventilar; discutir, airear.

ventilation, *n.* ventilación, *f.*

ventilator, *n.* ventilador, abanico, *m.*

ventricle, *n.* (anat.) ventrículo, *m.*

ventriloquist, *n.* ventrílocuo, *m.*

venture, *n.* riesgo, *m.*; ventura, *f.*; —, *vi.* osar, aventurarse; —, *vt.* arriesgar.

venturesome, **venturous**, *adj.* osado, atrevido; —**ly,** *adv.* osadamente.

veracious, *adj.* veraz; honrado.

veracity, *n.* veracidad, *f.*

veranda o verandah, *n.* veranda, terraza, galería, *f.*, mirador, *m.*

verb, *n.* (gram.) verbo, *m.*

verbal, *adj.* verbal, literal; —**ly,** *adv.* oralmente de palabra.

verbatim, *adv.* palabra por palabra.

verbiage, *n.* verbosidad, *f.*, ripio, *m.*

verbose, *adj.* verboso.

verdant, *adj.* verde.

verdict, *n.* veredicto, *m.*; sentencia, *f.*; dictamen, *m.*; fallo (del jurado), *m.*

verdure, *n.* verdura, *f.*, verdor, *m.*

verge, *n.* vara, *f.*; fuste, *m.*; borde, *m.*; margen, *m.* y *f.*; —, *vi.* inclinarse; tirar a, parecerse a (colores etc.).

verification, *n.* verificación, *f.*

verify, *vt.* verificar; sustanciar.

verily, *adv.* en verdad; ciertamente.

veritable, *adj.* verdadero, cierto.

vermilion, *n.* bermellón, *m.*; —, *vt.* teñir de bermellón, teñir de cinabrio.

vermin, *n.* bichos, *m. pl.*

vernacular, *adj.* vernáculo, nativo; —, *n.* lengua vernácula; jerga, *f.*, lenguaje propio de un oficio, etc.

versatile, *adj.* polifacético, hábil para muchas cosas; versátil, voluble.

versatility, *n.* habilidad para muchas cosas, flexibilidad, *f.*

verse, *n.* verso, *m.*; versículo, *m.*; **blank** —, verso blanco; **free** —, verso suelto o libre.

versed, *adj.* versado.

versify, *vt.* y *vi.* versificar, trovar, hacer versos.

version, *n.* versión, traducción, *f.*

versus, *prep.* contra.

vertebra, *n.* vértebra, *f.*

vertebral, *adj.* vertebral.

vertebrate, *n.* y *adj.* vertebrado, *m.*

vertex, *n.* cenit, vértice, *m.*

vertical, *adj.* vertical; —**ly,** *adv.* verticalmente.

vertigo, *n.* vértigo, vahído, *m.*

verve, *n.* estro poético; energía, animación, *f.*, entusiasmo, *m.*; numen, *m.*, inspiración, *f.*

very, *adj.* idéntico, mismo; verdadero; —,

adv. muy, mucho, sumamente.

vesicle, *n.* vesícula, vejiguilla, *f.*

vespers, *n. pl.* vísperas, *f. pl.*

vessel, *n.* vasija, *f.,* vaso, *m.;* buque, bajel, *m.*

vest, *n.* chaleco, *m.;* —, *vt.* vestir; investir.

vestal, *adj.* casto, puro; — **virgin,** vestal, *f.*

vested, *adj.* vestido, investido.

vestibular, *adj.* vestibular.

vestibule, *n.* zaguán, *m.,* casapuerta, *f.*

vestige, *n.* vestigio, *m.*

vestment, *n.* vestido, *m.;* vestidura, *f.*

vest-pocket, *adj.* propio para el bolsillo del chaleco; pequeño; — **dictionary,** diccionario de bolsillo; — **edition,** edición en miniatura.

vestry, *n.* sacristía, *f.*

veteran, *n.* y *adj.* veterano na.

veterinary, *n.* y *adj.* veterinario, *m.*

veto, *n.* veto, *m.*

vex, *vt.* vejar, molestar, contrariar; —**ed** *adj.* picado, molesto, contrariado.

vexation, *n.* vejamen, *m.,* vejación, molestia,

vexatious, *adj.* penoso, molesto, enfadoso.

v.g.: verbi gratia, for example, vg., verbigracia, por ejemplo.

via, *prep.* por la vía de; por; — **airmail,** por vía aérea; — **freight,** por flete o carga.

viaduct, *n.* viaducto, *m.*

vial, *n.* redoma, ampolleta, *f.,* frasco, *m.*

viand, *n.* vianda, *f.*

vibrant, *adj.* vibrante.

vibrate, *vt.* vibrar.

vibration, *n.* vibración, *f.*

vibrator, *n.* vibrador, *m.*

vicar, *n.* vicario, *m.*

vicarious, *adj.* vicario.

vice, *n.* vicio, *m.;* maldad, *f.;* deformidad física; mancha, *f.,* defecto, *m.;* — **versa,** viceversa, al contrario; —, *prep.* en lugar de.

vice-admiral, *n.* vicealmirante, *m.*

vice-chairman, *n.* vicepresidente (de una reunión, etc.), *m.*

vice-consul, *n.* vicecónsul, *m.*

vice-president, *n.* vicepresidente, *m.*

vicinity, *n.* vecindad, proximidad, *f.*

vicious, *adj.* vicioso; — **circle,** círculo vicioso; —**ly,** *adj.* de manera viciosa.

vicissitude, *n.* vicisitud, *f.*

victim, *n.* víctima, *f.*

victimize, *vt.* sacrificar; engañar.

victor, *n.* vencedor, *m.*

victorious, *adj.* victorioso, vencedor.

victory, *n.* victoria, *f.*

victual, *vt.* proveer, abastecer de comestibles.

victuals, *n. pl.* vituallas, viandas, *f. pl.,*

comestibles, *m. pl.*

video, *n.* televisión, *f.*

videotape, *n.* grabación televisada en cinta.

vie, *vi.* competir.

Vienna, Viena, *f.*

Viennese, *n.* y *adj.* vienés, esa.

view, *n.* vista, *f.;* perspectiva, *f.;* aspecto, *m.;* examen, *m.;* apariencia, *f.;* ver, *m.;* **bird's eye** —, vista a vuelo de pájaro; **in** — **of,** en vista de; **point of** —, punto de vista; —, *vt.* mirar, ver; examinar.

viewpoint, *n.* punto de vista.

vigil, *n.* vela, *f.;* vigilia, *f.*

vigilance, *n.* vigilancia, *f.*

vigilant, *adj.* vigilante, atento; —**ly,** *adv.* con vigilancia.

vigor, *n.* vigor, *m.;* robustez, *f.;* energía, *f.*

vigorous, *adj.* vigoroso; fuerte.

vile, *adj.* vil, bajo; —**ly,** *adv.* vilmente.

vilify, *vt.* envilecer; degradar.

villa, *n.* quinta, casa de campo.

village, *n.* aldea, *f.*

villager, *n.* aldeano, *m.*

villain, *n.* malvado, miserable, *m.*

villainous, *adj.* bellaco, vil, ruin; villano; —**ly,** *adv.* vilmente.

villainy, *n.* villanía, vileza, *f.*

vim, *n.* energía, *f.,* vigor, *m.*

vindicate, *vt.* vindicar, defender.

vindication, *n.* vindicación, *f.;* justificación,

vindictive, *adj.* vengativo; —**ly,** *adv.* por venganza.

vine, *n.* vid, *f.*

vinegar, *n.* vinagre, *m.*

vineyard, *n.* viña, *f.,* viñedo, *m.*

vinyl, *n.* vinilo, *m.;* —, *adj.* vinílico.

vintage, *n.* vendimia *f.*

viol, *n.* (mus.) violón, *m.*

viola, *n.* (mus.) viola, *f.*

violate, *vt.* violar.

violation, *n.* violación, *f.*

violator, *n.* violador, ra.

violence, *n.* violencia, *f.*

violent, *adj.* violento.

violet, *n.* (bot.) violeta, viola, *f.;* violeta (color), *m.*

violet ray, *n.* rayo violeta.

violin, *n.* (mus.) violín, *m.*

violinist, *n.* violinista, *m.* y *f.*

violoncello, *n.* (mus.) violoncelo, violonchelo, *m.*

viper, *n.* víbora, *f.*

virgin, *n.* virgen, *f.;* —, *adj.* virginal; virgen.

virginal, *adj.* virginal.

virginity, *n.* virginidad, *f.*

virile, *adj.* viril.

virility, *n.* virilidad, *f.*

virology, n. virología, f.

virtual, adj. virtual; **—ly,** adv. virtualmente.

virtue, n. virtud, f.

virtuous, adj. virtuoso.

virtuosity, n. virtuosidad, f., disposición extraordinaria para las bellas artes.

virulence, n. virulencia, f.

virulent, adj. virulento.

virus, n. (med.) virus, m.; — **pneumonia,** pulmonía a virus.

visa, n. visa, f., permiso para entrar en un país; visto bueno; —, vt. visar (un pasaporte) .

visage, n. rostro m., cara, f.

viscera, n. pl. vísceras, entrañas, f. pl.

viscose, n. viscosa, f ; —, adj. viscoso.

viscosity, n. viscosidad, f.

viscount, n. vizconde, m.

viscous, adj. viscoso, glutinoso.

vise, f.; tornillo, torno, m.

visé, vt. visar (un pasaporte).

visibility, n. visibilidad, f.

visible, adj. visible.

vision, n. visión, f., fantasma, m.; vista, f.

visionary, n. y adj. visionario, ria.

visit, vt. y vi. ver; visitar; —, n. visita, f.; **farewell —,** visita de despedida; **to pay a —,** hacer una visita.

visitation, n. visitación, f.; visita, f.

visiting card, n. tarjeta de visita.

visitor, n. visitante, m. y f., visitador, ra.

visor, vizor, n. visera, f.; máscara, f.

vista, n. vista, perspectiva, f.

visual, adj. visual.

visualize, vt. vislumbrar, percibir mentalmente percibir con clara visión.

vital, adj. vital; — **statistics,** estadística demográfica; **—ly,** adv. vitalmente; **—s,** n. pl. órganos vitales.

vitality, n. vitalidad, f.

vitamin, n. vitamina, f.

vitreous, adj. vítreo, de vidrio.

vitriol, n. vitriolo, m.

vituperate, vt. vituperar.

vivacious, adj. vivaz.

vivacity, n. vivacidad, f.

vivid, adj. vivo. vivaz; gráfico.

vividness, n. vivacidad, intensidad, f .

vivisection, n. vivisección, f.

vixen, n. zorra, raposa, f.; mujer regañona y de mal genio; mujer astuta, arpía, f.

viz.: namely, a saber, esto es.

vocabulary, n. vocabulario, m.

vocal, adj. vocal; — **cords,** cuerdas vocales.

vocalist, n. cantante, m. y f.

vocation, n. vocación, carrera, profesión, f.; oficio, m.

vocational, adj. práctico, profesional,

vocacional; — **school,** escuela de artes y oficios, escuela vocacional; — **training,** instrucción vocacional.

vocative, n. vocativo, m.

vociferate, vi. vociferar.

vociferous, adj. vocinglero, clamoroso.

vogue, n. moda, f.; boga, f.

voice, n. voz, f.; sufragio, m.

voiceless, adj. sin voz, mudo; que no tiene voz ni voto.

void, adj. vacío, desocupado; nulo; n. vacío, m.; —, vt. hacer nulo, anular; abandonar, salir; incapacitar; vaciar.

voile, n. espumilla (tela), f.

vol.: volume, vol. volumen.

volatile, adj. volátil; voluble.

volcanic, adj. volcánico.

volcano, n. volcán, m.

volition, n. voluntad, f.

volley, n. descarga de armas de fuego; salva, f.; andanada (de insultos, etc.), f.; (tenis) voleo, m.

volleyball, n. balonvolea, vólibol m.

volt, n. vuelta (entre jinetes), f.; elec.) voltio, m.

voltage, n. (elec.) voltaje, m.

voltaic, adj. voltaico.

voltameter, n. voltámetro, m.

voluble, adj. voluble; fluido, corriente; gárrulo.

volume, n. volumen, m.; libro, tomo, m.

voluminous, adj. voluminoso; muy grande.

voluntarily, adv. voluntariamente.

voluntary, adj. voluntario; —, n. (mus.) improvisación, f.; preludio, m.

volunteer, n. (mil.) voluntario, ria; —, vi. servir como voluntario; ofrecerse para alguna cosa.

voluptuous, adj. voluptuoso.

vomit, vt. y vi. vomitar; —, n. vómito, m.; vomitivo, m.

voracious, adj. voraz.

vortex, n. vórtice, remolino, torbellino, m., vorágine, f.

votary, n. persona consagrada a algún ideal, a algún estudio, religión, etc.

vote, n. voto, sufragio, m.; —, vt. votar.

voter, n. votante, m. y f.

votive, adj. votivo; — **offering,** exvoto, m.

vouch, vt. atestiguar, certificar, afirmar.

voucher, n. testigo, m.; documento justificativo; comprobante, recibo, m.

vouchsafe, vt. conceder, adjudicar; —, vi. dignarse, condescender.

vow, n. voto, m.; —, vt. y vi. dedicar, consagrar; hacer votos.

vowel, n. vocal, f.

voyage, n. viaje por mar; travesía, f.; —, vi. hacer viaje por mar.

voyager, *n.* navegador, ra, viajero, ra, navegante, *m.* y *f.*

V.P.: Vice President, V.P., vicepresidente.

vs.: verse, verso, versículo; **versus,** contra.

v.t.: transitive verb, v.tr. verbo transitivo.

vulcanite, *n.* ebonita, vulcanita, *f.*

vulcanize, *vt.* vulcanizar; **—ed rubber,** caucho vulcanizado.

vulgar, *adj.* vulgar, cursi.

vulgarity, *n.* vulgaridad, *f.;* bajeza, *f.*

vulgarize, *vt.* vulgarizar.

vulnerable, *adj.* vulnerable.

vulture, *n.* buitre, *m.*

vying, *adj.* competidor, emulador.

W

w.: week, semana; **west,** O. oeste; **width,** ancho; **wife,** esposa.

wad, *n.* atado de paja, heno, etc., *m.;* borra, *f.;* taco, *m.;* (coll.) rollo de papel moneda; riqueza en general; —, *vt.* acolchar, rellenar; atacar (una arma de fuego).

wadding, *n.* entretela, *f.;* taco, *m.;* recolchado, *m.*

waddle, *vi.* anadear.

wade, *vt.* vadear.

wafer, *n.* hostia, *f.;* oblea, *f.;* sello (en farmacias), *m.;* galletita, *f.*

waffle, *n.* barquillo, *m.;* hojuela, *f.*

waft, *vt.* llevar por el aire o por encima del agua; —, *vi.* flotar; —, *n.* banderín, gallardete, *m.*

wag, *vt.* mover ligeramente; **to — the tail,** menear la cola; —, *n.* meneo, *m.;* bromista, *m.* y *f.*

wage, *vt.* apostar, emprender; **to — war,** hacer guerra; **—s,** *n. pl.* sueldo, salario, *m.,* paga, *f.;* **monthly —s,** mesada, *f.;* **— earner,** jornalero, *m.;* asalariado, da.

wager, *n.* apuesta, *f.;* —, *vt.* apostar.

waggish, *adj.* chocarrero.

waggle, *vi.* anadear, menearse.

wagon, *n.* carro, *m.;* carreta, *f.*

wagonload, *n.* carretada, *f.*

waif, *n.* niño sin hogar, granuja, *m.;* algo *n.* acción de esperar; demora, *f.*

wail, *n.* lamento, gemido, *m.;* —, *vi.* lamentarse.

waist, *n.* cintura, *f.;* chaqueta, *f.*

waistcoat, *n.* chaleco, *m.*

waistline, *n.* cintura, *f.*

wait, *vi.* esperar, aguardar; quedarse; —, *n.* acción de esperar; demora, *f;* **— list,** lista de espera, *f.*

waiter, *n.* sirviente, mozo, servidor, mesero, camarero, criado, *m.*

waiting, *n.* espera, *f.;* **— room,** sala de espera.

waitress, *n.* camarera, criada, mesera, *f.*

waive, *vt.* abandonar, renunciar (a un derecho, privilegio, etc.); posponer.

waiver, *n.* renuncia (a un derecho o privilegio, etc.), *f.*

wake, *vi.* velar; despertarse; —, *vt.* despertar; —, *n.* vela, *f.;* vigilia, *f.;* velorio, *m.;* (naut.) estela, *f.*

wakeful, *adj.* vigilante; despierto.

waken, *vt.* y *vi.* despertar, despertarse.

waking, *n.* vela, *f.;* acto de despertar.

walk, *vt.* y *vi.* pasear, andar, caminar, ir a pie; —, *n.* paseo, *m.,* caminata, *f.;* esfera de acción; **to take a —,** dar un paseo, ir a caminar.

walker, *n.* paseador, ra; andador, ra; andaniño, *m.*

walkie-talkie, *n.* radioteléfono emisor-receptor portátil.

walking, *n.* acción de pasear; paseo, *m.;* **to go —,** dar un paseo, ir de paseo.

wall, *n.* pared, muralla, *f.,* muro, *m.;* —, *vt.* cercar con muros.

wallet, *n.* mochila, *f.;* cartera de bolsillo.

wallflower, *n.* (bot.) alhelí doble; (coll.) persona que se queda sin bailar en las fiestas; **to be a —,** quedarse sin bailar en una fiesta, (coll.) comer pavo.

wallop, *vt.* azotar, tundir; —, *n.* golpe, *m.*

wallow, *vi.* encenagarse.

wallpaper, *n.* papel de entapizar.

walnut, *n.* nogal, *m.;* nuez, *f.*

walrus, *n.* (zool.) morsa, *f.*

wall-to-wall, *adj.* de pared a pared (aplícase a una alfombra).

waltz, *n.* vals, *m.*

wan, *adj.* pálido.

wand, *n.* vara, varita, *f.;* varita mágica; batuta, *f.*

wander, *vi.* vagar, rodar; desviarse, extraviarse.

wanderer, *n.* vagamundo, *m.;* peregrino, *m.*

wane, *vi.* disminuir; decaer; menguar; —, *n.* decadencia, *f.;* **— (of the moon)** menguante (de la luna).

wangle, *vt.* engatusar, obtener algo bajo

pretexto o con dificultad.

want, *vt.* y *vi.* desear, querer, anhelar; faltar; —, *vi.* estar necesitado; sufrir la falta de algo; —, *n.* falta, carencia, *f.;* indifencia, *f.;* deseo, *m.;* necesidad, *f.*

want ad, *n.* anuncio de ocasión, anuncio clasificado en un periódico.

wanting, *adj.* falto, defectuoso, necesitado; menos.

wanton, *adj.* lascivo, licencioso; desenfrenado; —, *n.* persona lasciva; —, *vi.* hacerse lascivo o licencioso.

war, *n.* guerra, *f.;* —, *vi.* guerrear; —, *adj.* relativo a la guerra.

warble, *vi.* trinar; gorjear; —, *n.* trino, gorjeo, *m.*

warbler, *n.* cantante, *m.* y *f.;* persona o pájaro que trina o que gorjea; (orn.) cerrojillo, herreruelo, *m.*

ward, *vt.* repeler; **to — off,** evitar, desviar; —, *n.* guardia, defensa, *f.;* crujía de hospital; pupilo, *m.*

warden, *n.* custodio, guardián, *m.;* alcaide de una cárcel; bedel, *m.;* comandante, *m.*

wardrobe, *n.* guardarropa, *f.,* ropero, *m.;* ropa, *f.,* vestuario, *m.*

wardroom, *n.* (naut.) cuartel de la oficialidad.

ware, *n.* mercadería, *f.;* loza, *f. ;* —**s,** *n. pl.* efectos, *m. pl.,* mercancías, *f. pl.*

warehouse, *n.* almacén, depósito *m.,* bodega, *f.;* **— man,** guardaalmacén, almacenero, *m.*

warfare, *n.* guerra, *f.,* conflicto armado.

warhead, *n.* punta de combate.

warily, *adv.* prudentemente, con cautela.

warlike, *adj.* guerrero, belicoso, marcial.

warm, *adj.* cálido; caliente; abrigador; cordial, caluroso; **to be —,** hacer calor; tener calor; —, *vt.* calentar; —**ly,** *adv.* calurosamente.

warm-blooded, *adj.* de sangre ardiente; vehemente, entusiasta, fervoroso, apasionado.

warmhearted, *adj.* afectuoso, generoso, benévolo, de buenos sentimientos.

warmonger, *n.* propagador de guerra.

warmth, *n.* calor, *m.;* ardor, fervor, *m.*

warn, *vt.* avisar; advertir; prevenir.

warning, *n.* amonestación, *f.;* advertencia, *f.,* aviso, *m.*

warp, *n.* urdimbre, *f.;* comba, *f.;* —, *vi.* torcerse, alabearse, combarse; —, *vt.* torcer; pervertir.

warrant, *vt.* autorizar; privilegiar; garantir, garantizar, asegurar; —, *n.* testimonio, *m.;* justificación, *f.;* decreto de prisión; autorización, *f.*

warranty, *n.* garantía, seguridad, *f.*

warren, *n.* conejera, *f.,* conejar, *m.*

warrior, *n.* guerrero, soldado, batallador, *m.*

warship, *n.* barco de guerra.

wart, *n.* verruga, *f.*

wartime, *n.* época de guerra.

wary, *adj.* cauto, prudente.

was, 1ª y 3ª persona del singular del pretérito del verbo **be.**

wash, *vt.* lavar; bañar; —, *vi.* lavarse; —, *n.* lavadura, *f.;* loción, ablución, *f.;* lavado, *m.;* variedad de pintura para acuarela; **— bowl, — basin,** lavabo, *m.*

washable, *adj.* lavable.

wash-and-wear, *adj.* de lavar y ponerse, que no necesita plancharse.

washday, *n.* día de lavar.

washer, *n.* máquina de lavar ropa; lavadora, *f.;* (mech.) arandela, *f.*

washerwoman o **washwoman,** *n.* lavandera, *f.*

wash goods, *n. pl.* telas lavables.

washing, *n.* lavadura, *f.;* lavado, *m.;* ropa para lavar; **— machine,** máquina de lavar, lavadora, *f.*

washout, *n.* deslave, *m.;* socavación, *f.;* (coll.) fracasado, da.

washstand, *n.* lavabo, aguamanil, *m.*

wasp, *n.* avispa, *f.*

waste, *vt.* consumir, gastar; malgastar, disipar; destruir, arruinar, asolar; —, *vi.* gastarse; **to — away,** demacrarse; —, *n.* desperdicio, *m.;* estopa, *f.;* destrucción, *f.;* despilfarro, *m.;* merma, *f.;* desgaste, *m.;* limpiaduras, *f. pl.;* **— pipe,** tubería de desagüe; desaguadero, *m.*

wastebasket, *n.* cesto o cesta para papeles.

wasteful, *adj.* destructivo, pródigo, despilfarrador.

wastefulness, *n.* prodigalidad, *f.,* despilfarro, *m.*

wastepaper, *n.* papel de desecho.

waster, *n.* disipador, ra, gastador, ra.

watch, *n.* desvelo, *m.;* vigilia, vela, *f.;* vigía, *f.;* centinela, *f.;* reloj de bolsillo; **wrist —,** reloj de pulsera; **stop —,** cronógrafo, *m.;* **night —,** vela, *f.;* **— shop,** relojería, *f.;* **to be on the —,** estar alerta; —, *vt.* y *vi.* observar; velar, guardar, custodiar; espiar.

watchdog, *n.* perro guardián.

watchful, *adj.* vigilante; cuidadoso; observador.

watching, *n.* vigía, *f.;* observación, *f.*

watchmaker, *n.* relojero, *m.*

watchman, *n.* sereno, velador, *m.*

watchtower, *n.* atalaya, garita, vigía, *f.*

watchword, *n.* (mil.) santo y seña, contraseña, f.

water, n. agua, f.; **fresh** —, agua dulce; **hard** —, agua cruda; **high** —, mar llena; **lime** —, agua de cal; **low** —, baja mar; **mineral** —, agua mineral; **running** —, agua corriente; **salt** —, agua salada; **soda** —, agua de soda; **toilet** —, agua de tocador; — **cask,** bota, cuba, f.; — **closet,** común, inodoro, excusado, retrete, m., letrina, f.; — **color,** acuarela, f.; — **cress,** berro, m.; — **faucet,** grifo, grifón, caño de agua, m.; — **front,** barrio ribereño; ribera, f.; — **glass,** vidrio soluble, silicato de sosa; clepsidra, f.; reloj de agua; — **heater,** calentador de agua; — **lily,** nenúfar, m., lirio acuático; — **main,** cañería maestra de agua; — **meter,** medidor del agua; — **moccasin,** mocasín, f., culebra venenosa de agua; — **polo,** polo acuático; — **power,** fuerza hidráulica; — **tower,** torre para servicio de agua; — **wing,** nadadera, f.; —, vt. regar; abrevar; —, vi. llorar; hacer aguada.

water-cooled, adj. enfriado por agua.

watercourse, n. corriente de agua; lecho de un río; conducto natural de agua; canal para conducir agua.

water cress, n. (bot.) berro, m.

waterfall, n. cascada, catarata, f., salto de agua; caída de agua.

watering, n. riego, m.; —, adj. que riega; — **pot,** regadera, f.

watermark, n. filigrana o marca en el papel que indica su procedencia; señal de agua.

watermelon, n. sandía, f.

waterproof, adj. impermeable, a prueba de agua.

watershed, n. vertiente de las aguas; cuenca, f.

water ski, n. esquí acuático.

waterspout, n. manga, f., bomba marina.

waterway, n. cañería, f.; corriente de agua; vía fluvial.

waterworks, n. establecimiento para la distribución de las aguas.

watt, n. vatio, m.

wave, n. ola, onda, f.; **short** —, onda corta; **sound** —, onda sonora; — **length,** longitud de onda; —, vi. fluctuar; ondear; flamear; **to** — **(to some one),** saludar (a alguien) agitando la mano.

wavering, n. titubeo, m.

waving, n. ondulación, f.

wavy, adj. ondeado, ondulado.

wax, n. cera, f.; — **candle,** vela de cera; — **paper, —ed paper,** papel encerado; — **match,** cerilla, f., (Mex.) cerillo, m.; fósforo, m.; — **taper,** cerilla, f.; —, vt. ence-

rar; —, vi. aumentarse, crecer.

waxen, adj. de cera.

waxwork, n. figura de cera.

waxy, adj. ceroso.

way, n. camino, m., senda, ruta, f.; modo, m., forma, f.; medio, m.; **by the** —, a propósito; **in no** —, de ningún modo, de ninguna manera; **on the** —, al paso, en el camino; **this** —, por aquí; así; **to force one's** —, abrirse el paso; **to give** —, ceder; **right of** —, derecho de vía; **—s and means,** orientación y fines; — **station,** (rail.) estación intermediaria; **to lose one's** —, perderse, extraviarse.

wayfarer, n. pasajero, ra, transeúnte, m. y f.

waylay, vt. insidiar, poner asechanzas.

wayside, n. orilla o borde del camino o sendero; **by the** —, a lo largo del camino o sendero.

wayward, adj. caprichoso; desobediente; delincuente.

we, pron. nosotros, nosotras.

weak, adj. débil, delicado físicamente; flojo; decaído; deleznable.

weaken, vt. debilitar; —, vi. aflojarse; ceder; debilitarse.

weakling, n. persona débil ya sea física o mentalmente; cobarde, m. y f.; (coll.) alfeñique, m.

weak-minded, adj. de poca mentalidad, sin carácter.

weakness, n. debilidad, f.

wealth, n. riqueza, f.; bienes, m. pl.; bonanza, f.

wealthy, adj. rico, opulento, adinerado; — **class,** clase acomodada, clase adinerada.

wean, vt. destetar.

weapon, n. arma, f.; **—s of war,** pertrechos de guerra.

wear, vt. gastar, consumir; usar, llevar, llevar puesto, traer; —, vi. consumirse, gastarse; — **and tear,** desgaste producido por el uso; **to** — **out a person,** fastidiar, aburrir o cansar a una persona; **to** — **well,** durar (una tela, etc.); —, n. uso, m.

weariness, n. cansancio, rendimiento, m., fatiga, f.

wearing apparel, n. ropa, f., ropaje, m., vestidos, m. pl.

wearisome, adj. cansado, tedioso; laborioso.

weary, vt. cansar, fatigar; molestar; —, adj. cansado, fatigado, fatigoso.

weasel, n. comadreja, f.

weather, n. tiempo, m., temperatura, f.; **bad** —, intemperie, f., mal tiempo; **the —is good,** hace buen tiempo; — **strip,** burlete, m.; —, vt. sufrir, aguantar (un temporal, adversidad, etc.).

weathercock, n. giralda, veleta, f.

weatherman, n. meteorologista, m.

weather report, n. boletín meteorológico.

weather-strip, vt. proteger con burlete.

weave, vt. tejer; trenzar; —, n. tejido, m.

weaver, n. tejedor, ra.

web, n. tela, f.; tejido, m.; red, f.; —, vt. unir en forma de red; enmarañar, enredar.

web site, n. sitio web, m.

wed, vt. y vi. casar, casarse.

wedded, adj. casado, desposado.

wedding, n. boda, f., casamiento, matrimonio, m., nupcias, f. pl.; **silver —,** bodas de plata; **golden —,** bodas de oro; **— cake,** torta o pastel de boda.

wedge, n. cuña, f.; —, vt. acuñar; apretar.

wedlock, n. matrimonio, m.

Wednesday, n. miércoles, m.

wee, adj. pequeñito.

weed, n. mala hierba; (coll.) cigarro, tabaco, m.; **—s,** pl. vestido de luto; —, vt. escardar.

week, n. semana, f.; **— end,** fin de semana.

weekday, n. día de trabajo; cualquier día de la semana que no sea domingo.

week-end, adj. de fin de semana.

weekly, adj. semanal, semanario; **— publication,** semanario, m.; —, adv. semanalmente, por semana.

weep, vi. llorar, lamentarse.

weeping, adj. llorón, plañidero; **— willow,** sauce llorón.

weigh, vt. y vi. pesar; examinar, considerar.

weight, n. peso, m.; pesadez, f.; **gross —,** peso bruto; **net —,** peso neto.

weightlessness, n. ausencia de gravedad, ingravidez, f.

weighty, adj. ponderoso; importante.

weird, adj. extraño, fantástico, sobrenatural, misterioso; que tiene que ver con el destino.

welcome, adj. recibido con agrado; **—!** ¡bienvenido!, n. bienvenida, f.; —, vt. dar la bienvenida.

weld, vt. soldar.

welding, n. soldadura autógena.

welfare, n. prosperidad, f.; bienestar, bien, m.; **— society,** sociedad benéfica, sociedad de beneficencia; **— state,** estado protector; **— work,** trabajo social, obra de beneficencia.

well, n. fuente, f.; manantial, m.; pozo, m., cisterna, f.; cacimba, casimba, f.; —, adj. bueno, sano; **to be —,** estar bien; —, adv. bien, felizmente; favorablemente; suficientemente; **as — as,** así como,

lo mismo que, también como; **— then,** conque; **very —!** ¡está bien! **—!** interj. ¡vaya!

well-behaved, adj. bien criado, cortés, bien portado.

well-being, n. felicidad, prosperidad, f.

wellborn, adj. bien nacido.

well-bred, adj. bien criado, bien educado.

well-defined, adj. bien delineado, bien definido.

well-disposed, adj. favorable, bien dispuesto.

well-done, adj. bien cocido.

well-groomed, adj. vestido elegantemente.

well-known, adj. notorio, bien conocido.

well-meaning, adj. de buenas intenciones.

well-nigh, adv. muy cerca, casi.

well-off, adj. acomodado, rico.

well-timed, adj. oportuno, hecho a propósito.

well-to-do, adj. acomodado, próspero, rico.

well-wisher, n. amigo, ga, partidario, ria.

welt, n. ribete, m.; roncha, f.; —, vt. ribetear; (coll.) golpear hasta causar ronchas.

welter, vi. revolcarse en el lodo; estar en un torbellino.

welterweight, n. peso medio ligero.

wen, n. lobanillo, m., lupia, f.

wench, n. mozuela, f.; sirvienta, f.

wend, vt. encaminar, dirigir; —, vi. ir, atravesar, pasar, encaminarse.

went, pretérito del verbo **go.**

were, 2ª persona del singular y todo el plural del pretérito del verbo **be.**

west, n. poniente, occidente, oeste, m.; —, adj. occidental.

westerly, western, adj. occidental.

westerly, westerly wind, n. viento del oeste, poniente.

West Indies, Antillas, f. pl.

westward, adv. hacia el poniente u occidente.

wet, adj. húmedo, mojado; **— blanket,** aguafiestas, m. o f.; **to get —,** mojarse, empaparse; **— nurse,** nodriza, nutriz, f.; —, n. humedad, f.; —, vt. mojar, humedecer.

wet-nurse, vt. servir de nodriza, amamantar a un hijo ajeno.

whack, vt. aporrear; —, n. golpe, m.; intento, m., prueba, f.; porción, participación, f.; **to take a — at it,** intentarlo, hacer la prueba para lograrlo.

whale, n. ballena, f.

whaling, n. pesca de ballenas; (coll.) tunda, zurra, f.

wharf, n. muelle, m.

wharves, n. pl. de **wharf.**

what, pron. qué; cuál; lo que; **— is the**

matter? ¿qué pasa?

whatever, whatsoever, pron. cualquier cosa que, lo que; — adj. cualquier.

wheat, n. trigo, m.; **winter** —, trigo mocho; — **field,** trigal, m.

wheedle, vt. sonsacar; engatusar; conseguir con lisonjas.

wheel, n. rueda, f.; — **chair,** silla de ruedas; — **base,** distancia entre ejes; — **and axle,** cabria, f.; **driving** —, rueda motriz; **gambling** —, rueda de la fortuna; **gear** —, rueda dentada; **paddle** —, rueda de paletas; **small** —, rodaja, f.; **water** —, rodezno, m.; — **rope,** (naut.) guardín, m.; — **track,** carril, m.; **steering** —, volante, m.; —, vt. rodar, hacer rodar, girar; —, vi. girar, dar vueltas.

wheelbarrow, n. carretilla, f., carretón de una rueda.

wheeling, n. rodaje, m.; **free** —, rueda libre.

wheeze, vi. resollar con sonido fuerte.

whelm, vt. y vi. dominar; cubrir; oprimir.

whelp, n. cachorro, cachorro de lobo; chiquillo (úsase en forma despectiva), m.; —, vi. parir (la perra, etc.).

when, adv. cuándo; —, conj. cuando, mientras que.

whence, adv. de donde; de quien.

whenever, conj. cuando quiera que, siempre que; — **you wish,** cuando quiera.

where, adv. dónde; en dónde; —, conj. donde; en donde.

whereabouts, n. paradero, m.; —, adv. por dónde, hacia dónde.

whereas, conj. por cuanto, mientras que; considerando que.

whereat, conj. a lo cual; por lo cual.

whereby, conj. con lo cual, por donde, por lo cual.

wherefore, conj. por lo que, por cuyo motivo.

wherein, conj. en donde, en lo cual, en que.

whereof, conj. de lo cual, de que.

whereon, conj. sobre lo cual.

whereupon, conj. sobre que; en consecuencia de lo cual.

wherever, conj. dondequiera que.

wherewith, conj. con que, con lo cual; por medio de lo cual.

wherewithal, n. medios, m. pl.; dinero necesario.

whet, vt. afilar, amolar; excitar; **to** — **the appetite,** incitar al apetito.

whether, conj. si; ora.

whetstone, n. aguzadera, piedra de afilar.

whey, n. suero, m.

which, pron. que, el cual, la cual, el que, la que; cuál; —, adj. cuál de los, qué.

whichever, whichsoever, adj. cualquier; —, pron. cualquiera que.

whiff, n. vaharada, f.; bocanada de humo, fumada, f.

while, n. rato, m.; vez, f.; momento, m.; **to be worth** —, valer la pena; —, conj. mientras, a la vez que; a medida que; en tanto.

whim, n. antojo, capricho, m.

whhnper, vi. sollozar, gemir; —, n. sollozo, gemido, m.

whimsical, adj. caprichoso, fantástico.

whimsy, n. fantasia, f., capricho, m.

whine, vi. lloriquear, lamentarse; —, n. quejido, lamento, m.

whining, n. (coll.) gimoteo, lloriqueo, m.

whinny, vi. relinchar los caballos.

whip, n. azote, látigo, m.; — **hand,** mano que sostiene el látigo; ventaja, f.; —, vt. azotar; —, vi. andar de prisa.

whipped cream, n. crema batida.

whipping, n. flagelación, paliza, f.

whippoorwill, n. (orn.) chotacabras, f. whir, n. zumbido, m.

whirl, vt. y vi. girar; hacer girar; moverse rápidamente; —, n. giro muy rápido; vuelta, f.

whirlpool, n. vórtice, remolino, m., vorágine, olla, f.

whirlwind, n. torbellino, remolino, m.

whisk, n. movimiento rápido como de una escobilla; escobilla, f., cepillo, m.; —, vi. moverse ligera y rápidamente; —, vt. batir (huevos, etc.).

whisk broom, n. escobilla, f., cepillo, m.

whisker, n. patilla, f., mostacho, m.; —s, pl. barba, f.

whiskey, whisky, n. whiskey, m., bebida alcohólica hecha de maíz.

whisper, vi. cuchichear, susurrar, hablar al oído; —, n. cuchicheo, susurro, m.

whistle, vt. y vi. silbar; chiflar; —, n. silbido, m.; pito, m.

whit, n. pizca, f.; **not to care a** —, no importarle un ápice.

white, adj. blanco, pálido; cano, canoso; puro; **to become** —, blanquearse; — **clover,** trébol blanco, m.; — **feather,** pluma blanca, señal de cobardía; — **gold,** oro blanco, oro aleado con níquel y cinco platino; — **heat,** incandescencia, f.; rojo blanco; estado de intensa conmoción fisica o mental; — **lead,** cerusa, f., blanco de plomo; — **lie,** mentirilla, f.; — **matter,** (anat.) tejido nervioso blanco (especialmente cerebral y medular); — **oak,** roble blanco, m.; — **pine,** pino blanco; — **poplar,** álamo blanco; — **sauce,** salsa blanca; — **slave,** víctima de la trata de blancas; —, n. color blanco; clara de huevo.

white-collar, *adj.* de oficinista; — **worker,** oficinista, *m.* y *f.*

white-haired, *adj.* canoso, de cabello blanco.

white-hot, *adj.* incandescente.

whiten, *vt.* y *vi.* blanquear; blanquearse, emblanquecerse.

whiteness, *n.* blancura, *f.;* palidez, *f.*

whitewash, *n.* jalbegue, blanquete, enlucimiento, *m.;* —, *vt.* encalar; jalbegar; encubrir.

whither, *adv.* adónde, a qué lugar.

whitish, *adj.* blanquizco, blanquecino.

whittle, *vt.* cortar con navaja; tallar, tajar, afilar, mondar, sacar punta.

whiz, *vi.* zumbar, silbar; —, *n.* zumbido, *m.*

W.H.O.: World Health Organization, *n.* O.M.S., Organización Mundial de la Salud, *f.*

who, *pron.* quien, que; quién.

whodunit, *n.* (coll.) novela policiaca.

whoever, whosoever, *pron.* quienquiera que, cualquiera que; quien.

whole, *adj.* todo, total; sano, entero; —, *n.* todo, total, *m.;* conjunto, *m.;* — **note** (mus.) redonda, semibreve, *f.;* — **number,** número entero.

wholehearted, *adj.* sincero, cordial.

wholesale, *n.* venta al por mayor; — **house,** casa al por mayor.

wholesaler, *n.* mayorista, *m.,* comerciante que vende al por mayor.

wholesome, *adj.* sano, saludable; **—ly,** *adv.* en forma sana.

whole-wheat, *adj.* de trigo entero.

wholly, *adv.* enteramente, totalmente.

whom, *pron.* quien, el que; quién.

whoop, *n.* gritería, *f.;* —, *vi.* gritar, vocear.

whooping cough, *n.* tos ferina, *f.*

whopper, *n.* (coll.) algo muy grande; mentirota, *f.*

whore, *n.* puta, *f.*

whose, *pron.* cuyo, cuya, de quien; de quién.

why, *adv.* ¿por qué? — **not?** ¿pues y qué? ¿por qué no?

W.I.: West Indies, Las Antillas, *f. pl.*

wick, *n.* torcida, mecha, *f.,* pabilo, *m.*

wicked, *adj.* malvado, perverso.

wickedness, *n.* perversidad, maldad, *f.*

wicker, *n.* mimbre, *m.;* —, *adj.* de mimbre.

wide, *adj.* ancho, vasto, extenso; remoto; **far and** —, por todos lados; **—ly,** *adv.* ampliamente.

wide-awake, *adj.* despierto, alerta, vivo.

wide-eyed, *adj.* asombrado, con los ojos muy abiertos.

widen, *vt.* ensanchar, extender, ampliar.

widespread, *adj.* extenso, difuso, esparcido, diseminado.

widow, *n.* viuda, *f.;* —, *vt.* privar a una mujer de su marido.

widower, *n.* viudo, *m.*

widowhood, *n.* viudez, viudedad, *f.*

width, *n.* anchura, *f.*

wield, *vt.* manejar, empuñar; ejercer.

wienerwurst, *n.* variedad de salchicha.

wife, *n.* esposa, consorte, mujer, *f.*

wifely, *adj.* propio de una esposa; — **duties,** deberes de esposa.

wig, *n.* peluca, *f.*

wiggle, *n.* meneo rápido, culebreo, *m.;* —, *vt.* y *vi.* menear, menearse.

wigwag, *vi.* menear; comunicarse por señales o banderolas; —, *n.* comunicación por señales o banderolas.

wigwam, *n.* choza típica de los indios norteamericanos.

wild, *adj.* silvestre, feroz; desierto; salvaje; —, *n.* desierto, yermo, *m.;* — **boar,** jabalí, *m.;* — **oats,** indiscreciones de la juventud.

wildcat, *n.* gato montés; (com.) negocio quimérico; (fig.) fiera, *f.;* —, *adj. (com.)* corrompido, quimérico.

wilderness, *n.* desierto, *m.,* selva, *f.* wildfire, *n.* fuego griego; conflagración destructiva; **to spread like** —, esparcirse como relámpago.

wile, *n.* dolo, engaño, *m.;* astucia, *f.*

wilful, *adj.* voluntarioso, obstinado.

will, *n.* voluntad, *f.;* albedrío, *m.;* testamento, *m.;* **at** —, a gusto; **against one's** —, contra la voluntad de uno; —, *vt* . legar, dejar en testamento; —, *vi.* verbo auxiliar que indica futuro.

willing, *adj.* deseoso, listo, dispuesto a servir; **—ly,** *adv.* de buen grado, de buena gana.

willingness, *n.* buena voluntad, deseo de servir.

willow, *n.* (bot.) sauce, *m.*

willowy, *adj.* que abunda en sauces; como un sauce; alto y esbelto.

wily, *adj.* astuto, insidioso.

win, *vt.* y *vi.* ganar, obtener, conquistar; alcanzar, lograr; **to** — **the favor (of),** caer en gracia (de).

wince, *vi.* encogerse.

winch, *n.* cabria, *f.,* torno, cabrestante, malacate, montacargas, *m.*

wind, *n.* viento, *m.;* aliento, *m.;* pedo, *m.;* **to break** —, peerse; — **instrument,** instrumento de viento; — **tunnel,** (avi.) túnel aerodinámico.

wind, *vt.* enrollar; dar vuelta, dar cuerda (a un reloj, etc.); torcer; envolver; —, *vi.* caracolear, serpentear; insinuarse; arrollarse; **to** — **up,** ultimar (un asunto).

winded, adj. desalentado, sin fuerzas.

windfall, n. fruta caída del árbol (por el viento); ganancia inesperada; acontecimiento feliz e inesperado.

winding, n. vuelta, revuelta, f.; arrollamiento (de un alambre); cuerda (de un reloj, etc.); —, adj. tortuoso, sinuoso; — **road,** camino sinuoso; — **sheet,** mortaja, f., sudario, m.; — **stair,** escalera de caracol; — **tackle,** (naut.) aparejo de estrelleras.

windlass, n. árgano, torno, m., grúa, f.; malacate, m.

windmill, n. molino de viento.

window, n. ventana, f.; — **frame,** marco de la ventana; **small** —, ventanilla, f.; — **blind,** celosía, f., persiana de ventana; — **shade,** visillo, m.; — **shutter,** puerta-ventana, contraventana, f.; —**sill,** repisa de ventana.

windowpane, n. vidrio de ventana.

windpipe, n. (anat.) tráquea, f.

windshield, n. guardabrisa, parabrisas, m.

windshield wiper, n. limpiaparabrisas, m.

windward, n. (naut.) barlovento, m.; **to ply to the** —, (naut.) bordear; —, adv. (naut.) a barlovento.

windy, adj. ventoso; **it is** —, hace viento.

wine, n. vino, m.; **red** —, vino tinto; — **cellar,** bodega, f.; — **merchant,** vinatero, m.

wing, n. ala, f.; lado, costado, m.; —**s,** pl. (theat.) bastidores, m. pl.; — **case,** élitro (de un insecto), m.; — **chair,** sillón con respaldo en forma de alas; —**spread,** extensión del ala de un aeroplano de un pájaro, etc; —, vt. herir superficialmente; —, vi. volar.

wink, vt. y vi. guiñar, pestañear; —, n. pestañeo, guiño, m.

winner, n. ganador, ra, vencedor, ra.

winning, n. ganancia, f.; lucro, m.; —, adj. atractivo, encantador; ganador.

winnow, vt. aventar, cerner (el grano).

winsome, adj. alegre, jovial; simpático.

winter, n. invierno, m.; — **wheat,** trigo mocho; —, adj. invernal; —, vi. invernar, pasar el invierno.

winterize, vt. preparar o acondicionar para el invierno.

wintry, adj. invernal.

wipe, vt. secar, limpiar; borrar; **to** — **out,** obliterar; arruinar financieramente.

wire, n. alambre, m.; **barbed** —, alambre de púas; **conducting** —, alambre conductor; **live** —, alambre cargado de electricidad; persona muy activa; **screen** —, alambre para rejas; **sheathed** —, alambre envuelto o forrado; — **fence,** — **fencing,** alambrado, m., cerca o cercado de

alambre; — **gauge,** calibrador de alambre; — **photo,** telefoto, f.; — **screen,** tela metálica; — **tapping,** conexión telefónica o telegráfica para interceptar mensajes; —, vt. alambrar; —, vi. (coll.) telegrafiar, cablegrafiar.

wireless, n. telegrafía sin hilos, telegrafía inalámbrica, radiotelefonía, f.; — **station,** radioemisora, estación radioemisora; — **transmission,** radioemisión.

wiring, n. instalación de alambres eléctricos.

wiry, adj. hecho de alambre; parecido al alambre; flaco pero a la vez fuerte.

wisdom, n. sabiduría, prudencia, f.; juicio, m.

wisdom tooth, n. muela del juicio, muela cordal.

wise, adj. sabio, docto, juicioso, prudente, sensato; —, n. modo, m., manera, f.; — **ly,** adv. sabiamente, con prudencia.

wisecrack, n. chiste o dicho agudo y gracioso; —, vi. decir cosas con agudeza y en forma chistosa.

wish, vt. desear, anhelar, ansiar, querer; **to** — **a happy Christmas, to** — **a happy** Easter, desear felices Pascuas; —, n. anhelo, deseo, m.

wishbone, n. espoleta, f.

wishful, adj. deseoso; ávido; — **thinking,** ilusiones, f. pl., buenos deseos.

wishy-washy, adj. débil, insípido.

wisp, n. manojo de paja, de heno, etc.; fragmento, m., pizca, f.

wisteria, n. (bot.) glicina, f.

wistful, adj. pensativo, melancólico, anheloso y sin esperanza de satisfacer sus deseos.

wit, n. ingenio, m., agudeza, sal, f.; **to** —, a saber.

witch, n. bruja, hechicera, f.; — **hazel,** carpe, m., loción de carpe.

witchcraft, n. brujería, f.; sortilegio, m.

witchery, n. hechicería, f.; encanto, m.; influencia fascinadora.

with, prep. con; por; de; a.

withdraw, vt. quitar; privar; retirar; —, vi. retirarse, apartarse, sustraerse.

withdrawal, n. retiro, m., retirada, f.; **bank** —, retiro de depósitos del banco.

wither, vi. marchitarse, secarse; —, vt. marchitar.

withhold, vt. detener, impedir, retener.

within, prep. dentro de; al alcance de; — **bounds,** a raya; —, adv. adentro.

without, prep. sin; fuera de; más allá de; —, adv. afuera.

withstand, vt. oponer, resistir.

withy, n. mimbre, m.; —, adj. flexible y tosco; flaco y ágil.

witness, *n.* testimonio, *m.;* testigo, *m.;* **eye —,** testigo ocular; **—,** *vt.* atestiguar; presenciar; **—,** *vi.* servir de testigo.

witty, *adj.* ingenioso, agudo, chistoso.

wives, *n. pl.* de **wife.**

wizard, *n.* brujo, hechicero, mago, *m.*

wk.: week, semana.

wobble, *vi.* bambolear; **—,** *n.* bamboleo, *m.*

wobbly, *adj.* instable, que se bambolea.

woe, *n.* dolor, *m.,* aflicción, *f.*

woebegone, *adj.* desolado, abatido.

woeful, *adj.* triste, funesto; **—ly,** *adv.* dolorosamente.

wolf, *n.* lobo, *m.;* **she- —,** loba, *f.;* **— pack,** manada de lobos.

wolfram, *n.* wolframio, tungsteno, *m.*

wolves, *n. pl.* de **wolf.**

woman, *n.* mujer, *f.*

womanhood, *n.* la mujer en general.

womankind, *n.* sexo femenino.

womanly, *adj.* mujeril, femenino.

womb, *n.* útero, *m.,* matriz, *f.*

women, *n. pl.* de **woman.**

wonder, *n.* milagro, *m.;* portento, *m.;* prodigio, *m.;* maravilla, *f.;* **—,** *vi.* maravillarse (de).

wonderful, *adj.* maravilloso, prodigioso; **—ly,** *adv.* maravillosamente.

wonderland, *n.* tierra maravillosa, país de las maravillas o de los prodigios.

wont, *n.* uso, *m.,* costumbre, *f.*

won't, contracción de **will not.**

woo, *vt.* cortejar, hacer el amor (a alguien).

wood, *n.* madera, *f.;* leña, *f.;* **— alcohol,** alcohol metílico; **— louse,** milpiés, *m.,* cochinilla, *f.;* **— pigeon,** paloma zorita; **— pulp,** pulpa de madera; **— thrush,** tordo americano; **— turning,** arte de trabajar la madera con el torno para sacar piezas de distintas formas; **—s,** *pl.* bosque, *m.*

woodbine, *n.* (bot.) madreselva, *f.*

woodchuck, *n.* (zool.) marmota, *f.*

woodcock, *n.* (orn.) chocha, becada, *f.*

woodcraft, *n.* destreza en trabajos de madera; conocimiento de la vida en el bosque.

woodcut, *n.* grabado en madera; estampa de un grabado en madera.

woodcutter, *n.* hachero, *m.;* leñador, *m.*

wooded, *adj.* arbolado.

wooden, *adj.* de madera.

woodland, *n.* bosque, *m.,* selva, *f.*

woodman, *n.* leñador, *m.;* guardabosque, *m.*

woodpecker, *n.* (orn.) picamaderos, picaposte, *m.,* pájaro carpintero.

woodpile, *n.* pila de leña.

woodshed, *n.* leñera, *f.,* sitio para guardar leña.

woodsman, *n.* leñador, *m.;* hachero, *m.;* maderero, *m.;* guardabosque, *m.*

woodwork, *n.* obra de madera, obra de carpintería, maderaje, m.; molduras, *f. pl.*

wool, *n.* lana, *f.;* **— merchant,** pañero, *m.*

woolen, *adj.* de lana, lanoso.

woolgathering, *n.* acto de soñar despierto o abstraerse; ensimismamiento, *m.*

woolly, *adj.* lanudo, lanoso.

word, *n.* palabra, voz, *f.;* **by — of mouth,** de palabra; **on my —,** a fe mía, bajo mi palabra; **to leave —,** dejar dicho; **—s (of a song)** letra (de una canción), *f.;* **in other —s,** en otros términos, en otras palabras; **—,** *vt.* expresar.

wordiness, *n.* verbosidad, *f.*

wording, *n.* dicción, *f.;* fraseología, *f.*

wordless, *adj.* sin habla, silencioso.

wordy, *adj.* verboso.

wore, *pretérito* del verbo **wear.**

work, *vi.* trabajar; laborar; funcionar; **—,** *vt.* trabajar, labrar; laborar; formar; **—,** *n.* trabajo, *m.,* obra, *f.;* gestión, *f.;* fatiga, *f.;* quehacer, *m.;* **metal —,** metalistería, *f.;* **— of art,** obra de arte.

workable, *adj.* laborable, explotable, factible; que se puede trabajar o hacer funcionar.

workaday, *adj.* laborioso, prosaico, ordinario.

workbag, *n.* saco de labor; bolsa de costura.

workbench, *n.* banco de taller.

worker, *n.* trabajador, ra, obrero, ra, operario, ria.

workhouse, *n.* casa de corrección.

working, *n.* funcionamiento, *m.;* trabajo, *m.;* explotación, *f.;* **— day,** día de trabajo.

workingman, *n.* obrero, *m.*

workman, *n.* labrador, *m.;* obrero, *m.;* artífice, *m.*

workmanship, *n.* manufactura, *f.;* destreza del artífice; trabajo, *m.*

workout, *n.* ensayo, ejercicio, *m.*

workroom, *n.* taller, *m.*

works *n. pl.* fábrica, *f.;* mecanismo, *m.*

workshop, *n.* taller, *m.*

world, *n.* mundo, *m.;* universo, *m.;* gente, *f.;* (fig.) mar, *f.*

wordly, *adj.* mundano, profano, terrenal.

world-wide, *adj.* mundial, del mundo entero.

worm, *n.* gusano, gorgojo, *m.;* **— gear,** (mech.) engranaje de tornillo sin fin, engranaje de rosca; **— of a screw,** rosca de tornillo; **—,** *vi.* moverse insidiosamente; —, vt. librar de gusanos; efectuar por medios insidiosos.

worm-eaten, adj. carcomido, apolillado.

wormwood, n. (bot.) ajenjo, m.

wormy, adj. agusanado.

worn, p.p. del verbo **wear.**

worn-out, adj. raído, gastado; cansado, rendido.

worry, n. cuidado, m.; preocupación, intranquilidad, f.; ansia, f., desasosiego, m.; —, vt. molestar, atormentar; —, vi. preocuparse; **to be worried,** estar con cuidado, estar preocupado.

worse, adj. y adv. peor; **to get —,** empeorarse; **so much the —,** tanto peor.

worship, n. culto, m.; adoración, f.; **your —,** vuestra merced; —, vt. adorar, venerar.

worst, adj. pésimo, malísimo; —, n. lo peor, lo más malo; —, vt. aventajar; derrotar.

worsted, n. variedad de estambre.

worth, n. valor, precio, m.; mérito, m., valía, f.; —, adj. meritorio, digno; **to be — while,** merecer o valer la pena; **to be —,** valer.

worthiness, n. dignidad, f.; mérito, m.

worthless, adj. indino, sin valor; **— effort,** esfuerzo inútil; **— person,** persona despreciable.

worth-while, adj. que vale la pena, digno de tenerse en cuenta.

worthy, adj. digno, benemérito; merecedor; —, n. varón ilustre.

would, pretérito de **will,** para expresar deseo, condición, acción.

would-be, adj. que aspira o desea ser; llamado, considerado; **— actress,** persona que pretende ser actriz.

wound, n. herida, llaga, f.; —, vt. herir.

wound, p.p. del verbo **wind.**

wove, pretérito del verbo **weave.**

woven, p.p. del verbo **weave.**

wrangle, vi. reñir, discutir; —, n. pelotera, riña, f.

wrangler, n. pendenciero, ra, disputador, ra.

wrap, vt. arrollar; envolver; **to — up,** abrigar, abrigarse; envolver.

wrapper, n. envolvedor ra; envoltura, f.; bata de casa; forro de un libro.

wrapping, n. envoltura, f.; cubierta, f., forro exterior.

wrath, n. ira, rabia, cólera, f.

wreak, vt. descargar (la cólera), etc.

wreath, n. corona, guirnalda, f.

wreathe, vt. y vi. torcer; enrollar; arrugarse; coronar.

wreck, n. naufragio, m.; destrucción, f.; choque, accidente, m.; naufragio, m.; —, vt. arruinar; destruir; —, vi. arruinarse.

wreckage, n. restos, despojos, m. pl., ruinas, f. pl.

wrecker, n. automóvil de auxilio.

wren, n. (orn.) reyezuelo, m.

wrench, vt. arrancar; dislocar; torcer; —, n. torcedura (del pie, etc.), f.; llave, f.; **monkey —,** llave inglesa.

wrest, vt. arrancar, quitar a fuerza.

wrestle, vi. luchar; (fig.) pelear; disputar; —, n. lucha, f.

wrestler, n. luchador, m.

wrestling, n. lucha, f.; **catch-as-catch-can —,** lucha libre; **Greco-Roman —,** lucha grecorromana.

wretch, n. pobre infeliz; infame, m.; **poor —!** ¡pobre diablo!

wretched, adj. infeliz, miserable; mezquino; mísero; deplorable, lamentable.

wriggle, vi. menearse, agitarse; culebrear.

wring, vt. torcer; arrancar; estrujar.

wringer, n. exprimidor de ropa.

wrinkle, n. arruga, f.; —, vt. arrugar.

wrinkleproof, adj. inarrugable.

wrist, n. muñeca (de la mano), f.; **— bandage,** pulsera, venda para la mano; **— watch,** reloj de pulsera.

wristband, n. puño de camisa.

writ, n. escrito, m.; escritura, f.; orden, f.

write, vt. escribir; componer; **— off,** cancelar; hacer un descuento por depreciación; **— up,** dar cuenta, completar; alabar en la prensa.

writer, n. escritor, ra, autor, ra; novelista, m. y f.; **prose —,** prosador, ra.

write-up, n. crónica de prensa.

writhe, vt. torcer; —, vi. contorcerse.

writing, n. escritura, f.; escrito, m.; manuscrito, m.; **in —,** por escrito; **to put in —,** poner por escrito; **— desk,** escritorio, bufete, pupitre, m.; **— paper,** papel de escribir.

written, p.p. del verbo **write.**

wrong, n. injuria, f.; injusticia, f.; error, m.; —, adj. malo, incorrecto, erróneo; injusto; **— side,** revés, m.; **to be —,** no tener razón; estar equivocado; —, vt. hacer un mal, injuriar; —, **—ly,** adv. mal, injustamente; al revés.

wrongdoer, n. pecador, ra, malvado, da.

wrongful, adj. injusto, inicuo.

wrote, pretérito del verbo **write.**

wrought, adj. labrado, hecho; **— iron,** hierro forjado.

wry, adj. torcido; tuerto; **— face,** mohín, m., mueca, f.

wt.: weight, P. peso.

W.T.O.: World Trade Organization, O.M.C., Organización Mundial del Comercio.

X

xerox, vt. fotocopiar.
Xmas: Christmas, Navidad, Pascua de Navidad.
X ray, n. rayo X; radiografía, f.

X-ray, adj. radiográfico; —**ing**, n. radiografía; —**specialist**, radiógrafo; —, vt. radiografiar.
xylophone, n. (mus.) xilófono, m., variedad de marimba.

Y

yacht, n. (naut.) yate, m.
yam, n. (bot.) batata, f., camote, m.
yank, vt. (coll.) sacudir, tirar de golpe; **Y—**, n. yanqui, m. y f.
Yankee, n. y adj. yanqui, m. y f.
yard, n. corral, m.; yarda (medida), f.; (naut.) verga, f.; patio, m.
yardmaster, n. (rail.) superintendente de patio.
yardstick, n. yarda o vara de medir.
yarn, n. estambre, m.; (coll.) cuento de aventuras por lo general exageradas o ficticias.
yawl, n. (naut.) canoa, f., sereni, m.
yawn, vi. bostezar; —, n. bostezo, m.
yd.: yard, yd. yarda.
ye, pron. (poet.) vos.
yea, adv. sí, verdaderamente; — **or nay**, sí o no.
year, n. año, m.; **all — round**, todo el año; **many —s ago**, hace muchos años.
yearbook, n. libro del año, anuario, m.
yearling, n. primal, m., animal de un año de edad.
yearly, adj. anual; —, adv. todos los años, anualmente.
yearn, vi. anhelar.
yearning, n. anhelo, m., deseo ferviente.
yeast, n. levadura, f.; giste, m.; — **cake**, pastilla de levadura.
yell, vi. aullar, gritar; —, n. grito, aullido, m.
yellow, adj. amarillo; —, n. color amarillo; — **fever**, fiebre amarilla.
yellowish, adj. amarillento.
yelp, vi. latir, ladrar; —, n. aullido, latido, m.
yen, n. yen (unidad monetaria del Japón), m.; (coll.) deseo intenso, anhelo, m.
yeoman, n. (naut.) contramaestre, pañolero, m.; alabardero, m.; guardaalmacén en la marina; hacendado, m.
yes, adv. sí.
yes-man, n. (coll.) persona servil, persona que siempre está de acuerdo con sus superiores ya sea con razón o sin ella.
yesterday, adv. ayer; **day before —**, anteayer.
yet, adv. todavía, aún; —, conj. sin embargo, con todo.
yield, vi. producir, rendir; ceder; sucumbir; darse por vencido; asentir; —, vt. producir, rendir; —, n. producto, rendimiento, m.; (mech.) rendimiento, m.
yielding, adj. condescendiente, que cede.
Y.M.C.A.: Young Men's Christian Association, Y.M.C.A., Asociación de Jóvenes Cristianos.
yodel, vt. cantar con modulación del tono natural al falsete; —, n. canto con modulación del tono natural al falsete.
yoke, n. yugo, m.; yunta, f.; férula, f.; —, vt. uncir; ligar; casar; sojuzgar.
yolk, n. yema (de huevo), f.
yon, yonder, adv. allí, allá; —, adj. de allí, de allá; aquel.
yore, n. tiempo antiguo, tiempo atrás; **in days of —**, en tiempo de Maricastaña.
you, pron. tú, usted; vosotros, vosotras, ustedes; te, le, lo, la; os, los, las; les; ti.
young, adj. joven, mozo; tierno; — **man**, joven, m.; — **woman**, joven, señorita, f.; — **people**, juventud, f.
youngster, n. jovencito, ta, chiquillo, lla, muchacho, cha, jovenzuelo, la.
your, adj. tu, su, vuestro, de usted, de vosotros, de ustedes.
yours, pron. el tuyo, el suyo, el vuestro.
yourself, pron. tú mismo, usted mismo; vosotros mismos; sí mismo; te, se.
yourselves, pron. pl. de **yourself**.
youth, n. juventud, mocedad, adolescencia, f.; joven, m.
youthful, adj. juvenil; —**ly**, adv. de un modo juvenil.
yr. yrs.: year, years, año, años.
yucca, n. (bot.) yuca, f.
Yule, n. Navidad, f.
Y.W.C.A.: Young Women's Christian Association, Y.W.C.A., Asociación de Jóvenes Cristianas.

Z

zany, *n.* y *adj.* tonto, ta, mentecato, ta, bufón, ona.

zeal, *n.* celo, ardor, ahínco, *m.*

zealous, *adj.* celoso, fervoroso; —**ly,** *adv.* fervorosamente.

zebra, *n.* zebra, cebra, *f.*

zenith, *n.* cenit, *m.*

zephyr, *n.* céfiro, favonio, *m.*

zero, *n.* cero, *m.;* — **hour,** (mil.) hora fijada para un ataque, etc.; hora del peligro, hora crítica.

zest, *n.* gusto, *m.*, sabor agudo; gozo, *m.*

zigzag, *n.* zigzag, *m.;* —, *vt.* y *vi.* hacer un zigzag, ir en forma de zigzag.

zinc, *n.* (chem.) cinc, zinc, *m.;* — **chloride,** cloruro de cinc; — **oxide,** óxido de cinc.

zinnia, *n.* (bot.) zinia, *f.*

zip gun, *n.* arma usada por pandilleros juveniles hecha de un trozo de tubo que lanza proyectiles con una tira de caucho.

zipper, *n.* cremallera, *f.;* cierre, *m.;* cierre relámpago.

zither, *n.* citara, *f.;* — **player,** citarista, *m.* y *f.*

zodiac, *n.* zodiaco, *m.*

zone, *n.* zona, *f.;* **danger** —, zona del peligro.

zoo, *n.* jardín zoológico.

zoological, *adj.* zoológico.

zoologist, *n.* zoólogo, *m.*

zoology, *n.* zoología, *f.*

zoom, *vi.* (avi.) levantar el vuelo repentinamente; subirse rápidamente o elevarse (como un aeroplano, etc.); zumbir.

zooming, *n.* subida vertical.

TRAVELER'S CONVERSATION GUIDE

GUÍA DE CONVERSACIÓN PARA EL VIAJERO

NOTE: In rapid speech, Spanish words often run together, causing a noticeable shift in the sound and position of letters at the junctures between words. Some examples from following pages: **no es mía** (no ez mē´â), **no tan aprisa** (no tâ nâ· prē´sâ), **con cuidado** (kong kwe·thâ´tho), **un poco** (ūm po´ko), **el agua de la llave** (e lâ´gwâ the lâ yâ´ve).

AT THE STATION (OR AIRPORT)	EN LA ESTACIÓN (O EL AEROPUERTO)	PRONUNCIATION
This is my passport.	Este es mi pasaporte.	(es´te ez mē pâ·sâ·por´te)
I need a porter.	Necesito un cargador (maletero).	(ne· se·sē´to ūng kâr·gâ·thor´ [mâ· le te´ro])
Where is my baggage?	¿Dónde está mi equipaje?	(don´de es·tâ´ mē e·kē·pâ´he)
Where is my porter?	¿Dónde está mi cargador?(maletero)?	(don´de es·tâ´ mē kâr·gâ·thor´ [mâ· le·te´ro])
Have you seen Porter No. 29?	¿Ha visto usted al cargador (maletero) No. 29?	(â vēs´to ūs·te´ thâl kâr· gâ·thor´ [mâ ·le·te´ro] nū´me·ro ve´en· te ē nwe´ve)
This is my baggage.	Este es mi equipaje.	(es´te ez mē e· kē·pâ´he)
There are five pieces in all.	Son cinco bultos en total.	(son sēng´ko būl´to sen to·tâl´)
I checked two trunks.	Tengo dos baúles facturados.	(teng´go thoz vâ·ū´les fâk ·tū·râ·thos)
I'll carry this valise.	Esta maleta la llevo yo.	(es´tâ mâ·le´tâ lâ ye´vo yo)
This suitcase isn't mine.	Esta maleta no es mía.	(es´tâ mâ·le´tâ no ez mē´â)
I want a cab, please.	Quiero un taxi, por favor.	(kye´ro ūn tâk´sē por fâ·vor´)

TAXICAB	TAXI	PRONUNCIATION
Take me to the — Hotel.	Lléveme al Hotel	(ye´ve·me â lo·tel´)
Is it very far?	¿Está muy lejos?	(es·tâ´ mwē le´hos)
How much do I owe you?	¿Cuánto le debo?	(kwân´to le the´vo)
How much is it to___?	¿Cuánto es para ir a´___?	(kwân´to es pâ´râ ēr â)
Here is five. Keep the change.	Aquí tiene cinco. Guarde el cambio.	(â·kē´ tye´ne sēng´ko gwâ·r´the el kâm´byo)
Do you have change?	¿Tiene usted cambio?	(tye´ne us·teth´ kâm´byo)
Take me to the Northwest Station.	Lléveme a la Estación del Noroeste.	(ye´ve·me â lâ es·tâ·syon´ del no ro·es´te)
Leave me here on the corner.	Déjeme aquí en la esquina.	(de´he·me â·kē´ en lâ es·kē´nâ)
I'm in a hurry.	Tengo prisa.	(teng´go prē´sâ)
Faster, please.	Más aprisa, por favor.	(mâ sâ·prē´sâ por fâ·vor´)
Not so fast.	No tan aprisa.	(no tâ nâ·prē´sâ)
Slow.	Despacio.	(des·pâ´syo)
Slower.	Más despacio.	(mâz thes·pâ´syo)
Drive carefully.	Maneje con cuidado	(mâ·ne´he kong kwē·thâ´-tho)
Stop.	Pare.	(pâ´re)
Go on.	Siga..	(sē´gâ)
Straight ahead.	Siga derecho.	(sē´gâ the·re´cho)
Turn to your right (left).	Voltee a la derecha (a la izquierda).	(bol·te´e â lâ the·re´châ [â lâ ēs·kyer´thâ)

HOTEL	HOTEL	PRONUNCIATION
Where is the front desk?	¿Dónde está la administración?	(don´de es·tâ´ lâ âth·mē·nēs·trâ·syon´)
I have a reservation.	Tengo un cuarto reservado.	(teng´go ūng kwâr´to rre·ser· vâ´tho)
My name is _____.	Mi nombre es _____.	(mē nom´bre es)
I want a single room with bath.	Quiero un cuarto sencillo con baño.	(kye´ro ūng kwâr´to sen·sē´yo kom bâ´nyo)

How much is it?	¿Cuánto cuesta?	(kwân´to kwes´tâ)
I want a front room.	Quiero un cuarto que dé a la calle	(kye´ro ūng kwâr´to ke the â lâ ká´ye)
Does the room have air conditioning?	¿Tiene el cuarto aire acondicionado?	(tye´ne el kwâr´to â´ē•re â•kon•dē•syo•nä´tho)
Do you have a special weekly (monthly) rate?	¿Tienen ustedes tarifa especial por semana (por mes)?	(tye´ne nūs•te´thes tâ•rē´fâ es•pe•syâl´ por se•mä´nâ
Do you have anything less expensive?	¿Tienen algo menos caro?	(tye´ne nál´go menos kâ´ro)
All right, I'll take this.	Está bien, tomaré éste.	(es•tâ´ byen to•mâ•re´ es´te)
Who will take my baggage to the room?	¿Quién me lleva el equipaje al cuarto?	(kyen me ye´vä e le• kē•pâ´he âl kwâr´to)
Where is the other bag?	¿Dónde está la otra maleta?	(don´de es•tâ´ lä o´trâ mâ•le´tâ)
Please bring me some towels and soap.	Tráigame toallas y jabón, for favor.	(trâ´ē• gâ•me to•â´yâ sē hâ•von´ por fâ•vor´)
Open that window, please.	Abra esa ventana, por favor.	(â´vrâ e´sâ ven•tâ´nâ por fâ•vor´)
Bring me some ice.	Tráigame hielo.	(trâ´ē•gâ•me ye´lo)
Is the water from the faucet safe?	¿Se puede tomar el agua de la llave?	(se pwe´the to•mâ´ re lâ´g-wâ the la yä´ve)
This pillow case doesn't look clean.	Esta funda no se ve limpia.	(es´tâ fūn´dâ no se ve lēm´pyâ)
Please call me at seven o'clock.	Favor de llamarme a las siete.	(fâ•vor´the yâ•mârʼme â lâs sye´te)
Can I have 24-hour laundry service?	¿Pueden lavarme la ropa en 24 horas?	(pwe´then lâ•vârʼ me lâ rro´-pâ em be´ēn•te ē kwâ´tro o´râs)
I want this suit pressed.	Quiero que me planchen este traje.	(kye´ro ke me plân´che nes´te trâ´he)
I want this dress cleaned.	Quiero que me limpien este vestido.	(kye´ro ke me lēm´pye nes´-te ves tē´tho)
When can I have it back?	¿Para cuándo lo tendré?	(pâ´râ kwân´do lo ten•dre´)
I'd like an extra blanket.	Quisiera otra cobija.	(kē•sye´râ o´trâ ko•vē´hâ)
How far is the post office?	¿A qué distancia está el correo?	(â ke thēs•tân´syâ es•tâ´ el ko•rre´o)
Can you sell me some stamps?	¿Puede venderme sellos de correo?	(pwe´the ven•derʼ me se´yoz the ko rre´o)

Please call me a cab.	¿Puede llamarme un taxi?	(pwe´the·yâ·mâr´me ūn tâk sē)
I'd like my bill, please.	Hágame el favor de la cuenta.	(ä´gä·me el fä·vor the lä kwen´ta)

RESTAURANTE	RESTAURANTE	PRONUNCIATION
Do you have a table for two?	¿Tiene una mesa para dos?	(tye´ne ū´nâ me´sâ pâ´râ thos)
I would prefer one closer to the window.	Preferiría una más cerca de la ventana.	(pre·fe·rē·rē´â ū´nâ mâs ser´kâ the lâ ven·tâ´nâ)
At what time do you serve meals?	¿A qué horas sirven ustedes las comidas?	(â ke o´râs sēr´ve nūs·te´-thez lâs ko·mē´thâs)
We serve breakfast from seven to nine.	Servimos el desayuno de siete a nueve.	(ser·vē´mo sel de· sä ·yū´no the sye´te â nwe´ve)
We serve dinner from one to three.	Servimos la comida de una a tres.	(ser·vē´moz lâ ko· mē´thâ the ū´nâ â tres)
We serve supper from eight to ten.	Servimos la cena de ocho a diez.	(ser·vē´moz lâ se´nâ the o´cho â thyes)
May I have a menu?	Me puede dar la lista (el menú)?	(me pwe´the thâr lâ lēs´tâ [el me·nū´])
Do you have a table d'hôte dinner?	¿Tienen comida corrida?	(tye´neng ko mē´thâ ko·rrē´thâ)
I would like to have some tomato juice.	Quisiera un poco de jugo de tomate.	(kē·sye´râ ūm po´ko the hū´go the to·mâ´te)
Is it included in the dinner?	¿Está incluido en la comida corrida?	(es·tâ´ ēng·klwē´tho en lâ ko·mē´thâ ko·rrē´thâ)
Charge it extra.	Cóbremelo aparte.	(ko´vre·me·lo â·pâr´te)
I want my steak well done (medium, rare).	Quiero mi bistec bien cocido (medio cocido, medio crudo).	(kye´ro mē vēs·tek´ vyeng ko·sē´tho [me´thyo ko·sē´tho me´thyo krū´tho)
What do you have for dessert?	¿Qué tiene de postre?	(ke tye´ne the pos´tre)

Bring me some more bread, please.	Tráigame más pan, por favor.	(trâ´ē·gâ·me mâs pân por fâ·vor´)
And more butter as well, please.	Y también más mantequilla, por favor.	(ē tâm·byen´ mâz mân·te·kē´yâ por fâ·vor´)
I want my coffee black.	Yo quiero el café negro	(yo kye´ro el kâ·fe´ ne´gro)
The lady wants hers with cream.	La señora lo quiere con crema.	(lâ se·nyo´râ lo kye´re kong kre´mâ)
I want my tea with lemon.	El té lo quiero con limón.	(el te lo kye´ro kon lē·mon´)
Check, please.	La cuenta, por favor.	(lâ kwen´tâ por fâ·vor´)
Do you pay here or at the cashier?	¿Se paga aquí o en la caja?	(se pâ´gâ â·kē´ o en lâ kâ´hâ)
I would like to wash my hands.	Quisiera lavarme las manos.	(kē·sye´râ lâ·vâr´me lâz mâ´nos)
Where is the ladies' room?	¿Dónde está el tocador de señoras?	(don´de es·tâ´ el to·kâ·thor´ the se·nyo´râs)
I want my lunch a la carte.	Quiero mi almuerzo a la carta.	(kye´ro mē âl·mwer´so â lâ kâr´tâ)
Would you like to have some fish (meat, turkey, chicken)?	¿Le gustaría un poco de pescado (carne, pavo, pollo)?	(le gūs·tâ·rē´â ūm po´ko the pes·kâ´tho [kâr´ne pâ´vo po´yo])
What kind of meat do you want, pork (beef, veal, lamb)?	¿Qué clase de carne desea, de puerco (de res, de ternera, de cordero)?	(ke klâ´se the kâr´ne the·se´â de pwer´ko [de rres de ter·ne´râ de kor·the´ro])
Do you have any breaded veal chops?	¿Tienen chuletas de ternera empanizadas?	(tye´nen chū·le´tâz the ter·ne´râ em·pâ·nēsâ´thâs)
I would prefer some spare ribs.	Preferiría unas costillas de puerco.	(pre·fe·rē·rē´â ū´nâs kos·tē´yâz the pwer´ko)
I want my eggs fried (scrambled, soft boiled, hard boiled, with ham, with bacon, with sausages).	Quiero mis huevos fritos (revueltos, pasados por agua, duros, con jamón, con tocino, con salchicas).	(kye´ro mē swe´vos frē´tos [rre· vwel´tos pâ sâ´thos por â´gwâ dū´ros kon hâmon´ kon to·sē´no kon sâl·chē´châs)

I'd rather have an omellete.	Preferiría una tortilla de huevos.	(pre·fe·rē·rē´â ū´nä tor·tē´yä the we´vos)
The coffee is cold.	El café está frío.	(el kâ·fe´ es·tä´ frē´o)
A glass of milk, please.	Un vaso de leche, por favor.	(ūm bä´so the le´che por fä·vor´)
All I want is toast and black coffee.	Quiero sólo pan tostado y café negro.	(kye´ro so´lo pân tos·tä´tho ē kâ·fe´ ne´gro)
I don't have a napkin.	No tengo servilleta.	(no teng´go ser·vē ye´tä)

MONEY	MONEDA	PRONUNCIATION
Is there a bank or currency exchange near here?	¿Hay algún banco o casa de cambio cerca?	(â´ ē âl·gūm´ bâng´ko o kä´sä the kâm´byo ser´-kä)
Where can I cash a check?	¿Dónde puedo cobrar un cheque?	(don´de pwe´tho ko·vrä´ rūn che´ke)
What is the rate of exchange today?	¿A cómo está el cambio hoy?	(â ko´mo es·tä´ el kâm´byo o·ē)
Give me small bills, please.	Hágame el favor de darme billetes chicos.	(â´gä·me el fâ·vor´ the thâr´me vē·ye´tes chē´kos)
Do I need identification to cash a check?	¿Necesito algún medio de identificación para cobrar un cheque?	(ne·se·sē´to âl·gūn´ me´th-yo the ē·then·tē·fē kä·syon´ pâ´râ ko·vrä´ rūn che´ke)
I left my passport in the hotel. I'll go get it.	Dejé mi pasaporte en el hotel. Voy a traerlo.	(de·he´ mē pâ·sä·por´te e ne lo·tel´ bo´ē â trâ·er´lo)
I left my tourist card in the hotel.	Dejé mi tarjeta de turista en el hotel.	(de·he´ mē tär·he´tä the tū·rēs´tä e ne lo·tel´)

SHOPPING	LAS COMPRAS	PRONUNCIATION
I want to go shopping. What store do you recommend?	Quiero ir de compras. ¿Qué tienda me recomienda?	(kye´ro ēr the kom´prâs ke tyen´dä me rre·ko·mye·n´dä)
How much is this?	¿Cuánto cuesta esto?	(kwân´to kwes´tâ es´to)
It's too expensive.	Es demasiado caro.	(ez the·mâ·syâ´tho kâ´ro)
Do you have something cheaper (better)?	¿Tiene usted algo más barato (mejor)?	(tye´ne ūs·te thâl´go mâz vâ·râ´to (me·hor´)

Do you accept personal checks?	¿Aceptan cheques personales?	(â·sep´tân che´kes per·so·nâ´les)
May I return it if my wife doesn't like it?	¿Puedo devolverlo si no le gusta a mi esposa?	(pwe· tho the·vol·ver´lo sē no le gūs´tâ â mē es·po´sâ)
Do you accept returned goods?	¿Aceptan devoluciones?	(â·sep´tân de·vo·lū·syo´nes)
I'll come back with her, then.	Entonces regresaré con ella.	(en·ton´sez rre·gre·sâ·re´ ko ne´yâ)
Show me some shirts, please.	Hágame el favor de enseñarme unas camisas.	(â´gâ·me el fâ·vor´ the en se·nyâr´me ū´nâs kâ·mē´sâs)
Neck, 14 1/2 sleeve, 33.	Cuello catorce y medio, manga treinta y tres.	(kwe´yo kâ·tor´se ē me´thyo mâng´gâ tre´ēn·tâ ē tres)
I'd rather have white.	Las prefiero blancas.	(lâs pre·fye´ro vlâng´kâs)
I'd rather have a solid color.	Las prefiero de color entero.	(lâs pre·fye´ro the ko·lo´ ren·te´ro)
I'll take this one.	Me quedaré con ésta.	(me ke·thâ·re´ ko nes´tâ)
I'd like to see some ladies' dresses.	Me gustaría ver algunos vestidos de señora.	(me gūs·tâ·rē´â ve râl·gū´noz ves·tē´thoz the se·nyo´râ)
What size?	¿De qué talla?	(de ke tâ´yâ)
Where can I buy a good hat?	¿Dónde puedo comprar un buen sombrero?	(don´de pwe´tho kom·prâ´ rūm bwen som·bre´ro)
How much do I owe you?	¿Cuánto le debo?	(kwân´to le the´vo)
Could you send it all to the hotel?	¿Podrían mandármelo todo al hotel?	(po·thrē´ân mân·dâr´me·lo to´tho â lo ·ter´)
THE MARKET	**EL MERCADO**	**PRONUNCIATION**
Where is the market?	¿Dónde está el mercado?	(don´de es·tâ´ el mer·kâ´tho)

When does the market open?	¿A qué hora abren el mercado?	(â ke o´râ â´vre nel mer·kâ´tho)
At what time does the market close?	¿A qué hora cierran el mercado?	(â ke o´râ sye´rrâ nel mer·kâ´tho)
I want a dozen of your best eggs.	Quiero una docena de huevos, de los mejores.	(kye´ro ū´nâ tho·se´nâ the we´vos de loz me·ho´res)
Also a kilo of cheese and a liter of milk.	También un kilo de queso y un litro de leche.	(tâm·bye´ nūng kē´lo the ke´so yūn lē´tro the le´che)
Do you have canned fruit juices?	¿Tienen jugos de fruta en latas?	(tye´nen hū´goz the frū´tâ en lâ´tâs)
Do you have fresh vegetables?	¿Tienen legumbres frescas?	(tye´nen le·gūm´bres fres´kâs)
How much is a bunch of asparagus?	¿Cuánto cuesta el manojo de espárragos?	(kwân´to kwes´tâ el mâ·no´ho the es·pâ´rrâ·gos)
Do you sell meat?	¿Venden ustedes carne?	(ben´de nūs·te´thes kâr´ne)
I would like a leg of lamb.	Quisiera una pierna de cordero.	(kē·sye´râ ū·nâ pyer´nâ the kor·the´ro)
I don't have change.	No tengo cambio.	(no teng´go kâm´byo)
I'm going to the corner to change this bill.	Voy a la esquina a cambiar este billete.	(bo´ē â lâ es·kē´nâ a kâm·byâ´ res´te vē·ye´te)
Are you open on Sundays also?	¿Abren ustedes los domingos también?	(â´vre nūs·te´thez loz tho·mēng´gos tâm·byen´)

THE POST OFFICE	EL CORREO	PRONUNCIATION
I want to send this letter air mail.	Quiero mandar esta carta por correo aéreo.	(kye´ro mân·dâ´ res´tâ kâr´tâ por ko·rre´o â·e´re·o)
How much will it cost?	¿Cuánto cuesta?	(kwân´to kwes´tâ)
Give me ten more air mail stamps.	Déme otros diez sellos de correo aéreo.	(de´me o·troz thyes se´yoz the korre´o â·e´re·o)

How much is it by regular mail?	¿Cuánto cuesta por correo ordinario?	(kwân´to kwes´tâ por ko•rre´o or•thē•nâ´ryo)
I want a stamp for this letter.	Quiero un sello para esta carta.	(kye´ro ūn se´yoz pâ´râ es´tâ kâr´tâ)
I'd like to send this package insured.	Deseo enviar este paquete asegurado.	(de• se´o em•byâ´ res´te pâ•ke´te â se•gū•râ´tho)
I'd like to register this letter.	Quiero certificar esta carta.	(kye´ro ser•tē•fē•kâ´ res´tâ kâr´tâ)
I'd like to send this letter special delivery.	Quiero mandar esta carta con entrega inmediata.	(kye´ro mân•dâ´ res´tâ kâr´tâ ko nen•tre´gâ ēn•me•thyâ´tâ)
Are there any letters for me?	¿Hay alguna carta para mí?	(â´ē âl• gū´nâ kâr´tâ pâ´râ mē)
Give me about five postcards.	Déme unas cinco tarjetas postales.	(de´me ū´nâs sēng´ko tar•he´tâs pos•tâ´les)
At what time does the post office close on Saturdays?	¿A qué horas cierra el correo los sábados?	(â ke o´râs sye´rrâ el ko•rre´o los sâ´vâ•thos)

TRAVELING BY RAILROAD	VIAJE POR FERROCARRIL	PRONUNCIATION
Is this the train to —?	¿Es éste el tren para —?	(e ses´te el trem pâ´râ)
Does it have a sleeping car?	¿Lleva vagón dormitorio?	(ye´vâ vâ• gon´ dor•mē•to´r yo)
I would like to have a lower (an upper) berth.	Quisiera una cama baja (alta).	(kē• sye´râ ū´nâ kâ´mâ vâ´hâ [âl´tâ])
How much is a section?	¿Cuánto cuesta la sección?	(kwân´to kwes´tâ lâ sek•syon´)
When do we arrive in —?	¿A qué horas llegamos a —	(â ke o´râz ye gâ´mo sâ)
Are we on time?	¿Vamos a tiempo?	(bâ´mo sâ tyem´po)
How late are we?	¿Qué retraso llevamos?	(ke rre•trâ´so ye•vâ´mos)

I want a first class ticket to___.	Quiero un boleto (un billete) de primera clase a —.	(kye´ro ūm bo•le´to [ūm bē•ye´te] the prē•me´râ klâ´se â)
Does this train have a dining car?	¿Tiene este tren vagón comedor?	(tye´ne es´te trem bâ• gong´ ko•me•thor´)
How late do they serve breakfast?	¿Hasta qué horas sirven el desayuno?	(âs´tâ ke o´râs sēr´ve nel de•sâ•yū´no)
When do they start to serve lunch?	¿A qué horas comienzan a servir el almuerzo?	(â ke o´râs ko•myen´sâ nâ ser•vē´ re lâl• mwer´so)
I want to go to bed. Please make up my berth.	Quiero acostarme. Hágame la cama, por favor.	(kye´ro â•kos•târ´me â´gâ•me lâ kâ´mâ por fâ•vor´)
Please take down that large valise.	Bájeme esa maleta grande, por favor.	(bâ´he•me e´sâ mâ•le´tâ grân´de por fâ•vor´)
Please call me at 6:30 a.m.	Hágame el favor de llamarme a las seis y media de la mañana.	(â´gâ•me el fâ •vor´ the yâ•mâr´me â lâs se´ê sē me´thyâ the lâ mâ•nyâ´nâ)
Will we have time for breakfast before we arrive?	¿Tendremos tiempo para desayunar antes de llegar?	(ten• dre´mos tyem´po pâ´râ the•sâ•yū•nâ´ rân´- tez the ye•gâr´)
Please let me know when we pass ----.	Avíseme, por favor, cuando pasemos por.	(â•vē´se•me por fâ•vor´ kwâ- n´do pâ•se´mos por)
Is there an air conditioned car here?	¿Hay algún vagón con aire acondicionado?	(â´ē âl•gūm´ bâ•gong´ ko nâ´ē•re â•kon•dē•syo•nâ´- tho)
I feel a draft. Would you turn off the fan?	Siento una corriente de aire. ¿Puede apagarme el ventilador?	(syen´to ū´nâ ko•rryen´te the â´ē•re pwe´the â• pâ•gâr me el ven•tē•lâ thor´)

TRAVEL BY PLANE	VIAJE POR AVIÓN	PRONUNCIATION
When does the plane leave?	¿A qué hora sale el avión?	(â ke o´râ sâle e lâ•vyon´)
Where is my plane?	¿Dónde está mi avión?	(don´de es•tâ mē â•vyon´)
I'd like to check my baggage.	Quiero dejar depositado mi equipaje•	(kye´ro the•hâr´ the•po•sē•tâ´tho mē e•kē•pâ´he)
What is my flight number?	¿Cuál es el número de mi vuelo?	(kwâ le sel nū´me•ro the mē vwe´lo)
Do you serve meals on this flight?	¿Sirven comidas en este vuelo?	(sēr´veng ko•mē´thâ se nes´te vwe´lo)

Where is the men's room?	¿Dónde están los lavabos para hombres?	(don´de es·tân´ loz lâ·vâ´vos pá´râ om´bres)
At what altitude are we flying?	¿A qué altura volamos?	(â ke âl·tū´râ vo·lâ´mos)
I feel airsick.	Me siento mareado.	(me syen´to mâ· re· â´tho)

TRAVEL BY CAR	VIAJE POR AUTOMÓVIL	PRONUNCIATION
I need some gas (oil).	Necesito gasolina (aceite).	(ne·se·sē´to gâ·so·lē´nâ [a·se´ē·te])
Fill her up.	Llene el tanque.	(ye´ne el tâng´ke)
Give me forty liters of your best gas.	Déme cuarenta litros de la mejor gasolina que tenga.	(de´me kwâ·ren´tâ lē´troz the lâ me·hor´ gâ·so·lē´nâ ke teng´gâ)
Do you have any light oil?	¿Tiene aceite delgado?	(tye´ne â·se ē·te thel·gâ´tho)
I have a flat tire.	Tengo un neumático desinflado (una llanta baja).	(teng´go ūn neū·mâ´tē·ko the·sēm·flâ´tho [ū´nâ yân´tâ bâ´hâ])
Check the water, please.	Vea cómo está el agua, por favor.	(be´â ko´mo es·tâ´ e lâ´gwa por fâ·vor´)
Check the tires too.	Revise también los neumáticos (las llantas).	(rre·vē´se tâm· byen´ loz neū·mâ´tē·kos [lâz yân´tâs])
Where can I get gas again?	¿Dónde puedo tomar gasolina otra vez?	(don´de pwe´tho to·mâr´ gâ·so·lē´nâ o´trâ ves)
I want to leave the car here tonight.	Quiero dejar aquí el auto esta noche.	(kye´ro the·hâr´ râ·kē´ e lâ´ū·to es´tâ no´che)
Can you wash it for me?	¿Pueden lavármelo?	(pwe´then lâ·vâr´me·lo)
I want the oil changed also.	También quiero que le cambien el aceite.	(tâm·byeng´ kye´ro ke le kâm´bye nel â·se´ē·te)
At what time do you open in the morning?	¿A qué hora abren ustedes en la mañana?	(â ke o´râ â´vre nūs·te´the sen lâ mâ· nyâ´nâ)
The engine gets hot very quickly.	El motor se calienta muy pronto.	(el mo·tor´ se kâ·lyen´tâ mwē pron´to)
Is the road in good condition?	¿Está bueno el camino?	(es ·tâ´ vwe´no el kâ·mē´no)

| Is it a paved road? | ¿Es camino pavimentado? | (es kâ·mē´no pâ·vē·men·tâ´tho) |

PHOTOGRAPHY	FOTOGRAFIA	PRONUNCIATION
Are we allowed to take pictures here?	¿Se permite tomar fotografias aquí?	(se per·mē´te to·mâr´ fo·to·grâ· fē´â sâ·kē´)
May I take my camera into the museum?	¿Puedo entrar con mi cámara en el museo?	(pwe´tho en·trâr´ kon mē kâ´mâ·râ e nel mū·se´o)
Are we allowed to take pictures inside the church?	¿Se nos permite tomar fotografias dentro de la iglesia?	(se nos per·mē´te to·mâr´ fo·to·grâ·fē´âz then´tro the lâ ē·gle´syâ)
Where can I buy camera supplies?	¿Dónde puedo comprar artículos fotográficos?	(don´de pwe´tho kom·prâ´-râr·tē´kū ·los fo·to·grâ´fē·kos)
I need some film for my camera.	Necesito películas para mi cámara.	(ne·se·sē´pe·lē´kū·lâs pâ·râ mē kâ´mâ·râ)
Here is my camera.	Aquí tiene usted mi cámara.	(â·kē´ tye´ne ūs ·teth´ mē kâ´mâ·râ)
It doesn't work. Can you fix it?	No funciona. ¿Pueden ustedes componérmela?	(no fūn·syo´nâ pwe´thenūs·te´thes kom·po·ner´me·lâ)
Can you develop these rolls of film for me?	¿Pueden revelarme estos rollos de películas?	(pwe´then rre·ve·lâr´mees´-toz rro´yoz the pe·lē´kū·lâs)
How much do you charge for developing a roll?	¿Cuánto cobran por revelar un rollo?	(kwân´to ko´vrân por rre·ve·lâ´ rūn rro´yo)
What does each print cost?	¿Cuánto cuesta cada copia?	(kwân´to kwes´tâ kâ´thâ ko´pyâ)
I want three prints of each negative.	Quiero tres copias de cada negativa.	(kye´ro tres ko´pyâz the kâ´thâ ne· gâ·tē´vâ)
Do you have color film?	¿Tienen películas a colores?	(tye´nem pe·lē´kū·lâ sâ ko·lo´res)
I need some rolls of movie film as well.	Necesito también algunos rollos para sacar películas.	(ne·se·sē´to tambye´ nâl·gū´noz rro´yos pâ´râ sâ· kâr´pe·lē´kū·lâs)

| Can I have these enlarged? | ¿Pueden ampliarme éstas? | (pwe´the nâm ·plyâr´me es´tâs) |
| When will they be ready? | ¿Cuándo estarán listas? | (kwân´do es·tâ·rân´ lēs´tâs) |

COMMUNICATIONS	COMUNICACIONES	PRONUNCIATION
Is there a public telephone close by?	¿Hay un teléfono público por aquí cerca?	(â´ē ūn te·le´fo·no pū´vlē·ko po râ·kē ser´kâ)
Does it take coins or phone cards?	¿Acepta monedas ó tarjetas telefónicas?	(â·sep´tâ mo·ne´thâ so târ·he´tâs te·le·fo´nē·kâs)
Where can I buy a phone card?	¿Dónde puedo comprar una tarjeta telefónica?	(thon´de pwe´tho kom prâ´ rūn´â târ·he´tâ te·le·fo´nē·kâ)
What is the phone number?	¿Cuál es el número de teléfono?	(kwâ´le sel nū´me·ro the te·le´fo·no)
How do I dial the number?	¿Cómo marco el número?	(ko´mo mâr´ko el nū´me·ro)
Is there internet access?	¿Hay acceso al internet?	(â´ē âk·se´so â lēn·ter·net´)
Do you have e-mail?	¿Tiene usted correo electrónico?	(tyen´e ūs·teth´ ko·rre´o e· lek·tro´nē·ko)

GENERAL PHRASES	FRASES GENERALES	PRONUNCIATION
Good morning.	Buenos días.	(bwe´noz thē´âs)
How are you?	¿Cómo está usted?	(ko´mo es·ta´ ūs teth´)
Very well, thank you.	Muy bien, gracias.	(mwē byen grâ´syâs)
I don't speak Spanish (English).	No hablo español (inglés).	(no â´vlo es ´pâ· nyol´ [ēng·gles´])
I understand it quite well, but I don't speak it.	Lo entiendo bastante, pero no lo hablo.	(lo en·tyen´do vâs·tân´te pe´ro no lo â´vlo)
I speak a little Spanish.	Hablo un poco de español.	(â´vlo ūm po´ko the es·pâ·nyol´)
I feel much better today.	Me siento mucho mejor hoy.	(me syen´to mū·cho me·ho´ro´ē)

Where are you going?	¿A dónde va?	(â thon´de vâ)
Come here, please.	Venga acá, por favor.	(beng´gâ â·kâ´ por fâ·vor´)
I want to show you something.	Quiero mostrarle algo.	(kye´ro mos· trâr´le âl´go)
Speak slowly, please.	Hable despacio, por favor.	(â´vle thes· pâ´syo por fâ·vor´)
Good-bye. I'll see you later.	Adiós. Nos veremos más tarde.	(â·thyos´ noz ve·re´moz mâs tar´the)
Wait here.	Espere aquí.	(es·pe´re â·kē´)
I have no time today.	Hoy no tengo tiempo.	(o´ē no teng´go tyem´po)
What do you wish?	¿Qué desea usted?	(ke the·se´â ūs·teth´)
What can I do for you?	¿En qué puedo servirle?	(eng ke pwe´tho ser·vēr´le)
Can you tell me —?	¿Puede usted decirme —?	(pwe´the ūs·teth´ the· sēr´- me)
I think so (not).	Creo que sí (no).	(kre´o ke sē [no])
Is there a doctor near here?	¿Hay médico por aquí cerca?	(â´ē me´thē·ko po râ· kē´ ser´kâ)
Is there a dentist around here?	¿Hay algún dentista por aquí?	(â´ē gūn´ den·tēs´tâ po râ·kē´)
Where is the beauty parlor?	¿Dónde está el salón de belleza?	(don´de es·tâ´ el sâ·lon´ de ve·ye´sâ)
With pleasure.	Con mucho gusto.	(kon mū´cho gūs´to)
What do you think?	¿Qué le parece a usted?	(ke le pâ·re´se â ūs ·teth´)
You know what I mean.	Usted sabe lo que quiero decir.	(ūs teth´ sá´ve lo ke kye´ro the·sēr´)
How do you say that in Spanish?	¿Cómo se dice eso en español?	(ko´mo se thē´se e´so e nes·pâ·nyol´)
What is this for?	¿Para qué es esto?	(pâ´râ ke e ses´to)
Do you understand me?	¿Me entiende usted?	(me en·tyen´de ūs·teth´)

I understand you when you speak slowly.	*Le entiendo cuando habla-despacio.*	(le en·tyen´do kwân´do â´vlâ thes·pâ´syo)
Of course.	*Por supuesto.*	(por sū·pwes´to)
Sorry, but I didn't under-stand you.	*Perdón, pero no le entendí.*	(per·thon´ pe´ro no le en·ten·dē´)
Please repeat the question.	*Favor de repetir la pregun-ta.*	(fâ·vor´ the rre·pe·tēr´ lâ pre·gūn´tâ)
Now I understand.	*Ahora sí entiendo.*	(â·o´râ sē en·tyen´do)
Think nothing of it.	*No se preocupe.*	(no se pre·o·kū´pe)
Don't bother.	*No se moleste.*	(no se mo·les´te)
You're very kind.	*Es usted muy amable.*	(e sūs·teth´ mwe â·mâ´vle)
Many thanks.	*Un millón de gracias.*	(ūn mē· yon´ de grâ´syâs)
Don't mention it.	*No hay de qué.*	(no â´ē the ke)
You're welcome.	*De nada.*	(de nâ´thâ)
May I speak to you for a moment?	*¿Me permite usted una palabra?*	(me per·mē´te ūs·te´thū´nâ pâ·lâ´vrâ)

TIME	LA HORA	PRONUNCIACION
What time is it?	*¿Qué hora es?*	(ke o´râ es)
It's two o'clock.	*Son las dos.*	(son lâz thos)
It's three o'clock sharp.	*Son las tres en punto.*	(son lâs tre sem pūn´to)
It's half past four.	*Son las cuatro y media.*	(son lâs kwâ´tro ē me´thya)
It's ten minutes to five.	*Faltan diez minutos para las cinco.*	(fâl´tan dyez mē·nū´tos pâ´râ las sēng´ko)
It's 11:45.	*Son las once y cuarenta.*	(son lâ son´se e kwâ·ren´-tâ)
It's a quarter to twelve.	*Falta un cuarto para las doce.*	(fâl´tâ ūng kwâr´to pâ´râ lâz tho´se)
My watch is fast (slow).	*Mi reloj está adelantado (atrasado).*	(mē rre·lo´ es·tâ´ â·the·lân·tâ´tho [â·trâ·sâ´tho])

WHEATHER	ESTADO DEL TIEMPO	PRONUNCIACION
What a beautiful day!	*¡Qué lindo día!*	(ke lēn´do thē´â)
It's cloudy.	*Está nublado.*	(es·tâ´ nū·vlâ´tho)
It looks like rain.	*Parece que va a llover.*	(pâ·re´se ke va â yo·ver´)
Is it very cold?	*¿Hace mucho frío?*	(â´se mū´cho frē´o)
On the contrary, it's warm.	*Al contrario, hace calor.*	(âl kon·trâ´ryo â·se kâ·lor´)

Pesas y Medidas
(Weights and Measures)

Medidas Métricas		Medidas de E.U.A.	
Kilómetro	0.62137 millas	Milla	1.6093 kms.
Metro	39.37 pulgadas	Milla marina	1.853 kms.
Decímetro	3.937 pulgadas	Yarda	0.9144 ms.
Centímetro	0.3937 pulgadas	Pie	0.3048 ms.
Milímetro	0.03937 pulgadas	Pulgada	2.54 cms.
Superficie		**Superficie**	
Kilómetro cuadrado	247.104 acres	Acre	0.4453 hectáreas
Hectárea	2.471 acres	Milla cuadrada	259 hectáreas
Metro cuadrado	1550 pulg.^{2}	Yarda cuadrada	0.8361 m.^{2}
Decímetro cuadrado	15.50 pulg ^{2}	Pie cuadrado	929.03 cms.^{2}
Centímetro	0.155 pulg.^{2}	Pulgada cuadrada	6.4516 cms.^{2}
Volumen		**Volumen**	
Metro cúbico	1.308 yardas^3	Pulgada cúbica	16.387 cm.^{3}
Decímetro cúbico	61.023 pulg.^{3}	Pie cúbico	0.0283 m.^{3}
Centímetro cúbico	0.0610 pulg.^{3}	Yarda cúbica	0.7646 m.^{3}
Capacidad		**Capacidad**	
Hectolitro	2.838 bushels ó 26.418 galones	Cuarto de gal. (líquido)	0.9463 litros
Litro	0.9081 cuarto de galón (áridos) ó 1.0567 cuarto de galón (líquido)	Cuarto de gal. (áridos)	1.101 litros
		Galón	3.785 litros
		Bushel	35.24 litros
Pesas		**Pesas**	
Tonelada	2204.6 lb.	Onza (avoirdupois)	28.35 gms.
Kilograma	2.2046 lb.	Libra	0.4536 kgs.
Gramo	15.432 granos	Tonelada larga	1.0161 ton. met.
Centigramo	0.1543 granos	Tonelada corta	0.9072 ton. met.
		Grano	0.0648 gms.

Weights and Measures

(Pesas y Medidas)

US Measures		Metric Measures	
Mile	1.6093 kms.	Kilometer	0.62137 miles
Naut. mile	1.853 kms.	Meter	39.37 inches
Yard	0.9144 ms.	Decimeter	3.937 inches
Foot	0.3048 ms.	Centimeter	0.3937 inches
Inch	2.54 cms.	Milimeter	0.03937 inches
Surface		**Surface**	
Acre	0.4453 hectares	Sq. kilometer	247.104 acres
Square mile	259 hectares	Hectare	2.471 acres
Square yard	0.8361 sq. meters	Square meter	1550 sq. inches
Square foot	929.03 sq. cms	Square decimeter	15.50 sq. inches
Square inch	6.4516 sq. cms.	Square centimeter	0.155 sq. inches
Cubic		**Cubic**	
Cubic inch	16.387 cu. cm.	Cubic meter	1.308 cu. yards
Cubic foot	0.0283 cu. ms.	Cubic decimeter	61.023 cu. inches
Cubic yard	0.7646 cu. ms.	Cubic centimeter	0.0610 cu. inches
Capacity		**Capacity**	
Liquid quart	0.9463 liters	Hectoliter	2.838 bushels
Dry quart	1.101 liters		or 26.418 gallons
Gallon	3.785 liters	Liter	0.9081 dry qu.
Bushel	35.24 liters		or 1.0567 liq. qts.
Weights		**Weights**	
Ounce (avoirdupois)	28.35 grams	Ton	2204.6 lbs.
Pound	0.4536 kgs.	Kilogram	2.2046 lbs.
Long ton	1.0161 met. tons	Gram	15.432 grains
Short ton	0.9072 met. tons	Centigram	0.1543 grains
Grain	0.0648 grams.		

Monetary Units
of America and the Iberian Peninsula

Country	Monetary Units (as of 2004)
Argentina	Argentine Peso
Bolivia	Boliviano
Brazil	Real
Canada	Canadian Dollar
Chile	Chilean Peso
Colombia	Colombian Peso
Costa Rica	Costan Rican Colón
Cuba	Cuban Peso
Dominican Republic	Dominican Peso
Ecuador	U.S. Dollar / Sucre
El Salvador	U.S. Dollar / Colon
Guatemala	Quetzal / U.S. Dollar
Haiti	Gourde
Honduras	Lempira
Mexico	Mexican Peso
Nicaragua	Gold Córdoba
Panama	Balboa / U.S. Dollar
Paraguay	Guaraní
Peru	Nuevo Sol
Portugal	Euro
Spain	Euro
United States of America	U.S.Dollar
Uruguay	Uruguayan Peso
Venezuela	Bolívar